Chicano Studies

Survey and Analysis

Third Edition

Dennis J. Bixler-Márquez
Carlos F. Ortega
Rosalía Solórzano Torres
University of Texas at El Paso

KENDALL/HUNT PUBLISHING COMPANY
4050 Westmark Drive   Dubuque, Iowa 52002

El Mural de Senecú

Lupe Casillas-Lowenberg, Artist/Muralist
and Ysleta Independent School District Youth Muralists

Main assistant: Student artist Jesús Meléndez

Las Leyendas de El Mural de Senecú

"Tree Lined Alameda
Temporary Tianguis,
Oasis of Life's offerings,
Haven to Desert Dwellers,
Midst El Paso-Senecú-Ysleta...
Tejidos, Estambres, Encajes
of life ever flowing,
ever weaving,
dynamically duplicating creators's creativity . . ."

Juan Contreras, Ysleta Independent School District
Artist-in-Residence,Chicano Studies
University of Texas at El Paso

Contents

Introduction

This anthology will begin your journey of introduction to the field of Chicano Studies as an academic discipline. This essay tells the story of the Mexican-origin community in the United States through the perspective of those who helped develop the field. Here, we analyze and interpret the diverse experiences of the Mexican community using interdisciplinary methods and theoretical schemes. The collection of readings is designed to prepare the first-time student in Chicano Studies with a basic foundation of almost forty years of research and teaching focus in the discipline.

The preparation of any anthology is always a precarious undertaking, largely due to what is left out of the collection rather than what goes in. As editors, we began the first edition of this project in 1996 with great enthusiasm. No introductory anthology in Chicano Studies had been published in over a decade. A need also arose in our introductory courses to have a set of standardized contemporary readings that reflected the breadth of Chicano Studies as a discipline. To that end, our primary goal is to provide students a foundation encouraging them to pursue in-depth studies on Chicanos from the perspective of the social sciences, education, the humanities, and the arts. With respect to the preparation of students in various professions, especially those who intend to live and work in the Southwest and the U.S.-Mexico border, the acquisition of pertinent knowledge on the history, culture, current socioeconomic, and political issues affecting Chicanos, is paramount. Our hope is this text will provide a fruitful experience to the readers as they embark on their study of the largest ethnic minority group in the Southwest and the United States.

But what is Chicano Studies? How did it come about? What purpose does it serve? This essay will attempt to answer these questions. By addressing the origins, intellectual focus, the contributions and issues within Chicano Studies, the reader will better understand the role and the significance of this book. While a complete and critical history of Chicano Studies has yet to be written—one that will examine the development of Chicano programs, departments and centers, assess the ideological relationships between institutions, the innovation of curriculum, and the relationship of undergraduate degrees and the workplace—insight of the workings and development of the discipline will provide the reader with a background and understanding of its political significance.

The Origins of Chicano Studies

The field of Chicano Studies is born during the tumultuous decade of the 1960s, during a period of U.S. history when the very structure of society is changing, or pressured to change. Issues such as race, inequality, opportunities in education and work, health, inclusion, and the war in Viet Nam lead groups throughout the country to question their social status and that of dominant elites. Initially, Chicano Studies is largely a California product for at least two reasons: 1) the large Mexican origin population in the state and 2) the Chicano student movement makes Chicano Studies its top priority and wages constant struggles to have programs developed and, later, defends their existence. The push in California, however, influences similar struggles in the Southwest and Midwest. Politically, students involve themselves with organizations such as the United Mexican American Students (UMAS), the Mexican American Youth Organization (MAYO), the Mexican American Student Council (MASC), or Movimiento Estudiantil Chicano de Aztlán (MEChA), to name only a few. Involvement with the United Farm Workers of America and local community politics, as seen through the Crusade for Justice in Denver, Colorado, provides the foundation for practical and ideological work. Racism and a legacy of discrimination in Southwestern universities also lead students to confront these institutions for their lack of social responsibility.[1]

Before the 1960s, few Chicanos are enrolled in universities and even fewer Chicano intellectuals with professional standing teach and publish their research. Those Chicanos attending college come from a small middle-class. Members of the working class who attend college often do so with the help of the Catholic and Protestant clergy and, to some extent, the Mormon Church and the Young Men's Christian Association (YMCA). This is the type of experience first-generation, Mexican-American college students encounter. Through the G.I. Bill and the Civil Rights Movement, the experience of exclusion is overcome and large numbers of Mexican American, working class students are able to obtain a higher education.

The students who attend college during the 1960s find, for the most part, no intellectual tradition with a distinct Mexican focus. It is a cultural dimension ignored in the curriculum and faculty makeup. The lone exception is the University of Texas at Austin, where some of the early Mexican American scholars and intellectuals are present: Carlos E. Castañeda; George I. Sánchez; perhaps the first Mexican American scholar to wage battle against racism in the schools, when in the 1930s he challenges the validity of IQ tests and their bias against Mexican students; and folklorist Américo Paredes, founder of the Center for Mexican American Studies (CMAS), who is best known for his book, *With His Pistol in His Hand.*[2]

At the University of New Mexico, Arthur Campa conducts historical and cultural studies while Sabine Ulibarri publishes early Chicano literature. At the University of Notre Dame, Julián Samora, a sociologist, was the first scholar to focus attention on political leadership in the Mexican American community and the co-optation of community leaders. He also founds the Mexican American Studies Center at Notre Dame. In California, Ernesto Galarza, who came from a migrant family, receives his Ph.D. in economics from Columbia University in 1929, but never pursues a university career—he does not believe universities care about Mexican workers. Instead, he becomes an independent scholar and a union organizer. His best-known book is *Merchants of Labor.*

As the student movement of the 1960s comes into its own, some militant students see the work of these first-generation scholars as too traditional, too academic, and too removed from the needs of the community. Instead, the kind of scholar in demand is one whose research would critically examine American society and, at the same time, shape the emerging consciousness based on cultural nationalism. The Chicano scholar would reject assimilationist and integrationist ideologies and embrace a strong Mexican identity with an activist orientation.

The emergence of Chicano Studies becomes, in part, the product of mass student protests on university and college campuses throughout the United States. The radicalism of the period is generated by numerous social and political issues of the time: Poverty, civil rights, political and economic inequality, racism, and the war in Viet Nam. Chicano youth are also concerned with access to institutions of higher education that traditionally exclude them. Their demands call for a university education that would 1) teach them about their culture and history and 2) offer training and knowledge needed to create change in their communities.[3]

By 1967, a Chicano student group by the name of Quinto Sol at the University of California at Berkeley begins publishing *El Grito: a Journal of Contemporary Mexican American Thought* under the leadership of Octavio Romano. The assumption guiding the Quinto Sol group is that Chicanos have the responsibility of challenging the assimilationist policies of the university, which perpetu-

ates racist stereotypes.[4] But the work of *El Grito* is more than an intellectual exercise. The writings are a direct response to conditions in the Mexican community, bleak educational experiences, the exploitation of farm workers, and the virtual exclusion from mainstream society. UC Berkeley, which is at the center of student protest against the war in Viet Nam, is not entirely supportive of the venture, since Romano was on the faculty of Anthropology and many of the staff and writers are students at the university.

During the latter part of the 1960s, especially in 1968, Chicano students apply pressure to colleges and universities to institutionalize the study of the Mexican-origin population in general and Chicanos in particular, as well as admit and retain Chicano students. Ironically, there is nothing uniform in these proposals. According to Carlos Muñoz:

> There was a consensus of the relevance and need for those programs for Chicano students but there was a lack of coherence in expectation and emphasis. Some emphasized the potential for such programs to contribute to the solution of student's cultural identity crisis caused by the assimilationist process. Others expected that these programs would develop into meaningful academic alternatives to traditional departments. Still others perceived such programs as training grounds for community organizers. Ideologically, the spectrum ran from those who identified Chicano Studies as curricula that would emphasize the contributions of Americans of Mexican descent to American culture and society to those who defined it as curricula that would focus attention on racism and the structure of class oppression.[5]

Nineteen-sixty-eight is a tumultuous year in higher education. Campuses throughout the United States are caught in the middle of student strikes addressing the Viet Nam War and the Civil Rights Movement. The situation in the country is also intensified by the assassination of Robert Kennedy and Martin Luther King, Jr. Added to this are student strikes in Europe and Mexico, the latter drawing much attention in the Chicano community after the massacre of university students at Plaza Tlaltelolco, October 2, 1968.

These events shape the demands of Chicano Studies programs. In Los Angeles, student strikes become a regular occurrence, with UMAS leading the way. At their 1968 statewide conference, they discuss such topics as colonialism, international solidarity, organizational structure, legal defense, and the establishment of Chicano Studies programs. At one point, there are at least 35 UMAS chapters in Southern California, with a combined membership of 2,000 and over 50 chapters in the state.[6] Their efforts and pressure lead to the first Chicano Studies program at California State College, Los Angeles.[7] By 1969, a Chicano Studies department is established at San Fernando State

College, (now California State University, Northridge) after students clash with the university administration. Similarly, MEChA-orchestrated student unrest and MAYA-led community activism from 1968 to 1972 results in the establishment of Chicano Studies at the University of Texas, El Paso (UTEP).

Some of these programs are more successful than others, for reasons shaped by their relationships with university administration, the quality of faculty and curriculum, and their relationship with the Chicano community. That Chicano Studies is a priority in academia, albeit a forced one, is evidenced by the development of programs across the country. Chicano Studies programs are established in California, New Mexico, Arizona, Texas, Colorado, and Washington. Chicano and Puerto Rican students help establish joint Chicano/Boriqua Studies programs in Indiana, Michigan, Illinois, Minnesota, and Iowa. Early Chicano Studies programs are still found at the University of Minnesota, the University of Wisconsin, and Michigan State University.[8]

A key moment in the development of Chicano Studies comes as a result of a three-day conference in Santa Barbara, California in April of 1969. The conference, according to Mario Barrera, is built upon the themes and goals discussed at the Denver Youth Leadership Conferences (1969 and 1970). The programs are a call to Mexican youth to organize their communities in order to liberate them through nationalism. Specifically, the resolutions call for political action, economic control of Chicano communities, and development of Chicano Studies programs. These resolutions include what came to be known as El Plan Espiritual de Aztlán (1968), composed by the poet Alurista, a manifesto that serves as a guide for cultural and political action, as well as, introducing the idea of Aztlán—a word that comes to reflect 'homeland:' The Southwest. The aim is to apply these goals on college campuses by developing a plan for Chicano higher education, which includes the development of a Chicano student movement. The essence of the Plan is communitarian and anti-assimilation.[9]

El Plan de Santa Bárbara, as the final document of the conference comes to be known, calls for the creation of Chicano Studies programs, sets forth curriculum approaches, and stresses the reinforcement of cultural heritage and the formation of a political community. While the plan recognizes that in elite-controlled institutions of higher education, Chicanos, who are attempting to gain access, face the reality of co-optation. While the Plan addresses such issues, how to deal with these realities is left unresolved.[10] In essence, it is left up to individual campuses to negotiate their academic presence. The document itself asserts that obtaining the American Dream is achieved at the cost of assimilation, while for the 'non-meltable,' it means a life of cheap labor. Thus the call is made for the self-determination of the community and the term Chicano[11] becomes the source of a new cultural identity.

From these perspectives, Chicano Studies comes to represent the Chicano community's aspirations revolving around higher education. The focus of El Plan de Santa Bárbara is a mandate to the university and college systems in California—although the directives become applicable to other areas as well. The directives call for 1) admission and recruitment of Chicano students, faculty, administrators and staff, 2) a curriculum program and academic major relevant to the Chicano cultural and historical experience, 3) support and tutorial programs, 4) research programs, 5) publication programs, and 6) community and cultural and social action centers.[12]

This also places Chicano Studies within the context of political change, which makes the link with the student movement. The resulting academic and community orientation became the cornerstone of Chicano Studies. However, the document does not define the curricula as either alternative to, or part of, the traditional university curriculum. Nor does it spell out the ideological direction other than that of "Chicanismo" or cultural nationalism. The developers of El Plan did not seem as concerned with changing the university as they apply its resources to the needs of the Chicano community.[13] Some Chicano scholars, however, come to believe a significant transformation of the mission, goals, and curricula of universities is essential, particularly those in regional institutions with a substantial Chicano population base, such as the University of Texas, El Paso (UTEP). These concerns lead to strategies bent on reforming the institution. For example, in the early 1970s, Tomás Arciniega, until recently, President of California State University, Bakersfield, and Norma Hernández, the first Chicana Dean of Education (at UTEP), begin to modify the sociocultural training of future teachers (National Teachers Corps), regional scholars, and the University's own faculty, with the scholarship developed by the Quinto Sol group in California. Marie Esman Barker initiates the first bilingual education program in El Paso, Texas and its concomitant teacher-training program at UTEP. Along with prominent area educators, her organizational efforts lead to the formation of the Southwest Association of Bilingual Education (SWABE), which later becomes the National Association of Bilingual Education (NABE). These efforts can be traced to the early and mid-1960s and include the seminal scholarship of Phillip D. Ortego, the first director of Chicano Studies at UTEP, who provides a voice from Texas on Chicanos. Whether discussing immigration, education, or the Chicano Movement, his essays are in line with the developments in California. Moreover, research by Thomas Carter at UTEP leads to one of the early publications on Chicano education.[14]

The focus on curricula by the authors of El Plan is on undergraduate education. It is to address the identity crisis of Mexican American youth through the teaching of Chicano culture and history and the development of Chicano activists who would return to the community.[15] The curriculum is viewed as a formal institutionalized and dynamic study of Chicano culture in all its diversity and unity; it is an academic examination of every facet of the Chicano experience—from language, education, literature, aesthetics and creative arts, philosophy, folklore, and ideology, to the objective conditions of its historical, social, cultural, psychological, political and economic socialization, development and existence. To this end, several dimensions to Chicano Studies exist: As an institutionalized discipline, it creates a body of critical and empirical knowledge. By utilizing multi-disciplinary approaches with a group of working practitioners in relation with one another, an emerging holistic portrait of the community's experience reflects not only past experience but also present realities, and also lays out a revolutionary strategy to change unequal conditions. In the words of José Cuellar, Chicano Studies "was originally conceived as a part of a people's struggle for equality and justice, and as a means to meet the growing need for accurate analysis of the strategic needs, progress, development, and self determination of the Mexican community in the United States."[16]

The Formation of a Discipline

Almost immediately, discussions arise regarding a Chicano paradigm reflecting a Chicano perspective of the world and based on new knowledge: Research needed to build a Chicano consciousness and research that would serve to liberate the Chicano community. The discussion of paradigm centers on a model contributing to the restoration of human dignity, leads to the socioeconomic transformation of the Chicano community, and contributes to the fullest potential of Chicano students. An important direction came from Octavio Romano, who publishes a series of important essays regarding the shortcomings of traditional social science, which casts a stereotyped and historically biased view of Chicanos. Romano's essays also become the foundation for the first stage of research in developing a Chicano paradigm. According to Romano, it is not just a question of Chicanos conducting social science, but rather introducing a "Chicano image" in social science. To do so, he suggests eight preliminary steps: 1) Chicanos are creators of social systems in their own right, having laid the foundation for cooperatives, mutual aid societies, and other examples; 2) Chicanos are participants in the historical process; 3) Chicanos have created social forms like dialects or music; 4) they have engaged in social issues such as the labor movement in the southwest and the struggle for bilingual education; 5) Chicanos are literate; having published over 500 newspapers in the southwest from 1848 through 1950; 6) Chicanos are capable of their own system of rationality; 7) intellectual ability has been part of the Chicano experience; and 8) the Chicano community has historically practiced and worked for an ecological balance within ecosystems.[17] This "image" then, becomes the foundation for research and deviated completely from traditional perspectives.

Two important journals also serve as outlets for this new research literature: the aforementioned *El Grito*, which begins publishing in 1967, and *Aztlán: A Chicano Journal of the Social Sciences and the Arts* (1970), based at the University of California, Los Angeles, strive to create more than mere critiques of social science, but also the formation of paradigms reflecting Chicano perspectives.[18] Eventually, this trend gives rise to Latino presses like the Bilingual Press and Arte Público Press and a federally funded clearinghouse on Mexican Americans sponsored by Educational Resources Information Center (ERIC). Established academic journals and university presses also begin to publish Chicano scholarship, gradually giving access to mainstream academia.

Just as important to the growth of Chicano Studies is the influence of the cultural renaissance taking place at the time. Armando Navarro writes:

> From 1967 to 1972 Chicano Student groups became increasingly supportive of Chicanismo. This cultural rebirth was predicated on Chicanos reconnecting to their Mexican roots. Rejecting assimilation and embracing cultural pluralism, Chicano students found pride, self-worth and greatness in their mestizo heritage. The spirit and symbolism of "indigenismo," the Mexican Revolution, La Raza Cósmica, and Che Guevara were echoed in their rhetoric, standards, and protest activities. The students embellished their vocabulary with nationalistic buzzwords, speaking of Maya, Toltec, Aztecs, Pancho Villa, the Magón brothers, Zapata, *Tierra y Libertad,* and Mestizo. Chicano Studies programs were by-products of the cultural renaissance. This was manifested in numerous courses that made-up the Chicano Studies curricula.[19]

One of the key areas in developing a Chicano paradigm comes from the social sciences. As more Chicanos earn doctorates, research and curriculum development come to illustrate this focus: History, labor history, sociology, politics, education, and anthropology are fields reflected in this early stage of work.[20] In time, research comes to take an even more diverse focus. Scholarship is published in folklore, literary criticism, biography, political economy, bilingualism, health, social services, economics, and music.[21]

The foundation of the Chicano Studies paradigm, an attempt to conceptualize and interpret the Chicano experience, begins with nationalistic perspectives that address concerns over identity and culture. In these early years, Chicano Studies passes through two very distinct phases: first, the Chicano image in the social sciences consists of critical reviews of the literature that assess social science work on the Chicano done by Anglo American social scientists. It is the starting point to the development of Chicano research and subsequent paradigm. The next stage is characterized by a collection of studies by Chicano scholars, particularly in the area of history. Most notable in this regard are the publications of *Occupied America* (1972) by Rodolfo Acuña, the essays of Juan Gómez-Quiñones addressing labor, culture and politics, and *Furia y Muerte (1973)* by Pedro Castillo and Alberto Camarillo. These publications reflect a revisionist approach to traditional historical interpretation. Another set of articles contains terms in their titles such as "Toward," "Tentative," and "Preliminary Remarks," which clearly reflect the early attempts at interpretation. Many of these revisionist interpretations also carry with them alternative theoretical approaches to Chicano research.[22]

By the early 1970s some Chicano scholars fall under the influence of Third World intellectuals such as Franz Fanon, Albert Memmi, and Pablo Casanova, who help develop the idea of their people as being "internally colonized;" the colonial experiences of Third World people made more sense to them than the traditional interpretations of the time. Those who assert this view include, Rodolfo Acuña, Carlos Muñoz, Mario Barrera, and Tomás Almaguer.[23]

By 1973, the internal colony analysis generates significant literature and, in many Chicano Studies programs, was the key paradigm for teaching and research—at least in the social sciences. At the same time, many scholars, including those who support the analysis, come to believe the internal colony model falls short. At a symposium at UCLA, it is agreed that in order to assure relevance of the model, "it should incorporate more aspects of Marxist analysis on colonialism." The internal colony model is an outgrowth of these movements and its purpose is to provide a theoretical framework for Chicano ideology. According to Carlos Muñoz:

> In the minds of the young movement scholars who developed it, internal colonialization had been meaningful not only as a concept that provided an alternative interpretation of the Mexican American experience more consistent with the historical and contemporary realities of a racist society, but also with the definition of the Chicano movement as a struggle for decolonialization and antiassimilation.[24]

Barrera comes to see the model as a form of dialogue, not as an absolute, however, there are those who come to view Marxist theory and class analysis as the major influence in understanding the Chicano experience, arguing that the internal colonial model is too deterministic and limited to the concept of racism, ignoring class experiences of Mexican oppression in U.S. capitalist society. Still others feel class analysis should be incorporated into the internal colonial model or rejected altogether. In the end, the internal colonial is viewed as limiting, because the oppression of Chicanos is based on a "legacy of colonialism," thus, Chicanos are, a postcolonial society.[25]

Originally, the basic premise of the Chicano paradigm is one that rejects: 1) explanations of the Chicano condition solely on the basis of genetics or cultural determinism; 2) romanticized descriptions of the Chicano; and, 3) use of improper and unethical research procedures in the process of developing a body of critical and empirical knowledge and data grounded in social reality. It accepts explanations based on theories of relationships between conditions of individuals in communities of Mexican descent and the economic, political, socio-cultural, and historical forces that mold and serve as their environments.[26]

Now, the paradigm of the internal colony becomes too narrow, deterministic and unsatisfactory. By the end of the 1970s new paradigms take hold. In the meantime, researchers move along the lines of their own disciplines creating a multi-disciplinary body of literature. One study suggests social science and literary output are connected in spirit to the goals of Chicano Studies.

> Each component of this creative explosion is related to all of the others in two ways. First, each negates the assumptions made by Anglo writers that Chicanos have not made and will not or cannot make significant contributions to American social, cultural and intellectual life. Second, each is part of the Chicano's efforts to define their own reality.[27]

The interdisciplinary and comparative focus helps to define the uniqueness of Chicano Studies. While Chicano social scientists emphasize the internal colony model, course offerings cover a wide range of topics. While the notion of cultural, social, and ideological awareness reflects the academic examination called for by El Plan de Santa Bárbara, there is little done to explain what one would do with a degree in Chicano Studies. Perhaps because of the activist orientation of the day, it may have been assumed that graduates would automatically return to the community. Regardless of the campus, curriculum approaches are interdisciplinary utilizing the social sciences, humanities, education, the arts, as well as, a bilingual focus to analyze the experience of Chicanos. On many campuses, such as California State University, Northridge, the curriculum also emphasizes communication skills—writing, critical thinking, research, and public speaking. Spanish language courses are geared for the first time to Chicano students. Students are also encouraged to double-major in order to make the most of their professional interests. Finally, Operation Chicano Teacher (OCT), a partnership between the School of Education and Chicano Studies, is a commitment to develop a cadre of strong bilingual Chicano teachers of Southern California schools. At the University of Texas, El Paso, in addition to a double-major option, academic minors, special academic areas of concentration, and leadership development programs are eventually developed to meet the needs of prospective social workers, educators, pre-law students, and students interested in graduate school.

Moreover, a necessity in bringing scholars and students together to discuss the many issues facing Chicano Studies lead to the creation of the National Association for Chicana/o Studies (NACCS) in 1974. Later, Chicana feminists help create Mujeres Activistas en Letras y Cambio Social (MALCS). These organizations sponsor annual conferences, help to create partnerships among Chicano researchers, and share the latest research and advocate support for Chicano Studies.[28]

Issues and Contribution in Chicano Studies

Into the late 1970s, issues surface that bring forth questions about the directions of Chicano Studies programs. One flaw surfaces when Chicana feminists raise the issue of male domination. According to Cynthia Orozco, Chicanas are being undermined; "Chicano intellectuals argued that race and class were the determining factors in understanding the subordinate position of Mexicans in the United States," but in the literature or in academic programs, women are nonexistent.[29] Orozco also criticizes El Plan de Santa Bárbara for its lack of relevance to women in Chicano Studies. Specifically, El Plan lacks mention of courses on Chicana Studies or awareness of sexism and the importance of gender.[30] As Alma García argues, Chicanas need to be a vital component of a Chicano Studies program, not a last minute discussion. Chicano scholars need to develop a consciousness about the elusiveness of Chicanas in the discipline.[31] García also points out that while courses on La Chicana developed throughout the seventies and eighties, providing a framework for the study of Chicanas in U.S. society, in many cases courses fall short due to a lack of gender analysis in Chicano Studies, "which focuses on the structure of patriarchy as a form of oppression affecting Chicanas as women."[32]

Teresa Córdova writes that to counteract the flaws in gender curriculum within Chicano Studies, gender must be placed as a central component in the study of the community, we must study the diversity of sexuality in the community, challenge patriarchy within and outside of the Chicano community, and support the pursuit of Chicana dreams and aspirations.[33]

Another set of issues revolves around the reassessment of El Plan de Santa Bárbara, "not because of any fundamental inadequacy in the principles, but because of the doubt that exists within our movement concerning their applicability to Chicano Studies today."[34] Despite the soundness of the principles they fall into disuse for three reasons: 1) the co-optation of Chicano Studies programs; 2) the sell-out of Chicano faculty to the world of academia, and 3) the contested value of Chicano nationalism as a driving force in Chicano Studies. The intent is to regenerate the founding principles of Chicano Studies—the necessity of self-determination, the link between Chicano Studies and the Chicano community, and the role of education in training students and developing plans, policies, and strategies to meet the needs of the community.

Ironically, years earlier, Juan Gómez-Quiñones outlines the very dilemmas hindering the success of Chicano Studies that remains evident today: The teaching and research objectives found in El Plan de Santa Bárbara are based on cultural resistance and social change; counter to what the university does.[35]

With the advent of the twenty-first century, concern over the preparation of a new generation of Chicano scholars begins to arise. While many of us enter graduate school pursuing our academic and intellectual interests, we do so because graduate programs in Chicano Studies do not exist. There is no choice. The strength of Chicano Studies is found in its teaching components at the undergraduate level. Whether at two-year institutions, state universities or research institutions, Chicano Studies exists in some form but always at the undergraduate level. According to Rodolfo Acuña (1998):

> The discipline itself is divided into teaching and research fields. The teaching field is much more developed than the research field, partly because research fields evolve from teaching fields and partly because of the failure of research institutions to initiate doctoral programs in Chicana/o Studies.[36]

The result of this trend is the appointment of Chicano faculty to joint positions, where the home department is based on the doctoral degree (history, sociology, etc.) and then splits time with Chicano Studies. In these situations, Chicano faculty are paid from the home department, get tenure in the home department, and in those cases where Chicano Studies programs close their doors due to political and financial reasons, faculty return to full-time teaching in the home department. In these cases, there is no commitment to Chicano Studies and research in the field is not fully developed.

A related trend currently found on some campuses reveals an attempt to develop policy where faculty must teach in departments where they earned their doctorates. If a Chicano faculty member with a doctorate in Education—so the policy goes—is teaching in Chicano Studies, such a policy could force the faculty member to abandon Chicano Studies and by virtue of their highest degree, thus find himself or herself teaching in an education department. It could also mean the end of Chicano Studies. It is a double-edged sword: How can one get a doctorate in Chicano Studies when research institutions do not develop graduate programs to train new faculty in this field? While doctorates in Ethnic Studies have become one alternative, these programs do not always focus on Chicano Studies, but rather on mastering key concepts in Ethnic Studies that can later be applied to the study of different ethnic groups.

Still, Chicano Studies is making important contributions to higher education. As the demographics of the Southwest continue to change, access to higher education remains a key issue for local communities. This point is explicit in El Plan de Santa Bárbara. By the late 1980s, Chicano Studies accomplishes the following: Maximizes the presence of Mexican American students, faculty, and administrative personnel; participates in the development of professionals—from teachers to lawyers to community workers to counselors; initiates the development of Chicano intellectuals; promotes an increase of knowledge in all fields from which ideological ideas, critiques, and empirical knowledge shapes perspectives and community action, and perhaps most importantly, placed in the context of a larger historical process, promotes the political and intellectual development of an oppressed working class.[37] Finally, Chicano Studies reaches the position of a serious "area study," as evidenced by the interest of international scholars from Europe, not to mention Mexico.[38]

Moreover, the presence of Chicano Studies Research centers is also important. These programs provide faculty with a vehicle for conducting research, providing funding and a location where researchers can concentrate on their work. Undergraduates can also benefit through internships, which can be a source of income and gaining much needed experience in research and program coordination. Centers at University of California, Los Angeles, University of California, Santa Barbara, Arizona State University, University of Texas, Houston, and University of Texas, Austin, among others, provide a strong base for Chicano Studies research.

Looking to the Future

The 1980s and 1990s are a period of survival and resurgence for Chicano Studies. Some programs in California are shut down completely or decimated by university administrations. But as Chicana feminists challenge the first stage of research, the factors of race, class, gender, sexual orientation and geographic location, they force a modification in interpretation of Chicano history and culture. It is a direct challenge to the "us vs. them" paradigm. These factors of diversity lead to the utilization of new alternative theories. This is evident in the use of 'Chicana/o'—an indication of gender recognition and the minimizing of patriarchal perspectives.

As we move into the twenty-first century, Chicana/o scholars have turned to theories such as cultural studies, postmodern theory, ethnographic, Marxist, and postcolonial. There is even a return to the internal colony model and many researchers concerned with higher education are using the notion of academic colonialism as a means of analyzing the experience of Chicana/o faculty. One outgrowth of these alternate approaches can be found in Border Studies, an approach that examines the often exciting and contradictory world of life 'on the line,' as

well as a method of analysis, which theoretically offers new investigations and metaphors while explaining the world of the border.[39] Those who focus on this approach concern themselves with cultural, social and political events as they play out at a transnational level. These and many other approaches demonstrate that Chicanas/os are not a homogeneous community as once assumed. The diversity of this group provides ample space and exciting time for investigating the ever-changing social and cultural climate of the Mexican-origin community.

In addition, the demographic surge of the Latino population in general brings a renewed interest in Chicana/o Studies. Enrollment doubles on some campuses, large numbers of Anglo students begin taking courses, and most importantly, Chicano faculty and students renew a commitment to the ideals of El Plan de Santa Bárbara. Texas scholar Tatcho Mindiola, commenting on the status of Chicana/o Studies at the end of the 1980s, claimed: "we've institutionalized our courses and wrested control over what is said about us."[40]

In recent years we have begun to see the development of graduate programs in Chicana/o Studies. This trend will help establish a group of scholars trained in the field, be able to land appointments in centers and departments, as well as carry out their research in their areas of training. This will also help the teaching process. Already, for example, one can enroll in master's programs in Chicano Studies at the following institutions: California State University, Northridge, San Jose State University, San Diego State University, and the University of Arizona. In 2003, a master's and doctoral program in Chicana/o Studies is established at the University of California, Santa Bárbara.

In a recent development, the Texas Legislature establishes a policy that would allow any two or four-year institution to create a program in Chicana/o Studies. Depending on the institution and the commitment to such a program, we are already beginning to see these developments.

And so, as you read the following pages, consider how Chicana/o Studies is the product of its times, specifically, the product of student activism. In its almost four decades of existence, the issues and problems confronting Chicana/o Studies do not destroy its mission. And though problems remain, Chicana/o Studies carries on: At times, in traditional academic fashion, in others, with a clear scholar/activist orientation.

The essays herein reflect a Chicana/o Studies perspective. The research reflects current situations or conditions with implications for Chicana/o Studies. Characterized by a diversity of perspective, approaches and theoretical frameworks, the collection strives to capture the cornucopia of perspectives—although we as editors recognize it is by no means complete. The information herein is relevant not just to the historian but to those entering the private sector or the human service professions—social work, education, and the non-profit sector. It can also be useful to individuals in policy-making positions.

A Note on Research

The articles and essays that comprise this anthology reflect perspectives in Chicana/o Studies research. Historically, these approaches have been opposed to traditional mainstream perspectives. And since Chicana/o Studies has always been interdisciplinary in scope, it may help to briefly mention some of these areas of research that make up this anthology, thereby giving the reader a better sense of the nature of scholarship and the curriculum.

Chicana/o Studies is comprised of dominant subfields of research, each with its thematic areas. This anthology addresses seven of the nine dominant fields of research as compiled by Macías.[41] These fields and their areas of work included herein are: Political Economy (labor, history, demography, migration, and politics); Social and cultural studies (change, tradition and folklore, social organization, and community studies); Critical semiotics (literature studies); Gender (Chicana feminism); Institutional impact and participation studies (schooling and health); Cultural production (painting, art and its mural dimension, film, literature, and music); and Space and location (environmental racism and justice, and the border). Macías states: "These nine sub-fields are not mutually exclusive, nor are the types of studies identified within each one. There is no single, reigning, dominant theory driving the field at the moment. Chicana and Chicano Studies is a broad area of study *qua* discipline."

Carlos F. Ortega
Chicano Studies Program
University of Texas, El Paso

Endnotes

1. Carlos Muñoz, Jr., *Youth, Identity, Power: The Chicano Movement* (New York: Verso Press, 1989) 127–128.
2. Muñoz, 130.
3. Carlos Muñoz, Jr., "The Development of Chicano Studies, 1968–1981," *Chicano Studies: A Multidisciplinary Approach*, eds. Eugene E. García, Francisco Lomelí, and Isidro D. Ortiz (New York: Teachers College Press, 1984) 5.
4. Muñoz , *Development* 9.
5. Muñoz, *Development* 9.
6. Juan Gómez-Quiñones, *Mexican Students Por La Raza: The Chicano Student Movement in Southern California, 1967–1977* (Santa Barbara: Editorial La Causa, 1978) 5.
7. Armando Navarro, *Mexican American Youth Organization: Avant Garde of the Chicano Movement in Texas* (Austin: University of Texas Press, 1995) 59–60.
8. Rodolfo Acuña, *Occupied America*. 4th ed. (New York: Longman, 2000) 414–417.
9. Mario Barrera, *Beyond Aztlán: Ethnic Autonomy in Comparative Perspective* (New York: Praeger Publishers, 1988) 42.
10. Barrera, 42–44.
11. The term 'Chicano' has always been a topic of controversy, but to some extent, this was quelled in the 1980s when the term was used interchangeably with Mexican American and vice versa. At the time of El Plan de Santa Bárbara, 'Chicano' had a specific meaning to those who identified with the term. In a seminal paper published one month after the Santa Barbara conference, Ysidro Ramón Macías characterized a Chicano as someone with a high degree of self respect, "because this individual accepts his Mexican culture and languages;" the individual had a sense of responsibility to Chicano communities, which in part was due to the rejection of the Puritan ethic of self improvement; that is, the Chicano did not reject the idea of self improvement rather the idea of self absorption and individualism. Finally, being a Chicano meant the continued maintenance and enrichment of one's Mexican heritage. See, Ysidro Ramón Macías, "Evolution of the Mind: a Plan for Political Action," *El Pocho Che*, May, 1969 (mimeo copy).
12. Chicano Coordinating Council in Higher Education, *El Plan de Santa Bárbara* (Santa Barbara: La Causa Publications, 1970) 9–10. See also, Juan Gómez-Quiñones, "To Leave to Hope or Chance," *Parameters of Institutional Change* (eds.), Southwest Network (Hayward: Southwest Network, 1974) 154–56.
13. Muñoz, *Development* 10–14.
14. Phillip D. Ortego, "The Mexican-Dixon Line," *El Grito* 1 (4) (1963) 29–31; "Moctezuma's Children," *El Grito* 3(3) (1970) 38–50; and "Chicano Renaissance," *Social Casework* 52 (1971). See, Thomas Carter, *Mexican Americans in School: A History of Educational Neglect* (New York: College Entrance Examination Board, 1970).
15. Muñoz, *Youth* 141.
16. José Cuellar, no title, no date, 8–9 (mimeo copy).
17. Octavio Romano, "Social Science, Objectivity, and the Chicano," *El Grito* 4 (1) (1970). The writings most often mentioned in Chicano critiques of social science include, but are not limited to: Munro Edmonson, *Los Manitos: A Study of Institutional Values* (New Orleans: Middle American Research Institute/Tulane University, 1957); Celia Heller, *Mexican American Youth: Forgotten Youth at the Crossroads* (New York: Random House, 1968); Florence R. Kluckhohn and Fred L. Strodbeck, *Variations in Value Orientations* (New York: Row, Peterson, and Co., 1961); and William Madsen, *Mexican Americans of South Texas* (New York: Holt, Rinehart, and Winston, 1964).
18. Muñoz, *Youth* 143–146.
19. Navarro, *Mexican* 71–72.
20. See, Isidro D. Ortiz, (ed.), *Chicanos and the Social Sciences: A Decade of Research and Development (1970–1980)* (Santa Barbara: Center for Chicano Studies/University of California, Santa Barbara, 1983).
21. Ricardo Romo and Raymund Paredes, eds. *New Directions in Chicano Scholarship* (La Jolla: Chicano Studies Program/University of California, San Diego, 1978).
22. Tomás Almaguer, "Interpreting Chicano History: The World Systems Approach to 19th Century California" Working Papers Series # 101, Institute for the Study of Social Change/University of California, Berkeley, 1977.
23. Muñoz, *Youth* 146–48.
24. Muñoz, *Youth* 153.
25. Muñoz, Youth 154; Fred A. Cervantes, "Chicanos as a Postcolonial Minority: Some Questions Concerning the Adequacy of the Paradigm of Internal Colonialism," *Perspectivas en Chicano Studies*, ed. Reynaldo Flores Macias (Los Angeles: Chicano Studies Center/University of California, Los Angeles, 1977) 123–35.
26. Cuellar 11–12.
27. Rudolph de la Garza and Rowena Rivera, "The Socio-Political World of the Chicano: A Comparative Analysis of Social Scientific and Literary Perspectives," *Minority Language and Literature: Retrospective and Perspective*, (ed.) Dexter Fisher (New York: Modern Language Association of America, 1977) 43.
28. Teresa Córdova, "Agency, Commitment and Connection: Embracing the Roots of Chicano and Chicana Studies," *International Journal of Qualitative Studies in Education* 18 (2) (2005): 221–33.
29. Cynthia Orozco, "Sexism in Chicano Studies and the Community," *Chicana Voices: Intersections of Race, Class, and Gender*, (eds.) Teresa Córdova, Norma Cantú, Gilberto Cárdenas, Juan García, and Christine M. Sierra (Austin: Center for Mexican American Studies/University of Texas, Austin, 1986) 12.
30. Orozco 13.
31. Alma García, "Studying Chicanas: Bringing Women into the Frame of Chicano Studies," *Chicana Voices*, 25–26. Also see the essays by Driscoll and Chabrán in the same volume.
32. García 13.
33. Reynaldo Flores Macías, "El Grito en Aztlán: Voice and Presence in Chicana/o Studies," *International Journal of Qualitative Studies in Education* 18 (2) (2005): 174.

34. René Núñez and Raoúl Contreras, "Principles and Foundations of Chicano Studies: Chicano Organizations on University Campuses in California," *Chicano Discourse* (eds.), Tatcho Mindiola and Emilio Zamora (Cheney: National Association for Chicano Studies, 1992) 32.

35. Gómez-Quiñones 173.

36. Rodolfo Acuña, *Sometimes There Is No Other Side* (Notre Dame: University of Notre Dame Press, 1998) 104.

37. Muñoz, *Youth* 165–67; Gomez-Quiñones, 158–59.

38. For example, in Germany, there is the work of Wolfgang Binder and Gustave Blanke; in Italy, Lia Tessarolo; in Poland, Herner Bus; in France, Genevieve Fabre, Yves-Charles Grandjeat and Marcienne Rocard; and in Hungary, Laszlo Scholz. See Renate von Bardeleben, Dietrich Briesmeister, and Juan Bruce-Novoa, (eds.) *Missions in Conflict* (Tubingen: Gunter Narr Verlag, 1988).

39. See, for example, Gloria Anzaldúa, *Borderlands: the New Mestiza* (Aunt Lute Books, 1987); Carl Guitiérrez Jones, *Rethinking the Borderlands: Between Chicano Culture and Legal Discourse* (Berkeley: University of California Press, 1995); Carlos G. Vélez-Ibáñez, *Border Visions* (Tucson: University of Arizona Press, 1996); and Jose David Saldívar, *Border Matters: Remapping American Cultural Studies* (Berkeley: University of California Press, 1997).

40. Karen Winkler, "Scholars Say Issues of Diversity Have Revolutionized Field of Chicano Studies," *Chronicle of Higher Education* 26 Sept. 1990: A1.

41. Macías 179–81.

Historical Perspectives

I t has often been said that people without knowledge of their roots are usually people without a sense of direction. People who do not know where they come from often do not know where they are going. Without a sound basis of their origins, rootless people find it harder to incorporate into their society. These insights were at the root of Chicano history during its infancy and provided a guide to the perspectives, methods, and conclusions in the late sixties. Today, these insights are still important but Chicano history has matured and the insights are more important than ever. In this section, an understanding of the history and heritage of the Chicano is a prerequisite for learning about the contemporary dimensions of the group and its future in American society.

Due to space limitations, the historical period preceding the annexation of the Southwest by the United States is not included. However, the reader is strongly encouraged to explore that historical period, which dates back to the Pre-Columbian period, via the readings and audio-visual resources suggested at the end of this section. In addition, most universities offer courses that specialize in certain segments or dimensions of relevance to the Chicano (The Mexican Revolution, the Borderlands, etc.) that would enhance the reader's background on the Chicano experience.

Of the six essays that comprise this section, two are new and overall, offer basic foundations for the study of Chicano history and at the same time provide specific examination of these experiences. The section is initiated by Gilbert González and Raúl Fernández who discuss migration to the United States from a new interpretive framework: Using the concept of 'empire', they conclude that Mexico's economy, controlled by the United States and other foreign powers, has created a state of affairs that has historically bled the rural areas of any form of stability and thus forcing individuals and families to head north to the U.S. Given the numerous debates surrounding immigration, this essay will provide students with insightful arguments regarding migration. This essay is followed by Griswold del Castillo's insights on the Treaty of Guadalupe Hidalgo and its implications for the Chicano Movement. The importance of this piece is that it links the Treaty to contemporary issues and restores the document's relevance to the present-day.

The next four essays provide information on community studies related to El Paso. Mary Romero extends this analysis by exploring the events leading to the confrontation between an Anglo "entrepreneur" and the Mexican "salineros" near El Paso, Texas. She examines both sides of the story in order to determine if this event was a mob action or a political struggle. The essay by Mario T. García, "Border Culture," focuses on the El Paso-Ciudad Juárez borderlands and how Chicanos survived and evolved in a region of political and cultural confluence. Vicki Ruiz examines how Chicanos living in the Segundo Barrio of El Paso were also able to adjust and organize their lives in ways that enabled them to survive a period when they were essentially segregated from the rest of the city's social, political, and cultural life. Finally, Laurie Coyle and her colleagues examine an important organized labor history milestone in the Southwest, one that, to this day, reverberates among El Paso's residents: The Farah Strike.

Empire and the Origins of Twentieth-Century Migration from Mexico to the United States

Gilbert G. González and Raúl A. Fernández

In this chapter we show how the twentieth-century appearance of a Chicano minority population originated from the subordination of the nation of Mexico to U.S. economic and political interests. We argue that, far from being marginal to the course of modern U.S. history, the Chicano minority, an immigrant people, stand both at the center of that history and of a process of imperial expansionism that originated in the last three decades of the nineteenth century and that continues today.

Several observations that challenge conventional interpretations of Mexican migration and of the Chicano experience derive from this approach. This century-long exodus of Mexicans to the United States has often been perceived as an "American" problem, affecting welfare, education, culture, crime, drugs, budgets, and so on, and solved through get-tough measures ranging from California's Proposition 187 to softer views such as those taken by immigrant rights agencies. In contrast, we take the position that migration is a Mexican national crisis. We argue that migration reflects Mexico's economic subordination in the face of U.S. hegemony and of the limitations placed on its national sovereignty by that domination. A century of mass border crossings signifies the breaking apart of the social fabric of the Mexican nation and its resettlement in enclaves across the United States as a national minority. Finally, the story of U.S. domination of Mexico dates to the last three decades of the nineteenth century.

The sociopolitical repercussions of this subordination were enormous. Domination of a new type by the United States increasingly undermined the social and political cohesion of Mexico, causing dislocation to its domestic agriculture and industry as well as migration to the United States-Mexico border and to the United States itself. In

his 1911 classic exposé *Barbarous Mexico,* John Kenneth Turner addressed the dismantling of the Mexican nation. "The partnership of Díaz and American capital," he argued, "has wrecked Mexico as a national entity. The United States government, as long as it represents American capital . . . will have a deciding voice in Mexican affairs."[1] Washington preferred economic domination by U.S. corporations to the direct annexation of Mexico. As John Mason Hart has persuasively demonstrated, U.S. capital realized that policy objective and reigned supreme in the Mexican economy by the late nineteenth century.[2] Mexico became the first foreign country to fall under the incipient imperial umbrella of the United States.

The practice of territorial conquest and expansion in pursuit of, or as a consequence of, commercial developments is very old; from the Romans to the Aztecs to nineteenth-century Britain, this characteristic is shared by nearly every imperial power in the history of the world. Over the past hundred-plus years, however, the United States, along with other global powers, developed an empire of a new type, a transnational mode of economic domination similar to yet different in important respects from previous imperial regimes.

While the United States has throughout its history engaged in numerous acts of territorial aggression and conquest—like other historical centers of power—its particular mode of empire building and maintenance emerged when the growth of large corporations and financial institutions included their direct involvement in alliance with local elites with the formally independent economies and politics of other countries. Simultaneously, these large conglomerates of finance and production had come to effectively dominate the government of the United States and freely used the power of the state to jockey for position with other world powers. The new twist in the practice of empire construction and management was aptly captured by the late U.S. secretary of state John Foster Dulles—who was directly involved in U.S. aggression against Guatemala and Iran in the 1950s—when he stated that "there [are] two ways of dominating a foreign nation:

Gilbert G. González, Raúl Fernández, "Empire and the Origins of Twentieth-Century Migration from Mexico to the United States," *Pacific Historical Review*, Vol. 71, No. 1: 19–57. © 2002, The Pacific Coast Branch, American Historical Association. Used by permission. All rights reserved.

invading it militarily or controlling it financially."[3] In the case of Mexico, U.S. policy preferred financial control over military options.

Mexico and the U.S. Model of Empire Building

A transnational mode of imperial hegemony defined U.S. relations with the rest of the world throughout the twentieth century. Mexico provided the first testing ground. The United States first began to engage new mechanisms of empire in the late 1870s, when it became the senior partner in an alliance with the local Mexican elite personified in the figure of dictator Porfirio Díaz. Using a governmental threat of military intervention, large U.S. capital interests invested heavily in the construction of railroads in Mexico. The initial intrusions were quickly followed by massive investments in mining, especially copper, cattle farming, and cotton production. After Mexico, the United States would move swiftly to establish economic control and political influence over the rest of the continent, turning the landmass into its backyard. The United States launched the War of 1898 for a variety of motives: to make sure that no sovereign and independent nation appeared in Cuba upon the defeat of the Spanish empire; to establish a military presence guaranteeing the security of its investments while denying it to others; and to establish strategic outposts to secure and control commerce and investments in the Caribbean and in East Asia. U.S. political leaders defended the war with the rhetoric of providing support for the underdog—as in the case of recent interventions in Somalia, Bosnia, and Iraq—a rationale to allay public unease over war and to manipulate public opinion. The War of 1898 was followed quickly by the U.S.-supported secession of the province of Panama from Colombia, ensuring U.S. control of interoceanic trade. At the same time, large U.S. investments took place via the company town model in agriculture, railroad construction, and mining in Mexico and Cuba.[4]

The investment of U.S.-based corporations in Latin America, beginning at the turn of the twentieth century, in cooperation with archaic land-based elites and bolstered by the U.S. military and the threat of annexation, would transform the hemisphere into a series of neocolonial republics. Mexico became something of a laboratory for the imperial experiments; few events of significance in the history of twentieth-century Mexico were not decisively influenced by the power of United States economic, political, and, as a last recourse, military intrusion.[5] A few examples will suffice: the United States played a determining role in the outcome of the 1910 Mexican Revolution; after World War II the United States provided the money, propaganda, and logistics to control the labor and social movements in which the ideas of socialism were taking root not only in Mexico but throughout Latin

America.[6] In the 1990s the United States established NAFTA to further secure its investments in Mexico and to restrict the use of that country for investments by its competitors. The freedom and security of U.S. capital remained a constant in U.S. policy toward Mexico in the twentieth century.

The establishment of U.S. imperial hegemony over Mexico and later Latin America at about the turn of the twentieth century has long been acknowledged in Latin America as central to local histories and identity. From the 1880s to the 1930s major Mexican and Latin American thinkers, including Vasconcelos, Martí, Rodó, de Hostos, and others, placed U.S. presence in Latin America as central to their essays on Latin America's future. The profound public awareness of the United States that pervades the lives, history, politics, and economics of Latin American countries is not matched by a parallel knowledge in the United States of its southern neighbors. In the academy, official U.S. historiography dates national emergence into the global scene with World War I, privileging U.S. activity in Europe over the decades of investment, interference, and invasions into Mexico and other southern neighbors. As a subset of official U.S. history, the study of the Chicano national minority has largely been constructed in an atmosphere in which "race matters," and culture, too, but empire does not. Insofar as the U.S. transnational mode of hegemony is acknowledged, it is not seen as essential, or even related, to understanding the origins and development of the Chicano national minority.[7]

The Push-Pull Thesis: The "Official" Line on Mexican Migration

The academic wisdom on Mexican migration to the United States established—since the first decade of the twentieth century—one basic theoretical construct: the push-pull thesis modeled upon conventional supply and demand economics. The thesis reduced the causes to sets of conditions within the sending country and the host country, conditions that *functioned independently* of each other. In one country a push (supply), or too many people and too few resources, motivated people to consider a significant move; in the other country a pull (demand), usually a shortage of labor, operated to attract the disaffected. In tandem they synergistically led to transnational migration.

Following the political militancy and cultural nationalism of the late 1960s, numerous studies focused great attention on the origins of the Mexican population in the United States. The Chicano theme aroused the interest not only of the Chicano activists but also of academics attracted to the issues raised by the regional political rebellion. Inevitably, immigration struck a chord among nearly everyone involved and became a major topic of discussion in the burgeoning field of Chicano studies. As the Chicano studies, research agenda matured, immigration, particularly in the 1900–1930 period, held a central place in many studies.[8] The original push-pull thesis as enunciated by the U. S. Industrial Commission on Immigration in 1901, repeated by Victor S. Clark in 1908, and Manuel Gamio and Paul S. Taylor in the early 1930s, became an article of faith among the new generation of academics destined to dominate the field to the end of the century.[9]

Many, if not most, academics simply made the 1910 Revolution the principal push factor operating in the 1900–1930 era.[10] Consequently, when in the late 1960s the UCLA Mexican-American Study Project engaged the question of immigration, the theoretical scenario had been set and the authors followed conventional wisdom: "The Mexican revolutionary period beginning in 1909–1910 spurred the first substantial and permanent migration to the United States. . . . By liberating masses of people from social as well as geographic immobility, [the Revolution] served to activate a latent migration potential of vast dimensions."[11]

To be sure, not every research study repeated previous studies verbatim. Research projects often emphasized particular conditions that modified the form in which push-pull would manifest. There *were* variations on the theme. A number of authors viewed the policies of Porfirio Díaz as similar if not parallel to the European elites' expropriation of peasants' lands and the simultaneous depeasanting of the countryside. Some see the extension of railroads throughout the nations as the key element that made migration possible. For others, the devastation of the 1910 Revolution and its aftermath precipitated the 1900–1930 migrations. A survey of the more significant studies of the past twenty years reveals the identification of a collage of factors that propel migration; seldom is the push viewed as the result of one factor alone. Currently, most students of Mexican migration and border studies agree that a complex of "push" factors operated at various times to create the conditions leading to Mexican migration over the course of the twentieth century.[12]

But regardless of the number of factors included in the push, the varying emphases, and the interrelations of factors within the push side of the equation, the crux for explaining Mexican migration during the 1900–1930 period focuses on a series of conditions exclusive to Mexico. Some authors point to Porfirian economic policies as the major push agent; others identify the Porfirian era as one that kept peasants tied to the land and subject to the power of hacendados. Beyond that, whether it was Porfirio Díaz's land policies or the 1910 Revolution, or both, that created the push, the consequences of either one comprised the immediate supply conditions leading to migration: low wages, unemployment, poverty, or political oppression. The "pull" factors—high wages and labor demand in the United States—are taken as givens.

In about 1970 the push-pull thesis came under widespread critical scrutiny, resulting in some modification but primarily refinement, rather than substantial overhaul. Condemned as a neoclassical artifact, the push-pull thesis was ostensibly supplanted by a coterie of theoretical approaches to explain Mexican migration. The new paradigms—social capital theory, segmented market theory, new economics theory, and world systems theory—challenged push-pull. The first three contend that the old economic categories—wages, poverty, surplus population, and unemployment—inadequately explain the "push" of Mexican migration, particularly the long-term trends appearing since roughly 1970. World systems theory, on the other hand, contends that global capitalism reaching into the remotest corners of Mexico uprooted peasants from land and caused unemployment; both conditions drive migration. In spite of the constant disclaimer that push-pull can no longer explain migration, we shall argue below that the basic premises that comprised push-pull have not been completely uprooted by these modifications.

One is immediately struck by the longevity of that theoretical "model" first developed by government officials to interpret European immigration to the United States in the late nineteenth century. With some modifications, push-pull has been utilized throughout the twentieth century. Applied to the Mexican case soon after the rising border crossings during the early 1900s, the push-pull thesis survives to this day in altered form as the nearly exclusive theoretical design for understanding Mexican migration.

Most analysts of migration seem to view the "push" factors—Porfirian policies, the 1910 revolution, wages, surplus population, and so forth—as operating independently of the economic power of the United States. Implicit in the argument is the contention that an autonomous modernization process, not unlike that which occurred in Europe, led to Mexican migration to the United States. In short, older versions and modern variations of push-pull inherently presume that Mexican migration—from 1900 to the present—followed from independently stimulated economic progress in Mexico. Largely absent in discussions of migration are two questions: Is it appropriate to conflate all migrations into a single "one size fits all" paradigm? And if the forces of supply and demand work to eliminate economic disequilibria, why has there been an apparent permanent disequilibrium that no amount of migration from Mexico (or modernization therein) has been able to root out and that remains in effect after one hundred years?[13]

Economic Conquest: Porfirian Mexico, 1880–1910

A critical examination of the push side of the thesis requires that we analyze the economic policies carried out by the Mexican government in the 1880–1910 period and their social consequences. To investigate the origins of this migration flow from Mexico to the United States it is necessary to take another look at four processes at work in Mexico in the latter part of the nineteenth century: first, the building of Mexico's railroads by U.S. companies; second, the investment of U.S. capital in mining and smelting; third, the effects of the above modernization projects on Mexico's agriculture; and fourth, the displacement of large segments of Mexico's peasant population as a consequence of the foreign-inspired modernization.

We intend to show that foreign monopolistic economic interests—not the much-vaunted *científicos*—were the principal architects of the policies implemented by the administrations of Porfirio Díaz, and that these policies resulted in the subjection of Mexico to foreign economic domination. It was a domination of a new type: a transnational mode of economic colonialism. While Porfirian policies forcibly removed peasants from ancestral village lands, it would be wrong to assume that these were policies wholly designed in Mexico City. Like the construction of railroads, oil exploration and exploitation, mining, and agricultural investments by foreign capital, the removal of peasants from village lands emanated from the integration and exploitation of Mexican natural resources into foreign, primarily U.S., industrial production.

Not only its southern neighbor, but also all of Latin America fell under the gaze of U.S. foreign policy at the end of the nineteenth century. Mexico, it was believed, was the doorway to all of Latin America's riches, but only if the neighbor remained under U.S. economic tutelage. U.S. policy essentially followed the dictum of no less a patron of imperialism than Cecil Rhodes, who envisioned Mexico as the material fountain of empire. "Mexico," he once said, "is the treasure house from which will come the gold, silver, copper, and precious stones that will build the empires of tomorrow, and will make the future cities of the world veritable Jerusalems."[14] The United States changed the plural "empires" to the singular "empire."

The victory of the U.S. Union armies in 1865 failed to deter the cry for "all of Mexico" that lingered in the minds of adventurous entrepreneurs and their supporters in the U.S. Congress. In 1868 a spate of articles in the *New York Herald* and other metropolitan newspapers called on the United States to establish "a protectorate over Mexico." Voices of opposition to such a policy were heard; not all were enthralled by the easy victories of 1848 and the imagined expansion to the isthmus. Antiannexationists responded with an economic alternative free of any humanitarian impulses. William S. Rosecrans, speculator and promoter in Mexican railroads, while serving as minister to Mexico anticipated future U.S. policy toward Mexico in his response to the newspaper articles. Rosecrans urged that Americans abandon the notion of "all of Mexico." "Pushing American enterprise up to, and within Mexico wherever it can profitably go," he claimed, "will give us advantages which force and money alone would hardly

procure. It would give us a peaceful conquest of the country."[15]

Rosecrans was not alone in contemplating a "peaceful conquest"; a number of his contemporaries engaged the discussion as to whether U.S. economic interests required annexation. One prominent American investor, Edward Lee Plumb, wrote, "If we have their trade and development meanwhile we need not hasten the greater event [annexation]." The attitude of former president Ulysses S. Grant, an investor in Mexico's railroads, leaned toward the Rosecrans position. According to David M. Pletcher, "Grant's fragmentary writings about Mexico, however, suggest that in the last years of his life he developed toward that country an ideology of economic imperialism closely similar to that of other promoters."[16] Former U.S. commercial attaché Chester Lloyd Jones reiterated Rosecrans', Grant's, and Plumb's policy proposal decades later in a book, *Mexico and Its Reconstruction* (1921). "The economic advantage that would result to the United States from annexation," he contended, "as contrasted to that which may follow independence and friendship is doubtful. Mexican trade, both import and export, is already almost inevitably American and investments will be increasingly so. . . . A friendly, strong, and independent Mexico will bring greater economic advantages than annexation that certain classes of Mexicans fear and some citizens of the United States desire."[17] However, when Jones set down his policy recommendations, Mexico was well on the way to being "an economic satellite of the United States."[18]

Invading U.S. capital first conquered the Mexican railroad system (which for all practical purposes was an extension of the American system), then the mining and petroleum industries, and, concurrently, trade between the two countries. The social consequences of this conquest reverberated throughout Mexico in the form of mass removal of peoples from village lands, the ruin of former artisans and other craftsmen, the creation of a modern working class subject to the business cycle, and the appearance of a migratory surplus population. That migratory population first appears within Mexico in a rural-to-urban movement and a south-to-north movement; as the tide of U.S. investments grows, the migratory distances increase and cross over to the United States.

Mexico began to build its railroads during the administration of Benito Juárez (1867–72), who granted a concession to a British company to build a railroad between Mexico City and Veracruz. His successor, Sebastián Lerdo de Tejada, continued the Juárez policies but refused to allow railroad lines to be built toward the north for fear that they might become a military advantage to the United States. Following a period of political instability, military strongman Porfirio Díaz took over Mexico's government in 1876. Díaz inaugurated the period of economic liberalism—forerunner of the current NAFTA-style neoliberalism—by selling railroad concessions to large U.S. railroad companies in the northern states. Within three years after Díaz came to power, concessions to the United States provided for the construction of five railroads in Mexico—some twenty-five hundred miles—and carrying subsidies of more than $32 million. These lines went from south to north and provided a route to the interior of Mexico from which mineral ores and agricultural products was transported to the United States.[19]

These developments occurred simultaneously with the further development of railroads in the southwestern United States by the same corporate interests, who often competed against each other. Thus the Southern Pacific extended to Yuma, Arizona, by 1877, and in 1881 reached Deming, New Mexico, and El Paso, Texas, connecting at Deming with the Atchison, Topeka, and Santa Fe. By 1902, U.S. investments in Mexican railroads amounted to $281 million, with the northern states of Sonora, Coahuila, and Chihuahua the main recipients. By 1910 U.S. corporate capital had largely financed the building of fifteen thousand miles of track, providing a basic infrastructure that would ensure the transport of raw materials northward and technology south.

By the dawn of the new century the United States controlled the Mexican economy. According to U.S. consul-general Andrew D. Barlow, 1,117 U.S.-based companies and individuals had invested $500 million in Mexico. Railroads were the cornerstone of the modernization process—initiated, designed, and constructed via foreign capital. Fully 80 percent of all investments in railroads emanated from the United States.[20]

Railroads enabled a myriad of economic activities, principally those under foreign control, including mining, the export of agricultural products, and oil production. In 1902 Walter E. Weyl observed that railroads "permitted the opening up of mines" and stimulated "agriculture, and manufacturing by establishing foreign markets. . . ."[21] While foreign investments entered Mexico "at an astonishing rate," Mexican national markets for raw materials such as copper were practically nonexistent, or, in the case of coffee, sugar, and henequen, were severely limited. Consequently, U.S. enterprises, and those owned by Mexicans, marketed their commodities primarily in foreign outlets. Thus the railroads were indispensable for the increased export of extractive raw materials and agricultural products and the import of tools, machinery, and other products supporting the modernized sectors of the economy.

Previous to 1880, for example, copper was processed through the centuries-old patio method for deriving precious metals from ore. "Railroads," commented Marvin Bernstein, "aided mining from their very inception."[22] Aid, that is, to the detriment of established miners using archaic techniques. According to mining engineer H. A. C. Jenison, writing in the *Engineering and Mining Journal-Press* in 1921, railroads "made the more remote regions accessible, made the transportation of heavy machinery possible, and the shipment of low-grade ores to smelters profitable." Consequently, about a sixth of rail mileage was "mineral railroad," but in general "most railroads counted upon mineral shipments."[23]

Under the stimulus of terms largely favorable to corporate investors rather than smaller individual stakeholders, U.S. capital assumed near-complete control in railroads, oil, agriculture, and mining, and had a large share of the financial structure in telegraphs, telephones, and urban transport. Mexico had passed into the hands of foreign economic interests. Related to Mexico's sovereignty, historian Robert G. Cleland wrote "[L]arge numbers of foreign companies, most of them which were American, entered Mexico. As the foreigner became interested in the industry, the Mexican gradually withdrew; little by little the important properties passed out of his control, until by 1912 of a total investment in the mining business estimated at $323,600,000 he could lay claim to less than $15,000,000." American investors held $223,000,000.[24] And of the total invested in that country, nearly 68 percent originated from foreign sources, its power multiplied by its control of key areas of the economy.

Every review of the evidence came to the same general conclusion: "Foreign investment [almost entirely of U.S. origin] was on the order of two-thirds of the total for the decade of 1900–1910; foreign ownership by 1910 has been estimated at half the national wealth."[25] U.S. interests were both dominant and strategically located in the economy: "American interests—the Hearsts, the Guggenheims, United States Steel, the American Corporation, Standard Oil, McCormick, Doheny—owned three-quarters of the minerals and more than half of the oil fields; they owned sugar plantations, coffee fincas, cotton, rubber, orchilla, and maguey plantations, and—along the American border—enormous cattle ranches."[26] For all practical purposes, the regional elites—the *comprador caciques*—and their representatives serving as the Mexican government provided the midlevel managing agency for foreign capital.[27]

Internal Migration: The First Step Toward Emigration

As in the past, Mexican wealth was concentrated in the semifeudal hacienda and remained so even as the railroads made the export of agricultural products to the United States and Europe a lucrative possibility. Enrichment without social change encouraged hacendados to transfer production from subsistence to cash crops for export. Coffee, fruits, henequen, hides, cattle, sugar, cotton, and other goods were traded beyond the local market to enter the international marketplace. For good measure, the large exporters received favorable transit rates that discriminated against domestic traders and forced the latter to produce for local consumption or not at all.[28] Hacienda export production, developed by and dependent on railroads, was equally significant for the effects on the peasantry. Evidence shows that the economic spur of the railroad promoted land expropriation laws, under the aegis of liberal land reform, and effected the legalized transfer of free peasant village holdings to nearby haciendas. Based on the locations of recorded violent peasant rebellions contesting land seizures between 1880 to 1910, *the majority of land expropriations during the Díaz era occurred along or nearby planned or operating railway routes.*[29] These activities, however, were entirely dependent on the effects of rail transport and production geared to foreign markets. Evidence points to similar patterns in other parts of Mexico. For example, studies have shown that in the northern state of Sonora, sales of empty public lands to speculators "faithfully mirror the history of the Sonora railroad."[30]

Interestingly, the railroads, which had little effect on industrial development, strengthened the precapitalist economic form, the hacienda. However, the hacienda, originally organized for self-sufficiency, engaged cash crop production on an extended scale to the detriment of staple crops, causing shortages of basic foodstuffs. Corn production fell by 50 percent and bean production declined by 75 percent between 1877 and 1910, forcing the nation to rely on costly imported staples. Yet, exports of raw materials such as henequen, coffee, sugar, hides, oil, and ores grew at an annual rate of 6.5 percent over the same period and dominated the rail traffic.[31] In 1910 Mexico was exporting 250,000 pounds of henequen a year, supplying midwestern farmers with twine for binding hay. While Mexico's foreign trade grew "tenfold between the mid-1870s and 1910," the average Mexican's diet fell below the levels of the pre-Díaz period as prices for staples rose much faster than wages.[32] The state-sponsored expropriations, the mass removal of hundreds of thousands of peasants from former village subsistence holdings, was the first phase toward the transnational migration that would occur a few years later. The first victims of Mexico's modernization—that is, economic conquest—were the peasants. As Friedrich Katz explained: "The expropriation of village lands as well as the demographic increase created large segments of unemployed laborers...."[33] The army of dispossessed moved from village to town and city, and, as the northern mining districts opened up, the migrations moved from north to south.

By 1910 a total of 90 percent of the central plateau's villages owned no communal land; meanwhile, the haciendas "owned over half of the nation's territory."[34] No wonder that over the course of the Porfiriato the village-to-city migration would lead to a dramatic population growth in the provincial capitals, 89 percent, which outstripped the national increase of 61 percent.[35] The most dramatic increase occurred in the nation's capital.

Toward the end of the nineteenth century, migrating peasants began to settle in Mexico City in substantial numbers, forming communities of shacks and tenements in the impoverished zones there. The landed aristocracy, who preferred the amenities of the capital to life on their rural estates, lived apart, along wide, appealing avenues lined with town homes and palacelike residences. Large numbers of railroad "men" made their base of operations in the capital and comprised the city's American section. But it was the peasants who made the largest impact on the city. According to Michael Johns, "Railroads and expanding haciendas threw so many off their lands in the 1880s and 1890s that nearly half of the city's five hundred thousand residents . . . were peasants."[36] Daily, the new arrivals searched for quarters as best they could, cramming into overcrowded lodgings. An estimated twenty-five-thousand homeless moved into *mesones*, a form of nightly shelter for transients. Men, women, and children could be found sleeping on mats in single rooms, huddled against the cold. Others lived in more permanent quarters, tenements, or *vecindades*, which, while not as inhospitable as the *mesones*, were nonetheless overflowing. John Kenneth Turner estimated that at least a hundred thousand "residents" were without a stable shelter—that is, were homeless.[37]

From this pool, the city's aristocracy and foreign (mainly American) businesspeople selected their domestic servants: drivers, cooks, baby-sitters, housecleaners, laundresses—some sixty-five thousand who in 1910 made up 30 percent of the capital's workforce.[38] This growing labor pool not only supplied the city with workers but also would eventually supply other regions. Labor recruiters working for textile manufacturers, henequen plantations, railroads, mining, and oil operations also targeted displaced peasants. Many ended up in Yucatán henequen estates as virtual slaves working alongside many thousands of Yaqui Indians forcibly removed from their Sonoran homelands to make room for land speculators and railroad builders.[39] As railroads expanded their radius of operations and as ownership of mines shifted from small prospectors to Americans, the search for labor became a key element in the modernization process. Ironically, the very same modernization projects that removed peasants from the land also removed many more thousands from traditional occupations. Moises Gonzalez Navarro remarked that "the progressive disintegration of artesanal production wrought by modern industry was a novel occasion for men that, in effect, would allow him to sense the weight of personal circumstances."[40]

The northern trade routes from the central region, which normally occupied sixty thousand pack mules, underwent a profound change with the advent of railroads. Fred Powell, an authority on railroads, wrote, "Until the railroads, Mexico was the paradise of the packer."[41] Early Latin Americanists noted this change. Frank Tannenbaum wrote that in the past the "surplus crop was . . . loaded upon the backs of pack mules or in some instances on the backs of men and carried to the nearest trading center, often days of travel away. More recently it has been delivered to the nearest railroad station."[42] Walter E. Weyl confirmed the gradual displacement in his study. He wrote, "the muleteer is now relegated to a lesser sphere of activity and a lower position in the national economy. The driver of the mule car is slowly giving way to the trained motorman, and before long the vast army of *cargadores*, or porters, will go the way which in other cities has been trod by the *leñadores* and *aguadores*—'the hewers of wood and drawers of water.'"[43] Others besides mule packers were cast aside as wagon drivers, weavers, shoemakers, tanners, soapmakers, and others found that they could not compete against the new enterprises and imported goods and joined the army of dispossessed and unemployed, the burgeoning migrant labor pool. More recent work uncovered evidence for that pattern. Historian Rodney Anderson writes, ". . . the artisans added to the growing numbers of rural people forced off their lands by enclosure."[44]

Victor Clark noted in his 1908 study for the U.S. Bureau of Labor that underemployment and unemployment, interrelated with the internal demand for labor, caused a northward migration from the central plateau of Mexico along the railroad routes:

> The railroads that enter Mexico from the United States run for several hundred miles from the border through a desert and very sparsely settled country, but all of them ultimately tap more populous and fertile regions. Along the northern portion of their routes resident labor is so scarce that workers are brought from the south as section hands and for new construction. This has carried the central Mexican villager a thousand miles from his home and to within a few miles of the border, and American employers, with a gold wage, have had little difficulty in attracting him across that not very formidable dividing line.

Later in this study, Clark noted the demand for labor in the mines: "Like the railways, the mines have had to import labor from the south; and they have steadily lost labor to the United States." Clark interviewed one mining operator who brought eight thousand miners in one year from the south to work several mining properties in Chihuahua. Thus, on the whole, continued Clark, "there is a constant movement of labor northward inside of Mexico itself to supply the growing demands of the less developed states and this supply is ultimately absorbed by the still more exigent demand . . . of the border States and Territories of the United States."[45]

In his review of the Porfiriato, Mexican historian González Navarro wrote that the internal migrations were a "phenomenon seen for the first time" whose origin was found in the "human displacement from the countryside."[46] Approximately 300,000 persons left the south to settle in the north during the Porfiriato, a massive and permanent shift in the nation's population generated by foreign-controlled modernization.[47] One mining engineer lamented, "The call for labor is greater than can be supplied by the

native population. . . ."[48] Another remarked, "The increase in number of mining operations in recent years has been so great as to make the securing of an adequate supply of labor a difficult problem."[49] Nonetheless, the employment statistics show a tremendous increase in the number of workers employed in the mines and smelters from roughly 1850 to 1900. At midcentury, scattered mines operated by small contingents of laborers toiled intermittently, often in a "hand-to-mouth affair," but by the century's end some 140,000 worked the mines and smelters, and most of these were internal migrants.[50] Another 30,000 to 40,000 were employed annually on the railroads in the 1880s and 1890s. It is no wonder that the population growth in the north superseded that of any other area of Mexico.[51]

Along the rail routes, cities such as Torreon and Gomez Palacio expanded enormously, as did ports such as Guaymas and Tampico, due to the transport of people and/or the export of goods. In 1883 Torreon was classified as a *ranchería*, a collection of ranches. By 1910 it had earned the title "city" with a population of more than 43,000. Nuevo Laredo grew from 1,283 in 1877 to 9,000 in 1910; and Nogales, which could not claim anything more than desert and some tents, blossomed into a thriving border port of 4,000 two years after the train passed through. Ciudad Lerdo offers an example of the power of the railroads to determine population placement—in this case, by their absence. In 1900 the city contained 24,000 inhabitants, but when the railroad bypassed it, the population declined to fewer than 12,000.[52]

The growth (or urbanization) of the city was the other side of the demographic shift from the central plateau to the north. In the case of the north, the population growth was most pronounced in the mining areas. Company towns such as Cananea, El Boleo, Nacozari, Navojoa, Copola, Concordia, Santa Eulalia, Santa Rosalía, Batopilas, and Esperanzas sprang from virtual wilderness into thriving mining camps within a few years. Albeit segregated, with Americans living apart from the Mexican labor force, the American employers believed that company housing was necessary to attract and control labor.[53] Cananea offers an example of one localized change occurring over a wide area of Mexico. A mining engineer reviewing the Greene Consolidated mining operations in 1906 wrote, "La Cananea presents a wonderful contrast to its earlier appearance . . . where eight years ago their were no persons other than a few warring prospectors . . . is now a camp of 25,000 persons with all the necessities and most of the comforts of civilization."[54] The Cananea operations required the labor of 5,500 regular men, with 8,000 to 9,000 listed as employees.

The Esperanza mining region in Coahuila experienced a similar profound change. In surveying the original site, the developer of the region found "cactus and mesquite desert with no trees, no houses (except a few 'jackals' [*jacales*, shacks]), and no water." In five years the area had grown to a population of 10,000, the mines employing 2,000. In roughly the same period, Batopilas grew from 300 to 4,000, employing 900 miners. Mulegè, a port near the copper boomtown of El Boleo, Baja California, demonstrates the secondary effects that mining had on the region. The small port grew from 1,500 in 1880 to 14,000 in 1910. Similarly, Nogales, Hermosillo, El Paso, and other cities that depended on mine-driven commerce paralleled the growth in the mining enterprises.

The reconfiguration of the centuries-old demographic pattern in Mexico comprises the first step in migrations to the United States. However, the economic forces that propelled the population shifts were not indigenous to Mexico; rather they emanated from foreign large-scale corporate enterprises operating under the protection of their home government's foreign policy.

Migration and Emigration

"In the southern section of the Western division immigration from Mexico has become an important factor," stated the 1911 *Report* of the Immigration Commission. Indeed, even before the launching of the full-scale battles of the 1910 Revolution (which were not to occur until 1913 to 1915), emigration had become a part of Mexican life. According to the available statistics, Mexican labor began to enter the United States in sizable numbers after 1905, partly as a result of the south-to-north internal migrations in Mexico. Later, migrations occurred in response to the

economic depression in the United States that caused a slowdown of mining, motivating a northward migration. Data on Mexican migration show that the numbers declined between 1905 and 1907 from 2,600 to 1,400. However, the numbers rose steeply in 1908 to 10,638, reaching 16,251 in 1909 and 18,691 in 1910. But this tells only part of the story. In 1911 the Immigration Bureau noted that at least 50,000 Mexicans crossed the border annually without documentation. The cyclic pattern of migration of superfluous labor from Mexico began to take root.

The argument made for the "push" of the Revolution does not answer why the migrations, documented and undocumented, appear before the onset of the Revolution or why the migrations slow during the Revolution and spur in the 1920s, well after the fighting had terminated.[55] Again, the data show that the rise in migration occurred well before the intense period of civil war and that the numbers of emigrants declined with the onset of violence and major battles associated with the war. Thereafter, emigration returned to the pattern of the pre-civil war years but continued to grow more acute, corresponding with the pre-1910 movement. It is entirely probable, even without the 1910 civil war, that emigration would have moved in the same upward direction. This is precisely what has happened from the 1940s to the present day, without the violence of war. Thus the war probably exacerbated a preexisting condition rather than created it. (See figure 1.)

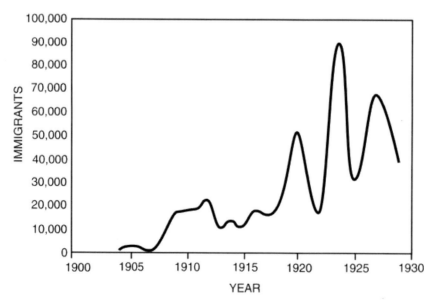

Figure 1. Mexican Migration to the United States, 1900–1929

Year	Immigrants	Year	Immigrants	Year	Immigrants	Year	Immigrants
1904	1,009	1911	18,784	1918	17,602	1925	32,378
1905	2,637	1912	22,001	1919	28,844	1926	42,638
1906	1,997	1913	10,954	1920	51,042	1927	66,766
1907	1,406	1914	13,089	1921	29,603	1928	57,765
1908	6,067	1915	10,993	1922	18,246	1929	38,980
1909	16,251	1916	17,198	1923	62,709		
1910	17,760	1917	16,438	1924	87,648		

Moreover, the argument that the railroads as a transportation system inspired migration cannot withstand scrutiny. If railroads per se fostered the mass movement, then why did the migrations begin a quarter of a century *after* trains began running from Mexico City to the U.S. border? Second, if wages were the stimulant, then emigration should have occurred earlier rather than in the middle of the first decade, since wages were always lower in Mexico than in the United States. (This was particularly true during the Depression of the 1930s.) In addition, abundant evidence suggests that a major impetus to emigrate was the hacendado class, who perceived the dispossessed peasants as a potential political hazard and financed migration journeys. In El Paso, Victor Clark interviewed several young migrants and was surprised to find evidence of lending by "patrons" in support of emigration, "sometimes a political officer—in one case a judge—and sometimes a merchant, possibly also a landowner."[56] Years later, Paul S. Taylor also found evidence of lending to the unemployed. In Jalisco, Taylor noted, "Anyone with money engaged in the business of assisting persons to migrate" and that the "hacendados prefer to let the workers get away so they won't congregate in pueblos and ask for land."[57] Clearly, there are serious problems with the conventional mode of analysis. The usual "push" arguments together with the recent modifications simply cannot hold up to the evidence.

Recent "Refinements" to Push-Pull

In supporting their assertions, recent research by sociologists has pointed out that migration continued unabated over the post-1960 period when economic conditions in Mexico were relatively good. Studies analyzed noneconomic factors and questioned whether these factors impacted the decision to migrate. Framed in such a perspective, emphasis swung to the role of "agency" or the independent decision making of the migrants as they "negotiated" their migratory treks. Based on these premises, social capital theory configured transnational migrant networks linking communities divided by national borders. Migrants summoned motivations, constructed pathways, and provided the resources that propelled migrations over the long term. Theoretically, an institutionalized culture of migration embedded in the psyche of potential migrants establishes a social network across borders that feed migrations. Migration, in other words, exists autonomously above the economic and political life of Mexico. As migrants cross the border, they allegedly define the border on their own terms, thereby reconfiguring sociopolitical spaces. Ultimately, recent sociological models celebrated migration as "transnational resistance" to internationalized economic and political imperatives.

Accordingly, migration evolved into an institutionalized "self-feeding process" having a life of its own. Tautological in essence, migration is explained by migration; migrants migrate because, as "historical actors," they have voluntarily chosen to create a culture of migration. Nevertheless, the question of origins, or the factors that send the first migration, which leads to the second and subsequent migrations, is left by default to push-pull. The original sin, push-pull, prompts the first migrations, but once the sin is committed, the migration assumes a *self-generating* state. The only true national and/or transnational factor of significance of this theoretical construct is the migration itself. Rational choices made by migrants to acquire commodities, or to reestablish community, cultural lifestyle, and family ties, motivate migrations. International economic relations are relegated to the margins, and the economic domination we address here is ignored while the "independent" decision making of the migrants is centered.[58]

A second theoretical design arising from the critique of push-pull, the segmented labor market model, emphasizes an aspect of economics of the receiving country, precisely the structured dependence of the modernized, "postindustrial" forms of production, on the continued flow of cheap immigrant labor. The demand to satisfy an economic addiction, an insatiable thirst for cheap labor, drives migration. As in the previous theoretical construct, the adherents to this position contend that the old push conditions, wage differentials, a surplus population, and so on, are irrelevant. However, while the push side of the equation evaporates, the pull side—that is, the demand for labor in the receiving country—functions as before. Note that both theoretical models view the two economically interconnected countries as *economically independent of each other* and ignore transnational financial *domination* with respect to the process of migration. Like the original push-pull theory, its revisions separate the process of migration into two interacting but independent operations.[59]

A third model, new economics theory, contends that migration is explained "by measures of risk and the need for access to capital" rather than by the workings of the labor market.[60] According to Douglas Massey, "Considerable work suggests that the acquisition of housing, the purchase of land, the establishment of small businesses constitute the primary motivations for international labor migration."[61] Here the push argument seems to have been supplanted by factors other than wages; however, this theoretical model, as in the case with social capital theory, stands well within the old model. New economics theorists argue that the sending country fails to supply needed capital, land, and business opportunities. These contentions fit into the push-pull model as it was first articulated nearly a century ago: the host country has something that the sending country lacks, hence people migrate to satisfy a felt need, and a neoclassical equilibrium is established (or should be established).

Ultimately, the several critiques of push-pull theory fail to extricate migration theory from the former's clutches. Several basic assumptions replicate the old model. For one, migrants have a felt need, and Mexico cannot meet that need; thus a push. Second, the United States has the conditions and wherewithal to satisfy the migrants' yearnings; therefore a pull. Last, the national economies of Mexico and the United States are interactive (often described as "interdependent") but without domination exerted by either party; hence independently functioning push and/or pull.[62]

Finally, the world systems model causally links global capitalism with migrations. In this view, direct foreign investments generate economic development in sending countries that removes natives from farming lands or causes unemployment in traditional occupations, creating a body of migrants within the country. Saskia Sassen, perhaps the best-known theoretician of migration from a world systems paradigm, rightly points out how a foreign investment interested in export agriculture modernizes production, which simultaneously upsets traditional farming practices, removes small farmers from the Mexican countryside, and resettles them in cities. Some migrate to the northern states, where foreign-owned assembly plants advertise employment. Ultimately that same surplus labor migrates to the United States, where immigrant labor is in constant demand.[63]

Our basic differences with world systems theory as applied to Mexican migration to the United States stem from (1) the emphasis on direct investments, (2) the implicit argument that modernization via foreign financing equals the development experienced by Europe in the nineteenth century, and (3) the exclusive attention to the post-1960 period in theoretical presentation. First, direct investments are only one type of foreign capital that has affected the national economy of Mexico; other types of capital have serious consequences for the economy and society as well. For example, U.S. government lending programs; private philanthropic organizations such as the Rockefeller Foundation and others; and economic development programs (loans) run by the IMF and the World Bank, and the trade policies of the World Trade Organization, have a decided impact on the economy and society of Mexico. Second, world systems theory implicitly parallels notions of the great nineteenth-century European migrations that occurred via an indigenous capitalist modernization and consequent depeasanting of the land. We contend that foreign economic incursions led to a colonial status, resulting in neither an indigenous capitalist-driven nor dependent modernization, but rather one under foreign control that depeasants the land, removing them to other parts of Mexico and into the United States. Our third criticism responds to the notion that the post-1960s migrations are distinct from those of earlier decades. We argue that U.S. economic domination over Mexico remained more or less constant during the twentieth century. While world systems theory does point to the significance of foreign investments in the removal of people from the coun-

tryside and their migration to cities and northern assembly plants, the roots of migration accrue to global capital, or direct foreign investments, which "modernize" the Mexican economy. In essence, Mexico and the United States are sovereign nations as in the first versions of the push-pull thesis, each in their own way subject to the nuances of global capital and interdependent in the process. They ignore government-to-government lending programs, bank capital, massive foreign debts, and empire in that theoretical design; the world system is all one expansive undulating capitalist plain in which issues of inequality and domination become obscured.

Even though a general discussion of world systems theory is beyond the purview of this study, we would like to note the following points. We believe that the Achilles heel of world systems theory, and its predecessor, dependency theory, can be traced to their definitions of capitalism and of capitalists. According to these theories, the essence of capitalism lies not in the social relations, property patterns, ideology, and political institutions of society but rather in the existence of commercial relations. By this definition, most of Mexico was capitalist in the nineteenth century. By assumption Mexican elites become—in this view—capitalists—that is, people with potential for entrepreneurship and national independence, rather than obsequious comprador middlemen and hacendados who carry the bags for U.S. finance capital. By definition world systems theory grants the Mexican elites of the nineteenth century characteristics that assume a penchant for independence and self-reliance. The pitfalls of dependency theory were addressed in a series of debates in sociology, political science, and Marxist economics in the 1970s before the dependency model began to be used, all too uncritically, by Latin American historians. In particular, a modality of dependency theory—labeled "right dependency" (advocated by Brazilian sociologist Fernando Henrique Cardoso)—was critiqued for defending capitalist development behind a facade of "leftist" rhetoric.[64] It is a similar concept of capitalism and capitalists in world systems theory, which ipso facto elevates the degree of "agency" of Third World elites. It accords them, axiomatically, a higher degree of freedom and independence in their dealings with stronger nations, as in the case of Mexico's nineteenth-century advisers to dictator Díaz, the notorious *cientificos*. In this manner, this theory obscures and obfuscates a history of imperial domination.[65] Lamentably, the major criticisms of world systems theory—in particular the criticisms of Eric Wolf and Peter Worsley—have not been appreciated by Latin American historians.

The core premise of push-pull—the imbalance of independent conditions in sending and host countries—still obtains in spite of critiques hurled against it. A real alternative to push-pull requires a reconceptualization of migration within the context of empire.

The Ebb and Flow of Migration, 1950–70

Analysis of the data on migration indicates that the flows are cyclical as well as long-term in nature. The push-pull thesis and its newer versions gloss over what accounts for this pattern of cycles, as it is unable to explain them. A "constant"—that is, a steady disparity in the level of income and wages, nor migrant networks and the like—cannot logically account for variations in the pace of migration. Rather, one must turn again to concrete historical developments to explain those changes.

Despite the upheaval of the 1910 civil war, U.S. investments in the 1920s either retained their position garnered during the Díaz years, or increased in significance.[66] With the coming of the global Depression that began in the early 1930s, economic activity by U.S. companies at home and abroad diminished. The evidence shows that migration from Mexico declines after 1930, following the 1910–30 generally upward pattern. The slowdown in migration lasts until the early 1950s, when it picks up again, with renewed vigor. To look for the causes of this rebound we once again turn to the pattern of U.S. economic activity in Mexico.

Beginning in the early 1940s, U.S. investments in Mexico began to rise once again but under new manifestations. The Depression of the 1930s brought to power in Mexico the incipient leadership of the future Partido Revolucionario Institucional under its paternalistic leading figure, Lázaro Cárdenas. Similar to the pattern established by Roosevelt's New Deal administration, the Cárdenas government used the economic power of the state as never before in Mexico to maintain and protect the free market/private property social contract.

Under the Partido Revolucionario Mexicano (forerunner of the PRI), foreign investment flowed once again: it tripled from 1940 to 1950, and doubled again by 1958.[67] But the profile of the investment was different. Guided by the governing party, the national government instituted in 1934 a major public finance and development institution, Nacional Financiera, which became the economic pillar of the economy. Nacional Financiera invested heavily in works of irrigation, highways, and electric power. Of the decades 1940 to 1970, a period of rapid economic growth in Mexico, it has been said that "[n]o financial institution in Mexico has contributed more to the economic growth of that country than Nacional Financiera."[68]

From the early 1940s on, U.S.-based banks and financial institutions began to invest in Mexico by way of loans to Nacional Financiera. Some of the lending institutions included the U.S. Export-Import Bank, the Bank of America, Chase Manhattan Bank, and eventually the International Bank for Reconstruction and Development (the World Bank). Between 1942 and 1959 more than $900 million (mostly of U.S. origin) had been invested in major works of infrastructure in Mexico by way of Nacional Financiera.[69] An analysis of Nacional Financiera funds reveals that, by 1953, foreign loans accounted for the single largest—about one-third—source of equity funds available to the institution.[70] This allowed U.S. capital to maximize its leverage over decision making while minimizing risks: U.S. financial institutions were in the driver's seat of the economic policies of Nacional Financiera.

The investments financed by Nacional Financiera would have a tremendous impact on the structure of Mexico's economic and demographic patterns with consequences for migration to the United States. A significant proportion of the investment went into major irrigation projects, the most important of which were in the northern border states of Mexico. Development of the irrigation projects began in the early 1940s and included the Falcón Dam in the Rio Grande and the Rio Fuerte Irrigation Project in the state of Sonora. A tremendous increase in agricultural production took place in northern Mexico, simultaneous with the development of irrigation projects between 1940 and 1960. High rates of growth in cotton production in areas such as the Mexicali Valley made Mexico the largest cotton exporter in the world and brought the value of cotton production from 8 percent in 1940 to 24 percent in 1958.[71] Cotton production itself developed under the close control, through credit and marketing channels, of a major U.S. agribusiness giant, Anderson Clayton.

Control over Mexican cotton production was made effective because Mexican growers did not sell their product in the international market but through Anderson Clayton (and other U.S. enterprises), which monopolized the harvest and provided credit, seed, and fertilizers to the producers (much like Anderson Clayton did in California's San Joaquin Valley in the 1930s). This company also managed cotton production in the countries with which Mexico competed in the world market: Brazil and the United States. In the late 1960s this control enabled Anderson Clayton to engage in cotton "dumping," reminding the Mexican government who was boss.[72] The opening up of irrigated lands in Sinaloa and Sonora also allowed for the production of "winter vegetables" in those states beginning in late 1940, creating a few small pockets of U.S-agribusiness control. The opening up of the Pan-American Highway—another Nacional Financiera project—facilitated the marketing of Mexican vegetables in the United States. Thus the export of tomatoes from Mexico's northeast increased from fewer than 1 million pounds in 1942 to 14 million pounds in 1944.[73] But the denationalized character of this production was evident as other U.S. corporations joined Anderson Clayton in effectively taking over Mexico's agribusiness, from the production and sale of machinery and fertilizers to the processing and merchandising of agricultural goods. Among the better-known companies in control of Mexico's northern agriculture were John Deere, International Harvester, Celanese, Monsanto, Dupont, American Cyanamid, Corn Products, United Fruit, and

Ralston Purina.[74] The method of political control that John Foster Dulles described was complete: Mexico was borrowing money from U.S. banks to develop irrigation projects and transportation, thereby making possible the growth of U.S.-controlled agriculture in the northern tier of Mexican states.

With the growth of agriculture came population shifts, continuing the pattern begun in the late nineteenth century. Outside of the tourist-driven economies of Acapulco and Quintana Roo, only three Mexican states, all border states, showed an astonishing rate of growth of 45 percent or more in the 1950–60 period: Baja California, 232 percent; Tamaulipas, 61 percent; and Sonora, 45 percent.[75] Between 1950 and 1960 the total population of the eight major *municipios* of the Mexican border—Tijuana, Mexicali, Nogales, Ciudad Juárez, Piedras Negras, Nuevo Laredo, Reynosa, and Matamoros—increased by 83 percent, from fewer than 900,000 to 1.5 million. By 1970 the population had reached a total of 2.3 million. Between 1960 and 1969 the population rise in the northern border states—Baja California, Sonora, Chihuahua, Coahuila, Nuevo Leon, and Tamaulipas—grew by 45 percent, in contrast with a figure of 31 percent for the nation as a whole. In 1970 fully 29 percent of the border population came from other parts of the country.[76] It is interesting to note that during the cotton boom years (1940–60), the border municipios where cotton was the main agricultural product—Mexicali, Cuidad Juárez, Reynosa, and Matamoros—registered the highest rates of population growth. On the other hand, during the years of the cotton crisis (1960–70), the same municipalities suffered a sharp drop in their populations.[77]

During the 1950–70 period further ties developed between countries formally equal and sovereign, but with one in a subordinate position while the other administered the transnational hegemony. The subordinated status of Mexico and specifically the changes in its political economy brought about by the economic and political activities of U.S. corporations and the U.S. government provided the opportunity to construct a giant agribusiness economy on both sides of the border that relied on the ready supply of cheap labor from the interior of Mexico. An evident consequence of this relationship was one of the most spectacular mass movements of people in the history of humanity. The northward migration of people from all corners of Mexico to its north, and for many, eventually to the United States, was motivated by the same general force, *the economic dislocation caused by U.S. capital—not an amorphous "global" capital—in Mexico*, the pace of the movement modulated in a cyclical manner by the relative intensity of U.S. economic intrusion. This movement turned the border area into a highly urbanized region. Simultaneously, migration constantly propelled the growth of the Chicano minority in the United States in a variety of forms: regulated and unregulated, legal and illegal, cyclical and long-term.

The Current Cycle, 1970–2000

As in the previous cycle, U.S. investments in Mexico shifted away from mining and railroads toward industrial manufacturing. U.S. corporations made their way through direct purchase into the most dynamic sectors of local industry, especially in the 1960s. This trend occurred most notably in consumer durables, chemicals, electronics, department stores, hotels and restaurants, and the food industry, in which United Fruit (later known as Dole), Heinz, Del Monte, and General Foods became very visible. Of the subsidiaries of U.S.-based corporations, 225 operated in the manufacturing sector.[78] U.S. investment in manufacturing concentrated around the Federal District, which accounted for 50 percent of the total manufacturing production of the country in 1975. As we will see, this would change in the ensuing years, but in the meantime Mexico's dependence on foreign loans continued to increase. Between 1950 and 1972 the foreign debt grew at an average annual rate of 23 percent, reaching $11 billion by the latter year.

A chronic balance-of-payments problem, a side effect of Mexico's reliance on the export of primary commodities and on foreign loans, made the situation worse. Beginning in the late 1960s, Mexico's hardly independent government had no choice but to accept lenders' terms. At the behest of international creditors, economic policies once again resulted in massive economic and demographic dislocation, contributing to a further increase of migration into its northern region, which became not only highly urbanized but also acquired a new role as a major "staging area" for further migration to the United States.

The Maquiladora Program

In 1967 Mexico took a giant step in the complete abdication of its economic sovereignty when it established the Border Industrial Program along its northern border. This program began the transformation of the entire area into a gigantic assembly operation. The sad story of the maquiladora program in all its sordid details has been told elsewhere.[79] Suffice it to say that, like a narcotic drug, which does not solve your problems while making you into an addict, Mexico has become dependent on its maquilas, which do not solve its unemployment problems nor allow the country to become self-sufficient, developed, and modern.

For the purposes of our argument, the maquiladora program served to make the border states of Mexico, and specifically its border cities, into entrepôts for the poverty-stricken, unemployed masses of the country. One cursory look at the employment figures and accompanying graph tell the tale. (See figure 2.)

The maquiladoras turned Mexico's northern border into an enclave with few links to the rest of the economy. Into the border area flowed duty-free manufacturing

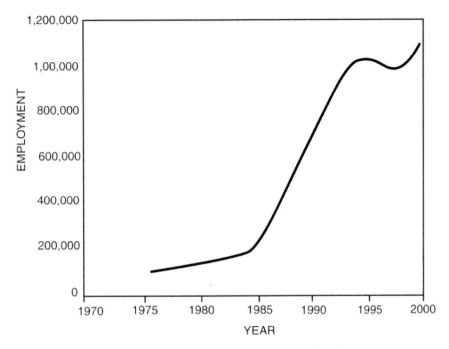

Figure 2. Maquiladora Employment, 1970–1999

Year	Employment	Year	Employment
1975	67,214	1993	546,433
1980	119,546	1998	983,272
1985	217,544	1999	1,100,000

inputs to be assembled into final products, using cheap labor for entry into the United States or export to other countries. The northern tier of Mexico became a direct appendage of U.S. manufacturing, replicating the examples of railroads and mining in the Mexican economy during the early 1900s.

Simultaneous with the development of the maquiladora program, other significant changes began to affect Mexican agriculture. Between 1940 and the late 1960s, Mexico's countryside provided the basic food staples to its growing urban population. However, pressure from international lenders and agribusiness multinationals would change that. Mexico's central government began a policy of eliminating subsidies to small agricultural producers, who then began to abandon their farm plots to join the migration streams. Into the breach moved the United States, which turned the same agricultural lands into mechanized farms, producing export commodities to the United States. In the 1970s the rate of growth of basic staples such as corn, beans, and wheat began to fall behind the population growth. To cover the precipitous decline in food production, a problem not seen since the Porfiriato, the country was forced to import basic food supplies.[80] However, imports could not feed Mexico's people satisfactorily. Infectious diseases and other illnesses linked to malnutrition and economic underdevelopment became rampant by the late 1980s.[81]

NAFTA

The 1990s witnessed the signing of the North American Free Trade Agreement (NAFTA), the most recent and devastating example of how U.S. domination over Mexico continues to misdevelop and tear apart the socioeconomic integrity of that society. The U.S. government and major corporate interests promoted the NAFTA concept as a weapon in their trade competition with Europe, and especially Japan. Under the "free trade" slogan the proposed treaty would serve two purposes. First, it would guarantee a free hand to U.S. enterprises willing and able to invest in Mexico to take advantage of that country's cheaper wages. Mexico was to become an export platform of manufactured commodities for the United States and other markets around the world. Major U.S. corporations, in particular automobile manufacturers, stood to benefit greatly from this scheme. Second, the treaty would simultaneously deny in various forms and degrees to other economic powers the advantage of operations in and exporting from Mexico. Briefly put, the United States sought to create with Mexico (and Canada) an economic bloc to compete against Europe and Japan.

In their quest the United States could count on the leadership of Mexico's governing party, the PRI, and then-president Carlos Salinas. Under his leadership Mexico undertook a wide-ranging set of measures designed to make NAFTA a reality. First, to demonstrate resolute support for market-oriented policies and to attract foreign capital, the Mexican government began to break up numerous government enterprises and to lay off thousands of employees. Hundreds of state companies and institutions were sold or "privatized." The government enacted laws to "flexibilize" the labor market, including restrictions on wage increases, curtailment of vacation and sick-leave time, extension of the workweek, and increased management powers over firings and hiring of temporary workers (known in the United States as downsizing). The elimination of trade protection meant that by 1993, nearly 50 percent of Mexico's textile firms and 30 percent of manufacturers of leather products had gone bankrupt. By the time of the signing of the treaty, Mexico's population had become severely polarized in terms of wealth and income.[82]

The actual signing of NAFTA revealed that Mexico was only as strong a bargainer as the weakest of the 435 U.S. congressmen. U.S. president Bill Clinton could only succeed in obtaining a majority vote in Congress by guaranteeing each and every representative protection for his or her district against any competition that might result from NAFTA. A Texas congressman agreed to vote in favor of NAFTA only after Clinton promised that the Pentagon would add two more cargo planes to a production order previously awarded to his electoral district by the Department of Defense. A Florida representative voted for the treaty only after the State Department agreed to seek the extradition of an individual residing in Mexico who was accused of a crime in the United States. A lawmaker from Georgia opted for the treaty in exchange for promises by the Agriculture Department that limits would be imposed on increasing imports of peanut butter from Canada. In this manner even small U.S. producers of brooms were protected from Mexican competition. Throughout the entire humiliating process not a peep was heard from the Salinas government. In the end, "free trade" meant that Mexico would be completely open to U.S. goods, but U.S. producers were safely guarded against Mexico's products.

Rather than a free trade agreement, NAFTA could be better described as a "free investment" agreement. During the previous decade, tariffs levied by Mexico against the United States had steadily declined. NAFTA codified these changes, and, more important, it opened up investment opportunities in Mexico, protected against nationalizations, and eliminated all restrictions against U.S. ventures in Mexico. Of course, the "free investment" part would be limited under a section of the treaty titled Rules of Origin. These rules defined as domestic any inputs originating in Canada, the United States, and Mexico. Others (e.g., Japanese inputs) were henceforth classified as "foreign," and any products assembled with them were liable to export limits. In other words, after NAFTA it became more difficult for Japanese or European investors to ship products for assemblage into Mexico and export to the United States.

NAFTA was never envisioned as a developmental policy for Mexico. All announced plans, forecasts, and decisions of U.S. multinationals relied on the low wages prevalent in Mexico as the key variable involved. Further displacement of peasants, massive migration, and the destruction of what remains of domestic Mexican agriculture will follow on the heels of the complete opening to competition with the large U.S. agribusiness consortiums. Via NAFTA, Mexico agreed to subject all land to privatization—that is, sale and speculation. It returned, for example, Indian lands to the same juridical status that gave rise ninety years ago to Mexico's famed agrarian revolt.[83]

Almost to the day of the first anniversary of the signing of NAFTA, the newly installed administration of Ernesto Zedillo faced a catastrophic devaluation of the national currency. Mexico's image changed from an investor's paradise to a disheveled financial hulk, a virtual economic protectorate of the United States. The United States set up conditions for a bailout that were, according to newspaper reports, too sensitive to be published in Mexico. Eventually it became known that the U.S. plan required Mexico to hand over all revenues from its oil sales, and gave to U.S. banks a right to supervise and enforce further measures of austerity and privatization. Everything went up for sale—for example, bridges, airports, toll roads, ports, and telephones. In the meantime, thousands of farmers, businesspeople, and consumers went broke because they could not pay their debts and mortgages. Contemporary estimates indicated that in the first two months of 1995 nearly 600,000 jobs were lost. A whopping 30 percent of Mexico's labor force, 11 million people, was reported unemployed in mid-1995.[84]

The American embassy in Mexico, demonstrating the U.S. resolve to remain committed to its plans for Mexico, referred positively to rising unemployment and bankruptcies as the "Darwinian effects" of NAFTA. Embassy officials praised its "stabilizing" effects on the economy and called it the "bright spot" in the Mexican catastrophe. The United States, taking advantage of the plummeting wage levels in Mexico relative to the dollar, benefited enormously as 250 companies opened up shop in the border area in the first three months of 1995. Apparently Mexico should have been grateful that, in exchange for millions of unemployed and thousands ruined, a handful of Mexicans—a new generation of migrants—obtained jobs toiling for a miserable wage assembling products in border cities for reshipment to the United States. In the long run, the devastating effects of NAFTA on Mexico's remaining agricultural production and national urban manufacturers will throw into the migration highways an even larger number of people desperately looking to make a living, thereby enlarging at a faster pace the mass of Mexican migrants in the United States. NAFTA is a particularly telling example of the unity of push and pull, and the role of U.S. domination in dismembering Mexico and creating a Chicano national minority in the United States.

Conclusion: A Network of Domination

Under NAFTA, a steadily dropping manufacturing employment (outside of the maquila sector) points to the deindustrialization of Mexico. While in 1981 manufacturing employment stood at 2,557,000, it fell to 2,325,000 in 1993 and to 2,208,750 by 1997, a 13.6 percent drop from 1981. This also brought lower living standards, as many workers moved from permanent to lower-wage contingency work that lacked benefits and union protection. The destruction of Mexico's industrial base is particularly pronounced in the area of capital goods. From 1995 to 1997 alone, following the peso debacle, 36 percent of the 1,100 capital goods plants closed down. In all, 17,000 enterprises of all kinds went bankrupt shortly after the crisis exploded. Meanwhile, employment opportunities in the lowest-paying categories ballooned by 60 percent, dragging 5 million people to the official "extreme poverty" category. Manufacturing production has been reduced to the maquiladora sector, situated largely in the northern confines of the country, and to an increasingly concentrated manufacturing system dominated by a few U.S. industrial giants involved in production for export.[85]

The debacle in national industry repeated in agriculture with catastrophic consequences. According to a Mexican analyst, the opening of the agricultural markets by the NAFTA treaty led to the rapid ruin of what remained of Mexico's production of basic staples, and to the dumping of cheap U. S. corn, wheat, and beans into Mexico. One hundred years of U.S. empire building has produced what three hundred years of Spanish rule could not accomplish: the complete inability of the Mexican nation to produce enough to feed its own people. The migratory conse-

quences are staggering: millions will be forced to leave Mexico's countryside in the next decade.[86]

The demographic impact of U.S. transformations in Mexico's economy has already caused a dramatic shift in the nation's population distribution. Since the 1960s, the northern municipios have featured one of the fastest-growing populations in the world. There appears no end in sight to this phenomenon: the population, which topped 4 million in 1995, is expected to double by 2010 and to more than triple by 2020. Ciudad Juárez, for example, has grown five times since 1970, reaching a population of 1 million. According to an Associated Press report, each day "an estimated 600 new people arrive from Mexico's poor provinces hoping for work" in Ciudad Juárez, or nearly 220,000 new arrivals a year. Internal migrants in desperate straits will later surface as international migrants confronting the dangers of the militarized border.[87]

Today this process intensifies the Mexicanization in the many barrios across the United States, forging a distinct demographic form with immigrants either outnumbering the second generation or reaching a level of parity not seen since the 1930s. Migrants are the fastest-growing sector of the Chicano population, approximately 40 percent born in Mexico, up from 17 percent four decades ago.[88] (See figure 3.) Had it not been for the Great Depression and World War II, the migratory movement of the 1900–1930 period would have proceeded without respite. That interruption made possible a distinctive Mexican-American generation and later the Chicano generation. However, once migration resumed its previous pace, a cultural pattern that first surfaced in the 1920s reappeared in the 1960s. We foresee that Mexicanization is overwhelming the older enclaves, remaking older barrios into immigrant centers and thus reforming the older ethnic politics,

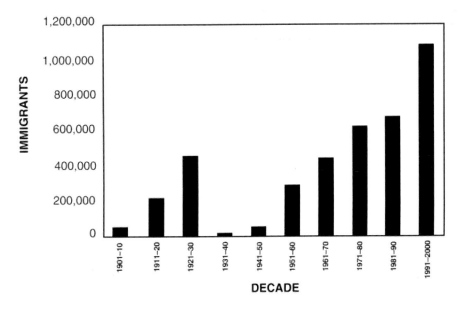

Figure 3. Twentieth-Century Immigration from Mexico to the United States.

Source: U.S. Immigration and Naturalization Service Statistical Yearbook 2000.

particularly the Chicano version forged out of the 1960s. Migration elbows out the 1940s-to-1960s variations of ethnic politics and replaces it with a politics deeply affected by an immigrant society.[89]

If there were any theoretical doubts about the false dichotomy between push-and-pull factors in the case of Mexico, the maquila program, NAFTA, and the agricultural collapse have erased them. For the most part, historians and social scientists have not chosen to critique push-pull in this manner. Rather, as we discussed above, social science perspectives have chosen, in head-in-sand fashion, to focus away from these "macro" factors toward the agency of migrants who, having constructed networks of migration, are regarded as the self-generators of migration. To be sure, Mexican immigrants have taken on active roles and made significant choices in the construction of their lives, families, and communities. But it defies common sense and the evidence to suggest that the explanation for Mexican migration to the United States lies within the immigrants' subjectivity. A simpler and more powerful explanation for Mexican migration to the United States, and the consequent development of the Chicano national minority, should focus on the one hundred years of economic domination by centers of transnational economic power in the United States. Bit by bit, this tighter and tighter network of domination has succeeded in disarticulating the Mexican economy, destroying its domestic industry as well as local agricultural production, creating demographic dislocation, and, in the process, turning an increasing portion of its population into a nomadic mass of migrant workers who eventually emerged as the Chicano national minority. The rise of the Chicano national minority was not an event marginal to U.S. history; quite the opposite, it was central to the construction of a U.S. neocolonial empire.

Epilogue

In our book, we challenged the widespread view that contemporary Chicano history originates in the aftermath of the 1848 conquest.[90] By focusing on economic transformations we questioned the conventional periodization of Chicano history and argued that the nineteenth- and twentieth-century Spanish-speaking populations of the Southwest were largely two different populations. A focus on the War of 1848—the presumed starting point of Chicano history—obscures the relationship between the establishment of U.S. hegemony over Mexico, which comes many decades later, and the development of the Chicano national minority in the United States in the twentieth century.

One needs to distinguish the annexation of 1848 and the ensuing institutional integration of the territory into the United States from the economic conquest of the late nineteenth and early twentieth centuries. Rather than the commonly held belief that the Mexican-American War of

1848 led to the construction of the Chicano minority, this study proposes that the origins of the Chicano population evolved from economic empire led by corporate capitalist interests with the backing of the U.S. State Department. The political and economic repercussions of the war virtually ended by the last decade of the nineteenth century. Furthermore, at no time did the 1848 annexation cause continuous internal migration, the mass population concentration along the border, the bracero program, low-wage maquila plants, Mexico's agricultural crisis, and, more important for this study, the decades of migrations to the United States. Those historical chapters, derived from the economic subordination of Mexico, forged the modern Chicano national minority.

Notes

1. John Kenneth Turner, *Barbarous Mexico* (Chicago: Charles H. Kerr, 1911), 256–57.
2. John Mason Hart, *Revolutionary Mexico: The Coming Process of the Mexican Revolution* (Berkeley: University of California Press, 1997), chapters 5 through 7.
3. As quoted in *The Monitor* (Ottawa, Canada), September 1995.
4. See, for example, the following: Jonathan C. Brown, *Oil and Revolution in Mexico* (Berkeley: University of California Press, 1993); William E. French, *A Peaceful and Working People: Manners, Morals, and Class Formation in Northern Mexico* (Albuquerque: University of New Mexico Press, 1996); G. M. Joseph, *Revolution from without: Yucatán, Mexico, and the United States, 1880–1924* (Durham, N.C.: Duke University Press, 1988); Ramon Eduardo Ruiz, *The People of Sonora and Yankee Capitalists* (Tucson: University of Arizona Press, 1988); Mark Wasserman, *Capitalists, Caciques, and Revolution: The Native Elite and Foreign Enterprise in Chihuahua, Mexico, 1854–1911* (Chapel Hill: University of North Carolina Press, 1984).
5. A number of studies look at the characteristics of the cooperation between Mexico's elites and powerful U.S. monopolies that descended on Mexico at the end of the nineteenth century. In addition to those listed in note 4, see Robert Freeman Smith, *The United States and Revolutionary Nationalism in Mexico, 1916–1922* (Chicago: University of Chicago Press, 1972) and Hart, *Revolutionary Mexico*, chapters 5 and 6.
6. See, e.g., Clarence Clendenen, *The United States and Pancho Villa: A Study in Unconventional Diplomacy* (Ithaca, N.Y.: Cornell University Press, 1961); Friedrich Katz, *The Secret War in Mexico: Europe, the United States, and the Mexican Revolution* (Chicago: University of Chicago Press, 1981); Gregg Andrews, *Shoulder to Shoulder? The American Federation of Labor, the United States, and the Mexican Revolution* (Berkeley: University of California Press, 1991); and Hart, *Revolutionary Mexico*.
7. Gilbert G. Gonzalez, *Mexican Consulates and Labor Organizing: Imperial Politics in the American Southwest* (Austin: University of Texas Press, 1999).
8. On this see Mario Barrera, *Race and Class in the American Southwest: A Theory of Racial Inequality* (Notre Dame, Ind.: University of Notre Dame Press, 1979), 68–69.
9. U.S. Industrial Commission, *Reports of the Industrial Commission on Immigration,* vol. 15 (Washington, D.C.: U.S. Government Printing Office, 1901), lxxxix. The report's conclusions about the cause of migration were based on the testimony of a former commissioner of immigration of the Port of New York. As a witness before the U.S. Industrial Commission he stated, "Those people who come for settlement in this country have a desire and feel the ability in themselves to expand, to look out for larger and better fields for their activity than they can find at home," p. 183; Victor S. Clark, *Mexican Labor in the United States,* Department of Commerce and Labor, Bureau of Labor Bulletin, no. 78 (Washington, D.C., 1908), 505; Manuel Gamio, *Migration and Immigration to the United States: A Study of Adjustment* (Chicago: University of Chicago Press, 1930), 171; and Paul S. Taylor, *A Spanish-Mexican Peasant*

Community, Arandas in Jalisco, Mexico (Berkeley: University of California Press, 1933), 40.

10. For a summary of sociological critiques of the "push-pull" theories see Alejandro Portes and Robert L. Bach, *Latin Journey: Cuban and Mexican Immigrants in the United States* (Berkeley: University of California Press, 1985); Stephan Castles and Mark J. Millen, *The Age of Migration* (New York: Guilford Press, 1993); Ewa Morawska, "The Sociology and Historiography of Immigration" in *Immigration Reconsidered: History, Sociology, and Politics,* edited by Virginia Yans-McLaughlin (New York: Oxford University Press, 1990), 192.

11. Leo Greble, Joan W. Moore, and Ralph C. Guzman, *The Mexican-American People: The Nation's Second-Largest Minority* (New York: Free Press, 1970), 63.

12. The examples of push-pull are many; the following are but a few: Leo R. Chavez, "Defining and Demographically Characterizing the Southern Border of the U. S." in *Demographic Dynamics of the U. S.-Mexico Border,* edited by John R. Weeks and Roberto Ham-Chande (El Paso: Texas Western Press, 1992); Douglas Massey et al., *Return to Aztlan: The Social Process of International Migrations from Western Mexico* (Berkeley: University of California Press, 1987), 108; Mark Reisler, *By the Sweat of Their Brows: Mexican Immigrant Labor in the United States, 1900–1940* (Westport, Conn.: Greenwood Press, 1976), 14; Arthur F. Corwin and Lawrence A. Cardoso, "*Vamos al Norte:* Causes of Mass Migration to the United States," in *Immigrants and Immigrants: Perspectives on Mexican Labor Migration to the United States,* edited by Arthur F. Corwin (Westport, Conn.: Greenwood Press, 1978), 39; David Maciel and Maria Herrera Sobek, "Introduction," in *Culture across Borders: Mexican Immigration and Popular Culture,* edited by David Maciel and Maria Herrera Sobek (Tucson: University of Arizona Press, 1998), 4; Camille Guerin Gonzales, *Mexican Workers and American Dreams: Immigration, Repatriation, and California Farm Labor, 1900–1939 (New* Brunswick: N.J.: Rutgers University Press, 1994), 27–30; George J. Sanchez, *Becoming Mexican American: Ethnicity, Culture, and Identity in Chicano Los Angeles, 1900–1945* (New York: Oxford University Press, 1993), 20, 39; Richard Griswold del Castillo and Arnoldo de Leon, *North to Aztlan: A History of Mexican Americans in the United States* (New York: Twayne Publishers, 1996), 60–61; Antonio Rios-Bustamante, ed., *Mexican Immigrant Workers in the United States* (Los Angeles: UCLA Chicano Studies Research Center Publications, 1981); Frank D. Bean, Rodolfo de la Garza, Bryan Roberts, and Sidney Weintraub, eds., *At the Crossroads: Mexico and U.S. Immigration Policy* (Lanham, Md.: Rowman & Littlefield, 1997).

13. There are a few exceptions. Mario Barrera's 1979 work *Race and Class in the Southwest: A Theory of Inequality* (Notre Dame, Ind.: University of Notre Dame Press) briefly pointed out that the push-pull notions were difficult to separate. Alejandro Portes also points to weaknesses in his chapter "From South of the Border: Hispanic Minorities in the United States" in Virginia Yans-Mclaughlin, ed., *Immigration Reconsidered.* Portes generally identities the role of U.S. expansion and intervention in Mexico, which he lumps with "postcolonial" societies. Upon closer examination he appears to be referring to the territorial acquisition following the Mexican-American War of 1846. He specifically places the origin of the northward migration on the activities of labor recruiters, not on the social dislocations caused by U.S. investments. Interestingly, Saskia Sassen also emphasizes the "emergence of multinational labor market" consequent to the "internationalization of capital." She writes that the investments by U.S. railroad and agricultural corporations and the Border Industrial Program "are all processes which created a labor market." The U.S.-Mexico border artificially divides this "labor market"; hence migration responds to the international labor marketplace. Saskia Sassen, "U.S. Immigration Policy toward Mexico in a Global Economy," in *Between Two Worlds: Mexican Immigrants in the United States,* edited by David Gutierrez (Wilmington, Del.: Scholarly Resources Books, 1996).

14. Quoted in P. Harvey Middleton, *Industrial Mexico: Facts and Figures* (New York: Dodd, Mead, 1919), frontispiece; for a slightly different version see Alfred Tischendorf, *Great Britain in Mexico in the Era of Porfirio Díaz* (Chapel Hill: University of North Carolina Press, 1961), 75.

15. David M. Pletcher, *Rails, Mines, and Progress: Seven American Promoters in Mexico, 1867–1911* (Ithaca, N.Y.: Cornell University Press, 1958), 38.

16. Ibid., 38, 79–80.

17. Chester Lloyd Jones, *Mexico and Its Reconstruction* (New York: D. Appleton, 1921), 299, 310. Mexican elites anticipated the policy design. One-time Mexican representative in Washington Matias Romero proposed an economic conquest in an 1864 speech before a gathering of New York City's prominent citizens. Guests included the largest capitalists: names such as Aspinwall, Astor, Fish, and Clews filled the list. Romero advised: "The United States are the best situated to avail themselves of the immense wealth of Mexico. . . . We are willing to grant to the United States every commercial facility. . . . This will give to the United States all possible advantages that could be derived from annexation, without any of its inconveniences." Matias Romero, *Mexico and the United States* (New York: G. P. Putnam's Sons, 1898), 385.

18. Pletcher, *Rails, Mines, and Progress,* 3.

19. Ruiz, *The People of Sonora,* 14–15; also, Wasserman, *Capitalists, Caciques, and Revolution,* 108–9.

20. In his authoritative 1921 review of Mexican railroads Fred Wilbur Powell stated, "Mexican railroad development was *the result of foreign capital and enterprise,* attracted by national franchises or 'concessions' and encouraged by subsidies [emphasis added]." Fred Wilbur Powell, *The Railroads of Mexico* (Boston: Stratford, 1921), 1.

21. Walter F. Weyl, *Labor Conditions in Mexico,* Bulletin 38, U.S. Department of Labor (January 1902), 52.

22. Marvin U. Bernstein, *The Mining Industry in Mexico, 1890–1950* (Albany: State University of New York Press, 1964), 35.

23. Ibid., 33. Booster advertising offering sure bets on Mexican investments cajoled American investors. Railroads, it was said, guaranteed lucrative profits and vast wealth awaiting the enlightened administration of the American investor. David M. Pletcher, "The Development of the Railroads in Sonora," *Inter-American Economic Affairs 1* (1948): 1–2. One pamphlet published by the U.S. government announced that ". . . the opening up of new mining districts is largely due to Americans, both through the improved mining methods and through the development of railroads built by our capital." International Bureau of the American Republics, Mexico: *Geographical Sketch, Natural Resources, Laws, Economic Conditions, Actual Development, Prospects of Future Growth* (Washington, D.C.: U.S. Government Printing Office, 1904), 233.

24. Robert G. Cleland, "The Mining Industry of Mexico: A Historical Sketch," *Mining and Scientific Press* (July 2, 1921), 13; also, Wasserman, *Capitalists, Caciques, and Revolution,* 76.

25. John Sheahan, *Patterns of Development in Latin America* (Princeton, N.J.: Princeton University Press, 1987), 297.

26. Henry Bamford Parkes, *A History of Mexico* (Boston: Houghton Mifflin, 1970), 309, cited in Barrera, *Race and Class in the Southwest,* 69.

27. On this see G. M. Joseph, *Revolution from without,* 30, 51, 62; also, Wasserman, *Capitalists, Caciques, and Revolution,* 46.

28. John Coatsworth, *Growth against Development: The Economic Impact of Railroads in Porfirian Mexico* (DeKalb: Northern Illinois University Press, 1981), 123–24.

29. Ibid., 158 (our emphasis); John Mason Hart makes this same point in his classic *Revolutionary Mexico.* Hart writes: "In the midst of land seizures associated with the planning of the new railroad system, peasant uprisings ranged from Chihuahua in the north to Oaxaca in the south," 41.

30. Coatsworth, *Growth against Development,* 170. See also French, *A Peaceful and Working People,* 37–47; Ruiz, *The People of Sonora,* 16–17; and Wasserman, *Capitalists, Caciques, and Revolution,* 109.

31. Coatsworth, *Growth against Development,* 145.

32. Michael Johns, *The City of Mexico in the Age of Díaz* (Austin: University of Texas Press, 1997), 14.

33. Friedrich Katz, "The Liberal Republic and the Porfiriato, 1867–1910," in *Mexico since independence,* edited by Leslie Bethel (New York: Cambridge University Press, 1991), 101; see also Hart, *Revolutionary Mexico,* 169.

34. Roger D. Hansen, *The Politics of Mexican Development* (Baltimore, Md.: Johns Hopkins University Press, 1971), 27; Nathan L. Whetten, *Rural Mexico* (Urbana: University of Illinois Press, 1948), 89.

35. Gonzalez Navarro, *El Porfiriato*, 20.

36. Johns, *The City of Mexico*, 64

37. Turner, *Barbarous Mexico*, 116.

38. Johns, *The City of Mexico*, 30.

39. Evelyn Hu-Dehart, "Pacification of the Yaquis in the Late Porfiriato: Development and Implications," *Hispanic American Historical Review* 54, no. 1 (February 1974): 77.

40. Moises Gonzalez Navarro, *Historia Moderna de Mexico, El Porfiriato,* vol. 4 (Mexico City: Editorial Hermes, 1957); see also Hart, *Revolutionary Mexico.*

41. Fred Wilbur Powell, "The Railroads of Mexico," in Robert Glass Cleland, *The Mexican Yearbook, 1920–1921* (Los Angeles: Times-Mirror Press, 1924), 164.

42. Frank Tannenbaum, *The Mexican Agrarian Revolution* (Washington, D.C.: Brookings Institution, 1929), 126.

43. Walter E. Weyl, *Labor Conditions in Mexico,* Bulletin 38, U.S. Department of Labor (January 1902), 91.

44. See Rodney D. Anderson, *Outcasts in Their Own Land: Mexican Industrial Workers, 1906–1911* (De Kalb: Northern Illinois University Press, 1976), 48–50.

45. Clark, *Mexican Labor in the United States,* 470–71; see also French, *A Peaceful and Working People,* 42–43.

46. Gonzalez Navarro, *El Porfiriato,* XVII, 25.

47. Friedrich Katz, "The Liberal Republic and the Porfiriato, 1867–1910," 89.

48. E. A. H. Tays, "Present Labor Conditions in Mexico," *Engineering and Mining Journal* 84 (October 5, 1907): 622.

49. Allen H. Rogers, "Character and Habits of Mexican Miners," *Engineering and Mining Journal* 85 (April 6, 1906): 700.

50. See Robert G. Cleland, "The Mining Industry of Mexico: A Historical Sketch," *Mining and Scientific Press* (July 2, 1921): 640.

51. J. Fred Rippy, *Latin America and the Industrial Age,* 2nd ed. (New York: G.P. Putnam's Sons 1947). Quote cited in Jonathan Brown, "Foreign and Native-Born Workers in Porfirian Mexico," *American Historical Review* 98 (June 1993): 798.

52. González Navarro, *El Porfiriato,* 23.

53. Rogers," Character and Habits of Mexican Miners," 701. See also Brown, *Oil and Revolution in Mexico,* 80–81. Brown writes that the Veracruz state population increased by 280,000 between 1890 and 1910, the oil boom years cited by personages such as Edward Doheny, developer of the Veracruz area oil explorations.

54. Dwight E. Woodbridge, "La Cananea Mining Camp," *Engineering and Mining Journal* 82 (October 6, 1906): 623.

55. See French, *A Peaceful and Working People, Brown, Oil and Revolution in Mexico;* Wasserman, *Capitalists, Caciques, and Revolution;* Ruiz, *The People of Sonora*; Smith, *The United States and Revolutionary Nationalism in Mexico.*

56. Clark, *Mexican Labor in the United States,* 472.

57. Taylor, *A Spanish-Mexican Peasant Community,* 44.

58. See, e.g., Nestor Rodriguez, "The Battle for the Border: Notes on Autonomous Migration, Transnational Communities, and the State" in *Immigration: A Civil Rights Issue for the Americas*, edited by Suzanne Jonas and Suzie Dod Thomas (Wilmington, Del.: Scholarly Resources Books, 1999); for a variation on the theme see David M. Reimers, *Still the Golden Door: Third World Comes to America* (New York: Columbia University Press, 1985), 128–29; Vicki Ruiz, *From out of the Shadows: Mexican Women* in *Twentieth-Century America* (New York: Oxford University Press, 1998), 163; Pierette Hondagneu-Sotelo, *Gendered Transitions: Mexican Experience of Migration* (Berkeley: University of California Press, 1994); Douglas Massey, "The Social Organization of Mexican Migration to the United States" in *The Immigration Reader: America in Multidisciplinary Perspective*, edited by David Jacobsen (New York: Oxford University Press, 1998), 213–14; and David Jacobsen, "Introduction," in *The Immigration Reader.* Jacobsen writes: "Mexican migration reflects the earlier development of social networks that sustain it."

59. See, e.g., Wayne Cornelius, "The Structural Embeddedness of Demand for Mexican Immigrant Labor: New Evidence from California," in *Crossings: Mexican Immigration in Interdisciplinary Perspective,* edited by Marcelo M. Suarez-Orozco (Cambridge, Mass.: Harvard University Press, 1998), 141–42; and Smith, "Commentary," in *Crossings.*

60. Massey, "What's Driving Mexico-U.S. Migration," 953.

61. Ibid., 954.

62. See the following: Reimers, *Still the Golden Door*; also, Frank D. Bean, W. Parker Frisbie, Edward Telles, and B. Lindsay Lowell, "The Economic Impact of Undocumented Workers in the Southwest of the United States," in *Demographic Dynamics of the U.S.-Mexico Border*, edited by John R. Weeks and Roberto Ham-Chande (El Paso: Texas Western Press, 1992).

63. Saskia Sassen, "Foreign Investment: A Neglected Variable," in Jacobsen, ed., *The Immigration Reader*; also, Saskia Sassen, *Globalization and Its Discontents: Essays on the New Mobility of People and Money* (New York: New Press), 1998, chap. 6.

64. Mr. Cardoso has long since shed the facade and openly advocates the neoliberal open-door investment policy prescribed by the United States as the preferred model for economic development.

65. The critiques of world systems theory are numerous, but see in particular Eric Wolf, *Europe and the People without History* (Berkeley: University of California Press, 1981) and Peter Worsley, *Three Worlds of Culture and Development* (Chicago: University of Chicago Press, 1984).

66. Smith, *The United States and Revolutionary Nationalism*, 34.

67. Howard F. Cline, *Mexico: Revolution to Evolution, 1940–1960* (New York: Oxford University Press, 1963), 244.

68. Benjamin Higgins, *Economic Development: Problems, Principles, and Policies* (New York: W. W. Norton, 1968), 643.

69. Cline, *Mexico*, 245.

70. Higgins, *Economic Development*, 645.

71. W. Whitney Hicks, "Agricultural Development in Northern Mexico, 1940–1960," *Land Economics* (November 1967): 396.

72. Raul Fernandez, *The United States-Mexico Border* (Notre Dame, Ind.: University of Notre Dame Press, 1977), 108.

73. Ibid., 123.

74. See David Barkin, "Mexico's Albatross: The U.S. Economy," *Latin American Perspectives* 2, no. 2 (1975); see also Hart, *Revolutionary Mexico,* epilogue.

75. Cline, *Mexico*, 86.

76. Raul Fernandez, *The Mexican-American Border Region Issues and Trends* (Notre Dame, Ind.: University of Notre Dame Press, 1989), 61.

77. Ibid.

78. Fernandez, *The United States-Mexico Border*, 108.

79. See Fernandez, *The United States-Mexico Border*, and *The Mexican-American Border Region.*

80. David Barkin and Blanca Suarez, "El Fin de la Autosuficiencia Alimentaria," in *Mexico: Nuevo Imagen* (Mexico City: Centro de Ecodesarrollo, Editorial Nueve Imagen, 1982); Ruth Rama, "Some Effects of the Internationalization of Agriculture on the Mexican Agricultural Crisis," in Stephan E. Sanderson, *The Americas in the New International Division of Labor* (New York: Holmes & Meier, 1985).

81. Hart, *Revolutionary Mexico.* Hart writes on p. 378, "Mexico in 1987 constitutes an economic and social disaster . . . 70 percent of the children suffer from malnutrition. . . . The World Health Organization estimates that 107,000 Mexican children died in 1983 from three diseases for which immunization is available."

82. Carlos Heredia and Mary E. Purcell, "The Polarization of Mexican Society," paper prepared for the NGO Working Group on the World Bank, Development Group for the Alternative Policies, December 1994.

83. Gonzalez, *Mexican Consuls and Labor Organizing*, 12, 14–15; see also James D. Cockcroft, *Mexico: Class Formation, Capital Accumulation, and the State* (New York: Monthly Review Press, 1983), 91.

84. Gonzalez, *Imperial Politics*, chap. 6.

85. *International Report*, issue 34, vol. 12, no. 1, (March 1994); issue 35, vol. 12, no. 2 (June 1994); issue 37, vol. 13, no. 1 (February 1995); and issue 38, vol. 13, no. 2 (July 1995). Raul Fernandez, "Perspectivas del Tratado de Libre Comercio de Norteamerica," *Deslinde*, 13 (March–April 1993). James Cypher, "Developing Disarticulation within the Mexican Economy," *Latin American Perspectives* 28, no. 3 (May 2001), 11–37.

86. Victor S. Quintana, "La Catástrofe Maicera," *La Opinión* (April 17, 1999); Chris Kraul, "Growing Troubles in Mexico," *Los Angeles Times* (January 17, 2000). Kraul writes that due to corn imports from the United States, "one-fifth of the 250,000 families who were

working the land in Guanajuato in 1990 have since left their farms . . . a population shift that has been repeated across Mexico." The Free Trade Agreement "mandated the end of the costly subsidy program." John Coatsworth, "Commentary," in Suarez-Orozco, ed., *Crossings*, 75–78; Philip Martin, "Do Mexican Agricultural Policies Stimulate Emigration?" in *At the Crossroads: Mexico and U.S. Immigration Policy*, edited by Frank D. Bean, Rodolfo O. de la Garza, Bryan R. Roberts, and Sidney Weintraub (Lanham, Md.: Rowman & Littlefield, 1997).

87. "A Call to Action Is Needed at U.S. Border," *Los Angeles Times* (May 9, 1999); Mark Stevenson, "Border Factories Target of Fury over Mass Killings of Women," *Orange County (Calif.) Register* (April 4, 1999); see also Roberto Ham-Chande and John R. Weeks, "A Demographic Perspective of the U.S.-Mexico Border," in *Demographic Dynamics of the U.S.-Mexico Border*, edited by John R. Weeks and Roberto Ham-Chande.

88. Frank D. Bean and Marta Tienda, *The Hispanic Population in the United States* (New York: Russell Sage Foundation, 1987), 110; Marcelo M. Suarez-Orozco, "Introduction: Crossings: Mexican Immigration in Interdisciplinary Perspectives," in Suarez-Orozco, ed., *Crossings*, 7; Gilda Laura Ochoa, "Mexican Americans' Attitudes and Interactions toward Mexican Immigrants: A Qualitative Analysis of Conflict and Cooperation," *Social Science Quarterly* (March 2000).

89. James P. Allen and Eugene Turner, using data available to 1990, have shown that in several enclaves of high concentrations of Mexicans and Mexican Americans in Los Angeles and Orange Counties (Consolidated Metropolitan Statistical Area), nearly 64 percent of those age 25 to 64 are immigrants out of a total population numbering 1.6 million. They also demonstrate that more than 37 percent of the same age group immigrated between 1980 and 1990. In other words, at least a third of the age group in these enclaves entered the United States in the post-1980 period. That such a high concentration of adults are immigrants will have a decided effect on the political orientation of the group. See James P. Allen and Eugene Turner, "Spatial Patterns of Immigrant Assimilation," *Professional Geographer*, 48, no. 2 (1996).

90. Gilbert G. Gonzalez and Raul Fernandez, "Chicano History: Transcending Cultural Models," *Pacific Historical Review*, 23, no. 4 (1994).

The Chicano Movement and the Treaty

Richard Griswold del Castillo

The Treaty of Guadalupe Hidalgo is the most important document concerning Mexican Americans that exists. From it stem specific guarantees affecting our civil rights, language, culture, and religion.

Armando Rendón
Chicano Manifesto

During the 1960s and 1970s a new generation of Mexican Americans sought to redefine their position within the United States using, in part, the Treaty of Guadalupe Hidalgo. They called themselves Chicanos, a term previously used as a derogatory reference to working-class Mexican immigrants. Sparked by a growing civil rights and anti-war movement, Chicano political militants sought to focus world attention on the failed promises of the Treaty of Guadalupe Hidalgo. Beginning with an agrarian revolutionary movement in New Mexico and a farm workers' strike in California, the newly born Chicano movement resurrected the treaty as a primary document in the struggle for social justice. This generation of Mexican Americans learned of the legal basis for reclaiming their lost lands. The political aims of the Chicano movement, to gain representation and recognition, generated a more critical interpretation of the meaning of the Mexican War and the treaty. A lasting legacy of Chicano awareness in the 1960s and 1970s was a consciousness of their history dating from 1848 and the Treaty of Guadalupe Hidalgo.

The Alianza Movement and New Mexican Lands

One of the first activists to provoke a reassessment of the treaty was Reies López Tijerina. Originally a fundamentalist preacher from Texas, Tijerina became part of the struggle of the Hispanos of New Mexico to regain the community land grants that had been taken from them after 1848 in violation of the treaty. Representing New Mexican land claimants, Tijerina traveled to Mexico City in 1959 and again in 1964 to present memorials to the Mexican authorities, including the president of Mexico. Thousands of Hispanos whose families had lost their lands in violation of the terms of the treaty signed the petitions. Tijerina and the delegation asked the government of Mexico to demand that the United States fulfill the terms of the treaty. On both occasions the Mexican government listened respectfully but did nothing.[1]

During the early 1960s Tijerina traveled throughout New Mexico, organizing La Alianza Federal de Mercedes Libres. The purpose of the organization was "to organize and acquaint the heirs of all Spanish land-grants covered by the Guadalupe Hidalgo Treaty" with their rights.[2] This organization became the catalyst for a number of militant actions by the Hispano villagers: the occupation of Kit Carson National Forest, the proclamation of the Republic of San Joaquín de Chama, the courthouse raid and shootout at Tierra Amarilla, a massive military manhunt for Tijerina and his followers, and lengthy legal battles. Lost in the sensational publicity surrounding Tijerina and the Alianza during the late 1960s was the fact that Alianza leaders justified their movement on the basis of historical and legal interpretations both of the constitutions of New Mexico and the United States and of the Treaty of Guadalupe Hidalgo. Much like the American Indian Movement of the same period, the Alianza claimed that legitimate treaty rights had been violated and demanded compensation. Tijerina's analysis of the land-grant question appeared in a booklet that the Alianza published and distributed throughout the Southwest.[3] Tijerina based his arguments for the reclamation of lost Hispano lands on two documents, the *Recopilación de leyes de las Indias*, which had been the legal framework for the Spanish land grants prior to the nineteenth century, and the Treaty of Guadalupe Hidalgo. He contended that the United States had violated Articles VIII and IX of the treaty, which had guaranteed property and citizenship rights to Mexicans. Ultimately, Tijerina's claims were presented before the U.S. Supreme Court as a class action lawsuit in 1969. Denied a hearing two times in 1970, the case finally received a favorable recommendation, but it was not presented, probably because Tijerina lacked sufficient funding to pursue the issue.[4]

One of the little-known episodes in the Alianza's history was Tijerina's effort to forge an alliance with Mexican popular and governmental organizations.

Early in January 1964 Tijerina and his wife, Rosita, went to Mexico City to meet with Mexican officials. On January 9th he met with a labor leader, Lic. Javier Rojo Gómez, who was the secretary general of the Confederación Nacional Campesina. Tijerina reported that he felt encouraged and that the interview was a great success. On January 14th he met with a secretary who worked with the Relaciones Exteriores (foreign relations) where he left a memorandum for president Adolfo López Mateos. On January 29 he sent a telegram to Lic. Donato Miranda Fonseca, secretary to the president in the National Palace, asking for a meeting, and on February 4 he met with the secretary. Tijerina had a lengthy meeting where he explained the various violations and aggressions suffered by Mexicans in the United States since the Treaty of Guadalupe Hidalgo.

Back in New Mexico, Tijerina set to work to organize a caravan to Mexico City. While doing this he began a letter-writing campaign to remind both the U.S. and Mexican governments of their obligations under the treaty.

In July, Tijerina again went to Mexico with his wife. In Chihuahua he attended a student meeting to promote the upcoming caravan. While he was speaking he was arrested by the Mexican Judicial Police. He was released from jail after a number of strategic phone calls were placed to Mexico City and Washington, D.C. He continued his journey to Mexico City undaunted, making a map for the later caravan. In Mexico City he sent a letter to Luis Echeverría, the secretary of Gobernación, along with memoranda to the president, Adolfo López Mateos, informing them of the caravan's purpose. He received a "positive impression" that the caravan would be permitted to travel to Mexico. He visited the offices of all the political parties in Mexico City, the left as well as the right, explaining his position on the treaty and "pueblo olvidado": "We, the Mexicans in the United States, only want that all Mexico, in the name of the Treaty of Guadalupe, would receive us so that the United States would know of the dear brotherhood between the Mexicans of the South and of those north of the Rio Grande." [5] Tijerina's speeches were reported in the Mexican media and he even appeared

before the national syndicate of publishers in Mexico City (Sindicato Nacional de Redactores de la Prensa), where he talked about the upcoming caravan.

Tijerina held a meeting of interested Mexican officials to discuss the caravan, emphasizing that the purpose was to seek Mexican support for Chicanos and their struggles in New Mexico. Mexican federal agents also attended. The next day Tijerina was detained by the police and questioned about his activities. Finally they decided to deport him with the threat that if he returned he would be put in prison for ten years. They took him to the airport and saw him off on the plane. Tijerina was convinced that he had been set up by the U.S. government. Back in New Mexico, with a heavy heart, Tijerina called off the caravan. Tijerina's activities in attempting to gain the support of the Mexican people for the plight of the Hispano villagers had threatened the Mexican government. It was possible that the U.S. government had influenced the deportation but ultimately the Mexican government was responsible. This episode put an end to the Alianza's dream of having the Mexican government act as an advocate within the United Nations.[6]

A few years later the legal and moral issues raised by Tijerina's Alianza movement influenced domestic politics. Senator Joseph Montoya of New Mexico introduced a bill in the U.S. Senate to create a Special Commission on Guadalupe Hidalgo Land Rights. Simultaneously Representative Manuel Luján (New Mexico) introduced a similar bill in the House. Montoya proposed that the federal government establish a temporary commission that would review violations of property rights guaranteed in the treaty and make recommendations to Congress and the president regarding restitution. One of the first tasks of the commission would be to "make a comprehensive study of the provisions of the Treaty of Guadalupe Hidalgo" to determine violations of the treaty. Senator Montoya, by no means a political ally of Reies Tijerina, adopted what seemed to be a radical plan of questioning established land tenures in his home state. He justified his measure as a means of rectifying past injustices: "If certain lands have been wrongfully taken from people, we must make amends."[7] Montoya's bill reflected the degree to which the long and bitter history of land-grant conflict in New Mexico had emerged as an issue for federal concern. Senator Montoya's bill died in the Insular and Interior Affairs Committee, as did a similar bill introduced the same year by Congressman Augustus Hawkins of California.

Hawkins proposed that Congress establish a Community Land Grant Act targeted specifically at the villages of New Mexico. Like Montoya, he envisioned the establishment of a commission that would hear petitions from members of villages whose community land grants had been lost through corruption or deceit. The commission was to have the power to "reconstitute the community land-grant" under the Laws of the Indies where it was consistent with the Constitution or state laws. Additionally the

Hawkins Bill provided for 10 million dollars to finance the operations of the commission.

Unfortunately there are no records of the debate surrounding either Montoya's or Hawkin's bill in these committees. That these measures were defeated is not too surprising, because any federal investigation into land tenure in New Mexico would be bound to unsettle powerful commercial and speculative interests. Nevertheless congressional interest in investigating the violations of the treaty's provisions continued. Throughout the 1970s at least three bills were introduced. In 1977 Representative Henry B. González (Texas) introduced a resolution to create a special congressional committee "to investigate the legal, political, and diplomatic status of lands which were subject to grants from the King of Spain and the Government of Mexico prior to the acquisition of the American Southwest as a result of the Treaty of Guadalupe Hidalgo." In 1979, Representative Ronald V. Dellums (California) introduced a similar proposal, but a House committee rejected it. Finally, in 1979, as a result of lobbying by Reies Tijerina, the New Mexico legislature instructed its representatives to introduce legislation to establish a board of review to investigate the theft of communal lands in northern New Mexico.[8] This move, like others before it, was killed by conservative interests in Congress.

The motivation for the continued legislative attempts to rectify the land-grant situation in New Mexico came primarily from increased public awareness and pressure originating from a revitalized Alianza movement. Again, the public records are silent on the debates surrounding these measures, because each was squashed without a lengthy hearing.

◦ The Urban Chicano Movement

Knowledge of the treaty and its violations was widespread among New Mexicans. Collectively they had been fighting for a return of their pueblo lands for more than a century. On the other hand millions of urban Chicanos—sons and daughters of Mexican immigrants who had entered the United States after 1910—had yet to be educated about the treaty. In the 1960s and 1970s this process took place in informal meetings, discussions, and rallies.

In the spring of 1968, urban and rural Mexican-American leaders found a common ground for dialog. Rudolfo "Corky" Gonzales, leader and organizer of the Denver Crusade for Justice, joined forces with Reies Tijerina to participate in the Poor People's March on Washington, D.C. Together with other urban leaders they issued a joint statement, entitled *We Demand,* listing the needs of Mexican Americans throughout the nation. These included bilingual education, adequate housing, job development, more sensitive law enforcement, economic opportunities, and agricultural reforms. The demand for agricultural reforms, inspired by Tijerina's struggle in New Mexico, called not only for a return of lands stolen from the pueblos in violation of the treaty, but also for "compensation for taxes, legal costs, etc., which pueblo heirs spent trying to save their land."[9]

The Treaty of Guadalupe Hidalgo and its implications became a topic of discussion at the first Annual Youth Conference in Denver, Colorado, which was organized by Gonzales in 1969. Knowledge of treaty violations became a driving force behind the final statement of the conference in "El Plan Espiritual de Aztlán," a document of Chicano solidarity and a declaration of independence. During the 1970s, surveys and critiques of the treaty, and especially of Articles VIII and IX, began to appear in anthologies and books being published to satisfy the demand for more printed materials dealing with Chicanos. One of the most popular of these was Armando Rendón's *Chicano Manifesto.* In the section of the book dealing with the treaty, Rendón summarized his view of the importance of the treaty: "The Treaty of Guadalupe Hidalgo is the most important document concerning Mexican Americans that exists."[10] The terms and spirit of the treaty, he said, had been systematically violated by the U.S. government. Rendón called for Chicanos to become aware of the "exact processes by which the Treaty of Guadalupe Hidalgo was made meaningless over the past century and a half." He had in mind a detailed documentary case that could be made against the federal government so that some kind of compensation could be exacted. He hinted that Chicanos could seek, as the American Indian tribes had, monetary settlements or even a return of territory to Mexico.[11] The probability that the latter would occur was nil, but the prospect of a monetary settlement did not seem wholly impossible, given the political atmosphere of the time. For many militants of the 1970s the treaty legitimized their demands for social and economic justice and provided a cause for radical action.

The Brown Berets' Occupation of Catalina Island

The same year that Rendón's *Chicano Manifesto* appeared, the most dramatic attempt to publicize the importance of the treaty took place. In September 1972 the Brown Berets in California began a twenty-four-day occupation of Santa Catalina Island, claiming that it had never been included in the original treaty and thus was still part of Mexico.

The Brown Berets were founded in 1967 by David Sánchez, a former chairman of the Los Angeles Mayor's Youth Council. Eventually the Berets claimed five thousand members nationwide. The goal of the Berets was to fulfill the ideals articulated in "El Plan Espiritual de Aztlán," that is to control or at least have a voice in the policies of major institutions in the barrio that affected Chicanos: the schools, police, welfare offices, and the immigration service. As an action-oriented militant organization, the Berets participated in and helped organize most of the major landmarks of the Chicano movement: high-school "blowouts" (walkouts) and moratorium marches in East Los Angeles, La Marcha and Caravana de la Reconquista, as well as other local actions in southern California designed to raise public awareness of oppression and racism.[12]

A particular interpretation of the meaning of the Treaty of Guadalupe Hidalgo influenced the Brown Berets' decision to stage a symbolic occupation of Santa Catalina Island. None of the nine channel islands off the coast of southern California had been mentioned in the treaty as part of the territory ceded to the United States in 1848. According to popular beliefs in Mexico and in many U.S. barrios, the islands remained part of Mexico until the 1870s, when Benito Juárez, then president of Mexico, leased Catalina Island to Americans. William Wrigley, Jr., of the chewing-gum empire, eventually acquired the ninety-nine-year lease on the property, which expired in 1970. The true history of Catalina Island's title contradicted this folk history. On July 4, 1846, Pio Pico, the last Mexican governor of California granted the island of Catalina to Tomás Robbins. Robbins sold the island to José María Covarrubias of Santa Bárbara in 1850, and Covarrubias sold it to Albert Roshard of San Francisco in 1853. Thereafter the title to the island is traceable up to Mr. Wrigley's purchase in 1919.[13]

Although the claim that Catalina had been leased from Mexico had no historical basis, the story reflected a need to keep alive the issue of the illegal seizure of community lands. The legend also reflected a real ambiguity in the treaty regarding the status of the offshore islands. This vagueness had been a source of sporadic public discussion in the 1950s and 1960s.[14]

Some legal experts in Mexico were prepared to argue that the island could be reclaimed by Mexico. A partial basis for argument was that Governor Pico's grant of the island was made after the declaration of war and hence was considered invalid by both the U.S. and the Mexican governments.[15] Late in the nineteenth century the Mexican government had considered making the ownership of the islands an international issue. In 1894 the United States asserted control over Clipperton Island in the Pacific Ocean (called Medanos or La Pasión by Mexico), a small island some thousand miles off the coast of southern Mexico. Mexican newspapers claimed that this island was rightfully Mexico's and that the Catalina Islands should be reclaimed by the Mexican government in retaliation. The issue became an item for official private correspondence but soon died for lack of presidential support.[16]

The Brown Berets did not seriously believe that they could regain Catalina for Mexico. The real purpose of the occupation was to provide a forum for discussion of the problems confronting Mexican Americans arising from their colonized status.

After several weeks of planning at a base near Lancaster, California, the offensive against the island, code named Tecolote, was ready. A primary concern was secrecy. From previous scouting expeditions the Berets knew that there was a Mexican barrio of about four hundred persons on the island. The leaders flew to Catalina and the rest of the contingent took the boat and acted as tourists. On August 30th the Berets assembled twenty-five men and one woman at the Waikiki Motel on Catalina. From there, they rented a jeep, and drove to the top of the hill above the town of Avalon Harbor. At nine o'clock the next morning the citizens of the small town awoke to see a huge Mexican flag flying from the hilltop. Campo Tecolote had been established.[17] The Beret contingent carried no arms but stood in formation, dressed in military fashion. At first some residents, recalling folktales about the controversial title to the islands thought they had been invaded by the Mexican army.[18]

The mayor of Avalon, Raymond Rydell, a former vice-chancellor of the California State College system, had dealt with student militants during the 1960s. He encouraged the sheriff's department to use a low-key approach to the Beret encampment and to leave them alone as long as they caused no trouble. The vice-president of the Santa Catalina Island Company was a Mexican American named Renton. He too advised the sheriffs to leave the Berets alone; and to show his good will he sent the Beret contingent cold drinks and box lunches. David Sánchez, the Beret leader, issued a press release, which read in part: "As gentlemen who may try to understand other gentlemen, how about a peaceful resolution? . . . We have begun an occupation plan, which is by means of peaceful occupation only. By this plan, we wish to bring you the true plight of the Chicano, and the problems of the people of Mexican descent living in the United States."[19]

The occupation lasted twenty-four days. During that time the Brown Beret camp became something of a tourist attraction. The small Mexican-American population of the island helped provide food and drink for the Chicano demonstrators. Local restaurateur Mike Budd gave them a free meal at his restaurant. As the occupation stretched into weeks, the Berets had a chance to talk to some of the island's Chicano residents. Their message was that the United States was illegally occupying not just Catalina but all of the American Southwest. Mexican Americans were a colonized people, they said, victims of an unjust war of aggression. The occupation of Catalina ended peacefully on September 23, when the city council decided to enforce a local camping ordinance and threatened jail unless the Berets abandoned their campground. The Berets left, vowing to return to occupy other islands at some future date and to engage in more legal research. As it turned out, however, the Catalina occupation was the last organized action of the Brown Berets. A few weeks later their leader, David Sánchez, citing the pervasive presence of police informants within the organization, announced that the Brown Berets had been disbanded.[20]

The Treaty of Guadalupe Hidalgo provided a basis for legitimizing the occupation of Catalina Island, both for the presentation of grievances and the dramatization of *la causa*. In comparison to the Alianza's occupation of Kit Carson National Forest and the shootout at Tierra Amarilla, Catalina Island was a relatively minor incident. Nevertheless, the Santa Catalina occupation demonstrated the degree to which some were willing to take militant action based on the historical violations of the Treaty of Guadalupe Hidalgo.

Interpretation by Chicano Intelligencia

American Indians and Mexican Americans are the only segments of U.S. society that have kept alive the issues raised by the Treaty of Guadalupe Hidalgo. Because of the popular movements of the 1960s and 1970s as well as the institutionalization of Chicano Studies classes in major universities, larger numbers of Mexican Americans have been introduced to the treaty and its significance. More often than not, however, this familiarity did not go beyond a belief that the treaty guaranteed certain rights for Mexican Americans and that these rights had been violated.

Only a few scholars writing about Chicano history have attempted to go beyond this generalized view of the implications of the treaty. Perhaps the most detailed, scholarly, and realistic appraisal of the meaning of the treaty for human rights appeared in 1978 as a doctoral dissertation by Fernando Chacón Gómez. Before Gómez, no one had analyzed how the treaty influenced subsequent court cases involving Mexican Americans. This work was a conscious blending of scholarly training and Chicano activism.

Gómez's main argument was that despite decades of "invisibility" and general neglect, the Treaty of Guadalupe Hidalgo had real legal implications for the present. He wanted to explore the legal history of the treaty after 1848 to determine "to what extent it could be used to compel enforcement of contemporary civil rights." He analyzed the cultural and historical background of the legal battles waged in the nineteenth and early twentieth centuries to secure property and civil rights for former Mexican citizens. On a case-by-case basis he pointed to the ethnocentric and racist basis of the arguments and decisions. Manifest Destiny, he concluded, had found its way into the courtroom. This was especially true in New Mexico where, because of the judge's ignorance of local tradition, "the century-old concept of flexibility of the common law may indeed have been 'bastardized.'" Elsewhere in the United States, judges relied on local precedent in making decisions. Not so in New Mexico. Thus, although the treaty

was a "rights conferring document," in the courts it remained a dead letter. Chacón Gómez concluded that the most viable avenues for redress were largely in the international arena because the Supreme Court had consistently ruled against interpretations of the treaty that would protect Mexican-American rights. A legal attack on the injustices and inequalities confronted by people of Mexican origin, he thought, could best be pursued in such international forums as the United Nations and the World Court.[21] This approach is currently being followed by a handful of activists.

Internationalization of the Treaty

Since World War II the plight of the Mexican Americans within the United States as been presented before various international forums, primarily agencies of the United Nations concerned with human rights. The Treaty of Guadalupe Hidalgo has figured prominently in these formal presentations; indeed the treaty has provided the legal rationale for discussing Mexican American rights within international bodies.

The earliest attempt to use an international forum to redress wrongs vis à vis Mexican Americans was by the American Committee for the Protection of the Foreign Born in 1959. The committee was a leftist organization that split from the American Civil Liberties Union in 1942. Carey McWilliams, a progressive newspaper reporter, editor, author, and activist was one of its first directors during the 1940s. In the 1950s the committee fell onto the U.S. attorney general's list of subversive, communist infiltrated organizations, and committee members were questioned by the House Un-American Activities Committee in the early 1960s. In 1959 the American Committee for Protection of the Foreign Born submitted a petition to the United Nations entitled "Our Badge of Infamy: A Petition to the United Nations on the Treatment of Mexican Immigrants."[22] The petition was signed by more than sixty individuals, most of them Anglo-American professionals. They charged that the United States had violated provisions of the Universal Declaration of Human Rights, specifically Articles II, III, IV, VII, IX, XV, XXII, and XXV. In their opening statement they stated that U.S. government committees and agencies had investigated the plight of the Mexican immigrant in the United States but no change had come about. "We feel that the United Nations should consider this problem only because repeated attempts over the years by agencies of the United States government and public and private organizations have failed to overcome the serious deprivation of the human rights of the Mexican immigrants living in the United States."[23]

The petition was not limited to defending Mexican immigrants; it also dealt with the violations of the Treaty of Guadalupe Hidalgo affecting the native-born Mexican Americans. "While rights to property, especially land, were safeguarded by the provisions of the Treaty of Guadalupe Hidalgo, in practice Mexicans and Mexican Americans were cheated of most of their properties in a short while."[24] The main orientation of the petition was to present concrete evidence, in the form of historical examples, of how the human rights of Mexicans in the United States had been violated. Instances of mistreatment and murder of bracero workers were documented to show violations of Article III of the U.N. declaration guaranteeing freedoms regardless of race. Cases of wage discrimination were related to violation of Article IV, which forbade slavery and involuntary servitude. The operations of the Immigration and Naturalization Service during Operation Wetback (a repatriation program of 1954) were presented as violations of Article IX, which provided for equal protection under the law.

The significance of the committee's petition was that it was the first attempt to go beyond the domestic system to seek redress under international law. It was over twenty years before another organization attempted to internationalize the issues raised by the treaty.

During the 1980s various Native American groups discovered the Treaty of Guadalupe Hidalgo and began to forge alliances with Mexican American organizations and individuals. In July 1980, at the Sixth Annual Conference of the International Indian Treaty Council (IITC) meeting at Fort Belnap, Montana, a resolution was introduced by native delegates to support the Treaty of Guadalupe Hidalgo and Mexican-American rights to self-determination.[25] The International Indian Treaty Council was a San Francisco-based organization dedicated to working for the rights of native peoples throughout the Western Hemisphere. Since 1977 it had been recognized by the United Nations as a Non-Government Organization (N.G.O.) and had traveled numerous times to Geneva to present petitions and interventions on behalf of Indian people. In 1981 the IITC introduced the Treaty of Guadalupe Hidalgo as one of the North American treaties that affected Indian peoples before the International Conference of Non-Government Organizations concerning Indigenous Populations and Land. Several U.S. Indian tribes considered the treaty an important part of their claims for redress. The Hopi people, for example, presented a statement at a 1981 Geneva Conference where they cited Article IX and XI of the treaty to support their opposition to the relocation of the Navajo (Dineh) and Hopi elders from their ancestral lands near Big Mountain, Arizona.[26]

According to Hopi prophecy, "most important information" bearing on the fate of their nation would be found at the bottom of a "high stack of papers." The elders reported that they had found this "important information"—Disturnell's 1847 map, which had been appended to the Treaty of Guadalupe Hidalgo. That map contained a notation, "Los Moquis [Hopis] has conservado su independencia desde el año 1680." The meaning of this notation on the treaty map was clear: the Hopis had not been considered subjugated by the Spanish; they were independent and sovereign. In the words of the elders, "From that time forward, the power of the Hopi and our right to sovereign independence should never have been questioned."[27] The 1981 Hopi statement as delivered to the United Nations went on to assert that their rights as Mexican citizens under Article VIII of the treaty had been violated by the U.S. courts and that their religious rights under Article IX had not been protected.

Other Indians also considered the Treaty of Guadalupe Hidalgo as bearing on their claims for compensation. The Tohono O'odham, or Papago, for example, have interpreted the treaty as bearing on their desire to reclaim lands.

The IITC continued to be active in bringing the Treaty of Guadalupe Hidalgo before international bodies. In June 1982 the position of the Chicano Caucus regarding the treaty at the IITC annual conference was presented before the General Assembly, and in September of that year Chicanos presented their case before the First American Indian International Tribunal held at D-Q University near Sacramento, California. In 1984, the IITC representatives presented the Chicano and Indian positions on the treaty before the 40th session of the U.N. Commission on Human Rights meeting in Geneva, Switzerland, and in 1985 the Treaty Council presented a document outlining the Chicano situation before a U.N. Working Group on Indigenous Populations at Geneva.

Working with the IITC during these years was a small group of Chicano and Mexican-American activists who saw a community of interest. For years the Chicano movement leaders had attempted to educate Mexican Americans regarding their indigenous roots. Almost every barrio had its contingent of nativists who strongly identified with and attempted to preserve Mexican and Southwestern Indian traditions through song, dance, paintings, and rituals. For them the spiritual lessons of the Indian peoples were all important. One statement of this position during these years was an anonymous pamphlet entitled "Aztlán vs. the United States." It argued that Chicanos in the United States were Indians by blood as well as heritage; they had suffered the same second class treatment as Indians. Aztlán, the Aztec name for their homeland, was a spiritual and biological nation that included Indians as well as Chicanos. "This is the nation of RAZA INDIGENA, and the INDIAN NATIONS, or in other words nosotros los indios de Aztlán."[28]

In the 1980s Chicano intellectuals also began to conceptualize the Treaty of Guadalupe Hidalgo in terms of its potential for mobilizing the declining activism of _el movimiento_. Armando Rendón, the noted author of *Chicano Manifesto*, wrote an essay in 1982 arguing that "the Treaty of Guadalupe Hidalgo is in fact an international human rights document, extending guarantees through the decades which have not been asserted on an international level."[29] He recommended that Chicanos seek redress in forums such as the International American

Commission on Human Rights and the Inter-American Court of Human Rights. Rendón argued that the development of human rights law since the 1960s had made the treaty a viable tool for seeking justice.

Rendón's perspective found elaboration and development in the writings of Roberto Barragán, a young undergraduate at Princeton who consulted with Rendón in writing his senior thesis in the Politics Department.[30] In a lengthy, 200-page thesis Barragán argued that in light of the pronouncements of various international bodies, the treaty conferred on Chicanos particular international human rights. "Rights guaranteed by the Constitution as regards Chicanos are no longer solely of domestic character. As they are additionally protected by the Treaty, they are now of international character. As such they are under the jurisdiction of various Inter American forums."[31] Barragán's view was that the effort to protect the human rights of Mexican Americans under the treaty should be part of a three-pronged project aimed toward self-determination. The organized effort to internationalize the treaty would be known as the Treaty of Guadalupe Hidalgo Project that would integrate the various Chicano communities into an organization that would use international forums to support Chicano self determination. Among his many proposals was one that this organization could request that member states of the Organization of American States ask for an advisory opinion on the Treaty of Guadalupe Hidalgo and the status of the land grants. He also opined that the language of Article IX (relating to citizenship) could be construed to apply to Mexican immigrants in the Southwest. Barragán's thesis found a small audience because it was not published but only circulated among interested parties. It did, however, become part of the archive of contemporary thought about the international aspects of the treaty.

Recent events have shown a maturation of Indian-Chicano efforts to internationalize the issues raised by the treaty. In 1986 the IITC hosted the first National Encuentro on the Treaty of Guadalupe Hidalgo at Flagstaff, Arizona. During the three day meeting, which was attended by over 100 representatives of Indian tribes and Chicano organizations, commitments emerged that led to subsequent planning meetings the next year in Denver, Colorado, and Jemez Springs, New Mexico. The Flagstaff Encuentro also resulted in a commitment to send a delegation of Chicano observers with the IITC delegates to the Geneva U.N. Commission on Human Rights meeting in early 1987.

This was a major step in introducing a small group of Mexican Americans to international politics. For the first time a delegation of Chicano delegates spoke before a U.N. body about the Treaty of Guadalupe and contemporary problems confronting Chicanos. The IITC allowed a Chicano delegate to present an intervention before the commission. It read in part:

That same Treaty of Guadalupe Hidalgo, in which Mexico tried to guarantee human rights to indigenous people, is continually being violated by injustices toward the Chicano indigenous people by the United States. These people have suffered since the military conquest of their indigenous land of AZTLAN. The treaty right to maintain their language and culture have been denied to Chicanos: their human rights and dignity have been subverted through racism, intended to undermine the cultural ethnicity of indigenous people.[32]

The Chicano delegates presenting formal documents also held press conferences with representatives of the media of Mexico, Brazil, Argentina, and various European nations, where they presented Chicano perspectives on the treaty and issues affecting Mexican Americans. At Geneva, the representatives learned about diplomatic protocol and lobbying to expand their views regarding the role of Mexican Americans within the world community.[33]

The first national attempt to form an organization that would regularize Chicano participation within international forums took place in Santa Cruz, California, on October 10–12, 1987. This meeting brought together international lawyers with Chicano community activists and tribal representatives. The treaty became a point of organizing a larger number of people than had previously participated. Commissions on land grants, international law, and cultural violations were established. As a result of this endeavor further Encuentros were planned to solidify the directions that were established.

The Treaty of Guadalupe Hidalgo became a focal point for claims of social and economic justice during the activist 1960s and 1970s through militant action, popular books, and scholarly studies. An important legacy of the Chicano movement is its fostering of a particular historical awareness: the Southwest is really "occupied Mexico," and Mexican Americans and Indians are a "colonized people" whose rights have been violated despite the guarantees of the treaty. In the 1980s, attempts to use the Treaty of Guadalupe Hidalgo to reach international audiences has increased, primarily through the organizing energies of the International Indian Treaty Council. The result has been that the Chicano movement has gained new international dimensions.

Notes

1. Patricia Bell Blawis, *Tijerina and the Land Grants* (New York: International Publishers, 1970), p. 37; see also Richard Gardner, *Grito!: Reies Tijerina and the New Mexican Land Grant Wars of 1967* (New York: Harper & Row, 1970), and Peter Nabokov, *Tijerina and the Courthouse Raid* (Albuquerque: University of New Mexico Press, 1969). For Tijerina's own account of the trip and the Alianza, see Reies Tijerina, *Mi lucha por tierra* (Mexico: Fondo de Cultura Económica, 1978).
2. Richard Gardner, p. 96.
3. Reies Tijerina, *The Spanish Land Grant Question Examined* (Albuquerque: Alianza Federal, 1966).
4. See *Tijerina et al. vs. U.S.* 396 U.S. 843; 396 U.S. 990; and 396 U.S. 922.

5. Tijerina, *Mi Lucha*, p. 106.

6. Ibid., pp. 104–110.

7. See Senate Bill 68 and House Resolution 3595 (need exact citation); *Congressional Record,* vol. 21, pt. 1, January 15, 1975, pp. 321–22.

8. The summaries of these bills were provided by the Library of Congress as follows: HR2207, 94th Congress 1/28/75; HRES 585, 95th Congress 5/18/77; HRES 16, 96th Congress 1/15/79; *Albuquerque Journal,* March 16, 1979, 8:6.

9. "We Demand," in Luis Valdez and Stan Steiner, eds., *Aztlán: An Anthology of Mexican American Literature* (New York: Alfred A. Knopf, 1972), p. 220.

10. Armando Rendón, *Chicano Manifesto* (New York: Macmillan Publishing Co., 1972), p. 81.

11. Ibid., pp. 84–85.

12. María Blanco, "A Brief History About the Brown Beret National Organization," unpublished ms., November 10, 1975, San Diego State University, Love Library, pp. 4–6.

13. Adelaide Lefert Daron, *The Ranch That Was Robbins': Santa Catalina Island, California* (Los Angeles: Arthur Clark Co., 1963), ch. 6.

14. See J. N. Bowman, "California's Off-Shore Islands," *Pacific Historical Review* 31, No. 3 (August 1962): 291–300.

15. In Mexico, J. Antonio Rosete Murgía, produced a master's thesis arguing that the islands were still part of Mexico. It is entitled "El Tratado de Guadalupe y el problema de las islas Catalina" (Master's thesis, UNAM, 1957). Rosete Murgía recommended that Mexico reopen negotiations over the status of the Catalina islands under Article 21 of the Treaty of Guadalupe Hidalgo. See *Los Angeles Times,* August 31, 1972, for details of the initial occupation.

16. Luis Zorrilla, *Historia de la relaciones entre México y los Estados Unidos de América, 1800–1958,* vol. 2. (México: Editorial Porrúa, 1977), P. 85.

17. David Sánchez, *Expedition Through Aztlán* (La Puente: Perspectiva Publications, 1978), p. 174. Sánchez provides a detailed account of the invasion in this book.

18. *Los Angeles Times,* August 31, 1972, 1, 1: 2.

19. Sánchez, pp. 180–81; *Los Angeles Times,* September 2, I, 1: 5; *Los Angeles Times,* August 31, 1972, loc. cit.

20. *Los Angeles Times,* September 23, 1972, II, 1:2.

21. Fernando Chacón Gómez, "The Intended and Actual Effects of Article VIII of the Treaty of Guadalupe Hidalgo: Mexican Treaty Rights Under International and Domestic Law," (Ph.D. diss., University of Michigan, 1977), p. 197.

22. For a history of the American Committee for the Protection of the Foreign Born, see Louise Pettibone Smith, *Torch of Liberty: Twenty-Five Years in the Life of the Foreign Born in the U.S.A.* (New York: Dwight-King Publishers, 1959); American Committee for the Protection of the Foreign Born, "Our Badge of Infamy: A Petition to the United Nations on the Treatment of Mexican Immigrants," (New York: American Committee for Protection of Foreign Born, 1959).

23. Ibid., p. 5.

24. Ibid., p. 10.

25. International Indian Treaty Council, "Plans for Treaty of Gudalupe Hidalgo Conference," 1986, Mimeograph.

26. IITC, "General Working Paper," 1986, Hopi Nation, "The Treaty of Guadalupe Hidalgo: A Native American Perspective," 1981, Mimeograph. The Indians were being relocated following an agreement that the Bureau of Indian Affairs had arranged with opposing factions with the two tribes.

27. Ibid., p. 2.

28. "Aztlán vs. the United States," 198?, Mimeograph.

29. Armando B. Rendón, "The Treaty of Guadalupe Hidalgo and its Modern Implications for the Protection of the Human Rights of Mexican Americans," 1982, p. 27, Mimeograph.

30. Roberto E. Barragán, "The Treaty of Guadalupe Hidalgo and the American Convention on Human Rights: A Political Analysis for Chicano Self Determination," Senior thesis, Politics Department, Princeton University, 1984. Barragán's thesis and Rendon's essays have been circulated by the Tonantzin Land Institute in New Mexico as part of the Treaty of Guadalupe Hidalgo Project.

31. Ibid., p. 44.

32. International Indian Treaty Council, "Question of Violation of Human Rights or Fundamental Freedoms in Any Part of the World," Agenda Item 12, Commission on Human Rights, 43 Session, Geneva, Switzerland.

33. Ron Sandoval, "Diary," 1987, Mimeograph. Most of the xerox materials relating to the IITC and the treaty are available through the Tonantzin Land Institute, 1504 Bridge Blvd., Albuquerque, New Mexico.

El Paso Salt War:
Mob Action or Political Struggle?

Mary Romero

The border area between the United States and Mexico plays an important role in popular culture. Beginning in pulp magazines and western novels, later thundering across the silver screen, the larger than life images of heroic Texans and sneaky Mexicans have played out a distorted view of American history as manifest destiny. In films like "The Alamo" and "Red River," we learn how John Wayne brought law and order to the border, subduing the Indians and pacifying the Mexicans. Only recently has the other side of the story been considered. Native American and Chicano historians have begun the laborious process of uncovering what happened from the point of view of those who were conquered. Recent films like "Little Big Man" and "The Ballad of Gregorio Cortez" have dared to suggest to the Anglo-American[1] population that a different view is possible. This essay examines a littleknown but revealing conflict between the Spanish-speaking population near El Paso, Texas and the Anglo-Americans who were seeking to move into the area.

In 1877 there were 12,000 persons living along the Rio Grande near El Paso. All but eighty were of Mexican descent. San Elizario (twenty five miles south of El Paso) had a population of 2,000 of whom only 12 to 15 were Anglo-Americans.[2] Although the Mexican population constituted the numerical majority, Anglos controlled the political positions and the majority of the wealth. Most people along the border were engaged in subsistence agriculture. Large scale cattle ranching was not yet profitable because of Indian raids and the difficulty of transporting livestock to distant markets. Salt was one of the few commodities which could be obtained locally and traded to produce supplementary income.

As long as anyone could remember there had been cattle trails to the salt licks at Guadalupe Lakes, but prior to 1824, there was no evidence of wagon tracks. The

Guadalupe Lakes became an important source of salt after access to the San Andrés saline lakes, a hundred miles north of El Paso, was ended by the claim of private ownership by Anglo entrepreneurs. The *salineros* turned to the Guadalupe salt deposits as an alternative site. In 1863, a seventy-two mile road to the salt lakes was built as a co-operative undertaking by Mexicans from both sides of the border.[3]

The two cultures, Mexicano and Anglo-American, held diametrically opposed concepts of property. Prior to 1848, the area was under Spanish law. The *pueblo* or community used the land adjacent to it freely; the common land was held in trust while the *alcalde* (mayor) portioned out to each man as much land and river water as needed for his family use. Natural resources were similarly held in common; they belonged to the community and were not owned privately.[4] This crucial difference in land usage and ownership explains how Anglo developers were able to appropriate the salt beds. Under American law, they were unclaimed lands, available to anyone who filed a proper deed.

In 1877, Charles Howard, a Missouri lawyer and Texas District Judge, filed deeds and claims of ownership to the Guadalupe Salt Lakes in El Paso County. Previously the salt deposits had been communal property used by the Mexican population on both sides of the border. Howard's claim was disputed by the local population who organized to fight what they saw as a land grab and a threat to their economic survival. Although the movement was issue-oriented and lacked a specific ideology, Mexican citizens and Mexican Americans armed themselves and fought against the Texas Rangers. In the events which came to be called the El Paso Salt War, Howard was killed as were several Rangers and Mexicanos living in the border region. The event was more an insurrection or peasant revolt then a "riot" as some historians have portrayed it.

The Salt War became the object of a congressional investigation which yielded both a majority and a minority report on the causes of the disturbances. Major Jones,

El Paso Salt War: Mob Action or Political Struggle?" by Mary Romero. Taken from *Aztlán*, Vol. 16. No. 1–2, 1985. Reprinted by permission.

the governor's appointee to the committee, filed the Minority Report disputing points made by the four-member Congressional board that highly criticized the action of the Texas Rangers and local authorities. Both reports stressed cultural distinctions of land usage; however, the minority report presented the cultural interpretations of the local Mexican community as evidence of their anti-American ideology. Furthermore, the minority report analyzed the incident as an international affair in which Mexican citizens attacked the Texas Rangers and U.S. citizens. The Majority Report recommended that the United States government establish a permanent 200-man garrison to prevent further trouble over the salt beds and the usage of Rio Grande water for irrigation purposes. Fort Bliss was thus established on January 1, 1878 and still "protects" the Rio Grande Valley.

The two major histories of the El Paso Salt War have been written by Anglo-American historians. Walter Prescott Webb and C.L. Sonnichsen characterized the incident as a mob action instigated by local politicians against Charles Howard and the Texas Rangers. Both historians interpreted the event as stemming from the isolation of the region and cultural differences separating the participants. Webb emphasized that "outside agitators" were responsible for the trouble and used the terms "mob" and "riot" to describe the event. He recognized the crucial economic importance of the salt, yet failed to understand that the private appropriation of the salt lakes was the primary cause of the event. Sonnichsen pointed out "the greed and jealousy of the Americans."[5] He disputed Webb's view that the Spanish-speaking population was "docile and stupid," by drawing attention to the different concepts of property held by the two cultures. Both historians speculated on cultural values as causing a misinterpretation of events resulting in escalation of violence.

Contemporary Chicano writers[6] have referred to the Salt War as the people's revolt rather than a mob action. They analyze the event within the context of an economy in the process of transformation from feudalism (based on common ownership of certain lands and resources) to capitalism (based on private ownership of all means of production). This perspective shifts the focus from cultural misunderstanding to structural and economic differences leading to conflict. What has been lacking in the scholarly analysis thus far is an assessment of the Mexican community's interpretation of conditions leading to the conflict. This essay will reconstruct the Mexican community's understanding and political intentions in the event by comparing testimonies made by members of the community to the testimonies of Anglos. It will also consider the relationship between the Mexican community and local politicians, and investigate the treatment of U.S. citizenship by local officials and the Mexican-American population along the border.

Description of the Event

In the early 1800's, El Paso's economy was mostly subsistence agriculture. Cattle ranching was unprofitable because of Indian raids and the distance to market. Mexicans from both sides of the border needed salt for their personal use. Furthermore, salt was a commodity which could be bartered in the interior of Mexico. Therefore, salt selling was an essential element of El Paso's commerce.[7] The salt lake road was completed in 1863; attempts to appropriate the lake as private property began almost immediately. In 1866, Sam Maverick of San Antonio made the first private claim to portions of the Guadalupe Lakes. Maverick's claim marked the first occasion in which a fee or duty was charged for obtaining salt. Local citizens complained about the private benefit Maverick reaped from the wagon road they had built. Mexicans on both sides of the border responded by ceasing to take salt. When they realized that Maverick claimed only a portion of the salt beds, the people began to mine salt from areas not privately owned.

Problems arose again when S.J. Fountain and W.W. Mills joined to form a "Salt Ring" to acquire possession of the salt beds in order to monopolize the salt and "collect a revenue upon each bushel or *fanega* that was taken away."[8] The founders of the Salt Ring were prominent Anglo developers and major figures in the El Paso County Company. The Salt Ring's first attempt to claim the area failed because their certificate, "known as the Jett certificate, proved defective and the company fell into two factions which carried the Salt Lakes into El Paso County Politics."[9] Sonnichsen relates the split between Mills and Fountain to divisions within the Republican party: "Fountain was a strong supporter of Radical Republicanism and Mills was a conservative."[10] Mills continued to represent the El Paso Salt Ring. Fountain led the opposition, later called the Anti-Salt Ring, whose goal became to secure the land for the people of El Paso.

In 1870, Fountain was elected state senator. His first order of business was an attempt to push a bill through the Legislature.

> calling for the relinquishment of the County of El Paso, for the use of her citizens forever, all right, title and interest of the State of Texas in and to the unlocated portion of the Guadalupe Salt Lake in El Paso County.[11]

However, a petition containing four hundred signatures against any legislation on the salt question was presented to the Texas Senate, and Fountain withdrew his bill. Apparently, disapproval was based on the desire of the local community to keep the salt beds open to Mexicans who lived on the other side of the border.

In 1872, the split in the Republican party provided Charles H. Howard, the lawyer from Missouri, the opportunity he needed to move into El Paso politics. After forming an alliance with Luis Cardis, a local stage contractor and politician, Howard campaigned for the Mexican vote and was elected to the position of county judge in 1875. Edmund Stine, a local official, proved this description of Cardis and Howard:

> both were alike ambitious, and alike unscrupulous. They worked together very harmoniously for awhile, and profited by their partnership, for, while one became district judge, the other was sent to the legislature and constitutional convention.[12]

The relationship prospered from 1872 to 1875, and then turned into a bitter feud with repeated threats of violence.

The situation was aggravated when Howard placed all the salt beds under his father-in-law's name, Zimpleman, and enforced an immediate halt to persons entering the area. When an attempt was made to collect fees for the salt removed, only three persons signed contracts with Howard. Juan Armendáriz later testified to the terms:

> Judge Howard authorized me to pay for hauling salt from the salines at the rate of $1.25 per fanega. I sold the salt after it was hauled here at $1.75 and $2 per *fanega*.[13]

Sonnichsen makes clear the seriousness of Howard's actions on the local economy:

> He might as well have told the Mexicans that he intended to sell air at so much a breath. The salt was all that stood between some of them and starvation. The river had been dry for a month; the corn drying; the people were desperate; and now the little they could pick up by hauling salt was about to be taken away from them.[14]

Angrily, the Mexican people questioned the legality of the claim. Padre Ramón Ortiz, from the parish of Paso Del Norte, testified that the Spanish government had established communal usage of the land and its resources in 1656 and the law was upheld by the Mexican authorities. The Treaty of Guadalupe Hidalgo was intended to preserve Mexican American citizens' land rights. But, after the Mexican American War, the new American citizens were unable to legitimize the same rights and privileges surrounding communal resources granted to them under Spain and Mexico. This was partly because U.S. courts did not recognize communal property, and partly because the United States delayed the demarcation of the U.S./Mexico border. The situation was further complicated by the theft of the titles of property from the El Paso and Mexican archives during the Doniphan expeditions.[15]

Local authorities responded by requesting the *salineros* to pay Howard; later, if Howard's claim was found to be illegal, their money would be returned. On September 29th, José María Juárez and Macedonio Gándara were arrested for having threatened to enter the area for salt. Judge García dismissed the case against Gándara due to lack of evidence; however, Juárez was placed under a peace bond of $200 and incarcerated for making an outburst in the courtroom.[16] Several hundred Mexicans from San Elizario and Ysleta rallied at the jail and freed Juárez. Later they held a mass meeting demanding their rights. Led by Chico Barela and León Granillo of San Elizario, they marched to Judge García's home and demanded a warrant for Howard's arrest on the basis that "it is the will of the people that he should go to jail."[17] While this argument had precedence in the Spanish legal system, the judge refused to issue the warrant. Judge García and his older brother, Porfirio García (the Justice of the Peace), were subjected to a "citizen's arrest." Later Howard and his agent, McBride, were arrested along with Sheriff Kerber. All were held prisoner for three days except Kerber, who escaped.

Padre Bourgard, the parish priest of San Elizario, and Cardis worked out a plan for the prisoner's release in which Judge García and the justice of the peace were forced to resign from public office. The terms agreed upon for Howard's release were that he:

1. relinquish all claims to the salt lakes;
2. assign claims to the people;
3. set up a $12,000 bond insuring that he would never return to the county;
4. agree not to prosecute persons involved in this incident;[18] and
5. confess to the unjust and inproper prosecution of Juárez and Gándara.[19]

In Mills' account of the event, he noted that the arrest and trial by "the people" were no more a lawless act "than defrauding people of an election fairly won, or many other things that are common."[20]

Howard agreed to the above and on October 5th he was released and fled to New Mexico where he immediately began to agitate for a counter attack with the assistance of the Texas Rangers. Howard convinced Governor Hubbard of Texas that there had been an invasion from Mexico. Major Jones of the Rangers was sent to investigate the situation. Mills characterized Howard's action as having fired the "Texas heart" with many telegrams about lawless work, war of races, invasion from Mexico, etc., etc. He charged that Cardis was the chief conspirator and marplot who had created all the trouble and had sought to have him (Howard) assassinated.[21] Although he had accused Cardis of being an assassin, Howard struck first. On his return to the salt beds, Howard shot and killed Cardis. Throughout the border region, Anglos waited for trouble to result from Howard's action. Immediately rumors began to circulate of "midnight messengers, secret conclaves, and even some drilling in military formation."[22] To escape possible retaliation, Howard quickly placed himself under the protection of the custom-house officer.

On November 6th, a group assembled to collect the bond which had been forfeited by Howard when he returned to the area. Representatives from the Mexican community met with Major Jones and the Texas Rangers in an attempt to clarify their actions. According to Webb, the group

> produced a copy of the constitution to show that they had a right to assemble and bear arms. . . . They said they had the right to collect the bond. The Mexicans declared that Howard had forfeited his bond by returning to El Paso, that they had no hope of collecting it in court, and they had a right to collect it by force.[23]

Major Jones assured the Mexican community that Howard would be arrested. However, Jones's credibility eroded quickly when he organized local Anglos into a company of Texas Rangers.

Local Mexicanos were apprehensive about the neutrality of the Rangers. Another meeting was held with Jones to request that Mexicanos be allowed to form their own company of Rangers, and elect their own officers. When Jones denied the request, the people demanded that U.S. troops be called upon instead of creating a local Anglo vigilante battalion. Later reports proved the reality of community fears about the Rangers. Sonnichsen described the men selected for the company as "assembled out of holes and corners. Not one of them would have been a Ranger under normal circumstances."[24]

On November 16th, Howard voluntarily surrendered to Major Jones. With the assistance of the collector of customs, Joseph Magoffin, Howard was able to persuade the local justice of peace to set bail at $4,000. During the investigation, this action was criticized:

> the death of Cardis at the hands of Howard seems to have been premeditated murder, a crime for which there is no bail provided by law. . . Yet Howard, after its commission, and without being confined, or examined in the presence of a prosecuting officer, either on the part of State, district, or county, was suffered to give bail and go free.[25]

Around the first of December, a train of about sixteen carts and wagons was rumored to be moving toward the salt lakes. Howard, a murderer and illegally out on bail, was accompanied by the Texas Rangers under Lieutenant Tays, to serve "writs of sequestration on the parties having the salt."[26] Later, Captain Blair of the U.S. Army identified Howard's move towards San Elizario as the signal to awaiting Mexicans to arm themselves and prepare to fight.

On December 12, Howard and the Texas Rangers arrived at San Elizario where they were surrounded by Chico Barela and his armed followers. Tays wired for assistance to Captain Blair who had been instructed by the federal government to investigate the participation of citizens of Mexico in this struggle. Blair was intercepted by armed Mexicans who wanted to know why Howard was being protected. Blair denied a personal interest in Howard's welfare and claimed Tays was not Howard's hired protector. The Mexicans were assured that the Army would not intervene in the question of the salt bed ownership and usage, and Blair demonstrated this by returning to El Paso.

For the next week, Howard and the Texas Rangers were held under siege by local Mexican Americans and their Mexican comrades. Charles Ellis, a former sheriff and tax collector, was killed. Shortly afterwards, Sergeant E.E. Montier of the Frontier Battalion States troops was killed. Realizing that the army was not coming to rescue the tired and restless Rangers, Lieutenant Tays arranged to meet with the Mexicano leaders, who demanded Howard's surrender.

Lieutenant Tays assured Howard that the Texas Rangers would defend him to the death; nevertheless, Howard eventually surrendered. Some reports suggest that Howard's decision to surrender may have been influenced by the other besieged men who feared for their own lives. The events surrounding Howard's surrender are unclear. Tays claimed John Atkinson, one of Howard's bondsmen, negotiated a deal with the Mexican leaders behind Howard's back. Whatever the case, Atkinson returned to the Ranger quarters and instructed them to surrender. He paid eleven thousand dollars of Howard's bond on the condition that Atkinson, Howard and McBride be freed. Apparently the agreement was not kept because a public execution was called for, and Howard, McBride and Atkinson were put to death. The Ranger troops were released the following day after being "asked whether they were employed by the governor of Texas or by Howard, and then each one was required to sign a black paper."[27] Sonnichsen awarded Tays the dubious distinction of being "the only officer of the rangers who ever surrendered to an enemy."[28]

The Rangers regrouped at Franklin, New Mexico under Sheriff Charles Kerber and Captain Moore. They were reinforced by volunteers from Silver City, New Mexico, and were authorized by the governor to return to San Elizario "to prevent further outrages, to restore peace and quiet, and to assist the civil officers in preserving and enforcing the law."[29] Their pacification program began on December 22nd.

At Ysleta, Crecencio Irigoyen and Santiago Durán were arrested during a "round up" because they had "Ranger guns" in their possession. A later report indicated they were killed while attempting to escape. The same "round up" process was used in Socorro. In the first house of the town, a man named Núñez was killed and his wife wounded. Jesús Telles, identified as a participant in the seige, was killed and Cruz Chávez was wounded. Mexicans evacuated the area in anticipation of more violence.

Incidents of rape and general harassment were uncovered during the Congressional investigations. Even though many Mexicans refused to testify to the congressional committee and others had already fled across the border, state officials made the volunteers from Silver City responsible for all atrocities. On March 25th, Lieutenant Tays resigned from the Texas Rangers.

The basis for the official investigation requested by Congress and Governor Hubbard of Texas was that "Texas had been invaded by armed forces from Mexico."[30] The committee had to determine if Mexican-American land rights had been violated and whether Mexican or U.S. citizens had fought against the Texas Rangers. The actions of public officials and military personnel were also under question. Areas of dispute included the issue of the citizenship of participants, the actual date of the salt lakes' discovery, the reputation of civil law in the area, the legality of action taken by Texas Rangers and others under their command, the amount of damage, and the legality of waiving examination and permitting Howard to be released on bail. Major Jones's major concern was that "the inter-national aspect of the affair" had been ignored. He argued that the United States should demand that the Mexican government punish its own criminals and make reparations for looting. He estimated the amount of damage at $31,000 against the Board's $12,000.[31]

The issue of ownership of the salt lakes was resolved on behalf of Zimpleman who was permitted to retain his private claim. Sergeant J.D. Ford of the Texas Rangers was assigned to protect Zimpleman's private property. The local community had to submit to his authority in order to obtain the salt needed to survive.

Interpretations of the El Paso Salt Wars

A review of historians' treatment of the El Paso Salt War reveals Anglo ethnocentrism which distorts Chicano history. Both Webb and Sonnichsen identified the isolation of the region as a contributing factor permitting the incident to occur. Sonnichsen made the claim on the basis that the U.S. had pulled troops out of Fort Bliss and Fort Quitman in 1872. El Paso was in fact geographically isolated from other U.S. establishments. However, Webb's concept of isolation was restricted to Anglo Americans. The El Paso region was not isolated from Mexico. Consequently, isolation must be considered an ethnocentric term. Webb justified economic and political domination by Anglos by arguing that Mexicans were un-American, and thus not trustworthy to hold office. Webb further suggested that the Mexican population engaged in the Salt War incident were simply sheep, acting under the guidance of evil leaders. Padre Antonio Borrajo, the parish priest of San Elizario and Socorro (about ninety miles from the salt lakes), and Luis Cardis were identified as the evil leaders of the Mexican people. Webb emphasized their role by relying heavily upon Fountain's testimony given during the congressional investigation.

Fountain claimed that Padre Antonio Borrajo offered him the Mexican people's cooperation if he entered into a profit-making agreement with Borrajo over the salt beds. Borrajo suggested purchasing the land and imposing a tax on the salt obtained, thus creating a profit that could be divided between the two men. Fountain also claimed that Padre Borrajo and Luis Cardis campaigned against the passage of his bill "to have the Salt Lakes delivered to the people, under the management of a board of trustees selected by them."[32] However, it is unlikely that Padre Borrajo played a major role in the insurrection. According to Ward B. Blanchard, the deputy surveyor at the time the salt lakes were surveyed for Zimplemen, the priest had been removed from the church of San Elizario and Socorro when El Paso became part of the bishopric of Arizona.

Webb's claim of outside agitators as the cause of the Salt War was consistent with his labeling of participants of the insurrection as the "mob" and their actions as "rioting." However, Webb recognized the role of community leaders, pointing out that the governor of Texas sent a telegram to Chico Barela, the Mexican leader, demanding that he give up.

Sonnichsen also over-emphasized the role Cardis and Borrajo played in the incident. However, Sonnichsen introduced several other items of vital background information. For instance, he pointed out the existence of different attitudes toward private property. Similarly, Webb failed to recognize the private appropriation of the salt lakes as the major cause of the El Paso Salt War. The Mexican people were not, as Webb claimed, "docile and stupid;" rather they were acting in accordance with deeply-held cultural beliefs about communal land ownership and usage. Another cultural distinction identified by Sonnichsen was the idea of participatory democracy:

> They knew that power originates in the people and they reasoned that what the people agree on must be right regardless of the law books . . . they were the people, and the people were the law. That was the argument used more than once to justify what Americans called mob action.[33]

This notion of democracy and the political participation of the Mexican community account for the fact that Luis Cardis and Padre Borrajo needed to make deals to claim the salt beds, rather than simply seizing ownership. Fountain's testimony recognized that continuing support of the Mexican people could only be maintained by manipulating their interests. In his later book, *Pass of the North,* Sonnichsen provided further information about Cardis' relationship to his Mexican constituents. For instance, when the Rio Grande flooded the farm area in El Paso in 1874, Cardis introduced a bill to provide more irrigable land for the people.[34] Therefore, the Mexican population did not follow blindly, as Webb suggested, but rather responded to economic and political circumstances.

Conflicting interpretations appearing in the House Executive Document clearly reflect interest groups involved in the incident. In order to justify the actions of the Texas Rangers, Major Jones had to establish the incident as an international affair. Notice was issued by the Mexican government warning its citizens that persons crossing the border to participate in the riot at San Elizario would be punished. Guards were placed along the border to turn back all armed persons. Since the Mexican government was obviously not involved in the conflict over the salt beds, the issue of citizenship among the participants in the rebellion was the only argument that could be made to support this perspective. Howard obtained military protection from the Texas Rangers by claiming a Mexican invasion had occurred.

Captain Blair, on the other hand, maintained throughout the investigation that this was not an international affair, thus justifying his action in retreating. Blair claimed the reports made by other officials concerning the presence of Mexican citizens were exaggerated, and noted that many Mexicans, regardless of citizenship had lived on both sides of the border. Mills commented on the argument over labeling the incident as an international affair by pointing out that "If 'all Americans' were in danger, why was only one man selected to be protected by the Rangers?"[35]

The issue of citizenship is an interesting one. The area had formerly been Mexican territory, and many Mexicans chose U.S. citizenship in order to keep their homes after the war. Testimonies and description of other political events indicate that citizenship was a distinction that was socially meaningful only to Anglos (politicians, merchants and Texas Rangers). It benefited local Anglos to recognize the border population's citizenship during a political campaign, whereas it was to their advantage to deny the border population U.S. citizenship during incidents of economic exploitation or military suppression. For instance, the establishment of El Paso as the permanent county seat in 1883 illustrates the uses of citizenship:

> When the score was in, El Paso had 2,252 votes; Ysleta had 475. Since every Mexican who could be rounded up on either side of the river had been induced to vote at least once, the number of ballots was far in excess of the number of qualified voters of the county.[36]

Very little evidence can be given to indicate that there was any practical reason for the border population to make citizenship distinctions among themselves. J.P. Hague, a Texas lawyer during the incident, described the significance of the Rio Grande as an international boundary:

> The people of one are bound to those of the other by more than ordinary obligations of race and hospitality. They have married and intermarried; their interests are in many respects identical . . . it should not be a matter

of surprise that 300 armed persons, residents of Mexico . . . united with others of El Paso County and aided them in their attack upon the Rangers . . ..[37]

Remarks made during the investigation clearly show that Anglos were aware of the Mexican community's relationship on the border. Zabriskie, El Paso's district attorney at the time expressed his understanding of the community's mutual response to Howard:

> It was but natural, therefore, when the dispute over the salt lakes culminated in open war, that the entire Mexican people (on both sides) should be greatly excited and deeply interested in the result. Nor is it strange that the civil authorities in El Paso, Mexico, and their supporters, being in a hopeless minority, were unable to restrain their citizens from rushing to the assistance of their brethren on this side.[38]

The Minority Report based its international affair argument on the claim that Mexican Americans opposed the U.S. method of government. For instance, the sheriff's problem in collecting taxes was cited as an example of local opposition.[39] However, the argument is weakened by several events. First of all, Mexicans requested membership in the Texas Rangers for the purpose of capturing Howard, a wanted criminal. However, Major Jones refused the offer and proceeded to recruit known Mexican haters who served to protect Howard while he was attempting to protect his capital. Therefore, the Texas Rangers were perceived as Howard's hired army. Secondly, Chico Barela clearly indicated to Captain Blair that the subject of his attack was Howard, not the United States government. As a matter of fact, the Mexican community requested the intervention of federal troops because of the lawlessness of state officials who protected Howard's interests regardless of legality. At the same time, the Texas Rangers' insistence that Mexican Americans opposed the U.S. system of government was correct. The opposition was not an attempt to overthrow U.S. imperialism in the newly conquered territory; however, they were opposed to paying tribute as a conquered people. Protection of citizenship rights had been guaranteed by the Treaty of Guadalupe Hidalgo and therefore, Mexican-Americans resisted being relegated to an inferior position.

Conclusion

Although land ownership and land usage were culturally defined in the Spanish and Mexican land grants, the struggle over previously community-owned lands was not a cultural conflict. The transformation from community ownership of the salt beds to private ownership changed how the salt beds were used and ultimately threatened the economic survival of the people. Howard's claim threatened the economic survival of the Mexican border population which had built the wagon road, and thus had a vested interest in the future of the salt beds. Blair described the members of the insurection as "350 sober, well-organized, well-armed determined men, with a definite purpose. Howard they wanted; nothing else, nothing less."[40] Even though the border people armed themselves and fought against the Texas Rangers, their purpose and goals were aimed at eliminating Howard, and thus alleviating economic and political oppression. At no time were border Mexican-Americans and Mexicans attacking the United States government. The *salineros* understood that private ownership of the salt beds would result in severe economic exploitation. Furthermore, the border community understood Howard to have committed criminal acts under U.S. law, and they recognized that preferential treatment of Howard (or any other Anglo) would result in further political oppression by establishing two sets of codes. The Texas Rangers were seen as a capitalist private army and not representative of the U.S. government. Acuña appropriately defined this incident as a people's revolt, rather than a riot or mob action.[41] Leaders, as well as a specific plan of action, were visible throughout the incident.

Historians and social scientists have emphasized cultural differences between Mexican and Anglo Americans and have assigned these differences as causes of land loss among the Mexican population. Historians frequently ignore the effects of transformation of land ownership on the people's economy because their evolutionary perspective of history has glossed over incidents of insurrection as "growing pains" along the road to modernization. The El Paso Salt War of 1878 is an incident of Chicano struggle against Anglo efforts to exploit natural resources on community land. Testimonies taken after the El Paso Salt War provide evidence that the local Mexican American community, with the assistance of their Mexican friends and relatives, organized and fought against Charles W. Howard's efforts to claim private ownership of salt beds formerly authorized as communal resources. The Mexican population clearly supported the insurrection as Sonnichsen noted:

> The Grand Jury of El Paso County indicted six of the leaders of the mob, and later the Governor offered rewards for Chico Barela, Sisto Luciano Frésquez, Agatón Porras, Desiderio Apodaca and Jesús García. Not a Mexican turned a finger to collect the money.[42]

Although the United States government agreed to protect the Mexican people's land rights, the grantees were subjected to new rules and laws. Legal tactics used in the judicial system supported the interests of U.S. capitalists. Mexicanos could have learned new land grant rules, but they were unable to win in a system owned by the conqueror. Frequently, taking up the gun was the last recourse in an attempt to retain usage of the community land.

Yale College

Notes

1. My use of the term "Anglo" follows Carey McWilliams' statement that "two or more ethnics always implies the existence of another. In most portions of the Southwest, the term 'Anglo' and 'Hispanic' are the heads and tails of a single coin, a single ethnic system; each term has meaning only as the other is implied. The terms do not define homogeneous entities; they define a relationship." Carey McWilliams, *North From Mexico* (New York: Greenwood Press, 1948) p. 8.
2. McWilliams, p. 110.
3. C.L. Sonnichsen, *Ten Texas Feuds* (Albuquerque: University of New Mexico Press, 1957) p. 123.
4. Congress, Second Session, House Executive Document No. 93 (Washington, D.C.: GPO, 1878), p. 2. Henceforth, this document will be cited as H.E.D.
5. Sonnichsen, p. 112.
6. Rodolfo Acuña, *Occupied America, The Chicano's Struggle Toward Liberation* (San Francisco: Canfield Press, 1972; second edition, 1981), p. 37–40. The August Twenty-Ninth Movement (Marxist-Leninist) organization published the pamphlet "Fan the Flames, A Revolutionary Position on the National Question," (1976) which historically documents that Chicanos are an oppressed nation. This document is largely a response to the CUPUSA's 1930s position that denied the existence of a Chicano National Movement.
7. Walter Prescott Webb, *The Texas Rangers, A Century of Frontier Defense* (Austin: University of Texas Press, 1935).
8. Ibid., p. 347.
9. Ibid.
10. C.L. Sonnichsen, *Pass of the North: Four Centuries on the Rio Grande* (El Paso: Texas Western Press, 1968) p. 181.
11. Sonnichsen, *Ten Texas Feuds*, p. 117.
12. H.E.D., p. 65.
13. Ibid., p. 112.
14. Sonnichsen, *Ten Texas Feuds*, p. 123.
15. H.E.D., p. 68.
16. Sonnichsen, *Ten Texas Feuds*, p. 128.
17. Ibid., p. 129.
18. Webb, p. 351–52.
19. Sonnichsen, *Ten Texas Feuds*, p. 131.
20. W.W. *Mills, Forty Years at El Paso, 1858-1898* (El Paso: Carl Hertzog, 1898), p. 151.
21. Ibid.
22. Sonnichsen, *Ten Texas Feuds*, p. 135.
23. Webb, p. 355.
24. Sonnichsen, *Pass of the North*, p. 138.
25. H.E.D., p. 17.
26. Ibid., p. 56.
27. Ibid., p. 57.
28. Sonnichsen, *Ten Texas Feuds*, p. 154.
29. H.E.D., p. 28.
30. Webb, p. 336.
31. Sonnichsen, *Ten Texas Feuds*, p. 155.
32. Webb, p. 348.
33. Sonnichsen, *Ten Texas Feuds*, p. 112.
34. Sonnichsen, *Pass of the North*, p. 197.
35. Mills, p. 155.
36. Sonnichsen, *Pass of the North*, p. 347.
37. H.E.D., p. 143.
38. Ibid., p. 53.
39. H.E.D., p. 143.
40. H.E.D., p. 56.
41. Acuña, p. 37.
42. Sonnichsen, *Ten Texas Feuds*, p. 155.

Border Culture

Mario T. García

Working among themselves as manual laborers and living in segregated barrios adjacent to their homeland, Mexican immigrants in El Paso and throughout the Southwest, like other newcomers to the United States, maintained native customs that helped provide a sense of community. As one historian has correctly written of the northern movement of Mexicans: "Mexican immigration bore little resemblance to the 'uprooting' experience which Oscar Handlin depicted as characteristic of European immigration. Indeed, continuity rather than alienation, marginality and social disorganization, characterized Mexican immigration." Yet, within El Paso's large Mexican population, cultural differences also existed. Mexican Americans, educated and sophisticated political refugees, and the mass of poor immigrants comprised diverse cultural enclaves although they were linked by a common language and certain Mexican traditions. Moreover, cultural continuity coexisted with some cultural change. The immigrants' adjustment to new working conditions, especially in urban areas, their relationship with more Americanized Mexican Americans, and the impact of certain gringo institutions such as the schools introduced a gradual acculturation. Cultural change among Mexican immigrants, especially children, likewise occurred because, as Ernesto Galarza indicates, working class immigration brought "no formal institutions to perpetuate its culture." Cultural continuity as well as cultural change, the two in time developing a Mexican border culture, can be detected in the family, recreational activities, religion, and voluntary associations. The family represents the most basic cultural institution transferred by Mexican immigrants and was the most resistant barrier to American assimilation. Besides young single males who entered the United States seeking work, many families also arrived. The Dillingham Commission report of 1911 observed that a high percentage of Mexican laborers in western industries had brought

their wives from Mexico. According to the commission, 81.5 percent of Mexican railroad shop workers in the survey reported their wives in the United States. Investigators discovered a similar condition in urban related work. Sixty percent of Mexicans employed as construction workers by street railways stated they had their wives with them. Although no substantial research has been done on the composition and nature of working-class or peasant families in Mexico during the late nineteenth and early twentieth centuries, nevertheless it appears that the family formed a strong social and economic unit. Galarza in his autobiography, *Barrio Boy,* recalls that his family in rural Nayarit included not only his mother (who had divorced his father prior to Galarza's birth) but also his aunt, three uncles, and two cousins. In the Galarza household the men went to labor in the fields during the day while the women and children performed the housework and cooking.

Although some Mexican women in El Paso and throughout the urban Southwest contributed to household incomes by taking in wash or lodgers, no disintegration took place in the traditional pattern of men being the chief wage earners and women doing household work (of course, certain lower-class women in Mexico were wageworkers). The 1900 El Paso census sample shows that no mothers and almost no daughters, most being too young, worked outside the home in an immigrant family headed by the father (although no data exist, some women may have worked part-time). Nevertheless, the necessity of more women having to become wage-workers over the years no doubt affected family patterns. This appears to be true as daughters grew to working age throughout the region. According to a Los Angeles survey by Paul S. Taylor in 1928, the majority of Mexican women took jobs in ministry because "of poverty, due either to irregular work of the male members of the family, or to the combination of large families, low wages, high rents." However the entrance of women into the job market constituted, as Taylor put it, a process "contrary to their customs and traditions." Taylor believed that "such radical changes" in the daily lives of Mexican women could not help but produce cultural changes, especially within the family. The University of California scholar observed both older as well as younger women in industrial jobs, but he detected more profound alterations in the habits of younger Mexicans. Not only did they adapt to the work routine better, but what little education they secured in American schools, especially the learning of English, made them more productive and efficient. "They look upon some sort of industrial work" Taylor wrote, "as soon as they have completed the minimum amount of schooling as the natural course of events." Besides acquiring some new material and cultural tastes that they introduced into the home, by the 1920s young Mexican working women appear to have begun to exhibit a desire for greater independence from strict family practices. "Her parents are apt to be ignored," Taylor stressed, "she tends to break away from the old custom of parental authority." Whether Taylor's observations would also pertain to El Paso cannot be determined due to a lack of similar studies in the border city. Certainly, young Mexican women who worked in the laundries and garment factories, and possibly even as domestics, may have displayed parallel characteristics.

The economic necessity for Mexican women to find jobs likewise appears to have challenged to a degree the traditional male-dominated Mexican family structure. Although perhaps Mexican fathers could more easily accept their daughters than their wives working outside the home, a pattern not uncommon in Mexico, still Taylor noticed that Mexican men resented women working or wanting to work. One man stated that women should not work because that was a man's duty, whereas women's consisted of keeping house. Another husband told Taylor that he could not allow his wife to work because his friends would then think he could not adequately provide for his family. Another insisted that his wife could not have a job outside the home since no women in his family had ever worked; moreover, it was neither necessary nor correct. The pressure of higher living costs north of the border, however, eventually forced many Mexican women into the job market. While more research needs to be conducted into the full impact that this process had on family culture, it seems that traditional patterns slowly changed over the years. One Mexican man who had lived in the United States for over 25 years told anthropologist Manuel Gamio in the 1920s that he disliked the transformation Mexican women underwent in the Southwest. According to Carlos Ibáñez, he disliked American laws that allowed women too many rights and made them less subordinate to men. "Now the Mexican women who come here," Ibáñez emphasized, "also take advantage of the laws and want to be like the American women." Because of the change, Ibáñez concluded that if he ever married it would be in Mexico.

Within the family, Mexicans preserved many native cultural traditions that aided them in their transition to a new American setting by providing a familiar cultural environment. It is difficult to arrive at an accurate picture of family life in El Paso, but anthropologist Manuel Gamio noted certain customs being practiced in the late 1920s by Mexican immigrant families in El Paso and other southwestern locations. Gamio observed that despite the fact that Mexican immigrants accepted American material goods such as housing, clothing, domestic utensils, and machinery, they still retained earlier popular customs. These included folklore, songs and ballads, birthday celebrations, saints' days, baptisms, weddings, and funerals in the traditional style. Owing to poverty, a lack of physicians in the barrios plus traditional customs the Mexican scholar witnessed the continued use of medicinal herbs by both Mexican immigrants and Mexican Americans. "In almost all parts of America where there are Mexicans and Mexican-Americans," he stressed, "there are Mexican drug stores in which there is a great sale of every sort of medicinal plant." Mexicans along the border could also find remedies for their physical and emotional ailments by visiting Mexican healers known as *curanderos*. "I cure by means of herbs" one *curandera* in Tucson informed Gamio, "but I never promise to cure this one or that one because that is something of God. . . . I have cured many Mexicans of syphilis and tuberculosis and other diseases. I have also helped to assist at childbirth many times, when the doctors have let me. The existence of such popular traditions illustrates what scholars have discovered in studies of migration patterns: the persistence of earlier preindustrial cultural practices within an industrializing society—or what one sociologist refers to as an "urban village."

Immigrant families interviewed by Gamio further acknowledged that for the most part they continued to cook Mexican style. "I don't suffer in the matter of food," one woman told him in Los Angeles, for my mother cooks at home as if we were in Mexico. There are some dishes which are different but we generally eat Mexican style and rice and beans are almost never lacking from our table." According to a report one of Gamio's associates, however, Mexican families in certain areas purchased items such canned chile, canned sauces, and canned tomatoes from California. Obtaining food processed in the United States often led to complaints about the inadequacy and poor quality of American products in the cooking of Mexican dishes. "The foodstuffs, besides costing a lot," another woman informed Gamio, "are no good for making good Mexican food . . . so that it might be said that the food is half-Mexican and half-American, being neither the one nor the other." Most Mexican families in El Paso avoided this dietary problem by apparently purchasing much of their food in Juárez.

Outside the home, Mexicans patronized various other forms of entertainment and recreation. Men visited Mexican bars, pool halls, and gambling establishments in both El Paso and Juárez. At the turn of the century, some Mexicans sponsored horse rides in Washington Park with attendance from not only the city but the surrounding area as well. On its visits to the border the circus stood out as a special treat for Mexican children and their parents. The *Times* recorded in 1887 that many Mexicans as well as Americans had attended John Robinson's Great Circus in back of the Santa Fe depot. Elephants, camels, and other strange beasts, a reporter observed, captured the attention of the Mexican spectators. Mexicans from the adjacent territory also came in large numbers. They camped next to the circus tents, the *Times* man wrote, and everyone spent their *dinero* freely. Mexicans along with Americans eagerly awaited the arrival of such special attractions as the Ringling Brothers' "Greatest Show on Earth" and Barnum and Bailey's circus. Besides American circuses, small Mexican traveling shows with acrobats and sideshows called *carpas* visited El Paso and performed in Chihuahuita. According to one Mexican American critic, these carpas included improvised satirical skits. "The brief, topical skits of la carpa," he proposes, "with their focus on physical movement and rapid verbal gymnastics are the progenitors of today's [Chicano] 'actos.'" Mexicans also spent their limited leisure time at spectator sports that helped distract their minds from homesickness, work, and harsh living conditions. Bullfights in Juárez, for example, were a cultural link with la patria. Boxing matches on both sides of the border enticed many males. Mexican boxers such as Benny Chávez and Mexican Americans like lightweight Aurelio Herrera held special attraction for the Mexican fans. By 1900 Mexicans also began to show an interest in American baseball. In addition to its attraction as a spectator event, some Mexicans, mostly Mexican Americans, organized baseball teams of their own. The Internationals stood out as the earliest and most popular Mexican baseball team in the border city. With an all Mexican lineup and playing against Anglo-American teams, the Internationals proved to be one of the finest clubs in El Paso for several years and played games throughout the Southwest. Sportswriters considered the Mexican American players among the finest athletes. José "Curly" Villarreal, playing for a local team in 1917, was regarded as the best pitcher in the city league. One writer commented that with Curly on the pitching mound "it is a safe bet that a large number of Mexican fans will be out Sunday to see their favorite in action."

The allure of American baseball for Mexicans transcended the border and began to have a cultural impact in Mexico. "Baseball is showing promise," the *Times* proudly reported in 1908, "of becoming the national game of Mexico as well as the United States." Admitting that other foreign sports such as cricket, field hockey, and polo had some following in the neighboring republic, the *Times* believed that those cultural imports could not compare with the "grand old game." The newspaper subjectively concluded that the sport physically suited the Mexicans due to their "natural quickness." Moreover, it recognized the language influence that baseball had on Mexicans with the acceptance of baseball terms such as "You're out." The

Times further understood the political objective American baseball served in Mexico. Baseball would create a sympathetic link between Americans and Mexicans. Two men cheering for the same team, it emphasized, would find it difficult to disagree on other matters. At the same time that the United States had become Mexico's principal trade partner and investor, the *Times* boasted that south of the border American baseball had outdistanced British, French, German, and other European sports. The border publication predicted that it would be only a matter of time before the "better classes" in Mexico would stop bullfighting and then baseball would become the national sport. "When the mob can no longer have it [bull-fighting]," the *Times* stressed, "baseball will be the national game from Central America to the Great Lakes."

In spite of strong Mexican cultural influences in El Paso owing to increased Mexican immigration and the city's proximity to the border, Mexicans underwent subtle cultural changes. After 1910, for example, they faced the acculturating influence of American mass culture through the silent movies. Although it does not appear that the early movie houses such as the Crawford, the Grand, the Little Wigwam, and the Bijou specifically excluded Mexicans, the attendance of Mexicans at the movies grew when several Mexican theaters opened by the period of World War I. The International Amusement Company of El Paso, Owned and managed by Mexican businessmen including Mexican American politico Frank Alderete, operated seven theaters in the border city. These included the Alcazar, the Eureka, the Hidalgo, the Paris, the Iris, and Rex movie houses on South El Paso Street. By 1917, these theaters showed some films produced in Mexico but for the most part Mexican audiences paid 6 or 11 cents admission, depending on where one sat, to see American movies featuring such stars as Charlie Chaplin, Mary Pickford, and Fatty Arbuckle. "Regardless of what some may say ," *La Patria* commented in reviewing a Chaplin film at the Teatro Rec, "Carlos Chaplin is a magnificent artist; he is not a vulgar clown, but rather a refined and competent comic actor, whose every gesture, every graceful pose, brings forth joy not only for children, but for adults."

Besides exposing Mexicans to some American material and cultural values and mores, the movies also may have influenced their ability to understand some English. Mexicans employed by the movie houses translated English subtitles to Spanish ones, which appeared at the bottom of the screen below the original dialogue. American slang was no problem, remarked a *Times* reporter, for the translators of slapstick comedies screened at Mexican theaters. Even Americans studying Spanish took advantage of the process and visited Mexican theaters to improve their Spanish reading ability. The reporter further noted that the technique of imposing the Spanish translation on the films had been invented by a Mexican employee of the International Amusement Company and "is now in use wherever American films are used for Spanish-speaking audiences. Guillermo Balderas recalls that his own brother Eduardo worked as a translator in one of the Mexican movie houses. "These were 'silent movies,'" Balderas remembers, "that were translated into Spanish." By the 1920s American movies were an important acculturating agent, especially on the first generation native born, on both sides of the border. As one Mexican immigrant explained in a corrido, Hollywood films had enticed him to leave Mexico for the "promised land:"

> I dreamed in my youth of being a movie star
> And one of these days I came to visit Hollywood.

For Mexican immigrants, Catholicism provided a familiar cultural environment as well as institutional support for their adjustment north of the border. The Catholic Church in El Paso, under the control of Irish Americans, recognized quite early that it would have to establish separate facilities for its Mexican members. Consequently, it organized Mexican parishes in the barrios to serve the particular religious and social needs of the immigrants. Unlike many national churches in the United States, however, those in El Paso were not staffed, for the most part, by Mexican priests, of whom there was an apparent shortage in the Southwest, but by Italian and American clergy. As a result the Church not only took into consideration Mexican cultural traditions but also became an agent of Americanization among its parishioners, especially those families, many of them political refugees, who could afford to send their children to Catholic schools. Still, the mass of Mexican immigrants retained their popular religious beliefs and practices by transferring them across the border. Regardless of economic or political background, first generation immigrants and political refugees, through their reestablishment of spiritual societies common in Mexico as well as the reenactment of native Mexican religious celebrations, successfully maintained cultural continuity and helped create a sense of community in the barrios.

As an institution, the Catholic Church in El Paso pursued a bicultural approach in its treatment of Mexican immigrants. The south-side parochial schools, for example, under the direction of the American Sisters of Loretto emphasized, as one part of their curriculum, the Americanization of their students and attempted to change what they considered to be the Mexicans' bad cultural habits.

In addition to a basic curriculum emphasizing religious and academic subjects with some industrial and domestic training, Sacred Heart School presented performances displaying both the talents of young Mexicans as well as the influences of American middle-class culture. The *Times* reported in 1895 that Sacred Heart School students would offer a musical and dramatic entertainment at the old stone church on North Oregon Street. Mainly performed in English, the school's closing exercise in 1904 took place at Myar's Opera House, where a large audience assembled. According to the *Times* critic, the entertainment not only proved to be interesting but also reflected great credit on the nuns who taught at Sacred Heart. The best acts included the singing of "The Poor Old Tramps" by a male choir and an instrumental performance by the Mandolin Club that "was rendered without a single discord, and gave promise that El Paso will have a number of skillful musicians, who, with light touch, will call forth the music that stirs men's souls." Some of the girls who presented a drama in three acts entitled "The Little Waiters" received "round upon round of applause, and demonstrated the fact that several of the young ladies had real dramatic ability." Impressed, the *Times* gave credit to the students' teachers and praised the Catholic Church for its work among the Mexican children of the city. The performance had demonstrated, the paper concluded, "that there is an efficient and practical movement on foot to educate the Catholic youths and young girls of El Paso and teach them how to become good citizens and dutiable daughters and faithful wives."

Yet English and middle-class American customs at Sacred Heart shared the curriculum with Spanish and Mexican cultural traditions. Cleofas Calleros, who attended Sacred Heart during the first decade of the century, remembered that although there were only two Mexican teachers in a faculty of ten, both English and Spanish were used in instruction along with American and Mexican history. Years later, lecturing to the 1919 graduating girls of Sacred Heart, the Italian pastor of the parish encouraged them to adopt the best of other cultures but to never forget who they were: young Catholic Mexican girls, who were obliged to follow Christ and as Mexicans, to conserve the beautiful customs and traditions of *la raza*. Hence, Sacred Heart as well as the other Mexican parochial schools served a two-fold purpose. They helped transmit Mexican ethnicity and, at the same time, provided lessons in English and American culture in order to assist students to adjust and hopefully succeed in the United States.

Next to Sacred Heart, the religious and cultural activities of St. Ignatius Church at Park and Second perhaps best exemplified the Church's interest in the Mexicans' adjustment. For the spiritual needs of its members, St. Ignatius sponsored a variety of religious groups popular in Mexico. In 1905 some women formed the League of the Sacred Heart and Congregation of the Daughters of Mary (Congregación de las Hijas de María). That same year a group of young people and children organized the Congregation of San Luis Gonzaga as a prayer union for youth. Care of the church sacristy led to the beginning of the Altar Society. Still other parishioners, especially women, belonged to additional religious associations such as the Society of Good Death (Buena Muerte), the Society of Our Lady of Guadalupe, the Society of Divine Providence, and the Association of Christian Mothers. Besides their specific devotions, many of these organizations assisted in the more popular religious ceremonies among the Mexican working class such as the Feast of Our Lady of Guadalupe and, of course, at Christmas, when parishioners performed the Shepherds' Play (Los Pastores). The Corpus Christi procession held every June, however, was the most impressive popular religious feast day, clearly fostering a communal spirit among the entire Mexican population of El Paso. Although this event centered around Sacred Heart Church, all Mexican parishes participated. In 1919, for example, between 10,000 and 20,000 Mexicans marched in the annual procession with thousands more watching, making the Revista Católica, the Spanish-language Jesuit newspaper in the city, declare that the Mexican colony saw Corpus Christi as an ethnic holiday.

St. Ignatius supported various other cultural and recreational activities as well. Shortly after the church opened, it hired Trinidad Concha to assemble a young women's orchestra, which by 1908 appeared in public concerts. Concha further directed the church's well-known choir. In 1912 St. Ignatius obtained the benefit of another musical group when a boys band at Sacred Heart had to leave that parish because it made too much noise and instead moved to St. Ignatius. This marked the start of the young people's band, which gained much prominence under the direction of Professor Melitón Concha. By 1918 St. Ignatius also had one of the largest Mexican athletic clubs in the city. Founded by the church to counter the success of the Mexican YMCA, the Association of Catholic Youth (Asociación Católica de Jóvenes), better known as the Club Anahuac, sponsored both athletic and cultural events. It possessed the best baseball, football, tennis, and basketball teams in south El Paso and won several city-wide contests. Moreover, its 100 members aided in the building of athletic and playground facilities for the children of the area. And, as part of its expression of loyalty to the United States during World War I, the club held picnics and athletic exhibitions to raise money for the war fund of the Knights of Columbus. "The young members of this club," it appealed to other Mexicans, "moved by a sense of duty and humanitarianism. and not being able to contribute in any other way to relieve the suffering of our own brothers, have decided to help through this exhibition. Won't you help us by attending? *Remember:* It will benefit our brothers who are fighting on the front lines."

Indeed, the war gave St. Ignatius and the Catholic Church of El Paso another opportunity to stress the Americanization of the Mexicans, especially youth. After the United States declared war in 1917, the priests of St. Ignatius explained to their parishioners the alien registration provisions of the draft law, and urged them to cooperate with the civil and military authorities. The church also requested Mexicans to buy Liberty Bonds (Bonos de la Libertad). Yet the parish's proudest contribution to the war came when more than 40 young Mexican men, both native born and foreign born, enlisted for military service, despite the fact that most Mexicans in the city claimed

draft exemptions owing to their alien status. A few of the Mexican soldiers, moreover, served with distinction. Marcos B. Armijo, who died in battle, received the Distinguished Service Cross, while the French government honored Manuel J. Escajeda with the Croix de Guerre. Marcelino Serna, however, represented not only St. Ignatius' most distinguished soldier but one of the most decorated in El Paso and Texas. Serna received the American Distinguished Service Cross, the French Croix de Guerre and Military Medal, the Italian Cross of Merit, and the British medal of Bravery. This demonstration of American patriotism on the part of St. Ignatius' youth revealed the conviction of the Catholic Church in El Paso that, regardless of native sentiments, Mexicans for their own economic benefits should learn the language, customs, and values of the United States as quickly as possible. After the war the Church strongly supported the city's Americanization program, which included night school for Mexican adults. In an editorial even the sometime Anti-American *Revista Católica* encouraged its Mexican readers to avail themselves of this education in order to help them obtain better jobs. "The movement initiated in Washington," the Mexican Catholic paper pointed out, "to 'Americanize' all foreigners in the United States has reached El Paso, and all indicators show that it will prove more fruitful in this city than in other places. The name of this program will scare off many Mexicans and perhaps because of this fear many will not take advantage of this excellent opportunity to improve their conditions."

Hence, by 1920 the Catholic Church in El Paso through its endorsement of postwar Americanization programs as well its own efforts in the parochial schools served, along with the public schools, as a major American institution of socialization, especially for the children of Mexican immigrants. Based on a viewpoint stressing loyalty to both Church and country, which by the 1920s and 1930s increasingly meant the United States, the Catholic Church in the Southwest assisted Mexicans not only to adjust to border life but, ultimately, to believe in the American Dream. Still, the constant stream of additional immigrants into El Paso and other southwestern areas after 1920, as well as the proximity of Mexico, meant that Mexican immigrant parishes were never completely Americanized. Rather than examples of an earlier past, many of them, due to continued immigration from Mexico, remain viable through poor institutions helping to link Mexican immigrant communities in the United States with the mother country and culture.

As a form of ethnic self-protection as well as an expression of ethnicity. Mexican social organizations in El Paso revealed the Mexicans' accommodation to their new American setting. Forced to organize in a sometimes hostile society, some of El Paso's Mexicans, especially more skilled and educated ones, formed several mutual and fraternal associations that helped provide organized leadership in the Mexican settlement. Similar societies, moreover, existed in Mexico and hence were familiar forms of association. As mediating institutions the mutual and fraternal organizations, besides aiding in the preservation and encouragement of Mexican ethnic consciousness among the immigrants, helped form a more permanent and cohesive Mexican community.

As early as 1893 the Mexican newspaper *El Hispano-Americano* printed a notice from La Unión Mexicana (the Mexican Western Union), which was one of the first Mexican mutual aid societies in El Paso. "It is neither more nor less than what it's name implies a group of persons of Mexican origin," stated organizer and political exile Víctor L. Ochoa. He went on to explain that the unión had several objectives: to aid and defend its members, to "unalterably" maintain the Spanish language, to protect the morality of its members, and to spread fraternal bonds among Mexican nationals in the United States. In addition, when a member died, his wife and children would receive $2.50 from each unión member. One year later another mutual aid society, Los Caballeros del Progreso (the Gentlemen of Progress), stressed that the poor economic conditions of Mexicans in the United States resulted from a lack of unity and that in order to alleviate this problem Los Caballeros had been organized. *El Defensor* noted that when one of the society's members who had not kept up his dues died, Los Caballeros refused to pay the funeral costs as a lesson to other negligent members.

One Mexican newspaper also urged unity through organizations when it observed in 1899 that despite the large numbers of Mexicans in El Paso, the city's oldest Mexican mutual benefit society (1888), the Sociedad Mutualista Mexicana "La Protectora," had only 40 members. It pointed out the validity of the motto "Unity Makes Force" and informed its readers that only through organization had the United States become a great power. "'If it is true then that unity makes force," it added, "then we do not understand why Mexicans do not develop those relationships that will unite us. The Sociedad Mutualista Mexicana "La Protectora," the paper asserted, aimed to unite and protect Mexicans who lived in El Paso. Had it not been for this society, the paper believed that Mexicans in the city would have been deprived of a common meeting place where they "could exchange impressions of our beloved country." *Las Noticas* further reminded Mexicans of their obligation to one another as members of the same race "and sons of the same mother: Mexico." Among its benefits, "La Protectora" assisted members who required hospitalization and paid for funeral costs. *Las Dos Américas,* another Mexican newspaper in El Paso, expressed its gratitude in 1898 to "La Protectora's" Mexican American president, A. J. Escajeda, and its vice-president C. Aguirre, for their consideration during the funeral of Antonio G. Gallardo, who had been killed by a Southern Pacific train at Deming, New Mexico. Although it appears that the membership of "La Protectora" remained small, it met regularly every second and fourth Monday of the

month. Its leadership seems to have come from Mexican Americans like Escajeda, but the entire composition of its membership cannot be determined.

As more Mexicans arrived in El Paso by the turn of the century, several other benefit and fraternal groups appeared. The *Times* announced in 1907 that seven Mexican societies of El Paso would participate in that year's 16th of September celebrations honoring Mexican independence. These included La Benéfica patriotic society from the smelter, the Sociedad Unión Constructora, La Mutualista, Los Hijos de Hidalgo, and the Sociedad Filarmónica. "Few Americans if any," a Mexican told a *Times reporter,*

> are aware of the wonderful growth and activity to be found in the Mexican fraternal orders now existing in the Southwest.
>
> While the chief element of these orders is made up of the common working class, it must be remembered that there are also affiliated with these societies many Mexicans of culture—among them professional and business men. El Paso has the distinction of having the largest number of these lodges; Tucson ranking next, it being the place where two of the most important orders, the "Sociedad Zaragoza" and the "Sociedad Hispano-Americana" have their home offices.

He further explained that the Hispano-American society paid $1,000 to the family of a deceased member and $200 to a member upon the death of his wife. In addition he declared that although the Sociedad Zaragoza had been operating for a shorter time than other societies, it had a larger membership with 28 branches throughout Arizona, New Mexico, and Texas. In El Paso it was represented by Lodge No. 18, founded that year with 90 members.

The growing numbers of Mexican immigrants and refugees in El Paso after 1910 also influenced the expansion of these societies. "Mexicans in El Paso are interested in lodge work to an extent probably not generally known," member Pedro A. Candelaria stated in an interview in 1915. Candelaria observed that the Sociedad Mutualista Mexicana had a membership of 115 and La Constructora had 300 members. Both represented the two largest societies in the city and intended to protect the widows and orphans of deceased members. Each of these organizations assessed every member $3 whenever a death occurred and turned the amount over to the widow. Candelaria pointed out that still another lodge, La Benéfica, operated in East El Paso. These organizations had developed substantially in recent years, he concluded, owing to the arrival of Mexican refugees.

The sharp rise in the Mexican population of the Southwest during the years of the Mexican Revolution encouraged consolidation among Mexican mutual aid societies and increased their emphasis on insurance practices. The best example of the change can be seen in the activities of

La Sociedad Alianza Hispano-Americana. Organized in 1894 in Tucson, it grew from a small numbers of lodges to 88 in 1919 with more than 4,000 members from California to Texas, and with additional lodges in northern Mexico. It hoped to unite all Mexicans and Latin Americans in the United States into one "family" under the principles of "protection, morality, and education." According to the Alianza's historian, its membership consisted of both lower-middle-class and working-class people. In one of the largest demonstrations of Mexican social organization in the United States, El Paso hosted a national convention of the Alianza in 1910 attended by close to 200 delegates from New Mexico, Arizona, Southern California, and Texas. At their opening session the mayors of both El Paso and Juárez welcomed the delegates and assured them they would not be molested by the police of either border town. One of the main items in the convention's agenda dealt with changes in insurance payments. Every member paid a flat rate of $1 each month for $1,000 insurance without regard to age or other conditions. However, the *Times* reported that the supreme lodge had $16,790 on hand of which $14,000 had been put in the reserve fund. Although the convention voted to retain a flat rate for present members, it approved a new classified assessment for future ones but kept the amount of insurance that could be secured at $500 or $1,000, with $100 and $200 funeral benefits.

Nine years later *La Patria* published an advertisement for the Alianza containing both its insurance provisions and a list of its lodges in the Southwest. The notice emphasized that the Alianza had no political or religious qualifications for membership, that it treated every member equally, that each received the same benefits, and that it spent none of its members' funds for amusements. The Alianza also stressed that women could purchase a policy, "for we believe them to be as worthy and as entitled to the same right to protect their children who depend on them." Despite the fact that most of its members were "humble workers," the Alianza proudly announced that since its formation it had paid out a million and a half dollars in benefits. To share in the Alianza's protection, a Mexican had to pay $3.50 admission fee plus $1 to $2 for a medical examination. Monthly payments would then be determined by the amount of the policy and the age of its holder. "We respectfully invite you and your family to join the 'Alianza,'" the ad told the readers of *La Patria*. In 1919 three of its lodges, apparently located in Chihuahuita, functioned in El Paso. *La Patria* observed that members of the different lodges could attend one another's meetings. In addition Jesús M. Ortiz, who had been named Alianza organizer for Texas, believed that a new chapter could be established in East El Paso since many Mexicans there had expressed an interest in the society. Besides El Paso, lodges could be found in nearby New Mexico in Silver City, Hillsboro, Santa Rita, Las Cruces, and Hurley.

Like other immigrant organizations in the United States, the Mexican mutual and fraternal societies of El Paso provided social and cultural activities for their members. Many of these social functions consisted of dances sponsored by different lodges. In 1911, for example, the Mexican secret societies held a grand ball at the Fraternal Brotherhood Hall. "The national colors of Mexico will be flying," the *Times* commented, "and those who cannot have one of the most enjoyable times of their life . . . will be hard to please." In 1919 the Logia Morelos held its Second Grand Ball at Liberty Hall and in 1920 the Sociedad Mutualista Zaragoza Independiente sponsored a literary and dance show to celebrate its twelfth anniversary. That same year the Alianza hosted an artistic presentation to raise funds. Moreover, the lodges sponsored the 16th of September celebrations as well as other Mexican patriotic holidays. When William Howard Taft met Porfirio Díaz in El Paso in 1909, the city's Mexican societies turned out in force to honor both leaders and the nations they represented. "As the president's carriage neared the position occupied by the Mexican societies," a reporter noticed of Taft's parade down El Paso street, "there was a tumult of applause, cheers and cries of "Viva Taft! Viva Taft!'" After Taft had visited Díaz in Juárez, the Mexican organizations joined the parade up El Paso Street to downtown Cleveland Square. "Four different Mexican societies," the *Times* observed, "numbering about 1,000 men and all wearing natty uniforms comprised the divisions."

For Mexican Americans, the social activities of the lodges became quite important because participation in Anglo-Saxon society remained limited. Although the Women's Club, the El Paso Country Club, and other American social organizations had no clear policy on the exclusion of Mexican members, businessman Félix Martínez, who belonged to the Toltec Men's Club, appears to have been one of the few persons of Mexican descent throughout the period who claimed membership in an America social group. Social intercourse between Mexicans and Americans on an organized level seems to have occurred only during special political or patriotic events or the arrival of major Mexican dignitaries such as Díaz. Because of this de facto social separation as well as their own cultural affinity, Mexican Americans either formed their own clubs or joined immigrant organizations. In 1907 the Logia Fraternal No. 30, composed exclusively of Mexican Americans, held a banquet in honor of Mexican Independence Day at the Sheldon Hotel attended by 132 persons including 35 prominent American politicians. The walls of the big dining room had been decorated with a number of Mexican and American flags, while at the south end of the hall facing the toastmaster was an immense Mexican and a huge American flag leaning so close together that their folds embraced each other." After some of the American guests spoke, lodge officer Agapito Martínez emphasized that it gave him great pride to say that every member of the lodge held American citizenship and yet could also be proud of Mexico's achievements. "Freedom," said editor Lauro Aguirre, "started the fire at Philadelphia, at Paris and in Mexico." Z. M. Oriza ended the speeches by a toast to the menu motto "After All, What is Better than Friendship."

The annual 16th of September celebration proved to be not only the most important Mexican cultural event in El Paso, and throughout the Southwest, but also an indication of the level of social organization and cooperation that could occur among the different Mexican societies. The 1897 ceremonies, for example, stood out as one of the most successful holidays in El Paso and revealed the various cultural activities that often took place during this community fiesta. As early as July, the Mexican newspaper *El Monitor* announced a meeting of La Junta Patriótica Mexicana (the Mexican Patriotic Council) to select a board of directors and decide on the best format for the 16th of September celebration. One month later the paper criticized some Mexican Americans who did not believe that the 16th of September had any meaning for them and refused to support the festivities: "To these 'Agringados' (Americanized Mexicans) who negate that they are Mexicans because they were born in the United States, we ask: what blood runs through their veins? Do they think they are members of the Anglo-Saxon race who only happen to have dark skins because they were born on the border! What nonsense! (Qué barbaridad!)." *El Monitor* went on to add that this did not mean that Mexican Americans should not be good citizens of the United States and even fight for "Tio Samuel" if it went to war against a European or an Asiatic nation. However, in the event of conflict between the United States and Mexico or a Latin American nation, *El Monitor* believed that every Mexican living north of the border should go to the defense of their "blood brothers" and the country of their parents' birth. The paper concluded by asking: "Why should there be any reason now for us to feel ashamed of being a Mexican?"

Led by the Junta Patriótica, the Mexicans of El Paso prepared to celebrate the independence of Mexico. In its September 12th edition, *El Monitor* dedicated its coverage to the Mexican workers of the city, "to whom we wish all kinds of happiness during these glorious days." It also reminded its readers of the events to be held on both the fifteenth and sixteenth, and commented that the prepared program left nothing to be desired, thanks to the work of the Junta. Similar festivities would occur in other areas of Texas, as well as in New Mexico, Arizona, and California, but the paper predicted that one of the best 16th of Septembers would be held in El Paso. To stimulate patriotic sentiments, *El Monitor* retold the story of the fathers of Mexican independence, Hidalgo and Morelos, and the independence struggle against the "tyranny of Spain." "Long live the illustrious Liberator," the article eulogized Hidalgo, "and, 'Viva México!"

Organized in honor of the Mexican colony, especially the Junta Patriótica and the Mexican consul Francisco Mallén, only rain spotted an otherwise flawless event. The celebration began on the morning of the fifteenth, when Consul Mallén dedicated the observance to Don Porfirio Díaz. That evening the Junta, the Mexican mutual benefit society "La Protectora," and the Mexican students of Sacred Heart School marched from Fifth Street, bordering the downtown area, to Sacred Heart Church in Chihuahuita preceded by a Mexican band. Throughout the route the homes and businesses of both Mexicans and Americans had been decorated with the Mexican tricolors. At 8:00 P.M. Consul Mallén and the president of the Junta, Dr. Reehy, accompanied by their wives arrived at the platform in front of the church and the program commenced by the playing of the Mexican national anthem. The more than 3,000 people who attended also heard recitations by several young people as well as songs and piano recitals. A speech in English by lawyer T.J. Beall that praised Mexican independence and Hidalgo received much applause. After several songs, Don Esteban Gómez del Campo delivered the main speech touching on various Mexican historical themes. The band then played both the Mexican and American anthems followed by two tunes originally composed by Trinidad Concha entitled "On the Shores of the Rio Grande" and "Through El Paso." At last the secretary of the Junta read Hidalgo's act of independence (El grito de Dolores") and Consul Mallén said a few words. The program concluded with the Mexican national anthem sung by a chorus of young Mexican women. The following morning of the sixteenth, a parade through downtown El Paso containing both Mexican and American units ended the independence day celebrations.

As the 16th of September festivities partly indicated, different cultural influences touch the Mexican population of El Paso. Given diverse cultural levels within the Mexican settlement, these influences also had varied effects and responses. More acculturated than the immigrants, the minority of Mexican Americans felt the pull of both cultures much more strongly. "This civilization is American nominally," Gamio observed of Mexican Americans in the 1920s, "and exhibits the principal material aspects of modern American civilization, but intellectually and emotionally it lives in local Mexican tradition." On the other hand, the recently arrived immigrants retained to a considerable degree their native traditions in the form of language, folklore, superstitions, songs, and religious holidays, which expressed their national origins.

However, the impact of American industrialization and urbanization forced the immigrants to adjust to changed conditions. In the process many of El Paso's Mexicans formed relationships with one another through family, recreational, mutual aid, fraternal, and patriotic organizations that, on the one hand, provided a cultural security and continuity and, on the other, revealed new American conditions and influences. Moreover, the schools, both public and parochial, American material goods, and to a degree, churches represented institutions and attractions within the barrios that affected the subtle and gradual Americanization of the Mexicans.

Although their culture underwent some transformation as they adjusted to immigrant life, Mexicans, as Gamio further recognized, "never became integrally assimilated to American civilization." He believed that the problem retarding the complete Americanization of the Mexicans lay in the large gulf between what he called "purely American culture" and "purely Mexican culture." The economic discrimination and segregation aimed at Mexicans in El Paso also made it difficult to assimilate them as well as Mexican Americans because employers desired to keep them as a source of cheap labor. Furthermore, unlike European immigration, which slowed to a trickle in the 1920s, Mexican immigration persisted and reinforced a distinct Mexican presence in El Paso. Too, most Mexicans believed they would soon return to their homeland and therefore felt no strong motivation to discard their cultural traditions. Mexico, of course, was right next door. Consequently, a dialectical relationship existed between the immigrant's native culture and the attempt by American institutions and reformers to restructure earlier habits and instill a new urban-industrial discipline among the Mexicans. The eventual result: a Mexican border culture, neither completely Mexican nor American, but one revealing contrasting attractions and pressures between both cultures. Yet Mexican border culture was and is by no means monolithic because different experiences are represented. Recent arrivals display what Galarza calls "the most authentic transplant of Mexican working-class culture," whereas middle-class newcomers, such as many of the political refugees during the Revolutionary period, bring with them a more sophisticated bourgeois, one of both Mexican and European origins. Finally, Mexican Americans, especially the children and grandchildren of immigrants, have faced an erosion of their Mexican culture as American institutions, including an acculturated family environment, bring them into the fold of American mass culture.

Confronting "America"

Vicki L. Ruiz

As a child Elsa Chávez confronted a "moral" dilemma. She wanted desperately to enjoy the playground equipment close to her home in El Paso's Segundo Barrio. The tempting slide, swings, and jungle gym seemed to call her name. However, her mother would not let her near the best playground (and for many years the only playground) in the barrio. Even a local priest warned Elsa and her friends that playing there was a sin—the playground was located within the yard of the Rose Gregory Houchen Settlement, a Methodist community center.[1]

While one group of Americans responded to Mexican immigration by calling for restriction and deportation, other groups mounted campaigns to "Americanize" the immigrants. From Los Angeles, California, to Gary, Indiana, state and religious-sponsored Americanization programs swung into action. Imbued with the ideology of "the melting pot," teachers, social workers, and religious missionaries envisioned themselves as harbingers of salvation and civilization.[2] Targeting women and especially children, the vanguard of Americanization placed their trust "in the rising generation." As Pearl Ellis of the Covina City schools explained in her 1929 publication, *Americanization Through Homemaking*, "Since the girls are potential mothers and homemakers, they will control, in a large measure, the destinies of their future families." She continued, "It is she who sounds the clarion call in the campaign for better homes."[3]

A growing body of literature on Americanization in Mexican communities by such scholars as George Sánchez, Sarah Deutsch, Gilbert González, and myself suggest that church and secular programs shared common course offerings and curricular goals. Perhaps taking their cue from the regimen developed inside Progressive Era settlement houses, Americanization projects emphasized classes in hygiene, civics, cooking, language, and vocational education (e.g., sewing and carpentry). Whether

seated at a desk in a public school or on a sofa at a Protestant or Catholic neighborhood house, Mexican women received similar messages of emulation and assimilation. While emphasizing that the curriculum should meet "the needs of these people," one manual proclaimed with deepest sincerity that a goal of Americanization was to enkindle "a greater respect . . . for our civilization."[4]

Examples of Americanization efforts spanned the Southwest and Midwest from secular settlements in Watts, Pasadena, and Riverside to Hull House in Chicago. In addition, Catholic neighborhood centers, such as Friendly House in Phoenix, combined Americanization programs with religious and social services. Protestant missionaries, furthermore, operated an array of settlements, health clinics, and schools. During the first half of the twentieth century, the Methodist Church sponsored one hospital, four boarding schools, and sixteen settlements/community centers, all serving a predominately Mexican clientele. Two of these facilities were located in California, two in Kansas, one in New Mexico, and sixteen in Texas.[5] Though there are many institutions to compare, an overview, by its very nature, would tend to privilege missionary labors and thus, once again, place Mexican women within the shadows of history. By taking a closer look at one particular project—the Rose Gregory Houchen Settlement—one can discern the attitudes and experiences of Mexican women themselves. This chapter explores the ways in which Mexican mothers and their children interacted with the El Paso settlement, from utilizing selected services to claiming "American" identities, from taking their babies to the clinic for immunizations to becoming missionaries themselves.

Using institutional records raises a series of important methodological questions. How can missionary reports, pamphlets, newsletters, and related documents illuminate the experiences and attitudes of women of color? How do we sift through the bias, the self-congratulation, and the hyperbole to gain insight into women's lives? What can these materials tell us of women's agencies within and against larger social structures? I am intrigued (actually obsessed is a better word) with questions involving decision-making, specifically with regard to acculturation. What have Mexican women chosen to accept or reject? How have the economic, social, and political environments influenced the acceptance or rejection of cultural messages that emanate from the Mexican community, from U.S. popular culture, from Americanization programs, and from a dynamic coalescence of differing and at times oppositional cultural forms? What were women's real choices and, to borrow from Jürgen Habermas, how did they move "within the horizon of their lifeworld"?[6] Obviously, no set of institutional records can provide substantive answers, but by exploring these documents through the framework of these larger questions, we place Mexican women at the center of our study, not as victims of poverty and superstition as so often depicted by missionaries, but as women who made choices for themselves and for their families.

As the Ellis Island for Mexican immigrants, El Paso seemed a logical spot for a settlement house. In 1900, El Paso's Mexican community numbered only 8,748 residents, but by 1930 this population had swelled to 68,476. Over the course of the twentieth century, Mexicans composed over one-half the total population of this bustling border city.[7] Perceived as cheap labor by Euro-American businessmen, they provided the human resources necessary for the city's industrial and commercial growth. Education and economic advancement proved illusory as segregation in housing, employment, and schools served as constant reminders of their second-class citizenship. To cite an example of stratification, from 1930 to 1960, only 1.8 percent of El Paso's Mexican workforce held high white-collar occupations.[8]

Segundo Barrio or South El Paso has served as the center of Mexican community life. Today, as in the past, wooden tenements and crumbling adobe structures house thousands of Mexicanos and Mexican Americans alike. For several decades, the only consistent source of social services in Segundo Barrio was the Rose Gregory Houchen Settlement House and its adjacent health clinic and hospital.

Founded in 1912 on the corner of Tays and Fifth in the heart of the barrio, this Methodist settlement had two initial goals: (1) provide a Christian roominghouse for single Mexican wage earners and (2) open a kindergarten for area children. By 1918, Houchen offered a full schedule of Americanization programs—citizenship, cooking, carpentry, English instruction, Bible study, and Boy Scouts. The first Houchen staff included three Methodist missionaries and one "student helper," Ofilia [sic] Chávez.[9] Living in the barrio made these women sensitive to the need for low-cost, accessible health care. Infant mortality in Segundo Barrio was alarmingly high. Historian Mario García related the following example: "Of 121 deaths during July [1914], 52 were children under 5 years of age."[10]

Houchen began to offer medical assistance, certainly rudimentary at first. In 1920, a registered nurse and Methodist missionary Effie Stoltz operated a first aid station in the bathroom of the settlement. More important, she soon persuaded a local physician to visit the residence on a regular basis and he, in turn, enlisted the services of his colleagues. Within seven months of Stoltz's arrival, a small adobe flat was converted into Freeman Clinic. Run by volunteers, this clinic provided prenatal exams, well-baby care, and pediatric services and, in 1930, it opened a six-bed maternity ward. Seven years later, it would be demolished to make way for the construction of a more modern clinic and a new twenty-two-bed maternity facility—the Newark Methodist Maternity Hospital. Health care at Newark was a bargain. Prenatal classes, pregnancy exams, and infant immunizations were free. Patients paid for medicines at cost and, during the 1940s, $30 covered the hospital bill. Staff members would boast that for less than $50, payable in installments, neighborhood women could give birth at "one of the best equipped maternity hospitals in the city."[11]

Houchen Settlement also thrived. From 1920 to 1960, it coordinated an array of Americanization activities. These included age and gender graded Bible studies, music lessons, Campfire activities, scouting, working girls' clubs, hygiene, cooking, and citizenship. Staff members also opened a day nursery to complement the kindergarten program. In terms of numbers, how successful was Houchen? The available records give little indication of the extent of the settlement's client base. Based on fragmentary evidence for the period of 1930 to 1950, perhaps as many as 15,000 to 20,000 people per year or approximately one-fourth to one-third of El Paso's Mexican population utilized its medical and/or educational services. Indeed, one Methodist from the 1930s pamphlet boasted that the settlement "reaches nearly 15,000 people."[12]

As a functioning Progressive Era settlement, Houchen had amazing longevity from 1912 to 1962. Several Methodist missionaries came to Segundo Barrio as young women and stayed until their retirement. Arriving in 1930, Millie Rickford would live at the settlement for thirty-one years. Two years after her departure, the Rose Gregory Houchen Settlement House (named after a Michigan schoolteacher) would receive a new name, Houchen Community Center. As a community center, it would become more of a secular agency staffed by social workers and at times Chicano activists.[13] In 1991 the buildings that cover a city block in South El Paso still furnish day care and recreational activities. Along with Bible study, there are classes in ballet fólklorico, karate, English, and aerobics. Citing climbing insurance costs (among other reasons), the Methodist Church closed the hospital and clinic in December 1986 over the protests of local supporters and community members.[14]

From 1912 until the 1950s, Houchen workers placed Americanization and proselytization at the center of their efforts. Embracing the imagery and ideology of the melting pot, Methodist missionary Dorothy Little explained:

Houchen settlement stands as a sentinel of friendship
. . . between the people of America and the people of
Mexico. We assimilate the best of their culture, their
art, their ideals and they in turn gladly accept the best
America has to offer as they . . . become one with us.
For right here within our four walls is begun much of
the "Melting" process of our "Melting Pot."[15]

The first goal of the missionaries was to convert Mexican
women to Methodism since they perceived themselves as
harbingers of salvation. As expressed in a Houchen report, "Our Church is called El Buen Pastor . . . and that is
what our church really is to the people—it is a Good Shepherd guiding our folks out of darkness and Catholocism
[sic] into the good Christian life." Along similar lines, one
Methodist pamphlet printed during the 1930s equated
Catholicism (as practiced by Mexicans) with paganism
and superstition. Settlement's programs were couched in
terms of "Christian Americanization" and these programs
began early.[16]

Like the Franciscan missionaries who trod the same
ground three centuries before, Houchen settlement workers sought to win the hearts and minds of children. While
preschool and kindergarten students spoke Spanish and
sang Mexican songs, they also learned English, U.S. history, biblical verses—even etiquette a la Emily Post.[17] The
settlement also offered various after-school activities for
older children. These included "Little Homemakers,"
scouting, teen clubs, piano lessons, dance, bible classes,
and story hour. For many years the most elaborate playground in South El Paso could be found within the outer
courtyard of the settlement. Elsa Chávez eventually got
her playground wish. She and her mother reached an agreement: Elsa could play there on the condition that she not
accept any "cookies or koolaid," the refreshments provided
by Houchen staff. Other people remembered making similar bargains—they could play on the swings and slide, but
they could not go indoors.[18] How big of a step was it to
venture from the playground to story hour?

Settlement proselytizing did not escape the notice of
barrio priests. Clearly troubled by Houchen, a few predicted dire consequences for those who participated in any
Protestant-tinged activities. As mentioned earlier, one priest
went so far as to tell neighborhood children that it was a
sin even to play on the playground equipment. Others,
however, took a more realistic stance and did not chastise
their parishioners for utilizing Methodist child care and
medical services. Perhaps as a response to both the Great
Depression and suspected Protestant inroads, several area
Catholic churches began distributing food baskets and establishing soup kitchens.[19]

Children were not the only ones targeted by Houchen.
Women, particularly expectant mothers, received special
attention. Like the proponents of Americanization programs in California, settlement workers believed that
women held a special guardianship over their families'
welfare. As head nurse Millie Rickford explained, "If we
can teach her [the mother-to-be] the modern methods of
cooking and preparing foods and simple hygiene habits
for herself and her family, we have gained a stride."[20]

Houchen's "Christian Americanization" programs
were not unique. During the teens and twenties, religious
and state-organized Americanization projects aimed at the
Mexican population proliferated throughout the Southwest.
Although these efforts varied in scale from settlement
houses to night classes, curriculum generally revolved
around cooking, hygiene, English, and civics. Music
seemed a universal tool of instruction. One Arizona schoolteacher excitedly informed readers of *The Arizona Teacher
and Home Journal* that her district for the "cause of Americanization" had purchased a Victorola and several records
that included two Spanish melodies, the "'Star Spangled
Banner,' 'The Red, White, and Blue,' 'Silent Night,'. . .
[and] 'Old Kentucky Home.'"[21] Houchen, of course, offered a variety of musical activities beginning with the
kindergarten rhythm band of 1927. During the 1940s and
the 1950s, missionaries provided flute, guitar, ballet, and
tap lessons. For fifty cents a week, a youngster could take
dance or music classes and perform in settlement recitals.[22] Clothing youngsters in European peasant styles was
common. For instance, Alice Ruiz, Priscilla Molina, Edna
Parra, Mira Gómez, and Aida Rivera represented Houchen
in a local Girl Scout festival held at the Shrine temple in
which they modeled costumes from Sweden, England,
France, Scotland, and Lithuania.[23] Some immigrant traditions were valorized more than others. Celebrating Mexican heritage did not figure into the Euro-American
orientation pushed by Houchen residents.

In contrast, a teacher affiliated with an Americanization program in Watts sought to infuse a multicultural perspective as she directed a pageant with a U.S. women's
history theme. Clara Smith described the event as follows:

Women, famous in the United States history as the
Pilgrim, Betsy Ross, Civil War, and covered wagon
women, Indian and Negro women, followed by the
foreign women who came to live among us were portrayed. The class had made costumes and had learned
to dance the Virginia Reel. . . . They had also made
costumes with paper ruffles of Mexican colors to represent their flag. They prepared Mexican dances and
songs.[24]

Despite such an early and valiant attempt at diversity,
the teacher did not think it necessary to include the indigenous heritage of Mexican women. Indeed, stereotypical
representations of the American Indian "princess" (or what
Rayna Green has termed "the Pocahantas perplex"[25]) supplanted any understanding of indigenous cultures on either side of the political border separating Mexico and the
United States.

Like Americanization advocates across the Southwest, Houchen settlement workers held out unrealistic notions of the American Dream as well as romantic constructions of American life. It is as if the Houchen staff had endeavored to create a white, middle-class environment for Mexican youngsters complete with tutus and toe shoes. Cooking classes also became avenues for developing particular tastes. Minerva Franco, who as a child attended settlement programs and who later as an adult became a community volunteer, explained, "I'll never forget the look on my mother's face when I first cooked 'Eggs Benedict' which I learned to prepare at Houchen."[26] The following passage, taken from a report dated February 1942 outlines, in part, the perceived accomplishments of the settlement:

> Sanitary conditions have been improving—more children go to school—more parents are becoming citizens, more are leaving Catholicism—more are entering business and public life—and more and more they are taking on the customs and standards of Anglo people.[27]

Seemingly oblivious to structural discrimination, such a statement ignores economic segmentation and racial/ethnic segregation. Focusing on El Paso, historian Mario García demonstrated that the curricula in Mexican Schools, which emphasized vocational education, served to funnel Mexican youth into the factories and building trades. In the abstract, education raised expectations, but in practice, particularly for men, it trained them for low-status, low-paying jobs. One California grower disdained education for Mexicans because it would give them "tastes for things they can't acquire."[28] Settlement workers seemed to ignore that racial/ethnic identity involved not only a matter of personal choice and heritage but also an ascribed status imposed by external sources.[29]

Americanization programs have come under a lot of criticisms from historians over the past two decades and numerous passages and photographs in the Houchen collection provide fodder for sarcasm among contemporary readers. Yet, to borrow from urban theorist Edward Soja, scholars should be mindful of "an appropriate interpretive balance between space, time and social being."[30] Although cringing at the ethnocentrism and romantic idealizations of "American" life, I respect the settlement workers for their health and child care services. Before judging the maternal missionaries too harshly, it is important to keep in mind the social services they rendered over an extended period of time as well as the environment in which they lived. For example, Houchen probably launched the first bilingual kindergarten program in El Paso, a program that eased the children's transition into an English-only first grade. Houchen residents did not denigrate the use of Spanish and many became fluent Spanish speakers. The hospital and clinic, moreover, were important community institutions for over half a century.[31]

Settlement workers themselves could not always count on the encouragement or patronage of Anglo El Paso. In a virulently nativist tract, a local physician, C. S. Babbitt, condemned missionaries, like the women of Houchen, for working among Mexican and African Americans. In fact, Babbitt argued that religious workers were "seemingly conspiring with Satan to destroy the handiwork of God" because their energies were "wasted on beings . . . who are not in reality the objects of Christ's sacrifice."[32] Even within their own ranks, missionaries could not count on the support of Protestant clergy. Reverend Robert McLean, who worked among Mexicans in Los Angeles, referred to his congregation as "chili con carne" bound to give Uncle Sam a bad case of "heartburn."[33]

Perhaps more damaging than these racist pronouncements was the apparent lack of financial support on the part of El Paso area Methodist churches. Accessible records reveal little in terms of local donations. Houchen was named after a former Michigan schoolteacher who bequeathed $1,000 for the establishment of a settlement in El Paso. The Women's Home Missionary Society of the Newark, New Jersey, Conference proved instrumental in raising funds for the construction of both Freeman Clinic and Newark Methodist Maternity Hospital. When Freemen Clinic first opened its doors in June 1921, all the medical equipment—everything from sterilizers to baby scales—were gifts from Methodist groups across the nation. The Houchen Day Nursery, however, received consistent financial support from the El Paso Community Chest and later the United Way. In 1975, Houchen's Board of Directors conducted the first community-wide fund-raising drive. Volunteers sought to raise $375,000 to renovate existing structures and build a modern day care center. The Houchen fund-raising slogan "When people pay their own way, it's your affair . . . not welfare" makes painfully clear the conservative attitudes toward social welfare harbored by affluent El Pasoans.[34]

The women of Houchen appeared undaunted by the lack of local support. For over fifty years, these missionaries coordinated a multifaceted Americanization campaign among the residents of Segundo Barrio. How did Mexican women perceive the settlement? What services did they utilize and to what extent did they internalize the romantic notions of "Christian Americanization?"

Examining Mexican women's agency through institutional records is difficult; it involves getting beneath the text to dispel the shadows cast by missionary devotion to a simple Americanization ideology. One has to take into account the selectivity of voices. In drafting settlement reports and publications, missionaries chose those voices that would publicize their "victories" among the Spanish speaking. As a result, quotations abound that heap praise upon praise on Houchen and its staff. For example, in 1939, Soledad Burciaga emphatically declared, "There is not a person, no matter to which denomination they belong, who hasn't a kind word and a heart full of gratitude towards the Settlement House."[35] Obviously, these documents have their limits. Oral interviews and informal discussions with people who grew up in Segundo Barrio give a more balanced, less effusive perspective. Most viewed Houchen as a Protestant-run health care and after-school activities center rather than as the "light-house" [sic] in South El Paso.[36]

In 1949, the term Friendship Square was coined as a description for the settlement house, hospital, day nursery, and church. Missionaries hoped that children born at Newark would participate in preschool and afternoon programs and that eventually they and their families would join their church, El Buen Pastor. And a few did follow this pattern. One of the ministers assigned to El Buen Pastor, Fernando García, was a Houchen kindergarten graduate. Emulating the settlement staff, some young women enrolled in Methodist missionary colleges or served as lay volunteers. Elizabeth Soto, for example, attended Houchen programs throughout her childhood and adolescence. On graduation from Bowie High School, she entered Asbury College to train as a missionary and then returned to El Paso as a Houchen resident. After several years of service, she left settlement work to become the wife of a Mexican Methodist minister. The more common goal among Houchen teens was to graduate from high school and perhaps attend Texas Western, the local college. The first child born at Newark Hospital, Margaret Holguin, took part in settlement activities as a child and later became a registered nurse. According to her comadre, Lucy Lucero, Holguin's decision to pursue nursing was "perhaps due to the influence" of head nurse Millie Rickford. According to Lucero, "The only contact I had had with Anglos was with Anglo teachers. Then I met Miss Rickford and I felt, 'Hey, she's human. She's great.'" At a time when many (though certainly not all) elementary schoolteachers cared little about their Mexican students, Houchen residents offered warmth and encouragement.[37]

Emphasizing education among Mexican youth seemed a common goal characterizing Methodist community centers and schools. The Frances De Pauw School located on Sunset Boulevard in Los Angeles, for example, was an all-girls boarding school. Frances De Pauw educated approximately 1,800 young Mexican women from 1900 to 1946 and a Methodist pamphlet elaborated on its successes. "Among [the school's] graduates are secretaries, bookkeepers, clerks, office receptionists, nurses, teachers, waitresses, workers in cosmetic laboratories, church workers, and Christian homemakers." While preparing its charges for the workaday world, the school never lost sight of women's domestic duties. "Every De Pauw girl is graded as carefully in housework as she is in her studies."[38] With regard to Friendship Square, one cannot make wholesale generalizations about its role in fostering mobility or even aspirations for mobility among the youth of Segundo Barrio. Yet it is clear that Houchen missionaries strived to build self-esteem and encouraged young people to pursue higher education.

Missionaries also envisioned a Protestant enclave in South El Paso; but, to their frustration, very few people responded. The settlement church, El Buen Pastor, had a peak membership of 150 families. The church itself had an intermittent history. Shortly after its founding in 1897, El Buen Pastor disappeared; it was officially rededicated as part of Houchen in 1932. However, the construction of an actual church on settlement grounds did not begin until 1945. In 1968, the small rock chapel would be converted into a recreation room and thrift shop as the members of El Buen Pastor and El Mesias (another Mexican-American church) were merged together to form the congregation of the Emmanuel United Methodist Church in downtown El Paso. In 1991, a modern gymnasium occupies the ground where the chapel once stood.[39]

The case histories of converts suggest that many of those who joined El Buen Pastor were already Protestant. The Dominguez family offers an example. In the words of settlement worker A. Ruth Kern:

> Reyna and Gabriel Dominguez are Latin Americans, even though both were born in the United States. Some members of the family do not even speak English. Reyna was born . . . in a Catholic home, but at the age of eleven years, she began attending the Methodist Church. Gabriel was born in Arizona. His mother was a Catholic, but she became a Protestant when . . . Gabriel was five years old.[40]

The youth programs at Houchen brought Reyna and Gabriel together. After their marriage, the couple had six children, all born at Newark Hospital. The Dominguez family represented Friendship Square's typical success story. Many of the converts were children and many had already embraced a Protestant faith. In the records I examined, I found only one instance of the conversion of a Catholic adult and one of the conversion of an entire Catholic family.[41] It seems that those most receptive to Houchen's religious messages were already predisposed in that direction.

The failure of proselytization cannot be examined solely within the confines of Friendship Square. It is not as if these Methodist women were good social workers but incompetent missionaries. Houchen staff member Clara Sarmiento wrote of the difficulty in building trust among the adults of Segundo Barrio. "Though it is easy for children to open up their hearts to us we do not find it so with the parents." She continued, "It is hard especially because we are Protestant, and most of the people we serve . . . come from Catholic heritage."[42] I would argue that the Mexican community played an instrumental role in thwarting conversion. In a land where the barrio could serve as a refuge from prejudice and discrimination, the threat of social isolation could certainly inhibit many residents from turning Protestant. During an oral interview , Estella Ibarra, a woman who participated in Houchen activities for over fifty years, described growing up Protestant in South El Paso:

> We went through a lot of prejudice . . . sometimes my friends' mothers wouldn't let them play with us. . . . When the priest would go through the neighborhood, all the children would run to say hello and kiss his hand. My brothers and I would just stand by and look. The priest would usually come . . . and tell us how we were living in sin. Also, there were times when my brother and I were stoned by other students . . . and called bad names.[43]

When contacted by a Houchen resident, Mrs. Espinosa admitted to being a closet Protestant. As she explained, "I am afraid of the Catholic sisters and [I] don't want my neighbors to know that I am not Catholic-minded." The fear of ostracism, while recorded by Houchen staff, did not figure into their understanding of Mexicano resistance to conversion. Instead, they blamed time and culture. Or as Dorothy Little succinctly related, "We can not eradicate in a few years what has been built up during ages."[44] Their dilemma points to the fact historians Sarah Deutsch and George Sánchez have noted: Americanization programs in the Southwest, most of which were sporadic and poorly financed, made little headway in Mexican communities. Ruth Crocker also described the Protestant settlements in Gary, Indiana, as having only a "superficial and temporary" influence.[45] Yet even long-term sustained efforts, as in the case of Houchen, had limited appeal. This inability to mold consciousness or identity demonstrates not only the strength of community sanctions, but, more significant, of conscious decision-making on the part of Mexican women who sought to claim a place for themselves and their families in American society without abandoning their Mexican cultural affinities.

Mexican women derived substantive services from Friendship in the form of health care and education; however, they refused to embrace its romantic idealizations of American life. Wage-earning mothers who placed their children in the day nursery no doubt encountered an Anglo world quite different from the one depicted by Methodist missionaries and thus were skeptical of the settlement's cultural message. Clara Sarmiento knew from experience that it was much easier to reach the children than their parents.[46] How did children respond to the ideological undercurrents of Houchen programs? Did Mexican women feel empowered by their interaction with the settlement or were Methodist missionaries invidious underminers of Mexican identity?

In getting beneath the text, the following remarks of Minerva Franco that appeared in a 1975 issue of *Newark-Houchen News* raise a series of provocative questions. "Houchen provided . . . opportunities for learning and experiencing. . . . At Houchen I was shown that I had worth and that I was an individual."[47] Now what did she mean by that statement? Did the settlement house heighten her self-esteem? Did she feel that she was not an individual within the context of her family and neighborhood? Some young women imbibed Americanization so heavily as to reject their identity. In *No Separate Refuge*, Sarah Deutsch picked up on this theme as she quoted missionary Polita Padilla: "I am Mexican, born and brought up in New Mexico, but much of my life was spent in the Allison School where we had a different training so that the Mexican way of living now seems strange to me." Others, like Estella Ibarra and Rose Escheverría Mulligan, saw little incompatibility between Mexican traditions and Protestantism.[48]

Which Mexican women embraced the ideas of assimilation so completely as to become closet Mexicans? As a factor, class must be taken into consideration. In his field notes housed at the Bancroft Library, economist Paul Taylor contends that middle-class Mexicans desiring to dissociate themselves from their working-class neighbors possessed the most fervent aspirations for assimilation. Once in the United States, middle-class Mexicanos found themselves subject to racial/ethnic prejudice that did not discriminate by class. Due to restrictive real estate covenants, immigrants lived in barrios with people they considered inferiors.[49] By passing as "Spanish," they cherished hopes of melting into the American social landscape. Sometimes mobility-minded parents sought to regulate their children's choice of friends and later marriage partners. "My folks never allowed us to be around with Mexicans," remembered Alicia Mendeola Shelit. "We went sneaking around, but my Dad wouldn't allow it. We'd always be with white." Indeed, Shelit married twice, both times to Euro-Americans.[50] Of course it would be unfair to characterize all middle-class Mexican women immigrants as repudiating their mestizo identity. Working in a posh El Paso department store, Alma Araiza would quickly correct her colleagues when they assumed she was Italian.

> People kept telling me 'You must not be Mexican.' And I said, 'why do you think I'm not?' 'Well, it's your skin color. Are you Italian?'. . . I [responded] 'I am Mexicana.'[51]

Or as a young woman cleverly remarked to anthropologist Ruth Tuck, "Listen, I may be a Mexican in a fur coat, but I'm still a Mexican."[52]

The Houchen documents reveal glimpses into the formation of identity, consciousness, and values. The Friendship Square Calendar of 1949 explicitly stated that the medical care provided at Houchen "is a tool to develop sound minds in sound bodies; for thus it is easier to find peace with God and man. We want to help people develop a sense of values in life." Furthermore, the privileging of color—with white as the pinnacle—was an early lesson. Relating the excitement of kindergarten graduation, Day Nursery head Beatrice Fernandez included in her report a question asked by Margarita, one of the young graduates. "We are all wearing white, white dress, slip, socks and Miss Fernandez, is it alright if our hair is black?"[53] Sometimes subtle, sometimes overt, the privileging of race, class, culture, and color taught by women missionaries had painful consequences for their pupils.

Houchen activities were synonymous with Americanization. A member of the settlement Brownie troop encouraged her friends "to become 'an American or a Girl Scout' at Houchen." Scouting certainly served as a vehicle for Americanization. The all-Mexican Girl and Boy Scout Troops of Alpine, Texas, enjoyed visiting El Paso and Ciudad Juárez in the company of Houchen scouts. In a thank-you note, the Alpine Girl Scouts wrote, "Now we can all say we have been to a foreign country."[54]

It is important to remember that Houchen provided a bilingual environment, not a bicultural one. Spanish was the means to communicate the message of Methodism and Christian Americanization. Whether dressing up children as Pilgrims or European peasants, missionaries stressed "American" citizenship and values; yet, outside conversion, definitions of those values or of "our American way" remained elusive. Indeed, some of the settlement lessons were not incongruous with Mexican mores. In December 1952, a Euro-American settlement worker recorded in her journal the success of a Girl Scout dinner. "The girls learned a lot from it too. They were taught how to set the table, and how to serve the men. They learned also that they had to share, to cooperate, and to wait their turn."[55] These were not new lessons.

The most striking theme that repeatedly emerges from Houchen documents is that of individualism. Missionaries emphasized the importance of individual decision-making and individual accomplishment. In recounting her own conversion, Clara Sarmiento explained to a young client, "I chose my own religion because it was my own personal experience and . . . I was glad my religion was not chosen for me."[56]

In *Relations of Rescue*, Peggy Pascoe carefully recorded the glass ceiling encountered by "native helpers" at Protestant rescue homes. Chinese women at Cameron House in San Francisco, for example, could only emulate Euro-American missionaries to a certain point, always as subordinates, not as directors or leaders. Conversely, Mexican women did assume top positions of leadership at Methodist settlements. In 1930, María Moreno was appointed the head resident of the brand new Floyd Street Settlement in Dallas, Texas. Methodist community centers and boarding schools stressed the need for developing "Christian leaders trained for useful living."[57] For many, leadership meant ministering as a lay volunteer; for some, it meant pursuing a missionary vocation.

The Latina missionaries of Houchen served as cultural brokers as they diligently strived to integrate themselves into the community. Furthermore, over time Latinas appeared to have experienced some mobility within the settlement hierarchy. In 1912, Ofilia [sic] Chávez served as a "student helper"; forty years later Beatrice Fernandez would direct the preschool. Until 1950, the Houchen staff usually included one Latina; however, during the 1950s, the number of Latina (predominately Mexican American) settlement workers rose to six. Mary Lou López, María Rico, Elizabeth Soto, Febe Bonilla, Clare Sarmiento, María Payan, and Beatrice Fernandez had participated in Methodist outreach activities as children (Soto at Houchen) and had decided to follow in the footsteps of their teachers. In addition, these women had the assistance of five full-time Mexican laypersons.[58] It is no coincidence that the decade of greatest change in Houchen policies occurred at a time when Latinas held a growing number of staff positions. Friendship Square's greater sensitivity to neighborhood needs arose, in part, out of the influence exerted by Mexican clients in shaping the attitudes and actions of Mexican missionaries.

So, in the end, Mexican women utilized Houchen's social services; they did not, by and large, adopt its tenets of Christian Americanization. Children who attended settlement programs enjoyed the activities, but Friendship Square did not always leave a lasting imprint. "My Mom had an open mind, so I participated in a lot of clubs. But I didn't become Protestant," remarked Lucy Lucero. "I had fun and I learned a lot, too." Because of the warm, supportive environment, Houchen Settlement is remembered with fondness. However, one cannot equate pleasant memories with the acceptance of the settlement's cultural ideals.[59]

Settlement records bear out Mexican women's *selective* use of Houchen's resources. The most complete set of figures is for the year 1944. During this period, 7,614 people visited the clinic and hospital. The settlement afternoon programs had an average monthly enrollment of 362 and 40 children attended kindergarten. Taken together, approximately 8,000 residents of Segundo Barrio utilized Friendship Square's medical and educational offerings. In contrast, the congregation of El Buen Pastor included 160 people.[60] Although representing only a single year, these figures indicate the importance of Houchen's medical facilities and Mexican women's selective utilization of resources.

By the 1950s, settlement houses were few and far between and those that remained were run by professional social workers. Implemented by a growing Latina staff, client-initiated changes in Houchen policies brought a realistic recognition of the settlement as a social service agency rather than a religious mission. During the 1950s, brochures describing the day nursery emphasized that while children said grace at meals and sang Christian songs, they would not receive "in any way indoctrination" regarding Methodism. In fact, at the parents' request, Newark nurses summoned Catholic priests to the hospital to baptize premature infants. Client desire became the justification for allowing the presence of Catholic clergy, a policy that would have been unthinkable in the not too distant past.[61] Finally, in the new Houchen constitution of 1959, all mention of conversion was dropped. Instead, it conveyed a more ecumenical, nondenominational spirit. For instance, the goal of Houchen Settlement was henceforth "to establish a Christian democratic framework for—individual development, family solidarity, and neighborhood welfare."[62]

Settlement activities also became more closely linked with the Mexican community. During the 1950s, Houchen was the home of two LULAC chapters—one for teenagers and one for adults. The League of United Latin American Citizens (LULAC was the most visible and politically powerful civil rights organization in Texas.[63] Carpentry classes—once the preserve of males—opened their doors to young women, although on a gender-segregated basis. Houchen workers, moreover, made veiled references to the "very dangerous business" of Juárez abortion clinics; it appears unclear whether or not the residents themselves offered any contraceptive counseling. During the early 1960s, however, the settlement, in cooperation with Planned Parenthood, opened a birth control clinic for "married women." Indeed, a Houchen contraception success story was featured on the front page of a spring newsletter. "Mrs. G__, after having her thirteenth and fourteenth children (twins), enrolled in our birth control clinic; now for one and one half years she has been a happy and nonpregnant mother."[64] Certainly Houchen had changed with the times. What factors accounted for the new directions in settlement work? The evidence on the baptism of premature babies seems fairly clear in terms of client pressure, but to what extent did other policies change as the result of Mexican women's input? The residents of Segundo Barrio may have felt more comfortable expressing their ideas and Latina settlement workers may have exhibited a greater willingness to listen. Indeed, Mexican clients, not missionaries, set the boundaries for interaction.

Creating the public space of settlements and community centers, advocates of Americanization sought to alter the "lifeworld" of Mexican immigrants to reflect their own idealized versions of life in the United States. Settlement workers can be viewed as the narrators of lived experience as Houchen records reflected the cognitive construction of missionary aspirations and expectations. In other words, the documents revealed more about the women who wrote them than those they served. At another level, one could interpret the cultural ideals of Americanization as an indication of an attempt at what Jürgen Habermas has termed "inner colonization."[65] Yet the failure of such projects illustrates the ways in which Mexican women appropriated desired resources, both material (infant immunizations) and psychological (self-esteem) while, in the main, rejecting the ideological messages behind them. The shift in Houchen policies during the 1950s meant more

than a recognition of community needs; it represented a claiming of public space by Mexican women clients.

Confronting Americanization brings into sharp relief the concept I have termed cultural coalescence. Immigrants and their children pick, borrow, retain, and create distinctive cultural forms. There is no single hermetic Mexican or Mexican-American culture, but rather permeable *cultures* rooted in generation, gender, region, class, and personal experience. Chicano scholars have divided Mexican experiences into three generational categories: Mexicano (first generation), Mexican American (second generation), and Chicano (third and beyond).[66] But this general typology tends to obscure the ways in which people navigate across cultural boundaries as well as their conscious decision-making in the production of culture. However, people of color have not had unlimited choice. Race and gender prejudice and discrimination with their accompanying social, political, and economic segmentation have constrained aspirations, expectations, and decision-making.

The images and ideals of Americanization were a mixed lot and were never the only messages immigrant women received. Local *mutualistas*, Mexican patriotic and Catholic pageants, newspapers, and community networks reinforced familiar legacies. In contrast, religious and secular Americanization programs, the elementary schools, movies, magazines, and radio bombarded the Mexican community with a myriad of models, most of which were idealized, stylized, unrealistic, and unattainable. Expectations were raised in predictable ways. In the words of one Mexican-American woman, "We felt that if we worked hard, proved ourselves, we could become professional people."[67] Consumer culture would hit the barrio full force during the 1920s, exemplified by the Mexican flapper. As we will see in the next chapter, even Spanish-language newspapers promoted messages of consumption and acculturation. Settlement houses also mixed in popular entertainment with educational programs. According to historian Louise Año Nuevo Kerr, the Mexican Mothers Club of the University of Chicago Settlement "took a field trip to NBC radio studios in downtown Chicago from which many of the soap operas emanated."[68]

By looking through the lens of cultural coalescence, we can begin to discern the ways in which people select and create cultural forms. Teenagers began to manipulate and reshape the iconography of consumer culture both as a marker of peer group identity and as an authorial presence through which they rebelled against strict parental supervision. When standing at the cultural crossroads, Mexican women blended their options and created their own paths.

Notes

1. Interview with Elsa Chávez, April 18, 1983, conducted by the author. *Note*: Elsa Chávez is a pseudonym used at the person's request.
2. Recent scholarship on Americanization programs aimed at Mexican communities includes George J. Sánchez, "Go After the Women:

Americanization and the Mexican Immigrant Woman, 1915–1929," in *Unequal Sisters: A Multicultural Reader in U.S. Women's History*, 2nd ed., eds. Vicki L. Ruiz and Ellen Carol DuBois (New York: Routeledge, 1994), pp. 284–97; Sarah Deutsch, *No Separate Refuge: Culture, Class, and Gender on the Anglo-Hispanic Frontier in the American Southwest, 1880–1940* (New York: Oxford University Press, 1987), pp. 63–86; Gilbert González, *Chicano Education in the Era of Segregation* (Philadelphia: Balch Institute Press, 1990), pp. 30–61; Ruth Hutchinson Crocker, "Gary Mexicans and 'Christian Americanization': A Study in Cultural Conflict," in *Forging a Community: The Latino Experience in Northwest Indiana, 1919–1975*, eds. James B. Lane and Edward J. Escobar (Chicago: Cattails Press, 1987), pp. 115–34; Susan Yohn, *A Contest of Faiths: Missionary Women and Pluralism in the American Southwest* (Ithaca: Cornell University Press); Vicki L. Ruiz, "Dead Ends or Gold Mines?: Using Missionary Records in Mexican American Women's History," *Frontiers: A Journal of Women's Studies*, 12:1 (1991): 33–56.

3. Pearl Idella Ellis, *Americanization Through Homemaking* (Los Angeles: Wetzel Publishing Co., 1929), preface [no page number].

4. *Ibid.*, p. 13.

5. M. Dorothy Woodruff, "Methodist Women Along the Mexican Border" (Women's Division of Christian Service pamphlet, ca. 1946) [part of an uncatalogued collection of documents housed at Houchen Community Center, El Paso, Texas; heretofore referred to as HF for Houchen Files]. This pamphlet provides brief descriptions of each of the twenty one "centers of work" operated by Methodist missionaries. For a celebratory overview of Methodist women's missionary endeavors throughout the United States, see Noreen Dunn Tatum, *A Crown of Service* (Nashville, Tenn.: Parthenon Press, 1960).

6. Steven Seidman, ed., *Jürgen Habermas on Society and Politics: A Reader* (Boston: Beacon Press, 1989), p. 171.

7. Oscar J. Martínez, *The Chicanos of El Paso: An Assessment of Progress* (El Paso: Texas Western Press, 1980), pp. 6, 17.

8. Martínez, *Chicanos*, pp. 10, 29–33. Mario García meticulously documents the economic and social stratification of Mexicans in El Paso. See Mario T. García, *Desert Immigrants: The Mexicans of El Paso, 1880–1920* (New Haven: Yale University Press, 1981). *Note:* In 1960, the proportion of Mexican workers with high white-collar jobs jumped to 3.4 percent. [Martínez, *Chicanos*, p. 10.]

9. "South El Paso's Oasis of Care," *paso del norte*, Vol 1 (September 1982): 42–43; Thelma Hammond, "Friendship Square," (Houchen Report, 1969) [HF]; "Growing with the Century" (Houchen Report, 1947) [HF].

10. García, *Desert Immigrants*, p. 145; Effie Stoltz, "Freeman Clinic: A Resume of Four Years Work" (Houchen Pamphlet, 1924) [HF]. It should be noted that Houchen Settlement sprang from the work of Methodist missionary Mary Tripp who arrived in South El Paso in 1893. However, it was not until 1912 that an actual settlement was established. ["South El Paso's Oasis of Care," p. 42].

11. Stoltz, "Freeman Clinic"; Hammond, "Friendship Square"; M. Dorothy Woodruff and Dorothy Little, "Friendship Square (Houchen Pamphlet, March 1949) [HF]; "Friendship Square" (Houchen Report, circa 1940s) [HF]; *Health Center* (Houchen Newsletter, 1943) [HF]; "Christian Health Service" (Houchen Report, 1941) [HF]; *El Paso Times*, October 20, 1945.

12. "Settlement Worker's Report" (Houchen Report, 1927) [HF]. Letter from Dorothy Little to E. Mae Young dated May 10, 1945 [HF]. Letter from Bessie Brinson to Treva Ely dated September 14, 1958 [HF]; Hammond, "Friendship Square"; Elmer T. Clark and Dorothy McConnell, "The Methodist Church and Latin Americans in the United States" (Board of Missions pamphlet, circa 1930s) [HF]. My very rough estimate is based on the documents and records to which I had access. I was not permitted to examine any materials then housed at Newark Hospital. The most complete statistics on utilization of services are for the year 1944 in the letter from Dorothy Little to E. Mae Young. *Note*: Because of the deportation and repatriation drives of the 1930s in which one-third of the Mexican population in the United States were either deported or repatriated, the Mexican population in El Paso dropped from 68,476 in 1930 to 55,000 in 1940. By 1960 it had risen to 63,796. [Martínez, *Chicanos*, p. 6]

13. *El Paso Herald Post*, March 7, 1961; *El Paso Herald Post*, March 12, 1961; "Community Centers" (Women's Division of Christian Service Pamphlet, May 1963); *Funding Proposal* for Youth Outreach and Referral Report Project (April 30, 1974) [Private Files of Kenton J. Clymer, Ph.D.]; *El Paso Herald Post*, January 3, 1983; *El Paso Times*, August 8, 1983.

14. Letter from Tom Houghteling, Director, Houchen Community Center to the author December 24, 1990; Tom Houghteling, telephone conversation with the author, January 9, 1991.

15. Dorothy Little, "Rose Gregory Houchen Settlement" (Houchen Report, February 1942) [HF].

16. *Ibid.*; "Our Work at Houchen" (Houchen Report, circa 1940s) [HF]; Woodruff and Little, "Friendship Square"; Jennie C. Gilbert, "Settlements Under the Women's Home Missionary Society pamphlet, circa 1920s) [HF]; Clark and McConnell, "Latin Americans in the United States."

17. Anita Hernandez, "The Kindergarten" (Houchen Report, circa 1940s) [HF]; *A Right Glad New Year* (Houchen Newsletter, circa 1940s) [HF]; Little, "Rose Gregory Houchen Settlement"; "Our Work at Houchen"; Woodruff and Little, "Friendship Square." For more information on the Franciscans, see Ramón Gutiérrez, *When Jesus Came, the Corn Mothers Went Away: Marriage, Sexuality, and Power in New Mexico, 1500–1846* (Stanford: Stanford University Press, 1991).

18. Settlement Worker's Report (1927); Letter from Little to Young; letter from Brinson to Ely; *Friendship Square Calendar* (1949) [HF]; interview with Lucy Lucero, October 8, 1983, conducted by the author; Chávez interview; discussion following presentation, "Settlement Houses in El Paso," given by the author at the El Paso Conference on History and the Social Sciences, August 24, 1983, El Paso, Texas [tape of presentation and discussion is on file at the Institute of Oral History, University of Texas, El Paso].

19. Chávez interview; discussion following "Settlement Houses in El Paso." *Note:* The Catholic Church never established a competing settlement house. However, during the 1920s in Gary, Indiana, the Catholic diocese opened up the Gary-Alerding Settlement with the primary goal of Americanizing Mexican immigrants. The bishop took such action to counteract suspected inroads made by two local Protestant settlement houses. See Crocker, "Gary Mexicans," pp. 123–27.

20. "Christian Health Service"; "The Freeman Clinic and the Newark Conference Maternity Hospital" (Houchen Report, 1940) [HF]; *El Paso Times*, August 2, 1961; *El Paso Herald Post*, May 12, 1961. For more information on Americanization programs in California, see George J. Sánchez, "Go After the Women," pp. 250–63. *Note:* The documents reveal a striking absence of adult Mexican male clients. The Mexican men who do appear are either Methodist ministers or lay volunteers.

21. Sánchez, "Go After," pp. 250–83; Deutsch, *No Separate Refuge*, "Americanization Notes," *The Arizona Teacher and Home Journal*, 11:5 (January 1923): 26. *Note:* The Methodist and Presbyterian settlements in Gary, Indiana, also couched their programs in terms of "Christian Americanization." [Crocker, "Gary Mexicans," pp. 118–20]

22. "Settlement Worker's Report" (1927); *Friendship Square Calendar* (1949) [HF]; letter from Brinson to Ely; Chávez interview.

23. "News Clipping from *The El Paso Times*" (circa 1950s) [HF].

24. Clara Gertrude Smith, "The Development of the Mexican People in the Community of Watts" (M.A. thesis, University of Southern California, 1933), p. 104.

25. Rayna Green, "The Pocahontas Perplex," in *Unequal Sisters*, pp. 15–21.

26. Sánchez, "Go After the Women," p. 260; *Newark-Houchen News*, September 1975. I agree with George Sánchez that Americanization programs created an overly rosy picture of American life. In his words: "Rather than providing Mexican immigrant women with an attainable picture of assimilation, Americanization programs could only offer these immigrants idealized versions of American life." [Sánchez, *loc. cit.*]

27. Little, "Rose Gregory Houchen Settlement."

28. García, *Desert Immigrants*, pp. 110–26; Paul S. Taylor, *Mexican Labor in the United States*, Vol. 1 (Berkeley: University of California Press, 1930, rpt. Arno Press, 1970), pp. 79, 206–206. [Quote is from Taylor, *Mexican Labor*, p. 79.]

29. Margarita B. Melville, "Selective Acculturation of Female Mexican Migrants," in *Twice a Minority: Mexican American Women*, ed.

Margarita B. Melville (St. Louis: C.V. Mosby, 1980), pp. 159–60; John García, "Ethnicity and Chicanos: Measurement of Ethnic Identification, Identity, and Consciousness," *Hispanic Journal of Behavioral Sciences*, Vol. 4 (1982): 310–11. For an insightful, brief overview of Mexican-American ethnic identification, see David Gutiérrez, *Walls and Mirrors: Mexican Americans, Mexican Immigrants, and the Politics of Ethnicity in the Southwest, 1910–1986* (Berkeley: University of California Press, 1995), pp. 1–11.

30. Edward Soja, *Postmodern Geographies: The Reassertion of Space in Critical Social Theory* (New York and London: Verso Press, 1989), p. 23. Gracias a Matthew García for bringing this text to my attention.

31. "Settlement Worker's Report" (1927); Hernandez, "The Kindergarten" [HF]; *A Right Glad New Year*; Little, "Rose Gregory Houchen Settlement"; "Our Work at Houchen"; Woodruff and Little, "Friendship Square"; "South El Paso's Oasis of Care," *loc. cit.*; *El Paso Herald Post*, March 7, 1961; *El Paso Herald Post*, March 12, 1961; *El Paso Herald Post*, May 12, 1961.

32. C.S. Babbitt, "The Remedy for the Decadence of the Latin Race" (El Paso: El Paso Printing Company) (Presented to the Pioneers Association of El Paso, Texas, July 11, 1909, by Mrs. Babbitt, widow of the author), p. 55. Pamphlet courtesy of Jack Redman.

33. George J. Sánchez, *Becoming Mexican American: Ethnicity, Culture, and Identity in Chicano Los Angeles, 1900–1945* (New York: Oxford University Press, 1993), p. 156; Robert McLean, *That Mexican! As He Is, North and South of the Rio Grande* (New York: Fleming H. Revell Co., 1928), pp. 162–63, quoted in E.C. Orozco, *Republican Protestantism in Aztlán* (Santa Barbara: The Petereins Press, 1980), p. 162. *Note*: Immigration has frequently been linked with food from the "melting pot" of assimilation to the "salad bowl" of cultural pluralism. McLean's metaphor of Uncle Sam as a diner at the immigration cafe follows:

Fifty and one hundred years ago Uncle Sam accomplished some remarkable digestive feats. Gastronomically he was a marvel. He was not particularly choosy! Dark meat from the borders of the Mediterranean or light meat from the Baltic equally suited him, for promptly he was able to assimilate both, turning them into bone of his bone, and flesh of his flesh—But this chili con carne! Always it seems to give Uncle Samuel the heartburn; and the older he gets, the less he seems to be able to assimilate it. Indeed, it is a question whether chili is not a condiment, to be taken in small quantities rather than a regular article of diet. And upon this conviction ought to stand all the law . . . as far as the Mexican immigrant is concerned.

34. *Account Book for Rose Gregory Houchen Settlement* (1903–1913) [HF]; Hammond, "Friendship Square"; "Growing with the Century"; *El Paso Times*, September 5, 1975; Stoltz, "Freeman Clinic": Woodruff and Little, "Friendship Square"; *El Paso Times*, October 3, 1947; "Four Institutions. One Goal. The Christian Community" (Houchen pamphlet, circa early 1950s) [HF]; Houghteling conversation; "A City Block of Service" (Script of Houchen Slide Presentation, 1976) [HF]; *El Paso Times*, January 19, 1977; "Speech given by Kenton J. Clymer, Ph.D." (June 1975) [Clymer Files]; *El Paso Times*, May 23, 1975; *Newark-Houchen News*, September 1975. It should be noted that in 1904 local Methodist congregations did not contribute much of the money needed to purchase the property on which the settlement was built. Local civic groups occasionally donated money or equipment and threw Christmas parties for Houchen children. [*Account Book; El Paso Herald Post*, December 14, 1951; *El Paso Times*, December 16, 1951]

35. Vernon McCombs, "Victories in the Latin American Mission" (Board of Home Missions pamphlet, 1935) [HF]; "Brillante Historia De La Iglesia 'El Buen Pastor' El Paso," *Young Adult Fellowship Newsletter*, December 1946 [HF]; Soledad Burciago, "Yesterday in 1923" (Houchen Report, 1939) [HF].

36. This study is based on a limited number of oral interviews (five), but they represent a range of interaction with the settlement from playing on the playground to serving as the minister for El Buen Pastor. It is also informed by a public discussion of my work on Houchen held during an El Paso teachers' conference in 1983. Most of the educators who attended the talk had participated, to some extent, in Houchen activities and were eager to share their recollec-

tions. [C.f. note 13]. I am also indebted to students in my Mexican-American history classes when I taught at the University of Texas, El Paso, especially the reentry women, for their insight and knowledge.

37. Woodruff and Little, "Friendship Square"; Hammond, "Friendship Square"; *Greetings for 1946* (Houchen Christmas Newsletter, 1946) [HF]; Little, "Rose Gregory Houchen Settlement'; Soledad Burciaga, "Today in 1939" (Houchen Report, 1939) [HF]; "Our Work at Houchen"; "Christian Social Service" [Houchen Report, circa 1940s] [HF]; Interview with Fernando García , September 21, 1983, conducted by the author; *El Paso Times*, June 14, 1951; Lucero interview; Vicki L. Ruiz, "Oral History and La Mujer: The Rosa Guerrero Story," in *Women on the U.S.-Mexico Border: Responses to Change* (Boston: Allen and Unwin, 1987), pp. 226–27; *Newark-Houchen News*, September 1975.

38. Woodruff, "Mexican Women."

39. *Spanish-American Methodist News Bulletin*, April 1946 [HF]; Hammond, "Friendship Square"; McCombs, "Victories"; "El Metodismo en La Ciudad de El Paso," *Christian Herald*, July 1945 [HF]; "Brillante Historia"; "The Door: An Informal Pamphlet on the Work of the Methodist Church Among the Spanish-speaking of El Paso, Texas" (Methodist pamphlet, 1940) [HF]; "A City Block of Service" (script of slide presentation); García interview; Houghteling interview. *Note*: From 1932 to 1939, services for El Buen Pastor were held in a church located two blocks away from the settlement.

40. A. Ruth Kern, "There is No Segregation Here," *Methodist Youth Fund Bulletin* (January–March, 1953): 12 [HF].

41. *Ibid.*; "The Torres Family" (Houchen Report, circa 1940s) [HF]; interview with Estella Ibarra, November 11, 1982, conducted by Jesusita Ponce; Hazel Bulifant, "One Woman's Story" (Houchen Report, 1950) [HF]; "Our Work at Houchen."

42. Clara Sarmiento, "Lupe" (Houchen Report, circa 1950s) [HF].

43. Ibara interview.

44. Bulifant, "One Woman's Story"; letter from Little to Young.

45. Deutsch, *No Separate Refuge*, pp. 64–66, 85–86; Sánchez, "Go After the Women," pp. 259–61; Crocker, "Gary Mexicans," p. 121.

46. Sarmiento, "Lupe." In her study, Ruth Crocker also notes the propensity of Protestant missionaries to focus their energies on children and the selective uses of services by Mexican clients. As she explained, "Inevitably, many immigrants came to the settlement, took what they wanted of its services, and remained untouched by its message." [Crocker, "Gary Mexicans," p. 122.]

47. *Newark-Houchen News*, September 1975.

48. Deutsch, *No Separate Refuge*, pp. 78–79; Ibarra interview; interview with Rose Escheverría Mulligan, Volume 27, of *Rosie the Riverter Revisited: Women and the World War II Work Experience*, ed. Sherna Berger Gluck (Long Beach: CSULB Foundation, 1983), p. 24.

49. Paul S. Taylor, "Women in Industry," field notes for *Mexican Labor in the United States*, Bancroft Library, University of California, Berkeley, Box 1. *Note*: Referring to Los Angeles, two historians have argued that "Mexicans experienced segregation in housing in nearly every section of the city and its outlying areas." [Antonio Ríos-Bustamante and Pedro Castillo, *An Illustrated History of Mexican Los Angeles* (Los Angeles: UCLA Chicano Studies Research Center, 1986), p. 135.]

50. Interview with Alicia Mendeola Shelit, Volume 37, *Rosie the Riveter Revisited*, p. 32; Mulligan interview, p. 14. Anthropologist Ruth Tuck noted that Euro-Americans also employed the term "Spanish" to distinguish individuals "of superior background or achievement." [Ruth Tuck, *Not with the Fist* (New York: Harcourt, Brace and Co., 1946; rpt. Arno Press, 1974), pp. 142–43.]

51. Interview with Alma Araiza García , March 27, 1993, conducted by the author.

52. Tuck, *Not with the Fist*, p. 133.

53. *Friendship Square Calendar* (1949); Beatrice Fernandez, "Day Nursery" (Houchen Report, circa late 1950s) [HF].

54. "Friendship Square" (Houchen pamphlet, circa 1950s) [HF]; letter to Houchen Girl Scouts from Troop 4, Latin American Community Center, Alpine, Texas, May 18, 1951 [HF].

55. *A Right Glad New Year*; News clipping from the *El Paso Times* (circa 1950s); "Our Work at Houchen"; Little, "Rose Gregory Houchen Settlement"; "Anglo Settlement Worker's Journal" (entry for December 1952) [HF].

56. *Newark-Houchen News*, September 1975; Sarmiento, "Lupe."

57. Peggy Pascoe, *Relations of Rescue: The Search for Moral Authority in the American West, 1874–1939* (New York: Oxford University Press, 1990), pp. 112–39; Woodruff, "Methodist Women."

58. *Datebook for 1926* (entry: Friday, September 9, 1929) (Settlement Worker's private journal) [HF]; "Brillante Historia"; "Report and Directory of Association of Church Social Workers, 1940" [HF]; "May I Come In?" (Houchen brochure, circa 1950s) [HF]; "Friendship Square" (Houchen pamphlet, 1958) [HF]; Mary Lou López, "Kindergarten Report" (Houchen Report, circa 1950s) [HF]; Sarmiento, "Lupe"; "Freeman Clinic and Newark Hospital" (Houchen pamphlet, 1954) [HF]; *El Paso Times*, June 14, 1951; "Houchen Day Nursery" (Houchen pamphlet, circa 1950s) [HF]; *El Paso Times*, September 12, 1952.

59. Chávez interview; Martha González, interview with the author, October 8, 1983; Lucero interview; *Newark-Houchen News*, September 1974.

60. Letter from Little to Young; "The Door"; Woodruff and Little, "Friendship Square."

61. "Houchen Day Nursery"; "Life in a Glass House" (Houchen Report circa 1950s) [HF].

62. *Program* for First Annual Meeting, Houchen Settlement and Day Nursery, Freeman Clinic, and Newark Conference Maternity Hospital (January 8, 1960) [HF]. It should be noted that thirty years later, there seems to be a shift back to original settlement ideas. Today, Houchen Community has regularly scheduled bible studies. [Letters from Houghteling to the author.]

63. *Program* for Houchen production of "Cinderella" [HF]; letter from Brinson to Ely. For more information on LULAC, see Mario T. García, *Mexican Americans: Leadership, Ideology, and Identity, 1930–1960* (New Haven: Yale University Press, 1989).

64. Bulifant, "One Woman's Story"; *News from Friendship Square* (Spring newsletter, circa early 1960s) [HF].

65. My understanding and application of the ideas of Jürgen Habermas have been informed by the following works. Jürgen Habermas, *Moral Consciousness and Communicative Action*, trans. Christian Lenhardt and Sherry Weber Nicholsen, introd. Thomas McCarthy (Cambridge: MIT Press, 1990); Seidman, ed., *Jürgen Habermas on Society and Politics*; Nancy Fraser, *Unruly Practices: Power, Discourse, and Gender in Contemporary Social Theory* (Minneapolis: University of Minnesota Press, 1989); Seyla Benhabib and Drucilla Cornell, "Introduction: Beyond the Politics of Gender," in *Feminism as Critique*, eds. Seyla Benhabib and Drucilla Cornell (Minneapolis: University of Minnesota Press, 1987).

66. As an example of this typology, see Mario García, *Mexican Americans*, pp. 13–22, 295–302. Richard Griswold del Castillo touches on the dynamic nature of Mexican culture in *La Familia: Chicano Families in the Urban Southwest, 1848 to the Present* (Notre Dame: University of Notre Dame Press, 1984).

67. Escheverría Mulligan interview, p. 17.

68. Louise Año Nuevo Kerr, "The Chicano Experience in Chicago, 1920–1970" (Ph.D. dissertation, University of Illinois, Chicago Circle, 1976), p. 104.

Women at Farah: An Unfinished Story

Laurie Coyle, Gail Hershatter and Emily Honig

Introduction

When four thousand garment workers at Farah Manufacturing Company in El Paso, Texas went out on strike for the right to be represented by a union, many observers characterized the conflict as "a classic organizing battle."[1] The two-year strike, which began in May 1972 and was settled in March 1974, was similar in many ways to earlier, bloodier labor wars.

There was a virulently antiunion employer, Willie Farah, who swore in the time-honored manner that he would rather be dead than union. There was a company which paid low wages, pressured its employees to work faster and faster, consistently ignored health and safety conditions, and swiftly fired all those who complained. There was a local power structure which harassed the strikers with police dogs and antipicket ordinances, denied them public aid whenever possible, and smothered their strike and boycott activities with press silence for as long as it could. There were strikebreakers, and sporadic violence was directed at the striking workers. On the side of the strikers there was a union, the Amalgamated Clothing Workers of America, which mustered national support for the strikers and organized a boycott of Farah pants. There was support from organized workers and sympathizers throughout the United States. Finally, there was a victory—an end to the strike and a union contract.

However, any account of the Farah strike which focuses exclusively on its "classic" characteristics misses most of the issues which make it an important and unfinished story. The Farah strikers were virtually all Chicanas. They were on strike in a town whose economy is profoundly affected by proximity to the Mexican border, in a period when border tensions were on the rise. They were workers in an industry plagued by instability and runaway shops. They were represented by a national union committed to "organize the unorganized," but which often resorted to tactics which undermined efforts to build a strong, democratic local union at Farah. Perhaps, most important, 85 percent of the strikers were women. Their experiences during and since the strike changed the way they looked at themselves—as Chicanas, as wives, and as workers—and the way they looked at their fellow workers, their supervisors, their families, and their community.

The account which follows does not focus on Willie Farah's flamboyant antiunion capers. Instead, it attempts to explore the effect of the strike on the women who initiated and sustained it. This article is based on extensive interviews (approximately seventy hours) conducted during the summer of 1977. In these interviews the women described their working conditions, events leading to the strike, the strike itself, the development of the union, and their lives as Mexican American women in the Southwest. In an effort to accurately place the Farah strike in perspective, this article also deals with the social and economic context in which the strike took place. The account appears here primarily as it was told by the Farah strikers themselves—eloquently, sometimes angrily, and always with humor.

Before the Strike

The history of the Farah Manufacturing Company exemplifies the myth and reality of the American success story. Unlike many other Southwest garment plants that ran away from the unionized Northeast, Farah got its start in El Paso. During the depression, Mansour Farah, a Lebanese immigrant, arrived in El Paso and set up a tiny shop on the South side. Farah, together with his wife and two sons, James and Willie, and a half-dozen Mexican seamstresses, began to turn out the chambray shirts and denim pants that were the uniform of the working West.

The authors wish to thank the real authors of this oral history—the women workers at Farah who generously shared their lives and opinions with three outsiders. Many of them asked to remain anonymous because they still live and work in El Paso, Texas.

"Women at Farah: An Unfinished Story" taken from *Mexican Women in the United States* by Coyle, Hershatter and Honig. Chicano Studies Research Center, 1980. Reprinted by permission of the authors.

When Mansour died in 1937, James was twenty-one and Willie only eighteen, but they were well on the way to becoming kingpins of the needle trade. Winning government contracts for military pants during the war mobilization effort enabled the company to expand, and it emerged from World War II in the top ranks of the garment industry. In the postwar period, the rapid expansion of the garment industry transformed the South into the largest apparel-producing region of the United States. The Farah brothers shifted production to meet the growing demands of the consumer trade, and sold their product to the major chain stores, J.C. Penneys, Sears, and Montgomery Ward for retail under the store names. In 1950, the Farah brothers began marketing pants under their own name, and built a loyal and growing clientele in men's casual and dress slacks. The company expanded until it employed 9,500 workers in Texas and New Mexico.[2] Before the strike, it was the second largest employer in El Paso.

Farah's major role in developing El Paso's industry and expanding the employment ranks made the family prominent in town. At least among some sectors of the population, Farah had the reputation of being a generous boss who lavished bonuses on his workers, gave them turkey at Thanksgiving, bankrolled an elaborate party each Christmas, and provided health care and refreshments on the job. The company's hourly wages, however low they were, seemed generous in comparison to the piece rates which were standard in the garment world. Farah was the only garment plant in El Paso that would hire the inexperienced. In a town where the overwhelming number of unskilled Chicanas had to find work in retail or as domestic servants, many women considered themselves fortunate to work at Farah.

After the sudden death of James Farah in 1964, Willie undertook a major expansion of the company, constructing or acquiring a plant in Belgium, in Hong Kong, and five in El Paso the Gateway, Paisano, Northwest, Clark Street and Third Street plants. Within ten years, from 1960 to 1970, Farah's share of the market for men's casual and dress slacks rose from 3.3 percent to 11 percent.[3] In 1967, the company went public and qualified for the New York Stock Exchange. The booming growth, new capital investment, and increased planning and control of marketing resulted in major changes within the plant, including increased pressure on workers to produce more, higher quotas, and greater impersonality on the job.

Working Conditions

Many workers felt that the expansion ruined what had been warm relations between management and employees. One woman remarked on the changes:

> In 1960, there were only two plants. They had time for you. But it started growing and they didn't give a damn about you, your health, or anything. They just kept pushing.

While some workers saw these changes as significant departures from happier days, many felt that the public image of Farah as one big happy family had never accorded with the reality on the shop floor. Willie ran his business like a classic patron, conducting unannounced plant inspections and instructing women in how best to do their jobs. The most minute aspects of production, down to a seamstress's technique for turning corners, were matters of near fanatical personal concern for Farah. His overbearing presence led many workers to feel that he assumed responsibility for work problems.

In fact, he would shower the workers with promises of liberal pay raises which never materialized. One woman who began working in 1953 recollected:

> I used to tell my kids, work hard and your boss will love you and treat you well. So years and years passed, and though I was one of the fastest seamstresses, nothing was repaid, neither to me nor to the other workers. One day before the organizing drive began, I met Willie Farah and I asked him why he worked us so hard and never gave us a raise. He told me to come along to the office, and when we got there he said, "Listen, I don't know a thing about what happens to the workers on the floor. If it will make you happy, I will go myself to your supervisor and check to see if you are getting your due." Well, great, I thought, being sure of the quality of my work. Time went on and nothing happened. Seven months passed and no Willie. I asked, what happened, Willie doesn't want to give me my due?

For many, wages were never raised above the legal minimum, and workers were often misled to believe that legislated increases in the minimum wage were raises granted by management. Wages remained low under the quota system; since pay increases were based upon higher and higher production rates, workers' wages continually lagged behind spiralling quotas. Women were pitted against one another in the scramble to meet management demands and protect their jobs. As one women observed:

> They would threaten to fire you if you didn't make a quota. They would go to a worker and say, "This girl is making very high quotas. It's easy, and I don't know why you can't do it. And if you can't do it, we'll have to fire you." So this girl would work really fast and if she got it up higher, they'd go to the other people and say, "She's making more. You'll get a ten cent raise if you make a higher quota than she." They would make people compete against each other. No one would gain a thing—the girl with the highest quota would make a dime, but a month later the minimum wage would come up. I knew a girl who'd been there for sixteen years, and they fired her, and another who was there for sixteen years and still making the minimum.

In the garment industry where labor comprises a major portion of a firm's expenditures, southwestern companies like Farah keep their competitive edge over unionized plants in the Northeast by these cutthroat pay practices.

Many women who were pretty and willing to date their supervisors received preferential treatment. One seamstress, who had worked on a particular job operation for twenty years, received less than the attractive young woman who had begun the operation only a year before. The less favored women were subjected to constant harassment:

> Every day they would come around to your machine to see how much you'd make. If you didn't make your [quota of] 300, they would hurl things at us, yell at us like, "You don't do nothing, you don't do your job, I'm gonna fire you." Embarrass me in front of all those guys pressing seams next to me. I was so embarrassed, but I said nothing. I got to the point where I dreaded going to work.

Rather than hire Chicanos who had worked on the shop floor, it was standard practice for the company to hire Anglo males as supervisors. Their treatment of Chicana workers was frequently hostile and racist. Women were humiliated for speaking Spanish. When they could not understand a supervisor's orders, he would snap his fingers, hurl insults, bang the machines and push them. One worker remembered that:

> In my department, the cafeteria, there was a supervisor. . . . This man didn't like Latinos—he had a very brusque manner when talking to us. He wasn't a supervisor; he was an interrogator! He would talk to me in English, which I can't speak, and insist upon it, even though he knew I didn't understand. The others would tell me what he said—things that offended, hurt me. But I couldn't defend myself.

The close cooperation of authorities on both sides of the border, as well as the special privileges granted to twin plants, allows for the optimum flow of labor and goods between El Paso and Juárez. The state of Texas has protected these privileges by establishing the right-to-work law. This law stipulates that no worker in a plant be required to join a union, and furthermore that all workers, whether they are union members or not, are entitled to the benefits provided by a union contract. Collective bargaining efforts have frequently been undermined by this law, and El Paso remains a largely nonunion town.

The availability of unorganized workers on the El Paso side, many of whom are Mexican nationals without rights of permanent residence, and many others who are unskilled Chicanos, has created an ideal situation for companies investing in labor-intensive operations such as electronics and garments. El Paso has become the last frontier of U.S. industry on the move south and out of the United States.

"Runaways?" asked one Farah worker incredulously. "Industries in El Paso don't need to move. They have the advantage that they can get people from Juarez to work for less."

The United States government participates actively in depressing wages by manipulating the migrant work force to meet the needs of industry. The issuance of green cards, which are temporary permits for Mexicans to work in the U.S., guarantees business an abundant supply of labor which can be curtailed or expanded when necessary. In addition, the H-2 program of the U.S. Department of Labor allows an individual employer to bring in a specified number of workers from Mexico if he can prove that a labor shortage exists. This program has been used to strikebreak in the cotton industry in the South, and more recently, against union strikers in Texas. The Immigration and Naturalization Service (INS) also plays a role in regulating the presence of Mexican workers without documents. It allows them to enter during critical harvest periods or when there are labor disputes, and at the same time deports those undocumented workers who have joined strikes. "The INS knows that there are illegals," one Farah worker complained,

> . . . because when they need them, they send them in by the hundreds to the U.S. When they need them they look the other way. But when they don't need them, they get them out of there *fast*, They *know* they're there.

Even in normal times, and particularly in the last eight years with unemployment on the rise, there is intense competition for jobs in the El Paso area. The complexity of the El Paso labor market has the built-in potential for conflicts among United States-born Mexicans and Mexican nationals with or without documents. Employers in El Paso use the competition for jobs to create and exacerbate conflict among these groups whenever labor troubles arise.

Many Farah strikers maintained close ties with friends and family in Juárez. Women who had extensive personal contact with life in Mexico, either because their parents had crossed the Rio Grande or because they themselves had grown up there and come to the United States as adults, tended to see the Mexicans and Chicanos as one people. When they looked at the undocumented workers of today, they saw the experiences of their own parents. "I was born over there and raised here," one striker recalled.

> I was seven when we came here. I remember, when we were living in Juárez my father had to come back and forth every fifteen days. He used to live on a farm in the U.S. I don't have any grudges against wetbacks. I do support the Texas farmworkers. If they want to sign up the whole border I don't mind. I understand how it is over there. I understand what it is to have a father as a wetback. I understand what people are trying to do with the border situation.

Many workers at Farah, as children, took part in the pilgrimage North to find work. Some of their families crossed the border illegally. "My father was a laborer," one woman recollected. "There was no work in Mexico. My parents were having a picnic one day, and zoom-they came across." Families contracted to work seasonally, harvesting cotton and pecans. Some never intended to make the United States their home, but they became permanent residents when they found that the money they earned during temporary work visits to the United States could not sustain them when they returned to the increasingly constricted economy of rural Mexico.

Other women at Farah came north as adults to seek work. Even when they succeeded in finding a stable job, the relocation entailed severe hardships and demanded major readjustments. Most of the women had grown up in the poverty-stricken rural areas of northern Mexico. They had almost no formal education, and many married very early in life. While the daily struggle to survive prepared them for the grinding labor of the factory, nothing in their backgrounds had prepared them to assume roles traditionally restricted to male heads-of-household: to leave the home, enter the industrial work force, and, for some, become the major breadwinner of the family. That the move was a radical departure from their upbringing can best be understood from the childhood recollections of the women who experienced these changes. "My childhood?" a striker reminisced:

> I was born in a village where they mine silver, Cusinichi. My father worked there, as did his father and his grandfather. It was a company town. The company was American and there was a union. My family helped build the union. My father wanted to have schools, to have benefits. My father spoke to me often about how the company was very rich and that we were all making the company rich and it was just that the company give us a part for our children. My father talked a lot about this, and sometimes they would throw him out of the mine. After great fights, my father would be back in the mine.
>
> He was a product of his times. He thought that only men should go to school, that we women should only learn to write. Men are the ones who support the family, and so the women don't need anything more.
>
> My father named me after his mother, and even though I had two brothers and three sisters, I was my father's favorite. I was the only child until age four, when my brother arrived. Everything was for me. They took me to work, to the mines, to visit my father. He had a little office where they kept records of people injured on the job, etc. And they also took me to the paymaster. In those days they paid cash. I went everywhere with my father and uncles, to union meetings where everyone didn't stop talking shouting and discussing their problems. A child learns when it is born. When a child begins to breathe a child begins to learn.

> Thus I spent all my time with my father and uncles, but when I'd learned to read and write at nine years, I was not sent to school any more. "No, Papa," I began to cry and shout. When he saw me sitting with a long face and asked me why, I said, "Why can't I go to school anymore?" So he said to go ahead. So they cut my hair and I went. I finished elementary.
>
> Afterwards, I would look up at the mountains, so high. The mines were in the mountains. What more is there? I was dying to know. What's beyond the mountains? What are the people like? Of course my father wouldn't consider my leaving home. He wanted me to get married and have children.
>
> One day my cousin went to the city of Chihuahua. When he returned, I asked him, "What is it like there?" Oh, the buildings are tall, very tall, and the streets-some of them are paved." Here they were made of dirt. "Imagine! The streets are wide—wide as from here to the next village." The more he said, the more I wanted to know.
>
> I thought and thought and one day I asked my father, "Don't we have any relatives in Chihuahua?" He answered that my godfather was there. I told him, "Father, I want to meet him. Maybe I can write." "Go ahead, write him," he agreed. I wrote the letter and asked my father, "Papa, isn't it true that the mail is sacred? You can't open a sealed envelope? Right?" "Yes," he answered. So I said, "Here's the letter for my godfather," and sealed it. He could do nothing but send it. In the letter I told my godfather that I wanted to come meet him and his wife. He wrote back saying that he'd love to have me come and visit for a while. "My wife is expecting a baby and it would be fine." I wrote again asking him to ask my father for his permission, or to come if possible. He arrived. "How long it has been since we've seen each other, how great, couldn't she go with me for a while. My wife is having a baby, and it would be great if your daughter would accompany her." Since he was my godfather, my father accepted.

This woman came to the city, finished her studies and became a teacher. She married, had a family and decided once again to leave her home—this time for the United States. Hardship in Mexico pushed her, and promises of a better future for herself and her children drew her. Upon arriving in El Paso, she had to give up her teaching and enter Farah's factory. This was an immense shock to her hopes; the hardships continued. In making all of these decisions she made a radical departure from her upbringing and grew stronger as a woman. Part of this strength was her intense attachment to her origins.

> Of course I still go back to Mexico frequently to see my parents in Cuateque. My father can no longer get papers to come here, but when he comes to Juárez, to visit my brother, I go to see him. My children go all the time. They love the ambiente there. I believe that this is a good country, but I don't want them to become Americanized so that they don't want to see their

own people. Our roots are there. I became an American citizen by my own choice. This was my decision, but I don't want to negate my roots, or say that I don't want to be there [Mexico]. I love this country as much as I love my own [Mexico]. For that reason I live here. But my children should love both equally: the land is one and the same.

Many other women experienced profound physical and emotional changes; yet their ties to Mexico remained powerful.

A major change for those who came from Mexico involved no longer being a "native" but being stigmatized as an "alien." This identification was applied to all Mexican people regardless of citizenship, and included a population indigenous to the region and more "native" than the later white settlement.

The pride of many Farah workers in their Mexican heritage—a pride often fostered by their parents—protected them somewhat from this hostility and enabled them to stand up to it. "For not having much of an education my father was a pretty smart man," one striker remembered.

> I wish I was like him. He kept up in his history . . . He used to say, "Americanos? We are the Americanos, we're the Indians, we were the first ones here." He was an Indian. He always argued about people calling an Anglo "Americano" and a Mexican "Mexicano." That really got him mad. He'd say, "We are Americanos; *they* are Anglos." That was one thing he always argued about.

Like their sisters in Mexico, Chicanas growing up in El Paso were expected to share responsibility for la familia at an early age. They were raised in poverty, received little formal education, began working when they were still children, married young, and spent their working lives in low status, low paying jobs.

Most of the Chicana workers at Farah had grown up in the barrio in south El Paso's Second Ward. Squeezed between the downtown area and the border, residents of "El Segundo" faced street violence, police indifference, or brutality, rip-offs from slumlords, and racism from uptown whites.

The violence in the streets was inescapable. "When I grew up," one woman recalled,

> life was a lot different at that time. Everything was harder . . . At that time there were no youth centers. There was nothing to do for the kids, no recreation or things like that. So they would hang around on the corners, they would have gangs and fight against each other. You know it became a *barrio* where policemen were there all the time. That kind of reputation. I guess that's one reason why the police didn't care what happened to them because they had that reputation. So they [the police] would beat them up and a lot of times they would just be sitting there with a quart of beer

and the [police] would break it and kick them and take them to jail for nothing.

The unrelieved poverty operated as brutally on residents as attacks by the police. Many a childhood ended prematurely as young girls quit school to help support their families.

> I grew up in the Second Ward. It was a poor neighborhood. We used to live in the projects. Some Mexican Americans try to help each other; others are selfish. My mother used to have three jobs: at Newark Hospital, at night, and at Levi's. After school I worked at Newberry's, babysitting, and as a maid when I was nine. With three young children and myself, I had to help my mother. It was a hard childhood. I didn't have a father. My mother had to work day and night. I told her to let me work for her at the Newark Hospital—so I cleaned the beds and floors.

While many quit school because of economic necessity, even more were driven out by systematic discrimination. They were penalized for being brown-skinned and Spanish speaking. Like the Anglo supervisors at Farah, Anglo teachers in El Paso schools instilled deepseated feelings of inadequacy, humiliation, and disaffection in their Chicano students. Chicanos were discouraged from finishing high school, and the strict tracking system prohibited college and career aspirations. "To me it was hard in school," one woman recalled.

> People making fun of you, especially the way you talked. Your English or your understanding [of English]. I believe my older brothers and sisters had the most difficulty getting adjusted here because they couldn't speak any English. Neither could I, but I was put in kindergarten so it didn't matter to me. People in that small village [outside of El Paso] didn't know how to speak English so we talked Spanish, but it was very difficult for them because they were put in the fourth or fifth grade and they were fourteen. People were making fun of them. I just went to eighth grade, then I quit and got married. I was sixteen and I'm still married to the same man. I was sixteen and I was still in eighth grade. I used to get very disappointed that most of my friends were fourteen or thirteen in the same grade. I was supposed to be in tenth grade at the age of sixteen. That used to bother me a lot. Because of the language problem I had when I came across the border [sic].

Whether at home, in the streets, at school, or on the job, there was no refuge from personal hostility or institutionalized discrimination. Mature women workers are still nursing their childhood wounds, looking back on childhood dreams which were crushed and scorned whichever way they turned.

Yet growing up Chicana in El Paso also provided these women with sources of strength, pride and courage. They drew strength from El Segundo's sense of community, which was formed in response to confrontations with the Anglo power structure of El Paso. Their families transmitted to them pride in Mexican culture, as well as countless individual examples of courage in difficult circumstances.

Whether they were raised in the U.S. or Mexico, these women by no means suffered passively. To survive they had to struggle. They responded with anger to the racism, deprivation, and systematic oppression which they experienced as Raza women. While this anger was seldom expressed openly, it was always present and potentially explosive. The advent of a unionization campaign helped to give organized expression to this anger.

Early Organizing

Despite the fact that most workers in the El Paso region were not organized into unions, some of the women had been exposed to labor organizing drives. Women from Mexico had parents who had fled to the United States after their attempts to organize workers in Mexico had failed. They had lost everything in the process. Some women, as children, had witnessed bloody strikes in the textile mills and mines of northern Mexico. Among those women, some had even worked as children in these industries. Others had undergone the dislocation and hardship of migrant life in the United States.

Among Chicanas at Farah, some had fathers, mothers, brothers, and husbands who belonged to unions in El Paso's smelting and packing plants. There was the example of the prolonged and successful strike of garment workers for union recognition at the Top Notch clothing plant in the 1960s. But experience with organized labor was by no means widespread among workers at Farah. The overwhelming majority of the women in the plant during the day-to-day activities of a union, and virtually no examples of working women's struggles in unions to guide them. Yet, Farah workers from both sides of the border had grown up in working class families, and many had had tragic personal experiences which dramatized for them the need for unionization. One woman recalled the early death of her father from lung cancer.

> He died when he was young, only forty-four years old. Because where he was working, they didn't have no union and he was doing dirty work, smashing cans and bumpers. When you smash them, smoke comes up and he inhaled it and that's what killed him. He didn't have no protection; they didn't even give him a mask. He put only a handkerchief to cover his face. He died of cancer because of all the things he was inhaling. That's what the doctor told us . . . He died before I turned seventeen. They operated and said he had only half a lung and wasn't going to live long. He lasted three weeks. I'd do anything for him, I was very close

> to him. He told me it was too late to have another job. I couldn't stand it and would go into the next room to cry so that he wouldn't hear me. He was so husky until the sickness ate him away.

This woman never lost the conviction that her father's life could have been prolonged if he'd had a union's protection on the job. "When I started to know about the union," she concluded grimly, "I joined right away because of my father."

The earliest attempt by workers at Farah to present an organized response to management attacks was a brief petition campaign among markers at the Gateway plant in 1968. A more systematic effort to address workers' grievances began in 1969 when male workers from the cutting and shipping departments contacted organizers from the Amalgamated Clothing Workers of America (ACWA).[4] They acted in spite of Farah's repeated violent tirades against unions. Farah presented films about union corruption on company time and pronounced to his workers, "See what a union does? You don't want anything to do with that!" But Farah overestimated the impact of his blitz on organizing. He was sufficiently confident of union defeat in an upcoming election that he urged cutters to vote, insisting that not to vote was to vote for the union. The cutters turned out in force for the election, and on October 14, 1970, they voted overwhelmingly to affiliate themselves with the union. Not about to accept the unexpected turn of events, Farah immediately appealed the election result with the National Labor Relations Board (NLRB). The cutting room election was tied up in court until 1972, when the election victory was set aside on grounds that the cutting room was not an appropriate bargaining unit. But by that time, organizing had long since spread to the rest of the plant.

Soon after this first election, a handful of cutters began attempts to sign up workers in other departments. Reactions to the organizing drive varied. Most women had little idea of what the activists hoped to gain from union recognition. Others were fearful—with good cause—of supervisors' retaliation. Furthermore, many workers believed what Willie Farah said about labor unions taking their money and benefits.

Even so, some women were moved by their fellow workers' persistence in the face of personal harassment and threats to their jobs. Several workers signed cards and began to talk to their coworkers about the new organizing drive. Efforts to sign up workers took place clandestinely because of the virulence of management tactics against the organizers. Women hid union cards in their purses, met hurriedly in the bathrooms and whispered in the halls to persuade the indifferent. The cafeteria was the heart of the organizing efforts. During lunch time, workers circulated among the tables to sound out each other's sentiments about the union. The first union meetings in people's homes were a completely new experience. "Oh, I did like them," a striker reminisced. "There was a lot of—you know, talking about new things, about the union. And especially, I felt that somebody was talking for us."

Management responded to organizing activities with a series of repressive measures. Supervisors were stationed in the halls to monitor sympathizers and interrogate employees concerning their union loyalties. "They would say, 'What are they saying in there?' and I would respond, 'Who? I don't know what they're saying,'" a striker recalled.

> They'd say, "Don't believe about the union, the union's a bunch of bullshit. They only want to take your money away." That's what they'd say. And I just heard them, and I didn't say anything . . . But once they knew you were involved with the union, they'd start pressuring you . . . Some of us just quit, some were fired.

All personal conversations were restricted during work time, and conditions worsened even for those not involved in organizing. "When we began organizing," one woman recalled," [the company] put even harsher supervisors who tried to humiliate people more. If there was a shortage of work on a line, they made me sweep. I refused, but other workers were afraid of being fired and obeyed. They did it to humiliate us and to assure that no organization would succeed."

Company intimidation frightened many people away. Workers treated union organizers as if they had some kind of disease. Union sympathizers were fired, among them four women. One woman described her firing, saying, "My supervisor, Héctor Romero, sent me to Salvador Ibarra's line because my line had no work."

> After lunch, Héctor Romero told me to go back to my machine because now there was work, and I worked at the machine the rest of the afternoon. About half an hour before quitting time, Ernest Boeldner, another foreman, asked me what I was doing at my machine since I had been told to work in Ibarra's line. I told him that I was only following Romero's orders. Without another word he sent me to the office where they asked me to turn in my badge and scissors. I still did not know what was going on but the bell rang and I went home. The following day when I returned to work, Victor Chamali did not let me punch in and told me I was fired. Farah says I was fired for disobedience. Some people have spread the rumor that I was fired because I was lazy or that I quit to go to work for the union. But none of this is true. I was fired to stop me from organizing and to scare other people.

The firings intimidated workers, but also angered them. As one of the women who was fired observed, "It did give them some courage. They wanted to know why I was fired after all these years, with no earlier work problems." Few workers were willing to openly confront their supervisors, but as their anger grew they discussed the union among themselves more frequently.

Organizing continued at the Gateway plant, though there were no immediate plans to take action. The activists who were fired went down to the union office and vowed to continue the struggle. One woman organized a group of students from a nearby high school to distribute leaflets in front of the Gateway, Paisano, and Third Street plants. They were insulted, their leaflets were torn up and thrown in their faces, and some of them were assaulted. But the woman came every day at 6:00 a.m. and stood her ground until the day of the walkout.

The Walkout

The campaign to unionize the Farah plants intensified in the spring of 1972. In March, twenty-six workers were fired when they attempted a walkout at the Northwest plant in El Paso. But it was a series of events in San Antonio that triggered the large-scale strike in El Paso.

One weekend, members of the union organizing committee in El Paso sponsored a march. Farah workers from San Antonio made the twelve-hour drive between the two cities to join the demonstration. Some of them did not return to San Antonio in time for work on Monday morning. On Tuesday, a supervisor confronted a worker with pictures of him marching under union banners in El Paso and then promptly fired him. Workers who objected to his dismissal were also fired. More than 500 San Antonio Farah workers walked out in protest.

Six days later, when El Paso Farah workers learned of the San Antonio strike, their frustration with working conditions and with Farah's continued suppression of union activity exploded into a spontaneous strike. On May 9, the machinists, shippers, cutters, and some of the seamstresses walked out. The walkout, which continued for almost a month, initially took the company by surprise. Women who had worked docilely at their machines for years, women who had been reduced to tears by a supervisor's reprimand, women who had never openly spoken a word in favor of the union, suddenly began to speak up.

> That day that we walked out, the supervisor saw that I had a little flag on. He went over and he looked at me, sort of startled, and he said, "You?" And I said, "Yes!" And he said, "What have we done to you?" I said, "Oh, I wouldn't know where to begin." He said, "We haven't done anything to you." I said, "But you have done a lot to all of the people around me. I've seen it going on."

The startled management soon rallied with a skillful combination of promises and threats. On the first day of the walkout, as activists walked through the factory urging the workers to join them, supervisors followed them, telling the workers to let the dissidents go out on strike and suffer and lose their jobs. The loudspeaker system broadcasted "La Golondrina," a Mexican song of farewell, in a sardonic gesture to the strikers. The shop floor and the cafeteria were full of people shouting, arguing, or quietly trying to decide what to do. For many women, the decision was a difficult one which took several days to make, while the management did its best to frighten or cajole the women who were still undecided. For all of the strikers, the day on which they decided to walk out remains a vivid and memorable one.

> I remember the first time of the walkout we were all in break, eating, having some coffee. And then suddenly there was a whole bunch in the cutting room—the girls and everything. They went over to my table and said, "Alma, you've got to come out with us!" And I just looked at them. I was so scared I didn't even know what to do. What if I go and lose my thirteen years? So long, having seniority and everything. I just looked at them and said, "Yeah, yeah, I'll go. I'll go." That's all I said. And I had a whole bunch of people sitting there with me and I said, "Let's go!" And one of them said, "Well, if you go, we'll go."

> So the next day I went and put pants on. I always wear dresses. I used to love to wear dresses. So I put some pants on and said, "I don't know what's going to happen. Maybe there's going to be fighting or something." You know, we were scared . . . We were scared maybe they would beat us and everything.

> But I remember that day. When I was passing, the girls started yelling at me, "Alma, you'd better go out! We need you out here!" And I said, "Yeah, yeah, yeah. Wait, wait." "No, you're happy. That's what's the matter with you. You're just a happy one. The way they treat you in there, and you're still in there."

> So around nine o'clock I started gathering everybody. "We're going out! Right now! When you see me get off my machine." So you should have seen all those supervisors around me. Somebody pinched a finger on me and told them I was going to go out. You should have seen them all around me. They said, "Alma, you're a good worker. We'll pay you what you want. Alma, the way you sew, the way you work, the way you help us." And I would just say, "Yeah, I know. I know." They thought I was going to stay there.

> At nine o'clock I got off [the machine]. I went to the restroom and I started telling everybody, "Let's go!" So some of them just didn't go. I took a lot of people out with me.

> Then I started walking through the middle of the— where all the people were working—they thought I was very happy [with work at Farah]. And they started, "Alma! Alma!" And everybody started getting off the machines. I couldn't believe it. It was something so beautiful. So exciting.

> And then suddenly a supervisor got a hold of me on my shoulder, and he says, "Alma, we need you! Don't go!" So everybody started . . . I took a lot of people that were real good. I took them all out with me.

> When I started walking outside, all the strikers that were out there, yelling, they saw me, and golly, I felt so proud, 'cause they all went and hugged me. And they said, "We never thought you were one of us" And I said, "What do you think? Just because I'm a quiet person?"

> But it was beautiful! I really knew we were going to do something. That we were really going to fight for our rights.

As the walkout continued and spread beyond the shipping and cutting rooms, it began to include a wide variety of women. Some came from families with histories of union involvement, while others had no previous contact or experience with unions. Some who walked out had taken an active role in the union organizing campaign leading up to the strike, while others had never even signed a union card. For all of them, however, the act of walking out began a process of change in the way they looked at themselves and their work. "For me," one striker recalled,

> [The day of the walkout] was something out of this world. I was pleased with myself, but at the same time I was afraid. That night I couldn't sleep. I couldn't see myself out of Farah. So many years.

The Strike

The Amalgamated Clothing Workers of America quickly moved to support the Farah workers; the strike was declared an unfair labor practice strike. One month later a national boycott of Farah products was begun, endorsed by the AFL-CIO. In El Paso the strikers began to picket the Farah plants and local stores which carried Farah products. But in a town where many regarded Willie Farah as a folk hero, the strikers found that public reaction to the walkout was often hostile. One woman remembers that:

> People were just very cruel. Everybody thought that Farah was a god or something . . . . I swear, they'd even turn around and spit on you if they could. There was one lady, I was handing out some papers downtown . . . and she got her purse and started striking me . . . . When she started hitting me, she said, "Ah, you people, a bunch of dumb this and that! Farah's a great man!"

Passers-by told the picketers that they were lazy bums who just wanted welfare and food stamps. The strikers were repeatedly reminded that Farah was a major employer in an area where unemployment was high, and that they should be grateful to him for giving them jobs.

Antiunion sentiment was not limited to random comments on the street. It was also expressed in a virtual blackout in the local media. A reporter for the *El Paso Times* who wanted to write a series of feature articles on the strikers was told that the strike was a "private affair" between Farah and his workers. The editor added, "Maybe if we let Willie Farah run his business he'll let us run our newspaper." It wasn't necessary for Farah himself to exercise direct censorship. His importance in the El Paso business community ensured that no newspaper would print material which was damaging to him. A striker describing the extent of his informal influence wryly observed, "Willie Farah conquered El Paso."

There was also considerable racism in the antiunion sentiment. Some members of the Anglo community felt that Mexican Americans were "aliens" and that Mexican American strikers were ungrateful troublemakers who should be dealt with severely. One woman angrily remembers:

> When we were on strike there was a program on TV and anybody could call up. You know, one man called the TV station and told them why didn't they send all the Mexicans back to Mexico? How ignorant! Here I was born in the United States and this stupid man has the nerve to say to send them all back to Mexico because we were on strike!

Racial tensions between Anglos and Chicanos, an ever-present feature of life in El Paso, were exacerbated by the strike and the political mobilization of Chicana workers which accompanied it.

However, opinions about the strike did not simply divide along racial or ethnic lines. The strike split the Chicano community. Many workers at Farah crossed picket lines and continued to keep the plant operating. They were known as the "happies" because they wore buttons which featured a smiling face and the slogan, "I'm happy at Farah." Especially at Farah's Third St. plant, where many of the people had worked for Farah since World War II, vehement opposition to the strike was expressed.

> There was this woman who was married to one of the supervisors . . . . She even yelled at us that we were going to starve. She said, "Don't worry! We'll give you the cockroaches!"
>
> They used to call us a lot of names . . . . You should be ashamed after so many years that Willie has been supporting you with work." "Why don't you start working? All you want is to be loafing around. At your age!"

The strike divided families. Several women told of walking out while their sisters remained inside the plant. There was even one family where the husband was on strike and his wife was continuing to work at Farah. "He'd drive his wife up to the door," one striker recalled, "and get out of there as fast as he could. Now this was ridiculous!"

Striking workers were quickly replaced by strikebreakers from El Paso and the neighboring Mexican city of Juárez. There was no lack of applicants for the jobs: El Paso unemployment figures have soared as high as 14 percent in recent years, while Juarez, like much of Mexico, has a current unemployment rate of 40 percent.

Until shortly before the strike, Willie Farah, who liked to style himself as a superpatriot, had refused to hire Mexi-

cans to work in his plant even if they had green cards. But when the strike began and he needed workers, he abruptly changed his policy, and became willing to hire Mexican nationals. Large numbers of greencarders appeared in the plant. Farah's hiring practices were partly successful in pitting workers against each other. Some Chicano strikers blamed Mexican workers for being hired by Farah, rather than blaming Farah and other employers along the border for using job competition to divide workers. However, many of the strikers recognized that the economic situation in Juarez forced people to find work wherever they could. And in spite of the economic squeeze, a small number of Juarez residents joined the strikers.

People on the picket lines faced continuing harassment from company personnel. Farah hired guards to patrol the picket line with unmuzzled police dogs. Several strikers were hit by Farah trucks, and one woman was struck by a car driven by Willie Farah's mother. Farah obtained an injunction limiting pickets to one every fifty feet; 1,008 workers were cited for violations, and many were ordered to report to the police station in the middle of the night and required to post four hundred dollar bonds. One woman was jailed six times. (The Texas law which permitted such injunctions was later declared unconstitutional, and all charges were dropped.)

Support

Although the strikers suffered physical and psychological harassment from opponents of the strike, they also discovered new sources of support. The Amalgamated Clothing Workers of America sent organizers to El Paso, gave weekly payments of thirty dollars to each striker, administered a Farah Relief Fund, and sponsored classes for the strikers on labor history and union procedures. For many workers, the films shown by the union were their first exposure to the history of labor struggles in the United States. One woman was deeply moved by a film about a strike in Chicago; another striker especially liked the movie "Salt of the Earth," because it showed the role of Chicanas in a strike in New Mexico.

Immediately after the strike began, the union organized a national boycott of Farah pants which became a crucial factor in the success of the strike. By January 1974, forty union representatives were working on boycott campaigns in more than sixty cities.[5] The Amalgamated issued leaflets, posters, and public relations kits, and worked closely with other unions, church and student groups to implement the boycott. Many Farah workers went on speaking tours to promote the boycott. All of these efforts transformed the Farah strike from an isolated local struggle to a national campaign with widespread support.

The Catholic Church was another source of help for the strikers. Father Jesse Muñoz, a priest at Our Lady of the Light Church, made church facilities available for union meetings and participated in several national speaking tours to promote the boycott of Farah products. He also came to the picket line at the Gateway plant to bless the strikers on Ash Wednesday. Bishop Sidney Metzger of El Paso publicly endorsed the boycott in a letter to his fellow bishops. Metzger said, "The fact that today over 3,000 workers are on strike is evidence that both grievances and resentment are real. And by listening to the people over the years one gradually became aware that things at Farah were not actually as they were made to appear."[6]

In El Paso, a town with a large and devout Catholic population, the approval of the church was a source of emotional as well as organizational support for the strikers and a setback for their opponents. Muñoz received threatening letters from unknown sources, and he contends that Farah hired someone to put LSD in his Coca-Cola at a union dinner.

When a group of happies announced that they planned to picket the church, the strikers quickly organized a counteraction. The happies arrived to find the church surrounded by strikers. One striker spotted the black ribbons worn by the protesters and called out, "What happened, did Willie die already?" The happies took stock of the situation and retreated.

Father Muñoz suggests that there were many reasons why the church chose to back the strikers in spite of the continuing controversy. He points out that the church has a commitment to social justice, which he personally had supported by joining the southern civil rights protests of the 1960s. "So when I came here and there was a roaring tiger in my backyard, I wasn't going to ignore it." Muñoz was also concerned that the strikers would be incited to violence by "communists from Red China, Cuba, and Berkeley," whom he charges came to town to disrupt the strike. By inviting the strikers to use church facilities, he hoped to isolate them from what he viewed as dangerous influences.

Workers at Asarco and the few other union plants in town also expressed their support for the strikers. Even more surprising to the strikers, given the prevailing mood of hostility, was the support given them by some local businesses.

> We got on that truck . . . and we went to ask everybody if they could give us some food. . . . That was when, I tell you, my life started changing. There you know who your good friends are and who cares about people. . . . We went to that fruit stand on Alameda. . . . He gave us, I guess, about twenty bags of potatoes. . . . Then we went to that Peyton [meat] packing company, and they gave us wienies. . . . Mostly we went to the stores to ask for baby food. Then we went to the *tortillería* in Ysleta [east of El Paso] . . . and that man gave us about twenty dozens of tortillas . . . and tamales, and some juice. . . . Then we went back to report to the people, to tell them that we had support.

The strikers were also encouraged by messages of solidarity and financial support from other unions around the country. Particularly important to them was the visit to El Paso of César Chávez. In addition, a variety of Chicano, student, and leftist organizations in El Paso and around the country supported the strike by publicizing the boycott and the conditions at Farah.

New Responsibilities

But the most profound changes among the Farah strikers began when they took on new responsibilities for organizing strike activities. Some women went to work for the union on a volunteer basis, writing strike relief checks, keeping records, and distributing the goods that arrived from outside El Paso. Almost immediately they began to realize that their capabilities were not as limited as they had been taught to believe. One striker asserted, "if I had not walked out, I would not have been able to realize all those things about myself."

> You know, when we used to register the people from the strike, would you believe that we organized all those cards, all those people on strike? And you know, not realizing, here you can do this anywhere! You can go to any office and sit down and work! You know, you think to yourself, "How in the world did I ever think I couldn't do anything?" This is one of the things that's held us back. We didn't think we could do it. . . . Until you actually get there and sit down and do it, and you find out, "I'm not so dumb after all!"

Other strikers went on speaking tours organized by the union or by strike support groups to publicize the boycott and raise funds.

> I had never travelled as much as I did when I was on strike. The only place I had gone was to L.A., one time, but that was about all. But I never thought that I could go to New York, or Seattle, or all these places. To me it was just like a dream, something that was just happening and I was going through, but I couldn't stop to think about it. I just had to go and talk to those people about the strike. . . . The first week it was hard [to get used to talking to groups of people]. Because over here I just used to talk to one or two persons when I was working they hardly let you talk at all . . . . Sometimes I would try to talk just as though I was talking to the strikers right here. I just didn't think that they were other people that I didn't know.

One woman observed that anti-union harassment took similar forms all over the country; when she stopped to talk to workers at a non-union plant, a supervisor appeared and shooed the workers back inside. When she spoke on the East Coast she noticed that racial and ethnic differences often kept workers isolated from one another. She returned to El Paso with a heightened perception of the difficulties involved in building a strong union.

Financial Troubles

As the months wore on, strikers faced increasing financial hardship. The union strike relief payments of thirty dollars a week were inadequate for many families. In one household both husband and wife were on strike, and there were eight children to feed and clothe. Unable to handle their house payments, the family moved in with the husband's mother. The uncertainties of the strike, the financial troubles, and the change in living arrangements were a strain on the marriage:

> My husband was worried too, because of the financial [situation], and he would start to drinking to take it off his mind. I . . . even told him to go to the hospital, because he was getting awful. And I had an operation too at that time. And he did, he went to the hospital and he got cured. . . . [Drinking was a big problem among the strikers) because there was nothing for them to do. . . . He had to be there [on the picket line] from 7:30 until 4:30 in the afternoon, because he was the [picket] captain. Mostly the kids wouldn't see him at all, and neither did I, until two in the morning when he got home.

For single women workers living with their parents, the situation was somewhat easier. Their parents supported them, and working brothers and sisters often helped with car payments and other bills. But many single women were themselves working to support widowed parents and younger siblings. For them the strike meant financial desperation.

Women who could find work in other clothing factories did so, continuing to picket at Farah before and after work and on Saturdays. Only the small number of unionized plants in El Paso were willing to hire Farah strikers. At nonunion plants, however, the jobs only lasted as long as the striker's identity was unknown.

In working-class areas, particularly in the sprawling eastern end of town, many workers felt a sense of solidarity with their neighbors.

> Here the whole neighborhood, you know, the majority of us were on strike! . . . The guy on the corner was on strike, the girl across the street, the one on the corner over there, then there was Virgie and all her sisters, and then we had one lady down the other corner that was working. . . . my neighbors in front—her father's always been fighting for unions. A lot of these things, I think, kind of made you feel good.

The Home

As women became more and more involved in running strike support activities, and as they developed new friendships among the strikers, they began to spend more time outside the home. This was a source of tension in many households.

> I was so involved that I was forgetting everything. My husband started getting very angry at me, and I was giving him a hard time. You know, at the time I didn't realize that I was hurting my kids and my husband. At the time I just felt that this was something I had to do, and if my husband liked it or didn't like it he was going to have to accept it. . . . Lucky that he was able to accept [it], because this went on and on during the strike. . . . Now I stop to think, and I tell myself, good grief, he really did put up with a lot! How would I like it if he was gone every day of the week! . . . So I'm just glad that he was able to stand behind me, and it didn't destroy our marriage, but it did destroy a lot of marriages. . . .

In some cases, differences of opinion about the merits of the walkout were fueled by financial insecurity. In other homes the husbands did not think that attending public meetings was an appropriate way for their wives to spend their time.

> Well, at the beginning they didn't like it. They thought [the women) should be at home, because here they were kind of old-fashioned, the women were always supposed to be at home. The only time she'd be working was if she had to work to keep up with the bills, and both wife and husband had to work. Otherwise there was no way that the man himself could support the house. But that's about all they thought about, just for them to work—they didn't think they could go to meetings.

But the women felt strongly enough about their involvement in the strike to put up a spirited defense of their activities.

> My ex-husband told me, "You're not gonna make it, and I'm not gonna help you!" And I said, "if God made it, and his followers made it, like Peter, he left his boat behind, his wife . . . everything, he left everything behind, all his belongings to follow God, yet he didn't die! Right now he's in better shape than we are. He's in heaven, holding that door—isn't that true!

For many women the changes in their marriages were more profound than a few disagreements over meetings or money. The strike made them more confident of their ability to make decisions, and they began to question their own attitudes toward their husbands.

> Maybe it's just the Mexican woman, maybe it's just that the Mexican woman has been brought up always to do what somebody tells you, you know, your father, your mother. And as you grow up, you're used to always being told what to do. . . .

For years I wouldn't do anything without asking my husband's permission. . . . I've been married nineteen years, and I was always, "Hey, can I" or "Should I. . . ." I see myself now and I think, good grief, having to ask to buy a pair of underwear! Of course, I don't do this anymore . . . . [The time of the strike was] when it started changing. All of it. I was able to begin to stand up for myself, and I began to feel that I should be accepted for the person that I am.

Most marriages survived the ordeals of the strike, and many women feel that their growth as individuals has strengthened their relationships with their husbands. But it was also not uncommon for husbands threatened by the new eloquence, assertiveness, and political awareness of their wives simply to walk out.

The strike also transformed the relationship of women workers to their children. Many brought their children to meetings and to the picket line. "My little boy was only three months, and you should have seen me, I had him always in my arms, going everywhere," remembers one striker. Children who were slightly older took an active part in strike support work, and formed their own opinions about unionization.

See my little boy? . . . I used to take him with me to go picket. We [adults] used to go give people . . . papers, and they would hold their papers, or throw them at us right in the face, or say "Shove it down your you-know-what." He would get them—you know, he's a small boy. People would not pay attention to him. So he would say, "Here, sir!" "OK!" He would put it in his pocket, or read it. . . . He was always out with me, always out picketing. He was about seven or eight. . . . Anybody talks about unions, he'll tell you, "Go out there and join the union." Tell him, "Unions are no good." "They're good. They educate. They educated my mother."

One teenager commented, "Mom used to be a slave. But since the strike she thinks for herself. It's a lot better."

Women also consciously reevaluated their ideas about child-rearing and their hopes for their children.

I used to be a very nervous person when my kids were little. I almost had a nervous breakdown. . . . My husband used to drive me batty, you know. The kid couldn't be bawling over there in the other room—I had to get up and run and see what's the matter with the kid! Because my husband was an overly protective person with his children. . . . So here's the idiot wife, running like crazy to look after these kids, and it was driving me batty! . . .

These are the things that I was able to begin to stand up for. It was crazy, you couldn't watch the kid constantly . . . And I've come to where now I don't feel this . . . pressure. I don't feel this anymore. I'll look out for my kids the best I can. . . .

My ideas are a whole lot different than they used to be. I want my kids to be free. I never want them to feel oppressed. I want them to treat everybody as an equal . . . . I don't think they should slight someone because he's black or he's any different than they are. And this is what I want—I want them to be free people. And to be good people . . . .

I want my daughter to be able to do what she's gotta do . . . and not always comply to whatever her boyfriend or her husband [wants] . . . that she should be the person that she is. And I want my boys to be the person that they are.

You know, it's very funny, when my daughter and my son were little, you know my husband wouldn't let my boy wash dishes? . . . So he grows up never washing a dish! And I tell my husband, "I think it's your fault that he doesn't know how to wash dishes . . ."

You know, I think it [the strike] has made my kids more outspoken . . . . Maybe some people would call it disrespect. I don't. I think that being outspoken is not harmful if you do it in the right way. Like my son—if someboy, if an adult, gives him a hard time, I expect him to stand up and speak for his rights.

Unidad Para Siempre

Women strikers turned a critical eye on their personal lives and their home; as they became more experienced they developed criticisms of the union campaign as well. Some women felt that the Amalgamated Clothing Workers of America was not promoting the strike and boycott actively enough, particularly in El Paso.

The union, hard-pressed to pay each striker thirty dollars a week, stopped encouraging more workers to come out on strike. (The union organizers felt that the strike could not be won unless there was a successful national boycott, and that funds should be channeled into boycott organizing rather than support of additional strikers.) There were squabbles about eligibility for emergency funds and relief payments. More important, many strikers felt that they were not being encouraged to take independent action to raise funds or publicize the strike. They wanted the process of education which had begun with the walkout to continue. One woman remembers that she and her fellow activists "were trying to get those people to reorganize not only the union, but actually to really try to stand on their own two feet . . . trying to talk things out for yourself without having somebody else talk them out."

Some strikers began to meet independently of the union, in a group which was known simply as the rank-and-file committee. (This group took the name Unidad Para Siempre—Unity Forever—when it was reactivated after the strike.) The members of the group—about forty—shared a strong sense of themselves as workers and a desire to build a strong and democratic union. They put out their own leaflets, participated in marches and rallies, helped to found the Farah Distress Fund, and talked to other strikers about the need for a strong union. "We wanted a union with action, not just words. That's why we were having meetings and going out, really doing more, making our own papers . . .

Politicization of Women

For the women on strike at Farah there was no artificial separation between personal and political change. Their experiences during the strike altered the way they looked at themselves as women and as workers.

Of course, we never did anything wrong, really. What we were fighting for was our rights, because we were very oppressed. For one thing, I was a very insecure person way back then. I felt that I was inferior to my supervisors, who were at the time only Anglo. None of this affects me anymore. I have learned that I am an equal. I have all the rights they have. I may not have the education they have, and I may not earn the money they earn . . . . But I am their equal regardless. And it's done a lot for me, it's changed a lot for me. It made me into a better person. . . .

It used to be if a supervisor got after me for anything I'd sit there and cry. Well, they don't do this to me anymore. They don't frighten me anymore. Two of them can take me into the office—it does not affect me at all. I have my say, and if they like it or not, I'm going to say so. . . . Before I wouldn't say anything. I would just hold it in and cry it out, and stay and stay. . . .

And I believe very much in fighting for your rights, and for women's rights. . . . I don't believe in burning your bra, but I do believe in our having our rights, that even if you're married you can make your marriage work. I know that sometimes we have to put up with a little bit more, but it has changed a lot of things for me. . . .

Maybe the company doesn't feel this way, but it's done a lot for us. . . .

The strike made women more conscious of political and social movements which they had regarded as "outside" and irrelevant to their own lives. These ranged from the support of local union struggles to the struggles of the UFW and Texas Farmworkers to the women's movement.

"During the strike," says one woman, "every place I turned around there'd be a strike. They [other strikers] used to go to the stores where they were selling Farah pants, and they used to picket at the stores, and in return we used to go and help them picket." Farah workers have supported recent strikes at a local cannery and the municipal bus lines. Some of them joined the picket lines when Asarco, a nearby smelting plant, went on strike in the summer of 1977.

Recently, ex-strikers have also been involved in other unionizing drives. One woman who now works in a hospital is contemplating an organizing campaign among health care workers. Another has helped her father and uncles to begin signing up people at a bread factory. Several other women have joined a Texas Farmworkers support committee, which publicizes the working conditions of the farm workers and tries to raise funds for their unionizing campaigns.

People have also begun to discuss the women's movement in their homes. Although it is still perceived as a movement that is taking place somewhere outside of El Paso, it evokes both sympathy and support.

Well, all of us women, we like it. And we sure would like to join them. Some of the husbands they don't like it at all. They're not happy about it. . . . [My husband] doesn't like it . . . . Sometimes [we argue] and my daughters help me, my daughters back me up. [My sons] like it too.

For all of the women, the strike made them more conscious of themselves as working people with interests distinct from other classes. One woman began to argue with her dentist, who complained to her that her strike was causing him to lose money he had invested in Farah Manufacturing Company. She commented that he could afford to lose money, and added,

It's like I tell him, "Just because you happen to be one Mexican out of many that made it to the top—and I bet you worked your butt off to get up there. I'll respect you for your ideas as long as you respect me for mine. I happen to be of the working class, and I happen to be one of the minority (i.e. Chicana), that I feel work at the lowest type of job there is, and I feel that we have a right to fight.

For others the strike altered the way they looked at their jobs, and for the first time made them feel that their workplace was the site of an important struggle.

For myself, I would like to continue working where I am. I think about going to school and getting a secretarial job, and I think it would be a boring thing. I like to be where the action is. For my kids, if they want a college education, I expect to give it to them. . . . I'd rather have them have a better job than me.

But I like being there. I like the challenge. You don't know what the next day's going to bring you. You might get fired! . . . I don't think I could see myself sitting there in back of a desk, answering phones. When you could be fighting somewhere else, in a grievance, fighting with your supervisors, giving them hell. . . .

[Before the strike] it was just a job to go to. Now it is kind of challenging, you know, you can never tell what's going to happen.

Inside the Plant: The Pressure Builds

By the beginning of 1974, the nationwide boycott organized by the ACWA was having a noticeable effect on Farah's business. Sales, which were $156 million in 1972, dropped to $126 million in 1974.[7] By the end of 1973 four Farah plants outside of El Paso had been closed, and the El Paso plants had been put on a four-day week.

The five El Paso plants, which had been operating with scab labor throughout the strike, began to resemble ghost towns. One striker who maintained a close friendship with a strikebreaker recalls:

> She told me all the things that happened in there. That sometimes there wasn't even work and they would send them home. She said sometimes they would just play tic tac toe for hours. . . . She said she used to get tired of staying waiting hours in there for material. And they would just sit down and talk, or go into a bathroom and spend thirty minutes in there. . . . I think that their orders weren't coming in [because of] the boycott.

Even among the business community in El Paso, there was concern that the city was acquiring a reputation as a bad place to invest, and there was embarrassment at the outrageous and frequently racist statements that Farah periodically made to the press. When Farah publicly blamed the Catholic Church for his problems with the union, national press coverage was not sympathetic.

The final blow came at the end of January 1974, when an Administrative Judge of the National Labor Relations Board issued a decision which accused Farah of "flouting the (National Labor Relations) Act and trampling on the rights of its employees as if there were no Act, no Board, and no Ten Commandments." Farah was ordered to offer reinstatement to the strikers (whom the company asserted had voluntarily quit), to reinstate with back pay several workers who had been fired for union activity, and to allow the union access to company bulletin boards and employee lists.

Farah initially indicated that he would appeal the decision, but several weeks later he abruptly changed course. On February 23, apparently after preliminary discussion with union officials, he recognized the Amalgamated Clothing Workers of America as the bargaining agent for Farah employees. The union simultaneously announced that it would terminate the boycott.

The strikers, exultant and relieved, celebrated the fact that they had outlasted El Paso's major business figure.

> It's like Rome. Remember, at that time, Caesar and all of them, he had a big throne. He said, "I am a god. I make these people do that and and I make these people do this." Yet his throne, his empire, crumbled down. That's what happened to Farah. It was an empire. . . . And yet, his empire came down. Farah's empire came down. . . .

However, for many strikers the feeling of triumph was marred by a confusion about who had decided to end the strike. They resented the fact that they were not involved in the discussions which preceded Farah's capitulation. Many people first heard the news on the picket line.

> All of a sudden the strike was over. [We heard about it] the day before, because they said, "Nobody's gonna picket tomorrow." After I got out of the check committee I went out picketing. . . . [The picket captain] knew, I'm pretty sure he did, because he's working now as a business agent. . . .
>
> We really didn't know what was going on. "We don't picket tomorrow." "Why don't we picket?" "I don't know. The strike is over, I guess." "Oh, really?" And then the newspaper, the headlines. . . . I didn't like it, because I thought it was something they had already made up their minds to it, you know. We were not involved. . . . I wasn't really pleased about it, but I said, "Well, at least we got the union in."

Most strikers believed that the decision to end the strike had been made in New York.

When the negotiating committee for the first contract was elected, strikers discovered to their dismay that happies were to be represented on the committee. In the few weeks before Farah recognized the union, his supervisors had been ordering people to sign union cards, telling them that if they didn't comply the factory would close. As nominal union members, these people had the right to participate in contract negotiations. The committee was thus badly split.

> You know, we were strikers, and they told us we were going to have a committee for the negotiations as strikers. And I believe that as long as you're on strike, that you have the right to decide what contract you want. . . . They [the union officials] decided that it was only fair that the people that were inside [should] have another committee.
>
> So there was the table, this side were happies, and this side was strikers. We wanted something, they voted against us. We wanted thirty cents, they wanted five cents. That's where I believe we got screwed. If we had the chance, not having that committee there, I believe we would have gotten a better . . . contract.

Other strikers on the negotiating committee felt that they were powerless, that the union officials had decided what they wanted before they held meetings with the workers. "The negotiating committee never really had much to say. . . . [The officials] say they know what is right and what isn't." If a member of the negotiating committee raised a question about a specific contract provision in negotiations, recalls one committee member, the senior union official would say: "Well, let's have a little break now." And he would talk to the people and say, "You shouldn't do that, you know. They know how much they can give you."

The final contract included pay increases of fifty-five cents an hour over three years, a medical insurance plan financed by the company, job security and seniority rights, and a grievance procedure. It also gave union representatives the right to challenge production quotas for individual operations. It was ratified at a meeting of employees on March 7.

Many workers were angry that there was little time taken to explain the contract or hear people's questions and objections.

> They put us all in the cafeteria of one of the factories. And we were in there along with all the people. There was a lot of people, a lot of noise. Some of the clauses that were in there, we didn't even get to understand them very well. He [a union official would explain it in English, and Sánchez [the ACWA Joint Board Manager] would just translate it. . . . But he was going so fast with it that we didn't have a chance to really understand it. But then they said that we had to take that contract regardless because Mr. Farah had said that if that contract was not signed he wasn't about to change his mind and go for another contract. That contract had to be taken or else he would just close down the factory and that was that. . . .
>
> So he read the contract real fast and then he asked, "Does anybody disapprove?" and then a few of the people raised their hands and they were ignored. . . . He said, "OK, this means we go back to work." . . . We didn't vote on it.

Strikers felt that two years of suffering entitled them to a stronger contract. But Farah was in financial trouble as a result of the boycott and a series of management mistakes, and his threat to close the factory was a real one. The strikers, inexperienced at contract negotiations, felt outmaneuvered by a process in which the company set the terms and the union lawyers made most of the decisions.

After the Strike

In spite of their misgivings about the contract, and a pervasive feeling that the situation was no longer under their control, most strikers concluded that the contract was "all right for a first try," and that it was "a beginning." They realized that their fight for better working conditions was by no means over, but at least they now had the protection of a union and a grievance procedure. They were determined that they would no longer be intimidated by supervisors; if they were mistreated they were going to climb off their machines and protest. "I'm going to say something if I have to say it," one striker insisted. "And I'll be nice if they're nice. If they're not very nice I can also be very unnice."

When they returned to work in the spring of 1974, the strikers faced tremendous obstacles. Texas was (and still is) a right-to-work state, so workers were not required to join the union. If enough workers took the benefits with-

out joining the union, the company could move to have the union decertified. This made the task of organizing the unorganized at Farah both very necessary and immensely difficult. It was complicated by the fact that the conclusion of the strike did not dilute Willie Farah's notorious antiunion sentiment. He had recognized the union with great reluctance, and was determined to break it. Finally, there were serious divisions among the workers in the plant. Strikers determined to build a strong union would have to overcome tensions between themselves and the "happies," as well as divisions between Chicanas and Mexicanas which had been created during the strike.

When the strikers returned to the factory, they found that the organization of production had changed dramatically during the two years of the strike. In an attempt to keep up with the changing men's clothing market, Farah was diversifying production to include men's leisure suits and jackets. Workers were placed in new production lines without adequate retraining. Women who had been sewing straight seams for ten years were suddenly expected to set sleeves. One woman said, "They just sat me on the machine and said, 'Try to do this.' That was my training."

Workers who previously had been working with a six-piece pattern for pants were now working with a thirty-piece pattern for jackets. Seamstresses accustomed to sewing cotton fabric suddenly had to adjust to sewing brushed denim, plaids and double-knits-fabrics which were much more difficult to handle. In addition, sewing collars and cuffs of jackets were much more delicate and time-consuming work than most operations involved in the production of pants.

These changes in materials, patterns and techniques were not taken into account when new production quotas were established. Women whose wages had been based on their ability to produce a certain number of pieces at one operation were expected to produce just as many at a new operation. As a result, quotas were often impossibly high. Unable to meet their new quotas within the prescribed time limit, many women suffered wage reductions and eventually were fired for low production. Some ex-strikers believe that by selectively assigning them to the most difficult new operations and establishing outrageous quotas, the company hoped gradually to weed them out of the plant.

At the same time that Farah was changing production, the company plunged into a serious financial disaster. The recession of 1974-1975 hurt the company, and in addition, Willie Farah made major miscalculations in production and marketing.[8] He had always been able to stockpile his most dependable styles and sell them on a stable market year after year. Lightning changes in styles meant that Farah could no longer predict the market. For example, one year he would corner the market in leisure suits, stockpile thousands of leisure suits, and then find that the next year no one was wearing leisure suits. In 1974 Farah decided he wanted to produce his own fabrics, and opened a textile mill in El Paso. The venture was a six million dollar flop.

Farah's financial predicament was exacerbated by marketing problems. In the past, Farah had been known for the high quality of its merchandise. But under severe pressure to meet quotas on new operations, workers were simply unable to concern themselves with perfection. "When you're pushing people they can't get their work out right," one ex-striker commented.

> So they were getting it out as fast as they could, without caring how it was coming out . . . They made all these jackets lopsided and crooked. Who are you going to sell them to once the stores see how they are? They are definitely going to return them. And that is what started happening. They were sending back truckloads of jackets, sportcoats, and pants.

In addition, retailers who disliked Farah's highhanded business practices had gladly removed Farah pants from their shelves during the boycott, and were reluctant to resume dealing with the company again after the strike.

All of these management problems resulted in a 40 percent decline in sales and a $3.5 million loss in the last quarter of 1976. Five thousand of the original 9,000 employees were laid off. Several of the Farah plants were closed, including plants in San Antonio, Victoria, and Las Cruces, New Mexico.

Union Troubles

These financial setbacks hindered the efforts of union activists to continue organizing. First, there was a visible cutback in services provided for the workers by the company. Bus service to and from the plant was curtailed, coffee and donuts no longer were served during breaks, the already inadequate medical care available to workers was cut back, and Thanksgiving turkeys and Christmas parties were no longer provided. Many workers complained that the plants were dirtier and more dust-covered than they had ever been in the past. Since these cutbacks coincided with the end of the strike, many nonunion members blamed the union, not Farah, for the decline in their working conditions.

A more serious consequence of Farah's financial setback was that it required a drastic reduction in the size of the workforce. This need to layoff workers provided Farah with an opportunity to harass and eliminate his most vocal opponents among the union activists. Some were given extremely erratic work schedules. Some days they would be required to work until noon, other days until three o'clock, and frequently they were called to work on Saturdays. They were rarely given much advance notice of their hours. Some ex-strikers were switched to production lines which were scheduled to be phased out. Others were placed on extended layoff and after one year were let go by the company.

Farah's management devised several further strategies which undercut the ability of union activists to organize. One was to isolate union members. At the end of the strike almost all of the strikers were assigned to the large Gateway plant. (By keeping them all in one place the company apparently hoped to prevent strikers from "infecting" other workers in the various plants.) After the strike, one woman recalled,

> We were closer. We didn't let our chain break. They tried to break it. At first they put us all together. And then suddenly they knew that we were so strong, they started separating us. They went to Northeast, and the other ones went to Paisano. So then suddenly you were all separated . . . Then they put "happies" with you. It was hard to make them understand.

While, in the past, an effort had been made to assign women to the plant nearest their homes, after the transfers many workers found themselves working at plants across the city from their residence.

Grievances

It is against this background of changes in production, financial setbacks, the establishment of high quotas, and transfers of workers that many grievances were filed. (During negotiations for the second contract in March 1977, union officials stated that more grievances were filed at Farah than at all other ACWA plants in the United States combined.) When workers had grievances it was up to the shop stewards to investigate the complaint, collect all the necessary information, discuss it with the immediate supervisor, fill out the forms and deliver them to the union office. If a grievance could not be resolved on the shop floor it would be turned over to a business agent.

Most of the shop stewards were inundated with grievances. Some were responsible for lines of a hundred workers, stretched out over a quarter mile. Unlike the supervisors, they did not have roller skates and bicycles at their disposal to traverse the distances within the plant. They had to do all union-related work during lunch hours and breaks. One ex-striker said:

> I'm a very active person and I love to help people. They wouldn't let you talk during work, they wouldn't let you talk about the union or anything. At breaktimes I would go real fast, I would go in the plant and start talking to the people, start going line by line.

Work for the union did not end with the end of the working day at Farah, and most shop stewards spent several hours each day driving to and from the union office. "Some people don't understand the time you put into it," one shop steward complained,

> . . . the time you have to leave your kids to go fight their cases . . . We don't get paid for being shop stew-

ards, we don't get gas money, we still pay our union dues, everything. We get nothing out of it, other than our self-satisfaction that we are helping our people.

In addition to being overworked, shop stewards were systematically harassed. One union activist noticed that every time she went to the bathroom a supervisor followed her, and if she took time to smoke a cigarette, the supervisor would hurry her back to work. Another found that whenever she had problems with her sewing machine and signalled the supervisor, he would consistently ignore her, and it would be hours before the machine was repaired.

The ability of shop stewards to effectively solicit and process grievances was further hindered by their isolation from other union activists and from workers in general. "They have a great big cutting room," one shop steward commented

> And on the corner where all the machines start, that's where I'm at, on the very corner. They kind of keep me isolated from the other people . . . I had one woman tell me-she saw me in the bathroom. She said, "Are you the shop steward here?" I said, "Yeah." And she said, "You know, I'd never seen you before here." I said, "Yes, I've been here, but I've never been on the other side." She said, "Well, they keep telling me there was one [shop steward, but I never saw you."

There is at least one case of a steward being fired for carrying out her duties. In this instance, an ex-striker who had filed a grievance was being harassed by the supervisor. The entire production line had stopped work to watch the argument. The shop steward stepped off her machine and walked down the line to investigate. The supervisor started yelling at her to return to her machine. Outraged that she had climbed down from her machine in the first place, and then refused to go back, he phoned the plant manager who fired her for disobedience. She had witnesses and was rehired after her case went to arbitration.

A final factor which made the shop stewards less effective than they might have been was the continuing apathy of nonunionized workers. The ex-strikers clearly understood that they had to organize to defend their interests, and were continually frustrated by the complacence and lack of support from workers who refused to act on their own behalf.

There were never enough women willing to serve as shop stewards. When shop stewards were laid off, or transferred from one plant to another, there was rarely another worker willing to take their place.

The effectiveness of the grievance procedure depended largely on the resources of the union staff. The business agents, hired by the union, were chosen from among the ex-strikers. Inexperienced and inadequately trained, they were overwhelmed by the volume of grievances. In addition, some ex-strikers charge that the union carefully selected the most passive and malleable strikers to work full-time for the union.

Another union staff member who played a decisive role in implementng the grievance procedure was the union engineer. Because of the changes in production from pants to leisure suits and the introduction of new operations, many of the grievances dealt with allegedly unfair quotas assigned to those operations. Quotas for new operations were initially set by company engineers. If they were to be challenged, a grievance had to be filed within thirty days; then a union engineer would be sent to the plant to determine whether or not the quota set by the company for that operation had been reasonable.

There was only one union engineer for the five Farah plants, and he was responsible for all the other ACWA plants in El Paso as well. Not only was the union engineer overworked and unable to investigate every dispute, but all too often, ex-strikers complained, the union engineer would back up the quotas set by the company.

One union activist, switched to a new production line and given an impossibly high quota, received a pink slip for low production. She called in the union engineer to observe the operation. She could not even produce half of the quota, and another person he observed was also not able to make the quota. Nonetheless, he agreed with the company that the quota was a reasonable one. The repeated occurrence of similar cases led many strikers to conclude that the union engineer could not be counted on as an advocate for the workers.

Many ex-strikers felt victimized by a combination of the company's determination to manipulate and undermine the union and the union's reluctance to actively challenge the company. The union seemed willing to take to arbitration only those cases in which a favorable decision was certain. Only a small percentage of all the grievances filed were taken to arbitration.

Decline of Unidad Para Siempre

Militant union members were left in a particularly vulnerable position. The rank-and-file group, Unidad Para Siempre, pushed for reforms which had not been included in the contract. These reforms included elimination of the quota system, compensation and training for shop stewards, and greater rank-and-file participation in settling grievances between workers and the company. In this way, they hoped to build a stronger and more responsive union. The continued growth of Unidad was hampered by the fact that a large number of its members—the most vocal and militant union activists—were among the first to be laid off by Farah during his cutbacks in production. Unidad members feel that the union did not actively prosecute their cases because, like the company, it felt threatened by their presence. By 1977, few members of Unidad still worked in Farah plants.

Unidad's ability to form a strong organization was further inhibited by fundamental divisions among the workers. There were differences among the ex-strikers and nonstrikers about how much and when to criticize the union. Among the workers at Farah, there were some who still actively opposed the union. They blamed the union for Farah's financial predicament; they blamed the union for the termination of services they had previously enjoyed. They did their best to aggravate union activists in the plant. "Oh, I had so many things done to me," one shop steward remarked.

> They [workers hostile to the union] used to get into my car, put gum on my chair . . . . One time I was setting the cuff. People would come by and knock them all down. They would take all my union papers and leaflets. They'd take them off or throw them on the floor . . . . One time somebody cut all the threads off my machine. Can you imagine?

Other workers were simply indifferent to the union. As far as they were concerned they could take advantage of union benefits without paying dues or suffering the harassment inflicted upon union activists. Some Mexicans feared that they might lose their green cards if they became union activists.

Union members viewed the union in a variety of ways. Some uncritically supported it. In their view the major obstacle to the growth of a strong union was the apathy of the workers who refused to share the responsibility of working to improve conditions. There was another group of union activists who expressed frustration with passive, nonunion workers in the plant, but who attached equal importance to the weaknesses of the union machinery. There was still another group, many of whom belonged to Unidad, who emphasized the extent to which the union had collaborated with the company, and who saw democratizing the union as the major requirement. Finally, there was a small group of ex-strikers who became disillusioned with the union, and simply signed out.

The Second Contract

The continuing layoffs, loss of rank-and-file activists, tensions among workers in the plant, and inadequate support from the international union all combined to weaken the position of the workers during contract negotiations in early 1977.

Negotiations took place with both sides assuming that Farah was in serious financial difficulties. Workers on the negotiating committee spent several days listening to detailed descriptions of Farah's woes, and finally were told, "You can ask for the moon, but if we give it to you we'll fold tomorrow and you'll all be out on the street."

This bleak picture was accepted by union lawyers, who urged the negotiating committee to accept Farah's terms. The union officials clearly were worried about

Farah's financial status, and felt that no further challenges to the company's authority should be mounted. Instead of giving an organized voice to workers' grievances, they tried to devise a strategy which would help the company back to financial health. As one union official put it, "Once Farah was a union plant, it was in the union's interest to sell pants." If selling pants more cheaply meant accepting a serious setback in working conditions, the union officials were willing to pay that price to keep Farah from going under.

The 1977 contract granted the workers a scanty thirty-cent pay raise over a three-year period. It eliminated dental benefits and retained the hated quota system. Most damaging of all, it permitted Farah to lay off experienced workers and call them back to work on a different production line-at the minimum wage. Some members of the negotiating committee reluctantly voted to accept the contract, certain that once it was taken to the workers for ratification it would be rejected.

Many workers now believe that the company exaggerated its problems so that the union would settle for a weak contract. Although it is still uncertain whether Farah Manufacturing Company will recover from its economic crisis, it is already clear that under the terms of the 1977 contract, the workers are paying for Farah's problems.

The contract was hastily presented in a short meeting held in the cafeteria at the Gateway plant. The meeting was called at the end of the working day, and most workers did not know until the last minute that the meeting was to take place. The contract was read in legalistic Spanish which few workers could understand, and questions from the floor were discouraged. When a vote was called, Tony Sánchez (the ACWA Joint Board Manager) requested that those in favor of the contract stand up. Since the room was packed, most people were already standing up. There is a great deal of controversy about what happened at this point. Many who attended the meeting say that a clear majority of workers raised their hands in opposition to the contract. No formal count was made, however, and Tony Sánchez declared that the contract had passed.

Before workers could raise their objections to the terms of the contract and the way in which the vote was conducted, the bell signalling the end of work rang. Workers swarmed out of the Gateway cafeteria, many angrily pulling their union buttons off their shirts and throwing them onto the ground. Lacking experience as well as the presence of a strong rank-and-file organization, the remaining union activists were unable to challenge the proceedings. This created even greater divisions among the workers, as many felt that they had been sold out by union militants.

Since March 1977, Farah has closed another of its El Paso plants. The number of workers at Farah, particularly union members, continues to decline.

Conclusion

Events at Farah since the strike show the continuing difficulty of union organizing in the Southwest. The right-to-work law, the consolidated opposition of powerful employers, the timidity of union officials, and the many incipient tensions in the border area which employers can use to divide the workforce—all of these are formidable obstacles in the way of a strong workers'organization.

The story of the ACWA at Farah also illustrates some of the problems specific to organizing workers in the garment industry. In contrast to relatively monopolized, capital-intensive industries such as auto and steel, the garment industry is highly competitive, volatile, and labor-intensive. In this context of constant business fluctuations, it is possible for a large and established company like Farah to suffer a dramatic decline within a period of several years.

The development of runaway shops during the last decade has made this instability even more pronounced. Increasing workers' organization and the relatively high cost of American labor have prompted labor-intensive industries such as garments and electronics to move south across the border, or to southeastern Asian countries, where labor is cheaper and less organized than in the United States. In border cities such as El Paso, industries have been able to take advantage of the proximity of an abundant supply of documented and undocumented workers from Mexico.

In an attempt to prevent industries from leaving the country, many unions such as the ACWA have adopted the strategy of bailing out the company in times of financial hardships. As recent events at Farah suggest, this may often be done at the expense of the workers. Although this is not a problem whose ultimate solution lies solely within the borders of the United States, current union strategy has not even provided a partial answer. Instead, it has failed to prevent runaway shops and simultaneously has helped to undermine the development of a strong union movement.

It is clear from the Farah experience that a successful unionization effort does not end when the union wins a contract. Organizing and training of workers in everything from a grievance procedure to labor history must continue on a long-term basis. In addition, workers must develop a strong rank-and-file movement-one which can overcome divisions among the workers, build a democratic local union, and encourage women workers to develop leadership skills and an analysis of their working situation.

While the Farah strike did not produce a strong, mature rank-and-file movement, it did help to create the conditions in which one can develop. The workers who made the strike were irreversibly changed by it. All of them say that they would organize and strike again; most of them recognize the need for strong support from an international union like the ACWA, as long as it does not undermine the independent organization of rank-and-file workers. "We're sticking in there and we're not going to get out and we're not giving up!" one ex-striker insisted.

In the words of one striker:

> I believe in fighting for our rights, and for women's rights . . . When I walked out of that company way back then, it was like I had taken a weight off my back. And I began to realize, "Why did I put up with it all these years? Why didn't I try for something else?" Now I want to stay here and help people to help themselves.

The Chicanas who comprise the majority of strikers learned that they could speak and act on their own behalf as women and workers, lessons they will not forget.

Notes

1. El Paso, Texas is located on the western tip of the Texas panhandle, near the point where the boundaries of Texas, New Mexico, and Mexico intersect. In July 1975, the population was estimated by the U.S. Bureau of Census at 414,700 people, of whom 57 percent were "Spanish American." El Paso is directly across the U.S.-Mexico border from Ciudad Juárez, which has an estimated population of 600,000.
2. General Executive Board Report "Farah Boycott: Union Label," to the 1974 Convention, Amalgamated Clothing, Workers of America, p. 1.
3. Allen Pusey, "Clothes Made the Man," *Texas Monthly* (June 1977), p. 135.
4. In June 1976, ACWA merged with the Textile Workers Union of America, and became the Amalgamated Clothing and Textile Workers Union. Since the events in this article occurred before the merger, the union will be referred to as ACWA.
5. "Farah Boycott: Union Label," General Executive Board Report, op. cit.
6. Bishop Sidney Metzger to Bishop of Rochester, October 31, 1972, reprinted in *Viva La Huelga: Farah Strike Bulletin No. 15* (Amalgamated Clothing Workers of America, AFL-CIO).
7. *Moody's Industrial Manual,* 1975, p. 1099.
8. Critics of the union have blamed the strike and boycott for the company's business troubles. However, the boycott never actually destroyed Farah's profit margin. In fact, some analysts argue that the short-term effect of the strike was beneficial because it forced the company to stop overproduction. They note that "during the only full year of the boycott (1973), the company jumped from $8 million in losses to a modest $42,000 profit." Pusey, loc. cit. The losses predate the union and can be traced to management errors on Farah's part.

Section I: Historical Perspectives
Assessment and Application

1. According to González and Fernández, how has the idea of empire-building by the United States—in terms of economic and political interests—created the need for migration?

2. Discusss the "push-pull" thesis with respect to migration. What shortcomings do González and Fernández see in this argument?

3. Under what pretenses were the Mexicans and their descendants in the "New American Southwest" deprived of their lands and possessions after the Treaty of Guadalupe Hidalgo was signed?

4. What are the implications of the Treaty of Guadalupe Hidalgo for Chicanos in the Southwest according to Griswold del Castillo?

5. Describe the concepts of "Aztlán" and "Chicanismo" and their major features.

6. Who were the major leaders of the Chicano Movement of the late 1960s and early 1970s, their geographic area of operation, and their major political accomplishments?

7. Outline the facts leading to the El Paso Salt War in 1877. In your opinion, was it a mob revolt or were the citizens of San Elizario justified in defending the salt flats from 'privatization'?

8. What are your impressions about family life in El Paso as discussed by García? What can these activities teach us about our own family experiences in the 21st century?

9. After reading Vicki Ruiz' chapter, locate and interview Chicanas who received social and educational services from missionary institutions as adolescents. Determine if those experiences contributed to their Americanization.

10. What were the key factors, local and national, that led to the successful unionization of the Farah Garment factories?

Section 1: Suggested Readings

Acosta, Teresa Palomo. (2003). *Las Tejanas 300 Years of History*. Austin, TX: University of Texas Press.

Acuña, Rodolfo. (2004). *Occupied America: A History of Chicanos* (5th ed.). New York, NY: Pearson and Longman.

Barrera, Mario. (1979). *Race and Class in the Southwest*. Notre Dame, IN: University of Notre Dame Press.

Cárdenas, Gilberto. (2004). *La Causa: Civil Rights, Social Justice and the Struggle for Equality in the Midwest*. Houston, TX: Arte Público Press.

Chávez, Ernesto. (2002). *"¡Mi Raza Primero!" (My People First!): Nationalism, Identity, and Insurgency in the Chicano Movement in Los Angeles, 1966–1978*. Berkeley, CA: University of California Press.

Department of Defense. (1990). *Hispanics in America's Defense*. Washington, D.C.: U.S. Government Printing Office.

Driscoll, Barbara A. (1999). *The Tracks North: The Railroad Bracero Program of World War II*. Austin, TX: Center for Mexican-American Studies, University of Texas at Austin.

Durán, Livie Isauro and Russell, Bernard H. (1982). *Introduction to Chicano Studies* (2nd ed.). New York, NY: Macmillan Publishing.

García, Mario T. (1994). *Memories of Chicano History: The Life and Narrative of Bert Corona*. Berkeley, CA: University of California Press.

García, Mario T. (1989). *Mexican Americans: Leadership, Ideology, & Identity, 1930–1960*. New Haven, CT: Yale University Press.

Gonzales, Manuel G. and Gonzales, Cynthia M. (2000). *En Aquel Entonces: Readings in Mexican American History*. Bloomington, IN: Indiana University Press.

Gonzales, Manuel M. (1999). *Mexicanos: A History of Mexicans in the United States*. Bloomington, IN: Indiana University Press.

González, Gilbert G. and Fernández, Raúl A. (2003). *A Century of Chicano History: Empire, Nations, and Migration*. New York, NY: Routledge.

Gonzáles, Gilbert and Fernández, Raúl. (1998). Chicano History: Transcending Cultural Models. In Antonia Darder & Rodolfo Torres, (Eds.). *The Latino Studies Reader: Culture, Economy and Society*. Malden, MA: Blackwell Publishers.

Gonzales, Rodolfo "Corky." (2001). *Message to Aztlán: Selected Writings*. Houston, TX: Arte Público Press.

Gutiérrez, David. (1998). LULAC and the Assimilationist Perspective. In Richard Delgado & Jean Stefancic, (Eds.) *The Latino Condition: A Critical Reader*. New York, NY: New York University Press.

Gutiérrez, José Angel. (1998). *The Making of a Chicano Militant: Lessons from Cristal*. Madison, WI: University of Wisconsin Press.

Gutiérrez, José Angel. (2005). *The Making of a Civil Rights Leader*. Houston, TX: Arte Público Press.

Gutiérrez, José Angel. (2000). *They Called Me "King Tiger": My Struggle for the Land and Our Rights*. Houston, TX: Arte Público Press.

Gutiérrez, José Angel. (2005). *We Won't Back Down: Severita Lara's Rise from Student Leader to Mayor*. Houston, TX: Arte Público Press.

Johnson, Benjamin Heber. (2003). *Revolution in Texas: How a Forgotten Rebellion and its Bloody Suppression Turned Mexicans into Americans*. New Haven, CT: Yale University Press.

Kearney, Milo and Knopp, Anthony. (1995). *Border Cuates: A History of U.S.-Mexican Twin Cities*. Austin, TX: Eakin Press.

Maciel, David R. (1996). *El México Olvidado: La Historia del Pueblo Chicano Vol. I and II*. Cd Juárez, Chih.: Universidad Autónoma de Ciudad Juárez.

Mariscal, George. (Ed.) (1999). *Aztlán and Vietnam: Chicano and Chicana Experiences of the War*. Berkeley, CA: University of California Press.

Mariscal, George. (2005). *Brown–Eyed Children of the Sun: Lessons from the Chicano Movement, 1965–1975*. Albuquerque, NM: University of New Mexico Press.

Martínez, Oscar J. (Ed.). (1996). *The U.S.-Mexico Borderlands: Historical and Contemporary Perspectives*. Wilmington, DE: Scholarly Resources.

McWilliams, Carey. (1990). *North from Mexico: The Spanish-Speaking People of the United States*. New York, NY: Praeger Publishers.

Meier, Matt S. and Rivera, Feliciano. (1972). *The Chicano: A History of Mexican Americans*. New York, NY: Hill & Wang.

Menchaca, Martha. (2001). *Recovering History, Constructing Race: The Indian, Black and White Roots of Mexican Americans*. Austin, TX: University of Texas Press.

Moquin, Wayne and Van Doren, Charles. (1972). *A Documentary History of the Mexican Americans*. New York, NY: Praeger Publishers.

Navarro, Armando. (2004). *Mexicano Political Experience in Occupied Aztlán: Struggles and Change*. Lanham, MD: Altamira Press.

Noriega, Chon A. et al. (Ed.). (2001). *The Chicano Reader: An Anthology of Aztlán, 1970–2000*. Los Angeles, CA: Chicano Studies Research Center Publications.

Oropeza, Lorena and Espinoza, Dionne. (2006). *Enriqueta Vásquez and the Chicano Movement: Writings from El Grito del Norte*. Houston, TX: Arte Público Press.

Pérez, Emma. (1999). *The Decolonial Imaginary: Writing Chicanas into History*. Bloomington, IN: Indiana University Press.

Rendón, Armando. (1971). *Chicano Manifesto: The History and Aspirations of the Second Largest Minority in America*. Berkeley, CA: Ollin & Associates.

Rivas-Rodríguez, Maggie; Torres, Juliana; Dipiero-D'sa, Melissa, and Fitzpatrick, Lindsay. (2006). *A Legacy Greater Than Words: Stories of U.S Latinos & Latinas of the World War II Generation*. Austin, TX: U.S. Latino & Latina WWII Oral History Project.

Rosales, F. Arturo. (2006). *Dictionary of Latino Civil Rights History*. Houston, TX: Arte Público Press.

Rosales, F. Arturo. (1999). *¡Pobre Raza!: Violence, Justice, and Mobilization among México Lindo Immigrants, 1900–1936*. Austin, TX: University of Texas Press.

Ruiz, Vicki L. (1998). *From Out of the Shadows: Mexican Women in Twentieth-Century America*. New York, NY: Oxford University Press.

Sánchez, George J. (1993). *Becoming Mexican American: Ethnicity, Culture, and Identity in Chicano Los Angeles, 1900–1945*. New York, NY: Oxford University Press.

Sepúlveda Jr., Juan A. (2003). *The Life and Times of Willie Velásquez: Su Voto es Su Voz*. Houston, TX: Arte Público Press.

Sheridan, Thomas E. (1986). *Los Tucsonenses: The Mexican Community in Tucson, 1854–1941*. Tucson, AZ: University of Arizona Press.

Vigil, Ernesto B. (1999). *The Crusade for Justice: Chicano Militancy and the Government's War on Dissent*. Madison, WI: University of Wisconsin Press.

Villanueva, Tino. (1980). *Chicanos* (Selección). México, D.F.: Fondo de Cultura Económica.

Section 1: Suggested Films and Videos

The American Experience: Los Mineros
PBS
1320 Braddock Avenue, Alexandria, VA 22314-1698

Adelante Mujeres, 1992
National Women's History Project
Santa Rosa, CA

Border Bandits, 2004
Trans-Pecos Productions
P.O. Box 4124, Dallas, TX 75208

Cesar Chávez: The Hispanic and Latin American
    Heritage
Library Video Company
P.O. Box 580, Wynnewood, PA 19096

Chicano! History of the Mexican American Civil Rights
    Movement (parts 1–4), 1996
NLCC Educational Media

Harvest of Shame, 1960
CBS Productions

Hero Street USA, 1985
Innervision Studies

The Mexican Americans, 2000
New York

One of the Hollywood Ten
Morena Films, Saltire Entertainment, ESICMA
Productions, Bloom Street Productions

La Raza: History and Heritage, 1976
La Raza Series
Moctezuma Productions
McGraw-Hill Broadcasting

Salt of the Earth, 1953
Independent Productions and the International
Union of Mine, Mill & Workers
Oak Forest, IL

Soldados Chicanos in Vietnam, 2003
Chusma House Publications
P.O. Box 467, San Jose, CA 95103

The Buried Mirror, 1991
Sogeted Productions/The Smithsonian Institute
San Antonio, TX

The U.S.-Mexican War
PBS Home Video
1320 Braddock Avenue, Alexandria, VA 22314-1698

Viva La Causa: 500 Years of Chicano History,
    Parts 1 & 2, 1995
Collision Course Video Productions
Southwest Organizing Project
San Francisco, CA/Albuquerque, NM

Zoot Suit Riots
PBS Home Video
1320 Braddock Avenue, Alexandria, VA 22314-1698

Demographics, Society and Culture

ime Magazine initiates this section with a concise yet highly informative portrait of the Hispanic population. It covers with informative graphics a wide range of indicators that can quantitatively guide the reader in this and subsequent sections on the Hispanic presence in various sectors of American society. Rogelio Sáenz, María Cristina Morales and Janie Filoteo expand on the aforementioned portrait with a historical demographic examination of the Mexican origin population. This chapter includes a breakdown by state, family composition, nativity, etc. that will also help explain the content of future chapters.

Marta Tienda *et al* showcase four major realms of social integration by Hispanics in American society: Family, education, work, and health. Of the utmost importance is the structure of the family and concepts like "familismo" that inform the group's participation in the labor force, the educational arena and other societal domains. This chapter is the result of a Project by the National Research Council's Panel on Hispanics in the United States. The chapter is followed by examinations of those social and/or regional spheres.

Pablo Vila and John Peterson reveal the environmental problems and challenges faced by the binational metroplex formed by El Paso, Texas and Ciudad Juárez, Chihuahua, and the implications for transnational policy formulation. David Hayes-Bautista presents the state of Latino health, in comparison to other ethnic groups, and the research agenda required to understand and address the needs of the Latino population. He emphasizes the need to develop and employ Latino metrics that disaggregate the various Latino sub-groups to better measure their individual status. Certainly the connection between environmental justice and health issues can be better understood by consulting the recommended readings and documentaries that support this section.

Arturo González presents an overview of the Mexican origin population in the labor market. Ultimately, the Chicano rate and level of participation in the labor market determines their socioeconomic status. It is critical to determine how Chicanos interface across generations in key societal dimensions like education, home ownership, health, gender, etc. Miriam Ching Yoon Louie delves into the role of Mexican immigrant women's participation in the labor force, in the transnational context of the U.S.-Mexico border. She explores in an ethnographic manner the struggles and complexities of factory employment in the midst of "NAFTA the SHAFTA," job outsourcing, and inadequate government support for displaced workers, some of whom actually started their odyssey in "maquiladoras" in Mexico. Pierrette Hondagneu-Sotelo closes out this chapter and the section with a probe into the complex dynamics of immigrant Latina domestic employment. She reveals the challenges of a subordinate and invisible population that is an important dimension of the immigration debate.

Inside America's Largest Minority

Origins and Immigration

Today Hispanics are 14% of the U.S. population. About half were born outside the U.S., but most want to blend into American society.

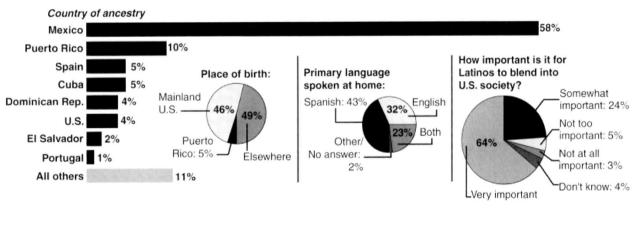

Country of ancestry

Mexico	58%
Puerto Rico	10%
Spain	5%
Cuba	5%
Dominican Rep.	4%
U.S.	4%
El Salvador	2%
Portugal	1%
All others	11%

Place of birth:
Mainland U.S. 46%
49% Elsewhere
Puerto Rico: 5%

Primary language spoken at home:
Spanish: 43%
English 32%
23% Both
Other/No answer: 2%

How important is it for Latinos to blend into U.S. society?
Somewhat important: 24%
Not too important: 5%
Not at all important: 3%
Don't know: 4%
64%
Very important

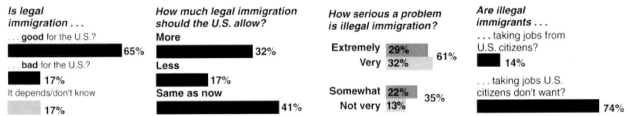

Is legal immigration...
...**good** for the U.S.? 65%
...**bad** for the U.S.? 17%
It depends/don't know 17%

How much legal immigration should the U.S. allow?
More 32%
Less 17%
Same as now 41%

How serious a problem is illegal immigration?
Extremely 29% / Very 32% = 61%
Somewhat 22% / Not very 13% = 35%

Are illegal immigrants...
...taking jobs from U.S. citizens? 14%
...taking jobs U.S. citizens don't want? 74%

By the Numbers

The U.S. Hispanic population has increased **17%** in the past four years, to **41.3 million**. Hispanics are projected to account for **46%** of all U.S. population growth over the next 20 years. Although only **62%** of all U.S. Hispanic adults have finished high school, **84%** of U.S.-born Hispanics graduate. The median net worth of Hispanic households is **$7,932**, less than one-tenth the figure for non-Hispanic whites, $88,651. There were **1.6 million** Hispanic-owned firms in the U.S. in 2002, a **30%** increase since 1997. U.S. Hispanic workers sent an estimated **$30 billion** home to Latin American countries in 2003.

Politics and Issues

Hispanics tend to be Democrats, but President Bush grabbed a significant share of their votes in 2004. Education and jobs are top concerns.

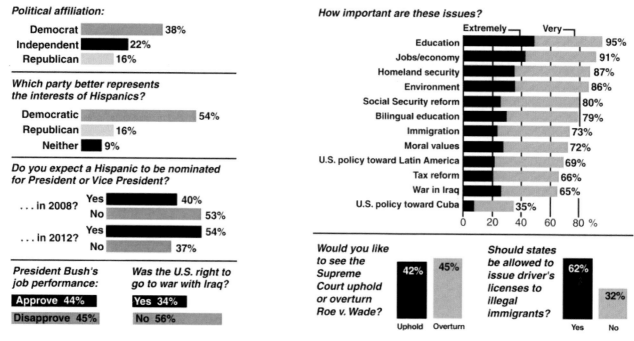

Political affiliation:

Democrat	38%
Independent	22%
Republican	16%

Which party better represents the interests of Hispanics?

Democratic	54%
Republican	16%
Neither	9%

Do you expect a Hispanic to be nominated for President or Vice President?

... in 2008?
| Yes | 40% |
| No | 53% |

... in 2012?
| Yes | 54% |
| No | 37% |

President Bush's job performance:

Approve 44%
Disapprove 45%

Was the U.S. right to go to war with Iraq?

Yes 34%
No 56%

How important are these issues?

Extremely — Very —

Education	95%
Jobs/economy	91%
Homeland security	87%
Environment	86%
Social Security reform	80%
Bilingual education	79%
Immigration	73%
Moral values	72%
U.S. policy toward Latin America	69%
Tax reform	66%
War in Iraq	65%
U.S. policy toward Cuba	35%

0 20 40 60 80 %

Would you like to see the Supreme Court uphold or overturn Roe v. Wade?

42% Uphold
45% Overturn

Should states be allowed to issue driver's licenses to illegal immigrants?

62% Yes
32% No

This TIME poll was conducted by telephone July 28–Aug. 3 among 503 Latino adults throughout the U.S. by SRBI Public Affairs. Interviews were conducted in both English (60%) and Spanish (40%). Margin of error for the entire sample: approximately ± 5 percentage points. "Don't know" omitted for some questions. Sources for "By the Numbers" statistics: Census Bureau, Pew Hispanic Center

The Demography of Mexicans
in the United States

Rogelio Sáenz, María Cristina Morales, and Janie Filoteo

The Mexican-origin population is one of the most dynamic ethnic groups in the United States.[1] During the twentieth century it grew more rapidly than any other group. While the country's total population tripled from 92 million in 1910 to 281.4 million in 2000, the Mexican population expanded from 367,500 to 20.6 million in the same time span. Over the past decade, the Mexican population increased four times faster (52.9 percent) than the overall U.S. total population (13.2 percent). Few other ethnic groups in the nation can match this contemporary growth pattern. Today, Mexicans—the largest segment of the Latino population—represent the second largest specific minority group in the nation, trailing only African Americans.

Mexican population growth has been caused by three factors: (1) Mexicans tend to be relatively young compared to other groups in the nation, (2) Mexicans traditionally have higher fertility rates, and (3) the Mexican population has been supplemented by large flows of immigrants, both legal and illegal, especially since the 1960s. Population estimates by the U.S. Census Bureau (2000a,b) suggest that immigrants accounted for nearly two-thirds (65.2 percent) of the growth of the overall Latino population between 1990 and 1999. These three demographic factors supply the potential for further growth in the Mexican population over the coming decades.

Historically, the Mexican population has been disproportionately located in the Southwest region. Approximately three-fourths of the country's Mexicans were found in the Southwest in 2000, down from more than four-fifths in 1990. Clearly a significant shift away from the Southwest took place in the 1990s. Unfortunately, much of our knowledge of the Mexican population has been based almost solely on the Southwest.

This chapter seeks to provide an in-depth overview of the demographic attributes of the Mexican population in the United States overall and in five regions of the country. Before undertaking the analysis, however, we will establish a historical demographic perspective.

Historical Demographic Context

The Mexican-origin ethnic group has a long history in this country. Its ancestors explored and established settlements in parts of the Southwest long before European immigrants landed in Plymouth Rock (Saenz 1999). The incorporation of Mexicans into the United States came about through conflict between the United States and Mexico—first with the annexation of Texas in 1845 after the independence of Texas from Mexico, and later with the signing of the Treaty of Guadalupe Hidalgo in 1848 at the conclusion of the Mexican-American War. The Mexican-origin population has grown significantly since the initial cohort of Mexicans who became U.S. citizens during this period. Unfortunately, there is a dearth of historical demographic statistics enumerating the Mexican-origin population, with specific data for Mexicans completely lacking or plagued by inconsistent definitions. For example, the definition of persons of Mexican origin has varied over time from Mexicans being treated as a racial category, to the presence of a Spanish surname, to the use of the Spanish language. Fortunately, since the 1980 census, people have been allowed to identify themselves as Hispanic-origin and the specific Hispanic subgroup to which they belong.

While historical information on the population size of Mexicans in the United States is lacking, much of the growth has been due to immigration. According to the U.S. Immigration and Naturalization Service (2000), slightly more than 5.8 million Mexicans immigrated to the United States legally between 1820 and 1998 (table 1), making Mexico the second largest sender of immigrants during the period behind Germany (nearly 7.2 million immigrants). This figure, however, does not include the large

Table 1. Number of Mexican Legal Immigrants Entering the United States, 1820–1998

Period	Number Mexican Immigrants	% of Total Mexican Immigrants Over 1820–1998	Cum.% Immigrants 1820–1998
1820	1	0.00	0.00
1821–1830	4,817	0.08	0.08
1831–1840	6,599	0.11	0.20
1841–1850	3,271	0.06	0.25
1851–1860	3,078	0.05	0.31
1861–1870	2,191	0.04	0.34
1871–1880	5,162	0.09	0.43
1881–1890	1,913	0.03	0.46
1891–1900	971	0.02	0.48
1901–1910	49,642	0.85	1.33
1911–1920	219,004	3.76	5.10
1921–1930	459,287	7.89	12.99
1931–1940	22,319	0.38	13.37
1941–1950	60,589	1.04	14.41
1951–1960	299,811	5.15	19.56
1961–1970	453,937	7.80	27.36
1971–1980	640,294	11.00	38.37
1981–1990	1,655,843	28.45	66.82
1991–1998	1,931,237	33.18	100.00
Total	5,819,966	100.00	100.00

Source: U.S. Immigration and Naturalization Service, 2000.
Note: The data are based on country of last residence rather than country of birth.

number of Mexicans who arrived as undocumented immigrants. Yet Mexican immigration to the United States is a twentieth-century phenomenon. Of the slightly more than 5.8 million Mexicans who immigrated to the United States legally from 1820 to 1998, only 0.5 percent (or about 28,000) immigrated between 1820 and 1900. The first major wave of Mexican immigration to the United States occurred in the 1910s and 1920s when many Mexicans fled the Mexican Revolution. Mexican immigrants coming legally at this time accounted for approximately one-eighth (11.7 percent or about 678,000) of all legal Mexican immigrants between 1820 and 1998. The flow of immigrants coming to this country during the period, however, continued to be dominated by Europeans.

The ethnic composition of U.S. immigration has changed dramatically since the 1960s. From 1961 to 1998, Mexico has been the major sender of immigrants to the United States, with nearly 4.7 million Mexicans (or 80 percent of all Mexicans who have entered legally between 1820 and 1998) immigrating legally to the United States during the period. The heavy immigrant flow was due in part to the Immigration Act of 1965 and its emphasis on family reunification. Furthermore, the Immigration Reform and Control Act (IRCA) of 1986 allowed many Mexican undocumented immigrants to legalize their status (Bean, Edmonston, and Passel 1990; U.S. Immigration and Naturalization Service 1992). Mexicans accounted for approximately three-fourths of the three million persons who gained legal status through IRCA (Chavez 1996). Between 1991 and 1998, slightly more than 1.9 million Mexican immigrants entered the country legally, accounting for one-

third of all Mexican legal immigrants between 1820 and 1998. Moreover, the March 2000 Current Population Survey (U.S. Census Bureau 2001a) indicated that Mexicans made up 28 percent of the foreign-born population living in the United States in 2000, the highest level since the 30 percent mark of Germans in 1830.

This historical demographic perspective illustrates the unique position of the Mexican-origin population. This population is one that has a long, well-established presence in this country, but it also accounts for the majority of recent immigrants (Saenz 1999). This combination of newcomers and old-timers is largely responsible for the diverse nature of the Mexican population. The Mexican-origin population includes people who trace their roots in this country back to the late 1840s as well as those who have recently crossed the border into the United States.

Analysis Plan and Data Sources

The following analyses provide a general overview of the demography of the Mexican population in the United States. First, we examine the population and geographic distribution patterns among Mexicans for the 1990–2000 period. Data for this part of the analysis come from the 1990 and 2000 censuses and are obtained directly from the Inter-University Program for Latino Research (2001, 2002). The analysis is conducted at the national, regional, state, and place levels. Second, we use data from the American Community Supplementary Survey 2000 Public Use Microdata Sample (PUMS) (U.S. Census Bureau 2002) and from the March 2000 Current Population Survey (CPS)

(U.S. Census Bureau 2001a,b) to develop a profile for Mexicans with respect to demographic attributes (e.g., metropolitan residence, nativity, age/sex distribution, and marriage/family characteristics).

The data for the Mexican-origin population are based on individuals who defined themselves as "Hispanic/ Latino" and more specifically as "Mexican." For comparative purposes, we present data for the U.S. total population to assess the similarities and differences between the demographic patterns of Mexicans and the overall national population.

The analysis will present data for the Mexican population at the national and regional levels. Although the U.S. Census Bureau categorizes the U.S. states and the District of Columbia into four regions (Midwest, South, West, and Northeast), we make some alterations to develop an additional region, the Southwest, to account for the concentration of Mexicans in the five states (Arizona, California, Colorado, New Mexico, and Texas) that compose this region. The reader should keep in mind that the West region as used here does not include Arizona, California, Colorado, and New Mexico, while the South region does not contain Texas.[2]

The Demography of the Mexican-Origin Population

In this section, we provide an overview of the population and geographic distribution patterns of Mexicans as well as a demographic profile of Mexicans in the coun-try and in the five regions. We begin the analysis with an analysis of the population and geographic distribution patterns of the Mexican population.

Population and Geographic Distribution Patterns

According to the 2000 Census, there were approximately 20.6 million Mexicans in the United States in 2000 (table 2). Thus, in absolute numbers the Mexican population increased by 7.1 million between 1990 and 2000, with about 58 percent (or 4.1 million) of this growth centered in the Southwest region. During the same period, the entire U.S. population increased almost 32.7 million. This suggests that although Mexicans accounted for only 7.3 percent of the nation's population in 2000, they accounted for 21.8 percent of the 32.7 million inhabitants added to the U.S. population through natural increase and immigration between 1990 and 2000.

The growth in the Mexican population during the 1990s can be further illustrated by examining the relative growth during the decade (figure 1). Overall, the Mexican population increased at a rate (52.9 percent) that was four times faster than that of the U.S. total population (13.2 percent) between 1990 and 2000. The rapid growth of the Mexican population relative to the total population is also apparent across the different regions. The Mexican population grew the most rapidly in the South (226.1 percent), where the number of Mexicans more than tripled, the Northeast (173.8), the West (132.6 percent), and the

Table 2. Population Characteristics for Mexican and U.S. Population by Region, 1980–2000

Region	Mexican		U.S. Total	
	1990	2000	1990	2000
Population Size				
Southwest	11,237,325	15,374,276	55,221,222	65,974,407
Midwest	1,153,296	2,200,196	59,668,632	64,392,776
West	477,618	1,110,952	14,551,370	18,075,345
South	452,703	1,476,118	68,459,420	79,385,000
Northeast	174,996	479,169	50,809,229	53,594,378
Total	**13,495,938**	**20,640,711**	**248,709,873**	**281,421,906**
% Distribution				
Southwest	83.3	74.5	22.2	23.4
Midwest	8.5	10.7	24.0	22.9
West	3.5	5.4	5.9	6.4
South	3.4	7.2	27.5	28.2
Northeast	1.3	2.3	20.4	19.0
Total	**100.0**	**100.0**	**100.0**	**100.0**
% Region's Population				
Southwest	20.3	23.3	—	—
Midwest	1.9	3.4	—	—
West	3.3	6.1	—	—
South	0.7	1.9	—	—
Northeast	0.3	0.9		

Source: Inter-University Program for Latino Research (2001).

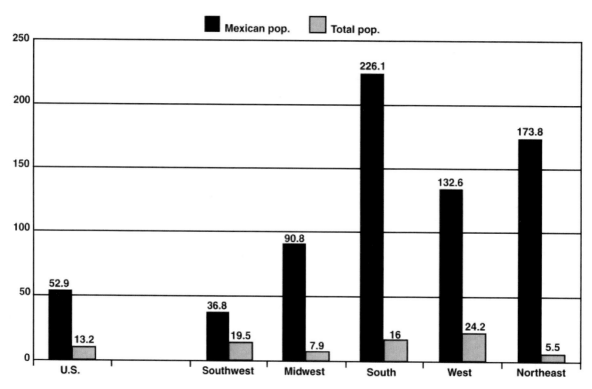

Figure 1. Percentage Change in the Mexican and Total Population for the U.S. and Regions, 1990–2000

Midwest (90.8 percent) during the decade. In contrast, the Mexican population grew the most slowly in the Southwest (36.8 percent), although the growth was much more rapid than the region's overall population growth (19.5 percent).

The Mexican population continues to be predominately located in the Southwest region, with 74.5 percent of all Mexicans making their home in the region in 2000 (table 2). Close to 11 percent live in the Midwest, slightly more than 7 percent live in the South, and more than 5 percent live in the West. Relatively few (2.3 percent) Mexicans live in the Northeast. Proportionately speaking, Mexicans are over three times more likely to be located in the Southwest compared to the total population. However, it is clear that the geographic distribution of the Mexican population shifted significantly during the 1990s. Indeed, the Southwest region's share of the Mexican population in the nation dropped from 83.3 percent in 1990 to 74.5 percent in 2000, while the share of each of the other regions rose. Remarkably, in the South the regional share of Mexicans doubled from 3.4 percent in 1990 to 7.2 percent in 2000.

Nonetheless, the Mexican-origin population composes a significant portion (23.3 percent) of the total population of the Southwest (see table 2). The Mexican population makes up a relatively small share of the populations of the other four regions, with Mexicans having the highest proportional representation (about one of every 16 residents) in the West and the lowest (about one of every 100 residents) in the Northeast.

Population Patterns at the State Level

The number of Mexicans at the state level varies greatly from a low of 1,174 in Vermont to nearly 8.5 million in California (table 3). The top ten most populous states with respect to Mexicans include California (8,455,926), Texas (5,071,963), Illinois (1,144,390), Arizona (1,065,578), Colorado (450,760), Florida (363,925), New Mexico (330,049), Washington (329,934), Nevada (285,764), and Georgia (275,288). Together, these ten states contain 86 percent (or nearly 17.8 million) of the nation's Mexican-origin population. However, California and Texas together contained nearly two-thirds (65.5 percent) of Mexicans in the nation.

In a relative sense, Mexicans accounted for one-fourth of the populations of California and Texas and one-fifth of the inhabitants of Arizona. They made up at least one-tenth of the populations of three other states: New Mexico (18.1 percent), Nevada (14.3 percent), and Colorado (10.5 percent). In sixteen states located in the Northeast, South, and Midwest, Mexicans accounted for less than 1 percent of the population.

States varied greatly, however, in the absolute and relative growth in the Mexican-origin population between 1990 and 2000. In absolute terms, California and Texas together accounted for one of every two of the additional 7.1 million Mexicans added to the national population between 1990 and 2000. However, states outside of the Southwest tended to grow more rapidly in a relative sense. Twenty-eight states saw their Mexican populations more than double between 1990 and 2000, none located in the

Table 3. Total and Mexican Population by State, 2000

State	Total Pop.	Mexican Pop.	State	Total Pop.	Mexican Pop.
Alabama	4,447,100	44,522	Montana	902,195	11,735
Alaska	626,932	13,334	Nebraska	1,711,263	71,030
Arizona	5,130,632	1,065,578	Nevada	1,998,257	285,764
Arkansas	2,673,400	61,204	New Hampshire	1,235,786	4,590
California	33,871,648	8,455,926	New Jersey	8,414,350	102,929
Colorado	4,301,261	450,760	New Mexico	1,819,046	330,049
Connecticut	3,405,565	23,484	New York	18,976,457	260,889
Delaware	783,600	12,986	North Carolina	8,049,313	246,545
Dist. of Col.	572,059	5,098	North Dakota	642,200	4,295
Florida	15,982,378	363,925	Ohio	11,353,140	90,663
Georgia	8,186,453	275,288	Oklahoma	3,450,654	132,813
Hawaii	1,211,537	19,820	Oregon	3,421,399	214,662
Idaho	1,293,953	79,324	Pennsylvania	12,281,054	55,178
Illinois	12,419,293	1,144,390	Rhode Island	1,048,319	5,881
Indiana	6,080,485	153,042	South Carolina	4,012,012	52,871
Iowa	2,926,324	61,154	South Dakota	754,844	6,364
Kansas	2,688,418	148,270	Tennessee	5,689,283	77,372
Kentucky	4,041,769	31,385	Texas	20,851,820	5,071,963
Louisiana	4,468,976	32,267	Utah	2,233,169	136,416
Maine	1,274,923	2,756	Vermont	608,827	1,174
Maryland	5,296,486	39,900	Virginia	7,078,515	73,979
Massachusetts	6,349,097	22,288	Washington	5,894,121	329,934
Michigan	9,938,444	220,769	West Virginia	1,808,344	4,347
Minnesota	4,919,479	95,613	Wisconsin	5,363,675	126,719
Mississippi	2,844,658	21,616	Wyoming	493,782	19,963
Missouri	5,595,211	77,887			

Source: Inter-University Program for Latino Research (2001).

Southwest. In North Carolina the Mexican population increased more than sevenfold from 32,670 in 1990 to 246,545 in 2000, and in Georgia it increased by a factor of 5.5 from 49,182 in 1990 to 275,288 in 2000. Five other states saw their Mexican populations more than quadruple during the period: Tennessee (457.5 percent increase from 13,879 to 77,372), Arkansas (389.8 percent increase from 12,496 to 61,204), South Carolina (379.4 percent increase from 11,028 to 52,871), Alabama (368.2 percent increase from 9,509 to 44,522), and Delaware (321.2 percent increase from 3,083 to 12,986). Much of this growth in the South and Midwest was due to their recruitment into beef, pork, and poultry processing jobs (Gouveia and Saenz 2000; Stull, Broadway, and Griffith 1995).

Population Patterns at the Place Level

The large presence of Mexicans in the Southwest, however, can also be illustrated at the place level. The left-hand part of table 4 contains a list of the twenty places with the largest Mexican-origin populations in 2000, with all but two (Chicago and New York) located in the Southwest and fifteen of the twenty located in California and Texas. The ten places with the largest number of Mexicans include Los Angeles, CA (1,091,686), Chicago, IL (530,462), Houston, TX (527,442), San Antonio, TX (473,420), Phoenix, AZ (375,096), El Paso, TX (359,699), Dallas, TX (350,491), San Diego, CA (259,219), Santa Ana, CA (222,719), and San Jose, CA (221,148). It should

be noted that the populations of these places are for the city itself and do not include the population of surrounding communities that compose the metropolitan statistical area (MSA). Thus, the populations of the MSAs would be larger than those of the individual places.

There are numerous places, especially in the Southwest, where Mexicans represent the numerical majority population. Mexicans make up at least half of the populations of 308 of the 1,661 cities, census designated places (CDPs), towns, and villages across the United States that contained at least one person of Mexican origin in 2000. Of these 308 geographic places, the greatest number are in Texas (129) and California (127), with the remainder located in Arizona (20), Washington (13), New Mexico (8), Florida (5), Illinois (2), Colorado (1), Georgia (1), Nevada (1), and Oregon (1).

The right-hand part of table 4 contains the top twenty places having the highest levels of Mexican proportional representation. Note that the list excludes CDPs, towns, and villages due to their relatively small population sizes, with the one exception being East Los Angeles (a large CDP), which is included in the list. Mexicans compose at least 82.7 percent of the populations of these places, located in Texas (11), California (6), Arizona (2), and New Mexico (1). However, the top-twenty list is dominated by places located in the Lower Rio Grande Valley of Texas, the southernmost part of Texas, with eight of the twenty located in this region. The top ten places where Mexicans

Table 4. Top Twenty Places in the United States with the Largest Absolute and Relative Mexican Populations, 2000

Rank	City	Mexican Population	City	% Mexican
1	Los Angeles, CA	1,091,686	Progresso, TX	93.6
2	Chicago, IL	530,462	Presidio, TX	89.9
3	Houston, TX	527,442	Alton, TX	89.6
4	San Antonio, TX	473,420	Hidalgo, TX	89.4 (4)
5	Phoenix, AZ	375,096	Cactus, TX	89.4 (4)
6	El Paso, TX	359,699	Penitas, TX	89.4 (4)
7	Dallas, TX	350,491	Palmview, TX	89.2
8	San Diego, CA	259,219	Roma, TX	88.8
9	Santa Ana, CA	222,719	Calexico, CA	87.7
10	San Jose, CA	221,148	Somerton, AZ	87.4
11	New York, NY	186,872	Coachella, CA	87.2
12	Austin, TX	153,868	Huron, CA	86.9
13	Tucson, AZ	145,234	Parlier, CA	86.4
14	Fresno, CA	144,772	San Juan, TX	84.5
15	Laredo, TX	133,185	La Joya, TX	83.9
16	Fort Worth, TX	132,894	East Los Angeles, CA	83.9
17	Long Beach, CA	127,129	San Joaquin, CA	83.2
18	Anaheim, CA	126,017	San Luis, AZ	83.0
19	Denver, CO	120,664	Sunland Park, NM	82.7 (19)
20	East Los Angeles, CA	104,223	Palmhurst, TX	82.7 (19)

Source: Inter-University Program for Latino Research (2002).

account for the highest proportion of the population include Progreso, TX (93.6 percent), Presidio, TX (89.9 percent), Alton, TX (89.6 percent), Hidalgo, TX (89.4 percent), Cactus, TX (89.4 percent), Penitas, TX (89.4 percent), Palmview, TX (89.2 percent), Roma, TX (88.8 percent), Calexico, CA (87.7 percent), and Somerton, AZ (87.4 percent).

Demographic Characteristics of Mexicans Across Regions

This section analyzes the demographic characteristics of the Mexican population with respect to metropolitan residence, nativity, age/sex distribution, and marriage/family characteristics. This part of the analysis is based on data from the American Community Supplementary Survey 2000 Public Use Microdata Sample (PUMS) and the March 2000 Current Population Survey (CPS). It introduces data for Mexicans living in the United States overall and the five regions, as well as reference data for the U.S. total population.

Metropolitan Residence

The Mexican population tends to be overwhelmingly located in metropolitan areas. Overall, approximately 90 percent of Mexicans make their homes in metropolitan areas, compared to about 81 percent of the nation's entire population (table 5). Mexicans tend to be concentrated in the central cities while the total population is more likely to reside in suburbs. Across the regions, Mexicans have the highest degree of metropolitan residence in the Northeast (98.2 percent) and Southwest (91.2 percent). In contrast, slightly over one-fourth of Mexicans in the West and

roughly one-seventh of those in the South and Midwest are located in nonmetropolitan areas.

Nativity

As noted earlier, immigrants represent a major portion of the Mexican-origin population. Overall, foreign-born persons make up two-fifths (40.7 percent) of the Mexican population in the country (table 5), compared to only one-ninth (11.1 percent) of the overall U.S. population. Foreign-born persons are the most represented in the South (57.7 percent) and Northeast (57.4 percent), where they compose nearly three-fifths of the Mexican populations of each of these regions. By way of contrast, less than two-fifths (38.2 percent) of Mexicans in the Southwest are foreign-born.

Age/Sex Distribution

Given the unique demographic patterns of Mexicans, the age/sex structure of the Mexican population differs noticeably from that of the national population. The Mexican population is quite young. About one of every three (31.9 percent) Mexicans in the United States was under fifteen years of age in 2000 (table 5). In contrast, this age-group made up only slightly more than one of every five (21.9 percent) in the overall U.S. population. On the other hand, elderly persons sixty-five years and older accounted for only one of every twenty-five (4 percent) persons in the Mexican population, while seniors constituted about one of every eight (12.1 percent) in the overall U.S. population. Within the Mexican population, persons less than fifteen years of age accounted for approximately one-third of the populations of the West (32.9 percent), Southwest (32.2 percent), and Midwest (32.2 percent), while the elderly were most well represented in the Southwest (4.5 percent).

The age composition of the Mexican-origin population can be illustrated graphically with an age/sex pyramid, a bar graph containing bars for successive age-groups from the youngest at the base to the oldest at the top, with males represented on the left side of the graph and females on the right side. The width of each bar denotes the size of a given age/sex group relative to the total population according to the percentage scale on the horizontal axis.

The age/sex pyramid for the Mexican population in the nation and the U.S. total population in 2000 appear in figures 2a and 2b. The shape of the two pyramids differs significantly, reflecting major differences in the age/sex structure of the two populations. The youthfulness of the Mexican population is evident by the wide bars at the base. For example, males and females less than five years of age together account for 11 percent of the entire Mexican population (compared to 7 percent in the case of the U.S. total population). The immigration influence is evident in the wide bars associated with the 20–24 and 25–29 age-groups for Mexicans. Males in these age-groups represent a significantly larger proportion of the entire population (11.2 percent) than do their female counterparts (9.2 percent), with the respective percentages being smaller even among the U.S. total population (males, 6.5

percent; females, 6.6 percent). The pointed top of the Mexican pyramid reflects the relative scarcity of the elderly in this population, while the comparatively wider top in the U.S. total population shows the older structure of the overall national population.

Sex distribution data reveal that males outnumber females within the Mexican population. Demographers use the sex ratio (number of males per 100 females) to assess the sex distribution of given populations. The overall sex ratio for the Mexican population is 109.8, a figure that is quite different from that of the U.S. total population (95.4), where females outnumber males (table 5). This discrepancy is due to the young age structure and large prevalence of immigrants among the Mexican population. Males outnumber females within the Mexican population to the greatest extent in three regions that have sex ratios of at least 125: South (132.1), Northeast (126.5), and Midwest (125.0).

Marriage/Family Characteristics

The marriage and family characteristics of Mexicans also tend to differ from those of the general population. Overall, one-fifth of Mexican families had female householders without a husband present (table 5), whereas such families formed a somewhat lower percentage (18.4 percent) of families among the U.S. total population. This

Table 5. General Demographic Characteristics of Mexicans by Region, 2000

Selected Characteristics	Total	Southwest	Midwest	West	South	Northeast
Metro residence:						
% in Metro areas	89.8	91.2	86.5	74.1	85.2	98.2
Nativity:						
% Foreign-born	40.7	38.2	44.1	41.3	57.7	57.4
Age/sex:						
% Less than 15	31.9	32.2	32.2	32.9	28.7	30.1
% 65 and older	4.0	4.5	2.8	2.2	2.1	2.4
Sex ratio	109.8	105.5	125.0	113.4	132.1	126.5
Marriage/family:						
% Fam. HHs with Fem. householder, No husband present	20.0	21.5	12.6	15.6	15.9	18.6
% 25–44 Age-group Currently married:						
Males	65.2	65.6	64.0	68.4	57.7	74.0
Females	66.7	65.8	71.2	73.2	66.4	68.7
% Females 15–49 Having baby within the last year	10.0	9.7	10.6	7.2	14.7	10.6

Sources: The metro residence data are obtained from the 2000 Current Population Survey March 2000 Supplement (U.S. Census Bureau 2001) and the remaining data are obtained from the American Community Survey Supplementary Survey 2000 Public Use Microdata Sample (PUMS) (U.S. Census Bureau 2002).
Note: The metro residence data are based on persons sixteen years of age and older.

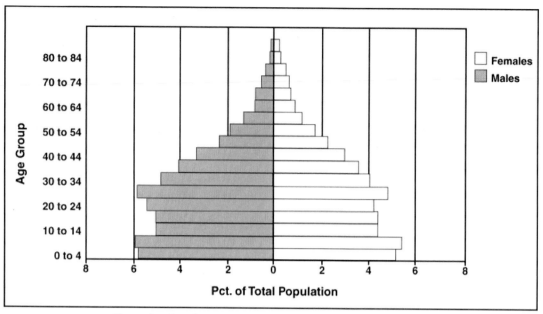

Figure 2a. Age-Sex Pyramid for the Mexican Population, 2000

type of family is the most prevalent among Mexicans in the Southwest (21.5 percent) and the least prevalent in the Midwest (12.6 percent).

We also use data to assess the prevalence of marriage among Mexicans 25–44 years of age. Two-thirds of Mexican men and women in this age-group are currently married, compared to about three-fifths of their peers in the U.S. total population (table 5). The subgroups within the Mexican population that are the most likely to be currently married include men in the Northeast (74.0 percent)

and women in the West (73.2 percent) and Midwest (71.2 percent). In contrast, less than three-fifths of Mexican men in the South (57.7 percent) are currently married.

Other data indicate the extent to which Mexican women of childbearing age (15–49) gave birth within one year of the 2000 census. Overall, one-tenth of Mexican women in the 15–44 age category had a baby in the previous year, compared to a lower percentage (5.9 percent) among women in the overall national population (table 5). Within the Mexican population, the level of fertility

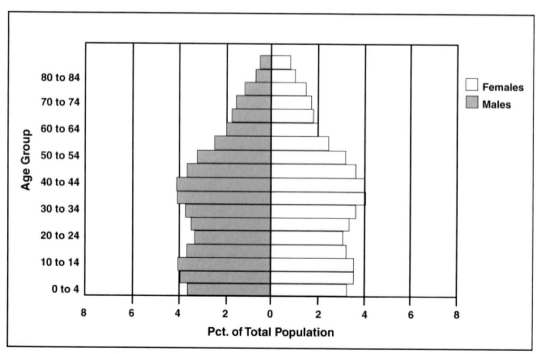

Figure 2b. Age-Sex Pyramid for the Total U.S. Population, 2000

within the last year ranged from a low of 7.2 percent among Mexican women in the South to a high of 14.7 percent among those in the West.

Conclusion

This chapter has presented an overview of the demography of the Mexican-origin population in the United States. The Mexican population has grown tremendously during the twentieth century and continues to grow at a rapid rate, outpacing the growth of most other ethnic groups in the country. While Mexicans accounted for only 7.3 percent of the nation's population, they were responsible for nearly 22 percent of the 32.7 million people added to the overall U.S. population through natural increase and immigration between 1990 and 2000.

The large-scale growth of the Mexican population is likely to continue through the twenty-first century due to the group's young age structure, high fertility rates, and continued immigration from Mexico. Under this realistic scenario, the Mexican population is likely to continue to account for major portions of the future growth of the national population. In addition, the group's relative share of the U.S. population is likely to rise as well. People in both the public and private sectors will have to pay increasing attention to the Mexican population because of its tremendous growth and related impact on different societal institutions. We call on policymakers in particular to devote more attention to the plight of Mexicans in such areas as education, training, and employment. The combination of a young age structure along with a low level of education requires immediate attention to address the problems that members of this group encounter. Failure to deal with the problems of this population today could potentially result in massive social and economic problems in the future, with Mexicans ill prepared to compete effectively in an increasingly technological workforce.

Undoubtedly the most important trend arising in the 1990s has been the shifting geographic distribution of the Mexican population. While it is still true that Mexicans continue to be clustered in the Southwest, this region experienced a drop in its share of the national Mexican population from 83.3 percent in 1990 to 74.5 percent in 2000. All other regions increased their share of the Mexican population. The Mexican population is increasingly fanning out to points beyond the Southwest. Between 1990 and 2000, the Mexican population more than tripled in the South, nearly tripled in the Northeast, more than doubled in the West, and nearly doubled in the Midwest. This suggests that other regions of the country, aside from the Southwest, are likely to experience varying patterns of population change associated with the growth of the Mexican-origin population. Mexicans in the five regions vary to a certain extent on the different characteristics examined here. Clearly immigration continues to be a prominent feature in the experience of Mexicans in the United States. Thus, the Mexican-origin population is quite diverse. This chapter has provided a demographic knowledge intended to enhance the reader's understanding of the more substantive aspects of the Mexican-origin population presented in the remainder of the book.

Notes

1. In this chapter the terms "Mexican" and "Mexican-origin" are used interchangeably to refer to the population under study. These terms do not take into account nativity status and are meant to capture the diverse nature of the Mexican-origin population.
2. The Southwest includes Arizona, California, Colorado, New Mexico, and Texas. The Midwest comprises Illinois, Indiana, Iowa, Kansas, Michigan, Minnesota, Missouri, Nebraska, North Dakota, Ohio, South Dakota, and Wisconsin. The West is made up of Alaska, Hawaii, Idaho, Montana, Nevada, Oregon, Utah, Washington, and Wyoming. The South is composed of Alabama, Arkansas, Delaware, the District of Columbia, Florida, Georgia, Kentucky, Louisiana, Maryland, Mississippi, North Carolina, Oklahoma, South Carolina, Tennessee, Virginia, and West Virginia. The Northeast includes Connecticut, Maine, Massachusetts, New Hampshire, New Jersey, New York, Pennsylvania, Rhode Island, and Vermont.

References

Bean, Frank D., Barry Edmonston, and Jeffrey S. Passel, eds. 1990. *Undocumented Migration to the United States: IRCA and the Experience of the 1980s.* Washington, DC: Urban Institute Press.

Chavez, Leo R. 1996. "Borders and Bridges: Undocumented Immigrants from Mexico and Central America." In *Origins and Destinations: Immigration, Race, and Ethnicity in America,* ed. Silvia Pedraza and Ruben G. Rumbaut, 250–62. Belmont, CA: Wadsworth.

Gouveia, Lourdes, and Rogelio Saenz. 2000. "Global Forces and Latino Population Growth in the Midwest: A Regional and Subregional Analysis." *Great Plains Research* 10: 305–28.

Inter-University Program for Latino Research. *Population Change for Mexican by State.* 2001. Notre Dame, IN: Inter-University Program for Latino Research, Census Information Center, 2001. www.nd.edu/ percent7Eiuplr/cic/origin_data.html (September 7, 2001).

———. *Population Change for Mexican by Place.* 2002. Notre Dame, IN: Inter-University Program for Latino Research, Census Information Center. www.nd.edu/ percent 7Eiuplr/cic/ethnic_place htmlfiles/ethnic_place_data.html (revised January 20, 2002).

Saenz, Rogelio. 1999. "Mexican Americans." In *The Minority Report: An Introduction to Racial, Ethnic, and Gender Relations,* ed. A. Gary Dworkin and Rosalind J. Dworkin, 209–29. Fort Worth, TX: Holt, Rinehart & Winston.

Stull, Donald D., Michael J. Broadway, and David Griffith, eds. 1995. *Any Way You Cut It: Meat Processing and Small Town America.* Lawrence, KS: University Press of Kansas.

U.S. Census Bureau. 2002. *American Community Survey Supplementary Survey 2000 Public Use Microdata Sample (PUMS).* Washington, DC: U.S. Census Bureau. www.census.gov/acs/www/Products/PUMS (revised August 22, 2002).

———. 2001a. *Current Population Survey March 2000 Supplement.* Washington, DC: U.S. Census Bureau and the Bureau for Labor Statistics, 2001. www.bls.census.gov/cps/ads/2000/sdata.htm (July 6, 2001).

———. 2001b. *Profile of the Foreign-Born Population in the United States.* Current Population Reports, P23–206. Washington, DC: U.S. Bureau of the Census.

———. 2000a. *Foreign-Born Resident Population Estimates of the United States by Sex, Race, and Hispanic Origin: April 1, 1999 to July 1, 1999.* Washington, DC: U.S. Census Bureau. http://eire.census.gov/popest/archives/national/us_nativity/fbtab003.txt (April 11, 2000).

———. 2000b. *Native Resident Population Estimates of the United States by Sex, Race, and Hispanic Origin: April 1, 1999 to July 1, 1999.* Washington, DC: U.S. Census Bureau, 2000b. http://eire.census.gov/popest/archives/national/us_nativity/nbtab003.txt (April 11, 2000).

U.S. Immigration and Naturalization Service. 2000. *1998 Statistical Yearbook of the Immigration and Naturalization Service.* Washington, DC: U. S. Department of Justice.

———. 1992. *Immigration Statistics: Fiscal Year 1991 (Advanced Report).* Washington, DC: U.S. Department of Justice.

Realms of Integration:
Family, Education, Work, and Health

Panel on Hispanics in the United States, National Research Council of the National Academies

This chapter examines four aspects of the Hispanic experience—family and living arrangements; schools and education; employment and economic well-being; and health status and access to care. These attributes not only portray current terms of belonging, but also highlight risks and opportunities that will ultimately define the future of the U.S. Hispanic population. A focus on features that set Hispanics apart from other groups—notably language use, youthfulness, and large shares of unskilled immigrants—helps assess whether the identified risks are likely to be enduring.

Family and Living Arrangements[1]

Hispanic families are often extolled as a source of strength and cohesion that derives from their "familism"—a strong commitment to family life that values collective goals over individual well-being. Indicators of familism that differentiate Hispanics from whites include early childbearing and higher average fertility levels, large family households that often extend beyond nuclear members, and a greater overall tendency to live with kin rather than with unrelated individuals or alone. As a source of support for relatives in the extended network of kin relationships, familism can help mitigate economic and social risks in the face of adversity. These sentiments were echoed across the generational spectrum in focus groups conducted for the panel:

> Sometimes families here, white families, are not as united as Hispanic families are. We're always famous for having aunts and uncles and relatives. Americans, it's just mom and dad and kids. (Mexican immigrant. Raleigh)

* * *

> Typically, we have close families. Family is a really big part of our culture. (third-generation Hispanic, Houston)

At the same time, consistent with their varied immigration histories and social conditions, Hispanic families are highly diverse. Specific aspects of family behavior, such as intermarriage patterns, cohesion among relatives, and the content of social exchanges, differ by nationality and generation. Mexican Americans are considered particularly familistic, possibly because the large numbers of immigrants among them bring cultural traditions into sharper relief.

Most observers agree that the positive aspects of familism are worth keeping, yet there is no consensus on what can be preserved in the face of the rapid Americanization of second-generation youth. Whether ideals of collective support and other positive features of familism will endure and what forms family structure among Hispanics will take in the future are open questions with far-reaching implications for the evolution of group identity and social well-being.

If Hispanics follow the paths of other immigrant groups, their familism would appear to be in jeopardy as they acculturate, experience socioeconomic mobility, and adopt U.S. norms, which includes many behaviors that tend to erode kinship patterns and traditional family behavior. The rise in divorce and nonmarital childbearing among Hispanics, evident in the growth of mother-only families, signals what some scholars term "family decline."[2] In 1980, fathers were absent in 12 percent of white families, 38 percent of both Dominican and Puerto Rican families, and 40 percent of black families. By 2000, approximately 14 percent of white families had a single female head, compared with about 20 percent of Mexican and Cuban families, 25 percent of Central and South American families, 36 percent of Dominican and Puerto Rican families, and 45 percent of black families.[3] Because mother-only families are significantly more likely to be poor, this trend signals new vulnerabilities for the growing numbers of youths reared by single parents.

Generational transitions also dilute familism, although apparently not uniformly among Hispanic subgroups. For example, among Mexicans and Puerto Ricans born in the United States, the percentage of married-couple households is smaller and the percentage of female-headed households larger than among first-generation immigrants. Compared with the immigrant generation, U.S.-born Mexican Americans exhibit higher divorce rates. Only 56 percent of third-generation Mexican children (those who have American-born parents) live with both parents, compared with about 73 percent of children with Mexican-born parents. Another sign of dwindling familism is the shrinking size of extended families, which often results in reduced safety nets for related individuals.[4]

Rising nonmarital childbearing is another sign of eroding Hispanic familism. Between 1980 and 2000, the percentage of births to unmarried women more than doubled for whites (134 percent), Mexicans (101 percent), and Cubans (173 percent), and increased by more than half for Central and South Americans (64 percent) and other Hispanics (97 percent). Out-of-wedlock childbearing among Puerto Ricans rose more slowly because, as with blacks, their share of nonmarital births was already high in 1980. By 2000, the percentage of births to unmarried Hispanic mothers was between that of whites (22 percent) and blacks (69 percent). The rate for Cubans was closer to that for whites at 27 percent, and the Puerto Rican rate was closer to that for blacks, at 59 percent. At 44 percent, the out-of-wedlock birth rate for Central and South Americans lay between the extremes.

Finally, the cultural mergers produced by rising rates of intermarriage—between Hispanics and non-Hispanics and among Hispanic nationalities—can diminish or redefine the content of familism. As a measure of social distance between groups, an indicator of assimilation, and a force that shapes racial and ethnic boundaries, intermarriage can either redefine or erode Hispanic familism over generations. For all Hispanics, the tendency to marry, cohabit, and procreate with members of their own ethnic group declines across generations, though notable differences exist across groups. Mexican Americans not only are considered to be more familistic than other Hispanics, but also, given their large numbers, are far more likely to be paired with a member of the same ethnic group in marriage, cohabitation, or parenthood than are Puerto Ricans, Cubans, Central/South Americans, or other Hispanics.[5] One possible explanation for this is that high levels of immigration, buttressed by residential segregation, help preserve Mexican familism in the face of erosion from other sources.

Whether traditional Hispanic familistic orientations will persist beyond the third generation, whether they will take the same forms, and whether they will serve similar protective functions is unknown. Trends in marriage, co-

habitation, and parenthood offer provocative insights. Hispanics are more likely to partner with another Hispanic in marriage than in cohabitation and nonmarital parenthood. Although generally less common, relationships with white partners frequently involve marriage. U.S.-born Hispanics are more likely than Hispanic immigrants to have a white, or other non-Hispanic spouse.[6] Unions among partners of different Hispanic origins or between Hispanics and blacks are more likely to involve cohabitation and unmarried childbearing. Hispanic-black unions quite frequently produce children out of wedlock.

Hispanics' interethnic unions foreshadow changing ethnic boundaries through childbearing. In particular, children of mixed unions face complex identity issues: Will they retain a mixed identity, adopt the ethnic (or racial) identity of one parent, or perhaps opt for a panethnic identity? Unions between Hispanic women and white partners can facilitate assimilation into mainstream white society, because these mixed marriages are more common among the better educated. Whether and how Hispanics' ethnic mixing will redraw racial and ethnic boundaries in the United States is uncertain because the prevalence of intermarriage depends on even greater uncertainties, such as the effect of geographic dispersal on the incidence of mixed unions, future levels of immigration, and the way persons of mixed ancestry self-identity ethnically.[7] Because of their sheer numbers and relatively high residential concentration, Mexican Americans are likely to retain a relatively distinct ethnic identity, although generational transitions will blur boundaries through unions with whites. Smaller in size, other Hispanic subgroups are less likely to sustain discrete identities over time because of their higher levels of ethnic mixing with other Hispanic groups and with blacks, which creates greater ambiguity about the place of their offspring in the evolving racial spectrum. How settlement patterns recontour marriage markers will also decide the viability of Hispanicity as a panethnic identity.

Schools and Education[8]

The United States houses some of the most outstanding universities in the world, which coexist with countless highly dysfunctional primary and secondary schools. Thousands of young Hispanics must pursue inter- and intragenerational social mobility predominantly via segregated inner-city schools that feature dropout rates well above the national average. The vastly unequal opportunities for academic achievement they confront in the lower grades contribute to widening disparities at higher levels of the education system.

Although most demographic groups have experienced significant increases in educational attainment since the 1960s, Hispanics are distinguished by their historically low levels of completed schooling, currently completing less formal schooling than any other demographic group.[9] In the context of the rising demand for skills in today's economy, this liability is cause for concern.

In 2000 working-age Hispanics averaged nearly 3 years less of formal schooling than U.S.-born whites and blacks. Moreover, there are large disparities in educational attainment among Hispanic groups, mainly between the native- and foreign-born. On average, foreign-born Hispanics of working age complete 2.5 years less of formal schooling than their U.S.-born compatriots, with negligible differences between men and women. As figure 1 shows, the educational standing of foreign-born Hispanics has eroded since 1980 compared with both whites and blacks. By contrast, U.S.-born Hispanics have closed the school attainment gap with whites by more than half a year— from 2 to 1.3 years over the same period.

Educational disparities between foreign- and native-born Hispanics play out as inequities among national-origin groups of working age because of the changing volume and composition of immigration in recent decades. Not only do foreign-born Mexicans feature the lowest educational levels of any Hispanic subgroup, but the gap in completed schooling between the foreign and native born is larger for Mexicans than for Hispanics of other nationalities—rising from 3 years in 1980 to 4.4 years in 2000— owing to substantial educational advances among the U.S.-born rather than declining attainment of recent immigrants (see figure 2). For other Hispanics, the birthplace gap in education rose more modestly during the same period—from 1 to 1.6 years—while for Puerto Ricans it was reduced by half. Cubans are distinguished from other Hispanic ethnicities because their average education level exceeds that of other subgroups, because foreign-born Cubans average more schooling than native-born Hispan-

ics, and because the educational attainment of U.S.-born Cubans equals (in the case of men) or surpasses (in the case of women) that of white men and women.[10]

If the schooling deficits of foreign-born Hispanics are imported from Latin America, the disparities among the native-born are produced in the United States. Scholastic disadvantages result from a myriad of social and family circumstances—mainly low parental education levels— and are compounded by schools that fail to deliver quality education.[11] Fortunately, educational disadvantages can be prevented for Hispanic youths that have not yet begun their school careers and reversed for those already enrolled.

Early Beginnings

Hispanic students' educational disadvantages begin in the early grades for two main reasons—their delayed entry into formal school settings and their limited opportunities to acquire preliteracy skills. Parents of Hispanic preschoolers are less likely than black, white, or Asian parents to be fluent in English and, because many have poor educational levels themselves, to have the resources necessary to promote their children's prescholastic literacy. This is highly significant because reading to preschool children fosters their language acquisition, enhances their early reading performance and social development, and may promote their future academic success.

Participation in home literacy activities such as telling stories or visiting libraries is especially low for children reared in Spanish-dominant homes. In 1999, children of Spanish monolinguals were only half as likely as white children to participate in such activities; if both parents were fluent in English, the gap was just 15 percentage

Figure 1. Mean Years of Education by Race/Ethnicity and Nativity, 1980–2000.

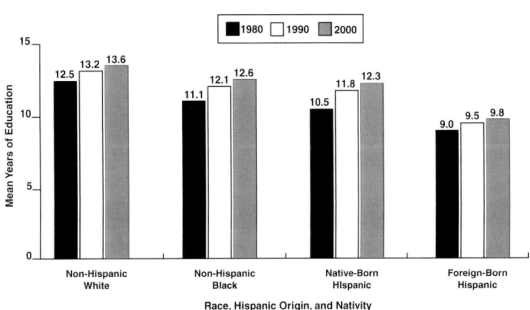

Note: For ages 25 to 64.
Source: U.S. Bureau of the Census (2000b), Integrated Public Use Microdata Series (IPUMS) 1 percent samples for 1980–2000.

Figure 2. Mean Years of Education of Hispanics by Ethnicity.

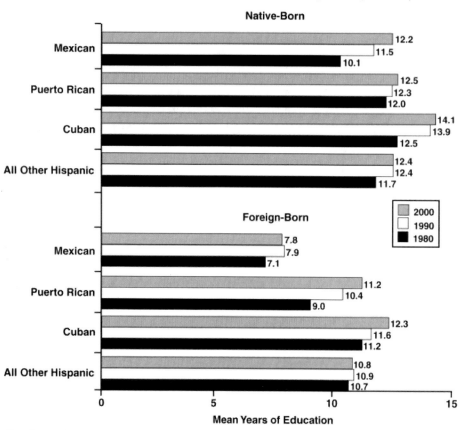

Note: For ages 25 to 64.
Source: U.S. Bureau of the Census (2000b), Integrated Public Use Microdata Series (IPUMS) 1 percent samples for 1980–2000.

points. The lack of exposure to preschool literacy activities, particularly among children from Spanish-dominant households, often creates literacy disadvantages in the early grades. A 1999 study by the U.S. Department of Education showed that Hispanic kindergarten students trailed their Asian and other non-Hispanic classmates in both reading and math skills.[12] Only Native American students had lower preschool reading literacy rates than Hispanics whose parents spoke little English (although Hispanic children exhibited lower math skills).

Household language partly reflects social class divisions and recent immigrant status—two attributes that influence children's exposure to literacy activities before kindergarten. Yet differences in school readiness between Hispanic youth reared in Spanish-dominant homes and English-dominant homes are not an indictment of Spanish-language use per se. Moreover, programs such as Head Start appear to raise Hispanic children's low average preschool literacy rates. Yet quality preschool programs often are either unavailable where the neediest children live or too costly for family budgets. Thus disadvantaged Hispanic children are left to make their way in the public schools, increasing their vulnerability to failure in the years ahead.

Primary and Middle Years

The academic achievement gap evident when Hispanics first enter school continues through the primary grades. During the first two years, teachers' perceptions of their Hispanic students' academic abilities often skew scholastic assessments, regardless of the children's actual aptitude. Results of the Early Childhood Longitudinal Study revealed that kindergarten teachers systematically rated Hispanic students below white students when first enrolled. As Hispanic children performed above their teachers' initial expectations, the gap between test-based abilities and teacher assessments decreased by half to two-thirds during kindergarten and was eliminated by the end of the first grade. Such teacher biases are compounded by a shortage of staff who understand Hispanic children's cultural backgrounds. Nationally, Hispanic students constitute approximately 15 percent of elementary school students—and nearly 20 percent of all school-age students—yet only 4 percent of public school teachers are Hispanic.[13]

Although Hispanic elementary school children have made steady progress in reading and math, greater gains by other groups have sustained or in some cases widened Hispanic achievement gaps. A 20-year comparison of test scores reported in the National Assessment of Educational

Progress shows that Hispanic students continue to lag behind whites in their scholastic achievement throughout middle and high school.[14] Evident for all Hispanic subgroups, these gaps are decidedly largest for Mexican Americans, the fastest-growing segment of the elementary school population. Carried into future grades, accumulating deficits in literacy and math competencies inhibit the learning of other academic subjects.

Middle school Hispanic students often encounter two circumstances that limit their chances for scholastic success: large, urban schools, generally considered suboptimal for learning in the middle grades,[15] and weak ties with their teachers.[16] Weak relations with teachers diminish students' motivation to pursue academic work, and in turn lower teachers' expectations in a self-perpetuating cycle of academic disengagement and underachievement. That students who become disengaged from school during the middle years cannot well appreciate the practical relevance of what is being taught in the classroom bodes ill for their academic performance in high school and dampens their aspirations for college.

Secondary School and Beyond

Even under optimal circumstances, the transition from middle to high school is a taxing experience for most students. This passage is especially difficult for Hispanic and black adolescents destined for oversized, resource-poor urban high schools staffed with many inexperienced or uncertified teachers.[17] Moreover, students whose parents lack a high school education are most in need of early guidance in course planning and preparation for college. Such guidance is in short supply in the schools these students attend. Given their parents' limited experience with the U.S. educational system and the blind trust many Hispanic parents are willing to place in teachers' authority, Hispanic eighth graders are more likely than any other demographic group to express uncertainty about the classes they will take in high school.[18] Mexican immigrant parents are especially likely to defer to teachers and administrators, rarely questioning their decisions.

High school experiences are vital in shaping students' educational expectations and occupational aspirations. Yet a recent study found that, compared with 25 percent of blacks, 31 percent of whites, and 37 percent of Asian Americans, only 23 percent of Hispanic eighth graders planned to enroll in a college preparatory curriculum.[19] These findings underscore the urgency of effective counseling on course selection in secondary school, particularly for students whose parents may be unfamiliar with the complexities of the U.S. educational system.

Despite modest improvements in recent years, rates of school failure among Hispanics remain unacceptably high. Even counting only those who actually attended U.S. high schools, the share of Hispanic high school students 16 to 19 years old who failed to graduate fell only marginally during the 1990s, from 22 to 21 percent.[20] The numbers involved are sobering because the school-age population in the United States has been growing rapidly as the children of baby boomers and recent immigrants make their way through the education system. That dropout rates for whites and blacks fell even more than for Hispanics—from 10 to 8 percent and from 14 to 12 percent, respectively—widened racial and ethnic disparities in secondary school success. Nor is the General Equivalency Diploma (GED) a viable route for Hispanics to close their high school achievement gap. In 1998, 7.9 percent of white 18- to 29-year-olds achieved high school equivalence by passing the GED test, as compared with 7 percent of Hispanics.[21] Moreover, those with exam-certified high school equivalency fare no better in the labor market than high school dropouts.[22]

Although foreign-born Hispanic youths ages 16 to 19 are significantly more likely than those who are native born to leave high school without a diploma—34 versus 14 percent in 2000—being foreign born is not the main factor explaining their failure to graduate. Many are recent arrivals who were already behind in school before arriving in the U.S.[23] Once here, they are likely to attend urban schools—such as those in Los Angeles, Chicago, and New York—that serve large numbers of low-income minority students and for which low graduation rates are typical. Fully 40 percent of Hispanic students attend high schools that graduate less than 60 percent of entering freshmen.[24]

Popular allegations that Hispanics value education less than do other groups are contradicted by evidence that large numbers of Hispanic high school students aspire to attend college. A study conducted by Public Agenda, a New York-based nonprofit public opinion research organization, found that 65 percent of Hispanic parents, compared with 47 percent of black and 33 percent of white parents, believed a college education is the single most important factor for economic success.[25] Yet Hispanics trail all other groups in their ambitions to pursue 4-year college degrees because of their disadvantaged beginnings, limited home educational resources, concentration in scholastically weak high schools, and lack of concrete information about how to prepare for college.[26]

Compared with whites and blacks, more second-generation Hispanic youths are the first in their family to attend college. But college prospects are limited for many because they fail to take courses or exams required for college entrance—another consequence of their poor guidance counseling during high school. Compared with other subjects, achievement in mathematics is the strongest predictor of college enrollment. That Hispanic students are about 20 percent less likely than whites to complete advanced mathematics, as well as less likely than both whites and blacks to take advanced science courses, compromises their post-high school educational options.[27]

Hispanic high school graduates are also less likely than whites, Asians, and blacks to take college entrance examinations or apply to college.[28] Spanish-language use per se does not explain this gap because bilingual Hispanics are more likely than whites to complete Advanced Placement courses and to take College Board exams. And parents who are proficient in both English and Spanish often can advance their children's educational prospects by bridging cultural and language divides.[29]

Despite the above obstacles, college enrollment among Hispanics has been on the rise. There is evidence that Hispanic high school graduates are more likely than white or black students to enroll in some form of college, but Hispanics also are significantly less likely to obtain a 4-year degree because they are more likely to enroll in 2-year colleges, to attend college only part-time, or to work while enrolled full-time.[30] This is especially true for Mexicans. In 2000, Hispanics were 11 percent of high school graduates.[31] They accounted for only 7 percent of students enrolled in 4-year institutions, but 14 percent of enrollees in 2-year colleges. Differences in college attendance between native- and foreign-born Hispanics contribute somewhat to these outcomes, but they are not the driving force.

Major reasons why Hispanics are more likely than whites to enroll in 2-year rather than 4-year colleges are poor academic preparation, weak counseling, and cost. Hispanics from Spanish-speaking families (for whom the risks of dropping out of high school are higher) are nearly as likely as blacks to attend 4-year colleges if they receive adequate academic preparation.[32] Like many students who begin their college careers at community colleges, Hispanics intend to transfer to 4-year institutions, but they are less successful than other groups in making the transition.[33] Furthermore, enrollment in a 4-year institution does not guarantee a degree. Compared with other high-achieving youths who enroll in 4-year institutions, Hispanics are less likely to receive baccalaureate degrees, unless they are among the select few who attend a highly selective college.[34]

Economic Well-Being

As in so many other ways, Hispanics are highly diverse with respect to economic well-being. On the one hand, lacking the protections afforded by legal status, millions of undocumented Hispanics fill low-wage jobs; many make ends meet by holding multiple jobs and pooling incomes from several household members. On the other hand, rising rates of home ownership attest that both established immigrants and native-born citizens are increasingly joining the ranks of the middle class.[35] This section reviews two aspects of economic well-being—employment and earnings, and household income—among Hispanics, as well as their experience of the extremes of poverty and wealth.

Employment and Earnings[36]

Hispanics' success in the U.S. labor market depends on their propensity to work, their skills, the kinds of jobs they secure, and, because many U.S. employers discount human capital acquired abroad, where they were born (see figure 3).[37] On average, Hispanic men's employment rate (87 percent) is somewhat lower than that for U.S.-born whites (92 percent), but well above that for U.S.-born blacks (77 percent).[38] Also among men, the average employment rate for both Cubans and Mexicans (both foreign- and U.S.-born) is similar to that for whites, but that for Puerto Rican men is appreciably lower, while that for island-born Puerto Ricans is similar to that for U.S.-born blacks.[39]

Birthplace differences in employment rates are much larger for Hispanic women than men. Overall, some 61 percent of immigrant Hispanic women were employed in 2000, compared with 76 percent of their U.S.-born counterparts. With just over one in two employed, Mexican immigrants have the lowest employment rate of all women, but the rate for island-born Puerto Ricans is only slightly higher at 61 percent. Average employment rates for U.S.-born Mexicans and Puerto Ricans are close to those for blacks (78 percent) and whites (80 percent), while Cubans have the highest rate of all, at 83 percent.

Owing to differences in educational attainment and language skills between native- and foreign-born Hispanics, the types of jobs they hold vary more on this dimension than by nationality. Foreign-born Hispanic men work disproportionately in agriculture (11 percent) and construction (18 percent), while foreign-born Hispanic women are overrepresented in manufacturing (19 percent)—mainly in production of nondurable goods.[40] Consistent with their education and English-language skills, Hispanic men and women born abroad are underrepresented in managerial/professional and technical/sales occupations, and overrepresented in service and operator/laborer occupations.

Hispanics' lower levels of education and English proficiency largely explain their lower employment rates compared with whites.[41] The 6 percentage point employment gap between native-born Mexican and white men would narrow to a mere 2 percentage points if their education and language skills were similar. With education and English proficiency levels comparable to those of whites, the employment rates of foreign-born Mexican immigrants also would be similar.[42] Foreign-born Mexican women provide an even more dramatic example, as their average employment deficit of 25 percentage points would shrink to just 3 with education and English proficiency levels comparable to those of white women. Puerto Ricans and Dominicans are an exception to this pattern because sizable employment gaps persist for them even with human capital endowments comparable to those of whites.[43]

On average, native-born Hispanic men earned 31 percent and foreign-born Hispanic men 59 percent less than

Figure 3. Employment Rates for White, Black, and Hispanic Men and Women ages 25–59 by Nativity.

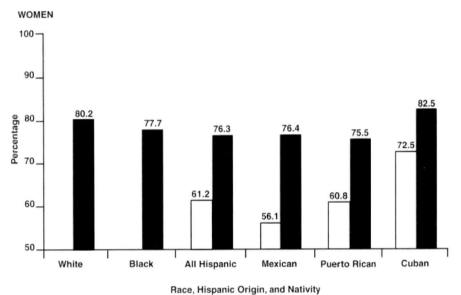

Source: U.S. Bureau of the Census (2000b), 5 percent samples Integrated Public Use Microdata Series (IPUMS).

whites in 1999. With similar human capital endowments, those earnings gaps would shrink to 13 and 5 percent, respectively. By comparison, and despite their higher average education levels and better command of English relative to Hispanics, black men suffer a 44 percent earnings penalty. Foreign-born Hispanic women earn about half as much as white women on average, but this disparity, too, would shrink given comparable educational attainment and English fluency.

Hispanics' average earnings also differ by national origin. Native-born Cubans enjoy relatively high earnings: U.S. born Cuban men earn as much as white men, and native-born Cuban women earn 20 percent *more* than white women. By contrast, both Mexicans and Puerto Ricans—especially those born abroad—exhibit large gaps compared with whites. But if Mexican and Puerto Rican women born abroad—whose average earnings trail those of white women by 63 and 28 percent, respectively—were as flu-

ent in English and as well educated as white women, their earnings gaps would virtually disappear.[44] Legal status also affects wages, with legal immigrants earning substantially more than those who are undocumented, and wage inequality, as discussed below.[45]

Thus unlike black men, for whom continuing discrimination in the labor market creates and augments earnings disparities, Hispanics could dramatically reduce their earnings gap with whites by closing the education gap and becoming proficient in English.[46] This does not mean that Hispanics do not experience discrimination in the labor market. There is some evidence of differences in treatment at initial contact and interview and in outcomes based on accent and phenotype.[47]

To understand the origins of earnings differentials and accurately portray Hispanic socioeconomic progress over time, one must consider changes in the birthplace composition of the Hispanic workforce. Since 1980, high rates of immigration have changed the human capital profile of Hispanic workers and widened their earnings disparities with whites. For example, the foreign-born share among Mexican men aged 25 to 59 surged from 37 percent in 1980 to 51 percent in 1990 and 63 percent in 2000. Among Hispanics, Mexicans are the largest ethnic group, average the lowest levels of human capital, and include a sizable share of undocumented workers.[48] With average educational attainment levels of 12 years for the native born and less than 9 years for the foreign born, Mexicans have faced particularly bleak labor market prospects since 1980, as the wage premiums for high skills grew and income inequality widened.

Looking back six decades, in 1940 Mexican men earned just over half (56 percent) of white men's wages. That figure rose to nearly 70 percent in the postwar decade, a period of vigorous economic growth when strong unions protected the wages of laborers. Although the Mexican-white earnings gap remained unchanged during the next two decades, by 1990 Mexican men's wages had deteriorated to 45 percent of those of white men, and this gap persisted through the following decade.[49] By contrast, earnings of black men rose between 1990 and 2000, from 50 to 56 percent of white male earnings. Larger human capital gaps since 1980, especially among the foreign born, are responsible for the stagnation of Hispanic earnings through 2000, especially as the premium placed on work-related skills has continued to rise.[50]

Previous waves of predominantly unskilled immigrants, such as the Irish and Italians, enjoyed substantial intergenerational progress that ultimately enabled their descendants to join the middle class. For most, though, this process required two or three generations to accomplish; moreover, the skill endowments of the immigrant generation were instrumental in the labor market success of their children and grandchildren.[51] Generational comparisons are particularly instructive for envisioning possible economic destinies for Hispanics. But because Hispanic immigrants are so diverse with respect to their length of U.S. residence, and because native-born Hispanics represent multiple generations, comparisons by birthplace are too coarse to portray true intergenerational progress. Snapshots of the Hispanic population taken over time can only approximate such progress, but nonetheless provide rough measures of the direction and pace of change.

Substantial educational gains realized by the U.S.-born offspring of Hispanic immigrants have narrowed the white-Hispanic earnings gap across generations, with the most sizable convergence occurring between the first and second generations. A smaller wage convergence occurs between the second and third generations, which mirrors the apparent stagnation of Hispanics' educational progress relative to whites. For example, for the 1998–2000 period, the earnings gap between Mexican and white men dropped from 66 percent for immigrants to 38 percent for

the second generation and 31 percent for the third and subsequent generations combined. Second-generation Mexicans even reaped higher earnings than native-born black men with higher levels of education. Earnings deficits for Puerto Rican men were 46 percent for the first generation, 30 percent for the second generation, and 16 percent for later generations. Reflecting their higher-class origins at arrival, Cuban immigrants' 31 percent initial deficit disappeared by the second generation.[52]

The apparent slowdown in Hispanic socioeconomic progress after the second generation may be more imagined than real because it is impossible to match immigrant parents and grandparents of the first generation with their descendants in later generations.[53] In fact, substantial educational and earnings gains are evident when second-generation Hispanics are compared with their third-generation descendants 25 years later. For example, one study showed that not only are schooling gaps smaller in the second compared with the first generation, but they are always lower in the third generation.[54]

Educational gains of younger third-generation relative to older second-generation Hispanics are an encouraging sign of intergenerational progress, but they yield conservative estimates of mobility for two reasons. First, the pace of intergenerational progress may be more rapid than available data can accurately portray because of the uncertain volume, pace, and composition of immigrant flows. Decennial censuses can only approximate this highly dynamic process, which for Hispanics is further complicated by the presence of a large and growing undocumented population, whose integration prospects are highly uncertain. Second, selective opting out of Hispanic ethnicity by third and higher generations would lead to underestimation of intergenerational progress. If the most successful Hispanics are less likely to identify themselves or their children as Hispanic—either because they are more likely to marry non-Hispanics or for other reasons—available estimates of earnings gains achieved between the second and third generations are conservative. Studies focused on documenting the prevalence of such opting out of Hispanic identity are relatively recent, and consensus on this issue has not yet been established.[55]

Recent evidence for Mexicans supports the idea that the most economically assimilated Hispanics—predominantly those from the third and higher generations—may be less likely to self-identify as Hispanic.[56] U.S.-born Mexican Americans who marry non-Mexicans are substantially more educated, on average, than Mexican Americans who marry within their ethnic group (either U.S. or foreign born), as their higher employment levels and earnings attest. Moreover, the children of intermarried Mexican Americans are much less likely to self-identify as Mexican than are the children of two Mexican parents. This implies that children of Mexican-origin parents with low education, employment, and earnings may be more likely to self-identify as Mexican than the offspring of intermarriage, which would bias downward assessments of Mexican Americans' intergenerational progress beyond the second generation. The magnitude of such biases, however, has yet to be systematically assessed.[57]

Given these uncertainties, conclusions about intergenerational changes in the labor market experience of Hispanics remain tentative at best. The evidence is clear as to improvement in educational attainment and earnings growth between first- and second-generation Hispanics, both absolutely and relative to whites. But the evidence regarding progress between the second and third generations, and especially beyond the third, is less clear, because educational gains between the second and third generations are not matched by commensurate progress in earnings, particularly among younger Mexicans.[58] Less debatable is that deficiencies in education and language skills will remain a formidable obstacle to the labor market success of Hispanics, especially for immigrants, and will continue to hamper their economic progress—perhaps even more so in the years ahead than in the past—because of the higher premium placed on skills and because blue-collar jobs that traditionally served as gateways to the middle class have all but vanished. Whether the growing second generation makes sufficient progress in closing these two key obstacles to economic mobility will be decisive in the long-term positioning of the Hispanic population.

Household Income

For obvious reasons, the gaps in employment and earnings experienced by Hispanics are reflected in disparities in household income. On average, incomes of white households are larger than those of Hispanic households, just how much larger depending on the birthplace and ethnicity of the Hispanic householder. Again mirroring employment and earnings disparities, U.S.-born Hispanic householders of all national origins garner higher incomes than blacks, although this pattern does not hold for households headed by immigrants. In 1999, the median income of Hispanic households was just about 70 percent that of whites and about 10 percent higher than that of blacks.[59] At the top of the Hispanic household income ladder are South Americans and Cubans who were either born or raised in the United States.[60] Ranking lowest on median household income, as with most other measures of economic well-being, are Puerto Ricans and Dominicans, followed by Mexicans (see figure 4).

As noted, an obvious explanation for the low household incomes of immigrants, and particularly Mexicans, Dominicans, and Central Americans, is their low earnings. In addition, per capita household income depends on household size. Thus, for example, despite having higher average incomes compared with blacks, second-generation Mexicans, Puerto Ricans, and Dominicans have slightly lower median per capita incomes because of their larger households. Central Americans fare somewhat better than Mexicans because of both their higher earnings capacity and smaller average households.

Additionally, Hispanics experienced a deterioration in economic well-being over time relative to whites, whose incomes have risen more when times were good and fallen less during recessions.[61] The median household income of Hispanics averaged 74 percent of that of whites during the early 1970s, but eroded following the 1973 oil crisis-induced recession. On the heels of another economic downturn in the early 1980s, the Hispanic-white income ratio deteriorated further, falling below 70 percent in 1985–1988

Figure 4. Median Total Household Income by Hispanic National Origin or Race/Ethnicity and Generation.

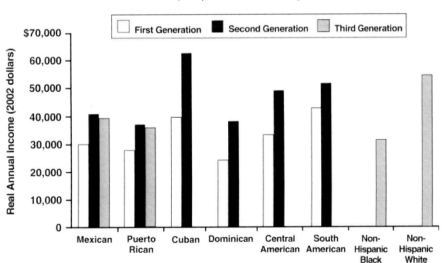

National Origin or Race/Ethnicity

Notes: Includes only households whose head is under age 65. Results for Hispanics are shown only for cells with at least 90 observations.
Source: Pooled March CPS flies, 1998–2002.

and again in 1992–1998, reaching its nadir in 1995 at 61 percent.[62] Although white-Hispanic median household incomes converged during the brisk economic growth of the late 1990s, there are signs that the relative income position of Hispanics is eroding yet again.[63] Median incomes of black households were consistently lower than those of Hispanics throughout the period, but over time their income position improved relative to both whites and Hispanics. In 1972, the median black household income was 77 percent that of whites, compared with 90 percent in 2003.[64] Because these comparisons do not separate out native- and foreign-born householders, it is difficult to distinguish changes related to increased numbers of low-skill immigrants from those related to business cycle variations. Yet the Survey of Income and Program Participation, one of very few surveys that record annual variation in income, poverty, and wealth, indicates a convergence of wealth between native- and foreign-born Hispanics between 1996 and 2001.[65]

Hispanics compensate for low household income through two strategies: income pooling based on extended living arrangements and reliance on public benefits (see figure 5). Relative to both whites and blacks, Hispanic households are more likely to include relatives outside the nuclear family, and extended members' average contributions to household income are higher. Extended living arrangements are most common among immigrant generations but decline thereafter. Mexicans, Central Americans, and Dominicans of the immigrant generation are especially reliant on extended-household members for income pooling, whereas Hispanics with U.S.-born parents largely resemble blacks in their tendency to rely on other relatives for support.

To what extent complex households reflect Hispanic cultural values (familism) versus economic need is unclear. Clearly, however, reliance on this multiple-source income pooling declines over time as the rising prosperity of second and higher generations reduces the need for such compensatory income strategies.

Among Hispanic subgroups, Dominicans and Puerto Ricans under age 65 rely most heavily on public assistance, the second key source of income supplementation. In the case of Puerto Ricans, this largely reflects their high share of single female heads of household; the scarcity of jobs and relatively generous benefit programs in the northeast where many Puerto Ricans live; and the fact that as U.S. citizens, Puerto Ricans (unlike new immigrants) are eligible for public benefit programs. Although second-generation Puerto Ricans rely less than the first generation on income from public benefits, even those born on the mainland depend more on this source of household income compared with other Hispanic subgroups—indeed, at rates more similar to those of blacks. Puerto Ricans' high rates of welfare participation reflect their elevated poverty rates.

Poverty and Wealth Among Hispanics

Trends in median household income conceal the poverty of those at the low end and the prosperity of those at the high end of the income ladder. Indeed, poverty rates dramatize the consequences of poor employment and earnings capacities more effectively than does median household income. Although poverty rates declined during the 1990s—by 3 and 4 percentage points for Hispanics and blacks, respectively—Hispanic poverty held fast at more

Figure 5. Sources of Median Total Household Income by Hispanic National Origin or Race/Ethnicity and Generation.

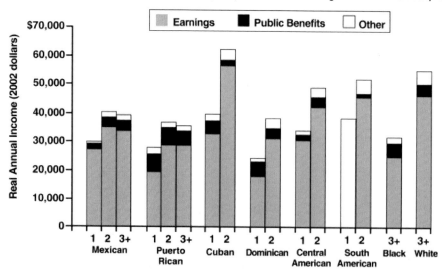

Notes: Includes only households whose head is under age 65. Means are simple averages across households, using household weights. Households with zero or negative total income or containing persons with negative income from any source are excluded. Results for Hispanics are shown only for cells with at least 90 observations.
Source: Pooled March CPS files, 1998–2002.

than 2.5 times the rate among whites.[66] In 1999, more than one in five Hispanics lived below the official poverty line ($16,895 for a family of four or a meager $12 per day per person).[67] Broken out by birthplace, declines in poverty were smallest for Puerto Ricans and greatest for Dominicans, who witnessed the largest drop in absolute poverty during the 1990s.[68] Central American immigrants were less likely to be poor than were Mexicans, Puerto Ricans, and Dominicans of the same generation, but their poverty rates were higher than those of South Americans.[69]

The similar overall poverty rates for first-generation Mexicans, Dominicans, and Puerto Ricans have different sources. As the least-educated group, Mexicans have the lowest overall earning capacity, a liability that persists beyond the second generation. Predominantly recent immigrants with limited skills, Dominicans are, like Puerto Ricans, further handicapped by a high incidence of female-headed households. Having only one potential earner exacerbates the effects of women's low average earnings in depressing household income. Combined, these conditions produce income shortfalls that are only minimally compensated by benefit programs.[70]

Poverty is especially pernicious for children because it is associated with many deleterious outcomes, such as low scholastic achievement, adolescent parenting, substance abuse, and violence.[71] In 1999, more than one in four Hispanics under the age of 18 were poor, compared with nearly one in ten whites. Child poverty rates among Dominicans and Puerto Ricans—35 and 33 percent, respectively—were comparable to those of blacks. Cuban and South American youths experienced the lowest rates of poverty, between 16 and 17 percent. Child poverty rates of Mexicans and Central Americans approached the Hispanic population average—28 and 24 percent, respectively—which is well above the 17 percent overall U.S. poverty rate for those under 18.[72] Elevated Hispanic child poverty rates are particularly disturbing because the relatively young age structure of the population implies large and growing numbers of the youthful poor, and because poverty magnifies the challenges of assimilation and integration for the burgeoning second generation.

Poverty levels are also elevated among elderly Hispanics. The elderly are only a small proportion of the Hispanic population today, but their numbers will grow rapidly in the future. Today's elderly provide a glimpse of how current Hispanic workers are likely to fare at advanced ages, depending on whether the present Social Security and Medicare safety nets remain intact. Overall, about one in five elderly Hispanics was poor in 1999, compared with fewer than one in ten whites and one in four blacks. The poverty risk for Hispanic elderly varies according to national origin, reflecting incomes and types of jobs held at younger ages, as well as length of time in the U.S. labor market. Mirroring child poverty differentials, elderly poverty rates are highest for Puerto Ricans and Dominicans—24 and 29 percent, respectively—and lowest for South

Americans, at 16 percent.[73] Poverty rates for other groups are close to the elderly Hispanic population average of 20 percent.

Because Hispanics tend to work for employers that do not offer pensions, elderly Hispanic householders rely more on other sources of income than do either blacks or whites. Moreover, except for Puerto Ricans and Cubans, foreign-born Hispanics rely less on Social Security than do whites and blacks because they are less likely to qualify for the benefits even if they work beyond the required 40 quarters. Until recently, the sectors in which many elderly Hispanics worked, such as agriculture and household service, were not covered by Social Security, which accounts for 42 percent of household income for elderly Central and South American immigrants, but close to 60 percent for blacks and island-born Puerto Ricans.[74]

Elderly immigrants who have not completed the required 10 years in covered jobs to qualify for Social Security benefits or whose benefits are low because of a lifetime of low-wage work often qualify for Supplemental Security Income (SSI), which offers less generous benefits than those provided by Social Security.[75] Elderly foreign-born Hispanics (with the exception of South Americans) derive a larger share of their income from SSI than do blacks, signaling their greater vulnerability to poverty, especially during inflationary periods. By qualifying for Social Security at higher rates, U.S.-born elderly Hispanics mitigate this risk to some extent and face better economic prospects relative to blacks.

Less well documented than trends and disparities in Hispanic poverty are changes at the high end of the income distribution—namely wealth. Net worth is a pertinent indicator of economic well-being because it represents assets that can be tapped in times of financial distress. Recent estimates of Hispanic wealth range from 3 to 9 percent of white median wealth.[76] Home equity constitutes the largest component of Hispanic household wealth, about 50 to 60 percent of net worth during the 1996–2002 period.[77] Less easily converted to cash than other assets in the event of financial crisis, home equity is the source of last resort to offset fluctuations in household income. The reversal of nearly two decades of wage stagnation in the late 1990s also allowed Hispanics to participate in the stock market, albeit to a much lesser extent than whites.[78]

Not only is home equity the largest component of household wealth, but it is also a key marker of middle-class status. Home ownership provides access to myriad social amenities that influence overall well-being, including school quality, neighborhood safety, recreation facilities, and access to health care organizations (see below).[79] Although Hispanic home ownership rates rose from 33 to 44 percent between 1983 and 2001, they have been relatively stagnant since the mid-1990s, even as the rates for white householders have climbed.[80] Consequently, the Hispanic-white ownership ratio, which rose from 48 to 64 percent from the mid-1980s to the mid-1990s, eroded to 60 percent by 2001.[81]

Whether the geographic dispersal of Hispanics from areas with higher to those with lower housing costs will reverse this trend remains unclear. Census data for the largest 100 metro areas indicate that both native- and foreign-born Hispanics participated in rising rates of home ownership during the 1990s owing to favorable interest rates, rising incomes, and the pace of housing construction relative to employment growth.[82] For the foreign born, however, ownership rates increased in the traditional settlement hubs while declining in the new destinations. Because the dispersal of Hispanics to new destinations is a relatively recent phenomenon that involves many recently arrived, low-skill immigrants, it is conceivable that their lower average home ownership rates will improve over time as they acculturate in their new locales.[83]

Health Status and Access to Care

Like other forms of human capital, health status—both physical and psychological—is an asset that requires investments for improvement and maintenance.[84] In addition to nutritious food, regular exercise, and a toxin-free environment, health status depends on a variety of circumstances—some unique to Hispanics and others shared with populations of similar socioeconomic status, some linked to behavior that compromises or promotes health, and others associated with access to care.

Health Status and Behaviors[85]

Like other indicators of integration, Hispanic health status differs according to subgroup, immigrant generation, English proficiency, and degree of acculturation. Puerto Ricans are less healthy, on average, than other Hispanic subgroups, while Mexicans, Central Americans, and South Americans often compare favorably with whites on several health indicators, despite their low average socioeconomic status. For example, the age-adjusted mortality of Hispanics is lower than that of blacks or whites; the exception is Puerto Ricans, whose mortality rates are higher than those of other Hispanic subgroups (see figure 6). Dubbed the Hispanic "epidemiological paradox" or "immigrant health paradox" by researchers, the lower mortality rates of Hispanics relative to those of whites with more favorable socioeconomic status have puzzled social and health scientists since the 1980s. Precise findings differ, but most studies show that foreign-born Mexicans, Central Americans, and South Americans are most likely to experience this advantage. One factor that contributes to their lower mortality is that healthier people are more likely to migrate than the sickly, but it is not a sufficient explanation. Why mortality rates are comparable for U.S.-born Hispanics and whites, however, remains a puzzle.

Hispanics also experience favorable birth outcomes in terms of birthweight and infant mortality, another case in which they fare much better than would be expected given their socioeconomic status. In 2001, Hispanics' infant mortality rate of 5.4 per 1,000 live births compared favorably with those of 5.7 for whites and 13.5 for blacks. Cubans (4.2), Central and South Americans (5.0), and Mexicans (5.2) all had lower infant mortality rates than whites, while Puerto Ricans (8.5) fared better than blacks but worse than whites.[86]

Experts often invoke protective cultural and social behaviors of immigrants to explain their advantage in birth outcomes relative to their U.S.-born counterparts. However, since second-generation Hispanic women also have relatively favorable birth outcomes compared with white women of comparable socioeconomic status, cultural explanations do not suffice. Other assets in the Hispanic health ledger include a lower incidence of several major cancers and relatively low rates of activity limitation (e.g., climbing stairs, getting dressed) compared with whites, along with mental health profiles that resemble those of whites. In 2000, for example, the age-adjusted death rate from cancer was 134.9 per 100,000 for Hispanics, compared with 200.6 per 100,000 for whites. Hispanics also smoke less than whites; the exception is Puerto Ricans, who smoke at similar rates.[87]

Hispanics also experience several health liabilities, diabetes and hypertension being by far the most severe. The rising prevalence of Hispanic adults considered overweight or obese likely contributes to higher rates of both conditions, as well as to cardiovascular disease. Although the U.S. epidemic of overweight and obese adults affects all racial and ethnic groups, it is particularly severe for Hispanics. Among Mexicans, 29 percent of men and 40 percent of women are considered obese, compared with 27 percent and 30 percent, respectively, of white men and women.[88]

Trends in overweight among Hispanic youths are particularly worrisome. Hispanic children and adolescents—Mexican and Puerto Rican girls in particular—are much more likely than whites to be overweight. Girls of Mexican origin are nearly twice as likely as white girls to be overweight, while Mexican-origin boys are more than twice as likely as white boys to be overweight. Even more troubling, rates of overweight have risen faster for Hispanic than for white youths (see figure 7). Over the last quarter century or so, the prevalence of overweight pre-adolescent (ages 6–11) Mexican youths doubled—rising from 13 to 27 percent for boys and from 10 to 20 percent for girls. The rate of adolescents (ages 12–19) considered overweight more than trebled for both boys (from 8 to 28 percent) and doubled for girls (from 9 to 19 percent) over the same period.[89]

Those who claim that acculturation contributes to the rise in Hispanic overweight and obesity point to immigrants' diets, which are richer in fruits and vegetables and

Figure 6. Age-adjusted Mortality for Whites, Blacks, and Hispanics by Sex, 2001.

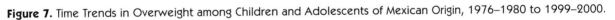

Source: Arias et al. (2003).

lower in fats compared with those of native-born youths, who are more prone to consume high-fat processed and fast foods. Generational differences in diet are mirrored in the prevalence of overweight adolescents, as about one in four first-generation adolescent Hispanics is at risk of being overweight, compared with about one in three second- and third-generation youths.[90]

Several other differences in the health circumstances of Hispanic youths are worth noting. With the exception of Puerto Ricans, Hispanic youths have low rates of asthma,

the major chronic disease of childhood. This health asset is offset by their worse oral health compared with their white peers. Hispanic youths also register higher blood lead levels than white children, which places them at greater risk for the adverse effects of lead poisoning on cognitive development.[91]

Hispanic adolescents engage in many health-compromising behaviors, such as use of alcohol and illicit drugs and early sex, at rates comparable to those of white teens, although their tobacco use is lower. Cuban-origin youths

Figure 7. Time Trends in Overweight among Children and Adolescents of Mexican Origin, 1976–1980 to 1999–2000.

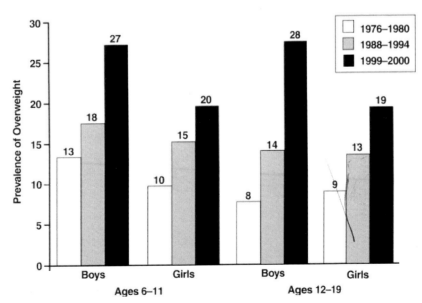

Source: National Center for Health Statistics (2003) (see Escarce et al., 2006).

have the highest levels of tobacco, alcohol, and drug use, followed by those of Mexican and Puerto Rican origin. By comparison, youths from other Hispanic subgroups have low rates of drug use—probably because larger shares of these subgroups are first-generation immigrants, which means they are less acculturated. In general, acculturated youths engage in such health-compromising behaviors more often than the less acculturated. Hispanic young people also experience poor mental health, exhibiting the highest prevalence of depression of any ethnic group. Although Hispanic adolescent girls are as likely as white adolescents to consider suicide, they are twice as likely to attempt it. Their suicide completion rate, however, is lower than that of other ethnic groups.

The significance of these and other health-compromising behaviors among adolescents transcends their own physical well-being. In 2003, Hispanics had the highest teen birthrate, with 82.2 births per 1,000 adolescent females ages 15–19. In comparison, the birthrate for teens of all backgrounds was 41.7, while that for white teens was 27.5 and for black teens was 64.8.[92] Such statistics bode ill for the educational prospects of Hispanic adolescents, who are more likely than either blacks or whites to withdraw from school if they become mothers.[93] Indeed, all health conditions and behaviors that affect scholastic performance—including not only adolescent childbearing, but also drug and alcohol use and exposure to lead and other environmental contaminants—are especially worrisome because of the lifelong consequences of educational underachievement discussed above.

Access to Quality Care

Hispanics face a variety of financial and nonfinancial obstacles to obtaining appropriate health care. Low rates of insurance coverage are perhaps most notable, but lim-

ited access to providers, language barriers, and uneven quality of care exacerbate inequities in health outcomes between Hispanics and whites and between native- and foreign-born Hispanics.

The lack of insurance coverage is greater among foreign-born compared with U.S.-born Hispanics, Spanish compared with English speakers, recent compared with earlier immigrants, and noncitizens compared with citizens. Undocumented immigrants are least likely to be insured; one estimate of their uninsured rates ranges between 68 and 84 percent.[94] Owing to their large shares of recent immigrants, Mexicans and Central and South Americans have the highest uninsured rates. Puerto Ricans and Cubans have the highest insurance rates, with sources of coverage differing between the two groups. Puerto Rican children and working-age adults are much more likely than their Cuban counterparts to obtain health coverage through public insurance programs such as Medicaid and the State Children's Health Insurance Program (SCHIP), but they are less likely to obtain it through an employer (see figures 8a and 8b). For Hispanic seniors, eligibility for the Medicare program keeps insurance coverage rates relatively high.

Compared with whites, Hispanics have lower access to employer-provided health insurance because they are more likely than whites to work in small firms, in seasonal occupations, and in part-time jobs.[95] Limited eligibility for public insurance programs, such as Medicaid and SCHIP, further accentuates Hispanics' low coverage rates (with the exception of Puerto Ricans). Many Hispanics—especially Mexicans and Cubans—live in states with restrictive eligibility rules for Medicaid and SCHIP. The federal welfare reforms of 1996 placed further limitations on access to public health insurance programs for all recent legal immigrants.[96] General confusion about how the

Figure 8a. Health Insurance Coverage for White, Black, and Hispanic Children, 1997 to 2001.

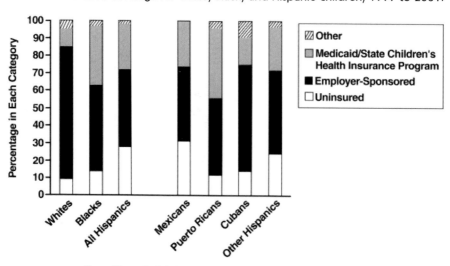

Race, Hispanic Origin, and Nativity

Source: 1997 to 2001 Medical Expenditure Panel Survey.

Figure 8b. Health Insurance Coverage for White, Black, and Hispanic Working-Age Adults, 1997 to 2001.

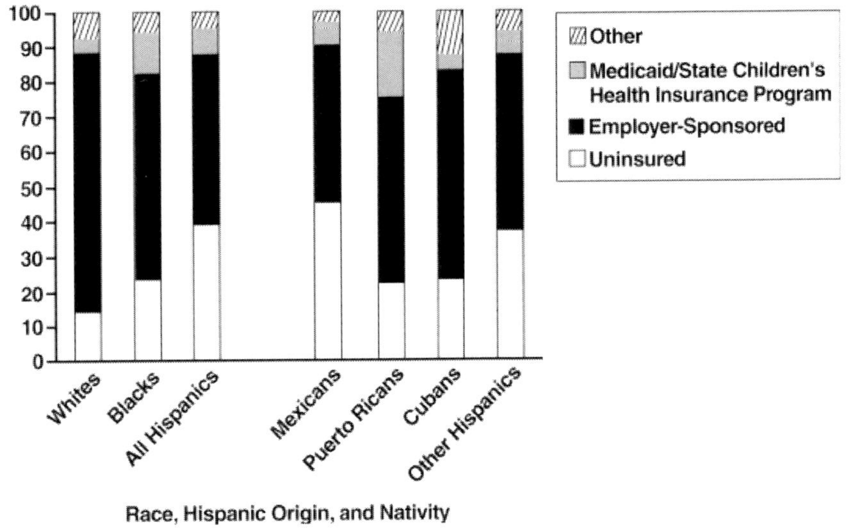

Race, Hispanic Origin, and Nativity

Source: 1997 to 2001 Medical Expenditure Panel Survey.

new laws affected immigrants triggered declines their overall utilization of public insurance programs.

Partly because of low rates of health insurance coverage, Hispanics are less likely than whites to have a usual source of care or regular health care provider, which in turn restricts their access to more specialized forms of care. The relatively low number of Hispanic physicians, especially in Hispanics' new destinations, further hinders access to care because Hispanic physicians are more likely than their non-Hispanic counterparts to care for Hispanic patients. Given their large share of recent immigrants, Mexicans are less likely than Puerto Ricans or Cubans to have a usual source of care, as are Spanish speakers compared with English speakers. Furthermore, language barriers undermine quality health care, even among groups with similar demographic and socioeconomic characteristics, by hindering patient-provider communication; by reducing access to health information; and in the worst case, by decreasing the likelihood that sick patients will seek needed care.[97]

Hispanics' low rates of insurance and reduced likelihood of having a regular health care provider mean less preventive care, fewer ambulatory visits, and higher rates of emergency room use compared with whites, although Hispanics' rates of inpatient care are equivalent to those of whites. The preventive services on which Hispanics trail whites include pneumococcal and influenza vaccinations for seniors; mammography, pap smears, and colon cancer screening; blood pressure and cholesterol measurements; and prenatal care for the general population. In 2001, just 75 percent of Mexican and 79 percent of Puerto Rican women received prenatal care in their first trimester, compared with 92 percent of Cuban and 89 percent of white women. Hispanic-white differences in childhood vaccination rates are trivial.[98]

Evidence on the quality of care received by Hispanics is inconclusive, partly because current assessments are based on populations that are not truly representative, such as low-income Medicaid recipients, and partly because results from satisfaction surveys are inconsistent. Nonetheless, Hispanics' reported satisfaction with health care delivery reveals large differences, depending on the degree of English proficiency. In general, Hispanics who speak only Spanish report worse experiences with health care than either whites or Hispanics who speak English. Satisfied patients are more likely to seek care when needed, to comply with provider recommendations, and to remain enrolled in health plans and with specific providers. Paradoxically, and for reasons not fully understood, Spanish-speaking Hispanics rate their physicians and health plans higher than do English-proficient Hispanics, despite admitting to worse care experiences.

To reduce language barriers to health care, the Department of Health and Human Services issued a directive in August 2000 requiring all federally funded programs and providers to offer interpreter services at no cost.[99] Yet only about half of Hispanic patients who need an interpreter receive one. In most cases, the interpreter is a staff person, relative, or friend rather than a trained medical interpreter; in such cases, reported satisfaction rates remain below those of whites.

Conclusion

Hispanic integration experiences are as diverse as the eclectic subgroups subsumed under the panethnic identity, but some general trends are discernible. Hispanic families converge in form and function with those of the white majority and rising intermarriage blurs the boundaries of nationality groups. The rise in divorce and nonmarital childbearing over time and across generations signal family decline. The rise of mother-only families bodes ill for economic prospects of the swelling second generation.

There are clear signs of educational progress at all levels both over time and across generations. That other groups also have improved their educational standing has widened attainment gaps, particularly at the college level. Because the fastest-growing and best-paying jobs now require at least some postsecondary education, Hispanics stand to lose economic ground even as their educational attainment rises. Still, employment and earnings trends show clear evidence of economic assimilation, with the greatest gains between the first and second generation. If the most successful third-generation Hispanics "opt out" of Hispanic identity, as available data suggest, economic progress for the third and later generations may well be understated.

Trends in Hispanic home ownership and median household income signal a growing middle class, although the dollar growth of Hispanic household assets is small compared with that recorded by white households.[100] Variation in financial status by immigrant and citizenship status, by age (favoring middle-aged over young householders) and especially by earnings capacity and educational attainment, largely explains the significant gap in economic well-being between Hispanics and whites. As long as this gap persists, however, Hispanics will remain more vulnerable to economic cycles because they have less of a cushion on which to draw during periods of financial distress.

Finally, recent health trends paint the picture of a Hispanic population burdened by the complications of obesity, diabetes, hypertension, and cardiovascular disease, which Americanization appears to worsen rather than improve. The deleterious effects of acculturation are especially evident among second-generation youths and in birth outcomes. Most striking is the high incidence of type 2 diabetes—usually a disease of adults—among young Hispanics and the increased prevalence of multiple risk factors for developing atherosclerosis among children of Mexican origin.[101] These trends foreshadow much higher rates of diabetes and its complications in the future, as large cohorts of Hispanic youths become adults.

The growing number of uninsured Hispanics will place particular stress on the health care safety net—a loosely organized system for delivering care to the uninsured that includes nonprofit organizations, government agencies, and individual providers. By default, some of the responsibility to health care delivery will shift to states and local communities, many of which are already struggling to compensate for shortfalls created by declining federal funding. Experts in both the public and private sectors consider cultural competence—the ability of health systems to provide care to patients with diverse values, beliefs, and behaviors, including tailoring delivery to meet patients' social, cultural, and linguistic needs—to be a crucial component of strategies to reduce disparities in care.[102] Compliance with the federal directive to provide interpreter services at care facilities is especially warranted in new immigrant destinations.

Notes

1. These findings are documented in greater detail in Landale et al., 2006.
2. Popenoe, 1993.
3. Landale and Oropesa, 2002.
4. Landale and Orepesa. 2002. The evidence for declines in familism among Central and South American nationalities is less clear than is the case for Mexicans because the generational depth is lower.
5. Landale et al., 2006.
6. Lee and Edmonston, 2005.
7. Edmonston et al., 2002, note that all population projections involve higher rates of intermarriage.
8. These findings are documented in greater detail in Schneider et al., 2006.
9. Mare, 1995.
10. See Duncan et al., 2006:Table 6-1.
11. Crosnoe, 2005; Crosnoe et al., 2004; Valencia, 2000.
12. U.S. Department of Education, National Center for Education Statistics, 1999.
13. U.S. Department of Education, National Center for Education Statistics, 1997.
14. U.S. Department of Education, National Center for Education Statistics, 2003b.
15. Carnegie Council on Adolescent Development, 1989.
16. Bryk and Schneider, 2002.
17. U.S. Department of Education, National Center for Education Statistics, 2003b; Valencia, 2002.
18. Bryk and Schneider, 2002.
19. Schneider and Stevenson, 1999.
20. Fry, 2003. This distinction is important because the Hispanic high school dropout rate has been inflated by the presence of foreign-born adolescents who withdrew from school before entering the United States.
21. U.S. Department of Education, National Center for Education Statistics, 2003a: Table 106.
22. Cameron and Heckman, 1993.
23. Fry, 2005; Hirschman, 2001.
24. Carnevale, 1999.
25. Tienda and Simonelli, 2001.
26. Kao and Tienda, 1998.
27. U.S. Department of Education, National Center for Education Statistics, 2002.
28. U.S. Department of Education, National Center for Education Statistics, 2003b.
29. Kim and Schneider, 2004; Portes and Rumbaut, 2001.
30. Fry, 2002, 2003.
31. College Enrollment and Work Activity of Year 2000 High School Graduates. Available: ftp://ftp.bls.gov/pub/news.release/History/hsgec.04132001.news [accessed December 23, 2005].
32. Schneider et al., 2006.
33. Velez, 1985.
34. Alon and Tienda, 2005; Fry, 2004.
35. Clark, 2003; Kochhar, 2004; Wolff, 2004.
36. These findings are documented in greater detail in Duncan et al., 2006.
37. Chiswick, 1978; Schoeni, 1997.
38. The annual employment rate is defined as the percentage of individuals who worked at all during the calendar year preceding the census. Similar results are obtained using annual hours of work as a measure of labor supply.
39. Dominican men also have relatively low employment rates, but nativity differentials for them are small.
40. Duncan et al., 2006:Table 6-4.
41. The estimated deficits are for persons ages 25 to 59 who worked during calendar year 1999, based on regressions by Duncan et al., 2006:Appendix Table A6-7.
42. This is not the case for black men, however, as their 15 percentage point employment deficit would shrink to only 13 percent-

age points if their human capital endowments were comparable to those of whites.

43. The employment gaps for Puerto Ricans and Dominicans may be due, in part, to their concentration in goods-producing industries in the northeast that have been hurt by deindustrialization, and in part to the fact that their employment patterns are more similar to those of blacks than to those of other Hispanic groups. See DeFreitas, 1991.

44. In contrast to black men, black women's modest earnings disadvantage relative to white women would disappear if they had comparable levels of human capital.

45. Phillips and Massey, 2000; Rivera-Batiz, 1999.

46. See Duncan et al., 2006.

47. Specifically, there is some evidence that darker, more Indian-looking Mexican Americans are vulnerable to discrimination based on skin color. See Allen et al., 2000.

48. Lowell and Fry, 2002.

49. Smith, 2001.

50. Duncan et al., 2006: Table 6–7.

51. Borjas, 1994; Chiswick, 1977; Neidert and Farley, 1985; Perlmann and Waldinger, 1997.

52. Duncan et al., 2006:Figure 5–8.

53. Borjas, 1993; Smith, 2003.

54. Smith, 2003, reports a 4.94-year mean education gap among all first-generation Mexicans (Table 3). This deficit fell to 2.95 years among second-generation Mexicans.

55. Alba and Nee, 1997; Duncan and Trejo, 2005; Telles et al., 2002.

56. Duncan and Trejo, 2005; Duncan et al., 2006; Reimers, 2006.

57. Edmonston et al., 2002; Rutter and Tienda, 2005.

58. Smith, 2003; see Duncan et al., 2006; Reimers, 2006.

59. U.S. Census Bureau; Income 1999. Available: http://www.census.gov/hhes/www/income/income99/99tablea.html [accessed December 27, 2005].

60. Those who were born in the United States have income levels similar to those of whites.

61. U.S. Bureau of the Census, 2004b.

62. U.S. Bureau of the Census, 2004b.

63. Wolff, 2004.

64. The Hispanic-black median income differential exceeded 90 percent between 1995 and 1997, hovering around 94 to 98 percent. See Wolff, 2004:Tables 7 and 8.

65. Kochhar, 2004.

66. Saenz, 2004:Table 11.

67. U.S. Bureau of the Census, 2000c. Poverty thresholds are not adjusted for cost-of-living differences. That large shares of Hispanics live in high-priced cities magnifies the welfare consequences of poverty-level incomes.

68. Saenz, 2004.

69. See Reimers, 2006:Table 7-2.

70. See Reimers, 2006.

71. McLanahan and Sandefur, 1994.

72. U.S. Bureau of the Census, 2000a.

73. U.S. Bureau of the Census, 2000a.

74. Reimers, 2006.

75. Social Security is an "earned" benefit that automatically increases with the cost of living, but SSI is a minimal, means-tested safety net for those elderly who have no other income. Unlike SSI, Social Security is not viewed as "welfare" by the general public. Persons who qualify for Social Security benefits by working most of their adult years in covered jobs, even at a low wage, receive more generous Social Security retirement benefits than persons forced to rely on SSI, the benefit rates of which are below the poverty line.

76. Using the Federal Reserve Board's Survey of Consumer Finances, Wolff, 2004, estimates Hispanic median net worth at 3 percent of the white median for 2001, but Kochhar, 2004, estimates the 2002 median gap at 9 percent—$8,000 versus $89,000—based on the Survey of Income and Program Participation. One source of the difference is that Wolff excludes equity in vehicles and other consumer durables from his estimate of wealth. However, both sets of estimates reveal similar trends, if not levels, for their overlapping period, namely mid-1990s to 2001–2002.

77. Kochhar, 2004:Table 9.

78. Wolf, 2004:26. Stock ownership is concentrated among households in the top quintile of the wealth distribution, accounting for 90 percent of all stock holdings.

79. Clark, 2003.

80. Wolff, 2004.

81. This estimate is close to the .62 for 2000 reported by Fischer and Tienda, 2006, on the basis of census data for the largest 100 metro areas.

82. Fischer and Tienda, 2006; Myers et al., 2005.

83. See Kochhar, 2004.

84. Grossman, 1972.

85. Our emphasis on Mexican-white comparisons reflects the paucity of research comparing other Hispanic nationalities in terms of specific health outcomes. This section draws from Escarce et al., 2006.

86. National Center for Health Statistics, 2003.

87. National Center for Health Statistics, 2003.

88. National Center for Health Statistics, 2003. National data are unavailable on the epidemiology of cardiovascular disease for Hispanics. Moreover, experts disagree about the differences in death rates from heart disease between Hispanics and whites because regional studies have yielded conflicting findings, Escarce et al., 2006.

89. National Center for Health Statistics, 2003.

90. Escarce et al., 2006.

91. Escarce et al., 2006. The Centers for Disease Control and Prevention is currently lowering the threshold blood lead level for intervention from 10 μg/dL to 5 μg/dL. More than one-fourth of preschool-age children and one-fifth of elementary school children of Mexican origin would meet the revised threshold.

92. Ryan et al., 2005.

93. Ahituv and Tienda, 2000.

94. Berk et al., 1999.

95. See Brown and Yu, 2002; Dushi and Honig, 2005; Schur and Feldman, 2001.

96. The 1996 Personal Responsibility and Work Opportunity Reconciliation Act (the Federal welfare reform law) barred legal immigrants who entered the United States after August 1996 from receiving federal Medicaid or SCHIP benefits for their first 5 years in the country. Although states can offer coverage for legal immigrants during the 5-year moratorium imposed by the federal regulations, few have elected to do so.

97. Langer, 1999; Ruiz et al., 1992.

98. Escarce and Kapur, 2006. A likely explanation for the shrinking gap in childhood vaccination rates is the Vaccines for Children program, created in 1994, which provides vaccines free of charge to eligible children, including the uninsured.

99. Department of Health and Human Services, 2000.

100. Kochhar, 2004:Tables 17 and 19.

101. Escarce et al., 2006. Other consequences of the overweight epidemic among Hispanic youth include elevated blood pressure and high rates of insulin resistance, hyperinsulinemia, glucose intolerance, and abnormalities in serum lipids. Hispanic youth also have higher triglyceride levels and lower levels of high-density lipoprotein cholesterol than white youth.

102. Betancourt et al., 2002.

Environmental Problems in Ciudad Juárez-El Paso: A Social Constructionist Approach

Pablo Vila and John A. Peterson

In the past few years the U.S.-Mexico border has become known as one of the most contaminated areas in the world, given the feverish industrial development that has characterized it as a result of the establishment of the twin plant industry (*maquiladoras*). Ciudad Juárez-El Paso, one of the main border industrial centers, participates fully in this characterization. The El Paso area has become a dumping ground for hazardous wastes, from toxic chemicals involved in *maquiladora* manufacturing to the Sierra Blanca Nuclear Waste Dump proposed for development within ninety miles of El Paso and only twelve miles from the Rio Grande border with Mexico. Air pollution from automobiles and point sources, including brick kilns and dust from quarries and unpaved roads, has plagued the region. Water suffers both in quality and in supply, with major groundwater sources expected to diminish within twenty-five years. Wastewater both in U.S. colonias and throughout Ciudad Juárez poisons the groundwater as well as the Rio Grande through dumping into the Aguas Negras ditch of the Lower Valley of Ciudad Juárez. If the region seems out of control, it is especially so to the low-income and immigrant communities that make up the largest population of the region, who problematize their plight quite differently from the public and expert discourses, and whose actions and responses reflect these different perspectives.

Despite this dilemma, there has been little research until now concerning area inhabitants' perceptions about environmental issues. This absence is not by chance but is framed within a larger problematic that afflicts environmental sociology and anthropology, which has only quite recently developed a focus that prioritizes the point of view of social actors in relation to the solution of environmental problems (Hannigan 1995). Thus only in the 1980s and 1990s did sociologists and anthropologists working on environmental issues begin using a constructionist ap-

proach to the issue (Gould 1991, 1993; Kottak and Costa 1993; Krauss 1993; Cable and Benson 1993). These studies examined the interplay of environmentalist discourse and local communities largely in an effort to understand how the attitudes and risk perceptions of disenfranchised groups could be integrated into larger and global environmental concerns and movements. From this perspective arose an interest in environmental justice, where Bullard (1994), Peña (1997), and Pulido (1996) discuss landscapes of inequality and focus on the relation between labor and gender in these contexts. Their emphasis is on the roles and empowerment of social actors rather than the process of social construction.

Gould's articles basically state that whereas the visibility of the sources of environmental pollution in a region can be extremely high (in the Juárez-El Paso case, the ASARCO smokestack, heavily contaminated drainage ditches, colonia water drums, uncollected trash, vehicle emissions, brick-manufacturing smoke, etc.), the visibility of *environmental deterioration* as produced by those sources varies substantially from source to source. In addition, it is important to keep this difference in mind, given the social visibility of a particular environmental problem that makes local residents become conscious of the existence of contaminants in their city (Gould 1993). Despite this, as Gould notes, consciousness does not necessarily bring about the definition of such contamination as a "problem." Thus what for some is the "horrible stench of pollution" is for others "the sweet smell of money" (Gould 1991).

Kottak and Costa's work also proposes to investigate the relationship between ecological risk, collective perception of that risk, and the development of an environmental conscience and action. According to these authors, even though the real presence of a contaminant enhances the perception of environmental risk, such perception does not necessarily originate from a rational cost-benefit analysis of that risk. On the contrary, the perception of environmental risk arises (or does not arise) within specific cultural, political, and economic contexts that are formed at the intersection of local ethnoecologies, imported ethnoecologies (often broadcast by mass media), and the changing circumstances linked to population, industrial growth, and migrations.

> An actual threat increases risk perception, but the threat does not cause the type of reaction that follows. Hazards may be accepted or avoided, emphasized or ignored. Risk assessment emerges or languishes in particular cultural contexts, and risk is culturally constructed. Recognizing cultural variations, it is important to consider that: (1) people react to dangers they perceive; (2) risk perception is selective; (3) sets of values determine the perception of threats; (4) values are culturally and politically determined; (5) the global spread of development and environmentalism is a political and economic process that entails cultural negotiation. (Kottak and Costa 1993, 338)

If this is so, an effective environmental strategy would, for these authors, involve one that listens to those afflicted and monitors their perceptions, reactions, needs and problems (336).

Celene Krauss emphasizes a feminist perspective concerning environmental issues. On the one hand, according to Krauss, this perspective values something that is put aside by the more traditional sociological analyses, that is, the subjective dimension of all social protest (Krauss 1993, 249). On the other hand, a feminist analysis would allow, according to Krauss, substantiation of the importance of environmental protests around specific issues (such as hazardous waste disposal in a particular community) showing how "ordinary women subjectively link the particulars of their 'private' lives with a broader analysis of power in the 'public' sphere" (249). In this manner, Krauss's article illuminates the way different groups of women, instead of constructing a *unique* truth concerning environmental problems that afflict them, construct partial visions or situational knowledge through their everyday narratives (251).

If the issue of situational knowledge is central to Celene Krauss, Sherry Cable and Michael Benson argue that the very idea of "environmental justice" is a historical and cultural construct: "Perceptions of environmental injustice arise when citizens come to believe that the state is failing to protect their lives and property from environmental pollution and that pollution costs are being unfairly imposed upon them" (Cable and Benson 1993, 464). According to these authors, local environmental action groups do not demand new environmental laws but rather press for the enforcement of already applicable laws. In this sense, these environmental activists are looking not for reform of environmental legislation but for environmental justice. This type of group arises when traditional, state-based environmental supervising mechanisms fail when trying to control what is popularly perceived as illegal and dangerous actions by local corporate actors. In this sense,

these local environmental groups represent replies, initiated within the citizenship, to what is interpreted as a failure of the state to control environmental pollution (465).

If the issue of social perception of environmental issues is something relatively new within the international literature on the subject, local research in this respect is almost nonexistent. The only manuscript-length work we could find on *any environmental issue* in the early 1990s was an interesting thesis written by Héctor Padilla (1993). He points out that it was as recently as the early 1990s when environmental issues emerged as an important matter in governmental agendas and in Juárez society. From the point of view of the government, "part of the Mexican environmental policy on the Northern border, besides aiming to remodel border cities in order to maintain their attractiveness for foreign investors, responded to local-scale environmental problems which were a source of binational conflicts" (Padilla 1993, 123). Thus, he notes, the lack of an "environmental discourse" can be exemplified by the theme's absence in municipal government annual reports during the 1980s. At the same time, according to Padilla, it would seem that the Panista government seeks particularly to emphasize the environmental issue. Nonetheless, as Padilla notes:

> Even though the government response to many problems arrived late, this fact did not place it totally out of concert with respect to the way civilian society demanded solutions on environmental problems. It can generally be asserted that civil society, through the action and discourse of social actors, was also late to perceive the dimension of the day-to-day problems that ail it, influenced by factors such as ignorance about the issue and its prioritization of other more pressing topics. In this sense . . . a possible explanation would be that the political agenda during the 1980s was engaged in political-electoral matters and that it was only toward the latter part of the decade when the electoral outlook was modified, that issues such as human rights, public services and the environment began to acquire political relevance. (Padilla 1993, 156)

Padilla identifies two well-defined phases in relation to civil society's participation in environmental issues. The first is characterized by a relative scarcity of "environmental" pronouncements, and the second phase outlines a discourse on the environment together with concrete action. What distinguishes both phases is also the type of ecological problem that concerned the social actors who brought them forth into the public arena. In this manner, the main points of the first phase, which would encompass 1983 to 1988, centered around the repercussions of the Cobalt 60 nuclear radiation accident, and pollution by the ASARCO smelter in El Paso. For the second phase, from 1988 to 1993, Padilla notes that the discussion centers around dwindling ecological resources, the brick-manufacturing problem, and, most of all, twin plant toxic waste disposal and its repercussions on the Juárez Valley. It is noteworthy that problems related to urban services were a constant presence in the civil society agenda during the entire 1983–1993 period (Padilla 1993, 163–64).

If on the one hand we will advance in this article a constructionist approach, on the other hand we fully realize that the "environment" has a phenomenological existence outside the perceptions of social actors in any milieu. These phenomena can sometimes be measured and monitored, and environmental discourses are replete with references to ozone, particulate matter, and toxic elements, for example, that can and do have real-world impacts on people as well as on ecosystems. Thus the plume of smoke wafting from the ASARCO smelter tower is not just a site of human perception or representation but also dumps real toxins such as lead and other materials on the environment downwind from the source.

However, the effects of these phenomena are themselves highly contingent on the perspective of those who are part of the environment, social actors ranging from scientists to bureaucrats to residents of barrios to academics toiling away in the ivory towers of the University of Texas at El Paso, also in the plume of ASARCO. Those perspectives each generate a variety of narratives that use these "data," from scientific to olfactory, to represent their own experience of the world and their own special interests. Environmentalists and pro-industry advocates obviously have their own vested interests in constructing, analyzing, and evaluating the data and the effects of the phenomena, and this has been treated recently to good effect by Ehrlich and Ehrlich (1996) in their masterful discussion of the rhetoric of industrialists, and, less convincingly, by Bailey (1995), regarding disinformation cast by environmentalists.

Research Project Objectives

Given the dearth of research on the issue of social perception of regional environmental issues in the region, it seemed important for us to contribute to this matter. Because we believe that the solution to environmental problems indubitably requires the active participation of diverse community actors, we thought that it was of great importance to be acquainted with the thoughts about the environmental problems afflicting those social actors. Thus, while there is no direct relationship between the visibility of environmental problems and social mobilization to arrive at its solution, this does not mean that social visibility of environmental problems in a region is not important. In this sense, we may argue that recognizing the existence of environmental problems is a *necessary* though not *sufficient* condition to explain the appearance and development of local environmental mobilizations (Gould 1993). If so, it should not be strange that private capital and governments often try to minimize social visibility of environmental pollution through diverse covert methods

(such as ASARCO's nighttime discharge of contaminating fumes). By the same token, people who are concerned about the environment should also resort to increasing social visibility of environmental problems if they seek to enable the social mobilization that will bring about their solution.

Because of all these factors, our research project intended first to investigate the level of social visibility of environmental problems in Ciudad Juárez-El Paso. To do so, we analyzed the commonsense discourse about environmental problems of diverse social actors in the region. Second, the study sketched the different ways social actors on the border addressed environmental problems. This seemed to us of great importance, because social actors are mobilized not by problems that are defined as such by experts but rather by those their own discursive universe defines as "priority problems." In other words, people can be conscious of environmental problems in their region and even so not mobilize, since the order of their priorities does not coincide with what environmental experts dictate. A Juárez colonia leader ably expressed this idea when asked about the main problems in his colonia: he pointed out that first came the land ownership problem and, second, the lack of water. "Once we succeed with the land problem, we tackle the water head on" (quoted in Padilla 1993, 183).

Main Research Findings

Visibility of Environmental Problems

What appears clearly in the analysis of the interviews is the high degree of social visibility of environmental problems among our interviewees. Most of the groups interviewed were generally acquainted with the principal environmental problems besetting the area.

If this was not surprising vis-à-vis officials and technicians we consulted, it was in the case of popular sectors we interviewed, who generally identified as problems the same ones singled out by the experts. Of course, our method in some respects *induces* people to identify the majority of the area's environmental problems, considering we showed them photographs that graphically illustrate those problems. Nonetheless, in most in-depth interviews, participants not only identified the problem but also demonstrated an even greater knowledge of it, referring to anecdotes, news stories, firsthand knowledge by way of family and friends, et cetera, concerning the shown photographs. In this sense, for instance, most of our Juárez interviewees not only knew about the brick-manufacturing pollution but also knew of the plan to change their brick-baking method, foregoing burning old tires as fuel in favor of natural gas. Also, it was common to see many interviewees remember contamination episodes on the part of the ASARCO, FLOUREX, and Candados Presto companies in vivid detail, or the pollution of untreated drainage ditch sewer water (aguas negras). Something similar happened in El Paso, proving that, at least with those we interviewed, most environmental problems were highly visible. The only exception to this visibility is the possible water shortage the area might face in the future. But this exception was once again shared by experts and common folk alike.

Environmental Problem Conceptualization: Priorities and Strategies

Another issue is how the various social actors characterize environmental problems and the place these occupy within their action agenda. We frequently heard in the area comments coming from both Mexicans and Americans, claiming that environmental problems do not recognize borders, that water contamination, air pollution, toxic waste, garbage collection, and so on are not just problems for El Paso or Juárez but that they are the blight of the border area in general. It is often argued that such problems do not recognize either the political delimitation of a national border or the social delineations that divide rich and poor, adults and children, women and men, Mexicans and Anglos.

However, this affirmation does not take into account that the mere definition of *what constitutes an environmental problem* is a cultural issue. If, on the one hand, borders and social classes are permeable to different cultures, on the other hand, the conceptualization of something as a "social problem" (as a "priority environmental problem" in this particular case) originates within the limits of a particular symbolic system. This symbolic system definitely determines whether an "obvious and urgent" problem, from a technical point of view, is (or is not) considered a priority environmental problem by the actors of a historically determined social space.

In this manner, what emerges in the in-depth interviews we conducted is that, from the point of view of the construction of meaning, many El Pasoans and Juarenses do not have the same environmental problems, and if they do, they do not usually bestow the same importance on them. Consequently border residents recognize and act on those environmental issues from the point of view of what their respective symbolic universes allow them to conceptualize as *priority problems*.

Same "Technical" Environmental Problem, Different Priorities

A good example of what we are discussing here is how, in some cases, national borders substantially modify the importance of environmental problems that would, from the technical point of view, affect El Pasoans and Juarenses to the same extent. This is the case of the Sunland Park landfill, which, according to complaints by the residents of this poor New Mexico suburb, gravely affects their health. Residents have mobilized to have the landfill relocated, and some of them have organized as an environmental group that meets periodically and has begun a structured battle to attain the relocation goal. According to Sunland Park residents, the landfill pollutes not only the groundwater but also the physical environment, as well as the air. As Guadalupe Contreras pointed out:

> The landfill is so close to the residential area and the schools . . . it's only five hundred feet away! So, when the wind is blowing, all of the contaminated soil . . . all that filth comes this way, all the dust, and the trash . . . comes to the community. There have been times when the teachers send their own children (so that the school will be very pretty), so they have the children pick up the trash. Even about a month ago they had the junior high students cleaning up the trash from along all the roads, when it's the obligation of the landfill to keep this whole area, all the sides of the roads, clean; because they come through here in their trucks and drop trash, but the mayor doesn't fine them or stop them, nor do the police say anything to them because it's all the same establishment, do you know what I mean?[1]

This pollution is particularly dangerous, as residents have claimed the trash that collects there is not only household trash (as the company contends) but highly contaminated trash that comes from Mexican twin plants, as well. As Guadalupe stressed:

> There are forty or fifty Juárez *maquiladoras* that bring their trash here. . . . Now, the men who run the landfill claim that it's household trash and that it's not dangerous. Then why don't they get rid of it in Juárez? We have stopped trailers, and when we opened them we found dangerous adhesives, for example, like the glue that is used for soldering; there are also different chemicals. So why don't they dispose of them in Juárez? This is the big riddle, you know what I mean?

Assorted health problems have resulted from this pollution since the landfill began operating, as documented by area residents:

> GUADALUPE: If we asked for a hearing, it was because they have to get rid of that dump, because the children complain that it always smells very bad there; that sometimes they don't even eat because of the odor, and they can't study because they have headaches, and things like that, right? So we asked for a hearing.

> AMELIA: And now I have a bunch of little bumps . . . especially on my chest and body, right? I went to the doctor, and he told me that it was a virus, but just going inside my house and not coming out makes them go away, and I just go outside to give the dog water or something and in just a little bit . . .[2]

> INTERVIEWER: The rash comes again.

AMELIA: And I also get very itchy. The doctor told me that it was a virus; and last night I got home at ten, and when I woke up at about one in the morning, I didn't have any, and when I got up this morning at seven I didn't have even one, and now I have them again, especially on my back . . . look . . .

INTERVIEWER: Oh! Yes, a rash . . .

Residents claim that the landfill jeopardizes not only their health but also their finances. Property values have depreciated considerably owing to the proximity of the landfill and to public knowledge about the high level of pollution it produces:

GUADALUPE: I consider this an injustice, for example that Mr. Margarito Ibáñez, having lived here for thirty years, and having built his house and some rental apartments, so that he could spend his later years comfortably . . . then how is it possible that a company like this, criminal, can come here and establish themselves, and then say, "Now we have contaminated your air; leave if you can." So where are all the assets the residents have worked for, will they go in the trash?

MARGARITO: I've been trying to sell that house for a year, and the people come and tell me, "Listen, I've heard about the dump, and . . . where is it located, and what's it doing to the environment?" Well, it's right up here, I tell them . . . Then they say to me, "Well, it's not worth it to me to invest ten, fifteen, or fifty thousand dollars . . . no, it's better for me to go elsewhere." Thus the dump is affecting our morals, our physical health, and our property.[3]

In the search for the cause of so much injustice, Sunland Park residents appeal to an ethnic discrimination discourse, emphasizing that it is not by chance that the landfill is located in an area with a high concentration of Hispanics.

GUADALUPE: But there is a problem; I don't know if the United States wants to get rid of Latinos, or I don't know why these companies, like the landfill, are only located where the communities are mostly Hispanic or black, why?

AMELIA: It would be good to see the dump in Coronado [the epitome of an Anglo neighborhood in El Paso]; do you believe they were going to put the landfill there? Even here the Country Club [another expression of rich and Anglo people of the city], they won't allow the toxic wastes to be transported through there, so they have to go through here, because Anglos unite and fight for what is theirs, and Mexicans tend to fight among themselves, do you know what I mean?

According to the Sunland Park residents, politics would be involved in the decision to install and maintain the landfill in their community, because they have de-nounced the existence of plotting between the landfill and several New Mexico authorities:

GUADALUPE: They have already run the dump out of four or five places where they've contaminated the area. If it continues here, . . . it's because now they are very well protected by the New Mexico governor, who knows about the problem, because we've talked to people who work for him. We've asked them to help, but nothing is done because the main person, the governor, turns out to be the one who is supporting them the most!

MARGARITO: And the landfill company's attorney was our senator, who represented us, and he came to defend them!

If this is going on in Sunland Park, something very different is happening just a few blocks away, on the Mexican side. The Juárez colonia immediately facing Sunland Park is called Puerto Anapra. From the point of view of experts who have investigated the area's problematic, there is no difference between the degree of health decline that Juarenses have suffered because of the landfill's presence in Sunland Park compared to what landfill neighbors on the American side have suffered. And the Mexican residents are fully conscious of the sanitary risks to which they are exposed because of the landfill's proximity.

ENRIQUETA: And we as neighbors, it makes . . . our skin crawl, right? To realize that sometimes our kids go there to play, and we know that they even dispose of human wastes there, right? . . . Infected body parts, and it's a huge danger that we have right here.[4]

CRISTINA: And here a neighbor of ours . . . her little children . . . the youngest one, right, Suquis? He has bald spots in his hair . . . he has blemishes here [signaling the head], and they haven't gone away.[5]

INTERVIEWER: And why do you think he has those pimples in his head?

CRISTINA: Because of . . . do you know what? They said in the news that it was because the landfills are here, and when . . . let's say the cloud of smoke that comes from there, it goes way up in the air, and it all falls on our hair. That's where the infections come from.

The residents of Puerto Anapra have also organized to battle environmental problems facing their colonia. Their most important fighting cause, however, is not landfill relocation but the provision of running water, which would allow them to get rid of the annoying system of (often contaminated) barrels they use to store water that a cistern truck delivers to them once every fifteen to twenty days.

INTERVIEWER: And in the meetings that you have, do you discuss this? For example, the dead dogs, the contamination that comes over here from the American dump, et cetera. In other words, is everyone aware of this, or is it only a few people who are worried?

ENRIQUETA: It's only a few people that . . . it's a few people, right? Really, our intention in having these meetings is . . . to protect ourselves here: our piece of land, working to have water—because we don't have water. That is another problem of contamination, right? They say there are contaminated barrels, right? . . . well, we have barrels, but thank God it hasn't affected us much. We're very careful, sometimes we even try to boil the water, right? But those barrels are dangerous. So in the meetings, yes, we do discuss the landfill, but we don't set aside a special time for it . . . only once in awhile . . .

Thus, what for residents on the American side is an environmental problem of such magnitude that some even declare, "If they don't go, we're going to have to," is for Puerto Anapra residents a secondary problem in relation to the more pressing one of water supply. In this fashion, while some are thinking of leaving (the Americans), others (the Mexicans) are thinking of securing a public service improvement in order to stay, with or without the landfill. This takes place within a context where Juarenses are fully conscious of the proximity of the landfill and of the health risks and have even met with their American counterparts to find a solution to the problem. As a Sunland Park leader declared:

GUADALUPE: We wanted to know if they had the same health problems that we do. They said they did. So we sought out their leaders, and we asked them to unite with us in protest, for example, a protest on both sides, they, being from Juárez, exposing their problems. Because its the same problem; they have the same health problems, skin allergies, their hair falling out, headaches, nausea, it's all the same. And we told them, "We want your help if times arrive to protest, can you join us?" And they said yes.

However, *their* priority environmental problem is water, not the landfill. Just as Guadalupe explains: "Do you know what happens? Water is such a huge necessity over there that they focus on that! Because what Enriqueta told me is that sometimes they go for months until the cistern trucks bring them any water, so it's a basic problem. That's why I think they focus more on the water problem, because it's a daily necessity."

Industrial Pollution: Neighbors versus Workers

Of course, we do not need to cross to the other side of the border to find divergent discourses relating to a particular environmental problem. In fact, living in such different countries as the United States and Mexico is a good

reason to have environmental discourses that are not precisely alike. But such conflicting discourses can still take the form of some neighbors even denying the existence of any problem at all, while others consider that such a problem is more than unbearable. This was what occurred precisely in a couple of interviews in Juárez and some others in El Paso. In this sense, for instance, we have found that the workers in several factories that have a particularly notorious polluting history had a totally different discourse from people who live close to the plants themselves.

Hence, in Juárez, for example, people from the colonia neighboring a *maquiladora* well known for contamination problems not only had full knowledge of the source of the pollution that affects them and of the environmental problems that the plant produced but had organized around their demands as well. They even occupied the plant for a brief time.

MODESTO: A *maquiladora* was set up here, right? Then later, I noticed that they were working with toxic products, very toxic. Then time passed, years, but we couldn't find the reason for our allergies. We saw a pipe there, close to the top, that gave off a kind of lime green smoke, like . . . yellowish . . . between yellow and green, and then the allergies started. Nasal allergies, a lot of nasal dryness, a lot of itching . . . a type of rash that broke out on our heads and all over our bodies. And then the nosebleeds started, and most of us complained of severe headaches, and I had read something about that, the contamination, and, well, those are the symptoms of toxic chemicals, right? And we had not organized here in the neighborhood until the accident happened with the little girl, because the factory disposed of the chemicals right here in the street, in a very irresponsible way, right? And there was nobody to tell them anything.[6]

WALKIRIA: And that little girl was burned because they had ditches there; they would open the ditches and throw all the wastes out here, and they left that ditch open and the little girl walked by and she put her little foot in there and was burned by the acid.[7]

WALKIRIA: Think about it: is it fair that we go to bed at night and in the morning we wake up vomiting, dizzy? Because they start working at four or five in the morning. So, for example now, when it's hot weather and we turned on the air conditioner, what happened? It pulled the smoke in. Did we wake up dizzy and with headaches!

In fact, some of the neighbors (or someone in their family) used to work at the factory and told about health problems that working there had brought them.

FLORENCIA: And my great-granddaughter was born with Down's syndrome, and it was my granddaughter's first child! And she was newly wed. Her husband doesn't smoke or drink, but the company has him working with the strongest chemicals. . . . So he quit when the baby was born like that, and the hospital told him that it was from handling so many chemicals. And they were still newlyweds! Since then he has two handicapped kids, so the chemicals damaged his blood . . .[8]

IRMA: I've had this illness for a long time now, I figure since I worked at the company. At first the scars weren't very noticeable, but for a while now, very much so! I thought they were fungus, but I went to a pharmacist, and he told me they weren't fungus, that it is a skin infection or maybe allergy, but not fungus. I have even noticed that since they've reopened the factory, my daughter has diarrhea often, and Sofia's little girl too, she's very sick with diarrhea, but no amount of medicine will get rid of it.[9]

IRMA: Oh, no! . . . I am just so itchy!

INTERVIEWER: It doesn't matter [laughs].

IRMA: Now that it's just us women, I have to tell you that I don't just have it only on my legs. The other day I showed Florencia . . . I told her I even have blood besides my streaks! But all this part is diseased; my breasts are the same way, it's not just my legs. That is the reason why I was telling you I can't sleep, my back, my butt, I won't show you that! But, can you believe it, it is not fair!

However, neither the factory owners nor the workers paid any attention to the neighbors' demands. The workers even went as far as to mock neighbors who hurt themselves because of contact with the chemicals that the factory had carelessly released into the surrounding streets. As one interviewee testified:

FLORENCIA: I have a grandson who was burned right here on the sidewalk, because they released the water with the acid here, under the door, and the acid was always coming out . . . then I sent my granddaughter . . . I sent her to the store, and she didn't notice that the little boy followed her and stepped in the water and got his feet burned—both his little feet were burned! Then, instead of helping him, they started laughing . . .

INTERVIEWER: Who started laughing? . . . The same people from . . . ?

FLORENCIA: Yes, the people from the factory . . . the workers!

INTERVIEWER: But why did they laugh at your grandson's problem?

FLORENCIA: Because they saw that he was burned, that he was screaming and jumping around there. Until my granddaughter came back and picked him up and brought him to my house. He was seriously burned.

Not only that, but at the moment of greatest tension between plant and neighbors (when the latter took over the plant), the workers stood behind the owners of the plant.

They also denied that the neighbors' claims held any truth, although they had similar health problems themselves. In this particular case, the digression among narratives about what was taking place came to a point of direct confrontation.

WALKIRIA: Yes, they have been rude to us, which is obvious, right? They are defending the positions they have in the factory, and we are defending our rights, no?

IRMA: When we occupied the factory, our children would pass by, and several factory workers would say, "Oh! Look at the contaminated little ones!" And then . . . they whistled at my sister-in-law and me, and then they said, "Oh, no, don't whistle at them because they're contaminated!"

FLORENCIA: "And there go the children without brains," that old hag that I was telling you about, the secretary would say, "There go the children without brains and the contaminated ones" . . . a mockery.

Consequently, as many of our interviews show, workers who labor at plants with a contamination history, when it comes to defending their source of income, often deny the truth of pollution charges. In those cases the mobilizations are usually effected by neighbors, without any support from the workers. And if it becomes extremely difficult to disavow the presence of pollution, there is always the resource of minimizing it or upholding the belief that it happened once but is not happening anymore. As a plant worker declared in another interview:

SECUNDINO: During the time that I have worked at the plant the necessity of educating the workers, providing them with adequate equipment, and modifying the machinery has been seen. All of that has greatly reduced the occupational risks and the pollution of the environment.[10]

What is odd is that many of these workers are entirely aware of the degree of environmental damage the company causes. Consequently, it is not that they support the company because they are unaware that it pollutes; rather, knowing that the company contaminates, they prioritize their source of work over the destructive effects on the environment.

INTERVIEWER: And what kinds of contaminants does the company produce?

SECUNDINO: Air pollution, because there are gaseous emissions, so mostly air pollution. And then also underground pollution. Because the factory produces acid, and due to leaks or spills the contaminated water goes underground. Or it used to go in the past.

INTERVIEWER: In other words, these days it's a little better controlled . . . and that wastewater that goes underground, would it reach the groundwater levels, or do you think that it wouldn't get that far?

SECUNDINO: Yes, it goes that deep, because the acid is very corrosive; it's contaminated water. All the chemical products are very concentrated, and the amount that goes underground depends on the size of the spill.

The economic incentives they collect from working in polluting plants are sometimes very significant and seem to outweigh not only the damage they know the company causes to the environment but also the risks to their own health.

INTERVIEWER: And, for example, in what way does the company protect you, as workers, so that you don't have problems? Or are there such good incentives that it's worth it?

SECUNDINO: Mainly that's the plant's attraction. In the past, there were barrels of applications turned in (in 1987 and 1988), because this plant was, and still is, considered high risk; so the people from this city went and made applications, as did people who came from other cities. . . . For example, they would make an application, come in and work, get to know the plant, and then leave and not come back . . . they never came back . . .

INTERVIEWER: And is it very risky for the workers to work there?

SECUNDINO: Last year, the worst accidents happened to workers when they were not working, outside the plant . . .

INTERVIEWER: But I'm referring to the risks of working with chemical substances, with the acids, and other things that can affect your health in the future.

SECUNDINO: Well, our work will definitely affect us in the future, just as many other kinds of work would . . .

We can therefore see how this interviewee is entirely conscious of the perils involved in working in such a polluting factory, and still he does not plan to change jobs. The question becomes what kind of narrative allows this worker to continue working at the plant in full knowledge of the jeopardy to his health. The logic emerges when the interviewee equates his work to his father's, who worked for years in a mine.

SECUNDINO: My work . . . I compare it to mining, because my father worked fifteen years in a mine, and I was very happy the day he decided to retire. They paid him, and he was very happy himself to leave the mine. He worked three more years as a bricklayer, because he knew how to work in construction too. It was about five years after he left the mine that he died after being run over on the highway in San Luis Potosí. So

his pleasure at having left the mine in one piece lasted a relatively short time, because he lived through the experiences of many people who died inside the mine. They stayed there, they got sick or suffered accidents in the mine; I imagine that it is still one of the places where there are more fatal accidents.

This worker develops an argument where he first recognizes the highly polluting and dangerous character of his work, because comparing his work with mining work is a kind of implicit question: what can be more dangerous and harmful to one's health than working in a mine? He then details how his father worked all his life in a mine where absolutely nothing happened to him, and how, finally, he died in a traffic accident. Therefore he wants to convince us that, for him, chance, not the kind of work you do, is the most important factor in determining people's destiny. If this is so, it does not make much difference whether one works in a dangerous place or in a nondangerous one.

National Discourses: "They Pollute More Than Us"

Another interesting aspect of the commonsense construction of environmental problems in Juárez and El Paso points to a particular attribute of the border: when it comes to finding a culprit for environmental problems, many people easily find it on the other side of the dividing line. Thus, in the majority of interviews in El Paso and Juárez, a certain logic of the "they pollute more than we do" type appeared prominently.

For this reason, many El Pasoans would, using various arguments, put almost all the burden of environmental problems that ail them on Juarenses' shoulders. Some interviewees believe that most of the pollution in the area is due to the lack of pavement in the streets of Juárez or the use of highly pollutive fuel to heat houses in the winter.

STEVEN: As much as the pollution, I think that in Juárez it's dust. There aren't, there aren't lawns in the neighborhoods like we have. I mean . . . Your backyard's a swimming pool, and what's gonna blow out of there? My front yard's all rocks, huh? And the roads aren't paved. I think that when you see that haze in the wintertime, you know, when it's the worst around here, it's 'cause of that. I think so. And then the other thing is they're poor people, so to heat their houses they use wood, they burn wood. And the other one really popular is the *calentones*. The little catalytic heaters with *petróleo*. Which is kerosene.[11]

Other El Pasoans interviewed argued that the most significant source of pollution on the border derives from the way Juarenses deal with their house trash, as well as the habit of burning tires to keep warm:

JEFF: You don't find garbage disposals in Mexico. I've always heard that the people that live right across from UTEP, in Mexico, they burn tires to keep them warm, as the fuel to their fires.[12]

For Jeff, sanitary conditions in Juárez are so catastrophic that they resemble those during the Middle Ages more than they do those of a developing country: "When I go to Juárez I take the back roads there. You actually see the sewage in the middle of the roads, and when an animal dies, like a cat . . . one time a cat got hit by a bus, and the dogs were fighting over eating that cat, it was . . . uh! It was uh! . . . barbaric! [laughs].

By contrast, for other El Pasoans, Juárez's stock of notoriously old and dilapidated cars is the main cause of the areas pollution.

SERENA: The cars over there, I don't know if they're inspected like they are here . . . to meet standards. You know, like Aníbal was telling me that I could go to Juárez and have that . . . catalytic converter removed, and they wouldn't even inspect it, and I go . . . see, I won't do that type of thing. Here in the United States you have to get your car inspected and it has to pass inspection, and I think that's important.[13]

In the account of many of our El Paso interviewees, Juarenses would be responsible not only for environmental pollution in their own city (pollution that has repercussions in El Paso's daily life as well—burning trash and tires, vehicular contamination, etc.) but also for much of the pollution generated in El Paso, prominently, the garbage generation.

SERENA: In Mexico . . . I think people tend to litter more even in their own city. I don't want to call it an attitude, but they carry it over here.

ETHEL: I understand the attitude she's saying, 'cause I went to the post office here and I was getting out of my car and there was this truck beside me with laborers from Mexico, I guess . . . and the guy in the front seat was gonna throw a can out the window, but he saw me and he stopped himself from doing that.[14]

This idea that Mexicans are the principal culprits for the trash present in El Paso was evident in many of our interviews. Not only that, but the issue was debated in a letter to the editor of the *El Paso Times*:

I would like to know why people across the border always leave their garbage here. We're trying to keep our city clean, even I feel guilty when I have a gum wrapper in my hand and want to throw it away. There's a lot of tourists that stop by and shop and see all that garbage and think the worst about us. They do not know its Mexicans who do it. The Mexicans come to shop in every one of our stores, especially Sam's, Kmart, Wal-Mart and Target. They unpack whatever they buy and leave all those big empty boxes lying all over the parking lot. Why in the world can't they put them in the garbage cans? That's one of the reasons I don't go over the border, I hate to see their dirty and filthy streets. (A. Delgado, *El Paso Times,* 26 February 1994)

As we can see, a whole arsenal of arguments was used by many El Pasoans to try to prove that, without a doubt, the greatest source of pollution came from the Mexican side.

Juarenses know very well of the "charges" against them, which is why it was not surprising to find a defensive attitude about the subject. For this reason, some of our Juarense interviewees "defended" their position, maintaining that while they admit Juárez creates a good part of the area's pollution, they also think that El Paso's pollution is much more conspicuous and dangerous than their own. In this manner, certain Juarenses argued that while it is true that brick manufacturing and other sources of air pollution are a serious problem, they do not compare to the degree of pollution produced by American sources such as the ASARCO or Chevron refineries. The arguments went from claiming that the latter work twenty-four hours a day, whereas burning tires or trash is only an occasional practice, to pointing out that lead emissions from ASARCO constitute a larger health hazard than the brick manufacturers' wastes.

ROBUSTIANO: I imagine that all that smoke [referring to the ASARCO refinery] pollutes more than anything else, because it's pure gas, from refineries and all that . . . it's pure, strong [dangerous] fumes. Because it's not the same as burning trash or something, the pollution from ASARCO is much worse.[15]

Other interviewees argued that vehicular contamination was not the Juarenses' fault, either. Thus they claim that even though it is true Mexican cars are very old, the source of most of the pollution would be the long waiting lines at the international crossing bridges, especially to cross to the American side, because of all the paper requirements American customs demand.

REFUGIO: Another serious problem occurs on the bridges: you often wait more than half an hour to cross. And it's not just one car, it's several![16]

INTERVIEWER: And in that case, who is responsible for the pollution from the bridges?

REFUGIO: People from over there, because they don't speed up the crossing process. It's less of a hassle to come over here . . . or maybe it's that when we go over there, they don't want us, that's why they give us a free way back to Juárez. Crossing from here to there, they search your car, open the trunk, raise the hood, and look at your passport; right there you lose maybe . . . three to five minutes. For them the search is quick, but it's not just one car, it's several, and several lines . . . and not just one bridge, there are several.

Further, although the majority of our interviewees on both sides of the border agreed in identifying *maquiladora* toxic refuse as a major source of area pollution, they did not agree on who is responsible for that pollution: Mexicans or Americans. In this manner, many El Pasoans blamed the Mexican government's lack of regulation for the American twin plant industry in Juárez, while some Juarenses we interviewed placed all the blame on the American companies that operate in Juárez to evade the strict American environmental regulation while benefiting from Mexicans' need for work. As we can observe, this "they pollute more than we do" logic has countless forms of expression on both sides of the border. It might even be one of the reasons for the lack of environmental mobilization found on the border.

The "Enlightenment" Discourse among Environmental Experts

We also think that this lack of mobilization is also somewhat related to the way many "experts" address the environmental problems of the region. We think that their usual approach to those problems is not the best suited to promote public mobilization in search of environmental solutions. Thus when we interviewed the "experts" (politicians, officials, contractors, and technicians who, directly or indirectly, have an environmental discourse), the most noticeable thing we found in their discourse was what can be termed as an "enlightenment approach to environmental discourse."[17] In this type of discourse, the need to create an environmental "conscience" for the population is understood as the number one priority in environmental issues. What is forgotten in this thematizing style of environmental problematic is that often "one sees what one wants to see and one does not see what one does not want to see." In addition, it is forgotten that discourse is an appropriate tool to enforce this divide between facts and perceptions. The point we wish to underline here is this: if it is impossible to live in situations of poverty without being able to simultaneously imagine a way out of these situations, where the vision of a brighter future is automatically incorporated into a vision of the present, thus making it more bearable, it is also impossible to live in an extremely polluted situation without resorting to some mechanism that, albeit symbolically, ameliorates it.

Thus the enlightenment posture to which we are referring—*see, know, acquire conscience, act*—also overlooks the *see, construct a particular narrative about what is seen, narrowly believe such a narrative, do not act* possibility. Is there anything more visible than the pollution that often floats around Ciudad Juárez-El Paso on winter mornings? We think not. Nonetheless, to illustrate how what we call an enlightenment discourse about environ-

mental problems fails to account for many of the people's attitudes about the environment, we shall refer to a specific interview. In that interview, Mexican UTEP students tried by any means possible to prove the smog they were being shown in a photograph was not really smog but something else that was not really pollution.

GRISELDA: This photograph . . . it seems to me that it isn't smog. I think that this city isn't as polluted as, say, Monterrey, where you go and it looks like this [like the photograph of Juárez]. That you can't really distinguish the . . . sometimes there are days when you can't see the mountains very clearly. So it seems to me that what the photo shows is very little . . . rather, I think . . . it's dust, or just a cloudy day or something. Because I've seen it when it's dusty, and that's how it looks.[18]

RODRIGO: Well, El Paso doesn't meet the standard that it should . . . the "safety zone" of air and . . . the biggest pollutant many times . . . is just dust particles. And the times that El Paso has not met the standard, it's because of that. Because the carbon monoxide and all that has almost always been at the required level, but . . . what ruins everything is exactly that, the dust.[19]

GRISELDA: I think that maybe it gives the impression that Juárez is very polluted . . . but I think it's just dust . . .

The idea of these interviewees is also to prove that smog is not really detrimental to one's health; that is, to argue that only air pollution originating from industrial or vehicular sources counts as pollution and that breathing suspended dust is not really an environmental problem. On the other hand, these students tried to remedy (although symbolically) the state of contamination they experience in the area by comparing it to other areas that supposedly are worse in that respect.

There is an additional example we would like to bring up for discussion to show how the *see, know, acquire conscience, act* logic often cannot account for why people do not organize around environmental issues even for the most grievous of them (at least from a technical point of view). What we want to mention here is how there are particular regional discourses that, although recognizing the existence of environmental problems, do not ask for any solution to them. This is the case of a religious discourse that is expanding quite rapidly on the northern border (one that comes from some Protestant denominations) that argues, among other things, that if there is pollution, it is due to God's will.

MAFALDA: Well, for example, about the pollution, I've heard people say that "the contamination is God's will" . . .[20]

ESTEFANÍA: Yes, a lot of people say that, that otherwise God had not allowed us to invent cars, factories, et cetera. Many people say, "If we are going to die from the pollution, it's because God wants it that way. "[21]

INTERVIEWER: But who would buy their God?

ESTEFANÍA: Well, only they know; it's the *ecoloco* [the crazy ecologist or the toxic man] [laughs].

As we can see, the possibility of *seeing, constructing a particular narrative about what is seen, narrowly believing such narrative, not acting* has many varieties, and all of them would be impermeable to the enlightenment logic many experts apply to environmental problems.

Implications for the Implementation of Public Policy

The present work has diverse implications for the design of public policy. First, dissonance in the conceptualization of problems and priorities of environmental questions, to which we referred earlier, poses an important obstacle to the solution of the innumerable problems that trouble the border. This is especially true because the execution of solutions does require a joint focus to be effective. So we are faced on the border with a myriad of environmental problems and priorities that are differently defined culturally and locally, and they can differ because of the definition of what a problem is or because of the importance that problem, once defined as such, has to different social actors. Nonetheless they require a unique implementation—transnational and transcultural—to arrive at a solution.

As we have noted, the problem is not that the area's environmental problems have a low social visibility or that "people are not environmentally conscious" in the sense that they do not know that they should not throw trash just anywhere, or waste water, or pollute drainage ditches with toxic substances, or contribute to the proliferation of clandestine garbage dumps. We do not want to affirm the opposite either, that is, that *all* people in the area possess an "environmental conscience." What we propose is something more complex, which has a significant effect on the design of public policy. We maintain that implementation of public policy that aims to solve environmental problems requires the active participation of the public, in one way or another. This can mean participating in a recycling program, wasting less water, disposing of industrial waste only where the law indicates, or organizing around some environmental problem that necessitates participation of the affected population (a polluting plant, an improperly located landfill, etc.). This citizen participation will only be achieved if the call for public involvement addresses the way people define which are the environmental issues that are problematic to them, and takes into account their order of priorities for their solution. In this way, people will participate or mobilize not in those issues or priorities that "technicians" define as such but rather in those the

people themselves define in their own terms as problems and priorities, given their particular perspective and their current priorities. In this sense, the technicians who design public policies should have something we can call "constructionism awareness."

The second point we want to address is closely linked to the first. We believe that just as it is necessary to "listen to the people" for the implementation of effective policies, so it is also imperative to "listen to the conflicting voices" of diverse social actors and to respect their particular narratives, even if many of these voices oppose each other. What we are proposing is to transform the cacophonous chorus we have right now on the border into a more tuneful one where, through public debate and narrative exchange, an environmental consensus can be reached that may eventually lead to the implementation of environmental policies that will solve at least the most urgent and important problems that the majority of the border population can negotiate discursively.

At the same time, an emergent awareness of the connectedness of human action within a broader framework must also be incorporated into discourses at all levels regarding the environment. In the process of analyzing the perceptions and representations of the environment in local discourses, we have tried to offer some insights about how the various conflictive voices can incorporate an awareness of our role(s) as interactive players within, and not apart from, the environment. As suggested in this chapter, "local" voices are often excluded from this dialogue, both because they have been disenfranchised and because their voices are not being systematically recorded. When they are, the conflict among the various discourses is often highlighted over local perceptions and concerns. As Hannigan (1995) concludes in his discussion of environmental sociology, the site of conflict often "involves a clash between opposing cultural constructions, one rooted in a vernacular, the other in a new ecological sensibility." In this project, we seek to document the commonsense or vernacular discourse from a constructionist perspective, not only to comment on the conflicts within a larger frame, but also to understand how players perceive and work out environmental concerns in their local contexts.

Notes

1. Guadalupe Contreras (a pseudonym, as are the other names used in this article) is a thirty-five-year-old Mexican national born in San Esteban, Durango. She migrated first to Ciudad Juárez in 1968 and later to El Paso nine years ago. She is a divorced housewife and mother of three children. Guadalupe identifies herself as "Christian" and has completed twelve years of school. She does not own her house at Sunland Park, but rents it. She is the leader of her neighborhood grassroots organization.
2. Amelia Rosales is a thirty-one-year-old native of Ciudad Juárez who has lived in El Paso for more than twenty years. She is married, has two children, and currently is a full-time housewife. Her religion is Catholicism, and she has completed her middle school education. She owns her house in Sunland Park.
3. Margarito Ibáñez is a Mexican immigrant who was born in Chihuahua sixty-seven years ago. He migrated to El Paso in 1958 and is

now retired. He is married and has two children. He does not recognize any religious affiliation and has only completed his elementary school education. He owns his own home.

4. Enriqueta Barrera is a thirty-eight-year-old Mexican national born in Sonora. She migrated to Ciudad Juárez when she was five. She is a single mother of four and a full-time housewife who has completed some secondary education. Enriqueta identifies herself as "Catholic," and she owns her house at Puerto Anapra. She is the leader of her neighborhood's grassroots organization.

5. Cristina is a thirty-five-year-old Mexican national born in Zacatecas. She is a recent migrant to Ciudad Juárez and has lived in Juárez for less than three years. She is married, has four children, and is a full-time housewife. Cristina identifies herself as "Catholic," and she owns her house in Puerto Anapra. She is illiterate.

6. Modesto is a fifty-four-year-old Mexican national born in Coahuila. He has lived in Juárez since he was twelve years old. He is married and is currently retired. Modesto is Catholic and has completed his high school education. He owns his house.

7. Walkiria is a thirty-four-year-old Mexican national born in Coahuila. She has lived in Juárez since she was two years old. She is married, and her occupation is housewife. Walkiria did not answer the question about religion, and she claimed she has completed her high school education. She owns her house.

8. Florencia is a fifty-four-year-old Mexican national born in Durango. She has lived in Juárez for the last thirty years. She is married, and her occupation is housewife. Florencia identified herself as "Christian," and she pointed out that she only went to the first three years of elementary school. She owns her house.

9. Irma is a twenty-nine-year-old native Juarense. She is married and has three children, and her occupation is housewife. Irma is Catholic and has completed her elementary school education. She owns her house.

10. Secundino is a twenty-eight-year-old native of San Luis Potosí. He migrated to Juárez four years ago to work in one of the most polluting *maquiladoras* located in the city. He is married, has three children, and listed his occupation as "worker." Secundino is Catholic and has completed less than half of his middle school education. He rents a house in a working-class neighborhood.

11. Steven is a forty-three-year-old native of New Mexico. He migrated to El Paso fifteen years ago. He is married, has two daughters, and is a manager in an American *maquiladora* in Juárez. Steven is a Baptist and has completed his high school education. He owns a house in a middle-class subdivision in west side El Paso.

12. Jeff is a twenty-seven-year-old native El Pasoan. He is single and self-employed. Jeff filled out "nonpreference" in the question about religion. He has completed his high school education and is a renter.

13. Serena was born twenty-one years ago in Costa Rica. She migrated to El Paso three years ago. She is single and currently studies at UTEP. Serena is Catholic and lives with her sister in a middle-class neighborhood on the west side of town.

14. Ethel is Serena's older sister. She is twenty-three and was also born in Costa Rica and migrated to El Paso three years ago. She is single, a student, and lives with her sister in a house that their parents own.

15. Robustiano, who is forty-three years old, came to Juárez from Parral, Chihuahua, more than twenty years ago. He lives in an extremely poor colonia in East Juárez and is self-employed. Robustiano, who never finished primary school, raises chickens on a small plot of land near his house. He used to work in the United States illegally. He is married and has a son. Robustiano is Catholic and owns his house.

16. Refugio is a fifty-two-year-old native Juarense. He lives in a poor colonia in East Juárez and is retired (he used to work as an elementary school teacher). He is single and Catholic.

17. Because of space restrictions, we can not analyze here the different variants of the "enlightenment" discourse.

18. Griselda was born twenty-one years ago in El Paso but has lived all her life in Juárez. She is single and currently studies at UTEP. Griselda is Protestant and lives with her family in a middle-class neighborhood.

19. Rodrigo was born twenty-five years ago in Ciudad Juárez and moved to El Paso when he was ten years old. He is married and is an electric engineer. Rodrigo is Catholic and rents the apartment where he lives.

20. Mafalda was born twenty-three years ago in Durango. She migrated to Ciudad Juárez three years ago. Mafalda works at home in a house that she shares with her parents and siblings in a working-class neighborhood. She is single and answered "Catholic" to the religion question. She has completed one year of adult education.

21. Estefanía was born twenty-nine years ago in Ciudad Juárez. She works at home but also, like Mafalda, does voluntary work at a small clinic in a very poor neighborhood. She lives with her husband and two children in a working-class neighborhood. Estefanía is not Catholic but Baptist. She owns her house.

References

Bailey, Ronald. 1995. *The True State of the Planet Earth: Ten of the World's Premier Environmental Researchers in a Major Challenge to the Environmental Movement*. New York: Free Press.

Bullard, Robert. 1994. *Unequal Protection: Environmental Justice and Communities of Color*. San Francisco: Sierra Club Press.

Cable, Sherry, and Michael Benson. 1993. "Acting Locally: Environmental Injustice and the Emergence of Grassroots Environmental Organizations." *Social Problems* 40 (4): 464–77.

Ehrlich, Paul R. and Anne H. Ehrlich. 1996. *Betrayal of Science and Reason: How Anti-environmental Rhetoric Threatens our Future*. Washington, D.C.: Island Press.

Gould, Kenneth A. 1991. "The Sweet Smell of Money: Economic Dependency and Local Environmental Political Mobilization." *Society and Natural Resources* 4 (2): 133–50.

———. 1991. "Pollution and Perception: Social Visibility and Local Environmental Mobilization." *Qualitative Sociology* 16 (2): 157–78.

Hannigan, John A. 1995. *Environmental Sociology: A Social Constructionist Perspective*. New York: Routledge.

Kottak, Conrad P., and Alberto C. G. Costa. 1993. "Ecological Awareness, Environmentalist Action, and International Conservation Strategy." *Human Organization* 52 (4): 335–43.

Krauss, Celene. 1993. "Women and Toxic Waste Protests: Race, Class, and Gender as Resources of Resistance." *Qualitative Sociology* 16 (1): 247–62.

Padilla, Héctor. 1993. "Ciudad Juárez en los ochenta: Medio ambiente, acción gubernamental y participación ciudadana." Thesis, Universidad Autónoma de Ciudad Juárez.

Peña, Devon. 1997. *The Terror of the Machine: Technology, Work, Gender and Ecology on the U.S.-Mexico Border*. Austin: CMAS Books, University of Texas at Austin.

Pulido, Laura. 1996. *Environmentalism and Economic Justice: Two Chicano Struggles in the Southwest*. Tucson: University of Arizona Press.

The Latino Health Research Agenda
for the Twenty-First Century

David E. Hayes-Bautista

Introduction

Until recently, medical research has been conducted overwhelmingly on non-Hispanic white male populations, with the result that baseline patterns of illnesses, behaviors, knowledge, and attitudes reflected the patterns of that population group. Under the prodding of the *Report of the Secretary's Task Force on Black and Minority Health* (USHHS 1987), gentle pressure has been exerted on investigators to include women and minorities in study populations. Current research guidelines now require that a principal investigator justify any exclusion of women and minorities from a research sample, and slowly these groups are becoming part of the nation's research focus. However, this prodding has been too little and too late for large states such as California, which have experienced rapid "minority" population growth in the years since the *Report of the Secretary's Task Force.*

In 1999 the non-Hispanic white population in the state of California became a minority population (49.7 percent), with Latinos making up the next largest group (31.3 percent), followed by Asian/Pacific Islanders (11.8 percent), African Americans (6.7 percent), and American Indians (0.6 percent). Among children, the changes are even more impressive. In 1998 nearly half of all the state's newborns (47.5 percent) were Latino, with non-Hispanic whites constituting barely a third (33.9 percent), Asian/Pacific Islanders 10.7 percent, and African American 6.8 percent of the state's births.

In spite of these dramatic population changes, health and medical research in California is still largely "normed" on the non-Hispanic white population, as it is in the rest of the country. But when theoretical models that explain patterns and variations of illnesses and disease are developed on the basis of non-Hispanic white populations and then applied to Latino populations, the results are confusing, seemingly paradoxical, and of little use in creating policies and programs aimed at the Latino population. In essence, non-Hispanic white metrics have been used to craft health policies and programs in a state in which barely a third of the state's children are non-Hispanic white. This approach is no longer suitable.

The Socioeconomic Status (SES) Model

The socioeconomic status model, which undergirds much thinking on health in general and minority health in particular, is one example of how a non-Hispanic white metric has been used for health policy. This model was developed from analysis of health patterns in different economic segments of the non-Hispanic white population. In this population, low socioeconomic status (SES) leads to poor health outcomes, whereas higher SES leads to good health outcomes. In other words, "wealth equals health."

When this model is applied to minority populations, who are generally poorer than non-Hispanic whites, even poorer health outcomes may be predicted. Minority health thus may be characterized as consisting of "health disparities" with indicators consistently worse than those of non-Hispanic whites. Here, for example, is a statement from the National Center for Health Statistics: "This chartbook documents the strong relationship between race, ethnicity and various measures of socioeconomic status: income, poverty status, level of education. . . . Racial and ethnic minorities are disproportionately represented among the poor . . . only the higher socioeconomic groups have achieved the target, while lower socioeconomic groups lag farther behind." (NCHS 1998, pp. 23–25)

So consistently has the association among race, low socioeconomic status and poor health outcomes been assumed that this model serves as the justification for national health policy, such as Healthy People 2010, which sets as its goal to reduce "health disparities among racial

From *Latinos: Remaking America* by Marcelo M. Suárez-Orozco & Mariela Páez, editors. Copyright © 2002 by the Regents of the University of California. Reprinted by permission of the University of California Press.

and ethnic subgroups of the population." (NCHS 1998, p. 23)

Naturally, the SES model has been applied to Latino populations, often without the support of good data. There is a consistent bias toward assuming that because Latinos are of low SES, their health must show adverse indicators. However, as this chapter will demonstrate, Latinos, nationally as well as in California, do not exhibit these adverse indicators; Latinos exhibit patterns that are not predicted by use of conventional metrics and models. With the growth in the Latino population, this paper argues, the development of Latino-based metrics and models is crucial for the formulating of sound health policies that accurately address Latino health dynamics.

Population Metrics and Modern Medicine

Population-Based Medicine

A major shift in medical research has been away from a nearly exclusive focus on the individual (and the constituent organs and systems) to a focus on larger groups of individuals. As providers become responsible for the care of large, enrolled populations, they need to understand better the patterns of health and disease in the groups for which they are responsible so that they can be prepared to deliver the appropriate levels of care in a timely fashion. It is no longer enough to implement heroic measures after a heart attack. It is now prudent medicine to understand how, when, and why heart attacks occur, and to whom and to work with patients to minimize their occurrence. While expanding the research focus from the individual to the group, it is important to acknowledge that not all groups exhibit the same profiles. Latinos, for example, are sufficiently distinct in health issues from non-Latinos (non-Hispanic whites and African Americans) that their health patterns warrant understanding.

Evidence-Based Medicine

Over the years, medicine has developed a number of protocols for treating specific diseases and conditions. Evidence based medicine requires that treatment protocols be measured against actual results, rather than used on the assumption that if they function in one population of patients, they will function equally well in another. Such protocols were almost never developed on Latino patient populations, although they have been applied to those populations. Do results justify their use?

To answer this question, the Center for the Study of Latino Health Culture of the School of Medicine, UCLA, has been studying the relationship between health and culture, with an eye to improving medical care research and practice. Among its goals are to

♦ Provide data on the dynamics of Latino health.
♦ Provide a conceptual model of Latino risk factors so that interventions can be developed.

♦ Develop educational curricula to train providers.
♦ Create policy models to better serve the needs of the Latino communities.
♦ Facilitate improvements in the delivery of services.

This may appear to be an ambitious research agenda. However, the need to manage the health of Latino communities effectively requires no less than this level of effort. Furthermore, as this research is slowly implemented, its findings may well make some key intellectual contributions to the scientific basis for the existence of Latino studies.

Statistical Basis for Latino Metrics

Large populations make possible the development of the statistical norms (Buttner 1996) on which policy prioritization and program setting are based. With Latinos becoming a large population, it is time now to consider developing Latino norms. Not only are there large Latino populations in many states, but these populations also present a health profile that is not consistent with the current thinking about "race/ethnic disparities" in program and policy development.

A brief overview of the Latino health profile will illustrate

♦ The need to understand Latino health *sui generis*—as constituting a unique phenomenon in its own right.
♦ The need for Latino-based norms of diseases and behaviors.
♦ The need for conceptual models that delineate the relationship between health and culture.

Latino Birth Outcomes

The "unpredictability" of Latino health norms is seen most comprehensively in birth outcomes. When we examine data from the National Center for Health Statistics (1998), extracted from birth certificates, the unusual contours of the Latino-based norms become clear.

Low Education

The Latinas who gave birth in 1996 were far less educated than non-Hispanic white, African American, and Asian/Pacific Islander mothers. Over half of Latina mothers (51.4 percent) had not completed high school at time of giving birth, whereas only 21.6 percent of non-Hispanic white mothers, 28.2 percent of African American mothers, and 15.0 percent of Asian/Pacific Islander mothers had not completed high school. See figure 1. A far lower percentage of Latina mothers were college graduates (6.4 percent) than were non-Hispanic white (23.9 percent), African American (10.0 percent), and Asian/Pacific Islander mothers (36.2 percent).

Figure 1. Maternal Education Less Than Twelve Years, U.S.A. 1996

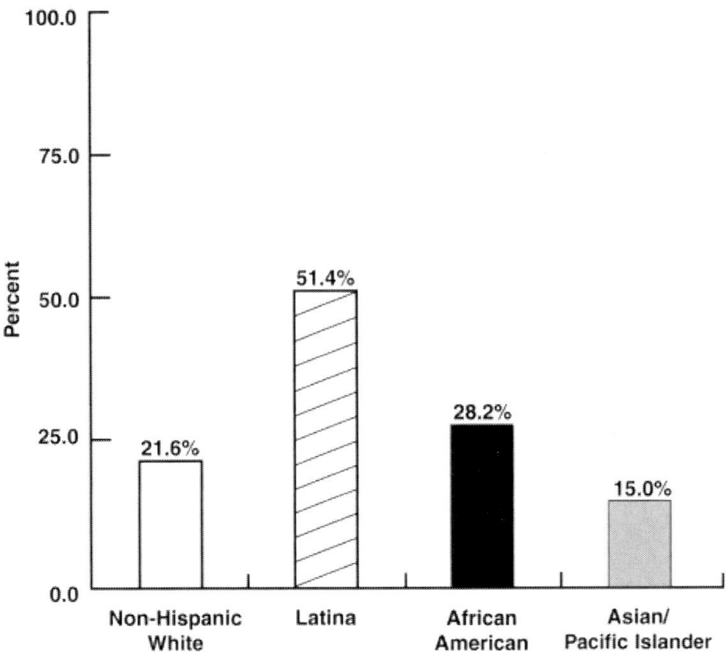

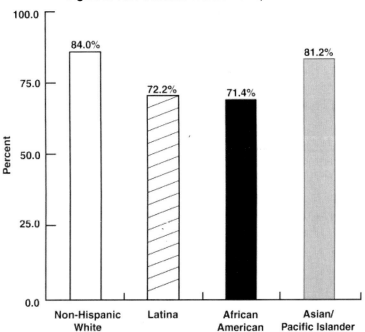

Low Access to Care

Numerous studies have pointed to the lower percentage of Latinos who have health insurance. This is reflected, in part, in the lower access to first-trimester prenatal care: 72.2 percent of Latina mothers received care in the first trimester of pregnancy, compared to 84.0 percent of non-Hispanic white and 81.2 percent of Asians/Pacific Islanders. Only African American mothers received less first-trimester care (71.4 percent). See figure 2.

Low Income

Income data are not captured on the birth certificate, but data from the 1998 Current Population Survey indicate that Latinas have the highest poverty rates, and the lowest income levels, of all groups. Thus it is indisputable that Latinas giving birth have one of the worst risk-factor profiles: lowest education, lowest income, low access to care.

Figure 2. First-Trimester Prenatal Care, U.S.A. 1996

In the conventional wisdom, this combination of risk factors should lead to adverse birth outcomes—specifically, to a high percent of low birthweight babies and elevated infant mortality. However, the birth outcomes of Latina mothers do not fit this expectation.

Little Low Birthweight. In spite of the risk factors, Latinas give birth to comparatively few low-birthweight babies. Only 6.28 percent of Latino babies born nationally in 1996 were of low birthweight (less than 2,500 grams). This is a lower percentage than that achieved by non-Hispanic white mothers (6.34 percent), African American mothers (13.01 percent) and Asian/Pacific Islander mothers (7.07 percent). See figure 3. This pattern also holds for very-low-birthweight babies (less than 1,500 grams), where Latinas had a percentage (1.12 percent) less than half that of African Americans (3.02 percent) and only slightly higher than non-Hispanic white (1.08 percent) and Asians/Pacific Islanders (0.99 percent).

Low Infant Mortality. Contrary to expectations, the Latina mothers, in spite of the high risk factors, have relatively low infant mortality. At 7.6 deaths per 1,000 live births, Latina infant mortality is less than half that of African Americans, at 17.1 deaths per 1,000 live births. Non-Hispanic white infant mortality is slightly lower than Latina, at 7.4. However, non-Hispanic white mothers have far more education, higher incomes, and better access to care. Asian/Pacific Islander mothers have the lowest infant mortality at 6.6 deaths per 1,000 live births. See figure 4.

This paradoxical pattern recurs in neonatal mortality (0 to 30 days after birth), where the Latino rate of 4.8 deaths per 1,000 live births is half that of the African American rate of 11.1 and only slightly higher than the non-Hispanic white rate of 4.6 and the Asian/Pacific Islander rate of 3.9. Likewise, in postneonatal mortality (31 to 365 days after birth), the Latino rate of 2.7 is half the African American rate of 6.1, equal to the non-Hispanic white rate of 2.7, and only slightly higher than the Asian/Pacific Islander rate of 2.6 deaths per 1,000 live births.

In birth outcomes alone, the need for Latino-based norms and models is obvious. In spite of the high risk factors, Latina birth outcomes more closely resemble those of the non-Hispanic white and Asian/Pacific Islander populations, which had higher income, more education, and better access to first-trimester care. None of this would be expected from the standard norms and models.

Latino "Epidemiological Paradox" or Latino Norm?

As Latinos become the majority population in many major urban areas, their health profile will become the statistical norm for those areas. If Latino health were no different from non-Hispanic white or African American health, this occurrence would be of little consequence. However, Latino health norms are distinctly at odds with the norms of those two populations.

Indeed, Latino health is so distinctive that it has received its own label: the Latino "epidemiological paradox." The paradox is this: although Latino populations may generally be described as low-income and low-education with little access to care, Latino health outcomes are generally far better than those of non-Hispanic whites. This paradox has been observed in so many Latino populations in so many regions over so many years that its existence

Figure 3. Low Birthweight (Percent of Live Births), U.S.A. 1996

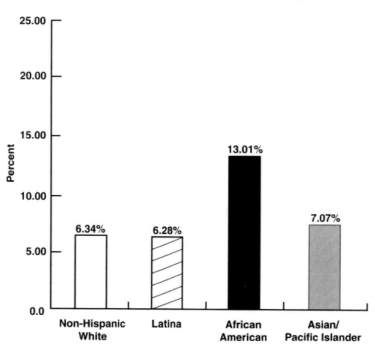

Figure 4. Infant Mortality, U.S.A. 1989–1991

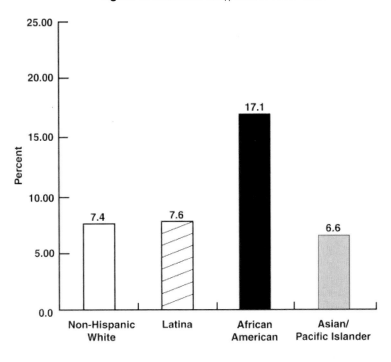

cries out to be explained. Yet no currently conceptual models can adequately explain its existence.

With nearly half the child population of California now Latino, the Latino pattern is no longer a "paradox"; it is the norm for most of the children in the state. The question should not be "Why are Latino children doing so well in spite of high risk factors?" but instead "Why are non-Hispanic white children doing so poorly in spite of all their advantages?"

Latino health patterns become more understandable if they are analyzed, not from the perspective of "white versus minority" metrics, but from the perspective of Latino-based metrics. Once Latino-based norms are understood, variations from the Latino norms can be understood, and Latino health can be understood on its own merits.

Latino Mortality Patterns: Diseases and Norms

Mortality data from the National Center for Health Statistics for 1996 (and, occasionally, other aggregated years) provide an illustration of the need for a Latino-based norm (NCHS 1998).

The Latino "epidemiological paradox" can also be seen at the opposite end of the life spectrum, in causes of death. Latino crude death rates are around 80 percent lower than non-Hispanic white rates, but because the Latino population is so much younger than the non-Hispanic white, the age-adjusted rates provide a more meaningful comparison. In order to age-adjust rates, the Latino population is artificially "aged" and the non-Hispanic white

population artificially "youthened" so that they have (artificially) the same age structure. This way, the effects of age are removed, and the death rates can be compared on a similar basis.

For all causes of death, the 1994–1996 Latino age-adjusted death rate of 376.1 deaths per 100,000 population is 20.5 percent lower than the non-Hispanic white rate of 473.6 deaths per 100,000 population. The Latino age-adjusted death rate is half (50.4 percent) that of the African American population, whose death rate is 758.7 deaths per 100,000 population. Only the Asian/Pacific Islander population rate of 282.8 deaths per 100,000 population is lower than the Latino rate, and this population has substantially higher income, more education and greater access to care. See figure 5.

In the aggregate, the lower Latino death rate in the face of higher risk factors appears paradoxical. This holds true generally for most causes of death. In fact, of the top eleven causes of death in the United States, Latinos have age-adjusted rates equal to or lower than those of non-Hispanic white for seven, including the top three causes of death: heart disease, cancer, and stroke. Again, given rapid Latino population growth, these patterns in many areas should be considered not a paradox but the new norm.

Latino Death Rates Equal to or Lower Than

Heart Disease

The number-one cause of death in the United States is heart disease. The Latino age-adjusted death rate of 88.6 per 100,000 population is 32.4 percent lower than the

Figure 5. Age-Adjusted Death Rates, U.S.A. 1994–96

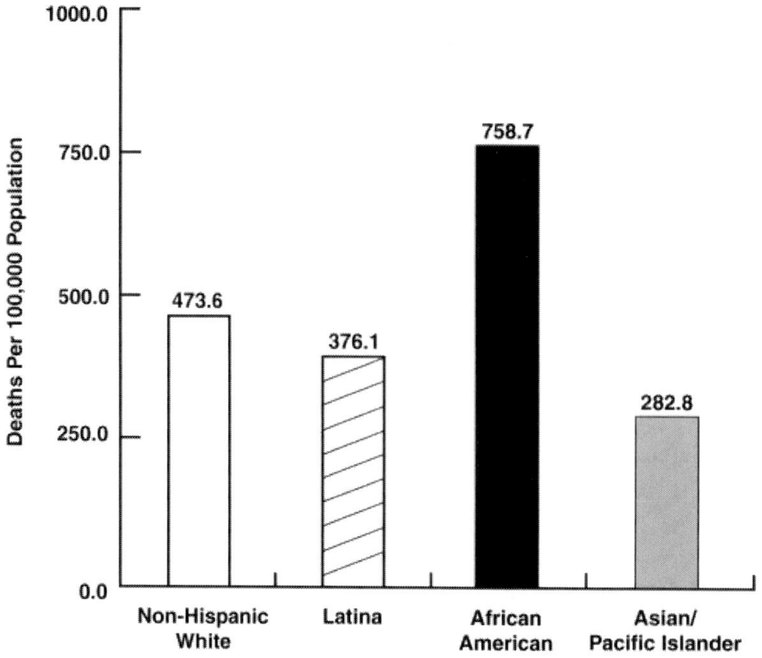

non-Hispanic white rate of 131.0 and 53.7 percent lower than the African American rate of 191.5. Only the Asian/Pacific Islander rate of 71.7 is lower than the Latino rate. See figure 6.

Cancer

The number-two cause of death in the United States is cancer. The Latino age-adjusted death rate of 77.8 deaths per 100,000 population is 39 percent lower than the non-Hispanic white rate of 127.6 and 53.6 percent lower than

the African American rate of 167.8. The Asian/Pacific Islander rate of 76.3 is slightly below the Latino rate. See figure 6. This lower Latino cancer mortality rate holds for most major sites.

For *lung (respiratory system) cancer*, the Latino rate of 15.4 is less than half the non-Hispanic white rate of 40.2 and is well under half the African American rate of 48.9. It is slightly lower than the Asian/Pacific Islander rate of 17.4. For *breast cancer*, the Latino rate of 12.8 is nearly one-third lower than the non-Hispanic white rate

Figure 6. Heart Disease, Cancer, and Stroke, Age-Adjusted Death Rates, U.S.A. 1996

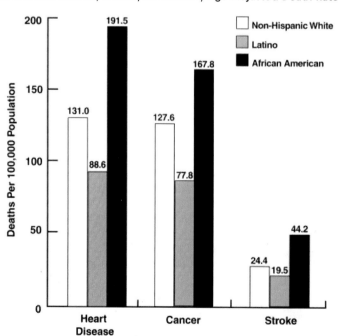

of 20.1 and is half that of the African American rate of 26.5. The Asian/Pacific Islander rate of 8.9 is somewhat lower than the Latino rate. For *prostate cancer*, the Latino rate of 9.9 is about one-third lower than the non-Hispanic white rate of 13.6. The African American rate of 33.8 is three times higher than the Latino rate. For *colorectal cancer*, the Latino rate of 7.3 deaths per 100,000 is lower than the non-Hispanic white rate of 12.1 and the African American rate of 16.8. It is also slightly lower than the Asian/Pacific Islander rate of 7.7.

Stroke

The number-three cause of death in the United States is cerebrovascular diseases. The Latino age-adjusted death rate of 19.5 deaths per 100,000 population is lower than the non-Hispanic white rate of 24.4, the African American rate of 44.2, and the Asian/Pacific Islander rate of 23.9. See figure 6.

Other Causes of Death

The number-four cause of death in the United States is chronic obstructive pulmonary disease. The Latino age-adjusted death rate of 8.9 per 100,000 population is 59.7 percent lower than the non-Hispanic white rate of 22.1, and is 50 percent lower than the African American rate of 17.8. The Asian/Pacific Islander death rate of 8.6 is slightly below the Latino rate. The Latino age-adjusted death rate of 9.7 for pneumonia and influenza is 20.4 percent lower than the non-Hispanic white rate of 12.2 and is 45.5 percent lower than the African American rate of 17.8. The Latino rate is also slightly lower than the Asian/Pacific Islander rate of 9.9. The Latino death rate for suicide of 6.7 deaths per 100,000 population is 44.2 percent lower

than the non-Hispanic white rate of 12.0. The African American rate of 6.6 and the Asian/Pacific Islander rate of 6.0 are slightly lower than the Latino rate.

Motor Vehicle accidents are one cause of death for which the Latino rate of 16.1 is virtually identical to the non-Hispanic white rate of 16.0 and to the African American rate of 16.7. The Asian/Pacific islander rate of 9.5 was lower than the rates for the other three groups.

Higher Latino Death Rates

There are four causes of death for which the Latino rate is higher than the rate for non-Hispanic white rate.

Diabetes

The Latino age-adjusted death rate of 18.8 per 100,000 population is 63.5 percent higher than the non-Hispanic white rate of 11. For some time, diabetes has been depicted as the "Latino disease." However, the African American rate of 28.8 is 53.2 percent higher than the Latino rate. The Asian/Pacific Islander rate of 8.8 is the lowest of all the groups. See figure 7.

HIV/AIDS

Nationally, the Latino death rate due to HIV/AIDS is 16.3, over twice the non-Hispanic white rate of 6.0. There are sharp regional variations, however, such that in the southwestern states, the Latino death rate due to HIV/AIDS is about half the rate for non-Hispanic whites. The African American death rate of 41.4 deaths per 100,000 population is more than twice the Latino rate. The Asian/Pacific Islander rate of 2.2 is the lowest of all four groups. See figure 7.

Figure 7. Diabetes, HIV/Aids, Homicide, and Cirrhosis Age-Adjusted Death Rates, U.S.A. 1996

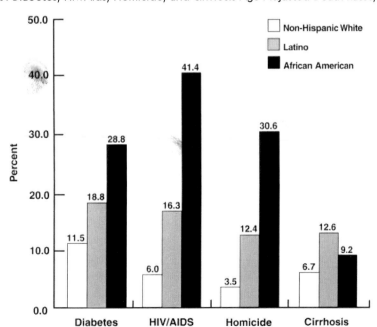

Homicide and Legal Intervention

The Latino age-adjusted death rate of 12.4 is over three times the non-Hispanic white death rate of 3.5. This finding is gender-linked, as will be discussed below. The African American rate of 30.6 is two and one-half times higher than the Latino rate. The Asian/Pacific Islander rate of 4.6 is slightly higher than the non-Hispanic white rate. See figure 7.

Chronic Liver Disease and Cirrhosis

This cause of death is the only one for which the Latino rate is simply the highest of all groups. The Latino death rate of 12.6 is nearly twice the non-Hispanic white rate of 6.7 and is 3.4 higher than the African American rate of 9.2. As will be discussed, this is due largely to male drinking patterns. See figure 7.

Illustrations could also be drawn from other data sets tracking other areas of Latino health: the hospital discharge summary, the National Health and Nutrition Evaluation Survey, the Behavioral Risk Factor Surveillance Survey, and similar population-based samples. The need for Latino-based norms is apparent in most large-scale studies; in spite of high risk factors, Latino health generally can be described as quite good.

This observation is so persistent, and so consistent, that it should no longer be viewed as a paradox, or as an interesting exception to a larger pattern. Instead, it should be considered a pattern in its own right—a pattern that is rapidly becoming the norm for large states such as California and Texas.

The Latino Health Research Agenda: Developing Latino Metrics

Identifying and Documenting Latino Norms

For too long, Latino health research has been an afterthought, given attention only after the health of the non-Hispanic white and African American populations were studied. At one point, when Latinos were a small minority, this oversight might have been understandable. However, Latino births currently account for nearly half of all births in California, Texas, Arizona, and New Mexico, and their outcome profile is quickly becoming the "norm" for all births. Yet Latino norms have not been clearly established. Indeed, the fact of the Latino "epidemiological paradox" is still surprising to many health services, researchers, and providers.

The basic epidemiological work of documenting Latino norms needs to occur in a number of areas:

Causes of Death

The preceding data on causes of death give only a glimpse into the uniqueness of Latino norms. These norms need to be tracked backwards for a number of years and established for states, counties, metropolitan areas, cities, and zip codes.

Birth Outcomes

Likewise, the Latino norms in birth outcomes need to be documented for past years and broken down by state, county, metropolitan area, city, and zip code.

Behavior

Latino behavioral patterns in smoking, drinking, drug use, exercise, seat belt use, and the like are not well established. There are contradictory data from a number of small-area studies. Norms for these and related behaviors need to be documented and established.

Access to and Utilization of Health Services

Very few data exist on Latino utilization of health services, including inpatient and outpatient services and physician office visits. Some data are available from the Current Population Survey on insurance coverage, but not enough to support a detailed analysis of patterns of coverage. The private insurance and HMO worlds have very little Latino data, because they have not had any place to indicate Latino ethnicity on their records.

Identifying Variations from Latino Norms

Once the norms for Latino populations are established, the variations from the norms can be identified, and then the risk factors that cause these variations can be sought. Several important variations need to be understood. They include variations that involve gender, geography, and Latino subgroup.

Gender

Generally, females of any ethnic group have a lower death rate than males. Latina females have a death rate that is 46% lower than that of Latino males. See figure 8. However, for specific causes of death, this can vary. Nationally, the Latino male rate for firearm-related deaths is nearly ten times as high as the Latina rate. See figure 9. However, for diabetes among adults in California, the female death rate does not follow the 40 percent lower pattern we would expect but, rather, is virtually identical to the Latino male rate. See figure 9. We need to understand such gender variations.

Geography

In the Southwest, the norm is for Latino mortality to be lower than non-Hispanic white mortality, but this pattern is not observed in New Mexico and Colorado (NCHS 1998). See figure 10. Another variation involves HIV/AIDS. Although nationally, the Latino incidence rate is higher than the non-Hispanic white incidence, there is great

Figure 8. All Causes, Age-Adjusted Death Rates, Male and Female, U.S.A. 1994–96

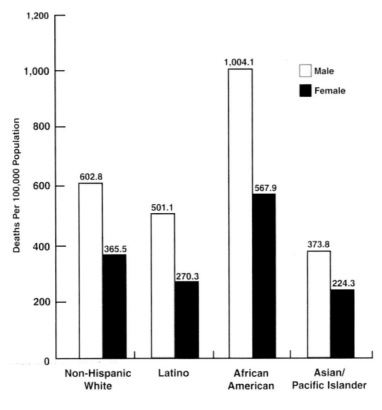

regional variation. In fact, in California and Texas, the Latino rate is consistently lower than the non-Hispanic white rate and is nearly one-fifth the rate observed among Latinos in New York and Connecticut (CDC 1993). See figure 11. Additionally, the major mode of transmission in the Southwest for Latino non-Hispanic whites, and Afri-

can Americans is male-male sex, with injection drug use being relatively minor, whereas in the Northeast, the major mode of transmission is injection drug use among Latinos, non-Hispanic whites, and African Americans, with male-male sex being relatively minor. See figure 12.

Figure 9. Latino Gender Variations: Homicide and Diabetes, 1996

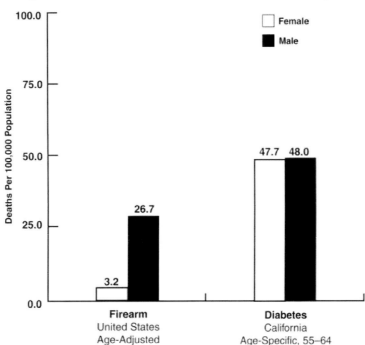

Figure 10. Geographic Variations, Latino and Non-Hispanic White Age-Adjusted Mortality, 1996

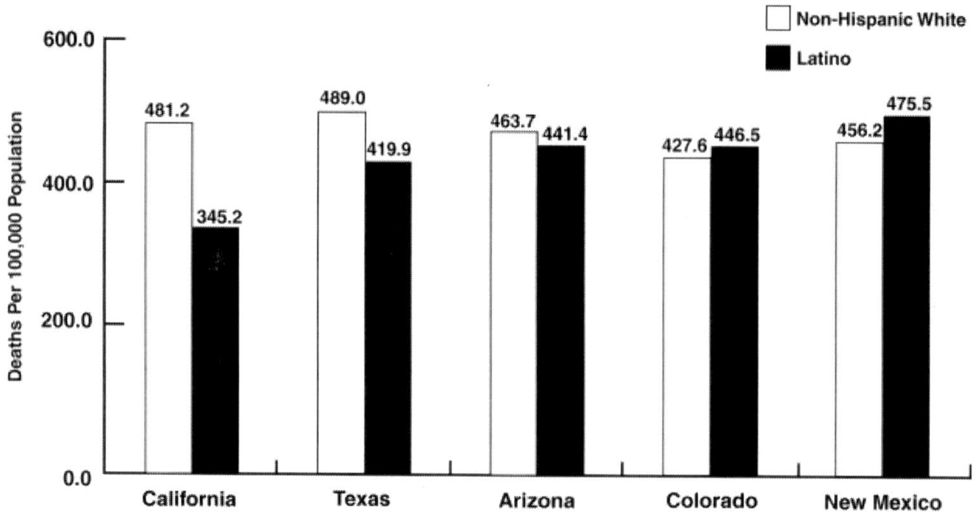

Latino Subgroup

We need to understand the differences between different Latino subgroups. In terms of birth outcomes, when we compare Mexican, Puerto Rican, Cuban, and Central/South American mothers, it is clear that mothers of Mexican origin have far lower educational levels and receive far less first-trimester prenatal care. Yet Mexican-origin Latinas also give birth to the lowest percentage of low-birthweight babies and have infant mortality 30.7 percent lower than that of mothers of Puerto Rican origin (NCHS 1998). See figure 13.

These are but a few examples of intra-Latino variation from Latino norms. Rather than comparing Latino subgroups to non-Hispanic whites or African Americans, it makes more sense to compare Latino populations to overall Latino norms. It has often been assumed that Latinos come in national-origin packages (Mexican, Cuban, etc.), but efforts to identify Latino subgroups may suggest new ways to segment Latino populations that will go further toward explaining the Latino "epidemiological paradox."

Using Latino Metrics for Latino Policies and Programs

Although investigators in health research frequently assume that the socioeconomic status (SES) model is applicable to Latino populations, generally it is not. More Latino-specific models need to be developed that can explain the Latino "epidemiological paradox" and harness its dynamics for better health outcomes. The relationship between culture and health needs to be understood, conceptualized, and operationalized. It may well be that the current SES-based models are but specific examples of larger, more comprehensive theoretical models that have not yet been developed.

Figure 11. Geographic Variations, in Incidence of HIV Among Latinos, 1993

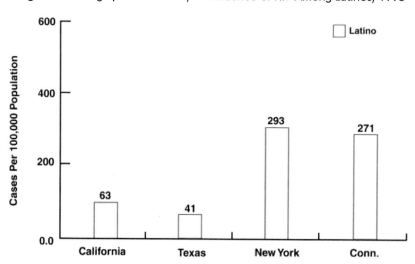

Figure 12. Geographic Variations in HIV Transmission via Intravenous Drug Use, 1996

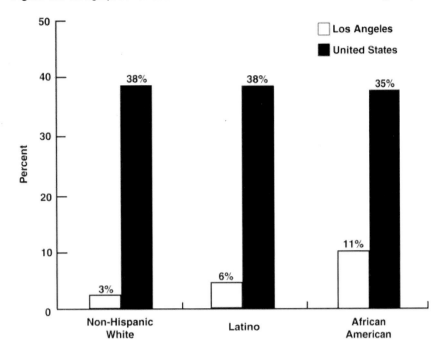

How do Latinos achieve such good health outcomes? What do Latinos have that can be shared with non-Latino populations to reduce their risk of heart disease, cancer, and stroke? It is our hypothesis that Latino culture, in some unknown way, plays a major role in the existence of the Latino "epidemiological paradox."

The study of Latino culture has largely been the province of researchers in history, literature, the arts, and the social sciences. The university resources provided for such study have usually been meager and the research results spotty and tentative—certainly not anything that the health sciences can use to explain the Latino "epidemiological paradox." There is no commonly agreed-upon conceptual construct for Latino culture, although cultural-sensitivity curricula have attempted to reduce it to a dozen or so characteristics applied uniformly to all Latinos everywhere.

Developing Educational Models

Once the basic data have been collected and analyzed to develop the underlying theoretical models, these findings need to be worked into educational curricula, especially those of health providers. The goal of "cultural competency" has often been held as an ideal, but there is very little evidence-based research to indicate exactly what that means in medical practice. Our recent book *Healing Latinos: Realidad y Fantasía: The Art of Cultural Competence in Medicine* (Hayes-Bautista and Chiprut 1999) is

Figure 13. Latino Infant Mortality, U.S.A. 1989–1991

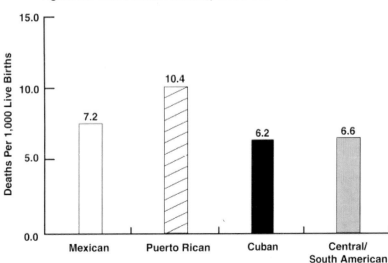

an initial attempt to offer guidance to physicians and other health care providers.

In the matter of health, culture matters. In the case of Latino populations, culture's significance can be appreciated in the case of diabetes. Given the higher Latino death rate for diabetes, this is a priority disease in California and other areas where many Latinos live. In a recent population-based survey of Latino and non-Hispanic white elderly in Los Angeles County, respondents were asked about the reasons for the onset of diabetes in adults. Latinos were as likely as non-Hispanic whites to cite the importance of heredity, diet, and overweight in the onset of diabetes. For Latinos, however, even more important than heredity, diet, and overweight was the role of *susto* (fright) in the onset of diabetes (Hayes-Bautista et al. 2000a). See figure 14.

Developing Policy Models

Health policy at the national, state, and county or municipal level needs to be informed by Latino-specific data and findings. Most health policy today is still based on assumptions about Latino norms and behavior, rather than on actual data. One such common assumption is the "minority health disparity" model, which overlooks the Latino "epidemiological paradox" and its implications for improving the health of non-Latino populations. Another common assumption is that low levels of Latino enrollment in Medicaid and other programs is due to fear of the I.N.S. However, a recent survey by the Field Institute showed that less than 9 percent of Latino respondents reported that they or any member of their family had avoided seeking services because of concerns about their immigration status. See figure 15. Far more important as barriers are the costs of care, lack of insurance coverage, and limited availability of services (California Healthcare Foundation 2000).

Designing the Delivery of Services

The design of delivery systems needs to reflect an understanding of Latino wants, needs, and desires. One major factor cited by Latino patients, especially immigrants, is the need for providers who speak Spanish. Recent work by our Center has confirmed this need. The shortage of Latino physicians, at least in California, is of nearly disastrous proportions. Latinos make up 30.4 percent of the state's population, but only 4.8 percent of California physicians are Latino. To express this another way, in non-Latino California, for every non-Latino physician there are 335 non-Latino Californians. In Latino California, for every Latino physician there are 2,893 Latino Californians (Hayes-Bautista et al. 2000b). This dismal ratio will get worse, in part because of declining first-year Latino matriculations.

Conclusions

The guiding maxim in health sciences research is that when the science is good, then all else follows. Latino health research is good science that can contribute in many areas: to the increased well-being of our nation's burgeoning Latino population, to the well-being of non-Latinos who can learn from the anomalies in Latino health that defy the dominant socioeconomic explanations of health, and to the scientific and intellectual foundations of Latino studies. Not only must Latinos be researched (and hence identified in records and samples) but research in Latino culture, in all its heterogeneity, must be understood, taught, and valued. Such a course might well lead to a reduction of deaths due to heart disease, cancer, and stroke in the entire population.

Latino studies does not exist just to make Latino undergraduate students feel good. Its findings are needed by all Americans.

Figure 14. Causes of Diabetes Among Latino and Non-Hispanic Whites, Los Angeles County, 1997

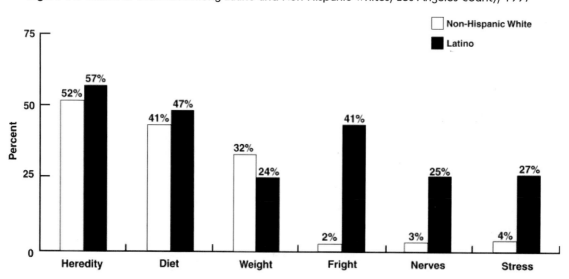

Figure 15. Field Institute: "Avoided getting medical care for selves or someone close because of immigration status concerns." California, 2000

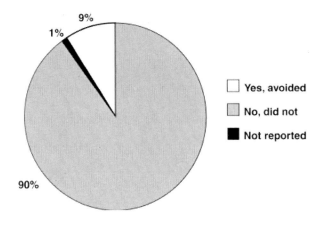

- ☐ Yes, avoided
- ☐ No, did not
- ■ Not reported

References

Buttner, J. 1996. Biological variation and quantification of health: The emergence of the concept of normality. *Clinical Chemistry and Laboratory Medicine*, 36 (1):69–73.

California Healthcare Foundation 2000. *A Political Profile of California Latinos and Their Views on Health Issues in the 2000 Primary Elections.* Oakland: Centers for Disease Control (1993). HIV/AIDS Surveillance Report. May: 5 (1).

Hayes-Bautista, D., E. and R. Chiprut. 1999. *Healing Latinos: Realidad y Fantasía: The Art of Cultural Competence in Medicine.* Los Angeles: Cedars-Sinai Health System.

Hayes-Bautista, D., E. P. Hsu, M. Hayes-Bautista, D. Iniguez, and D. Rose 2000a. *Latino elderly diabetes knowledge, attitudes and behavior in Los Angeles County* (in preparation).

Hayes-Bautista, D., E. P. Hsu, P. Dowling, R. Stein, R. Beltran, and J. Villagomez. 2001b. "Latino physician patterns in California: Sources, locations and projections." *Academic Medicine.* 75(7): 727–736.

National Center for Health Statistics 1998. *Health, United States, 1998, with Socioeconomic Status and Health Chartbook.* U.S. Department of Health and Human Services. DHHS Publication number (PHS) 98-1232.

USHHS 1987. *Report of the Secretary's Task Force on Black and Minority Health.* Washington, DC: USDHHS.

Trabajando
Mexican Americans in the Labor Market

Arturo González

Gerardo "Lalo" Medina was the road manager for Ozomatli, one of the more exciting and innovative music groups, as well as the tour manager for Dilated Peoples and Jurassic 5, both Los Angeles-based underground hip-hop groups. Medina was responsible for the everyday activities of the bands, from ensuring that their hotel reservations were correct to making sure that they made it to the next city on time to set up and prepare for the next show. He said "My job was to ensure the entire tour ran smoothly. This meant dealing with all details, large and small, and handling all the finances on the road. I was Daddy, Mommy, and friend." Medina did not set out to be a road and tour manager when he graduated from college. He graduated with a bachelor's degree from the University of California at Riverside and was an English teacher in Southern California. During this time, he was also involved in various creative activities, including contributions to the political satire group Pocho. Despite the monetary uncertainty of working in the entertainment industry, Medina thinks that the opportunities are worth the risks. The rewards have paid off: he has used his liberal arts education as well as his life experiences to make the bands' various tours successful ones—the bands consistently sell out their shows and leave a trail of happy concert-goers in their wake. Lalo is currently the road manager for the Latino music group The Mars Volta, which benefits enormously from Lalo's experience and managerial acumen.

In order to understand the underlying factors affecting the economic mobility, or lack thereof, of Mexican Americans, it is necessary to understand the labor market position of Mexican Americans, including unemployment, wages, and occupational status. This examination is the final component in the economic profile of Mexican Americans.

Workers provide their time to employers in the production of a service or product in exchange for some compensation, usually in the form of money. The labor market is comprised of all these elements: workers, employers, and the compensation workers receive for the labor they provide. Economic theory suggests that workers who acquire skills or knowledge are more productive. Furthermore, workers who are highly productive in some measurable way will earn more because they are more valuable to employers.

In this chapter, only the supply side of the labor market is examined; that is, the labor market activity and wages of workers. In addition to providing a general portrait of Mexican American workers, it explains their various labor market outcomes. In keeping with the overall theme, the chapter provides evidence that shows an improvement in the status of Mexican Americans from one generation to the next.

Labor economists measure labor supply in different ways, including labor force participation (LFP, also termed *labor force attachment*) and the number of hours worked during a specific amount of time, such as a week or a year. The amount of income earned by workers is also of considerable interest, and much effort is devoted to understanding why workers earn the amount they do. Therefore, this chapter profiles these different areas of the labor market for Mexican Americans.

Labor Market Activity

Activity in the labor market can take different forms, including part-time and full-time work, entry into and out of the labor market, search for employment, and the type of occupation workers are employed in. The majority of the working-age population not enrolled in school (that is, individuals sixteen to sixty-four years old) has two options with regard to the labor market: participate or not. Labor force participants are people who have a paying job or are looking for one. Therefore, LFP includes all unemployed people, because an unemployed person is defined as someone without a job but actively looking for one.

The definition of LFP excludes workers who do not receive compensation for their labor, such as family members who work in a family business for free or persons who volunteer their time to charitable organizations. Other individuals not participating in the labor force include those who wish not to work and those unable to work, such as persons with a physical disability, for example.

Table 1 presents labor market activity during the first week of March 1999. The four possible outcomes for an individual eligible to be in the labor force are as follows: non-participation in the labor force, full-time work, part-time work, or unemployment. The total number of Mexi-

Table 1. Labor Force Activity, by Generation and Gender, March 1999

	MALE				FEMALE			
	First	Second	Third	Total	First	Second	Third	Total
MEXICAN AMERICAN								
Not in labor force	7.8%	13.2%	12.8%	10.0%	50.6%	29.1%	27.1%	39.2%
Work full time	81.4%	76.2%	75.3%	78.9%	35.1%	50.7%	53.6%	43.8%
Work part time	6.1%	6.1%	6.4%	6.2%	9.6%	13.9%	14.4%	11.9%
Unemployed	4.7%	4.5%	5.5%	4.9%	4.7%	6.3%	4.9%	5.1%
Total labor force (in 1,000s)	3,236	833	1,591	5,660	2,637	921	1,704	5,263
NON-HISPANIC WHITE								
Not in labor force	11.0%	13.9%	10.9%	11.1%	34.2%	27.7%	24.9%	25.4%
Work full time	76.8%	75.7%	80.9%	80.4%	49.4%	51.8%	57.0%	56.5%
Work part time	6.9%	6.8%	5.3%	5.4%	13.7%	18.2%	15.9%	16.0%
Unemployed	5.3%	3.6%	3.0%	3.1%	2.7%	2.2%	2.2%	2.2%
Total labor force (in 1,000s)	2,235	2,890	50,122	55,247	2,253	2,866	51,212	56,331
BLACK								
Not in labor force	13.2%	27.4%	22.7%	22.0%	26.1%	25.1%	24.7%	24.8%
Work full time	79.5%	56.9%	64.8%	65.8%	56.8%	54.9%	59.0%	58.8%
Work part time	4.7%	10.9%	5.7%	5.7%	9.4%	13.8%	10.6%	10.6%
Unemployed	2.6%	4.8%	6.8%	6.5%	7.8%	6.2%	5.7%	5.8%
Total labor force (in 1,000s)	674	134	7,581	8,389	644	148	9,419	10,212
OTHER HISPANIC								
Not in labor force	10.5%	13.7%	17.4%	12.1%	35.7%	18.7%	29.0%	32.7%
Work full time	79.4%	69.2%	72.1%	76.8%	47.5%	63.5%	54.1%	50.3%
Work part time	5.2%	9.0%	5.7%	5.8%	13.1%	13.7%	13.6%	13.3%
Unemployed	4.9%	8.2%	4.8%	5.3%	3.7%	4.2%	3.2%	3.6%
Total labor force (in 1,000s)	1,612	300	383	2,295	1,877	283	429	2,589
ASIAN								
Not in labor force	13.4%	11.1%	11.6%	13.0%	33.6%	26.2%	21.7%	31.8%
Work full time	78.2%	72.3%	77.0%	77.6%	52.4%	57.9%	63.4%	54.0%
Work part time	5.9%	11.3%	7.3%	6.5%	11.7%	13.3%	11.4%	11.8%
Unemployed	2.5%	5.4%	4.1%	2.9%	2.3%	2.5%	3.5%	2.4%
Total labor force (in 1,000s)	2,254	220	325	2,799	2,565	236	330	3,130

Source: Author's weighted tabulations from the March 1999 Current Population Survey.
Notes: Includes persons age sixteen to sixty-four and not attending school, living in group quarters, or serving in the armed forces.

can American workers is 10.8 million, of which 5.7 million are men and 5.3 million are women.

One of the most revealing aspects of the labor activity of Mexican American workers is the fact that Mexican American men have the highest LFP rates in the country, with 90 percent working or looking for work, compared to 87 and 89 percent of Asian and non-Hispanic white men, respectively.

Full-time work is defined as working thirty-five or more hours per week, and part-time work as working fewer than thirty-five hours a week. Although full-time work is not necessarily the preferred type of employment, first- and second-generation Mexican American males have the highest percentage of full-time workers in their respective generations of any ethnic group (81.4 and 76.2 percent). Furthermore, third-generation Mexican Americans have the third-highest percentage of full-time workers after non-Hispanic whites and Asians. These LFP rates are consistent with those given in other studies (Borjas 1982; Borjas and Tienda 1985; DeFreitas 1985, 1991).

On the other hand, part-time employment is not a significant source of employment for Mexican American males, as only 6 percent work part time. Although this percentage is the second highest among all working men, it is not out of the ordinary compared to other groups.

In contrast to the high LFP rates of men, Mexican American women have the lowest rates of participation among women, with nearly 40 percent not being in the labor force. This is especially true among immigrant women, more than half of whom are not in the labor force. A much higher percentage of second- and third-generation Mexican American women, more than 70 percent, either work or are looking for work. Therefore, the immigrant experience, or perhaps the culture associated with the immigrant generation, is a significant factor in Mexican American females' decision about whether or not to seek employment (Segura 1992).

Yet, compared to other second- or third-generation women, Mexican American women are still less likely to be labor force participants. These generations of women in most other ethnic groups have LFP rates of around 75 percent. Non-Mexican Hispanic and white women have rates similar to these generations of Mexican American women.

Compared to men, a larger percentage of Mexican American working women have part-time jobs. Table 1 shows that 10 to 14 percent of Mexican American women work part time. Overall, table 1 shows that only white and non-Mexican Hispanic women are more likely to have part-time jobs than Mexican American women, a pattern also reported by Reimers (1992). Combined with the low labor force attachment of Mexican American women, the use of part-time employment suggests a strategic use of the labor market by Mexican American women and families (Segura 1992). That is, it is possible that Mexican American women balance economic issues with domestic and cultural expectations by working only part time. It could also be that Mexican American women have more difficulty finding work, as demonstrated by their high unemployment rate and by the greater number of weeks it takes them to find a job (see table 2).

Unfortunately, one reason why Mexican Americans have a strong labor force attachment is their high unemployment rate. Table 1 shows that Mexican Americans have unemployment rates between 5 and 6 percent, whereas whites and Asians have rates ranging from 2 to 5 percent. Only blacks have higher unemployment rates (6 percent or higher), and other Hispanics have somewhat comparable rates. High levels of unemployment may result from difficulty in finding a new job after losing one or from a higher frequency of job loss. DeFreitas (1985) finds evidence that the problem of unemployment lies in the duration, rather than the frequency, of unemployment: the unemployment rate for Mexican Americans is affected nearly twice as much by an inability to find a job than by the loss of a job. Table 2 supports this finding and shows that, on average, Mexican Americans spend more weeks than non-Hispanic whites looking for a job, although not as many as black workers do. Nevertheless, the 1.2 extra weeks spent by all Mexican American males and the 2.7 extra weeks spent by Mexican American females means that, relative to whites, Mexican Americans who lose their jobs are going to be unemployed for a longer time.

Table 2. Average Number of Weeks Spent Looking for Work in 1998

	MALE				FEMALE			
	First	Second	Third	Total	First	Second	Third	Total
Mexican American	8.6	7.7	8.6	8.5	6.3	7.3	7.5	6.9
Non-Hispanic white	5.7	6.4	7.4	7.3	4.3	3.8	4.2	4.2
Black	15.4	16.6	11.3	11.7	4.2	6.0	8.5	8.3
Other Hispanic	8.6	5.8	8.5	8.5	7.2	4.3	4.0	6.6
Asian	5.9	7.2	10.1	7.2	3.1	10.2	4.8	4.0

Source: Author's weighted tabulations from the March 1999 Current Population Survey.
Notes: Includes persons age sixteen to sixty-four and not attending school, living in group quarters, or serving in the armed forces. Includes those who worked for part of 1998 as well as those who did not work but looked for work.

Table 3. Average Number of Weeks and Hours per Week Worked in 1998, by Generation

	MALE				FEMALE			
	First	**Second**	**Third**	**Total**	**First**	**Second**	**Third**	**Total**
MEXICAN AMERICAN								
Weeks	47.6	47.8	47.4	47.6	42.4	43.6	44.7	43.5
Hours per week	41.5	42.0	41.7	41.6	37.3	37.7	36.9	37.3
NON-HISPANIC WHITE								
Weeks	48.8	48.8	49.1	49.0	46.4	46.4	46.2	46.2
Hours per week	44.9	43.9	44.2	44.2	37.7	36.8	37.4	37.4
BLACK								
Weeks	48.2	47.0	46.9	46.9	46.8	42.1	45.5	45.5
Hours per week	41.8	41.3	41.3	41.4	39.4	36.7	37.8	37.9
OTHER HISPANIC								
Weeks	48.7	48.7	48.7	48.6	45.7	46.7	47.3	45.8
Hours per week	42.5	41.8	42.0	42.2	37.6	39.2	37.8	37.8
ASIAN								
Weeks	49.2	47.0	48.0	48.7	45.9	43.2	46.0	45.6
Hours per week	42.5	39.2	43.1	42.2	39.0	37.9	39.1	38.9

Source: Author's weighted tabulations from the March 1999 Current Population Survey.
Notes: Includes persons age sixteen to sixty-four who are not attending school, living in group quarters, or serving in the armed forces.

Employment Patterns

Contrary to the stereotype of the "lazy Mexican" (Monroy 1999), Mexican Americans have a very strong work ethic as shown by their labor force activity. Table 3 provides further evidence that the work ethic and labor force attachment of Mexican Americans are higher than or at least comparable to those of other ethnic groups. Among the employed, the number of weeks worked during the year and the number of hours worked per week are indicative of how much workers work. Table 3 shows that, on average, Mexican American men work the second fewest number of weeks and hours per week of all ethnic groups (less than forty-eight weeks and forty-two hours per week), but the number of hours worked per week is only 0.7 hours less than the average for the other groups. Likewise Mexican American women work the fewest number of weeks of any group of women but work a similar number of hours per week. Thus, although a high percentage of Mexican Americans work, their longer unemploy-

ment spells reduce the number of weeks and hours they are able to work.

The ability to find and maintain a full-time job, defined as thirty-five or more hours per week year-round, is also an indicator of success and stability in the labor market. Although many individuals choose not to work full time, most workers are seeking full-time work. Table 4 examines the percentage of workers aged sixteen to sixty-four who worked full time. Among men, Mexican Americans have the second lowest percentage of year-round, full-time workers, barely ahead of blacks. In all, 71.9 percent of all Mexican American men were working full time, compared to 76.2 percent of non-Hispanic white men.

First-generation Mexican American males are the least likely immigrant group to work full-time year-round. This low percentage most likely is the result of low education and employment in occupations that are seasonal in nature. The second generation has an even lower percentage of full-time, year-round workers (67.4 percent), but this percentage is the second highest among all second-gen-

Table 4. Percentage of Full-Time, Year-Round Workers in 1998, by Generation

	MALE				FEMALE			
	First	**Second**	**Third**	**Total**	**First**	**Second**	**Third**	**Total**
Mexican American	73.4%	67.4%	71.3%	71.9%	51.8%	49.9%	57.4%	53.6%
Non-Hispanic white	76.4%	75.7%	76.2%	76.2%	61.5%	54.7%	56.6%	56.7%
Black	77.4%	63.2%	70.5%	71.0%	70.2%	48.0%	61.7%	62.0%
Other Hispanic	77.7%	66.3%	74.0%	75.5%	60.6%	59.2%	59.8%	60.3%
Asian	78.3%	56.5%	70.0%	75.0%	60.5%	38.3%	62.5%	58.1%

Source: Author's weighted tabulations from the March 1999 Current Population Survey.
Notes: Includes persons age sixteen to sixty-four who worked in 1998 and were not attending school or living in group quarters. Full-time, year-round work is at least fifty weeks and more than thirty-five hours per week.

eration male workers. Similarly, the percentage of full-time, year-round workers is lower for third-generation males than Mexican immigrants, but relative to other third-generation workers, Mexican American males have the third highest percentage of full-time work. Thus, among all ethnic groups, immigrant males are more commonly full-time, year-round workers than are either second- or third-generation workers.

Mexican American women, on the other hand, are generally the least likely of all women to work full-time year-round. Fewer than 54 percent work most of the year, whereas 57 to 62 percent of women of other ethnicities do so. Unlike Mexican American men, third-generation women are the most likely generation to be full-time, year-round workers.

The fact that many Mexican Americans did not work full time may be due either to an inability to find full-time work or to a preference for part-time work. Table 5 tabulates the reasons why Mexican Americans held part-time jobs in 1998. The major reason was slack work conditions, that is a reduction in work hours due to slow business. More than 50 percent of all part-time workers found themselves with part-time work because of this situation, and the second most common reason for part-time work was some unspecified reason. With the exception of the first generation, more part-time workers desired part-time work than were forced to accept it for lack of full-time employment. Nevertheless, the majority of those who work part time do so for reasons outside of their control.

Preference for part-time work grows with each generation. Among male immigrants, for example, the preference for part-time work is the lowest (2 percent) of all Mexican Americans (about 9 percent). The difference is most striking among women, however. Only about 6 percent of the first generation desired part-time work, but 18 and 27 percent of the second and third generations, respectively, sought such work. These outcomes may result in lower wages among third-generation workers.

Occupational Patterns

The type of job an individual holds determines not only the wages he or she earns, but also long-term job stability and prospects for economic mobility. At the same time, however, a person's job type is an outcome of the interplay of human capital variables, job search and job matching, social networks, and in certain cases, timing. Human capital variables include education and training, language ability, and other traits that enhance a worker's productivity. The search for a new job entails not only actively job hunting, but also using various technologies effectively to find the appropriate job. The search may be conducted by visiting employment agencies, phoning prospective employers, or "hitting the streets." The job search is successful if the employer and employee are matched in terms of qualifications and job requirements. Only when the job is agreeable to both parties is a job offered and accepted. Many workers learn about jobs through informal means, such as when a current worker either passes along information about job vacancies to friends or relatives, or recommends friends and relatives to fill a position. The importance of some of these variables is discussed in greater detail later in the chapter.

Table 6 presents the distribution of each generation of workers in all ethnic groups across seven broadly defined occupation types. Generally speaking, Mexican American males are concentrated in the blue-collar, labor-intensive occupations and are less visible in the white-collar, professional occupations. For example, 28 percent of second-generation Mexican Americans are operators, fabricators, or laborers, whereas only 13 percent work in professional or managerial occupations. On the other hand, the opposite is true of non-Hispanic whites and Asians—they are heavily concentrated in professional occupations.

Whereas table 6 contains a wealth of information for interethnic comparisons, figures 1 and 2 condense this information for Mexican American men and women, respectively. There are more Mexican American men in operator, fabricator, and laborer occupations (such as drilling and boring-machine operators) than in any other type of occupation, with about 30 percent of each generation of men employed in this sector. More than 20 percent of all Mexican American men work in precision production, craft, and repair occupations (such as cabinet making), making this the second most common type of occupation.

Table 5. Reasons for Working Part Time in 1998, by Generation

	MALE				FEMALE			
	First	**Second**	**Third**	**Total**	**First**	**Second**	**Third**	**Total**
Could find only part-time work	11.9%	3.8%	5.9%	9.8%	7.9%	11.9%	7.4%	8.6%
Wanted part-time work	2.0%	8.6%	9.2%	4.2%	5.5%	18.0%	26.8%	14.2%
Slack work	58.2%	62.1%	55.0%	57.9%	63.1%	52.3%	37.1%	53.4%
Other reason	27.9%	25.6%	29.9%	28.1%	23.6%	17.7%	28.7%	23.9%

Source: Author's weighted tabulations from the March 1999 Current Population Survey.
Note: Includes Mexican Americans age sixteen to sixty-four who worked part time and were not attending school or living in group quarters.

Table 6. Distribution of Occupation Type, by Generation and Gender in 1998

	MALE				FEMALE			
	First	**Second**	**Third**	**Total**	**First**	**Second**	**Third**	**Total**
PROFESSIONAL, MANAGERIAL, AND SPECIALIZED OCCUPATIONS								
Mexican American	4.1%	13.4%	14.3%	8.2%	6.2%	17.4%	22.5%	14.7%
Non-Hispanic white	42.7%	41.8%	31.0%	32.0%	36.1%	40.0%	35.6%	35.9%
Black	21.6%	20.1%	15.2%	15.9%	27.5%	45.5%	23.4%	24.0%
Other Hispanic	14.2%	32.5%	24.0%	18.0%	14.9%	33.5%	30.3%	19.9%
Asian	39.1%	30.8%	39.3%	38.5%	36.0%	45.3%	47.4%	38.1%
TECHNICAL, SALES, AND ADMINISTRATIVE SUPPORT								
Mexican American	6.4%	19.2%	17.3%	11.2%	19.5%	48.4%	42.0%	33.9%
Non-Hispanic white	16.8%	20.0%	19.7%	19.6%	31.9%	41.7%	40.9%	40.6%
Black	14.7%	34.0%	18.3%	18.2%	25.3%	32.4%	36.9%	36.2%
Other Hispanic	16.9%	34.0%	24.9%	20.2%	32.2%	47.5%	41.1%	35.7%
Asian	22.8%	30.2%	20.4%	23.2%	30.2%	43.2%	35.7%	31.9%
SERVICE								
Mexican American	16.3%	12.2%	12.5%	14.7%	34.5%	20.5%	24.9%	28.0%
Non-Hispanic white	9.5%	6.9%	7.2%	7.3%	20.1%	11.4%	14.1%	14.2%
Black	20.1%	13.7%	16.0%	16.4%	39.5%	16.0%	27.0%	27.6%
Other Hispanic	16.9%	11.5%	12.9%	15.6%	35.6%	11.6%	19.4%	29.8%
Asian	9.3%	16.3%	8.3%	9.8%	16.1%	9.9%	10.8%	15.0%
FARMING, FORESTRY, AND FISHING								
Mexican American	17.4%	6.2%	5.6%	12.6%	9.4%	2.7%	1.0%	4.8%
Non-Hispanic white	1.4%	2.1%	3.2%	3.1%	1.1%	0.5%	1.0%	1.0%
Black	2.7%	0.0%	2.7%	2.6%	0.8%	0.0%	0.2%	0.2%
Other Hispanic	4.0%	0.0%	1.4%	3.1%	0.6%	0.2%	0.2%	0.5%
Asian	1.0%	4.0%	2.9%	1.5%	0.4%	0.0%	1.7%	0.5%
PRECISION PRODUCTION, CRAFT, AND REPAIR								
Mexican American	23.5%	20.8%	22.0%	22.7%	4.3%	1.5%	1.9%	2.8%
Non-Hispanic white	16.1%	17.8%	21.1%	20.7%	2.4%	1.7%	2.1%	2.1%
Black	15.3%	9.7%	14.9%	14.9%	0.6%	2.1%	2.4%	2.3%
Other Hispanic	19.4%	7.7%	18.8%	17.9%	3.1%	1.6%	2.4%	2.8%
Asian	11.3%	7.3%	20.3%	12.0%	3.6%	0.0%	2.0%	3.1%
OPERATOR, FABRICATOR, AND LABORER								
Mexican American	32.3%	28.2%	28.3%	30.6%	26.1%	9.5%	7.7%	15.7%
Non-Hispanic white	13.5%	11.4%	17.9%	17.4%	8.4%	4.7%	6.2%	6.2%
Black	25.6%	22.5%	32.9%	32.1%	6.4%	4.0%	10.1%	9.8%
Other Hispanic	28.7%	14.3%	18.0%	25.2%	13.6%	5.5%	6.5%	11.4%
Asian	16.4%	11.5%	8.8%	15.1%	13.7%	1.7%	2.4%	11.3%

Source: Author's weighted tabulations from the March 1999 Current Population Survey.
Notes: Includes persons age sixteen to sixty-four who are not attending school and who worked in 1998. Occupation is for the job held longest in 1998. Excludes those who were unemployed or previously in the armed forces.

Mexican American men are least likely to work in farming, fishing, and forestry occupations. Although 17.4 percent of immigrants perform this type of labor, less than 7 percent of second- and third-generation Mexican American men do. The low percentage of Mexican American men (and women) in agriculture-related fields contradicts the stereotype of the Mexican worker as a fruit and vegetable picker.

Technical, sales, and administrative support occupations also represent another significant source of employment for Mexican American men, particularly in the second and third generations (19.2 and 17.3 percent, respectively); note that the level for immigrants is much lower, at 6.4 percent. Similarly, professional and managerial occupations account for 13 to 14 percent of second- and third-generation Mexican American male workers, but only 4.1 percent of Mexican immigrants. Lastly, significant percentages of Mexican American men also work in service occupations, with a range from 12 to 16 percent across all generations.

Figure 1 shows that there is a movement away from labor-intensive jobs and into white-collar and technical jobs from the first to the second and third generations. For example, the percentage of workers in operator, fabricator, and laborer occupations decreases from 32 to 28 percent between the first and third generations. Similarly, the percentage of workers in professional occupations rises from 4 to 14 percent from the first to third generations. Most of the movement into more prestigious occupations occurs between the first and second generations, although there continues to be an increase into the third generation. These movements are probably associated with the educational levels of each generation.

Figure 2 illustrates that Mexican American women are not as evenly distributed across occupations as men are. More than 40 percent of second- and third-generation Mexican American women work in technically oriented occupations. Another prominent occupation type for these generations is professional and managerial occupations: between 17 and 23 percent work in these types of jobs. Mexican American women are also likely to be employed in service-related occupations (ranging from 21 to 35 percent). Mexican immigrant women are especially likely to be employed in service occupations. Mexican American immigrant women also differ from later generations in that a significant percentage (26 percent) are employed in operator occupations, compared to less than 10 percent for the second and third generations.

Figure 2 also illustrates a shift in occupational composition across generations of women. The movement out of blue-collar and into white-collar occupations is more pronounced among Mexican American women than among men. For example, less than 3 percent of second- and third-generation Mexican American women work in agriculture-related occupations, as opposed to nearly 10 percent of immigrant women, and the percentage of professionals and managers increases from 6 to 23 percent between the first and third generations.

Annual Income

The desirability of a job is often highly correlated with its wages. A person's income is generally dependent on education, training, work experience, and other worker attributes that enhance productivity. Although the information in table 7 does not adjust fir differences in these

Figure 1. Occupational Distribution of Mexican American Males by Generation.

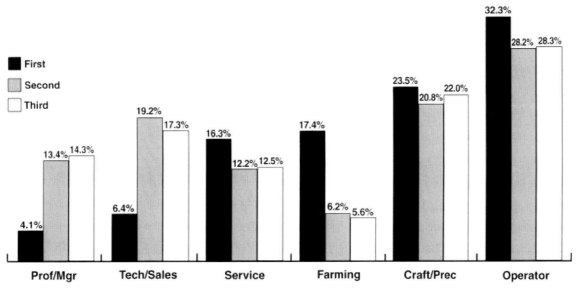

(Source: Author's weighted tabulations from the March 1999 Current Population Survey)

Figure 2. Occupational Distribution of Mexican American Females by Generation.
Plot from data in table 18.

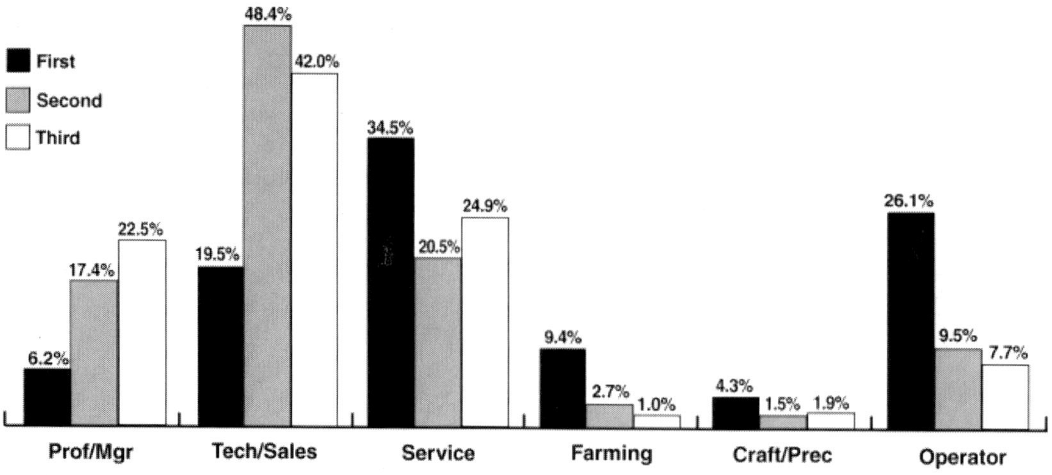

Source: Author's weighted tabulations from the March 1999 Current Population Survey.

human capital characteristics, the mean annual wage information is nonetheless useful.

With a few exceptions, Mexican Americans' annual income is the lowest of all ethnic groups, ranging from roughly $19,400 to $30,000 for men and $13,000 to $18,600 for women. The annual income of Mexican American men ranges from about 50 to 100 percent lower than the income of non-Hispanic white men, and the income of Mexican American women is 35 to 125 percent lower than that of white women.

Table 7 shows improvement in annual income for second- and third-generation Mexican Americans. The second generation earns an average of 35 percent more, and the third earns 31 percent more, than the first generation. The decline in income from the second to the third generation is unexpected. Comparing 1998 income to 1997 income (found in the March 1998 CPS) reveals an interesting outcome. Whereas the incomes of first- and third-generation Mexican Americans were comparable between 1997 and 1998, for unknown reasons the income of second-generation Mexican Americans grew substantially; the mean income of the second generation was $24,871 in 1997 but $29,965 in 1998, an increase of 20 percent.

Wages, Human Capital, and Discrimination

Why do Mexican Americans have lower incomes than other groups, especially non-Hispanic whites and Asians? Several possible explanations include discrimination, structural changes in the labor market, such as the loss of high-paying manufacturing jobs overseas, less familiarity with U.S. labor markets among immigrants, lower education levels, less work experience, and other productive characteristics.

Table 8 shows several demographic differences between Mexican-origin and non-Mexican-origin populations in education, work experience, union membership, and English ability. Comparing Mexican Americans to non-Hispanic whites, it is clear that Mexican Americans average less education and less experience, and are less likely to belong to a union or speak English very well. For example, third-generation Mexican American men average 12 years of education, 18 years of work experience, 3 percent union membership, and 91 percent speak English very well. In contrast, third-generation non-Hispanic whites average 14 years of schooling, 20 years of work experience, 4.1 percent union membership, and 100 percent speak

Table 7. Average Annual Salaries in 1998, by Generation

	MALE				FEMALE			
	First	Second	Third	Total	First	Second	Third	Total
Mexican American	$19,366	$29,965	$28,071	$23,276	$12,910	$18,299	$18,585	$16,194
Non-Hispanic white	$46,297	$51,306	$41,799	$42,441	$29,074	$27,961	$25,121	$25,389
Black	$27,178	$29,935	$27,081	$27,131	$20,927	$25,285	$21,127	$21,173
Other Hispanic	$27,564	$37,658	$32,672	$29,660	$17,849	$25,714	$25,299	$20,125
Asian	$41,410	$31,589	$41,318	$40,502	$25,917	$26,809	$31,098	$26,655

Source: Author's tabulations from the March 1999 Current Population Survey.
Notes: Includes persons age sixteen to sixty-four who are not attending school and who worked in 1998. Excludes persons who were self-employed, worked without pay, or lived in group quarters. Wages and salaries are top-coded by the CPS.

Topic Highlight: Opportunities in Real Estate

Humberto López is a developer who survived the real-estate crash of the late 1980s. López is back on top as one of the most prominent dealmakers and real-estate holders in Tucson, Arizona. He owns and manages four hotels totaling 800 rooms, owns and manages about 2,600 apartment units in twelve complexes, and is managing partner of 1,000 apartments in Phoenix, Yuma, and Dallas. Among his other holdings are two California land-development deals (a 420-home development in San Marcos and a 240-home development in Carlsbad), 40 percent ownership of TransAmerica, a mail-order company in Cleveland with $65 million in sales last year, and a 50 percent interest in the Dorado Country Club in Tucson.

Born in Nogales, Arizona, in 1946, López was raised across the border in Ciudad Obregón, Sonora, until he was twelve, when his father died without a will. The family went from middle class to poor because most of its wealth was lost to lawyers and the Mexican government during probate. His mother moved the family of six back to her native Nogales, Arizona, where López began working, selling newspapers and doing yard work. Throughout high school, he worked forty hours a week at a grocery store, bagging and making deliveries. "We did pretty well in Mexico," he recalled. "But when we came back to the States, our lifestyle changed."

Despite being advised by his high-school counselor to pursue a vocational course, he went to Cochise College with friends. "My counselor didn't think I was capable of going to college and recommended vocational school," Lopez explained. "Several of us who had him as counselor and didn't want to go to vocational school ended up at Cochise, which was new at the time." At Cochise, he took some business courses. He seemed to learn accounting most easily, so he stuck with it and transferred to the University of Arizona. Immediately after graduation, he left Tucson and took an accounting job at Deloitte, Haskins, and Sells in Los Angeles. "When I graduated from the [University of Arizona], I didn't interview in Tucson or Phoenix," he recalled. "I wanted the biggest business with the most exposure. That's because I wanted to find the business for me." As a certified public accountant, he began requesting real-estate accounts and eventually started getting into the field himself. His first deal involved borrowing $1,000 from an uncle to buy a $3,000 lot. He later sold it for $7,000. Thus began his career in real estate.

Throughout his career, López has found time for civic activities. He has helped not-for-profit organizations raise money and is chairman of the board of advisers for the University Heart Center in Tucson. He was also named Man of the Year by City of Hope and Father of the Year by the Juvenile Diabetes Foundation in Tucson. "I like to give back because the community has been good to me," he said. "I like to give not just money, but my time." (From Higuera 1998).

English very well. Therefore, it is not unreasonable to expect that these differences would account, at least to some extent, for the lower relative incomes of Mexican Americans.

Table 9 examines the effect of various demographic characteristics on the hourly wages of Mexican Americans and non-Mexican Americans. The Average Log Hourly Wage section gives the mean of the logarithm of hourly wage, the common economic measure of wages, and the Adjusted Log Hourly Wage section gives the log of hourly wage adjusted for demographic differences between non-Mexican-origin second-generation workers and all other workers. The bottom rows give the wage deficit of Mexican Americans after demographic differences between them and second-generation non-Mexican-origin workers are eliminated. Given that the average log hourly wage of non-Mexican American second-generation workers is 2.82, and second-generation Mexican Americans have a corresponding log hourly wage of 2.39, the implied difference in hourly wages (shown in the bottom panel) is -34.8 percent ($e^{2.39-2.82} = -0.348$). In other words, second-generation Mexican Americans earn an average of 34.8 percent less than non-Hispanic whites. Similarly, first- and third-generation Mexican Americans earn 39.7 percent and 24.5 percent less than non-Mexican-origin workers of the same generation. The results show that certain demographic factors—given in the notes of the table—

explain between 87 and 94 percent of the lower wages of Mexican Americans.

One reason why adjusted wages decline for Mexican Americans between the second and third generations is a difference in years of experience. As shown in table 8, second-generation Mexican Americans have less work experience than their third-generation counterparts. To calculate the adjusted wages, both generations are given the same years of experience as second-generation non-Mexican Americans (approximately 21.4 years). Doing so increases the experience of second-generation workers more than third-generation workers, resulting in a –0.04 log point lower in adjusted wages for the second generation (2.68 compared to 2.64).

In terms of relative adjusted wages, first- and third-generation Mexican Americans make the biggest gains: first-generation men and women earn 5 to 6 percent less than comparable non-Hispanic workers, whereas third-generation workers earn about 7 to 12 percent less. These figures are considerably less than the average wage deficits.

Unfortunately, the fact is that real-world observed wages (i.e., "average" wages) stagnate from the second to the third generation for both Mexican Americans and non-Hispanic whites. However, contrary to the experience of whites, whose income is significantly lower in the third generation, the wages of Mexican Americans do not

Table 8. Selected Worker Characteristics, by Generation and Gender

	MALE				FEMALE			
	First	**Second**	**Third**	**Total**	**First**	**Second**	**Third**	**Total**
MEXICAN AMERICAN								
Schooling (years)	9.1	12.1	12.1	10.4	9.2	12.3	12.4	11.1
Work experience (years)	19.3	16.1	17.5	18.4	20.9	15.8	17.9	18.7
Union membership	1.1%	1.7%	2.7%	1.7%	0.5%	2.1%	1.4%	1.2%
Speaks English very well	18.4%	85.7%	90.6%	57.7%	—	—	—	—
NON-HISPANIC WHITE								
Schooling (years)	14.1	14.3	13.6	13.6	13.8	13.9	13.6	13.6
Work experience (years)	20.3	21.4	20.0	20.1	22.4	22.0	20.2	20.4
Union membership	2.4%	4.2%	4.1%	4.0%	2.7%	3.4%	2.8%	2.8%
Speaks English very well	75.7%	99.5%	99.9%	99.2%	—	—	—	—
BLACK								
Schooling (years)	12.6	13.7	12.7	12.7	12.8	14.2	13.0	13.0
Work experience (years)	19.8	14.7	19.0	19.0	19.4	13.0	18.9	18.8
Union membership	6.8%	0.0%	4.7%	4.9%	4.6%	6.3%	2.9%	3.1%
Speaks English very well	—	—	99.8%	—	—	—	—	—
OTHER HISPANIC								
Schooling (years)	11.4	13.6	12.7	11.9	11.9	14.1	13.0	12.3
Work experience (years)	20.6	11.2	17.3	18.9	21.3	11.2	18.9	19.6
Union membership	1.3%	2.5%	2.8%	1.7%	1.4%	1.9%	1.4%	1.5%
ASIAN								
Schooling (years)	14.3	14.0	14.3	14.3	13.9	14.7	14.4	14.1
Work experience (years)	18.4	9.4	19.1	17.7	19.8	10.8	18.1	18.8
Union membership	2.7%	2.4%	3.2%	2.7%	2.5%	0.0%	6.3%	2.8%

Sources: English proficiency data are from Trejo (1997), based on the November 1989 Current Population Survey; all other data are author's weighted tabulations from the March 1999 CPS.
Notes: Includes persons age sixteen to sixty-four who are not attending school and who worked in 1998. Excludes persons who were self-employed or worked without pay. Sample weights are used.

Table 9. Average and Adjusted Hourly Wages, by Generation

	MALE			FEMALE		
	First	**Second**	**Third**	**First**	**Second**	**Third**
AVERAGE LOG HOURLY WAGE						
Mexican American	2.09	2.39	2.39	1.90	2.18	2.20
Non-Mexican American	2.59	2.82	2.67	2.33	2.54	2.39
ADJUSTED LOG HOURLY WAGE[1]						
Mexican American	2.58	2.68	2.64	2.43	2.43	2.42
Non-Mexican American	2.64	2.82	2.76	2.38	2.54	2.49
IMPLIED PERCENTAGE HOURLY WAGE DEFICIT[2]						
Average hourly wage	–39.7%	–34.8%	–24.5%	–14.1%	–29.4%	–18.0%
Adjusted hourly wage	–5.7%	–13.2%	–11.9%	5.4%	–11 %	–7.0%

Source: Author's weighted estimates from the March 1999 Current Population Survey.
Notes: Sample includes persons age sixteen to sixty-four who are not enrolled in school and who worked in 1998. Excludes persons who were self-employed, worked without pay, or lived in group quarters.

[1]Estimates are from regressions for males and females of log hourly wages on state of residence, central-city/MSA residence, marital status, work experience (quartic), union membership in March 1999, education, Mexican American identifier for each generation, non-Mexican American identifier for each generation, and a constant. Second-generation non-Mexican Americans are the reference group. Hourly wage is defined as total wage and salary earnings divided by the product of number of weeks worked and usual hours worked per week. Wages and salaries are top-coded by the CPS.
[2]If x is the log wage difference between Mexican Americans and non-Mexican Americans, then the implied wage differential is $e^x - 1$.

decline, and in the case of women, they actually increase. Undoubtedly, the reduction in wages is partly due to a higher percentage of part-time workers in the third generation. For this reason, the adjusted wage deficit of Mexican Americans shows improvement from the second to the third generation.

Discussion

Two possible explanations exist for the wage differential between Mexican Americans and European Americans: systematic discrimination against Mexican Americans in the labor market or differences in workers' productive characteristics. Several other studies have reached the same conclusion presented here; namely, that worker characteristics explain about 95 percent of the wage differential between European Americans and Mexican Americans (Cain 1986; Ehrenberg and Smith 1994; Reimers 1985; Trejo 1997). One particularly significant characteristic distinguishing Mexican American from European American men is high English proficiency. Trejo (1997) suggests that factoring in English language proficiency further reduces the wage differential by about 5 percentage points to almost nothing. (English proficiency was not considered in the present analysis due to data limitations.) Trejo also suggests that any remaining wage difference is explained by the ethnic composition of whites—whites of British descent, for example, earn the same as Mexican Americans with the same characteristics, but both groups earn less than whites of Russian descent. He concludes that third-generation Mexican Americans earn lower wages because of lower productive characteristics, especially education and English proficiency, and that there is no evidence of systematic discrimination in wages. In contrast, he does find evidence of wage discrimination against blacks.

This evidence suggests that improving the educational levels of Mexican Americans is one of the most effective ways to reduce the wage gap between them and non-Mexican-origin workers. Improved English language proficiency will also reduce wage differentials, but this variable is highly correlated with education levels. At the same time, the maintenance of Spanish may result in highly sought-after bilingual workers; these workers may experience labor market rewards that are generally not available to monolingual English speakers.

Furthermore, improved education levels are likely to change the industrial and occupational distribution of Mexican Americans—a high-school graduate would not be expected to be an architect or engineer. The labor market can be divided into two markets, primary and secondary, with the primary market being distinguished by better wages, prestige, and stability (Cain 1986; Schiller 1989). Not surprisingly, entrance into the primary labor market is highly correlated with education. Increases in education, English ability, and work experience will more than

likely result in more Mexican Americans moving out of the secondary and into the primary labor market.

Even though wage discrimination is not a significant issue for the majority of Mexican Americans, there is evidence of other types of discrimination. Delgado Bernal (1998) and Monroy (1999) provide evidence of pre-labor market discrimination in terms of Mexican American children receiving a lower-quality education. Unfortunately, no definitive study has been undertaken that measures educational discrimination in a statistically meaningful way. For example, is the lower quality of education provided to Mexican American children due simply to the fact that they are poorer, on average, than middle-class Americans? After all, poor whites also suffer from low educational levels. Poor populations live in neighborhoods that cannot fund school districts to the same extent as wealthier neighborhoods. The solution to this inequality is unclear. Attempts to equalize spending across school districts actually have had the perverse result of reducing per-pupil spending, which may end up hurting rather than helping poor students (Silva and Sonstelie 1995).

At the hiring stage, Kenney and Wissoker (1994) found that Hispanics and European Americans with nearly identical qualifications applying for entry-level jobs had different outcomes. In particular, European American applicants were more likely to be asked to file a job application, to obtain a job interview, and to be offered the job than Hispanics were. Kenney and Wissoker's study covered only two cities and was not a representative sample of employers, however, so we should be cautious in assuming that the results provide evidence of systematic job discrimination. Nevertheless, these findings indicate that it is imperative to continue enforcement of anti-discrimination laws at all levels.

Summary

The labor market situation of Mexican Americans is in some ways encouraging: they are hard working and dedicated to work. On the other hand, they suffer from higher than average levels of unemployment and spend more time looking for work than most other workers. For those who are working, their occupational profile tells a mixed story. The first generation is likely to be concentrated in labor-intensive manufacturing work, but a fair percentage of the second and third generations moves out of these jobs and into white-collar occupations. Still, fewer Mexican Americans work in prestigious jobs than is true for other ethnic groups.

Mexican Americans earn more than 25 percent less than non-Mexican-origin workers, although the wage deficit decreases across generations. The adjusted averages for Mexican Americans improve into the third generation relative to non-Hispanic whites. Much of the gap can be accounted for by differences in education, English language ability, and other worker characteristics. This suggests that a prescription for attaining economic equality is to eliminate educational inequalities. Although the employment and income statistics are bleak, current education information available provides some encouraging signs that educational levels are increasing among Mexican Americans. I hope that these educational gains will continue and result in even greater economic gains for the next generation of Mexican Americans. Current Mexican American workers will also see their wages rise as they become older, acquire more work experience, maintain the same levels of labor force attachment, and continue their quest for *buenos días*.

References

Borjas, George J. 1982. The Labor Supply of Male Hispanic Immigrants in the United States. *International Migration Review* 17, 343–53.

Borjas, George J., and Marta Tienda. 1985. Introduction. In *Hispanics in the U.S. Economy*, edited by George J. Borjas and Marta Tienda. Orlando, Fla.: Academic Press.

Cain, Glen G. 1986. The Economic Analysis of Labor Market Discrimination: A Survey. In *Handbook of Labor Economics*, edited by Orley Ashenfelter and Richard Layard. Vol. 2. New York: Elsevier Science Publishers.

DeFreitas, Gregory. 1985. Ethnic Differentials in Unemployment among Hispanic Americans. In *Hispanics in the U.S. Economy*, edited by George J. Borjas and Marta Tienda. Orlando, Fla.: Academic Press.

———. 1991. *Inequality at Work: Hispanics in the U.S. Labor Force*. New York: Oxford University Press.

Delgado, Bernal, Dolores. 1998. Chicana/o Education from the Civil Rights Era to the Present. In *The Elusive Quest for Equality: 150 Years of Chicana/Chicano Education*, edited by José F. Moreno. Cambridge, Mass.: Harvard Educational Review Publishing Group.

Ehrenberg, Ronald G., and Robert S. Smith. 1994. *Modern Labor Economics: Theory and Public Policy*. 5th ed. New York: HarperCollins College Publishers.

Higuera, Jonathan J. 1998. Developer Stands Tall after Crash: Local Mogul 'Toughed' It Out, Hitting the Top of the Market. *Tucson Citizen*, May 18, p. IA.

Kenney, Genevieve M., and Douglas A. Wissoker. 1994. An Analysis of the Correlates of Discrimination Facing Young Hispanic Job-Seekers. *American Economic Review* 84, 674–83.

Monroy, Douglas. 1999. *Rebirth: Mexican Los Angeles from the Great Migration and the Great Depression*. Berkeley: University of California Press.

Reimers, Cordelia W. 1985. A Comparative Analysis of the Wages of Hispanics, Blacks, and Non-Hispanic Whites. In *Hispanics in the U.S. Economy*, edited by George J. Borjas and Marta Tienda. Orlando, Fla.: Academic Press.

———. 1992. Hispanic Earnings and Employment in the 1980s. In *Hispanics in the Workforce*, edited by Stephen B. Knouse, Paul Rosenfeld, and Amy Culbertson. Newbury Park, Calif.: Sage.

Schiller, Bradley. 1989. *The Economics of Poverty and Discrimination*. 5th ed. Englewood Cliffs, N.J.: Prentice Hall.

Segura, Denise A. 1992. Walking on Eggshells: Chicanas in the Labor Force. In *Hispanics in the Workforce*, edited by Stephen B. Knouse, Paul Rosenfeld, and Amy Culbertson. Newbury Park, Calif.: Sage.

Silva, Fabio, and Jon Sonstelie. 1995. Did Serrano Cause a Decline in School Spending? *National Tax Journal* 48, 199–215.

Trejo, Stephen J. 1997. Why Do Mexican Americans Earn Low Wages? *Journal of Political Economy* 105, 1235–68.

¡La Mujer Luchando, El Mundo Transformando!
Mexican Immigrant Women Workers

Miriam Ching Yoon Louie

At their *Día de Los Muertos* [Day of the Dead] celebration on November 1, 1994, *las mujeres* [the women] look gaunt but on a spiritual high. The women are members of Fuerza Unida, the organization they created with their own hands and hearts when Levi Strauss & Co. laid them off and ran away to Costa Rica in 1990. They have trekked all the way from San Antonio with sleeping bags to haunt Levi's plaza and corporate headquarters in San Francisco, California.

So that CEO Robert Haas will hear their cries for corporate responsibility loud and clear, the women shout at the tops of their lungs, *¡No tenemos hambre de comida; tenemos hambre de justicia!* [We're not hungry for food; we're hungry for justice!]. The women gently break their 21-day hunger strike savoring the miracle of *pan dulce* [sweet rolls] and steaming cups of coffee carted in by their many supporters. Their *comadre* [girlfriend] Puerto Rican activist Luz Guerra calls these *huelgistas de hambre* [hunger strikers] *las nuevas revolucionarias* [the new revolutionaries] who picked up where Emiliano Zapata, Pancho Villa, the *soldaderas* and *adelitas* [women soldiers and companions] of the 1910 Mexican Revolution left off.

Throwing back their heads in laughter, they clap and tap their feet as Chicano *poeta/músico/activista* Arnoldo García serenades them with his new rendition of a traditional Mexican song:

La Fuerza Unida

En los frentes de liberacíon
de este pueblo de trabajadores
Existen mujeres fuertes y valientes
Existen mujeres que saben luchar

En ciudades y campos se forman
dando fuerza y visión a los pueblos
Son trabajadoras radientes de luchas
Son trabajadoras de justicia y paz

Su cultura y trabajo respeten
Con la fuerza de su dignidad
Son las costureras pidiendo justicia
Son las costureras que saben luchar

Son las desplazadas de la Levis
Luchadoras del gran movimiento
Son las costureras de la Fuerza Unida
Son las costureras de liberacíon[1]

As Mexico's former dictator Porfirio Díaz lamented, "Poor little Mexico, so far from God, so close to the United States."[2] Mexico's fateful proximity to the developing "Colossus of the North"[3] has long shaped the destiny of its working people and the national, race, and class formation of the United States. Ever since the United States annexed half of Mexico's territory by seizing Texas in 1836 and launching the Mexican-American War (1845–1848), Mexican workers have served as a giant labor reserve and shock absorber for the bumps and potholes of US economic development.[4] Sharing a 2,000-mile border with its powerful neighbor to the north, Mexico is the homeland of an estimated 40 percent of US immigrants.[5] Migration to the United States also serves as a safety net for Mexico's economic and political system, yielding remittances of at least $6 billion a year, one of the largest sources of Mexico's foreign exchange, along with the oil, tourism, and maquiladora industries.

Chicana labor historian Vicki Ruiz says that Mexicanas crossed the border as "farm worker mothers, railroad wives, and miners' daughters" to join male relatives recruited by those burgeoning industries during the spate of post-Civil War US industrial expansion.[7] Especially since the 1920s, Mexican immigrant women and US-born Chicanas have emerged as the backbone of many of the lowest paying, most back-breaking jobs in Texas, California, New Mexico,

From *Sweatshop Warriors: Immigrant Women Workers Take on the Global Factory* by Miriam Ching Yoon Louie. Copyright © 2002. Reprinted by permission of the publisher, South End Press.

Colorado, Arizona, and Illinois, such as the agribusiness, cannery, pecan shelling, food processing, garment, and domestic service industries. Mexicana labor migration has also increased to the US Northwest, Midwest, East, and South.[8] By the end of 1996 there were 9.6 million Latinas in the United States, including 5.7 million women of Mexican origin, 1.1 million Puerto Rican women, 485,000 Cuban women, and another 2.3 million women of Latin American descent.[9] Latinas continue to have the highest concentrations of workers in "blue collar" operative jobs and the lowest in management and professions among all races of women.[10]

The rise in export-oriented production for transnational corporations along the US-Mexico border since the 1960s and other aspects of economic restructuring have accelerated Mexicanas internal and cross-border labor migration. Many of today's *nuevas revolucionarias* started working on the global assembly line as young women in northern Mexico for foreign transnational corporations. Some women worked on the US side as "commuters" before they moved across the border with their families. Their stories reveal the length, complexity, and interpenetration of the US and Mexican economies, labor markets, histories, cultures, and race relations. The women talk about the devastating impact of globalization, including massive layoffs and the spread of sweatshops on both sides of the border. *Las mujeres* recount what drove them to join and lead movements for economic, racial, and gender justice, as well the challenges they faced within their families and communities to assert their basic human rights. The women featured in this chapter play leadership roles in La Mujer Obrera [The Woman Worker] in El Paso, Texas, Fuerza Unida [United Force] in San Antonio, Texas, and the Thai and Latino Workers Organizing Committee of the Retailers Accountability Campaign in Los Angeles, California.

Growing Up Female and Poor

Mexican women and girls were traditionally expected to do all the cooking, cleaning, and serving for their husbands, brothers, and sons. For girls from poor families, shouldering these domestic responsibilities proved doubly difficult because they also performed farm, sweatshop, or domestic service work simultaneously. Refugio "Cuca" Arrieta, the only daughter of farm worker parents in Ciudad Jiménes, Chihuahua, reluctantly left school early:

> I stayed home because I had to take care of my younger brothers. I went to school and finished no more than the first, second, and third grade. At the nearby *ranchitos* [little farms] we learned how to read and write. Before starting school I had already learned how to read and write. I taught myself.[11]

Petra Mata, a former seamstress for Levi's whose mother died shortly after childbirth, recalls the heavy housework she did as the only daughter:

> Aiyeee, let me tell you! It was very hard. In those times in Mexico, I was raised with the ideal that you have to learn to do everything—cook, make tortillas, wash your clothes, and clean the house—just the way they wanted you to. My grandparents were very strict. I always had to ask their permission and then let them tell me what to do. I was not a free woman. Life was hard for me. I didn't have much of a childhood; I started working when I was 12 or 13 years old. [12]

Neoliberalism and Creeping Maquiladorization

These women came of age during a period of major change in the relationship between the Mexican and US economies. Like Puerto Rico, Hong Kong, South Korea, Taiwan, Malaysia, Singapore, and the Philippines, northern Mexico served as one of the first stations of the global assembly line tapping young women's labor. In 1965 the Mexican government initiated the Border Industrialization Program (BIP) that set up export plants, called maquiladoras or maquilas, which were either the direct subsidiaries or subcontractors of transnational corporations. Mexican government incentives to US and other foreign investors included low wages and high productivity; infrastructure; proximity to US markets, facilities, and lifestyles; tariff loopholes; and pliant, pro-government unions.[13]

Many of the women worked in electronics and garment maquiladoras before crossing the border to work in US plants. María Antonia Flores describes her co-workers in the Juárez electronics plant where she worked as *puras jovenes* [all young women], while the supervisors were *puros varones* [all male]. Describing her quarter-century-long sewing career in Mexico, Celeste Jiménez ticks off the names of famous US manufacturers who hopped over the border to take advantage of cheap wages:

> I sewed for twenty-four years when I lived in Chihuahua in big name factories like Billy the Kid, Levi Strauss, and Lee maquiladoras. Everyone was down there. Here a company might sell under the brand name of Lee; there in Mexico it would be called Blanca García.[14]

Many of the women worked in the maquilas because of the unstable economic status of male family members— where men are either absent, unemployed, or earning well below the "family wage," i.e., the wage sufficient to support a family. Marta Martínez, a laid-off Levi's worker first learned to sew from her mom:

I was born in Mexico City in 1959. My mom was a seamstress who ran a little workshop about this size. [She points to Fuerza Unida's small sewing coop production area.] Once in a while she was able to get a contract and work for a maquiladora. Dad worked as a *campesino* [farm worker]. I had four sisters and three brothers. I'm in the middle. But I was able to finish 12 years of school so I got to be a teacher. . . . In 1983, I worked for the Castro company on this side, making baby clothes. It wasn't hard to learn. I already knew from my mom how to use an industrial machine.[15]

Transnational exploitation of women's labor was part of a broader set of policies that critical opposition movements in the Third World have dubbed "neoliberalism," i.e., the new version of the British Liberal Party's program of laissez faire capitalism espoused by the rising European and US colonial powers during the late 18th and 19th centuries. The Western powers, Japan, and international financial institutions like the World Bank and International Monetary Fund have aggressively promoted neoliberal policies since the 1970s.[16] Mexico served as an early testing ground for such standard neoliberal policies as erection of free trade zones; commercialization of agriculture; currency devaluation; deregulation; privatization; outsourcing; cuts in wages and social programs; suppression of workers', women's, and indigenous people's rights; free trade; militarization; and promotion of neoconservative ideology.

Neoliberalism intersects with gender and national oppression. Third World women constitute the majority of migrants seeking jobs as maids, vendors, maquila operatives, and service industry workers. Women also pay the highest price for cuts in education, health and housing programs, and food and energy subsidies and increases in their unpaid labor.[17]

The human costs of Mexico's neoliberal program and extended economic crisis are evident in the 60 percent drop in real minimum wages between 1982 and 1988 and the 30 percent drop in internal consumption of basic grains during the 1980s.[18] In 1986, some 62 percent of the economically active population of Mexico earned sub-minimum wages.[19] In 1994, the World Bank estimated that 38 percent of the total population of Mexico lived in absolute poverty. Two out of five households had no water supply, three out of five had no drainage, and one in three had no electricity.[20]

The deepening of the economic crisis in Mexico, especially under the International Monetary Fund's pressure to devaluate the peso in 1976, 1982, and 1994, forced many women to work in both the formal and informal economy to survive and meet their childrearing and household responsibilities.[21] María Antonia Flores was forced to work two jobs after her husband abandoned the family, leaving her with three children to support. She had no choice but to leave her children home alone, *solitos*, to look after themselves. Refugio Arrieta straddled the formal and informal economy because her job in an auto parts assembly maquiladora failed to bring in sufficient income. To compensate for the shortfall, she worked longer hours at her maquila job and "moonlighted" elsewhere:

We made chassis for cars and for the headlights. I worked lots! I worked 12 hours more or less because they paid us so little that if you worked more, you got more money. I did this because the schools in Mexico don't provide everything. You have to buy the books, notebooks, *todos, todos* [everything]. And I had five kids. It's very expensive. I also worked out of my house and sold ceramics. I did many things to get more money for my kids.[22]

In the three decades following its humble beginnings in the mid-1960s, the maquila sector swelled to more than 2,000 plants employing an estimated 776,000 people, over 10 percent of Mexico's labor force.[23] In 1985, maquiladoras overtook tourism as the largest source of foreign exchange. In 1996, this sector trailed only petroleum-related industries in economic importance and accounted for over US$29 billion in export earnings annually.[24] The maquila system has also penetrated the interior of the country, as in the case of Guadalajara's electronics assembly industry and Tehuacán's jeans production zones.[25] Although the proportion of male maquila workers has increased since 1983, especially in auto-transport equipment assembly, almost 70 percent of the workers continue to be women.[26]

As part of a delegation of labor and human rights activists, this author met some of Mexico's newest proletarians—young indigenous women migrant workers from the Sierra Negra to Tehuacán, a town famous for its refreshing mineral water spring, in the state of Puebla, just southeast of Mexico City. Standing packed like cattle in the back of the trucks each morning the women headed for jobs sewing for name brand manufacturers like Guess?, VF Corporation (producing Lee brand clothing), The GAP, Sun Apparel (producing brands such as Polo, Arizona, and Express), Cherokee, Ditto Apparel of California, Levi's, and others. The workers told US delegation members that their wages averaged US$30 to $50 a week for 12-hour work days, six days a week. Some workers reported having to do *veladas* [all-nighters] once or twice a week. Employees often stayed longer without pay if they did not finish high production goals.

Girls as young as 12 and 13 worked in the factories. Workers were searched when they left for lunch and again at the end of the day to check that they weren't stealing materials. Women were routinely given urine tests when hired and those found to be pregnant were promptly fired, in violation of Mexican labor law. Although the workers had organized an independent union several years earlier, Tehuacán's Human Rights Commission members told us that it had collapsed after one of its leaders was assassinated.[27]

Carmen Valadez and Reyna Montero, long-time activists in the women's and social justice movements, helped found Casa de La Mujer Factor X in 1977, a workers' center in Tijuana that organizes around women's workplace, reproductive, and health rights, and against domestic violence. Valadez and Montero say that the low wages and dangerous working conditions characteristic of the maquiladoras on the Mexico-US border are being "extended to all areas of the country and to Central America and the Caribbean. NAFTA represents nothing but the 'maquiladorization' of the region."[28]

Elizabeth "Beti" Robles Ortega, who began working in the maquilas at the age of fourteen and was blacklisted after participating in independent union organizing drives on Mexico's northern border, now works as an organizer for the Servicio, Desarrollo y Paz, AC (SEDEPAC) [Service, Development and Peace organization]. Robles described the erosion of workers rights and women's health under NAFTA:

> NAFTA has led to an increase in the workforce, as foreign industry has grown. They are reforming labor laws and our constitution to favor even more foreign investment, which is unfair against our labor rights. For example, they are now trying to take away from us free organization which was guaranteed by Mexican law. Because foreign capital is investing in Mexico and is dominating, we must have guarantees. The government is just there with its hands held out; it's always had them out but now even more shamelessly. . . . Ecological problems are increasing. A majority of women are coming down with cancer—skin and breast cancer, leukemia, and lung and heart problems. There are daily deaths of worker women. You can see and feel the contamination of the water and the air. As soon as you arrive and start breathing the air in Acuña and Piedras Negras [border cities between the states of Coahuila and Texas], you sense the heavy air, making you feel like vomiting.[29]

Like Casa de La Mujer Factor X in Tijuana, and the women workers' centers and cooperatives whose work the Frente Auténtico del Trabajo (FAT) has prioritized especially since 1992, SEDEPAC also participates in national networks of Mexican women workers such as the Red de Trabajadores en Las Maquilas, which meets annually in different cities in the northern border region, as well as in binational networks like the Southwest Network for Environmental and Economic Justice.[30]

Maquiladorization Accelerates Migration

Many of the Mexicanas migrated to the United States in a two-stage migration process, similar to many of the Asian women workers. Migration to the northern border region offered women proximity to family members working on the other side, and after the initiation of the Border Industrialization Program in 1965, potential employment opportunities as well. Patricia Fernández-Kelly has suggested that by recruiting mainly young female workers, the border maquiladora program ended up drawing even more migrants to the border, yet failed to reduce male farm workers' unemployment caused by termination of the Bracero Program as the Mexican government had originally planned. Many migrants to the northern border eventually cross into the United States.[31]

For example, La Mujer Obrera organizer Irma Montoya Barajas was born in the central Mexican state of Aguascalientes. At age ten she moved with her parents to Juárez in northern Mexico, where her father found work as a carpenter while her mother took care of her nine brothers and sisters. Similarly María Antonia Flores was born in the central state of Zacatecas, but moved with her family to Juárez when she was eight years old. There her parents found odd jobs working in maquilas, restaurants, and as food vendors. Petra Mata of Fuerza Unida traces her roots to Nuevo Laredo, Tamaulipas, across from Laredo, Texas. But she and her parents were actually born in the little village of Bustamante, Nuevo León. They moved when they could no longer survive through farming, and Petra's grandfather and father, like many Mexican and Chinese immigrant men, got jobs working for the railroad.

Over time Mexican migration networks have become more regionally diverse. María Antonia Flores explains that while many workers migrate from areas adjacent to the border:

> People come here from almost all of the states in the south of Mexico to find work due to the economic problems throughout the nation and precisely because of the pull of all the maquiladoras located on the border. So every day people arrive at the maquilas from the south looking for work and trying to better their struggle to survive. But they find *nada, nada* [nothing]. Around here many people come from Coahuila, Durango, Zacatecas, and Chihuahua, but over there in Tijuana, there are also people from Chiapas, Oaxaca, San Luis Potosí, that is to say almost all of the states.[32]

Alberta "Beti" Cariño Trujillo, a dedicated organizer for the human rights commission in Tehuacán, Puebla, originally comes from the southern coastal state of Oaxaca. With her mother and siblings, Cariño struggled to survive in Oaxaca while her father worked as a migrant laborer picking oranges up in California.

Cariño is anxious to make contact with US immigrant and workers' rights groups to develop an information network. She and her co-workers teach a night school for garment workers and their children in Tehuacán. The human rights workers are concentrating on the fight for better wages and working conditions locally, and against toxic-waste dumping and water contamination by the maquilas, lack of childcare and educational opportunities, domestic and street violence, unwanted pregnancies, and high stress levels, especially among single mothers. They also want to provide accurate information about what life is like for immigrant workers in the United States to dispel any illusions potential migrants might have.[33]

Indeed the information "grapevine" extends into the farthest corners of Mexico. In the *colonia* [newly built, poorly served, suburban settlement] of Nezahuacoyotl on the outskirts of Mexico City, members of a local poor women's group shared their knowledge of the United States during a visit from international participants of a November 1989 garment workers' conference in Mexico City. Many of the women were themselves internal migrants to the world's largest city and they proudly told conference delegates of a free breakfast and milk program they developed so that poor children would not go to school on empty stomachs.

A Chicana activist's description of her work with immigrants in Los Angeles, unleashed an animated exchange with the Mexicana *colonia* organizers. "Chicago is a bad place for Mexican workers." "Don't go to Fresno, they already have too many Mexicans; you can't find a job anymore." "Orange County is very conservative and does not like Mexicans." "Go to Washington to pick apples. My cousin got a job there, and she likes it so much, she's going to send for her two daughters."[34] Perhaps some of such Mexicana organizers contributed their experience to the United Farm Workers Union efforts in the 1990s to organize Mexican immigrants in Washington's apple orchards.[35]

When the Border Was Just a Bridge between Neighborhoods

The wide variety in the immigration and citizenship status of the women and their family members reflects the permeability of a border that workers of Mexican descent have criss-crossed since US annexation in 1848. After centuries of relatively free movement within the region, only in 1924 did the US government create the Border Patrol and the notion of the "illegal alien," thus transforming Mexican workers into potential fugitives of the law unless they could secure official permits. Yet employers escaped responsibility and often used the fear of deportation to lower the wages of undocumented workers.[36]

The period from World War I until the Great Depression marked the first big wave of migration when the US government launched a contract-labor program for male migrant workers, the predecessor of the Bracero Program.[37] Mexican government recruitment efforts initially targeted men from the central western states of Michoacán, Jalísco, and Guanajuato. These workers served as the links of mi-

gration chains stretching between rural Mexican communities to specific US farms and towns.[38] Over time, tributaries from all the Mexican states contributed to the flow of Mexican workers across the border.

The elder relatives of many of the women interviewed for this book had worked in the United States, especially as farm workers, railroad workers, and miners. Some had been born in the United States or had become US citizens at other times in their lives, yet continued to migrate across the border in both directions. For example, Celeste Jiménez was born in the northern state of Chihuahua in 1939. Yet she explains:

> My father was born in Candelario, Texas, and my mom in Sierra Blanca. I'm 100 percent Mexican. My father worked raising cattle and my mom was a housewife. There were ten children, eight girls and two boys. I was born in Mexico. I'm the third oldest among the kids. My dad was a US citizen. My mom was a Mexican citizen. She was born in California but lived in Chihuahua most of her life. My mom's parents came here [to the US] in 1942. In 1964, my mom and dad came here too, but they didn't work anymore because they were getting too old. In 1982, I came here directly from Chihuahua. I'm a permanent legal resident.[39]

Similarly María del Carmen Domínguez describes the peripatetic wanderings of her farm worker father and how her mother moved closer to the border, anchoring the family:

> My father was born in California and lived and worked in Mexico many, many years. He also worked in El Paso, Texas and traveled to Los Angeles to work in the fields with machines and doing other jobs. My mother was born in Chihuahua, Mexico. She bore and raised four children. She stayed in Ciudad Juárez most of her life.[40]

Although Carmen "Chitlan" Ibarra Lopéz was born in Chihuahua where her father worked as a miner and her mother as a homemaker, she traces her cross-border roots to her grandparents' generation:

> I became a naturalized US citizen through my mother because my mother was born in the US. She was born in the US but she went back to live in Mexico. What I heard was that during the Mexican Revolution [1910–1920] my grandparents came to live in California. They went to Wasco. They were farm workers. They picked cotton. My mother and her brothers and sisters were born in Wasco. Me and my sister lived with one of mom's sisters for a while.[41]

Following the trail of Mexican migrant chili workers, long-time Juárez residents Alicia and Carlos Marentes packed up their belongings and crossed the international bridge separating Juárez and El Paso in 1971. After serving a stint in the Texas Farm Workers Union, they helped found the Border Agricultural Workers Union in El Paso in 1984. After a decade of struggle, the union opened a beautiful center in 1995. This shelter acts as an oasis for chili workers who are hired through a humiliating human auction system to toil 12-hour days in Texas and New Mexico under a haze of toxic pesticides at temperatures that alternate between scorching and freezing. Women and undocumented workers get paid the lowest of the low, averaging a scant $5,300 a year, while even male workers with documents earn only $6,000.

Alicia coordinates classes where women learn to make handicrafts that they can sell during the dead season when they can find no work in the fields. Her friendly face clouds with sadness as she reminisces, "So many of the campesinos Carlos and I started working with back in 1980 have already passed away because of their hard lives. We have lost whole generations of farm workers." Carlos says that workers must become visible within the broader society if they are to improve their lives. Yet the anti-immigrant backlash is dehumanizing and criminalizing these workers. He shakes his head saying, "I remember when the border was nothing more than a bridge you crossed from a poor neighborhood to a richer one. That was before they started enacting all the anti-immigration legislation, rounding up immigrants, and militarizing the border."[42]

Ironically, and some insist intentionally, cross-border movement of people is increasingly restricted precisely during an unprecedented flow of capital, trade, goods, services, information, and culture, especially since the enactment of the North American Free Trade Agreement (NAFTA) in 1994. According to immigrant rights and environmental justice activist Arnoldo García, NAFTA has proven a total disaster for Mexican workers, farmers, and small business people and spurred more migration:

> During NAFTA's first year and a half, the US trade deficit with Mexico grew by a whopping $4 billion and some 80,000 US jobs were lost. Mexican workers' wages declined 40 to 50 percent, ravaging their buying power. While the cost of living has risen by 80 percent in Mexico, salaries only increased by a mere 30 percent. Mexico's inflation rate runs over 51 percent; 2.3 million Mexican people have lost jobs and the peso has been severely devalued—from 3.1 pesos to the dollar in January 1994 to 7.6 pesos in March 1996. Over 20,000 small and medium businesses have gone belly-up in the face of increased multinational competition. And NAFTA's much touted labor and environmental side agreements have proven to be weak and ineffective.[43]

The Clinton administration doubled the budget of the INS after enacting NAFTA. The 1996 "Illegal Immigration Reform and Immigrant Responsibility Act" then mandated hiring another thousand border patrol agents. According to the Urban Institute, only four out of ten individuals who are in the US illegally crossed the southern border while the other six entered with legal visas as visitors, students, or temporary employees who failed to leave when their visas expired. These immigrants have documents and have been in contact with the INS. Only about one-third of the undocumented population is from Mexico. Yet 85 percent of all the resources of the INS, including the Border Patrol, are trained on the border with Mexico—reflecting both racist backlash against Mexican workers and the INS's evidently unquenchable thirst for money and military hardware.[44]

Mexico's extended economic crises prompted a major demographic shakeup in migration to the United States. These new stresses forced workers from large industrial urban centers without previous traditions of US migration; more people from the urban and middle classes; and more women, children, and elderly people to risk crossing the border. Political scientist and immigration expert Wayne Cornelius dubbed this new, more heterogeneous pool of migrants *los migrantes de la crisis*.[45] Commenting on the utility of the border to politicians and employers, La Mujer Obrera organizer Carmen Ibarra Lopéz reflects:

> It's very hard for us as Mexican workers to understand the line on the border. I think that's why nobody has really, really put attention on the border's workers because it's a very different situation. It's like another world when you come through El Paso. I think the kinds of problems we are seeing workers come in with are not just because of the lack of good opportunities, but also because of a lot of discrimination. When I say discrimination, it's because we have a lot of members who under the amnesty law have a perfect right to come to the US and become citizens.[46]

Feminization of Migration

Women do not always migrate or stay home based on male family members' unchallenged decisions, but sometimes play the principal role in initiating migration. In her insightful study of the immigration of undocumented Mexican workers, sociology professor Pierrette Hondagneu-Sotelo warns that contrary to popular stereotypes, extensive research on Chicano and US-based Mexican families suggests that not all families are characterized by uniformly extreme patriarchy. Although sexism persists, she says that urbanization and women's growing role as income earners have begun to erode male dominance to varying degrees, and that traditional social relations and cultural resources neither disappear not stay the same but are being constantly reshaped through the processes of migration and resettlement.[47]

Indeed, women made decisions to cross the border under a variety of circumstances, including invitations from their partners, other relatives, and friends. Some initiated the move themselves. For example, María del Carmen Domínguez decided to move from Juárez to El Paso because she got tired of commuting to work:

> I came to El Paso in 1972 because I needed to work to support my family. At that time I had two children. Eight years later I had another child that is my baby right now who's 18 years old. I came to work in the factories. I was 15 years old when I was pregnant with my first boy and I got married when I was 17, almost 18 years old. I met my husband through friends and the family. He worked in the construction of houses and putting up fences. When I was living in Juárez, I worked for two years in El Paso, crossing the bridges everyday from Mexico. That was too hard so we decided to come to live in El Paso and I stayed here. During the time I was crossing the bridges, I was coming to work in a garment factory.[48]

Petra Mata also began working in the United States as a cross-border commuter. She started working as a maid when she was 12 or 13 years old after the tragic death of her mother and subsequent abandonment by her father. Although she worked hard and scrubbed floors on her hands and knees, she only made $10 a week. She recalls, "During the five years I worked for the same family, the highest pay I ever got was $16 a week." Later Petra moved to the United States permanently after she got married. She and her husband took up their friends' invitation to come, first as undocumented immigrants. Later Petra and her husband got US citizenship to "have a voice, a right to vote."[49]

Lucrecia Tamayo, a garment worker and leader in the Thai and Latino Workers Organizing Committee of the Retailer Accountability Campaign decided to make the big move from Acapulco, Guerrero to Los Angeles after her marriage failed. During her "stopover" in Tijuana, that famous "travelers advisory and transit center," she secured the means to make the crossing and picked up information on possible job leads in Los Angeles, the metropolis with the second largest Mexican population in the world, after Mexico City. Lucrecia relied on a female relative, the well-developed migrant "underground railroad," and a waiting job market:

> I got married in Mexico, but the person I married was treating me bad, so I moved here 15 years ago in 1982. I came by myself. (laughs) I came by *el cerro* [through the mountains], with a coyote. Oh, it was scary! There were so many people, I was in the front with the driver, and over there, a mountain of people. And the driver was very nervous about running into immigration. I only had one sister who was living here.
>
> I came to the United States because after [my former husband] left, I had a little girl to take care of. It wasn't my parents' obligation to raise her. So I had to find a new life. I came straight to Los Angeles. I lived with

my sister for about a year. About six months after coming here, I started working in garment. When I was in Tijuana I heard about this kind of job by word of mouth. The people who came back to Mexico told us all about how life is here, about the kinds of work you can get. If you don't know about it, they teach you.[50]

Working *al Otro Lado* [on the Other Side]

Until recently women who crossed the border were frequently able to land jobs in *El Norte* [the North], often performing work similar to what they had done in Mexico. Arriving in such well-established Mexican immigrant communities as El Paso, San Antonio, and Los Angeles, the women found jobs fairly quickly, in some cases even before they settled permanently in the United States. They heard about work through family members, friends, and neighbors. Women changed jobs as they got adjusted to US working conditions and "learned the ropes."

After moving from Juárez to El Paso with her husband, Irma Montoya of La Mujer Obrera got a job working as an electronics assembler and inspector at a plant that made thermometers:

> My cousin's husband told me about the job. I worked there from 1987 until they laid us off in 1995. I made good money there, $6.30 an hour and the working conditions were good, too. But in 1995 they shut us down and moved to Mexico. There were about 400 of us who lost our jobs. My husband lost his job after working for 20 years making Tony Lamas boots. Now he can only find work as a janitor.[51]

María del Carmen Domínguez heard about jobs through the grapevine. After commuting from Juárez, she changed to better jobs as she gained more experience and learned what was available:

> I worked for 15 years in garment factories. The first one was Rudy's Sportswear where I worked for almost five years. I worked for one year at Emily Joe and almost nine years at CMT Industries as a seamstress.
>
> My friends told me about the job in the first factory. I think I got paid minimum wage there. In the last one I got paid more, sometimes up to $5.50 or $6 an hour because it was by the quota. At the other factories I was paid by the hour. I didn't get paid for overtime. In the last factory, at CMT, we got some benefits, like vacations and some holidays.
>
> The first shop I worked at was so small. It expanded, but then they had a problem about wages and their contracts and it went bankrupt. The second one was a small factory, but it was too ugly! I didn't like it, so I quit. (laughs).[52]

Tina Mendoza of Fuerza Unida started working in Mexico when she was 16 years old as a secretary. After she came to the United States, it took her some time to adjust and find the right job:

> At first I did not like it here. I come from a family that is very close so I felt really alone here. After I made friends I got used to the life here. First I got a job working with chemicals that they put on animals [insecticides] for about two years. After that I got a job working as a cook frying chicken. Then I got a job at a maquiladora factory. After that I started working at Levi's. I stayed for eight years until they laid us off.[53]

Like many US-born Chicanas who work in low-waged industries alongside Mexican immigrant women,[54] Viola Casares, a third-generation Chicana, started out doing farm work. Her father had picked cotton in Lubbock, Texas, and worked in Arizona. Over her husband's objections, she eventually landed a sewing job:

> In a year [after getting married at 18] I got pregnant, then had my first daughter Sandra. After six months, I went back to work in the fields. We went to Michigan and picked strawberries and tomatoes. When I was pregnant I used to get morning sickness at my job packing onions. . . . My husband was real macho and jealous and would not let me work. I was supposed to stay home. The kids were grown and going to school. . . . Because of his jealousy I stayed home for a while. But the children really needed extra things. . . .
>
> I [started] work[ing] for Farah making pants for a couple of months. Then it was the same thing again with my husband. He [began] harassing me until I quit. But I really needed to work. He had started drinking. I began working at Levi's in 1980. I thought I was finally going to have a secure job. I told myself that I had to work and that I was not going to let him stop me again. With work, I could make a better home and get things for the kids. . . . At Levi's I thought it would be okay, that I would be able to work and support us until I could retire some time. But all of sudden we lost our jobs. I was so worried, "Wow, what are we going to do?" It's so hard being a single mother.[55]

Wages, working conditions, and benefits tended to be better at the larger factories than the smaller shops. For example, even though the Farah Manufacturing Company in El Paso was the target of a major struggle and national boycott by the Amalgamated Clothing and Textile Workers Union (1972–1974), as a large factory of some 4,000 workers, wages and working conditions were better than what women had experienced in Mexico or in smaller US shops.[56] Carmen Ibarra López learned about job openings at Farah through her younger sister.

> It was good pay at the time. The minimum wage I think was $1.60 an hour. I got paid by the hour. We worked

in very good conditions especially because the Farah on Gateway was in a new building.

> I was there when the strike began. I just remember I didn't pay too much attention. First of all, in Mexico everything was different. I just remember one day at noon at lunch time I saw the workers walking out. And I was trying to find out about it and asked "What's going on?" But we didn't have too much information about it even though I worked inside. Probably they had a workers' or union committee to lead the strike, but I know. That's why it's not until now that I realized how unions work. I think it was just because the unions select a few workers, but they don't give out as much information as other organizations do, like La Mujer Obrera does. Yes, that is what you need, a lot of information.[57]

Despite low wages and less than optimal working conditions, many of the women expressed satisfaction with being able to work outside their homes and contribute to their family's well-being. They were proud of their skills and job performance and enjoyed the friendships and camaraderie they developed with their co-workers. Refugio Arrieta worked in a variety of restaurants and garment factories in El Paso:

> The garment factories were small, maybe about 100 people. It's small to me. I worked at Tex-Mex International. They made jeans. I worked as a seamstress, an operator. They paid us the minimum by the hour. Sometimes we worked overtime. There were no benefits there. Sometimes I worked 40 hours a week, sometimes 50 hours when I put in overtime. At the last one it was 20 hours because that's how it was before they closed. I worked at Tex-Mex four years. We were all friends there. (laughs) It was like we were all school-mates.[58]

María del Carmen Domínguez's close relations with co-workers deepened as they banded together to confront the boss on failure to pay holiday leave as promised:

> The CMT factory was large and busy. I was working very well. It was comfortable for me, and I liked it a lot. When I was working there I think there were about 250 workers. Right now they have maybe 1,000 workers. They sew garments like tuxedos. It's more skilled work. Devon was one of the labels. I don't remember the others. We also sewed vests. I think you get paid more money for sewing men's clothes. . . . I was the organizer in my area and we had ten women and I controlled it. (laughs). Yes, *ellas* [they] would say "I love you." And I would say, "I love you, too." We were all partners. Yeah. I love to help the people. And I would fight, fight, fight in CMT, every day. (laughs) Yes, that's a long time to fight![59]

Since she's now a highly skilled and vivacious organizer, one can easily imagine Petra Mata as a highly competent and outgoing worker before she lost her job at Levi's:

> I did the hard, more difficult operations, like sewing the pockets on the sides of the coat. For three and a half years I sewed this way before they put me on utility so I could do any operation. Then they made me a trainer to teach the new people. I liked working with the girls and helping out. Finally they made me a supervisor for eight years. I was very happy with my job because I got to work closely with my co-workers. [60]

NAFTA the SHAFTA

Like the Hong Kong and Korean workers who transnational corporations dumped during the second stage of globalization, hundreds of thousands of US manufacturing workers, many of them women of color, also found themselves out on the street as their jobs ran away to Mexico, Central America, the Caribbean, and Asia. After the Border Industrialization Program had begun in 1965, the Reagan administration launched the Caribbean Basin Initiative in 1983 during the height of US military adventures in Central America. US military intervention in and capital export to the region accelerated the migration of workers, including Salvadoran, Guatemalan, Honduran, Nicaraguan, Dominican, and Haitian women who subsequently found jobs working in the garment industry in Los Angeles, New York, and Miami.

Prior to the enactment of NAFTA in 1994, US-based companies utilized Item 807 of the US Tariff Code, which specified that tariffs applied only to the value-added portion of products assembled abroad. If US apparel firms cut their garments at home and had them sewn offshore, they only had to pay tariff on the labor value added by sewing—which could be very small, given the low wages of Third World women workers. Item 807 was principally used to exploit seamstresses in Mexico, Central America, and the Caribbean because of the region's proximity and the political clout the United States has exercised in the hemisphere since the days of the Monroe Doctrine. Thus, government trade policies effectively encouraged corporations to take jobs overseas to bolster US foreign policy objectives.[61] In 1960, 2 percent of apparel was imported; in 1980, 30 percent; and in 2000, 60 percent. Conversely the number of US manufacturing jobs plummeted. While apparel employment peaked in 1970 with 1,363,800 jobs, by 1999 the figure had fallen to 696,000.[62]

In 1990, Levi's, whose brand name jeans together with Coca-Cola and McDonald's hamburgers have become practically synonymous with the "American way of life" around the world, closed its San Antonio plant and moved to Costa Rica where workers earned in *a day* what the average San Antonio seamstress had made in *half an hour.* The San Antonio factory was Levi's largest US manufacturing facility at the time. Overnight some 1,150 mainly Mexican-American women suddenly lost their jobs. Fuerza Unida, the fight back organization the laid-off San Antonio workers founded in 1990, asserts that "we were early victims of NAFTA." With direct experience in the consequences of "free trade" policies, Fuerza Unida actively organized against the passage of NAFTA, sporting "AFTA NAFTA the SHAFTA!" and "Levi's, button your fly, your greed is showing!" picket signs. Between 1981 and 1990 the company had already closed 58 plants laying off 10,400 people.[63] But the San Antonio workers were the first to organize a sustained fight back demanding corporate responsibility.

Under Republican and Democratic administrations alike, beginning with Reagan's, corporation-friendly politicians extolled the virtues of globalization and free trade policies while maintaining a conspicuous silence on the devastating impact of these policies on workers and their communities. The San Antonio workers' painful testimony gave voice to the economic and psychological trauma workers go through every single time a plant closes or a company "downsizes."[64] Denied useful retraining and other assistance, the former Levi's workers lost not only their jobs, but also their cars, homes, and peace of mind. Viola Casares says she will never forget the moment Levi's company representatives announced the plant closure:

> In less than 15 minutes, the men in suits ruined our whole lives. As long as I live, I'll never forget how the white man in the suit said they had to shut us down to stay competitive. The funny thing is that no one said anything. We stood there like mummies. I heard some people fainted. They didn't even tell us in Spanish, just in English. We didn't want to lose our jobs. Nothing can replace a job with dignity. [65]

Petra Mata says she experienced the trauma twice, first at a secret preparation session management convened for supervisors, and again on the plant floor with the rest of the workers. Staff were told to keep the company's plans secret pending a general announcement to all the workers. Petra recalls:

> At 7:30 a.m. BOOM! they called for a general meeting in the middle of the plant. A guy got upon one of the tables and announced it. *¡Hijole!* That was something that we'll never forget for the rest of our lives, like it just happened yesterday. When everybody heard the announcement we started screaming, hugging each other, crying and asking, "Why? Why: Why?" But they have never answered. They never told us why. There was no reason to shut us down really. We made good quality clothes and high quotas every week. In May 1989 we got the $200 Miracle Bonus because we made such high production levels. . . .
>
> A lot of people went crazy because they didn't know how they were going to live without a job. When you

lose your job you feel like nothing but trash, a remnant, a machine to be thrown out. They take away your dignity. You get scared. How are you going to pay for the car, the house, the kids to eat and go to school? *¡Hijole!* After so many years of working for Levi's, overnight we had nothing.[66]

Levi's now sends work to some 700 sewing and finishing subcontractors in 50 countries. From 1997 to 1999, Levi's closed 29 of its manufacturing and finishing plants in North America, slashing some 18,500 employees— nearly half its remaining work force.[67] Levi's also sacked workers in Belgium and France. Over the protests of human rights groups the company announced plans to restart production in China.[68] CEO Robert Haas told the *San Francisco Chronicle* that most of the work from the closed plants would be moved to contractors elsewhere in the Americas, most likely to Mexico and the Caribbean.[69]

In another example of what "Made in America" now means, in March 2000, Levi's, Calvin Klein, Brooks Brothers, Abercrombie & Fitch, Talbots, and Woolrich were added to a class action lawsuit alleging violations of garment workers' rights in Saipan, the Marianna Islands, a US "trust" in the Western Pacific where over 13,000 garment workers typically work 12-hour days for $3.10 or less an hour, seven days a week, often without overtime pay. The $1 billion-a-year industry in Saipan relies on "guest workers" mostly from China and the Philippines, many of whom must pay a cash bond up to $5,000 for a one-year contract to work.[70]

El Paso has also been devastated by plant closures. The Labor Department said some 10,000 workers in El Paso had lost their jobs because of NAFTA by 1998, the most anywhere in the United States.[71] For example, Levi's, which had been El Paso's largest private employer, closed three of its six plants, laying off some 1,400 workers in 1997.[72] On August 29, 1997, the Greater Texas Finishing Corporation, a division of Sun Apparel, Inc., closed its El Paso operations to send production to Mexico, including the Tehuacán free trade zone. At the time Sun Apparel's largest contracted label was Ralph Lauren's Polo brand. Some 200 laid-off workers included veterans who had served the company for more than 18 years. In a statement calling for support, the laid-off workers said, "Most of us were let go with little more than a good-bye and directions to the NAFTA training and unemployment offices to join the more than 7,000 other workers in El Paso who have lost their jobs to NAFTA and have been unable to get new jobs."[73]

La Mujer Obrera (LMO) is a Mexicana/Chicana women workers' organization founded by garment workers and Chicana/o movement organizers in El Paso in 1981. LMO fought hard against the passage of NAFTA, having first hand experience with maquiladorization enacted under the "twin city" arrangement between El Paso and Juárez during the Border Industrialization Program. Since NAFTA's passage LMO has organized the thousands of workers laid off by NAFTA. LMO says that of the 20,000 displaced workers in El Paso by 2000, 97 percent were Latino; two-thirds, women; one third, single mothers; 50 percent, between 30–45 years of age with the majority of the rest over 45 years old; and 4,000 were in job training programs.[74] After a running battle with state and federal agencies, NAFTA-displaced workers won a $3 million extension in government-funded training for laid-off workers in addition to the original $4.2 million allocated. But María del Carmen Domínguez says that workers in El Paso remain in a profound state of crisis:

> The economic crisis is the big, big problem right now. The women come to La Mujer Obrera because of unemployment. The factories are closing left and right now, and more of the women are becoming single parents. Problems within the families are rising because of this situation. It's hard when women don't have the money to pay the utilities, the rent, or food. When they are confronted with the denial of public services—no welfare, no food stamps.[75]

While workers in large and medium-sized plants lost their jobs to globalization, like their Chinese counterparts, Mexican immigrant women working in small sweatshops also reported declining wages and working conditions. Los Angeles, the apparel manufacturing center of the Untied States, employed some 122,500 employees in April 1998.[76] Lucrecia Tamayo, an undocumented worker from Mexico, describes her experience working in Los Angeles sweatshops:

> The first day I started working I felt like I was working the whole 24 hours! O *sea* [that is to say], ever since I worked in this country I have worked over 12 hours a day, from 7 a.m. to 8 p.m. at night, without Sundays off, *siempre, siempre trabajando* [always, always working]. I earned $100 a week, working from 7 a.m. to 8 p.m. every day. I worked in four factories over a 15-year period. In the first place I worked there were about 30 people, in another about 60.
>
> I worked six years in the El Monte shop. . . . There were about 20 Latinos working there, with Thai workers in another room. . . . We were paid by the piece, so the pay varied. Sometimes I made about $260 a week. Oh, that owner! I used to only get off twice a year, like for a two-hour break if I had to take my child to the doctor. In the case of emergencies, I had to ask my sister to take my child or else the owner would start screaming at me.[77]

Joining the Movement

Much of the education and leadership training the women received took place "on the job." The women talked about how much their participation in the movement had changed them. They learned how to analyze working conditions and social problems, who was responsible for these conditions, and what workers could do to get justice. They learned to speak truth to power, whether this was to government representatives, corporate management, the media, unions, or co-ethnic gatekeepers. They built relations with different kinds of sectors and groups and organized a wide variety of educational activities and actions. Their activism expanded their world view beyond that of their immediate families to seeing themselves as part of peoples' movements fighting for justice.

The women joined the movement through a variety of routes. Some women sought out workers' centers when they experienced a particular grievance at work. María del Carmen Domínguez just showed up at La Mujer Obrera with over a hundred co-workers one day. People packed into the tiny office, soon spilling out into the street. Workers complained that the boss was trying to cheat them out of holiday pay promised in the personnel policy. La Mujer Obrera provided an infrastructure of support for the workers during their wildcat strike and negotiations with management. Through this process the organization gained new leaders and members, including Domínguez. She recalls:

> We won! They had to give us back pay for our holidays and vacations, yes, for everything, for all the workers. I knew about La Mujer Obrera before the strike because their organizers used to come to the factory, outside the doors, and bring leaflets. So when we had problems (laughs and snaps her fingers), we remembered them.[78]

For a long time Domínguez felt angry that she had not known the law and about what women workers could do to defend their rights. Through her participation in the movement, she developed her skills, leadership, and awareness:

> When I stayed at work in the factory, I was only thinking of myself and how am I going to support my family—nothing more, nothing less. And I served my husband and my son, my girl. But when I started working with La Mujer Obrera I thought, "I need more respect for myself. We need more respect for ourselves." (laughs) *Pero* [but] this also meant big changes for my husband, too! (laughs). But he supported me so much through many, many years. He died three years ago.
>
> I also learned so much about how to use the computer and communicate with other people because the kind of communication you need to work in an organization is different from in a factory. I learned about the law and I learned how to organize classes with people, whether they were men or women like me. I learned how to develop curriculum and citizenship material in Spanish. I made a book, yeah![79]

Domínguez also cherishes her friendships with women worker organizers from communities across the United States and overseas:

I did a lot of traveling for the organization. This is very good because now I know more about where and how we are living in the United States. I got the opportunity to meet with other women, worker women, which is very important to me. Projects like the Lucy Parsons Initiative [a collaborative of Mexican, Chinese, and Dominican women leaders from workers' centers supported by the Funding Exchange] are very good. I love it! And I got to know different organizations, who is doing what kind of work, and who are the women representing these groups.

I have also gone to international meetings. . . . I represented La Mujer Obrera in 1989, after there was the big *temblor* [earthquake] in Mexico. We participated in a giant march. It was very good with so many women in the streets. We worked with the September 19th Garment Workers Union.[80]

In other instances, women first came into contact with the workers' centers through family members, friends, and recruitment into specific programs and activities organized by the centers. Carmen Ibarra López learned about La Mujer Obrera from her aunt Esperanza Rodríguez, a veteran seamstress who labored 37 years in the garment industry and continues to work as a janitor:

> She invited me to come to the meetings so I started coming. I began doing a lot of volunteer work, and I was a member of the Board of Directors and of the *Comité de Lucha*. Finally Cecilia [the group's former director] asked me to work here. . . . When I started out, I just gave away flyers and La Mujer Obrera's newspaper. I participated in meetings, and when no one from La Mujer Obrera could attend a meeting I was in charge of going. And also I helped in ordinary ways, cleaning, mopping, doing the bathroom. I don't mind doing it. I still do it because I like the workers to come and see this place clean.[81]

The confidence and skills women gained while standing up for their rights at work spilled over into other jobs. Ibarra adds:

> I remember, about six years ago, Larry, the boss, sent his daughter to talk to us. She said that Larry was having a lot of problems paying his IRS bills. She asked us in the name of Larry if we wanted to support him. So we asked how he wanted us to support him. And she said if we could work eight hours but he was going to just pay us for seven hours. By that time I had just become a member of La Mujer Obrera and I said, "No way! I'm not going to do it. Why?" She said, "Well, *es que* [it's that] he doesn't want to close the factory. You can keep your job." But I said, "No way!" So a few of us said no, but the rest said yes. But even with that he shut down in March 1991.[82]

Irma Montoya came to a special summer camp that La Mujer Obrera organized for NAFTA-displaced workers after the electronics plant where she worked fled to Mexico. Montoya stayed on and became an organizer. One day when she went to testify to state and federal legislators about the impact of NAFTA and workers' need for quality job training and placement, her picture appeared in the *New York Times*.[83]

Refugio Arrieta first became involved with La Mujer when she came to attend English classes:

> I came to classes one or two days a week for two hours each, and I ended up staying. Some of my friends from the factory also came here to attend the classes. We worked a lot to help out. We have demonstrations, we have meetings with the politicians. I am the president of *La Mesa Directiva* [Board of Directors] here. I received the La Mujer Obrera award.[84]

In some cases the organizations conducted systematic political education to consolidate a core of women worker leaders. María Antonia Flores, María del Carmen Domínguez, and Eustolia Olivas were trained as the initial worker leadership core of La Mujer Obrera. Flores recalls:

> On some occasions Cecilia gave the training, at other times Guillermo, people who came from different parts of the city, and political teachers, including from Mexico. [Cecilia Rodríguez and Guillermo Domínguez Glenn helped launch La Mujer Obrera and the Centro Obrero in El Paso.] They gave classes in politics and everything related to study, from Paolo Freire's methods to the political economy of Mexico. Trainings lasted two or three weeks, a month, three months, or sometimes daily when the teachers were here. What we got first from study we later put into practice.[85]

If one meets Flores today, it is hard to imagine her as the person she describes before her involvement in the movement:

> I have learned so much here. I used to be shy. I hardly spoke. I was a submissive housewife. I had all the characteristics of a Mexican woman who was only made for marriage. But once we came here to this organization, we all learned something. For working class women it's harder to develop ourselves as leaders. I did not have these experiences in mind when I first came here. At least I did not know what it meant to be part of an organization. I got my liberation after being suppressed for 15 years and limited to the house and home labor. I came out in the world. Before that I did not even know that such a thing as women's oppression even existed; one just thinks its normal.
>
> When you are just sitting there listening to your husband, you think it's perfectly natural that you have no rights as a woman, as a person. Your rights are violated and you don't know it. When you go out into the outside world, you find another reality. I think that's what has made me so protective of this organization.[86]

"I Don't Want Other People to Go Through What We Went Through"

The government raid on the El Monte sweatshop on August 2, 1995, marked a turning point in Lucrecia Tamayo's life. She transformed from being a frightened worker to the campaign nerve center who relishes speaking out and going to demonstrations against big name retailers that profited from her labor:

> The second of August woke me up. It was like I was a blind woman before that. I like going to the actions and demonstrations. Before when the owners screamed at me, I got real small. I wondered what I had done wrong to make them so mad. Now I know we have rights.
>
> I have had two jobs since the raids at El Monte. Because of the publicity around our case, the owner knows who I am. The owner would call at six a.m. in the morning telling you whether or not you could come in. I didn't like it. There is no written contract. Everything is just done by his word. I was only getting paid $80 a week. But since I started working there I wrote down the hours I worked and how many pieces I sewed, like I learned to do. After a year, I took my calculations to KIWA [Korean Immigrant Workers Advocates]. Paul [Lee, a KIWA organizer] went with me to talk to the owner and they paid what they owed me soon after.
>
> I'm the information source for our group of workers. If a problem comes up, I call everyone up to let them know what's going on. Ever since the raid on the El Monte shop, I have kept track of all the paper work and keep workers informed. I no longer have any fear. My only fear is immigration. But the rest, no. I do not want other workers to suffer. I don't want other people to go through what we went through. This experience opened up my eyes. It made me conscious. It gave me the motivation to speak up and fight against the owners. My husband thinks I'm crazy. I always ask Paul "When are we going to have the next demonstration?" I like to yell and scream at the retailers in the stores that made so much money off of us.[87]

"This Is the Best School You Could Have"

Fuerza Unida allowed laid-off Levi's workers to channel their anger and sense of betrayal, while building on the friendships and ties they had relished in their jobs. A combination of curiosity and revenge first attracted Viola Casares to Fuerza Unida:

> I remember when people were passing out information. I was curious and wanted to find out what they wanted to tell us. Because of my curiosity, I started going to the meetings. At first there were 25 to 30 ladies who started meeting at a small church hall. We

began talking about how we have to do something. We needed to get more information about what is really going on. We needed to find out what the company was going to give us. We needed to do something because of the awful way they shut down the plant. I got interested. I was angry about what they did to us without warning. At first I just wanted to get back at them. I started as a volunteer, then became a board member, then a co-coordinator.[88]

Casares expanded her vision and network of friends through her involvement with Fuerza Unida:

I've done a lot of traveling and met wonderful people. I've learned that I am not the only one who has had problems. This experience has opened up my mind and views. For example, because of lack of information and education and the way I was raised by my family, I used to think that being gay, being homosexual was a sin. But I don't believe that any more. We are all human beings. . . . I learned from my broken marriage, my job, and Fuerza Unida. I have a second chance to pass on what the movement taught me. I never thought I could have done the things that I have. Losing my job opened my eyes. I used to work and live in my own little world. We were taught to just look out for our own family and to compete with other people. Levi's taught us to compete against other workers to be part of their machine. Fuerza Unida taught us that we are part of a bigger family, that we should care about our sisters.[89]

Marta Martínez ran into problems making her way through the company rehiring and government job training program after the layoffs but stuck with Fuerza Unida through thick and thin:

I've been with Fuerza Unida from the beginning. They offered some of us work at the other plants. I worked there for three months. I had to quit because they treated us so bad. Even the other workers there were mad at us. They said we were stealing their jobs. The supervisors accused us of being lazy, saying that's why the plant shut down and moved out. They were very rude to those of us who came in from the old plant. I went through the ESL, GED, and job training classes. The training mainly helped the people who could speak English. But they didn't really help people find jobs. With Fuerza Unida, I worked on the protests, the hunger strikes, everything.[90]

Similarly, Tina Mendoza put her energy into Fuerza Unida after the Levi's layoffs:

I've been working with Fuerza Unida for eight years. The first two years I just went to meetings, but after that I started coming to the office regularly to help out. We work on everything. We never say we can't do it. Our biggest problem is with English. We do all these things so that Fuerza Unida can live on, so our struggle can continue, so that we can serve as an example to women about what is possible. We work to build pride that we are women. I have learned a lot here. I met so many different people and learned about what they do, about different struggles. For me I feel great pride to be a part of this struggle.

At first I was afraid and ashamed to go to the demonstrations. I tried my best to cover my face so that I would not be seen. Now when I go, I scream as loud as I can. I do not cover my face. Fuerza Unida injects you with a lot of energy. *Ojala* [I hope to God/Allah] that we will continue to move ahead.[91]

Fuerza Unida members later reached out to low-waged workers in other plants and industries. Obdulia "Obi" Segura first came to Fuerza Unida after hearing about the food bank available for unemployed workers and low-income families in need:

I try to help out at Fuerza Unida, doing whatever kind of work I can. I started coming here about two and a half years ago, first because I heard about the food bank. Now I help with sweeping, office work, and whatever needs to be done. Even though the women have their own families and homes to take care of, they all give a lot to the work of Fuerza Unida, to help other people in need. There are women in this world who will not do anything for anyone else, who are very egotistical. But that is not the way of Fuerza Unida. Petra and Viola do everything they can to help the people, to build cooperation. That is the character of working with Fuerza Unida. Here we are always ready to help, to love each other, to work together. This is what moves me to volunteer here in whatever way I can.[92]

Petra Mata, who had already picked up many leadership skills as a daughter, wife, mother, and seamstress, got baptized in the fire of fighting the world's largest garment manufacturer:

I learned so much at Fuerza Unida. This is the best school you could have, working with people, listening, chairing meetings—all the things you have to understand to carry out the struggle. Here we are not just individuals. We go to support and participate in all struggles in the movement. We work with Asian, Filipino, African American, Mexican, white. We are part of the same vision, the same movement. In the past when Levi's said, "blah blah blah," we said, "yes sir." Now we ask, "Why? Wait a minute. I don't like it." They should do what's right, or fair at least. Companies cannot do without workers, it should be half and half, 50-50, not just 100 percent going to one side. That's what we learned through Fuerza Unida.[93]

"Sometimes God Knocks Us Around a Little Bit"

For some of the women, showing compassion, solidarity, and faith in the face of hardships is sustained by deeply held religious beliefs. Viola Casares says she tells Petra Mata, "I think sometimes God knocks us around a little bit to make us think and to remind us to be thankful for what we have." Casares reaffirmed her faith during a visit to maquiladoras in Honduras with a US delegation hosted by the Mennonite Church:

> Sometimes when I get discouraged I pray for God to give me a sign to let me know if what I am doing is right. One day we were scheduled to visit different maquilas including a place called Interfashion. No one knew what we would find there. But when we got there, the first thing we saw when we walked through the door was women sewing Levi's and Dockers label pants. God had given me a big sign to see that what we were doing was right. He showed us exactly what was going on in the factories our jobs had run away to. It was a miracle!
>
> We saw just what Levi's was doing to our sisters in Central America. We saw that their chairs and working conditions were really uncomfortable and that they got paid so much less, with no benefits. The place looked just like a prison and workers were treated like prisoners. I saw that with my own eyes. It made me really angry. That company just cares about profits.[74]

Similarly Carmen Ibarra López of La Mujer Obrera explains: "All the time I like to do my job with *fé* [faith]. Yes, I have a lot of faith in God—period. I feel very, very respectful of all the religions. I do my job because I have faith in God."[95]

Bringing Home the Fight for Women's Rights

Work, migration, and activism are all threads that run through the women's histories. But as working class women, they also endured distinct challenges as daughters, lovers, wives, mothers, sisters, and grandmothers. With their participation in movements seeking to overturn oppressive class, gender, and racial practices have come changes in their views of gender and family roles.

Viola Casares complained that her husband had run around with *sus mujeres de la cantina* [his women of the bars], while projecting his jealousy on to her. He refused to let her work outside the home despite their poverty. Casares swears that 1990 was absolutely the worst year in her life. That dark time she lost not only her job of nine years, but also her marriage. She finally separated from her husband who had become a jealous alcoholic and broken her nose during a beating. The stress from the loss of her job and marriage, combined with her declining health, put Casares in the hospital:

> I told him, "If you want to get back together it's got to be 50-50, not 90 percent going to your side." But by that time his drinking had gotten really bad. We never got a divorce although we were separated for six years. He didn't want to give me a divorce. He'd come and stay for a couple of weeks. Our oldest daughter loved him dearly. He was such a strong man with his macho image. When we were living together he would run around with other women. I was a good wife and faithful, but I told him, "One of these days, I'm going to leave." He would come back and cry. He had his regrets. I think a lot of it was because of his drinking. I've lost a lot of uncles and cousins to drinking. His father used to drink. My husband died from drinking when he was only 46 years old. I guess that's why I loved, hated, and pitied this man all at the same time. He lived in his own way. Maybe he did not know how to show love because he was not shown love since his father also drank a lot and ran around with women. [96]

Casares managed to climb out of the well of depression by channeling her energy into taking care of her children and grandchildren and building Fuerza Unida as a support center for women like herself. She explains:

> I'm glad that I became part of Fuerza Unida. It's really changed my life. What I went through with the plant closure and my marriage prepared me for the work I am doing right now, even for the death of my husband and coping with the loss of my job. I think that if I didn't have this organization, I would be completely lost now. Fuerza Unida made us strong women, strong mothers. I like to be independent. I told my husband when he tried to come back, "You have to want the new Viola, not the old Viola that only stayed home."[97]

The barriers women had to surmount because of their gender status were made doubly difficult because of economic hardships they faced as working class women. The women worry about their children, grandchildren, parents, and siblings. A number had experienced the loss of family to substance abuse and violence. The workers' centers acted as a women's support network. Remedios García tried to manage her stress and loss by staying active:

> It's been almost seven years that my oldest son was murdered. That affected me greatly. Since that time I've gone from illness to illness to illness. (starts crying) I haven't been able to recuperate. It's been seven years or more that I've stayed like this. *Aieee!* He was out with his friends. When the telephone rang that night and I thought it must be an emergency as soon as I heard it. *Aieee!* The doctor said I must not always think about this and move on to do other things. But it's my son, I told him. So a lot of problems have come from

this. I started having problems with my husband, with a lot of things because it affected me personally. But, nevertheless, one has to go on living. I can't recuperate so that's why I've been like this, do you understand? I feel a lot of guilt, that I didn't spend enough time with my son. I've had one complication after another. For this it is good to have a lot of friends and continue working. . . . I have my mama, my children, and people who need me. And they have me. [98]

Many of the women met their partners, had children, and started working outside the home when they were teenagers. They described a range of positive and negative experiences with partners. A number of the women had separated from their first husbands. Despite her high levels of skills, Elena Alvarez is suppressed by a jealous husband who will not permit her to work for pay. She can only leave the house with his permission, even though their household is in dire financial condition. Carmen Ibarra López experienced a serious bout of depression when her first marriage did not work out, so she started going to beautician school and worked as a manicurist for many years before she returned to the garment industry. Still in the "honeymoon" phase of her new marriage, Carmen is crossing her fingers and says that she is praying that God will give her "a second chance."[99]

Tina Mendoza says her husband has been very supportive of her involvement with Fuerza Unida. She just tries to make sure she has his meals ready and makes sufficient time for her family:

> I no longer have babies at home. My children are grown. My husband supports my work with Fuerza Unida. He wants me to be useful, not just staying home watching TV. I make sure I get my husband's meals ready and make his life easier. I try to spend as much time with the family as possible. He's a second level supervisor after working for the city for over 25 years. Where he works is unionized. Before the union came in there used to be a lots of discrimination against Mexicans. But thanks to the union, minorities have been able to raise their positions.[100]

Petra Mata also says her husband has been very supportive of her work at Fuerza Unida. Indeed, he has continued to work at two low-paying jobs to support the family, especially when funding runs out and she and her co-coordinator Viola Casares stop getting paid. She says that sometimes his friends rib him when they see her speaking at some demonstration on TV, but she says, "at least he can see what I'm doing."[101]

María del Carmen Domínguez takes pride in her scrapper stance towards her father, brothers, and schoolmates growing up, as well as in her children's strength:

> My family made it possible for me to organize the strike at the factory and work here. (laughs) I started out fight-

ing with my father. I fought in school. I fought with my husband. (laughs) *¡Aiiyaiiyaii!* Yes, because I am very strong! Come on! With the boys at school I played baseball. (laughs) First I wanted to bat, to pitch. . . . My daughter has some of the same personality as me. Well, I think, no, not only my daughter, but my boys, too, yeah. My daughter is a very, very fighting woman. (laughs) Yes, but she is also crying, fighting, crying.[102]

Carmen Ibarra López is both critical of her own upbringing as well as proud to break the mold in raising her daughter and son:

> You know, I was born and grew up in a culture where the women didn't have a voice. So I said I'm not going to do the same with my children. I want to teach them to be different. I'm not the kind of a person who wants to do the same thing that my family does, did with me. No, I'm not. Especially with my daughter. You know my son is the oldest, and my daughter is the youngest. I taught my son how to clean house, wash dishes, and all kinds of tasks because I said, "Your sister is not going to be your maid. She is just going to be your sister and a human being." So they both respect each other very much. They are not just brother and a sister but very, very good and close friends. Yes, I don't want to keep doing the same thing that my family did. No, no way! [103]

Through participation in their organizations and *el movimiento,* the women gained new skills and awareness, underwent major transformations, provided leadership to communities under siege, built working friendships with Asian immigrant women and other low-waged workers across the globe, and won victories.

During a protest at Levi's posh glass, steel, and brick corporate headquarters in San Francisco, to the surprise, consternation, then chagrin of management, *las mujeres* suddenly chain themselves to the front door. Calmly awaiting the arrival of police paddy wagons, over the bullhorn they issue a friendly Texas home-style invitation to their upcoming benefit dance with Dr. Loco's Rockin' Jalapeño Band. *Las mujeres luchando* inspire stanzas in the band's catchy *cumbia* rhythm, "El Picket Sign" (1992):

> *From San Anto to San Francisco Fuerza Unida has been saying*
> *Desde San Anto hasta San Francisco Fuerza Unida anda diciendo*
> *Don't buy Dockers or Levi's jeans and stop the Free Trade Agreement*
> *¡Boicot Dockers y Levi's jeans y alto al libre comercio!*
>
> *El picket sign, el picket sign*
> *¡Qué Viva La Mujer Obrera!*
> *El picket sign, el picket sign*
> *¡Queremos Justice for Janitors!*
> *El picket sign, el picket sign*

We say ¡Chale con Coors!
El picket sign, el picket sign
¡Porque la unión es La Fuerza! [104]

María Antonia Flores

La Mujer Obrera Director, Popular Educator

I was born in 1954 in Zacatecas, Mexico. My family moved to Ciudad Juárez in 1962. I have eight sisters and brothers, and I am the oldest. In Juárez my parents worked in maquilas, restaurants, [and] as vendors selling food.

I studied through middle school, then a year to be a secretary, and in a school for teachers. I was an adult literacy teacher while I was studying to become a teacher, but I didn't finish and get a diploma. I worked for two years as an educator, and later two years in a maquila.

The maquila was a rather large electronics factory called Centra Labs Components; about 400 people worked there. I was 19 years old then. For that period of time the pay was good—minimum wage, and one could earn 700 pesos, but it was very hard work. I started work at three in the afternoon, left at 11 p.m., and we worked Saturdays. I don't know the name, but we also used a paste, mixed like a dough to cover the capacitors, and it smelled really bad. We attached different components between the two edges so the current could pass through. Then we carried the capacitors and dipped them in alcohol or acetone. That work gave you a lot of headaches because sometimes when we handled such tiny capacitors, we had to use a big lens to see the small pieces well enough to grab them. After a while they changed me to a department where I worked at a machine that cut the capacitor wires, squared them, and sent them to be packaged in boxes for shipping. The majority of workers almost *puras jovencitas* [all young women]; the supervisors were *puros varones* [all male].

I got married when I was 18, almost 19, on August 21, 1971. My daughter Paula was born August 18, 1972, a year after I got married. My son Gerardo was born in July 1973, my other daughter in February 1977, and my youngest son in July 1988. Now I have five grandchildren, four girls and one boy. [laughs] They're from my two daughters.

My husband and I came to the US from Juárez to El Paso in 1974 because his parents had residency here, and we lived with them for two years. Then he left the house and us to live with his mama until 1985, when I moved out of my in-laws' house. Already he had gone running around with other women. I was separated from him, almost since 1977. We got to know each other because he lived near me and came to a *fiesta* [party] at my house. He used to work as a factory operative in El Paso.

I came here when I was about 22, 23 years old. During the first years I was only a housewife, not doing anything but taking care of the family, the in-laws. But afterwards I started to work in small factory workshops,

cleaning offices, doing homecare for adults. I got special training to take care of a sick person who could not move. I was with this person for two years and after that I worked at a factory for another year. Then I returned to cleaning offices and from 1986 to 1990 I did both jobs. During the day I worked in the factory, and at night and weekends I cleaned offices. [groans]

Aiiee! I never got any sleep! The garment factory was so difficult. I left my children home *solitos* [alone]. They went to school and we didn't see each other because I didn't get home from work until one or two in the morning.

The first factory where I worked was named Emily Joe. Later I worked at CMT and at other small shops, Elias Lavalla. The last one I worked at was Eddy Wad. With the first job I still didn't have my papers because my husband left me while he ran around with his friends and sweet young things. But because he was always working in these different industries he knew about jobs and told me where to go. On other jobs I had my own references, people that I worked with and knew. I always came with good recommendations. I found the last job because the factory was near where I lived.

After I got off from the factory I started coming to La Mujer Obrera. I volunteered because I enjoyed it. In March or April of 1985 a friend of mine who was a neighbor first brought me for a women's meeting on topics given by Cecilia [Rodríguez, La Mujer Obrera's co-founder], workshops on the oppression of *la mujer,* and planning for a festival for children. During those days I only participated in small meetings and visited, not as a member. In 1986 I became a member, worked on committees, then part of the leadership. After a year they started to organize special workshops to train me and two other compañeras, María del Carmen [Domínguez] and Eustolia [Olivas] as the first three organizers trained to advance the organization.

On some occasions Cecilia gave the training; at other times, Guillermo [Domínguez Glenn, Cecilia's husband]. People who came from different parts of the city, and political teachers, including from Mexico. They gave classes in politics and everything related to study, from Paolo Freire's methods to the political economy of Mexico. Trainings lasted two or three weeks, a month, three months, or sometimes daily when the teachers were here. What we got first from study we later put into practice.

Since about 1988 we began to develop more activities and a bit stronger membership. We started the first cooperative food project through a committee organized by María del Carmen. She also created the newspaper for educational work. It was about eight pages long and came out every month. María del Carmen developed all the educational material, leaflets and brochures, and gave classes. I was a teacher, yes, from my past training in Mexico.

There were big problems in the factories during this period so we leafleted them in 1988, 1990, 1991. We had over a thousand members, with educational meetings four times a week. Fifty workers came to every meeting. It was so busy! We were running *La Cooperativa* [the food cooperative] and also *La Clinica* [free workers health clinic]. Fifteen to twenty people helped us operate our educational program and the coop. There was a *huelga* [strike] in November. That's when we had all the problems with the union, the divisions.

I was in charge of political education. In 1995 and 1996 we also moved into economic development. I prepared the curriculum based on what we were planning, for the workers, volunteers, and people who came from outside El Paso. We even had a volunteer from Spain. We made presentations according to the needs of the group, whether it was religious, progressive, or more conservative. We conducted political education in our *Escuela Popular* [People's School]. The courses lasted three months, two hours a week, with one hour in English or citizenship, and then one hour on economics, politics, and social issues. We made murals, drawings, and leaflets to reinforce the learning process. We do more murals and *dinamícas* [skits] and show videos. We developed plans for the *Comité de Lucha* and when the people developed as stronger leaders, they took on more responsibility for planning.

We have to design the curriculum so that everyone can understand. We do not rely much on writing because a lot of our people do not know how to read. Doing murals together is so people don't go to sleep like in church; they're so colorful. Workers come here tired and hungry so we have to capture their interest and keep them engaged. When people first come, we start with very basic stories and simple questions. If they go on to the second level, we cover more political economy and advanced topics. We talk about what money is, what transnational corporations are, why factories are closing, and neoliberalism. We draw pictures of the transnational corporations and their activities around the world and ask what does this have to do with us? We talk about what is happening to people in Chiapas and what that poor people's struggle has to do with workers in this community.

I love doing educational work! We started before the big garment factories started closing, while the women were still working. Then the different corporations began setting up twin plants along the border in the 1970s here in Juárez and El Paso; later the biggest factories started to leave. Through our relations with workers in Canada we learned more about the disasters workers went through in Canada and the United States. We made many trips and shared stories with other workers. One of the most beautiful of all experiences is when workers support each other. Different people from La Mujer Obrera participate in these exchanges. It sets a good base of information. But the governments still passed NAFTA.

We started working [in solidarity] with the [independent Mexican labor union federation] Frente Auténtico del Trabajo [FAT], founded in 1960.[105] The FAT works in four sectors. First, it works in the workers sector, which now has various national level unions, like the unions of iron and steel, farm, textile, and shoemaker workers, from northern Mexico to the southwest part of the central valley. Second, the cooperative sector organizes savings, credit, consumers, and producers cooperatives, including a glass factory that the workers won after a strike. Third, people living in the *colonias* [neighborhoods] developed similar consumer cooperatives; in the urban sector *colonia* residents organize around all kinds of questions, like water, electricity, and sewage. Finally, the *campesino* sector is conducting a survey of the people in the countryside to estimate the results of the harvest so they don't get exploited by some company. They work with the *ejidatarios* [owners of communal land]. The fundamental goal is to improve the conditions of life of all the people.

Our groups are organizing independently because we belong to no political party or government, and the workers themselves are the ones who feel this [is important]. . . . The FAT had to develop completely independently from the unions [that are] working in collaboration with the government. We are based in self-determination where workers are the ones who decide what we want and who is going to represent us. The situation in Mexico is very different from that of the US AFL-CIO unions; the CTM [Confederación de Trabajadores Mexicanos] is part of the official government and ruling party. The government's physical repression can't stop the workers, but does place many obstacles before them. For example, when workers really start organizing, the first thing they [the Mexican government] do is fire everyone [in the union]. Or the government labor commissions give false counts of the election votes. They bring in people to vote who really don't work there. Through these same laws and government bodies that are supposed to protect the workers, the administration carries out many tricks.

Since around 1963 they started to establish maquiladoras along the border and added many more in the 1980s and 1990s. So it became necessary for the FAT to establish a workers' center on the border, *Centro de Estudios y Taller Laboral,* to train women maquiladora workers about everything related to their labor rights to defend themselves whether at the individual or collective level. Especially here in the United States where there is no understanding of what an independent union or organization is, we want workers to know how things could be different.

In general people who work in the maquilas have no previous experience in these kinds of jobs. Some maquiladoras require that workers have completed primary school, but in others, many do not know how to read and write. Workers receive no study or training because all the work in the maquiladoras is very easy and routine, so one needs only a certain amount of manual aptitude. They contract mostly young people, from 16 to 35 years old, depending on the factory. If the work involves a lot of tiny pieces, they greatly prefer women's labor; when the work is a little more heavy, they contract more men. The ratio is about 60 percent women and 40 percent men. About 50 percent of the workers in Juárez are not from here, but from all the other states of the republic. Some 55 percent of the women also have children, averaging one or two. People often cannot secure the necessities of life. There are not enough childcare centers to accommodate so many people. Many times parents have to leave their children by themselves.

Most of the factories are transnational, headquartered in the United States, Canada, and Japan, [and more recently, subcontractors from South Korea and Taiwan] with also some Mexican-owned maquilas. The average pay is $4 a day. [exclaims] Yes, that's what it is! That includes bonuses for productivity, good attendance, punctuality, so that workers will work even harder to survive. They give some prizes, but the pay offered is so low because it benefits them to keep us needy. Many maquilas have people who worked ten, twelve years doing the same thing, but have not been trained to do anything else.

At La Mujer Obrera we have classes twice a week. We try not to lose hold of our education program, or we will have no power. We need to motivate the workers so they can struggle for their rights. Before NAFTA passed we helped organize a big march on the bridge between here and Mexico and had problems with the police. It was very cold! We stayed in the Plaza all night together with so many groups, including from Canada and Mexico.

Now the education we do is on the results of the crisis, the disaster, the unemployment, the people out in the streets, the treating of workers like they didn't exist. Workers are invisible in Mexico, here, and whatever part of the world. But how can workers become more visible and take on this problem? The problem we are having with NAFTA is not just a local one affecting El Paso; it is also the worldwide problem of neoliberalism. We have to educate workers, both immigrants and non-immigrants. We must understand the roots of the problems. We need to know not just that we don't have work, but *why* we don't have work.

Women are not the only ones who come for help, but yes, the working woman is the one who is in the worst need. You can hear it in our name, La Mujer Obrera [The Woman Worker]; it comes out in our methods of organizing, initiatives, development of women's leadership. La Mujer Obrera is a name people know so women come here directly to see how we can support them. When a woman comes with her needs, we should be ready to help her, whether she stays or not, because she is unprotected. But we also want women to participate in this organization because it is in our interest to strengthen the group to promote the development of women. We don't want to continue to be used as objects, like furniture, right?!

We have been through so many experiences that were good, strong, and brave. One of the most important things for us as leaders of this organization is to have the support of our families. One way they do this is by accepting our schedules, since there is no fixed routine. If a husband or children oppose our activities, we would have to leave our work only half done. Working together with women through hard times like the hunger strike or the organizing of Camp Dignity [a popular education, two-week summer camp LMO organized for NAFTA-displaced workers and their families] have been great learning experiences. [There] we saw how far each of us as an organizer could go and how the organization could grow. We have the experiences of building relationships among workers to better express themselves and communicate with others.

Now I can say what I want, what I expect, what I do or do not want done in the organization, in the family, for myself. But if you're only inside your home, you don't learn anything. Development is very important. Lots of good and bad things happen as one goes through life. The negative ones affect your health and psyche so we must be prepared to know how to get the strength to face problems and whatever lies ahead. If I know that my health could affect the organization, then I have to think not only of myself, but also of the group, of my co-workers. I think that once one joins an organization, one is not completely free because one has to think about the organization, the family, and the self. So you turn into many parts and you are not alone. You have to think about how you are going to respond to these different parts of your life because you cannot abandon them.

Our priorities for workers are in three areas: the economic, political, and ideological. In the future, I hope that we will reach our goal of having an economic base from which we can live and support the community and ourselves, so workers will be able to take care of their families. I hope that we will achieve the best for the workers, the dreams we've always had about creating a bilingual school and cultural plaza, which would be the greatest, most fabulous thing. Our political priority is to strengthen the workers to confront the bureaucrats to make them implement workers' rights. We must be conscious of what is happening so we can defend ourselves. We know what kind of politics we want and that we must exert efforts so that the voices of the community will be heard. Ideologically I will continue to uphold my ideals for the organization and my family to build a better future.

If the conditions of the community improve, then my family's condition will also improve. If the community's conditions do not improve, then my family will continue to live in the same poor situation they are in now. Without this organization we cannot have a better future for our children or our grandchildren. We have to keep fighting all three fights. If we are conscious of our goals, we won't lose our way, our vision. Any woman who is a real leader has to be in the forefront of continuing to struggle to better our conditions.

—El Paso, Texas, February 24, 1997

Petra Mata

Former Levi's Garment Worker,
Fuerza Unida Organizer and Miracle Maker

I was born on May 31, 1946 in a little town called Bustamente, Nuevo León, Mexico. My parents worked as farmers. When there was no more money in farming, they moved. My mother died at the very early age of 28 years old, when I was only 5. She had a baby in this small town they say is only a *rancho*. The hospital services were very poor, no doctors, nobody. In those days women had their babies at home. I think they did not take care of my mom very well, so she developed problems.

My little sister, the baby that my mom bore, died. A few days later my mom died, too. That left us five kids, my four brothers and myself. I was in the middle. When my mother died, my father felt lost. He couldn't stand that my mother had died, so he left us. After that, my grandfather moved me and my brothers to Nuevo Laredo. He took care of us kids until we got married.

It was sad for me. I made a lot of sacrifices and suffered when I was young because my ma died. I don't think anybody cares about you the way your mother does because you are born from her. That's what I tell my kids now, "You only have one mother in your life." I didn't have a mother. [eyes water] But in a way, my grandparents did something good for me because now I can live with dignity. When I was young I had to respect myself. I was always praying that I would not do something that was going to degrade me. I always tell my girls, "Respect yourself no matter what. You've got to have respect to receive respect."

After years and years my father came back and we accepted him. But I don't have the kind of love for him I would like to have because he never lived with us when we were little, when we needed him. When I got married I had all this sadness stored up in my heart that I had to let go of, that used to bother me. But now I have my family and a wonderful husband. He helps me a lot. I've got my four kids. My daughter turned 27 in August. My oldest boy is 26, my small boy is 22, and my girl is 17.

I met my [future] husband in *el mercado* [the market] in Nuevo Laredo when I was 15. Then I left to work in the United States for three or four years. We knew this family very well in Laredo, Texas. They asked my aunt if I could work for them. I worked in their house for two straight years without going to see my family. I had to clean the floors on my hands and knees and wash windows and change everything every month.

When I was 17, I was able to go home to Nuevo Laredo on the weekends, then come back to work by Monday. I went back and forth like that. I cleaned the house because I just went to six years of school in Mexico. At that time there was no opportunity to go to school or college. So I had to *¡Hijole!* work as a maid and serve them. They had two kids, and I had to put them to bed every night, give them their clothes, prepare them for school, make breakfast, and do all the housework. There was a wife, but of course I was the maid! [laughs] I only made $10 a week.

I went back to Nuevo Laredo to the same place where I had worked and started talking with my [future] husband. One time, when I was getting off from work, I called his house and asked, "What are you going to do today?" He said, "Well, nothing." I said, "Well, I'm going to go to the movies. Do you want to go with me?" He said right away, "Yeah!" My sister-in-law told me, "The day you called, we were all ready to go out, but he got so excited because he was going to go with you." So I'm the one who took the first step. [laughs] But it was only for that one day that he was just like a little chicklet with me. We have a very good relationship. We got married when I was 23 years old and Domingo was 27.

Three months later we came to the United States. All the kids were born here. I remember the first days were very bad because it was very cold. We didn't even have blankets to cover ourselves and the house didn't have any windows. Oooh! Then little by little we saved and began buying things. We are still in this house now.

After my third child was born I started working in a tortilla factory, counting tortillas on the night shift and taking care of my kids during the day. Then I moved to a restaurant where I was in charge of the kitchen and they paid me a very, very low wage, about $60 or $70 a week. I was hired three years and worked 6am to 4pm everyday, even Saturdays, making tortillas and everything. I was unsatisfied and felt like this was not all I could do.

People said that they were hiring at the Levi's factory on Zarzamora Street. The pay was very good. I said, "Well, wow! I would like to do this!" and decided to apply. I went one morning and took the test. I didn't even get back home before I already got a call. They told me to come in for an interview. So I went right away, and they hired me in 1976.

When I started working there, they were paying by levels A to D, with D getting higher pay—which I qualified for. I did the hard, more difficult operations, like sewing the pockets on the sides of the coat. For three and a half years I sewed this way before they put me on utility so I could do any operation. Then they made me a trainer to teach the new people. I liked working with the girls and helping out. Finally they made me a supervisor for eight years. I was very happy with my job because I got to work closely with my co-workers.

The layoff happened on January 16, 1990. The Friday before the Martin Luther King holiday, they told us that all the supervisors and trainers had to go downtown for a meeting. We suspected something was wrong because we had heard a lot of rumors. Usually at Christmas they gave us a $500 bonus, but not that year. We found out later that they decreased our hours because they were planning to shut us down. Nobody got the benefit of a pay increase based on 40 hours because we were working less hours.

We [supervisors] went downtown to a very fancy hotel on Tuesday. Everyone sat down around tables in a big room. Then all of a sudden we saw a lot of people coming with folders. We thought, "What's going on?" Finally, the person from Levi's started to speak and said that they were planning to shut us down because Levi's had to be competitive in the market. Everything turned black. We started screaming and saying "Why?"

They already had the package ready, knew who we were, and took us to different, individual rooms. Then they start explaining, "This is what you're going to get." I was very sad. I started crying. They told us, "Yeah, yeah, calm down. I know how you feel, I know." Ahhh! I told her [eyes water], "How in the hell do you know how I feel?" I mean I *love* my job. After the 14 years I worked for this company, they just turn us out like this. Our jobs are over. "You're going to tell me you know how I feel? You still have a job!"

We came back and went outside. We hugged each other and said, "What are we going to do?" "Ahhh!" "I just bought my car." "I just got my credit card to buy Christmas gifts." A lot of people were buying houses, then lost them. They lost their cars. I had two cars at the time. We lost everything because we couldn't pay no more, *sabes* [you know]? When they turned us away they said, "Oh, we want you to cooperate with us. We want you to help us to work with the people tomorrow." Everybody went back and said, "Oh no! You want us to help you when you are doing this to us?"

They had a lot of advisors [who] told us, "You poor lady, you're going to be all right." They gave some money to the city to provide services, but those services did not help Levi's workers directly, but instead went to the whole city with close to 10,000 people out of jobs. They [also] mishandled that money by renting a big office and buying a lot of things. We didn't get anything. About 1,150 workers were displaced.

When Levi's closed, it was a disaster for most of the families. My husband has had to work at two jobs since they shut us down. In the evening he's a cook at the Marriott Hotel and in the morning he's working with vegetables in a lot of grocery stores. Before I lost my job I sent one of my kids to college. My two older kids had everything that they needed, not what they wanted, but at least what they needed. The ones who suffered most were the small ones. They remember that we could buy five pairs of pants, one for each day. When I lost my job my small boy said, "Mom, how come we can only buy two pants, one to use today and the other one tomorrow?" He asked, "Why did Junior have this and I cannot?" It was hard for them to understand.

About two months before they shut us down, they started reducing personnel. They paid us whatever they wanted. Workers didn't know how to calculate their pay. So we started comparing. "How much do you have?" "How much did you get?" And they said, "Well, look I got less than you and I was working more years." That's when we started to get together, decided to form Fuerza Unida, and declared the boycott against Levi's.

At first we didn't have any office. We did all of the work from Rubén's house. Rubén [Solís of the Southwest Public Workers Union] was the one who helped us start to put together Fuerza Unida. The first day they made the shut down announcement. Rubén was there protesting in front of the plant. We got a lawyer right away. We had meetings and formed the *Concilio* [Board of Directors]. The workers got involved, and we decided to put together our demands. Then we got a very little place at the Esperanza Peace and Justice Center on South Flores Street.

For six months we got unemployment benefits, $200 every two weeks. After that ran out, we felt very bad. We put more and more attention and time into Fuerza Unida. We put aside our personal and family problems. We used to cry *noches* [nights] to see the people with no food. We started having trainings and participating in conferences—locally, nationally, internationally. We moved again to 3946 South Zarzamora and stayed for almost two years until we moved over here [to 710 New Laredo Highway] where the rent is cheaper. We're low on income. The owner is a very good, cooperative man.

Viola, Irene [Reyna], and I were the co-coordinators at that time. . . . For the first year or two the people worked for free, nominated by the Board. First, there was Frances Estrella, Raquelina, and another lady whose name I don't remember, and Margie Castro, who volunteered so much. A lot of girls got involved and put in a lot of time. Then they decided to make Fuerza Unida a non-profit organization with papers and everything, and get a grant to pay full-time coordinators. They nominated Viola and Irene, and, because I was putting in my time volunteering, me in February 1992. We worked as a team, Viola, Irene, and myself. Irene had to leave when we ran out of money. I wish we had resources to hire technical assistance. We need someone to sit down and use the computer. Then we could move more quickly, with our sewing cooperative, food bank, and everything.

Every several weeks, we went to San Francisco to organize the campaign at Levi's corporate headquarters. We had to leave our families. It was good but hard. We needed to walk so far and learn to be good leaders to head the campaign. We have learned that if we want to do something, we just need to develop our own goals. I have a lot of friends who do not know what they can do. They see themselves as a wife and mother, washing dishes, cooking dinner, or making clothes only for their own families. A lot of women are heads of households; not enough attention is paid to the problems they face. San Antonio is very poor. Sometimes women fall deep down into that depression they must learn to cross so they can get to the other side. We also need to be motivated by other issues and aware of other people's problems to make changes. We tell women that if someone is trying to abuse you, you must speak up.

Of course, we learned these things. When we started picketing and going to protests, I held the poster up to cover my face. I was afraid. Now if people don't call me, I call them. If you are denied opportunities, you have to look for and create opportunities.

My two oldest [children] got married when I lost my job. I missed them a lot. With the two small ones I did not spend too much time at home. My son is very independent, but my little girl has always wanted to be with me. If I go to town and work late, she comes here to help me. It's hard for me to decide how many hours to work a day. You plan your day, but something comes up, people come in the door. Most of the time my family supports me. My husband's friends say, "Hey, I saw your wife on TV."

I learned so much at Fuerza Unida. This is the best school you could have, working with people, listening, chairing—all the things you have to understand to carry out the struggle. Here we are not just individuals. We go to support and participate in all struggles in the movement. We work with Asian, Filipino, African American, Mexican, white. We are part of the same vision, the same movement.

People come here to cry if they want to cry, complain if they want to complain, laugh if they want to laugh, and get recommendations and advice about what to do. We started a food bank two years ago, after the Levi's layoffs, to help people during emergencies with groceries. We didn't have many resources. We suffered and made sacrifices. We know what many people who are out of work need—flour, oil, rice, juices, canned goods, beans, crackers, laundry detergent, bread, tortillas. We pay 12 cents a pound to the food bank and give the bags away for free. People come to volunteer and sew in exchange.

We have a good group of volunteers working closely with us. The group is mixed between ex-Levi's and other workers. Our sewing coop sells ready-made items such as bedspreads, tablecloths, curtains, and aprons. We bought sewing machines after many fundraising events. We really need two more commercial machines with a single needle. We also need a new truck to pick-up the materials for the sewing coop and the food coop.

When sales are good, we try to give volunteers a little something for their gas expenses. Through our *Loteria Mexicana* [bingo] everyone can take something home. Everyone brings something in and we cook and eat together. Anyone who comes here goes away with something. When women get frustrated we tell them, "Hey, come over here!" They leave with a piece of material, bingo prize, advice, and friendship to make them feel good. We are trying to expand the work of the organization. Our dream is to make pants. Now we are making miracles.

We never knew we were going to be around this long. When we met with La Mujer Obrera years ago, we asked "how could you survive so long?" They told us, "You have to think about and plan how you are going to survive that long." We have survived this long. Six years from now, I would like to see a stronger, more established organization that can keep going boom, boom, boom! We need technical assistance to stabilize the organization. I want to see Fuerza Unida do not only local, but more global projects together with other women.

When we first came here my husband and I were undocumented. Then my husband got his citizenship. About two years ago I made myself a citizen, too, because I felt that it was not right for me to be in this struggle when I didn't have a voice, a right to vote. I got to be somebody in the United States. I want to continue to work for our people to have a better life. I want to teach my grandchildren to go to school and college, to be good citizens, and participate in making decisions.

My health bothers me. I want to talk more with the people, to sew, to pray, and get the power to sit down for a while. But God knows what he's doing. Maybe he uses my health to make me slow down and take a rest. My husband and kids are in good shape. My husband works at two jobs. He does not go out to drink. He talks to me. He helps me clean house, wash, and cook. What else could I want? I only want to see Fuerza Unida become an established organization working especially for gender equality.

—San Antonio, Texas, October 7, 1997

Notes

1. English Translation:
   In the liberation fronts
   of working people
   There are women who are strong and valiant
   There are women who know how to struggle
   They are women developing
   In the city and the countryside
   Giving strength and vision to the people
   They are working class women luminous with struggle
   They are working class women for justice and peace
   Respect their culture and work
   With the force of their dignity
   They are garment workers demanding justice
   They are garment workers who know how to struggle
   They are the women displaced by Levis
   The strugglers of the great movement
   They are the seamstresses of La Fuerza Unida
   They are the seamstresses of liberation.
   Traditional music with lyrics adapted by Arnoldo García (1994)
2. Porfirio Díaz ruled Mexico with an iron hand from 1877 until the 1910 Mexican Revolution.
3. José Martí, Cuba's beloved poet, writer, and leader who died May 19, 1895, fighting Spanish colonialism, coined this term and warned against US designs on Latin America. See Roig de Leuchsenring, 1967.
4. For example, while an estimated half million people of Mexican origin, including US citizens, were deported during the Great Depression, World War II brought Mexican workers back to the United States on a massive scale via the US government-sponsored "*bracero* [working arms] program," a contract labor project designed to address wartime labor shortages in agriculture. In 1954 during the post-Korean War recession, the Immigration and Naturalization Services (INS) implemented "Operation Wetback," which deported over one million undocumented Mexican

workers. At the same time nearly five million temporary labor contracts were issued to Mexican citizens between 1942 and 1964, while apprehensions of Mexican workers without documents also numbered over five million The bracero program ended in December 1964 due to strong opposition to abuses of migrant farm workers. (Hondagneu-Sotelo, 1994: 22–23. Fernández-Kelly, 1983:26). As of this writing, immigrant rights organizers feared that the George W. Bush administration will enact a new version of the bracero program to use guest migrant workers to work for one-year periods, making it difficult for them to organize without being deported, and forcing them to leave their families home in Mexico (Interview with Eunice Cho, National Network for Immigrant and Refugee Rights, February 26, 2001).

5. Fix and Passel, 1994:24–25.
6. Falk, 2001; McDonnel, 1999.
7. Ruiz, 1998:7; Hondagneu-Sotelo, 1994:20.
8. By the 1920s many growers sought a more stable supply of immigrant workers, including Mexican women and children. (Hondagneu-Sotelo, 1994:21–22). During the war years many Mexican and Chicana/o families migrated from Texas to California. As the population became increasingly urban, women moved from the fields into garment factories in the Southwest. (Amott and Matthei, 1996: 79–80; Blackwelder, 1997:71–72). For more on the role of Mexicana and Chicana labor, see feminist researchers like Zavella, 1987; Mora and Del Castillo, 1980; Ruiz, 1987 and 1998; Mary Romero, 1992; Leeper, 1993; Blackwelder, 1984 and 1997; Soldatenko, 1993; Rose, 1990 and 1995; Calderón and Zamora, 1990: 37–40; Vargas, 1997; Honig, 1996; Blackwelder, 1997:71–72; Ruiz, 1998; Amott and Matthei, 1996; and Fernández-Kelly and García, 1989 and 1992; Fernández-Kelly and Sassen, 1991.
9. US Department of Labor, Women's Bureau, 1997:1.
10. US Department of Labor, Women's Bureau, 1997: 6–7. According to US government statistics, leading occupations for "Hispanic Origin" women were as cashiers, secretaries, sales, retail and personal service workers; janitors and cleaners; nursing aids, orderlies, and attendants; textile sewing machine operators, cleaners and servants in private households, and cooks in 1996. Segregation into lower-paying, secondary labor market jobs, layoffs and high unemployment, and lower educational attainment all combined to keep incomes low and poverty rates high for Mexicanas and Chicanas. The 1995 median incomes for full-time workers put Latinas at the bottom of the income scale averaging $17,178. While Mexicanas and Chicanas earned only half as much as Anglo men, their male counterparts also made only 61 percent of white male earnings in 1990 (Amott and Matthei, 1996: 91).
11. Interview with Refugio "Cuca" Arrieta, February 26, 1997.
12. Interview with Petra Mata, October 7, 1997.
13. Fernández-Kelley, 1983:4 and 19–46. For more on the border economy, see Southwest Network for Environmental & Economic Justice, 1996.
14. Interview with Celeste Jiménez, February 26, 1997.
15. Interview with Marta Martínez, October 9, 1997.
16. The neoliberal program was designed to address systemic problems of the 1970s, such as the falling rates of profit, global recession, oil crisis, slump in commodity prices and markets, and ballooning rates of foreign debt which international banks feared deeply indebted nations would be forced to default. See Martínez and García, 1997; Vickers, 1991; García, Arnoldo, 1996; Asian Migrant Centre, 1996b; Zamora, 1995; National Commission for Democracy in Mexico, 1997b.
17. See Sparr, 1994; Vickers, 1991; Rivera, 1996; Suárez Aguilar, 1996; Louie and Burnham, 2000.
18. Stephen, 1997: 115.
19. Chant, 1991:41, cited in Stephen, 1997:115.
20. Economist Intelligence Unit, 1994:13, cited in Stephen, 1997:115.
21. See Benería and Roldan, 1987; Stephen, 1997:111–157; and Thompson, 1999.
22. Interview with Refugio "Cuca" Arrieta, February 26, 1997.
23. Human Rights Watch, 1996:2.
24. Fernández-Kelly, 1994:263.
25. Bustos and Palacio, 1994:19; Louie, Miriam, 1998.
26. Fernández-Kelly, 1994:265.

27. Delegation meetings organized by National Interfaith Committee for Worker Justice and hosted by the *Comisión para la Defensa de los Derechos Humanos del Valle de Tehuacán, Cetilizchicahualistli* (Tehuacán Human Rights Commission), February 22–23, 1998. Interviews with "María" and "Araceli," February 22, 1998. See National Interfaith Committee for Worker Justice, 1998; Louie, Miriam, 1998.
28. Interview with Carmen Valadez and Reyna Montero, February 17, 1998 in Tijuana, Mexico. Interview with Beatriz Alfaro, November 8, 1998. See also Valadez and Cota, 1998. Valadez and Montero explained that their group chose the feminist name "Factor X," after the X chromosomes which distinguishes females from males.
29. Interview with Elizabeth "Beti" Robles Ortega, July 10, 1998.
30. Author interviews with Elizabeth Robles of SEDEPAC, July 10, 1998; Mathilde Arteaga of FAT, February 20, 1998; Carmen Valadez and Reyna Montero, February 17, 1998; and Beatríz Alfaro of Factor X, November 8, 1998.
31. Fernández-Kelly, 1983: 62–63, 70–71. Between 1995 and 2000, for example, more than 1 million Mexicans moved to the northern border, largely in search of work in the maquila industry (Thompson, 2001:A1).
32. Interview with María Antonia Flores, February 24, 1997.
33. Delegation meeting organized by the National Interfaith Committee for Worker justice with the *Comisión para la Defensa de los Derechos Humanos del Valle de Tehuacán, Cetilizchicahualistli* (Tehuacán Human Rights Commission in Tehuacán), February 22, 1998.
34. Louie, Miriam, 1990.
35. Egan, 1997.
36. Gomez-Quinones and Maciel, 1998:37–38.
37. Hondagneu-Sotelo, 1994:21.
38. Monto, 1994.
39. Interview with Celeste Jiménez, February 26, 1997.
40. Interview with María del Carmen Domínguez, February 24, 1997.
41. Interview with Carmen "Chitlan" Ibarra Lopéz, February 24, 1997.
42. Interview with Alicia and Carlos Marentes, February 25, 1997.
43. García, Arnoldo, 1996:6.
44. Fix and Passel, 1994:25. For more on militarization of the border see Palafox, 1996. See also Michael Moore's spoof on the inconsistencies of US immigration policy, "Not on the 'Mayflower? Then Leave!," 1996:33–42.
45. Cornelius, 1988, cited in Hondagneu-Sotelo, 1994:31.
46. Interview with Carmen "Chitlan" Ibarra Lopéz, February 24, 1997. The 1986 Immigration Reform and Contract Act contained provisions for an amnesty-legalization program for undocumented immigrants who could prove continuous residence in the United States since January 1, 1982, and for those who could prove they had worked in US agriculture for 90 days during specific periods (Hondagnue-Sotelo, 1994:26.)
47. Hondagneu-Sotelo, 1994:2–20.
48. Interview with María del Carmen Domínguez, February 24, 1997.
49. Interview with Petra Mata, October 7, 1997.
50. Interview with Lucrecia Tamayo, March 3, 1997.
51. Interview with Irma Montoya Barajas, February 28, 1997.
52. Interview with María del Carmen Domínguez, February 24, 1997.
53. Interview with Ernestina "Tina" Mendoza, October 8, 1997.
54. For more on second and third generation Chicanas' labor, see Romero, 1992; Zavella, 1987; and Ruiz, 1987 and 1998.
55. Interview with Viola Casares, October 7, 1997.
56. See Coyle, Hershatter and Honig, 1980; Honig, 1996.
57. Interview with Carmen "Chitlan" Ibarra Lopéz, February 24, 1997. For more on race and gender insensitivity and top-down leadership within the union during the Farah strike, see Coyle, Hershatter and Honig, 1980.
58. Interview with Refugio "Cuca" Arrieta, February 26, 1997.
59. Interview with María del Carmen Domínguez, February 24, 1997.
60. Interview with Petra Mata, October 7, 1997.
61. Bonacich and Walker, 1994:86–87.
62. Sweatshop Watch, 2000:1.
63. Kever, 1990.
64. See Bluestone and Harrison, 1982; Moore, 1996.
65. Interview with Viola Casares, October 7, 1997.

66. Interview with Petra Mata, October 7, 1997.
67. Colliver, 2000; Schoenberger, 2000.
68. Landler, 1998; Frost, 1998, Emert, 1998.
69. Emert, 1999.
70. Sweatshop Watch, 1998:1–2. UNITE had initially requested that Levi's and Liz Claiborne not be included in the original suit.
71. Verhovek, 1998.
72. For information on the lawsuit filed by injured workers at Levi's plants in El Paso, see Tanaka, Wendy. 1997.
73. Greater Texas Workers Committee, 1997.
74. La Mujer Obrera, "Desastre causado por NAFTA-caused Disaster," Flyer, 2000.
75. Interview with María del Carmen Domínguez, February 24, 1997.
76. Bonacich and Appelbaum, 2000:16.
77. Interview with Lucrecia Tamayo, March 3, 1997.
78. Interview with María del Carmen Domínguez, February 24, 1997. After becoming an LMO organizer, Domínguez in turn leafleted factory gates to inform workers of their rights during impending NAFTA closures.
79. Interview with María del Carmen Domínguez, February 24, 1997. See Centro de Trabajadores and La Mujer Obrera. 1993.
80. Interview with María del Carmen Domínguez, February 24, 1997. The independent union adopted as its name the day in 1985 when angry workers launched the group as Mexico City sweatshop owners retrieved machines first, instead of injured seamstresses trapped under the earthquake's rubble.
81. Interview with Carmen "Chitlan" Ibarra Lopéz, February 24, 1997.
82. Interview with Carmen "Chitlan" Ibarra Lopéz, February 24, 1997.
83. Verhovek, 1998.
84. Interview with Refugio "Cuca" Arrieta, February 26, 1997. LMO holds an annual awards dinner honoring outstanding women labor and community leaders.
85. Interview with María Antonia Flores, February 24, 1997. For discussion about popular education, see Freire, 1990; Bell, Gaventa and Peters, 1990.
86. Interview with María Antonia Flores, February 24, 1997.
87. Interview with Lucrecia Tamayo, March 3, 1997.
88. Interview with Viola Casares, October 7, 1997.
89. Interview with Viola Casares, October 7, 1997.
90. Interview with Marta Martínez, October 9, 1997.
91. Interview with Ernestina "Tina" Mendoza, October 11, 1997.
92. Interview with Obdulia "Obi" Segura, October 8, 1997.
93. Interview with Petra Mata, October 7, 1997.
94. Interview with Viola Casares, October 7, 1997.
95. Interview with Carmen "Chitlan" Ibarra Lopéz, February 24, 1997.
96. Interview with Viola Casares, October 7, 1997.
97. Interview with Viola Casares, October 7, 1997.
98. Interview with Remedios García, February 26, 1997.
99. Interview with Carmen "Chitlan" Ibarra Lopéz, February 24, 1997.
100. Interview with Ernestina "Tina" Mendoza, October 8, 1997.
101. Interview with Petra Mata, October 7, 1997.
102. Interview with María del Carmen Domínguez, February 21, 1997.
103. Interview with Carmen "Chitlan" Ibarra Lopéz, February 24, 1997.
104. Dr. Loco's Rockin' Jalapeño Band, 1992. Reprinted with permission.
105. The FAT started organizing on the northern border at the General Electric plant in Júarez in 1993. On September 28, 1996, the FAT inaugurated its new center for maquila workers, the *Centro de Estudios y Taller Laboral*, A.C. (CETLA) [Labor Workshop and Study Center]. Interview with Beatríz E. Lujan Uranga, CETLA organizer, Ciudad Júarez, February 25, 1997. Interview with Mathilde Arteaga, in charge of national women's organization within the FAT, Mexico City, February 20, 1998. For more information on the FAT, see Hathaway, 2000.

Maid in L.A.

Pierrette Hondagneu-Sotelo

The title of this chapter was inspired by Mary Romero's 1992 book, *Maid in the U.S.A.,* but I am also taking the pun to heart: most Latina immigrant women who do paid domestic work in Los Angeles had no prior experience working as domestics in their countries of origin. Of the 153 Latina domestic workers that I surveyed at bus stops, in ESL classes, and in parks, fewer than 10 percent reported having worked in other people's homes, or taking in laundry for pay, in their countries of origin. This finding is perhaps not surprising, as we know from immigration research that the poorest of the poor rarely migrate to the United States; they simply cannot afford to do so.

Some of the Latina immigrant women who come to Los Angeles grew up in impoverished squatter settlements, others in comfortable homes with servants. In their countries of origin, these women were housewives raising their own children, or college students, factory workers, store clerks, and secretaries; still others came from rural families of very modest means. Regardless of their diverse backgrounds, their transformation into housecleaners and nanny/housekeepers occurs in Los Angeles. I emphasize this point because images in popular culture and the media more or less identify Latinas with domestic workers—or, more precisely, as "cleaning gals" and "baby-sitters," euphemisms that mask American discomfort with these arrangements. Yet they take on these roles only in the United States, at various points in their own migration and settlement trajectories, in the context of private households, informal social networks, and the larger culture's racialized nativism.

Who are these women who come to the United States in search of jobs, and what are those jobs like? Domestic work is organized in different ways, and in this chapter I describe live-in, live-out, and housecleaning jobs and pro-

file some of the Latina immigrants who do them and how they feel about their work. The chapter concludes with a discussion of why it is that Latina immigrants are the primary recruits to domestic work, and I examine what they and their employers have to say about race relations and domestic work.

Live-in Nanny/Housekeeper Jobs

For Maribel Centeno, newly arrived from Guatemala City in 1989 at age twenty-two and without supportive family and friends with whom to stay, taking a live-in job made a lot of sense. She knew that she wouldn't have to spend money on room and board, and that she could soon begin saving to pay off her debts. Getting a live-in job through an agency was easy. The *señora,* in her rudimentary Spanish, only asked where she was from, and if she had a husband and children. Chuckling, Maribel recalled her initial misunderstanding when the *señora,* using her index finger, had drawn an imaginary "2" and "3" in the palm of her hand. "I thought to myself, well, she must have two or three bedrooms, so I said, fine. 'No,' she said. 'Really, really big.' She started counting, 'One, two, three, four . . . two-three rooms.' It was twenty-three rooms! I thought, *huy!* On a piece of paper, she wrote '$80 a week,' and she said, 'You, child, and entire house.' So I thought, well, I have to do what I have to do, and I happily said, 'Yes.'"

"I arrived on Monday at dawn," she recalled, "and I went to the job on Wednesday evening." When the *señora* and the child spoke to her, Maribel remembered "just laughing and feeling useless. I couldn't understand anything." On that first evening, the *señora* put on classical music, which Maribel quickly identified. "I said, 'Beethoven.' She said, 'Yeah,' and began asking me in English, 'You like it?' I said 'Yes,' or perhaps I said, '*Si,*' and she began playing other cassettes, CDs. They had Richard Clayderman and I recognized it, and when I said that, she stopped in her tracks, her jaw fell open, and she just stared at me. She must have been thinking, 'No schooling, no

From *Doméstica: Immigrant Workers Cleaning & Caring in the Shadow of Affluence* by Pierrette Hondagneu-Sotelo. Copyright © 2001 by the Regents of the University of California. Reprinted by permission of University of California Press.

preparation, no English, how does she know this music?"'
But the *señora*, perhaps because of the language difficulty,
or perhaps because she felt upstaged by her live-in's knowledge of classical music, never did ask. Maribel desperately wanted the *señora* to respect her, to recognize that
she was smart, educated, and cultivated in the arts. In spite
of her best status-signaling efforts, "They treated me," she
said, "the same as any other girl from the countryside."
She never got the verbal recognition that she desired from
the *señora*.

Maribel summed up her experiences with her first live-
in job this way: "The pay was bad. The treatment was,
how shall I say? It was cordial, a little, uh, not racist, but
with very little consideration, very little respect." She liked
caring for the little seven-year-old boy, but keeping after
the cleaning of the twenty-three-room house, filled with
marble floors and glass tables, proved physically impossible. She eventually quit not because of the polishing and
scrubbing, but because being ignored devastated her socially.

Compared to many other Latina immigrants' first live-
in jobs, Maribel Centeno's was relatively good. She was
not on call during all her waking hours and throughout the
night, the parents were engaged with the child, and she
was not required to sleep in a child's bedroom or on a cot
tucked away in the laundry room. But having a private
room filled with amenities did not mean she had privacy
or the ability to do simple things one might take for granted.
"I had my own room, with my own television, VCR, my
private bath, and closet, and a kind of sitting room—but
everything in miniature, Thumbelina style," she said. "I
had privacy in that respect. But I couldn't do many things.
If I wanted to walk around in a T-shirt, or just feel like I
was home, I couldn't do that. If I was hungry in the evening,
I wouldn't come out to grab a banana because I'd have to
walk through the family room, and then everybody's
watching and having to smell the banana. I could never
feel at home, never. Never, never, never! There's always
something invisible that tells you this is not your house,
you just work here."

It is the rare California home that offers separate
maid's quarters, but that doesn't stop families from hiring
live-ins; nor does it stop newly arrived Latina migrant
workers from taking jobs they urgently need. When live-
ins cannot even retreat to their own rooms, work seeps
into their sleep and their dreams. There is no time off from
the job, and they say they feel confined, trapped, imprisoned.

"I lose a lot of sleep," said Margarita Gutiérrez, a
twenty-four-year-old Mexicana who worked as a live-in
nanny/housekeeper. At her job in a modest-sized condominium in Pasadena, she slept in a corner of a three-year-
old child's bedroom. Consequently, she found herself on
call day and night with the child, who sometimes went
several days without seeing her mother because of the

latter's schedule at an insurance company. Margarita was
obliged to be on her job twenty-four hours a day; and like
other live-in nanny/housekeepers I interviewed, she
claimed that she could scarcely find time to shower or brush
her teeth. "I go to bed fine," she reported, "and then I wake
up at two or three in the morning with the girl asking for
water or food." After the child went back to sleep, Margarita
would lie awake, thinking about how to leave her job but
finding it hard to even walk out into the kitchen. Live-in
employees like Margarita literally have no space and no
time they can claim as their own.

Working in a larger home or staying in plush, private
quarters is no guarantee of privacy or refuge from the job.
Forty-four-year-old Elvia Lucero worked as a live-in at a
sprawling, canyon-side residence where she was in charge
of looking after twins, two five-year-old girls. On numerous occasions when I visited her there, I saw that she occupied her own bedroom, a beautifully decorated one
outfitted with delicate antiques, plush white carpet, and a
stenciled border of pink roses painstakingly painted on
the wall by the employer. It looks serene and inviting, but
it was only three steps away from the twins' room. Every
night one of the twins crawled into bed with Elvia. Eliva
disliked this, but said she couldn't break the girl of the
habit. And the parents' room lay tucked away at the opposite end of the large (more than 3,000 square feet),
L-shaped house.

Regardless of the size of the home and the splendor
of the accommodations, the boundaries that we might normally take for granted disappear in live-in jobs. They have,
as Evelyn Nakano Glenn has noted, "no clear line between
work and non-work time," and the line between job space
and private space is similarly blurred.[1] Live-in nanny/
housekeepers are at once socially isolated and surrounded
by other people's territory; during the hours they remain
on the employer's premises, their space, like their time,
belongs to another. The sensation of being among others
while remaining invisible, unknown and apart, of never
being able to leave the margins, makes many live-in employees sad, lonely, and depressed. Melancholy sets in and
doesn't necessarily lift on the weekends.

Rules and regulations may extend around the clock.
Some employers restrict the ability of their live-in employees to receive telephone calls, entertain friends, attend evening ESL classes, or see boyfriends during the
workweek. Other employers do not impose these sorts of
restrictions, but because their homes are located on remote hillsides, in suburban enclaves, or in gated communities, their live-in nanny/housekeepers are effectively kept
away from anything resembling social life or public culture. A Spanish-language radio station, or maybe a
telenovela, may serve as their only link to the outside world.

Food—the way some employers hoard it, waste it,
deny it, or just simply do not even have any of it in their
kitchens—is a frequent topic of discussion among Latina
live-in nanny/housekeepers. These women are talking not

about counting calories but about the social meaning of food on the job. Almost no one works with a written contract, but anyone taking a live-in job that includes "room and board" would assume that adequate meals will be included. But what constitutes an adequate meal? Everyone has a different idea, and using the subject like a secret handshake, Latina domestic workers often greet one another by talking about the problems of managing food and meals on the job. Inevitably, food enters their conversations.

No one feels the indignities of food more deeply than do live-in employees, who may not leave the job for up to six days at a time. For them, the workplace necessarily becomes the place of daily sustenance. In some of the homes where they work, the employers are out all day. When these adults return home, they may only snack, keeping on hand little besides hot dogs, packets of macaroni and cheese, cereal, and peanut butter for the children. Such foods are considered neither nutritious nor appetizing by Latina immigrants, many of whom are accustomed to sitting down to meals prepared with fresh vegetables, rice, beans, and meat. In some employers' homes, the cupboards are literally bare. Gladys Villedas recalled that at one of her live-in jobs, the *señora* had graciously said, "'Go ahead, help yourself to anything in the kitchen.' But at times," she recalled, "there was nothing, nothing in the refrigerator! There was nothing to eat!" Even in lavish kitchens outfitted with Subzero refrigerators and imported cabinetry, food may be scarce. A celebrity photographer of luxury homes that appear in posh magazines described to a reporter what he sees when he opens the doors of some of Beverly Hills' refrigerators: "Rows of cans of Diet Coke, and maybe a few remains of pizza."[2]

Further down the class ladder, some employers go to great lengths to economize on food bills. Margarita Gutiérrez claimed that at her live-in job, the husband did the weekly grocery shopping, but he bought things in small quantities—say, two potatoes that would be served in half portions, or a quarter of a watermelon to last a household of five all week. He rationed out the bottled water and warned her that milk would make her fat. Lately, she said, he was taking both her and the children to an upscale grocery market where they gave free samples of gourmet cheeses, breads, and dips, urging them all to fill up on the freebies. "I never thought," exclaimed Margarita, formerly a secretary in Mexico City, "that I would come to this country to experience hunger!"

Many women who work as live-ins are keenly aware of how food and meals underline the boundaries between them and the families for whom they work. "I never ate with them," recalled Maribel Centeno of her first live-in job. "First of all, she never said, 'Come and join us,' and secondly, I just avoided being around when they were about to eat." Why did she avoid mealtime? "I didn't feel I was part of that family. I knew they liked me, but only because of the good work I did, and because of the affection I showed on the boy; but apart from that, I was just like the gardener, like the pool man, just one more of their staff." Sitting down to share a meal symbolizes membership in a family, and Latina employees, for the most part, know they are not just like one of the family.

Food scarcity is not endemic to all of the households where these women work. In some homes, ample quantities of fresh fruits, cheeses, and chicken stock the kitchens. Some employer families readily share all of their food, but in other households, certain higher-quality, expensive food items may remain off-limits to the live-in employees, who are instructed to eat hot dogs with the children. One Latina live-in nanny/housekeeper told me that in her employers' substantial pantry, little "DO NOT TOUCH" signs signaled which food items were not available to her; and another said that her employer was always defrosting freezer-burned leftovers for her to eat, some of it dating back nearly a decade.

Other women felt subtle pressure to remain unobtrusive, humble, and self-effacing, so they held back from eating even when they were hungry. They talked a lot about how these unspoken rules apply to fruit. "Look, if they [the employers] buy fruit, they buy three bananas, two apples, two pears. So if I eat one, who took it? It's me," one woman said, "they'll know it's me." Another nanny/housekeeper recalled: "They would bring home fruit, but without them having to say it, you just knew these were not intended for you. You understand this right away, you get it." Or as another put it, "*Las Americanas* have their apples counted out, one for each day of the week." Even fruits growing in the garden are sometimes contested. In Southern California's agriculture-friendly climate, many a residential home boasts fruit trees that hang heavy with oranges, plums, and peaches, and when the Latina women who work in these homes pick the fruit, they sometimes get in trouble.[3] Eventually, many of the women solve the food problem by buying and bringing in their own food; early on Monday mornings, you see them walking with their plastic grocery bags, carting, say, a sack of apples, some chicken, and maybe some prepared food in plastic containers.

The issue of food captures the essence of how Latina live-in domestic workers feel about their jobs. It symbolizes the extent to which the families they work for draw the boundaries of exclusion or inclusion, and it marks the degree to which those families recognize the live-in nanny/housekeepers as human beings who have basic human needs. When they first take their jobs, most live-in nanny/housekeepers do not anticipate spending any of their meager wages on food to eat while on the job, but in the end, most do—and sometimes the food they buy is eaten by members of the family for whom they work.

Although there is a wide range of pay, many Latina domestic workers in live-in jobs earn less than minimum wage for marathon hours: 93 percent of the live-in workers I surveyed in the mid-1990s were earning less than $5 an hour (79 percent of them below minimum wage, which was then $4.25), and they reported working an average of sixty-four hours a week.[4] Some of the most astoundingly low rates were paid for live-in jobs in the households of other working-class Latino immigrants, which provide some women their first job when they arrive in Los Angeles. Carmen Vasquez, for example, had spent several years working as a live-in for two Mexican families, earning only $50 a week. By comparison, her current salary of $170 a week, which she was earning as a live-in nanny/housekeeper in the hillside home of an attorney and a teacher, seemed a princely sum.

Many people assume that the rich pay more than do families of modest means, but working as a live-in in an exclusive wealthy neighborhood, or in a twenty-three-room house, provides no guarantee of high salary. Early one Monday morning in the fall of 1995, I was standing with a group of live-in nanny/housekeepers on a corner across the street from the Beverly Hills Hotel. As they were waiting to be picked up by their employers, a large Mercedes sedan with two women (a daughter and mother or mother-in-law?) approached, rolled down the windows, and asked if anyone was interested in a $150-a-week live-in job. A few women jotted down the phone number, and no one was shocked by the offer. Gore Vidal once commented that no one is allowed to fail within a two-mile radius of the Beverly Hills Hotel, but it turns out that plenty of women in that vicinity are failing in the salary department. In some of the most affluent Westside areas of Los Angeles—in Malibu, Pacific Palisades, and Bel Air—there are live-in nanny/housekeepers earning $150 a week. And in 1999, the *Los Angeles Times* Sunday classified ads still listed live-in nanny/housekeeper jobs with pay as low as $100 and $125.[5] Salaries for live-in jobs, however, do go considerably higher. The best-paid live-in employee whom I interviewed was Patricia Paredes, a Mexicana who spoke impeccable English and who had legal status, substantial experience, and references. She told me that she currently earned $450 a week at her live-in job. She had been promised a raise to $550, after a room remodel was finished, when she would assume weekend housecleaning in that same home. With such a relatively high weekly salary she felt compelled to stay in a live-in job during the week, away from her husband and three young daughters who remained on the east side of Los Angeles. The salary level required that sacrifice.

But once they experience it, most women are repelled by live-in jobs. The lack of privacy, the mandated separation from family and friends, the round-the-clock hours, the food issues, the low pay, and especially the constant loneliness prompt most Latina immigrants to seek other job arrangements. Some young, single women who learn to speak English fluently try to move up the ranks into higher-paying live-in jobs. As soon as they can, however, the majority attempt to leave live-in work altogether. Most live-in nanny/housekeepers have been in the United States

for five years or less; among the live-in nanny/housekeepers I interviewed, only two (Carmen Vasquez and the relatively high-earning Patricia Paredes) had been in the United States for longer than that. Like African American women earlier in the century, who tired of what the historian Elizabeth Clark-Lewis has called "the soul-destroying hollowness of live-in domestic work,"[6] most Latina immigrants try to find other options.

Until the early 1900s, live-in jobs were the most common form of paid domestic work in the United States, but through the first half of the twentieth century they were gradually supplanted by domestic "day work."[7] Live-in work never completely disappeared, however, and in the last decades of the twentieth century, it revived with vigor, given new life by the needs of American families with working parents and young children—and, as we have seen, by the needs of newly arrived Latina immigrants, many of them unmarried and unattached to families. When these women try to move up from live-in domestic work, they see few job alternatives. Often, the best they can do is switch to another form of paid domestic work, either as a live-out nanny/housekeeper or as a weekly housecleaner. When they do such day work, they are better able to circumscribe their work hours, and they earn more money in less time.[8]

Live-out Nanny/Housekeepers

When I first met twenty-four-year-old Ronalda Saavedra, she was peeling a hard-boiled egg for a dog in the kitchen of a very large home where I was interviewing the employer. At this particular domestic job, the fifth she had held since migrating from El Salvador in 1991, she arrived daily around one in the afternoon and left after the children went to bed. On a typical day, she assisted the housekeeper, a middle-aged woman, with cleaning, laundry, and errands, and at three o'clock she drove off in her own car to pick up the children—a nine-year-old boy, whom she claimed was always angry, and his hyperactive six-year-old brother.

Once the children were put to bed, Ronalda Saavedra drove home to a cozy apartment that she shared with her brother in the San Fernando Valley. When I visited her, I saw that it was a tiny place, about half the size of the kitchen where we had first met; but it was pleasantly outfitted with new bleached oak furniture, and the morning sunshine that streamed in through a large window gave it a cheerful, almost spacious feel. Ronalda kept a well-stocked refrigerator, and during our interview she served me *pan dulce*, coffee, and honeydew melon.

Like many other women, Ronalda had begun her work stint in the United States with a live-in job, but she vastly preferred living out. She slept through the night in peace, attended ESL classes in the morning, ate what she wanted when she wanted it, and talked daily on the phone with her fiancé. All this was possible because live-out jobs are firmly circumscribed. Even when women find it difficult to say no to their employers when they are asked, at the last minute, to stay and work another hour or two, they know they will eventually retreat to their own places. So while the workday tasks and rhythms are similar to those of live-ins, the job demands on live-outs stop when they exit the houses where they work and return to their own homes, usually small and sometimes crowded apartments located in one of Los Angeles' many Latino neighborhoods. For such women with husbands or with children of their own, live-out jobs allow them to actually live with their family members and see them daily.

Live-out nanny/housekeepers also earn more money than live-ins. Most of them work eight or nine hours a day, and of those I surveyed, 60 percent worked five days a week or fewer. Their mean hourly wages were $5.90—not an exorbitant wage by any means, but above the legal minimum, unlike the wages of their peers in live-in jobs. Ronalda earned $350 for her forty-hour workweek, making her hourly wage $8.75. On top of this, her employer gave her an additional $50 to cover gasoline expenses, as Ronalda spent a portion of each afternoon driving on errands, such as going to the dry cleaners, and ferrying the children home from school and then to and from soccer practices, music lessons, and so on. In the suburban landscape of Los Angeles, employers pay an extra premium for nanny/housekeepers who can provide this shuttling service. Only Latina nanny/housekeepers with experience, strong references, English skills, and an impressive array of certificates and licenses enjoy earnings that reach Ronalda's level.

Today, most Americans who hire a domestic worker to come into their homes on a daily basis do so in order to meet their needs for *both* housecleaning and child care. Most Latina nanny/housekeepers work in households where they are solely responsible for these tasks, and they work hard to fit in the cleaning and laundry (most of them don't cook) while the children are napping or at school. Some of them feel, as one woman said, that they need to be "octopuses," with busy arms extended simultaneously in all directions. A big part of their job requires taking care of the children; and various issues with the children present nanny/housekeepers with their greatest frustrations. Paradoxically, they also experience some of their deepest job satisfaction with these children with whom they spend so much time.

After what may be years of watching, feeding, playing with, and reprimanding the same child from birth to elementary school, day in and day out, some nanny/housekeepers grow very fond of their charges and look back nostalgically, remembering, say, when a child took her first steps or first learned nursery rhymes in Spanish. Ronalda, an articulate, highly animated woman who told stories using a lot of gestures and facial expressions, talked a great deal about the children she had cared for in her various jobs. She imitated the voices of children she had taken care of, describing longingly little girls who were, she said, "*muy* nice" or "*tan* sweet," and recalled the imaginary games they would play. Like many other nanny/housekeepers, she wept freely when she remembered some of the intimate and amusing moments she had spent with children she no longer saw. She also described other children who, she said, were dour, disrespectful, and disobedient.

Many live-out nanny/housekeepers made care work—the work of keeping the children clean, happy, well nourished, and above all safe—a priority over housecleaning duties. This sometimes created conflicts with their employers, who despite saying that their children should come first still expected a spotless house. "The truth is," explained Teresa Portillo, who looked after a child only on the weekends, "when you are taking care of children, you can't neglect anything, absolutely nothing! Because the moment you do, they do whatever little *travesura*, and they scrape their knees, cut themselves or whatever." Nanny/housekeepers fear they will be sent to jail if anything happens to the children.

Feeding the children is a big part of the job. Unlike their live-in peers, when live-out nanny/housekeepers talk about food, they're usually concerned with what the children eat or don't eat. Some of them derive tremendous pleasure and satisfaction from bringing the children special treats prepared at their own homes—maybe homemade flan or *pan con crema*, or simply a mango. Some nanny/housekeepers are also in charge, to their dismay, of feeding and cleaning the children's menagerie of pets. Many feel disgusted when they have to bathe and give eyedrops to old, sick dogs, or clean the cages of iguanas, snakes, lizards, and various rodents. But these tasks are trivial in comparison to the difficulties they encounter with hard-to-manage children. Mostly, though, they complain about permissive, neglectful parents.

Not all nanny/housekeepers bond tightly with their employers' children, but most are critical of what they perceive as their employers' careless parenting—or, more accurately, mothering, for their female employers typically receive the blame. They see mothers who may spend, they say, only a few minutes a day with their babies and toddlers, or who return home from work after the children are asleep. Soraya Sanchez said she could understand mothers who work "out of necessity," but all other mothers, she believed, hired nanny/housekeepers because they just didn't like being with their own kids. "*La Americana* is very selfish, she only thinks about herself," she said. "They prefer not to be with their children, as they find it's much easier to pay someone to do that." Her critique was shared by many nanny/housekeepers; and those with children of their own, even if they didn't live with them, saw their own mothering as far superior. "I love my kids, they don't. It's just like, excuse the word, 'shitting kids,'" said Patricia Paredes. "What they prefer is to go to the salon, get their nails done, you know, go shopping, things like that. Even if they're home all day, they don't want to spend time with the kids because they're paying somebody to do that for them." For many Latina nanny/housekeepers, seething class resentments find expression in the rhetoric of comparative mothering.

When Latina immigrant women enter the homes of middle-class and upper-middle-class Americans, they encounter ways of raising children very different from those with which they are familiar. As Julia Wrigley's research has shown, the child-rearing values of many Latina and Caribbean nannies differ from those of their employers, but most are eager to do what middle-class parents want—to adopt "time out" discipline measures instead of swatting, or to impose limits on television viewing and Nintendo.[9] Some of them not only adapt but come to genuinely admire and appreciate such methods of child rearing. Yet they, too, criticize the parenting styles they witness close up in the homes where they work.

Some nanny/housekeepers encounter belligerent young children, who yell at them, call them names, and throw violent temper tantrums; and when they do, they blame the parents. They are aghast when parents, after witnessing a child scratch or bite or spit at them, simply shrug their shoulders and ignore such behavior. Parents' reactions to these incidents were a litmus test of sorts. Gladys Villedas, for example, told me that at her job, a five-year-old "grabbed my hair and pulled it really hard. Ay! It hurt so much I started crying! It really hurt my feelings because never in my own country, when I was raising my children, had this happened to me. Why should this happen to me here?" When she complained to her employer, she said the employer had simply consulted a child-rearing manual and explained that it was "a stage." Not all nanny/housekeepers encounter physically abusive children, but when they do, they prefer parents who allow them the authority to impose discipline, or who back them up by firmly instructing their children that it is not okay to kick or slap the nanny. Nanny/housekeepers spoke glowingly about these sorts of employers.

When nanny/housekeepers see parent-child interactions in the homes where they work, they are often put off and puzzled by what they observe. In these moments, the huge cultural gulf between Latina nanny/housekeepers and their employers seems even wider than they had initially imagined. In the home where Maribel Centeno was working as a live-out nanny/housekeeper, she spent the first few hours of her shift doing laundry and housecleaning, but when a thirteen-year-old boy, of whom she was actually very fond, arrived home from school, her real work began. It was his pranks, which were neither malicious nor directed at her, and parental tolerance of these, that drove her crazy. These adolescent pranks usually involved items like water balloons, firecrackers, and baking soda made to look like cocaine. Recently the boy had tacked up on his parents' bedroom door a condom filled with a small amount of milk and a little sign that read, "Mom and Dad,

this could have been my life." Maribel thought this was inappropriate behavior; but more bewildering and disturbing than the boy's prank was his mother's reaction—laughter. Another nanny/housekeeper had reacted with similar astonishment when, after a toddler tore apart a loaf of French bread and threw the pieces, balled like cotton, onto the floor, the father came forward not to reprimand but to record the incident with a camcorder. The regularity with which their employers waste food astounds them, and drug use also raises their eyebrows. Some nanny/housekeepers are instructed to give Ritalin and Prozac to children as young as five or six, and others tell of parents and teens locked in their separate bedrooms, each smoking marijuana.

Nanny/housekeepers blame permissive and neglectful parents, who they feel don't spend enough time with their own children, for the children's unruly behavior and for teen drug use. "The parents, they say 'yes' to everything the child asks," complained one woman. "Naturally," she added, "the children are going to act spoiled." Another nanny/housekeeper analyzed the situation this way: "They [the parents] feel guilty because they don't spend that much time with the kids, and they want to replace that missed time, that love, with toys."

Other nanny/housekeepers prided themselves on taming and teaching the children to act properly. "I really had to battle with these children just to get them to pay attention to me! When I started with them, they had no limits, they didn't pick up their toys, and they couldn't control their tempers. The eldest—oof! He used to kick and hit me, and in public! I was mortified," recalled Ronalda Saavedra. Another woman remarked of children she had looked after, "These kids listened to me. After all, they spent most of the time with me, and not with them [the parents]. They would arrive at night, maybe spend a few moments with the kids, or maybe the kids were already asleep." Elvia Areola highlighted the injustice of rearing children whom one will never see again. Discussing her previous job, she said, "I was the one who taught that boy to talk, to walk, to read, to sit! Everything! She [the child's mother] almost never picked him up! She only picked him up when he was happy." Another nanny/housekeeper concluded, "These parents don't really know their own children. Just playing with them, or taking them to the park, well, that's not raising children. I'm the one who is with them every day."

Nanny/housekeepers must also maneuver around jealous parents, who may come to feel that their children's affections have been displaced. "The kids fall in love with you and they [the parents] wonder, why? Some parents are jealous of what the kids feel toward you," said Ronalda Saavedra, "I'm not going to be lying, 'I'm your mommy,' but in a way, children go to the person who takes care of them, you know? That's just the way it is." For many nanny/housekeepers, it is these ties of affection that make it possible for them to do their job by making it rewarding. Some of them say they can't properly care for the children without feeling a special fondness for them; others say it just happens naturally. "I fall in love with all of these children. How can I not? That's just the way I am," one nanny/housekeeper told me. "I'm with them all day, and when I go home, my husband complains that that's all I talk about, what they did, the funny things they said." The nanny/housekeepers, as much as they felt burdened by disobedient children, sometimes felt that these children were also a gift of sorts, one that parents—again, the mothers—did not fully appreciate. "The babies are so beautiful!" gushed Soraya Sanchez. "How is it that a mother can lose those best years, when their kids are babies. I mean, I remember going down for a nap with these little babies, how we'd cuddle. How is it that a person who has the option of enjoying that would prefer to give that experience to a stranger?" Precisely because of such feelings, many Latina immigrants who have children try to find a job that is compatible with their own family lives. Housecleaning is one of those jobs.

Housecleaners

Like many working mothers, every weekday morning Marisela Ramírez awoke to dress and feed her preschooler, Tomás, and drive him to school (actually, a Head Start program) before she herself ventured out to work, navigating the dizzying array of Los Angeles freeways. Each day she set off in a different direction headed for a different workplace. On Mondays she maneuvered her way to Pasadena, where she cleaned the stately home of an elderly couple; on Tuesdays she alternated between cleaning a home in the Hollywood Hills and a more modest-sized duplex in Glendale; and Wednesdays took her to a split-level condominium in Burbank. You had to keep alert, she said, to remember where to go on which days and how to get there!

By nine o'clock she was usually on the job, and because she zoomed through her work she was able to finish, unless the house was extremely dirty, by one or two in the afternoon. After work, there were still plenty of daylight hours left for Marisela to take Tomás to the park, or at least to take him outside and let him ride down the sidewalk on his kid-sized motorized vehicle before she started dinner. Working as a housecleaner allowed Marisela to be the kind of wife and mother she wanted to be. Her job was something she did, she said, "because I have to"; but unlike her peers who work in live-in jobs, she enjoyed a fairly regular family life of her own, one that included cooking and eating family meals, playing with her son, bathing him, putting him to bed, and then watching *telenovelas* in the evenings with her husband and her sister. On the weekends, family socializing took center stage, with *carne asadas* in the park; informal gatherings with her large Mexican family, which extended throughout Los Angeles; and music from her husband, who worked as a gardener but played guitar in a weekend *ranchera* band.

Some might see Marisela Ramírez as just another low-wage worker doing dirty work, but by her own account—and gauging by her progress from her starting point—she had made remarkable occupational strides. Marisela had begun working as a live-in nanny/housekeeper in Los Angeles when she was only fifteen years old. Ten years later, the move from live-in work to housecleaning had brought her higher hourly wages, a shorter workweek, control over the pace of work, and flexibility in arranging when she worked. Cleaning different houses was also, she said, less boring than working as a nanny/housekeeper, which entailed passing every single day "in just one house, all week long with the same routine, over and over."

For a while she had tried factory work, packaging costume jewelry in a factory warehouse located in the San Fernando Valley, but Marisela saw housecleaning as preferable on just about every count. "In the factory, one has to work very, very fast!" she exclaimed. "And you can't talk to anybody, you can't stop, and you can't rest until it's break time. When you're working in a house, you can take a break at the moment you wish, finish the house when you want, and leave at the hour you decide. And it's better pay. It's harder work, yes," she conceded, "but it's better pay."

"How much were you earning at the factory?" I asked.

"Five dollars an hour, and working in houses now, I make about $11, or even more. Look, in a typical house, I enter at about 9 A.M., and I leave at 1 P.M. and they pay me $60. It's much better [than factory work]." Her income varied, but she could usually count on weekly earnings of about $300. By pooling these together with her husband's and sister's earnings, she was able to rent a one-bedroom bungalow roofed in red tile, with a lawn and a backyard for Tomás's sandbox and plastic swimming pool. In Mexico, Marisela had only studied as far as fifth grade, but she wanted the best for Tomás. Everyone doted on him, and by age four he was already reading simple words.

Of the housecleaners I surveyed, the majority earned, like Marisela, between $50 and $60 per housecleaning, which usually took about six hours. This suggests an average hourly wage of about $9.50, but I suspect the actual figure is higher.[10] Women like Marisela, who drive their own cars and speak some English, are likely to earn more than the women I surveyed, many of whom ride the buses to work. Marisela was typical of the housecleaners whom I surveyed in having been in the United States for a number of years. Unlike nanny/housekeepers, most of the housecleaners who were mothers themselves had all their children with them in the United States. Housecleaning, as Mary Romero has noted, is a job that is quite compatible with having a family life of one's own.

Breaking into housecleaning is tough, often requiring informal tutelage from friends and relatives. Contrary to the image that all women "naturally" know how to do domestic work, many Latina domestic workers discover that their own housekeeping experiences do not automatically transfer to the homes where they work. As she looked back on her early days in the job, Marisela said, "I didn't know how to clean or anything. My sister taught me." Erlinda Castro, a middle-aged woman who had already run her own household and raised five children in Guatemala, had also initially worked in live-in jobs when she first came to Los Angeles. Yet despite this substantial domestic experience, she recalled how mystified she was when she began housecleaning. "Learning how to use the chemicals and the liquids" in the different households was confusing, and, as friends and employers instructed her on what to do, she began writing down in a little notebook the names of the products and what they cleaned. Some women learn the job by informally apprenticing with one another, accompanying a friend or perhaps an aunt on her housecleaning jobs.

Establishing a thriving route of *casas* requires more than learning which cleaning products to use or how to clean quickly and efficiently. It also involves acquiring multiple jobs, which housecleaners typically gain by asking their employers if they have friends, neighbors, or acquaintances who need someone to clean their houses; and because some attrition is inevitable, they must constantly be on the lookout for more *casas*. Not everyone who wants to can fill up her entire week.

To make ends meet when they don't have enough houses to clean, Latina housecleaners in Los Angeles find other ways to earn income. They might prepare food—say, tamales and *crema*—which they sell door-to-door or on the street; or they might sell small amounts of clothing that they buy wholesale in the garment district, or products from Avon, Mary Kay cosmetics, and Princess House kitchenware. They take odd jobs, such as handing out flyers advertising dental clinics or working at a swap meet; or perhaps they find something more stable, such as evening janitorial work in office buildings. Some housecleaners work swing shift in garment factories, while others work three days a week as a nanny/housekeeper and try to fill the remaining days with housecleaning jobs. Some women supplement their husband's income by cleaning only one or two houses a week, but more often they patch together a number of jobs in addition to housecleaning.

Housecleaning represents, as Romero has written, the "modernization" of paid domestic work. Women who clean different houses on different days sell their labor services, she argues, in much the same way that a vendor sells a product to various customers.[11] The housecleaners themselves see their job as far preferable to that of a live-in or live-out nanny/housekeeper. They typically work alone, during times when their employers are out of the home; and because they are paid "by the job" instead of by the hour, they don't have to remain on the job until 6 or 7 P.M., an advantage much appreciated by women who have

families of their own. Moreover, because they work for different employers on different days, they are not solely dependent for their livelihood on one boss whom they see every single day. Consequently, their relationships with their employers are less likely to become highly charged and conflictual; and if problems do arise, they can leave one job without jeopardizing their entire weekly earnings. Since child care is not one of their tasks, their responsibilities are more straightforward and there are fewer points of contention with employers. Housecleaning is altogether less risky.

Housecleaners also see working independently and informally as more desirable than working for a commercial cleaning company. "The companies pay $5 an hour," said Erlinda Castro, whose neighbor worked for one, "and the women have to work their eight hours, doing up to ten, twenty houses a day! One does the vacuuming, the other does the bathroom and the kitchen, and like that. It's tremendously hard work, and at $5 an hour? Thank God, I don't have to do that." Two of the women I interviewed, one now a live-out nanny/housekeeper and the other a private housecleaner, had previously worked for cleaning services, and both of them complained bitterly about their speeded-up work pace, low pay, and tyrannical bosses.

Private housecleaners take enormous pride in their work. When they finish their job, they can see the shiny results, and they are proud of their job autonomy, their hours, their pay, and, most important, what they are able to do with their pay for themselves and for their families. Yet housecleaning brings its own special problems. Intensive cleaning eventually brings physical pain, and sometimes injury. "Even my bones are tired," said fifty-three-year-old Lupe Vélez; and even a relatively young woman like Celestina Vigil at age thirty-three was already reporting back problems that she attributed to her work. While most of them have only fleeting contact with their employers, and many said they work for "good people," just about everyone has suffered, they said, "inconsiderate persons" who exhort them to work faster, humiliate them, fail to give raises, add extra cleaning tasks without paying extra, or unjustly accuse them of stealing or of ruining a rug or upholstery. And the plain old hard work and stigma of cleaning always remain, as suggested by the answer I got when I asked a housecleaner what she liked least about her job. "The least?" she said, with a wry smile. "Well, that you have to clean."

Domestic Job Trajectories and Transnational Motherhood

As we have seen, private paid domestic work is organized into suboccupations, each with different pay scales, tasks, and hours.[12] Although they share many similarities, each job arrangement has its own different problems and rewards. In this section I discuss the movement between

Table 1. Type of Domestic Work, Length of Residence in the United States, and Mean Hourly Wages

	Live-ins (percent) (n = 30)	Live-outs (percent) (n = 64)	Housecleaners (percent) (n = 59)
Five years or less in the United States	60	31	17
More than five years in the United States	40	69	83
Mean hourly wage	$3.80	$5.90	$9.50

the three suboccupations and some of the family characteristics of the women who fill these jobs.

Some researchers have called live-in domestic work "the bridging occupation," because in various periods and places, it allowed rural migrant women to acculturate to the city and learn new ways of living.[13] Unlike Irish immigrant women or the black women who went from the South to the North to work as domestics in the early twentieth century, and unlike many private domestics in Europe and Latin America in the past, most Latina immigrants doing paid domestic work in the United States are *not* new to the city. Yet for many of them in Los Angeles today, especially those who are single and have very limited options for places to work and live, live-in jobs do serve as an initial occupational step. As table 1 shows, new arrivals and women who have lived in the United States five years or less concentrate in live-in jobs (60 percent). In contrast, the majority of housecleaners (83 percent) and live-out nanny/housekeepers (69 percent) have lived in the United States for more than five years. Some begin their live-in jobs literally within forty-eight hours after arriving in Los Angeles, while some housecleaners have lived in the United States for twenty years or more. For newly arrived immigrant women without papers, a live-in job in a private home may feel safer, as private homes in middle- and upper-middle-class neighborhoods are rarely, if ever, threatened by Immigration and Naturalization Service raids.[14]

As the years pass, the women who took live-in jobs learn some English, gain knowledge of other job possibilities, and learn to use their social networks to their occupational advantage. Most of them eventually move out of live-in work. Some return to their countries of origin, and others look to sales, factory work, or janitorial work. But given the low pay of those jobs—in 1999, garment workers in Los Angeles were earning $5.00 an hour, and nonunion janitors with six years of experience were earning $6.30 an hour—many of them transition into some form of domestic day work.[15] As they abandon their live-in positions for live-out nanny/housekeeper and housecleaner jobs, their wages increase. For these women, the initial misery suffered in their live-in jobs makes other domestic work look if not good then at least tolerable—and certainly better than where they started.

For Latina immigrants in Los Angeles today, live-in domestic work does serve as an occupational bridge of sorts, but it often leads only to other types of domestic jobs. These individual trajectories match historical transformations in the occupation. Much as live-in jobs were once the dominant form of paid domestic work, and then gave way to arrangements in which domestics continued to work daily for one employer but lived with their own families, and finally to modernized "job work" or periodic housecleaning, so many Latina immigrants today traverse these three different types of jobs. Some roughly follow the historical order, moving from live-in to live-out nanny/housekeeper jobs, and then to housecleaning, but their modest occupational mobility does not always follow such a linear course.

As Mexican and Central American immigrant women move into live-out and housecleaning jobs, their family lives change. With better pay and fewer hours of work, they become able to live with their own family members. Among those I surveyed, about 45 percent of the women doing day work were married, but only 13 percent of the live-ins were married. Most women who have husbands and children with them in Los Angeles do not wish to take live-in jobs; moreover, their application for a live-in job is likely to be rejected if they reveal that they have a husband, a boyfriend, or children living in Los Angeles. As one job seeker in an employment agency waiting room put it, "You can't have a family, you can't have anyone [if you want a live-in job]." Live-out nanny/housekeepers often face this family restriction too, as employers are wary of hiring someone who may not report for work when her own children come down with the flu.

Their subminimum wages and long hours make it impossible for many live-in workers to bring their children to Los Angeles; other live-ins are young women who do not have children of their own. Once they do have children who are either born in or have immigrated to Los Angeles, most women try to leave live-in work to be with them. Not all the women can do so, and sometimes their finances or jobs force them to send the children "back home" to be reared by grandmothers. Clearly, performing domestic work for pay, especially in a live-in job, is often incompatible with caring for one's own family and home.[16]

The substantial proportion of Latina domestic workers in Los Angeles whose children stay in their countries of origin are in the same position as many Caribbean women working in domestic jobs on the East Coast, and as the Filipinas who predominate in domestic jobs in many cities around the globe. This is what I labeled "transnational motherhood"; in a 1997 article Ernestine Avila and I coined this term as we examined how Latina immigrant domestic workers are transforming their own meanings of motherhood to accommodate these spatial and temporal separations." As table 2 suggests, these arrangements are most common among women with live-in jobs, but live-in domestic workers and single mothers are not the only ones who rely on them.[18]

These transnational arrangements are not altogether new. The United States has a long history of incorporating people of color through coercive systems of labor that do not recognize family rights, including the right to care for one's own family members. As others have pointed out, slavery and contract labor systems were organized to maximize economic productivity, and offered few supports to sustain family life.[19] Today, international labor migration and the job characteristics of paid domestic work, especially live-in work, virtually impose transnational motherhood on many Mexican and Central American women who have children of their own.

At the other end of the spectrum are the housecleaners, who earn higher wages than live-ins (averaging $9.50 an hour vs. $3.80) and who work fewer hours per week than live-ins (twenty-three vs. sixty-four). The majority of them (76 percent) have all their children in the United States, and they are the least likely to experience transnational spatial and temporal separations from their children. Greater financial resources and more favorable job terms enhance housecleaners' abilities to bring their children to the United States. As we have seen, weekly housecleaning is dominated by relatively well-established women with more years of experience in the United States, who speak some English, who have a car, and who have job references. Because their own position is more secure, they are also more likely to have their children here. And because they tend to work fewer hours per week, have greater flex-ibility in scheduling, and earn higher wages than the live-ins, they can live with and care for their children.

With respect to their ability to care for their own children, live-out nanny/housekeepers fall between live-ins and weekly cleaners—predictably, since they are also in an intermediate position in their earnings, rigidity of schedule, and working hours. Live-out domestic workers, according to the survey, earn $5.90 an hour and work an average workweek of thirty-five hours, and 42 percent of those who are mothers reported having at least one of their children in their country of origin.

The Dominance of Central American and Mexican Immigrant Women

Paid domestic work has long been a racialized and gendered occupation, but why today are Central American women hugely over-represented in these jobs in Los Angeles in comparison with Mexicans (whose immigrant population is of course many times larger)? In the survey I conducted of 153 Westside Latina domestic workers, 75 percent of the respondents were from Central America; of those, most were from El Salvador and Guatemala. And in census counts, Salvadoran and Guatemalan women are, respectively, twelve times and thirteen times more likely than the general population to be engaged in private domestic work in Los Angeles.[20] Numerous studies paint a similar picture in other major U.S. cities, such as Washington, D.C., Houston, and San Francisco; one naturally wonders why this should be so.[21]

In Los Angeles, the heavy concentration of Central American women in paid domestic work is partially explained by the location of L.A.'s primary Central American immigrant neighborhood, the Pico-Union/Westlake area, just west of the small, high-rise downtown. As UCLA sociologist David Lopez and his colleagues explain, "A large proportion of Central Americans tend to reside closer to the middle-class neighborhoods of the Westside and the San Fernando Valley . . . while Mexicans are concentrated

Table 2. Type of Domestic Work, Marital Status, and Location of Children

	Live-ins (percent) (n = 30)	Live-outs (percent) (n = 64)	Housecleaners (percent) (n = 59)
Single (includes the widowed, divorced, or separated)	87	55	54
Married	13	45	46
Domestic Workers with Children	*(n =16)*	*(n = 53)*	*(n = 45)*
All children in United States	18	58	76
At least one child "back home"	82	42	24

in the more isolated areas east and south of Downtown Los Angeles."[22] It is certainly quicker to drive or take a bus to the Westside from the Pico Union area than it is from East L.A. But there is more to this story than spatial location and L.A. transportation systems: distinct migration patterns have also influenced these occupational concentrations.

Mexican migration to the United States goes back over a hundred years, initially driven by labor recruitment programs designed to bring in men to work in agriculture. Since the late 1960s, it has shifted from a primarily male population of temporary or sojourner workers to one that includes women and entire families; these newcomers have settled in rural areas, cities, and suburbs throughout the United States, but disproportionately in California. Many Mexican women who migrated in the 1970s and 1980s were accompanied by their families and were aided by rich social networks; the latter helped prevent the urgency that leads new immigrants to take live-in jobs. Even those unmarried Mexican women who did migrate on their own, despite being opposed and sometimes stigmatized by their family and community, were often assisted by friends and more sympathetic family members. By the 1990s, more unmarried Mexican women were going north, encouraged in part by help from female friends and kin. When Mexican women arrive in the United States, many of them enjoy access to well-developed, established communities whose members have long been employed in various industries, particularly agriculture, construction, hotels, food-processing plants, and garment factories. Compared to their Central American peers, Mexican women are more likely to have financial support from a husband; because fewer Mexican immigrant women *must* work outside their home, they have lower rates of overall participation in the labor force than do Central American women.[23] Their social networks also give Mexican women greater variety in their employment options; paid domestic work is only one of their alternatives.

Salvadoran and Guatemalan women migrating to the United States have done so under different circumstances than Mexican women. For Central Americans coming to *el norte*, there was no long-standing labor program recruiting men who could then bring, or encourage the migration of, their wives and daughters. In fact, as Terry Repak's study shows, some of the early pioneers of Salvadoran migration to Washington, D.C., were women, themselves informally recruited by individual members of the diplomatic corps precisely because they were desired as private domestics.[24] More significantly, Salvadoran and Guatemalan women and men left their countries in haste, often leaving their children behind, as they fled the civil wars, political violence, and economic upheaval of the 1980s. Theirs are immigrant communities that subsisted without legal status for nearly two decades, grew rapidly, and remain very poor. Even Guatemalan and Salvadoran women who arrived in the United States in the late 1980s and early 1990s could not count on finding communities of well-established compatriots who could quickly and efficiently situate them in jobs in restaurants, hotels, factories, or other industries. In fact, as some of the most compelling ethnographies of Salvadorans in San Francisco and on Long Island have shown, Central Americans' relatively shallow U.S. roots have left their social networks extremely impoverished and sometimes fractured.[25] For Central American women arriving on their own, without husbands and children in tow, desperate and lacking information about jobs—and at a crucial historical moment when American families were seeking to resolve their own child care and housekeeping problems—live-in jobs were both attractive and available.

Family structures and marriage patterns may have also contributed to the preponderance of Central American women in paid domestic work. El Salvador has traditionally had one of the lowest marriage rates in the hemisphere, especially among the urban poor, where common-law marriages and legacies of internal and intra-Central America labor migration—mostly for work on coffee plantations—have encouraged the formation of female-headed households.[26] Thus Salvadoran women have been more likely to migrate on their own and accept live-in jobs.[27] Their large numbers in this lowest rung of domestic work would then explain their eventual disproportionate concentration in all types of private paid domestic work, following the pattern discussed above.

The experience of Central American women might also be compared to that of Asian immigrant women, who have been entering the United States at increasing rates. The latter are an extremely heterogeneous group, but on average—and this is particularly true of Chinese, Indian, and Filipina women—they arrive with much higher levels of education, better English language skills, and more professional credentials than do their Latina peers. They are also more likely to have legal status; and members of some groups, especially Korean immigrant women, enjoy access to jobs in family businesses and ethnic enclaves.[28] At the same time, the generally poorer and less-educated women from Vietnam, Laos, and Cambodia have been able to withstand periods of underemployment and unemployment because they are officially sanctioned political refugees and therefore enjoy access to welfare and resettlement assistance from the federal government. While some individual Asian immigrant women are working in paid domestic work, they have not developed social networks that channel them into this niche.

It is particularly striking that Filipina immigrants predominate in this occupation elsewhere around the globe, but not in the United States. Worldwide, about two-thirds of Filipina migrants in countries as different as Italy, Canada, Hong Kong, Taiwan, Singapore, Saudi Arabia, and Jordan, do paid domestic work; but in the United States, their high levels of education and fluent English enable most of them to enter higher status occupations that require more skills than does domestic work. In 1990, 71 percent of the Filipinas in the United States were working in managerial, professional, technical/sales, and administrative support jobs, and only 17 percent were employed in service jobs.[29] They are disproportionately concentrated in the health professions, the result of formal recruitment programs designed to fill U.S. nursing shortages.[30] Experience in the health professions leads many Filipinas to take jobs in elder care; and though some work as nanny/housekeepers in Los Angeles, many of them as live-ins, in my numerous discussions with employers, Latina employees, attorneys, and owners and employees of domestic employment agencies, no one ever mentioned Filipina housecleaners.

Nevertheless, Filipina immigrants are doing paid domestic work in the United States. Interviews conducted by Rhacel Parreñas with twenty-six Filipina domestic workers in Los Angeles reveal that many of these women have college diplomas and are working in homes because they are older and face age discrimination; they tend to earn more as care providers for the elderly ($425 per week) and more as nanny/housekeepers ($350 per week) than do Latina immigrants in these same jobs.[31] When it comes to caring for their children, some employers prefer Filipina nanny/housekeepers because they speak English well (English is the official language of schools and universities in the Philippines), and because they tend to be highly educated. Paradoxically, these qualities may predispose some employers to *not* choose Filipinas as domestic employees. At three domestic employment agencies, the owners told me that they rarely placed Filipina job applicants, because they were deemed "uppity," demanding, and likely to lie about their references. Racial preferences, as the next section suggests, shape the formation of Latina domestic workers and their employment in Los Angeles.

Narratives of Racial Preferences

In a race-conscious society, everyone has racial preferences and prejudices, and Latina domestic workers and the women who employ them are no exception. When choosing someone to work in their homes, many employers prefer Latinas, because as "others" in language, race-ethnicity, and social class, they are outside white, English-speaking, middle-class social circles and are thus seen as unlikely to reveal family secrets and intimacies. If they do tell someone about the family fight they witnessed, that someone is likely to be another Latina nanny or a member of their own family—in either case, no one who matters to the employers. This fear of exposure sometimes prevents employers from choosing white, English-speaking job candidates. "She was non-Hispanic, and I wasn't sure if I could trust her," said one woman of a prospective employee. Another employer had been advised not to hire a white woman as a nanny/housekeeper because an immigrant would be less likely to recognize a philanthropic

family's name and to engage in bribery or kidnapping. Other women told me that they did not want a European au pair or midwestern (white) teenager taking care of their children because they would probably be young, irresponsible teens, more interested in cavorting with boyfriends, cruising the beach, and stargazing in Hollywood than in doing their job. Employers may also prefer to hire Latina nannies, as research conducted by Julia Wrigley suggests, because they view them as more submissive than whites.[32]

While some of the older employers I interviewed had hired African American housecleaners and domestics in the past, none were now doing so. Of the relatively few black women working in paid domestic work in contemporary Los Angeles, most are immigrants from Belize and Brazil, and some employers remain adamantly opposed to hiring black women to work in their homes. One domestic employment agency owner told me that some clients had requested than he never send black women to interview for a job. And at an informal luncheon, arranged by one of the employer interviewees, one of them cleared her throat and then offered, with some awkward hesitation, "Uhm, ah, I would never hire a black woman. I'd be too scared to, and I'd be especially scared if her boyfriend came around." The women, all of them relatively upper-class white matrons, had nodded in silent agreement. The old stereotype of the bossy black maid is apparently alive and well, now joined by newer terrifying images associated with young black men; but since African American women are not pursuing domestic work jobs in Los Angeles, most employers need never confront their own racial fears directly. It is, after all, Latina immigrant women who are queuing up for domestic jobs in private homes.

When I talked with them, most employers expressed genuine appreciation for the effort, dedication, and work that these women put into their homes and children. They viewed Latina domestic workers as responsible, trustworthy, and reliable employees who have "a really strong work ethic." And while plenty of employers spoke at length about Latina women as ideally suited to caring for children, relying on images of Latinas as exceptionally warm, patient, and loving mothers, there was no similar racialized image of cleanliness. No one said, for instance, "She cleans like a Mexican." Such a phrase may sound offensive, but the absence of any such generalization is striking when nearly everyone hired to do cleaning in Los Angeles is Mexican or Central American.

Indeed, some of the employers I interviewed did make this kind of statement—to associate their own northern European heritage with superior cleaning and hygiene. A few of them offered remarks such as "People associate very clean homes with Dutch people," or "My mother's German and she cleans, you know, like Germans clean." These women did not necessarily claim that they were excellent cleaners, only that they belonged to racial-ethnic groups associated with cleanliness. None of them described their domestic employees as "dirty," but the adjective has been commonly featured in racial epithets directed at Mexicans in the Southwest and at domestic workers just about everywhere. The historian Phyllis Palmer, who has written compellingly about dirt, domesticity, and racialized divisions among women, notes that while dirt and housework connote inferior morality, white middle-class women transcend these connotations by employing women different from themselves to do the work. "Dirtiness," Palmer notes, "appears always in a constellation of the suspect qualities that, along with sexuality, immorality, laziness, and ignorance, justify social rankings of race, class and gender. The 'slut,' initially a shorthand for 'slattern' or kitchen maid, captures all of these personifications in a way unimaginable in a male persona."[33]

Employers are not the only ones who hold strong racial-ethnic preferences and prejudices. Latina domestic workers at the bus stops, at the agencies, and in the public parks readily agreed on who were their worst employers: Armenians, Iranians, Asians, Latinos, blacks, and Jews, especially Israeli Jews. "I'll never work again for *un chino!*" or "*Los armenios* [Armenians] are the worst," they tell each other. These statements were echoed in the individual interviews, as well as by the preferences job candidates register at employment agencies, and they seem to mirror what Latino men who work as day laborers think about their similarly racialized employers in Los Angeles.[34] Anyone marked as "nonwhite," it seems, is at risk of being denounced as a cheap, abusive, and oppressive employer, one to be avoided at all costs.

There are a number of factors at work here. Many of the employers in these racial-ethnic groups are immigrants themselves, albeit entrepreneurial and professional immigrants with substantially more resources than the Latinas they hire to care for their homes and children. Many had belonged to elites in their countries of origin, accustomed to having servants in their homes who would be expected to perform all sorts of jobs on demand. Some of them bring these expectations with them when they come to the United States. When Latina domestic workers are expected to massage the *señora's* feet with oil, or scrub the kitchen floor on their hands and knees, they take offense. Others are wholly unprepared to iron Hindu saris, or to follow kosher food preparation and serving practices in the homes of Orthodox Jews. At the same time, the immigrant and ethnic employers may have been accustomed in their countries of origin to paying slave wages, and the tenuous financial situations of some makes them unable to pay minimum wage. Some newly arrived women who find their first job working as a live-in for other working-class Latino immigrant families may receive as little as $25 or $50 a week in exchange for their round-the-clock services.

Latina immigrants also operate under racist assumptions, many of which they learn in the United States. They quickly pick up the country's racial hierarchies and racist stereotypes. "Jews are cheap," "Mexican Americans and blacks are lazy," or "*Los chinos* are too bossy," they say.

The regional racial hierarchy also fixes Jews, Armenians, and Iranians in low positions. "*Los Americanos,*" the term they typically use to refer to employers marked only "white," are almost never singled out by ethnicity and are rarely criticized or negatively labeled as a group.

Conversely, Latina domestic workers single out the race of particular employers who happen to be both "bad employers" and "racialized" as nonwhite. One Mexican housecleaner who maintained that Latino employers were among the most exploitative was Lupe Vélez. When I probed why she felt this way, she cited as evidence her experiences with one employer, a man from Monterrey, Mexico. A large, verbally abusive man, he had called her a pig, he went out of his way to deny her food when she sat down to eat with his family, and he had unfairly accused her of scratching and ruining a stove top. These deeply felt, painful experiences were recounted tearfully.

Yet as we talked longer, I discovered that in Los Angeles, Lupe had worked in three different Latino homes; she spoke of a Mexican American teacher who had treated her well and paid her fairly. Mutual fondness, respect, and closeness had grown between the two, who had unsuccessfully conspired at matchmaking between their young adult children. How could she maintain that Latinos were the "worst" employers when in fact a Mexican American had been among her best employers? In recalling her bad experience with the Mexican man, Lupe Vélez singled out his racial-ethnic identity. As she recalled that painful experience, his being Mexican and consistently acting abusively toward her became the most salient features about him. She applied "Latino," a racial marker, to this man, labeled an abusive, bad employer, but not to the teacher whom she had favored.

I suspect that when Latina domestic workers denounce Jewish employers, a similar process is at work. In those cases, they may only identify as Jewish those employers who are abusive and who are, as Orthodox Jews or recently emigrated Israeli Jews, unambiguously marked as Jewish. They might not recognize the other Jews for whom they work. Or perhaps Latina domestic workers' disdain for Jewish employers is testimony to the force of contemporary anti-Semitism. It is no small irony that a major provider of legal services for Latina domestic workers in Los Angeles is a Jewish nonprofit organization.[35]

Some Latina domestic workers related counter-narratives, criticizing their peers for relying on racial stereotypes and hasty racial judgments. One Salvadoran housecleaner cited her Moroccan employer as one of the most gracious because she always served her a hot lunch, sitting down to chat with her; another related her appreciation of an African American bachelor, an ex-basketball player, who kept a messy house but paid her very generously; still another felt warmly toward her Korean employer who did not pay well, but who passed many choice housecleaning jobs on to her. Yet the voices of these women were drowned out by the louder, frequently blanket condemnations that other Latina domestic workers offered about their racially marked minority and immigrant employers. Amid the public clamor of racialized nativism that propelled California ballot initiatives against health and education services for undocumented immigrants and their children, against affirmative action, and against bilingual education (Propositions 187, 209, and 227 respectively), Latina immigrant domestic workers learn their own version of regional racism.

In this chapter, I conveyed briefly some of the life textures and the daily trials and triumphs experienced by Latina immigrants who work as housecleaners, live-out nanny/housekeepers, and live-in nanny/housekeepers. The Mexican, Salvadoran, and Guatemalan women who occupy these jobs come from diverse class, regional, and cultural locations, and they bring different expectations to their jobs. Once in the United States, however, they share a set of similar experiences, in part because of the way that their domestic work is structured.

Notes

1. Glenn 1986:141.
2. Lacher 1997:E1.
3. One nanny/housekeeper told me that a *señora* had admonished her for picking a bag of fruit, and wanted to charge her for it; another claimed that her employer had said she would rather watch the fruit fall off the branches and rot than see her eat it.
4. Many Latina domestic workers do not know the amount of their hourly wages; and because the lines between their work and nonwork tend to blur, live-in nanny/housekeepers have particular difficulty calculating them. In the survey questionnaire I asked live-in nanny/housekeepers how many days a week they worked, what time they began their job, and what time they ended, and I asked them to estimate how many hours off they had during an average workday (39 percent said they had no time off, but 32 percent said they had a break of between one and three hours). Forty-seven percent of the women said they began their workday at 7 A.M. or earlier, with 62 percent ending their workday at 7 P.M. or later. With the majority of them (71 percent) working five days a week, their average workweek was sixty-four hours. This estimate may at first glance appear inflated; but consider a prototypical live-in nanny/housekeeper who works, say, five days a week, from 7 A.M. until 9 P.M., with one and a half hours off during the children's nap time (when she might take a break to lie down or watch television). Her on-duty work hours would total sixty-four and a half hours per week. The weekly pay of live-in nanny/housekeepers surveyed ranged from $130 to $400, averaging $242. Dividing this figure by sixty-four yields an hourly wage of $3.80. None of the live-in nanny/housekeepers were charged for room and board—this practice is regulated by law—but 86 percent said they brought food with them to their jobs. The majority reported being paid in cash.
5. See, e.g., Employment Classified Section 2, *Los Angeles Times*, June 6, 1999, G9.
6. Clark-Lewis 1994:123. "After an average of seven years," she notes in her analysis of African American women who had migrated from the South to Washington, D.C., in the early twentieth century, "all of the migrant women grew to dread their live-in situation. They saw their occupation as harming all aspects of their life" (124). Nearly all of these women transitioned into day work in private homes. This pattern is being repeated by Latina immigrants in Los Angeles today, and it reflects local labor market opportunities and constraints. In Houston, Texas, where many Mayan Guatemalan immigrant women today work as live-ins, research by Jacqueline Maria Hagan (1998) points to the tremendous obstacles they face in leaving live-in work. In Houston, housecleaning is dominated by better-established immigrant women, by Chicanas and, more recently, by the commercial cleaning companies—so it is hard for the Maya to secure those jobs. Moreover, Hagan finds that over time, the Mayan women who take live-in jobs see their own social networks contract, further reducing their internal job mobility.
7. Several factors explain the shift to day work, including urbanization, interurban transportation systems, and smaller private residences. Historians have also credited the job preferences of African American domestic workers, who rejected the constraints of live-in work and chose to live with their own families and communities, with helping to promote this shift in the urban North after 1900 (Katzman 1981; Clark-Lewis 1994:129–35). In many urban regions of the United States, the shift to day work accelerated during World War I, so that live-out arrangements eventually became more prevalent (Katzman 1981; Palmer 1989). Elsewhere, and for different groups of domestic workers, these transitions happened later in the twentieth century. Evelyn Nakano Glenn (1986:143) notes that Japanese immigrant and Japanese American women employed in domestic work in the San Francisco Bay Area moved out of live-in jobs and into modernized day work in the years after World War II.
8. Katzman 1981; Glenn 1986.
9. Wrigley 1995.
10. Keep in mind that the survey questionnaire was administered at three different types of sites: bus stops, ESL evening classes, and parks where nannies congregate with the children in their charge. Housecleaners who drive and have their own cars, and who speak some English, typically earn more money and are able to clean more houses per week. Because my survey is biased toward Latina domestic workers who ride the buses and attend ESL classes, those housecleaners earning higher wages are not taken into account.
11. Romero 1992.
12. In addition to the jobs of live-in nanny/housekeepers, live-out nanny/housekeepers, and weekly or biweekly housecleaners, an increasingly important and growing segment of the domestic workforce is engaged in elder care. That, too, is organized in different ways; and though the occupation lies beyond the parameters of this study (much of it is formally organized and contracted for by the state or medical organizations), some Latina immigrants are privately contracted for jobs as elders' companions and caretakers, as *damas de compañía.*
13. Smith 1973; McBride 1976.
14. The only news report of INS raids involving nannies working in private homes in Los Angeles that came to my attention as I did this research involved a nanny working for a top-ranking Latino INS agent, Jorge Guzman. In 1996 armed plainclothes INS agents illegally raided Guzman's home, and allegedly fondled and made sexual advances toward the domestic worker. Guzman claimed that the raid was part of a ten-year program of internal anti-Latino harassment directed at him. After he filed suit, the U.S. Justice Department agreed to pay him $400,000 to settle (McDonnell 1999).
15. Personal communication, Cynthia Cranford, March 1999; and Cleeland 1999a.
16. Rollins 1985; Glenn 1986; Romero 1992. See Romero 1997 for a study focusing on the perspective of domestic workers' children. Although the majority of respondents in that study were children of day workers, and none appear to have been children of transnational mothers, they still recall that their mothers' occupation had significant costs for them.
17. Hondagneu-Sotelo and Avila 1997.
18. Central American women seem more likely than Mexican women to leave their children in their country of origin, even if their husbands are living with them in the United States, perhaps because of the multiple dangers and costs associated with undocumented travel from Central America to the United States. The civil wars of the 1980s, continuing violence and economic uncertainty, greater difficulties and costs associated with crossing multiple national borders, and stronger cultural legacies of socially sanctioned consensual unions may also contribute to this pattern for Central Americans.
19. Glenn 1986; Dill 1988.
20. The figures on Salvadoran and Guatemalan women are taken from an analysis of the 1990 census data by the sociologists David E. Lopez, Eric Popkin, and Edward Telles (1996); they also found that Mexican immigrants were only 2.3 times as likely as those in the general population to be engaged in paid domestic work.
21. See Salzinger 1991; Hagan 1994, 1998; Repak 1995.
22. Lopez, Popkin, and Telles 1996:298.

23. According to 1990 PUMS Census data, about 70 percent of Central American women between the ages of 24 and 60 in Los Angeles County are in the labor force, while only 56 percent of their Mexican peers are. Among this same group, 71 percent of Mexican immigrant women but only 56 percent of their Central American peers are married and living with a spouse. To put it even more starkly, 28 percent of Mexican immigrant women and 43 percent of Central American women report living with family members or adults other than their spouses.

24. Repak 1995.

25. Mahler 1995; Menjívar 2000.

26. Some studies estimate that as many as 50 percent of poor households in San Salvador were formed by "free unions" rather than marriage by law. This pattern is related not just to internal and intra-Central American labor migration but also to urban poverty, as there is no need to secure inheritance rights when there is no property to share (Nieves 1979; Repak 1995).

27. Countries with traditions of consensual marriages afford women more migration opportunities (Donato 1992).

28. A survey conducted in Los Angeles and Orange County in 1986 revealed that 45 percent of Korean immigrants were self-employed; many were business owners in the Korean ethnic economy (Min 1996:48).

29. Mar and Kim 1994

30. Between 1966 and 1985 nearly 25,000 Filipina nurses came to work in the United States, and another 10,000 came between 1989 and 1991. Filipinas who were formally recruited through government programs then informally recruited their friends and former nursing school classmates (Ong and Azores 1994).

31. Parreñas, in press.

32. Wrigley 1995.

33. Palmer 1988:140.

34. Personal communication with UCLA professor Abel Valenzuela, fall 1998.

35. Bet Tzedek Legal Services.

Section 2: Demographics, Society and Culture
Assessment and Application

1. Compare and contrast two issues important to Hispanics in the *Time Magazine* Hispanic portrait that are also critical to a Chicano community in your area.

2. What are the future implications for public education given the current age distribution of Hispanics?

3. What regional settlement trends can you discern for the Hispanic population based on the article on Mexican demography in the U.S.?

4. Trace the academic achievement gap of Hispanics in Marta Tienda's *et al* chapter and compare and contrast that with the achievement data in a school district in your area?

5. How would you characterize Hispanic integration in the four social realms examined in Marta Tienda's *et al* chapter?

6. What are some of the major environmental problems faced by the transnational metroplex formed by El Paso, Texas-Ciudad Juárez, Chihuahua?

7. How extensively should environmental organizations include community members in the formulation of policy and specific interventions?

8. Identify a major environmental issue in a community and the principal actors involved in its public portrayal.

9. What are the leading health problems facing the Hispanic population?

10. Why is it important to develop a Latino health agenda based on Latino metrics?

11. What are some explanations for the lower incomes of Mexican Americans?

12. How do Mexican-American women in the labor force address economic and domestic issues and cultural expectations?

13. Characterize the experience of Mexican **immigrant** workers in the U.S., in terms of their ability to attain upward socioeconomic mobility within their generation.

14. How has NAFTA and the "maquiladora" industry in northern Mexico affected the rate of Mexican female immigration to the U.S.?

15. Is the success of Mexican immigrant women worker organizations like Mujer Obrera transportable to other communities? Why?

16. Why do Mexican and Central American women predominate in the domestic worker economy?

17. How do Latina immigrant nannies view American parenting practices? Why?

18. How do Latina immigrant domestic employees manage to care for their own children while employed?

Section 2: Suggested Readings

Abalos, David T. (2002). *The Latino Male: A Radical Redefinition*. Boulder, CO: Lynne Rienner.

Aguirre-Molina, Marilyn and Molina, Carlos W. (2003). *A Public Health Reader: Latina Health in the United States*. San Francisco, CA: Jossey–Bass.

Aldama, Arturo J. and Quiñonez, Naomi H. (2002). *Decolonial Voices: Chicana and Chicano Cultural Studies in the 21st Century*. Bloomington, IN: Indiana University Press.

American Cancer Society. (2003). *Cancer Facts & Figures for Hispanics/Latinos 2003–2005*. Atlanta, GA: American Cancer Society.

Anzaldúa, Gloria. (1987). *Borderlands/La Frontera: The New Mestiza*. San Francisco, CA: Aunte Books.

Arreola, Daniel D. (2004). *Hispanic Spaces, Latino Places: Community and Cultural Diversity in Contemporary America*. Austin, TX: University of Texas Press.

Bach, Robert. (1993). *Changing Relations, Newcomers and Established Residents in U.S. Communities*. New York, NY: The Ford Foundation/The National Board of the Changing Relations Project.

Barry, Tom and Sims, Beth. (1994). *The Challenge of Cross-Border Environmentalism: The U.S- Mexico Case*. Albuquerque, NM: Resource Center Press.

Bonilla, Frank; Meléndez, Edwin; Morales, Rebecca, and Torres, María de Los Angeles. (1998). *Borderless Borders: U.S. Latinos, Latin Americans, and the Paradox of Interdependence*. Philadelphia, PA: Temple University Press.

Briggs, Vernon N.; Fogel, Walter, and Schmidt, Fred H. (1977). *The Chicano Worker*. Austin, TX: University of Texas Press.

Byrne, John; Glover, Leigh, and Martínez, Cecilia. (2002). *Environmental Justice: Discourses in International Political Economy, Energy and Environmental Policy*. Somerset, NJ: Transaction Publisher.

Cafferty, Pastora San Juan and Engstrom, David W. (2004). *Hispanics in the United States: An Agenda for the Twenty-First Century*. New Brunswick, NJ: Transaction Publisher.

Dohan, Daniel. (2003). *The Price of Poverty: Money, Work, and Culture in the Mexican American Barrio*. Berkeley, CA: University of California Press.

Flores, Estevan T. (1983). Chicanos and Sociological Research: 1970–1980. In Isidro D. Ortiz, (Ed.). *Chicanos and the Social Sciences: A Decade of Research and Development (1970–1980)* (pp. 9–18). Santa Barbara, CA: Chicano Studies Center, University of California, Santa Barbara.

Garza, Hedda. (2001). *Latinas: Hispanic Women in the United States*. Albuquerque, NM: University of New Mexico Press.

GAO. (2000). *U.S.-Mexico Border: Despite Some Progress, Environmental Infrastructure Challenges Remain, GAO/NSIAD-00-26*, March. Washington, D.C.: United States Government Accounting Office.

González, Arturo. (2002). *Mexican Americans & the U.S. Economy: Quest for Buenos Días*. Tucson, AZ: University of Arizona Press.

González, Manny and González-Ramos, Gladys. (2005). *Mental Health Care for New Hispanics Immigrants: Innovative Approaches in Contemporary Clinical Practice*. Binghamton, NY: Haworth Press.

González, Norma. (2005). *I Am My Language: Discourses of Women and Children in the Borderlands*. Tucson, AZ: University of Arizona Press.

González, Ray. (Ed.). (1996). *Muy Macho: Latino Men Confront Their Manhood*. New York, NY: Anchor Books.

Griswold del Castillo, Richard. (1984). *La Familia: Chicano Families in the Urban Southwest, 1848 to the Present*. South Bend, IN: University of Notre Dame Press.

Gutiérrez, David G. (1995). *Walls and Mirrors: Mexican Americans, Mexican Immigrants, and the Politics of Ethnicity*. Berkeley, CA: University of California Press.

Herzog, Lawrence M. (Ed.). (2000). *Shared Space: Rethinking the U. S.-Mexico Border Environment*. San Diego, CA: Center for U.S.-Mexican Studies, University of California, San Diego.

HispanTelligence. (2005). *The U.S. Hispanic Economy in Transition: Facts, Figures and Trends*. Santa Barbara, CA: Hispanic Business.

Hispanic Health Concerns. (2005). *The Hispanic Outlook in Higher Education*. Vol. 15, (18).

Jenning, James. (2003). *Welfare Reform and the Revitalization of Inner City Neighborhoods*. Ann Arbor, MI: Michigan State University Press.

Jourdane, Maurice. (2005). *The Struggle for the Health and Legal Protection of Farm Workers: El Cortito*. Houston, TX: Arte Público Press.

Kaplan, Caren; Alarcón, Norma, and Moallem, Minoo. (1999). *Between Woman and Nation: Nationalism, Transnational Feminisms, and the State*. Durham, NC: Duke University Press.

Keefe, Susan E. and Padilla, Amador M. (1987). *Chicano Ethnicity*. Albuquerque, NM: University of New Mexico Press.

Kingsolver, Barbara. (1996). *Holding the Line: Women in the Great Arizona Mine Strike of 1983*. Ithaca, NY: Cornell University Press.

Kopinak, Kathryn. (2004). *The Social Costs of Industrial Growth in Northern Mexico*. San Diego, CA: Center for U.S.-Mexican Studies, University of California, San Diego.

Lorey, David. (1999). *The U.S.-Mexican Border in the Twentieth Century*. Wilmington, DE: Scholarly Resources Books.

Lui, Meizhu; Gluckman, Amy; Collins, Chuck; Leodar-Wright, Betsy; Offner, Amy and Scharf, Adria. (2004). *The Wealth Inequality Reader*. Boston, MA: Dollars and Sense.

Martínez, Oscar I. (2001). *More Thorns than Roses: Mexican American-Origin People in the United States Since 1900*. Tucson, AZ: University of Arizona Press.

Milkman, Ruth and Wong, Kent. (2000). *Voices from the Front Lines: Organizing Immigrant Workers in Los Angeles*. Los Angeles, CA: Center for Labor Research and Education.

Mumme, Stephen P.; Pineda, Nícolas, and Cruz Pineiro, Rodolfo. (2001). *The Future of the U.S.-Mexico Border: Population, Development, and Water*. Washington, D.C.: Woodrow Wilson International Center for Scholars.

Ochoa, Gilda L. (2004). *Becoming Neighbors in a Mexican American Community: Power, Conflict and Solidarity*. Austin, TX: University of Texas Press.

Oehmke Loustaunau, Martha and Sánchez-Bane, Mary. (Eds.). (1999). *Life, Death, and In-Between on the U.S.-Mexico Border: Así es la Vida*. Westport, CT: Greenwood Publishing Group.

Passel, Jeffrey S. (1994). *How Much do Immigrants Really Cost?* Claremont, CA: Tomás Rivera Center.

Peña, Devon G. (1998). *Chicano Culture, Ecology, Politics: Subversive Kin*. Tucson, AZ: University of Arizona Press.

Portes, Alejandro and Rumbaut, Rubén G. (1996). *Immigrant America: A Portrait* (2nd ed.). Berkeley, CA: University of California Press.

Rothenberg, Daniel. (1998). *With These Hands: The Hidden World of Migrant Farmworkers Today*. New York, NY: Harcourt Brace & Company.

Romano, V., Octavio I. (1968). The Anthropology and Sociology of the Mexican Americans. *El Grito.II* (1).

Romano, V., Octavio I. (1968–69). The Historical and Intellectual Presence of Mexican Americans. *El Grito. II* (2).

Romano, V., Octavio I. (1970). Social Science Objectivity, and the Chicanos. *El Grito, IV* (1).

Russel, Joe; Corvalán, Marcos, and Guadalupe, Patricia. (2006). Elite Women Series. *Hispanic Business Magazine*. Pp. 27–58.

Treviño, Roberto R. (2006). *The Church in the Barrio: Mexican American Ethno-Catholicism in Houston*. Chapel Hill, NC: University of North Carolina Press.

Segura, Denise A. and Pesquera, Beatriz M. (1995). Chicana Feminisms: Their Political Context and Contemporary Expressions. In Antonia Darder and Rodolfo Torres, (Eds.), *The Latino Studies Reader: Culture, Economy and Society*. Malden, MA: Blackwell Publishers.

Spalding, Mark J. (1999). *Sustainable Development in San Diego-Tijuana*. San Diego, CA: Center for U.S.-Mexican Studies, University of California, San Diego.

Staudt, Kathleen A. (1998). *Free Trade?: Informal Economies at the U.S.-Mexico Border*. Philadelphia, PA: Temple University Press.

Tienda, Martha and Mitchell, Faith, (Editors, Panel on Hispanics in the United States). (2006). *Multiple Origins, Uncertain Destinies: Hispanics and the American Future*. Washington, D.C.: National Academies Press.

Tinjacá, Mabel. (2001). *¡Visión!: Hispanic Entrepreneurs in the United States*. Pleasant Hill, MO: Heritage Publishing Company.

Tobar, Héctor. (2005). *Translation Nation: Defining a New American Identity in the Spanish-Speaking United States*. New York, NY: Penguin Group.

United States-Mexico Border Health Commission. (2003). *Healthy Border 2010: An Agenda for Improving Health on the United States-Mexico Border*. El Paso, TX: United States-Mexico Border Health Commission. <www.borderhealth.org>

Valle, Víctor M. and Torres, Rodolfo D. (2000). *Latino Metropolis*. Minneapolis, MN: University of Minnesota Press.

Velásquez, Roberto J.; Arellano, Leticia M., and McNeill, Brian W. (2004). *The Handbook of Chicana/o Psychology and Mental Health*. Mahwah, NJ: Lawrence Erlbaum Associates.

Vélez-Ibáñez, Carlos and Sampaio, Anna. (2002). *Transnational Latina/o Communities: Politics, Processes, and Cultures*. Lanham, MD: Rowman & Littlefield Publishers.

Vila, Pablo. (2005). *Border Identifications: Narratives of Religion, Gender, and Class on the U.S.- Mexico Border*. Austin, TX: University of Texas Press.

Williamson, Jeffery G. (2006). Global Migration. *Finance and Development Magazine*. Pp 23–27.

Section 2: Suggested Films and Videos

American Jobs
Spottsfilm
1223 Wilshire Blvd. #1565, Santa Monica, CA 90403

La Batalla de las Cruces: Protesta Social y Acciones
Colectivas en Torno de la Violencia Sexual en Ciudad
Juárez
CIESAS y Campo Imaginario

Cadillac Desert Series pt 1-4
PBS Home Video
1320 Braddock Avenue, Alexandria, VA 22314-1698

California and the American Dream
Berkeley Media LLC
2600 Tenth Street, Suite 626, Berkeley, CA 94710

The Changing Role of Hispanic Women
Films for the Humanities and Sciences
P.O. Box 2053, Princeton, NJ 08543-2053

De Mujer a Mujer, 1992
Women Make Movies
New York, NY

Desert Semaphore: The Chihuahuan Desert Trilogy:
Part III
Chihuahuan Desert Research Institute
P.O. Box 1334, Alpine, TX 79831

Environmental Racism
Third World Newsreel
545 Eighth Avenue, 10th Floor, New York, NY 10018

The Forgotten Americans, 2000
Galán Incorporated Television and Film
5524 Bee Caves Rd. Suite B-5 Austin, TX 78746

Hispanic Americans, 2000
Insight Media
2162 Broadway, New York, NY 10024-0621

Hispanic Americans: The Second Generation
Films for the Humanities and Sciences
P.O. Box 2053, Princeton, NJ 08543-2053

I Am Joaquín! 1969
El Teatro Campesino
San Juan Bautista, CA

Immigrants in New York
PBS
1320 Braddock Avenue, Alexandria, VA 22314-1698

The Invisible Mexicans of Deer Canyon
Gatekeeper Productions
8484 Harold Way, Los Angeles, CA 90069

IMPACT: Environmental Pollution on the U.S.-Mexico
Border, 1997
CNN
New York, NY

Latinos: The Life of the Spirit, 1992
Films for the Humanities and Sciences
P. O. Box 2053, Princeton, NJ 08543-2053

The Latino Family
Films for the Humanities and Sciences
P.O. Box 2053, Princeton, NJ 08543-2053

Maquilapolis: City of Factories
California Newsreel
P.O. Box 2284, South Burlington, VT 05407

Mixed Feelings: San Diego/Tijuana
PBS
P.O. Box 86738, 900 N. Alameda Ave.,
Los Angeles, CA 90086

Rancho California (Por Favor)
Berkeley Media LLC
2600 Tenth Street, Suite 626, Berkeley, CA 94710

The Three Stages of Latino Life, 1992
Films for the Humanities and Sciences
P. O. Box 2053, Princeton, NJ 08543-2053

What's Going On?: Poverty in America
Zenger Media
P.O. Box 802, Culver City, CA 90232

Yo Soy Chicano, 1972
The Cinema Guild
New York, NY

Political and Socioeconomic Perspectives

This section provides an overview of the salient Chicano issues in American politics and efforts to address them, in a cumulative continuation of the historical, demographics and sociocultural sections. While Chicano involvement in American politics dates back to the Mexican-American War, the contemporary orientation of this text forces a more recent point of departure-the Chicano Movement.

Ignacio García initiates this section by analyzing the academic reinterpretation of the Chicano experience during the 1960s and 1970s that lead into, among other things, a positive and emancipating view of Chicanos, an interpretation of the Chicano experience by Chicanos, and the academic development of Chicano Studies. In tandem, Alma M. García discusses the Development of Chicana Feminist Discourse, bringing into focus the origins of Chicana feminism within the context of the Chicano Movement. Not only did women question traditional roles within the family, Chicana feminists drew up their own political agenda, which emerged from their own political activity and their intellectual movement. Chicana feminists were the first to question the Chicano paradigm and insisted that scholars examine not only race and class, but also gender.

David Engstrom tackles the critical issue of Hispanic immigration and its political importance to the nation and the Hispanic population. A summary of American immigration policy and a historical analysis of large-scale Hispanic immigration are followed by a presentation of issues like NAFTA, welfare utilization, fiscal impact, and the highly controversial border enforcement policy and practice, which change almost by the day. An examination of current immigration trends and politics by Mortimer B. Zuckerman, Editor-in-Chief of the *U.S. News & World Report* concludes the immigration segment of this chapter. He complements Engstrom's portrayal of Hispanic immigration with a succinct analysis of the integration of Hispanics in American society, in the midst of national controversy and political upheaval. He concludes that the new waves of Hispanic immigrants will "enrich our nation, as million of immigrants before have."

The third stage of this section focuses on electoral politics, not at all unrelated to Hispanic immigration politics. First, Kim Geron broaches the question of what will be the face of Latino politics in the new millennium by connecting past struggles with contemporary gains. He examines strategies like the accommodation of other groups through coalition building and addressing class interests. Lisa Magaña incorporates the often missing, feminist perspective into the electoral debate. She captures the struggle for Latinas to attain elected office by relating the trajectories of Latina elected officials. She highlights the importance of community activism and Chicana activists in the political process, going so far as to probe binational activism. The 2005 mapping of the political landscape by the Pew Research Center brings the reader up-to-date with the major Hispanic political participation trends. Key findings covering the 2000–2004 period are followed by a data-based interpretation of the characteristics of Hispanics eligible to vote and their voting level in the 2004 elections. Perhaps this barometer may predict future levels of participation and political party affiliation in a fluid political environment that includes the variables and actors identified by Geron and Magaña.

Reinterpreting the Chicano Experience

Ignacio M. García

After Chicano activists rejected the liberal agenda and its prescription for integration, they set out to tackle another major obstacle to *la gente's* progress: history. They understood that the treatment of Mexican Americans was partly the result of the distorted view of them perpetuated by historians, social scientists, essayists, and the media in general. Although Mexican American middle-class reformers had taken on many of the stereotypes, few of them had ever attempted a fundamental reinterpretation of the history of Mexican Americans.[1] They had been content with emphasizing inclusion and telling "their" side of American history. Chicano activists believed, however, that for the barrios to develop the type of self-esteem and pride necessary for political action, Mexican Americans had to see themselves in a new light. They also had to shift the blame for their condition from themselves to mainstream society. Said José Angel Gutiérrez: "We're called apathetic, disorganized. We drink beer. Like to make babies. That we fight. That we're slow learners. That we're not . . . as 'ambitiously motivated' as an Anglo. That we're weird in terms of art and music. And everything that is applied to us is really a commentary on society, the Anglo. The problem is not us. The problem is white society."[2]

To Gutiérrez and other activists, the problems of the community were most often caused by external forces. Chicanos, after all, did not create low-paying jobs, did not build inadequate housing, did not set up inefficient schools, and did not write condescending or racist advertising jingles. They also did not hire policemen with violent streaks or transport powerful drugs from South America or Asia to the barrios. These problems had been forced upon a community that was faced with a relentless attack on its identity. Social scientists, according to Chicano activists, had continued to perpetuate stereotypes that were destructive to the self-esteem of the Mexican American community. Chicanos who chose to read the academic literature or the popular press came across countless references to their "apathy," "laziness," and self-victimization.[3] For many, Mexican Americans were either emotionally or intellectually unable to lift themselves up from their difficult conditions of poverty and illiteracy. They had been so socialized to accept their disadvantaged status that it had become part of the culture. This culture of poverty, argued social scientists, provided few, if any, of the tools to help Mexican Americans pull themselves out of the cycle of hopelessness in which they were caught.[4]

Chicanos also saw themselves as victims of history, though they did not see culture as at fault. Luis Valdez, founder of the Teatro Campesino, saw Mexican Americans as being treated as, and consequently acting like, a "colonized race . . . [whose] uniqueness . . . lies buried in the dust of conquest." The conquest had been not only a military one but a psychological one, since Mexican Americans had been cut off from their history.[5] The solution to this condition, according to Valdez, was to "reach into our people, in the . . . memory of their beginning."[6] Chicanos had to find a past unmarred by the conquest, and within that past find the prototype society where the early "Chicano" was unspoiled by Anglo-American society. David Sánchez, prime minister of the paramilitary group the Brown Berets, described it thus: "In the beginning . . . there were beautiful lands with all the living resources. . . . It was a paradise where the balance of nature kept everyone alive. . . . We were a proud people who perfected medicines . . . until strange ships came from an old world. . . . They came not to build, but to rule . . . at the cost of our blood."[7]

In that past, Chicanos searched for a reinterpretation of their existence that would uncover the myths and legends of the struggle for survival and provide the basis for a cultural and political renaissance. This new interpretation of the Chicano experience also sought to undo the years of biased scholarship that formed the core of what was known about the Mexican American. In 1968, Enriqueta Longeaux y Vásquez wrote: "The raza in the southwest . . . wants our history back. . . . Our cities, our mountains, and rivers were explored and settled by Indians and Spaniards, not pilgrims and wagon masters. The first cattle raisers, cowboys and farmers were raza. We weren't waiting here to be saved by the great white fathers."[8]

Octavio Romano was one of the first Chicano scholars to promote the new interpretation. An anthropologist at the University of California, Berkeley, he attacked much of the traditional scholarship on Mexican Americans by social scientists. In his most influential article, "The Anthropology and Sociology of the Mexican-American: The Distortion of Mexican-American History," Romano took on the academy: "Social science studies have dealt with Mexican Americans as an ahistoric people—with a place in history reserved for them only when they undergo some metamorphosis usually called acculturation. . . . Mexican Americans are never seen as participants in history, much less as generators of the historical process."[9] For activists, Chicano history was a recollection of events, of ideas, and of people who had resisted the American conquest of the Southwest and the subsequent colonization that followed. They believed that to "deprive man of his heritage was the worst form of oppression."[10] So they set out to uncover facts long forgotten or ignored and to debunk the Anglo-American version of their history. To do so required more than a different retelling, it meant framing the discovered history within a new interpretation that challenged the traditional literature. This interpretation presented Chicanos as active participants in "their" history.

Romano chided social scientists who wrote that Mexican Americans had a difficult time dealing with the conflict between two cultures. This conflict, one anthropologist argued, often led them to "retreat" into their "conservative . . . world," to "escape to larger cities" or into alcoholism, or to engage in antisocial behavior. Their only hope rested on their acculturating "more and more."[11] Although offended by the belittling descriptions of Mexican Americans, Romano reacted more angrily to the implication that only acculturated Mexican Americans were active participants in their lives. Romano rebutted, "Contrary to the ahistorical views . . . Mexican Americans as well as Mexican immigrants have not . . . wallowed passively in some teleological treadmill, awaiting the emergence of an acculturated third generation before joining in the historical process."[12] He cited numerous instances when Mexican Americans had engaged in strikes in the agricultural fields and the mines of eight different states. These had been intense, even violent acts of labor resistance that had incurred a "massive counter-action" that included widespread deportations. Romano pointed to Carey McWilliams, who wrote in 1949: "Long charged with a lack of 'leadership' and talent for organization, they proved all too effectively that neither talent was lacking. . . . By 1930 the myth of the docility of Mexican labor had been thoroughly exploded."[13]

Romano took on the anthropologist Ruth Tuck, who in 1946 wrote: "For many years the (Mexican) immigrant and his sons made no effort to free themselves. They burned with resentment over a thousand slights, but they did so in private. . . . Perhaps this passivity is the mark of any minority which is just emerging."[14] With that statement, said Romano, Tuck wiped away decades of resistance and set a tone for anthropologists and sociologists to emulate in describing Mexican Americans and their condition. Romano then took on Munro Edmonson, Celia Heller, Julian Samora, Lyle Saunders, and others whose work only reaffirmed Tuck's conceptualization of the Mexican American as a victim of his or her cultural deficiencies.[15] In summarizing their work, Romano accused the aforementioned scholars of making Mexican Americans the generators of their problems, thus freeing Anglo-Americans from most responsibility. Calling upon his readers to reject these perceptions of traditional Mexican culture, he urged them to learn about the intellectual history of Mexican Americans.

That led to another important article, "The Historical and Intellectual Presence of Mexican Americans."[16] Although not as influential as his first one, this article sought to provide a picture of the pluralistic nature of the Mexican American community and to point out that there were important philosophical and ideological currents that influenced the thinking of most Mexican Americans. Romano posited that three main streams of thought permeated the Mexican American community. These were "indianist philosophy," "historical confrontation," and "cultural nationalism." "At times," wrote Romano, "they [the three philosophies] coincide with actual historical occurrences. Other times they lie relatively dormant, or appear in a poetic metaphor, a song, a short story told to children, or in a marriage pattern."[17] Indianist philosophy dealt with the indigenous origin of most Mexican Americans; historical confrontation dealt with protest and popular action against tyranny and oppression; and cultural nationalism concerned itself with the development of the cultural characteristics of being a *mexicano*.

These philosophies came from the Mexican Revolution, an event that Romano believed influenced most Mexicans who crossed the border at the turn of the century. The philosophies were passed on from generation to generation and remained an active intellectual element within an extremely diverse community. These philosophies were responsible for the resistance that Chicanos continually waged against opposition. They were also responsible for the nationalistic or ethnocentric response of the working class toward Anglo-American encroachment into their community. Romano concluded his article by warning Chicanos to avoid being "permanently entombed in the histories of the past."[18] As a young recruit to the Movement, I read Romano's first article and felt outraged over the academic scholarship on Mexican Americans. It became a hotly discussed and debated article in my "Introduction to Mexican Americans" course at Texas A & I

University in Kingsville. It would be quoted over and over in Chicano newspapers, lectures, and rallies, and in other academic articles and papers during the early years of the Movement.[19] Romano had, in a few short pages, identified what most Chicano activists perceived to be the most damaging assault on the Mexican American community. Said Romano, "Mexican Americans are [seen as] simpleminded . . . children who . . . choose poverty and isolation instead of assimilating into the American mainstream."[20]

The teaching of such perceptions had served to perpetuate stereotypes and thus kept mainstream society unsympathetic and often hostile toward Mexican Americans. The racist feelings and remarks had, in part, been rationalized by liberal social scientists who saw Mexican Americans as passive, unmotivated, and responsible for accepting much of their own suffering.[21] The biased scholarship had also served to perpetuate feelings of inferiority among many Mexican Americans and to cause some of the more educated to remove themselves culturally and physically from their communities. For me, and many like me, the article revealed a condescending attitude by social scientists who—we believed—would not have written about blacks in the same manner. We were under the impression that blacks, through the civil-rights movement, were freed from much of this type of scholarship. It was a false assumption but one that led many of us to the next phase of our politicization. Although we were always conscious of discrimination, many of us often abdicated the role of "oppressed minority" to blacks because few of us had ever understood the extent of the discrimination and racism perpetrated against Mexican Americans. To find that Mexican Americans were also victims of intellectual racism, and then to realize that there was no civil-rights movement for Mexican Americans, made many of us anxious to get involved in a movement of our own. The seeming lack of Anglo-American sympathy caused the Chicano Movement to become more nationalistic and separatist in nature than it might have been.[22]

Following Romano's lead, many other Chicano college students and professors picked up the discussion of the portrayal of Mexican Americans in the academic and popular literature. Juan Gómez-Quiñones, a young scholar at the University of California at Los Angeles at the time, called for a reconceptualization of Mexican American history, arguing that the history of Chicanos was not simply a history of the "Anglo oppressor" and the "Chicano oppressed."[23] He attempted to construct the first framework for retelling the story of the Mexican American. In an article entitled "Notes on Periodization, 1900–1965," Gómez-Quiñones broke Mexican American history into several definable periods.[24] Carlos Muñoz, a graduate student at the University of California, called on Chicanos scholars and students to be more than academicians. The Chicano scholar, said Muñoz, "must commit himself to the emancipation of his people."[25] Journals such as *Aztlán, De Colores, Caracol, Regeneración, Encuentro Femenil,*

and Romano's *El Grito* followed the lead of these writers and charged ahead with a scathing scholarship that sought to disprove stereotypes that had become part of the mainstream in academia.[26] All of the aforementioned were academic journals with the exception of *Caracol*, which was a popular magazine for the masses that published a hodgepodge of articles, poems, theater acts, and essays.[27] These and other periodicals became self-imposed required reading for college students and Chicano activists in the community. Whereas many Chicanos were attracted to the Movement by the rhetoric and passion of the leaders, others less passionate were attracted by the intellectual discourse on the status of Chicanos, their past, and what might lie ahead. For many students coming to universities with little knowledge of their past, it became an intellectual culture shock to read the new Chicano scholarship.[28]

If Romano's article began the debate, Rodolfo Acuña's *Occupied America* heightened its intensity. No other academic work caused the controversy that Acuña's history of Chicanos did. Beginning with the premise that Chicanos were an internal colony still suffering from the legacy of the American conquest, Acuña went on to describe in detail many of the atrocities committed against La Raza. He introduced the book in this manner: "*Occupied America* has evolved from my belief that the history of Chicanos . . . must be reexamined. . . . As my research progressed, I became convinced that the experiences of Chicanos in the United States parallel that of other Third World people who have suffered under the colonialism of technologically superior nations. Thus, the thesis of this monograph is that Chicanos . . . are a colonized people. The conquest of the Mexicans, the occupation of their land and the continued oppression they have faced document this thesis."[29]

For Chicano activists, Acuña's work was a godsend. No longer did they have to piece together accounts of discrimination and racism. In several hundred pages, Acuña documented more than enough incidents to confirm almost anything that activists chose to blame on American society.[30] Chicano academicians also quickly endorsed the book because it provided them with a text for their courses. In it they found a comprehensive and panoramic view of Chicano history. Its model of "internal-colonialism" also provided a framework by which to explain the Chicano experience. The internal-colony model posited that the Southwest had been subjected to a conquest and a ruthless process of colonization that left Mexican Americans in circumstances similar to those of nations that had been colonized by imperialist powers. A dual-wage system, rampant segregation, exploitation of natural resources, coaptation of the native elites, and other characteristics of a foreign colony were present in the Southwest, according to Acuña. The internal-colony social structure also placed racial conflict at the center of Mexican and Anglo-American relationships.[31] Chicano students were immediately attracted to the book by the information, much of it new to them, and by its academic "legitimacy." They also liked its militancy. Far from being esoteric, it invited the reader to action, to be an active participant in history. It also provided heroes and heroines and allowed Chicano students to see that Mexican Americans had never been passive. Rather, they had resisted domination. In a time of lettuce and grape boycotts, land-grant battles, urban street militancy, and school walkouts, *Occupied America* became the intellectual bible that rationalized the heightened militancy.

In Acuña's account of the conquest of the Southwest, nothing had come by chance, or by a spontaneous desire by Anglo-American settlers to live free under a democratic government. Instead, these settlers, in collusion with merchants, land speculators, businessmen, and government officials, had plotted to take Mexico's land. "Remember the Alamo" was not the defiant cry of a ragtag army of freedom-loving men but that of a band of ruffians and outlaws who had come to Texas to engage in their own brand of frontier conquest. Acuña, in this short monograph, rewrote the histories of Texas, Arizona, California, and New Mexico, documenting the methods used to conspire for revolution and war as well as how, once attaining victory, these invaders conspired to steal the lands from the Mexicans who had chosen to stay behind. In Acuña's account there were no tough, democratically inclined cowboys who tamed the West with courage, integrity, and a single six-gun. Instead, Acuña painted a picture of fraud, violence, and lawlessness—of a time when all Mexican possessions were an open target; when the law was exclusively on the side of the Anglo-Americans; and when a heterogeneous Mexican society had, for the most part, been violently compressed into a powerless, poor rural caste. But Mexicans and their Chicano offspring fought back, wrote Acuña. In California, social bandits such as Joaquín Murrieta and Tiburcio Vásquez fought violence with violence of their own. In New Mexico, "Las Gorras Blancas" cut the wire fences of land-grabbing land barons, and the Partido del Pueblo Unido fought the Anglo-American political machines in the electoral arena. In Texas, *revolucionarios* such as Catarino Garza and Juan Cortina led several uprisings against the landed and urban elites in South Texas. The battles against the Texas Rangers and the union strikes in the mines of Arizona and the pecan factories in San Antonio became part of the border mythology. The Mexican American community had finally succumbed to oppression, but these men and numerous women became heroes through Acuña's book.

In his concluding chapter, Acuña reaffirmed the prevailing rejection of American society articulated by the leaders of the emerging movement: "Chicanos who actively participated in the political life of the nation took a hard look at their assigned role in society, evaluated it, and then decided that they had had enough, so they bid good-bye to America."[32] In this chapter, Acuña depicted the rise of a new generation of leaders who had lost hope of finding solutions through the traditional channels of protest and litigation. Although the book ended on a somber, almost pessimistic note, Acuña nonetheless succeeded in setting the tone for the intense struggle for Chicano liberation. No other book before or since has carried the powerful message that Mexican Americans are an exploited and oppressed minority but one that has fought and continues to fight back.

I would never look at American society in the same way after reading *Occupied America*. For many like myself, our historical roots had been torn from the American soil, and we set out in a quest to find identity and to learn history—"our" history. Romano and Acuña led the search for more Chicano history. The new heroes became those who resisted the American conquest of the Southwest. Mexican military men who fought against the Texas rebels or who defended Mexico against the American invasion became men to admire. Particularly admirable were men like Catarino Garza and Juan Cortina, who rose up in arms to defend their Mexican compatriots. As inspiring were Emma Tenayuca, who led the pecan shellers' strike in San Antonio in the 1930s, and Luisa Moreno, an organizer for the United Cannery, Agricultural, and Packing Workers of America and a founder of El Congreso de los Pueblos de Habla Español in 1938.[33] The search for heroes did not end with larger-than-life men and women. With time, our heroes became those individuals who survived the daily struggles in a society still foreign to them.

Romano and Acuña were not the only ones writing this new interpretation. After the initial attack on the Anglo-American academy, Chicano scholars began to write their own history. Gómez-Quiñones wrote about the labor struggles of Chicanos and their early political activism. And he provided an in-depth view of the first ideological hero of the Chicano Movement when he wrote a biography of Ricardo Flores Magón, the Mexican anarchist and intellectual precursor of the Mexican Revolution. For the more ideological radicals in the Movement, Magón became and remained the most influential historical figure in Mexican history.[34] Gómez-Quiñones also pioneered the field of Chicano studies and served as a mentor for many graduate students who wrote about Chicanos in the pages of *De Colores*, *Aztlán*, *El Grito*, and other academic journals. His influence, through his writings and the students he mentored, was felt strongly in California and on college campuses nationwide. There were others. Renato Rosaldo promoted Mexican American studies at the University of Arizona and compiled the work *Chicanos: The Beginnings of Bronze Power*, one of the first anthologies of articles on Mexican Americans produced by a major publisher. Alberto Camarillo wrote about urban Chicanos in California; Américo Paredes and José Limón wrote about folklore, *corridos*, and the Rio Grande Valley; Emilio Zamora wrote about Chicano socialist activists at the turn of the century; Margarita Melville, Adelaida del Castillo, and other women scholars wrote about Chicanas in labor, politics, and letters. Anglo-American scholars such as Stan Steiner, Joan C. Moore, and David Weber also wrote works relevant to the study of Chicanos. Still others involved in this work were amateur historians, many of them poets, dramatists, and artists who incorporated history within their art. Each of them sought to reinterpret history and to create the necessary heroes, heroines, and myths needed to add flames to the Chicano cultural renaissance. Social scientists could not fill the void on the Chicano experience fast enough, so many essayists and fiction writers contributed to the reinterpretation.

These new writers created an image of themselves and their people that did not integrate into mainstream society. In the past, Mexican American writers had struggled to force themselves into the American literary mainstream. Most wrote of their people and themselves as marginalized individuals awaiting the acculturation of their community. Marcienne Rocard has written of the contrast between these two generations: "The older Mexican American poets and short-story writers were isolated; though they sometimes attacked the dominant society harshly and felt themselves to be marginal, they were part of it in spite of themselves. They had no separate image of themselves. By contrast, Chicano writers had a will to define and assert themselves with respect to the Anglo world, a will conditioned by ethnic allegiance."[35] They were, she added, obsessed with identity.

While historians sought to discover the history of Chicanos and sociologists worked to correct the stereotypes, Chicano writers attempted to give meaning to the Chicano experience by blending the social science with folklore and mythmaking. They were at times historians, social critics, seers, and political cheerleaders. More than anyone else, Chicano writers created, expanded, and exported their "new" history as they traveled throughout the barrios of the Southwest reading their works.[36] Their topics ranged from the Aztec gods to the Mexican Revolution; from the *pachuco* to the migrant farmworker; and from the young Chicano militants to Che Guevara, Augusto Sandino, Lucio Cabañas, and Fidel Castro. Most of the poetry dealt with identity and pride in being Chicano.[37] Poetry took the Chicano mind where history could not. Whereas historians wrote of brave men and women who resisted oppression, and of short-lived victories against the Anglo-American, poems provided the ultimate victory. In them, history and the present were described not as they were but as they could and would become. It was in the realm of literature that Chicanos had full control of their lives. There were no facts to contradict Chicano liberation. In poetry Anglo-Americans were simpletons; policemen cowardly; American culture degenerate; and Chicanos organic, brave intellectuals with a rich and moral culture.[38]

Art was another form of history, since most of it depicted the Chicano's Indian heritage and the community's legacy of struggle. Many Mexican American children first learned about Pancho Villa, Emiliano Zapata, Benito Juárez, Cuauhtémoc, and other Mexican heroes from the murals in the barrio. Art was another form that transcended historical facts and provided a new view of La Raza. The murals were larger than life, and the people in them could not help but be seen as heroic. Much of the impetus for this "new" art came from the Mexican revolutionary muralists like Diego Rivera and David Alfaro Siqueiros.

Probably as important as the poetry and art was Chicano *teatro*. With the founding of the Teatro Campesino at the start of the farmworkers' struggle in the mid-1960s, theater became an important tool in the development of identity and militancy. In the case of Teatro Campesino, as well as other Chicano theater groups, the playwright and the actors were part of the social movement. Their topics were usually discrimination, racism, police brutality, workers on strike, or Chicano culture. The goal went beyond entertainment. Theater became a way by which people came to terms with their condition. The tradition of *teatro* in the barrio had been an entrenched one up until about the 1950s. Traveling theater troupes called *carpas*, whose name referred to the tents under which they performed, were a common feature in the Mexican American communities of the Southwest.[39] The skits were usually satires that presented a working-class view of the world. It made gentle fun of people in the barrio, while being particularly cutting toward middle- and upper-class *sociedad*. Props and scenery were kept to a minimum, and most skits were improvised. Few were political in a partisan or ideological way, but they nonetheless provided commentary on people's lives. For parents, these *variedades* (variety shows)[40] were a way to keep their children immersed in the culture and to strengthen their language skills in Spanish. It was also a way to keep the family together, because parents understood that American culture and the public schools were pulling their children away from them. The theater groups kept them close to their culture and *patria*. Although some parents had left Mexico willingly and had no desire to return, they nevertheless felt estranged from their country, and the *carpas* provided some relief from the alienation that they felt in the United States.[41]

Chicano theater groups emulated many aspects of the early Mexican troupes. They were not particularly ideological as much as they were critical of American society. In its early development, Chicano theater proved to be more critical of Anglo-American culture and of those Mexican Americans who sought assimilation than of the political system. With time that changed, and the country's policies at home and abroad became the targets of Chicano satire. Its most significant function, however, remained its promotion of the "new" Chicanos.

Teatro Campesino served as the model for most of these Chicano theater groups. Founded in 1965, it sought to teach farmworkers about the union activities of César Chávez and to attract them to union membership. In 1972, Luis Valdez, the Teatro's founder, wrote the following about its use of skits and funny scenes to further *la causa*: "Our use of comedy stemmed from necessity—the necessity of lifting the strikers' morale. We found we could make social points [commentary] not in spite of the comedy, but through it. Slapstick can bring us . . . close to the underlying tragedy . . . that human beings have been wasted for generations."[42] For two years after its founding, Teatro Campesino worked alongside the union in the picket lines. Its actors performed in the fields, in the labor camps, at rallies, at union meetings, and at strike benefits. They also toured the country and at each stop publicized the union boycotts, informing Mexican American and Anglo-American audiences about the plight of the farmworkers. They advocated a rural culturalism that sought to tie all Chicanos to the land. This culturalism promoted the family as the unit of struggle, since in farmworkers families everyone worked in the fields to help out. Once unionized, all members of the family became connected to the strike, boycott, or picket line. For Teatro Campesino there existed a new Chicano, willing to work for *la causa*. This Chicano shunned materialism and looked to the land and his or her history for meaning.

The founders of Teatro Campesino, as well as those of the union, knew there existed another kind of Mexican American. He was the *vendido*, the Mexican American willing to sell out his people to the highest bidder. In the rural areas he was the Mexican labor contractor, in the urban barrios he was the *politico*, and at the university he was the acculturated Chicano who believed in the system and in education for the professional advantages it brought. The theater became the place to expose this type of character, and thus the *vendido* became one of the stock characters of most Chicano plays. It was the United Farm Workers Union (UFW)[43] that first identified the dichotomy within the Chicano community. Union organizers quickly labeled as "sell-outs" those Mexican Americans who were afraid to challenge the growers or those who worked for them. In identifying a character such as the *vendido*, Chicano theater provided a contrast for the new Chicano. It also was a way to belittle and discredit those who straddled the fence or sided against the Movement. In time, it became a way to keep discipline within the ranks, since the threat of being designated a *vendido* intimidated many a wavering Chicano activist.[44]

Chicano theater groups appeared throughout the Southwest. The Crusade for Justice had its own theater group, and so did many other organizations. But although they were supportive of the Movement, most Chicano theater groups were independent of control from activists. This freedom gave them the ability to transcend local or regional issues and allowed them artistic freedom. Much as in the Chicano Movement, their ideological base resulted from a hodgepodge of ideas and concerns. The underlying theme of all their work, and the one with which all Chicanos could identify, was the threat of cultural genocide and its economic, social, and spiritual legacy. The *teatros* provided a simple message: Chicanos and their culture were under attack; they had to resist by knowing their history and maintaining their culture and they had to

root out the *vendidos* from among them. That theme served Chicano activists from the California college campuses to the migrant shanty towns of Hidalgo County in Texas. Chicano theater, much like Chicano literature, provided a more positive view of the Mexican American community. Although the history and experience depicted in the plays often defied historical accuracy, they nevertheless projected a positive image and created new myths, something of which Chicanos seemed so much in need.

Two other institutions promoted a new interpretation of the Chicano experience: Chicano studies programs and centers, and the Chicano press. Both Chicano studies, as a political and academic movement, and the Chicano press, as a conveyor of information, proved to be crucial to the reinterpretation of the Chicano experience. More Chicanos learned about "their" history and about brown militancy from these two institutions than from any other source. Their importance to the Movimiento cannot be overemphasized.

Chicano studies programs began appearing on college campuses in the mid-1960s in response to student demands that Mexican American history and culture be taught as part of the academic curriculum. These programs first appeared in California as a result of the student strikes occurring in Los Angeles and other major cities. The main impetus for the growth of Chicano studies, however, came from a conference at the University of California at Santa Barbara in April 1969. There, over one hundred delegates from 29 campuses met under the sponsorship of the Chicano Coordinating Committee on Higher Education to develop a master plan for Chicanos in higher education.[45]

In El Plan de Santa Bárbara, which came out of the conference and became the Movement's design for educating the Chicano masses, the authors declared: "We recognize that without a strategic use of education that places value on what we value, we will not realize our destiny. . . . Throughout history the quest for cultural expression and freedom has taken the form of a struggle."[46] This "strategic use of education" meant Chicano students and faculty were to be involved in the development of curriculum and in the administration of programs. It also meant that these programs would be within what Carlos Muñoz called "the context of a politics for change."[47] The Plan's authors express this context in the following manner: "Now Chicano university students, not unmindful of the historic price of assimilation, take charge within the community as the point of departure for their social and political involvement. . . . At this moment we do not come to work for the university, but to demand that the university work for our people."[48] Many of those hired to teach and direct the programs used the classroom to expound their version of Chicano history. For those who found themselves in areas where there were no major Movement organizations, the courses in Chicano studies allowed them to participate, at least emotionally, in the Movement. Also, many of these programs sponsored trips to large protest activities, marches, and militant conferences.

In Kingsville, many joined the Movement through the efforts of José Reyna, head of the Ethnic Studies program at Texas A&I University. In his classroom, students read Romano's articles, Acuña's book, and the countless other articles, books, and periodicals that were surfacing during the early 1970s. Self-identity usually became the main topic of the courses offered there and in other places. In class environments made up mostly of Chicanos, students often discussed and debated issues that would have been deemed inappropriate in other classrooms.[49] In places such as California State University at Northridge, degrees were offered in Chicano studies, and students graduating from these programs were expected to have some fluency in both Spanish and Náhuatl (the language of the Aztecs) and to know their Mexican and Chicano history. In other places, like Kingsville, where lack of university support limited the programs, students were provided the basics of Chicano thought and were then exhorted to join community grassroots organizations that were involved in some form of activism. The Chicano studies programs provided a sense of legitimacy for many and a place in which Chicano intellectual debates were appreciated.[50] It was also for many a place where the correct "history" of La Raza could be learned. According to an editorial in *El Grito*, "The responsibility upon the shoulders of those in Chicano programs is great, for should the end product be disfigured in any way whatsoever, they will have turned victory into defeat, self-expression into self-denial, a dream into a nightmare, and a promise into . . . purposeless mouthings."[51] For Chicano academicians, Chicano studies programs were a personal responsibility. They sought to eliminate "past distortions." The "future image" was now in their hands, and they set out to craft that image.[52]

Through the efforts of Chicano studies and ethnic studies programs, many Chicanos rediscovered their culture, learned about their history, and regained an identity many had lost or had never acquired at home. Through these programs, students participated in local community activities such as Diez y Seis de Septiembre and Cinco de Mayo celebrations (Mexican patriotic holidays) and local elections and protests. It was not uncommon for groups associated with a Chicano studies program to sponsor Christmas parties, food drives, or picnics for the local Chicano community.[53] Students who had often been unaware of cultural events in their hometowns, or who had simply not been interested in participating, now became involved. With the mentoring of their professors, they saw the community in a different light. Herbal remedies, cultural traditions, and other barrio survival techniques became symbols of resistance to an alienating urban world. No longer were students ashamed of the cure-all *hierbas*, the *parteras*, the *salsa picante* and *tacos*, and *quinceañeras*, and other cultural "anomalies" in which the barrio participated. Rather than blame La Raza for its poverty, dropout

rates, or juvenile delinquency, many college students, tutored by their Chicano instructors, shifted the blame to mainstream Anglo-American society. Chicano culture became all good, healthy, and moral; problems encountered were those that had been inflicted on the barrios by external forces. For many Chicano students, the Chicano experience took on a different character than even the one they had experienced themselves. Isolated in a university environment often foreign to them, they saw the community as warm and familiar. Although they were in reality separated by education and status from the community, they felt a greater connection to it than ever before. Nostalgia had become history.

For those who did not attend the university, the Chicano press served as the catalyst for intellectual discussion. "*El Gallo* was born out of frustration and determination for the truth," wrote "Corky" Gonzales of the Crusade's newspaper, in 1967.[54] One year later, the editors of *El Grito del Norte* would declare their intent to promote the "course of justice of the poor people . . . and conserve the cultural heritage of la raza."[55] Chicano newspapers carried bits of history, literature, current news, commentary, and a strong dose of cultural polemics.

There were three kinds of newspapers and magazines that formed the nucleus of the Chicano press. The first were newspapers that represented specific organizations and usually promoted particular political philosophies. There were the UFW's *El Malcriado*, La Raza Unida Party's *Para la Gente*, the Brown Berets' *Regeneración*, the newspapers of other major Chicano Movement groups, and other smaller periodicals representing smaller organizations. These were initially the most influential and most scathing in their polemics. The second category of newspapers included those published by university student groups. These were mostly disseminated within the local university community and to other college campuses throughout the country. These newspapers dealt with issues of academic freedom, Chicano studies, and student politics and published a fair amount of commentary on international issues. They were often the most brash and used language deemed inappropriate for the other two categories of newspapers. Some of these were *El Chile* from Texas A & I University at Kingsville and *El Chingazo* from San Diego State University. The third kind of publication was the independent newspapers directed toward the community, even though some came from university groups or particular partisan groups. These periodicals tended to publish for a longer period of time and were as popular outside the locality where they were published as they were within. Examples were *El Grito del Norte* from Denver; *La Raza* from Los Angeles; and *Caracol* from San Antonio, Texas.

These news sheets were in essence the wire service for Chicano activists throughout Aztlán. Articles that originated in the pages of these periodicals were reprinted in other newspapers, duplicated, and passed out during rallies or political discussions. This kept the flow of ideas going and bound all of the peripheries to the centers of Chicano activism. Through them, Chicanos learned what issues were of greatest importance to the greatest number of Chicanos. From them also came word as to which leaders were rising in the Movement and which were fading. Much like radio and television for American society, the Chicano press developed a "mainstream" image of what a Chicano or Chicana in the Movement did or said.

None of the aforementioned periodicals, nor most of the others, had rigid ideological lines to present. They were nationalistic, anticapitalist, and geared toward action. *El Grito del Norte* tended to concentrate on the work of the Alianza, *El Gallo* on the politics of the Crusade for Justice, and *La Raza* on the California activities of the Chicano student movement and later La Raza Unida Party. *Caracol* tended to be the most independent. It also became the most diversified, with over half of its pages devoted to poems, autobiographical essays, plays, and short stories. These newspapers and magazines provided a view of local, national, and international events from a Chicano perspective. The war in Vietnam was important in relation to how many Chicanos were being killed. The national liberation movements in Asia, Africa, and Latin America were analyzed to identify strategies that Chicanos could use in their own liberation. And American foreign policy received critical scrutiny to confirm the Chicano condemnation of American imperialism. Locally, the coverage revolved around daily occurrences of discrimination; local laws, ordinances, or practices that treated Chicanos as second-class citizens; and political victories by community groups.[56]

The periodicals evolved politically with time. Most went from covering the local community to commenting on national and international events. As time went by, and political victories at home became more difficult to obtain, the newspapers increased their polemical discussions on ideology and "Yankee imperialism." They also moved away from cultural events and histories that had been the mainstay of the first issues. Nevertheless, the newspapers remained the promoters of the new image of the Chicano. And they continued to interpret the Chicano experience in a separatist mode, where aggression and resistance were the main themes of that experience. Some of these newspapers later made the transition to becoming community newspapers, while others spurned more traditional periodicals that were in business to make money and not political commentary.

By the mid-1970s, for those who took time to notice, Chicanos had created a historical image for themselves. This image of a historical people with heroes, legends, intellectual foundations, and culture differed dramatically from that which came from the academic and popular literature. Mexican Americans no longer had to accept the view of the Chicano as a lazy, unambitious, violent individual with insatiable sexual desires and a culture that bred

poverty and delinquency. They also did not have to accept the image of passivity. This new outlook became important as Chicano activists rejected the liberal approach to solving the problems of the community. A failure to replace the image of the nonachieving Chicano at a time when the liberal approach was rejected would have meant that Chicanos were worse off than they believed. When they had been unable to develop a mass protest movement, the liberal approach had been a safety net for Mexican Americans. The piecemeal approach had had its benefits. Once that approach was rejected, Chicanos needed a stronger self-image in order to embark on their own program of self-help. Historical identity became crucial for activists. This identity developed through the efforts of academicians, who rejected stereotypes and dug out the real history; poets and playwrights, who presented culturally militant Chicanos and Chicanas as the prototypes of the new Mexican American; Chicano studies programs, which involved students and created a reservoir of Chicano intellectuals; and newspapers and magazines, which kept Chicanos informed of what was happening in Aztlán and which served to develop a cultural and political "homogeneity" among Chicano activists.[57] The reinterpretation of the Chicano experience affected the way particular sectors within the Chicano community saw themselves. Even in segments of the community where radicalism did not dominate the mode of operations, the new view of Chicanos caused considerable change. The Church—as used here, denoting religious groups within the community, predominantly the Catholic Church—was one such entity deeply affected by the Chicano Movement's activism and its interpretation of history.[58]

For many Chicano activists, the Church had been one of those institutions that had cooperated in the oppression of the Chicano masses by teaching them subserviency and by encouraging them to be happy with their lot on Earth, as heaven would bring celestial rewards.[59] For others, the Church represented a financial and social power that refused to intervene on behalf of the poor Chicano. "The religious dollar must be invested, without return expected, in the barrios," declared an editorial in *El Grito del Norte*.[60] César Chávez, a man of deep religious loyalty, also called for a more sensitive Church. "It is our duty" to appeal to the church for the poor, he told readers of *El Grito* in 1968. "It should be as natural as appealing to government . . . and we do that often enough."[61] The Mexican American Youth Organization (MAYO) had even responded to the Church's passivity with sacrilege in 1969 when its members spray-painted brown a statue of Our Lady of the Immaculate Conception that stood on the grounds of an old seminary building in Mission, Texas. They had done so to protest the Church's refusal to give them the building for their "university without walls" and for its overall lack of support for the Movement.[62] Other activists who were Marxist-oriented, or disciples of anarchy, saw the Church as reactionary.

There were others, however, who saw that the Church was an important institution in the barrio and that many Mexican Americans remained faithful to it. "God is alive and well in the heart of the Chicano," Luis Valdez would write during the height of the grape and lettuce boycott.[63] They also saw within it a number of Chicano and Anglo-American priests ready to join the Movement. While preaching against the Church's hierarchy, many activists united with lay leaders and clergy to promote Movement activities. In New Mexico, Reies López Tijerina, a former Pentecostal preacher, would lead the land-grant movement with a religious zeal and place it within the context of a spiritual crusade. In Robstown, Texas, a number of early Movement candidates were Baptist lay leaders. At Brigham Young University, A Chicano from San Antonio's Spanish-speaking Mormon congregation established the university's first ethnic studies club. In Tucson, a Methodist parish provided the meeting space for the Mexican American Liberation Committee. And in New York, Protestant churches, responding to lay leaders' demands, established the National Farm Workers Ministry.[64]

Chávez was the most adept at using the Church as a powerful ally. In the UFW union hall in Delano, California, a large banner reminded the farmworkers daily that "God is beside you on the picket line." In rallying the poor Chicanos to continue their strikes and their organizing amid arrests, intimidation, and seemingly unbeatable odds, Chávez continually used religious symbolism and rhetoric to inspire his followers. The march to Sacramento became a religious pilgrimage. "They [the farmworkers] hope to set themselves at peace with the Lord, so that the justice of their cause will be purified of all lesser motivations."[65] The fasts became petitions for "nonviolence and a call to sacrifice." They also became a way to attract national attention to the nobleness of the cause. For the UFW, the Virgen de Guadalupe became the patron saint of the Movement, accompanying its strikers on the picket lines, marches, and rallies. Organizations such as Católicas por La Raza, PADRES, HERMANAS, and other arose.[66]

Movement activists learned to acknowledge that religious affiliation remained important for many Mexican Americans. To make that affiliation beneficial for the Movement meant reinterpreting the Church's historical role in the community. To do so, these activists looked back in history to find those religious leaders who had sided with the oppressed and the Indians. They found Fathers Miguel Hidalgo y Costilla and José María Morelos y Pavón of the Mexican War for Independence, and they found religious revolutionaries such as Rubén Jaramillo, a lay Methodist preacher, who fought alongside the famous Mexican peasant leader of the Revolution of 1910, Emiliano Zapata. Others simply reinterpreted the role of Christ, making him a revolutionist. "For it is from him that we draw our strength," said an activist calling herself Dolores del Grito.[67] Tijerina would compare his actions to those of an angry god: "The revolution of Tierra Amarilla was like Christ entering the temple and clearing out the Pharisees."[68] This interpretation was fanned by the development of liberation theology and the rise of guerrilla-priests in Latin America.

The moral tone of the Movement attracted a number of religious individuals to the struggle. In my own Mormon parish In San Antonio, a number of members joined La Raza Unida Party and a number of the other community organizations active at the time. The Movement to me, and many others like me, represented a variation of the social gospel. We were to work for the poor, to preach higher moral and political values, and to empower communities to challenge an evil society. Attending political masses, working with priests and lay leaders to empower poor parishioners, and placing the Movement within the context of a moral crusade served to radicalize religious life for many of us. We then interpreted many of our religious leaders' actions within a historical context of resistance against Anglo-American racism or paternalism.

The Church—as a religious entity—did not change drastically, notwithstanding many challenges to its ministries. But many Chicano followers did change. They saw the Church as having a role beyond the four walls of the chapel or the cathedral. They saw the gospel going beyond personal values to providing a framework for a just society. The moral authority of the Church was to be used to teach against the evils of poverty, discrimination, and capitalism. For activists, the changing role of the faithful in the Church, an institution that had functioned for decades as the maintainer of culture, helped in the reinterpretation of the Chicano experience. Taking the collective cultural experience of the Church as a basis, Chicano activists not only provided historicity to their struggle but also gave it a moral impetus. The intellectual dichotomy between those who accepted religion and those who rejected it remained significant throughout the Movement period, but for those who remained faithful, the new interpretation made them more adamant about working for social justice. This added to the new view of an active and resisting community.

Chicanas proved to be another sector of the community deeply affected by the reinterpretation of history. If Mexican American males suffered the burden of stereotypes, then Mexican American women suffered a double burden. What could be expected of the mothers, wives, and daughters of those men who were ahistorical, passive, lazy, and *mañana*-oriented? Arthur Rubel, one of those social scientists that Romano had taken to task for stereotyping Mexican American males, wrote about the Chicana: "[They are] ideally submissive, unworldly, and chaste."[69] They were possessions to be guarded and protected from the outside world. William Madsen went further in denigrating Mexican American women: "The Latin woman plays the perfect counterpart to the Latin male. Where he is strong, she is weak. Where he is aggressive, she is submissive. While he is condescending toward her, she is respectful toward him. A woman is expected to always display those subdued qualities of womanhood that make a man feel the need to protect her."[70] Spousal abuse, continued Madsen, was seen as deserved and as proof of profound love.

Gloria Molina de Pick argued that Chicanas suffered from the depiction of being chaste and submissive as well as seductive and representing the "most provocative of sexual adventures."[71] This contradiction, wrote Adaljiza Sosa Riddell, served to free American society from any responsibility for the Chicanas' oppression, and it kept Chicanas "preoccupied" with their "shortcomings." This conflictive dichotomy blamed Chicanas "for not being good mothers, for not keeping the family together, for working instead of staying home, or conversely, for being too oriented to their family, for having too many children, for not working, for staying home."[72] Mexican American women simply could not win. Either seen as submissive and passive or as seductive and responsible for familial shortcomings, they were even less a rational entity than their husbands, fathers, or sons.

Initially, the Movement's interpretation of women centered on their relationships to the family. At the Chicano Youth Liberation Conference, Chicanas, anxious to be seen as part of a united front, voted to declare that they did not want to be "liberated."[73] But the Movement, notwithstanding the chauvinism of some of its leaders, could not help but challenge patriarchy through its liberation rhetoric and through the opportunity it gave women to become involved in protest activities. Women, through their clerical skills, their willingness to do tedious jobs well, and their ability to follow through on assignments, became the organizational backbone of the Movement.

When Movement activities began in the early 1960s, precursors were few. Although they tended to be predominantly male, there were a significant number of women. A few women were known Movement-wide, but many others were part of the rank and file, whose influence remained at the local and regional level.

These women, once in the Movement, began to argue for inclusion in the new interpretation. "When we talk equality," wrote Longeaux y Vásquez , "we better be talking about total equality."[74] But rather than wait for the men to dominate the process, they set out to do the interpretation. Chicano activists often saw the historical Mexican woman as self-sacrificing—as the *abuelita*, or the Adelita who followed the man during times of upheaval. The poet José Montoya wrote:

When I remember the *campos* [fields]
. . . I remember my *jefita's* [mother's]
palote [rolling pin]
(I swear, she never slept)
Es tarde mi hijito [it's late my son]
cover up
. . . a maternal reply mingled with
the hissing of the hot *planchas* [iron]

. . . *y la jefita* slapping tortillas
. . . *y en el fil* [in the field], pulling
her *cien* [one hundred]
libras del algodón [pounds of cotton]
. . . that woman—she only complains
in her sleep.[75]

Chicanas saw themselves as more than self-sacrificing spouses or mothers. Like the male activists, they saw themselves as having a strong historical legacy but a diverse one. They accepted the role of the self-sacrificing woman as a legitimate part of the Chicana experience but complemented it with that of the labor leader who fought for the rights of working people, of the *soldadera* who fought with guns and rifles for freedom, and of the ideologue who wrote and spoke against injustices. Women were to be found wherever there was struggle.[76]

Most Chicana activists felt a need to remain within the mainstream of the Movement. They saw the liberation of community as the first goal. They argued, at least initially, that Chicanas first became ideologically conscious of discrimination as Chicanas rather than as women. But within the Movement, they demanded the room to deal with issues that affected them as mothers and as women. And they also sought an influential role in defining the direction of the community's liberation. Many men responded to the women's concerns positively. Activist scholar Martha Cotera remembered that most of the male leaders in La Raza Unida Party tended to be supportive. "I don't really remember the men as obstacles," she would say years later.[77]

The women's dialogue, first among themselves and then publicly in the publications such as *Regeneración*, *Encuentro Femenil*, and other Chicano journals of the time, sought to define a new place for Chicanas. The new Chicana would stand alongside her man as the *soldadera* of the Mexican Revolution did, but she expected the partnership to be equal. And the definition of liberation now had to include freedom from *machismo* and the full freedom to participate in all aspects of the Chicano community's decision making. The political agenda had to concern itself with child care, employment and training for women, and a redefinition of familial roles.[78] Chicano activists, faced with a need for dedicated workers and confronted with their own "ideologically progressive" rhetoric, found themselves forced to open the Movement to women. Although the opening oftentimes seemed scarcely a crack to many, the women took advantage of it and reinterpreted their historical role within the Chicano community. If the men had struggled and resisted conquest and discrimination, then Chicanas had done the same. Chicana scholars, artists, essayists, and poets made sure that those within and without the Movement did not forget.

Chicanas also began exploring the special burden that they carried as women. Declared the platform of La Raza Unida Party in Colorado: "For our women . . . there exists a triple exploitation, a triple degradation; they are exploited as women, as people of *La Raza*, and they suffer from the poverty that straitjackets all of *La Raza*. We feel that without recognition . . . of their special form of oppression . . . our movement will suffer greatly."[79] Like their black counterparts, these Chicanas sought to expand beyond the ideological boundaries set for them by male activists and white feminists. Chicanas saw their struggle in terms of community and family, even as they fought for equality at the personal level. Unbridled by the males' concept of honor, which saw political defeat as humiliating, these women continued to push for an end to racism and for collective empowerment in the face of strong opposition. Once they reinterpreted the Chicana experience as positive and heroic, they found the historical impetus to continue their activism.

Scholarly works of high quality, with a few exceptions, would come after the decline of the Movement. Some of them would even contradict the romanticism of the Movement-inspired histories. But most continued to offer a new and positive interpretation of the Chicano experience. Chicano Movement historians, trained or otherwise, had engaged in a historical discourse to discredit stereotypes and to combat the crisis of identity that many Mexican Americans confronted. Their history often worked chronologically backward. Their premise was that Chicanos were a strong and courageous people who had survived conquest, colonization, and racial brutality. Working back from that premise meant interpreting the "facts" to support the thesis. This new view of history allowed Chicanos to become the evaluators and legitimizers of their history and provided them the opportunity to define their historical significance and importance. Historical reinterpretation would be one of the most significant products of the Chicano Movement.

Notes

1. One who did was Carlos E. Castañeda, who wrote what historian Mario T. García calls a "complementary history" of the Mexican American. This history attempted to underscore the similarities between Mexican Americans and Anglo-Americans. It also sought to dispel the stereotypes that Anglo-Americans had about Mexican Americans. For a further explanation of Castañeda's work, see Mario T. García, *In Search of History: Carlos E. Castañeda and the Mexican American Generation*, Renato Rosaldo Lecture Series Monograph 4 (Tuscon: Mexican American Studies and Research Center, University of Arizona, 1988), 1–20.
2. John C. Hammerback, Richard J. Jensen, and José Angel Gutiérrez, *A War of Words* (Westport, Conn.: Greenwood Press, 1985), 51.
3. See the following works for an example of this type of scholarship: Celia S. Heller, *Mexican-American Youth. Forgotten Youth at the Crossroads* (New York: Random House, 1968); William Madsen, *Mexican-Americans of South Texas, Case Studies in Cultural Anthropology* (New York: Holt, Rinehart and Winston, 1964); Ruth Tuck, *Not with the Fist* (New York: Harcourt, Brace and Co., 1946); and Edmonson S. Munro, *Los Manitos: A Study of Institutional Values* (New Orleans: Middle American Research Institute, 1957).
4. "Poverty of culture" was developed as a concept from the writings of men like Oscar Lewis, Michael Harrington, and Daniel Moynihan. Ironically, all three authors claimed to write on behalf of the disadvantaged but ended up coining concepts that were used to blame the victims of poverty. See Oscar Lewis, *La Vida: A Puerto Rican Family in the Culture of Poverty* (New York: Random House, 1966);

and Michael Harrington, *The New American Poverty* (New York: Penguin Books, 1984).
5. Valdez referred to the Spanish Conquest of Mexico, but other activists would us the term "conquest" to describe the occupation of the American Southwest by the U.S. military, which is what it refers to here. Whereas Anglo-American scholars often describe the Spanish Conquest as having created a legacy of problems for Mexicans, Chicano scholars would see the later conquest as being more significant.
6. Luis Valdez and Stan Steiner, eds., *Aztlán: An Anthology of Mexican American Literature* (New York: Alfred A. Knopf, 1972), xiii, xiv.
7. See David Sánchez, "Chicano Power Explained" (mimeographed booklet), Special Collections, Stanford University Libraries, 1.
8. Enriqueta Longeaux y Vásquez, "Despierten hermanos," *El Grito del Norte*, August 24, 1968, p.6.
9. Octavio Romano, "The Anthropology and Sociology of the Mexican American: The Distortion of Mexican-American History," *El Grito* 2 (1968): 13–14.
10. Enriqueta Longeaux y Vásquez , "A nuestros lectores," *El Grito del Norte*, September 15, 1968, p. 2.
11. William Madsen, *The Mexican American in South Texas* (New York: Holt, Rinehart and Winston, 1964), 109.
12. Romano, "Anthropology and Sociology," 14.
13. Carey McWilliams, *North from Mexico: The Spanish-Speaking People of the United States* (New York: Greenwood Press, 1968), as quoted in Romano, "Anthropology and Sociology."
14. Tuck, *Not with the Fist*, 198.
15. Interestingly, Julian Samora was both praised and criticized during this period.
16. Octavio Romano, "The Historical and Intellectual Presence of Mexican Americans," *El Grito* (winter 1969): 32–46.
17. Ibid., 40–44.
18. Ibid., 46.
19. Romano's articles and his publication *El Grito* became required reading for Chicano activists. A Chicano student would have been hard pressed to discuss Chicano identity and history without discussing Romano's work.
20. Editorial, *El Grito* 1, no. 1 (fall 1967): 4.
21. Many liberal scholars, in trying to empathize, often added to the stereotypes of being overly sensitive about Chicano issues to the point of condescension. See Américo Paredes, "On Ethnographic Work among Minority Groups," in *New Directions in Chicano Scholarship*, ed. Raymond Romo and Raymond Paredes (La Jolla, Calif.: Chicano Studues Monograph Series, 1978). See also Octavio Romano, "Minorities, History and Cultural Mystique," *El Grito* 1, no. 1 (1967).
22. It is also because of the scarcity of Anglo-American liberal supporters that the Chicano Movement has not been a major theme explored by Anglo-American academicians. Few Anglo-American activists or scholars ever received training in the struggles of Chicanos for equal rights as many did in the black civil-rights battles. See Renato Rosaldo, Jr., *When Natives Talk Back: Chicano Anthropology Since the Late Sixties*, Renato Rosaldo Lecture Series Monograph 2 (Tucson: Mexican American Studies and Research Center, University of Arizona, 1986), 3–20, for a discussion of the early abandonment of Chicano scholarship by Anglo-American scholars, who were unwilling to face Chicano critique of their work.
23. See Juan Gómez-Quiñones, "Toward a Perspective on Chicano History," *Aztlán* (fall 1971): 1–49.
24. Juan Gómez-Quiñones, "Notes on Periodization, 1900–1965," *Aztlán* (spring 1970): 115–118.
25. See Carlos Muñoz, "Toward A Chicano Perspective of Political Analysis," *Aztlán* (fall 1970).
26. Many of the articles published in these journals were reprinted in numerous community and underground newspapers and magazines and thus became accessible to those communities and campuses where the journals were not available.
27. *Caracol* is in itself a work worthy of study, since it is served as a vehicle for many artists and essayists to get started. Everything that was submitted was published, and so it encouraged many to continue to pursue their dreams of writing, drawing, and publishing. Headed by Cecilio García-Camarillo, *Caracol* proved to be the most important popular literary magazine of the Movement.

28. More research has to be conducted on those who rediscovered their ethnicity during the years of the Chicano Movement. Many of these "born-again" Chicanos became the most passionate of all the activists.

29. See Acuña, introduction to *Occupied America*, 1st ed.

30. The other book to appear at about the same time was by Matt S. Meier and Feliciano Rivera, *The Chicanos: A History of Mexican Americans* (New York: Hill and Wang, 1972), which was a milder version popular among Anglo-American historians who chose to include the history of Mexican Americans in their courses. That book never quite gained a place in Chicano studies.

31. The theory would eventually come under attack from Chicano Marxist scholars for having no class-analysis component. Other mainstream Chicano historians would also question the model. As mentioned above, by the second edition of his *Occupied America* in 1981, Acuña had also rethought his political model and so did not include it. Still, the internal-colony model remains influential even today, much in the same manner that Frederick Jackson Turner's discredited theory of the development of the West remains influential among western historians. For a more in-depth explanation of the internal-colony model, see Mario Barrera, Carlos Muñoz, and Charles Ornelas, "The Barrio as Internal Colony," *Urban Affairs Annual Review* 6 (1972): 465–98; see also Tomás Almaguer, "Toward the Study of Chicano Colonialism," *Aztlán* 2, no.1 (spring 1971): 7–20.

32. Acuña, *Occupied America*, 3d. ed., chapter 11.

33. For information on Emma Tenayuca and Luisa Moreno, see Carlos Larralde, *Mexican American Movements and Leaders* (Los Alamitos, Calif.: Hwong, 1976); for information on El Congreso de los Pueblos de Habla Español, see M.T. García, *Mexican Americans*, 145–74.

34. Juan Gómez-Quiñones, *Sembradores, Ricardo Flores Magón y el Partido Liberal Mexicano: A Eulogy and Critique* (Los Angeles: Aztlán Publications, Chicano Studies Center, University of California, 1973).

35. Marcienne Rocard, *Children of the Sun*, 213.

36. Ibid.

37. Ibid., 213–15.

38. In the works of the Teatro Campesino, La Raza would win its economic battle; in Nephthali De Leon's plays, the Chicano struggle had the blessings of Che Guevara and other fallen revolutionaries; in Rudy Anaya's novels, all answers came from within the Chicano family; and in Evangelina Vigil's poems, the Chicana won her struggles against Anglo society and Chicano men.

39. Nicolas Kanellos, *Mexican American Theater Then and Now* (Houston: Arte Público Press, 1983), 41–51.

40. Most working-class drama was composed of a series of skits and musical numbers; thus they were called variety shows. See Kanellos, *Mexican American Theater*, 19–40.

41. Kanellos deals with this type of sociological dilemma facing Mexican Americans in his discussion of Chicano theater groups; see *Mexican American Theater*, 35–38.

42. Luis Valdez, "Notes on Chicano Theater," in *Aztlán: An Anthology of Mexican American Literature*, ed. Luis Valdez and Stan Steiner (New York: Alfred A. Knopf, 1972), 353–54.

43. The NFWA had become the United Farmworkers Union, or UFW.

44. The taxonomy or lexicon, as some called it, of the Chicano Movement served a useful purpose for activists seeking to change the way the community perceived itself and Anglo-American society. See Valdez, "Notes on Chicano Theater," 354–59.

45. Carlos Muñoz, *Youth, Identity, Power*, 134–35.

46. Ibid., 191–202.

47. Ibid., 138.

48. Ibid., 192.

49. It is important to note that, unlike today, when many Anglo-American students are "forced" to take these courses because of degree requirements, few Anglo-American students took them when they first became part of the college curriculum.

50. In Kingsville, the Chicano Movement depended on the limited facilities of the ethnic studies program and used students to do much of the campaigning, leafleting, and protest marching.

51. Editorial, *El Grito* 3, no. 3 (spring 1970): 2.

52. Ibid.

53. In Kingsville, La Raza Unida Club sponsored Christmas parties for children, Cinco de Mayo celebrations for the community, lectures series, art exhibits, Tejano music concerts, and Chicano plays.

54. Editorial, *El Gallo*, July 28, 1967, p.2.

55. Longeaux y Vásquez , "A nuestros lectores," 2.

56. For a discussion of Chicano newspapers, see Stephen Casanova, "La Raza Unida Press," 1986, personal collection of I.M. García.

57. This homogeneity did not spill over into political strategies or even rigid ideologies, but it did provide an image of Chicanos deeply committed to struggle for liberation.

58. For a discussion of the changes that took place in the American Catholic Church after the activism of the 1960s and 1970s, see Jay P. Dolan and Allan Figueroa Deck, S.J., eds., *Hispanic Catholic Culture in the U.S.: Issues and Concerns* (Notre Dame, Ind.: University of Notre Dame Press, 1994).

59. See "Católicos por la raza," *La Raza* (February 1970).

60. Editorial, *El Grito del Norte*, February 11, 1970, p.2.

61. César Chávez, "The Mexican Americans and the Church," *El Grito* 2, no. 4 (summer 1968).

62. Navarro, "El Partido," 250–52.

63. Luis Valdez, "The Church and the Chicanos," in *Aztlán: An Anthology of Mexican American Literature*, ed. Luis Valdez and Stan Steiner (New York: Alfred A. Knopf, 1972), 387–88.

64. Leo D. Nieto, "The Chicano Movement and the Churches in the United States," *Perkins Journal* (fall 1975).

65. See "Peregrinación, Penitencia, Revolución," by César Chávez (mimeographed; reprinted in Luis Valdez and Stan Steiner, eds., *Aztlán: An Anthology of Mexican American Literature* [New York: Alfred A. Knopf, 1972], 389–90.)

66. See Dolan and Deck, *Hispanic Catholic Culture*, 224–36.

67. See "Jesus Christ as a Revolutionist," *El Grito del Norte*, February 11, 1970.

68. "Day of Triumph in Tierra Amarilla," *El Grito del Norte*, January 1969, p.7.

69. Arthur Rubel, "The Family," in *Mexican Americans in the United States*, ed. John H. Burman (New York: Shenkman Publishing Co., 1970), 214.

70. William Madsen, *Mexican American*, 20.

71. Gloria Molina de Pick, "Reflexiones sobre el feminismo y la raza," *La Luz* (August 1972): 58.

72. Adaljiza Sosa Riddell, "Chicanas and el Movimiento," *Aztlán* 5, nos. 1 and 2 (1974): 160.

73. Enriqueta Longeaux y Vásquez , "The Woman of La Raza," in *Aztlán: An Anthology of Mexican American Literature*, ed. Luis Valdez and Stan Steiner (New York: Alfred A. Knopf, 1972), 272.

74. Enriqueta Longeaux y Vásquez, "The Women of La Raza," *El Grito del Norte*, July 6, 1969.

75. José Montoya, "La Jefita," in *El Espejo—The Mirror: Selected Mexican American Literature*, ed. Octavio V. Romano (Quinto Sol Publications: 1969).

76. See "Our Feminist Heritage," in Martha P. Cotera's *The Chicana Feminist* (Austin, Tex.: Information Systems Development, 1977), 1–7.

77. Martha Cotera made this statement on September 12, 1994, in Austin, Texas at a training session for producers and writers of an upcoming Public Broadcasting System special on the Chicano Movement.

78. Enriqueta Longeaux y Vásquez , "Woman of La Raza," 274–77.

79. "La Chicana," *El Grito del Norte*, June 5, 1971, special section.

The Development of Chicana Feminist Discourse

Alma M. García

Between 1970 and 1980 a Chicana feminist movement developed in the United States that addressed the specific issues that affected Chicanas as women of color. The growth of the Chicana feminist movement can be traced in the speeches, essays, letters, and articles published in Chicano and Chicana newspapers, journals, newsletters, and other printed materials.

During the sixties American society witnessed the development of the Chicano movement, a social movement characterized by a politics of protest. The Chicano movement focused on a wide range of issues: social justice, equality, educational reforms, and political and economic self-determination for Chicano communities in the United States. Various struggles evolved within this movement: the United Farmworkers unionization efforts, the New Mexico Land Grant movement, the Colorado-based Crusade for Justice, the Chicano student movement, and the Raza Unida Party.

Chicanas participated actively in each of these struggles. By the end of the sixties, Chicanas began to assess the rewards and limits of their participation. The 1970s witnessed the development of Chicana feminists whose activities, organizations and writings can be analyzed in terms of a feminist movement by women of color in American society. Chicana feminists outlined a cluster of ideas that crystallized into an emergent Chicana feminist debate. In the same way that Chicano males were reinterpreting the historical and contemporary experience of Chicanos in the United States, Chicanas began to investigate the forces shaping their own experiences as women of color.

The Chicana feminist movement emerged primarily as a result of the dynamics within the Chicano movement. In the 1960s and 1970s, the American political scene witnessed far-reaching social protest movements whose political courses often paralleled and at times exerted

influence over each other. The development of feminist movements have been explained by the participation of women in larger social movements. Macías, for example, links the early development of the Mexican feminist movement to the participation of women in the Mexican Revolution. Similarly, Freeman's analysis of the white feminist movement points out that many white feminists who were active in the early years of its development had previously been involved in the new left and civil rights movements. It was in these movements that white feminists experienced the constraints of male domination. Black feminists have similarly traced the development of a Black feminist movement during the 1960s and 1970s to their experiences with sexism in the larger Black movement. In this way, then, the origins of Chicano feminism parallel those of other feminist movements.

Origins of Chicana Feminism

Rowbotham argues that women may develop a feminist consciousness as a result of their experiences with sexism in revolutionary struggles or mass social movements. To the extent that such movements are male dominated, women are likely to develop a feminist consciousness. Chicana feminists began the search for a "room of their own" by assessing their participation within the Chicano movement. Their feminist consciousness emerged from a struggle for equality with Chicano men and from a reassessment of the role of the family as a means of resistance to oppressive societal conditions.

Historically, as well as during the 1960s and 1970s, the Chicano family represented a source of cultural and political resistance to the various types of discrimination experienced in American society. At the cultural level, the Chicano movement emphasized the need to safeguard the value of family loyalty. At the political level, the Chicano movement used the family as a strategic organizational tool for protest activities.

Dramatic changes in the structure of Chicano families occurred as they participated in the Chicano movement. Specifically, women began to question their

Alma M. García. From *Gender & Society*, Vol. 3, No. 2, June 1989, pages 217-238. Reprinted by permission of Sage Publications.

traditional female roles. Thus, a Chicana feminist movement originated from the nationalist Chicano struggle. Rowbotham refers to such a feminist movement as "a colony within a colony." But as the Chicano movement developed during the 1970s, Chicana feminists began to draw their own political agenda and raised a series of questions to assess their role within the Chicano movement. They entered into a dialogue with each other that explicitly reflected their struggles to secure a room of their own within the Chicano movement.

Defining Feminism for Women of Color

A central question of feminist discourse is the definition of feminism. The lack of consensus reflects different political ideologies and divergent social-class bases. In the United States, Chicana feminists shared the task of defining their ideology and movement with white, Black, and Asian American feminists. Like Black and Asian American feminists, Chicana feminists struggled to gain social equality and end sexist and racist oppression. Like them, Chicana feminists recognized that the nature of social inequality for women of color was multidimensional. Like Black and Asian American feminists, Chicana feminists struggled to gain equal status in the male-dominated nationalist movements and also in American society. To them, feminism represented a movement to end sexist oppression within a broader social protest movement. Again, like Black and Asian American feminists, Chicana feminists fought for social equality in the 1970s. They understood that their movement needed to go beyond women's rights and include the men of their group, who also face racial subordination. Chicanas believed that feminism involved more than an analysis of gender because as women of color, they were affected by both race and class in their everyday lives. Thus, Chicana feminism, as a social movement to improve the position of Chicanas in American society, represented a struggle that was both nationalist and feminist.

Chicana, Black and Asian American feminists were all confronted with the issue of engaging in a feminist struggle to end sexist oppression within a broader nationalist struggle to end racist oppression. All experienced male domination in their own communities as well as in the larger society. Ngan-Ling Chow identifies gender stereotypes of Asian American women and the patriarchal family structure as major sources of women's oppression. Cultural, political, and economic constraints have, according to Ngan-Ling Chow, limited the full development of a feminist consciousness and movement among Asian American women. The cross-pressures resulting from the demands of a nationalist and a feminist struggle led some Asian American women to organize feminist organizations that, however, continued to address broader issues affecting the Asian American community.

Black women were also faced with addressing feminist issues within a nationalist movement. According to

Thornton Dill, Black women played a major historical role in Black resistance movements and, in addition, brought a feminist component to these movements. Black women have struggled with Black men in nationalist movements but have also recognized and fought against the sexism in such political movements in the Black community. Although they wrote and spoke as Black feminists, they did not organize separately from Black men.

Among the major ideological questions facing all three groups of feminists were the relationship between feminism and the ideology of cultural nationalism or racial pride, feminism and feminist baiting within the larger movements, and the relationship between their feminist movements and the white feminist movement.

Chicana Feminism and Cultural Nationalism

Throughout the seventies and in the eighties, Chicana feminists have been forced to respond to the criticism that cultural nationalism and feminism are irreconcilable. In the first issue of the newspaper, *Hijas de Cuauhtémoc*, Anna Nieto Gómez stated that a major issue facing Chicanas active in the Chicana movement was the need to organize to improve their status as women within the larger social movement. Francisca Flores, another leading Chicana feminist, stated:

> [Chicanas] can no longer remain in a subservient role or as auxiliary forces in the [Chicano] movement. They must be included in the front line of communication, leadership and organizational responsibility. . . . The issue of equality, freedom and self-determination of the Chicana—like the right of self-determination, equality, and liberation of the Mexican [Chicano] community—is not negotiable. Anyone opposing the right of women to organize into their own form of organization has no place in the leadership of the movement.

Supporting this position, Bernice Rincón argued that a Chicana feminist movement that sought equality and justice for Chicanas would strengthen the Chicano movement. Yet in the process, Chicana feminists challenged traditional gender roles because they limited their participation and acceptance within the Chicano movement.

Throughout the seventies, Chicana feminists viewed the struggle against sexism within the Chicano movement and the struggle against racism in the larger society as integral parts of Chicana feminism. As Nieto Gómez said:

> Chicana feminism is in various stages of development. However, in general, Chicana feminism is the recognition that women are oppressed as a group and are exploited as part of *"La Raza"* people. It is a direction to be responsible to identify and act upon the issues

and needs of Chicana women. Chicana feminists are involved in understanding the nature of women's oppression.

Cultural nationalism represented a major ideological component of the Chicano movement. Its emphasis on Chicano cultural pride and cultural survival within an Anglo-dominated society gave significant political direction to the Chicano movement. One source of ideological disagreement between Chicana feminism and this cultural nationalist ideology was cultural survival. Many Chicana feminists believed that a focus on cultural survival did not acknowledge the need to alter male-female relations within Chicano communities. For example, Chicana feminists criticized the notion of the "ideal Chicana" that glorified Chicanas as strong, long-suffering women who had endured and kept Chicano culture and the family intact. To Chicana feminists, this concept represented an obstacle to the redefinition of gender roles. Nieto stated:

> Some Chicanas are praised as they emulate the sanctified example set by [the Virgin] Mary. The woman *par excellence* is mother and wife. She is to love and support her husband and to nurture and teach her children. Thus, may she gain fulfillment as a woman. For a Chicana bent upon fulfillment of her personhood, this restricted perspective of her role as a woman is not only inadequate but crippling.

Chicana feminists were also skeptical about the cultural nationalist interpretation of machismo. Such an interpretation viewed machismo as an ideological tool used by the dominant Anglo society to justify the inequalities experienced by Chicanos. According to this interpretation, the relationship between Chicanos and the larger society was that of an internal colony dominated and exploited by the capitalist economy. Machismo, like other cultural traits, was blamed by Anglos for blocking Chicanos from succeeding in American society. In reality, the economic structure and colony-like exploitation were to blame.

Some Chicana feminists agreed with this analysis of machismo, claiming that a mutually reinforcing relationship existed between internal colonialism and the development of the myth of machismo. According to Sosa Riddell, machismo was a myth "propagated by subjugators and colonizers, which created damaging stereotypes of Mexican/Chicano males." As a type of social control imposed by the dominant society on Chicanos, the myth of machismo distorted gender relations within Chicano communities, creating stereotypes of Chicanas as passive and docile women. At this level in the feminist discourse, machismo was seen as an Anglo myth that kept both Chicano and Chicanas in a subordinate status. As Nieto concluded:

> Although the term "machismo" is correctly denounced by all because it stereotypes the Latin man . . . it does

a great disservice to both men and women. Chicano and Chicana alike must be free to seek their own individual fulfillment.

While some Chicana feminists criticized the myth of machismo used by the dominant society to legitimate racial inequality, others moved beyond this level of analysis to distinguish between the machismo that oppressed both men and women and the sexism in Chicano communities in general, and the Chicano movement in particular, that oppressed Chicana women. According to Vidal, the origins of a Chicana feminist consciousness were prompted by the sexist attitudes and behavior of Chicano males, which constituted a "serious obstacle to women anxious to play a role in the struggle for Chicana liberation."

Furthermore, many Chicana feminists disagreed with the cultural nationalist view that machismo could be a positive value within a Chicano cultural value system. They challenged the view that machismo was a source of masculine pride for Chicanos and therefore a defense mechanism against the dominant society's racism. Although Chicana feminists recognized that Chicanos faced discrimination from the dominant society, they adamantly disagreed with those who believed that machismo was a form of cultural resistance to such discrimination. Chicana feminists called for changes in the ideologies responsible for distorting relations between women and men. One such changes was to modify the cultural nationalist position that viewed machismo as a source of cultural pride.

Chicana feminists called for a focus on the universal aspects of sexism that shape gender relations in both Anglo and Chicano culture. While they acknowledged the economic exploitation of all Chicanos, Chicana feminists outlined the double exploitation experienced by Chicanas. Sosa Riddell (1974, p. 159) concluded: "It was when Chicanas began to seek work outside of the family groups that sexism became a key factor of oppression along with racism." Francisca Flores (1971a, p. 4) summarized some of the consequences of sexism:

> It is not surprising that more and more Chicanas are forced to go to work in order to supplement the family income. The children are farmed out to a relative to baby-sit with them, and since these women are employed in the lower income jobs, the extra pressure placed on them can become unbearable.

Thus, while the Chicano movement was addressing the issue of racial oppression facing all Chicanos, Chicana feminist argued that it lacked an analysis of sexism. Similarly, Black and Asian American women stressed the interconnectedness of race and gender oppression. Hook (1984, p. 52) analyzes racism and sexism in terms of their "intersecting, complementary nature." She also emphasizes that one struggle should not take priority over the other. White (1984) criticizes Black men whose nationalism limited discussions of Black women's experiences with sexist oppression. The writings of other Black feminists criticized a Black cultural nationalist ideology that overlooked the consequences of sexist oppression (Beale 1975; Cade 1970; Davis 1971; Joseph and Lewis 1981). Many Asian American women were also critical of the Asian American movement whose focus on racism ignored the impact of sexism on the daily lives of women. The participation of Asian American women in various community struggles increased their encounters with sexism (Chow 1987). As a result, some Asian American women developed a feminist consciousness and organized as women around feminist issues.

Chicana Feminism and Feminist Baiting

The systematic analysis by Chicana feminists of the impact of racism and sexism on Chicanas in American society and, above all, within the Chicano movement was often misunderstood as a threat to the political unity of the Chicano movement. As Marta Cotera (1977, p. 9), a leading voice of Chicana feminism pointed out:

> The aggregate cultural values we [Chicanas] share can also work to our benefit if we choose to scrutinize our cultural traditions, isolate the positive attributes and interpret them for the benefit of women. It's unreal that *Hispanas* have been browbeaten for so long about our so-called conservative (meaning reactionary) culture. It's also unreal that we have let men interpret culture only as those practices and attitudes that determine who does the dishes around the house. We as women also have the right to interpret and define the philosophical and religious traditions beneficial to us within our culture, and which we have inherited as our tradition. To do this, we must become both conversant with our history and philosophical evolution, and analytical about the institutional and behavioral manifestations of the same.

Such Chicana feminists were attacked for developing a "divisive ideology"—a feminist ideology that was frequently viewed as a threat to the Chicano movement as a whole. As Chicana feminists examined their roles as women activists within the Chicano movement, an ideological split developed. One group active in the Chicano movement saw themselves as "loyalists" who believed that the Chicano movement did not have to deal with sexual inequities since Chicana men as well as Chicano women experienced racial oppression. According to Nieto Gómez (1973, p. 35), who was not a loyalist, their view was that if men oppress women, it is not the men's fault but rather that of the system.

Even if such a problem existed, and they did not believe that it did, the loyalists maintained that such a matter would best be resolved internally within the Chicano movement. They denounced the formation of a separate Chicana feminist movement on the grounds that it was a politically dangerous strategy, perhaps Anglo inspired. Such a move-

ment would undermine the unity of the Chicano movement by raising an issue that was not seen as a central one. Loyalists viewed racism as the most important issue within the Chicano movement. Nieto Gómez (1973, p. 35) quotes one such loyalist:

> I am concerned with the direction that the Chicanas are taking in the movement. The words such as liberation, sexism, male chauvinism, etc., were prevalent. The terms mentioned above plus the theme of individualism is a concept of the Anglo society; terms prevalent in the Anglo women's movement. The *familia* has always been our strength in our culture. But it seems evident . . . that you [Chicana feminists] are not concerned with the *familia*, but are influenced by the Anglo woman's movement.

Chicana feminists were also accused of undermining the values associated with Chicano culture. Loyalists saw the Chicana feminist movement as an "anti-family, anti-cultural, anti-man and therefore an anti-Chicano movement" (Gómez 1973, p. 35). Feminism was, above all, believed to be an individualistic search for identity that detracted from the Chicano movement's "real" issues, such as racism. Nieto Gómez (1973, p. 35) quotes a loyalist as stating:

> And since when does a Chicana need identity? If you are a real Chicana then no one regardless of the degrees needs to tell you about it. The only ones who need identity are the *vendidas*, the *falsas*, and the opportunists.

The ideological conflicts between Chicana feminists and loyalists persisted throughout the seventies. Disagreements between these two groups became exacerbated during various Chicana conferences. At times, such confrontations served to increase Chicana feminist activity that challenged the loyalists' attacks, yet these attacks also served to suppress feminist activities.

Chicana feminist lesbians experienced even stronger attacks from those who viewed feminism as a divisive ideology. In a political climate that already viewed feminist ideology with suspicion, lesbianism as a sexual lifestyle and political ideology came under even more attack. Clearly, a cultural nationalist ideology that perpetuated such stereotypical images of Chicanas as "good wives and good mothers" found it difficult to accept a Chicana feminist lesbian movement.

Cherríe Moraga's writings during the 1970s reflect the struggles of Chicana feminist lesbians who, together with other Chicana feminists, were finding the sexism evident within the Chicano movement intolerable. Just as Chicana feminists analyzed their life circumstances as members of an ethnic minority and as women, Chicana feminist lesbians addressed themselves to the oppression they experienced as lesbians. As Moraga (1981, p. 28) stated:

> My lesbianism is the avenue through which I have learned the most about silence and oppression[1] . . . . In this country, lesbianism is a poverty—as is being brown, as is being a woman, as is being just plain poor. The danger lies in ranking the oppressions. The danger lies in failing to acknowledge the specificity of the oppression.

Chicana, Black, and Asian American feminists experienced similar cross-pressures of feminist-baiting and lesbian-baiting attacks. As they organized around feminist struggles, these women of color encountered criticism from both male and female cultural nationalists who often viewed feminism as little more than an "anti-male" ideology. Lesbianism was identified as an extreme deviation of feminism. A direct connection was frequently made that viewed feminism and lesbianism as synonymous. Feminists were labeled lesbians, and lesbians as feminists. Attacks against feminists—Chicanas, Blacks, and Asian Americans—derived from the existence of homophobia within each of these communities. As lesbian women of color published their writings, attacks against them increased (Moraga, 1983).

Responses to such attacks varied within and between the feminist movements of women of color. Some groups tried one strategy and later adopted another. Some lesbians pursued a separatist strategy within their own racial and ethnic communities (Moraga and Anzaldúa 1981; White 1984). Others attempted to form lesbian coalitions across racial and ethnic lines. Both strategies represented a response to the marginalization of lesbians produced by recurrent waves of homophobic sentiments in Chicano, Black, and Asian American communities (Moraga and Anzaldúa 1981). A third response consisted of working within the broader nationalist movements in these communities and the feminist movements within them in order to challenge their heterosexual biases and resultant homophobia. As early as 1974, the "Black Feminist Statement" written by a Boston-based feminist group—the Combahee River Collective—stated (1981, p. 213): "We struggle together with Black men against racism, while we also struggle with Black men against sexism." Similarly, Moraga (1981) challenged the white feminist movement to examine its racist tendencies; the Chicano movement, its sexist tendencies; and both, their homophobic tendencies. In this way, Moraga argued that such movements to end oppression would begin to respect diversity within their own ranks.

Chicana feminists as well as Chicana feminist lesbians continued to be labeled *vendidas* or "sellouts." Chicana loyalists continued to view Chicana feminism as associated, not only with melting into white society, but more seriously, with dividing the Chicano movement. Similarly,

many Chicano males were convinced the Chicana feminism was a divisive ideology incompatible with Chicano cultural nationalism. Nieto Gómez said that "[with] respect to [the] Chicana feminist, their credibility is reduced when they are associated with [feminism] and white women." She added that, as a result, Chicana feminists often faced harassment and ostracism within the Chicano movement. Similarly, Cotera stated that Chicanas "are suspected of assimilating into the feminist ideology of an alien [white] culture that actively seeks our cultural domination."

Chicana feminists responded quickly and often vehemently to such charges. Flores answered these antifeminist attacks in an editorial in which she argued that birth control, abortion, and sex education were not merely "white issues." In response to the accusation that feminists were responsible for the "betrayal of [Chicano] culture and heritage," Flores said, "Our culture hell"—a phrase that became a dramatic slogan of the Chicana feminist movement.

Chicana feminists' defense throughout the 1970s against those claiming that a feminist movement was divisive for the Chicano movement was to reassess their roles within the Chicano movement and to call for an end to male domination. Their challenges of traditional gender roles represented a means to achieve equality. In order to increase the participation of and opportunities for women in the Chicano movement, feminists agreed that both Chicanos and Chicanas had to address the issue of gender inequality. Furthermore, Chicana feminists argued that the resistance that they encountered reflected the existence of sexism on the part of Chicano males and the anti-feminist attitudes of the Chicana loyalists. Nieto Gómez, reviewing the experiences of Chicana feminists in the Chicano movement, concluded that Chicanas "involved in discussing and applying the women's question have been ostracized, isolated and ignored." She argued that "in organizations where cultural nationalism is extremely strong, Chicana feminists experience intense harassment and ostracism."

Black and Asian American women also faced severe criticism as they pursued feminist issues in their own communities. Indeed, as their participation in collective efforts to end racial oppression increased, so did their confrontations with sexism. Ngan-Ling Chow describes the various sources of such criticism directed at Asian American women:

> Asian American women are criticized for the possible consequences of their protests: weakening the male ego, dilution of effort and resources in Asian American communities, destruction of working relationships between Asian men and women, setbacks for the Asian American cause, co-optation into the larger society, and eventual loss of ethnic identity for Asian Americans as a whole. In short, affiliation with the feminist

movement is perceived as a threat to solidarity within their own community.

Similar criticism was experienced by Black feminists.

Chicana Feminists and White Feminists

It is difficult to determine the extent to which Chicana feminists sympathized with the white feminist movement. A 1976 study at the University of San Diego that examined the attitudes of Chicanas regarding the white feminist movement found that the majority of Chicanas surveyed believed that the movement had affected their lives. In addition, they identified with such key issues as the right to legal abortions on demand and access to low-cost birth control. Nevertheless, the survey found that "even though the majority of Chicanas . . . could relate to certain issues of the women's movement, for the most part they saw it as being an elitist movement comprised of white middle-class women who [saw] the oppressor as the males of this country."

Nevertheless, some Chicana feminists considered the possibility of forming coalitions with white feminists as their attempts to work within the Chicano movement were suppressed. Since white feminists were themselves struggling against sexism, building coalitions with them was seen as an alternative strategy for Chicana feminists. Almost immediately, however, Chicana feminists recognized the problems involved in adopting this political strategy. As Longeaux y Vásquez acknowledged, "some of our own Chicanas may be attracted to the white woman's liberation movement, but we really don't feel comfortable there. We want to be a Chicana *primero* [first]." For other Chicanas, the demands of white women were irrelevant to the Chicana movement.

Several issues made such coalition building difficult. First, Chicana feminists criticized what they considered to be a cornerstone of white feminist thought, an emphasis on gender oppression to explain the life circumstances of women. Chicana feminists believed that the white feminist movement overlooked the effects of racial oppression experienced by Chicanas and other women of color. Thus, Del Castillo maintained that the Chicana feminist movement was "different primarily because we are [racially] oppressed people." In addition, Chicana feminists criticized white feminists who believed that a general women's movement would be able to overcome racial differences among women. Chicanas interpreted this as a failure by the white feminist movement to deal with the issue of racism. Without the incorporation of an analysis of racial oppression to explain the experiences of Chicanas as well as of other women of color, Chicana feminists believed that a coalition with white feminists would be highly unlikely. As Longeaux y Vásquez concluded: "We must have a clearer vision of our plight and certainly we cannot blame our men for the oppression of the women."

In the 1970s, Chicana feminists reconciled their demands for an end to sexism within the Chicano movement and their rejection of the saliency of gender oppression by separating the two issues. They clearly identified the struggle against sexism in the Chicano movement as a major issue, arguing that sexism prevented their full participation. They also argued that sexist behavior and ideology on the part of both Chicano males and Anglos represented the key to understanding women's experiences that focused exclusively on gender oppression.

Chicana feminists adopted an analysis that began with race as a critical variable in interpreting the experiences of Chicano communities in the United States. They expanded this analysis by identifying gender as a variable interconnected with race in analyzing the specific daily life circumstances of Chicanas as women in Chicano communities. Chicana feminists did not view women's struggles as secondary to the nationalist movement but argued instead for an analysis of race and gender as multiple sources of oppression. Thus, Chicana feminism went beyond the limits of an exclusively racial theory of oppression that tended to overlook gender and also went beyond the limits of a theory of oppression based exclusively on gender that tended to overlook race.

A second factor preventing an alliance between Chicana feminists and white feminists was the middle-class orientation of white feminists. While some Chicana feminists recognized the legitimacy of the demands made by white feminists and even admitted sharing some of these demands, they argued that "it is not our business as Chicanas to identify with the white women's liberation movement as a home base for working for our people."

Throughout the 1970s, Chicana feminists viewed the white feminist movement as a middle-class movement. In contrast, Chicana feminists analyzed the Chicana movement in general as a working-class movement. They repeatedly made reference to such differences, and many Chicana feminists began their writings with a section that disassociated themselves from the "women's liberation movement." Chicana feminists as activists in the broader Chicano movement identified as major struggles the farmworkers movement, welfare rights, undocumented workers, and prison rights. Such demands of the white feminist movement, and Chicana feminists could not get white feminist organizations to deal with them.

Similar concerns regarding the white feminist movement were raised by Black and Asian American feminists. Black feminists have documented the historical and contemporary schisms between Black feminists and white feminists, emphasizing the socioeconomic and political differences. More specifically, Black feminists have been critical of the white feminists who advocate a female solidarity that cuts across racial, ethnic, and social class lines. As Thornton Dill states:

The cry "Sisterhood is powerful!" has engaged only a few segments of the female population in the United States. Black, Hispanic, Native American, and Asian American women of all classes, as well as many working-class women, have not readily identified themselves as sisters of the white middle-class women who have been in the forefront of the movement.

Like Black feminists, Asian American feminists have also had strong reservations regarding the white feminist movement. For many Asian Americans, white feminism has primarily focused on gender as an analytical category and has thus lacked a systematic analysis of race and class.

White feminists organizations were also accused of being exclusionary, patronizing, or racist in their dealings with Chicanas and other women of color. Cotera states:

> Minority women could fill volumes with examples of put-down, put-ons, and out-and-out racism shown to them by the leadership in the [white feminist] movement. There are three major problem areas in the minority-majority relationship in the movement: (1) paternalism or materialism, (2) extremely limited opportunities for minority women . . . , (3) outright discrimination against minority women in the movement.

Although Chicana feminists continued to be critical of building coalitions with white feminists toward the end of the seventies, they acknowledged the diversity of ideologies within the white feminist movement. Chicana feminists sympathetic to radical socialist feminism because of its anticapitalist framework wrote of working-class oppression that cut across racial and ethnic lines. Their later writings discussed the possibility of joining with white working-class women, but strategies for forming such political coalitions were not made explicit.

Instead, Del Castillo and other Chicana feminists favored coalitions between Chicanas and other women of color while keeping their respective autonomous organizations. Such coalitions would recognize the inherent racial oppression of capitalism rather than universal gender oppression. When Longeaux y Vásquez stated that she was "Chicana *primero*," she was stressing the saliency of race over gender in explaining the oppression experienced by Chicanas. The word *Chicana* however, simultaneously expresses a woman's race and gender. Not until later—in the 1980s—would Chicana feminist ideology call for an analysis that stressed the interrelationship of race, class, and gender in explaining the conditions of Chicanas in American society, just as Black and Asian American feminists have done.

Chicana feminists continued to stress the importance of developing autonomous feminist organizations that would address the struggles of Chicanas as members of an ethnic minority and as women. Rather that attempt to overcome the obstacles to coalition building between Chicana feminists and white feminists, Chicanas called

for autonomous feminists organizations for all women of color. Chicana feminists believed that sisterhood was indeed powerful but only to the extent that racial and class differences were understood and, above all, respected. As Nieto concludes:

> The Chicana must demand that dignity and respect within the women's rights movement which allows her to practice feminism within the context of own culture. . . . Her approaches to feminism must be drawn from her own world.

Chicana Feminism: An Evolving Future

Chicana feminists, like Black, Asian American and Native American feminists, experience specific life conditions that are distinct from those of white feminists. Such socioeconomic and cultural differences in Chicano communities directly shaped the development of Chicana feminism and the relationship between Chicana feminists and feminists of other racial ethnic groups, including white feminists. But dialogue among all feminists will require mutual understanding of the existing differences as well as the similarities. Like other women of color, Chicana feminists must address issues that specifically affect them as women of color. In addition. Chicana feminists must address those issues that have particular impact on Chicano communities, such as poverty, limited opportunities for higher education, high school dropouts, health care, bilingual education, immigration reform, prison reform, welfare, and, most recently, United States policies in Central America.

At the academic level, an increasing number of Chicana feminists continue to join in a collective effort to carry on the feminist legacy inherited from the 1970s. In June 1982, a group of Chicana academics organized a national feminist organization called Mujeres Activas Letras y Cambio Social (MALCS) in order to build a support network for Chicana professors, undergraduates, and graduate students. The organization's major goal is to fight against race, class, and gender oppression facing Chicanas in institutions of higher education. In addition, MALCS aims to bridge the gap between academic work and the Chicano community. MALCS has organized three Chicana/Latina summer research institutes at the University of California at Davis and publishes a working paper series.

During the 1982 conference of the National Association for Chicano Studies, a panel organized by Mujeres en Marcha, a feminist group from the University of California at Berkeley, discussed three major issues facing Chicana feminists in higher education in particular and the Chicano movement in general. Panelists outlined the issues as follows:

1. For a number of years, Chicanas have heard claims that a concern with issues specifically affecting Chicanas is merely a distraction/ diversion from the liberation of Chicano people as a whole. What are the issues that arise when women are asked to separate their exploitation as women from the other forms of oppression that we experience?

2. Chicanas are confronted daily by the limitations of being a woman in this patriarchal society; the attempts to assert these issues around sexism are often met with resistance and scorn. What are some of the major difficulties in relations amongst ourselves? How are the relationships between women and men affected? How are the relationships of women to women and men to men affected? How do we overcome the constraints of sexism?

3. It is not uncommon that our interests as feminists are challenged on the basis that we are simply falling prey to the interests of white middle-class women We challenge the notion that there is no room for a Chicana movement within our own community We, as women of color, have a unique set of concerns that are separate from white women and from men of color.

While these issues could not be resolved at the conference, the panel succeeded in generating an ongoing discussion within the National Association for Chicano Studies (NACS). Two years later, in 1984, the national conference of NACS, held in Austin, Texas, adopted the theme "Voces de la Mujer" in response to demands from the Chicana Caucus. As a result, for the first time since its founding in 1972, the NACS national conference addressed the issue of women. Compared with past conferences, a large number of Chicanas participated by presenting their research and chairing and moderating panels. A plenary session addressed the problems of gender inequality in higher education and within NACS. At the national business meeting, the issue of sexism within NACS was again seriously debated as it continues to be one of the "unsettled issues" of concern to Chicana feminists. A significant outcome of this conference was the publication of the NACS 1984 conference proceedings, which marked the first time that the association's anthology was devoted completely to Chicanas and Mexicanas.

The decade of the 1980s has witnessed a rephrasing of the critical question concerning the nature of the oppression experienced by Chicanas and other women of color. Chicana feminists, like Black feminists, are asking what are the consequences of the intersection of race, class, and gender in the daily lives of women in American society, emphasizing the simultaneity of these critical variables for women of color. In their labor-force participation, wages, education, and poverty levels, Chicanas have made few gains in comparison to white men and women and Chicano men. To analyze these problems, Chicana femi-

nists have investigated the structures of racism, capitalism, and patriarchy, especially as they are experienced by the majority of Chicanas. Clearly, such issues will need to be explicitly addressed by an evolving Chicana feminist movement, analytically and politically.

Note

1. For bibliographies on Chicanas see Balderama (1981); Candelaria (1980); Loeb (1980); Portillo, Ríos, and Rodríguez (1976); and Baca Zinn (1982, 1984).

References

Almaguer, Tomás. 1974. "Historical Notes on Chicano Oppression." *Atlas* 5:27–56.

Baca Zinn, Maxine. 1975a. "Political Familism: Toward Sex Role Equality in Chicano Families." *Aztlán* 6:13–27.

———. 1975b. "Chicanas: Power and Control in the Domestic Sphere." *De Colores* 2/3:19–31.

———. 1982. "Mexican-American Women in the Social Sciences." *Signs: Journal of Women in Culture and Society* 8:259–72.

———. 1984. "Mexican Heritage Women: A Bibliographic Essay." *Sage Race Relations Abstracts* 9:1–12.

Balderama, Sylvia. 1981. "A Comprehensive Bibliography on La Chicana." Unpublished paper, University of California, Berkeley.

Barrera, Mario. 1974. "The Study of Politics and the Chicano." *Aztlán* 5:9–26.

———. 1979. *Race and Class in the Southwest.* Notre Dame, IN: University of Notre Dame Press.

Beale, Frances. 1975. "Slave of a Slave No More: Black Women in Struggle." *Black Scholar* 6:2–10.

Cade, Toni. 1970. *The Black Woman.* New York: Signet.

Candelaria, Cordelia. 1980. "Six Reference Works on Mexican American Women: A Review Essay." *Frontiers* 5:75–80.

Castro, Tony. 1974. *Chicano Power.* New York: Saturday Review Press.

Chapa, Evey. 1973. "Report from the National Women's Political Caucus." *Magazín* 1:37–39.

Chávez, Henri. 1971. "The Chicanas." *Regeneracion* 1:14.

Cheng, Lucie. 1984. "Asian American Women and Feminism." *Sojourner* 10:11–12.

Chow, Esther Ngan-Ling. 1987. "The Development of Feminist Consciousness Among Asian American Women." *Gender & Society* 1:284–99.

Combahee River Collective. 1981. "A Black Feminist Statement." Pp. 210–18 in *This Bridge Called My Back: Writings by Radical Women of Color*, edited by Cherrie Moraga and Gloria Anzaldúa. Watertown, MA: Persephone.

Córdova, Teresa et al. 1986. *Chicana Voices: Intersections of Class, Race, and Gender.* Austin, TX: Center for Mexican American Studies.

Cotera, Marta. 1973. "La Mujer Mexicana: Mexicano Feminism." *Magazín* 1:30–32.

———. 1977. *The Chicana Feminist.* Austin, TX: Austin Information Systems Development.

———. 1980. "Feminism: The Chicana and Anglo Versions: An Historical Analysis." Pp. 217–34 in *Twice a Minority: Mexican American Women*, edited by Margarita Melville. St. Louis, MO: C.V. Mosby.

Davis, Angela. 1971. "Reflections on Black Women's Role in the Community of Slaves." *Black Scholar* 3:3–13.

———. 1983. *Women, Race and Class.* New York: Random House.

Del Castillo, Adelaida. 1974. "La Vision Chicana." *La Gente*: 8.

Dill, Bonnie Thornton. 1983. "Race, Class, and Gender: Prospects for an All-Inclusive Sisterhood." *Feminist Studies* 9:131–50.

Dunne, John. 1967. *Delano: The Story of the California Grape Strike.* New York: Strauss.

Fallis, Guadalupe Valdés. 1974. "The Liberated Chicana—A Struggle Against Tradition." *Women: A Journal of Liberation* 3:20.

Flores, Francisca. 1971a. "Conference of Mexican Women: Un Remolino. *Regeneración* 1(1):1–4.

———. 1971b. "El Mundo Femenil Mexicana." *Regeneración* 1(10):i.

Fong, Katheryn M. 1978. "Feminism Is Fine, But What's It Done for Asia America?" *Bridge* 6:21–22.

Freeman, Jo. 1983. "On the Origins of Social Movements." Pp. 8–30 in *Social Movements of the Sixties and Seventies*, edited by Jo Freeman. New York: Longman.

———. 1984. "The Women's Liberation Movement: Its Origins, Structure, Activities, and Ideas." Pp. 543–56 in *Women: A Feminist Perspective*, edited by Jo Freeman. Palo Alto, CA: Mayfield.

García, Alma M. 1986. "Studying Chicanas: Bringing Women into the Frame of Chicano Studies." Pp. 19–29 in *Chicana Voices: Intersections of Class, Race, and Gender*, edited by Teresa Córdova et al. Austin, TX: Center for Mexican American Studies.

García, F. Chris and Rudolph O. de la Garza. 1977. *The Chicano Political Experience*. North Scituate, MA: Duxbury.

Gómez, Anna Nieto. 1971. "Chicanas Identify." *Hijas de Cuauhtémoc* (April):9.

———. 1973. "La Femenista." *Encuentro Femenil* 1:34–47.

———. 1976. "Sexism in the Movement." *La Gente* 6(4):10.

González, Sylvia. 1980. "Toward a Feminist Pedagogy for Chicana Self-Actualization." *Frontiers* 5:48–51.

Hernández, Carmen. 1971. "Carmen Speaks Out." *Papel Chicano* 1 (June 12):8–9.

Hooks, Bell. 1981. *Ain't I a Woman: Black Women and Feminism.* Boston: South End Press.

———. 1984. *Feminist Theory: From Margin to Center.* Boston: South End Press.

Joseph, Gloria and Jill Lewis. 1981. *Common Differences: Conflicts in Black and White Feminist Perspectives.* Garden City, NY: Doubleday.

Kushner, Sam. 1975. *Long Road to Delano.* New York: International.

LaRue, Linda. 1970. "The Black Movement and Women's Liberation." *Black Scholar* 1:36–42.

Loeb, Catherine. 1980. "La Chicana: A Bibliographic Survey." *Frontiers* 5:59–74.

Longeaux y Vásquez, Enriqueta. 1969a. "The Woman of La Raza. "*El Grito del Norte* 2(July):8–9.

———. 1969b. "La Chicana: Let's Build a New Life." *El Grito del Norte* 2(November):11.

———. 1970. "The Mexican-American Woman." Pp. 379–84 in *Sisterhood Is Powerful*, edited by Robin Morgan. New York: Vintage.

———. 1971. "Soy Chicana Primero." *El Grito del Norte* 4(April 26):11.

Macías, Anna. 1982. *Against All Odds.* Westport. CT: Greenwood.

Márquez, Evelina and Margarita Ramírez. 1977. "Women's Task Is to Gain Liberation." Pp. 188–94 in *Essays on La Mujer*, edited by Rosaura Sánchez and Rosa Martínez Cruz. Los Angeles: UCLA Chicano Studies Center.

Martínez, Elizabeth. 1972. "The Chicana." *Ideal* 44:1–3.

Matthiesen, Peter. 1969. *Sal Si Puedes: César Chávez and the New American Revolution.* New York: Random House.

Meier, Matt and Feliciano Rivera. 1972. *The Chicanos.* New York: Hill & Wang.

Moraga, Cherrie. 1981. "La Guera." Pp. 27–34 in *This Bridge Called My Back: Writings by Radical Women of Color*, edited by Cherrie Moraga and Gloria Anzaldúa. Watertown, MA: Persephone.

———. 1983. *Loving in the War Years.* Boston: South End Press.

Moraga, Cherrie and Gloria Anzaldúa. 1981. *This Bridge Called My Back: Writings by Radical Women of Color.* Watertown, MA: Persephone.

Moreno, Dorinda. 1979. "The Image of the Chicana and the La Raza Woman." *Caracol* 2:14–15.

Mujeres en Marcha. 1983. *Chicanas in the 80s: Unsettled Issues.* Berkeley, CA: Chicano Studies Publication Unit.

Muñoz, Carlos, Jr. 1974. "The Politics of Protest and Liberation: A Case Study of Repression and Cooptation." *Aztlán* 5:119–41.

Nabokov, Peter. 1969. *Tijerina and the Courthouse Raid.* Albuquerque, NM: University of New Mexico Press.

Navarro, Armando. 1974. "The Evolution of Chicano Politics." *Aztlán* 5:57–84.

Nelson, Eugene. 1966. *Huelga: The First 100 Days.* Delano, CA: Farm Workers Press.

Nieto, Consuelo. 1974. "The Chicana and the Women's Rights Movement." *La Luz* 3(September):10–11, 32.

———. 1975. "Consuelo Nieto on the Women's Movement." *Interracial Books for Children Bulletin* 5:4.

Orozco, Yolanda. 1976. "La Chicana and 'Women's Liberation.'" *Voz Fronteriza* (January 5):6, 12.

Piven, Frances Fox and Richard A. Cloward. 1979. *Poor People's Movements: Why They Succeed, How They Fail.* New York: Vintage.

Portillo, Cristina, Graciela Ríos, and Martha Rodríguez. 1976. *Bibliography on Writings on La Mujer.* Berkeley, CA: University of California Chicano Studies Library.

Riddell, Adaljiza Sosa. 1974. "Chicanas en el Movimiento." *Aztlán* 5:155–65.

Rincón, Bernice. 1971. "La Chicana: Her Role in the Past and Her Search for a New Role in the Future." *Regeneración* 1(10):15–17.

Rowbotham, Sheila. 1974. *Women, Resistance and Revolution: A History of Women and Revolution in the Modern World.* New York: Vintage.

Ruiz, Vicki L. 1987. *Cannery Women, Cannery Lives: Mexican Women, Unionization, and the California Food Processing Industry*, 1930–1950. Albuquerque: University of New Mexico Press.

Segura, Denise. 1986. "Chicanas and Triple Oppression in the Labor Force." Pp. 47–65 in *Chicana Voices: Intersections of Class, Race and Gender*, edited by Teresa Córdova et al. Austin, TX: Center for Mexican American Studies.

Shockley, John. 1974. *Chicano Revolt in a Texas Town.* South Bend, IN: University of Notre Dame Press.

Vidal, Mirta. 1971. "New Voice of La Raza: Chicanas Speak Out." *International Socialist Review* 32:31–33.

White, Frances. 1984. "Listening to the Voices of Black Feminism." *Radical America* 18:7–25.

Wong, Germaine Q. 1980. "Impediments to Asian-Pacific-American Women Organizing." Pp. 89–103 in *The Conference on the Educational and Occupational Needs of Asian Pacific Women.* Washington, DC: National Institute of Education.

Woo, Margaret. 1971. "Women + Man = Political Unity." Pp. 115–16 in *Asian Women*, edited by Editorial Staff. Berkeley, CA: University of California Press.

Zavella, Patricia. 1987. *Women's Work and Chicano Families: Cannery Workers of the Santa Clara Valley.* Ithaca, NY: Cornell University Press.

Hispanic Immigration at the New Millennium

David W. Engstrom

Hispanics were among the first immigrants to the United States. More than twenty years before the Pilgrims established a foothold near Plymouth Rock, the Spanish had already created settlements in New Mexico. Yet Hispanics are also among the most recent immigrants. For the past thirty years, well over one-third of foreign nationals emigrating to the United States have come from Latin American and Spanish-speaking Caribbean countries. Like all immigrants, Hispanics have encountered in their adopted country a host of conflicting perceptions and government policies about immigrants. At times, United States policy has encouraged Hispanic immigration, in order to meet labor shortages and serve foreign policy objectives. At other times, the United States has tried to close the gate to Hispanic immigration and even forcibly returned not only legal residents, but also Hispanic citizens to their countries of origin. Some Americans view Hispanic immigrants as hard workers who add to the diversity of the country. Others perceive Hispanic immigrants as a population that drains the public coffers and contributes to the Balkanization of the United States.[1]

Scholars have developed various theories to explain the flow of immigration and the mechanisms for maintaining it. This chapter reviews Hispanic immigration in the context of current immigration theory, making comparisons between historic and present-day immigration to the United States. The history of United States policies to screen and channel immigration flows is examined, as are instances in which those policies have produced unanticipated results.

To aid comprehension of the vast terrain of Hispanic immigration and the issues it raises, this chapter also briefly discusses the recent volume of immigration, the provisions by which immigrants enter the United States, where immigrants settle, and the problems inherent in immigration statistics.

The chapter concludes by exploring several contentious issues surrounding Hispanic immigration, including border enforcement, fiscal effects, and the backlash against immigrants (particularly Hispanic immigrants) that has resurfaced as the twentieth century draws to a close. Efforts to restrict immigrant use of social services, welfare programs, and other public services are examples of that backlash.

The Importance of Hispanic Immigration to the United States

In 1990, Congress authorized the creation of a commission to study immigration and to make recommendations to reform United States immigration policy. The United States Commission on Immigration Reform asked the distinguished National Research Council (NRC) to convene a panel of demographers to study the demographic implications of immigration for the population of the United States and to estimate what the population will look like at the year 2050. Employing a sophisticated model for examining population change, the NRC predicted that if the current volume of immigration continues in the future, the United States can expect to have a population of 387 million residents by 2050.[2] Fertility and mortality changes partially explain the 120-million-person growth in population, but the NRC identified immigration—and specifically Hispanic immigration—as the major factor. Whereas one in eleven Americans in 1995 claimed Hispanic ancestry, in 2050 about one in four Americans will identify themselves as Hispanic. Clearly, Hispanic immigration is transforming the United States.

What Has Created and Maintained the Flow of Hispanic Immigration

The classic model of immigration is referred to as *push-pull*. Conditions in country "A" push people to emigrate, while conditions in country "B" pull them to immigrate. Put another way, people leave their country of origin because they believe that their lives will be improved by settling in another country. Jorge Castaneda wrote, "The 'push-pull' effect is truly the decisive determinant of the intensity, size, and evolution of migratory flows."[3] The model seems wonderfully simple. However, the model masks the tremendous complexity of the forces that create the push-pull dynamic.

Historically, immigration to the United States has been caused in part by economic transformation or economic development in sending countries. However contradictory this may seem, much of nineteenth- and early twentieth-century immigration from Europe actually occurred when countries such as England, Germany, and Italy industrialized. This weakened the social and economic importance of agriculture and created large-scale population movements to urban areas. But not every urban migrant found employment, so many emigrated. Improvements in communication and transportation facilitated emigration.

Not surprisingly, Hispanic immigration has been moved by similar currents. Economic development and political instability (often, the two go hand-in-hand) have been the major push factors behind Hispanic emigration.[4] The intrusion of worldwide markets into rural areas, the introduction of more efficient agricultural techniques, the development of transportation facilities, the rapid growth and improvement of communications, and population increases are among the contributing factors in the exodus from rural Latin American communities. The growth of urban areas in Latin America and the economic opportunities found there have held some Hispanics to their homeland. However, like their European counterparts 100 years ago, tens of thousands have chosen to emigrate. As Douglas Massey reminded us, "In the short run . . . [economic] development does not reduce the impetus for migration, but only increases it."[5]

Nevertheless, even in the era of unrestricted immigration to the United States, most people chose to stay in their homelands rather than leave them. The same is true today. The overwhelming majority of Latin Americans never attempt to immigrate—legally or illegally—to the United States. As Portes and Rumbaut observed, "The questions can thus be reversed to ask not why many come, but why so few have decided to undertake the journey, especially with difficult economic and political conditions in many sending countries."[6]

The United States has been, and continues to be, the major magnet of Hispanic immigration. American policies have triggered immigration through labor recruitment, military intervention, and foreign policy. Additionally, higher wages, better employment and educational opportunities, regional economic development, political freedom, family reunification, and the lure of the "good life" have all contributed to pull Hispanic immigrants to the United States.

Changes in economic and political institutions create incentives to immigrate, but the act of emigrating remains an individual or family decision. Immigrants have been and continue to be self-selected. People do not leave their homeland if they are content and satisfied with their lives. Generally, it is not the advantaged or the poor of a society who decide to leave. Blocked opportunity often provides the classic reason to emigrate. Portes and Rumbaut wrote:

> The basic reason [to emigrate] is the gap between life aspirations and expectations and the means to fulfill them in the sending countries. Different groups feel this gap with varying intensity, but it clearly becomes a strong motive for action among the most ambitious and resourceful. Because *relative*, not absolute deprivation lies at the core of most contemporary immigration, its composition tends to be positively selected in terms of both human capital and motivation.[7]

It is clear that relative deprivation plays a role in Hispanic immigration. Describing the interaction of poor economic prospects and political instability on Central American emigration, Sergio Diaz-Briquets wrote:

> These changes result in rising individual aspirations not likely to be satisfied in countries of origin, given limited domestic opportunities that stand in stark contrast to what emigrants can hope for in the far more tranquil and prosperous United States.[8]

Arguing a similar point, de la Garza and Szekely contended that Mexican immigrants leave to use their talent and energy in the United States because they are frustrated by their inability to advance economically, politically, and socially in their native country.[9] It takes initiative, resources, willingness to take risks, and skill to immigrate.

Several facts, however, differentiate recent Hispanic immigration from the European and Asian immigration streams of the nineteenth and early twentieth centuries. First, present-day Hispanic immigrants arrive in areas already long settled by Spanish descendants. It was through the Texas War for Independence, the Mexican-American War, and the subsequent Treaty of Guadalupe Hidalgo that the United States took possession of the present-day Southwest; indeed, military conquest and diplomatic treaty brought more Hispanics into the United States than did immigration during the nineteenth century. Prior settlement has contributed to a sense among many Hispanics, particularly in the Southwest, that the southern border is an artificial and arbitrary line. That sentiment is best characterized by the saying: "We didn't cross the border, the border crossed us."

Proximity also is fact. Mexico shares a 2,000-mile-long border with the United States, which makes it a relatively easy entry point for Mexicans and other Hispanic immigrants. The 90 miles of ocean that separate Cuba from the United States have proven too short a distance to dissuade Cubans from sailing to southern Florida. Second, modern transportation has made travel easy for those living further from the United States. Virtually all Hispanic sending countries have regular air service to the United States, placing those immigrants mere hours from their destination. This is in stark contrast to the weeks, if not months, it took nineteenth-century immigrants to leave their countries of origin and reach the shores of the United States. Distance and time are no longer the serious considerations they were a century ago.

Geographic proximity and the transportation revolution affect emigration in added ways. To emigrate from Europe or Asia 100 years ago meant separation from family and friends for years, if not a lifetime. Oscar Handlin's classic book, *The Uprooted*, eloquently spoke of the difficulty of severing links to the old country and starting life over in a far-off land.[10] An American mythology grew which held that every immigrant who came to the United States stayed permanently—the benefit of America more than outweighed the pain of separation. In fact, difficult as it was to make the journey back, as many as one-third of the European immigrants eventually returned to their homelands, although repatriation usually took years.

In contrast, contemporary Hispanic immigrants do not encounter the same circumstances. As Jorge Castaneda wrote, "Emigrating from next door produces sharply different effects on the mind-set and lifestyle of the migrant than does embarking on a long, once-in-a-lifetime voyage with no return."[11] Ties to family, friends, and community are presently much easier to maintain. Cyclical or temporary immigration occurs more frequently now than in the past. Studies of sending communities in Mexico consistently report that immigrants make multiple trips to and from the United States.[12] Proximity is an especially important factor in explaining the cyclical dynamics of undocumented immigrants who travel with relative ease between their homelands and the United States.

Social networks are important to the process of immigration. Networks start when immigrants permanently settle in an area and use their knowledge of local opportunities to help relatives, friends, and acquaintances from back home emigrate. As more people join the network, ethnic enclaves form and extend the network. Hispanic immigration to the United States is sustained by rich migration networks that have developed over several decades. Writing about certain migration networks, Massey observed that

networks consist of kin and friendship relations that link Mexican sending communities to particular destinations in the United States. People from the same family or town are enmeshed in a web of reciprocal obligations. New migrants draw upon these obligations in order to enter and find work in the United States. As these networks develop and mature, they dramatically reduce the costs of migration, inducing others to enter the migrant work force. The entry of additional migrants, in turn, leads to more extensive networks, which encourages still more migration.[13]

Individuals connected to networks are more likely to immigrate than those who have no such connection. Tapping into immigrant networks reduces the psychological, social, and economic costs of immigrating.[14] Many pressing questions are answered before the emigrant starts out: How will I get to my destination? Where will I live? Who do I know there? Where will I work? As Carlos Rico stated, "The existence of old and complex social networks gives a truly social character to the phenomenon of migration. . . . This breeds increased familiarity and very well established 'connections' for many Mexican sending communities."[15]

Once established, migrant networks facilitate and promote further immigration. Examples of this abound. The presence of Cuban enclaves in Florida and New Jersey has encouraged Cuban refugee flows for nearly four decades. Observing Guatemalan networks in Houston, Texas, Hagan and Gonzalez-Baker discovered the importance networks play in transmitting information about U.S. immigration policy.[16] Central American immigration during the 1980s was facilitated by existing networks used by Mexicans to gain entry into the United States.[17] Relatives of Central Americans already living in the United States played a role in fostering immigration. Commenting on Nicaraguan immigration, Lars Schoultz noted that "nearly two-thirds of the tickets from Managua to Mexico City are purchased in the United States by friends or relatives of the traveler, who picks up the ticket at a Managua travel agent or airline office."[18] A rich body of Mexican community studies has documented the importance of migration networks in the movement of Mexicans, particularly undocumented ones, into the United States.[19]

The existence of migration networks also explains why Hispanic immigrants, both legal and illegal, settle in so few states. Established in certain states, the extensive networks effectively guide immigrants to these areas. Settlement is generally not a random process. As Portes and Rumbaut noted, "Migration is a network-driven process, and the operation of kin and friendship ties is nowhere more effective than in guiding new arrivals toward preestablished ethnic communities."[20]

Migration networks are central to understanding immigration. Once established, networks create a self-sustaining dynamic. Community studies show that the migration decision became increasingly disconnected from the social and economic conditions in the sending community and determined more by the accumulation of migration-related human capital and social capital in the form of network conditions.[21]

In effect, the "push" part of the migration equation becomes less important as networks mature and expand. U.S. immigration policy has actually aided the creation of migrant networks by emphasizing family reunification (most recently) and temporary worker programs (in the past). Significantly, migrant networks have made it increasingly difficult for U.S. immigration policy to control the flow of persons coming to the United States. Research examining efforts to reduce undocumented immigration, by enhancing border enforcement and denying job opportunities through employer sanctions, has largely concluded that such policies have scarcely made a dent in the immigration flow. Donato, Duran, and Massey found that migration networks effectively countered attempts by the United States to clamp down on illegal immigration.[22]

Hispanic Immigration and U.S. Immigration Policy

Economic, political, and social conditions and immigration networks trigger and maintain immigration, but the movement of people across international boundaries is shaped, to some extent, by the immigration policies of nation states. During its first 100 years, the United States federal government, which has jurisdiction over immigration, allowed unrestricted immigration. Starting in 1875, the federal government began to screen out immigrants for various reasons, including lewd and immoral character and later on the basis of race. By the turn of the century, Congress had greatly increased the number of exclusion categories used to screen immigrants—yet such actions did little to stem the flow of the millions of immigrants who came to the United States. Not until 1921, and then with the Immigration Act of 1924 (commonly referred to as the National Origins Act), did the United States effectively restrict the total number of immigrants it would accept annually and allocate immigration visas on the basis of country of origin.

The National Origins Act exempted Western Hemisphere immigration from the quotas. The exemption meant that the United States placed no restrictions on Hispanic immigration, which had begun in earnest during the first three decades of the new century. Fueled by the instability created by the Mexican Revolution and encouraged by U.S. labor recruiters, more than 660,000 Mexicans streamed to the industrial Midwest and the rapidly developing Southwest. The United States encouraged this immigration in the 1910s and 1920s to meet industrial and agricultural labor shortages created by the diminished flow from Europe. However, U.S. immigration authorities deported hundreds of thousands of Mexicans during the Great Depression, in the first instance of a practice that would be followed time and time again.[23] During years of prosperity, the United States encourages Mexican immigration; during economic recessions, the United States attempts to limit Mexican immigration.[24] Interestingly, despite these fluctuations in policy and treatment, the social and economic networks developed by the initial Mexican immigrants survived.

The Start of Large-Scale Hispanic Immigration

Faced with growing labor shortages brought about by World War II, the United States and Mexico negotiated the Braceros Program in 1942, which allowed Mexicans to work temporarily in the United States. Between 1942 to 1964, the United States issued more than 4.5 million temporary work visas to Mexicans.[25] The Braceros Program had several unintended consequences. Because the terms of the bilateral agreement required U.S. employers to provide Braceros workers the same benefits and amenities as were provided to U.S. workers, U.S. employers had economic incentives to hire the cheaper, undocumented workers who found it easier to work illegally than wait for their applications for Bracero visas to be processed. Additionally, some Braceros workers overstayed their work visas and became illegal immigrants.[26] Perhaps most important, as Freeman and Bean noted, the Braceros Program "re-established the practice of seasonal agricultural work that had declined significantly during the depression."[27] The Braceros Program exposed tens of thousands of Mexican workers to employment and social networks in the United States. Not surprisingly, those networks facilitated immigration to the United States well after the Braceros Program ended in 1964.

During the 1950s and early 1960s, unforeseen consequences of immigration policy, coupled with the politics of the Cold War, had a profound impact on Hispanic immigration. In 1952 Congress passed the McCarren-Walters Act, which prohibited the entry of Communists into the United States, emphasized labor market criteria in allocating immigration visas, and codified existing immigration law. Two aspects of the law had direct bearing on Hispanic immigration. First, the McCarren-Walters Act included the "Texas Proviso," which made it perfectly legal to knowingly hire someone who had violated immigration law by entering the country illegally. In effect, the Texas Proviso acknowledged the dependence of Southwest agricultural interests on undocumented workers. The Texas Proviso greatly contributed to enlarging the stream of undocumented immigration in the following decades. Second, a little-known and little-discussed provision in the act granted the Attorney General the authority to parole foreign nationals into the United States. Parole allowed the Attorney General to admit foreign nationals without having to fit them into existing immigration categories. Congress clearly intended parole to be exercised only on an individual basis, but subsequent administrations used it as a means to admit hundreds of thousands of refugees. Parole ended up serving as the de facto refugee policy for several decades.

Among the prime beneficiaries of the parole provision were Cubans, who began to flee the Cuban Revolution in 1959. The postrevolutionary exodus settled in small, preexisting Cuban enclaves, primarily in south Florida and New Jersey. Like Mexican immigrants, Cuban refugees established social and economic networks that encouraged further immigration. Unlike Mexican immigrants, the United States rolled out the welcome mat for the Cubans. The United States encouraged immigration from the island because the Cubans were fleeing from a Communist government; Cuban immigration thus served the larger goals of U.S. foreign policy. From 1960 until 1980, the United States granted parole to hundreds of thousands of Cubans.[28]

Cold War concerns also played a major role in the creation of immigration from the Dominican Republic. Fearing the possibility of a leftist takeover of the Dominican Republic following the assassination of Trujillo in 1961, the United States freely granted both temporary and permanent immigration visas to middle-class Dominicans.[29] United States policy makers viewed immigration as a safety valve, reducing political instability and discontent.[30]

The 1965 Immigration Act

Social and political changes in the 1960s forced policy makers to reexamine immigration policy. Intense civil rights efforts and the containment of Communism made untenable a policy that banned or greatly limited the immigration opportunities of entire regions of the world. In 1965, Congress, at the urging of the Johnson administration, fundamentally altered policy by stressing the equality of all nations in the allocation of immigration slots. The Immigration Act of 1965 struck down the national origins quotas; ended the almost absolute ban on Asian immigration; and imposed, for the first time, numeric restrictions on immigration from the Western Hemisphere (120,000 visas per year). Although the 1965 reforms permitted no country in the Eastern Hemisphere to receive more than 20,000 restricted visas, it placed no limit on the number available to specific Western Hemisphere countries. Equally important, the law changed the criteria for selecting immigrants. Whereas the McCarren-Walters Act of 1952 had emphasized occupational skill as the primary selection criterion, the 1965 Act shifted the selection emphasis to family reunification.

Proponents of immigration reform had argued that the 1965 Immigration Act would not significantly increase immigration. Such predictions were wrong. Numbers of immigrants during the 1970s increased by more than one-third over the immigration flows of the 1960s. Switching to a kinship-based preference system meant that as families immigrated to the United States, they could sponsor more family members from "the old country." By encouraging families to immigrate, the United States created a dynamic that fostered more immigration. A little more than ten years after the 1965 Act, family reunification accounted for three-quarters of all immigrants.

The 1965 immigration reform addressed problems associated with previous policy, but it created a new set of problems. By placing a numeric ceiling on Western Hemisphere immigration, the United States restricted immigration from Latin American countries just when the pressure to immigrate had increased. Not surprisingly, applicants for immigration visas outstripped supply, and long waiting lists resulted. To deal with the fact that Mexican immigration dominated the 120,000 restricted visas awarded annually, Congress approved a measure in 1978 to impose a 20,000-visa limit for countries in the Western Hemisphere. Although this "freed up" more visas for countries like the Dominican Republic, the reform "had the effect of exacerbating the backlog of Mexican visa applications that had prompted the concern in the first place."[31] Additionally, the abrupt termination of the Braceros Program in 1964 withdrew the means by which Mexican workers could legally enter the United States—but it changed neither the supply of workers nor the demand for workers. Ultimately, U.S. immigration policy could not address the continuing demand for legal immigration. Immigrants continued to come, with or without visas, and created a growing illegal immigration flow.

Refugee Policy

The 1965 Immigration Act included, for the first time, statutory language creating an annual refugee admissions quota. However, refugee admissions were limited to the Eastern Hemisphere. Even before President Johnson signed the 1965 Immigration Act into law, these narrow refugee provisions were tested and found wanting. That year the Cuban government allowed Cuban exiles to sail to Cuba to pick up friends and relatives. The United States quickly negotiated an end to the boatlift from the village of Camarioca and established an immigration accord. The "Freedom Flights" brought almost 200,000 Cubans to the United States between 1965 and 1973.[32] Because of the 1965 Immigration Act, though, refugee slots were reserved solely for Eastern Hemisphere refugees, so the Johnson and Nixon administrations used the parole authority of the Attorney General to admit the Cubans.

Refugee flows from Cuba, and later the need to admit large numbers of Indochinese refugees following the fall of South Vietnam, pointed up the necessity for a more comprehensive refugee policy. In response, Congress passed the 1980 Refugee Act, which increased the number of refugee slots from 17,400 a year to 50,000 and removed the geographic restriction on admission. More importantly, the 1980 act altered the definition of *refugee* from one who is fleeing from Communism to anyone with a well-founded fear of persecution (political, racial, ethnic, religious) who is residing in a country of first asylum. The act created, for the first time, asylum provisions that allowed individuals to enter the United States and request asylum. Finally, it also provided an extensive array of resettlement benefits fully funded by the federal government.

As had happened fifteen years earlier with the 1965 Immigration Act, a large, uncoordinated boatlift from Cuba presented the first test to the newly passed Refugee Act. In 1980, boats chartered by Cuban exiles were again allowed to pick up Cuban nationals, this time at the port of Mariel. Approximately 125,000 Cubans were brought to the shores of the United States. The Carter administration fumbled and threatened in an effort to gain control over the massive human exodus, to no effect.[33] Unable to stop the flow of refugees, policy makers looked for means to legally admit them. Although members of Congress encouraged the Carter administration to use the newly created Refugee Act to handle the problem, the Carter administration rejected congressional advice and opted to parole the Cubans. The administration further angered policy makers in areas (such as south Florida) heavily impacted by the boatlift, by refusing to pay full federal reimbursement for the costs of resettling the Cubans, as had been done under the earlier Cuban Refugee Program.

Central American refugee flows to the United States further tested the Refugee Act. Sparked by economies unable to absorb growing numbers of workers, and social and political instability created by civil wars, immigration to the United States began in earnest from Central America in the late 1970s. The active involvement of the United States in suppressing leftist insurgency movements played a central role in creating a large-scale exodus. Many Nicaraguans, Salvadorans, and Guatemalans left their homelands seeking refuge in neighboring states. Over the years, well over a million Central Americans journeyed to the United States and entered the country as undocumented workers.[34] Once in the United States, growing numbers of Central Americans petitioned for asylum. By any standard, the number of asylum seekers was large: between 1985 and 1990, the Immigration and Naturalization Service (INS) received more than 225,000 asylum requests from Central Americans.

Policy makers had envisioned that the asylum provisions, included as almost an afterthought in the Refugee Act, would be used only occasionally. The arrival of so many Central Americans stirred considerable public debate. Human rights groups advocated for granting asylum to a majority of Central American applicants, while the Reagan and Bush administrations argued that most applicants were illegal immigrants who should be returned home. Asylum application was a useful survival strategy

for extending their stay in the United States. Because the initial asylum provisions had strong due process guarantees, asylees could stay in the United States while the immigration bureaucracy decided their cases.[35] The large number of asylum applicants completely overwhelmed the capacity of the INS and State Department to process and decide the validity of each case. It took years for cases to be finally decided.

Although the pace of processing worked to the advantage of many asylees, the decisions, once made, often did not. Advocates for reforming U.S. refugee policy had hoped that the new definition of *refugee/asylee* in the Refugee Act would depoliticize the determination of who was a refugee or asylee. In fact, ideology and politics played a huge role in asylum decisions regarding Central American applicants in the 1980s. Because the United States supported the governments of El Salvador and Guatemala, it seldom found in favor of asylum applicants from those countries. For example, only 5 percent of Salvadoran and 4 percent of Guatemalan asylum cases decided in 1987 granted asylum. In contrast, applicants from Nicaragua, whose government the United States opposed, fared well. Of Nicaraguan asylum cases decided in 1987, 86 percent were awarded asylum.

Central American refugee flows have remained high throughout the 1990s. Continued conflict in the region, coupled with changes in asylum policy, has contributed to the growing numbers of asylum seekers.[36] So, too, have the expanding enclaves of Central Americans that aid in the exodus. From 1990 to 1996, the INS received 441,305 applications for asylum from Central Americans. To deal with the continuing legal and asylum issues involving Central Americans, Congress passed the Nicaraguan Adjustment and Central American Relief Act in late 1997. The act established procedures to legalize the status of tens of thousands of Central Americans.

Illegal Immigration and the Immigration Reform and Control Act of 1986

Illegal immigration emerged as the dominant immigration issue in the late 1970s and 1980s.[37] By then, the consequences of restricting legal immigration had become obvious. More foreign nationals were illegally entering the United States. At the same time, many in the United States expressed concern over the perceived negative effects of illegal immigration. Undocumented workers were blamed for undercutting wages and taking jobs away from U.S. citizens, increasing crime, and fostering cultural divisions. In times of economic prosperity such charges would have had little resonance, but during a period characterized by economic recessions, high unemployment, and stagnant wages, arguments linking illegal immigration to the economic woes of the United States were powerful. As Espenshade and Calhoun noted, "Illegal immigrants are convenient scapegoats for a wide variety of societal ills."[38]

Several key themes surfaced in the discussion of what to do about illegal immigration. First, attention focused almost entirely on the southern border as the source of or entry point for undocumented immigration. Illegal immigration became synonymous with Mexico. Seldom did illegal immigration at the northern border enter into the debate. Second, policy making and debate were hampered by the absence of quality data on the size and characteristics of undocumented immigration. No official count of population, such as the census, measured illegal immigration. Lacking reliable data, the INS records of apprehension of undocumented immigrants became the proxy measure for illegal immigration, despite the inherent weakness of those statistics. Third, proponents of a tough stance on illegal immigration used the lack of solid estimates to make exaggerated claims about the size of the undocumented population. In particular, the INS and its supporters framed illegal immigration as a law enforcement issue and used concern over the problem to argue for a larger budget and more personnel.

Acknowledging illegal immigration as an issue proved far easier than developing a consensus on what to do about it. The Ford and Carter administrations formed interagency task forces to examine the problem. In 1978, Congress authorized the creation of the Select Commission on Immigration and Refugee Policy (SCIRP) to study immigration issues and make recommendations to Congress. In its 1981 final report to Congress, SCIRP recommended both restrictive and progressive measures to deal with illegal immigration, most notably employer sanctions and amnesty. After five years of failed attempts by advocates for immigration reform to secure legislation adopting SCIRP recommendations, the Immigration Reform and Control Act of 1986 (IRCA) cleared both the House and the Senate and was signed into law by President Reagan.

The IRCA adopted a law enforcement policy focused on creating disincentives to immigrate illegally. The law overturned the Texas Proviso by making it illegal for employers knowingly to hire undocumented workers. Employer sanctions operated on the premise that if the United States could cut off the employment opportunities for undocumented workers, there would be less incentive to immigrate illegally. The IRCA required that employers verify the work eligibility of all workers or face civil and criminal penalties. Additionally, the law authorized a sizable increase in the budget and personnel of the INS Border Patrol. Lawmakers reasoned that more border enforcement would make it more difficult to enter the country illegally. Virtually all the additional Border Patrol agents were assigned to police the southern border.

To garner enough votes to pass Congress, the IRCA created two amnesty, or legalization, programs that permitted eligible undocumented workers to apply for and receive legal immigration status. The Legally Authorized Workers (LAWs) program granted those undocumented workers with long-standing ties to the United States the opportunity to legalize their immigration status. Unlike the basic provisions of the LAWs program, which had existed in earlier immigration reform efforts, the Special Agricultural Workers (SAWs) program found its way into the IRCA relatively late in the congressional debate.[39] With its more liberal eligibility criteria, the SAWs program allowed agricultural workers to apply for legalization after working in the country for only one year. Both programs granted qualified applicants temporary legal status and outlined procedures for attaining permanent resident status and, ultimately, naturalization.

Despite initial difficulty and controversy in implementing the amnesty programs, the INS eventually developed extensive outreach efforts. The majority of applicants were processed within several years of the program's creation. Exceeding earlier estimates of the number of eligible undocumented workers, the INS legalized approximately 1.7 million LAWs and 1 million SAWs.[40] Although undocumented workers of any nationality could apply for amnesty, the legalization programs were used mostly by undocumented Hispanic immigrants. One study of the LAWs program found that Mexican and Central Americans accounted for 70 percent and 13 percent, respectively, of all applicants.[41]

The amnesty programs succeeded in legalizing the status of millions of undocumented workers, but the IRCA's attempt to regulate illegal immigration did not go according to script. Initially, the INS did report a drop in apprehensions along the Mexican borders. Some scholars attribute the decline to the legalization of several million undocumented workers who no longer had to cross the border illegally. Others suggest that many undocumented workers waited for a while to see how the INS would implement the law. Regardless, almost every long-term assessment of the IRCA has concluded that there is little evidence to suggest that employer sanctions and increased border enforcement substantially reduced the flow of undocumented workers. To begin with, the INS lacked sufficient personnel to enforce the employer sanctions. Too few inspectors meant that only a handful of the millions of U.S. businesses could anticipate having their employment records scrutinized. A preexisting market for fraudulent documents, such as Social Security cards, quickly expanded. Additionally, employers wishing to comply with the law had no way of determining the authenticity of documents. Researchers could not "uncover statistically reliable evidence that [the] IRCA had a significant effect in deterring undocumented migration from Mexico."[42]

Opponents of the IRCA feared that employer sanctions would create job discrimination. They reasoned that many employers would avoid the possibility of violating the law by hiring no foreign-born or minority workers. To address those concerns, lawmakers included a sunset provision in the IRCA, which would terminate employer sanctions if a "widespread" pattern of discrimination could be linked to the law. In its 1990 report to Congress, the General Accounting Office (GAO) estimated that 10 percent of employers engaged in "one or more practices that represent national origin discrimination."[43] The GAO concluded that "it is more reasonable to conclude that a substantial amount of discriminatory practices resulted from [the] IRCA rather than not."[44] Not surprisingly, given the perception that illegal immigrants are predominantly Hispanic, employment discrimination based on national origin frequently affected Hispanics. However, despite evidence pointing to widespread discrimination, Congress decided to keep the employer sanctions and instead make incremental improvements to the process of employment verification.

1990 Immigration Act and Current Immigration Policy

Once Congress had dealt with illegal immigration through the IRCA in 1986, it turned to the task of overhauling the system of legal immigration. The 1965 Immigration Act had created a number of problem areas for legal immigration. Long queues existed for family-based immigrant visas. The amnesty provisions of the IRCA meant that the waiting lists would only lengthen as greater numbers of legalized immigrants sponsored their family members. Some members of Congress raised the concern that legal immigration from Asia and Latin America had effectively "choked off" European immigration. Advocates for diversity wanted to continue efforts started in 1988 to encourage immigration from "traditional" sending countries. Also, concern over productivity and economic growth in the United States led some to advocate that U.S. immigration move to labor market criteria in awarding immigration visas, and away from family reunification criteria.

Congress eventually passed the Immigration Act of 1990, which, for the first time in twenty-five years, substantively altered legal immigration policy. Despite little public support for increasing the number of immigrants, the 1990 Immigration Act created a new, permanent ceiling of 675,000 per year. During the first two years of its implementation, Congress authorized higher ceilings to shorten the backlog of immigrant visas. To deal further with the effects of the IRCA, policy makers granted 55,000 additional visas from 1992 to 1994 for immediate family members of IRCA-legalized immigrants. The Immigration Act increased the per-country quota immigrants from 20,000 to 28,000. Addressing concerns that the United States should admit more skilled immigrants, the act narrowed the type of categories available for family reunification and greatly expanded employment-based immigrant

visas. Finally, the act reserved 55,000 diversity slots for immigrants coming from "unrepresented countries."

It is too soon to assess the overall impact of the 1990 Immigration Act. It is clear that family-based preferences continue to be the primary basis on which immigrants enter the country. In 1996, approximately two out of every three immigrants were family sponsored. Immigrants coming to the United States by means of employment-based preferences make up around one-eighth of all immigrants. Contrary to the intention of the 1990 Immigration Act, waiting queues for immigration visas remain high. In 1996, the Visa Office at the State Department reported a worldwide waiting list of 3,692,506 persons.[45]

Finally, responding to continuing concern over illegal immigration and prompted by the findings of the U.S. Commission on Immigration Reforms, Congress passed the Illegal Immigration Reform and Immigrant Responsibility Act of 1996 (IIRIRA).[46] The return of Congress to the issue of undocumented immigration signified that its previous efforts at reform had not solved the problem. The IIRIRA framed undocumented immigration almost solely as a law enforcement problem. It gave the INS more resources and personnel for law enforcement, expanded the agency's authority to remove "illegal aliens," weakened the role of the courts in reviewing enforcement decisions, and increased the civil and criminal penalties associated with illegal immigration (such as smuggling and creating and using fraudulent documents).[47] In a move away from amnesty, the IIRIRA required that undocumented immigrants leave the United States to adjust their immigration status. The act further barred undocumented immigrants from returning to the United States for periods of three to ten years, depending on how long they had lived illegally in the country.

Recent Hispanic Immigration

Legal Immigration

Since the late 1960s, the United States has experienced a surge in immigration. From 1971 to 1996, approximately 18 million persons have come to the United States as immigrants.[48] The legal immigration numbers come close to matching the peak years of immigration to the United States, at the turn of the twentieth century. At that time, from 1890 to 1915, slightly more than 21 million persons, mostly from Europe, immigrated to the United States. That large European immigration had a proportionately greater effect on the peopling of the United States than the most recent immigration wave. In 1910, nearly one in seven United States residents was foreign born, compared with one in thirteen in 1990.

Of the 18 million immigrants from 1971 to 1996, nearly 7 million have been Hispanics. Thus, roughly 39 percent of all immigrants in the past 25 years have been Hispanic. The large number of Hispanic immigrants is not an aberration in the annals of American immigration. Throughout the history of the United States, immigration has been dominated for periods of time by certain countries or regions. For example, from 1841 to 1850, the Irish constituted nearly half of all immigrants. During the immigration at the turn of the century, immigrants from Southern and Central Europe accounted for more than 60 percent of all immigrants.

Between 1986 and 1996, more than 2,969,000 Mexicans, 195,000 Cubans, 405,000 Dominicans, 678,000 Central Americans, and 604,000 South Americans legally immigrated to the United States. Immigration from Mexico dwarfs that from all other countries. In 1996, 18 percent of immigrants to the United States came from Mexico. In 1996, three of the top ten immigrant-sending countries to the United States were Hispanic.

Although immigration policy is almost exclusively the domain of the federal government, it has very real effects locally. Throughout the history of the United States, immigrants have concentrated in certain areas.[49] For example, Scandinavians settled almost exclusively in the upper Midwest. The Irish tended to settle in large urban areas such as New York, Boston, and Chicago. Immigrants from Poland and Croatia settled in the industrial areas of Illinois, Indiana, Ohio, and Pennsylvania. Like their immigrant predecessors, Hispanic immigrants also concentrate in certain states or regions. Cubans have stayed mostly in south Florida and northern New Jersey. The Dominicans have settled almost exclusively in the New York metropolitan area. Mexican immigrants are widely dispersed, but the majority of them can be found in a handful of states: California, Texas, Illinois, and, now, New York. In fact, 70 percent of all immigrants now settle in only 6 states: California, New York, Texas, Florida, Illinois, and New Jersey.[50]

Family reunification provisions are the most available and most-used means by which foreign nationals legally immigrate to the United States; certainly, family reunification is the dominant route for legal Hispanic immigration. In 1996, 65 percent of all immigrants and 85 percent of Hispanic immigrants were admitted under family reunification provisions. In the largest source country for immigrants, Mexicans overwhelmingly use family reunification to gain admission to the United States: approximately 95 percent of Mexican immigrants were sponsored by a family member. Dominican immigrants rely even more on family reunification: 99 percent immigrated to the United States using family reunification provisions.

Employment-based visas represent the other major method by which people may immigrate to the United States.[51] In 1996, approximately 13 percent of all immigrants, compared to 7 percent of all Hispanic immigrants, entered under employment-based visas. Within Hispanic sending countries, great variation exists. Of the top three Hispanic sources of immigration (Mexico, Cuba, and the Dominican Republic), employment preference provisions

account for 2 percent or less of immigrant visas. A greater percentage of immigrants from countries such as El Salvador (15 percent), Argentina (39 percent), Bolivia (33 percent), Chile (21 percent), and Venezuela (21 percent) rely on employment-based preferences to gain entry into the United States.

It is important to note that immigration data are often portrayed as measuring the yearly addition of foreign nationals living in the United States. When the statistic is presented that 915,900 foreign nationals were admitted to the United States in 1996, many people assume that the country's population just increased by that same number. Immigration statistics do not account for emigration *from* the United States. On average, approximately one-third of all immigrants eventually leave the United States to return to their homelands or to live in another country.[52] Emigration is even more of a factor with undocumented immigrants than with legal immigrants. Studies of sending communities in Mexico consistently find that a majority of Mexican undocumented immigrants living in the United States eventually return home.[53]

Additionally, immigration data are often used to suggest that the statistics are measuring new arrivals, when in fact they do not. Of the 915,900 immigrants admitted to the United States in 1996, only 46 percent were new arrivals. The rest were already residing in the United States—legally or illegally—prior to having their immigration status changed to that of "immigrant." The distinction between "adjustments" and "new arrivals" is particularly important in understanding immigration data from the years 1989 to 1994. Data from that five-year span imply an enormous jump in overall levels of immigration, especially from Mexico. Yet almost half of the 6 million persons classified as permanent resident aliens or immigrants during those years were already living in the United States as undocumented foreign nationals. As noted earlier, the provisions in the 1986 Immigration Reform and Control Act gave millions of undocumented workers the means to legalize their immigration status.

Undocumented Immigration

The issue of undocumented immigration adds to the complexity of any study of Hispanic immigration. Legal immigrants have permission from the federal government to enter and live in the United States. Undocumented or illegal immigrants do not. Generally, there are three ways for foreign nationals to enter the United States and remain as undocumented immigrants. First, a foreign national may slip across the border of the United States undetected by the Border Patrol of the INS. In immigration jargon, such persons are *EWIs* (enters without inspection). Second, a foreign national may have temporary permission to enter the United States, for example, as a student or tourist, but then not return to the country of origin once his or her entry visa has expired. That group is called *visa overstayers.* Third, a foreign national may violate the terms of the entry visa. For example, tourists who take jobs violate the conditions of their visas and become illegal immigrants.[54] Visa overstayers and visa violators are a significant proportion of the undocumented immigrants, representing slightly more than 40 percent of that population.[55] Undocumented immigrants are a difficult population to count. Thomas Espenshade wrote:

> For numerous reasons, illegal immigration is a difficult issue to study. Not the least of the obstacles is the fact that the number of unauthorized immigrants entering the United States is unobserved and therefore not precisely known. In addition, no census or other federally sponsored survey asks respondents about their legal status, so the impact of undocumented immigration is often inferred from other indicators.[56]

Over time, demographers have developed more precise methods to estimate the size of the undocumented population. Research by demographers from the Census Bureau and the INS have produced estimates that consistently place the size of the undocumented immigrant population as between 3 to 5 million persons. This is considerably less than estimates in the 1970s and 1980s, which reported this population as 8 to 12 million.

According to the most recent estimates, Hispanics make up more than two-thirds of the undocumented immigrant population. Representing more than 50 percent, Mexico is far and away the single largest source of undocumented immigrants, followed by El Salvador (6.7 percent) and Guatemala (3.3 percent). The NRC estimated that between 200,000 and 300,000 undocumented immigrants settle in the United States each year.[57] Based on available data, it is estimated that between 138,000 to 207,000 Latin Americans yearly enter the United States as undocumented immigrants.

Undocumented immigrants tend to concentrate in the same handful of states that legal immigrants do. The only difference between the two groups is that undocumented immigrants are even more likely to reside in California, New York, Texas, Florida, Illinois, and New Jersey than are legal immigrants. Roughly 70 percent of legal immigrants are found in those states, compared to 80 percent of undocumented immigrants.[58] The concentration of both types of immigrants in so few states goes a long way toward explaining why the issue is so important to California but not to Maine.

Current Issues with Hispanic Immigration

NAFTA and Emigration Policy

In studies of Hispanic immigration, the emigration policies of sending countries are often ignored as a factor in shaping the characteristics and volume of immigration.

Virtually all nation-states place some restrictions on the ability of their citizens to travel to foreign states. Christopher Mitchell noted that until the overthrow of the Trujillo regime in the Dominican Republic in 1961, it was almost impossible for any but very wealthy Dominicans to obtain exit permits to leave the island.[59] The difficulty of securing exit visas from Cuba and the absence of normal immigration channels from Cuba to the United States effectively blocked large-scale immigration for years.[60]

Emigration policy, however, is more than just granting or withholding permission to leave. Through domestic policy, states can intentionally or unintentionally develop incentives for people to emigrate. For example, civil war and persecution in states such as El Salvador, Guatemala, and Nicaragua during the 1980s created the impetus for tens of thousands to leave. Rodolfo O. de la Garza and Gabriel Szekely argued that the domestic policies of the Mexican government have played a direct role in promoting emigration.[61] One could argue that the most significant emigration policy in recent years is the North American Free Trade Agreement (NAFTA) among Mexico, the United States, and Canada.

One of the selling points of NAFTA for Mexico and the United States was that it would reduce undocumented immigration. For Mexico, NAFTA represented a clear emigration policy. Mexican President Salinas stated, "Without the free-trade agreement you will witness millions of Mexicans crossing the border and looking for work."[62] The link between NAFTA and emigration is based on the assumption that free trade will create economic growth and economic growth will create enough jobs to employ the growing number of Mexicans now entering their working years. NAFTA is meant to keep more Mexicans in Mexico.

The long-term impact of NAFTA on Mexican immigration is the subject of much speculation. Cornelius and Martin argued, "In the long term . . . economic dynamism in Mexico stemming from a free trade agreement could deter substantial future emigration." Others have argued that the free-trade agreement will produce large-scale emigration.[63] There is general consensus, however, that economic development policies such as NAFTA will produce short-term increases in immigration. NAFTA has removed many of the trade protections for sheltered areas of the Mexican economy, such as small business and agriculture. International competition in those areas is likely to create, at best, temporary economic dislocations resulting in greater underemployment and unemployment. Such economic problems will increase migratory pressures.

United States policy makers have not used immigration policy to soften the economic transitions within Mexico resulting from NAFTA. Massey argued, "If it is in the U.S. interest to promote rapid economic development in Mexico, then it is also in the U.S. interest to accept relatively large numbers of Mexican immigrants."[64] But in the four years since the passage of NAFTA, the opposite has occurred. The Clinton administration never pushed Congress for a short-term increase in the number of immigration visas available for Mexico. In fact, the administration implemented the toughest policies in recent memory to deter illegal immigration (discussed later in this section) from Mexico. There is evidence that since NAFTA was approved in 1994, efforts to legally and illegally immigrate to the United States from Mexico have increased. In its most recent report, the Visa Office noted a backlog for immigration visas from Mexico of more than 1 million.[65] The most recent INS apprehension data reveal that the Border Patrol apprehended nearly 1.6 million Mexicans in 1996, a 46 percent increase since 1994.

Border Enforcement

Just as demand for immigration opportunities has increased in Mexico, the United States has engaged in a series of policy initiatives designed to curtail undocumented immigration. Since entering office in 1992, the Clinton administration has devoted more attention to, and directed more resources at, law enforcement along the southern border than have prior administrations. Congress has authorized a 5,000-person increase in the number of Border Patrol agents over a 5-year period, making the INS the largest federal law enforcement agency. The 1996 Illegal Immigration Reform and Immigrant Responsibility Act gave the INS added legal means to deter illegal immigration. High-profile initiatives, such as Hold-the-Line (El Paso) and Gatekeeper (San Diego), have attempted to stem the flow of undocumented immigration by making it more difficult to illegally enter the United States.

Increased border enforcement along the southern border perpetuates the perception and bias that only Mexico supplies the U.S. with undocumented immigrants.[66] For example, Canada shares a longer border with the United States than does Mexico, yet Canadians accounted for less than 1 percent of all apprehensions in 1996. According to INS data, the INS apprehends 500 Mexicans for every 1 Canadian. That Mexico has approximately three times the population of Canada may account for some of the difference in this ratio. That the economic and social incentives to immigrate illegally are fewer in Canada than in Mexico may also explain the ratio. However, it is telling that the United States positions 82 percent of its Border Patrol officers on the Mexican border, compared with 7 percent at the Canadian border.[67] This is despite estimates suggesting that more than 120,000 Canadians live in the United States illegally, making Canada the fourth largest source country for undocumented immigrants. It is a rare day when the media or policy makers focus on the northern border as a source of undocumented immigration. Nor does the press acknowledge that several million "undocumented immigrants" did not sneak across the southern border, but are, in fact, visa overstayers.

Welfare and Fiscal Impact

One of the ongoing assumptions Americans have about immigrants is that they come to the United States to use welfare programs.[68] Indeed, one of the first categories created to screen immigrants was the provision barring the entry of immigrants "likely to become a public charge." That provision was established in 1882, long before the existence of modern entitlement programs. A recent Gallup poll reported that 60 percent of those surveyed thought that Latin American immigrants ended up on welfare.[69] Despite the tenacity of this perception there is little evidence that immigrants disproportionately rely on welfare programs. For example, major welfare entitlement programs have excluded undocumented workers from receiving benefits. Even when legal immigrants were eligible for welfare services and benefits, prior to 1996, relatively few immigrants used them.

Of all types of immigrants, refugees rely the most on welfare programs, because the conditions under which they flee their countries of origin usually leave them with few resources. Using data from the 1990 census, Fix and Passel reported that once refugees are factored out only 2.8 percent of recent adult immigrants received welfare, compared to 4.2 percent of native-born adults. Including refugees, all foreign born adults have a welfare rate of 4.7 percent, only slightly higher than native born.[70] Research points to the immigrant elderly as the one sub-group with relatively high rates of welfare use. Van Hook and Bean found that 31 percent of immigrant elderly relied on Supplemental Security Income (SSI), compared to only 5.9 of native-born elderly.[71] Because many immigrant elders have not worked in the United States long enough to qualify for Social Security retirement, they rely on SSI in relatively large numbers.

Hispanic immigrant use of welfare programs is hard to determine, because many studies do not account for the ethnicity of immigrant welfare recipients. Examining census data, researchers from the University of Texas found that a greater number of Mexican, Guatemalan, and Salvadoran immigrant households relied on public assistance in 1990 than in 1980. Most of the increase was attributed to "the increasing size of the sub-group rather than to changes in sub-group rates." Immigrants from those Latin American countries had higher welfare rates than all other immigrant households. Interestingly, in 1990, native-born Mexican households (13.9 percent) reported greater use of welfare than Mexican and Central American immigrant households (11.7 percent). The researchers concluded that "Mexican/Central American immigrants . . . are not pronouncedly welfare-prone and do not manifest increases during the 1980s in either AFDC [Aid to Families with Dependent Children] or SSI recipiency."[72]

Despite the lack of compelling evidence of widespread welfare abuse by immigrants, Congress passed legislation in 1996 to restrict immigrant use of welfare. The Illegal

Immigration Reform and Immigrant Responsibility Act required that all family-based immigrants have an "affidavit of support" from a sponsor before they enter the United States. The affidavit of support means that sponsors commit to supporting each petitioned immigrant at 125 percent of the poverty level. If individuals cannot meet this financial commitment, they are prevented from sponsoring family members as immigrants. The law assigned public welfare agencies the responsibility of enforcing the affidavit of support requirement, which went into effect in 1997. Given the generally low income levels of Hispanic households, it is likely that the affidavit of support will prevent many Hispanics, immigrant and citizen alike, from sponsoring the immigration of their relatives.[73]

The Personal Responsibility and Work Opportunity Reconciliation Act (PROWA) is one of the best known of the recent immigrant welfare reforms. PROWA made immigrants ineligible for SSI and food stamps and allowed states to restrict eligibility to Medicaid and TANF (the replacement program for AFDC). Immediately after signing the welfare bill into law, President Clinton said he would work to reverse the prohibition against immigrants qualifying for welfare benefits. Clinton was not alone in arguing for repealing the provisions denying immigrants use of welfare. In 1997, the U.S. Commission on Immigration Reform, created to advise Congress on immigration, voiced its opposition to the recent legislation. The commission wrote that "the denial of safety net programs to immigrants solely because they are noncitizens is not in the national interests."[74] Soon after passage of that legislation, some of the most restrictive elements were repealed. In addition, many states continue to provide welfare to immigrants.[75]

Welfare use by immigrants is part of a larger debate on the overall fiscal impact of immigrants on the United States. Assessments of this impact vary greatly according to the models used, the sources of revenue attributed to immigrants, and the cost associated with providing public services to them. Passel estimated that immigrants bring in a net $25–30 billion in revenue; Huddle contended that immigrants cost the United States slightly more than $42 billion per annum.[76] Despite the differences in estimates, most research acknowledges that immigration has different effects locally and nationally. As Fix and Passel noted, "While most of the taxes paid by immigrants go to federal coffers, the costs of providing social services fall to state and local governments."[77]

The National Research Council has explored the local fiscal effects of immigration. Using two states with large numbers of immigrants as case studies, the NRC found that the fiscal burden on native-headed households in New Jersey was $232 and in California $1,178 per year (in 1996 dollars). The NRC attributed these results to three primary reasons:

(1) immigrant-headed households include more school-age children than native households on average, and they currently consume more educational services; (2) immigrant-headed households are poorer than native households on average, and therefore receive more state and locally funded income transfers; and (3) immigrant-headed households have lower incomes and own less property than native households on average, and thus pay lower state and local taxes.[78]

The NRC found that immigrants make a small but positive contribution to the federal government. Studying the long-term fiscal implications of immigration, the NRC stated, "Under most scenarios, the long-run fiscal impact is strongly positive at the federal level, but substantially negative at the state and local levels."[79]

Few research studies exist that focus on the fiscal impact of Hispanic immigration. In their comprehensive review of research on the topic, Gonzales-Baker and her colleagues noted, "None of the studies provide detailed information on the fiscal impact of specific national-origins populations."[80] Studies have concluded that undocumented workers "generate more expenses than revenues across all levels of government."[81] Given that Hispanics make up a large percentage of undocumented immigrants, it can be concluded that that particular sub-group of Hispanic immigrants creates fiscal costs largely in the areas of law enforcement, education, and health services. The NRC study mentioned earlier did examine the fiscal impact of immigrants from Europe/Canada, Asia, Latin America, and other regions. It estimated that Latin American immigrant households in New Jersey and California used, respectively, $3,396 and $4,977 per year more in public services than they paid in taxes.[82] The negative fiscal impact of Latin American immigrants is largely explained by the fact that their low household income means they pay less in taxes. However, it must be pointed out that Hispanic immigrants contribute to the local economy by buying housing, food, and other goods and services.

Attempts to measure the fiscal impact of immigration serve political agendas. Immigrants have been easy targets on which to pin the blame for federal and state budget deficits.[83] Findings that associate negative costs with immigrants are used to bolster assertions that too many immigrants enter the country and use too many public services; the country, it is said, cannot afford immigrants. The fiscal impact of immigration is of particular concern to the handful of states that receive large numbers of legal and illegal immigrants. There is nothing new about that concern. In the 1960s, Florida successfully lobbied Washington to reimburse it for the costs of resettling Cuban refugees. In recent years, California has claimed that it is bearing almost the entire fiscal burden for the consequences of federal immigration policy. In 1994, Californians approved Proposition 187, which sought to save revenue by denying almost all public services to undocumented workers. A court challenge eventually overturned Proposition 187, but the sentiment remains. At the national level, efforts to restrict welfare benefits to immigrants are often justified as one way to reduce the federal deficit.

Conclusions and Policy Recommendations

The United States can anticipate strong immigration flows from Latin America and the Spanish-speaking Caribbean well into the twenty-first century. Wage differentials, employment opportunities, and political stability will continue to attract Hispanic immigrants to the United States. Underemployment, unemployment, low wages, and political and economic instability will continue to foster emigration. Recent efforts to promote a Western-Hemisphere equivalent of NAFTA will create economic transformations in Latin America and will increase immigration pressure on the United States. Already established and extensive Hispanic migration networks will continue to facilitate Hispanic immigration.

The reality is that immigration policy can only partially control and shape Hispanic immigration. The United States can choose between making the immigration flow mostly legal or retaining policies that legalize only parts of it. Suggestions to construct hundreds of miles of walls along the Mexican border and to deploy military personnel to patrol the border are likely to run into strong political resistance and legal challenges. Moreover, there is strong evidence that while enhanced border enforcement may make entry more difficult, it will not prevent undocumented immigration. It is difficult to imagine that a country that so effectively used the image of the Berlin Wall to combat Communism will create a wall of its own to keep people out. Reducing the incentives to immigrate illegally have proven difficult to implement. So far, the federal government seems unwilling to put enough resources into the enforcement of employer sanctions to give the policy much credibility let alone effectiveness. Employers who rely on undocumented workers find ways around the law, and those who wish to comply with the law do not have the expertise to identify fraudulent identification papers. A national identification card might aid the latter group, but thus far Americans have resisted instituting such a system of identification.

It must first be recognized that there are no easy answers to immigration problems. However, the United States can choose options that reflect American values and interests. Through its immigration policies, the United States could reaffirm the special relationship it has with Latin America and Spanish-speaking countries of the Caribbean. For countries such as Mexico, where there is great emigration pressure, the per-country ceiling on immigration creates tremendous backlogs in visa requests. Long waits for immigration visas force families to make difficult choices by obeying the law and being apart or disobeying the law and being together. Periodically passing time-limited legislation to clear up visa backlogs would help ensure that people who have the opportunity to legally immigrate do so. It is equally clear that placing even greater emphasis on labor market criteria, at the expense of family reunification, will reduce the opportunity for many Hispanics to immigrate. Devaluing family reunification will turn legal immigrants into illegal immigrants.

A country that so values the rule of law must develop policies that establish incentives for prospective immigrants to immigrate legally. The issue of illegal immigration obviously defies simple policy remedies. The continuing stream of undocumented workers to the United States demonstrates strong demand for their labor.

One controversial policy that recognizes this symbiotic relationship would be for the United States to reinstitute a guestworker program that would permit short-term immigration. Learning from problems with the Braceros and guestworker programs in Europe, a U.S. version could provide temporary legal status for most undocumented immigrants. Any guestworker program should contain strong incentives to reward those who eventually return home. For example, once workers have returned to their countries of origin, their contributions to the Social Security system could be refunded. The issue in such a policy would be withholding enough to encourage return but not too much to make the program unattractive to would-be participants. A guestworker program has other benefits as well. It would greatly reduce discrimination based on national origin, because workers would have work authorization. Also, a guestworker program would provide some administrative review of participants before they enter the United States. A guestworker program will reduce but not eliminate illegal immigration. It is clear that some recipients of guestworker visas will overstay their visas and permanently settle in the United States. That dynamic is really no different from the one that now characterizes illegal immigration.

In recent years, through legislation and court decisions, the United States has created a growing distinction between citizen and immigrant. Until recently, citizenship primarily conferred the right to participate in the political dimension of American life. Citizenship now confers greater economic, social, and legal rights. It is too soon to assess the long-term implications of these changes. The increasing advantage of citizenship may prompt more and more immigrants, particularly Hispanic immigrants who have low naturalization rates, to petition for naturalization. The emphasis on citizenship may add to the marginalization of immigrants and increase the difficulty of adjusting to American life and institutions.

One of the key needs regarding immigration in the next millennium is to better address the local effects of immigration. The nation as a whole benefits from immigration, while states and localities incur very real costs.

One way to reduce the divisions and tensions that produced Proposition 187 is for the federal government to offer more economic aid to areas heavily settled by immigrants. In the past, the United States has offered impact aid to communities that resettle refugees; the same can be done for immigrants. It is counterproductive to ignore the reality that localities seldom have the resources to provide adequate educational and social services to immigrants. How well immigrants and their children do in their communities will ultimately determine the health and well-being of the United States. Assuring that immigrants become incorporated into the fabric of American life at the local level is an investment in America's future.

Notes

1. David M. Kennedy, "The Price of Immigration." *Atlantic Monthly* 278, no. 3 (November 1996): 51–68.
2. James P. Smith and Barry Edmonston, eds. *The New Americans: Economic, Demographic, and Fiscal Effects of Immigration* (Washington, D.C.: National Academy Press, 1997).
3. Jorge Castaneda, *The Mexican Shock: Its Meaning for the United States* (New York: New York Press, 1995), 16–17.
4. Scholars looking at Mexican immigration have noted that economic changes created by the Mexican Revolution ushered in the first wave of large-scale Mexican immigration to the United States.
5. Douglas Massey, "Economic Development and International Migration in Comparative Perspective," in *Determinants of Emigration from Mexico, Central America, and the Caribbean,* ed. Sergio Diaz-Briquets and Sidney Weintraub (Boulder, Colo.: Westview Press, 1991), 15.
6. Alejandro Portes and Ruben G. Rumhaut, *Immigrant America: A Portrait* (Los Angeles, Cal.: University of California Press, 1990), 8–9.
7. Ibid., 12.
8. Sergio Diaz-Briquets, "The Central American Demographic Situation: Trends and Implications," in *Mexican and Central American Population and U.S. Immigration Policy,* ed. Frank D. Bean, Jurgen Schmandt, and Sidney Weintraub, 34 (Austin, Tex.: University of Texas Press, 1989).
9. Rodolfo O. de la Garza and Gabriel Szekely, "Policy, Politics and Emigration: Reexamining the Mexican Experience," in *At the Crossroads: Mexican Migration and U.S. Policy,* ed. Frank D. Bean, Rodolfo O. de la Garza, Bryan R. Roberts, and Sidney Weintraub (Lanham, Md.: Rowman & Littlefield, 1997).
10. Oscar Handlin, *The Uprooted* (Boston: Little, Brown, 1951).
11. Casteneda, *The Mexican Shock,* 19.
12. Katharine M. Donato, "U.S. Policy and Mexican Migration to the United States: 1942–92," *Social Science Quarterly* 75. no. 4 (December 1994): 707–29: Douglas Massey, Rafael Alarcon, Jorge Durand, and Humberto Gonzalez, *Return to Aztlan: The Social Process of International Migration from Western Mexico* (Berkeley, Cal.: University of California Press, 1987).
13. Douglas Massey, "The Social Organization of Mexican Migration to the United States," *Annals* 487 (September 1986): 103.
14. Douglas Massey, Joaquin Arango, Graeme Hugo, Adela Pellegrino, and J. Edward Taylor, "An Evaluation of International Migration," *Population and Development Review* 20, no. 4 (December 1994): 728.
15. Carlos Rico, "Migration and U.S.-Mexican Relations, 1966–1986," in *Western Hemisphere Immigration and United States Foreign Policy,* ed. Christopher Mitchell (University Park, Pa.: Pennsylvania State University Press, 1992), 236.
16. Jacqueline Maria Hagan and Susan Gonzalez-Baker, "Implementing the U.S. Legalization Program: The Influence of Immigrant Communities and Local Agencies on Implementing Policy Reform," *International Migration Review* 27, no. 3 (Fall 1993): 513–36.
17. Lars Schoultz, "Central America and the Politicization of U.S. Immigration Policy," in Mitchell, *Western Hemisphere Immigration and United States Foreign Policy,* 182.
18. Ibid., 185.
19. For a review of studies documenting the importance of networks to Mexican migration, see Massey et al., "An Evaluation of International Migration."
20. Portes and Rumbaut, *Immigrant America.*
21. Massey et al., "An Evaluation of International Migration." 729.
22. Katherine M. Donato, Jorge Durand, and Douglas Massey, "Stemming the Tide? Assessing the Deterrent Effects of the Immigration Reform and Control Act," *Demography* 29 (May 1992): 155.
23. George C. Kiser and Martha Woody Kiser, eds., *Mexican Workers in the United States* (Albuquerque, N.M.: University of New Mexico Press, 1979).
24. One can argue that the recent efforts to counter illegal Mexican immigration during prosperous times contradicts the historic norm. It must be remembered that California's recent and influential role in lobbying for tighter border enforcement occurred when the state—but not the nation—was recovering from the effects of economic recession.
25. Larry C. Morgan and Bruce L. Gardner, "Potential for a U.S. Guest-Worker Program in Agriculture: Lessons from the Braceros," in *The Gateway: U.S. Immigration Issues and Policies,* ed. Barry R. Chiswick (Washington, D.C.: American Enterprise Institute, 1982).
26. Frank D. Bean, George Vernez, and Charles Keely, *Opening and Closing the Doors: Evaluating Immigration Reform and Control* (Washington, D.C.: Urban Institute Press, 1989), 7.
27. Gary P. Freeman and Frank D. Bean, "Mexico and U.S. Worldwide Immigration Policy," in Bean, de la Garza. Roberts, and Weintraub, *At the Crossroads,* 25.
28. David W. Engstrom, *Presidential Decision Making Adrift: The Carter Administration and the Mariel Boatlift* (Lanham, Md.: Rowman & Littlefield, 1997).
29. Christopher Mitchell, "U.S. Foreign Policy and Dominican Migration to the United States," in Mitchell, *Western Hemisphere Immigration and United States Foreign Policy,* 100.
30. Massey et al., "An Evaluation of International Migration," 728.
31. Freeman and Bean, "Mexico and U.S. Worldwide Immigration Policy," 27.
32. For an excellent history of Cuban immigration, see Felix Roberto Masud-Piloto, *From Welcome Exiles to Illegal Immigrants: Cuban Migration to the U.S.* (Lanham, Md.: Rowman & Littlefield, 1996).
33. Engstrom, *Presidential Decision Making Adrift.*
34. Schoultz noted that the emigration represented up to 6 percent of the region's population. Schoultz, "Central America and the Politicization of U.S. Immigration Policy," 168.
35. Norman L. Zucker and Naomi Flink Zucker. *The Guarded Gate: The Reality of American Refugee Policy* (New York: Harcourt. Brace, Jovanovich, 1987).
36. Class-action lawsuits, such as *American Baptist Churches v. Thornburgh,* and congressional action granting temporary protected status have allowed hundreds of thousands of Central Americans to remain in the United States. Growing concern over the volume of asylum applications has led Congress to streamline asylum provisions and increase the number of officers, to speed up processing asylum claims.
37. Illegal immigration has existed since the United States began imposing restrictions on immigration. The predecessor to the Border Patrol was established in 1906, to patrol the border of the southwest to prevent the illegal entry of Chinese immigrants. The first large-scale effort to deal with illegal immigration occurred during the recession of the early 1950s. The Immigration and Naturalization Service (INS) tightened its enforcement at the southern (but not northern) border; this campaign culminated in the implementation of Operation Wetback in 1954. That year the INS apprehended more than 1 million undocumented immigrants.
38. Thomas J. Espenshade and Charles A. Calhoun, "An Analysis of Public Opinion Toward Undocumented Immigration," *Population Research and Policy Review* 12 (1993): 191–92.
39. Susan Gonzalez-Baker, "The 'Amnesty' Aftermath: Current Policy Issues Stemming from the Legalization Programs of the 1986 Immigration Reform and Control Act," *International Migration Review* 31, no. 1 (Spring 1997): 5–27.
40. United States Department of Justice, *Immigration Reform and Control Act: Report on the Legalized Alien Population* (Washington, D.C.: Government Printing Office, 1992).

41. Gonzalez-Baker, "The 'Amnesty' Aftermath."

42. Donato, Durand, and Massey, "Stemming the Tide?," 155. Other immigration scholars reached similar conclusions. Jeffrey S. Passel, Frank D. Bean, and Barry Edmonston, "Assessing the Impact of Employer Sanctions on Undocumented Immigration to the United States," in *The Paper Curtain: Employer Sanctions' Implementation, Impact, and Reform*, ed. Michael Fix (Washington, D.C.: Urban Institute Press, 1991).

43. United States Congress, Senate Committee on the Judiciary, *The Implementation of Employer Sanctions: Hearings before the Subcommittee on Immigration and Refugee Affairs*, 102d Cong., 2d sess, April 3–10, 1992.

44. Quote from Lindsay B. Lowell, Jay Teachman, and Zhongren Jing, "Unintended Consequences of Immigration Reform: Discrimination and Hispanic Employment," *Demography* 32 (November 1995): 618.

45. United States Department of State, *Report of the Visa Office 1996* (Washington, D.C.: Government Printing Office, 1998).

46. United States Commission on Immigration Reform, *U.S. Immigration Policy: Restoring Credibility* (Washington, D.C.: Government Printing Office, 1994).

47. Peter Schuck argued that the 1990 and 1996 immigration legislation "radically limited the procedural and substantive rights that aliens had come to enjoy." See Peter H. Schuck, *Citizens, Strangers, and In-Between* (Boulder, Colo.: Westview Press, 1998), 14.

48. These numbers do not reflect undocumented or illegal immigration. Unless otherwise indicated, all immigration data are drawn from the United States Department of Justice, *1996 Statistical Yearbook of the Immigration and Naturalization Service* (Washington, D.C.: Government Printing Office, 1998).

49. Portes and Rumbaut, *Immigrant America.*

50. U.S. Commission on Immigration Reform, *Becoming an American: Immigration and Immigrant Policy* (Washington. D.C.: Government Printing Office, 1997).

51. For an analysis of employment-based preferences, see Demetrios G. Papademetriou and Stephen Yale-Loehr, *Balancing Interests: Rethinking U.S. Selection of Skilled Immigrants* (Washington, D.C.: Brookings Institution, 1996).

52. Bean, Vernez, and Keely, *Opening and Closing the Doors*, 19; Smith and Edmonston, *The New Americans,* 39–40.

53. Massey et al., *Return to Aztlan*; Donato. "U.S. Policy and Mexican Migration."

54. For example, Christopher Mitchell wrote: "A good many Dominicans entered the United States on visitor's visas and remained to work, violating the terms of those visas. Although it is not possible to measure this 'undocumented' migrant flow precisely, it may have totaled between one-third and one-half the size of the legal immigrant stream from the Dominican republic." Mitchell, "U.S. Foreign Policy and Dominican Migration," 93–94.

55. Jeffrey S. Passel, "Undocumented Immigration," in *The Debate in the United States over Immigration*, ed. Peter Duignan and Lewis H. Gann (Stanford, Cal.: Hoover Institution Press, 1998).

56. Thomas J. Espenshade, "Unauthorized Immigration to the United States," *Annual Review of Sociology* 21 (1995): 196.

57. Smith and Edmonston, *The New Americans*, 51.

58. United States Commission on Immigration Reform, *Becoming an American*, 35.

59. Mitchell, "U.S. Foreign Policy and Dominican Migration."

60. Block migration opportunities did result in three dramatic boatlifts from Cuba to the United States in 1965, 1980, and 1994. For a discussion of the boatlifts, see Engstrom, *Presidential Decision Making Adrift.*

61. They noted that most commentators on Mexican immigration "have ignored or dismissed the role politics and policy have played in shaping emigration policy." De la Garza and Szekely, "Policy, Politics and Emigration."

62. Quoted in Wayne A. Cornelius and Philip L. Martin, "The Uncertain Connection: Free Trade and Rural Mexican Migration to the United States," *International Migration Review* 27, no. 3 (Fall 1993): 485.

63. For a balanced discussion of NAFTA and Mexican immigration, see Peter H. Smith, "NAFTA and Mexican Migration," in Bean, de la Garza, Roberts, and Weintraub, *At the Crossroads*, 263–82.

64. Massey, "Economic Development and International Migration in Comparative Perspective," 15.

65. United States Department of State, *Report of the Visa Office 1996.*

66. Jeffrey S. Passel and Michael Fix, "Myths about Immigrants," *Foreign Policy*, no. 95 (Summer 1994): 154.

67. The remaining 11 percent of INS Border Patrol agents are assigned to patrolling the coastal areas. United States General Accounting Office, *Border Patrol: Staffing and Enforcement Activities*, Report to Congressional Committees, GAO/GGD-96-65 (Washington, DC: Government Printing Office, 1996).

68. Michael Katz noted that immigrants were blamed for rising taxes when taxes were used to fund poor relief in the early nineteenth century. Michael Katz, *In the Shadow of the Poorhouse* (New York: Basic Books, 1996).

69. As reported in Thomas J. Espenshade and Maryann Belenger, "U.S. Public Perceptions and Reaction to Mexican Migration," in Bean, de la Garza, Roberts, and Weintraub. *At the Crossroads*, 227–62.

70. Michael Fix and Jeffrey S. Passel, "Setting the Record Straight," *Public Welfare* 52, no. 2 (Spring 1994): 10.

71. Jennifer V. W. van Hook and Frank Bean, "The Growth in Non-Citizen SSI Caseloads During the 1980s: Immigration versus Aging Effects," Texas Population Research Center Papers No. 96-97-12 (Austin, Tex.: Texas Population Research Center, 1996–97).

72. Frank D. Bean, Jennifer V. W. van Hook, and Jennifer E. Glick, "Mode-of-Entry, Type of Public Assistance and Patterns of Welfare Reciepency Among U.S. Immigrants and Natives," Texas Population Research Center Papers No. 94-95-17 (Austin, Tex.: Texas Population Research Center, 1994–95), 20.

73. An individual sponsoring the immigration of three family members must have a total yearly income of $20,050. Many individuals and families will lack the financial resources to be sponsors. For example, data from Chiswick and Hurst (see chapter 6) indicate that the average yearly earnings of many Hispanic male subgroups are insufficient to meet the $20,050 sponsorship threshold; male Mexican immigrants average only $15,994 in yearly wages.

74. United States Commission on Immigration Reform, *Becoming an American*, 22.

75. Congress gave states the discretion on whether to allow legal immigrants the opportunity to continue participating in various programs such as TANF, food stamps, and Medicaid. Some observers argued that states would disenroll immigrants from welfare programs to save revenue. A recent GAO study found that most states have continued to provide welfare benefits to immigrants who entered the United States before August 22, 1996. The GAO found that "about a third of the states provide state-funded temporary assistance to needy immigrants, medical assistance, or both to new immigrants during their 5-year bar from federal programs." United States General Accounting Office, *Welfare Reform: Many States Continue Some Federal or State Benefits for Immigrants*, Report to the Ranking Minority Member, Subcommittee on Children and Families, Senate Committee on Labor and Human Resources, GAO/HEHS-98-132 (July 1998), 8.

76. Cited in Susan Gonzales-Baker, Robert G. Cushing, and Charles W. Haynes, "Fiscal Impacts of Mexican Migration to the United States," in Bean, de la Garza, Roberts, and Weintraub, *At the Crossroads*, 145–76.

77. Michael Fix and Jeffrey S. Passel. "Setting the Record Straight," 8.

78. Smith and Edmonston, *The New Americans*, 293.

79. Ibid., 12.

80. Gonzales-Baker, Cushing, and Haynes, "Fiscal Impacts of Mexican Migration to the United States," 146.

81. Passel and Fix, "Myths about Immigrants," 158; Gonzales-Baker, Cushing, and Haynes, "Fiscal Impacts of Mexican Migration to the United States."

82. Smith and Edmonston, *The New Americans.*

83. Papademetriou and Yale-Loehr, *Balancing Interests.*

Bibliography

Bean, Frank D., Rodolfo O. de la Garza, Bryan R. Roberts, and Sidney Weintraub, eds. *At the Crossroads: Mexican Migration and U.S. Policy.* Lanham, Md.: Rowman & Littletield, 1997.

Bean, Frank D., Jurgen Schmandt, and Sidney Weintraub, eds. *Mexican and Central American Population and U.S. Immigration Policy.* Austin, Tex.: University of Texas Press, 1989.

Bean, Frank D., Jennifer V. W. van Hook, and Jennifer E. Glick. "Mode-of Entry, Type of Public Assistance and Patterns of Welfare Recipiency Among U.S. Immigrants and Natives." Texas Population Research Center Papers, No. 94-95-17. Austin, Tex.: Texas Population Research Center, 1994–95.

Bean, Frank D., George Vernez, and Charles Keely. *Opening and Closing the Doors: Evaluating Immigration Reform and Control.* Washington, D.C.: Urban Institute Press, 1989.

Castaneda, Jorge. *The Mexican Shock: Its Meaning for the United States.* New York: New York Press, 1995.

Chiswick, Barry R.. ed. *The Gateway: US. Immigration Issues and Policies.* Washington, D.C.: American Enterprise Institute, 1982.

Cornelius, Wayne A., and Philip L. Martin. "The Uncertain Connection: Free Trade and Rural Mexican Migration to the United States." *International Migration Review* 27, no. 3 (Fall 1993): 484–512.

de la Garza, Rodolfo O., and Gabriel Szekely. "Policy, Politics and Emigration: Reexamining the Mexican Experience." In *At the Crossroads: Mexican Migration and U.S. Policy,* edited by Frank D. Bean, Rodolfo O. de la Garza, Bryan R. Roberts, and Sidney Weintraub. Lanham, Md.: Rowman & Littlefield, 1997.

Diaz-Briquets, Sergio. "The Central American Demographic Situation: Trends and Implications." In *Mexican and Central American Population and U.S. Immigration Policy,* edited by Frank D. Bean, Jurgen Schmandt, and Sidney Weintraub. Austin, Tex.: University of Texas Press, 1989.

Diaz-Briquets, Sergio, and Sidney Weintraub, eds. *Determinants of Emigration from Mexico, Central America, and the Caribbean.* Boulder, Colo.: Westview Press, 1991.

Donato, Katharine M. "U.S. Policy and Mexican Migration to the United States: 1942–92." *Social Science Quarterly* 75, no. 4 (December 1994): 707–29.

Donato, Katherine M., Jorge Durand, and Douglas Massey. "Stemming the Tide? Assessing the Deterrent Effects of the Immigration Reform and Control Act." *Demography* 29 (May 1992): 139–57.

Duignan, Peter, and Lewis H. Gann, eds. *The Debate in the United States over Immigration.* Stanford, Cal.: Hoover Institution Press, 1998.

Engstrom, David W. *Presidential Decision Making Adrift: The Carter Administration and the Mariel Boatlift.* Lanham, Md.: Rowman & Littlefield, 1997.

Espenshade, Thomas J. "Unauthorized Immigration to the United States." *Annual Review of Sociology* 21 (1995): 195–216.

Espenshade. Thomas J., and Maryann Belenger. "U.S. Public Perceptions and Reaction to Mexican Migration." In *At the Crossroads: Mexican Migration and U.S. Policy,* edited by Frank D. Bean, Rodolfo O. de la Garza, Bryan R. Roberts, and Sidney Weintraub, 227–62. Lanham, Md.: Rowman & Littlefield, 1997.

Espenshade, Thomas J., and Charles A. Calhoun. "An Analysis of Public Opinion Toward Undocumented Immigration." *Population Research and Policy Review* 12 (1993): 189–224.

Fix, Michael, ed. *The Paper Curtain: Employer Sanctions' Implementation, Impact, and Reform.* Washington, D.C.: Urban Institute Press, 1991.

Fix, Michael, and Jeffrey S. Passel. "Setting the Record Straight." *Public Welfare* 52, no. 2 (Spring 1994): 6–15.

Freeman, Gary P., and Frank D. Bean. "Mexico and U.S. Worldwide Immigration Policy." In *At the Crossroads: Mexican Migration and U.S. Policy,* edited by Frank D. Bean, Rodolfo O. de la Garza, Bryan

R. Roberts, and Sidney Weintraub. Lanham, Md.: Rowman & Littlefield, 1997.

Gonzales-Baker, Susan. "The 'Amnesty' Aftermath: Current Policy Issues Stemming from the Legalization Programs of the 1986 Immigration Reform and Control Act." *International Migration Review* 31, no.1 (Spring 1997): 5–27.

Gonzalez-Baker, Susan, Robert G. Cushing, and Charles W. Haynes. "Fiscal Impacts of Mexican Migration to the United States." In *At the Crossroads: Mexican Migration and U.S. Policy,* edited by Frank D. Bean, Rodolfo O. de la Garza, Bryan R. Roberts, and Sidney Weintraub, 145–76. Lanham, Md.: Rowman & Littlefield, 1997.

Hagan, Jacqueline Maria, and Susan Gonzalez-Baker. "Implementing the U.S. Legalization Program: The Influence of Immigrant Communities and Local Agencies on Implementing Policy Reform." *International Migration Review* 27, no. 3 (Fall 1993): 513–36.

Handlin, Oscar. *The Uprooted.* Boston: Little, Brown, 1951.

Katz, Michael. *In the Shadow of the Poorhouse.* New York: Basic Books, 1996.

Kennedy, David M. "The Price of Immigration." *Atlantic Monthly* 278, no. 3 (November 1996): 51–68.

Kiser, George C., and Martha Woody Kiser, eds. *Mexican Workers in the United States.* Albuquerque, N.M.: University of New Mexico Press, 1979.

Lowell, Lindsay B., Jay Teachman, and Zhongren Jing. "Unintended Consequences of Immigration Reform: Discrimination and Hispanic Employment." *Demography* 32 (November 1995): 617–28.

Massey, Douglas. "Economic Development and International Migration in Comparative Perspective." In *Determinants of Emigration from Mexico, Central America, and the Caribbean,* edited by Sergio Diaz-Briquets and Sidney Weintraub. Boulder, Colo.: Westview Press, 1991.

———. "The Social Organization of Mexican Migration to the United States." *Annals* 487 (September 1986): 102–13.

Massey, Douglas, Rafael Alarcon, Jorge Durand, and Humberto Gonzalez. *Return to Aztlan: The Social Process of International Migration from Western Mexico.* Berkeley, Cal.: University of California Press, 1987.

Massey, Douglas, Joaquin Arango, Graeme Hugo, Adela Pellegrino, and J. Edward Taylor. "An Evaluation of International Migration." *Population and Development Review* 20, no. 4 (December 1994): 699–751.

Masud-Piloto, Felix Roberto. *From Welcome Exiles to Illegal Immigrants: Cuban Migration to the US.* Lanham, Md.: Rowman & Littlefield, 1996.

Mitchell, Christopher. "U.S. Foreign Policy and Dominican Migration to the United States." In *Western Hemisphere Immigration and United States Foreign Policy,* edited by Christopher Mitchell. University Park, Pa.: Pennsylvania State University Press, 1992.

Mitchell, Christopher, ed. *Western Hemisphere Immigration and United States Foreign Policy.* University Park, Pa.: Pennsylvania State University Press, 1992.

Morgan, Larry C., and Bruce L. Gardner. "Potential for a U.S. Guest-Worker Program in Agriculture: Lessons from the Braceros." In *The Gateway: U.S. Immigration Issues and Policies,* edited by Barry R. Chiswick. Washington, D.C.: American Enterprise Institute, 1982.

Papademetriou, Demetrios G., and Stephen Yale-Loehr. *Balancing Interests: Rethinking U.S. Selection of Skilled Immigrants.* Washington, D.C.: Brookings Institution Press, 1996.

Passel, Jeffrey S. "Undocumented Immigration." In *The Debate in the United States over Immigration,* edited by Peter Duignan and Lewis H. Gann. Stanford, Cal.: Hoover Institution Press, 1998.

Passel, Jeffrey S., Frank D. Bean, and Barry Edmonston. "Assessing the Impact of Employer Sanctions on Undocumented Immigration to the United States." In *The Paper Curtain: Employer Sanctions' Implementation, Impact, and Reform,* edited by Michael Fix. Washington, D.C.: Urban Institute Press, 1991.

Passel, Jeffrey S., and Michael Fix. "Myths about Immigrants." *Foreign Policy*, no. 95 (Summer 1994): 151–60.

Portes, Alejandro, and Ruben G. Rumbaut. *Immigrant America: A Portrait.* Los Angeles, Cal.: University of California Press, 1990.

Rico, Carlos. "Migration and U.S.-Mexican Relations, 1966–1986." In *Western Hemisphere Immigration and United States Foreign Policy*, edited by Christopher Mitchell. University Park, Pa.: Pennsylvania State University Press, 1992.

Shoultz, Lars. "Central America and the Politicization of U.S. Immigration Policy." In *Western Hemisphere Immigration and United States Foreign Policy*, edited by Christopher Mitchell. University Park, Pa.: Pennsylvania State University Press, 1992.

Schuck, Peter H. *Citizens, Strangers, and In-Between.* Boulder, Colo.: Westview Press, 1998.

Smith, James P., and Barry Edmonston. eds. *The New Americans: Economic, Demographic, and Fiscal Effects of Immigration.* Washington, D.C.: National Academy Press, 1997.

Smith, Peter H. "NAFTA and Mexican Migration." In *At the Crossroads: Mexican Migration and U.S. Policy*, edited by Frank D. Bean. Rodolfo O. de la Garza, Bryan R. Roberts, and Sidney Weintraub, 263–82. Lanham, Md.: Rowman & Littlefield, 1997.

United States Commission on Immigration Reform. *Becoming an American: Immigration and Immigrant Policy.* Washington, D.C.: Government Printing Office, 1997.

United States Commission on Immigration Reform. *U.S. Immigration Policy: Restoring Credibility.* Washington. D.C.: Government Printing Office, 1994.

United States Congress. Senate Committee on the Judiciary. *The Implementation of Employer Sanctions: Hearings before the Subcommittee on Immigration and Refugee Affairs.* 102d Cong., 2d sess., April 3–10, 1992.

United States Department of Justice. *Immigration Reform and Control Act: Report on the Legalized Alien Population.* Washington, D.C.: Government Printing Office, 1992.

United States Department of Justice. *1996 Statistical Yearbook of the Immigration and Naturalization Service.* Washington, D.C.: Government Printing Office, 1998.

United States Department of State. *Report of the Visa Office 1996.* Washington, D.C.: Government Printing Office, 1998.

United States General Accounting Office. *Border Patrol: Staffing and Enforcement Activities.* Report to Congressional Committees. GAO/GGD-96-65. 1996.

United States General Accounting Office. *Welfare Reform: Many States Continue Some Federal or State Benefits for Immigrants.* Report to the Ranking Minority Member, Subcommittee on Children and Families, Senate Committee on Labor and Human Resources. GAO/HEHS-98-132. July 1998.

van Hook, Jennifer V. W., and Frank Bean. "The Growth in Non-Citizen SSI Caseloads During the 1980s: Immigration versus Aging Effects." Texas Population Research Center Papers No. 96-97-12. Austin, Tex.: Texas Population Research Center, 1996–97.

Zucker, Norman L., and Naomi Flink Zucker. *The Guarded Gate: The Reality of American Refugee Policy.* New York: Harcourt Brace Jovanovich, 1987.

Land of Opportunity

Mortimer B. Zuckerman

We are a nation of immigrants, neatly epitomized in Franklin Delano Roosevelt's ironic remark to the Daughters of the American Revolution: "Welcome, fellow immigrants." Immigrants come to America for many reasons, but mainly they come because it's the land of opportunity and upward mobility where achievement is more important than inheritance. Uprooting themselves from the familiarity of family, community, and even language and culture, they are self-selected risk-takers, which is why they tend to be hardworking, self-starting, creative, and smart. It's also why immigration has been such an economic plus for America and why so many of us look so favorably on legal immigrants.

Some Americans, however, have reservations, and some, perhaps driven by nativist, anti-immigrant sentiment or concern over the cost of illegal immigrants, decry the huge waves of legal and illegal Hispanic immigration we've seen over the past 50 years: Eleven million illegals live in a shadow world within our borders, reinforced annually by an influx of hundreds of thousands more. They are mainly from Mexico, just a car ride away, so they can maintain real and emotional ties to their home country. The anxiety is that Hispanics will retain their language and culture and thus remain separate from and isolated within America. The popular phrase is that they will acculturate rather than assimilate, for Hispanics can remain within their own culture given the easy accessibility to Spanish TV networks, newspapers, and radio stations—and the fact that many tend to live in large Spanish-speaking enclaves, in places like California—all of which raises the concern that we might become a bilingual country.

Roots. The concerns are understandable, but the thing to really watch is not how much Hispanics are changing America but how much America is changing Hispanics. They are learning English as fast as any immigrant group. True, they are retaining their native language longer, but the transition from Spanish to English is virtually completed in one generation, on average. Of the children born here to immigrants, only 7 percent rely on Spanish as their primary language, and nearly half have no Spanish skills at all. Of the third generation, that is, Latinos born of U.S.-born parents, virtually none speak only Spanish, and less than a quarter are bilingual. According to the Pew Hispanic Center poll of 2004, 96 percent believe English is fundamental to their future. By the third generation, 60 percent of Mexican-American children speak only English at home.

When Hispanics have children in America, they tend to sink deeper roots here and lose touch with the homes they left behind. That's why there is little difference, for example, between Mexican-American lifestyles and other American lifestyles. Hispanics are embracing the American way. Their goals are the essence of the American dream: economic opportunity and security, health and education, and home ownership. They place as much emphasis on the American values of hard work and family as any group in America.

They are also intermarrying at a rate similar to that of other immigrant groups. By the third generation, a third of Hispanic women marry non-Latinos. They serve and die in the military as much as any other group in proportion to their population and now compose about 10 percent of the U.S. military. They have also done relatively well financially for a community that came here with virtually nothing. Nearly 80 percent live above the poverty line, and 68 percent of those who have lived here for 30 years or more own their own homes. Their culture of hard work, in other words, has enabled them to climb out of poverty, and they are going through the same powerful process of change as any of the immigrant groups that have come to the United States, melting gradually but inexorably into our middle and working classes.

The one area where they lag is education. Roughly 60 percent of Hispanics graduate from high school, compared with 90 percent of nonimmigrant Americans; only

8 percent get college degrees, compared with 26 percent of whites. Their strong work ethic compounds the problem by drawing many young Latinos into the workforce before they finish high school, keeping high school graduation rates lower and trapping too many in low-wage service jobs. In fairness, the urban public schools that they typically attend have failed them, as they have failed so many others, for these are no longer the best schools with the best teachers, as they were a century ago.

Yes, the challenges of this wave of Hispanic immigration are daunting, especially the illegals. But there's no reason to be pessimistic. The evidence suggests strongly that we will be able to absorb the Hispanics—as we have earlier generations from Europe—and weave them into a dynamic American society. Not only that. Every new wave of immigrants has taught our nation something new and enriched our culture. This, in other words, is an opportunity, not a problem.

The Hispanic Vote
Electoral Strength Lags Population Growth

Overview

Between the elections of 2000 and 2004, Hispanics[1] accounted for half of the population growth in the United States but only one tenth of the increase in the total votes cast.

This difference between overall growth in population and growth at the ballot box is primarily the result of the two demographic factors that distinguish Latinos from whites and blacks in the electoral arena: A high percentage of Hispanics are too young to vote or are ineligible because they are not citizens.

As a result, a population increase of 5.7 million Latinos between 2000 and 2004 yielded only 2.1 million new eligible voters. In addition, Hispanic voter participation rates lag those of whites or blacks, so that the number of Hispanic voters increased by just 1.4 million.

The combination of demographic factors and participation rates meant that just 18% of the total Latino population (adults as well as children, citizens and non-citizens) went to the polls in 2004, compared with 51 % of all whites and 39% of all blacks. This gap in size between the Latino population and the Latino vote has been developing for decades and has widened considerably in recent years.

Despite these factors, however, the Hispanic population has been growing at such a strong rate that it still has led to an increase—albeit a small one—in the Hispanic share of the overall electorate. In November 2004, Hispanics accounted for 6.0% of all votes cast, up from 5.5% four years earlier. During the same period, the Hispanic share of the population rose from 12.8% to 14.3%.

This section uses Census Bureau data to analyze the relationship between Hispanic population growth and voting strength. In addition, it addresses a lingering question about the extent of Hispanic support for President George W. Bush last year. An analysis of 2004 exit poll data in conjunction with census data suggests that Bush's share

of the Hispanic vote was probably closer to 40% than to the 44% widely reported last year by news organizations that had relied on national exit poll data.

The key findings are:

◆ Between the 2000 and 2004 elections, the Hispanic population grew by 5.7 million, accounting for half of the 11.5 million increase in the U.S. population. This growth was fueled both by immigration and by high birth rates among Latinos already living in this country.

◆ Of those 5.7 million Hispanics added to the U.S. population between the last two presidential elections, 1.7 million persons or 30% were younger than 18 and thus not eligible to vote. Another 1.9 million or 33% were adults not eligible to vote because they were not citizens.

◆ As a result of these factors, only 39% of the Latino population was eligible to vote, compared with

Figure 1. The Growing Divergence between the Hispanic Population and Hispanic Voters, 1970–2004

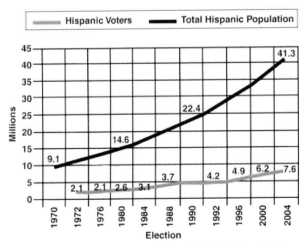

Source: *Hispanic Americans: A Statistical Sourcebook*, Pew Center tabulations of 2004 November Current Population Survey, and decennial censuses for 1970–2000.

Table 1. Political Participation by Hispanics and Total U.S. Population, 2004

	Hispanic	**All Persons**
Total Population, regardless of age or citizenship status	41,300,000	289,362,000
Not Eligible to Vote—Total	25,212,000	92,357,000
Youths under 18	14,171,000	73,668,000
Adults without U.S. citizenship	11,041,000	18,689,000
Eligible Voters—U.S. citizens age 18 and above	16,088,000	197,005,000
Registered Voters—Adult U.S. citizens registered to vote	9,308,000	142,070,000
Reported Voters—Adult U.S. citizens who reported voting	7,587,000	125,736,000

Source: Pew Hispanic center tabulations of 2004 November Current Population Survey. All figures rounded independently.

76% of whites and 65% of the black population (figure 2).

◆ Both the number of Latinos registered to vote (9.3 million) and the number of Latinos who cast ballots (7.6 million) in November 2004 marked increases of political participation over the 2000 election that were larger than those for any other ethnic or racial group in percentage terms.

◆ However, both registration and turnout rates for Latinos were lower than for whites or blacks. As a result, only 47% of eligible Hispanics went to the polls compared with 67% of whites and 60% of blacks. Differences in registration rates explain most of the gaps.

◆ The combination of demographic factors and participation rates meant that only 18% of the Latino population voted in 2004, compared with 51 % of whites and 39% of blacks.

◆ In November 2004, Hispanics accounted for 14.3% of the total population but only 6.0% of the votes cast. In the previous election, Hispanics accounted

for 12.8% of the population and 5.5% of the votes cast.

◆ The large number of Hispanic young people will eventually add to the Latino electorate as they reach voting age. But, if immigration flows continue adding to the number of Latino females of childbearing years and Hispanic fertility rates and immigration flows persist at current levels, even larger numbers of youths will be added each year to the population not eligible to vote. And, if participation rates remain unchanged, the young people added to the electorate will register and vote at relatively low levels.

◆ There are significant demographic differences between the total Hispanic population and the Hispanic electorate. The foreign-born account for 56% of the Latino adult population but only 28% of 2004 Latino voters. As a result, 27% of Latino adults live in households where only Spanish is spoken, compared with only 9% of Latino voters.

◆ An analysis of census and exit poll data suggests that President Bush took 40% of the Hispanic vote in 2004 rather than the 44% as originally reported from the major news media exit poll.

◆ Religion appears to be linked to President Bush's improved showing among Hispanics in 2004 over 2000, when he took 34% of Latino votes. Hispanic Protestants made up a larger share of the Latino vote last year (32% in 2004 compared with 25% in 2000), and 56% of these voters supported the president in 2004, compared with 44% in 2000. The president's share of the Hispanic Catholic vote remained essentially unchanged between 2000 and 2004.

Figure 2. Eligible Voters as a Share of Total Population for Major Racial/Ethnic Groups, 2004

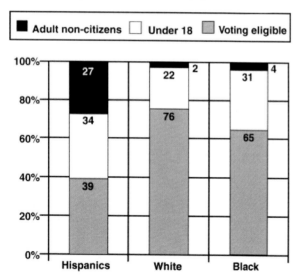

Source: Pew Hispanic Center tabulations of 2004 November Current Population Survey

A Note on the Current Population Survey

This section relies primarily on a supplement of the Current Population Survey (CPS) that is conducted every November of an election year by the U.S. Census Bureau. The November supplements ask people whether they were registered to vote and whether they actually voted.

All surveys are subject to discrepancies due to margins of error and other factors. This is true of the CPS, even though it is a very large survey regularly conducted of the American public with an average monthly sample of about 140,000 individuals.

Historically, the November election year supplements of the CPS show a larger number of persons voting than the actual count. This was the case again last year: The November 2004 CPS showed that 125.74 million persons reported voting in the 2004 national election while the official count of votes

in the Federal Register for the 2004 presidential contest was 122.28 million. The discrepancy is 3.5 million votes—about 3 percent of the official count. The CPS supplement is taken after Election Day and relies on individuals' self-reporting of their voting behavior. According to the Census Bureau, the difference between the CPS numbers and the official count results primarily from two factors: Some people report having voted when they did not, and some ballots do not get counted for various reasons, such as being marked improperly by a voter or being misread by a voting machine.

The CPS covers the civilian, non-institutional population resident in the country. It excludes almost all active-duty military in the United States and abroad, as well as persons in institutions, including nursing homes and correctional facilities.

Demographic Characteristics of the Hispanic Population and Electorate

The differences between the Hispanic population and the Hispanic electorate are more than just a matter of size. Latinos who are eligible to vote and those who actually do vote have distinctly different characteristics from the Latino population as a whole.

The most obvious difference involves nativity. Because so many Latino immigrants are not eligible to vote, a far greater share of the Hispanic adult population (56%) is foreign-born than is the case among those who reported voting in 2004 (28%).

Differences in nativity bring with them differences in language use. Surveys show that virtually all native-born Latinos speak English fluently while about a third are bilingual and almost none speak only Spanish. Meanwhile, virtually all of the foreign-born speak Spanish, about a quarter are bilingual and almost none speak only English.[2] The Census Bureau's Current Population Survey, from which most of the data in this section are drawn, does not measure bilingualism, but it does identify people who live in households where only Spanish is spoken. Fewer than 11% of eligible voters and fewer than 9% of actual voters live in Spanish-only households, compared with 27% of the entire Hispanic adult population and 50% of adult non-citizens.

Given that the growth of the immigrant population is fed by the arrival of young adults, it is not surprising that the population as a whole is somewhat younger than the electorate. In the entire adult population, 58% of Hispanics are younger than 40 compared with 52% of eligible voters. Two thirds of adult non-citizen Hispanics are under 40.

Hispanic eligible voters are somewhat more affluent than nonvoters. For example, 34% earn family incomes of more than $50,000 a year, compared with 27% of the Hispanic adult population as a whole. And the electorate is better educated. Among eligible voters, just 28% failed to complete high school, compared with 40% of the entire adult population.

How Latinos Voted in 2004

Although the CPS does not ask respondents how they voted, it does shed some light on a lingering question about how Hispanics voted in the 2004 presidential race and suggests that Latino support for President Bush may have been slightly lower than initially reported.

The uncertainty over the partisan breakdown of the Latino vote last year stems from questions about whether the Hispanic sample in the national exit poll was in fact representative of the Hispanic vote. The National Election Pool (NEP) was conducted on behalf of a consortium of news organizations using a well-established methodology that involves interviewing voters at a sample of precincts chosen to be representative of all polling places across the nation. The NEP national exit poll indicated that President Bush had taken 44% of the Hispanic vote—a 10 percentage point increase over his share in 2000. This 44% figure was widely reported by news organizations.

In this national poll, which was conducted at 250 precincts designed to be representative of the nation as a whole, 1,037 respondents identified themselves as Hispanics. At the same time as the national poll was being conducted on Election Day, the NEP was also conducting 51 individual polls designed to produce results representative in each of the 50 states and the District of Columbia. These polls were taken at 1,469 precincts at which

Table 2. Characteristics of the Hispanic Adult Population by Voting Eligibility, November 2004 CPS (percentages)

	Eligible Voters	18 & over, non-citizen	All Hispanic Adults
Age			
18 to 29	31	35	32
30 to 39	21	32	26
40 to 49	20	18	19
50 to 64	18	11	15
65	11	4	8
Sex			
Male	49	55	51
Female	51	45	49
Nativity			
Foreign born	25	100	56
Native born	75	0	44
Spanish only spoken in household?			
No	89	50	73
Yes	11	50	27
Family income			
Under $15,000	17	24	20
$15,000 to 29,999	22	33	27
$30,000 to 49,999	26	27	26
$50,000 to 74,999	19	10	15
$75,000 or more	16	7	12
Education			
Less than 9th grade	13	39	73
9th to 12th grade	16	20	17
11.S. graduate or some college	59	35	49
Bachelor's degree or more	13	7	10

Source: Pew Hispanic Center Tabulations of 2004 November Current Population Survey

4,469 Hispanics were interviewed. The Pew Hispanic Center has aggregated data from the 51 state polls and weighted the results to produce results for the nation as a whole. As first noted by Ana Maria Arumi, a polling specialist then with NBC who offered fresh insights on the exit poll at an event hosted by the National Association of Hispanic Journalists (NAHJ) on Dec. 2, 2004, the 51 state polls show that Bush drew 40% of the Hispanic vote rather than the 44% in the national poll.

A comparison of the profiles of Hispanic voters in the national and the combined state polls offers several clues why the national poll indicated a higher level of Latino support for President Bush. Compared to the combined sample in the 51 state polls, the national NEP data have fewer young Latino voters, fewer voters residing in cities with more than 50,000 residents, fewer women, fewer voters who identified themselves as Democrats and fewer who said they disapproved of the war in Iraq. All of these characteristics are shared by Hispanics who voted for Sen. John F. Kerry, the Democratic candidate. The national poll also had more Cuban voters in the Miami area, a traditionally Republican voting bloc.

It is impossible to determine definitively whether the national or the 51 state exit polls more accurately captured Hispanic voter preferences. However, the Latino voter profile in the 51 state polls more closely matches the

CPS on a few important points. For example, the CPS has 27% of the Hispanic vote coming from California, which is in line with the 26% in the state exit poll rather than the 21% in the national poll. And both the CPS and the state polls have the male share of the Hispanic vote at about 46% compared with more than 48% in the national exit poll (Table 3). The state polls (7.5%) come closer to the CPS finding on the Hispanic share of the total vote (6.0%) than the national exit poll (8.4%).

President Bush's Gains Among Hispanics

Whether he received 40% or 44% of the Hispanic vote last year or something in between, President Bush improved his showing from 2001 to 2004 among Hispanics by a bigger margin than he did among the population as a whole. Data from the combined state exit polls suggest that religion may have played a role in President Bush's greater success with Hispanics. Hispanic Protestants, who are mostly evangelicals rather than members of mainline Protestant denominations, comprised 32% of the Latino vote in 2004, up from 25% in 2000, according to the 51 state polls conducted during those elections.[3] In addition, this segment of the Latino electorate tilted more heavily

Table 3. Characteristics of Hispanic Voters, 51 State Exit Polls 2004 (percentages)

Sex			**Political party identification**	
Male	47		Democrat	49
Female	53		Republican	27
			Independent	24
Age			**Political philosophy**	
18 to 29	32		Liberal	26
30 to 39	20		Moderate	45
40 to 49	22		Conservative	30
50 to 64	19			
65 and over	7		**Size of place**	
			City over 50,000	44
Family Income			Suburbs	42
under $15,000	10		Small city or rural	14
$15,000 to 29,999	18			
$30,000 to 49,999	24		**State**	
$50,000 to 74,999	22		Arizona	3
$75,000 or more	25		California	26
			Florida	13
Religion			Illinois	5
Protestant/other Christian	32		New Jersey	4
Catholic	55		New York	7
Jewish	1		Texas	17
Something else	4		Other	26
None	8			

Source: Pew Hispanic Center tabulations of 2004 Combined State Exit Polls, National Election Pool

Table 4. Support for Bush Among Hispanic Voters, 2000 and 2004, from 51 State Exit Polls (percentages)

	2004	2000	Change To 2004
All Hispanic Voters	40	34	6
Sex			
Male	43	39	3
Female	37	30	7
Age			
18 to 29	34	33	1
30 to 39	40	39	1
40 to 49	43	33	10
50 to 64	43	33	10
65 and over	45	26	20
Family Income			
Under $15,000	28	26	2
$15,000 to 29,999	30	25	6
$30,000 to 49,999	37	32	5
$50,000 to 74,999	45	40	5
$75,000 or more	47	46	0
Religion			
Protestant/other Christian	56	44	12
Catholic	33	33	0
Political party identification			
Democrat	12	10	2
Republican	90	84	6
Independent	39	42	-3
Political philosophy			
Liberal	17	12	5
Moderate	35	33	2
Conservative	66	66	0
Size of place			
City over 50,000	36	26	10
Suburbs	43	38	4
Small city or rural	43	50	-8

Source: Pew Hispanic Center tabulations of 2004 Combined State Exit Polls, National Election Pool

toward Bush in 2004, giving him 56% of their votes last year compared with 44% in 2000. Thus, Hispanic Protestants were both a growing and increasingly pro-Republican constituency between the two elections. Meanwhile, Bush's share of the Hispanic Catholic vote held steady at 33% in the state exit polls.

Aside from his strong support from Hispanic Protestants, President Bush also gained some ground among nearly all segments of the Hispanic vote (table 4). His share of the vote increased among female Hispanic voters and across all age categories and income groups. He did better among big-city Hispanic voters. The only Hispanic vote segments of the Hispanic electorate where his share did not increase were among Catholics, political independents, conservatives, and rural voters.

The data from the combined state exit polls also shed some light on the issue of Latino realignment in political party leanings. Surveys of registered Latino voters typically reveal that Latinos identify with the Democratic Party over the GOP by at least a two-to-one advantage.[4] However, in the 2004 exit poll, the margin was somewhat smaller: 49% of Hispanic voters identified with the Democrats, 27% with the Republicans, and 24% indicated independent leanings. Hispanic Democratic affiliation declined

from the 2000 election, where the comparable NEP exit poll data indicate a 55%-to-24% split in favor of Democratic over Republicans. Whether the decline in the fortunes of the Democrats among Hispanic voters from 2000 to 2004 reflects the relative popularity of President Bush among Hispanic voters or marks a more permanent shift in Hispanic party loyalties remains an open question.

Notes

1. The terms "Hispanic" and "Latino" are used interchangeably. The terms "white" and "black" refer to non-Hispanics in those racial categories.
2. Pew Hispanic Center & Kaiser Family Foundation. 2002. *The 2002 National Survey of Latinos.* Washington, D.C.: Pew Hispanic Center.
3. The combined state NEP exit poll data do not reveal whether a voter was a "born-again or evangelical" Christian. The Protestant designation in the text refers to non-Catholic Christians; that is, it includes Hispanics identifying themselves as Protestant, Mormon/ Latter Day Saints and "other Christian" (excluding Catholic). Pre-election surveys reveal that the bulk of Hispanic non-Catholic Christian registered voters are evangelical or born-again Christians. Five out of six Hispanic non-Catholic Christian registered voters are evangelical Christians, as opposed to mainline Protestants (Leal, David L., Matt A. Barreto, Jongho Lee, and Rodolfo A. de la Garza. 2005. "The Latino Vote in the 2004 Election," *Political Science and Politics,* January, pages 41-49).
4. Pew Hispanic Center & Kaisesr Family Foundation. 2004. *The 2004 National Survey of Latinos: Politics and Civic Participation.* Washington, D.C.: Pew Hispanic Center.

Latino Politics in the New Millennium

Kim Geron

The aim of this book is twofold: to describe the transition by Latinos from disenfranchised outsiders to political leaders and policymakers, and to explain to what degree Latino elected officials are sensitive to ethnic community concerns and seek to deliver policy benefits to their communities. Stated another way, the story that has been presented explored the historical struggle of Latinos to overcome discriminatory barriers to full participation and to achieve political incorporation and obtain policy benefits. This book makes a contribution to the larger study of Latino politics. First, it shows through case studies the different ways Latino communities have mobilized to achieve and consolidate Latino political incorporation. Second, it explores the demographics of Latino political leaders, the pathways they used to win elective office, and their views on contemporary policy matters. Third, it has summarized the more than 150 years of struggle by Latinos to receive, in the words of the Voting Rights Act, "an equal opportunity to participate in elections and to elect a candidate of their choice." This struggle is far from over for Latinos. Discriminatory barriers have been made illegal, yet high rates of noncitizenship, low voter registration and turnout rates, combined with continuing racially polarized voting patterns, have limited Latinos' access, full participation, and election to office. Relative to the majority population, Latinos still do not have equal opportunity to participate in the electoral process.

While some argue that Latinos have entered a post-civil rights era in which they are no longer victims of the political system and no longer in need of legal protection through court-ordered boundaries, others contend that Latinos still need the protection of the Voting Rights Act and its amendments to obtain their fair share of elected positions in a society that remains bounded by racial politics. One thing that is not in dispute is the fact that Latinos continue to live in residentially segregated areas that are densely populated and have underfunded schools, and that they have lower average levels of education and income than the average American. Social struggles are still required for Latinos and other racial minorities to achieve full equality in our democracy. These battles must continue to be waged, while others in the Latino community push forward the boundaries of who can be elected and where they can be elected.

The core of majority-Latino districts that have elected Latinos should be viewed as a base, not a ceiling, for Latino electoral aspirations. The dilemma faced by Latino political strategists is how to expand the number of districts in each state where Latinos will have the opportunity to elect the representative of their choice. Should a certain percentage of majority-minority districts be broken up and district lines redrawn to create more non-Latino-majority electoral districts where Latino candidates can compete? This assumes that non-Latino voters will vote for Latinos. While there is some evidence for this in certain areas of the country, the legacy of prejudice and discrimination against Latinos still hangs heavy over the political process. As the Mexican American Legal Defense Fund (MALDEF) noted recently about one state: "Unfortunately, racially polarized voting persists in California, thus demonstrating the continued need for and enforcement of the Voting Rights Act. MALDEF's consultants have conducted preliminary racial polarization analysis of elections occurring during the decade and have found evidence of polarization, particularly in Southern California."[1]

While for the foreseeable future the preservation of existing Latino-majority districts is a necessary part of Latino efforts for equal opportunity in the political process, this should not restrict Latino attempts to win elections in areas and regions where historically they have had only a limited presence. How to hold on to existing seats and expand into new electoral districts has become a controversial issue.

Drawing Conclusions and Seeking Clarity from Latino Politics

Latinos have overcome enormous barriers to achieve elected office and are now institutionalized in the very structures that previously excluded them. This seeming contradiction between societal biases toward Latinos and Latino electoral successes has mainly occurred through the group efforts of Latinos to modify electoral structures to allow them to elect candidates of their choice. Before the 1980s, in most cases, only Latinos elected Latinos to office. By the 1990s, this pattern was beginning to break down as non-Latinos in some locations began to help elect Latinos to office. The election of Latinos in diverse locations has allowed for a more systematic study of the attitudes and patterns of Latino officeholders and their policy beliefs. This chapter will suggest some tentative conclusions that can be drawn from an analysis of the history of Latino political efforts and the case studies of contemporary Latino political incorporation efforts, and it will offer some suggestions for students and activists involved in the study and practice of Latino politics.

In spite of attempts to exclude them from participating in fundamental political activities such as voting and running for office, Latinos have overcome marginalization and discriminatory practices by the dominant majority to achieve numerous political milestones. Beginning in the eighteenth and nineteenth centuries, pioneer Latino politicians became involved in American-style electoral politics. During the Jim Crow segregation era, from the late 1800s to the 1950s, nonwhites in most communities were prevented from voting, seeking office, and fully participating in the democratic process, yet Latinos remained active in political affairs, built middle-class civil rights groups, and organized labor and political activities.

Beginning in the 1960s, Latinos organized outside the mainstream political arena, built alternative organizations, and framed new political ideologies that reflected the militancy of the times. They also used legal methods and insider politics within the political parties and at the grassroots level to have a voice in mainstream American politics. Longtime Latino ethnic groups such as Mexicans and Puerto Ricans and new immigrants from the Caribbean Islands, Central America, and South America became more engaged in domestic and homeland politics. Foreign policy in Latin America became not just an issue for U.S. foreign policy planners; now Latin American governments and their supporters and critics within the Latino Diaspora are more actively engaged. Several Latin American nations have established dual nationality provisions for their former residents who live in the United States. Remittances from Latinos to their families and towns of origin in Latin America have become a multibillion-dollar effort and are critical for the economic development of our neighbors in the Western Hemisphere.

The stakes are high in a globalized economy. With the U.S. Hispanic market already larger than all but the eleven richest countries, there is potential for economic and political influence. The interrelationships between the United States and Latin America is illustrated by recent events: the Elian Gonzalez controversy in 2000, the efforts of George W. Bush and Vicente Fox to regularize Mexican immigrants to the United States, and U.S. government involvement in the internal politics of Venezuela. The U.S. government also provided $1.3 billion in foreign aid to the Colombian government (third largest after Israel and Egypt at the time) as part of Plan Colombia in 2000.[2] Eighty percent of the aid was earmarked for the military and police, which helped fuel Colombia's long civil war whose victims were almost all civilians. The growing interrelationships among the nations and peoples of the Western Hemisphere require ongoing attention and the active involvement of the Latino community and its leadership.

Learning from the Incorporation Process

A few general conclusions can be drawn regarding how the process of political incorporation unfolds and how political governing coalitions are constructed at the local level. The first conclusion is that a singular major event that sparks protests and demands for change, leading to movements for political representation, is not required. In our case studies, usually several events combined to trigger a reaction leading to movements for political incorporation. In Salinas, there was not one decisive trigger event but a string of events that culminated in political incorporation.

Another conclusion that can be drawn from these case studies relates to the role of community organizations in the incorporation process. Community organizations that mobilized to achieve the inclusion of Latinos have had an important impact on the character of the political incorporation process in various places. Community-led efforts to win district elections in San Antonio, Miami-Dade County, and Salinas built a strong foundation to carry forward the demand for full political incorporation. In Los Angeles, while district elections already existed when Latinos began to seek inclusion, the struggle took the form of drawing district boundaries that enabled Latinos to have a fair chance at winning elected office. In Salinas, the strength of Latino political incorporation was due to a strong grassroots community organization, the Alisal Betterment Committee (ABC), that fought to win district elections for community representatives who would reflect the values and beliefs of the Latino community. The formation of this organization and the mobilization of the Chicano community, combined with the sophistication of

Chicano community activists, were indispensable to the campaigns to win district elections.

Another conclusion that can be drawn is that a biracial coalition to achieve political incorporation is a tactic, not a strategic necessity. Where Latinos are a minority of the population, Latino politicians will continue to work with an array of allies, including labor, African Americans, Asian and Pacific Islanders, and Native Americans, to build electoral coalitions. Where Latinos are the dominant majority in locations such as Miami and Salinas, the role of white liberals was not critical in Latinos' ascent to political leadership, and sometimes other potential allies were not evident. In Salinas, the political incorporation efforts of Latinos were carried out without strong support from the white community, yet there was a critical minority that consistently supported Latino efforts. In Miami, white liberals and the conservative Cuban American community were at odds over many issues and failed to work together. A biracial coalition was not necessary in the political incorporation efforts within either of these communities.

This finding is similar to conclusions others have drawn regarding some Latino-majority cities in the Southwest. The point is that where Latinos are the majority of voters, they are less likely to seek or need the assistance of white liberals, although they will want to work closely with whites and with other minority groups where there is agreement on policy aims and goals. This certainly was the case with the 2001 Ed Garza mayoral victory in San Antonio, where Garza won the support of both white and Mexican American voters. In many other cities, the achievement of political incorporation for Latinos and other racial minorities was based on the forging of biracial and multiracial coalitions.[3]

Political Incorporation and Class Interests

Another conclusion that can be drawn from the efforts of Latinos to achieve political incorporation is that governing coalitions encompass multiple class interests. Urban government involves a complex mix of influences as commercial development, labor, neighborhood, environmental, and Latino and other minority community interests seek to steer local policy. The dominant governing coalition in cities where Latinos have been electorally successful does contain Latinos, often as members of the city council and as city bureaucrats; however, a combination of factors has limited the level of policy benefits being delivered to the working poor in the Latino community. These factors include slow economic investment, systemic poverty in the Latino community produced by a low-wage labor market, and differing land use and environmental policy agendas of elected Latinos and other local elected officials. Issues such as crime reduction, public safety, and

no-growth versus progrowth tend to receive the most attention and budgetary consideration in cities; meanwhile, services desperately needed in the Latino community, such as more varied employment opportunities, training for better-paying jobs, easing of school overcrowding, improved educational services, and after-school programs have received inadequate resources.

Latino political incorporation has meant, for the first time, not only the representation of Latinos in general but, more specifically, the inclusion of low-wage Latino workers and the urban poor in the dialogue in some communities. Latino worker interests are usually involved in the electoral coalition that elects Latinos to office. Previously, local governments rarely addressed labor issues. Today, these concerns are likely to be openly discussed and debated, since they relate to water issues, housing, education, and other social policies. In many cities, policies have been created that have benefited the working poor in Latino communities; these policies appear to be much stronger than those of previous governing coalitions, which were dominated exclusively by downtown business interests. For example, the city of Los Angeles passed a living-wage ordinance in 1997 after a community coalition that included numerous Latino worker organizations carried out a grassroots campaign. The ordinance requires that any contractor doing business with the city provide health benefits and pay salaries that are substantially higher than the state's current minimum wage of $6.75 per hour.

Another observation from the case studies and history of political incorporation efforts is that Latino community stakeholders and officeholders have not always acted with a common vision. The need for an ongoing community-based movement of Latinos that can articulate demands for policy equity, hold city leaders (including Latino council members) accountable for their actions, and push for a greater share of policy benefits in the future was an important lesson learned by community activists in places like San Antonio and Los Angeles. However, Latinos are not the dominant economic players in most communities, and thus they remain economically dependent on the same economic interests that have controlled local and regional politics for decades. In cities such as Salinas and San Antonio, where Latinos are the majority of the governing coalition, the Latino community must negotiate a relationship with the dominant economic forces that shape the policy agenda. In these locations, the governing coalition must deal with the dual pull of corporate influences and the need to redistribute resources to the working poor in Latino and other communities.

In Miami, where Latino business interests are quite powerful, Cuban American politicians are also brokers for the wealth and power of their community's members in the business world. Here there appears to be a more equitable relationship between race and class forces; however, this is highly unusual. In most cities, the role of Latino politicians is to negotiate policy benefits for the Latino community in the context of supporting large economic development projects. This usually involves obtaining agreements from private developers to build affordable housing, hire from the community, and fund urban education or parks and recreation areas in Latino communities as part of development efforts.

Economic interests will remain significant where there are investment opportunities. This requires that they deal with the political forces that occupy the seats of power. Economic interests must find ways to compromise to achieve their financial goals or use their economic strength to negotiate a deal most favorable to them. This is the logic of the market system. Latinos in power in local and higher levels of government should continue to leverage their political power to obtain the best possible economic deals for their communities and for others in need of community development and social services.

Levels of Political Incorporation and Policy Benefits

The results of these case studies indicate that the level of political incorporation is not an accurate predictor of the strength of Latino political power. The more important question is, how does political power manifest itself in the strength of policy benefits returning to local Latino communities? The level of political incorporation alone does not determine the answer to this question. Particularly in cities that use district elections, where candidates are elected from different neighborhoods with widely divergent socioeconomic conditions and issue formation, there are different types of Latino officeholders.

At least in cities with district elections, the number of Latinos on a city council does not fully explain differences in policy formation among cities. Even in cities with at-large electoral systems, the ability of Latinos to get elected stems from the support of different voter bases. This will, in turn, affect the character and type of governing coalition that is created. A 1990s study of California Latina officeholders found that almost 100 percent of them were of working-class origins and "given [this], these elected officials may introduce policy perspectives more responsive to the needs of poor and working-class people."[4]

Not only is who is elected significant, but what type of administrators are hired into key positions, such as city manager, police chief, and head of economic development, are also important in the construction of a governing coalition. Those holding these positions, in conjunction with elected officeholders, have a powerful role at the local level. They shape local policy decisions and can steer cities in a variety of directions. These usually nonelected local government leaders can provide leadership regarding key issues and direct resources to solve long-standing problems.

A final conclusion of the case studies is that in addition to the important roles of economic interests, Latino politicians, and city administrators, an ongoing, organized community-led movement of Latinos must be vigilant to ensure that policy benefits are returned to the community. The key lesson from the many political incorporation efforts is the need for the Latino community to continue to mobilize to receive its fair share of resources and highlight broader social issues *after* Latinos are elected to office. This can take the form of a well-organized interest group such as Communities Organized for Public Service (COPS) in San Antonio, Texas, that regularly meets with elected officials and holds them accountable for the stands they take on local issues. Where it is absent, there is no mechanism other than electing different political actors to keep local government accountable to the needs of the Latino community. Latino politicians, even if they have run for office on a program to implement a Latino agenda, may soon lapse into a business-as-usual mentality that is disconnected from the most pressing needs of the community. This situation existed for a time in Los Angeles, where elements of the Latino elected leadership had grown removed and insulated from the grassroots needs of their communities.[5] This is a dangerous trend and adds to cynicism in the Latino community that elections are an ineffective and counterproductive arena for democratic action.

In a representative democracy, an overreliance on the electoral arena, on elected Latino officeholders, and on achieving the maximum numbers of Latinos in office will not solve the complex problems of Latino communities. In addition to maintaining the accountability of political leaders, issue-based neighborhood organizing in Latino communities is vital to address structural inequalities. Understanding the interplay between political incorporation efforts and empowerment efforts at the grassroots level is important for the study of Latino politics.

Community initiatives usually begin as small and seemingly insignificant actions but form the basis for later large-scale changes, such as the dramatic changes in the cities we explored. These efforts are difficult to maintain, as movements ebb and flow; yet the existence and maintenance of organized interest groups, neighborhood-based organizations, community activists, and local residents can extend inclusion in a governing coalition or force changes in policies of cities as small as Salinas and as large as Los Angeles.[6] More often than not, it is these efforts that provide the spark that ultimately leads to reevaluation of public policy, institutional changes, and the election of new leaders.

Final Thoughts

The diversity of the political experiences of Latinos makes broad generalizations difficult. For example, the rapid rise to local political power of Cuban Americans in south Florida is due to the combination of a favorable U.S. government policy and local political and economic underdevelopment in Miami that enabled Cubans to overcome the discriminatory obstacles created by the city's Anglo establishment.[7] The Cuban experience reflects a different process of political incorporation from that of Puerto Ricans, who are citizens by decree of the U.S. government; of Mexican Americans in the Southwest and Midwest, who have suffered a much longer history of entrenched structural discrimination and social ostracism; and of recent immigrants and refugees from Central and South America, who have only recently begun to achieve electoral office.

Latinos do not share an identical political experience in this country, and no one method is adequate to study such a diverse group of people. Although Latinos have a common history of conquest and colonization, their diverse paths to political officeholding and political power reflect a multiplicity of factors—the conditions they entered as ethnic immigrants, their social and political status upon entering this new environment, and the sorts of efforts they made to change their status. For these reasons, this book did not attempt to capture the totality of Latino political experience; rather, it is a more focused exploration of how racial politics have unfolded in the post-civil rights era, where racial identities, economics, and political power have been contested in various ways. While I did analyze the political conflicts with whites in some cities and the transition of power away from those who had held it for many decades, the book did not fully explore the dynamics of black and Latino political relationships. This is an important topic that others have more fully examined.[8]

This book sought to capture the contemporary thinking of Latino elected officials. The results of the survey of Latino elected officials demonstrate that LEOs exhibit significant concern for the needs of the Latino community in their political behavior. The interviews conducted with LEOs confirmed the initial finding of the mail survey that most Latino political leaders were committed to being substantive representatives of the Latino community. They consciously sought to set policy that would benefit this community.

With Latinos achieving political office, and in some cases dominating the local political power structure, have the limitation of Latinos' collective economic fortunes and lack of economic control reduced their officeholding to window dressing, merely giving the appearance that they have gained equality with whites? It is my belief that Latino politics, as it is played out in numerous locations, has the potential to create partnerships for the economic development of Latino communities. This will not be easy, as the Latino community does not control most of the economic resources in its regions; yet the sheer number of Latino voters is forcing global economic interests to address their needs. The U.S. Hispanic market is enormous, and the Latino community has the potential to shape economics and politics in the hemisphere. Within the constraints of an unequal economic system, Latino political power can at opportune moments redirect economic resources to solve some long-standing social problems.

As the numbers of Latinos continue to grow in urban, suburban, and rural communities, different pathways to political empowerment are becoming available. There will undoubtedly be a wider variety of Latino candidates from both major parties and as independents. More important, the ongoing poverty and social inequality in many communities will require the construction of new and varied forms of social movements to respond to new conditions. As many U.S.-born Latinos move away from the barrios to the suburbs, the growth of middle-class enclaves of Latinos and the integration of Latino families into non-Latino areas will also create new challenges and new voting patterns. Furthermore, the continuing growth of anti-immigrant forces that fan racial and cultural wars will also prompt new and varied responses within the Latino and other immigrant communities. As old alliances fray, new ones may emerge.

Undoubtedly this chapter is but one piece of a much larger puzzle. The types of electoral districts and candidates seeking office can be explored more systematically and compared in other qualitative studies. As part of the growing body of literature on racial politics in American cities, however, this study helps to validate the development of Latino politics at the local and national level. Latino politics is still a relatively new subfield of social science investigation, and as various social theories are tested in the context of the experiences of Latinos, and in interaction with others, these theories will be enriched.

In a society as diverse as the United States, equality for all remains an elusive goal. In a nation where physical and cultural differences have been used by a dominant majority to discriminate against and marginalize groups of people, symbolic and substantive representation are necessary steps in a long process of gaining full equality for historically underrepresented groups. The political representation of people of color, however, is not exclusively the responsibility of those of that particular racial or ethnic group. The historical divisions among peoples of color in this country require continued exploration of how minority representatives act to represent their own historically underrepresented group members and others. As Melissa Williams (1998) notes, "Although representation for marginalized groups is not in itself a cure for injustice, there is good reason to believe it is at least a healing measure."[9]

Notes

1. MALDEF (2001).
2. G. Leech (2000).
3. R. Hero (1997), p. 257.
4. P. C. Takash (1993).
5. J. Regalado (1997).
6. R. Rosales (2000); J. Regalado (1998); J. Anner (1996); P. Medoff and H. Sklar (1994).
7. D. Moreno (1997).
8. N. Vaca (2004); E. Morales (2004); J. Jennings (1994); C. P. Henry (1980); J. Miles (1992).
9. M. Williams (1998), p. 243.

References

Anner, John, ed. 1996. *Beyond Identity Politics: Emerging Social Justice Movements in Communities of Color.* Boston: South End.

Henry, Charles P. 1980. "Black-Chicano Coalitions: Possibilities and Problems." *Western Journal of Black Studies* 4: 202–232.

Hero, Rodney. 1997. "Latinos and Politics in Denver and Pueblo, Colorado: Differences, Explanations, and the 'Steady-State' of the Struggle for Equality." In *Racial Politics in American Cities*, 2nd ed., edited by Rufus P. Browning, Dale R. Marshall and David H. Tabb. New York: Longman.

Jennings, James, ed. 1994. *Blacks, Latinos, and Asians in Urban America: Status and Prospects for Politics and Activism.* Westport, CT: Praeger.

Leech, Gary. 2000. "Plan Colombia: A Closer Look." Colombia Journal Online, www.colombiajournal.org/plancolombia.html (accessed January 10, 2005).

Medoff, Peter, and Holly Sklar. 1994. *Streets of Hope: The Fall and Rise of an Urban Neighborhood.* Boston: South End.

Mexican American Legal Defense and Education Fund (MALDEF). n.d. "About Us: The Founding of MALDEF." http://www.maldef.org/about/index.htm (accessed December 8, 2001).

Miles, Jack. "Blacks vs. Browns." 1992. *Atlantic Monthly*, October, pp. 41–68.

Morales, Ed. 2004. "Brown like Me? Book Review." *Nation*, February 19. www.thenation.com/doc (accessed February 8, 2005).

Moreno, Dario. 1997. "The Cuban Model: Political Empowerment in Miami." In *Pursuing Power: Latinos in the Political System*, edited by F. Chris Garcia. Notre Dame, IN: Notre Dame University Press.

Regalado, Jaime. 1998. "Minority Political Incorporation in Los Angeles: A Broader Consideration." In *Racial and Ethnic Politics in California*, edited by Michael B. Preston, Bruce E. Cain, and Sandra Bass, 2: 381–409. Berkeley: Institute of Government Studies Press.

Rosales, Rodolfo. 2000. *The Illusion of Inclusion: The Untold Political Story of San Antonio.* Austin: University of Texas Press.

Takash, Paula Cruz. 1993. "Breaking Barriers to Representation: Chicana/Latina Elected Officials in California." *Urban Anthropology* 22, no. 3-4 (fall-winter): 325–360.

Vaca, Nicolás C. 2004. *The Presumed Alliance: The Unspoken Conflict between Latinos and blacks and What It Means for America.* New York: HarperCollins.

Williams, Melissa S. 1998. *Voice, Trust, and Memory: Marginalized Groups and the Failing of Liberal Representation.* Princeton, NJ: Princeton University Press.

Mexican American Women and Politics

Lisa Magaña

I wish there were more Latina elected officials. All you ever see is the same Anglo male elected official. If there were more Latinas, I think there would be more attention given to Latinas and their needs.

(Grace N., 46)

This chapter examines the presence of Mexican American women in elected office at the federal, state, and local levels, as well the motivating factors that sustain their participation. Also explored is the presence of Mexican American women in grassroots political movements. Research on Mexican American women, and women of color in general, shows that their participation in grassroots politics is innovative and effective. Their political behavior is not fully assessed, however, because their actions fall outside of traditional classifications of politics, and often these women do not define themselves as "political." Mexican-origin women are minorities in politics and they are non-traditional political actors, in that many do not speak English and are not U.S. citizens. Because much of the research focuses on Latinas in general, not Mexican-origin women specifically, in several locations I describe Latina political behavior.

Female Elected Officials

During the past forty years, the number of Latinas participating in electoral politics has grown substantially. Numerous factors contribute to this trend including unprecedented outreach by political parties and elected officials and the increasing importance of the expanding Latino population. However, the majority of Latino politicians remain men. One factor contributing to this gender gap may be cultural, in that Latinas have traditionally been expected to conform to traditional female gender roles.

Running for political office has not been a common trend or legacy. A Latina candidate, like women candidates generally, may still be viewed as unusual.

According to the Center for American Women and Politics (CAWP), there are fourteen women of all races (14 percent) in the U.S. Senate (CAWP, "Facts"). In 2004, of the 535 congressional seats, women held 74 (13.8 percent). At the state level, women held 81 of 315 elective executive-branch positions (25.7 percent). Of the 7,382 state legislators, 1,059 (22.5 percent) were women, breaking down as follows: 411 of 1,971 state senate seats (20.9 percent) and 1,248 of 5,411 of the state house seats (23.1 percent). CAWP reports that the number of females serving in state legislative positions has increased more than fourfold since 1969. The states with the highest percentages of women in their legislatures were Washington (36.7 percent), Maryland (34.0 percent), Colorado (34.0 percent), Vermont (31.1 percent), New Mexico and California (both 30.0 percent), Connecticut (29.4 percent), Delaware (29.0 percent), Oregon (28.9 percent), and Nevada (28.6 percent).

Of the seventy-four women in the U.S. Congress in 2004, eighteen (24.4 percent) were women of color. African American women and Caribbean American women served as delegates to the House of Representatives from the District of Columbia and the Virgin Islands. Of the eighty-one women serving in statewide executive-branch elective offices, five (6.2 percent) were women of color. Women of color constituted 18.4 percent of state legislators, with 85 senators and 221 representatives. All but eighteen of the female elected officials surveyed were Democrats (CAWP, "Facts").

Latina Elected Officials

The numbers of Latina elected officials are also promising and growing substantially. As of 2003 NALEO had 1,427 Latina elected and appointed officials in its registry (NALEO 2001). There were seven Latinas in the U.S. Congress. At the state level, there were three Latinas in state executive positions, and there were sixty-one at the state legislative level.

Latinas are represented in greater numbers at the local and county levels than at federal or state levels. In 2003, 167 Latinas held county positions, 150 Latinas were in judicial and law enforcement positions, and 335 Latinas held elective municipal offices. There were 605 Latinas serving on school boards, and a few were superintendents. Latina political participation is significant in Arizona, California, Colorado, Illinois, New Jersey, New Mexico, and New York, states with large Latino populations.

Why They Run

A study focusing on 150 Chicana/Latina elected representatives in California investigated the characteristics of Chicana/Latina elected officials (Takash 1993). Most of the respondents had graduated from college, with either a bachelor's or a master's degree, and most hailed from working-class backgrounds. They identified their fathers' occupations "as laborers, construction workers, gardeners, and agricultural workers; their mothers' occupations as housewives or service sector workers" (422). In line with their working-class backgrounds, common political agendas or interests focused on poverty and economic reform issues. Most of the respondents had experienced significant economic and social mobility, with family incomes of between $50,000 and $100,000. Most of the Chicana elected officials were born in the United States and defined themselves as Catholic, and 82 percent identified themselves as Democrats. (See topic highlight 1 for a profile of one Chicana elected official.)

Surprisingly, more than half of the respondents stated that their political role models were not women. When asked about the most important event, factor, or influence leading them to run for office the first time, the Mexican American women cited dissatisfaction with politics or the incumbents. The remaining respondents claimed a general concern with social change.

In terms of political experience, these women had never held elective or appointed positions, and more than half indicated they had never worked for political campaigns. Consistent with the experiences of many Mexican American elected officials, these women did say they had worked at the community level as a starting point of their political careers. Almost half said they had gained valuable experiences in women's organizations. The top two organizations in which these elected officials had participated were the National Women's Political Caucus and the National Organization of Women (Takash 1993). Another study confirmed the importance of political organizations, such as the Comisión Femenil Mexicana Nacional, the National Hispana Leadership Institute, MALDEF, and the Hispanic Steering Committee of the National Women's Political Caucus, as stepping-stones for political office (Montoya, Hardy-Fanta, and García 2000).

CAWP has created a web page that focuses on the growing number of Latina elected officials (CAWP, "Elección"). This information confirms that most elected officials are college graduates, have experienced socioeconomic mobility, are nominally Catholic, and come from working-class backgrounds. Most of the women also become involved in politics through a desire to mobilize change at the community level. Interestingly, perhaps because of the lack of female elected officials, most of the respondents stated that their role models were men.

Mexican American women are also personally committed to politics at a macro as well as micro level. As Joyce notes,

---

Topic Highlight 1. Lucille Roybal-Allard

Congresswoman Lucille Roybal-Allard began her political career as a member of the California State Assembly for three terms (United States House of Representatives). Born and raised in Boyle Heights, California, she is the eldest daughter of Lucille Beserra Roybal and retired Congressman Edward R. Roybal, who served as a member of Congress for thirty years. She graduated from California State University, Los Angeles, is married to Edward T. Allard III, and is the mother of two adult children.

Lucille Roybal-Allard is the first Mexican American woman to be elected to the U.S. Congress, and the first Latina to be appointed to the House Appropriations Committee, perhaps one of the most powerful committees in Congress.

Her other committee appointments oversee funding for small business development, international trade, the 2000 census, national security, labor relations, law enforcement, equal employment issues, and the restructuring of the INS.

In 1999, she became the first woman elected to chair the Congressional Hispanic Caucus. In this position, she focused on education, economic development, and access to health care. Roybal-Allard was also elected chairwoman of the California Democratic Congressional Delegation. She became the first woman, the first Latina, and the first member ever to assume this position through an election, rather than just being given the position based on her seniority.

I define politics on two levels. One level is personal conviction; this level is the foundation for the ways that I perceive the broader political realm. A personal political framework includes commitment to the groups one has investment in and strong beliefs in how those groups and individuals within those groups should be treated by and within social institutions. The second level, then, includes support and involvement with groups or individuals with power to take social action, make changes, make a public difference. Exercise of personal politics is daily, and that daily personal action should be reflected in involvement on this second level. Broader political involvement can range from the simple and necessary act of informed voting to involvement on the local level through volunteer work with church and civic groups geared toward social action and reform to writing letters to state government leaders and actively contributing, financially or otherwise, to a specific political party. (Joyce L., 31)

Political Attitudes and Expectations

The National Latino Political Survey surveyed Latinas and Latinos regarding the issues they were concerned with as constituents (de la Garza et al. 1998). This was perhaps the first political survey that identified the differences between Latinos and Latinas as well as among Cuban, Mexican, and Puerto Rican constituents. Questions addressed a variety of attitudes, such as whether men or women were more capable in public office during a crisis. The majority of respondents did not voice a strong opinion, but there were some important group differences. Mexican and Puerto Rican women were more likely to answer "women," whereas Mexican and Puerto Rican men were more likely to answer "men." Cuban male and female respondents alike were more likely to indicate that men were better suited than women to be in positions of political power during a crisis; clearly for them gender is an important feature in politics.

What do women generally and Latinas specifically expect from their elected officials? In a recent survey conducted by the League of Women Voters (LWV), women overall saw the necessity for reform and political action in the area of social issues. Most women, including Latinas, maintained that jobs that paid well and allowed a good quality of life were very important. Schools needed to be decent and safe, and these institutions should make a difference in eradicating many social problems. Reducing the crime rate and violence were other major concerns, as were guns in school and too much sex and violence in the media.

The women maintained that elected officials have made little progress in addressing issues concerning women. Nearly seven out of ten of all women described themselves as "feeling disgusted, frustrated, and disillusioned" with the lack of attention to women's issues. When these women were asked for whom they would vote and what characteristics were important in a political candidate, they responded as follows. First, a very small percentage of women would vote for a candidate based solely on political affiliation; for most women, the candidate's position on issues was more important. The other factors women considered were a candidate's integrity followed by his or her experience. Although a significant majority of women believed that more women should be elected to political office, only one in three would vote for a female candidate based simply on her gender.

The results of these surveys illustrate that Latinas vote on issues, not on party affiliation. They also want to trust their elected officials and feel that they are accountable to the community. Furthermore, Latinas are willing to support both male and female candidates, whereas Latinos are less likely to support female candidates. Social issues, such as school reform, gun control, and local safety are all important issues for Latinos. (See topic highlight 2 for biographies of two Latina congresswomen whose agendas focus on many of these issues.)

Feminism and Grassroots Politics

Irrespective of the patterns that discourage Latina participation in traditional political outlets, Latinas are not apolitical. On the contrary, women, in comparison to men and regardless of their ethnicity or socioeconomic status, are more likely to pursue politics at the local level and for personal reasons, actions that may not be fully recognized. Their activity is also not easily described within the bounds of mainstream feminism.

Theoretical feminism, from a political perspective, examines how women organize to counter sexual oppression. The feminism of white mainstream women does not always accurately describe the concerns and activities of Mexican American women, however. Critics note that defining the political actions of Mexican American women simply as a means to end sexual oppression does not take into account the unique cultural and ethnic factors that motivate or hinder their political participation. Furthermore, mainstream feminism does not provide a sufficiently inclusive agenda for Mexican American women. Because the founding members of the feminist movement came from middle-class backgrounds, mainstream feminist platforms do not meet all the needs of Mexican American women, who generally come from poorer backgrounds with strong ties to the Mexican immigrant community (Ruíz and DuBois 2000).

The Chicano Movement was important for Mexican American feminism because in many ways it opened the door to greater political participation. More Mexican American women began running for office, whereas others became involved in community-based activist and civic groups, as well as the political campaigns of their spouses. The Chicano Movement not only created a specific politi-

---

Topic Highlight 2. The Sánchez Sisters

Linda and Loretta Sánchez made history in 2003 as the first sisters ever to win seats in the U.S. Congress at the same time. The Sánchez sisters come from a family of seven children. Born in Lynwood, California, they are the daughters of Mexican immigrants.

Loretta Sánchez was born in 1960. She received her bachelor's degree in economics and master's degree in business from American University. Her congressional district covers Anaheim, Garden Grove, Santa Ana, and Fullerton. She has worked to develop greater economic opportunities for her constituents through enhancing community projects and job creation.

Linda Sánchez was born in 1969. She graduated from Berkeley with a bachelor of arts in Spanish literature with an emphasis on bilingual education. She later received a law

degree from the University of California at Los Angeles. Her district covers Artesia, Cerritos, Hawaiian Gardens, Lakewood, Paramount, Southgate, and parts of Whittier and Los Angeles.

Both congresswomen have prioritized policy issues that they believe are important for the growing Latino community, such as crime prevention, education, health care, unemployment, expanded economic opportunities, and job creation. They are members of important committees, including the judiciary and House Armed Services committees as well as the Select Committee on Homeland Security. They are also members of the Hispanic Caucus and the Women's Caucus and are important players in the Democratic National Committee (Chávez Candelaria, García, and Aldama; United States House of Representatives).

---

cal platform around race, gender, and class, it also socialized a large number of Mexican American women to participate in electoral politics. The Chicano Movement also championed several major objectives, such as labor rights and ending segregation, discrimination, and political repression. The fact that Chicana feminism was an offshoot of the Chicano Movement is not surprising to historians given that other women of color communities began their feminist organizing activities while participating within larger social and political movements. For instance, Asian American and African American women began organizing within the Civil Rights Movement.

During the Chicano Movement, Mexican American women were generally relegated to supporting the needs of the male activists, many of whom professed progressive ideals but operated in the patriarchal style of previous generations (Ruíz and DuBois 2000). In the early days of the movement, and still to some degree today, the issue of male machismo has produced tension between progressive Chicanas and the male-dominated hierarchy of Chicano grassroots and mainstream political organizations (Mirandé and Enríquez 1979). Feeling that Chicana needs were being overlooked, Mexican American women formed their own organizations to mobilize against racial, gender, and cultural oppression. Some Chicanos and Chicanas accused these women of being disloyal to the Chicano Movement, charging that Chicana feminism was akin to selling out to the whites and that their cause divided the Chicano Movement. Similarly, many Chicano males felt that Chicana feminism was a divisive ideology that was incompatible with the Chicano Movement (García 2000).

Mexican American women face a multitude of barriers from both American culture at large and their culture of origin. According to the "triple oppression" perspective, the sources of Chicana oppression are threefold: (1) Mexican American women are minorities and confront rac-

ism in the United States, (2) Mexican American women must cope with sexism and other barriers related to their gender, and (3) Mexican American women must also contend with oppression at the hands of males in their own community (Riddell 1974). That is to say, husbands, brothers, fathers, and boyfriends may not support women's efforts to participate as equals and may challenge their political participation, especially as leaders. Even today, the overwhelming majority of Hispanic members of Congress are males, many of whom launched their political careers during the Chicano Movement and subsequent grassroots political initiatives (Takash 1993).

Community Activism

Politics is not simply about assuming positions. A person usually becomes involved because of their life experiences. I became involved because I saw the lack of educational opportunities in California for Mexican Americans. My parents, who are seventy-one and seventy years old, attended segregated schools and experienced discrimination. My father, Frank, whose first language was Spanish, was hit by his teacher for speaking Spanish in his elementary school class. My mother, Celina, lived close to a school with nice equipment but was not allowed to attend because she was Mexican American. She was bussed to a school farther away from her home. I know that if they had had more positive educational experiences, they would have assumed professional careers. My parents are far more intelligent than I am, but I had better opportunities. I continue to see these inequities play out in the school system today. (Frances M., 36)

Frances illustrates how Latina feminist community activism, or the need to take a stand, is shaped by the importance of family and space for women, a motivation sometimes described as "activist mothering" (Naples

1998). Another common characteristic of women community activists is commitment to community work as part of a larger struggle for social justice. In short, women are committed to change in their community as a way to improve the quality of life for future generations. They feel a sense of promise in changing their communities for the better.

As is true of Latina elected officials, many of these community organizers are influenced by previous work in political organizations. These organizations shape their norms and values as well as set agendas or issues to be undertaken. The culture of the community greatly shapes the agendas women pursue. Some activists pursue agendas within their specific communities whereas others feel a commitment to work on behalf of their people in general, whether or not they live in the same community.

Because many Mexican American women are involved in their church, this can become a meaningful site for political involvement. Religious traditions of social justice and charity toward the poor make the church a strong political influence, a phenomenon called "liberation theology." The church also provides a good forum to disseminate information and take a stand on issues. Furthermore, church members are very familiar with what goes on and the needs that are present in their communities (Cadena and Medina 2004). Many activist women feel they are in a better position than elected officials to mobilize change in their communities. Generally, these women believe that elected officials are motivated by a desire for power not for social chance. Therefore, the women feel that they can make a bigger difference at the local level.

Chicana Activists

Perhaps the most important study on Mexican American women activists relates to Mothers of East Los Angeles (MELA). These nontraditional political players stopped the building in their community of a 1,700-inmate prison and a waste incinerator that would have been near thirty surrounding schools (Pardo 1997). Pardo concluded that "the women in MELA transformed their traditional networks and resources around family and culture into specific political assets to protect their communities" (Pardo 1997, 151). Because poor people are more likely to live in areas that have environmental risks, environmentalism has become an issue that has successfully mobilized many poorer communities (Prindeville and Bretting 1998).

Many MELA members described their previous political activism as being involved in their children's education or joining parent-school associations, the same background as one of the most famous Chicana activists, Dolores Huerta (see topic highlight 3). Pardo notes that it is in these school organizations that social networks were established. She continues, "They have defied stereotypes of apathy and used ethnic, gender, and class identity as an impetus, a strength, a vehicle for political activism. They have expanded their—and our—nderstanding of the complexities of a political system, and they have reaffirmed the possibility of doing something" (Pardo 1997, 164–65).

Binational Activism

Latinos in the United States are more interconnected with Latinos in other Latin American countries than ever before. These binational and multinational social and economic relationships are predicted to expand, promoting pan-ethnicity, an identity that transcends nation-states. Large multinational companies that operate in both the United States and Latin America, trade policies that encourage bilateral relationships, and immigration that creates international social networks all solidify a bond between U.S. Latinos and Latin Americans.

A growing area of research examines the cooperative organizing strategies of Mexican American women and women in other Latin American countries. In a study focusing on women's organizing at the grassroots level, Nancy Naples (1998) looked at how international investments influence local organizing strategies. She examined a coalition called Hermanas en La Lucha/Sisters, a group of women that organized based on Chicana feminism. They linked their struggles with those of the indigenous women of Latin America and Mexico, with whom they share the same needs by virtue of colonialism, globalization, race, and gender and class subordination. The Hermanas en La Lucha/Sisters helped generate solidarity on both sides of the U.S.-Mexico border for the Zapatista resistance in Chiapas, Mexico. For example, they initiated the Bread Project, with the proceeds from bread sales going to assist the women of Chiapas. Naples predicts that similar transnational organizing groups will continue to flourish.

Concluding Thoughts

Chicana feminism has been an important influence in U.S. politics. Many Mexican American women felt that mainstream feminism was important but did not take into account their particular needs. Today, confronting racism and sexism are important political agendas for Mexican American women in both traditional and nontraditional political venues.

The role of women in the political process is multifaceted and complex. Although the number of Mexican American women participating in traditional political outlets is relatively small, recent trends promise growing involvement and influence. A Chicana leader has several characteristics. She is typically from a working-class background, is educated, and has been politicized through participatory politics at the local level. She usually becomes involved in politics because of a personal commitment to issues that affect her community.

Topic Highlight 3. Dolores C. Huerta

Dolores C. Huerta is the mother of eleven children and a grandmother to fourteen. But she is far better known for helping to give birth to the United Farm Workers of America, the union she cofounded with César Chávez. Huerta was born in a mining town in northern New Mexico on April 10, 1930. Her father, Juan Fernández, was a miner, field worker, union activist, and member of the state assembly. Her parents divorced when she was three. She learned her management skills through watching her mother, Alicia, run a restaurant and seventy-room hotel in Stockton, California.

After a career teaching in the public schools, Huerta left her job because she said she could not stand to see children coming to class hungry and in need of shoes. So she moved on to community activism in 1955. Working for the Community Service Organization, she began to battle segregation and police brutality, to lead voter registration drives, to push for improved public services, and to fight for new legislation.

In 1960, Huerta organized and founded the Agricultural Workers Association. In 1961, she became a lobbyist and successfully pushed to remove citizenship requirements from pension and public assistance programs. Huerta was also instrumental in the passage of legislation that allowed people to vote in Spanish and to take their driver's license tests in their native language. In 1962, she went to Washington, DC, to help end what she described as the "captive labor" Bracero Program. Later that year, the Community Service Organization refused a request from its president, César Chávez, to start organizing farm workers. So Huerta, a single mother of seven children, moved to Delano, California, and helped Chávez

form the National Farm Workers Association, which later became the UFW. The pair traveled the California farm country, enlisting members along the way. As a result of a series of boycotts and strikes, the union negotiated labor contracts for tens of thousands of workers, often against stiff opposition by landowners.

In 1963, Huerta helped secure Aid for Dependent Families, which has become a critical assistance program for the unemployed and underemployed. In 1966, Huerta negotiated a collective bargaining contract with the Schenley Wine Company that made history. It was the first contract ever between farmworkers and an agricultural company.

During a strike in 1973, thousands of farmworkers were arrested for picketing, hundreds were beaten, and two were murdered. Despite such dangers, Huerta has continued her work. She has been arrested more than twenty times for her union activities. Her influence in politics also has been substantial. Robert F. Kennedy, moments before he was assassinated, praised Huerta for helping him win the California primary election in 1968. Huerta was inducted in the National Women's Hall of Fame in 1993. She received the American Civil Liberties Union Roger Baldwin Medal of Liberty Award, the Eugene V. Debs Foundation Outstanding American Award, and the Ellis Island Medal of Freedom Award. In 1998, *Ms* magazine chose Huerta as one of its three women of the year. In the same year, the *Ladies Home Journal* included her in its "100 Most Important Women of the 20th Century" (United Farm Workers of America).

Although it is important to highlight the need for greater Latina involvement in traditional politics, it is just as important to understand the local, participatory, and activist nature of their involvement as distinctive and no less important. As one scholar notes, the political mobilization of Latina women is more participatory because they have different perceptions of the nature of politics. Rather than focusing on elected officials, Latinas put their energy toward practical issues related to the community and interpersonal networks (Hardy-Fanta 1993).

There are a growing number of Latina leaders at the local level. The concerns of these women revolve around their community, their space, and their children. Also intriguing is the fact that Mexican American women's identity is being shaped not only by the country in which they reside but also by women in other Latin American countries. This political trend is predicted to continue given the interconnecting forces of immigration, technology, business, and overall pan-ethnicity.

Discussion Exercises

1. What is Chicana feminism and how is it different from mainstream feminism?
2. What are typical characteristics of Chicana/Latina elected officials? How are these important in shaping their political activities and agendas?
3. What are some of the issues Mexican American women want politicians to pursue?
4. How do you think politics has transformed women activists at the local, state, and federal levels?
5. What are some of the issues that have mobilized Mexican American women at the grassroots level? Why are these issues of particular importance to Chicanas?
6. What do you predict for the future of women's organizing at the grassroots level?

Section 3: Political and Socioeconomic Perspectives
Assessment and Application

1. Compare and contrast three aspects of Chicano history that were reinterpreted by Chicano scholars in the 1960s and 1970s.

2. How did the history of Chicanas fare initially in the process of reinterpreting Chicano history?

3. How did Chicana scholars reconcile Chicana feminism and cultural nationalism?

4. Identify the major goals of the Chicano Movement and describe to what extent these have been achieved at the present time.

5. How has Chicano cultural identity changed in your community since the 1960s?

6. How did the Mexican-American and Chicano generations influence the development of the Hispanic generation?

7. According to Kim Geron, what factors tend to account for Hispanic immigration to the U.S.?

8. How has immigration legislation and policy affected Hispanic immigration?

9. How have contemporary border enforcement policy and practice impacted Chicanos in your community?

10. Looking at the *Time Magazine* portrait of Hispanics in chapter two, what evidence supports Mortimer B. Zuckerman's assertion that new Hispanic immigrants are going to have a positive effect on American society?

11. Explain how the "politics of accommodation" affect Latino electoral politics.

12. Identify five national Latino organizations and describe how these currently attempt to shape national public policy.

13. During the last election, how did Chicana(o) candidates fare in your municipality and state?

14. Compare and contrast the senior citizen vote with the Latino vote in your community in the last municipal and/or school bond elections.

15. Select a community with a Chicano population and determine whether there is a substantial underclass of Chicanos, and describe how they are perceived and treated by middle-class Chicanos.

16. How is current immigration from Mexico impacting communities outside the Southwest?

17. What are the Pew Research Center's key findings about the Latino electorate between 2002–2004?

18. Explain why there is a growing divergence between the Hispanic population and the number of Hispanic voters.

19. What factors influence Latino support for political parties?

Please note that the chapter by Lisa Magaña contains an excellent set of questions at the end that you can tap to develop a better understanding of the role of Latinas in electoral politics.

Section 3: Suggested Readings

Acuña, Rodolfo. (1995). *Anything but Mexican: Chicanos in Contemporary Los Angeles*. New York, NY: Verso.

Akers Chacón, Justin and Davis, Mike. (2006). *No One is Illegal: Fighting Racism and State Violence in the U.S.-Mexico Border*. Chicago, IL: Haymarket Books.

Balderrama, Francisco E. and Rodríguez, Raymond. (2006). *Decade of Betrayal: Mexican Repatriation in the 1930s*. Albuquerque, NM: University of New Mexico Press.

Burke, John Francis. (2002). *Mestizo Democracy: The Politics of Crossing Borders*. College Station, TX: Texas A&M University Press.

Chang, Grace. (2000). *Disposable Domestic: Immigrant Women Workers in the Global Economy*. Cambridge, MA: South End Press.

Chicago Council on Foreign Relations. (2004). *Comparing Mexican and American Public Opinion and Foreign Policy*. Chicago, IL: Chicago Council on Foreign Relations.

Congressional Hispanic Caucus Institute. (2000). *1999 Issues Conference Policy Recommendations*. Washington, D.C.: Congressional Hispanic Caucus Institute.

De la Garza, Rodolfo O. and DeSipio, Louis. (Eds.). (1999). *Awash in the Mainstream: Latinos and the 1996 Elections*. Boulder, CO: Westview Press.

De la Garza, Rodolfo O.; DeSipio, Louis; García, Chris, F., and García, John. (1992). *Latino Voices: Mexicans, Puerto Ricans & Cuban Perspectives on American Politics*. Boulder, CO: Westview Press.

De la Isla, José. (2003). *The Rise of Hispanic Political Power*. Santa Maria, CA: Archer Books.

De la Torre, Adela. (2002). *Moving from the Margins: A Chicana Voice on Public Policy*. Tucson, AZ: University of Arizona Press.

Delgado Gaitán, Concha. (2004). *Involving Latino Families in School: Raising Students Achievement Through Home-School Partnerships*. Thousand Oaks, CA: Corwin Press.

Durán, Jorge and Massey, Douglas S. (2004). *Crossing the Border: Research from the Mexican Migration Project*. New York, NY: Rusell Sage Foundation.

Fry, Richard. (2006). *Gender and Migration*. Washington, D.C.: Pew Hispanic Center.

García, Chris F. (Ed.). (1997). *Pursuit of Power: Latinos and the Political System*. Notre Dame, IN: University of Notre Dame Press.

García, John A. (2003). *Latino Politics in America: Community, Culture and Interests*. New York, NY: Rowman & Littlefield Publishers.

García, Mario T. (1995). *Rubén Salazar, Border Correspondent*. Berkeley, CA: University of California Press.

García, Mario T. (1998). *The Making of a Mexican American Mayor: Raymond L. Telles of El Paso*. El Paso, TX: Texas Western Press.

Geron, Kim. (2005). *Latino Political Power*. Boulder, CO: Lynne Rienner Publishers.

Gertner, Jon. (2006). What is a Living Wage? *The New York Times Magazine*. Jan 2006. Section 6. Pp 38–45.

Gómez-Quiñones, Juan. (1994). *Chicano Politics: Reality and Promise, 1940–1990*. Albuquerque, NM: University of New Mexico Press.

Gutiérrez, David. (1994). *Walls and Mirrors: Mexican Americans, Mexican Immigrants, and the Politics of Ethnicity*. Berkeley, CA: University of California Press.

Hero, Rodney E. (1992). *Latinos and the U.S. Political System: Two-Tiered Pluralism*. Philadelphia, PA: Temple University Press.

Johnson, Kevin R. (2004). *The Huddled Masses Myth: Immigration and Civil Rights*. Philadelphia, PA: Temple University Press.

Jones, Toni Griego and Fuller, Mary Lou. (2003). *Teaching Hispanic Children*. Boston, MA: Allyn and Bacon.

Latina Leaders. *Hispanic Trends*. Sept/Oct 2006.

Montejano, David. (Ed.). (1999). *Chicano Politics and Society in the Late Twentieth Century*. Austin, TX: Center for Mexican-American Studies, The University of Texas at Austin.

Navarro, Armando. (2000). *La Raza Unida Party: A Chicano Challenge to the U.S. Two-Party Dictatorship*. Philadelphia, PA: Temple University Press.

Navarro, Armando. (1998). *The Cristal Experiment: A Chicano Struggle for Community Control*. Madison, WI: University of Wisconsin Press.

Orozco, E.C. (1996). *The Chicano Labyrinth of Solitude: A Study in the Making of the Chicano Mind and Character*. Dubuque, IA: Kendall/Hunt Publishing.

Papademetriou, Demetrios G. and Meyers, Deborah Waller. (2001). *Caught in the Middle: Border Communities in an Era of Globalization*. Washington, D.C.: Carnegie Endowment for International Peace.

Portes, Alejandro. (Ed.). (1996). *The New Second Generation*. New York, NY: Russell Sage Foundation.

Ramos, Jorge. (2004). *The Latino Wave: How Hispanics Will Elect the Next American President*. New York, NY: HarperCollins Publishers.

Ramos García, José María. (2004). *La Gestión de la Cooperación Transfronteriza México-Estados Unidos en un Marco de Inseguridad Global: Problemas y Desafíos*. México, D.F.: Consejo Mexicano de Asuntos Internacionales.

Rodríguez Cadavid, Fresia. (2004). *The Hispanic Role in U.S. Hemispheric Policy*. Washington, D.C: Cuban American National Council/Hispanic Link Journalism Foundation.

Rosales, Arturo. (1996). *Chicano!: The History of the Civil Rights Movement*. Houston, TX: Arte Público Press.

Rosales, Francisco F. (1999). ¡*Pobre Raza!: Violence, Justice, and Mobilization among México Lindo Immigrants, 1900–1936*. Austin, TX: University of Texas Press.

Rosales, Rodolfo. (2000). *The Illusion of Inclusion: The Untold Political Story of San Antonio*. Austin, TX: University of Texas Press.

Skerry, Peter. (1993). *Mexican Americans: The Ambivalent Minority*. Cambridge, MA: Harvard University Press.

Staudt, Kathleen A. (1998). *Free Trade? Informal Economies at the U.S.-Mexico Border*. Philadelphia, PA: Temple University Press.

SVREP. (2000). Latino Vote 2000 Heats Up. *Latino Vote Reporter*, Vol. 5, (I). Pp. 1;6–7.

The Women Issue. *Latino Leaders: The National Magazine of the Successful American Latino*. May 2006.

Thornburgh, Nathan. (2006). Inside the Life of the Migrants Next Door. *Time Magazine*. Vol. 167, (6). Pp 36–45.

Vázquez, Carmen Inoa. (2004). *Parenting with Pride, Latino Style: How to Help Your Child Cherish Your Cultural Values and Succeed in Today's World*. New York, NY: HarperCollins Publishers.

Yoshino, Kenji. (2006). The Pressure to Cover. *The New York Times Magazine*. Jan 2006. Section 6. Pp 32–36.

Section 3: Suggested Films and Videos

Across the Bridge, 2004
Rank Film Distributor of America

Bread & Roses: When You Have Nothing, You Have Nothing to Lose, 2001
Lions Gate Home Entertainment
Santa Monica, CA

Crossing the Line/ Sobre pasando la línea
Las Lineas Media Library
P.O. Box 1084, Harriman, NY 10926

El Contrato: The Contract, 2003
Films for the Humanities and Sciences
P. O. Box 2053, Princeton, NJ 08543-2053

Dying to Get In: Illegal Immigration to the E.U., 2002
Films for the Humanities and Sciences
P. O. Box 2053, Princeton, NJ 08543-2053

Farmingville, 2004
Camino Bluff Productions, Inc., 752 W. End Ave, #2F, New York, NY 10025

Fighting for Political Power, 1996
Chicano: History of the Mexican American Movement Series
National Latino Communications Center

Hispanic Entrepreneurs: Against All Odds
Films for the Humanities and Sciences
P.O. Box 2053, Princeton, NJ 08543-2053

Immigrant Nation, Divided Country, 2006
CNN Programs

Latin and African Americans: Friends or Foes, 1998
Films for the Humanities and Sciences
P. O. Box 2053, Princeton, NJ 08543-2053

Letters from the Other Side, 2006
New Day Films
190 Route 17M, P.O. Box 1084, Harriman, NY 10926

Patrolling the Border: National Security & Immigration Reform, 2004
Films for the Humanities and Sciences
P. O. Box 2053, Princeton, NJ 08543-2053

Quest for a Homeland, 1996
Chicano!: History of the Mexican American Movement Civil Rights Movement
National Latino Communications Center

La Raza: Politics, 1976
La Raza Series
Moctezuma Productions
McGraw-Hill Broadcasting

Spanish in America, 2006
Films for the Humanities and Sciences
P. O. Box 2053, Princeton, NJ 08543-2053

The Time Has Come! An Immigrant Community Stands Up to the Border Patrol, 1996
The El Paso Border Rights Coalition
El Paso, TX

The Valley of Tears, 2005
Perry Films
135 West 29th Street #703, New York, NY 10001

The Wrath of Grapes, 1986
United Farm Workers of America
Keene, CA

Women of Hope: Latinas Abriendo Camino
Films for the Humanities and Sciences
P .O. Box. 2053, Princeton, NJ 08543-2053

Linguistic and Educational Perspectives

4

anguage and education issues are very important to the Chicano community. These issues are commonly intertwined in public policy formulation and implementation, hence their presence in this section. American schools are the official repositories and conveyors of American values, beliefs, language and culture. Schools are political arenas that have been traditionally contested by Chicanos in their quest for linguistic and cultural self-preservation, inclusion in American society, and socioeconomic and political empowerment. Therefore, the educational progress of Chicanos is an important gauge of the group's status in American society.

This section was designed to address the extant linguistic and educational issues facing the Chicano community, particularly in controversial themes such as bilingual education. To gain a thorough understanding of language and education issues in the nation, the reader also needs to examine some of the resources suggested at the end of this section. Additionally, we recommend the introduction and discussion of the topics by the course instructor, visits to educational programs and community centers, and attendance at forums in which language and education issues are discussed.

Peter Schmidt leads the section with an overview of the higher education challenges faced by Hispanics in the context of rapid demographic change in the nation. Salient Hispanic trends are examined, followed by an analysis of the K–12 educational pipeline and the factors that currently affect the success of Hispanics in their pursuit of a university education.

The next two chapters by Gilbert G. González and Dolores Delgado Bernal cover the educational experience of Chicanos from 1900–1940 and the Civil Rights era to the present, respectively. The former documents the struggle for educational equality by Chicanos striving to overcome segregation, race and ethnic bias, and attempts to relegate them to an underclass status. González also describes the political and legal actions by a politically aware, Mexican-American generation, in its initial quest of first-class citizenship. Delgado Bernal brings to the reader a chronicle of educational change during the Civil Rights Movement that builds on the politics of the previous decades. The social activism and social policy of the 1960s and the educational inequity of the 1970s are examined in the context of political upheaval and great society policies. Bernal Delgado covers recent educational changes and challenges via an analysis of issues such as bilingual education and higher education issues, particularly in California, that are now resonating dangerously in other states, such as meritocracy in higher education admissions and the reduction of funding for higher education in many states.

Nicolás C. Vaca contributes an important discussion of Chicano educational emancipation in his examination of the legal role that Chicanos played in civil rights issues related to segregation. His purpose is to erase the idea that Chicanos and Latinos were never involved in civil rights issues. To address this notion, perpetuated by academics and journalists, he analyzes the impact of the Méndez v. Westminster and Delgado v. Bastrop Independent School District cases. Nicolás Vaca reveals the historical and legal Chicano interface that shaped the legal arguments that were later heard in the Brown v. Topeka case that helped deflate the structure of school segregation.

James Crawford delineates the history of educational language rights in the United States. He provides the political, legal and linguistic context for the rise of a leading educational approach for linguistic minorities, bilingual education, which is now under siege in states like California.

Guadalupe Valdés brings the section to a close with an ethnographic portrait that partially informs the aforementioned Hispanic educational profiles in this and other sections. Explanations for the academic failure of Chicanos and other ethnic minorities are presented in a historical context, followed by an examination of educational interventions that have taken place to ameliorate said failure. Particular attention is paid to family intervention as a valid socio-educational strategy.

Academe's Hispanic Future

Peter Schmidt

The nation's largest minority group faces big obstacles in higher education, and colleges struggle to find the right ways to help.

If they haven't already, college professors and administrators should try to get accustomed to pronouncing names like Alejandro, Jorge, Nuria, and Pilar.

Hispanics have become the largest minority group in the United States and now represent about 13 percent of the country's population. They account for about half of the population growth in recent years and are expected, given immigration and their relatively high fertility rates, to represent a much larger share of the population and work force in years to come. Of the 5.6 million additional school-age children projected to be living in the United States in 2025, some 5.2 million, or 93 percent, will be Hispanic, the U.S. Census Bureau says.

Along with growing rapidly, the nation's Hispanic population is spreading out, quickly moving into communities in the South and Midwest where few Hispanics had settled before.

As they show up on campuses, Hispanic students are having a profound influence from the Mexican border to Minnesota, from California to the Carolinas.

In the past decade more than 240 colleges have been designated "Hispanic-serving institutions" by the federal government, meaning that at least a quarter of their enrollment is Hispanic and more than half of their students come from low-income backgrounds. While 49 of the institutions are in Puerto Rico, California has 73; Texas, 38; New Mexico, 20; and Arizona, Florida, Illinois, and New York each have at least 10. Others are located in Colorado, Massachusetts, New Jersey, Oklahoma, Oregon, and Washington. The list grows by about a half-dozen colleges each year.

"Relatively speaking, we are the newest kid on the higher-education block," says Antonio R. Flores, president of the Hispanic Association of Colleges and Universities, which represents Hispanic-serving institutions.

The federal government did not classify colleges as "Hispanic-serving" until 1992. By contrast, historically black colleges and universities date back to 1837. Now some Hispanic-serving institutions, especially in Texas, have such large Hispanic enrollments that they are seeking to make the education of those students a key part of their mission and identity, and they are looking to historically black colleges and universities as potential models, Mr. Flores says.

Many other colleges are establishing new courses geared toward Hispanic students; aggressively trying to recruit Hispanic students, faculty members, and administrators; and overhauling their admissions practices and student services to be more attentive to Hispanic needs. Meanwhile, the Bush administration says it is committed to helping more Hispanics get into college.

'Black and White Paradigm'

There is still plenty of room for improvement. Hispanic students remain severely underrepresented and underserved in higher education.

Colleges have made some progress. Since 1980, the number of Hispanics enrolled in colleges has more than tripled, to nearly 1.5 million, outpacing the rate of Hispanic population growth, which has more than doubled to about 38.8 million. Hispanics' share of all bachelor's degrees awarded has risen from about 2.3 percent to about 6.2 percent.

But though Hispanics represent about 18 percent of the college-age population, they account for just 9.5 percent of all students at the nation's higher-education institutions, and just 6.6 percent of enrollments at four-year colleges.

Over all, Hispanics are the least-educated major racial or ethnic group. Just 11 percent of those over the age of 25 have a bachelor's degree, compared with about 17 percent of black, 27 percent of white, and 47 percent of Asian-American adults in the same age bracket. More than two-fifths of Hispanic adults over 25 never graduated from high school, and more than one-fourth have less than a ninth-grade education.

In terms of overall Hispanic educational attainment, "we were doing better in the '70s than we are in the 21st century," says Raúl Yzaguirre, president of the National Council of La Raza, one of the nation's largest Hispanic-advocacy groups.

In many parts of the country, colleges' efforts to serve minority populations remain focused almost solely on black students, even where local Hispanic populations are burgeoning.

In Atlanta, the Hispanic population increased nearly tenfold, to about 290,000, during the 1990s. But Hispanics account for just a dozen of the 1,900 students enrolled at Atlanta Metropolitan College, which has a 95-percent-black student body. Harold E. Wade, the college's president, says predominantly Hispanic neighborhoods have cropped up "within walking distance" of his two-year public institution, but "a lot of Hispanic youngsters who have migrated into this area have not reached college age yet," and their parents don't enroll because they "have come here to work and to take care of families here and in Mexico."

Throughout the nation, "we are still seeing education through a black and white paradigm," Mr. Yzaguirre says. Hispanic students, he says, "are not being given the proper priority."

Hispanic men remain especially underserved. A report issued by the American Council on Education last month found that between the late 1970s and the late 1990s, the college-participation rate for Hispanic men remained essentially unchanged, at 31 percent. For Hispanic women, the college-participation rate increased from 27 percent to 37 percent.

Swimming Against the Tide

Several trends in higher education may be making it even harder for Hispanics to get a college education:

◆ Last year loans accounted for nearly 70 percent of all federal financial assistance available to college students, up from about 56 percent two decades ago. Raymund A. Paredes, vice president for programs at the Hispanic Scholarship Fund, the nation's largest private provider of scholarships to Hispanic students, says the shift from grants to loans "is having a very serious impact on the Latino community," which is relatively poor and leery of taking on debt. Many more Hispanics

would be attending college if they could get grants rather than loans, and many more would pursue advanced degrees "if they could get out from under this debt that they incur as undergraduates," he says.

◆ Given their relatively high rate of poverty, Hispanic students have been hit hard by the stiff increases in public-college tuition and the cuts in state financial aid that have come in recent years.

◆ Because many Hispanics inhabit the nation's fastest-growing regions (and are driving much of that growth), they are especially likely to live near colleges that have been resorting to enrollment caps to hold down costs. They are also disproportionately likely to be turned away when colleges raise their admissions standards to curtail enrollment growth or bolster their own reputations, since the standardized-test scores of Hispanics tend to be significantly lower than those of whites.

◆ Legal and political assaults on affirmative action may also be taking a toll on Hispanic enrollment. Wherever selective colleges have been forced to limit or abandon their use of race- and ethnicity-conscious admissions, the result has been an immediate drop in the share of Hispanic applicants they accept. Hispanic enrollment has rebounded somewhat when colleges have aggressively used alternatives to affirmative action, such as considering socioeconomic status or automatically admitting those near the top of their high-school classes. But the effectiveness of such policies toward ensuring Hispanic access, especially in graduate and professional schools, remains in dispute.

In the past two years, legal challenges have also been mounted against scholarship, internship, and academic-support programs reserved specifically for minority students. Several colleges have either abandoned the programs or opened them up to all races and ethnicities, based on their lawyers' advice that the programs are legally vulnerable.

Leaks in the Pipeline

Policy analysts often speak of the various sectors of education as pieces of a pipeline. At every stage of that pipeline, Hispanic students are getting stuck or spilling out.

Their problems begin in their early years, when many Hispanic children receive little exposure to English, and they are much likelier than white children and nearly as likely as black children to be living in poverty. Several studies have shown that the schools they enter tend to be some of the nation's most segregated and poorly financed, and are more likely than others to be staffed by teachers with little experience in their fields.

By the age of 17, Hispanic high-school students, on average, have the same reading and mathematics skills as white 13-year-olds. More than a third of the states recently surveyed by the National Center for Education Statistics said that their Hispanic students were significantly more likely than others to drop out of school. And those who earned their diplomas were less likely than their white peers to have taken rigorous college-preparatory courses such as Algebra II and chemistry, according to a report issued last month by the Education Trust, a nonprofit research and advocacy organization based in Washington, D.C.

"The curriculum matters hugely," says Paul Ruiz, one of the Education Trust's chief researchers. "A robust curriculum is the single greatest predictor of college success."

It is not that Hispanic families fail to see the value of education. Family surveys conducted by the Education Department show that more than 9 out of 10 Hispanic parents expect their children to attend college—a figure in line with the results for both black and white parents. But Hispanic children are much less likely than white children to have a parent who attended college.

"It is absolutely the case that they have parental support, but they don't have anybody in the family who really knows the ropes," says Tomás A. Arciniega, president of California State University at Bakersfield, which has an enrollment that is about 36 percent Hispanic, and serves the children of many Mexican and Central American migrant workers employed by local farms and food-processing plants. Like many colleges, his institution is collaborating with the local community-college district and public schools to try to get more Hispanic children to go on to college.

The educational problems of Hispanic Americans don't end at the college door. Hispanic freshmen are less likely than white students to progress to upper-division courses, and Hispanic students who make it to their third year of college are less likely to earn bachelor's degrees, according to the Inter-University Program for Latino Research, a national consortium of 18 Hispanic-focused research centers.

On the whole, Hispanic students are far likelier than white students to be enrolled in two-year colleges, to be working to support themselves or their families, or attending college part time—choices that they often can't help making but that reduce their chances of ever earning bachelor's or advanced degrees.

"The biggest challenge that these kids have to face is, How do they balance what they see as their responsibility to help out at home now that they are young adults and, at the same time, follow their dream of going on to college?" says Dr. Arciniega. He routinely urges faculty and staff members to sit down with students who also work and convince them of how much more money they will earn in a lifetime with a degree.

"We are constantly hitting on the note that college is important," he says.

Only black students have a worse college-graduation rate than Hispanics, and Hispanics have the lowest rate of graduate-school enrollment of any major racial and ethnic group. At the very end of the educational pipeline, Hispanics earn just 4 percent of the doctorates awarded by colleges. A report issued last month by the American Council on Education says that the number of Hispanics earning doctorates or professional degrees actually declined slightly in recent years.

Those statistics help explain why Hispanics account for just 2.9 percent of full-time college faculty members and just 3.2 percent of college administrators.

Repairs in just a few segments of the education pipeline could produce significant increases in the number of Hispanics earning degrees, according to the Inter-University Program for Latino Research. In a 2001 report, it crunched the numbers and determined that if Hispanic high-school students earned their diplomas and went on to four-year colleges at the same rate as white students, the result—all other things remaining equal—would be a 25-percent increase in the number who earn bachelor's degrees each year. Increases of 12 percent in the number of baccalaureates annually awarded to Hispanics could be produced by ensuring that those in two-year colleges transfer to four-year colleges at the same rate as white students, or by ensuring that those who are freshmen at four-year colleges graduate at the same rate as white students.

Among the institutions that have mounted concerted efforts to retain Hispanic students is Lehman College of the City University of New York system, which has about a 47-percent Hispanic enrollment. It operates a program that keeps freshmen together in groups of 25 to 30 to provide one another with support. The faculty members involved share information about particular students and seek to integrate the curriculums of their respective classes so that students in an English-composition class can be working on assignments that they can turn in to their sociology professor.

"This program is costly because you have to pay faculty for additional hours of meetings with each other and with students," Ricardo R. Fernández, president of Lehman College, says. But, he says, "the students like it," and he is confident that the program keeps many from dropping out during their crucial first year.

St. Philip's College, a public two-year institution in San Antonio, Tex., has the distinction of being classified as both historically black and Hispanic-serving, with an enrollment that is about a fifth black and half Hispanic. Angle S. Runnels, its president, says Hispanic students there clearly benefit from support services developed for black students, such as tutoring programs, instructional laboratories focused on reading, writing, and mathematics; and an approach to student advising that disperses counselors into academic divisions and departments to ensure adequate guidance.

"We are particularly interested in students who are the first generation in their families to experience college," Ms. Runnels says.

Partly because they offer night classes and training for specific jobs, the nation's for-profit colleges have proved especially adept at recruiting and retaining Hispanic students, even though they often charge more than public higher-education institutions.

Many experts on Hispanic college students believe that their educational attainment would improve, especially in graduate and professional schools, if they were more willing to travel long distances to colleges well suited to meet their needs. "An emphasis on close family ties is one characteristic shared by most Latinos regardless of national origin or income, and among Latino immigrants this often translates into an expectation that children will live with their parents until they marry," says a report by the Pew Hispanic Center.

A Diverse Group

Despite their linguistic and cultural similarities, the nation's Hispanic residents are very diverse. Experts on educating them generally agree that getting a larger proportion through college will require focusing on educational differences that the collective term "Hispanic" now masks.

For instance, Cuban-Americans ages 18 to 24 are slightly more likely than white students their age to be enrolled in college, and 90 percent attend full time, more than any other racial or ethnic group. They are also about as likely as white students to go on to graduate school. In contrast, Mexican-American students in that age bracket are about half as likely as their Puerto Rican or Cuban-American peers to be attending two-year colleges.

Puerto Ricans, many of whom travel back to the island often or for extended periods, as family or work needs dictate, can have distinct educational needs tied to their mobility. "You can have a kid who will start in Puerto Rico in September and be in New York in November," says Félix V. Matos Rodríguez, director of the Center for Puerto Rican Studies at Hunter College.

"It all depends on what circumstances they come here for," says Eduardo J. Padrón, president of Miami Dade College, where the enrollment is two-thirds Hispanic. "If they come here as a result of political circumstances, what you find is that some of them are better prepared than our native students. If the immigration is economic immigration, what you find is that most of these people come with a lack of knowledge of the culture and language. Even in their own language, they are not well prepared."

It also matters greatly whether Hispanic students or their parents were born in the United States or abroad.

Statistics that represent Hispanics as a group often are severely skewed by the foreign-born, who account for about 40 percent of the overall Hispanic population. One

example: On average, Hispanic males 25 and older have 10.6 years of schooling. When immigrants are taken out of the equation, however, Hispanics' educational attainment rises to 12 years.

About 44 percent of adult Hispanic immigrants dropped out of school before getting their high-school diplomas, compared with about 15 percent of those born here. More than half of foreign-born Hispanic children who had dropped out of schools in their native lands never set foot in schools in the United States.

The Pew Hispanic Center has found that foreign-born Hispanic teenagers are more likely than other immigrants their age to have come to the United States to work rather than study. They earn a lot more money than black people and white people their age—a reflection of long hours rather than high pay—and they're a key source of low-skilled, low-wage labor for agriculture and other industries. Because the nation's immigration policies place a heavy emphasis on bringing in the family members of legal U.S. residents, the current influx of the poor and uneducated props open the door for immigration by people with similar backgrounds.

"America needs a highly educated work force, but we have an immigration policy that is importing huge numbers of undereducated immigrants," says David Ray, a spokesman for the Federation for American Immigration Reform, a nonprofit advocacy group in Washington. "You get a cheap, exploitable employee for the business owner, and an additional tax burden for the American worker."

When Hispanic families come here illegally, paying for college can be especially tough. Many states' public colleges require undocumented immigrants to pay the same, comparatively high tuition as nonresidents, although a few states, including California, New York, and Texas, have agreed in recent years to let them pay in-state rates. They are ineligible for federal financial aid for college, and for many, scholarships and grants awarded by colleges and private foundations.

"A lot of donors are uncomfortable about helping undocumented students," says Mr. Paredes of the Hispanic Scholarship Fund, which provided more than $26-million in aid to more than 7,500 Hispanic college students during the 2002–3 academic year.

The educational prospects improve substantially for the U.S.-born children of Hispanic immigrants, who account for about 28 percent of the total Hispanic population and attend college at the same rate as whites.

That is especially true of people whose families came here from the Dominican Republic. Ramona Hernández, director of the Dominican Studies Institute at City College, in New York, says she believes, based on personal experience and anecdotes, that Dominican immigrants place an exceptionally high value on education.

"I used to show off my books on the train," says Dr. Hernández. "I wanted people to see I was going to college. I wanted to share that information on the subway train as I was commuting from Lehman College to my home in the Bronx."

As with other immigrant groups, members of the so-called "second generation" of Hispanics—the U.S.-born children of the foreign-born—tend to have a fire in the belly that makes them achieve at levels that their own children, the "third generation," can't match. Among the U.S.-born children of U.S.-born Hispanics—the children of the "third generation" and beyond—just 36 percent of 18- to 24-year-old high-school graduates are in college. The second generation of Hispanics catches up with the white population in terms of college attendance, but its descendants lose some of that ground.

Moving into New States

About half of the nation's Hispanics live in just two states, California and Texas. Eight other states—Arizona, Colorado, Florida, Illinois, Nevada, New Jersey, New Mexico, and New York—account for more than a fourth.

But Hispanics also are rapidly moving into states where relatively few had lived just a few decades ago. During the 1990s, their numbers more than doubled in Kentucky, Minnesota, and Nebraska, more than tripled in Alabama, Tennessee, and South Carolina, and more than quadrupled in Arkansas, Georgia, and North Carolina.

Many colleges in these states are just beginning to find ways to serve Hispanic students.

Carl V. Patton, president of Georgia State University, says his institution established a Hispanic-student-services office last spring and is working to increase Hispanic enrollment, now at about 3 percent, to 8 percent to reflect the size of Georgia's Hispanic population.

"We have found that the way you get these students is from word of mouth," he says. "A stream of students starts to come from the good schools, and those students will tell other students."

In Minnesota, Minneapolis Community and Technical College has joined with U.S. Bancorps to set up a program that trains Hispanic bank employees, in response to a threefold increase in that city's Hispanic population during the 1990s. Phillip L. Davis, the two-year college's president, says the program is popular because it trains students for existing jobs and is not just based on "off-in-the-distance speculation about what the job market will look like." In some states, like California, Florida, Illinois, and Texas, public colleges are feeling top-down pressure to better serve Hispanic students as Hispanic legislators grow in number and flex more muscle.

For public colleges in those states, improving services for Hispanic students is becoming "a budget issue," says Gilbert Cárdenas, director of the Inter-University Program for Latino Research. "They realize that if they are going to get the support of the elected officials, they have to be more sensitive to the broader needs of the state."

The Bush administration has taken note of the educational problems of Hispanic Americans. Since 2001 it has increased federal spending on colleges classified as "Hispanic-serving" by about 36 percent, to $93 million. It has also overseen a $39 million, or roughly 64 percent, increase in spending on grants to colleges of education to prepare teachers to work with students who do not speak English at home.

In October 2001, President Bush signed an executive order establishing the President's Advisory Commission on Educational Excellence for Hispanic Americans. In a report issued last March, the panel warned: "Hispanics are not maximizing their income potential or developing financial security. This leads to lost tax revenues, lower rates of consumer spending, reduced per-capita savings, and increased social costs."

Among its recommendations, the commission urged the federal government to conduct much more research on the needs of Hispanic students; hold colleges accountable for improving Hispanic graduation rates, and undertake a nationwide public-awareness campaign aimed at helping Hispanic parents navigate the nation's education system.

Upon the release of the commission's report, Secretary of Education Roderick R. Paige said: "We're not letting any more Hispanic kids slip through the cracks. It's a disgrace. And it's going to stop."

Ronald Reagan, and every president since, worked with similar panels on Hispanic education, with mixed results. Mr. Yzaguirre, of the National Council of La Raza, resigned as the head of such a commission under President Bill Clinton because, he says, in six years not a single federal agency had complied with an executive order instructing them to provide the panel with an inventory of programs for Hispanic students. The report from the newest commission says that it, too, had trouble getting federal departments and agencies to provide basic information about their services to Hispanic students.

Such developments have made many Hispanic advocates cynical about the prospect of the federal government's bringing about real improvements any time soon.

"We don't need any more reports," says Lauro F. Cavazos, who worked with such panels as secretary of education under Presidents Reagan and George H.W. Bush.

"We know what the problem is," Mr. Cavazos says. "We know what the solutions are. There just has to be a will to do it, to bring about the change."

For Many Hispanics, College Is an Obstacle Course

Hispanic high-school graduates are more likely to go on to college than their white peers, yet are less likely to earn bachelor's degrees. They are deterred by several obstacles tied to poverty and immigration, and others that they inadvertently create for themselves by focusing as hard on paying bills as they do on getting through college. Among the biggest obstacles:

♦ Poor academic preparation. On average, Hispanic students score 9 percent to 11 percent lower than white students on standardized college-admissions tests. More than one-fourth of Hispanics enter college needing remedial English courses, compared with one-tenth of white freshmen, and more than half need remedial mathematics, compared with less than one-third of their white peers. On average, Hispanic students' college grades are lower, and those who need to play catch-up generally end up taking longer to earn a degree.

♦ Parents who never attended college. More than two out of five Hispanic freshmen at four-year colleges are the first in their family to attend college, compared with about one out of five white freshmen. Those whose parents can't speak English are even less likely to get sound advice from their families about college.

♦ Worries about tuition. More than three-fourths of Hispanic freshmen at four-year colleges report having major concerns about paying for their education, compared with one-fifth of white freshmen. Hispanic students tend not to take advantage of all the financial aid that is available to them, particularly loans, which usually account for most of the available assistance.

♦ Not transferring from two-year colleges. About 40 percent of 18- to 24-year-old Hispanic college stu-

dents are enrolled in two-year institutions, compared with 25 percent of black and 25 percent of white students. Of those who do not start at four-year institutions, 39 percent have no degree and have dropped out within four years. Of those who begin at four-year institutions, just 18 percent leave college without a degree within four years.

♦ Enrolling in college part time. About 25 percent of traditional-age Hispanic college students are enrolled part time, compared with 15 percent of white students. Part-time college students of any race or ethnicity are more likely than full-timers to drop out.

♦ Enrolling later in life. Among the traditional college-age population, 33 percent of Hispanic high-school graduates and 42 percent of white high-school graduates are enrolled in undergraduate programs. Traditional-age college students are more likely than older students to earn their baccalaureates and go on to earn advanced degrees. About 4 percent of Hispanic high-school graduates 25 and older are enrolled in undergraduate programs, making them twice as likely as their white counterparts to still be working toward undergraduate degrees at that age when they are more likely to have children and other responsibilities distracting them from their studies.

Sources

U.S. Census Bureau; U.S. Department of Education; Higher Education Research Institute at the University of California at Los Angeles; Inter-University Program for Latino Research; Pew Hispanic Center

Segregation and the Education of Mexican Children, 1900–1940

Gilbert G. González

In the aftermath of the 1848 war between Mexico and the United States, the newly acquired U.S. territory in the Southwest underwent a radical social transformation. Using a variety of legal, extralegal, and generally violent means, Anglo-American capitalist society first dominated then decimated the pre-capitalist Mexican system. At the heart of the transformation was a continually expanding labor-intense production system that required an inexhaustible labor supply; this system replaced the old Mexican self-subsistence economy. As the new century opened to a national imperialist expansionism that engulfed the Caribbean, Mexico and Latin America, the entrenchment monopolistic economy of the Southwest demanded an army of cheap, mobile, unorganized, and dependable labor.

In Porfirian Mexico (1880–1910) and later in post-revolutionary Mexico, governmental policies complemented that demand and ensured the availability of labor for U.S. business. Porfirio Díaz's and revolutionary Mexico's open-door foreign investment policy (demanded by Washington), coupled with large-scale corporations' voracious appetite for Mexican labor, functioned as an international infrastructure that stabilized the Mexican immigrant community as a permanent component and ethnicity within the U.S. working class. An incipient sector of the regional working class was formed in the early 1900s, and it continued to grow with the help of legal and illegal immigration in response to capital's requirements for workers. More often than not, "illegal" immigration constituted a form of state-sanctioned labor crossing of the border to satisfy corporate demand.

Indeed, the Mexican community emerged as a major participant in the capitalist development of the Southwest. It became integrated into the corporate industries then experiencing unprecedented growth. These same economi-cally productive workers were segregated in terms of work, religion, occupation, recreation, housing, and education. An apparent irony was set in motion as they were integrated into a system of production dominated by monopolistic capital and yet segregated from nearly every other aspect of society. The social and economic conditions that have characterized the Mexican community in the United States throughout the twentieth century were especially evident during the first two decades, a period during which the modern Chicano community made its entrance.

Immigration and Settlement

Well over a million Mexican migrants streamed into the United States between 1900 and 1930. The majority arrived in the 1920s to settle in mining zones, irrigated agricultural valleys, manufacturing centers, and railroad construction sites. Laborers, with families in tow, were coveted and actively recruited by employers. They entered into the lowest-wage employment in the packing houses of Southern California, the sugar beet fields of Colorado, the smelters of El Paso, the garment factories of San Antonio, the copper mines of Arizona, the cotton farms of Texas, and railroad construction across the United States. As the Mexican community in the Southwest grew, a new lexicon entered the vocabulary of the dominant community. Mexicans, it was said, were naturally suited to physical labor, as their short stature made it easier for them to pick, hoe, and lift. Nature adapted them to a subordinate status in which they took orders from a paternalistic boss and lived on meager wages. Though humble, they nevertheless enjoyed the simple pleasures of life to the fullest.

Charles Teague, longtime CEO of the Southern California Fruit Growers Exchange (the forerunner of Sunkist) in the interwar years, casually remarked that "Mexicans are naturally adapted to agricultural work, particularly in the handling of fruits and vegetables. . . . Many of them have a natural skill in the handling of tools and are resourceful in matters requiring manual ability."[1] Teague knew where the interests of the corporation lay: over 90 percent of the picking force of twenty-five thousand were Mexican laborers.[2] Although Mexicans were praised for their manual dexterity, they were seldom compensated for it. "Mexican wage" meant working for less than Anglo-American workers, and "Mexican work" meant undesirable, lowest-paid manual labor.

A settlement pattern quickly formed along the U.S.-Mexican border, where about 85 percent of migrants put down roots. They established permanent communities in company towns sponsored by mining companies, citrus associations, and cotton farms; covenants forced them to live "across the tracks," where they created *colonias* in the cities' outskirts and *campos* on the edges of agricultural towns. Throughout the Southwest, the increasing number of Mexican settlements kept pace with the economic development of the region. Mexican customs, traditions, celebrations, organizations, and activities were transplanted into the inhospitable environment. Before long, the residents established a new identity embodied in their communities and, except for leaving to work or to find some form of recreation, life was spent within the colonia or campo.

Integration into the economic sphere carried a price: segregation in theaters, parks, politics, and restaurants marked relations between Mexican society and the dominant community. In spite of the strength of community organizations and structures, Mexican barrios became associated, in the popular mind, with the outcast: Mexicans were foreigners, immigrants, transients, poor, delinquent, uncultured, and unskilled. Soon enough, the "Mexican problem," which encapsulated a host of alleged dangers to society's fundamental institutions, became a topic of widespread discussion in public policy venues. Los Angeles City Schools Superintendent Susan B. Dorsey lamented having to administer the educational mission of the schools with high enrollments of Mexican children. In one talk to district administrators she addressed the widely deplored educational problem:

> It is unfortunate and unfair for Los Angeles, the third largest Mexican city in the world, to bear the burdens of taking care educationally of this enormous group. We do have to bear a spiritual burden quite disproportionate to the return from this great number of aliens in our midst. This burden comes to us merely because we are near the border.[3]

Another complaint expressed by many educators accused Mexicans of increased crime, welfare cases, schooling problems, vice, and threats to the racial and cultural homogeneity of the nation.[4]

Public Schools and the Segregation of Mexican Children

As these communities formed, the public education system underwent a major overhaul and assumed a prominent position among the institutions shaping the political culture and social structure of the nation. In the late nineteenth century, periodic labor strikes convulsed the nation, and socialism and communism made inroads among the working classes. In response to these threats, leading social theorists cautioned that modern society contained dangerous and volatile social elements that threatened cultural disintegration, even a political revolution, if not properly controlled and neutralized.[5] Indeed, the public education system emerged transformed from a small-scale volunteer endeavor to a centralized, mass, compulsory state agency organized to indoctrinate the citizenry with a common political culture aimed at strengthening political stability, while inculcating the skills necessary for optimal economic growth and profitability.[6] At no time, however, did the schooling enterprise propose to alter existing class relations. Schools actively represented the status quo, with all of its attendant public policies, inequalities, and prejudices, and shouldered the task of creating an efficient,[7] organic, clock-like society. Across the nation, expanding public schooling placed the maintenance of the status quo high on its agenda while simultaneously assimilating and unfolding social relations, including class and racial hierarchies, dominant political ideologies, and economic operations.[8] Within this context, the Mexican problem compelled Southwestern school districts, which were enrolling significant numbers of Spanish-speaking children, to design a curriculum adapted to Mexican children. Acceptance of schooling intended to resolve the Mexican problem ensured the reproduction of the Mexican community as a source of cheap labor.

How did school systems treat the Mexican problem? What objectives guided school administrators? What methods did they employ to realize those objectives? The first administrative proposal for solving the Mexican problem was simple: segregation into all-Mexican schools. Several reasons were proffered for separating Mexican children from Anglo-American children. First, educators and academicians claimed that segregation provided a fitting environment in which to meet the educational needs of the culturally distinctive Mexican child. Administrators and educators confidently insisted that Anglo-American and Mexican children were substantially distinct culturally. Moreover, the culture of the Mexican child diminished his or her capacity to learn to such a degree that it was unwise to place both in the same school setting. The crux of the learning problem pivoted around language. Slowed by speaking Spanish, Mexican children progressively fell behind through the grades. Simultaneously, segregation unburdened the Anglo-American child from the "slower"

Mexican pupils, who in turn benefited by avoiding competition with "faster students." Second, the inherited intelligence of Mexican children, as measured by IQ tests, purportedly fell well below that of the average Anglo child. This also required segregation to educate at the special ability levels of Mexican children. Third, the level of measured intelligence and the employment pattern peculiar to Mexicans (which parents seemed to pass on to their children) appeared to contain the seeds of a social inevitability. Educators therefore implemented a strict emphasis on vocational education in the segregated environment.

The Culture Concept

In school districts throughout the region, a variety of segregation practices appeared. Initially, separating children into "foreign" classrooms seemed to solve the educational problem; eventually the first experiments grew into complete separation. In urban school districts such as Los Angeles, district lines created officially named "neighborhood schools" that only "foreign" (i.e. Mexican) students attended. The procedure most often applied, however, was the classic "Mexican School." In towns and cities where a Mexican colonia had been established, a separate school for Mexican children became a high priority for boards of education. Nearly all school districts separated Mexican children in one fashion or another, ostensibly because of the need to cleanse them of cultural defects by means of proper guidance and control. School bore the responsibility for teaching them the English language and American customs, values, and norms—that is, of Americanizing them. Mexicans were alleged to hold a Pandora's box of cultural dilemmas that, if allowed to escape, could move beyond the confines of the colonia and subvert the desirable and healthy cultural norms of society. If Mexicans were left to themselves, it was believed that certain destruction would threaten the superior (Anglo) culture and all that it had created. Educators and political leaders worried over Mexican habits thought to be antithetical to the national culture: uncleanliness, shiftlessness, irresponsibility, lack of ambition, unthriftiness, fatalism, promiscuity, and proneness to alcohol abuse.

E.E. Davis of the University of Texas confidently asserted in a report on illiteracy in Texas that "there is but one choice in the matter of educating these unfortunate [Mexican] children and that is to put the 'dirty' ones into separate schools till they learn how to 'clean-up' and become eligible to better society."[9] A deeply perplexed Phoenix principal argued that Mexicans' propensity to "steal cars, break windows, wreck recreational centers"[10] required that "more time should be spent teaching the [Mexican] child clean habits and positive attitudes towards others, public property, and their community in general." One Southern California teacher of Americanization wrote that "Mexican apathy . . . the infirmity of the will, forever the promise of mañana [dragged] upon the wheels of such progress as might exist."[11] An assistant supervisor in the Los Angeles city schools bluntly summarized the widely discussed Mexican problem:

> The Mexican problem . . . is principally the product of poverty in the home, which, in turn, is largely the appendage of the influx of immigrants from the Republic south of us. . . . The infusions of Spanish blood into Aztec and Maya veins has Latinized later generations since the sixteenth century. The mixture of the two is fundamentally responsible for the carefree, if not indolent, characteristic of the race.[12]

At a meeting of administrators in 1925, Susan B. Dorsey, the Los Angeles School District superintendent, recommended to her supervisors the antidote most often applied: "We have these [Mexican] immigrants to live with, and if we can Americanize them, we can live with them . . .". She, like many of her colleagues, believed that Americanization controlled the cultural defects while bringing Mexicans "to the light" so that they could embark on the process of social betterment.

To fulfill the objectives of the Americanization program, however, proficiency in English and the elimination of Spanish were paramount, for language was considered the linchpin of culture. Backward cultural beliefs could be eliminated, it was claimed, once the core of the belief system, the Spanish language, was replaced by the heart of the superior culture, English. Thus, in district after district, English instruction via immersion and the forced removal of Spanish (and any traces of bilingualism) occupied the first two years of instruction in segregated schools. The first and second grades were generally known as the "Americanization" rooms, the locus of cultural change and guided entrance into American society.

Classroom rewards and punishments revolved around the child's willingness to adapt to speaking English exclusively. Schools incorporated practices that valued and rewarded proficiency in English, a practice that implicitly branded the language of the parents and the community as inferior and undesirable. Many an adult who lived through that era recalls the signs that warned "No Spanish" or "Speak English" and punishment by detention, corporal punishment, loss of privileges, or bad grades. One graduate of a segregated school bitterly recalled that "teachers warned us, 'I don't want to catch you speaking Spanish' . . . [but] we couldn't help it. That's all we knew at home. They'd tell us 'we're going to send you back to Mexico' because they wanted to scare us that way. . . . That's about all we used to hear. . . . I forced myself to learn English."[14] The curriculum of Mexican schools correlated with the identification of the language barrier as the internal enemy arrayed against America's basic institutions.

Language, however, encapsulated a complex pedagogical equation for the education of Mexican children.

Gender figured prominently. Females were considered the social "gene" that, when properly socialized, could transform Mexican colonias from islands of cultural degradation into solid, American enclaves in one generation. Towards this objective, Americanization classes for adult women and home economics for girls in school took center stage. Americanization teachers taught cooking, childrearing, housekeeping, thrift, and manners, and sponsored competitive projects like "Better Homes Week," during which women were urged to learn "acceptable" standards of housekeeping. Graduation ceremonies awarded diplomas to adult women able to speak a modicum of English. Schooling, however, did not have the interests of the women or of the community in mind.[15]

Beneath the educational surface, however, larger political issues were in command. Mexicans were alleged to harbor a culture that threatened not only to undermine prevailing norms, but also to create political mischief. The Americanization program in California, for example, initiated in 1915, targeted language because it was believed that all non-English-speaking sectors of the population held the potential to develop a class consciousness capable of evolving into radical, even communistic, organization and activities. In the Americanization agenda, more than ethnic rivalry was at stake; clear political objectives grounded the exercise.[16] Americanization, fundamental to the agenda of the segregated school, served as a preventive measure that promised the elimination of cultural disintegration and political disaster that loomed within the Mexican psyche.

The Bell Curve, 1920s Style

Justification of the selection of Mexican children for special education experiences went beyond culture to include genetic "stock." No other pedagogical device controlled classroom practice and curriculum as did the IQ test. Segregation may have accomplished the removal of Mexican children from the "normal" class, but it was the concept of intelligence and its operational contrivance, the IQ test, that "scientifically" legitimized and guaranteed unequal outcomes. Moreover, prevalent psychological theory laid the cultural "backwardness" of the Mexican immigrant community on the genetic material from which they descended.

The foremost psychologists and educators of the period, particularly in the 1920s, held that nature behaved in a most undemocratic fashion, bestowing intellectual abilities unequally. An ancillary premise of intelligence theory was that culture reflected intelligence; thus, a superior stock created a superior culture. Furthermore, a device called the IQ test could measure with great accuracy the mental variations among any population. The specter of race hovered over intelligence testing research that sought to define exactly how nature divvied up shares of intelligence. A politically saturated science that found nature's unfortunates—those endowed with degrees of intelligence be-

low the "norm"—predominated. If the theoretical novelty had been confined there, perhaps the grosser consequences of the widespread segregation of Chicano children might have been avoided. But there were social implications in intelligence theory that affected the curriculum as well.

William James, Lewis Terman, Henry Goddard, E.L. Thorndike, and a host of social scientists who embraced the commonly accepted doctrine of the racial distribution of intelligence contended that social inequality, the division of labor, and the gross disparities in wealth and political power were passed from one generation to the next via the genes.[17] Moreover, only those with superior intelligence were capable of entering the professional occupations; the less intelligent were fitted for slots suitable to their level of mental ability in the lower quarters of the division of labor. Thus, class structure mirrored the distribution of intelligence, and neither conscious choice nor institutional practice molded the social order.

Schools across the nation rapidly adopted IQ testing and ignored all of its theoretical shortcomings and heavy-handed biases. Departments of psychological testing and research were instituted between 1910 and 1920 in the school systems of Los Angeles, El Paso, Phoenix, and San Antonio to survey the intellectual ability of students and to adjust individual school curricula to group averages. In classic doublespeak, they also embraced a new definition of democratic education; unequals could not be given the same curriculum nor expected to learn at the same pace. Differing intellectual abilities meant differing educational experiences, and therefore unequal outcomes. Educators concluded that such results were inevitable when understood in the context of prevailing theories that identified the "low-mentality" individual with low achievement (and the working class).

The principal of a Southern California school repeated the message broadcast during the 1920s by many experts when he wrote that "stupid parents are apt to have stupid children." Sensing that a critic might suggest environment as a factor, he flatly denied the environment thesis, contending that environment "never made a stupid child intelligent." So it was not unexpected that, as one Los Angeles supervisor put it, "nothing is so unequal as the equal treatment of unequals."[18] The principal at an all-Mexican school joined the broadening denunciation of the notion of equality: "The doctrine that 'all men are born free and equal' applies to man's political equality . . . In no way can this idea of equality be applied to intellectual endowment."[19] Democratizing the schools mandated an internally differentiated schooling process accommodated to the intellectual diversity contained within any student universe. An entirely new lexicon gained footing in school administrative offices, as terms like "gifted," "bright," superior," "average," "subnormal," "dull," "moron," "low grade moron," "borderline moron," "low mentality," and "feebleminded" were used to describe the children under their charge. Accordingly, a twentieth-century democratic education required unequals to be prepared differently for the inevitable reality that faced them in later life. Effective schools trained the diverse pool of children to assume the kinds of occupations that their inherited intelligence presaged. Under such a charge, school systems became training grounds not only for the superiors, but also for the slow learners and the feebleminded.

But much more was at stake. Adherents of IQ theory postulated an antidemocratic corollary: nature destined intellectual superiors to occupy positions of political power as well. The genetically less well endowed required government by their genetic superiors. Those whom nature allocated substantially fewer mental abilities required a tailored education administered by a paternal state that trained (recruited?) manual labor for employment possibilities in the Southwest's burgeoning enterprises. Although the widespread use of IQ tests appeared to have particular bearing upon Mexican children in the region, we should not ignore the national scope of the testing movement. Racialized policies enforcing the use of testing, segregation, and tracking affected children across the United States.

In segregating Mexican children, unequal education justified by a theory of inborn racial traits (and therefore inborn cultural traits) assumed center stage in the nation's state-run schools. Racial inequality—the foundation for and consequence of widespread pedagogical practices—rested on the near religious acceptance and universal application of the intelligence test. But racially inspired educational theory and practice, buttressed by scientific claims, reflected existing social relations and the division of labor in the production of commodities and sought to maintain them over generations. Moreover, dominant political and economic classes tethered those discourses and schooling practices to their interests.

Dozens of research projects simulated the scientific racism of Lewis Terman at Stanford. They were set up to identify the intellectual level of Mexican children. Over nine thousand Mexicans served as research subjects for nearly forty intelligence studies between 1915 and 1950. In survey after survey, a dismal conclusion was reached. Mexican children consistently scored lower than the norm for Anglo-American children, that mythical average 1.00. And even when the language "handicap" was controlled for, the test results hardly varied. Scores clustered around the .90 range in study after study. According to investigations in Los Angeles completed during the 1920s, about 47 percent of Mexican children scored below the .90 level, and only 22 percent scored at the normal step (a figure that paralleled general studies carried out on Mexican children by a host of psychologists). In 1932, the statistician for the Los Angeles district offered her reasons for the poor performance of Mexican children: "There is some selection in the type of Mexican family who comes to Los Angeles. Most of the children represented in the group belong to the laboring class."[20]

A 1928 investigation in California concluded that Mexican children scored on average at .86 and that 60 percent scored in the nonacademically inclined range.[21] At Belvedere Junior High in Los Angeles, with a student population that was 50 percent Mexican, 55 percent of all students scored below .90. At Lafayette Junior High School, not far from Belvedere, over half of all Mexican students were channeled into the nonacademic group. Statistics gathered for 1929 by the Los Angeles School District reported that the majority of "mentally retarded children" came from districts with the largest number of immigrants: the reverse was true for the "children of superior mentality," who were found "most frequently in the Normal Type school" or neighborhood.[22]

Many educationists and policymakers thought like the vice-principal of an urban elementary school that enrolled only "low mentality" children. He wrote that the "pupil of low intelligence" was prone to "failure, tardiness, lying, cheating, truancy." He confidently asserted that "inheritance" explained the problem.[23] California State Superintendent of Public Instruction William J. Cooper offered similar advice to the teachers under his supervision. His 1927 public policy statements on the subject added little to contemporary views of the relationship of biology and social conditions, but they demonstrate the confidence in such theoretical discourse. Like his contemporaries, Cooper contended that "we build on a biological foundation. We cannot make a black child white, a deaf child hear, a blind baby see, nor can we create a genius from a child whose ancestors endowed him with a defective brain. Within the limits set by heredity we can do much." He then recommended that "teachers should study biology."[24]

These theoretical premises and racialized cultural stereotypes had important bearing on teacher training during the period under study. In some cases, administrators were trained by leading authorities in the field of intelligence psychology. Dr. Frances Gaw, psychologist with the Los Angeles City Schools' Division of Psychology and Educational Research, earned her doctorate under Cyril Burt at the University of London. The division's director, Elizabeth Sullivan, and the agency's statistician, Alice McAnulty, were tutored by Lewis Terman at Stanford University. The clinician in charge of social service, Dorothy Henry, completed her master's degree under E.L. Thorndike at Columbia.

Of course, not all had the opportunity to study under the masters; the next best thing was to read their books. Teachers' colleges commonly used texts by leading psychological and pedagogical authorities of the day. Works by eugenicist Lathrop Stoddard and psychologists Lewis Terman and E.L. Thorndike, together with a host of others, found their way into course reading lists. Included in the lists one finds titles relating to Mexico and interpretations of Mexican culture from the perspective of these same social scientists and like-minded visitors to Mexico. Common reference texts emerged from the first cohort of scholars dabbling in Mexico, later known as Latin Amercanists, which included Wallace Thompson (*The Mexican Mind*) and Edward A. Ross (*Social Revolution in Mexico*), both of whom disparaged all things Mexican, and the paternalistic and romanticized versions of Stuart Chase, Carleton Beals, Frank Tannenbaum, and Ernest Gruening, who found things of value in the Indian background and culture of Mexico. Neither the romanticized nor the racially inspired readings held any promise for enabling students to better understand Mexico and the Mexican immigrant. Both viewpoints essentially bolstered the belief in a fundamental distinction between Mexican and Anglo-American, a belief that corresponded with U.S. foreign policy in the region and provided the theoretical beginning point in the segregationist policy. One need read only a few of the dozens of master's theses on the education of Mexican children written by budding school administrators to appreciate their blind faith in the conventional pathway elaborated by the acknowledged experts.[25]

The scientific method held such sway over the education corps that the common contention that Mexican children, and the entire Mexican community, for that matter, comprised inferior genetic material appeared incontrovertible. In step with learned opinion, superintendents authoritatively cautioned principals, counselors, and teachers that the Mexican child could expect to achieve only two-thirds of the educational potential of the Anglo-American child. El Paso, Los Angeles, San Antonio, and Phoenix, like many smaller rural districts, adjusted their curriculum to the range of intelligence of the student body. All children who scored between .50 and .90 were considered "nonacademic types" who could excel with their hands but not their minds, fine material for manual labor but not the "book learning" type. In Los Angeles, the research and testing arm of the district, the Division of Psychology and Educational Research, found that at least half of all Mexican children fell into the slow-learning to feeble-minded categories and were ideal material for nonacademic course work "suited to their needs." And since the remaining half still fell below the norm, it was an easy solution to the Mexican problem to design a curriculum that revolved around below-average learners. School administrators believed that the problem of the slow learner was not that he or she learned at a slower pace, but that his or her capacity to learn limited the rate of curriculum that could be adequately mastered.

Industrial Education[26]

As segregated schools matured into the convention, a policy enforced by counselors armed with IQ tests affirmed that slow learners were quite capable of mastering the world of manual, nonacademic education; college-level preparation could never be considered for the slow learner. This conclusion became the bedrock of the education of Mexican children. In relation to Mexican children, school officials resolved that the curriculum would comprise

heavy doses of industrial education, and would derive in part from counselor surveys of the group's intelligence, the kinds of occupations open to Mexicans in the local area, and the cultural qualities attached to Mexicans.

Segregated schools resembled industrial schools, and in some districts these were (rightly) referred to as the "industrial school." These schools should not be confused with trade schools, however. Trade schools stipulated that applicants score at the norm on the intelligence test; in the trade classes of the Mexican schools, it was assumed that such courses were admirably suited to the intelligence and temperament of Mexican children. On the basis of scores on any intelligence test then in use, Mexican children found themselves placed in slow-learner tracks in numbers far out of proportion to their population. For boys, course work often included body shop, agriculture, basket weaving, upholstery, and animal husbandry. Girls learned to keep a neat house, care for children, serve as a domestic servant, keep house for an employer, and sewing and needlework.

In 1923, the copper mining enclave of Miami, Arizona, opened a school for the children of Mexican miners that was equipped "with a view to emphasizing industrial and homemaking courses for these children." Zavala Mexican School in Austin, Texas, paralleled Miami's plan; the school represented the "only elementary school in Austin . . . equipped with an industrial arts shop and home economics laboratory." Sidney Lanier Junior High School in San Antonio, Texas, attended exclusively by Mexican students, offered "special courses, flexible programs, home making, and industrial activities" based on courses in "sewing, cooking and art work for the girls; machine shop practice, auto repair, auto painting, top making, sheet metal work, plain bench and cabinet work in wood and a department in which type setting and job printing are taught to boys."[27] These examples from the 1920s and 1930s demonstrate the assumption that two goals were met simultaneously by industrial education: the cultural and intellectual needs of the Mexican community and the wider labor requirements of employers were satisfied in a single curriculum.

The assumption that Mexican children inevitably gravitated toward employment similar, if not identical, to that of their parents moved districts to begin the vocational experience in the early grades. The Arizona State Department of Education implemented early vocational curriculum because it found that "under present conditions" most Mexican children would enter unskilled or semiskilled positions, regardless of schooling; that being the case, vocational education was "to be introduced early and homemaking should be an important part of the elementary course for both boys and girls." One researcher who investigated the curriculum in Mexican schools throughout the Southwest found that the "sentiment of many teachers of Mexican children was known to favor an early introduction in the grades of these subjects [industrial education] for Mexicans."[28]

The degree and form of segregation did not end there, however. Vocational tracks absorbed the majority of children, but not all who were funneled into such classes attended the same course level. Some were judged to have an even lower mental ability than the majority of Mexican children and required a special vocational curriculum. An excessively large number of these children scored below .70, in the feeble-minded category. In Los Angeles, this group required a special education separate from their peers, which created a second level of segregation that funneled them en masse into schooling for the "mentally handicapped" (later "educationally mentally retarded") in sites named development centers and development rooms. These "less-capable" students could be trained for basic types of employment as unskilled and low-paid factory workers and workers in restaurants, hotels, laundries, private homes, agriculture, shoe-shine parlors, and the like. In 1929, some twenty-eight hundred children were assigned to ten development centers and thirty development rooms, located largely in working-class sections of the city, a substantial distance in terms of space and curriculum from the "normal" schools in Los Angeles. According to district reports, space in the centers and rooms accommodated only one-quarter of the "subnormals": many more waited for a transfer out of the normal classes.

By 1930, approximately one-fourth of the development schools and rooms were located in or near Los Angeles's Mexican colonia. One supervisor noted that "the subnormal child is apt to come from a low type home. . . . Often he comes from a foreign home," and thus the majority of recruits for the development centers and rooms attended near their neighborhoods.[29] By 1940 the population at these centers had increased to about five thousand, and throughout the era Mexican children composed approximately a quarter of the enrollees. As late as the 1960s, Chicano children still comprised one-quarter of students in the educationally mentally retarded classes, double their proportion of the school population.[30]

The Los Angeles City Schools, like most school districts administering Mexican schools, implemented a complex plan to adjust the subnormal child to the area's economic enterprises. District publications announced that at the Coronel Center, attended largely by Mexican children, courses were offered in "auto shop, tin shop, wood shop, paint shop, bakery, cookery, laundry work, power machine sewing, electric stitching, millinery, dressmaking, personal hygiene (including shampooing and manicuring), nursery maid training, cafeteria work, paper favor work, and trade ethics."[31] Every effort was made to correlate trade training with language instruction. Spelling and vocabulary words were selected from a list relating to words used in auto shops, laundries, cafeterias, and garment factories. Boys and girls received training suitable to their gender; for girls, employment in garment factories, laundries, bakeries, domestic service, and restaurants was determined adequate to their mental capacity. Beauty shop classes did not aim to prepare girls to become beauticians, but taught them grooming and personal hygiene— "to know how to keep themselves neat and clean"—which would make them more employable in their eventual search for work. Some girls were selected for training for day nursery work, not to care for children but to do the "unskilled tasks of cleaning, scrubbing, polishing, washing the dishes, etc." Particular emphasis was placed on laundry work for girls, training that, unlike beauty shop courses, had specific occupational objectives. The director of the elementary development centers reported in the 1929 *Yearbook* of the Division of Psychology and Educational Research that "several employers have told us that a dull girl makes a very much better operator on a mangle than does a normal girl. The job is purely routine and is irksome to persons of average intelligence, while subnormals seem to get actual satisfaction out of such a task. Fitting the person to the job reduces the turn over in industry and is, of course, desirable from an economic point of view."[32] Surrounded by agricultural fields, Los Angeles served as a harbor for many farmworkers, who migrated during some portion of the year. No surprisingly, enrollment in the development centers rose and fell with the harvests. According to a district publication:

> Enrollment in the Development classes is far from constant. The children enter in late Fall, due to the seasonal employment in the countryside, where the children and their parents are employed picking fruits and nuts. The enrollment reaches the peak in the Spring when many centers and Rooms have to maintain waiting lists. The month of June usually brings an appreciable exodus when the children and their parents go out into the fields to harvest the onion crop.[33]

While IQ tests appeared to wear the mantel of infallibility, not all choices in the strict vocational regimen for Mexican children were based on testing. Some elements of Mexican culture were thought to be superior, and many a smiling educator theorized that these innate abilities redeemed Mexicans and demonstrated that not all was lost. It was believed that Mexicans enjoyed an artisanal dexterity that could turn almost anything into a work of art. Unfettered by the frenzied materialism of industrial society, Mexicans supposedly harbored a love of music, poetry, and philosophy. They did have something to offer, claimed many teachers, but nothing that was essential or of primary importance in the schooling enterprise. Moreover, in asserting that Mexicans were naturally gifted in handwork, were happy and carefree, if rather indolent despite (or perhaps because of) their poverty, educators offered more reasons for segregation and nonacademic schooling for Mexican children.

We should not be surprised that prevailing opinion among educators and employers considered Mexicans, as a group, culturally and genetically destined to perform manual labor. In 1932, the Texas Department of Education urged teachers to gauge the occupational future of Mexican children and to measure the curriculum against the findings. One Texas teacher's method was selected as a good example of an effective and appropriate approach for teaching Mexican children. In her English-language instruction, she placed "special emphasis upon the words the child will use in his work-a-day life as a tiller of the soil."[34] Later in the decade, the California State Board of Education *Bulletin* made a similar recommendation when it warned that growth in the minority population "would seem to present a problem of which educators must take cognizance, that a minority group . . . may receive appropriate instruction, *especially in reference to their probable vocations*" (emphasis added).[35] Whether by way of the IQ test or by determining "probable vocations," industrial education anchored the curriculum in Mexican schools across the Southwest. Not only did industrial course work follow the child from elementary school to junior high, but for the small minority fortunate enough to graduate from the eighth grade and enter secondary school, it also followed them. As a consequence, many Mexican students experienced at least twelve years of manual training linked with heavy doses of Americanization.

Exclusion and the Migratory Child

Not all Mexican children were fortunate enough to attend school. Total and partial exclusion, a third level of segregation, affected Mexican children, principally in rural areas where migrant family labor predominated. In these cases, the opportunities for schooling were rare because the family relied on children's labor for income. In districts that depended heavily on the labor of the family, as in the cotton-growing region of Texas, the sugar beet fields of Colorado, and the farming areas of some California counties, school boards in effect hung signs on schoolhouse doors to warn "No Migrant Children Allowed." One study of Hidalgo County, Texas, reported a widespread "attitude that school attendance should not be allowed to interfere with the supply of cheap farm labor." A Texas school superintendent candidly justified the practice: "Most of our Mexicans are of the lower class. They transplant onions, harvest them, etc. The less they know about everything else the better contented they are. You have undoubtedly heard that ignorance is bliss; it seems that it is so when one has to transplant onions."[36] Economist Paul S. Taylor noted that in Dimmit County, Texas, not "more than 25 percent of the Mexican scholastics, i.e., children aged 7 to 17 inclusive" were enrolled in school and that "the average number in attendance [was] undoubtedly less."[37] In 1938, a study found that in Crystal City, Texas, "the average 18 year old [Mexican] youth has not completed the third grade of school." Carey McWilliams's observation that "so far as migratory children are concerned, the compulsory school attendance laws might just

as well never have been enacted" came as no surprise to those in the Southwest's agricultural belts.[38] A Texas district superintendent said as much when he testified that "the compulsory school attendance law is a dead letter—there is no effort to enforce it. Nobody cares."[39] In Texas, as late as 1945, only half of all Mexican school-age children actually attended any school, although school districts received state funds for the nonattending group. In short, Anglo-American children and corporate growers benefited from the nonenforcement of attendance laws in relation to Mexican children; meanwhile, thousands of children were denied their basic Constitutional right to equal protection of the laws.

It was not uncommon for a school district to allow migrant children into segregated schools, but this did not imply an invariable full school day. School hours, in another variation on the exclusion policy, were shortened to accommodate family labor needs during harvests. For the rural Mexican child, admission policies and the length of the school day were determined by the corporate agricultural interests. Education for the Mexican child under these conditions was a rare privilege. Obstacles to their education generated by growers shaped public policy and forced them into a kind of "hands-on" vocational education in the fields alongside their parents. The 1924 biennial report of California's superintendent for public instruction lauded the value of the special dispensation for migrant children: "There should be an adjusted school day beginning not later than the field work. This provides for the whole family leaving the camp at the same time, the adults going to the field and the children to school. . . . It also means that the school day is over when the mid-day meal is ready. It provides also that the children may work in the afternoon."[40] In school districts across Southern California, even in districts in Los Angeles County, schedules were modified throughout the 1920s to meet the demands of growers for the cheapest of all labor, that of children. County Superintendent of Schools John R. Hunt advised that the absence of Mexican children during the harvests was handled through "special migratory classes in each district whenever necessary." He continued:

> Harvesting of [walnuts] is peculiarly adapted to the Mexican family. . . . It provides them with a fine vacation, a camping experience under ideal conditions. . . . The walnut ranchers are particularly anxious to have the Mexican family do this work because of their adaptability [and because their availability] provides the rancher with the cheapest method of harvesting the crop. No other kind of labor could possibly be secured that could compete in price, and so it is an economic factor that the rancher faces.[41]

Hunt noted that students were bused to school at 8:00 a.m. and returned at noon in time to go to work in the orchards.

Despite admission into flexibly scheduled schools, the educational success of thousands of children from the migratory camps and rural colonias was affected by severe nutritional and health problems. A Depression-era study of California's migrant labor camps reported miserable wages, poor housing, irregular employment, malnourishment, and "children . . . growing up without an opportunity for normal education and recreation. . . . Medical care which they need is unavailable to them."[42] A report by the National Child Labor Committee commented that migratory "children are apt to have no schooling at all, or schooling of so poor a character and given under such adverse circumstances that it can not be effective, and the children are badly retarded."[43] Public officials, like the growers, could wash their hands of responsibility because, presumably, migrant children needed no formal preparation for the arduous agricultural tasks they would assume as adults. And if there were any doubts, IQ scores and "expert" opinion could be called upon in support of educational policy.

Teachers and Physical Resources

Despite the widely held contention that the Mexican school was but a temporary measure to ensure equality of opportunity, vast differences divided these schools from those attended by Anglo-American children. Teachers assigned to Mexican schools bore the stigma of the social inferiority attached to the school. Beginning teachers, older teachers, or poor teachers were commonly placed in Mexican schools. For novice teachers, their initiation into the profession required some experience before promotion "up" to a nonsegregated school. In Los Angeles, young graduates from teachers' colleges could expect to be assigned to the less-desirable sections of the city; if they proved competent, a spot somewhere in the better part of the city would be their reward. The Los Angeles assistant superintendent of assignments casually remarked in 1928 that teachers should expect a period of breaking in to demonstrate worthiness for assignment to one of the popular schools: "After two years of probation in the valley or harbor districts, the teacher transfers to the city proper. It is usually necessary to place her in the foreign, semi-foreign, or less convenient schools. After a few more years of satisfactory service, she may be placed in the more popular districts."[44] The all-Mexican Miguel Hidalgo School in Brawley, California, in the fertile Imperial Valley, rotated teachers every three years. One researcher wrote that "the best teachers from the Mexican school are 'promoted' to the American school in order to provide experienced teachers there." In 1935, for example, thirty teachers taught 1,551 students, over fifty per class, at Miguel Hidalgo, but only twenty-two classrooms were available. Seasonal harvests caused some classes to expand overnight to as many as eighty students.[45]

Ambition, or status consciousness, motivated teachers to leave the Mexican schools. Administrators regularly evaluated the teaching force by school assignment and level of classes taught. Teachers at Mexican schools were considered less qualified, found little respect from their peers across town, and earned considerably less for their efforts. The best teachers were assigned to the "best" schools and taught the "bright" students. Teachers of the superior or gifted classes not only earned the greatest respect, but also were rewarded with higher salaries.

Mexican school practice eventually became tradition, ingrained in a conventional wisdom that few educators challenged. The most visible signs of educational policy were found in the quality of the physical resources available to Mexican children compared to those of the Anglo-American child. Overcrowded, poorly designed and constructed buildings, insufficient recreational space, used and repaired furniture, and books handed down from the Anglo schools plagued the Mexican schools.

In conducting research for his master's thesis, Carlos Calderón studied a district in the Lower Rio Grande Valley of Texas in 1950 to gauge the differences between a Mexican school and an Anglo school. The distinctions stood out boldly. He found the pupil-to-teacher ratio to average 32 to 1 in the Anglo schools, but 47 to 1 in Mexican schools. In eight cases a Mexican classroom held over fifty pupils, and Calderón reported that one class held seventy pupils. Nearly five hundred Mexican children were taught in inferior facilities—old frame buildings that had once served as army barracks and were badly in need of paint and repair. Classrooms were illuminated by a single light bulb, or perhaps two, and ventilated by a screen door and two transom windows. A small wooden shack housed an outdoor restroom finished with a rough cement floor and two toilets without stalls. The boys and girls used identical back-to-back restroom facilities. Drinking fountains were outdoors and unprotected for use in inclement weather. Neither medical facilities nor a cafeteria was available. Calderón then described the school for the Anglo-American community: "a modern brick structure with rest rooms, drinking fountains, book rooms, principal's office and teacher's lounge." Restrooms were finished with tile floors and six toilet stalls with doors, and the school had an indoor water cooler. The only cafeteria in the district served the Anglo school.[46]

The investigations of reformer George J. Sánchez revealed that in district after district this pattern was repeated.[47] Mexican schools were inferior in every respect, from teachers to curriculum to physical plant. Board of education policies ensured that the inequalities would remain, despite pleas for a larger share of the budget. These pleas went unheard. The principal at both La Jolla elementary and junior high in Southern California (located on the same grounds) recalled:

They moved all the old buildings, all the old wooden shacks that they could move in and although we did get a few of the portable bungalows. . . . some of the other schools had them too, but not to the extent that we had them. And if they got rid of the furniture it was shipped down to us. After it didn't look good in the Anglo school, they would ship it down and we had no other say than to take what we were given. I was never glad to have it but we had to use it anyway.[48]

The board of education in La Jolla accepted the common belief that Mexican children were not capable of high school work and so curtailed instruction for them at tenth grade. The La Jolla school was considered a terminal school.

Struggles to Desegregate the Mexican Schools

If oppression is never permanent, it is only so because the victims rise up against their oppressors, and in the Southwest the Mexican community engaged in a political struggle to dismantle segregation. Despite segregation, the educational institution held a valued place within the Mexican communities, which manifested itself as a strong belief in the power of education as a means for social betterment. Bitterness arose from within the community. One observer noted, in relation to Brawley's Miguel Hidalgo School, that "Mexicans resent the crowded condition of the school, the double session, and the dearth of conveniences." A teacher commented that parents and children understood the underlying racial motives of the board of education: "Many times . . . our youngsters would say to me 'The reason they do it is because we're Mexicans.' The parents felt that way too."[49]

Formal assaults came from organizations and community leaders. In Texas, the League of United Latin American Citizens battled long for school reform and desegregation. One member expressed a sentiment shared by many in the organization in proclaiming that "WE MUST BATTLE SEGREGATION BECAUSE OF RACE PREJUDICES!"[50] George I. Sánchez and labor leader Ernesto Galarza criticized segregation throughout the 1930s and 1940s, calling the practice arbitrary, capricious, and racially motivated. Sánchez's trenchant criticisms expressed the community's growing sentiment for reviewing the injustice of segregation. In an unprecedented legal action, incensed Mexican parents in Lemon Grove, California, boycotted their school in 1930 before suing the board of education in the first successful desegregation case in the nation's history.[51] Although the case had only local impact, the rebellion augured the resistance to come in the 1940s.

Despite the post-1920s transition to a culture-based interpretation of IQ, the curriculum remained as before; little changed in administrative procedure. The consequences of a nonhereditary theoretical basis for IQ proved meager for the Mexican community. Through the late 1930s and into the 1940s, the culture of the community was still used to explain the "Mexican problem." Gradually a philosophy, freed from scientific race theory, took shape. In the new pedagogical environment, the culture of the Mexican community was defined as the cause of the tangle of pathologies that were alleged to plague it. It was believed that nothing could be gained until there was a transformation, either coerced or voluntary, from Mexican cultural standards to American standards. Nothing appeared to indicate that segregated schooling required modification, and it remained the prescription of choice for "remedying" Mexican culture.

It is within this atmosphere that the Mexican American community engaged in its civil rights struggles of the 1940s to desegregate schools. The Mexican community joined a national political struggle to force the democratization of the nation's schools. The first round of the conflict that eventually led to the historic *Méndez v. Westminster*[52] case occurred in 1943 in Santa Ana, California, the county seat of Orange County. The school board instituted segregated classes in 1913 and established the first Mexican school in 1919. Parents at the time opposed the move and appealed to the board, but without success. For two generations, the board, with few exceptions, directed Mexican children to attend one of three segregated schools. Throughout the county, fifteen Mexican schools were maintained and attended by nearly five thousand children. Chafing under decades of segregation, several Santa Ana parents appeared before the board of education in 1943 and vociferously demanded the right for their children to attend the school of their choice. An unbending board, upset at the strident tones of petitioners, refused.

Officials were negotiating with the politically aware second generation, however, a generation more cognizant of the injustices and harm generated by segregation. Many members of that generation had served in the armed forces during the Second World War, and many had relatives who had served. Returning veterans had tasted equality in the armed forces and were restive under the segregationist codes now governing their conduct. Leaders began to emerge and organize to challenge segregation. In Orange County, veterans founded the Latin American Organization and resolved to reform schools to serve the needs of the Mexican community. Meanwhile, parents joined the movement throughout the county.

In rural Westminster, Gonzalo and Felicitas Méndez, who had only recently moved into the area, sent their youngsters to the closest elementary school. Unknown to them, the school restricted admission to Anglos. When school officials discovered the nationality of the Méndez children, they were refused admission. Unfazed, the Méndezes took an unheard-of step and refused to send their children to the segregated school and protested to the board. The board recommended a "special admission" for the Méndezes. The Mexican parents, calling the special admission a slap in the face, refused the board's offer and organized a boycott of all parents until all children were allowed to enroll in the school of their choice. Mrs. Méndez later recalled that she and her husband organized the boycott because they got "tired of being pushed around." That sentiment became more widespread.[53]

In Garden Grove, Ruth and Cruz Barrios defied the board, and Santa Ana parents had already confronted the board in 1943. The stage was set when, in 1945, a class action lawsuit filed by five parents on behalf of five thousand children was filed in federal court to demand the desegregation of the county's schools. Assisted by the newly formed Santa Ana chapter of the League of Latin American Citizens, the plaintiffs argued that the Fourteenth Amendment's equal protection clause had been violated, as there were no laws enabling the segregation of Mexican children. The defendants answered that segregation in this case passed legal muster under the *Plessy*[54] doctrine, that is, separate but equal, and that schools for Mexican children were as good as those for Anglo children. Furthermore, argued the defendants, Mexican children required special courses in Americanization, particularly English, to prepare them for the higher grades, and thus segregation involved strictly educational objectives.

In February 1946, U.S. District Court Judge Paul L. McCormick ruled that the school districts were guilty of violating the Fourteenth Amendment in forcing Mexican children to attend segregated schools. Judge McCormick found that a "paramount requisite in the American system of public education is social equality. It must be open to all children by unified school association regardless of lineage."[55] The judge clearly broke with *Plessy* by maintaining that separation implied inferiority, and that inferiority was obtained through arbitrary administrative practices. He wrote that the country's practices "foster[ed] antagonism in the children and [suggested] inferiority among them where none exist[ed]."[56] The county counsel appealed to the U.S. Circuit Court of Appeals, but the appeals judges upheld the lower court's ruling. The county was ordered to begin the process of dismantling segregation in the fall of 1948.

The class action suit, known by the legal title *Méndez v. Westminster*, reverberated throughout the nation, particularly in the Southwest, and led to successful challenges in Arizona and Texas. Legal analysts quickly focused on the case. An article in the *Columbia Law Review* argued that the case strongly suggested that the *Plessy* doctrine might be in for a constitutional test. The author noted that the "courts in the [*Méndez*] case breaks sharply with this approach and finds that the Fourteenth Amendment requires 'social equality' rather than 'equal facilities.'" A piece in the *Yale Law Journal* affirmed that the Méndez decision "questioned the basic assumption of the Plessy Doctrine. . . . A dual school system even if 'equal facilities' were provided does imply social inferiority."[57]

Civil rights activists understood the significance of *Méndez*. The NAACP legal defense team of Thurgood Marshall and Robert C. Carter followed the case closely and filed amicus curiae briefs during the appeals process. According to Carter, the briefs were a "dry run for the future" and contained every one of the key arguments later used in the *Brown v. Board of Education* case (which followed *Méndez* by eight years). All the documents filed by the plaintiffs' lawyer were handed over to Marshall and Carter, who read them with great interest. Clearly, the struggle to desegregate the United States has many points of origin, but one that we must not ignore is the *Méndez* case of 1947.

Many districts, particularly in rural areas, ignored the decision, and even districts that desegregated maintained many discriminatory practices. Segregation reappeared in the form of gerrymandered neighborhood school districts, and schools with a majority of Chicano students increased notably. Strong reliance on IQ testing, heavy tracking into industrial education, Americanization, English immersion, and the generally negative perception of Mexican culture continued to guide education. Continuity and change marked the transition from the era of the Mexican school to the era of integration shaped by the culture concept. Continuity, however, maintained the dominant position.

Notes

1. Charles C. Teague, *Fifty Years a Rancher* (Los Angeles: Ward Ritchie Press, 1944), p. 143.
2. Gilbert G. González, *Labor and Community: Mexican Citrus Worker Villages in a Southern California County* (Urban: University of Illinois Press, 1994), p. 28.
3. Susan B. Dorsey, "Problems of the Los Angeles School Board," *Los Angeles City Schools Journal*, 6 (1923), 59.
4. See Charles Clifford Carpenter, "Segregation vs. Non-Segregation of the Mexican Student," Master's thesis, University of Southern California, 1935; see also Gilbert G. González, "Educational Reform in Los Angeles and Its Effect Upon the Mexican Community. 1990–1930." *Explorations in Ethnic Studies*, 1, No 2 (1978), 5–26.
5. Edward A. Ross, *Social Control: A Survey of the Foundations of Order* (New York: MacMillan, 1912,) p. 2; also, Charles Horton Cooley, *Social Process* (New York: Scribners, 1918).
6. See Samuel Bowles, "Unequal Education and the Reproduction of the Social Division of Labor," in *Schooling in a Corporate Society*, ed. Martin Carnoy (New York: David McKay, 1972), pp. 36–64; see also, Raymond E. Callahan, *Education and the Cult of Efficiency* (Chicago: University of Chicago Press, 1962); also, David Nasaw, *Schooled to Order: A Social History of Public Schooling in the United States* (New York: Oxford University Press, 1981).
7. In the early twentieth century the term "efficient" meant "scientific management," that is, Taylorisation in all spheres of society, the controlled utilization of all available resources, human and physical, for social and economic "uplift" or progress toward a harmonious society. In practice, efficiency meant that schools (and society) were to be managed by the same principles governing the large-scale business enterprise and employ the conveyorbelt system used in factories for processing students through their courses. Further, immigrants were a drag upon progress until Americanized and able to integrate into the bureaucratic social system. In this context, labor strikes were "inefficient" because they prevented the full and unfettered control of labor power in the production of commodities, and also because strikes "balkanized" society into classes, a great fear among adherents of efficiency.
8. See, for example, Samuel Bowles and Herbert Gintis, *Schooling in Capitalist America* (New York: Basic Books, 1976): see also,

Martin Carnoy, *Education as Cultural Imperialism* (New York: David McKay, 1974).

9. Gilbert G. González, *Chicano Education in the Era of Segregation* (Philadelphia: Balch Institute, 1990), p. 37

10. H.F. Bradford, "The Mexican Child in our American Schools," *Arizona Teacher Parent*, 27 (March 1939), 199.

11. Jessie Hayden, "The La Habra Experiment," Master's thesis, Claremont College, 1934.

12. Leonard John Vandenburgh, "The Mexican Problem in the Schools," *Los Angeles School Journal*, 11, No. 34 (1928), 15.

13. Susan B. Dorsey, "Mrs. Pierce and Mrs. Dorsey Discuss Matters Before the Principals Club," *Los Angeles School Journal*, 6, No. 25 (1925), 59.

14. González, *Labor and Community*, p. 101.

15. See Gilbert G. González, "The Americanization of Mexican Women and Family During the Era of De Jure Segregation," in *Ethnic and Gender Boundaries in the United States: Studies of Asian, Black, Mexican, and Native Americans*, ed. Sucheng Chan (Lewiston, NY: Edwin Mellon Press, 1989). pp. 55–79.

16. See González, *Labor and Community*, pp. 127–129.

17. See Gilbert G. González, "The Historical Development of the Concept Intelligence," *Review of Radical Political Economy*, 11, No. 2 (1979), 44–54.

18. See González, *Labor and Community*, pp. 127–129.

19. George K. Miller, "Birds of a Feather," *Los Angeles School Journal*, 9, No. 24 (1926), 17.

20. Ellen Alice McAnulty, "Achievement and Intelligence Test Results for Mexican Children Attending Los Angeles City Schools," *Los Angeles Educational Research Bulletin*, 11, No. 7 (1932), 89.

21. See Merton Hill, *The Development of an Americanization Program* (Ontario, CA: Board of Trustees of the Chaffey Union High School District and the Chaffey Junior College, 1928), p. 110.

22. Alma Leonhardy, "Slow-Learning Groups in High Schools," in *Third Yearbook*, ed. Los Angeles City School District (Los Angeles: Los Angeles City Schools, Division of Psychology and Educational Research, 1929), pp. 187–188.

23. Joseph M. Sniffen, "The Senior High School Problem Boy," *Los Angeles School Journal*, 11, No. 32 (1928), 14.

24. William John Cooper, "Character Education," *Los Angeles School Journal*, 10, No. 26 (1927), 18.

25. This observation is based on a selected number of master's theses written by students at the University of Southern California. I used the bibliographies to gauge the typical readings covered in the course work. In all the examples consulted, conventional distortions of Mexico, Mexican culture, and immigrants permeated the works. Teacher college training programs embraced and promulgated the scientific racism of day.

26. In this article, the terms "vocational" and "industrial" are used interchangeably; however, in the materials used to prepare this article, "trade" was sometimes synonymous with the two. In Los Angeles, the district Trade School carried out training for skilled trades, whereas industrial or vocational course work implied an unskilled or semi-skilled training curriculum. The distinctions were not always consistent. In relation to Mexican children, all job-oriented curriculum, whether termed trade, vocational, or industrial, meant training for the lower skilled categories of the work force.

27. González, *Chicano Education*, p. 87.

28. González, *Chicano Education*, pp. 87, 89.

29. Mary Florence Macredy, "The Mentally Handicapped Child for Wage-Earning and Citizenship," *Los Angeles Educational Research Bulletin*, 9, No. 6 (1930), 6.

30. James Vásquez, "Measurement of Intelligence and Language Differences," *Aztlán*, 3, No. 1 (1973), 155.

31. M. Frances Martin, "Development Centers and Rooms," *Third Yearbook*, ed. Los Angeles City School District (Los Angeles: Los An-

geles City School District, Division of Psychology and Educational Research, 1929), pp. 84–85.

32. Martin, "Development Centers and Rooms," p. 87.

33. "Development Centers," *Fourth Yearbook*, ed. Los Angeles City School District (Los Angeles: Los Angeles City Schools, Department of Psychology and Educational Research, 1931), p. 116.

34. González, *Chicano Education*, p. 87.

35. González, *Chicano Education*, p. 88.

36. Herschel Manuel, *The Education of Mexican and Spanish-Speaking Children in Texas* (Austin: University of Texas Press, 1930), pp. 76–77.

37. Paul S. Taylor, "Mexican Labor in the United States: Dimmit County, Winter Garden District, South Texas," *University of California Publications*, 6, No. 5 (1930), 372.

38. Carey McWilliams, *Ill Fares the Land: Migrants and Migratory Labor in California* (New York: Barnes and Noble, 1942), p. 256.

39. McWilliams, *Ill Fares the Land*, p. 256.

40. State of California Superintendent of Public Instruction, *Biennial Report of the School Years Ending 30 June 1923 and 30 June 1924* (Sacramento: California State Printing Office, 1924), p. 35.

41. John R. Hunt, "The Problem of the Migratory School Child," *Los Angeles School Journal*, 12, No. 14 (1928), 24.

42. Bertha Underhill, "A Study of 132 Families in California Cotton Camps with Reference to Availability of Medical Care" (Sacramento: California Department of Social Welfare, Division of Child Welfare Services, 1936), p. 18.

43. González, *Chicano Education*, p. 105.

44. Jessie A. Tritt, "The Problem of Elementary Assignments," *Los Angeles School Journal*, 12, No. 1 (1928), 15.

45. Jay Newton Holliday, "A Study of Non-Attendance in Miguel Hidalgo School of Brawley, California," Master's thesis, University of Southern California, 1935.

46. Carlos Calderón, "The Education of Spanish-Speaking Children in Edcouch-Elsa, Texas," Master's thesis, University of Texas, 1950.

47. See, for example, Virgil E. Strickland and George I. Sánchez, "Spanish Name Spells Discrimination," *Nation's Schools*, 41 (1948), 22–24.

48. Interview with Chester Whitten by Robin Rodarte and Richard Gutiérrez in *Harvest: A Compilation of Taped Interviews on the Minority Peoples of Orange County*, ed. Priscilla Oaks and Wacira Gethalga (Fullerton: California State University, Fullerton, 1974).

49. González, *Labor and Community*, p. 104.

50. Guadalupe San Miguel, Jr., *"Let Them All Take Heed": Mexican Americans and the Campaign for Educational Equality in Texas, 1910–1981* (Austin: University of Texas Press, 1987), p. 76.

51. Superior Court of the State of California, County of San Diego. *Robert Alvarez v. the Board of Trustees of the Lemon Grove School District*. February 13, 1931.

52. *Méndez et al. v. Wesminster School District of Orange County et al.* Civil Action Number 4292. District Court S.D., California. Central Division February 18, 1946. 64 F. Supp. 544 (S.D. California, 1946), (C.C.A., 9th April, 1947).

53. María Newman, "Tired of Being Pushed Around," *Celebrate*, 3 (1989), 75.

54. *Plessy v. Ferguson*, 163 U.S. 537, 1896.

55. González, *Chicano Education*, p. 153; also, Gertrude Staughton, "In California's Orange County Mexican Americans Sue to End Bias in School Systems," *People's World*, 16 (March 1945), 324; Mary M. Peters, "The Segregation of Mexican American Children in the Elementary Schools of California—Its Legal and Administrative Aspects." Masters thesis, University of California, Los Angeles, 1948.

56. González, *Chicano Education*, p. 153.

57. González, *Chicano Education*, p. 154

Chicana/o Education from the
Civil Rights Era to the Present

Dolores Delgado Bernal

The struggle of Chicanas/os for educational equity and the right to include their culture, history, and language in K–12 and higher education curricula predates the civil rights movements of the 1960s by decades. Although Chicanas/os have made significant progress in terms of educational inclusion over the last five decades, since the late 1970s hard-won gains have eroded. Many of today's most hotly debated educational issues are very similar to those discussed in Mexican communities since before the turn of the century: improvement of inferior school facilities; removal of racist teachers and administrators; elimination of tracking; and inclusion of Mexican history, language, and culture in the curriculum. Today's conditions can be better understood within a contextual and historical analysis that connects the present to earlier periods, and links belief systems to our judicial system and social policies.

This chapter addresses educational policies and practices and judicial decisions that have affected Chicana/o education from the 1950s through the 1990s. This period encompasses the early civil rights era, including the Chicana/o Movement, which brought significant improvements in Chicana/o schooling, and the more recent neoconservative era in which we have seen the deterioration of Chicana/o educational rights. I have included several educational themes that were especially prominent throughout the Southwest from the 1950s through the 1990s: continued school segregation, bilingual education, and higher education. During this period, school segregation and desegregation efforts took on a new form, and differ greatly from the era of de jure segregation that officially ended in 1954 with the *Brown* decision.[2] The bilingual education movement is unique to this period, and Chicana/o participation in higher education was virtually

nonexistent prior to the 1950s. Another common thread that weaves through this chapter (and the entire book) is the resistance and activism of Chicana/o communities, including their use of the judicial system in demanding educational equity. Though each of these themes was important throughout the Southwest, this chapter places an emphasis on California and Texas, where the majority of Chicanas/os live and where much of the research on Chicana/o education has focused. In addition, the contemporary focus on California at the end of this chapter is purposeful, as California seems to be setting a national public policy standard in regards to legislation that negatively impacts the schooling of Chicanas/os.

Starting with the 1950s and early 1960s, I examine the continued school segregation of Mexican students even after numerous court decisions found de jure segregation of Mexican students illegal. Next I turn to the social activism and social policies that positively influenced Chicana/o schooling during the late 1960s and early 1970s. Then I address the conservative retrenchment that began in the mid-1970s, specifically the tension between desegregation and bilingual education, the educational inequity in K–12 education, and the myth of meritocracy in higher education. Finally, I assess where we are today, acknowledge progress in some aspects of Chicana/o schooling, and briefly analyze recent California legislation that has or will have a negative impact on Chicana/o education.

De Facto School Segregation: The 1950s to the Early 1960s

In the 1950s and early 1960s, Mexicans saw the elimination of school segregation as the key to full economic and social mobility. Throughout the Southwest, however, judicial decisions outlawing the segregation of Mexican students were ignored; instead, school boards purposely overlooked desegregation, and de facto segregation of Mexican students actually increased (Bogardus, 1949; Rangel & Alcala, 1972; Salinas, 1971). Why were these judicial decisions ignored? I argue that the White social

Dolores Delgado Bernal, "Chicana/o Education from The Civil Rights Era to the Present," from *The Elusive Quest for Equality: 150 Years of Chicano/Chicana Education*, edited by José F. Moreno, pp. 53–76. Copyright © 1999 by the President and Fellows of Harvard College. All rights reserved. Reprinted with permission.

belief system about Mexicans helped support the many political and economic reasons for their continued segregation. Indeed, the images of Mexicans held by educators and the judicial system shared a common trait during this period: both were "premised upon political, scientific, and religious theories relying on racial characterizations and stereotypes about people of color that help support a legitimating ideology and specific political action" (Tate, 1997, p. 199). The ideologies of Anglo-Saxon superiority, capitalism, and scientific theories of intelligence proved the cornerstones of de jure segregated schooling for Mexicans throughout the Southwest during the first half of this century (González, 1990; Menchaca & Valencia, 1990). These theories, along with a belief system that viewed Mexicans as "culturally deficient" and characterized them as ignorant, backward, unclean, unambitious, and abnormal were unaffected by major judicial decisions in California and Texas (see González, 1974; Taylor, 1934).

In California, the *Méndez v. Westminster* (1946) landmark case officially ended de jure segregation for Mexican students and cast doubt on the "separate but equal" doctrine. Five Mexican families, including Felicitas and Gonzalo Méndez, claimed that their children and other children of Mexican descent were victims of unconstitutional discrimination in the segregated schools of Orange County. U.S. District Court Judge Paul L. McCormick's 1946 ruling in favor of the plaintiffs, upheld in the Court of Appeals in 1947, found that the segregation of Mexican children could be considered arbitrary action taken without due process of the law (Wollenberg, 1974). In Texas, just one year later, Minerva Delgado and twenty other parents filed a suit against several Texas school districts in *Delgado v. Bastrop Independent School District* (1948). As in California, the court ruled that placing Mexican students in segregated schools was arbitrary and discriminatory, and in violation of constitutional rights guaranteed by the Fourteenth Amendment (San Miguel, 1987). However, these cases, which ended de jure racial segregation for Mexican students, did not change the existing American belief system that portrayed Mexicans as inferior.

In Texas, even after the *Méndez* and *Delgado* decisions found de jure segregation of Mexican students illegal, segregation continued to be widely practiced (Bogardus, 1949; Menchaca, 1995). When state school officials were confronted with evidence of continued school segregation, there was little interest in seriously addressing the problem. For example, representatives from the League of United Latin American Citizens (LULAC) and the American G.I. Forum found this to be true when they appeared before the State Board of Education in 1950 with a list of twenty Texas cities that were still practicing segregation in spite of the recent judicial decisions (San Miguel, 1987).[3] In response, the State Board of Education proposed a policy statement on the illegality of the segregation of Mexican schoolchildren, but allowed local districts to handle the complaints and grievances of

discriminatory treatment. The Board's policy simply created a bureaucratic process that limited the number of grievances that could actually reach the state commissioner of education. As San Miguel stated, "Between 1950 and 1957 nine local school districts were brought to the commissioner of education for special hearings, although hundreds of school districts throughout the state were segregating Mexican American students" (p. 132).

Belief in the cultural deficiency of Mexicans remained in place and supported the political action that continued to segregate Mexican students. At the same time, school segregation itself perpetuated an ideology of inferiority. Critical race theorist Charles Lawrence (1993) argues that school segregation conveys an ideology of inferiority that denies equal citizenship based not just on the act of segregation (de jure or de facto), but also on the defamatory message it sends about students of color:

> *Brown* held that segregation is unconstitutional not simply because the physical separation of Black and white children is bad or because resources were distributed unequally among Black and white schools. *Brown* held that segregated schools were unconstitutional primarily because of the message segregation conveys—the message that Black children are an untouchable caste, unfit to be educated with white children. Segregation serves its purpose by conveying an idea. It stamps a badge of inferiority upon Blacks, and this badge communicates a message to others in the community, as well as to Blacks wearing the badge, that is injurious to Blacks. (p. 59)

Following this line of reasoning, the injurious message behind Mexican school segregation was that Mexican students were inferior and did not deserve society's investment in their education. For example, in the *Méndez* decision, Judge McCormick stated, "the methods of segregation prevalent in the defendant school districts foster antagonisms in the children and suggest inferiority among them where none exists" (64 Federal Supplement, 1946, cited in Harders & Gómez, 1998, p.8). In other words, school segregation itself suggested an inferiority that was greater than any attempt to provide equal school facilities, making them inherently unequal. Thus, even after the end of de jure segregation, Mexican students remained segregated in substandard schools and were labeled as members of an inferior group. The comments of a Los Angeles teacher in the 1960s reveal the cultural deficit beliefs many teachers held:

> The attitudes of my colleagues are negative toward the Mexican American. I have heard some remarks in the teachers' room made like, "I have never had a Mexican who could think for himself." I have heard others say, "These Mexican kids, why do they have to be here?" (Delgado Bernal, 1997, p. 83)

The historic devaluation of Spanish also promoted these beliefs. Prohibiting Spanish-language use among Mexican schoolchildren was a social philosophy and a political tool used by local and state officials to justify school segregation and to maintain a colonized relationship between Mexicans and the dominant society.[4] Bilingualism was seen as "unAmerican" and considered a deficit and an obstacle to learning. There were no formal bilingual programs for Spanish-speaking students prior to the late 1960s, and it was routine to segregate Mexican students into "Mexican schools" or "Mexican classrooms," using their perceived language deficiency as justification. Even after the end of de jure segregation, it was common to find Mexican students physically separated from other students within the same classroom. Los Angeles Unified School District board member Vickie Castro, who went through elementary school in the 1950s, recalls how she was physically separated from her peers:

> I do recall my first day of school. And I did not speak English. . . . I just recall being frightened and I recall not knowing what to do and I recall being told to just sit over there in the corner. And there was one other little girl and we were just scared out of our minds. (Castro, 1994, p. 2, 3)

It was also common to hold Mexican students back for several years while they learned English. This left them over age for their grade, and thereby more likely to quit school before graduating.[5] This "assimilationist" perspective viewed bilingualism as a cognitive disability that caused confusion and impeded academic development (Jensen, 1962). In other words, many educators believed that there was only so much room in the brain, and children would not be able to function if they were learning English and maintaining their native Spanish. In fact, during the 1950s and early 1960s, most educators, along with LULAC, strongly supported the idea of intensive English instruction without the maintenance of Spanish (Crawford, 1992). LULAC's motive in supporting this type of instruction was their desire for Mexican students to learn English as quickly as possible so they could be successful in the dominant society. Though the goal of LULAC leaders was not total assimilation of the Mexican population, they were drawn into the assimilationist language perspective, and only later recognized the damage this perspective had on Mexican students (San Miguel, 1987).

Some Mexican educators at the time also advocated for an English-only approach, prior to offering their support for bilingual education in the late 1960s. One interesting example is Joe Bernal, the Texas senator and former educator, who later sponsored the Bilingual Education Act of 1968. He grew up on the predominantly Mexican west side of San Antonio in the 1940s, and as a high school student leader helped enforce an English-only campus policy. Each student was given a ribbon that said, "I Am an American—I Speak English," and was urged to turn in classmates heard using Spanish. Those caught speaking Spanish faced corporal punishment, after-school detention, and other forms of discipline (Crawford, 1992). Later, as an elementary schoolteacher in the 1950s, Bernal fined his pupils a penny for each time they used Spanish, saving the proceeds for a class party. He remembers: "I used to collect a lot of money from these kids. The parents knew about it and they were supportive" because they believed that their children must learn English, whatever the cost (Crawford, 1992, p. 79). Suppressing Spanish was a way to degrade and control an entire cultural group without explicitly using force or violence. It was one strategy for sustaining a colonized/colonizer relationship between Mexicans and the dominant White society. Many Mexicans internalized these negative views of Spanish—and therefore a negative view of themselves and their families—in order to assimilate into the dominant society.

Although the relationship between Mexicans and the dominant White society is complex and beyond pedagogical issues, it was clearly a part of Mexican school segregation. Mexican boys and girls continued to be tracked into vocational classes that served an economic function and supported the unequal division of power, wealth, and status, just as in the era of de jure segregation. Young Mexican women were tracked into home economics and clerical or secretarial classes, which prepared them for low-paying domestic and subservient work. Mexican women had an additional hurdle to jump, for even if they were able to move beyond paid domestic work, their families usually did not expect them to pursue an education beyond the domestic skills they would need in their homes (García, 1997; López, 1977; Nieto Gómez, 1974). The sexist attitudes of the wider society were manifested in the Mexican culture through such common sayings as ¿Para que quieres educarte si de nada te va a servir cuando te cases? (Why do you want to educate yourself if it will not be of any use to you when you get married?) (López, 1977).

Throughout the 1960s, the message that both Chicana and Chicano students were inferior continued to translate into overcrowded and under-financed schools, low graduation rates, and the overrepresentation of Chicana/o students in special education classes, including classes for the mentally retarded and the emotionally disturbed (California State Advisory Committee, 1968). A 1967 Chicana high school graduate remembers the deplorable educational conditions at her urban high school:

> We had severely overcrowded classrooms. We didn't have sufficient books. We had buildings that were barrack type buildings that had been built as emergency, temporary buildings during World War II, and this was the late 1960s, and we were still going to school in those buildings. (Delgado Bernal, in press)

Demographic factors such as the expanding Chicana/o school-age population, immigration, urbanization, and White flight also contributed to the increased de facto segregation of Chicana/o students. In cities such as Los Angeles, San Jose, Phoenix, Denver, San Antonio, and Houston, the picture was especially stark. By 1960, more than 80 percent of California's 1.4 million Spanish-surnamed people lived in urban areas, and the number of Spanish-surnamed children attending inferior segregated schools had increased (Wollenberg, 1974). Nearly half of all Chicana/o students in the Southwest attended elementary and secondary schools in which the Chicana/o enrollment was over 50 percent of the total student body (U.S. Commission on Civil Rights, 1971). As educational conditions worsened, tension and resentment increased, and Chicanas/os became disillusioned with the "American Dream." In response, many Chicanas/os in the 1960s embraced a nationalist perspective and a militancy to bring about educational, political, and social reform.

Social Activism and Social Policy of the Late 1960s

The last half of the 1960s marked the first time that youth played a central role in the shaping of movements aimed against social institutions and those in power. Street politics and mass protests marked this period, and student movements helped shape larger struggles for social and political equity (Muñoz, 1989). During this period of social unrest, Chicana/o students were influenced by numerous social and political forces, such as the wider Chicana/o movement, the Black civil rights movement, the federal government's War on Poverty, anti-Vietnam War sentiments, the women's movement, and political struggles in Mexico and Latin America. At the same time, expanding economic opportunity for low-income citizens and people of color became the main focus of federal social policy, and education emerged as the fundamental mechanism for combating poverty and racial inequality (Wise, 1982).

Throughout the Southwest, Chicana/o students and their communities struggled to call attention to and improve the poor quality of public education offered to them. In March 1968, well over ten thousand Chicana/o students walked out of East Los Angeles high schools to protest inferior schooling conditions. The students boycotted classes and presented a list of grievances to the Los Angeles Board of Education. The list consisted of thirty-six demands, including smaller class sizes, bilingual education, an end to the vocational tracking of Chicana/o students, more emphasis on Chicano history, and community control of schools (McCurdy, 1968). The East L.A. walkouts focused national attention on the K–12 schooling of Chicanas/os and also set a precedent for school boycotts throughout the Southwest, including those in Crystal City and San Antonio, Texas; Denver, Colorado; and Phoenix, Arizona (Acuña, 1988).

Though their stories are often excluded in written historical accounts, Chicanas played crucial leadership roles in these mass demonstrations and were intimately involved in the struggles for educational justice. Celeste Baca, Vickie Castro, Paula Crisóstomo, Mita Cuarón, Tanya Luna Mount, Rosalinda Méndez González, Rachel Ochoa Cervera, and Cassandra Zacarías were but a few of the women who made up the East L.A. student leadership. They engaged in networking, organizing, and developing consciousness; held elected and appointed offices; and acted as spokespersons (Delgado Bernal, 1997). For example, Paula Crisóstomo and Rosalinda Méndez González both provided testimony to the U.S. Commission on Civil Rights regarding the education of Mexican American students. Méndez González described the racist curriculum and popular stereotypes of Chicanas/os in this way:

> From the time we first begin attending school, we hear about how great and wonderful our United States is, about our democratic American heritage, but little about our splendid and magnificent Mexican heritage and culture. We look for others like ourselves in these history books, for something to be proud of for being a Mexican, and all we see in books and magazines, films, and T.V. shows are stereotypes of a dark, dirty, smelly man with a tequila bottle in one hand, a dripping taco in the other, a serape wrapped around him, and a big sombrero. (California State Advisory Committee, 1968)

Chicana students resisted both racist school policies and sexist educational practices. Artist Patssi Valdez, who participated in the East L.A. walkouts, remembers what her home economics teacher told her and other Chicanas: "She would say. . . . 'You little Mexicans, you better learn and pay attention. This class is very important . . . most of you are going to be cooking and cleaning for other people'" (Valdez, 1994). The teacher's comments illustrate the intersecting forms of subordination that have historically influenced the schooling of Chicanas.[6] Because they were female, Mexican, and working class, the teacher expected Chicana students to prepare themselves for domestic labor that met the needs of White middle- and upper-class families. Chicana students struggled against sexism not only in the wider society, but also within the Chicana/o community. Within the movement and various student organizations, Chicanas had to actively reject the traditional roles to which they were often relegated by their male peers. One Chicana stated, "My male friends at the time, in the organization, would try to put me in female roles. Like be the secretary, make the sandwiches, do that. But . . . I always challenged. And when I would see that there were no women involved, boom, I made myself right there" (Delgado Bernal, in press).

Chicana/o student activism also played a crucial role in gaining access to institutions of higher education. As

Chicana/o students across the Southwest demanded equitable K–12 schooling, they likewise demanded their place in colleges and universities. Prior to this time, Mexican students were virtually absent from institutions of higher education. After World War II, the G.I. Bill gave a few Chicanao servicemen access to college, and by 1958, "California enrolled nearly 36,000 college freshman of Mexican-American origin, several more than in Texas" (Weinberg, 1977, p. 341, cited in Webster, 1984, p. 42).[7] Less than a decade later, in 1967, one of the first Chicana/o college student organizations, the Mexican American Student Association (MASA), was formed at East Los Angeles Community College (Gómez-Quiñones, 1978). College student organizations rapidly formed in California and throughout the Southwest, including organizations such as United Mexican-American Students (UMAS) in California and the Mexican-American Youth Organization (MAYO) in Texas. The primary issue of these organizations was the lack of Chicana/o access to quality education, and their activities revolved around the institutionalization of Chicano Studies and support programs for Chicana/o students (López, 1977).

As a result of the development of Chicana/o student organizations, the East L.A. school walkouts in 1968, and Chicana/o student activism in general, there was a statewide student conference in Santa Barbara, California, in 1969. Rosalinda Méndez González remembers that she, like many young Chicanas, actively participated in the conference and that "the Santa Barbara conference . . . was like everybody coming together to reconceptualize the schools and higher education for our communities" (Méndez González, 1995, p. 37). At this conference, students, faculty, administrators, and community representatives produced a 150-page document called *El Plan de Santa Bárbara: A Chicano Plan for Higher Education* (Chicano Coordinating Council, 1970). *El Plan* provided the theoretical rationale for the development of Chicano Studies, a plan for recruitment and admission of Chicano students, support programs to aid in the retention of Chicano students, and the organization of Chicano Studies curricula and departments. Another significant result of the Santa Barbara conference and *El Plan* was the unification of Chicano student organizations and the creation of Movimiento Estudiantil Chicano de Aztlán (MEChA). MEChA's goal was to link all Chicano student groups throughout the Southwest and "to socialize and politicize Chicano students on their particular campus to the ideals of the [Chicano] movement" (Chicano Coordinating Council, 1970, p. 60).

El Plan offered a vision and course of action for Chicanos in higher education, one of the first of its kind among the Chicana/o community. However, it was confined in its scope, reflecting a limited consciousness by not including references to women, female liberation, or Chicana Studies (Pardo, 1984). Some have called it a "*mani*festo" for its grounding in traditional cultural nationalism, rather than an ideology that works toward the elimination of all forms of oppression (Orozco, 1986). In the early 1970s, in response to the absence of women in the curriculum, Chicana activists at a Chicano Studies/MEChA conference at California State University, Northridge, proposed five courses on La Chicana, including The Chicana in Education, The Chicana and the Law, and Religion and la Mujer. They also proposed a requirement that all Chicano Studies majors take at least one class on La Chicana (Nieto Gómez, 1973).

At the national level, Chicanas were also addressing the unique needs of Chicana students in attaining high school and/or higher education. At the National Women's Political Caucus Convention in 1973, the Chicana Caucus consisted of sixty women from seven states, including Texas, New Mexico, Illinois, and California. The Chicana Caucus submitted a resolution requesting that legislative efforts of the organization include: a) research on the educational needs of Chicanas; b) recruitment of Chicanas to higher education; c) financial support for the education of Chicanas; d) tutorial and counseling programs designed for Chicanas; e) incorporation of Chicana culture into educational systems and textbooks; and f) inclusion of Chicanas in all affirmative action activity (Chapa, 1973). In this way, the women of the Chicana Caucus attempted to address the unique problems that confronted Chicana students by shaping national social policy.

Throughout the 1960s and early 1970s, Chicana/o activism and Chicana feminist ideas merged with social policies to better address the needs of Chicana/o students and increase their access to institutions of higher education. During the Kennedy administration and President Johnson's War on Poverty, affirmative action attempted to equalize the playing field in the realm of higher education. Federal legislation helped facilitate Chicana/o participation in higher education. The Higher Education Act of 1965, among other things, authorized several financial aid programs, and Title VII extended the Civil Rights Act of 1964 to include all educational institutions. Federal and state programs were created, such as the Educational Opportunities Program (EOP), which played a critical role in recruiting and retaining Chicana/o students into universities and colleges. EOP and programs similar to it were the initial bridges that brought Chicana/o students into higher education in more visible numbers (Acuña, 1988). At the same time, as social activism and social policies were opening the doors to higher education, a number of social forces were also shaping bilingual education.

Social Forces Shaping Bilingual Education

The struggle by Chicanas/os to obtain bilingual education in public schools began with the social activism and policies of the 1960s. Historian Guadalupe San Miguel (1985) proposes that two views on bilingualism came into conflict and contributed to the formation of policies on bilingual education. The "assimilationist" perspective, discussed earlier, continued to uphold the post-World War II belief that bilingualism was divisive and un-American, a disability rather than an asset. Shared by associations of school administrators and their supporters, this view held that language and culture were incidental to the teaching and learning process. It did not recognize the value or utility of incorporating the language and culture of limited-English-speaking students into the public school curriculum. As discussed earlier in this chapter, prior to the late 1960s there were no bilingual programs for Mexican students, and it was routine to segregate Mexican students based on their perceived language deficiency. In fact, during the 1940s and 1950s, LULAC and Mexican educators such as Joe Bernal did not support bilingual instruction in public schools. The assimilationist ideology left students believing that speaking Spanish in school was an evil they had to avoid at all costs. Writer and poet José Antonio Burciaga (1993) articulates the pain experienced by students when their schooling was regulated by the assimilationist beliefs that devalued Spanish:

> Perhaps the most memorable experiences one has in school are those that come into direct conflict with one's family's beliefs and traditions. . . . No learning experience was more painful or damaging than the silence imposed on our Mexican culture, history and beautiful Spanish language. To speak Spanish was not only illegal but also a sin: "Bless me father, for I have sinned. I spoke Spanish in class and during recess. . . . *Mea culpa, Mea culpa, mea máxima culpa!*" (pp. 36, 40)

A second view on bilingualism in the 1960s, the "pluralist" perspective, accepted the plurality of languages as a necessary ingredient in U.S. education. This view was embraced by most Chicana/o communities and political allies (San Miguel, 1985). Pluralists viewed the first language and culture of the child as essential to the instructional and learning process. During the late 1960s, some educators, sociolinguists, and Chicana/o communities created a philosophical force that openly challenged the commonly held assimilationist perspective. Chicana/o student activism focused on poor educational conditions, racist school policies, and the implementation of bilingual education. Chicanas/os began to regard language as a matter of self-determination and language as a basic human right. Educator Reynaldo Macías has suggested that language rights can be based on "the right to freedom from discrimination on the basis of language" and "the right to use your language(s) in the activities of communal life" (1979, pp. 88–89). For many Chicanas/os, the right to maintain Spanish was a way of declaring some control over their lives and rejecting the colonized relationship between Chicanas/os and the dominant society. Whatever the justification, bilingual education offered some hope that

Chicana/o schooling would be more meaningful and lead to educational equity.

With much political pressure from Chicana/o communities and liberal educators who held a pluralist perspective, the federal government, for the first time, funded bilingual education in 1968 through Title VII of the Elementary and Secondary Education Act of 1965 (Crawford, 1992). The 1968 Bilingual Education Act provided money to train teachers and aides, to develop instructional materials, and to establish parent-involvement projects (Loya, 1990). The Act was meant "to develop and carry out new and imaginative elementary and secondary school programs . . . [for] children of limited English-speaking ability" (Crawford, 1992, p. 85). However, the act did not impose teaching methods or even define the concept of bilingual education. In addition, the bill was viewed as a compensatory educational program in which linguistically "disadvantaged" children were assisted.

It is often argued that civil rights legislation has been very modest in its efforts to eliminate inequalities and often serves those in power as much if not more than those it is actually supposed to serve (Crenshaw, Gotanda, Peller, & Thomas, 1995; Matsuda, Lawrence, Delgado, & Crenshaw, 1993). For example, in most Chicana/o communities, bilingual education represented a way to maintain one's language and culture and was by definition a rejection of colonization. However, the official goals of bilingual education emanating from federal and state bilingual education guidelines from 1968 to the present have never included the maintenance of the student's first language. An early controversy in the House and Senate revolved around whether bilingual education was simply a better way to teach English or a means to preserve a student's first language, which might create unwanted ethnic pluralism. In fact, one of the sponsors of the original 1968 Bilingual Education Act was careful to state during the deliberation of the bill, "It is not the purpose of the bill to create pockets of different language throughout the country . . . not to stamp out the mother tongue and not to make their mother tongue the dominant language, but just to try to make these children fully literate in English, so that the children can move into the mainstream of American life" (Crawford, 1992, p. 84). Even during the mid-1970s, when bilingual education enjoyed its greatest level of support, native-language instruction was only seen as a necessary strategy that allowed a child to achieve competence in English (Roos, 1978). Never has federal or state legislation stated that bilingual education should help students maintain their first language to become bilingual and biliterate citizens. Yet, paradoxically, during the 1960s, the federal government spent millions of dollars trying to ensure a bilingual populace by calling for foreign-language requirements and well-funded foreign language departments in select high schools and most universities (Crawford, 1992; Schaller, Scharff & Schulzinger, 1992). These efforts, supported by the Cold War and the 1958

National Defense Education Act, certainly benefited middle-class Whites more than those Spanish-speaking students who started school already fluent in a "foreign" language.

In order to compel school officials to provide bilingual education, Chicanas/os have brought lawsuits under Title VI of the Civil Rights Act, which bans discrimination based "on the ground of race, color, or national origin" in "any program or activity receiving Federal financial assistance."[8] In the 1974 *Lau v. Nichols* case, non-English-speaking students of Chinese ancestry brought suit against the San Francisco Unified School District. The plaintiffs charged that where students were taught only in English, school officials had not taken significant action to provide a meaningful education. The U.S. Supreme Court unanimously found that by "failing to affirmatively overcome the English language deficiencies of national origin-minority group children with limited English-speaking ability, school officials violated Title VI of the Civil Rights Act" (Roos, 1978, p. 116). The court handed down this decision even though the school district had made an effort to remedy language difficulties by providing supplemental English instruction to about one thousand of the 2,856 Chinese students who did not speak English. About 1,800 students, however did not receive any special instruction, which was a violation of Title VI of the Civil Rights Act. The decision helped to establish a precedent, though it did not provide a specific remedy to assist students with limited English proficiency.

Chicanas/os in New Mexico used the *Lau* decision in *Serna v. Portales Municipal Schools* (1974) to seek an order requiring the district to provide bilingual and bicultural education under Title VI. Chicanas/os in the New Mexico community felt that the school district's English as a Second Language (ESL) remedy was an inadequate response to the educational needs of Chicana/o students. And expert witnesses testified that when a child "goes to school where he finds no evidence of his language and culture and ethnic group represented [she/he] becomes withdrawn and nonparticipating" (cited in Roos, 1978, p. 129). Using *Lau* as a precedent, the court held that the district's failure to offer a bilingual and bicultural educational program that provided Chicana/o students with a meaningful education deprived them of their rights under Title VI (Martínez, 1994). It is significant that the court once again decided against the school district, even though the latter was making an effort to provide a limited ESL program.

Legal indeterminacy has led to various judicial interpretations. Policies and law regarding bilingual education are indeterminate in that courts often permit a judge to exercise discretion in rendering vague standards and justifying multiple outcomes to lawsuits (Martínez, 1994). Such was the case in decisions that ignored or interpreted *Lau* and *Serna* differently. For example, *Keyes v. School District Number 1* (1973), although often thought of as a de-

segregation case, was similar to the *Lau* and *Serna* cases.[9] The Chicana/o plaintiffs "alleged that the Denver school board's failure to adopt a bilingual and bicultural program constituted a violation of Title VI" (Martínez, 1994, p. 608). In 1975 the 10th Circuit Court of Appeals found that the district had implemented various programs to address the needs of students with limited English proficiency (as did the school districts in *Lau* and *Serna*), and therefore was not in violation of Title VI. The *Keyes* decision, made by the same circuit that affirmed the extensive bilingual and bicultural education programs in *Serna*, failed to discuss the *Serna* and *Lau* decisions and did not explain how its ruling was consistent or inconsistent with those cases (Martínez, 1994). The *Keyes* case demonstrates that courts can and have exercised discretion to limit access to bilingual and bicultural education.[10]

Conservative Retrenchment

The sociopolitically conservative era that began in the mid-1970s and that hit hard during the Reagan and Bush administrations had a negative impact on Chicana/o schooling conditions. A strong backlash against the social equity programs of President Johnson's War on Poverty was accompanied by increased military spending, reduced educational spending, and a growing recession. The conservatives regained a strong voice, which was reflected in social ideas, educational policy, and judicial decisions. As tension between desegregation and bilingual education intensified, the funding for bilingual education was drastically reduced and public school finance was restricted for Chicana/o schools. This left Chicana/o students in underfunded, segregated schools that failed to adequately prepare them for post-secondary education. At the same time, the myth of meritocracy in higher education and a growing attack on affirmative action programs also limited Chicana/o students' access to colleges and universities.

The Tension between Desegregation and Bilingual Education

The desegregation process has usually been thought of as an issue pertinent only to African American communities, with Chicana/o students often being ignored in the process and in the educational literature. By the 1970s, more Chicana/o students attended second-rate segregated schools than at the time of the 1947 *Méndez* decision. In fact, many Chicana/o scholars and activists believe that the *Brown* decision had no effect on the schooling of Chicana/o students until the 1970s, when the courts were forced to decide how to treat Chicana/o students in the desegregation process (Acuña, 1988). *Cisneros v. Corpus Christi Independent School District* was filed in 1968 by Chicana/o labor activists in Corpus Christi, Texas, and was decided in 1970 at the federal district court level. The plaintiffs challenged the legal framework for future desegregation cases and the segregation of Chicana/o and African American school children in Corpus Christi. The court ruled that Chicanas/os were an identifiable ethnic minority and found them to be unconstitutionally segregated in the public schools. It also required that an appropriate desegregation plan that included Anglos, Chicanas/os, and African Americans be submitted (San Miguel, 1987). Prior to this case, the strategy employed in most successful school desegregation efforts was based on Chicanas/os' claim to "Whiteness."[11]

The U.S. Supreme Court reinforced how Chicana/o students were to be treated in the school desegregation process in the 1973 *Keyes v. School District Number 1* case. Before *Keyes*, Denver Public Schools, like many schools throughout the Southwest, integrated Chicana/o students with African American students and called it desegregation. The Court either had to define Chicana/o students as "Caucasians—and integrate them with African Americans or redefine their ethnic status (as a protected ethnic minority group) and integrate them with everyone else" (Donato, 1997, p. 124). In *Keyes*, the Supreme Court decided that Chicana/o students were an identifiable minority group and ruled that they had been denied their constitutional rights by the Denver Public Schools. The court authorized racial-balance remedies and required districts to integrate African Americans and Chicanas/os into White urban school districts.

It is important to note that after these decisions and throughout the 1970s, there was growing tension between the pursuit of bilingual education and school desegregation. During the 1930s and 1940s, Mexicans fought school segregation in the courts in such cases as *Alvarez v. Lemon Grove* (1931), *Del Rio Independent School District v. Salvatierra* (1931), *Méndez v. Westminster School District* (1947), and *Delago et al. v. Bastrop* (1948). A few decades later, Chicanas/os began to see bilingual education as key to the quest for equal education, and judicial decisions such as those in *Lau* and *Serna* placed responsibility for meeting the needs of students with limited English proficiency on the schools. After a difficult struggle to obtain the right to bilingual instruction, many Chicana/o communities were suspicious of desegregation efforts that might disperse Chicana/o students without considering their need for bilingual education.[12] Parents and policymakers argued that bilingual education and desegregation might not be fully compatible. Desegregation usually meant "scattering Black students to provide instruction in 'racially balanced' settings. Bilingual education, on the other hand, has usually meant the clustering of Spanish-speaking students so they could receive instruction through their native language" (Zerkel, 1977, p. 181, cited in Donato, Menchaca, & Valencia, 1991). By the mid-1970s, enforcement of both the *Brown* and *Lau* decisions led to more complications than policymakers originally anticipated, as Chicana/o students were resegregated based on language within desegregated schools (Donato et al.,

1991). This was an ironic result of desegregation and bilingual education efforts, and depending on one's educational philosophy, either desegregation or bilingual education could be openly supported. For example, education policymakers who opposed bilingual education could avoid it by scattering limited-English-proficient students throughout their districts in the name of desegregation. At the same time, someone who opposed mixing White and Chicana/o students in the same classroom could use the opportunity to segregate Chicana/o students in bilingual classrooms, thus using the same old racially motivated rationale for separating Mexican children from White students based on their perceived language deficiency (see Donato, 1997).

By the early 1980s, the tension between desegregation and bilingual education was receiving increasingly more attention. Though some educators throughout the Southwest were optimistic that the two could work together, there was little time to successfully produce meaningful results in meeting the needs of Chicana/o students. During the 1980s, assimilationist educators and politicians gained the upper hand; bilingual education was under strong attack, and financial support for it was being drastically reduced. The 1980s provided a political climate in which community activism was difficult and bilingual education suffered many setbacks. In the words of Chicana feminist writer Ana Castillo:

> In 1980 when the Republicans and the Reagan administration came to office, their tremendous repression quashed the achievements of the Chicano/Latino Movement.... Community projects and grassroots programs dependent on government funding—rehabilitation and training, child care, early education and alternative schooling, youth counseling, cultural projects that supported the arts and community artists, rehab-housing for low income families, and women's shelters—shut down. (1994, p. 31)

Under the Reagan administration, while the government spent billions of dollars on the military, Title VII bilingual education funding was cut from $167 million in 1980 to $133 million in 1986, representing more than a 20 percent reduction (Loya, 1990)—this at a time when the number of English learners was greatly increasing. In California alone, students with limited English proficiency increased nearly 75 percent, from 326,000 in 1980 to 568,000 in 1986 (California State Department of Education, 1993).

Educational Inequity in the 1970s and Beyond

At the same time that bilingual education was under attack and suffering reduced financial support, the conservative retrenchment also attacked public school finance. In order to compel school officials to provide educational equity, Chicanas/os brought lawsuits under the equal protection clause. In Colorado, Josie Luján, one of the lead plaintiffs in *Luján et al. v. Colorado State Board of Education* (1979), along with a handful of parents charged that the Colorado school finance system violated the equal protection clause of the U.S. and Colorado Constitutions because of the extreme funding disparities among school districts in the state. Lower per-pupil expenditures existed in districts with high Chicana/o student enrollment. Though the district court ruled in favor of the plaintiffs, in 1982 the State Supreme Court of Colorado held that the financing system was constitutionally permissible, thus leaving the system virtually unchanged. Luján did, however, win a seat on the local school board and she became an education advocate for Chicana/o students (Espinosa, 1979).

In another key school finance case, *Serrano v. Priest* (1971), John Serrano sued the California state treasurer on the grounds that his son received an inferior education in East Los Angeles because the state school finance system was based on financing schools through local property taxes. He alleged that, due to the differential property values and resulting tax base, children were given unequal treatment and resources in poor districts that did not have as high a tax base and funding as wealthier districts (Acuña, 1988). In 1971, the California Supreme Court ruled in his favor, finding that "financing primarily through local property taxes failed to provide equal protection under the law" (Acuña, 1988, p. 389). The U.S. Supreme Court upheld the *Serrano* decision in 1976, but limited its decision to California, stating that the finance system violated the state's equal protection clause by denying equal access to education. *Serrano*, however, brought few changes to Chicana/o schools because wealthier districts still had better facilities, more experienced teachers, and less overcrowding. Soon after, in 1978, California's Proposition 13 applied a taxation cap that in effect restricted funding for all districts in California. By the late 1980s, California ranked eighth nationally in per capita income, but spent only 3.8 percent of its income on public education—placing it forty-sixth among the fifty states (Kozol, 1991). Although educators and researchers do not agree about whether there is a causal relationship between educational expenditures and the quality of education, there is widespread agreement that Chicanas/os are generally subjected to inferior educational conditions in poorly funded schools (De La Roas & Maw, 1990; Valencia, 1991).

San Antonio Independent School District v. Rodríguez is a class-action suit filed in 1968 by Demetrio Rodríguez and other parents on behalf of their children who were students in the Edgewood School District, which was poor and 96 percent non-White. At the time, San Antonio had several school districts segregated along class and racial/ethnic lines. Edgewood was among the poorest, while Alamo Heights, with a predominately White student population was the richest (Acuña, 1988). The Mexican American Legal Defense and Educational Fund (MALDEF)

argued on behalf of the Edgewood parents that the Texas finance system taxed residents of the poor Edgewood district at a higher rate than it taxed residents of Alamo Heights. In addition, per-pupil spending was much lower in Edgewood than in the wealthier district. Even with the minimum provided by the state, Edgewood spent only $231 per pupil, while Alamo Heights was able to spend $543 on each pupil (Kozol, 1991). The state public school financing practices were challenged and presented as a violation of the federal equal protection clause of the U.S. Constitution. The district court ruled in favor of Rodríguez and the other parents, and found that Texas was in violation of the equal protection clause. However, the decision was overruled by the U.S. Supreme Court in 1973. The Court's five-to-four decision in *Rodríguez* is especially noteworthy because it signaled the end of an era of progressive change and set the tone for educational inequity during the 1980s and 1990s.

A number of other factors promoted the educational inequity of Chicana/o students in the 1980s and into the 1990s. For example, Chicana/o schools that were among the most severely underfunded were also the most overcrowded, offering a limited curriculum with few resources (Achievement Council, 1984; Assembly Office of Research, 1990). Chicana/o and other Latina/o students were disproportionately retained for at least one grade and were seldom exposed to enriched curricula or pedagogy (Achievement Council, 1984; Assembly Office of Research, 1985). There were few Chicana/o and other Latina/o teachers and administrators in California's schools (California State Department of Education, 1985, 1988). Throughout the Southwest, Chicana/o students were highly unlikely to have Chicana/o teachers to act as mentors, since Latinas/os made up only 2.9 percent of all public school teachers in the country (De La Rosa & Maw, 1990). Cassandra Zacarías, a high school counselor who went through school in the 1960s, remembers that as a student she too lacked role models in school:

> When I was in high school I never felt like there was anybody that was like me who was a teacher, or counselor, or principal. I mean there was, I don't know, maybe a couple of Latinos that were teachers and it always seemed really sad to me. (Delgado Bernal, 1997, p. 160).

Chicanas/os and other high school students of color continue to report that they feel their teachers, school staff, and peers neither like nor understand them, and many of their teachers admit to not always understanding ethnically diverse students (University of California, Latino Eligibility Task Force, 1995).

In addition, the continued school tracking of Chicana/o students into vocational programs and into special education programs for learning-disabled students has prompted educational, social, and economic inequities for such students, and has limited their access to higher education (Aguirre, 1980; González, 1990; Mitchell, Powell, Scott, & McDaid, 1994; Oakes, 1985). Throughout the Southwest, Chicana/o students in K–12 schools have been systematically tracked into courses that do not provide an environment or curriculum that prepares them for the postsecondary level (Aguirre & Martínez, 1993; Oakes, 1985). Indeed, 75 percent of all Latina/o high school seniors in 1980 had been enrolled in a curricular program that made a college education improbable (Orum, 1986). For those Chicanas/os who enrolled in a post-secondary institution, half attended a community college instead of a four-year institution (Astin, 1982; Durán, 1983).

The use of a "counterstory" (Delgado, 1989) demonstrates how the secondary school context continues to promote the educational inequality of Chicana/o students and limits access to higher education.[13] Gloria Martínez, a Chicana and first-generation college student, compares her journey to higher education with the path of her White, middle-class roommate.[14] Her story describes the secondary experiences of most Chicanas/os:

One day during first semester of my freshman year, my roommate and I were sitting in our dorm room talking about our high schools. I already knew that we had very different life experiences, but I could barely believe the huge contrast between our two schools. She had attended a suburban upper middle-class high school and I went to an urban high school in a predominantly working-class Chicano community. During high school my roommate took two years of Japanese and had her choice of Spanish, French, Italian, German, and Chinese. I took Spanish in high school. I was already semibilingual in Spanish before I took it, but my only other choice was French, and I figured I wouldn't have much need for it. She said her high school's science department was chaired by a former NASA scientist and offered biology, chemistry, physics, geology, biochemistry, and astronomy. I was in the honors track and I was only offered biology and chemistry. Most of my friends were told to just take general science. The math department at my school was limited as the science department, while hers offered algebra, geometry, algebra II, trigonometry, calculus, and statistics. Some of these were advanced placement [AP] courses so she was able to start our freshman year with several units of university credits. There were no AP classes at my high school, only honors courses that did not carry college credit. She enjoyed great electives like journalism and computer programming, because her school had up-to-date technology and lots of computers. They also had college counselors who helped students complete college and scholarship applications, enroll and take the college entrance exams, and get information materials from various in- and out-of-state colleges. The counselors at my high school had such a heavy student load that it was impossible to get an appointment with them, and college advising just wasn't their priority. My *tía* [aunt] who'd just started

going to a local community college is the one who advised me and helped me apply for college.

After that conversation with my roommate, I remember feeling like I'd been shafted, not by my roommate, but by my high school or maybe the whole educational system. It seemed really unfair that my roommate came to the university so prepared and here I was struggling with the lower division courses. I knew I was a really smart person, did really well in high school, and was dedicated to my studies. But sometimes I doubted myself, and I wondered if I really belonged in this university. I used to wonder if the only people who could actually succeed in college were the ones who had backgrounds similar to my roommate. Sometimes I questioned whether or not I deserved my spot in the university and if in fact I could succeed.

The precollege experience of Chicanas/os continues to differ vastly from that of middle-class White students, and Gloria's experience illuminates what numerous studies have found: college access and successful college participation for Chicana/o students is severely limited by an inferior secondary school education.[15] By tracking Chicana/o middle and high school students into low-ability classes, they are not given enough exposure to the academic subjects, critical thinking skills, and writing skills that are needed to do well on college entrance exams or in a college classroom (Durán, 1983). Access to college by Chicana/o students today is also limited by the myth of meritocracy and the attack on affirmative action.

Meritocracy and Chicana/o College Students

In higher education, meritocratic values often contradict the fundamental educational mission of developing students' knowledge. Meritocracy is a system of rewards presumably based solely on ability and talent, so that rewards go to those who "perform the best." Meritocratic values drive a wide range of educational practices such as testing, grading, admissions, and ability tracking, all in the spirit of "equality." Higher education scholar Alexander Astin (1982) points out that advocates of a meritocratic higher education system often view education as an open competition, analogous to an intellectual footrace. All contestants are allowed to enter the race, and rewards go to the swiftest; however, he argues, certain realities about the competition are distorted. For example, Chicanas/os often never get to the starting line because of poor secondary school conditions. Limited school resources and tracking into vocational programs mean that Chicanas/os often fail to show up at the competition because they lack reliable information about the race. Many Chicanas/os who do start the race do not run well and struggle to remain in the race because of their inferior training and the fact that they were never given the complete rules of the game. And many Chicanas/os who participate and run well may still end up with a second-class award, since the race they have entered (community college) offers a very different trophy than the race in an Ivy League college (Astin, 1982).

It seems that most Americans do not question the myth of meritocracy in higher education, believing that admissions decisions are fair and based solely on comparing one's qualifications to a universal standard of excellence. An important and often overlooked reality in a meritocratic system, however, is the fact that "merit" is socially constructed and standards of competition are set by those in power. For example, in higher education, SAT/ACT scores and a student's high school grade point average have traditionally been the standard by which students are admitted to college. SAT/ACT scores have been used as a standard despite an abundance of research that shows that these scores are not good predictors of college success for Chicanas/os, and that standardized testing in general has had a negative impact on Chicana/o students (Aguirre, 1980; Durán, 1983; Goldman & Hewitt, 1975; Goldman & Richards, 1974; González, 1974; Valencia & Aburto, 1991). In fact, high school preparation and testing and admission standards have been cited as two of the largest barriers to higher education for Chicanas/os and other Latinas/os (Orum, 1986). In California, the SAT has been a barrier for eligibility and participation in the University of California for Chicanas/os since it was incorporated into UC admissions requirements in 1968 (University of California, Latino Eligibility Task Force, 1997). Yet, it seems that many people perceive the UC system to be a fair and meritocratic one, based on a universal standard of excellence (the SAT).

"Reverse discrimination" is only claimed by Whites and conservatives when they perceive that an allegedly fair and meritocratic system is being threatened. During the late 1970s, *Regents of the University of California v. Bakke* (1978) popularized the discourse of "reverse discrimination" and the growing public opinion that higher education had overstepped its bounds in creating opportunities for women and students of color. After Alan Bakke, a 34-year-old White engineer, applied to and was rejected by thirteen medical schools, a White administrator at the University of California, Davis, suggested he sue, as presumably less qualified students of color had been admitted. Bakke challenged the special admissions program that set aside sixteen slots out of one hundred for "disadvantaged" students. The special admissions program had been initiated just six years before his lawsuit, and prior to the program only three students of color had been admitted (Acuña, 1988). In 1978, the U.S. Supreme Court issued a somewhat ambiguous opinion in the *Bakke* case. The university's set-aside program was found to be illegal, and the university was directed to admit Bakke. Yet, the Court also ruled that race could be used in admissions provided that it was not the sole selection factor. The *Bakke* decision reflected growing public opinion that higher education had "gone too far" in trying to accommodate the

special needs of "minorities" and was a precursor of the discourse of "reverse discrimination" today (Astin, 1982).

Where We Are Today

Today, there is evidence that points to modest progress. More Chicanas/os and other Latinas/os are going to college; most major universities in the Southwest offer some type of Chicana/o Studies courses; and more Chicana/o scholars are writing about and documenting the life experiences of Chicanas/os. In California, more Latina/o students are graduating from high schools, more are taking the SAT and ACT tests, and more are becoming eligible for the California community college and state university system (University of California, Latino Eligibility Task Force, 1995). These improvements are modest, however, particularly when contrasted with the proportional growth of the Chicana/o population over the last fifty years. Moreover, attacks continue on the educational opportunities of and the quality of education offered to Chicana/o students. Presently, Chicanas/os are still considered to be the most unlikely racial/ethnic group to finish high school, to attend college, and to graduate from college (Chapa, 1991; Gándara, 1994). From the civil rights era to the present, it is safe to say that public schools have continued to constantly fail Chicana/o students at every point in the educational pipeline. The current anti-Latino and anti-immigrant beliefs manifested in California's Propositions 187, 209, and 227 continue to shape public policy that directly affects Chicana/o communities' educational, economic, political, and social well-being. Although such legislation and policy initiatives seem to issue primarily from California, it is significant for all Latinas/os in the United States because California appears to be setting a national public policy standard (Brownstein, 1995; García, 1995).

An Extended Form of School Segregation: California's Proposition 187

Even the school segregation statistics of the late 1980s and the prediction that "the segregation of Chicano students will intensify in the years ahead" (Valencia, 1991, p. 7) did not prepare us for California's public referendum that attempted to push Chicana/o school segregation toward Chicana/o school exclusion. In the early 1990s, then Governor Pete Wilson and a group of "concerned" California residents tired of undocumented immigrants began the Save Our State (SOS) movement, which put Proposition 187 on the 1994 California ballot. Proponents of 187 argued that "illegal aliens" were unfairly benefiting from state resources and were crowding their children out of public schools. Proposition 187 attempted to extend the segregation of Chicana/o students by denying public education to anyone attending a public elementary, secondary, or post-secondary school who was "reasonably suspected" to be an "illegal alien" in the United States. In addition, Proposition 187 required teachers and other officials to report those who were suspected of being in this country without proper immigration documents. These educational sections of the initiative were in direct conflict with the U.S. Supreme Court's 1982 decision in *Plyler v. Doe*, which held that the state of Texas could not bar undocumented children from public elementary schools because doing so violates the Equal Protection Clause of the Fourteenth Amendment. The authors of Proposition 187 put forth the initiative knowing *Plyler* was a legal precedent that provided protection for undocumented students to attend public schools. In fact, one of the goals of the proposition's authors was to call on a more politically conservative Supreme Court to overturn the *Plyler* decision (Prince, 1994).

Supporters of Proposition 187 also contended that the measure had nothing to do with race/ethnicity, arguing that it was merely an attempt to save scarce state resources. However, opponents viewed the initiative as an attack on racial and cultural minorities, and saw it as part of a historical continuum of race-based immigration and education policies (García, 1995). For example, using the term "illegal alien" demonizes undocumented immigrants as criminals. Just as de jure segregation conveyed an idea of the inferiority of Mexican students, Proposition 187 criminalized undocumented immigrants and those who are suspected of being "illegal aliens": "If we assume that undocumented immigrants are a criminal element, then we are automatically accepting that the existing . . . laws are just and fair" (Bosco, 1994, cited in García, 1995, p. 118). Indeed, Proposition 187 was not a race-neutral law and would have disproportionately affected Chicanas/os, Latinas/os, and other people of color who are stereotyped as "illegal aliens."

Though the initiative passed by a margin of 59 percent to 41 percent, there was a tremendous amount of community action and mobilization against it. Students all over the state engaged in demonstrations, walkouts, and protests. Lilian Ramírez, a student who protested at San Francisco's city hall shortly after the passage of Proposition 187, believes that the proposition provided an "open season for racism" (Gutekunst, 1994). The 1994 student resistance to Proposition 187 was similar to the student resistance of the 1960s I have chronicled earlier in this chapter. In both cases, students were motivated to transform existing conditions (or a law) that devalued their sociocultural experiences and limited their access to quality education.

In fact, California's passage of Proposition 187 was the epitome of the educational segregation that Chicanas/os have historically resisted in their efforts to gain their constitutional right to an equal public education. The passage of Proposition 187 brought to the forefront a racist state law that attempted to dehumanize all Latina/o students and exclude them from public education. Similar measures followed in other states, as did calls for reduction in funding for bilingual education and the implementation of English-only policies (García, 1995). In California, MALDEF and the American Civil Liberties Union (ACLU) were key in pursuing legal action against the proposition, and the five lawsuits filed against the state were consolidated into one federal action. U.S. District Judge Mariana Pfaelzer recently ruled that the proposition was "unconstitutional from top to bottom" because the state has no power to regulate immigration ("Judge dumps," 1998). The 1994 student walkouts and assemblies in protest of Proposition 187 and the state and federal lawsuits filed against its passage illustrate the various actions taken by Chicanas/os to obtain equal access to public education. Certainly the legal challenges to Proposition 187, and its defeat in the courts, indicates that these grassroots and legal strategies can be successful and continue to be crucial in Chicanas/os pursuit for educational equity.

Limited Access to Higher Education: California's Proposition 209

Today, the discourse of "reverse discrimination" is as strong as ever, and California leads the national movement to dismantle affirmative action programs. In 1996, California voters passed Proposition 209, the California Civil Rights Initiative. Proposition 209 appropriates the language of early civil rights legislation to, in essence, eliminate all affirmative action in California, including that in higher education. It states that California shall not use "race, sex, color, ethnicity, or national origin as criterion for either discriminating against, or granting preferential treatment to any individual or group." While the legislation outlaws considerations of race/ethnicity in university admissions, outreach, and recruitment, it also ignores current societal inequalities. The anti-affirmative action legislation and its proponents adopted a narrow interpretation of the equal protection clause, embracing a colorblind constitution and the myth of meritocracy. Therefore, supporters are able to argue simultaneously that they strongly support equal opportunity for people of all color and that affirmative action policies violate a White man's right to equal protection, resulting in "reverse discrimination."

Proposition 209 legislates restricted access for Chicanas/os and other students of color at a time when college campuses remain racially stratified. Few middle- and upper-class Whites complain that throughout the Southwest at least 50 percent of all Chicanas/os who go to college go to a community college rather than a four-year institution (Astin, 1982; Olivas, 1986; Villalpando, 1996). The proposition is a specific political action supported by the meritocracy myth, and it validates a subjective and highly selective admissions process that tracks Chicanas/os into community colleges and keeps the gate to four-year campuses guarded. The admission policies at the "gatekeeper" schools, such as the University of California system, exert a powerful and controlling influence over who enters certain professions and who has access to positions of influence and economic and social reward.

Proposition 209's attack on affirmative action policies applies to the state's system of public employment, public education, or public contracting. Astin (1982, 1995) warns, however, that we should not confuse college admissions with employment and must acknowledge that discrimination in college admissions is often based on something other than a racial/ethnic classification:

> The employer seeks to exploit talent by hiring the best applicants; the public university seeks to develop the talents of the students it admits. University admissions are inherently discriminatory anyway, simply because there are not enough places for all applicants. . . . More than 95% of the 21,445 freshman admitted to the UC system last fall met . . . eligibility requirements. The 953 who did not meet them included athletes; students with artistic, musical, or other special talents; students with disabilities, and members of underrepresented minority groups. There were just as many white students among these 953 "special action" admits. (Astin, 1995, p. B5)

Proposition 209 limits access to education just as an increasing number of Chicana/o students are attending K–12 schools. In 1995, California's Latina/o student population was 2.3 million, and it is projected to reach 3.1 million by the year 2005 (University of California, Latino Eligibility Task Force, 1997). Yet only 3.9 percent of all Latina/o high school graduates were fully eligible for admission to the University of California, and the proportion of those admitted to four-year colleges appears to be declining nationally (Kerr, 1994; University of California, Latino Eligibility Task Force, 1997). These factors combine with the passage of Proposition 209 to create a great need for an overhaul in admission standards.

Legal scholar Richard Delgado (1995) argues for "an overhaul of the admissions process and a rethinking of the criteria that make a person a deserving . . . student" (p. 51). He and many others have argued for admission standards that would result in an increased number of women and students of color gaining admission, yet he points out that these recommendations are often ignored and have never instituted. In fact, the University of California Latino Eligibility Task Force (1997) recently recommended that the university system simply eliminate the SAT in determining eligibility without reducing overall admissions standards. The Task Force argued that the eligibility of Latina/o students could be greatly increased by eliminating the SAT and relying only on grade point average. Without the SAT, the proportion of Latina/o high school graduates achieving full eligibility to the University of California would rise by 59 percent (from 3.9 to 6.2 percent). So far the University system has not acted on the Task Force's recommendation, but throughout public

policy, university, and community circles, additional recommendations focusing on bringing in "educationally and economically disadvantaged" students are being proposed.

The Latest Threat to Bilingual Education: California's Proposition 227

Even with a growing number of students with limited English proficiency and expanding global borders that call for multilingual abilities, the threat to bilingual education is as strong as ever. In June 1998, California voters passed Proposition 227, the "English Language Education for Immigrant Children" initiative. The proposition was cosponsored by Ron Unz, a wealthy Silicon Valley businessman who unsuccessfully ran for governor of California in 1994, and Gloria Matta Tuchman, who failed in her first attempt to be elected State Superintendent of Public Instruction.[16] The proposition espouses the values of a just society while calling for the elimination of all bilingual education in the state of California. The proposition mandates that within sixty days of its passage, 1.38 million limited-English-speaking students be put into separate classrooms—regardless of age, language background, and/ or academic ability (Citizens for an Educated America, 1997). In these separate classrooms, these students will be taught English by a teacher who will be restricted, under the threat of a lawsuit, from speaking to them in their primary language.

Supporters of the proposition claim to have in mind the best interests of children "regardless of their ethnicity or national origins" (Article I: b, c, f). However, Article 2, the crux of the proposition, requires a 180-day English-only approach and states that "all children in California public schools shall be taught English by being taught in English during a temporary transition period not normally intended to exceed one year." This requirement counters educational research that demonstrates that English immersion is one of the least effective ways to teach children with limited English proficiency (Cummins, 1981; Gándara, 1997; Krashen, 1981; Wong Fillmore, 1991). The initiative does away with all bilingual education and English-language development programs that do not meet its rigid 180-day English-only approach. It also allows local schools "to place in the same classroom English learners of different ages but whose degree of English proficiency is similar" (Article 2). This means that twelve-year-old boys and six-year-old girls of any language group, for example, can be placed in the same classroom for a full year (180 days) to study English, without any instruction in content areas such as math, science, and social studies. Chicanas/os know from experience that placing all English-language learners into a separate classroom, regardless of age and academic abilities, and using rote memorization to teach English without academic instruction will fail because it was the standard process that failed miserably in the era of de jure segregation. Indeed, its failure was the reason why the federal Bilingual Education Act was passed just thirty years ago.

Today, Proposition 227 represents a distinct cultural attack on Chicanas/os and other Latinas/os, and creates yet another educational barrier imposed on Chicana/o students. For example, although Ron Unz and many other Proposition 227 supporters presented themselves as the voice of Latinos, arguing that Latinos supported the measure by an overwhelming majority, the actual Latino vote on the proposition was 63 percent "No" and 37 percent "Yes" (Pyle, McDonnell, & Tobar, 1998). The proposition was carried by a two-to-one vote among Whites in an electorate in which Whites represent a larger percentage than they represent in the general population. The victory of Proposition 227 will be a victory imposed on Latinos despite their opposition. In fact, Latino students will be disproportionately affected if the new law goes into effect because 80 percent of California's K–12 limited-English-proficient students are Spanish speakers (Gándara, 1997). There is, however, hope that the new law will not be enforced as a coalition of schoolchildren, and civil rights groups filed a lawsuit in federal court to challenge Proposition 227 the day after it was passed by voters. Three of the civil rights groups participating in the lawsuit are the California Latino Civil Rights Network, Mujeres Unidas y Activas, and the National Council of La Raza. Their lawsuit, which contends that Proposition 227 violates the U.S. Equal Educational Opportunities Act of 1974, Title VI of the Civil Rights Act of 1964, and the constitutional right to equal protection (Colvin & Smith, 1998), continues the historic tradition of Chicana/o community resistance and activism in their pursuit of an equitable and just educational system.

Conclusion

I have provided an overview of Chicana/o education from the 1950s through the 1990s and demonstrated a relationship between popular belief systems, judicial decisions, and educational policies and practices. Bilingual education, access to higher education, K–12 school equity, and continued school segregation have all been at the forefront during this period. Schooling for Chicanas/os has indeed improved since the era of de jure segregation, yet since the late 1970s there has been a deterioration of educational gains. Many of today's most important educational issues are similar to those voiced in Mexican communities before the 1950s. In fact, Jonathon Kozol states that in the realm of public schooling, "social policy has been turned back almost one hundred years" (1991, p. 4). In reality, the improvements in Chicana/o schooling have been modest and have not really kept pace with the demographic growth of the Chicana/o population.

Chicanas/os have a rich historical legacy that includes active struggles to gain equal access to quality education. A focus of the Chicana/o student movement was improv-

ing the quality of education at various points in the educational pipeline, and Chicanas were actively involved in and offered leadership to this movement. Over the past five decades, Chicano families have used the judicial system to fight educational practices that have limited the education of their children. They have utilized the courts to fight for bilingual education and school access and to fight against school segregation and schooling inequities. Today, Chicana/o students and their families have remained active in the pursuit of quality education through grassroots resistance and legal recourse. History is re-peating itself, and exclusionary laws such as California's Propositions 187, 209, and 227 contribute to an an-tagonistic sociopolitical climate that fosters the racist practices of the de jure segregation era. Inasmuch as the education of all Latina/o students is threatened, it is crucial that educators, policymakers, and Chicana/o communities continue to engage in strategies that combat this antagonistic sociopolitical climate and work toward educational equity.

References

Achievement Council. (1984). *Excellence for whom?* Oakland, CA: Author.

Acuña, R. (1988). *Occupied America: A history of Chicanos.* New York: Harper Collins.

Aguirre, A. (1980). *Intelligence testing education and Chicanos* (ERIC/ TM Report No. 76). Princeton, NJ: ERIC Clearing House on Tests, Measurement, and Evaluation, Educational Testing Service.

Aguirre, A., & Martínez, R.O. (1993). *Chicanos in higher education: Issues and dilemmas for the 21st century* (ASHE-ERIC Higher Education Report No. 3). Washington, DC: George Washington University, School of Education and Human Development.

Allsup, C. (1982). *The American G.I. Forum: Origins and evolution.* Austin: University of Texas, Center for Mexican American Studies.

Alvarez v. Lemon Grove School District (1931) Superior Court of the State of California, County of San Diego, Petition for Writ of Mandate, No. 66625.

Assembly Office of Research. (1985). *Dropping out, losing out: The high cost for California.* Sacramento, CA: Author.

Assembly Office of Research. (1990). *Education minority students in California: Descriptive analysis and policy implications.* Sacramento, CA: Author.

Astin, A.W. (1982). *Minorities in American higher education.* San Francisco: Jossey-Bass.

Astin, A.W. (1995, May 1). Perspective on affirmative action: Replace sound bites with discourse. *Los Angeles Times*, p. B5.

Barrera, M. (1979). *Race and class in the Southwest: A theory of racial inequality.* Notre Dame, IN: University of Notre Dame Press.

Biegel, S. (1994). Bilingual education and language rights: The parameters of the bilingual education debate in California twenty years after *Lau v. Nichols. Chicano-Latino Law Review*, 14, 48–60.

Bogardus, E.S. (1949, April). *School inspection report on fourteen schools* (American G.I. Forum Archives). Corpus Christi, TX: American G.I. Forum.

Brownstein, R. (1995, May 14). Immigration debate roils GOP presidential contest. *Los Angeles Times*, pp. A1, A18.

Burciaga, J.A. (1993). *Drink cultura: Chicanismo.* Santa Barbara, CA: Joshua Odell Editions.

California State Advisory Committee to the U.S. Commission on Civil Rights. (1968, April). *Education and the Mexican American community in Los Angeles county* (CR 1.2:ED8/3). Los Angeles: Author.

California State Department of Education. (1981). *Schooling and language minority students: A theoretical framework*. Los Angeles: California State University, Los Angeles, Evaluation, Dissemination and Assessment Center.

California State Department of Education. (1985). *Racial or ethnic distribution of staff and students in California public schools, 1984-85*. Sacramento, CA: Author.

California State Department of Education. (1988). *Racial or ethnic distribution of staff and students in California public schools, 1987–88*. Sacrament, CA: Author.

California State Department of Education. (1993). *R30-LC language census report*. Sacrament, CA: Author.

Castañeda v. Pickard, 648 F. 2d 989 (5th Cir. 1981).

Castillo, A. (1994). *Massacre of the dreamers: Essays on Xicanisma*. New York: Plume.

Castro, V. (1994, December). [Transcribed interview conducted by Susan Racho with Vickie Castro]. Unpublished data.

Chapa, E. (1973). Report from the National Women's Political Caucus. *Magazín*, 1 (9), 37–39.

Chapa, J. (1991). Special focus: Hispanic demographic and educational trends. In D.J. Carter & R. Wilson (Eds.), *Minorities in higher education: Ninth annual status report* (pp. 11–17). Washington DC: American Council on Education.

Chicano Coordinating Council on Higher Education. (1970). *El plan de Santa Bárbara: A Chicana/o plan for higher education*. Santa Barbara, CA: La Causa.

Citizens for an Educated America: No on Unz. (1997). Los Angeles: Citizens for an Educated America.

Cisneros v. Corpus Christi Independent School District, 324 F. Supp. 599 (S.D. Tex. 1970). appeal docketed, No. 71-2397 (5th Cir. July 16, 1971).

Colvin, R.L., & Smith, D. (1998, June 4). Prop. 227 foes vow to block it despite wide vote margin. *Los Angeles Times*, p. A1.

Crawford, J. (1992). *Hold your tongue: Bilingualism and the politics of English only*. Reading, MA: Addison Wesley.

Crenshaw, K.W., Gotanda, N., Peller, G., & Thomas, K. (Eds). (1995). *Critical race theory: The key writings that formed the movement*. New York: New Press.

Cummins, J. (1981). The role of primary language development in promoting educational success for language minority students. In California State Department of Education (Ed.), *Schooling and language minority students: A theoretical framework* (pp. 4–49). Los Angeles: California State University. Los Angeles, Evaluation, Dissemination and Assessment Center.

De La Rosa, D., & Maw, C.E. (1990). *Hispanic education: A statistical portrait 1990*. Washington, DC: National Council of La Raza.

Delgado Bernal, D. (1997). *Chicana school resistance and grassroots leadership: Providing an alternative history of the 1968 East Los Angeles blowouts*. Unpublished doctoral dissertation, University of California, Los Angeles.

Delgado Bernal, D. (in press). Grassroots leadership reconceptualized: Chicana oral histories and the 1968 East Los Angeles school blowouts. *Frontier: A Journal of Women Studies*.

Delgado, R. (1989). Storytelling for oppositionists and others: A plea for narrative. *Michigan Law Review*, 87, 2411–2441.

Delgado, R. (1995). The imperial scholar: Reflections on a review of civil rights literature. In K.W. Crenshaw, N. Gotanda, G. Peller, & K. Thomas (Eds.), *Critical race theory: The key writings that formed the movement* (pp. 46–57). New York: New Press.

Delgado et al. v. Bastrop Independent School District of Bastrop County et al., docketed, No. 388 (W.D. Tex. June 15, 1948).

Del Rio Independent School District v. Salvatierra, 33 S.W.2d 790 (Tex. Civ. App., San Antonio 1930), cert. denied, 284 U.S. 580 (1931).

Donato, R. (1997). *The other struggle for equal schools: Mexican Americans during the civil rights era*. Albany: State University of New York Press.

Donato, R., Menchaca, M., & Valencia, R.R. (1991). Segregation, desegregation, and integration of Chicano students: Problems and prospects. In R.R. Valencia (Ed.), *Chicano school failure and success: Research and policy agendas for the 1990's* (pp. 27–63). London: Falmer Press.

Durán, R.P. (1983). *Hispanics' education and background: Predictors of college achievement*. New York: College Entrance Examination Board.

Espinosa, A.L. (1979). Hispanas: Our resources for the eighties. *La Luz*, 8(4), 10–13.

Gándara, P. (1982). Passing through the eye of the needle: High-achieving Chicanas. *Hispanic Journal of Behavioral Sciences, 4*, 167–179.

Gándara, P. (1994). Choosing higher education: Educationally ambitious Chicanos and the path to social mobility. *Education Policy Analysis Archives, 2*(8).

Gándara, P. (1997). *Review of the research on instruction of limited English proficient students: A report to the California Legislature*. Davis: University of California, Linguistic Minority Research Institute, Education Policy Center.

García, R.J. (1995). Critical race theory and Proposition 187: The racial politics of immigration law. *Chicano-Latino Law Review, 17*, 118–154.

García, A. (Ed.). (1997). *Chicana feminist thought: The basic historical writings*. New York: Routledge.

Goldman, R.D., & Hewitt, B.N. (1975). An investigation of test bias for Mexican-American college students. *Journal of Educational Measurement, 12*, 187–196.

Goldman, R.D., & Richards, R. (1974). The SAT prediction of grades for Mexican-American versus Anglo-American students at the University of California, Riverside. *Journal of Educational Measurement, 11*, 129–135.

Gómez-Quiñones, J. (1978). *Mexican students por La Raza: The Chicano student movement in Southern California 1967–1977*. Santa Barbara, CA: Editorial La Causa.

González, G.G. (1974). *The system of public education and its function within the Chicano communities, 1910–1950*. Unpublished doctoral dissertation, University of California, Los Angeles.

González, G.G. (1990). *Chicano education in the era of segregation*. Cranbury, NJ: Associated University Presses.

Guadalupe Organization v. Tempe Elementary School District, 587 F.2d 1022 (9th Cir. 1978).

Gutekunst, L. (1994, November 21). Students protest passage of Prop. 187. *The Lowell*, p. 1.

Harders, R., & Gómez, M.N. (1998). Separate and unequal: *Méndez v. Westminster* and desegregation in California schools. In M. DeMartino (Ed.), *A family changes history: Méndez v. Westminster* (pp. 3–12). Irvine: University of California.

Jensen, V.J. (1962, February). Effects of childhood bilingualism, I. *Elementary English, 39*, 132–143.

Judge dumps rest of Proposition 187. (1998, March 19). *San Francisco Chronicle*, p. A15.

Kerr, C. (1994). *Troubled times for American higher education: The 1990s and beyond*. Albany: State University of New York Press.

Keyes v. School District Number 1 Denver Colorado, 413 U.S. 189 (1973), 521 F.2d 465 (10th Cir. 1975).

Kozol, J. (1991). *Savage inequalities: Children in America's schools*. New York: HarperCollins.

Krashen, S.D. (1981). Bilingual education and second language acquisition theory. In California State Department of Education, *Schooling and language minority students: A theoretical framework* (pp. 51–79). Los Angeles: California State University, Los Angeles, Evaluation, Dissemination and Assessment Center.

Lau v. Nichols, 414 U.S. 563 (1974).

Lawrence, C.R. (1993). If he hollers let him go: Regulating racist speech on campus. In M.J. Matsuda, C.R. Lawrence, R. Delgado, & K.W. Crenshaw (Eds.), *Words that wound: Critical race theory, assault-*

ive speech, and the First Amendment (pp. 53–88). Boulder, CO: Westview Press.

López, S. (1977). The role of the Chicana within the student movement. In R. Sánchez & R. Martínez Cruz (eds.), *Essays on a la mujer* (pp. 16–19). Los Angeles: University of California, Chicano Studies Research Center.

Loya, A.C. (1990). Chicanos, law, and educational reform. *La Raza Law Journal*, 3, 28–50.

Luján et al v. Colorado State Board of Education, 649 P.2d 1005 (Co. 1982).

Macías, R. (1979). Language choice and human rights in the United States. In J.E. Alatis (Ed.), *Georgetown University round table on languages and linguistics, 1979* (pp. 86–101). Washington, DC: Georgetown University Press.

Martínez, G.A. (1994). Legal indeterminacy, judicial discretion and the Mexican–American litigation experience: 1930–1980. *U.C. Davis Law Review*, 27, 555–618.

Matsuda, M.J., Lawrence, C.R., Delgado, R., & Crenshaw, K.W. (1993). *Words that wound: Critical race theory, assaultive speech, and the First Amendment.* Boulder, CO: Westview Press.

McCurdy, J. (1968, March 17). Frivolous to fundamental: Demands made by east side high school students listed. *Los Angeles Times*, pp. 1, 4–5.

Menchaca, M., & Valencia, R.R. (1990). Anglo-Saxon ideologies and their impact on the segregation of Mexican students in California, the 1920s–1930s. *Anthropology and Education Quarterly*, 21, 222–249.

Menchaca, M. (1995). *The Mexican outsiders: A community history of marginalization and discrimination in California.* Austin: University of Texas Press.

Méndez González, R. (1995, October). [Transcribed interview conducted by Dolores Delgado Bernal with Rosalinda Méndez González]. Unpublished data.

Méndez v. Westminster, 64 F. Supp. 544 (S.D. Cal. 1946), 161 F. 2d 774 (9th Cir. 1947).

Mitchell, D.E., Powell, R.J., Scott, L.D., & McDaid, J.L. (1994). *The impact of California's special education pre-referral intervention activities and alternative assessments on ethnolinguistically diverse students: Final report of a federal-state joint agreement evaluation feasibility study.* Riverside: University of California, California Educational Research Cooperative.

Morín, R. (1963). *Among the valiant: Mexican Americans in WWII and Korea.* Los Angeles: Borden.

Muñoz, C., Jr. (1989). *Youth identity, power: The Chicano movement.* New York: Verso.

Nieto Gómez, A. (1973). The Chicana: Perspectives for education. *Encuentro Femenil, 1*, 34–61.

Nieto Gómez, A. (1974). La feminista. *Encuentro Feminil, 1*, 34–47.

Oakes, J. (1985). *Keeping track: How schools structure inequality.* New Haven, CT: Yale University Press.

Olivas, M. (Ed.). (1986). *Latino college students.* New York: Teachers College Press.

Orozco, C. (1986). Sexism in Chicano studies and the community. In T. Córdova, N. Cantú, G. Cárdenas, J. García, & C.M. Sierra (Eds.). *Chicana voices: Intersections of class, race, and gender* (pp. 11–18). Austin, TX: Center for Mexican American Studies.

Orozco, C. (1992). *The origins of the League of United Latin American Citizens (LULAC) and the Mexican American Civil Rights Movement in Texas with an analysis of women's political participation in a gendered context, 1910–1929.* Unpublished doctoral dissertation, University of California, Los Angeles.

Orum, L.S. (1986). *The education of Hispanics: Status and implications.* Washington, DC: National Council of La Raza.

Otero v. Mesa County Valley School District Number 51, 408 F. Supp. 162 (D. Colo. 1975).

Pardo, M. (1984, March/April). A selective evaluation of El Plan de Santa Bárbara. *La Gente*, 14–15.

Plyler v. Doe, 457 U.S. 202 (1982).

Prince, R. (1994, September 6). Americans want illegal immigrants out. *Los Angeles Times*, p. B7.

Pyle, A., McDonnell P.J., & Tobar, H. (1998, June 4). Latino voter participation doubled since '94 primary. *Los Angeles Times*, p. A1.

Rangel, J.C., & Alcalá, C.M. (1972). Project report: De jure segregation of Chicanos in Texas schools. *Harvard Civil Rights-Civil Liberties Review*, 7, 348–359.

Regents of the University of California v. Bakke, 438 U.S. 265 (1978).

Roos, P. (1978). Bilingual education: The Hispanic response to unequal education opportunity. *Law and Contemporary Problems*, 42, 111–140.

Salinas, F. (1971). Mexican-Americans and the desegregation of schools in the Southwest: A supplement. *El Grito, 4*(4), 36–-69.

San Antonio Independent School District et al. v. Rodríguez et al., 337 F. Supp. 280 W.D. Tex. (1971), 36 L. Ed. 2d 16, 411 U.S. 1 (1973).

San Miguel, G., Jr. (1985). Conflict and controversy in the evolution of bilingual education in the United States: An interpretation. *Social Science Quarterly, 65*, 505–518.

San Miguel, G., Jr. (1987). *Let all of them take heed: Mexican Americans and the campaign for educational equality in Texas, 1910–1981.* Austin: University of Texas Press.

Sandoval, M. (1979). *Our legacy: The first fifty years.* Washington, DC: League of United Latin American Citizens.

Schaller, M., Scharff, V., & Schulzinger, R.D. (1992). *Present tense: The United States since 1945.* Boston: Houghton Mifflin.

Segura, D. (1993). Slipping through the cracks: Dilemmas in Chicana education. In A. de la Torre & B. Pesquera (Eds.), *Building with our hands: New directions in Chicana studies* (pp. 199–216). Berkeley: University of California Press.

Serna v. Portales Municipal Schools, 499 F.2d 1147 (10th Cir. 1974).

Serrano et al. v. Ivy Baker Priest, 487 P.2d 1241 (Cal. 1971).

Solórzano, D.G., & Delgado Bernal, D. (1998). *Critical race theory and transformation resistance: Chicana/o students in an urban context.* Unpublished manuscript.

Solórzano, D.G., & Villalpando, O. (in press). Critical race theory: Marginality, and the experiences of students of color in higher education. In C.A. Torres & T.R. Mitchell (Eds.), *Sociology of education: Emerging perspectives.* Albany: State University of New York Press.

Swarts, D. (1977). Pierre Bourdieu: The cultural transmission of social inequality. *Harvard Educational Review, 47*, 545–555.

Tate, W.F. (1997). Critical race theory and education: History, theory, and implications. *Review of Research in Education, 22*, 195–247.

Taylor, P.S. (1934). *An American-Mexican frontier: Nueces County, Texas.* Chapel Hill: University of North Carolina Press.

University of California, Latino Eligibility Task Force. (1995, March). *History of responses to Latino under-achievement* (Report No. 4). Berkeley, CA: Chicana/o/Latino Policy Project.

University of California, Latino Eligibility Task Force. (1997, July). *Latino student eligibility and participation in the University of California: Ya basta!* (Report No. 5). Berkeley, CA: Chicana/o/Latino Policy Project.

U.S. Commission on Civil Rights. (1971). *Mexican American education study, report 1: Ethnic isolation of Mexican Americans in the public schools of the Southwest.* Washington: DC: Government Printing Office.

Valdez, P. (1994, December). [Transcribed interview conducted by Susan Racho with Vickie Patssi Valdez]. Unpublished data.

Valencia, R.R. (1991). The plight of Chicano students: An overview of schooling conditions and outcomes. In R.R. Valencia (Ed.), *Chicano school failure and success: Research and policy agendas for the 1990's* (pp. 3–26). London: Falmer Press.

Valencia, R.R., & Aburto, S. (1991). The uses and abuses of educational testing: Chicanos as a case in point. In Valencia, R.R. (Ed.),

Chicano school failure and success: Research and policy agendas for the 1990's (pp. 203–251). London: Falmer Press.

Vásquez, M. (1982). Confronting barriers to the participation of Mexican American women in higher education. *Hispanic Journal of Behavioral Sciences, 4*, 147–165.

Villalpando, O. (1996). *The long term effects of college on Chicano and Chicana students: "Other oriented" values, service careers, and community involvement*. Unpublished doctoral dissertation, University of California, Los Angeles.

Webster, D.S. (1984). Chicano students in American higher education. *Integration Education, 22* (1–3), 42–52.

Wise, A.E. (1982). *Legislated learning: The bureaucratization of the American classroom*. Berkeley: University of California Press.

Wollenberg, C. (1974). *Westminster v. Méndez*: Race, nationality, and segregation in California schools. *California Historical Quarterly, 53*, 317–332.

Wong-Fillmore, L. (1991). Language and cultural issues in early education. In S.L. Kagan (ed.), *The care and education of American's young children: Obstacles and opportunities, the 90th yearbook of the National Society for the Study of Education* (pp. 39–50). Chicago: University of Chicago Press.

Zambrana, R. (1994). Toward understanding the educational trajectory and socialization of Latina women. In L. Stone & G.M. Boldt (eds.), *The education feminism reader* (pp. 135–145). New York: Routledge.

Zavella, P. (1991). Reflections on diversity among Chicanas. *Frontiers: A Journal of Women Studies, 12*, 73–85.

Notes

1. "Chicana/o" is used when referring to both females and males of Mexican origin living in the United States, irrespective of immigration or generation status. Chicana/o is meant to be inclusive of females and males, rather than using the Spanish masculine gender, Chicano, to refer to both genders. Terms of identification vary according to context, and Chicana/o is used here as a political term of self-determination and solidarity that was popularized during the Chicano Movement in the 1960s, and are used interchangeably with "Mexican" when referring to pre-1960s history. "Latina/o" is sometimes used when referring to contemporary issues in order to be more inclusive of all mestizo peoples whose families might originate in Central America, South American, the Caribbean, and Mexico, and who share geographic and sociopolitical space with Chicanas/os. Latina/o is also used when data on "Hispanics" has not been desegregated specifically for Chicanas/os.

2. "De jure" segregation refers to that which is supported by official policy or law, while "de facto" segregation refers to that which exists in reality, but without lawful authority.

3. LULAC was founded in Texas in 1929 by middle-class English-speaking Mexican Americans who stressed American patriotism. As a civil rights organization, LULAC led the fight for school desegregation in the 1930s and 1940s (see Sandoval, 1979; San Miguel, 1987; Orozco, 1992). In 1948, the American G.I. Forum was founded in Texas as a Mexican American veteran's organization that was interested in the welfare of veterans and their families. The organization became interested in fighting discriminatory practices in all public institutions, and educational issues were of primary importance (see Allsup, 1982; San Miguel, 1987). Today, LULAC and the G.I. Forum are national organizations that have often joined forces in their struggles for educational and social equity.

4. A colonized relationship in general is one of economic, political, and cultural domination and subordination of one group by another. The dominant and subordinate groups are defined along ethnic and/or racial lines, and the relationship is established to serve the interests of the dominant group. See Mario Barrera (1979) for a theoretical discussion of Chicanas/os and internal colonialism—a form of colonialism in which the dominant and subordinate groups are within a single society and there are no clear geographic boundaries of a "colony."

5. For historical and contemporary discussions of Chicana/o grade retention and risk factors for dropping out, see California State Advi-

sory Committee (1968), Assembly Office of Research (1985), and De La Rosa and Maw (1990).

6. See Segura (1993), Gándara (1982), and Vásquez (1982) for studies that examine barriers to education experienced by various groups of Chicanas.

7. The Servicemen's Readjustment Act of 1944, or the G.I. Bill, provided veterans and their families with various employment, health, economic, and educational benefits until the program ended in 1956. Veterans pursuing a college education received $110 a month, plus allowance for dependents and payment of tuition, fees, and books. Nationally, the G.I. Bill opened up a selective higher education system to working-class people by assisting over two million new students. Chicano servicemen also took advantage of the G.I. Bill's educational benefits (see Morín, 1963). However, because of the relatively small number of women who had served in the military and of active discrimination (i.e., women did not receive full benefits), Chicanas and other women received few direct educational benefits (see also Schaller, Scharff, & Schulzinger, 1992).

8. These lawsuits include Serna v. Portales Municipal Schools (1974); *Otero v. Mesa County Valley School District* (1975); *Guadalupe Organization v. Tempe Elementary School District* (1978). For more on these cases see, Martínez (1994).

9. In *Keyes v. School District Number 1*, plaintiffs alleged that the school board was practicing de jure segregation. The U.S. Supreme Court ruled that the school board had an unconstitutional policy of deliberately segregating Park Hill schools, one segment of the Denver school district, and mandated a desegregation plan. The Keys case did not address the issue of de facto segregation (see Martínez, 1994; San Miguel, 1987).

10. Later in 1981, the *Castañeda v. Pickard* case put forth a three-pronged test that the federal courts continue to follow today when evaluating a school districts' actions in overcoming the language barriers of students. In *Castañeda*, a group of Chicana/o children and their parents challenged the practices of a Texas school district under the Fourteenth Amendment, Title VI, and the Equal Educational Opportunity Act. The plaintiffs charged that the district failed to offer adequate bilingual education to overcome the linguistic barriers of students. The court ruled in favor of the plaintiffs and set forth the three-pronged analysis for courts to follow: 1) Ea court must determine whether the district is pursuing a program that is based on sound educational theory; 2) the court must establish whether or not the programs and practices effectively implement the educational theory adopted; and 3) the court must determine if the school's program actually results in overcoming language barriers of students (see Biegel, 1994).

11. In other words, since federal and state policies prior to 1954 had allowed for the segregation of Blacks and Whites and had not referenced Mexicans, the strategy had been to have Mexicans classified as part of the White race. If Mexicans were declared White, then segregating Mexican students from White students in the absence of a law allowing for their separation would be illegal. The Cisneros case was the first time a court officially recognized Mexicans as an identifiable minority group, thereby allowing them to use the equal protection strategy used in Black desegregation cases, rather than the claim to "Whiteness" strategy (see San Miguel, 1987).

12. See Donato (1997) for documentation of the tension between bilingual education and desegregation.

13. Critical race theorist Richard Delgado (1989) describes "counterstorytelling" as both a method of telling the story of those experiences not often told, and a tool for analyzing and challenging the dominant discourse and the stories of those in power.

14. Gloria Martínez is a composite character based on data from focus group interviews, individual conversations, and personal experiences. She was first introduced as an undergraduate student in an article by Daniel G. Solórzano and Octavio Villalpando (in press) and also appears in an article by Solórzano and Dolores Delgado Bernal (1998). In these articles, Gloria facilitates a technique of counterstorytelling.

15. The complex relationship between race/ethnicity, class, and gender, and how each of these categories contributes to the marginalization of Chicana/o students, cannot be fully dealt with here. However, it should be noted that even middle-class Chicana/o college students often experience a sense of marginalization, par-

ticularly when they are first-generation college students. These students may lack the kind of "cultural capital" valued by higher education systems. As Bourdieu has stated, "academic performance is linked to cultural background . . . and is more strongly related to parents' educational history than to parents' occupational status" (Swarts, 1977, p. 547). See Gándara, this volume, for a discussion of class, gender, and Chicana/o college students, and see Zavella (1991), Castillo (1994), Zambrana (1994), and García (1997) for a general discussion on how institutional and cultural differences based on sexism, racism, and classism create a different range of choices and options for Chicanas in particular.

16. In California's June 1998 primary election, Gloria Matta Tuchman once again ran for the position of State Superintendent of Public Instruction. She came in second with 25.5 percent of the votes, behind the incumbent Delaine Eastin with 43.3 percent of the votes. The two will face a run-off in the November 1998 election.

Who's the Leader of the Civil Rights Band?
Latinos' Role in *Brown v. Board of Education*

Nicolás C. Vaca

The fruits of the African American battle for civil rights are positions of power held by African Americans in the public and private sectors. And now we find ourselves in the position of defending that power against other people pushing for inclusion. Though we pride ourselves on our leadership role in civil rights, paradoxically, we guard the success jealously. "We're the ones who marched in the streets and got our heads busted. Where were they? But now they want to get in on the benefits."

Brenda Payton
Columnist for the *Oakland Tribune*

There is a Black perception that Latinos have not suffered discrimination to the same degree and in the same manner as they and are thus are not entitled to the benefits of the civil rights movements.\African Americans often assume that they were the pioneers in the area of civil rights. The actions of Martin Luther King, Roy Innis, and myriad other Black leaders would tend to confirm this belief. In addition to these inspirational leaders of the civil rights movement, Blacks reference the NAACP, the Congress of Racial Equality, and the Southern Christian Leadership Conference as leading examples of organizations that pushed for civil rights in the 1960s.

More specifically, African Americans point to their role in the passage of the Voting Rights Act of 1965 and the benchmark case of *Brown v. Board of Education* as demonstration of their leadership in the area of civil rights. While it is true that the historical deprivation of Black suffrage in the South was the impetus for passage of the Voting Rights Act of 1965, Latino civil rights litigation presaged the *Brown* decision by some eight years. Unfortunately, ignorance of Latino activism around this issue has led one scholar to conclude that the role of Latinos has been reduced to little more than a sidebar.[1]

The discrimination suffered by Mexican Americans in California and Texas and their response in the form of pioneering litigation gives Latinos a legitimate claim to being pioneers in the area of civil rights, as *Méndez v. Westminster* and *Delgado v. Bastrop Independent School District* make clear.

California: *Méndez v. Westminster*

The insatiable appetite for cheap Mexican labor in the Southwest did not come without social consequences. In the beginning most Mexican workers were single men who came to the United States with the goal of earning money and sending it back to Mexico. But later immigrant male workers arrived with their families. Inevitably, this had an impact on social service agencies and the education system as well. The impact was two-way. Historian George J. Sánchez writes: "In the 1930s, three institutions most clearly framed the experience of Mexican American adolescents and young adults in Los Angeles: the family, the school, and the workplace."[2] Mexican Americans, Sánchez argues, had accepted that education was the path to success in American society. In 1938 the Mexican American Movement (MAM), an organization comprised of second-generation Mexican Americans, published a piece in its newspaper, the *Mexican Voice*, that stressed the significance of remaining in school. "Education is the only tool which will raise our influence, command the respect of the rich class, and enable us to mingle in their social, political and religious life. . . . EDUCATION is our only weapon."[3]

But education facilities for Mexican American students were not only separate but also unequal—this was the harsh reality. The creation of separate schools for

Mexican American children existed throughout southern California. In 1913, Pasadena established a Mexican school. In 1921, the city of Ontario built its own Mexican school, and by 1928, the school was so overenrolled that another "Mexican" school had to be built. In 1924, Riverside built another "Mexican" school to accommodate the wishes of white parents to separate their children from Latino children.[4]

As the number of Mexican children who enrolled in school continued to increase, so did the degree of segregation. By 1927 over 65,000 Mexican American children were enrolled in California schools, and 88 percent were located in southern California with 50 percent concentrated in Los Angeles County. A study conducted in 1926 found that 80 percent of the Mexican American children were enrolled in 3 of the 14 elementary schools in East L.A. and 3 others had an enrollment of approximately 60 percent. The numbers had increased by 1939: each of the 6 schools enrolled more than 80 percent of their students from the Mexican American community. A survey conducted in 1931 discovered that 80 percent of school districts with significant Mexican student enrollment were segregated.[5]

The creation of separate schools for Latino children was not based on any statute or legal ruling. Up to 1947 California provided for the establishment of separate schools, but they were reserved for children of Native American, Chinese, Japanese, and Mongolian descent. Curiously, the statute did not mention Blacks or Mexicans. But even without a statutory basis, the school districts accomplished their goal of de facto segregation by two methods. The first was to gerrymander the school district. Gerrymandering was accomplished by arbitrarily creating school zone boundaries designed to include Mexicans only within those boundaries, thus assuring that the school that fell within that zone became a Mexican school. An example of how this gerrymandering was accomplished is reflected in a letter written by a "supervisory official" of the city of Los Angeles in 1933.

> Our educational theory does not make any racial distinction between the Mexican and native white population. However, pressure from white residents of certain sections forced a modification of this principle to the extent that certain neighborhood schools have been placed to absorb the majority of the Mexican pupils in the district.[6]

Such gerrymandering was not only the result of protest by white parents but also fit nicely into the pedagogy of the time. The segregation of Mexican American children was justified on several grounds, one being that they were naturally happier with their own kind. One educator described Mexican American students who sat in the same classroom as white students as "dull, stupid and phlegmatic." She contrasted this with the atmosphere in an all-Mexican American classroom, where the faces of the children "radiated joy, they had thrown off the repression that held them down when they were in school with other children."[7]

Another argument used by educators for segregated schools was the need to Americanize Mexican children. This push to assimilate the Mexican children could best be accomplished, educators argued, by segregating the students so that the special "assimilation" training that Mexican students needed would not hinder the white students' educational progress.[8]

An additional, and to many educators persuasive, argument for segregating Mexican children in separate classrooms or separate schools was the use and acceptance of standardized intelligence tests which ostensibly established that Mexican children were duller and slower than white students. The literature on the education of the Mexican-American in the early part of the 20th century emphasized their sub-normal intelligence. Study after "scientific" study established that Mexican children simply were not as intelligent as white students. In 1931 B. F. Haught conducted a study that concluded that the "average Spanish child has an intelligence quotient of .79 compared with 1.00 for the average Anglo child." O. K. Garretson concluded that "retardation of the Mexican child . . . is from three to eight times as great as that of the American child. . . ."[9] Leo M. Gamble conducted a study on Mexican-American children and found that "the average intelligence quotient for the Mexican was 78.75"[10] William Sheldon of the University of Texas administered the Cole-Vincent and Stanford-Binet tests to Mexican and American students in Texas. His results "scientifically" established that Mexicans had only 85 percent of the I.Q. of the white students. Thomas Garth, a professor at the University of Denver, administered the National Intelligence Test to more than 1,000 Mexican and Mexican-American students in Texas, New Mexico and Colorado and discovered that the median I.Q. was 78.1.[11]

This group was joined by numerous other scholars—Helen L. Koch, Rietta Simmons, Kimball Young, Ellen A. McAnulty, F. C. Paschal, C. R. Sullivan, and Florence L. Goodenough—in concluding that the intelligence of Mexican children was inferior to that of American children.

By the late 1920s and early 1930s the segregation of Mexican and Mexican American children was a fact of life. As Charles M. Wollenberg, a scholar who has examined the segregation of Mexican children in California schools, observed, "In Orange County . . . over 4,000 students, a quarter of total school enrollment, were Mexicans or Mexican-Americans in 1934. About 70 percent of the Spanish-surnamed total attended the fifteen Orange County elementary schools which had 100 percent Mexican enrollment." [12] It is this background of de facto segregation of Mexican children in Orange County that led to the groundbreaking case of *Méndez v. Westminster*—a case that helped lay the groundwork for the ruling in *Brown v. Board of Education* eight years later.

The Social Context of
Méndez v. Westminster

Orange County's economy in the early 1930s and 1940s was almost exclusively based on agriculture. Crops such as oranges, lemons, nuts, beans, and vegetables dominated the region's industry. And like the rest of Southwest agriculture, the preferred labor for these crops was Mexicans. Over time the Mexican population, instead of remaining migratory, established permanent residency in various cities in Orange County. González notes that in 1930, 17,000 Mexicans resided in these towns and cities.[13]

The Mexican population made an impact on the educational system as early as 1913 when a report revealed that school administrators had set aside a special room for "Spanish" children at one of the elementary schools. In time the number of Mexican children flowing into the school district forced the construction of a separate school building. Accompanying the physical segregation of Mexican children from white children was the creation of a separate curriculum for Mexican children. The school district emphasized manual training for the Mexican children, while it maintained academic preparation for white students.

In 1916, the Committee on Buildings recommended that a six-room building be constructed near the existing Fifth Street building, and that a separate two-room building be constructed to be used exclusively by Mexican children. Not only was there to be a separate physical facility for the Mexicans, and a different curriculum, but different criteria were used for selecting teachers assigned to the Mexican school and those assigned to the Anglo school. Responding to this resolution, the school board instructed the president to obtain bids for the construction of the building where all Mexican children would attend.

The proposed construction of the separate facility for Mexican children was criticized by both white and Mexican parents. The white parents did not believe that the construction was moving quickly enough, while the Mexicans demanded that it not proceed at all. In 1918, the all-Anglo Lincoln School PTA passed a resolution urging the school board to do something about the Mexican problem and advised that "segregation is eminently desirable from moral, physical and education standpoints." For its part, the Mexican community objected to the construction of the Mexican school. Pro Patria Club, a Mexican organization, objected strongly to the segregation of Mexican children and demanded they be returned to their respective schools.

Confronted with the two opposing parties, the superintendent of schools asked the city attorney to issue a legal opinion addressing the legal basis on which segregation of Mexican children could be justified. The city attorney conceded that the existing education statute did not provide for any basis for the creation of segregated schools for Mexican children. However, his opinion justified the creation of separate educational facilities for Mexicans based on language differences, age, and regularity of attendance. Based on this incorrect interpretation of the statute, the Santa Ana Board of Education passed a resolution that read, in part, "agreed that for the best interest of the Schools and especially for the great benefit to the Mexican children, to continue the Mexican school work at the present."[14] In other words, the school facilities would continue to be segregated.

Armed with what they believed was legal justification for segregating Mexican children, the Santa Ana Board of Education subsequently identified three schools as Mexican schools. González writes:

> On 5 June 1919, the "plans and specifications for the [just permanent] Mexican school buildings were approved and the secretary was instructed to advertise for bids. . . ." The temporary arrangement evolved into the first Mexican school building in Santa Ana, named the Santa Fe School. Thus, the process of segregation, begun in 1912 with separate classroom, reached its completed form in 1920 with the establishment of a separate Mexican school. In 1921 the district added Logan, another Mexican school, and incorporated a third, Delhi, in 1924.[15]

Mexican children were not only relegated to separate school buildings, but the teachers hired to instruct them also were paid anywhere from $90 to $100 less per year than teachers assigned to the Anglo schools.

The unequal nature of the education provided to the Mexican children was exemplified not only by the separate curriculum developed for them (emphasis on manual training for the boys and homemaking for the girls) and the lower-paid teachers assigned to them, but also by the decrepit structures in which they received their segregated instruction. In 1928 Osman R. Hull and Willard S. Ford, two University of Southern California professors, conducted an educational survey of the Santa Ana school district at the behest of the school district. Hull and Ford described the Mexican schools as follows:

> The Delhi school is a wooden structure which is a fire hazard and poorly constructed [and] provides less than one-third of the required amount of light. . . .
>
> The Grand Avenue School . . . is a two story frame structure entirely unsuited to school use . . . it has been condemned for years.
>
> The most unsatisfactory school that is now being used . . . is the Artesia school. . . . It is a frame building with no interior finish. It has a low single roof with no air space, which makes the temperature in many of the rooms almost unbearable. Since no artificial light is provided in the building, it is impossible to do satisfactory reading without serious eye strain on many days of the year."[16]

Based on these findings, they recommended that two of the Mexican schools be demolished and new schools be constructed. The reaction of the Anglo community to this recommendation was swift and forceful. Harvey Gardner, a member of the advisory committee of the Chamber of Commerce, objected to the monies that would have to be used to build two new Mexican schools when, he argued, there were not "proper facilities for the American school children." The board, cowed by the fierce reaction of the Anglo citizens, rejected Hull and Ford's recommendation and instructed them to provide a new set of recommendations.

Ford and Hull, in compliance with the board's request, provided a revised plan: they recommended that only one school be torn down instead of two, and they reduced from $170,000 to $112,000 the amount of money designated for repairs to the Artesia school. However, even these reduced figures did not satisfy the board, so Ford and Hull were instructed to provide a third revised plan.

Once again, the plan proposed by Ford and Hull did not meet with the approval of the board and advisory committee, and the contract with Ford and Hull was then terminated. In their stead a committee was appointed to decide what to do about a Mexican school. Ultimately, the committee recommended a new Artesia school building with a budget of $65,000; a new kindergarten for Delhi at a cost of $500; and instead of building a new Grand Avenue school, the committee recommended that the vacant Logan school be restored and an addition be appended at a cost of $32,000.

After considerable debate and input from Anglo citizens, who objected to the proposal for a variety of reasons, not the least of which was a desire to relocate the Artesia school within the boundaries of a Mexican neighborhood, the committee's plan was adopted. In the 1929–1930 school year, the new Artesia school (which was renamed Fremont School) opened: Logan enrolled 232 students and Delhi enrolled 319 students. The total number of Mexican children enrolled in these schools represented more than one-quarter of the district's total enrollment.

While segregation of Mexican children continued into the 1940s, by the early 1930s theories regarding the benefits of segregation were coming under attack. George I. Sánchez, at that time director of information and statistics for the New Mexico Department of Education, argued that the results of intelligence tests administered to Mexican children had to take into consideration the child's environment. Wollenberg notes that "California educator Simon Treff asserted that Mexican students in mixed schools seemed to be less 'retarded' than those in segregated schools. Herschel T. Manuel of the University of Texas claimed that reading and arithmetic problems of Mexican-American children were caused primarily by poverty and bilingualism."[17] By 1937, some educators were "call-

ing for an end to 'emotionalism' on the question of segregation; what was needed was more research."

It is generally accepted that soldiers who fought in World War II and returned to their towns were the impetus for many of the significant changes that occurred during the late 1940s in Mexican communities. Guadalupe San Miguel Jr., a Latino historian, writes:

> Despite these tremendous social and economic changes wrought by World War II, the status of Mexican Americans in the United States changed little . . . the majority continued to be denied equal opportunities, discriminated against, and treated as second-class citizens. . . .
>
> But change . . . was brewing within the Mexican American community. Much of this change was due to their experiences in the defense of American institutions and ideals. . . .
>
> The war experience gave Mexican Americans a new sense of dignity and responsibility. For the first time many of them were treated as first-class citizens and recognized for their contributions to the war effort.[18]

One of the issues that returning veterans confronted was the ongoing segregation in the school system. In 1943 Mexican veterans who returned to Santa Ana formed an organization, the Latin American Organization, whose main goal was combating school segregation. One of the first confrontations occurred on October 25, 1943, when Mrs. Leonides Sánchez and Mrs. Frank García appeared at a meeting of the Santa Ana Board of Education and argued that their children should be allowed to attend Franklin School, a largely Anglo school. The school board rebuffed the request, stating that while admitting that Anglo students were frequently transferred out of Mexican schools, the reverse was seldom the case. A year later Sánchez and García enrolled their children in the Franklin School, even though they had not been granted authorization to do so. The enrollment of the students was accomplished through a subterfuge, using false addresses that would allow the students to fall within the Franklin School zone. When this was discovered, the school board decided that, once the correct addresses for the two children were verified, they would be placed in the proper school—the Mexican school.

No sooner was the school board confronted with the Sánchez-García demand than an attorney representing Mr. and Mrs. William Guzmán and their son Billy Guzmán, along with several other parents, appeared before the board and requested leave to send Billy to the Franklin School. While the board initially indicated that it would study the problem and provide a response within 90 days, there was no change in the board's policy.

The struggle in which the Sánchez, García, and Guzmán families were engaged in Santa Ana was also going on in the town of Westminster. There, in 1944, Gonzalo and Felicitas Méndez attempted to enroll their three children in the school nearest their home—Westminster Elementary School. The school prevented them from enrolling on the basis of language deficiency. The Méndez family could have pursued the matter for their children alone, but the political atmosphere had changed by then. Instead, they organized a group of parents and petitioned the school board to end the segregation of Mexican children.

The superintendent maintained that Mexican children belonged in the Mexican schools, but that an exception would be made for the Méndez children: they would be allowed to enroll in Westminster Elementary School. Mr. and Mrs. Méndez rejected the offer and refused to allow their children into the school until such time as they could "regularly" enroll in the school. They were already of a mind to institute legal action, not only for the benefit of their own children but to challenge—and perhaps end—the existence of Mexican schools.

David Marcus, a Black attorney, represented the Méndez family. Marcus came to the Méndez case with an impressive résumé of court victories. In addition to having prevailed in litigation to desegregate the San Bernardino public parks and pools, he also handled matters for the Mexican consulates in Los Angeles and San Diego.

On March 2, 1945, Gonzalo Méndez, William Guzmán, Frank Palomino, Thomas Estrada, and Lorenzo Ramírez filed a class-action suit in Federal District Court, Southern District, against the Westminster, Garden Grove, and El Modeno school districts, the Santa Ana city schools, and the respective trustees and superintendents of the school districts (*Méndez et al. v. Westminster School District of Orange County et al.*).[19] The American Civil Liberties Union and the National Lawyers Guild filed amicus briefs, attesting to the importance of the case.

✳The complaint alleged that the school districts had engaged in a systematic and purposeful segregation of Mexican children whereby the Mexican children "are now and have been segregated and required to and must attend and use certain schools . . . reserved for and attended solely and exclusively by children and persons of Mexican and Latin descent, while such other schools are maintained, attended, and used exclusively by and for persons and children purportedly known as White or Anglo-Saxon children."[20] The plaintiffs in the action argued that such segregated schools violated the Mexicans' constitutional rights under the Fourteenth Amendment and asked, as part of their relief, that the court issue an injunction abating the segregation of the schools.

Both parties to the lawsuit stipulated to the court that while the segregation was not based on race, segregation per se was practiced by the defendant school districts beginning with the time that the Mexican children entered school and advanced through the grades. The parties further stipulated that this was the case even though the children were qualified to attend public schools in their own school zone.

Having stipulated that the segregation of Mexican children was not based on race, the defendant school districts justified their actions on the special educational needs of the Mexican children. The court noted that the Mexican children were "required to attend schools designated by the boards separate and apart from English-speaking pupils; that such group should attend such schools until they had acquired some proficiency in the English language."[21]

The Méndez family responded that the use of language as a basis for segregation of Mexican children was a subterfuge used by the school districts to arbitrarily discriminate against children of Mexican descent.

The court was careful to note that the "separate" educational facilities provided to the Mexican children were "equal" to if not superior to that offered to the Anglo children. The court noted, "The record before us shows without conflict that the technical facilities and physical conveniences offered in the schools housing entirely the segregated pupils, the efficiency of the teachers therein and the curricula are identical and in some respects superior to those in the other schools in the respective districts."[22] By so noting, the court dismissed any potential argument that its decision was influenced by "separate but unequal" educational access for the Mexican children.

Having set the record regarding the various stipulations by the parties and the "separate but equal" nature of the educational facilities provided to the segregated Mexican children, the court then framed the question before it as follows: "Does such official action of defendant district school agencies and the usages and practices pursued by the respective school authorities as shown by the evidence operate to deny or deprive the so-called non-English-speaking school children of Mexican ancestry or descent within such school districts of the equal protection of the laws?"

In presenting their case, plaintiffs relied heavily on social scientists who testified that segregation of Mexican children had a detrimental effect on them. The social science testimony was persuasive, leading the court to write:

> The evidence clearly shows that Spanish-speaking children are retarded in learning English by lack of exposure to its use because of segregation, and that commingling of the entire student body instills and develops a common cultural attitude among the school children which is imperative for the perpetuation of American institutions and ideals. It is also established by the record that the methods of segregation prevalent in the defendant school districts foster antagonism in the children and suggest inferiority among them where none exists.[23]

In addressing the districts' principal defense argument that the segregation of Mexican children was based on their lack of English, the court acknowledged that segregation of Mexican children could be justified on this basis, but that the facts before it did not warrant such a conclusion and sided with the plaintiff's position that language skills was a ruse for arbitrarily segregating Mexican children. As to the facts before it relating to the Santa Ana city schools, the court noted that "The tests applied to the beginners are shown to have been generally hasty, superficial and not reliable." In other instances, the court noted, the Santa Ana city schools simply used the "Latinized or Mexican name of the child" to determine the child's language skills. Such methods "of evaluating language knowledge are illusory," the court wrote.

The court went further to undermine the districts' argument that segregation of Mexican children in the elementary schools could be justified because of deficiency in English, by first stating that such deficiency had to be established by "credible examination by the appropriate school authority of each child." Furthermore, the court noted, if the segregation of a child was based on English-language deficiencies, then "such segregation must be based wholly upon indiscriminate foreign language impediments in the individual child, regardless of his ethnic traits or ancestry." Meaning, apparently, if children of Italian descent or German descent were appropriately tested and found to be deficient in English, then they too could be segregated for the sole purpose of improving their English.

At the end of the day, the court found that the school districts had, by virtue of arbitrarily segregating Mexican children, violated their rights under the Fourteenth Amendment and concluded that "the allegations of the complaint [petition] have been established sufficiently to justify injunctive relief affianced all defendants, restraining further discriminatory practices against the pupils of Mexican descent in the public schools of defendant school districts."[24]

The decision by Judge Paul McCormick was hailed as groundbreaking. *La Opinión*, a Los Angeles Spanish-language newspaper, reported that McCormick's decision was a "brilliant judicial exposition." And Marcus hailed the results as "one of the greatest judicial decisions in favor of democratic practices granted since the emancipation of the slaves."[25]

The celebration was short-lived because the defendants decided to appeal. The appeal to the Ninth Circuit attracted the attention of a number of major organizations: the NAACP, the American Jewish Congress, the Japanese-American Citizens League, and the State of California attorney general, in addition to the ACLU and the National Lawyers Guild. Not only did the NAACP submit an amicus brief, but it considered the case to be of such significance that it sent Thurgood Marshall to argue before the court. The *New York Times* reported that the case was being closely watched and considered a test case for addressing the constitutional validity of the "separate but equal" doctrine.

The *Times* was correct. Christopher Arriola, an attorney who has written on the *Méndez* case, notes that the civil rights organizations saw *Méndez* as a test case to attack the separate but equal underpinning of *Plessy v. Ferguson*. The amicus brief filed by the NAACP argued that "fundamental law" invalidated racial classification. It also argued that segregation prevents the achievement of due process and equal protection. Finally, it argued that *Plessy v. Ferguson* did not prohibit a finding that school segregation was invalid since that case was restricted to public transportation."[26]

The court of appeals did not take the NAACP bait and refused to rule on the "separate but equal" issue. The court wrote, "We are not tempted by the siren who calls to us that the sometimes slow and tedious way of democratic legislation is no longer respected in the progressive society."[27]

The school districts did not choose to appeal the case to the United States Supreme Court and the education commissioner of Orange County ordered that there be "some Anglo and Mexican children in every class." In the fall of 1947 the schools in Westminster, Garden Grove, El Modeno, and Santa Ana integrated their schools with few problems.[28]

While the impact of *Méndez was* not national in scope, its effect in California was both apparent and dramatic. In January 1947, a bill was introduced into the state legislature to repeal the state statutes that provided for the creation of segregated schools for Chinese, Japanese, Native Americans, and Mongolians. Some opposition was raised to the bill but it eventually passed, and on June 14, 1947, the bill was signed into law by Governor Earl Warren.

In Riverside, the school board members, reading McCormick's decision as writing on the wall, capitulated to the demands from the Mexican American community and integrated schools in the section of the city called Bell Town. Riverside closed an "all-white" school near a Mexican neighborhood, thus integrating a school that had previously been all Mexican. And the Ontario school board integrated a school in 1946.

Even though the effect of *Méndez* was not national in scope, its significance in preparing the ground for *Brown v. Board of Education* cannot be overemphasized. The use of social science testimony had a significant impact on McCormick and his decision. González writes that Robert Carter, one of the NAACP attorneys, was so impressed with the effective use of social science testimony that he suggested to Thurgood Marshall that such an approach would be the only way to "overturn segregation in the United States." González further notes:

> Later attorneys for the NAACP employed with success this particular strategy in the 1954 Supreme Court decision, *Brown v. Board of Education*. Carter . . . also

felt that the *amicus curiae* that he and Marshall filed in the appellate court in support of the district court's *Méndez* decision was a "dry run for the future." [29]

A note in the *Yale Law Journal* concurred: "However, a recent District Court decision, affirmed by the Ninth Circuit Court of Appeals, has questioned the basic assumption of the *Plessy* and may portend a complete reversal of the doctrine."[30] This conclusion was given further credence by Lester H. Phillips in an article published in the Black journal *Phylon*: "The observations of the judges in both the district and the appellate courts relative to segregation suggest that this case must be ranked among the vanguard of those making a frontal attack upon the 'equal separate' canon of interpretation of the equal protection clause."[31]

It is, therefore, not an exaggeration to state that *Méndez* was the first stage in the process of overturning the "separate but equal" doctrine in the 1896 *Plessy v. Ferguson* case.

Texas: *Delgado v. Bastrop Independent School District*

The discrimination and segregation that Mexicans experienced was not confined to California, as Chicano historian David Montejano makes clear in his highly acclaimed book *Anglos and Mexicans in the Making of Texas: 1836–1986*.[32] The parallels between California and Texas are clear. Like California, Texas had no state statute that provided for the creation of separate schools for Mexican children. In the absence of a statutory basis on which to segregate Mexican children, educators in Texas relied on administrative decrees. Reminiscent of statements in California, Texas school officials—administrators, school boards, trustees, superintendents—justified the creation and maintenance of separate Mexican schools because Mexicans suffered from mental retardation, did not speak English, had poor hygiene, did not really appreciate education, and, frankly, were just inherently inferior. And when a well-meaning school administrator happened to ignore the common lore regarding Mexican children, he was reminded by Anglo parents of the imperative to keep Mexican and Anglo children separate. As an example, in 1919 Mexican children in the town of Pharr-San Juan in Hidalgo County were initially allowed to attend school with Anglo children. However, they were quickly transferred to a "Mexican church" for separate instruction after Anglo parents protested the mingling of the Mexicans with Anglo children.[33]

Herschel T. Manuel, a professor of educational psychology at the University of Texas, conducted a study of Mexican children in Texas and published the results in 1930. He found that Mexican children were segregated into inferior schools. He describes one school for Mexican children as a run-down building that had previously been a church, and in southwest Texas he found four Mexican children using one tablet and one pencil, which they rotated among themselves.[34]

By the late 1920s and early 1930s segregation of Mexican children was widespread and institutionalized in areas of Texas. For example, during the 1930s it was believed that more than 40 school districts had created separate schools for Mexicans, and by 1942 it was estimated that 122 districts in 59 counties operated separate schools for Mexican American children.[35]

While there had been individual challenges to segregation, the legal challenges were made with the help and support of a new statewide Mexican organization, the League of United Latin American Citizens, generally referred to by its acronym, LULAC. LULAC's membership was uniquely different from other Mexican organizations in that all of its members were either born in the United States or naturalized citizens. Its goals were also different. While the other organizations existed primarily to provide social services to the Mexican community, LULAC's goal was to enable Mexicans to take advantage of U.S. political, social, and cultural institutions. This was reflected in LULAC's constitution, which had as one of its goals: "to assume complete responsibility for the education of our children as to their rights and duties and the language and customs of this country." Conjoined with this goal was LULAC's avowed purpose of eliminating all discriminatory practices based on race.[36]

The 1928 claim of Amanda Vela was one of the first challenges to the segregation of Mexican children in Texas. In the case of *Vela v. Board of Trustees of Charlotte Independent School District*, Felipe Vela, a Mexican American, had adopted Amanda Vela, a girl whose "race" was undetermined. Vela attempted to enroll Amanda in a school with white children. She was denied enrollment and transferred to the "Mexican school" by the board of trustees. Vela bypassed the local school board and made a direct appeal to the state superintendent of public instruction for a decision allowing his daughter to attend the "white school."

Much like the *Méndez* case, though not in a legal context, both sides agreed to certain facts. First, the parties agreed that the school district did not have any legal authority on which it could bar Amanda from attending the "white school." Second, the parties stipulated that Amanda did not live within the zone designated for the Mexican school, and that she was placed in the "Mexican school" simply because her parents were Mexican. Also, much like in the *Méndez* case, the local school officials defended their actions on pedagogical grounds, stating, "It is well understood that non-English-speaking children should be given special instruction and it is probably to the best interests of such children that they be placed in one room or in one school in order that the character of instruction given will be different from that given to English-speaking children."[37]

Like Judge McCormick in the *Méndez* case, the state superintendent of public instruction, S. M. N. Marrs, agreed that separation of Mexican children based on language difficulties could be used to justify segregating them into separate classes. In the case of Amanda, however, Marrs found that she not only spoke English well but was able to translate from Spanish to English and English to Spanish with great facility. As a consequence, he concluded, placing Amanda in the "white school" would not interfere with the progress of the white children and placing her in the "Mexican school" would disadvantage Amanda, since so many of the Mexican children did not speak English or, if they did, they did not speak it well. The school district, dissatisfied with the decision, appealed to the state board of education, but the board declined to reverse the state superintendent.

The first legal challenge to the practice of segregating Mexican children in the Texas education system was fostered by LULAC in 1930, two years after the Vela matter was resolved. *Independent School District v. Salvatierra* was a class-action suit filed against the Del Rio school district.[38] *Salvatierra* was also significant because it was a case of first impression, a fact the court acknowledged when it wrote, "The question of race segregation, as between Mexicans and other white races, has not heretofore found its way into the courts of the state, and therefore the decision of no Texas court is available in the disposition of the precise question present here." [39] Thus, its decision, if favorable to the plaintiffs, could be used to further challenge segregation in other school districts, but if favorable to the defendants could be devastating to any future challenges.

The Del Rio school district was composed of four school buildings and an athletic field, all of which were located on the same parcel of land. The white high school and two white elementary schools were at one end of the field and the Mexican school was located at the other end.

In 1930 the residents of Del Rio approved the sale of $185,000 in bonds to be devoted to the improvement of the existing school facilities. The school trustees earmarked the money to be used for constructing a new senior high school building, remodeling and enlarging the white elementary schools, and enlarging the Mexican school by adding five rooms, including an auditorium.

Mexican parents immediately objected to the plan not because of the quality or nature of the renovations to the Mexican school, but because such construction ensured the separation of the Mexican children from the white students.

The court, in deciding the case, concluded that the school district had not exceeded its administrative powers because the school board was not "arbitrarily" assigning Mexican children to the Mexican school. It also found that how Mexican students were identified as non-English-speaking for purposes of placing them in the Mexican school was not arbitrary or unconstitutional. Finally, it held that placement of Mexican children in the Mexican school was justified for additional pedagogical reasons. The first was the late enrollment and spotty attendance of the Mexican children. The second was, as in the *Méndez* case, the language issue. The school district argued that placing the Mexican children in the white school handicapped the Mexican students and thus they were better served by placing them in the Mexican school where their fellow students were more like them. Based on these grounds the court found that the school district had not violated any of the Mexican schoolchildren's constitutional rights.

The decision was a critical blow to LULAC and its zeal to eliminate segregation in the Texas school system. So devastating was the decision that LULAC concluded that, for the foreseeable future, the legal arena was not where the battle to end segregation in the school system should be fought. LULAC urged its members to take the battle to a different level and work informally with the various school districts to eliminate the discriminatory practices that they challenged in Del Rio.

While LULAC and the American G.I. Forum, another Mexican American organization that had as one of its goals the education of Mexican American children, continued to militate for equal educational opportunities for Mexican children, legal challenges to segregation in the Texas school system lay dormant until after the *Méndez* decision.

On April 8, 1947 the attorney general of Texas issued an opinion that prohibited segregation of Mexican children when such segregation was based solely on race. However, the decision provided an out to the local school districts by providing that separate placement of children could be justified based on language deficiencies and other needs, but only after these deficiencies and needs were determined by the administration of unbiased tests.

The attorney general's opinion turned out to be a paper tiger. It not only provided the school districts with an easy out—it also did not set forth a procedure to force compliance. The toothless nature of this decision was demonstrated when, several months after its passage, numerous challenges to school districts that continued to segregate Mexican schoolchildren were dismissed. A study of the Texas school system conducted by Virgil E. Stickland and George I. Sánchez found that segregation was practiced on "a purely arbitrary basis, determined solely by local custom, tradition and prejudice."[40]

Inspired by the *Méndez* case and assessing that the social and legal environments had changed, LULAC in 1948 assisted in filing a class-action suit against the Bastrop Independent School District. In *Delgado et al. v. Bastrop Independent School District of Bastrop County, Texas. et al.*[41] the complaint listed five arguments:

1. The defendants acted beyond the authority provided to them under the Texas constitution and

laws of the state by separate placement of Mexican children.

2. Nothing in the Texas constitution permitted the segregation of Mexican children into separate schools and/or classes.

3. The segregation of the Mexican children was based on custom, usage and/or common plan.

4. The segregation of the Mexican children was condoned by the state superintendent of public education and state board of education.

5. The segregation of Mexican children denied them due process and violated their rights under the Fourteenth Amendment.[42]

As in *Méndez*, the court found that placing Mexican students in separate buildings was arbitrary, discriminatory, and illegal. The judge further wrote, "The plaintiffs, as aforesaid, by the acts of the defendants complained of, were deprived of their rights under the Constitution of the United States and the Laws of the United States to be free from discrimination solely because of their ancestry."

The *Méndez* decision, rendered in 1946, presaged the *Brown v. Board of Education* decision rendered by the U.S. Supreme Court in 1954 by approximately eight years, and the *Delgado* case rendered in 1948 presaged it by approximately six years. While *Brown v. Board of Education* provided the Supreme Court with the factual basis and legal arguments to declare state-imposed de jure segregation in public schools a violation of the Fourteenth Amendment, Mexicans in California and Texas had fought similar battles and laid much of the legal groundwork for *Brown*'s eventual victory.

One plausible reason can be advanced to explain why *Méndez* and *Delgado* have received so little attention from legal scholars and historians. The decision in *Brown v. Board of Education* was rendered by the Supreme Court, making it the law of the land. So while *Méndez* and *Delgado* had significant regional impact, the ruling in *Brown v. Board of Education* blanketed the United States, radically altering the educational policies of every state of the Union. It was therefore reasonable for the general public, and scholars as well, to view *Brown v. Board of Education* as the natural reference point for the elimination of the "separate but equal" doctrine in *Plessy v. Ferguson*. All other decisions were regarded as having lesser significance.

However, the struggle by Mexican Americans in the Southwest to overcome the pernicious effect of segregated schools was no less significant and meaningful than was the parallel struggle of African Americans in the South. And the detrimental, and in some instances devastating, effect that segregated schools had on Mexican American students was no less than their impact on Blacks in the South. On these grounds alone, the Latino struggle to eliminate the insidious quality of the "separate but equal" doctrine should receive the recognition that it deserves.

Notes

1. Kenneth J. Meier and Joseph Stewart, Jr., *The Politics of Hispanic Education: Un paso pa'lante y dos pa'tras* (Albany: State University of New York Press, 1991), p. xvii.
2. George J. Sánchez, *Becoming Mexican-American*, New York: Oxford University Press, 1993, p. 255.
3. Ibid., p. 257.
4. Charles Wollenberg, *All Deliberate Speed: Segregation and Exclusion in California Schools, 1855–1975* (Berkeley: University of California Press, 1976), p. 112.
5. Sánchez, *Becoming Mexican-American*, p. 258.
6. Wollenberg, *All Deliberate Speed*, p. 112.
7. Ibid., p. 113.
8. Ibid.
9. Gilbert G. González, *Chicano Education in the Era of Segregation* (Cranbury, NJ.: Associated University Press, 1990), p. 72.
10. Ibid.
11. Wollenberg, *All Deliberate Speed*, p. 115.
12. Ibid., p. 116.
13. González, *Chicano Education in the Era of Segregation*, p. 137.
14. Ibid., p. 141.
15. Ibid., p. 142.
16. Ibid., p. 143.
17. Wollenberg, *All Deliberate Speed*, p. 120.
18. Guadalupe San Miguel Jr., *Let All of Them Take Heed: Mexican Americans and the Campaign for Education Equality in Texas, 1910–1981* (Austin: University of Texas Press, 1987), pp. 114–115.
19. *Méndez et al. v. Westminster School District of Orange County et al.* (1946), 64 F. Supp. 544.
20. Ibid., p. 545.
21. Ibid., p. 546.
22. Ibid.
23. Ibid., p. 549.
24. Ibid., p. 551.
25. Wollenberg, *All Deliberate Speed*, p. 128.
26. Christopher Arriola, "Knocking on the Schoolhouse Door: *Méndez v. Westminster:* Equal Protection, Public Education and Mexican Americans in the 1940s," *La Raza Law Journal* 8, no. 2 (1995): pp. 166–207.
27. *Westminster School District of Orange County et al. v. Méndez et al.*, 161 F. 2nd 774 (9th Cir., 1947), 780.
28. Wollenberg, *All Deliberate Speed*, p. 132.
29. González, *Chicano Education in the Era of Segregation*, p. 28.
30. "Segregation in Public Schools—A Violation of 'Equal Protection of the Laws'," *Yale Law Journal* 56, no. 6 (1947): 1059–1067; see also, "Segregation in Schools as a Violation of the XIVth Amendment," *Columbia Law Review* 47, no. 1 (1947): 325–329.
31. Lester H. Phillips, "Segregation in Education: A California Case Study," *Phylon* 10, no. 4 (1949): 407–413, p. 407.
32. David Montejano, *Anglos and Mexicans in the Making of Texas: 1836–1986* (Austin: University of Texas Press, 1987).
33. Ibid., p. 191.
34. Herschel T. Manuel, *The Education of Mexican and Spanish-Speaking Children in Texas* (Austin: University of Texas Press, 1930), p. 60.
35. Guadalupe San Miguel, *Let All of Them Take Heed*, p. 56.
36. Ibid., p. 71.
37. Ibid., p. 77.
38. *Independent School District v. Salvatierra*, 33 S.W.2d 790 (Tex. Civ. App. 1930), cert. Denied, 284 U.S. 580 (1931).
39. Guadalupe San Miguel, *Let All of Them Take Heed*, p. 78.
40. Ibid., p. 121.
41. *Minerva Delgado et al. v. Bastrop Independent School District of Bastrop County, Texas, et al.* (D.C. Texas Western District), June 15, 1948, Civil Action No. 388.
42. Guadalupe San Miguel, *Let All of Them Take Heed*, p.123.

Language Politics in the United States
The Paradox of Bilingual Education

James Crawford

Enacted at the apex of the Great Society, the Bilingual Education Act was passed by Congress and signed into law by President Lyndon B. Johnson without a single voice raised in dissent. Americans have spent the past thirty years debating what it was meant to accomplish. Was this 1968 law intended primarily to assimilate limited-English-proficient (LEP) children more efficiently, to teach them English as rapidly as possible, to encourage bilingualism and biliteracy, to remedy academic underachievement and high dropout rates, to raise the self-esteem of minority students, to promote social equality, or to pursue all of these goals simultaneously? The bill's legislative history provides no definitive answer.

It is hardly an idle question. Whether to continue teaching LEP students in two languages is now a matter of public debate throughout the United States. Since the mid-1980s, critics have won increasing support for the contention that this experiment, while well-intentioned, has failed to meet expectations. Now, in the late 1990s, policy makers are seriously considering demands to limit or even dismantle the program. California voters have already chosen the latter course. Proposition 227, a ballot initiative approved in June 1998, eliminates most native-language instruction in a state with 40 percent of the nation's LEP students.[1] The future of bilingual education is suddenly in doubt.

Ironically, research provides considerably more support for bilingual approaches today than it did in 1968, when few program models existed and almost none had been evaluated. What seemed reasonable in theory—that investing in children's native-language development should ultimately pay cognitive and academic dividends—has now been borne out in pedagogical practice. Not that success has been universal for all approaches labeled "bilingual." Nor has research proved conclusively, beyond a reasonable doubt, their superiority over English-only methodologies for all children in all contexts. By a more reasonable standard, however, a preponderance of the evidence favors the conclusion that well-designed bilingual programs can produce high levels of school achievement over the long term, at no cost to English acquisition, among students from disempowered groups (see, e.g., Ramírez, Yven, and Ramey 1991; Willig 1985; Greene 1998).

Pedagogically speaking, these research findings are excellent news. They confirm that developing fluent bilingualism and cultivating academic excellence are complementary, rather than contradictory, goals. Sacrificing LEP students' native language is unnecessary to teach them effectively in English. Moreover, the findings suggest that while language is not the only barrier to school success for these children, approaches that stress native-language instruction can be helpful in overcoming other obstacles such as poverty, family illiteracy, and social stigmas associated with minority status. These challenges are formidable, to be sure, requiring schools to replicate effective program models, adapt them to local conditions, train and retrain teachers, develop curriculum and materials, involve parents, and pay attention to a host of other practical details. Yet they are hardly insuperable—given a public commitment to improve programs for English learners.

Politically speaking, however, the research findings are less encouraging. They support an educational rationale for bilingual instruction that is both complex and counterintuitive to members of the public. They also imply a sociopolitical goal that few Americans are inclined to endorse: the legitimation of "bilingualism" in public contexts. Indeed, since the mid-1980s, many U.S. voters have reacted defensively against the racial, cultural, and language diversity brought by rising levels of immigration. A nationwide campaign for "the legal protection of English" has led to the passage of nineteen state laws designating English as the sole language of government.[2] Immigrant children's progress in acquiring English is now regarded as a matter of urgency, not only by many Anglo-Americans but also by a significant number of immigrant parents, hence the growing popularity of nostrums like "structured immersion" and "sheltered English," whose enthusiasts promise short-cuts to English proficiency. Conversely, bilingual approaches that feature a more gradual transition to the mainstream are vulnerable to legislative restrictions. In addition to Proposition 227, bills have been proposed in various states and localities, as well as the U.S. Congress, to impose arbitrary time limits on a child's enrollment in bilingual education (or, in some cases, in *any* special program to address limited English proficiency).

To understand how we arrived at this juncture, it is necessary to analyze the historical roots of today's language attitudes. Ethnic diversity is hardly a recent phenomenon in this country. Nor is bilingual education. How have Americans thought about and coped with these issues previously? How have current policies on language-minority education evolved? How are future ones likely to be determined?

Deconstructing Title VII

Let's begin by considering our original question. Was the Bilingual Education Act (also known as Title VII of the Elementary and Secondary Education Act) intended as an

- *antipoverty initiative* to overcome the educational disadvantages of language-minority students—that is, to remedy the problem of limited English proficiency?
- *antidiscrimination measure* to open up the curriculum for LEP students—that is, to guarantee their right to equal educational opportunity?
- *experiment in multicultural education* to foster bilingualism—that is, to develop linguistic and cultural resources other than those of the dominant society?

These alternatives correspond to Ruiz's (1984) "orientations in language planning": ways of framing language issues and the language policies adopted in response. *Language-as-problem* focuses on social liabilities, such as limited proficiency in the majority tongue and its academic consequences. From this perspective, Title VII was a way to ease LEP children's transition to the mainstream by teaching them English, raising their self-esteem, and thereby enabling them to progress in school. *Language-as-right* emphasizes questions of social equality, or lack thereof, such as whether members of minority groups enjoy unimpeded access to public institutions. In this view, Title VII was designed to overcome language barriers, make school meaningful for LEP students, and give them a chance to succeed. *Language-as-resource* takes a human capital approach, stressing the social value of conserving and developing minority-language skills. Seen

through this prism, Title VII was intended to promote fluency in two languages, exploit cultural diversity to meet national needs, and encourage ethnic tolerance.

Ruiz's orientations can help to illuminate the assumptions and implications of alternative language policies. For example, language-as-problem, by focusing on students' *language disability* is consistent with a quick-exit pedagogy (bilingual or otherwise) that places the rapid acquisition of English ahead of other academic goals. By contrast, language-as-resource, by focusing on students' *language ability* in a minority tongue, tends to support a late-exit enrichment model that continues native-language instruction after students are proficient in English.

As ex post facto descriptions, however, Ruiz's categories are less useful in explaining causality—that is, in analyzing the political and ideological factors that go into language policy decisions. Orientations in language planning, elaborated in "pure" form and focusing on sociolinguistic issues, may accurately summarize the policy alternatives as understood by experts in the field. Yet rarely do they correspond to the interests of contending factions or to the actual terms of political debate, which are never pure; usually they extend well beyond the realm of language. In short, orientations toward language per se are rarely determinant in policy decisions about language. This becomes evident in tracing the legislative history of Title VII.

Political momentum was strong from the outset, as thirty-seven different bilingual education bills were introduced in the Ninetieth Congress. Throughout 1967, a series of House and Senate hearings showcased the educational problems of LEP children and elicited virtually unanimous support for a solution involving bilingual instruction. Disagreements were confined to secondary issues, such as whether to cover all LEP students or just Spanish speakers. The witness lists included academic researchers, language educators, school administrators, teachers, psychologists, social workers, elected officials, and representatives of Hispanic, Asian American, and Native American organizations.[3] Some experts recommended bilingual education as a remedy for LEP students' "linguistic handicap" and resulting "educational problems." Others focused on the bill's potential to develop needed language resources, Spanish skills in particular. Many witnesses cited both objectives, describing them as educationally compatible. (Although the theme of language-as-right was barely detectable in deliberations over Title VII, that would soon change with a spate of litigation brought by language-minority parents.) José Cárdenas, a veteran educator from San Antonio, recalls that neither he nor his fellow experts worried about a contradiction between the "transition" and "maintenance" goals of bilingual instruction (Crawford 1992). These terms—yet to be coined in 1967—were the product of political, not pedagogical, necessity.

The most substantive, albeit brief, debate on the goals of the bill came on the Senate floor (*Congressional Record* 1967). Joseph Montoya of New Mexico urged his colleagues: "We must take advantage of thc language pluralism that exists in the Southwest. But it must be constructive pluralism. Comprehensive bilingual education programs are, to my way of thinking, one way we can give to all [Spanish-speaking students] the best of both worlds in terms of language, culture, and cooperation in daily life" (35053). Frank Lausche of Ohio was less enthusiastic about "the Federal Government pouring in . . . money" to help maintain minority tongues. A native speaker of Slovenian, he recalled, "I went to a grammar school where they taught English. They did not teach me Slovenian in order to learn English [sic]." He also worried about the precedent: "What are we to do if there is a Hungarian neighborhood in Toledo that finds it wants Hungarian taught in its schools?" (34702). The bill's chief sponsor, Ralph Yarborough of Texas, sought to finesse the differences by emphasizing transition while leaving the door ajar for maintenance:

> It is not the purpose of this bill to create pockets of different languages throughout the country. It is the main purpose of the bill to bring millions of school children into the mainstream of American life and make them literate in the national language of the country in which they live: namely, English. Not to stamp out the mother tongue and not to make their mother tongue the dominant language, but just to try to make these children fully literate in English, so that the children can move into the mainstream of American life. (34703)

This explanation appeared to satisfy Senator Lausche, who asked "whether all of us should not be expert in at least 2 languages—perhaps 3" and recommended "a knowledge of Latin" to everyone (34703). No further questions were raised, and the Bilingual Education Act passed as part of an omnibus education measure.[4]

Ambiguity served Senator Yarborough's purposes. In 1967, the political universe was perfectly aligned to create an antipoverty program serving Hispanic Americans, whose needs had thus far received little attention from the Great Society. Mexican American educators and the National Education Association (1966) had recently highlighted the plight of Spanish-speaking students, "the invisible minority." Yarborough, a populist Democrat, enlisted in the "bilingual movement" at the NEA's Tucson Conference in the fall of 1966. Senator George Murphy, a conservative California Republican, also endorsed the idea, noting that Governor Ronald Reagan had recently signed legislation repealing his state's mandate for English-only instruction. Still, there was no time to lose. Urban riots and a costly war in Southeast Asia were beginning to spoil the Johnson administration's appetite for social spending. Indeed, Yarborough had to twist arms to get its support for a new "title" of the Elementary and Secondary Education Act. (The administration initially favored funding bilingual approaches through existing programs.) Who knew when this opportunity would come again? Why risk it by raising sensitive matters like assimilation and pluralism? Better to pass a bilingual education bill today and clarify its goals at some future date.

As political strategy, Senator Yarborough's approach is hard to fault. As policy making, it left many loose ends. In particular, the unresolved question of goals would haunt Title VII for years to come. Reflecting on the legislative process long after the fact, many of the key players (including Yarborough) agreed that the law was conceived as an experiment not in language policy but in education policy, designed to tackle a problem of underachievement in which language happened to play a role (Croghan 1997). Conscious or not, the federal government's intervention on behalf of bilingual instruction was unprecedented and far-reaching. What did it mean? The program's administrators, members of Congress, school personnel, academic researchers, and the parents of LEP children all cherished their own interpretations.

The Office of Education included the following advice in its 1971 instructions for Title VII grant applicants: "It must be remembered that the ultimate goal of bilingual education is a student who functions well in two languages on any occasion." This was hardly the consensus view on Capitol Hill. Congressional committee members made it clear that "we were in there to overcome [students'] 'bilingual problem,'" Albar Peña, the program's first director, recalled two decades later. "There was an obsession that if they were not English-speaking at the end of the first grade that the world would come to an end" (quoted in Crawford 1992, 85). Appropriations for Title VII nevertheless remained modest—only $7.5 million in 1969. Although funding increased to $45 million by 1974, it was enough to support a mere 211 local programs (Crawford 1995).

As state legislatures began repealing English-only school laws and authorizing native-language instruction, they showed a similar ambivalence. In 1971, Massachusetts became the first state to require "transitional bilingual education" under certain circumstances—and the first to use the term—but its definition of the program omitted any mention of goals (*Mass. Gen. Laws,* Title XII, chap. 71A). A similar law, adopted two years later in Illinois, articulated the purpose of transitional programs: "to meet the needs of [LEP] children and facilitate their integration into the regular public school curriculum" (*Ill. Ann. Stat.,* chap. 122, art. 14C). By the mid-1970s, more than a dozen states had enacted bilingual education statutes; none drew sharp lines of demarcation between transition and maintenance.

Educators, for their part, continued to see the two goals as compatible. According to the American Institutes for Research (AIR) report (Danoff et al. 1977–1978), a nationwide study of Title VII's impact, 86 percent of local bilingual programs retained Spanish-speaking children even after they were deemed fluent in English. On the other hand, 50 percent of "bilingual" teachers lacked proficiency in the native languages of their students—casting doubts on whether Title VII was doing much to promote fluent bilingualism. Amid the furor over the first finding, however, the second was largely ignored. Critics charged the Office of Education with flouting both the melting-pot tradition and the intent of Congress by failing to "mainstream" children as quickly as possible (Epstein 1977). The language-as-resource approach was condemned as diametrically opposed to the goal of assimilation. In addition, AIR's mediocre report card for Title VII—"no consistent significant impact" on achievement—led opponents to question the program's effectiveness. This marked the first serious opposition to the bilingual experiment. Under the leadership of Senator S. I. Hayakawa of California, it would soon expand into an English-only movement seeking to restrict most uses of minority tongues by government (Crawford 1992).

In reaction to the controversy, Congress voted in 1978 to restrict federal support to transitional bilingual education programs. Henceforth, the native language could be used only "to the extent necessary to allow a child to achieve competence in the English language" (Public Law 95-561). While this statutory restriction was eased in 1984, for another decade only a tiny portion of federal funds flowed to maintenance—now known as "developmental bilingual education." Nevertheless, critics successfully portrayed Title VII as a program that emphasized the native language and "ethnic pride" at the expense of English. Led by the Reagan administration's secretary of education, William J. Bennett, they advocated "local flexibility" for districts to try English-only alternatives such as "structured immersion" (Bennett 1985). In response, defenders insisted that bilingual education was the most efficient solution to the problems of limited English proficiency and academic underachievement.

Thus, during the 1987–1988 reauthorization of Title VII, the debate involved means, not ends. Both sides embraced the language-as-problem orientation, which proved to be consistent with diametrically opposed policies for educating LEP students. Congress struck a compromise, diverting up to 25 percent of annual appropriations from bilingual to "special alternative instructional programs." Only a tiny share was made available for developmental programs, despite their promising academic outcomes and success in cultivating bilingualism.

Language-as-resource, while gaining hegemony among educational researchers and practitioners, was marginalized politically by the new terms of the debate. With any form of native-language instruction now condemned as a distraction from English—in effect, Title VII's critics portrayed transitional bilingual education as a language-maintenance approach—the program's defenders tended to downplay its potential to develop bilingual skills.

One exception was the Miami-based Spanish American League against Discrimination (SALAD). Troubled by Bennett's assimilationist rhetoric, in 1985 the group countered with the slogan "English Plus." While English is essential in the United States, SALAD argued, to succeed in a global economy, children need to learn more than one language and developmental bilingual education can be an effective means to that end. This philosophy was soon put into service as a programmatic alternative to the broader English-only campaign (Combs 1992). Again, however, its appeal has been limited mainly to language educators. English Plus has found few legislative champions outside of the Latino and Asian American caucuses (e.g., Serrano 1997).[5]

The Impact of *Lau v. Nichols*

Meanwhile, bilingual education had also become a civil rights issue. For militant Chicanos in particular, it emerged as a key demand—in no small part because of the suppression of Spanish in schools throughout the Southwest, a symbol of racial oppression. For La Raza Unida Party, which won control of the Crystal City, Texas, school board in 1970, bilingual education became a matter of self-determination, an assertion of ethnic pride, and a pedagogical approach to which high hopes were attached (Shockley 1974). Wherever language minorities were concentrated, school officials began to feel community pressure to adopt bilingual methods. Several districts became the target of lawsuits by parents who argued that failure to address students' language needs meant failure to provide them an equal opportunity to learn. As Mexican American students staged boycotts to protest their treatment by the schools in cities like Los Angeles, bilingual education was frequently among their demands.

In 1970, the U.S. Department of Health, Education, and Welfare responded with a memorandum on school districts' obligations toward LEP students. Under the Civil Rights Act of 1964, it warned, "sink or swim" was no longer permissible. Public schools would now have to take "affirmative steps" to help students overcome language barriers. Moreover, they would have to provide such assistance without segregating children on dead-end tracks of remedial education.

Few districts paid much attention. In San Francisco, for example, administrators insisted that by giving LEP students the *identical* education offered to all students—that is, instruction via the English language—schools were discharging their obligation to provide an *equal* education for all. Federal district and appeals courts agreed, rejecting a lawsuit brought on behalf of Chinese-speaking students and permitting sink-or-swim instruction. While this position may seem myopic today, in the early 1970s it was widely shared. The issue of desegregation had so dominated the civil rights struggle that any suggestion of "separate but equal" education was suspect even to progressives.

Unlike African Americans fighting exclusion, the language-minority plaintiffs in the San Francisco case sought to establish the principle that children with different needs are entitled to different treatment by the schools. They cited the words of Justice Felix Frankfurter a generation earlier: "There is no greater inequality than the equal treatment of unequals" (Steinman 1971).

The U.S. Supreme Court embraced the parents' reasoning in a unanimous opinion. Its ruling in *Lau v. Nichols* (414 U.S. 563 [1974]), while limited in scope, remains the major legal precedent on language rights in the United States—or, more precisely, on the obligation of government to provide appropriate language accommodations to safeguard (other) fundamental rights. Writing for the court, Justice William O. Douglas reasoned that

> there is no equality of treatment merely by providing students with the same facilities, textbooks, teachers, and curriculum; for students who do not understand English are effectively foreclosed from any meaningful education. Basic English skills are at the very core of what these public schools teach. Imposition of a requirement that, before a child can effectively participate in the educational program, he must already have acquired those basic skills is to make a mockery of public education. We know that those who do not understand English are certain to find their classroom experiences wholly incomprehensible and in no way meaningful. (565)

The decision stopped short of mandating bilingual education, leaving the door open to other pedagogical treatments for students' "language deficiency":

> No specific remedy is urged upon us. Teaching English to the students of Chinese ancestry who do not speak the language is one choice. Giving instructions to this group in Chinese is another. There may be others. Petitioner asks only that the Board of Education be directed to apply its expertise to the problem and rectify the situation. (563)

As interpreted by the U.S. Office of Education, however, *Lau v. Nichols* soon became a mandate for bilingual education: the remedy of choice whenever a school district was found to be violating the civil rights of LEP students. Aggressive enforcement of the so-called Lau Remedies from 1975 to 1981 imposed bilingual education on nearly five hundred school districts, mostly in the Southwest, through consent agreements known as Lau Plans. This period of federal oversight—or federal "heavy-handedness," in the view of many local officials—had contradictory results.

For the first time, large numbers of school districts were induced to pay attention to the language needs of LEP students and to serve them through bilingual education. Before the mid-1970s, few had done either of these

things—which required a thorough transformation of business as usual—without the carrot of federal or state subsidies. Now came the stick, as the federal Office for Civil Rights patrolled school systems with significant language-minority enrollments. Districts required to adopt Lau Plans, along with others that acted to pre-empt federal intervention, tended to accept the new pedagogy grudgingly at first. Over time, however, most came to regard bilingual instruction as, if not a panacea, at least a substantial improvement over "sink or swim." As pedagogical outcomes improved, community support usually increased.

Yet prescriptiveness also bred resistance. Bilingual education suddenly became a point of conflict between federal authorities and local school boards, a cause célèbre for opponents of Big Government—in short, a natural issue for conservatives of the period. First, the Lau Remedies were attacked as illegitimate because, as quasi-formal "guidelines," they had been issued without an opportunity for public scrutiny or comment. A federal court agreed. Labeling the rule-making process illegal, it ordered the Carter administration to develop formal Lau Regulations. When the new rules finally appeared, shortly before the 1980 election, they were greeted with near-unanimous opposition from the education community (other than the National Association for Bilingual Education and its affiliates).[6] Ronald Reagan, who had made attacks on federal red tape a major campaign theme, withdrew the Lau Regulations shortly after winning the presidency.[7] As a result, since 1981 the Office for Civil Rights has declined to articulate a preference for any pedagogical approach.[8]

Second, the Lau Remedies placed a new burden of proof on the federal government. Mandating bilingual instruction, rather than merely encouraging local school districts to try it, created pressure to offer "conclusive" evidence of its pedagogical benefits. A U.S. Department of Education review of the research literature, initiated by the Carter administration, found mixed results at best. Baker and de Kanter (1983) concluded that "no consistent evidence supports the effectiveness of [transition bilingual education (TBE)]. . . . An occasional, inexplicable success is not enough reason to make TBE the law of the land" (50–51). The report also speculated that alternative, all-English approaches might be promising. Yet the Baker-de Kanter study itself came under criticism for its methodology (e.g., Willig 1985). Many of the studies under review involved programs that were poorly designed and implemented, quick-exit models rather than the developmental approaches later found to be superior (Ramírez et al. 1991). The authors' claims for the promise of "structured immersion" were based on studies of Canadian programs (bilingual ones, at that) tailored to the needs of students who had little in common with language-minority students in the United States. Despite the study's limited credibility among researchers, however, it received considerable play in the news media. The debate lent credence to the argument, raised by Secretary of Education William Bennett (among others), that the experts are "divided" and thus the scientific evidence on bilingual education remains too "inconclusive" to support Title VII policy.

Hence the political paradox of bilingual education. It might well have remained a marginal experiment had it not been imposed on school districts via the Lau Remedies and assorted court orders. Today's most successful instructional models for LEP students might never have been developed; at best, they would likely be confined to a tiny number of schools. At the same time, however, federal and state mandates for bilingual education provoked a backlash and a fierce debate over the program's effectiveness. Critics charged that, however "well-intentioned," Title VII had failed to fulfill its promises—citing the persistence of high failure and dropout rates among Latino students in particular. Thus, its value as a civil rights remedy has come into question.

Increasingly, English-only advocates have appropriated the language-as-right approach for their own purposes. Chávez (1991) argues that if bilingual education segregates LEP children from the mainstream and discourages them from learning English, then it must limit their educational opportunities. Proposition 227, the so-called English for the Children (1997) initiative, made a similar pitch to California voters:

(a) WHEREAS the English language is the national public language of the United States of America and of the state of California, is spoken by the vast majority of California residents, and is also the leading world language for science, technology, and business, thereby being the language of economic opportunity; and

(b) WHEREAS immigrant parents are eager to have their children acquire a good knowledge of English, thereby allowing them to fully participate in the American Dream of economic and social advancement; and

(c) WHEREAS the government and the public schools of California have a moral obligation and a constitutional duty to provide all of California's children, regardless of their ethnicity or national origins, with the skills necessary to become productive members of our society, and of these skills, literacy in the English language is among the most important; and

(d) WHEREAS the public schools of California currently do a poor job of educating immigrant children, wasting financial resources on costly experimental language programs whose failure over the past two decades is demonstrated by the current high drop-out and low English literacy levels of many immigrant children; and

(e) WHEREAS young immigrant children can easily acquire full fluency in a new language, such as English, if they are heavily exposed to that language in the classroom at early age.

(f) THEREFORE it is resolved that: all children in California public schools shall be taught English as rapidly and effectively as possible. (Sec. 300)

Most fair-minded Americans would agree with most of these premises (although paragraphs [d] and [e] would receive few endorsements from experts in second-language acquisition). LEP children are surely entitled to "be taught English . . . as effectively as possible." Whether that also means "as rapidly as possible" is another matter. Still, no one disputes that English proficiency is crucial both to their academic success and to their "economic and social advancement" in the United States.

The question becomes one of means: How should these goals be pursued? Proposition 227 requires that "all children in California public schools shall be taught English by being taught *in* English." The initiative statute prohibits most uses of native-language instruction for LEP students and prescribes programs of "sheltered English immersion during a temporary transition period not normally intended to exceed one year" (English for the Children 1997, Sec. 305; emphasis added).[9]

Will this sweeping mandate serve the interests and safeguard the rights of English learners? Or will it do precisely the opposite? Laypersons are being asked to decide such questions not only in California but in other states as well—judgments that require sorting through complex and contradictory information. One might as well ask the electorate to mandate a treatment for AIDS or to select the design of the next space station.[10] How schools should teach LEP students has become a highly technical issue. It has also become a highly political one, which invites simplistic and demagogic answers.

Again, the paradox: In its path to acceptance, bilingual education followed the course of numerous reforms of the 1960s. Conceived as an innovative approach to a social problem, it was taken up as a demand by ethnic militants and parents' organizations, supported with federal funds, accepted by school boards, studied by researchers, embraced by practitioners, and sustained by a corps of experts, lawyers, and bureaucrats. In short, it became institutionalized. At the same time, however, these currents were eroding its political support. To the extent that bilingual education has become the domain of professionals, it is less of an activist cause, less of a community concern, less of a social movement.

Government agencies, educators' associations, and school districts have done little to explain the pedagogy to outsiders, including parents—many of whom are new to the United States and have no memory of earlier struggles for bilingual education. "The broader public, never clear about the rationale for native-language instruction, is increasingly skeptical of its results. With the rise of English-only activity, assimilationist rhetoric has won a growing acceptance. Now it is making inroads into language-minority communities. Polled by the *Los Angeles Times* on whether they would favor a ballot initiative to "require all public school instruction to be conducted in English and for students not fluent in English to be placed in a short-term English immersion program," 84 percent of Latinos answered in the affirmative, as compared with just 80 percent of all voters (Barabak 1997).[11]

There is no question that the parents of LEP students continue to feel strongly about the civil rights goals of bilingual education. Yet it is also clear that in the 1990s, language-minority communities are less vocal on its behalf than in the 1970s. Defending the program's effectiveness has become largely a job for professionals. Whether bilingual instruction provides an antidote for school failure, whether it teaches English effectively, whether it safeguards children's rights under *Lau*—these questions are usually left to specialists who can explain the complexities of educational research. Few members of the public seem interested in such explanations, which contradict cherished myths on how languages are learned and how immigrant ancestors "made it" without special help.

Moreover, the voters exhibit a growing impatience with government programs that benefit immigrants and racial minorities. By approving Proposition 187 in 1994, Californians instructed school officials to hunt down and expel the children of "illegal aliens." With Proposition 209 two years later, they chose to outlaw all forms of affirmative action. In 1998, disregarding the advice of professionals in the field, they voted to outlaw bilingual education. Meanwhile, Latino and Asian American politicians, who once rallied liberal supporters behind programs serving immigrants, now sense ambiguous feelings among their own constituents. Hence their wariness about countering attacks like Proposition 227.

Thus the political viability of bilingual education becomes increasingly tenuous to the extent it relies on expert opinion. This is true not only because experts are routinely divided on pedagogical matters. In addition, many researchers today are sensitive to the charge that their work has become "politicized"; so they are more guarded in expressing support for bilingual approaches than they were in the 1980s. A recent report by the National Research Council strived for even-handedness, noting the benefits of both native-language and English-only instruction, even though the panel comprised several prominent enthusiasts of "additive bilingualism" (August and Hakuta 1997).[12] Bilingual teachers and administrators continue to champion their programs without equivocation. Yet such views are easily dismissed as expressions of narrow self-interest—a perennial line of attack by conservative critics (see, e.g., Thernstrom 1980, Chávez 1991).

Without a broader and firmer political base, the future of bilingual education would appear uncertain, to say the least. Where is the needed support to be found? The most obvious undeveloped sources are language-minority families and communities. What has kept them from playing a larger advocacy role? Several factors have already been noted: professionalization of bilingual programs, poor communication by the schools, timidity among elected officials, and immigrants' inexperience in a new political system. Most important perhaps is the peculiar tradition of language rights—or lack thereof—in the United States.

Language Rights, American Style

In most of the world, language rights are understood in two ways: "(1) the right of freedom from discrimination on the basis of language; and (2) the right to use your language(s) in the activities of communal life" (Macías 1979, 41). International treaties to which the United States is a signatory, such as the United Nations Charter and the International Declaration of Human Rights, recognize either one or both varieties. Such treaty obligations make these language rights a part of U.S. law—at least, theoretically. Nevertheless, they remain largely foreign to our legal traditions.

Americans have frequently addressed the language needs of its citizens on political, economic, or moral grounds. During the nineteenth century, for example, a dozen states and territories authorized bilingual education in public schools; elsewhere it was often provided without official sanction (Kloss 1977). Yet there were no constitutional obstacles to terminating such policies and mandating English-only instruction, as most states chose to do during the World War I era. Some Hispanic advocates have argued that, under the 1848 Treaty of Guadalupe Hidalgo, Spanish-speakers are entitled to bilingual-bicultural education in the Southwest. In fact, the treaty makes no explicit mention of language rights, and such interpretations have been rejected by U.S. courts (e.g., *López Tijerina v. Henry* 389 U.S. 922[1969]).

Language rights exist in the United States only as a component of other rights, in particular the Fourteenth Amendment guarantee of "equal protection" under law without regard to race or national origin. *Lau v. Nichols* was decided on similar grounds, relying on Title VI of the Civil Rights Act of 1964. Taking another approach in *Meyer v. Nebraska* (262 U.S. 390 [1923]), the Supreme Court struck down restrictions on foreign-language instruction as an unconstitutional violation of "due process" guarantees.

> While this court has not attempted to define with exactness the liberty thus guaranteed . . . without doubt, it denotes not merely freedom from bodily restraint but also the right of the individual to contract, to engage in any of the common occupations of life, to acquire useful knowledge, to marry, establish a home and bring up children, to worship God according to the dictates of his own conscience, and generally to enjoy those privileges long recognized at common law as essential to the orderly pursuit of happiness by free men. The established doctrine is that this liberty may not be interfered with, under the guise of protecting

the public interest, by legislative action which is arbitrary or without reasonable relation to some purpose within the competency of the state to effect. (402)

Among these implicit rights, the Court enumerated a German language teacher's "right thus to teach and the right of parents to engage him so to instruct their children" (402).

Significantly, despite the breadth of constitutional "liberties" it found to be guaranteed by implication, the *Meyer* court said nothing about *community rights* to use and maintain a language other than English. Its omission is consistent with the Anglo-American tradition of common law, which almost always endows rights to individuals rather than to groups. This has tended to discourage the recognition of language rights, which have limited meaning outside a collective context. For example, the *Lau* decision defines an LEP student's right to special assistance designed to overcome the language barrier and make academic instruction comprehensible—not an ethnic group's right to perpetuate its language via vernacular (i.e., native-language) education. Restricted in this way, Magnet (1990) argues, language rights are ultimately meaningless:

> The right to utilize a language is absolutely empty of content unless it implies a linguistic community which understands the speaker and with whom that speaker can communicate. . . . *Language rights are collective rights.* They are exercised by individuals only as part of a collectivity or a group. Legal protection of language rights, therefore, means protection of that linguistic community, that community of speakers and hearers, vis-à-vis the larger community which would impinge upon it or restrict its right as a group to exist. (293; emphasis added)

Canada's policy of official bilingualism incorporates this philosophy. In essence, according to a former commissioner of official languages, it guarantees the Francophone minority's "right not to assimilate, the right to maintain a certain difference" (Yalden 1981). Besides entitling citizens to federal government services in both English and French, Canada provides subsidies to numerous indigenous and immigrant minorities for the purpose of linguistic maintenance. The United States, by contrast, has tended to resist such policies in principle, if not always in practice. Except in matters of religion, it would be hard to cite any collective "right not to assimilate" ever guaranteed by federal or state governments. Nor was there any formal recognition of a "right" to mother-tongue schooling for any non-Anglophone group, immigrant or indigenous.

Nevertheless, American linguistic minorities have succeeded in maintaining distinct communities, sometimes for several generations, with varying degrees of toleration or accommodation from authorities. Bilingual and vernacular education were widely, if inconsistently, available from the colonial era until World War I. In 1900, contemporary surveys reported that six hundred thousand elementary school children, public and parochial, were receiving part or all of their instruction in the German language. This figure—which Kloss (1977) regards as overly conservative—was equivalent to 4 percent of the elementary school population at the time,[13] probably larger than the proportion of children in all bilingual classrooms today.[14]

This era of accommodation ended following World War I, a period when speaking languages other than English, especially German, came to be associated with disloyalty to the United States. Such wartime fears strengthened a campaign to "Americanize the immigrant," especially in linguistic matters. This in turn had a major impact on the schools. By 1923, thirty-four states had adopted laws banning native-language instruction and, in some cases, foreign-language teaching in the early grades (Leibowitz 1969). As a result, bilingual education largely disappeared until the early 1960s, when it was revived by Cuban exiles in Dade County, Florida.

The Once and Future Politics of Bilingualism

While a thorough historical analysis is beyond the scope of this chapter, for our purposes the key question is: What can be learned from early American "traditions" of bilingual education that might be relevant to its present political plight? In particular, what were its ideological and political foundations before the modern era?

First, it should be noted that bilingual and vernacular schools were often the product of practical necessity or local choice. Before the twentieth century, fully English-proficient teachers were often unavailable in large expanses of the rural Midwest, New Mexico, southern California, Louisiana, and northern New England. Where language minorities commanded local majorities, they usually controlled their own education systems. The first public schools in the state of Texas, established by the municipality of New Braunfels in the 1850s, operated mostly in German (Kloss 1977). At about the same time, the Cherokee Nation of Oklahoma established a system of twenty-one bilingual schools and two academies, achieving higher literacy rates in English and Cherokee than the neighboring states of Arkansas and Texas could manage in English alone (U.S. Senate 1969).

Bilingual education also gained a foothold in major cities including St. Louis, Indianapolis, Milwaukee, and Cincinnati, which ran extensive German-English programs for several decades. School systems made conscious decisions to accommodate the wishes of immigrant parents. More than 5 million Germans arrived between 1830 and 1890, and most settled in the Ohio and Mississippi river valleys. Notwithstanding their religious, cultural, and political diversity, these immigrants were united on the value of German-language instruction as the key to a treasured heritage. For parents, language maintenance was usually the chief goal of bilingual instruction.

More important, school officials saw themselves in competition with parochial schools for immigrant students. Providing minority-language instruction became a way to entice parents to support the "common school." It was also conceived as a way to bring these groups into the mainstream of American life. William Torrey Harris, school superintendent in St. Louis and later U.S. commissioner of education, saw no contradiction in fostering bilingualism and assimilation simultaneously. Like other educational leaders—and unlike most immigrant parents—he saw the primary goal of bilingual education as teaching American culture, including the English language, as efficiently as possible. His rationale, however, was more political than pedagogical. "If separate nationalities keep their own [Lutheran and Catholic] schools," Harris wrote in 1870, "it will result that the Anglo- and German-American youth will not intermingle and caste-distinctions will grow up." On the other hand, "if the German children can learn to read and write the language of the fatherland in the public schools, they will not need separate ones" (quoted in Schlossman 1983, 152).

Harris believed strongly in the public schools' mission to "Americanize the immigrant." Yet he differed from later promoters of this cause in his conviction that the process would proceed more efficiently by voluntary rather than coercive means. In St. Louis, his approach proved successful. After fifteen years of German bilingual programs, the percentage of German-American children attending the public schools had increased from 20 percent to 80 percent (Schlossman 1983).

By offering bilingual instruction in St. Louis and elsewhere, schools recognized no language rights in the strict sense. Nevertheless, they paid homage to a strong tradition in American education: parents' prerogative to have a say in their children's schooling. However vaguely defined in legal terms, the right of parental choice has been revered as a political principle. Thus it has served at times as a powerful rallying cry for diverse groups of parents, including language minorities. In 1889, when German Americans learned that Wisconsin and Illinois had imposed English-only instruction on parochial as well as public schools, they put aside factional concerns, organized to defeat the ruling Republican Party at the next election, and soon repealed the legislation (Crawford 1992). In the 1960s, when Mexican Americans demanded an end to sink-or-swim neglect, they marshaled sufficient moral and legal authority to win bilingual education subsidies, court orders, and civil rights enforcement.

Parent activism can only flourish, however, when armed with clarity of purpose. To the extent that the parents of LEP children are uncertain about the rationale for bilingual education and alienated from the professionals who control it, they will remain passive players in the public policy debate. A majority of these parents may continue to favor the program. But without mass goals and leadership to rally behind, there can be no "bilingual movement" to provide needed political support. Indeed, parents' passivity may be taken for acquiescence to antibilingual policies—as it was in California's approval of Proposition 227.

If current trends continue, the consequences could be drastic: Bilingual educators find themselves increasingly isolated and hard-pressed to resist attacks. LEP students have fewer options, as many school districts limit access to native-language instruction and others convert to English-only models altogether. The nation's thirty-year experiment with bilingual education, despite its success in many schools and its benefits to many children, is branded a failure in the public mind. A generation of experience and research is discarded, as the pedagogy is relegated to marginal status.

The question for bilingual educators and advocates in the late 1990s is whether they can regain the confidence, understanding, and allegiance of their core constituency—language-minority communities—in time to rewrite this grim scenario.

Study Questions

1. What are the goals of bilingual education for various stakeholders? Which are primary and which are secondary? How successfully are they being met in practice and why? On what basis do you make these judgments?

2. What are the factors today that encourage public skepticism about teaching children in minority languages? To what extent do they reflect political concerns? Pedagogical concerns? Other concerns?

3. How have orientations toward U.S. language policy evolved as a result of Title VII, and what has been their impact? For example: How has "language-as-problem" affected the theory and practice of bilingual education? What contradictions in language rights have become evident in the public debate over the English-only movement? Why has the English Plus, language-as-resource strategy failed to appeal to significant numbers of Americans?

4. What accounts for the difference in the politics of bilingualism in the nineteenth century compared with the 1990s? What lessons can contemporary advocates draw from these differences?

5. Predict the future of bilingual education two decades from today. Will the field be stronger or weaker pedagogically? Will it stress the transition to English over the development of fluent bilingualism or vice versa? Will it continue to exist at all? Explain the early twenty-first century factors that led to these outcomes.

Notes

1. Proposition 227 was adopted on a vote of 61 percent to 39 percent. Immediately thereafter, the Mexican American Legal Defense and Educational Fund; Multicultural Education, Training and Advocacy, Inc.; American Civil Liberties union; and other advocates filed suit to block the initiative statute on civil rights and constitutional grounds. A federal district judge in San Francisco declined, however, to order a preliminary injunction. Although the lawsuit continued, Proposition 227 took effect as scheduled on August 2, 1998.

2. Three states had done so previously. In 1998, after a ten-year battle, Arizona's Article XXVIII was struck down by the state's supreme court as a violation of the First Amendment. This left a total of twenty-one states with active laws designating English as the official language.

3. Thernstrom (1980), a critic of bilingual education, claims: "The chairmen of the House and Senate committees did not call witnesses—in the sense of experts on the educational and political questions raised by the legislation—but (with few exceptions) lobbyists. Ethnic activists—mostly Hispanics—came to testify on the bill's necessity" (6). In fact, only twenty-six of the 144 witnesses were lobbyists for community and advocacy groups; about half had Hispanic surnames.

4. There was no separate recorded vote on bilingual education in either the House or the Senate.

5. This situation may be changing, as Republicans begin to make overtures to Hispanic voters. A new English Plus resolution was introduced in 1998 by John McCain of Arizona and nine other Republican senators.

6. Among interest groups, the National Education Association was the only major exception.

7. In a statement canceling the Lau Regulations, Terrel Bell, the new secretary of education, called them "harsh, inflexible, burdensome, unworkable, and incredibly costly" (quoted in Crawford 1995, 53).

8. The civil rights agency has relied instead on *the Castañeda* standard for determining whether school districts are meeting their obligations toward LEP students (Crawford 1996). This three-part test was developed by a federal appeals court in interpreting the Equal Educational Opportunities Act of 1974. Reaffirming the *Lau v. Nichols* decision, the law requires school districts to take "appropriate action to overcome language barriers that impede equal participation by its students in its instructional programs" (Sec. 1703[f]). More than vague "good faith" efforts are required, the court ruled in *Castañeda v. Pickard* (648 F. 2d 989 [5th Cir. 1981]). A program serving LEP students must meet the following criteria:

   It must be based on "a sound educational theory," endorsed by one or more experts.

   It must be "implemented effectively," with adequate resources and personnel.

   After a trial period, it must be evaluated as effective in overcoming language handicaps.

9. At parents' request, "waivers" of the English-only rule may be allowed for older LEP children and those with "special needs" but would be subject to many restrictions. Teachers, administrators, and school board members who failed to provide English-only instruction may be sued and held "personally liable" for financial damages (English for the Children 1997, Sec. 311 and 320).

10. These examples are not entirely far-fetched, considering California's attachment to government-by-initiative. In early 1998, there were five measures certified for the June ballot and forty others being circulated for the November ballot, ranging from a proposal to legalize casino gambling to an effort to ban the sale of horse meat for human consumption (Kershner 1998).

11. In fairness, it should be noted that this question poorly summarized the provisions of the "English for the Children" initiative, such as neglecting to mention its ban on bilingual education programs. Later polls showed contradictory results—for example, Spanish-language media in Los Angeles found that 88 percent of parents with children enrolled in bilingual programs were satisfied with the results. The major exit poll on June 2, 1998, concluded that Latinos had rejected Proposition 227 by 63 percent to 37 percent (Los Angeles Times-CNN Poll 1998). Yet even this level of support is substantially higher than in the past.

12. Several panel members had been part of the Stanford Working Group on Federal Programs for Limited-English-Proficient Students, which influenced the Clinton administration to expand support for developmental bilingual education (Hakuta et al. 1993).

13. Kloss (1977) argues that 1 million—or 7 percent—would be a more reasonable figure.

14. Unfortunately, today's data in this area have barely improved since 1900. Based on reports from forty-eight states and the District of Columbia, the U.S. Department of Education estimates that 3,018,042 students in public and private elementary and secondary schools were limited-English proficient in 1994–1995 (Macías and Kelly 1996). These counts vary in reliability, especially for private school enrollments. Information about the educational services provided to LEP children is especially fragmentary. California, the one state that conducts a thorough school-by-school language census each year, reports that only 30 percent of LEP students were enrolled in fully bilingual classrooms in 1994–1995. Extrapolated nationwide, that proportion would yield an estimate of 907,413 U.S. students in bilingual education—or less than 2 percent of the total elementary and secondary enrollment of 46,930,614.

References

August, Diane, and Kenji Hakuta, eds. 1997. *Improving schooling for language-minority students: A research agenda.* Washington, D.C.: National Academy Press.

Baker, Keith A., and Adriana A. de Kanter. 1983. The effectiveness of bilingual education. In *Bilingual Education,* ed. Keith A. Baker and Adriana A. de Kanter, 33–86. Lexington, Mass.: Lexington Books.

Barabak, Mark Z. 1997. Bilingual education gets little support. *Los Angeles Times,* 15 October, p. 1.

Bennett, William J. 1985. The Bilingual Education Act: A failed path. In *Language loyalties: A source book on the Official English controversy*, ed. James Crawford, 358–363, 1992. Chicago: University of Chicago Press.

Chávez, Linda. 1991. *Out of the barrio: Toward a new politics of Hispanic assimilation.* New York: Basic Books.

Combs, Mary Carol. 1992. English Plus: Responding to English Only. In *Language loyalties: A source book on the Official English controversy*, ed. James Crawford, 216–224. Chicago: University of Chicago Press.

Congressional Record. 1967. Debate on the Elementary and Secondary Education Amendments Act of 1967 (H.R. 7819), December 1, 5, pp. 34702–34703, 35053.

Crawford, James. 1992. *Hold your tongue: Bilingualism and the politics of "English Only."* Reading, Mass.: Addison-Wesley.

Crawford, James. 1995. *Bilingual education: History, politics, theory, and practice.* Los Angeles: Bilingual Educational Services.

Crawford, James. 1996. Summing up the *Lau* decision: Justice is never simple. In *Revisiting the* Lau *decision: 20 years later,* ed. Susan Sather, 81–86. Oakland, Calif.: ARC Associates.

Croghan, Michael Joseph. 1997. Title VII of 1968: Origins, orientations, and analysis. Ph.D. diss., University of Arizona.

Danoff, Malcolm N., et al. 1977–78. *Evaluation of the impact of ESEA Title VII Spanish/English bilingual education programs: vol. 1, Study design and interim findings,* and *vol. 3, Year two impact data, educational process, and in-depth analysis.* Arlington, Va.: American Institutes for Research.

English for the Children. 1997. *English language education for children in public schools.* California initiative statute (certified as Proposition 227 for the 2 June 1998, primary election).

Epstein, Noel, 1977. *Language, ethnicity, and the schools: Policy alternatives for bilingual-bicultural education.* Washington, D.C.: Institute for Educational Leadership.

Greene, Jay P. 1998. *A meta-analysis of the effectiveness of bilingual education.* Claremont, Calif.: Tomas Rivera Policy Institute.

Hakuta, Kenji, et al. 1993. *Federal education programs for limited-English-proficient students: A blueprint for the second generation.* Stanford, Calif.: Stanford Working Group.

Kershner, Vlae. 1998. Democracy gone awry. *San Francisco Chronicle*, 18 May, p. 1.

Kloss, Heinz. 1977. *The American bilingual tradition*. Rowley, Mass.: Newbury House.

Leibowitz, Arnold H. 1969. English literacy: Legal sanction for discrimination. *Notre Dame Lawyer* 45(7): 7–67.

Los Angeles Times-CNN Poll, "Profile of the Electorate," 4 June 1998. Available online: http://www.latimes.com/HOME/NEWS/POLLS/exitpollsuper.htm

Macías, Reynaldo Flores. 1979. Choice of language as a human right: Public policy implications in the United States. In *Bilingual education and public policy*, ed. Raymond V. Padilla, 39–57. Ypsilanti: Department of Foreign Languages and Bilingual Studies, Eastern Michigan University.

Macías, Reynaldo F., and Candace Kelly. 1996. *Summary report of the survey of the states' limited English proficient students and available educational programs and services, 1994–1995*. Washington, D.C.: National Clearinghouse for Bilingual Education.

Magnet, Joseph. 1990. Language rights as collective rights. In *Perspectives on official English: The campaign for English as official language of the USA*, ed. Karen L. Adams and Daniel T. Brink, 293–299. Berlin: Mouton de Gruyter.

National Education Association. 1966. *The invisible minority: Report of the NEA-Tucson Survvey*. Washington, D.C.: Author.

Ramírez, J. David, Sandra D. Yuen, and Dena R. Ramey. 1991. *Final report: Longitudinal study of structured innuersion strategy, early-exit, and late-exit transitional bilingual education programs for language-minority children*. San Mateo, Calif.: Aguirre International.

Ruiz, Richard. 1984. Orientations in language planning. *NABE Journal* 8(2):15–34.

Schlossman, Steven L. 1983. Is there an American tradition of bilingual education? German in the public elementary schools, 1840–1919. *American Journal of Education* 91(2): 139–186.

Serrano, José. 1997. English Plus resolution. H.Con.Res. 4, 105th Cong., 1st Sess.

Shockley, John Staples. 1974. *Chicano revolt in a Texas town*. Notre Dame, Ind.: University of Notre Dame Press.

Steinman, Edward H. 1971. *Kinney Kimmon Lau, et al., Appellants v. Alan H. Nichols, et al. Appellees: Appellants' reply brief*. U.S. Ninth Circuit Court of Appeals, 4 January.

Thernstrom, Abigail. 1980. *E pluribus plura*—Congress and bilingual education. *Public Interest 60* (summer): 3–22.

U.S. Senate, Labor and Public Welfare Committee, Special Subcommittee on Indian Education. 1969. *Indian education: A national tragedy, a national challenge*. 91st Cong., 1st Sess.

Willig, Ann C. 1985. A meta-analysis of selected studies on the effectiveness of bilingual education. *Review of Educational Research* 55: 269–317.

Yalden, Maxwell F. 1981. The bilingual experience in Canada. In *The new bilingualism: An American dilemma*, ed. Martin Ridge. New Brunswick, N.J.: Transaction Books.

School Failure:
Explanations and Interventions

Guadalupe Valdés

Mexican-origin children have not fared well in American schools. Their problems have been documented by many researchers (e.g., Arias, 1986; Bean & Tienda, 1987; Carter, 1970; Carter & Segura, 1979; Durán, 1983; Keller et al., 1991; Matute-Bianchi, 1986; Orfield, 1986; Olivas, 1986; Orum, 1986; U.S. Commission on Civil Rights, 1972a, b, c; 1973; 1974; Valencia, 1991 a, 1991 b). Many attempts have been made both to explain the reasons for the poor school performance of this particular group of children and to intervene in meaningful ways in their educational experiences. Within the last 20 years, for example, much attention has been given, by both the research and the policy communities, to the study of factors that appear to contribute to the school failure of Mexican-background students. In general, research on the condition of education for Mexican-origin students has focused on issues such as segregation, attrition, school finance, language and bilingual education, and testing.

Explanations of School Failure

Mexican-origin individuals are, in terms of their school performance, a part of a much larger population that includes the disadvantaged, the at-risk, and the underprivileged. A discussion of the school failure of Mexican-origin students must, therefore, be framed by a broader discussion that examines why other children who share similar backgrounds have also failed. It is important to first outline the causes of school failure among all children whom the educational establishment does not serve well and then to examine how the specific status of the Mexican-origin population might contribute in unique ways to this group's lack of educational success and achievement.

In general, explanations of poor academic achievement by non-mainstream children can be grouped into a number of categories. The three categories used by Bond (1981) are

1. the genetic argument,
2. the cultural argument, and
3. the class analysis argument.

The Genetic Argument

In the United States, the genetic argument—the view that certain groups are genetically more able than others (Eysenck, 1971; Herrnstein, 1973; Jensen, 1969)—had been out of favor for a number of years. Revisited recently by Herrnstein and Murray (1994), the genetic argument holds that academic talent is largely inherited and that society rewards these genetically inherited abilities. Supporters for this position argue that, given unequal innate capabilities, children of different ethnic or racial groups perform differently in school.

Strong views about the relationship between heredity and intelligence—which are largely based on the analysis of group performance on IQ tests—have been criticized by a number of scholars. Such scholars question the premises underlying psychometric testing (Figueroa, 1983, 1989; Gould, 1981; Kamin, 1977; Morrison, 1977; Schwartz, 1977; White, 1977; Zacharias, 1977), and specifically challenge the entire notion of IQ, a notion that is based exclusively on psychometric procedures and practices. A number of individuals (e.g., McClelland, 1974) have pointed out that IQ tests do not measure important features of intelligence. Others (e.g., Samuda, 1975) argue that efforts to produce culture-free tests have been disappointing. Still others (Roth, 1974) present evidence that procedures and practices in test administration may negatively affect the performance of minority children.

It is important to note that the genetic argument has failed to convince scholars within the research community who themselves may accept the assumptions under-

Reprinted by permission of the publisher from Valdés, Guadalupe, Con Respeto: *Bridging the Distance Between Culturally Diverse Families and Schools*, (New York: Teachers College Press, © 1984 by Teachers College, Columbia University. All rights reserved.), pp. 15–40.

lying ability testing. Some individuals (Goldberg, 1974a, b; Kamin, 1974), for example, have challenged specific aspects of research carried out by Jensen, one of the most prominent proponents of the genetic argument. Both Goldberg and Kamin question Jensen's findings based on available twin studies. Additionally, a number of scholars (e.g., Lewontin, Rose, & Kamin, 1984) have attacked the entire concept of race. They argue not only that from a biological perspective "race" is a fuzzy concept, but also that studies focusing on adoption across racial and class lines failed to separate the genetic from the social. More recently, a number of scholars (e.g., Sternberg, 1982, 1985; Sternberg & Detterman, 1986) have attempted to move "beyond IQ" and have endeavored to examine conceptions of intelligence from a variety of different perspectives.

The Cultural Argument

As opposed to the genetic argument, the cultural explanation is currently still drawn upon by many researchers and practitioners. In its strongest form, proponents of this position (e.g., Lewis, 1966) argue that poor children are trapped in a "culture of poverty" and locked into a cycle of failure that is, in essence, self-perpetuating. Those who subscribe to this position maintain that children succeed in school only if their many deficiencies are corrected and if they are taught to behave in more traditionally mainstream ways in specially designed intervention programs.

The less extreme forms of the cultural argument do not see poor children as directly playing a role in perpetuating their own circumstances. They nevertheless consider children who historically performed poorly in school to be either culturally deprived (Bereiter & Englemann, 1966; Deutsch et al., 1967; Hess & Shipman, 1965; Hunt, 1961; McCandless, 1952) or culturally different and therefore mismatched with schools and school culture (Baratz & Baratz, 1970). Language in particular has been used as a primary example of the ways in which children are mismatched with schools and school personnel (Au & Mason, 1981; Bernstein, 1977; Drucker, 1971; Erickson & Mohatt, 1982; Heath, 1983; Michaels & Collins, 1984; Philips, 1982).

Although the line between theories of cultural difference and cultural deprivation is a fine one, it can generally be said that advocates of the cultural difference or mismatch perspective ordinarily attribute value to the backgrounds of non-mainstream children. They do not speak of deprivation, but hold, instead, that rich and rule-governed as these children's experiences may be, they are not what educational institutions value and expect. Examples of work carried out from this perspective are those on Black English (Labov, 1973) and on children's socialization for literacy in the Appalachian region of the United States (Heath, 1983).

Closely related to the research on differences between mainstream and disadvantaged children is research on parents and their ability to "support" their children's education. This work has primarily focused on parental involvement in education, parental attitudes toward schools and education, and maternal teaching styles. In general, this research takes the perspective that at-risk children do poorly in school because of their parents' beliefs and behaviors. Non-mainstream parents either do not have the "right" attitudes toward the value of education; or they do not prepare their children well for school; or they are not sufficiently involved in their children's education. During the 1960s and early 1970s, much of this research focused on Black American families. Descriptions of the supposedly inadequate home environments of Black children were used by well-meaning social scientists to refute the arguments made by geneticists about the causes of school failure. In a review of the several streams of research on the achievement of Black children, for example, Baratz and Baratz (1970) discussed the findings of this research. Black children were found by some researchers (e.g., Hunt, 1961) to suffer from too little stimulation, while other researchers found them to be victims of too much stimulation (Deutsch, Katz, & Jensen, 1968). Others defined the problem as rooted in the inadequacy of parenting skills by Black mothers (Hess et al., 1968) and advocated compensatory programs that would teach Black women how to become "good" parents from the perspective of the majority society.

While perhaps less popular with theorists, cultural difference arguments continue to undergird a variety of practices currently being implemented in schools and communities around the country.

The Class Analysis Argument

The final explanation of school failure involves the analysis of the role of education in maintaining class differences, that is, in maintaining the power differential between groups. Proponents of this view argue that non-mainstream children do poorly in school because of the class structure of capitalist society. They argue that educational institutions function to reproduce the structure of production and that schools serve as sorting mechanisms rather than as true avenues for movement between classes. For these theorists, it is not accidental that the children of the middle classes are primarily sorted into the "right" streams or tracks in school and given access to particular kinds of knowledge (e.g., technology). The role of schools is to legitimize inequality under the pretense of serving all children and encouraging them to reach their full potential. The genius of the system resides in the fact that although the cards are clearly stacked against them, students come to believe that they are in fact given an opportunity to succeed. They leave school firmly convinced that they could have done better, perhaps achieved as much as their middle-class peers, if only they had tried harder or worked more. They are then ready to accept low-paying working-class jobs, and the working class is thus reproduced.

Explanations of school failure from this particular perspective, however, are more complex than I have outlined above. Essentially, as Giroux (1983) has argued, there are three different theories or models of reproduction: the economic-reproductive model represented by the work of Bowles and Gintis (1976), Althusser (1969), and Althusser and Brewster (1971); the cultural reproductive model represented by the work of Bourdieu and Passeron (1977, 1979, and Bourdieu, 1977); and the hegemonic-state reproductive model represented by the work of Dale and Macdonald (1980), David (1980), and Sarup (1982) and based largely on the work of Gramsci (1971).

The economic-reproductive model focuses on the relations between the economy and schooling and argues that schools reproduce labor skills as well as relations of production. The cultural reproductive model, on the other hand, attempts to link culture, class, and domination and argues that culture is itself the medium through which the ruling class maintains its position in society. Schools validate the culture of the ruling class and at the same time fail to legitimize the forms of knowledge brought to school by groups not in power. Finally, the hegemonic-state reproductive model focuses on the role of the state in organizing the reproductive functions of educational institutions.

A particular concern for a number of theorists has been the role of human agency in explaining societal reproduction. A number of individuals—although willing to agree that macro-level factors lead to a reproduction of class relations and that schools play an important role in such reproduction—seek to understand exactly how individual members of society in particular institutions actually bring about such reproduction. These scholars hypothesize that the relationship between schooling and the perpetuation of class status is re-created at the interpersonal level in the school setting and that students actively contribute to the perpetuation of their situation by viewing mainstream students and the life choices valued by this group as worthy of contempt. "Working-class" students thus band with others of their same background and present an oppositional stance to that of the "good" or successful student. This "resistance," however, rather than allowing them to break out of the "working-class" cycle, results in the replication and reproduction of their class status. This particular trend in the investigation of the ways in which schools reproduce class membership is an attempt to understand the contents of the "black box," that is, to understand what actually goes on in educational institutions in order to bring about "failure" for certain groups of individuals. Work in this tradition is represented by the investigations carried out in Great Britain by McRobbie and McCabe (1981), Robins and Cohen (1978), and Willis (1977).

Understanding School Failure

From a theoretical perspective, the understanding of the difficulties surrounding the education of non-mainstream children must of necessity involve, as Persell (1977) argued, the integration of four levels of analysis: the societal, the institutional, the interpersonal, and the interpsychic. According to Persell, an adequate theory of educational inequality must take into account the distribution of power within a particular society and the ideology that supports that distribution. It must then link these macro-concerns to both existing ideologies about education and the nature of educational institutions. As Cortes (1986) maintains, moreover, such a theory must also take into account the educational process itself. It must consider factors such as the knowledge, skills, and attitudes of teachers, administrators, and counselors and individual student qualities and background, as well as instruction and the instructional context.

Unfortunately, as the discussion above suggests, to date examinations and explorations of school failure by non-mainstream students in school settings have been explored primarily from a single perspective.

School Failure and the Education of Immigrants

Current discussions of differential achievement by "new" American immigrants (e.g., Asians and Latinos) have tended to suggest that the difficulties encountered in schools by these newcomers were surmounted easily by the immigrant groups that arrived in this country during earlier historical periods. Vehement arguments against special compensatory programs such as bilingual education, for example, are frequently couched in the supposition that non-English speakers who entered the United States in the early part of the century managed to succeed in school without special attention given to their language or cultural differences.[1]

A review of the work carried out on the educational experiences of those immigrants who came into this country in the mid-19th century as well as in the early 20th century, however, presents a very different picture. It is evident that school failure or lack of school success was common and that Italian, Irish, Polish, and many Jewish children left school early and did not enter high school. Recent work on New York public schools (Berrol, 1982), for example, points out that until the 1950s, immigrant and even first generation children in New York City received a very limited amount of formal education. This was the case not only for the "ignorant" Irish, but also for children (e.g., Jewish children) whose parents have consistently valued formal education. Indeed, the picture that emerges from the work of most researchers who have focused on the education of turn-of-the-century immigrants (e.g., Berrol, 1982; Bodnar, 1982; Fass, 1988; Handlin, 1982; LaGumina, 1982, Mathews, 1966; Olneck &

Lazerson, 1988; Perlmann, 1988; Weiss, 1982; Williams, 1938/1969) is one that does not support idealistic views about the power of education to help all children succeed. Instead, what emerges is a sense that between 1840 and 1940, immigrants, rather than immediately availing themselves of the "opportunities" offered by educational institutions, made choices for their children that were framed by their views about education in general, their economic position, and the success or failure experienced by their children in school.

As has been the case in the examination of school failure in general, numerous explanations have been offered to account for the differences in academic and economic achievement of the various ethnic groups represented among turn-of-the-century immigrants. In particular, much attention has been given to accounting for the differences between generally "successful" groups such as the Jews and generally "unsuccessful" groups such as the Italians, the Irish, and the Slavs. As Perlmann (1988) points out, however, most of these explanations have had a long and ugly history in American intellectual life. As was the case in the late 1960s and early 1970s, for example, there was much concern in the early 20th century about genetic differences. Indeed, interest in ethnic differences reflected a profound suspicion of new immigrants that took on what Fass (1988) has characterized as a "racist slant." For many individuals who wrote during the early part of this century and even as late as the 1930s, differences in economic achievements (and educational achievements) by new immigrants were considered to be the result of inborn "race traits." As Fass (1988) argues, however, race was confused with what we now would consider to be culture, and many discussions about race focused on the habits and values of immigrant families. According to Fass, the eager acceptance of IQ testing in this country after World War I occurred in response to educators' concerns about the "retardation" of large numbers of pupils. IQ testing supposedly provided a means for ranking individuals according to their innate and unchanging talent and for ordering a hierarchy of groups. It offered a "scientific" rationale for existing views about inherited endowment and provided educators with justification for creating different "opportunities" for different students.

For early-20th-century immigrants, the genetic argument was used not only to account for differences in school performance, but to argue for the development of differentiated curricula suited to the particular talents of the less able members of the population. As a result, children with lower IQs (largely children of foreign parentage who were also poor) were placed in vocational or commercial programs. According to Fass (1988), in New York City high schools, "as early as 1911-12, about one third of the population was enrolled in commercial tracks or in the two special commercial high schools." Moreover, "educators did not believe that the new masses were smart enough to benefit from traditional academic subjects" (p. 67).

The cultural difference or deficit argument has also figured prominently in discussions about educational attainment among immigrant/ethnic groups in the United States. As Perlmann (1988) points out, variations in the attainment levels of different ethnic groups have been attributed in large part to their premigration histories. Much attention has been given both to the occupational skills, resulting from the positions they occupied in their countries of origin, and to the cultural attributes (attitudes, habits, values, and beliefs) that newcomers brought with them. A number of scholars, for example, have argued that certain groups (e.g., Italians) did not improve their lot as rapidly as others because their cultural background did not allow them to take advantage of the opportunities offered to them by the educational system. These scholars generally maintain that other groups (e.g., the Jews) did indeed bring with them views and attitudes about education that were congruent with the focus on the importance of schooling present in this country. Dinnerstein (1982), for example, argues that the cultural heritage of the Jews (what he considers to be "their high regard for learning") was vital to their achieving social mobility through education. Agreeing with this general view of cultural deficit, LaGumina (1982) stresses that Italians did not enjoy similar rapid mobility through education because southern Italian peasants who immigrated to the United States were conservative, fatalistic, and family-oriented. A parallel argument is made by Sowell (1981) and others about the Irish and their cultural orientation. Miller (1985, cited in Perlmann, 1988) views the traditional Irish peasant culture as communally dependent and fatalistic, and Irish people as "feckless, child-like, and irresponsible" (p. 53).

For those individuals who support the cultural background explanations of differences in school attainment, the issues are straightforward. Certain groups of immigrants did not bring with them life experiences and cultural values that would have allowed or encouraged them to take advantage of the opportunities offered to them by American educational institutions. These immigrant parents failed because cultural "differences" prevented them from expecting their children to persevere and to succeed in school .

Scholars who take this perspective do not generally ask questions about the ways in which children of different groups were treated in schools, about whether the curriculum responded or failed to respond to these children's needs, or about the ways in which extreme poverty might have impacted on families' decisions to withdraw their children from school. The root of the problem is seen to reside in the shortcomings of the immigrants themselves.

Other scholars offer a different perspective. Steinberg (1981), in particular, argues that cultural explanations of differences in attainment are based on a "New Darwinism" in which cultural superiority and inferiority have replaced biological measures of superiority. For New Darwinists, he maintains, there are certain cultural traits associated with attainment and achievement (e.g., frugality, temperance, industry, perseverance, ingenuity), while others (e.g., familism, fatalism) are associated with limited success and social mobility. Steinberg contends that Horatio Alger stories about success and hard work are based primarily on New Darwinism and glorify the effect of tenacity and hard work without taking into account the many other factors that impact on people's lives. Specifically, such myths discount the importance of the structural locations in-which new immigrants find themselves in their new society.[2]

More recently, Perlmann (1988), in his work on ethnic differences in schooling among the Irish, Italians, Jews, and Blacks in Providence, Rhode Island, between 1880 and 1935, has presented evidence that supports the argument that differences in attainment among ethnic groups are the results of social processes that have long histories. He contends that an understanding of such differences involves "determining the specific manner in which these general factors—the pre-migration heritage, discrimination, and the place of the migrants in the new class structure—operated, and interacted, in the history of a given ethnic group" (p. 6). From the data that he examined, Perlmann concluded that "neither culture nor discrimination nor class origins in the American city can alone provide a credible summary" (p. 219). He further argues that there is not a single consistently primary factor or a single generalization that will account for differences in individual ethnic histories.

In sum, explorations of differences in school success among the various immigrant groups that entered this country between 1840 and 1940 have in general terms attempted to account for the inequality of their educational outcomes by using the same three arguments used to explain the educational failure of non-mainstream children in general. The genetic argument coupled with the cultural difference argument appears to have been used most frequently. However, it also appears that the cultural argument, with its perspective on desirable cultural traits and characteristics, was the most influential. To date, beliefs about desirable individual and family characteristics continue to be reflected in both research and practice.

Recent Immigrants, Minorities, and School Achievement

In present-day American society, the success or lack of success experienced by turn-of-the-century immigrants is often contrasted with that experienced by African-Americans as well as with that experienced by Latinos. While there are some parallels between the position occupied by African-Americans in this country with the positions occupied by both Latinos and earlier "problem" immigrant groups, there are also many significant differences.

A few scholars have attempted to understand these differences by focusing on the economic-reproductive ef-

fects of societal arrangements and taking into account the responses of oppressed or exploited populations to these societal arrangements. Ogbu (1978, 1983, 1987a, b), for example, has sought to identify important distinctions between different groups of present-day "minorities" in the United States. He discusses *immigrant minorities* and *caste minorities* and shows that there is a clear difference, for example, between newly arrived Korean immigrants (an immigrant minority) and Black Americans (a caste minority), who have suffered generations of discrimination and racial prejudice. He argues that immigrant minorities frequently achieve success in ways that caste minorities do not, because they are both not conscious of the limits the majority society would place upon them, and content to do slightly better than their co-nationals who remained at home. Caste minorities, on the other hand, are quite aware of the reality in which they live, of the jobs they will never get, and of the kinds of lack of success they will experience. Arguing that caste minorities develop folk theories of success based on the options available to them in that society, Ogbu suggests that these individuals justifiably reject education because they also reject the common view that it can provide them with true alternatives.

For Ogbu, the question of why different groups of non-mainstream children succeed while others fail is answered within the tradition of the class analysis argument and in particular from the economic-reproductive perspective. For Ogbu and for theorists who work in this tradition, premigration factors are of less importance than the discrimination that is experienced by different groups in this society, their particular location within the class structure, and their awareness or perception of the permanency of that location.

The Mexican-Origin Population

The Mexican-origin population of the United States, as opposed to other recently arrived immigrant groups, includes individuals who have been here for generations and who see themselves as the original settlers of parts of the United States as well as individuals who have arrived here relatively recently as both legal and illegal immigrants. Generalizations about the Mexican-origin population with regard to educational success or failure are difficult to make because there are important and significant differences (generational, regional, experiential, linguistic) among the various groups that make up the Mexican-origin population.

There is evidence to suggest, however, that a large majority of Mexican persons who emigrate to the United States do not come from the groups that have obtained high levels of education. There are problems, however, in generalizing about the class origins of both early and recent Mexican immigrants. According to Bean and Tienda (1987), Jasso and Rosenzweig (1990), Portes et al. (1978), and Portes and Bach (1985), Mexican-origin immigrants are poor and have low levels of educational attainment. However, Duránd and Massey (1992) have argued that generalizations about Mexican migration to the United States are inconsistent and contradictory. They maintain that case studies (e.g., Cornelius, 1976a, b, 1978; Dinerman, 1982; Massey et al., 1987; Mines, 1981, 1984; Mines & Massey, 1985; Reichert & Massey, 1979, 1980) of Mexican "sending" communities (communities from which large numbers of Mexican nationals have emigrated) have yielded very different views about a number of questions. Among other topics, these studies present contradictory evidence about the class composition of U.S. migration. Duránd and Massey (1992) argue that a few community factors, including age of the migration stream, the geographic, political, and economic position of the community within Mexico, and the distribution and quality of agricultural land, affect the class composition of migration. The authors stress the difficulties surrounding attempts at generalization, and they suggest that such generalizations can only be made when a number of communities are studied using a common analytical framework. What this means is that educational researchers must use caution in interpreting findings about Mexican immigrants and persons of Mexican background.

As might be expected, a number of researchers have attempted to be sensitive to intragroup differences when working with Mexican-origin populations in educational settings. Matute-Bianchi (1991), for example, proposes five different categories for students:

1. "recent Mexican immigrants," who have arrived in the United States within the last three to five years;
2. "Mexican-oriented" students, who are bilingual but retain a *Mexicano* identity and reject the more Americanized Mexican-origin students;
3. "Mexican-American" students, who are U.S.-born and highly acculturated;
4. "Chicanos," who are U.S.-born, generally second generation, and frequently alienated from mainstream society; and
5. "Cholos," who dress in a distinct style and are perceived by others to be gang-affiliated.

Consistently clear differentiations between members of these several categories are difficult to make, and because of this, the study of the causes of school failure for the different segments of this population becomes complex. The Mexican-American group does not fit neatly into the categories proposed by a number of researchers. For example, the Mexican-origin population cannot be classified adequately using Ogbu's (1978, 1983, 1987a, b) two categories, *immigrant and caste* minorities. The problem is that there are simultaneously both *immigrant* minorities and *caste* minorities within this single population. The former group includes those individuals who have recently

entered the United States and cyclical immigrants who have worked in this country for years at a time, but who return to Mexico for extended periods. The latter group could include children of recently arrived *Mexicanos* whether U.S.-born or not, as well as first-, second-, third-, fourth-, and fifth-generation residents of several regions of the country. In several areas (e.g., Texas), persons of Mexican origin were already residing in the area when the area was annexed by the United States. While these individuals were not indigenous to the areas, they were certainly more "indigenous," for example, than persons who have arrived in the area within the last 20 years.

In this book, I take the position that the distinction between Mexican-origin persons who can still be categorized as immigrants and those persons who must be considered "hyphenated Americans" (Mexican-Americans/Chicanos/Cholos) has to do with a number of factors. Those persons who can be categorized as "immigrants" from Mexico (whether born in this country or not) still have what can be termed an "immigrant mentality," that is, they are oriented toward the home country, identify with Mexico, and measure their success (as Ogbu has suggested) using Mexican nationals in Mexico as their reference group. Mexican-Americans or Chicanos, on the other hand, no longer look to Mexico for identification. Their ties with Mexico have weakened and they see their lives as being carried out exclusively in this country. In general, these persons consider themselves to be different from white Americans as well as from Mexican nationals. More importantly, however, members of this group have often experienced discrimination in this country as members of a low-status and stigmatized minority. They have frequently developed an "ethnic consciousness" and have a sense of sharing the same low status as other Mexican-origin people. Mexican immigrants are immigrant minorities, while Mexican-Americans/Chicanos are caste minorities. This latter group is conscious of discrimination and prejudice by the majority group directed at Mexican-origin people *in particular* rather than at new immigrants or at outsiders in general.

What I am suggesting is that the development of an awareness of being both different and unacceptable to the majority society is a key factor in the shift in identification from immigrant to caste minority by Mexican-Americans/Chicanos. I would argue that Mexican immigrant individuals can be considered full members of the caste minority group in the United States when they:

1. become conscious that they are no longer like Mexican nationals who have remained in Mexico,
2. feel little identification with these Mexican nationals,
3. self-identify as "Americans"
4. become aware that as persons of Mexican origin they have a low status among the majority society, and

5. realize the permanent limitations they will encounter as members of this group.

Mexican-Origin Students and Explanations of School Failure

According to a number of researchers (e.g., Arias, 1986; Durán, 1983; Fligstein & Fernández, 1988; Meier & Stewart, 1991; Rumberger, 1991), Mexican-origin students have experienced a long history of educational problems, including below-grade enrollment, high attrition rates, high rates of illiteracy, and under-representation in higher education. As might be expected, a coherent theory that takes into account the many factors that impact on the poor school achievement of Mexican-origin students has not been proposed. However, a number of factors have been identified as influencing the school achievement of Mexican-origin children. These include: family income, family characteristics, and language background (Macías, 1988; Nielsen & Fernández, 1981; U.S. Department of Education, 1987); teacher/student interaction (Buriel, 1983; So, 1987; Tobias, Cole, Zinbrin, & Bodlakova, 1982; U.S. Commission on Civil Rights, 1972b); school and class composition (i.e., segregation and tracking) (Espinosa & Ochoa, 1986; Fernández & Guskin, 1981; Haro, 1977; Oakes, 1985; Orfield, 1986; Orum, 1985; Valencia, 1984); and school financing (Domínguez, 1977; Fairchild, 1984).

As will be noted, of the factors that have been identified as influencing the school achievement of Mexican-origin students, one factor (family income) can be said to be indicative of the family's location in the social structure. Two factors (school composition and school financing) can be identified as involving the school or institutional context, and two other factors (family characteristics and language background) can be considered to refer to a set of "cultural traits" not unlike those discussed by the literature on immigrants written in the early part of this century.

Not surprisingly—given that the cultural difference explanation of school failure is still drawn upon—much attention has been paid by researchers and practitioners to both language differences and family characteristics. Although most researchers working on the language problems of Mexican-origin children do not see themselves as working primarily within the deficit/difference paradigm, language issues have come to dominate the debate surrounding the education of today's "new" immigrants. The literature that has concentrated on language background issues as they relate to Mexican-origin children is immense and encompasses the study of a number of different areas, including the investigation of the process of second-language acquisition, the sociolinguistic study of language use in Mexican-American communities, the study of the relationship between teacher behaviors and second-language acquisition, the instructional use of two languages (e.g., bilingual education, two-way immersion), and the effects of various types of language intervention programs on Mexican-origin children.[3]

As compared to the literature on language background, the study of family characteristics as they relate to the education of Mexican-origin children has, in general, attempted to discover whether and to what degree these characteristics are like or unlike those found in mainstream American families. One important trend in this research (e.g., Laosa, 1978; McGowan & Johnson, 1984) has been the study of socialization practices within Chicano families. Interestingly enough, in spite of clear evidence that research conducted in this country on child development and on "desirable" socialization practices is biased (Laosa, 1984b; Ogbu, 1985), recent implementation efforts focusing on parent involvement include family education components that are directly based on a deficit-difference paradigm. I will return to this point below.

In addition to the study of socialization practices, research on family characteristics has included work on the relationship between family constellation (size and sibling structure) and children's development, and on the relationship between single-parent families and children's development and scholastic performance (Henderson & Merritt, 1968; Laosa, 1984a; LeCorgne & Laosa, 1976; Valencia, Henderson, & Rankin, 1985).

In comparison to the work that has been carried out from the deficit difference paradigm, much less work has been carried out from the class analysis perspective on the causes of the low school attainment in the Mexican-origin population. Increasingly, however, broad examinations of the educational experiences of this population are being written that include attention to the power relationships between the dominant majority population and the Mexican or Chicano minority. These analyses (Meier & Stewart, 1991; San Miguel, 1987) take the perspective that policies resulting in segregation practices and in unequal school financing reflect the structural location of the Mexican-origin population.

Work in the tradition of the economic-reproduction model has been carried out by Ogbu and Matute-Bianchi (1986), Matute-Bianchi (1986, 1991), and Foley (1990). This work has been concerned with trying to understand differences in performance by Mexican-origin students of different generational backgrounds and has included an attempt to link factors such as premigration educational experiences, attitudes toward education, attitudes toward the majority group, and the like with academic achievement. Foley (1990), in particular, examined high school students' behaviors in school against a parallel study of discrimination and prejudice present in a Texas border city. For these researchers, societal arrangements themselves as reflected in teacher-student and student-student interactions in the classroom result in their reproduction.

In sum, research carried out on the causes of school failure in Mexican-origin students has followed the principal trends present in the research on non-mainstream populations in general. Less attention has been given to examining the genetic argument among this population, although interest in testing and test bias has been high.[4] For the most part, the research on this population can be categorized as falling within the cultural deficit-difference paradigm in that it attempts to explain low scholastic achievement by focusing on differences brought to school by the children themselves. What is evident is that single-factor explanations of school failure among the children of first-generation Mexican immigrants are inadequate and cannot account for the complexity of the experience. To attribute to language factors alone, for example, what is inextricably linked to elements such as children's non-mainstream behavior, teacher perceptions, and assumptions made by the schools about parents and by parent about schools, is simplistic. In order to account for the academic failure of Mexican-origin students from, for example, the perspective of theories of reproduction, researchers are faced with the challenge of having to account for the elements that lead to this reproduction using a binational framework.

Fixing the Problem: Educational Interventions

In spite of the complexity of the problem of school failure for non-mainstream children, those concerned about its remediation have focused on attempting to change particular aspects of the institutional and instructional contexts in the hope that such changes will bring about increased school success. While aware of the structural factors that frame the problem, these researchers and practitioners represent the tension that Carnoy and Levin (1985) have described as existing between "the unequal hierarchies associated with the capitalist workplace" and "the democratic values and expectations associated with equality of access to citizen rights and opportunities" (p. 4).

In comparison to theorists who have sought to explain the nature and circumstances of educational failure, practitioners and policymakers have focused on breaking the cycle of low educational achievement or bringing about change in schools and in school outcomes. It is interesting to note, however, that programs that have endeavored to alter or reverse educational outcomes for poor, disadvantaged, or at-risk children have reflected the thinking of theorists who have worked within the deficit-difference paradigm. Many of these theorists have tended to address single micro-level factors such as English language fluency, standardness of spoken English, or the blend and mix of students of different racial groups within a given school. These research and theoretical foci, in turn, have led to the implementation of programs that offer narrow solutions to far broader problems (e.g., bilingual education programs, desegregation programs, Head Start) and that have been marginally successful. Ironically, even though the theories that held that problems experienced

by at-risk children were their own "fault" or responsibility have been called into question, program implementation still responds to this fundamental view. With few exceptions, programs aimed at at-risk children are designed to address key shortcomings or "deficits" in these students in order to assist them in succeeding in the school environment.

It is not surprising that researchers working within the class analysis paradigm argue that such programs leave existing institutions largely untouched and that these institutions continue to reflect the power realities of the larger society. For that reason, they point out, compensatory programs have failed to meet the expectations of those policymakers and practitioners who sincerely hoped that correcting or compensating for key factors would bring about significant changes in total educational outcomes.

In the case of Mexican-origin students, the absence of a sound underlying perspective that brings together explanations with interventions is particularly evident. Not only is there a lack of a coherent theory about macro-level factors that can adequately explain the failure and success of these children in American schools, but there is also a lack of coherence among the many theories that have focused on micro-level variables. In general, the work of both policymakers and practitioners involved in the education of Mexican-origin children also reveals a very practical and problem-oriented focus. The focus for such individuals has been finding solutions, establishing policies, funding programs that will address the needs of these children, and implementing promising programs in spite of heavy local and national political fire.

While from the perspectives of class analyses of schooling and society the educational problems of Mexican-origin children cannot be alleviated without a major change in the societal structure that impacts on every level of students' lives, from the perspective of many policymakers and practitioners, what is needed is the right kinds of instructional solutions, the right kinds of school programs in order to bring about meaningful, if not lasting, change. Single and partial solutions, then, often take on extraordinary meaning, and these interventions become the focus of intense debate. The politics of bilingual education (a solution designed to focus on children's inability to profit from instruction carried out exclusively in English), for example, have been particularly acrimonious. Many practitioners, parents, and policymakers are convinced that good bilingual education programs *by themselves* will impact significantly on educational outcomes.[5]

The fact is that current educational outcomes—high drop-out rates, grade delay, low test scores, and low college enrollments by Mexican-origin students—demand solutions. Whatever the realities of the structures of inequality in this country may be, practitioners feel a strong pressure to find ways of helping their students to succeed in school.

The Concept of Family Intervention

In this book, I am concerned primarily with those examples of educational intervention that focus on families and their young children. I will argue throughout this book that this focus is problematic, and I will point out that this particular approach to equalizing educational outcomes is based directly on the deficit-difference paradigm.

In the section that follows, I will discuss a recently popular educational intervention perspective that has focused specifically on parents and families. This strategy, currently known as *parent involvement,* is considered by some researchers (e.g., Becker & Epstein,1982; Bennett, 1986; Díaz-Soto, 1988; Epstein, 1982, 1985, 1986b, 1991; Epstein & Dauber, 1991; Henderson, 1987; Simich-Dudgeon, 1986; Walberg, 1984) to result in various kinds of positive benefits for both parents and children. As I will point out below, this strategy is currently being implemented around the country, and its use is being advocated by both policymakers and practitioners.

The position I will take here is that, like many of the family intervention programs that came before it, parent involvement is an attempt to find small solutions to what are extremely complex problems. I am concerned that this "new" movement—because it is not based on sound knowledge about the characteristics of the families with which it is concerned—will fail to take into account the impact of such programs on the families themselves.

In order to provide a context for this position, which I will elaborate further in later chapters, I will discuss current thinking about parent education and provide a brief review of the literature that has focused on this notion.

Parent Education Programs for Mexican-Origin Families

Within the past decade, there has been a renewed interest in the impact of families and homes on children's education. Concern about parent "involvement" in children's learning has been expressed by educators, legislators, and religious leaders. The generally held view, as the publication *What Works* (U.S. Department of Education, 1987) made evident, is that schools depend directly on parents for assistance in educating children, and that without parental help the schools cannot carry out their work as effectively. The tone and direction of this publication reflects the thinking underlying many current attempts to solve what is perceived to be a serious problem. The section on the home within *What Works* (p. 5) makes the following statement:

Curriculum of the Home

Research: Findings: Parents are their children's first and most influential teachers. What parents do to help their children learn is more important to academic success than how well-off the family is.

Comment: Parents can do many things at home to help their children succeed in school. Unfortunately, recent evidence indicates that many parents are doing much less than they might. For example, American mothers on average spend less than half an hour a day talking, explaining, or reading with their children. Fathers spend less than 15 minutes.

They can create a "curriculum of the home" that teaches their children what matters. They do this through their daily conversations, household routines, attention to school matters, and affectionate concern for their children's progress.

Conversation is important. Children learn to read, reason, and understand things better when their parents:

• read, talk, and listen to them,
• tell them stories, play games, share hobbies, and
• discuss news, TV programs, and special events.

In order to enrich the "curriculum of the home," some parents:

• provide books, supplies, and a special place for studying,
• observe routine for meals, bedtime, and homework, and
• monitor the amount of time spent watching TV and doing after-school jobs.

Parents stay aware of their children's lives at school when they:

• discuss school events,
• help children meet deadlines, and
• talk with their children about school problems and successes.

Research on both gifted and disadvantaged children shows that home efforts can greatly improve student achievement. For example, when parents of disadvantaged children take the steps listed above, their children can do as well at school as the children of more affluent families.

At first glance, this statement appears to be straightforward and unproblematic. For middle-class practitioners, for middle-class parents, and for those who are familiar with middle-class standards and practices and who aspire to be middle class, there is not much to quarrel with in this set of recommendations. Of course parents should spend time with their children. Of course they should talk to them and engage them in conversations.

There are many activities on this list, however, that poor and newly arrived immigrant parents do not engage in. Moreover, there are assumptions in this seemingly innocuous statement about how families should live their lives. As I will endeavor to make clear in the descriptions of the 10 families that I will present here, for various important reasons, some families do not observe routines or discuss school events, or even tell their children stories. They cannot provide books or supplies, and they do not have hobbies. Many parents do not know how to read. Many others work late. Most have little understanding about school deadlines or about how to "monitor" their children's homework.

What is evident, however—given the above position about the role of families in education—is that many educators and policymakers believe that attention must be directed at educating or changing what I term here "nonstandard" families, that is, families that are non-mainstream in background or orientation (e.g., nonwhite, non-English-speaking, non-middle-class). This concern about nonstandard families and the widely held belief that these families—for the good of their children—must be helped to be more like middle-class families has led to a strong movement in favor of family intervention or family education programs.

In the case of Hispanic families, and in particular in the case of Mexican-origin families, the perception that these families must be brought into the mainstream is particularly strong. For example, while in office, the former Education Secretary, Lauro Cavazos, strongly criticized Hispanic families (Suro, 1990). Arguing that neither the language barrier nor economic difficulties completely explain the problems of Hispanic students, he stated that Hispanic parents deserve much of the blame for the high dropout rate among their children. According to Cavazos, Hispanics have stopped placing a high value on education. They have not acknowledged the problem, and they have not cared that youngsters have dropped out of school. For Cavazos, then, the first vital step in improving education for Hispanics involves, not obtaining increased funding for programs at every level, but obtaining a commitment from Hispanic parents that they will work to educate their children.

Inflammatory as Cavazos's remarks were, they simply echoed what has been generally believed by many American educators to be true: Hispanic parents are neither committed to nor involved in their children's education. These educators—because they have neither the experience nor the information that might help them make sense of the lives of people different from themselves—feel both angry and indignant at the seeming indifference of Mexican-origin parents.

Not surprisingly, many well-meaning educators have decided to intervene and to try to interrupt the pattern of failure. And like many educators, social workers, and policymakers in the past, they have decided to implement programs that have as their purpose teaching Mexican-origin mothers how to help their children succeed in school. As a result, many kinds of programs have been established around the country.[6] Most focus on mothers, and most hope to teach what middle-class professionals believe are valuable parenting skills: for example, how to prepare nutritional meals, how parents should talk to their children, how little ones should and should not be disciplined, and how

everyday household objects and activities can be used to teach children valuable school-related skills.

In one well-known and well-funded program established in the Southwest, for example, 2,000 low-income Mexican-origin families are being served under an umbrella of subprograms. In the parent-child education segment, mothers are visited at home and taken to receive instruction at a central program office while their children from birth to two years are cared for by others in a pleasant and well-designed child care center. They learn how to be "better" parents while they make toys for their children. They network with other parents, and they are encouraged to go to school, to learn English, and to aim for better jobs for themselves and for their children.

In another program established on the West Coast, the focus is home literacy in Spanish. Program organizers teach parents to read to their children and to encourage their writing of stories. Parents begin to write, too, and they take great pride in their children's stories. The program brings parents together to share their children's efforts and to support their "involvement" in their children's education. The aim of the organizers is to build parents' self-esteem and confidence, to develop their literacy skills, and to break the cycle of school failure for their children.

Initially, even without empirical evidence of their effectiveness, few would want to fault such programs. Indeed, as historians of education (e.g., Schlossman, 1976, 1978, 1983, 1986) have made clear, the tendency to solve perceived problems affecting families in this country by "educating" parents goes back to the turn of the century. As Schlossman (1986) has pointed out, the family-in-crisis motif is perennial and has led to a tendency "to see parent education as a solution for deeply rooted social problems" (p. 39).

A Brief Overview of Changing Goals and Purposes of Parent and Family Education

In this country parent education has been known by very different names and has had many goals. Movements to implement parent education programs have responded to varying perceptions about the existence of different problems and have been influenced by a wide variety of values or ideals about what should be. As Florin and Dokecki (1983) and Dokecki and Moroney (1983) have pointed out, an overview of the changing goals and purposes of parent and family education reveals that concern about families has periodically shifted its focus between "mainstream" and "troubled" families. From 1600 through 1800, for example, educational programs aimed at families sought to instill moral values and to combat immorality and corruption. From 1850 to 1880 and again from 1900 to 1920, the goal of parent education programs was to socialize new immigrants to this society's dominant values. During certain periods (e.g., 1880-1900 and 1920-

1940), parent education programs were aimed at the middle class and were mainly concerned with political corruption and moral responsibility. Beginning in the late 1950s, in an attempt to redress social inequalities, parent education programs were directed at the disenfranchised urban poor. The goals of such programs included the equalization of opportunities, the promotion of school success, and the early cognitive development of at-risk children. In the 1980s, in part as a result of the activities of the Barbara Bush Foundation for Family Literacy (1989), funding was made available to parent education programs that focused on developing the literacy skills of both parents and children.

According to Dokecki and Moroney (1983, pp. 56-59), the knowledge bases and theoretical/philosophical underpinnings as well as the specific purposes of parent education programs have shifted in important ways. Beginning in the early part of this century, for example, practices were directly influenced by theories about child development. According to Schlossman's (1983) overview of the first three decades of the 20th century, the nascent science of child development had a "tremendous popular appeal." In particular, "scientific" support for parent education was helped along by the efforts of foundation funding. Schlossman (1983) carefully documents how the Laura Spelman Rockefeller Memorial enlisted university researchers in the cause of child development research, in the publication of *Parents Magazine,* and in the cause of instructing women on how best to raise their children. Similarly, Laosa (1984b) traces the close relationship between these activities and the establishment of several government agencies: the National Institute of Mental Health in 1946, the National Institute of Child Health and Human Development in 1963, and the Office of Child Development in 1969. He comments that during the 1960s the public concern about children in particular led to an expansion of support for research in child development as well as to an expansion of funding for children's programming. Belief in the importance of education as well as in the need to equalize opportunities for the children of poor and immigrant families led to the implementation of compensatory programs. Early childhood intervention, according to Laosa (1984b), "was seen as having an unlimited potential not only for breaking the cycle of poverty, but also as a possibility for forging revolutionary changes in the entire educational system" p. 54). However, as Laosa also points out, professional knowledge and scientific expertise often greatly exceeded the available supply [of reliable data]." Sheldon White (1968, P. 204, cited in Laosa, 1984b, p. 54), for example, stated that "Placed in the uncomfortable role of experts without expertise, we are all in the business of trying to supply educated guesses about the nature of children's cognitive development."

During the 1960s and 1970s, that is, during the period in which the deficit-difference paradigm was widely supported, research on child development was designed to inform policies and practices that might improve educational opportunities for disadvantaged children. However, as Ogbu (1982) has argued, the underlying assumption of this research (e.g., Bloom, Davis, & Hess, 1965; Hunt, 1969; White et al., 1973) was that poverty, unemployment, and low attainment were caused by the inadequate childrearing practices of the poor themselves. Criticizing the process-product research paradigm, Ogbu (1982) contended that these studies were designed to show "causal relationships between family processes, especially parent-child interaction on the one hand and child rearing outcomes—generally the language cognitive, motivation and social competencies—on the other" (p. 253). For the most part, these studies compared particular kinds of skills and competencies found in minority parents with those found among middle-class white parents.

The problems with this particular orientation are more evident today than they were when this research was first conducted. Nevertheless, the view that there exists a universal model of human development and a set of particular competencies that all children should acquire if reared adequately still influences both policy and practice. Evidence from cross-cultural research on child socialization has had little impact on the notion that, as Ogbu (1981) maintains, sets up "white middle-class child rearing practices and competencies as the standard upon which all others are measured." Even though this research documents the fact that children around the world are socialized to develop those skills and competencies that are necessary for them to live as competent adults in their particular societies, child rearing strategies of minority populations have not generally been seen from that perspective. The socialization practices of these populations are seen as deficient or limited, rather than as based directly on the family and community's experience in providing their children with the competencies they will need in order to survive.

There is evidence, moreover, that in this country, notions about maternal competence and appropriate care for young children have changed dramatically during the last 85 years. Indeed, as Wrigley (1989) has demonstrated, the increasing emphasis on the cognitive stimulation of young children is not only recent but also rooted in the social context of the times. Her analysis of 1,017 articles drawn from the literature directed at parents written between 1900 and 1985 revealed that between 1900 and 1910, experts were concerned about hygiene, regular routines for baby management, and babies' physical care. Between 1900 and 1935, many articles argued that stimulation harmed babies and recommended leaving children strictly alone. By the 1930s, when child development had become a nascent science, experts began to be concerned about children's social and emotional development. Finally, in the 1960s, as poor children were targeted for special compensatory programs, interest in stimulating children's intellectual growth increased sharply. As a result, Wrigley (1989) argues, "middle-class families soon became interested in stimulating their young children's learning" (p. 65). By 1980, what Wrigley (1989) terms "better babies" were children "who were geared to perform academic feats at an unusually early age" (p.71). She argues that because education has become even more important in "sorting people into different occupations and class locations" parents must strive to foster in their children those competencies and skills that they will need in order to enter high-prestige professions.

Unfortunately for those who have worked to equalize opportunities for disadvantaged children by involving their parents in parent education, what emerges from the scholarship on parent education programs in general—especially those that were designed as part of an effort to equalize opportunities—is that there are no clear answers or formulas for providing early educational advantages for disadvantaged children. Research carried out on the effectiveness of many programs designed to provide an early start for non-mainstream children is contradictory. Different reviews of the literature (e.g., Boger et al., 1986; Bronfenbrenner, 1974; Goodson & Hess, 1975; Lazar, 1988; Lazar et al., 1977) provide different interpretations of the findings. Florin and Dokecki (1983), for example, present the findings of evaluations of parent education programs and begin by pointing out that the cross-study comparison of projects is exceedingly difficult. Using only studies that had a true or quasi-experimental design, they concluded that "as a group, parent education programs have demonstrated moderate to high immediate IQ gains in program children" (p. 41). They emphasize, however, that these gains gradually decrease over time but do persist into the elementary school years. They also report that evidence from objective measures of school achievement, special education placement, and grade retention is also not altogether consistent. They point out that even though results of evaluations focusing on both child and parent outcomes demonstrate a number of positive effects, "unbridled enthusiasm" should be tempered because of the possibility of biases in self-selected program samples, effects produced by non-treatment variables, and the lack of representation of the programs included in evaluation comparisons.

The Parent Involvement Movement

The currently popular term for family intervention/parent education programs appears to be *parent involvement*. Parent involvement in schools is being strongly advocated by both researchers and practitioners. Claims about the positive effects of such involvement (Becker & Epstein, 1982; Bennett, 1986; Clark, 1988; Díaz-Soto, 1988; Epstein, 1982, 1985, 1986a, 1991; Epstein & Dauber, 1991; Henderson, 1987; Simich-Dudgeon, 1986; Walberg, 1984) maintain that parent involvement results in raising student achievement among low-income and minority youngsters, developing parents' abilities to help their children, foment-

ing positive attitudes by children and parents toward teachers and schools, reducing absenteeism and dropout rates, and increasing home–school communication. McLaughlin and Shields (1987) suggest, however, that the involvement of disadvantaged parents may not have achieved what educators had hoped.

According to the NEA publication *Schools and Families: Issues and Actions,* the four currently popular parent involvement models are: (1) parents as volunteers, (2) parents as receivers of information about the school, (3) parents working at the school, and (4) parents working with their own children at home. Recent research, however, suggests that teachers' views about parent involvement seem to center around the notion that parents should receive training so that they can adequately work with their children at home. Olsen et al. (1994), for example, documented in their study of reform efforts in 32 schools in California that the "prevalent belief was that for teachers to do their job at school parents need to do their job at home" (p. 95). Teachers primarily wanted parents to support their children's school work. They had less interest in parents' becoming genuinely involved in restructuring efforts and only valued their ability to help out as volunteers, as advocates of the school, and or as fundraisers. Moreover, teachers generally expressed negative views about parents and thought of them as uneducated, poor, and dysfunctional.

Similarly, Lareau (1989) found in her research on parental involvement that there are important contrasts in home–school relationships between white middle-class and white working-class parents that raise questions about both the effectiveness of involvement and the degree to which teachers welcome such involvement. Lareau argues that rather than a question of degree or amount of involvement, it is the middle-class parents' ability to mobilize their cultural capital that accounts for differences in achievement between their children and the children of working-class whites. Even though white working-class mothers were found by Lareau to have high aspirations for their children, and even though they spend time working with their children, they do not have the resources available to middle-class mothers. They often do not know how to respond when their youngsters complain that their attempts at helping them are "all wrong," and they do not have friends who are members of the teaching profession. When talking to their children's teachers, working-class mothers often feel insecure and apprehensive.

According to Lareau's view of the middle-class "home advantage," children from this background succeed in school because their parents have power (social and occupational status), competence (knowledge about schools and school learning), education, income and material resources, a vision of the interconnectedness of home and work, and networks of individuals who have information about schools and school practices.

Working-class mothers' involvement is never quite satisfactory. Working-class parents must, therefore, depend much more on both teachers and schools. They cannot serve in the role of co-teachers as the schools would hope that they could. Lamentably, because of this, their home-school relationships will fall short of what school personnel have currently concluded is desirable for *all* families. Indeed, if teachers use the middle-class family as a standard, teachers will generally assume that all parents who are "committed to their children's education" will engage in the same kinds of activities and behaviors. They will often surmise quite erroneously that parents who do not do so are unsupportive of their children's academic performance.

Parental involvement, then, may not quite be what its supporters would hope. Relationships between parents and schools do, in fact, reflect the structural locations of these individuals in the wider society. Simply bringing parents to schools will not change the racist or classist responses that teachers may have toward them and their behaviors. Parenting classes alone will not equalize outcomes.

The View from Inside Ten Families

In the chapters that follow, my objective is to bring into focus the everyday lives of 10 women whose energies were primarily involved with the survival of their families and who viewed themselves as successes or failures in terms of their ability to contribute to that survival. By showing how these 10 families lived, what they thought about, believed in and aspired to, I hope to raise serious questions about current family education programs that seek to teach immigrant adults how to parent. What my data will show is that Mexican parents do indeed know how to parent, but that because their parenting styles are the product of their class, culture, and experiences, they are unlike those of the American model of the "standard" family.

As will be clear in my description of the parents and their children, I am not arguing here that their patterns of living and of socializing their children are unique or different from those found among people in many parts of the world. Instead, it is my contention that the Mexican-origin families that I followed are similar in many ways to the turn-of-the-century immigrants who were considered to be familistic, fatalistic, and otherwise unacceptable by the mainstream members of the population.

It is my position also that a view from inside the families may help to put into perspective old cultural-deficit theories in new clothing. By inviting readers to come to know 19 adults and 12 children, I want to offer a basis for examining and weighing carefully efforts ultimately designed to change stable, successful, and functioning households. By presenting the lives of 10 families, I hope to offer insights about how their lives and the lives of other people like them might be altered by well-intentioned intervention movements designed to help non-mainstream children to succeed in school. Very specifically, I contend that to date, we still lack the kinds of knowledge that Bronfenbrenner (1979) referred to when he wrote:

> I shall presume to speak for the procession in pointing out what we do know and what we don't. We know a great deal about children's behavior and development, and quite a bit about what can and does happen inside of families-parent child interaction, family dynamics, and all that. But we know precious little about the circumstances under which families live, how these circumstances affect their lives, and what might happen if the circumstances were altered. . . . Before we can engage in parent education of the kinds here proposed, we have to learn a good deal more than we know at present about the actual experience of families in different segments our society. (p. 220)

Notes

1. For a discussion of these arguments as they relate to bilingual education policy, the reader is referred to Crawford (1989, 1992a, 1992b).
2. Steinberg (1981) directly refutes the myth of Jewish intellectualism and Catholic anti-intellectualism and argues that many poor Jews in this country did not rapidly ascend the social ladder. He coincides with Berrol (1982) in his claim that poor Jews (like poor Italians, poor Irishmen and poor Slavs) dropped out of school quite early. He contends that cultural values were not the major or primary cause of school success and social mobility among jews, but that the economic success of the first and even second generation led to the educational success of succeeding generations.
3. The literature on the research carried out on the effectiveness of bilingual education is voluminous. For excellent reviews of this research, the reader should refer to Cazden and Snow (1990) and Casanova and Arias (1993). Both Hakuta (1986) and August and García (1988) include comprehensive overviews of language research as it relates to the education of linguistic minority students.
4. Two recent volumes contain excellent bibliographies on testing and Mexican-origin students; Keller et al. (1991) and Valdés and Figuerosa (1994).
5. For a discussion of the bilingual education debate in this country, the reader is referred to Crawford (1989), Cazden and Snow (1990), Porter (1990), and Hakuta (1986).
6. Because it is not my intention to criticize particular programs, I am deliberately not referring to these various efforts by name. I will point out, however, that many "parent education" programs focus on such areas as family literacy, family involvement in education, early learning, care and feeding of newborn children, etc. A general search of the ERIC system, for example, using the descriptors *Mexican and family education* yields an impressive number of articles describing such efforts.

Section 4: Linguistic and Educational Perspectives
Assessment and Application

1. Identify the major trends for Chicanos in higher education and determine how representative of those trends is your college or university.

2. How do undocumented immigrants fare in higher education based on the Pew study?

3. Select a community with a substantial Chicano population and identify key educational "pipeline leaks" in its school system.

4. Which of the major obstacles to higher education listed in Peter Schmidt's article are you facing personally and how are you planning to overcome them?

5. Analyze two salient legal decisions that have affected the educational standing of Chicanos.

6. What role has intelligence testing played in the education of Chicanos?

7. Identify and analyze the major changes in the education of Chicanos from the Civil Rights era to the present.

8. Select a major court decision on Chicano education and explain its educational importance.

9. How did legal decisions on Latinos relate the *Brown v. Board of Education* decision by the Supreme Court in 1954?

10. What is the relationship between earned income and educational attainment for Latinos?

11. Analyze the validity of three leading explanations for the school failure of Mexican-origin students.

12. Identify a "family intervention" program in the schools of your community and describe its structure, aims, and rate of success.

13. Determine the demand and availability of English-as-a-second language programs for adults in your community.

14. How would your community be impacted by an "English only" constitutional amendment?

15. What are the salient intentions or goals of Title VII, The Bilingual Education Act?

16. How do you foresee the standing of bilingual education in your community in the next five years?

Please note that the chapter by James Crawford contains an excellent set of questions at the end that you can tap to develop a better understanding of bilingual education in the United States and its future.

Section 4: Suggested Readings

Bennet, Christine I. (2007). *Comprehensive Multicultural Education* (6th ed.). Boston, MA: Allyn and Bacon.

Bermúdez, Andrea B. (1994). *Doing Our Homework: How Schools Can Engage Hispanic Communities.* Charleston, WV: ERIC Clearinghouse on Rural Education and Small Schools.

Bigelow, Bill. (2006). *The Line Between Us: Teaching about the Border and Mexican Immigration.* Milwaukee, WI: Rethinking Schools.

Bixler-Márquez, Dennis J. (1988). *Chicano Speech in the Bilingual Classroom.* New York, NY: Peter Lang Publishing.

Bixler-Márquez, Dennis J. (2005). La Preparatoria Bowie versus la Patrulla Fronteriza. *Aztlán: A Journal of Chicano Studies.* Vol. 30, (2). Pp. 157–168.

Bixler-Márquez, Dennis J. (2004). Tendencias de financiamiento de la educación superior en los Estados Unidos. Acta del 4to Congreso de la Educación Superior, Feb. 2–6, 2004. (PER-099). La Habana, Cuba. Pp. 1073–1092. www.universidad2004.cu

Bixler, Márquez, Dennis J. and Seda, Milagros. (1994). The Ecology of a Chicano Student at Risk. *The Journal of Educational Issues of Language Minority Students.* Vol.13. Pp. 195–208.

Brown, Santa. (1999). *What Works for Latino Youth* (1st ed.). Washington, D.C.: White House Initiative for Educational Excellence for Hispanic Americans.

Cockroft, James D. (1995). *Latinos in the Struggle for Equal Education.* New York, NY: Franklin Watts.

Donato, Rubén. (1997). *The Other Struggle for Equal Schools: Mexican Americans During the Civil Rights Era* Albany, NY: State University of New York Press.

Figueroa, Richard A. (1999). *A Report to the Nation on Policies and Issues on Testing Hispanic Students in the United States.* Washington, D.C.: President's Advisory Commission on Educational Excellence for Hispanic Americans.

Fisher, María; Pérez, Sonia M.; González, Bryant; Njus, Jonathan, and Kamasaki, Charles. (1998). *Latino Education: Status and Prospects.* Washington, D.C.: National Council of La Raza.

Foley, Douglas E. (1990). *Learning Capitalist Culture Deep in the Heart of Texas.* Philadelphia, PA: University of Pennsylvania Press.

Genesee, Fred. (1999). *Program Alternatives for Linguistically Diverse Students.* Washington, D.C.: Center for Research on Education, Diversity and Excellence.

Gibson, Margaret A.; Gándara, Patricia, and Koyama, Jill Peterson. (2004). *School Connections: U.S.-Mexican Youth, Peers and School Achievement.* New York, NY: Teachers College Press.

Ginorio, Angela and Huston, Michelle. (2001). *¡Sí, Se Puede! Yes, We Can: Latinas en la Escuela.* Washington D.C.: American Association of University Women Educational Foundation.

González, Gilbert G. (1990). *Chicano Education in the Era of Segregation.* Philadelphia, PA: Bach Institute Press.

Harvey, William B. and Anderson, Eugene L. (2005). *Minorities in Higher Education: Twenty-First Annual Status Report.* Washington, D.C.: American Council on Education.

Hill, Jane D. and Flynn, Kathleen M. (2006). *Classroom Instruction that Works with English Language Learners.* Alexandria, VA: Association for Supervision and Curriculum Development.

Jasinski, Jana L. (2000). Beyond High School: An Examination of Hispanic Educational Attainment. *Social Science Quarterly.* Vol. 81, (1). Pp 276–290.

Jones, Toni Griego and Fuller, Mary Lou. (2003). *Teaching Hispanic Children.* Boston, MA: Allyn and Bacon.

Koss-Chioino, Joan D. and Vargas, Luis D. (1999). *Working with Latino Youth: Culture, Development and Context.* San Francisco, CA: Jossey-Bass.

Montemayor, Robert and Mendoza, Henry. (2004). *Right Before Our Eyes: Latinos Past, Present & Future.* Tempe, AZ: Scholargy Publishing.

Moreno, José F. (Ed.). (1999). *Elusive Quest for Equality: 150 Years of Chicano/Chicana Education.* Cambridge, MA: Harvard Educational Review.

National Center for Education Statistics. (2003). *Status and Trends in the Education of Hispanics.* Washington, D.C.: National Center for Education Statistics.

Noguera, Pedro. (2003). *City Schools and the American Dream: Reclaiming the Promise of Public Education.* New York, NY: Teachers College Press.

Oakes, Jeannie and Lipton, Martin. (2006). *Learning Power: Organizing for Education and Justice.* New York, NY: Teachers College Press.

Orfield, Gary. (2004). *Dropouts in America: Confronting the Graduation Rate Crisis.* Cambridge, MA: Harvard Education Press.

Otto, Santa Anna. (2004). *Tongue Tied: The Lives of Multilingual Children in Public Education.* Lanham, MD: Rowman & Littlefield Publishers.

Reyes, Pedro; Scribner, Jay D., and Scribner Paredes, Alicia. (1999). *Lessons from High-Performing Hispanic High Schools: Creating Learning Communities*. New York, NY: Teachers College Press.

Reyes, Rogelio. (1988). The Sociolinguistic Foundations of Chicano Caló: Trends for Future Research. In Jacob L. Ornstein-Galicia, George K. Green & Dennis J. Bixler-Márquez, (Eds.). *Research Issues and Problems in United States Spanish*. Brownsville, TX: University of Texas at Brownsville.

Rippberger, Susan J. and Staudt, Kathleen A. (2003). *Pledging Allegiance: Learning Nationalism at the El Paso-Juárez Border*. New York, NY: Routledge.

Rosales, Arturo. (1996). *Chicano!: The History of the Mexican Civil Rights Movement*. Houston, TX: Arte Público Press.

San Miguel, Guadalupe, Jr. (1987). *Mexican Americans and the Campaign for Educational Equality in Texas, 1910–1981*. Austin, TX: University of Texas Press.

Sánchez, Rosaura. (1992–96). Mapping the Spanish Language Along a Multiethnic and Multilingual Border. *Aztlán: A Journal of Chicano Studies*. Vol. 21, (1, 2). Pp 49–104.

Vaca, Nicolás C. (2004). *The Presumed Alliance: The Unspoken Conflict Between Latinos and Blacks and What it Means for America*. New York, NY: HarperCollins.

Valencia, Richard R. (2002). *Chicano School Failure and Success: Past, Present and Future*. New York, NY: Routledge.

Valenzuela, Angela. (1999). *Subtracting Schooling: U.S.-Mexican Youth and the Politics of Caring*. Albany, NY: State University of New York Press.

Section 4: Suggested Films and Videos

School: The Story of American Public Education
(Episode 2), 2001
PBS Home Video
1320 Braddock Avenue, Alexandria, VA 22314-1698

Bilingualism: A True Advantage, 1992
Heritage Series
Films for the Humanities, Inc.
P.O. Box 2053, Princeton, NJ 08543-2053

Cada Cabeza es un Mundo/Every Mind is a World
AIMS Multimedia
9710 DeSoto Avenue, Chatsworth, CA 91311

Casting Calls: Racial and Ethnic Stereotypes on Screen,
2004
Discovery Channel

Closing the Achievement Gap: A Vision for Changing
Beliefs and Practices, 2004
ASCD
1703 North Beauregard Street, Alexandria, VA 22311

Common Miracles: The New American Revolution in
Learning, 1994
ABC News
P.O. Box 48, Howell, MI 48844

English Only in America
Films for the Humanities and Sciences
P.O. Box 2053, Princeton, NJ 08543-2053

La Raza: Education, 1976
La Raza Series
Moctezuma Productions
McGraw-Hill Broadcasting

Latino Education and Counseling, 1992
Heritage Series
Films for the Humanities, Inc.
P.O. Box 2053, Princeton, NJ 08543-2053

Latino Parents as Partners in Education
Films for the Humanities and Sciences
P.O. Box 2053, Princeton, NJ 08543-2053

No Saco Nada del Escuelín, 1972
El Teatro Campesino
San Juan Bautista, CA

Off Track: Classroom Privilege for All
Teachers College Press
Columbia University, New York, NY 10027

Our Hispanic Heritage—Strategies for Educators, 1986
Multicultural Media Corp.

Taking Back the Schools, Part 3, 1996
Chicano: History of the Mexican American Civil Rights
Movement
Series National Latino Communications Center
Los Angeles, CA

The Lemon Grove Incident, 1985
The Cinema Guild
130 Madison Ave., 2nd Floor, New York, NY 10016

So They May Speak . . . , 2003
California Tomorrow
1904 Franklin Street, Suite 300, Oakland, CA 94612

Walkout, 2006
HBO Films
New York, NY

Literature, Art, Folklore, Music, and Cinema

This section addresses literature, folklore, art, music, and cinema as dynamic avenues for cultural expression among Chicanas and Chicanos. Literature encompasses the rich, stimulating voices and histories of the Chicano people and their struggles for cultural affirmation. It also encompasses language, its application, and the creation of a multiplicity of subjectivities, which are written and expressed through oral tradition and folklore.

The literature of the Chicano goes back in time to the conquest and colonization of the Southwest. Chicanas and Chicanos, through their diverse narratives, continue to challenge and resist historical and economic forces of domination and subjugation. They address the dialectics of liberation and oppression through a process of *'concientización'* or social awareness. Hence, literature, in its many genres, becomes a multiplicity of lenses through which Chicanos confront, challenge, and transcend their daily situational limitations.

Literature by Chicanos and Chicanas writes "visible" the historical "invisibility" of a people's struggles for self-determination and political empowerment. Multiple identities emerge spiraling from within the prose, poetry, theater, novels, essays, journal entries, diaries, and historical accounts of "Chicanismo," "Xicanisma," Mexicanness, and bilingualism. Chicano literature includes Mexican and U.S. dominant Eurocentric values, and a complex separate identity formation emanating from the confluence of social and historical contexts.

Literature, while historically and socially situated, transcends time and space. It serves as a vehicle for cultural awareness, identity formation, as well as political power. Felipe de Ortego y Gasca provides a panoramic view of Chicano literature through a historical trajectory from the Spanish colonial environment to the Mexican independence and the Mexican-American War, which ended in 1848. This date marks, for some, the birth of the Chicano in the United States. Ortego traces Chicano letters from the beginning to the Chicano Movement and its concomitant cultural renaissance. He views the 1960s as a period of spiritual rebirth for Chicano literature that encompasses distinct historical stages or developmental phases of Chicano literature. He also addresses the interface of race, ethnicity, and nationality in constructing Chicano-based identities, which embrace their Indo-Hispanic roots partially with oral tradition and folklore. Yarbro-Bejarano provides an overview of the literary output of Chicanas. The feminist perspective is an important component to Chicano literature because Chicanas have taken gender and sexuality to shape voices that for a time had largely been ignored.

George Vargas provides an insightful historical overview of Chicano art and an analysis of its current status and directions. He reveals the various facets of Chicano art and traces its historical foundations and lines of development in a hemispheric framework. He employs portrayals of salient exponents of Chicano and Chicana art such as Gaspar Enríquez, Grunk, Mago Gándara, and Nora Mendoza to illustrate contemporary trends in Chicana/o art in various regions of the U.S., including the borderlands.

Amalia Mesa-Bains depicts the participation of Chicanas in redefining social and sexual roles, focusing on border and deconstructing "otherness" through artistic cultural representation. She introduces resistance as a characteristic of Chicana artistic expression, which also encompasses issues of cultural identity formation. Her well-documented and structured essay compiles an introduction to the Chicana aesthetic forms and narratives, where women are featured as figures of power and control that challenge a patriarchal system.

Mesa-Bains characterizes Chicana art as social defiance through the use of "inversion, satire, reversals and juxtapositions of resistant feminine commentary." The author provides an introduction to and critical analyses of the works of Chicana artists Judith Baca, Santa Barraza, Carmen Lomas Garza, Ester Hernández, Yolanda López, Patricia Rodríguez, and Patssi Valdez. These Chicana artists have challenged the established social and sexual role norms that yield gender inequalities between women and men in Chicano communities.

The piece by María Herrera-Sobek on Chicano Folklore examines oral traditions that have been handed down from generation to generation, such as narratives, folk songs, folk speech, proverbs and proverbial expressions, folk drama, children's songs and games, riddles, beliefs and folk medicine, folk festivities, folk arts and crafts, folk dance, and folk gestures.

Carlos F. Ortega examines the development of Chicano Music. By utilizing a working concept, he first discusses the foundations of the Chicano Music, then builds on the role of the Chicano Movement as the key architect of what we call Chicano Music. He also examines how popular musicians and styles were influenced by the *Movimiento* in the late 1960s so as to broaden the base of this musical style.

Finally, Chon Noriega discusses how the Chicano Movement also played a role in the development of Chicano cinema. He takes the reader through the stages that comprised the development of professional filmmakers as well as stylistic views.

Mexican American Literature: Reflections and a Critical Guide

Felipe de Ortego y Gasca

Prologue

Literature is not the product of a vacuum, nor is a literary text a divine inspiration as John Milton rhapsodized. Literature is *work*. It's a strand in a bundle of strands that comprise human activity. As such it is engendered by factors in a complex matrix of cultural production. And equally complex factors determine a reader's response to a text, depending on cultural affiliation or association. No one reader is privy to *the reading* of a text.

To understand a literature, a text, one must consider the backgrounds out of which a literature emerges. Writing is a cultural act surrounded and impacted by historical forces. What is written depends on the motivations of the writer. As readers and critics, we cannot accurately discern those motivations, we can only approximate them.

More to the point, however, is the question: What is Mexican American Literature? Simply, it's literary production by Mexican Americans, literary production which before the Chicano era had been marginalized by the hegemonic forces of the American literary establishment and its minions.

In the Summer of 1969, toward the end of the first decade of the Chicano era, I was on sabbatical at the University of New Mexico at Albuquerque from New Mexico State University at Las Cruces. Louis Bransford, Director of the fledgling Chicano Studies Program at the University of New Mexico at Albuquerque, asked me to organize a course in Mexican American literature for the Fall of 1969. I agreed, little realizing it would be the first course in Mexican American literature taught in the country, or so I have come to believe.

What was needed for the course were texts I naively assumed would be easy to find. Many of the Mexican American literary works I found and surveyed for that course were in various libraries whose nooks and crannies I scoured diligently, but many were in private collections difficult to get to. The wonder, though, is why no one before had looked at Mexican American writing as a literary tradition, studied it and given it a taxonomical structure from which to discuss it critically and historically as an integral part of the Mexican American experience and of American literature. There were bits and pieces of study but not an overview.

The course was successful beyond my expectations despite the paucity of works readily available for instruction. Many of the historical texts I thought suitable for the course were woefully out of print. Contemporary works were difficult to secure in quantities sufficient for the enrollment of the course since many of them were published ephemerally by "small" presses or in garage presses like Raymond Barrios' *The Plum Plum Pickers*.

After teaching that course I found validity for the proposition that there existed a body of Mexican American literature, in places amorphous in literary structure but there nevertheless. As a consequence of that course I undertook the study of *Backgrounds of Mexican American Literature* (University of New Mexico, 1971) in which I sought to provide some historical and taxonomic shape to Mexican American literature, a preliminary scaffold from which to start.

In the Preface of that study I pointed out that what was proffered therein represented but a skeletal view of Mexican American literature, that it was an exploration in literary archaeology akin to the representations we see of dinosaurs in museums, made life-like from inductions and deductions of the animal remains found here and there. We don't really know what woolly mammoths or mastodons looked like. Or saber-toothed tigers. Or pterodactyls. Or early man. The taxidermic models we see in museums are what we think they looked like from the way we've pieced together the scant evidence we've found.

In literary history, as in archaeology, there is always a lacunae (discontinuity) in need of exploration and interpretation. By and large, in 1969 our view of Mexican American literature was nominal. We know more about Mexican American literature in the year 2006 than we did in 1969. Thirty-seven years after Kitty Hawk we knew considerably more about heavier-than-air flight than when Wilbur and Orville Wright undertook their first flight.

Introduction

Mexican American literature begins in 1848 with the signing of the Treaty of Guadalupe Hidalgo on February 2, ending American hostilities against Mexico and ceding more than half of Mexico's territory to the United States including Mexican citizens living in the wrested area which now includes the states of Texas, New Mexico, Arizona, California, Nevada, Utah, Colorado, and parts of Wyoming, Kansas, and Oklahoma.

But that beginning did not mean Mexicans in the dismembered territory had no literature. Mexicans who became Americans by conquest had been nurtured by a literary tradition that stretched back hundreds of years. That was what I learned from the course and what I sought to infuse in my study.

Backgrounds of Mexican American Literature was not exhaustive. It was *a first effort* at a chronology of Mexican American literary history. Taxonomically I conceptualized Mexican American literature as a continuum of two pasts, welded together by the Treaty of Guadalupe Hidalgo. I dichotomized Mexican American literature into *Roots* and *Traditions*, pointing out that both the Spanish Colonial literature between 1527 (the year of Cabeza de Vaca's shipwreck on what is now Galveston, Texas) and 1821 (end of the war for Mexican independence) and the literature of the dismembered Mexican territory between 1821 and 1848 were part of the literary roots of Mexican American literature. As well as the indigenous works of greater Mexico (what is left of them), like the *Popul Vuh* of the Maya, for example. Most of the literary codices of indigenous Mexico were destroyed by zealous Spanish friars who thought them the works of the devil because of their pictographs. Ironically, no original works of indigenous Mexico are extant in the country; only copies.

What followed in the development of Mexican American literature after 1848 were the *traditions* the people developed in a series of periods which I proffered: the *Period of Transition,* 1848–1912, early Mexican American literature written mostly in Spanish by "the conquest generation" as Mario García identifies it (*Mexican Americans: Leadership, Ideology & Identity, 1931–1960,* 1989: 295); the *Period of Americanization,* 1912–1960, later Mexican American literature written in both Spanish and English; and the *Period of the Chicano Movement and the Chicano Renaissance,* 1960–1971/present, written in English, some Spanish, or a blend of both as a trans-border phenomenon.

In *Backgrounds of Mexican American Literature,* I contended that just as the English-language literature of New England and the Atlantic Frontier between 1607 and 1776 constitutes the British Colonial roots of American literature, so too the Spanish-language literature of New Spain and Mexico in what is now the United States constitutes the Spanish Colonial and Mexican National roots of American literature.

I also explained that the literary citations of the Spanish Colonial and Mexican National Periods which I referred to therein were just baseline citations, that future research would yield a trove of literature whose size would astonish us, as the University of Houston project in *Recovering the Hispanic Literary Heritage of the United States* has borne out in the last fifteen years. My rationale for bringing into American literature the Spanish Colonial and Mexican National roots of Mexican American literature emerged from the contention that, properly speaking, American Literature begins not with the founding of Jamestown in 1607 but with the Declaration of Independence in 1776: ergo, the literature of the British Colonies from 1607 to 1776 is really British Colonial literature. American literature is everything after 1776.

In the periodization of American literature there needs to be room for the literatures of populations which have been absorbed into the American hegemony by conquest. That includes the literatures of Native Americans (including Aleuts), of Mexican Americans, of Puerto Ricans, and of Pacific Islanders, all of them *territorial minorities.*

The histories of these *territorial minorities* did not begin *sui generis* at the moment of their conquest. They came into the American fold with a history, with customs, with roots. As I have already pointed out, in 1848 when the Mexicans of the Mexican Cession became Americans, they had been nurtured by a long literary tradition. The same is true of Puerto Ricans, of Native Americans, and of Pacific Islanders. In the case of Mexican Americans brought into the American fold in 1848 and Puerto Ricans brought into the American fold in 1898, their literary roots were in Spanish.

In large part, resistance to incorporating the literary traditions of *territorial minorities* has been because of language. But language should not be a bar to that incorporation as Thomas M. Pearce, professor of English at the University of New Mexico, argued in 1942 ("American Traditions and Our Histories of Literature," *American Literature,* November, 279).

In the history of the United States, not all American writers produced works in English. In the ethnic enclaves of America, there were publications in myriad languages. The Germans in America produced literary works in German; they produced newspapers and other information venues in German. The Italians of New York, the Poles and the Ukrainians of the Ohio Valley Crescent all produced literatures, respectively, in Italian, in Polish and in Ukrainian. The Jews of America, especially in New York, produced literature in Yiddish. The Norwegians and Swedes of the Midwest produced literature in their respective languages.

The American writer from Minnesota, Ole Rølvaag, wrote *Giants in the Earth* (1929) in Norwegian and was published in Norway for distribution there and in the Norwegian communities of the United States. Isaac Bashevis Singer, the Jewish writer from New York and a Nobel Prize winner for Literature, wrote principally in Yiddish. We know his works in English through translations. So too, Mexican American writers produced literary works by necessity in Spanish both during the Period of Transition (1848–1912) and by choice during the Period of Americanization (1912–1960) and the Chicano Period (1960 to the Present).

Foreign language venues have flourished from the beginning of the American experience, catering to the linguistic diversity of the American people. There are still large linguistic communities in the United States producing non-English language newspapers for scores of non-English language readers.

Period of Transition

The Period of Transition covers a span of 64 years, from 1848 to 1912, at least two generations. These were difficult years for Mexicans now Americans. Whatever social and political conditions wracked Mexico before 1848, its citizens had an identity with the country. Between 1527 and 1810, for example, most of the inhabitants of New Spain thought of themselves as Spaniards though not a few of them were called *criollos* (Spaniards born in the New World). And those who were not Spaniards in the Spanish caste system understood their political identity, nevertheless, as Spanish subjects.

Solomonically, hostilities severed their country, creating all at once a political diaspora that would stigmatize Mexican Americans into the 21st century. They would be strangers in their own land. But unlike non-contiguous immigrants to the United States, Mexican Americans were right next to their motherland. The 1800 mile U.S.-Mexico border was in large part a river of history from the Gulf of Mexico to the edge of Texas and only a line in the earth the rest of the way to the Pacific.

Though cut off politically from Mexico, the first Mexican Americans of the *conquest generation* continued to be succored linguistically, culturally, and intellectually by the motherland while participating in the activities of their new political context. The Chicano historian, Armando Alonzo, calls this *in situ* participation "agency." According to Leonard Pitt, between 1850 and 1856 in the Hispanic borderlands, Mexican Americans "obtained practically every imaginable public office, important or otherwise" (*Decline of the Californios*, 1966: 147).

Unfortunately, Mexican Americans were unprepared for the holocaust that was to befall them. The brutality of that holocaust caused them to cleave all the more to the motherland. And to remember, and pass on to their heirs, that the land they lived on had been their homeland before the conquest.

The force of that memory surged to consciousness a hundred years later during the Chicano Period when the sins of the Anglos would be called to account.

Despite the historical characterization of wholesale illiteracy in the Spanish and Mexican Southwest, the fact of the matter was that from the beginning Mexican Americans were a highly literate people as the inventories of personal and church libraries attest (Aurora Lucero-White Lea, *Literary Folklore of the Hispanic Southwest*, 1953: 4). There were scores of newspapers in the northern border states of New Spain, later Mexico. The Hispanic bent for documentation, suggests a substantial literate Spanish language public in Hispanic settlements.

Literary inventories affirm that Spanish language literature was read and written in Hispanic America. For example, the Spanish playwrights Calderón de la Barca and Lope de Vega extended their literary influence in Spanish America as did the Mexican playwright Juan Ruiz de Alarcón, the Mexican humanist-scholar Carlos de Sigüenza y Góngora, and the Mexican literary nun, Sor Juana Inez de la Cruz, often referred to as the 10th Muse of Mexico.

Mexicans who became Americans continued the Hispanic literary traditions not only by preserving the old literary materials but by creating new ones in the superimposed American political ambience. For example, in the Mexican and, later, Mexican American Southwest, liturgical pastorals depicting the creation and fall of man and of Christ's resurrection evolved into "cycle plays" similar to those of Spain and England.

By the time of the Civil War, there were a number of Mexican Americans engaged in the work of newspapers. In New Mexico alone, ten out of eighty journalists of the period were Mexican Americans (Porter A. Stratton, *The Territorial Press of New Mexico 1834–1912*, 1969: 12). Most Anglo American newspapers in the Hispanic Southwest published bilingual editions for their Spanish-language readers. And bilingual Mexican Americans were employed to translate English language news into Spanish.

There was a ferment of literary activity among Mexican Americans. Donaciano Vigil, editor of the newspaper *Verdad*, compiled a *History of New Mexico to 1851*. In 1859 Miguel Antonio Otero, who had been Assistant Professor of Latin and Greek at Pingree College at Fishkill-on-the-Hudson, essayed *The Indian Depredations in the Territory of New Mexico*. In California, Juan Bautista Alvarado completed a *History of California* which dealt chiefly with the Spanish and Mexican periods of California, its settlement, development, and commerce with the Indians. In Northern California, Mariano Guadalupe Vallejo wrote prolifically on a number of topics, composing sonnets for his children and for special occasions, culminating his literary activities with a five-volume *History of California* that became the source for Hubert Bancroft's

History of California (Nadie Brown Amparan, *The Vallejos of California*, 1968: 131). In Arizona, Estevan Ochoa reflected on his election as Chairman of the 1859 convention to organize the Arizona territory (Frank Lockwood, *Life in Old Tucson 1854–1864*, 1959: 237). When the Civil War came, men like Ochoa, Vallejo, Otero, and Vigil remained loyal to the Union. During the war, the bilingual *New Mexican* newspaper published accounts of Mexican American Union officers like the Diary of Major Rafael Chacón in both Spanish and English (September 24, 1864). It was common for Southwestern newspapers with large audiences of Spanish-language readers to publish letters bilingually from and for their Mexican American readers.

> Between 1880 and 1890, some forty new Spanish-language newspapers were introduced in the territory of New Mexico, with similar growth in Texas, Arizona, and California. Most of these Spanish-language newspapers carried a literary page or cultural supplement that contained poetry, short stories, and 'serial' novels (Tey Diana Rebolledo, *Women Singing in the Snow: A Cultural Analysis of Chicana Literature*, 1995: 20).

Political conditions in Mexico during the latter part of the 19th century caused many Mexican intellectuals to flee the country, finding refuge in Southwestern American cities like Los Angeles, El Paso, Laredo, San Antonio, and Brownsville. There was a special historical relationship between Mexicans and Mexican Americans that a border did not sunder. They were all members of *la raza*, the people.

Mexican writers like Ricardo Flores Magón, fleeing difficulties with Porfirio Díaz in Mexico, found ready sympathy in cities like El Paso and San Antonio. The presence of these writers in the United States significantly influenced Mexican American thought, particularly during the Chicano Period. The tremors of political stress in Mexico reached all the way to the American Southwest. And, indeed, it was from the Mexican American Southwest that Mexican leaders like Benito Juárez, Porfirio Díaz, and Francisco Madero launched their political careers.

So close were the ties between Mexicans and Mexican Americans that when Benito Juárez sought help in ousting the French puppet Maximilian, from Mexico, he contacted such Mexican Americans as Víctor Castro, Agustín Alviso, and Mariano Vallejo for help.

During the Period of Transition, Mexican Americans continued to bear the brunt of injustice after injustice in the American Southwest. Their lands were craftily secured by squatters, shyster lawyers and con artists who bilked them because of their disadvantage with the English language and American law. For example, in 1877 for $15 an Anglo American purchased from the Sheriff of Hidalgo County in Texas 3,027 acres of land confiscated from a Mexican American for back taxes. When the Mexican American Lugo family of southern California lost its

wealth, Benjamin Hayes quickly suggested it was the finger of providence that was responsible for the decay of Mexican Americans (*Pioneer Notes 1849–1875*, edited by Marjorie Tisdale Wolcott, 1929: 280). The providence of Anglos was fraught with peril for Mexican Americans despite the fact that Anglos had guaranteed Mexican Americans full citizenship and had agreed to regard them as equals rather than a conquered people. Anglo rationalization for broken promises was that Mexican Americans were culturally unsuited to the new order and that they had brought misfortune on themselves. According to Leonard Pitt, the American pretense at ethical behavior "appears all the more reprehensible because of the blatant bigotry" (284).

Despite the fact that Mexican Americans constituted the majority population in the Southwest at first, they were quickly eased down the social ladder with the increase of Anglos in the area. During these years, Mexican American literature was undergoing the rigors of change from one social order to another. Mexican American writers like Vallejo, Alvarado, Pico, and others, continued writing in Spanish, their sentiments and outlook still rooted in the literary tradition from which they sprang.

The transition from writing in Spanish to writing in English was a process encompassing the latter half of the 19th century. Only an occasional Mexican American writer like María Amparo Ruiz de Burton (1872), Andrew García (1877) or Miguel Antonio Otero (1896) wrote in English, although García and Otero's works did not appear until the 20th century.

How many works in English by Mexican American writers appeared in the last half of the 19th century is difficult to ascertain only because comprehensive efforts like the University of Houston Project have, thus far, yet to make that determination. What the University of Houston Project has made us aware of is that there were more Mexican Americans writing during the Period of Transition than we had been aware of.

In the meantime, American writers mischievously stereotyped Mexican Americans in their writings, casting them as indolent and afraid of hard work, adjudging a Mexican American's wealth as the product of connivance rather than of fortitude and application. One particularly mischievous work was *Ramona* by Helen Hunt Jackson, published in 1884. During the Chicano Period, Mexican Americans repudiated her portrait of their forebears just as Blacks repudiated their portrait in *Uncle Tom's Cabin* and *Huckleberry Finn*. The most objectionable aspect of *Ramona* is that it perpetuated the "pastoral fallacy" of nostalgia for a kind of life that never really existed. In *North From Mexico*, Carey McWilliams called that fallacy "the Templar Tradition." *Ramona* stressed the pintoresque at the expense of reality, for the fact of the matter is that life in the American Southwest during the days of the Dons was as strenuous as it was under American rule.

Unfortunately, the works of Anglo American writers "have glorified the heroic at the expense of the mundane" (Pitt, 290), the Spanish tradition at the expense of the Mexican, so much so that many of the descendants of the early Mexican Americans prefer to identify with the Spanish Templar Tradition (however fictitious) rather than with their Mexican-Indian roots. Why this dysphoria? one might ask. Was there anything in the existing literature of the Mexican Americans which might have reinforced an Anglo novelists's inaccurate picture of life in the Hispanic Southwest? Those were accepted by some Mexican Americans because, in retrospect, they saw the American occupation and annexation of their homeland as nothing more than broken promises.

Mariano Vallejo himself, last of the military governors of Mexican California who most eagerly welcomed the American takeover, asked bitterly:

> What has the state government done for the Californians since the victory over Mexico? Have they kept the promises with which they deluded us? I do not ask for miracles; I am not and never have been exacting; I do not demand gold, a pleasing gift only to abject peoples. But I ask and I have a right to ask for an answer ("At Six Dollars an Ounce" in *California: A Literary Chronicle*, edited by W. Storrs Lee, 1968: 183).

In the face of disappointment, Mexican American writers looked favorably and nostalgically upon their past ties with Mexico and Spain. Dysphorically, however, many Mexican Americans today insist on their Spanish ancestry, eschewing their Indian past even when they look more Indian than Spanish.

Toward the end of the 19th century there was a growing awareness about cultural pluralism in the United States. On July 20, 1883, for example, Walt Whitman wrote to New Mexico officials who had asked him for a poem commemorating the 333rd anniversary of the founding of Santa Fe. In response, Whitman wrote that Americans had yet to really learn about their own antecedents, to sort them, and to unify them. Whitman's reference was to the great diversity of the American experience and to the wide-ranging sources of its people. Whitman was responding positively to the New Mexicans when he reminded them that "impressed by New England writers and schoolmasters, we tacitly abandon ourselves to the notion that our United States have been fashion'd from the British Island only" (*Complete Poetry and Prose*, Deathbed Edition, 402–403). A decade later, in 1892, two short novels in Spanish by Eusebio Chacón were published in New Mexico but were to remain "undiscovered" until the Chicano era.

The strongest evidence for racial discrimination in the territorial Southwest occurred in 1904 in Arizona over an incident involving Anglo American foundlings from New York placed in Mexican American foster homes in the mining towns of Clifton and Morenci. The Anglo American residents of the two communities became so incensed at the thought of Anglo American children being placed in "half-breed Indian" families that they forcibly restrained placement of the children, taking them into their own homes instead, over the protests of the Foundling Hospital. The Territorial Supreme Court ruled in favor of the action by the Anglo American citizens of Clifton and Morenci, a decision later upheld by the U.S. Supreme Court.

It would be an egregious error to conclude that Mexican Americans were passive in defending themselves against Anglo American "aggressions." From 1848 to 1853, Father Martínez, a Catholic priest in New Mexico, led furious guerrilla resistance to Anglo American occupation of the state. In the 1880s, militia groups like *Las Gorras Blancas* (the White Caps), strenuously defended themselves against Anglo American depredations like that which in 1904 took the life of Colonel Francisco J. Chaves, a surgeon and Civil War veteran who had become a Mexican American spokesman, leader and territorial superintendent of Public Instruction. For their efforts they were called *marauders*.

In 1883, Mexican American agriculture workers struck for better wages and working conditions in the Panhandle of Texas, and in 1903, Mexican American sugar-beet workers struck for similar reasons in Ventura, California. To counter their exclusion from Anglo American schools, Mexican Americans formed private and parochial schools like *El Colegio Altamirante* in Hebbronville, Texas, in 1897. To overcome rural depredations, Mexican Americans founded the Knights of Labor in 1890, a mutual assistance and protective organization.

In 1894, a decade before formation of the NAACP, Mexican Americans in Tucson, Arizona, founded the *Alianza Hispano Americana*, a *mutualista* civil rights organization that persisted until the 1960s. In 1896 Manuel Cabeza de Baca published *Historia de Vicente Silva* as a commentary on another Mexican American "marauder" from New Mexico. In the last decade of the Period of Transition, Juan Caballería published in 1902 a *History of San Bernardino Valley, 1810–1851*, a nostalgic reminiscence of the Mexican national period of California through the early days of the American annexation. The story of *La Piedra Pintada* (a California legend) by Myron Angel in 1910 suggests the extent the allure of the mythic past of Mexican Americans still had on Mexican American writers.

For some years, Professor Aurelio M. Espinosa had been collecting Mexican American folklore at Stanford University. As early as 1910 one of his pieces on New Mexican folklore appeared in the *Journal of American Folk-Lore*. In the article, professor Espinosa pointed out the paucity of Mexican American folklore studies. Even earlier, in 1907, while he was professor of Romance languages at the University of New Mexico, he had edited a critical edition of *Los Comanches*, a dramatic composition of the latter half of the 18th century and very popular through the 1890s. In 1907, Professor Espinosa also undertook a study of New Mexican Spanish which was published by the University of New Mexico Press (December 1909). One could see in the steady progression of works by Mexican American writers during the Period of Transition that they were becoming American, shifting their texts from Spanish to English.

In summing up the *fin de siècle*: Mexican American labor helped forge and link the principal western rail lines and helped develop the Texas cotton and cattle industry. More than half of Teddy Roosevelt's Rough Riders were Mexican Americans. In 1897, Miguel Antonio Otero was appointed Governor of the New Mexico territory. Mexican Americans had served at Manila Bay and Guantanamo Bay. In the Hispanic Southwest, Mexican water and mining laws had been retained by Anglo American settlers and governments, Spanish words developed English equivalents: *la riata* became lariat; *juzgado* became hoosegow; *calabozo* became calaboose; *chapas* became chaps, and so on. While the American language absorbed Mexican vocabulary, Mexican Americans themselves were kept at arms length as outsiders, to be marginalized for another 60 years.

I chose 1912 as the end year for the Period of Transition instead of 1900 because the history of the American Southwest and the conquest generation comes to closure, it seems to me, with the admission of New Mexico and Arizona in 1912 as the final states of the forty-and-eight. Also, in 1910 the election and subsequent nullification of Francisco Madero as president of Mexico, ignited the Mexican Civil War of 1910–1921, creating so much turmoil in the country that one-and-a-half million Mexicans migrated to the United States between 1910 and 1930 in an exodus of unparalleled proportions in human history.

New Mexico and Arizona did not become states until 1912 owing to the vehement opposition of Senator Albert Beveridge of Indiana, a Catonist and an outright anti-Hispano, who led the resistance to statehood on grounds that Mexican Americans were unaspiring, easily influenced, and totally ignorant of American ways and mores; that despite the passage of more than fifty years since the Mexican War, Mexican Americans were still aliens in the United States, most of them having made no effort to learn English. The actual reason was based on racial prejudice and the number of Mexican Americans comprising the populations of New Mexico and Arizona. When the population shifted to Anglo Americans majority by 1912, Senator Beveridge dropped his objections, thus ushering in the era of the forty-and-eight, a nation that stretched from sea to shining sea. American euphoria endorsed manifest destiny.

Period of Americanization

The Period of Americanization starts in 1912 and ends in 1960, covering 48 years. But it did not begin automatically in 1912. The process of Americanization had been steady since 1848, becoming particularly noticeable during the first decade of the 20th century. The period of Americanization begins with the closing years of the presidency of William Howard Taft, a one-term president who left the turmoil of the Civil War in Mexico to his successor, Woodrow Wilson.

Not only did political conditions in Mexico force the flight of a million-and-a-half Mexicans to the United States, but World War I caused such severe manpower shortages in industrial and agricultural sectors of the United States that the U.S. government contracted for Mexican labor to ease the crunch. Once the war was over, the U.S. government hurried the return of those workers back to Mexico, as it did in the 1930s to repatriate almost a million Mexicans in the United States. Unfortunately, among the repatriated were American citizens of Mexican descent. That detail seemed to matter little to zealous immigration officers for whom all "Mexicans" looked alike in their racial profiling.

The U.S. battled with the border problem from 1912 to 1921 in an effort to contain the hostilities of the Mexican Civil War on the Mexican side of the border. The situation along the U.S.-Mexico border was perceived by Americans as so bad and the threat to American life and property in Mexico so grave that President Wilson ordered the occupation of Veracruz by United States Marines. That act of belligerency has been adjudged by both Mexican and American historians as hasty and indicative of the roughshod manner in which the United States has always dealt with its sister Republic.

After the 1916 raid on Columbus, New Mexico, by Pancho Villa, Wilson dispatched General Pershing to Mexico in pursuit of Villa. Public opinion against Mexico and Mexicans (including Mexican Americans) had been so whipped up by the American press that many factions in the United States clamored for war with Mexico and for further annexation of Mexican territory. Only the war in Europe prevented further hostility against Mexico.

Interestingly, sometime between 1910 and 1920 American literature 'came of age' (Robert E. Spiller, *The Cycle of American Literature*, 1955: 158). Before then only English literature was worthy of study in American colleges and universities. At the same time Mexican American literature was also coming of age. Mexican American scholars and writers like Aurelio M. Espinosa were seriously engaged in preserving the literary roots of their heritage. Mexican American creative writers were attempting poetry in both English and Spanish, nothing at all like the experimentally vibrant poetry of the Chicano Renaissance in the late 60s and early 70s where Spanish and English were used in binary syntactic structures. Still, this poetry was a harbinger of literary creativity to come.

In 1916, one year after his death, a collection of Vicente Bernal's poetry was edited and published under the title *Las Primicias* (First Fruits). Bernal, born in Costilla, New Mexico in 1888, was only 27 at the time of his death. What was particularly impressive about Bernal's poetry was his command of the English language. As was to be expected, Mexican American writers were becoming Americanized.

Throughout the country, however, Mexican Americans fared badly with their public image. In 1917, Edith Shatlo King wrote in *The Survey* magazine (March 3), "When there is no occasion for personal loyalty, the Mexican is bitter in hatred. He is supersensitive to insults and slights, quick tempered, proud and high spirited. He lacks a habit of sustained industry and a practical sense which Americans cannot accept" (626). And in *The Century Magazine*, almost a dozen years later in 1928, Erna Fergusson wrote patronizingly, "The Mexican frankly hates work and refuses to be bullied into believing that he loves it" (438). In 1930, a particularly vicious piece by C.M. Goethe describes Mexicans: "His standards are those of a Chinese coolie . . . his code of morals increases his undesirability . . . he is superstition-bound and has the revengeful instinct of the savage" (*The World's Work*, July-December, 47–48).

Avarice and prejudice did not distinguish between Mexicans and Mexican Americans. Avarice saw them as cheap, exploitable, and therefore necessary; prejudice saw them as alien, unnatural, and therefore undesirable. Both won, for Mexicans and Mexican Americans were discriminated as much as they were exploited. Many Mexican Americans were unaware that they too were contributing to their own oppression. In 1927, Emilie M. Baca contributed to the stereotypes about Mexicans and Mexican Americans. In a piece entitled "Pachita," she wrote: "Embued [sic] with the futile philosophy of the peon, she yields to whatever emotion is uppermost in her mind, taking her sorrows without much complaint as she takes her pleasures without comment—her outlook on life utterly apathetic" (*The Family*, April 1927: 44). So completely had the spurious profiles of Mexicans and Mexican Americans gained acceptance in the United States by the end of the 1920s that even Mexican Americans themselves had come to reiterate their assigned characteristics as articles of faith.

Unfortunately, these stereotypes were contributing to a pernicious theory of cultural determinism—"Mexicans" were the way they were because of their culture. Their improvement lay in changing their culture. The deficiencies of Mexican Americans could be eliminated simply by wringing all their Mexican culture out of them. But brave Mexican American voices were beginning to murmur their dissent and to express their disapproval of the distorted images of Mexican Americans being purveyed by Anglo American writers.

In 1929, some of those brave voices succeeded in forming the League of United Latin American Citizens (LULAC) in Corpus Christi, Texas, in the days when the law both east and west of the Pecos very much discriminated against Mexicans and Mexican Americans. The aim of LULAC was not only to improve the tarnished image of Mexican Americans but to hasten the process of Americanization, which to them seemed doubly slow for Mexican Americans. To this end LULAC advocated the primacy of the English language and special classes in citizenship. Americanization seemed to LULAC members to merit the emphasis.

But 40 years later the problem of Mexican Americans were as acute as they had always been. However, the great migration north from Mexico had just about come to an end by 1930. Indeed, Mexicans continued to emigrate to the United States in the 30s and 40s but not in the phenomenal numbers of the previous two decades. Later, during World War II, Mexicans were again courted to fill up the labor shortage of the United States, but this time the influx was more systematically controlled by what came to be known as "bracero pacts," that is, "labor agreements" between the United States and Mexico.

Perhaps the most important work by a Mexican American writer in the decade prior to the Second World War was George I. Sánchez' *Forgotten People: A Study of New Mexicans* (1939), a study undertaken for the Carnegie Corporation. At the time, his was almost the only voice in the American ethnic wilderness pointing out the special needs of Mexican Americans: "In this nation, there is no excuse for human misery . . . good intentions cannot substitute for good deeds" (viii). Another gifted Mexican American writer of this period is Josephina Niggli, whose plays from the 1930s have transcended time and space.

Prose works like *Mexican Immigration to the United States* (1930) by Manuel Gamio and *Old Spain in Our Southwest* (1936) by Nina Otero reflected the kinds of sociocultural perspectives held by some Mexican American writers during the 30s. Unwittingly, Dr. Gamio wrote:

> The majority of immigrants [Mexicans] continue to talk Spanish, but since they generally belong to the lower classes of Mexico and since in the United States they come in contact with the same grade of people, their poor Spanish becomes deformed and incrusted with English, and the result is a barbarous jargon which could not be understood in any Spanish-speaking country (231).

But linguistic science was still in the future, and Dr. Gamio was uttering what was commonplace about the mixture of languages among the linguistic elite. Prophetically the very language Dr. Gamio eschewed, *intrasentential alternation* or code switching (using

Spanish and English words in the same sentence), would become the language of choice for Chicano poets. More importantly, though, in Dr. Gamio's day, most people did not recognize the centrality of language in the lives of human beings, and that languages in contact are like consenting adults, creating new language wherever that contact occurs. That's how Latin produced Spanish, French, Italian, Portuguese and Romanian. Like human genealogy, linguistic genealogy is equally diverse.

As people still do today, Dr. Gamio equated *poor* Spanish with *poor* Mexican immigrants. For him, *good* language went with *good* breeding and background. It seems he was unaware that *good* and *bad* language are value judgments predicated on where one is on the socioeconomic scale. Fortunately, since then, works by linguists like Benjamin Whorf and Edward Sapir have dramatically enlightened our notions of linguistic propriety, as well as works by Rosaura Sánchez.

In the 1930s there were essentially two principal Mexican American literary outlets for Mexican American writers since, by and large, Anglo American literary outlets excluded them. The first was *Alianza Magazine* founded in 1907, published by the *Alianza Hispano-Americana* in Tucson; the second was *Lulac News* founded in 1933. The two publications differed in scope and purpose. The former dedicated itself to maintenance of Hispanic culture and language, running almost half, if not more, of its pieces in Spanish. The latter emphasized articles in English and was concerned with issues of citizenship and discrimination. Of the two, *Alianza Magazine* was the more literary. Occasionally, it published poetry and fiction, although *Lulac News* published poetry occasionally also. Interestingly, *Alianza Magazine* reported on events in Arizona and California while *Lulac News* covered Texas and New Mexico. Though *Lulac News* was radical from the beginning, the radicalization of *Alianza Magazine* did not occur until the 1950s. In general, both publications stressed the intense loyalty of Mexican Americans to the United States.

The 1930s also saw the emergence of such Mexican American writers as Arturo Campa, Juan Rael, Cleofas Jaramillo, and Jovita González, all of whom contributed significantly to the corpus of Mexican American literature as well as American literature. Campa, Rael, and González were avid collectors of folklore, but Campa also wrote fiction. One of his most celebrated short-stories, "The Cell of Heavenly Justice" (*New Mexico Quarterly*, August 1934) has been widely anthologized, particularly since the Chicano period. Though written in English, Campa's story is in the best tradition of the Hispanic *cuento* which stresses characterization over plot as in the Anglo American short story. Other Mexican American writers of the period were Bert Baca and Ely Leyba whose works appeared in the *New Mexico* magazine.

While Mexican American writers like Ernesto Galarza ("Without Benefit of Lobby," *Survey Graphic*, May 1,

1931) and George I. Sánchez were trying to break down the pernicious structures of stereotype, other Mexican American writers like Nina Otero and Emilie Baca only reinforced those structures.

Mexican American fiction of the 30s was generally characterized by themes and motifs of the past in which the characters are cast as gentle, peace-loving, and wise with the knowledge of things of the earth like Juan Sedillo's "Gentleman of the Río en Medio" (*New Mexico Quarterly*, August 1939: 183). In 1939 Robert Félix Salazar's poem "The Other Pioneers" about the Hispanic pioneers of the United States appeared in the July issue of *Lulac News*. The poem is noteworthy in view of the fact that Salazar had published poetry in such prestige magazines as *Esquire*, one of the few Mexican Americans poets who achieved that distinction.

World War II was a turning point for Mexican Americans as it was for Americans in general. On far-flung battlefields Mexican Americans were dying in their search for America. The tragedy for Mexican Americans was that even though they responded to the colors during the war, they were still considered as "foreigners" by so many of the Anglo American population, many of whom had themselves "recently" arrived from elsewhere, particularly Europe. But the irony of the Mexican American's situation was that the first draftee of World War II was Pete Despart, a Mexican American from Los Angeles.

In 1943 *Alianza Magazine* spoke out forcefully against what it called "the Mayflower Complex" of Anglo Americans, "a strange malady which may be contracted in the Northeastern section of the United States if one is not well inoculated against it by travel and study." Continuing the editorial, *Alianza Magazine* pointed out that Anglo Americans appear "surprised when a 'Martínez' or an 'Urías' brings down a Jap plane, sinks a Nazi U-Boat, or is promoted in rank" (January, 8).

In mid-century America, Mexican Americans were to emerge as the American ethnic group having won more medals of honor (17 altogether in World War II and Korea) than any other group of Americans except Anglos. Yet at the height of the war, just one month after Private José P. Martínez (U.S. Army) had been killed at the battle of Attu in the Aleutians, an action for which he was the first American awarded the Medal of Honor (posthumously), Mexican Americans were fleeing for their lives in Los Angeles in what came to be known nationally as "the Zoot-Suit Riots." American sailors didn't like the attire of Mexican Americans so they beat up on them. Sparked innocently enough, the roots of the incident lay deep in the strata of American racism of the kind that sent Japanese Americans to "detention" camps for the duration of the war and which kept African Americans segregated.

In 1942, on fabricated evidence 17 Mexican American youths were indicted for a murder that occurred in what was called "the Sleepy Lagoon" area of Los

Angeles. The case became notorious for the manner in which the Mexican American defendants were treated by the police and the California judicial system. Carey McWilliams, who served as Chairman of the Sleepy Lagoon Defense Committee, described the proceedings as "more of a ceremonial lynching than a trial in a court of justice" (*North From Mexico*, 1948: 231). The defendants had served two years in San Quentin before their convictions were reversed unanimously by the District Court of Appeals.

The events of the Sleepy Lagoon case and the Zoot-Suit Riots helped create an awareness on the part of Mexican Americans in California (as well as elsewhere) about the need for effective organizations capable of protecting their interests. The first such organizations to be founded in the wake of this awareness were the Unity Leagues, intended to achieve political objectives and to protect its members from harm.

The war years were to affect Mexican Americans as no other period in American history had, save the U.S. War with Mexico. While no accurate figures are available as to the number of Mexican Americans who served in the armed forces during World War II, estimates suggest that perhaps as many as half-a-million Mexican Americans were in uniform during the war years (McWilliams, 259).

Not only did Mexican Americans distinguish themselves on the battlefield, but for the first time they moved in large numbers into the industrial occupations made available by the war economy. At heart, the change in Mexican American attitudes was brought about by the fact that having fought to preserve the ideals of American democracy abroad, they would expect nothing less back home than first-class citizenship. The war sparked a growing resentment of all forms of discrimination.

The war rhetoric of "the good neighbor policy" and "hands across the border" quickly evaporated after the war. American amnesia obscured the fact that during the war Mexico had been an ally of the United States, declaring war on Germany, Italy, and Japan on May 22, 1942, and sending its troops to the principal theaters of war, including a Mexican air squadron in the Pacific. German and Italian prisoners of war interned in the United States received better treatment than Mexicans and Mexican Americans.

In the post-war years from 1946 to 1960, Mexican Americans discovered there were two Americas. The America of the 30s, 40s, and 50s had become a land of contradiction for them. Were they Mexicans or Americans? In 1946 Arturo Campa offered this explanation:

> Mexican Americans are not Mexicans, and they have not been since 1848; neither are they natives exclusively. Few can prove conclusively to be of Spanish descent, and none of them are Spanish-Americans, considering that such an adjective applies to people in Spanish-America, although legally and nationally they

are Americans; linguistically Spanish; Spanish-Americans, geographically; culturally Mexican (*Spanish Folk Poetry in New Mexico*, 15).

The dilemma would not be resolved until the efflorescence of the Chicano Renaissance. That event helped them understand they were both and need not be ashamed of either. But the post-war years were a struggle.

At every turn Mexican Americans had to go to the courts or establish alternative organizations for their well-being. On April 14, 1947, the Ninth Circuit Court ruled in *Méndez v. Westminster* (California) that it was unconstitutional to segregate Mexican American students. This was a precedent case for Thurgood Marshall's argument in *Brown v. Board of Education*. In 1947 the city of Three Rivers, Texas, refused to bury a Mexican American veteran in its municipal cemetery. The brouhaha led to the creation of a Mexican American veterans organization, the American GI Forum, by Dr. Héctor P. García in order to protect the rights of Mexican American veterans. A decade later an official of the Daughters of the American Revolution in Denver refused to let a Mexican American youth carry the American flag in a parade on grounds that only "American boys" should carry the flag, adding "I wouldn't want a Mexican to carry Old Glory, would you?" (*Alianza Magazine*, March 1957: 11).

In the meantime, Mexican American literature changed hardly at all in character from what it had been prior to World War II. With some exceptions, the emphasis was still on reflective pastoral themes highlighting "the hacienda syndrome," as Raymond Paredes called it. ("The Evolution of Chicano Literature" in *Three American Literatures*, 1982: 52). *We Fed Them Cactus* (1954) by Fabiola Cabeza de Baca and *Romance of a Little Village Girl* (1955) by Cleofas Jaramillo signaled the end of pastoral themes in Mexican American literature.

One cannot fault the writers (male or female) of these idyllic accounts for seeking refuge in their culture. They were writing about the verities they knew: about the loss of a Hispanic Eden as they remembered it. Rebolledo regards this writing as acts of resistance to Anglo domination (*Women Singing in the Snow*, 29). I can see that, but what is important is that they were writing and that their works demonstrated not just mastery of literary techniques, but comprehension of the historical dynamics engulfing them.

Not all works during this period dealt with the Spanish Templar Tradition. Arnold Rojas was writing about the equestrian tradition in the Hispanic Southwest with works like *California Vaquero*, 1953. During this time, Fray Angélico Chávez was a master of technique in poetry, prose, and fiction. His eye may have been on the past but his grasp was on the future. In *New Mexico Triptych*, 1959, a trio of stories, he weaves for us the meaning of perseverance and faith. The story abounds with sensitivity and *gravitas*.

On occasion short stories like Mario Suárez' "Señor Garza" appeared in such literary publications as the *Arizona Quarterly* (Summer 1947), stories which reflect more realistically the actuality of Mexican American life in the *colonias* and *barrios* of the Southwest.

At the close of the Period of Americanization, a seminal work of scholarship on the *corrido* in the Southwest, *With His Pistol in His Hand: A Border Ballad* by Américo Paredes (1958), appeared and transcended this period to become a key work in the development of Mexican American thought during the Chicano period. Paredes was more than a folklorist. "Throughout his early writings," Leticia Garza-Falcón explains, "Paredes gives voice to experiences of characters who had never been written into [Walter Prescott] Webb's story," supplying "the text missing from Anglo histories" of Mexican Americans (*Gente Decente: A Borderlands Response to the Rhetoric of Dominance*, 1998: 164–165).

Harbingers of things to come were on the horizon. Few, if any, Mexican Americans could foresee just how dramatic a change was in the offing. But it was not a change without consequences.

Period of the Chicano Movement and the Chicano Renaissance

No one can say with certainty when the Chicano Movement began, but most commentators trace its beginnings to 1960 and the political ferment of presidential elections that year. Some memoirists point to the founding of the United Farm Workers Association by César Chávez in 1962 as the beginning of the Chicano Movement. According to Alfredo Cuellar, "there is some evidence that [it] grew out of conferences held at Loyola University in Los Angeles in the summer of 1966" ("Perspectives on Politics," in *Mexican Americans* by Joan Moore, 1970: 149). The movement was happening everywhere.

Mexican Americans certainly honed their political skills in the election year of 1960. Viva Kennedy clubs sprang up everywhere as Democrats forged ties with Mexican American communities, recognizing their potential political strength. Though the election of 1960 produced little political patronage, it provided Mexican Americans with the expertise to get Edward Roybal elected to the U.S. House of Representatives in 1962, making him the first Mexican American to be elected to the federal legislature from California. That same year, Mexican Americans in Crystal City, Texas, captured the city government. In New Mexico, Reies López Tijerina founded the Alianza Federal de Mercedes as a means to reclaim land promised sacrosanct per the Treaty of Guadalupe Hidalgo. In Denver, Corky Gonzales was laying the foundation of his Crusade for Justice.

Chicano literature began, more or less, in tandem with the Chicano (Civil Rights) Movement of the 1960s as a reaction to exclusion by the American literary mainstream. Before 1960 few Mexican American writers were published by mainstream literary outlets. Concerned by that exclusion, in 1966 Octavio Romano, professor of anthropology at the University of California at Berkeley, gathered a cohort of Mexican Americans to organize *El Grito: Journal of Mexican American Thought*, a publication that was a manifesto and a shot across the bow of the American literary juggernaut that Mexican American writers would no longer look to the American literary mainstream for intellectual validation. *El Grito* (the cry) was a line in the sand.

Before *El Grito*, the literature of Mexican Americans was what the American literary mainstream said it was; after *El Grito*, Mexican Americans would say what Mexican American literature was. *El Grito* would be dedicated solely to the Mexican American experience. Chicano readers would be judges of Chicano literature which would create its own critical strictures and its own critical aesthetic.

Discourse-specific, Chicano texts would generate their own dynamics from which a critical criteria would emerge. That was a radical departure. And yet, necessary. For *El Grito* was the manifesto of Chicano liberation from Anglo American intellectual traditions that marginalized non-privileged perspectives. Publication of *El Grito* in the Spring of 1967 ushered in "The Chicano Renaissance"—a period of literary ferment that forever changed the intellectual relationship between Mexican Americans and the American literati. The promise of *El Grito* was that it would be the forum for Mexican Americans to articulate their own sense of identity.

Prior to the Chicano Renaissance, the American literary mainstream perceived Mexican American literary production as little more than folklore (like the folktale of *La Llorona*) and ballads of banditry (like the *Corrido of Gregorio Cortez*). In 1967, I was asked to submit a short story for an anthology of fiction, only to have it returned with the explanation that it wasn't the kind of story they were expecting from me. Along with the explanation they sent me a copy of J. Frank Dobie's "The Straw Man" as an example of the kind of story they wanted. They wanted a quaint story about the stereotypical culture of Mexican Americans. I had sent them "Chicago Blues," a story about a contemporary Mexican American jazz musician in Chicago. The story had won an international story competition in 1957 judged by Richard Wright.

The dynamics of the stereotypes about Mexican Americans have been engendered by pernicious Anglo characterizations of Mexican Americans, especially men, as untrustworthy, villainous, ruthless, tequila-drinking, philandering *machos,* indolent and afraid of hard work or else as courteous, devout and fatalistic peasants who were to be treated more as pets than as people. More often than not Mexicans were cast as either bandits or loveable rogues;

as hot-blooded, sexually animated creatures or passive, humble servants.

In one report to Washington, DC in the 19th century, Mexican Americans were described as "thoroughly debased and totally incapable of self-government," with "no latent quality about them that can ever make them respectable." Adding that "they have more Indian blood than Spanish, and in some respects are below the Pueblo Indians, for they are not as honest or as industrious" (*Congressional Globe*, 32nd Congress, 2nd Session (January 10, 1853), Appendix, p. 104). The pejorations and generalizations were deplorable, and the Chicano Renaissance gave rise against the perpetuation of such slanderous stereotypes.

Perhaps the main significance of the Chicano Renaissance lay in the identification of Chicanos with their Indian past. Chicanos cast off the meretricious externally imposed identification with the Spanish Templar tradition foisted on them by Anglo American society because of its preference for things European. In the 1930s, Mexican Americans turned to the label "Latin Americans" because Anglo America blanched at the word "Mexican."

Significantly, a literature draws from the history and myths of its people's past; and Chicanos turned to their Indian past for their most meaningful symbols and metaphors. For example, one of the key symbols of the Chicano Movement was the icon of the 5th Sun celebrated by the Aztecs in the form of the great calendar stone. The Aztecs considered themselves people of the Fifth Sun (*Quinto Sol*). According to their mythology, there had been four previous epochs, each governed by a sun. The first epoch ended with the inhabitants of earth devoured by ocelots; the second world and sun were destroyed by wind; the third by a rain of fire; and the fourth, by water. According to the Aztecs, the sun and world in which they lived—the fifth sun—was destined to perish as a result of earthquakes, famine, and terror.

The publishing enterprise that would produce *El Grito* was named *Quinto Sol* Publications. At the same time, the name of the publication, *El Grito*, celebrated the essence of the Mexican War for Independence, the start of which was initiated by the literal cry of Dolores by Father Hidalgo, spiritual leader of Mexican resistance against the Spaniards. Cuauhtémoc, not his brother Moctezuma, was apotheosized as the champion of indigenous resistance to Cortez and the Spaniards who vanquished Mexico City in 1521. That was not the conquest of Mexico as is popularly accepted, only the conquest of the city. Indigenous resistance to Spanish hegemony persisted into the 19th century ushering in the Mexican war for independence.

In the same manner, the Chicano Movement elevated Pancho Villa and Emiliano Zapata to the pantheon of Chicano populist heroes instead of any person or persons from the victorious cohort of the Mexican Civil War (1910–1921). Chicano mural painters depicted the "common folk" of Mexico and greater Mexico in their art, splashed vibrantly across any available wall. Chicano art was art for the people; just as Chicano literature was literature for the people. However, beyond the goal of equity, the significance of the Chicano Movement and the Chicano Renaissance was, as I have pointed out, the identification of Chicanos with their Indian past. They would be who they said they were, not who the mainstream said they were.

In 1969 Quinto Sol Publications brought out its first book entitled *El Espejo—The Mirror: Selected Mexican American Literature* edited by Octavio Romano. *El Espejo* was a brown paperback book reflecting "brown" literary hopes and aspirations in the United States. *El Espejo* represented the first efforts of a nascent literary boom, probing for its relevance in the Mexican American experience which had theretofore been articulated only at the margins of American literature, if at all. Explanation of the title of the anthology was given in the preface:

> To know themselves, to know who they are, some need nothing more than to see their own reflection. Therefore . . . *The Mirror—El Espejo*. May this book serve as a mirror for the many who see themselves herein.

From the beginning, Mexican American literature was a body of intellectual production looking for a form. I offered a form in *Backgrounds of Mexican American Literature*, to my knowledge, the first historical inquiry in the field and out of which grew my concept of "The Chicano Renaissance" a term that may, indeed, have been premature, as Juan Bruce Novoa has pointed out, considering the scarcity of Chicano materials available. For me, the term "Chicano Renaissance" signified the beginning of a boom in the literary production of Mexican Americans. That I contrasted it to other historical renaissances was a way of validating it as a historical movement.

In the 1960s Chicano literature emerged as a means by which Chicanos could find their own voice, their own sense of being Chicano, not Spanish, not Mexican, not American, but Chicano. As it emerged from the cauldron of cultural nationalism, the role of Chicano literature was to reflect Chicano life and Chicano values, drawing from an imagination distinctively Chicano.

That during this *incunabula* many of the early works of Chicano literature were inspired by ideological needs did not lessen the expectations that the responsibilities of Chicano writers were ultimately to create a literature so essentially Chicano that it stood on its own merits apart from other literatures. Chicano literature was to free Chicanos from the burden of American history and its libelous account of Chicanos and their ancestors. Like the disciples of Senchan Torpeist, the fabled Irish poet of myth, who were sent out to recover the whole of the *Tain*–the great Irish saga—which none of them could remember entirely, Chicano writers were the "disciples" through whom the lost inheritance of Chicanos would be recovered.

Literature means many things to many people. In literature as in other human endeavors there are problems with definitions. A piece of literature is not just a speech act—it's a social act; it has cultural connotations that reveal a writer's relation to his or her group and to the entire fabric of society. As a cultural manifestation, a literary work inheres a sense of audience, its language (whether English, Spanish or a combination of both) is part of a *weltanschauung* shared by a community of readers. The significance of a literary work lies not only in the social reality in which the writer participates but grows out of the culture which nourishes him or her.

What most characterized Chicano literature, early on, were its countertexts—the textual backgrounds against which Chicano literature was superimposed, the texts of Chicano reality. Chicano writers were expositing not just Chicano views but countertexts of Anglo views by which Chicanos were judged socially; countertexts which showed how Chicanos were contained within the apodictic value framework of mainstream culture and subjected cruelly and brutally to it.

Through countertexts, Chicano writers showed the insidious ways by which mainstream culture exercised hegemony over the Chicano community. Chicano countertexts pointed out how having been subjected to coercive Anglo texts and having internalized the values inherent in them, Chicanos had inadvertently been instruments in their own oppression. It was this ploy of text and countertext that provided Chicano literature with its most enduring quality—process. Chicano literature was a process, not an outcome, a process of imagining and figuring out the world, as Henry Louis Gates would have put it (*Black Literature and Literary Theory*, 1984: 71).

As products of process, Chicano texts were not finalities of truth but limns by which Chicano liberation could be achieved. Chicano literature was thus envisioned in the service of the cause, the people. It was not an end in itself. This meant Chicano texts were not self-sufficient but required the help of Chicano readers to actualize their meanings.

In 1971 when Tomás Rivera, José Reyna, and I took part in the first national symposium on Chicano Literature and Critical Theory at Pan American University, our presentations were not as arbiters nor as *dicta* in the development of Chicano literature. Chicano literature was a barely emerging field then. My essay on "The Chicano Renaissance" had just appeared in the May 1971 issue of *Social Casework*. Our presentations sought to show how Chicano writers were looking for forms discrete to the Chicano experience by which to articulate that experience; that Chicano writers were searching for textual structures of meaning unique to the Chicano experience through which the meaning of the Chicano experience would be validated—by Chicanos, not Anglos. Or as Ramón Saldívar has put it:

the function of Chicano narrative is . . . to produce creative structures of knowledge to allow its readers to see, feel, and understand their social reality (*Chicano Narrative: The Dialectics of Difference*, 1990: 6).

In this sense, the Chicano Renaissance functioned for Chicano writers much the way the Irish Renaissance functioned for Irish writers who cut their ties to British literature and turned to the roots and traditions of Irish literature for sustenance. Chicanos cast adrift the privileged norm of Anglo American literature. At that moment, Chicano literature embodied what Georg Simmel identifies as that process in life by which it generates forms demanding "a validity which transcends the moment" (*On Individuality and Social Forms*, 1971: 346).

What we can say about Chicano literature is that it's a literature in process, drawing from different literary traditions (American, Mexican, global), sometimes from one or the other, and sometimes in a unique synthesis of Mexican and American that is truly startling and innovative.

The earliest manifestation of that synthesis appeared in what has since come to be called "the first Chicano novel"—*Pocho* by José Antonio Villarreal, published in 1959. It's a "coming of age" novel in which the boy, Richard Rubio, experiences growing up in two cultures, feeling rejected by both because in both he's an outsider: in the United States, he's a "Mexican" and to the Mexicans he's a *pocho*, a Mexican who lives beyond the pale of Mexican culture, a Mexican who has become Americanized, foregoing his patrimony. Interestingly, the word *pocho* comes from the Nahuatl word *pochteca*, which means "he who wanders abroad." For the Aztecs this identified the trader who sold and bought wares in regions beyond the borders of their homeland which they called *Aztlán*.

The novel *Pocho* begins in Mexico at the end of the Mexican Civil War (1921) and traces the flight of Juan Rubio, ex-revolutionary colonel, from Mexico to the United States. Having killed a man in a brawl over a prostitute in *Ciudad Juárez*, Juan Rubio seeks safety north of the border, first in Texas then in California where he suffers silently the debilitating effects of acculturation upon his children, especially Richard, the *pocho* of the novel. Ambivalent about his identity, at the end of the novel, Richard Rubio goes off to war and to an uncertain future.

The novel received scant attention initially and lay in remainders until the early 1970s when it was used extensively in Chicano literature courses. A slew of novels by Mexican American writers appeared during the 60s, some of which ran into ideological quagmires. Were they Chicano novels consistent with the aims of Chicano literature as first advanced by the cultural nationalism driving the Chicano Movement? Not all of those novels passed muster. John Rechy's novel *City of Night* (1963) ran into ideological difficulties because of its homosexual implications. There was some question about Floyd Salas' *Tattoo the Wicked Cross* (1967). Ray Barrios' novel *The Plum*

Plum Pickers (1969) became a favorite Chicano novel of the 60s principally because the author drew his characters lifelike as migrant workers. But it was an experimental novel looking for an audience.

The Chicano novels of the 70s ran the gamut of thematic diversity but the majority of them were actuated by the mnemonic impulse, that is, their autobiographic thrust was linked to the collective memory of a displaced people, scratching out a living in a land dismembered from its self. Like Villarreal's *Pocho*, Richard Vásquez' novel *Chicano* (1970) details the odyssey of Héctor Sandoval from Mexico to the United States during the Mexican Civil War (1910–1921) and the travails of his children, Neftalí, Jilda, Hortencia, and their heirs in California. Like Chicano novels that were to follow, *Chicano* is a novel about a family, an immigrant Mexican family striving to survive in a place that does not welcome them.

In 1970, Tomás Rivera (now deceased) won the first *Premio Quinto Sol* for his episodic novel *And the Earth did not Part*, a work which has grown in stature over the last 30 years because of its enduring qualities. In 1972, Rolando Hinojosa won the *Premio Quinto Sol* and in 1976 the *Premio Casa de las Américas* for his novel *Klail City*. In 1973, Estela Portillo Trambley (now deceased) won the *Premio Quinto Sol* for fiction though she is better known for *Day of the Swallows*, a powerful play about strong women. She went on to publish other plays, collections of short fiction, and the novel *Trini* (1986). That same year one of the most enigmatic of the Chicano novelists, Oscar Zeta Acosta, published *Autobiography of a Brown Buffalo*, and like Ambrose Bierce disappeared from public view not long thereafter. The most successful novelist of the 70s still writing is Rodolfo Anaya whose novel, *Bless Me, Ultima* (1973), has become a landmark of Chicano literature. Another landmark novel of Chicano literature is *Peregrinos de Aztlán* (1974) by Miguel Méndez. *The Road to Tamazunchale* (1975) by Ron Arias was the first novel by a Chicano to employ the literary techniques of *magical realism*; that same year Alejandro Morales' novel *Caras Viejas y Vino Nuevo* (1975) was published in Mexico in Spanish; also that year Aristeo Brito's novel *El Diablo en Tejas* appeared in Spanish, later in a bilingual edition; another work of magical realism appeared in 1976 with Orlando Romero's *Nambé-Year One*. And in 1977, Nash Candelaria published *Memories of the Alhambra*.

During the 80s, Chicanos and Chicanas produced a range of novels. By and large, though, the novels produced by Chicanos and Chicanas during the 80s and early 90s still dealt with the verities of Chicano life in a hostile American environment. Significantly, during the 80s a surge in Chicana literary production engendered a wave of creativity that regenerated the Chicano Renaissance.

From the start, Mexican American women played prominent roles in literary production but, unfortunately, their texts have been "inaccessible" as Annie Eysturoy has pointed out (*Daughters of Self-Creation: The Contempo-* *rary Chicana Novel*, 1996: 35). Also, their contributions were little bruited in the masculine tsunami of early Chicano letters. That situation has been put aright by scores of Chicana writers who in the 1990s seem to have eclipsed their male counterparts.

In Chicana fiction, Sandra Cisneros, *The House on Mango Street*, 1985, has become the most visible and equally visible in public controversy. Other Chicana novelists include Isabella Ríos, *Victuum*, 1976; Sheila Ortiz Taylor, *Faultline,* 1982; Cecile Piñeda, *Face*, 1985; Ana Castillo, *The Mixquiahuala Letters*, 1986; Mary Helen Ponce, *The Wedding*, 1989; Roberta Fernández, *Intaglio*, 1990; Lucha Corpi, *Eulogy for a Brown Angel*, 1992; Beatriz de la Garza, *The Candy Vendor's Boy*, 1994; and Helena María Viramontes, *Under the Feet of Jesus*, 1995.

Chicano novels since the 70s include Ed Vega, *The Comeback*, 1985; Lionel García, *Hardscrub*, 1990; Víctor Villaseñor, *Rain of Gold*, 1992; Graciela Limón, *The Memories of Ana Calderón*, 1994; Alejandro Grattan-Domínguez, *Breaking Even*, 1997; and others.

Scores of Chicanos have written short (stories) fiction, starting with cuentos during the Period of Transition and the Period of Americanization. But the genre exploded among Chicanos during the Chicano Period. In 1967, Felipe de Ortego y Gasca won the NEA-Reader's Digest Foundation award for fiction with "Soledad," a short story about Mexican American high school students and their first experience with a Mexican American teacher of English. In 1968 his short story "The Coming of Zamora," a fictive rendering of the trial of Reies López Tijerina appeared in *El Grito* (Spring 1968), "Chicago Blues," *ARX Magazine* (Spring 1969), "The Dwarf of San Miguel," *New England Review*, April–May 1970, and "Rosemary, For Remembrance," *La Luz*, October and November 1974. Collections of short stories/cuentos by Chicano writers have appeared less often than novels by Chicano writers. In 1971, Sabine Ulibarrí published *Tierra Amarilla*; other short story collections include Alonso M. Perales, *La Lechuza: Cuentos de Mi Barrio* in Spanish, 1972; *Cachito Mío* by José Acosta Torres, 1973; *Blue Day on Main Street* by J. L. Navarro, 1973; *Rain of Scorpions* by Estela Portillo Trambley, 1975; *Requisa Treinta y Dos* edited by Rosaura Sánchez, 1979; *There are no Madmen Here* by Gina Valdés, 1981; *The Adventures of the Chicano Kid and Other Stories* by Max Martínez, 1982; *Tales of Huitlacoche* by Gary Keller, 1984; *The Iguana Killer* by Alberto Ríos, 1984; *The Last of the Menu Girls*, by Denise Chávez, 1986; *Days of Plenty, Days of Want* by Patricia Preciado Martin, 1988; and *Weeping Woman* by Alma Luz Villanueva, 1994.

In prose, one of the most influential books of the 70s was Marta Cotera's *Diosa y Hembra*, an exposition of the Hispanic woman as both goddess and *female*. There have been many Mexican American writers of prose over the years; but many more, it seems, during the Chicano period, many of them producing countertexts to dispel the protocols of racism that characterized Mexican Americans.

A text of profound significance, "The Space of Chicano Literature" by Juan Bruce Novoa in 1974 would become the standard for the expansion of Chicano Literature. In an open letter to me when I was Editor and Associate publisher of *La Luz* magazine in Denver (September 1973), he called for the space of Chicano literature to include the sum of its parts without canonical restrictions. I argued for that same inclusion.

Having written extensively on the educational condition of Mexican Americans since the 60s, the *Center Magazine* published my piece on "Montezuma's Children" as a cover story in its November/December issue of 1970. The piece was an exposé on the deplorable conditions of Mexican American education. In 1972, *The Saturday Review* ran a follow up piece of mine on "Schools for Mexican Americans" (April 17). In 1974, I teamed up with Marta Sotomayor for the study on *Chicanos and American Education* funded by the Ford Foundation through the National Council of La Raza. The study was released in 1976.

Richard Rodríguez' *Hunger of Memory* appeared in 1982 and quickly encountered a firestorm of controversy for its lack of political correctness. In 1987, Gloria Anzaldúa's *Borderlands*, a text of remarkable proportions, swept the emerging field of Chicana studies, staking out new markers in the intellectual field traversed by Chicanos and Chicanas. That same year, Al Martínez, the *Los Angeles Times* columnist, published *Ashes in the Rain (Selected Essays)*. And in 1990 the gifted theoretician, Ramón Saldívar published *Chicano Narrative*, a work that brought into sharper focus the narratology of Chicano texts. In autobiographic prose, *Barrio Boy* (1971) by Ernesto Galarza continues its preeminence. Anthony Quinn's *The Original Sin* (1972) has held up equally well. However, Chicano autobiographic prose is scant, although much of Chicano prose has biography embedded in it. See, for example, Richard Rodríguez' *Hunger of Memory* and *Days of Obligation*; or Linda Chávez' *Out of the Barrio*. Also, many Chicano novels are thinly veiled biographies. One biography of some years ago but only published recently is *The Rebel* (1994) by Leonor Villegas de Magnón, edited by Clara Lomas.

In addition to Estela Portillo Trambley in drama during this period, Luis Valdez is by far the most renowned both for his plays (*actos*) and for creation of *El Teatro Campesino*, the agitprop arm of César Chávez' United Farmworkers Organization. From plays like *Los Vendidos* (The Sellouts), Valdez went on to produce films like *Zoot Suit* and *La Bamba*. The playwright Carlos Morton came into drama out of the Chicano generation of the 70s. Prolific, Morton is nevertheless identified with *The Many Deaths of Danny Rosales* (1983), a message play about Anglo oppression of Chicanos in the criminal justice system. Other Chicano/a playwrights include Denise Chávez (who studied with Mark Medoff, author of *Children of a Lesser God*) and Felipe de Ortego y Gasca whose play about Cortez, Moctezuma, and the *Virgin de Guadalupe*,

Madre del Sol/Mother of the Sun, premiered in San Antonio in 1981 and was performed at the Teatro Antonio Casso in Mexico City in 1982. His play *Voces de Mujeres* was presented in 1993 at the 5th International Conference on Women at the University of Costa Rica in San José.

The work, *Mexican American Theatre: Then and Now* (*Revista Chicano Riqueña*, Spring 1983) edited by Nicolás Kanellos advances our historical understanding of Mexican American theater. And the works of drama critic and teacher, Jorge Huerta, extend our comparative knowledge of Chicano theater and its relationship to Latin American theater. Huerta was one of the principal organizers of TENAZ (*Teatro Nacional de Aztlán*), an international coalition of *teatros*.

Chicano/a poets abound. Some of the early poets were Felipe de Ortego y Gasca, *Sangre y Cenizas*, 1964; "the Poet Laureate of Aztlán," Abelardo Delgado, "Stupid America," 1968; Luis Omar Salinas, *Crazy Gypsy*, 1970; "the Walt Whitman of the Chicano Movement," Ricardo Sánchez, *Canto y Grito mi Liberación*, 1971; José Montoya, *El Sol y los de Abajo*, 1972; Raymundo "Tigre" Pérez, *The Secret Meaning of Death*, 1972; Juan Felipe Herrera, *Rebozos of Love*, 1974; and Reyes Cárdenas, *Chicano Territory*, 1975. Though not as productive in poetry as his compatriots, Rodolfo "Corky" Gonzales is best known for *I am Joaquín* (1968), perhaps the most celebrated poem of the early Chicano era, full of sound and fury signifying everything. Chicano poets vented the anger of the Chicano community in a range of protest poetry which Francisco Lomelí calls "instigative poetry with strong political overtones" ("An Overview of Chicano Letters: From Origins to Resurgence" in *Chicano Studies: Survey and Analysis*, 1997: 289).

Poets like Alurista (Alberto Urista) experimented with binary lines of poetry in "Mis Ojos Hinchados," for example, using English and Spanish in non-standard syntactic structures, intrasententially alternating Spanish and English—code switching. Rosaura Sánchez' work in linguistics (*Chicano Discourse: Sociolinguistic Perspectives*, 1983) illuminates this sphere of Chicano cultural production.

Other poets of the early Chicano renaissance include Tino Villanueva, *Hay Otra Voz Poems*, 1972; Sergio Elizondo, *Perros y Antiperros*, 1972; Nephtali De León, *Chicano Poet*, 1973; José Antonio Burciaga, *Un Torero*, 1974; Juan Gómez Quiñones, *5th and Río Grande*, 1974; Angela de Hoyos, *Arise, Chicano and Other Poems*, 1975; Dorinda Moreno, *La Mujer es la Tierra*, 1975; Ricardo Aguilar, *Caravana Enlutada*, 1975; Bernice Zamora, *Restless Serpents*, 1976; Leroy Quintana, *Hijo del Pueblo*, 1976; Gary Soto, *The Elements of San Joaquín*, 1977; Jesús Rafael González, *El Hacedor de Juegos*, 1977; Ana Castillo, *Otro Canto*, 1977; Juan Bruce-Novoa, *Inocencia Perversa*, 1977; and Marina Rivera, *Sobra*, 1977.

In the 80s, a new wave of Chicano/a poets emerged which included Raúl Salinas, *A Trip Through the Mind*

Jail, 1980; Olivia Castellano, *Blue Mandolin, Yellow Field*, 1980; Evangelina Vigil, *Thirty an' Seen a Lot*, 1983; Carmen Tafolla, *Curandera*, 1983; Cheri Moraga, *Living in the War Years,* 1983; Teresa Palomo Acosta, *Passing Time*, 1984; Rosemary Catacalos, *As Long as it Takes*, 1984; Leo Romero, *Celso*, 1985; Naomi Quiñónez, *Sueños de Colibrí*, 1985; Francisco Alarcón, *Tattoos*, 1985; Pat Mora, *Borders*, 1986; Ray González, *Twilights and Chants*, 1987; Jimmy Santiago Baca, *Black Mesa Poems*, 1989; and Alfred Arteaga, *Cantos*, 1991.

Fin de Siecle and the New Millennium

Toward the end of the 20th century, the esthetic philosophy of the pioneer activist writers of the Chicano Renaissance had given way to a wave of Chicano/a writers with tempered views of Chicano life mitigated by legal and social victories that made access to the American literary mainstream less difficult than it had been. This did not mean, however, that Chicano/a writers were swept up *en masse* by mainstream presses. On the contrary, while more Chicano/a writers were being published by mainstream presses, the competition for those writers focused on works that satisfied the institutional standards of those presses. In other words, nothing much changed. For Chicano/a writers seeking mainstream literary recognition, they had to pass the literary muster of mainstream presses. This had been the situation that had activated the Chicano Renaissance in the first place: in order to be published by a mainstream press, Chicano/a writers had to write in the public mould acceptable to mainstream publishers. The aspirations of the Quinto Sol writers to be free from the strictures of mainstream presses which suppressed the realities of Chicano life ebbed. The need for Chicano/a literary independence made the presence of Arte Público Press, the Bilingual Review Press, and other independent Chicano/a presses all the more necessary. This is not to diminish the artistry of those Chicano/a writers who have found outlets for their works with mainstream presses. But those outlets are finite, sustaining only a small number of Chicano/a writers. That is to say, Chicano/a literary voices are more numerous than mainstream presses seem able to handle—or are willing to handle.

What redeems this whole process of selection by mainstream presses is that, by and large, the Chicano/a works published by mainstream presses represent the high quality of writing produced by Chicanos and Chicanas and heretofore published elsewhere—oftentimes ephemerally in those garage presses of the 60s and 70s now transformed electronically into desktop publishing. The need for Chicano/a literary outlets as Octavio Romano foresaw in 1967 continues. While many Chicano/a writers are being featured by mainstream publishers, many more Chicano/a writers are being featured by a still lingering thread of

"pick-up presses" established for the purpose of publishing a particular book—much the way Mictla Press was organized in El Paso in 1971 to publish *Canto y Grito mi Liberación* by Ricardo Sánchez. Interestingly, university presses have stepped in to provide outlets for Chicano/a literary production. A quick survey reveals the significance of university presses to Chicano/a writers.

In this period of the last 16 years (1990–2006) the most surprising surge of literary production among Chicano/a writers has been in expository/argumentative prose and what the Mayborn Institute of Journalism at the University of North Texas calls "literary non-fiction." More Chicano/a scholars have turned to the production of critical works in Chicano Literature like *Decolonial Voices: Chicana and Chicano Studies in the 21st Century* (2002), edited by Arturo J. Aldama and Naomi Helena Quiñónez.

The works that have most inspired Chicano/a literary non-fiction are Gloria Anzaldúa's *Borderlands/La Frontera: The New Mestiza* (1987) and an earlier work (with Cherrie Moraga) *This Bridge Called my Back* (1981). Both are "bridge" works where the "bridge" becomes an enthymeme of hope in bridging two borderland cultures and a bridge of communal knowledge "where our paths converge." Anzaldúa's work is in the vein of "countertexts," which came into being early in the Chicano Renaissance as contestatory texts, refuting the historical images of Chicanos in mainstream texts and also setting the record straight about Chicanos in the United States.

In the main, the most notable Chicano/a writers of this *fin de siecle* phase and the start of the new millennium are those Chicano/a writers who started writing in the 80s, hitting their stride in the 90s and maturing in their art in the first decade of the new millennium. Among others, the newest Chicano/a novelists and novels of this period are Demetria Martínez (*Mother Tongue*, 1994), Benjamín Alire Sáenz (*Carry Me Like Water*, 1994 and *In Perfect Light*, 2005), Denise Chávez (*Loving Pedro Infante*, 2001), and Manuel Luis Martínez (*Drift*, 2003). From a nominal beginning of some nine novels in the first Chicano decade (1960–1969), Chicano/a novelists burst into flower in the second (1970–1979) and third (1980–1989) Chicano decades. That boom in the Chicano novel diminished somewhat in the fourth (1990–1999) and millennial (2000–2010) Chicano decades.

As a genre, the short story receives short shrift as fiction, but the exception is a superb collection of short stories *Mirrors Beneath the Earth: Fiction by Chicano Writers* (1992) edited by Ray González who is often compared with Raymond Chandler as a master of the genre. Some representative short story writers of this period are Luis Rodríguez (*Republic of East L.A.: Stories*, 2002), Rick Yáñez (*El Paso del Norte: Stories on the Border*, 2003) who also appears in *Mirrors Beneath the Earth*, and Daniel Chacón (*And the Shadows Took Him*, 2004). Chicano *literateurs* opine that the short story is the strongest genre of Chicano writers of fiction. Writers of the genre contend that it is the toughest of the literary genres to control and to master because of Aristotelian strictures defining its architecture and Edgar Alan Poe's successful formula for the genre.

A remarkable book that challenges generic classification but bearing a resemblance to *Like Water for Chocolate* is *Voices in the Kitchen: Views of Food and the World from Working-class Mexican and Mexican American Women* (2006) by Meredith Abarca.

Poetry is the most enduring genre for Chicanos though the least remunerative. Among the earliest Chicano poets still at the plough is Tino Villanueva who won an American Book Award for *Scene From the Movie Giant* (1993). One of the most overlooked Chicano pioneer poets whose productivity is prodigious is Rafael Jesús González from the San Francisco Bay Area but originally from El Paso, Texas. While his poems have appeared in countless reviews, journals, and anthologies he has produced only one tome *El Hacedor de Juegos* (1977). Many of the Chicano novelists, short-story writers, and literary non-fictionists (prose) also publish individual poems here and there, no books or chapbooks.

In drama and theater, Carlos Morton is still the most productive Chicano playwright, though a crop of Chicano playwrights have emerged as scriptwriters and directors for film and television, among them Jesús Treviño (*Raíces de Sangre*, film, 1976), Octavio Solís (*Man in the Flesh*, play, 1988), and Josefina López (*Real Women Have Curves*, play, 2002). No Chicano Neil Simon looms in the wings, though a plethora of Chicano actors now appear on screens.

Trends and the Future of Mexican American Literature

Two trends are discernable in Mexican American literature at the moment: (1) the mnemonic impulse generating scores of memoirs, autobiographies, and biographies like *Capirotada: A Nogales Memoir* by Alberto Ríos, 1999; *Thirteen Senses: A Memoir* by Víctor Villaseñor, 2001; *Man of Aztlán: A Biography of Rudolfo Anaya* by Abelardo Baeza, 2001; and (2) works like Denise Chávez's *Loving Pedro Infante* (2001) that deal more explicitly with borderland themes, locales, and issues. There is a growing corollary trend in works of social and literary history and criticism. It's in this corollary trend that I sense the vulnerability of Mexican American literature. Current critical analysis of Mexican American literature seeks to validate its presence and legitimacy by subjecting it to critical templates of other literatures or esoteric formulas not engendered from Mexican American literature. When Chicano literature emerged from the cauldron of Chicano nationalism in the 60s there was an expectation on the part of Chicano writers and critics that Chicano literature would develop *sui generis* an esthetic and criticism uniquely Chicano. In other words, Chicano literature would be what

Chicanos said it was, not what others said it was. Chicanos would validate their own texts. What has emerged in Chicano literary studies is a critical elitism that judges Chicano literature in terms of over-arching strictures advanced by literary theoreticians like Derrida, Foucalt, DeMan, Bhabha, et al, a new form of Edward Said's orientalism but now practiced by Chicano/a scholars and critics unaware they are aiding in their own literary oppression.

My hope for Chicano literature today, as it was 30 years ago, is its integration into the body of American literature. About those early aspirations of mine for Chicano literature, José Aranda, Jr. writes: "[Ortego] foresaw what would become by the 1990s, a whole industry from editors to academic scholarship redefining 'American literature as a fabric woven not exclusively on the Atlantic frontier by the descendants of New England Puritans and southern Cavaliers'. . . Ortego imagined the day this politically awakened ethnic group would participate more directly in the nationalist revision of American literature and culture. Ortego's generation of Chicano/a scholars thus fashioned a literary history faithful to a broad Chicano social politic" (*When We Arrive: A New Literary History of Mexican America*, 2005: 59).

I still think that revision of American literature is an important objective, though it's no longer as pressing as it once was despite the fact that not long ago I received a desk copy of an anthology purporting to be *The American Tradition in Literature* from McGraw Hill. It's a text of some 2300 pages. It seems to reflect the diversity of the American mosaic with the exception of Mexican Americans. Not till page 2199 do we see a Hispanic writer, Isabel Allende, a Chilean who now lives and writes in the United States. This is the editorial myopia so prevalent in mainstream presses: they don't see the distinctions among Hispanics. This is not to depreciate Isabel Allende's art but she is not a Mexican American and for the editors of the McGraw Hill anthology to offer her as the token U.S. Hispanic is tantamount to offering Chinua Achebe as the token African American.

The most disturbing development in Mexican American literature is the divide that distinguishes Chicana literature from Chicano literature. That divide was precipitated, of course, by Chicanos in the early days of the Chicano Renaissance when Chicanas were excluded from the initial literary burst—not all of them, but the disparity was evident. The backlash was inevitable. To tell their stories, Chicanas rallied around the rubric of Chicana literature. The strategy was effective. By the 1990s Chicana writers had so revitalized Mexican American literature that by the end of the decade they eclipsed their male counterparts and reignited the smoldering fire of the literary renaissance of the 60s and 70s, pushing its spike to an apogee surpassing the pioneer Chicano writers, a spike still sustained and climbing. It seems to me the future of Chicano/a literature lies in the hands of Chicanas whose current productivity is prodigious. But the situation creates a bifurcation that keeps the two strands of Chicano/a literature identifiably separate and confounds presentation. Despite cooperative efforts in the field, the division poses considerations not only for teaching the conspectus of Chicano/a literature vis-a-vis texts but for developing an integrated perspective of the field that enfolds the bifurcation. This is not an insurmountable task but it will require genuine intra-ethnic deliberations to establish a historical baseline for Mexican American literature that recognizes and acknowledges both Chicano and Chicana writers as *trabajadores de la raza*. In the film *The Dark Crystal*, wholeness embraces all the parts.

Chicano literature has transcended the bounds of American literature. It is studied in Paris, Munich, Rome, Moscow, and Mexico City. It is part of a new world order in which the Eurocentric view of literary canon is being scrutinized for its relevance to non-European-based literatures.

This is a critical juncture for Chicano literature. No longer necessary now is the need to juxtapose Chicano text and countertext, no need to identify the enemy, praise the people and promote the revolution. Chicano texts must manifestly stand on their own—not for the benefit of Anglo mainstream readers but for the benefit of Chicano readers with whom Chicano literature has a pact of long-standing. For it is Chicano literature, after all, whose responsibility it is to proffer the verities of Chicano life to Chicano readers and, ultimately, to a universal audience.

There are many Chicanos who argue that Chicano literature is so much of a piece that it has a distinctive center of gravity as well as its own ground of being and, therefore, its own esthetic. There are norms and patterns in Chicano writing that are common to mainstream American literature and to world literature while at the same time different. Not because of innate Chicano characteristics but because Chicano writers, by and large, have emerged from a distinctive group experience in the United States.

This is not to say that that experience is uniquely different. Most writers, I daresay, have emerged from comparable group experiences: Jewish writers, Black writers, and others. While each group experience may be comparable (and thus not unique), the experiences of each group are different. For instance, Jews have not been slaves in the United States nor did their ancestors lose a war to the United States. Blacks have not suffered religious pogroms in the United States nor have they been prohibited from speaking their home language in the schools. Yet Jews, Blacks, and Chicanos have suffered outrageous bigotry and discrimination in the United States. But that is not enough to say that their group experiences have been the same.

Chicano readers have come to understand intellectually what they knew all along intuitively: that Chicano literature is not value-free; that language and culture—what Taine called *moment, race, and milieu*—are key factors in literary (cultural) production. The Anglo American mainstream lost sight of that, believing that its appointed mission was to pass on to generation after generation of Americans of all colors the "truths" embedded in the literary works of the Western Tradition: what is fitting for us is fitting for them. Thomas Macaulay's words about the literature of India and Arabia reverberate in our consciousness as words about black and Chicano literature spoken by or subscribed to by white heirs of Macaulay's literary imperialism:

> I have no knowledge of either Sanskrit or Arabis, but I have done what I could to form a correct estimate of their value. I have read translations of the most celebrated Arabic and Sanskrit works. I have conversed both here and at home, with men distinguished by their proficiency in the Eastern tongues. I am quite ready to take the oriental learning at the valuation of the orientalists themselves. I have never found one among them who could deny that single shelf of a good European library was worth the whole native literature of India and Arabia. The intrinsic superiority of the Western literature is indeed fully admitted by those members of the committee who support the oriental plan of education . . . It is, I believe, no exaggeration to say that all the historical information which has been collected in the Sanskrit language is less valuable than what may be found in the paltry abridgements used at preparatory schools in England. (*Selected Writings*, 1972: 241).

The distinguished men identified by Macaulay as proficient in the Eastern tongues were non-Easterners. The Orientalists were non-Oriental, as Edward Said has pointed out. They were all English, expounding on the Eastern and the Oriental from the perspective of British imperialism.

The import of this perspective is that, with the exception of the Heath Anthology of American Literature, in the United States information about the literary accomplishments of Mexican Americans has been nil in literary texts. Like Macaulay's non-Easterners and non-Orientals, editors and writers of American literary texts have excluded and marginalized the literary achievements of Mexican Americans, first, and Chicanos, later, for reasons ranging from jingoism and racism to ignorance, disdain, and imperialism.

Epilog

Much research remains to be undertaken in Mexican American letters. For example, there is yet no comprehensive study of the Mexican American press or Mexican American journalists, showing their contributions to the development of Mexican American thought. My role in that area was the 10 year stint I put in *La Luz* magazine from 1972 to 1982 as Associate Publisher. At its peak, *La Luz* (first national Hispanic public affairs magazine in

English published in Denver) reached a readership of 500,000. Our editorial aim was to represent the diversity that made up Hispanics in the United States. When Dan Valdés, founder and publisher died in 1982 I withdrew from the enterprise. I went on to be Editor-in-Chief and Publisher of the *National Hispanic Reporter* from 1983 to 1992, first national Hispanic newspaper in English published in Washington, DC. Again, our aim was to represent the diversity of American Hispanics. There are many Hispanic publications in the United States now but so many of them lack the bite of their activist predecessors as they paddle to stay afloat in the Anglo mainstream. Only *Hispanic Link*, a weekly newsletter out of Washington, DC continues the journalistic tradition of Hispanic representation.

But the still greater work remaining is the reconstruction of American literary history. For only then will the literature of *los de abajo* (the marginalized) be available for all Americans and the world. In 1973, José Carrasco and I argued for that reconstruction in our piece "Chicanos and American Literature" published in *Searching for America* by the National Council of Teachers of English. What I marvel at today is how much each generation of Mexican Americans progresses because of the work of the previous generation. The panorama of Mexican American literature gives me hope.

Notes

This work includes some commentary that also appears in "The Labyrinth and the Minotaur" by the author published in *Aztlán*, Spring 2001.

The absence of some Mexican American writers herein does not mean their works are not worthy of inclusion or discussion. There are many Mexican Americans who have contributed significantly to Mexican American letters mention of whom was a question of length limitations for this presentation. Most of the authors cited have produced considerably more works than cited.

Chicana Literature from a
Chicana Feminist Perspective

Yvonne Yarbro-Bejarano

What are the implications of a Chicana feminist literary criticism? The existence of a Chicana feminist literary criticism implies the existence, first of all, of a tradition or body of texts by Chicana writers, which in turn implies the existence of a community of Chicanas and ideally of a Chicana feminist political movement. In other words, I do not see the development and application of a Chicana feminist literary criticism as an academic exercise. Like white feminism, Chicana feminism originates in the community and on the streets as political activism to end the oppression of women. This political movement is inseparable from the historical experience of Chicanos in this country since 1848, an experience marked by economic exploitation as a class and systematic racial, social and linguistic discrimination designed to keep Chicanos at the bottom as a reserve pool of cheap labor.

Within this collective experience, the facts and figures concerning Chicanas' education, employment categories and income levels clearly delineate the major areas of struggle for Chicana feminist movement.[1] There have always been Chicanas involved in political activism aimed at the specific situation of Chicanas as working-class women of color, objectified by economic exploitation and discrimination. Lucy González Parsons, the Liga Femenil Mexicanista, Dolores Hernández, Emma Tenayuca, the miners' wives in the strike in Santa Rita, New Mexico, in the early 50s, Alicia Escalante and many, many more—these names evoke community, Chicanas who have laid the groundwork for a contemporary movement.

The Chicana feminist critic, then, does not work in isolation, alone with her texts and word processor, typewriter or pad and pencil. She is a Chicana-identified critic, alert to the relationships between her work and the political situation of all Chicanas.[2] The exclusion of Chicanas from literary authority is intimately linked to the exclusion of Chicanas from other kinds of power monopolized by privileged white males. Their struggle to appropriate the "I" of literary discourse relates to their struggle for empowerment in the economic, social and political spheres.

The term "Chicana feminist perspective" also implies certain similarities with and differences from either an exclusively "feminist" or "Chicano" perspective. While sharing with the feminist perspective an analysis of questions of gender and sexuality, there are important differences between a Chicana perspective and the mainstream feminist one with regard to issues of race, culture and class. The Chicano perspective, while incorporating these important facets of race, culture and class, has traditionally neglected issues of gender and sexuality. The Chicana feminist is confronted with a dilemma, caught between two perspectives which appeal strongly to different aspects of her experience. In 1981, the publication of *This Bridge Called My Back* documented the rage and frustration of women of color with the white women's movement, not only for the racism, the tokenism, the exclusion and invisibility of women of color, but also for ignoring the issues of working-class women of color (such as forced sterilization).[3] The creative way out of this dilemma is the development of a Chicana feminism in coalition with other women of color dedicated to the definition of a feminism which would address the specific situation of working-class women of color who do not belong to the dominant culture. While recognizing her Chicana cultural identity and affirming her solidarity with all Chicanos and other Third World men and women to combat racial and economic oppression, the Chicana feminist also spearheads a critique of the destructive aspects of her culture's definition of gender roles. This critique targets heterosexist as well as patriarchal prejudice. Above all, Chicana feminism as a political movement depends on the love of Chicanas for themselves and each other as Chicanas.

Perhaps the most important principle of Chicana feminist criticism is the realization that the Chicana's experience as a woman is inextricable from her experience as a member of an oppressed working-class racial minority and a culture which is not the dominant culture. Her task is to show how in works by Chicanas, elements of gender, race, culture and class coalesce. The very term "Chicana" or "mestiza" communicates the multiple connotations of color and femaleness, as well as historical adumbrations of class and cultural membership within the economic structure and dominant culture of the United States. While this may seem painfully obvious, the assertion of this project in Chicana writing is crucial in combatting the tendency in both white feminist and Chicano discourse to see these elements as mutually exclusive. By asserting herself as Chicana or *mestiza*, the Chicana confronts the damaging fragmentation of her identity into component parts at war with each other. In their critique of the "woman's voice" of white feminist theory, María C. Lugones and Elizabeth V. Spelman suggest that being invited "to speak about being 'women' . . . in distinction from speaking about being Hispana, Black, Jewish, working-class, etc." is an invitation to silence.[4] The Chicana-identified critic also focuses on texts by Chicanas that involve a dual process of self-definition and building community with other Chicanas. In these works, Chicanas are the subjects of the representations, and often relationships between women form their crucial axes. In the 70s and especially the 80s, their works explore the full spectrum of Chicanas' bonds with Chicanas, including lesbianism. The process of self-definition involves what Black critic bell hooks calls moving from the margin to the center.[5] White male writers take for granted the assumption of the subject role to explore and understand self. The fact that Chicanas may tell stories about themselves and other Chicanas challenges the dominant male concepts of cultural ownership and literary authority. In telling these stories, Chicanas reject the dominant culture's definition of what a Chicana is. In writing, they refuse the objectification imposed by gender roles and racial and economic exploitation.

Chicana writers must overcome external, material obstacles to writing, such as limited access to literacy and the means of literary production, and finding time and leisure to write, given the battle for economic survival. But they must also overcome the internalization of the dominant society's definition of women of color. As Black writer Hattie Gossett phrases it, "who told you anybody wants to hear from you? you ain't nothing but a black woman!"[6] In her essay "Speaking in Tongues: A Letter to Third World Women Writers," Gloria Anzaldúa affirms that they must draw power from the very conditions that excluded them from writing in the first place, and write from what she calls the deep core of their identity as working-class women of color who belong to a culture other than the dominant one.[7]

By delving into this deep core, the Chicana writer finds that the self she seeks to define and love is not merely an individual self, but a collective one. In other words, the power, the permission, the authority to tell stories about herself and other Chicanas comes from her cultural, racial/ethnic and linguistic community. This community includes the historical experience of oppression as well as literary tradition. In spite of their material conditions, Chicanas have been writing and telling their stories for over a century. The Chicana writer derives literary authority from the oral tradition of her community, which in turn empowers her to commit her stories to writing.

Since this specific experience has been traditionally excluded from literary representation, it is not surprising that writing that explores the Chicana-as-subject is often accompanied by formal and linguistic innovation. In her essay "Speaking in Tongues," Anzaldúa stresses the need for women of color writers to find their authentic voice, to resist "making it" by becoming less different, to cultivate their differences and their tongues of fire to write about their personal and collective experience as Chicanas (166). The search is for a language that consciously opposes the dominant culture. Poet Cherríe Moraga has written: "I lack language. / The language to clarify / my resistance to the literate. / Words are a war to me. / They threaten my family." This search for an authentic language may include the fear of incomprehensibility, as the poem goes on to articulate: "To gain the word / to describe the loss / I risk losing everything. / I may create a monster . . . / her voice in the distance / unintelligible illiterate. / These are the monster's words."[8] "Visions of Mexico . . . ," by poet Lorna Dee Cervantes, also speaks of the urgent need to dominate the written word in order to smash stereotypes and rewrite history from the perspective of the oppressed:

> *"there are songs in my head I could sing to you*
> *songs that could drone away*
> *all the mariachi bands you thought you ever heard*
> *songs that could tell you what I know*
> *or have learned from my people*
> *but for that I need words*
> *simple black nymphs between white sheets of paper*
> *obedient words obligatory words words I steal*
> *in the dark when no one can hear me."*[9]

As evidenced by the poems quoted above by Moraga and Cervantes, the theme of writing itself may appear as mediator between individual and collective identity in works by Chicanas.

Writing is central to Sandra Cisneros' work of fiction *The House on Mango Street.*[10] *Mango St.* and Helena María Viramontes' collection of stories *Moths*,[11] are innovative in opposite directions—*Moths* characterized by formal experimentation, *Mango St.* by a deceptively simple, accessible style and structure. The short sections that make up this slim novel, *Mango St.*, are marvels of poetic language that capture a young girl's vision of herself and the world she lives in. Though young, Esperanza is painfully aware of the racial and economic oppression her community suffers, but it is the fate of the women in her *barrio* that has the most profound impact on her, especially as she begins to develop sexually and learns that the same fate might be hers. Esperanza gathers strength from the experience of these women to reject the imposition of rigid gender roles predetermined for her by her culture. Her escape is linked in the text to education and above all to writing. Besides finding her path to self-definition through the women she sees victimized, Esperanza also has positive models who encourage her interest in studying and writing. At the end of the book, Esperanza's journey towards independence merges two central themes, that of writing and a house of her own: "a house as quiet as snow, a space for myself to go, clean as paper before the poem" (100).[12]

Esperanza's rejection of woman's place in the culture involves not only writing but leaving the barrio, raising problematic issues of changing class:

> I put it down on paper and then the ghost does not ache so much. I write it down and Mango says goodbye sometimes. She does not hold me with both arms. She sets me free. One day I will pack my bags of books and paper. One day I will say goodbye to Mango. I am too strong for her to keep me here forever. One day I will go away. Friends and neighbors will say, what happened to Esperanza? Where did she go with all those books and paper? Why did she march so far away? (101–02)

But Esperanza ends the book with the promise to return: "They will not know I have gone away to come back. For the ones I left behind. For the ones who cannot get out" (102).

The House on Mango St. captures the dialectic between self and community in Chicana writing. Esperanza finds her literary voice through her own cultural experience and that of other Chicanas. She seeks self-empowerment through writing, while recognizing her commitment to a community of Chicanas. Writing has been essential in connecting her with the power of women and her promise to pass down that power to other women is fulfilled by the writing and publication of the text itself.

Mango St. is not an isolated example of the importance of writing in Chicana literature. The *teatropoesía* piece *Tongues of Fire*, scripted by Barbara Brinson-Pineda in collaboration with Antonio Curiel (1981), broke new ground in focusing on the Chicana subject as writer, drawing from Anzaldúa's essay which gave the play its title. The text did not privilege one Chicana voice, but created a collective subject through the inclusion of many individual voices speaking to multiple facets of what it means to be Chicana. The tongues of fire of the Chicana writers in the play exposed oppression from without as well as from within the culture, denouncing exploitation and racism but also the subordination of Chicanas through their cultures rigid gender roles and negative attitudes towards female sexuality. Writing emerged as the medium for the definition of the individual subjectivity of the Chicana writer through the articulation of collective experience and identity.

In *The Mixquiahuala Letters*,[13] Ana Castillo plays with the conventions of the epistolary novel, undermining those conventions by inviting the reader to combine and recombine the individual letters in Cortázar fashion. At the same time, the epistolary form calls attention to the role of writing in sifting through and making sense of experience. The narrative voice not only engages in a process of self-exploration through writing, but the form of the writing-letters-foregrounds an explicit exchange with a reader to whom the writing is directed. The novel defines subjectivity in relation to another woman, and the bond between the two women further cemented by the epistolary examination of their relationship is as important as the exploration of self through writing.

In *Giving Up the Ghost*, Cherríe Moraga broke a twenty-year silence in the Chicano theater movement by placing Chicana lesbian sexuality center stage. The text explores the ways in which both lesbian and heterosexual Chicanas' sense of self as sexual beings has been affected by their culture's definitions of masculinity and femininity. The theme of writing emerges at the end of the play. Marisa's writing is both provoked and interrupted by her memories of Amalia and sexual desire, just as the text itself. Marisa's secular "confession" to the audience is the product of her need to exhume and examine her love for this woman and all women. The text presents both the failures and the promises of building community. Just before Marisa speaks of her "daydream[s] with pencil in . . . mouth," she articulates the need for "familia," redefined as women's community: "It's like making familia from scratch / each time all over again . . . with strangers / if I must. / If I must, I will."[14]

The love of Chicanas for themselves and each other is at the heart of Chicana writing, for without this love they could never make the courageous move to place Chicana subjectivity in the center of literary representation, or depict pivotal relationships among women past and present, or even obey the first audacious impulse to put pen to paper. Even as that act of necessity distances the Chicana writer from her oral tradition and not so literate sisters, the continuing commitment to the political situation of all Chicanas creates a community in which readers, critics and writers alike participate.[15]

Notes

1. Elizabeth Waldman, "Profile of the Chicana: A Statistical Fact Sheet," in *Mexican Women in the United States*, Eds. Adelaida del Castillo & Magdalena Mora (Los Angeles: Chicano Studies, U.C.L.A., 1980), 195–204.

2. My understanding of the similarities and differences between Black and Chicana feminist criticism is indebted to Barbara Smith's "Towards Black Feminist Criticism" (1977), reprinted in *The New Feminist Criticism*, Ed. Elaine Showalter (N.Y.: Pantheon, 1985), 168–85.

3. *This Bridge Called My Back. Writings by Radical Women of Color*, Eds. Cherríe Moraga & Gloria Anzaldúa (Watertown, Ma.: Persephone Press, 1981).

4. "Have We Got a Theory for You! Feminist Theory, Cultural Imperialism and the Demand for 'the Woman's Voice,'" *Women's Studies International Forum*, 6:6 (1983), 574.

5. *Feminist Theory: From Margin to Center* (Boston: South End Press, 1984).

6. *This Bridge Called My Back*, 175–76.

7. In *This Bridge*, 165–74.

8. "It's the Poverty," in Anzaldúa, *This Bridge*, 166.

9. *Emplumada* (Pittsburgh: University of Pittsburgh Press, 1981), 45–46.

10. *The House on Mango Street* (Houston: Arte Público Press, 1985).

11. *The Moths and Other Stories* (Houston: Arte Público Press, 1985).

12. Sonia Saldívar-Hull includes a discussion of *Mango St.* in "Shattering Silences: The Contemporary Chicana Writer," forthcoming in *Women and Words: Female Voices of Power and Poetry*, Ed. Beverly Stoelbe (University of Illinois Press).

13. (Binghamton, N.Y.: Bilingual Press, 1986).

14. (Los Angeles: West End Press, 1986), 58.

15. The concept of a "Black writing community" is developed by Hortense J. Spillers in "Cross-Currents, Discontinuities: Black Women's Fiction," in *Conjuring. Black Women, Fiction and Literary Tradition*, Eds. Marjorie Pryse and Hortense J. Spillers (Bloomington: Indiana University Press, 1985).

A Historical Overview/Update on the State of Chicano Art

George Vargas

Chicano Art as North American Art

Whether of a political or an art-for-art's-sake intent, Chicano art is a visual manifestation of Chicano society, serving the Chicano community and, increasingly, the broader American culture. It represents an American expression born from the unique social and political conditions that have motivated and confined Chicanos in their struggle to become accepted as Americans while maintaining allegiance to their sense of Mexicanness. Though commonly perceived as mural or protest art, Chicano art reflects a great range of techniques, media, and content. Today, Chicano artists communicate both political and personal statements, utilizing traditional artistic expressions, as well as new vehicles such as conceptual/performance art, film/video, and installation art.

Despite denial and prejudice, Chicano art does exist, as do Chicanos who increasingly are cultivating the arts to validate their dual identities as Americans who are proud of their Mexican heritage. José Narezo (art teacher/muralist/painter from Grand Rapids, Michigan), who migrated with his family from Anáhuac, Mexico, to work in the fields and factories of Michigan, embraces both Mexican and Chicano/American cultural identities. "I have been interested in the customs and traditions of my homeland. I feel that an artist must be aware of his roots in order to be more profound in making a visual statement."[1] Many of the most talented Chicano artists are unknown outside their communities. Their art will become more recognized when Chicanos themselves become accepted as a people and as Americans in the United States. Until that transformation occurs, Chicano art will not be accepted or understood in the mainstream art market.

This chapter organizes Chicano art into categories relating to role and purpose: art as a visual document or text, art as a political vehicle, and art as personal expression. (Remember that some artists may defy categorization, and this is true for Chicano artists, too.) It then looks at the history of Chicano art, underscoring the importance of the individual artist's creativity by exploring the lives, works, and ideas of seven contemporary Chicano artists who have diversely participated in the history of Chicano art. Thus, the present state of Chicano art will be examined, as well as speculation regarding its future.

This chapter hopes to stimulate dialogue, if not answer questions, regarding the development of Chicano art within a historical framework. What is the new face of Chicano art, and how is it different from its original identity? Why has Chicano creativity increased when the Chicano movement is practically nonexistent? Can revolutionary art exist without patronage to a political movement? What is the future of Chicano art? These are questions that both the artists and the community help the historian answer.

A Study of Chicano Art

New scholars in various fields have made recent contributions to our knowledge of the Chicano experience, beginning with the Spanish conquest through the Chicano Movimiento (a political civil rights movement born in the 1960s, in which the production of art was dedicated to the Chicano ideology of political resistance and cultural affirmation) and into recent years. With the inevitable crossover of Chicano culture into American popular culture, there is a need to further investigate and document Chicano creative expression. As we gain a visual literacy of the Chicano experience, we come to know the struggles and successes of Chicanos as Americans and to learn more about the rich tapestry of the greater American experience.

The present Chicano experience of American culture is rich and broad, often transcending a strict political perspective and appealing to a more diverse audience. Chicano

"A Historical Overview/Update on the State of Chicano Art" by George Vargas from *Chicano Renaissance: Contemporary Cultural Trends* by David R. Maciel, Isidro D. Ortiz, and María Herrera-Sobek, editors. © 2000 The Arizona Board of Regents. Reprinted by permission of the University of Arizona Press.

artists have evolved, along with the Chicano community-at-large (largely blue-collar and white-collar urban dwellers), interpreting American history and constructing a new frontier through unique artistic forms that reflect their cultural reality of struggle, resistance, and change. Chicano art as a visual metaphor describes the continuity and change in the very nature of Chicano consciousness.

Chicanos represent a great and imminent change in the racial/ethnic balance of the United States. Demographic studies indicate that Mexican/ Chicano people, as the largest Latin(o) American population subgroup in the United States, soon will become a majority population, dramatically changing the face of U.S. society. By examining Chicano visual art, we can gain insight into the physical and psychological forces at play in the evolution of Chicano consciousness. We can then begin to get a personal portrait of a cultural environment that is regularly affected by both the United States and Mexico.

Chicano Art as Visual Text

Art can serve as a visual text or document for historians when other expressions of material culture are limited or yet undiscovered. As such, artworks are signposts of consciousness that reveal the condition of humanity in a particular culture at a particular time. In the case of Chicano history, the exhibition and preservation of Chicano art is critical because it represents one of the few accessible visual records documenting the Chicano presence in American history.

Chicano art speaks in a visual language that incorporates signs and symbols derived from the ancient civilizations of Mesoamerica and the more recent Mexican Mural Movement (which combined images of indigenous cultures with the political rhetoric of postrevolutionary Mexico) to create visual texts that portray the history, cultural heritage, memories, and visions of a contemporary Chicano culture. The artist constantly innovates or (re)invents meaning and form for traditional images by adding accents of his or her contemporary environment. Carlos Díaz (photographer/college teacher from Pontiac, Michigan) explains, "Through the photographic document [that pertains] to the common man/woman, my choice is to engage the issues rather than escape them. . . . Visual symbols and words serve as clues or signals offering a means by which the viewer can be a participant. The contents of these [cityscape photos] not only reflect upon the people who are its occupants but also speak about our species as a whole."[2]

Abstract thoughts and ideas come to life as creative expression through the artist, and in the case of Chicano art, its artists speak specifically from a Chicano perspective to address a specific Chicano state of mind or psychology. As cultural workers, Chicano artists facilitate the social production of art, constructing signposts in the form of murals, sculptures, and other visual expressions for the beautification and enlightenment of the local, national, and international community.

As one of the most accessible popular expressions, the murals of the Chicano art movement have their own fluid language of visual environmental communication that must integrate with the architectural environment as well as communicate its message. Murals give us information about the people who live and work in that environment, how they interact or communicate, and what they think. Some neighborhoods and regions have developed distinct mural styles or approaches that can be easily identified by the knowing eye.

Chicano Art as Political Art

Many Chicano artists of the sixties and seventies supported the Chicano Movimiento by creating posters and murals dealing with issues such as inequality in education and employment. Also a vital component of the People's Art Movement (a grassroots movement composed largely of women and people of color), Chicano art of this period interpreted the Chicano experience with a radical or militant political perspective. Marry Chicano artists identified with the revolutionary art of France and Russia and especially with the great art movement of social realism and intellectual expression of postrevolutionary Mexico. The posters and murals of this period portray popular Mexican and Chicano revolutionary heroes such as Emiliano Zapata and César Chávez and well-known Mexican icons such as Quetzalcoatl and the Virgen de Guadalupe, but the message was meant for Indians, *mestizos*[3] (meaning "mixed blood," which characterizes the racial/ethnic profile of Chicanos as well as Mexican and other Latin American populations), and poor and working class Americans of all colors.

Today, Chicano art no longer serves a formal political ideology, but it persists as a cultural agent of social change, especially in the continued production of mural art. The unresolved issues challenged by artists in the People's Art Movement and the Movimiento are still questioned by many Chicano artists who continue to speak out against persisting social injustice. San Francisco painter Ester Hernández. supports using the arts to promote activism: "As a Xicana-Azteca, I feel we must continue to use our creative skills to give strength to our political, cultural, and spiritual struggle. We must make visible our resistance to deception and the celebration of genocide."[4]

Chicano Art as Personal Expression

Chicano art, fortunately, also acts as a popular vehicle for self-expression and can be examined within the context of an emerging Chicano aesthetic that is independent of the Chicano political ideology associated with the sixties and seventies. A personal expression of the Chicano experience may have social or emotional impact without engaging in the polemics that accompany political art. Regarding a pure Chicano art of emotional appeal, José Narezo contends, "I believe that art needs to be pure in the sense that it comes from the emotions within."[5]

Personal expression in Chicano art is complex in style and iconography, serving as a mirror for the nature and condition of Chicano artists, reflecting their hopes, fears, political concerns, achievements, and aspirations. The diversity found in Chicano art can be traced to the growing range of Chicano artists, either trained or self-taught, who are exploring individual expression with innovative techniques and styles. Many Chicano artists possess a sharp universal sensibility, comparing their human ideas and feelings with other artists throughout the world.

A History of Chicano Art

Chicano visual art intertwines Mexican and American history into a unique historical perspective that, by its very nature, is political and therefore provocative because it challenges our preconceived notions about Chicanos. It chronicles the evolution of Chicano consciousness in a people who have had to survive as second-class citizens, outsiders living inside a rapidly changing American society. It interprets the life story of real Mexicans and Chicanos who, having lost land, language, and culture as consequences of the conquest, the U.S.-Mexican War, and the Mexican Revolution, nevertheless prevailed in American society. Chicano art portrays a people's cultural history within the context of a new American history.

Historical Background

In the 1960s Chicano art mass-communicated its unique perspective primarily through mural art, posters, and graffiti. It has since expanded its boundaries into virtually all forms of artistic expression. Regardless of style or time frame, Chicano artists draw from their *mestizaje*[6] (mixed culture or multicultural) experiences in synthesizing ideas and making artistic forms. Santa Barraza (painter/feminist living in Kingsville, Texas) exalts the mestizo as a powerful symbol of the people's revolution, liberation, and duality, representing a new hybrid:

> Chicanos identified with the peón mestizo of the Revolutionary Mexico of 1910 not only because of biological heritage, but also because of similar economic, working-class social status and political experience. The Chicanos utilized experiences from their history and art to create a unique culture of liberation, through which a language of expression resulting from the symbiosis of mainstream United States culture and traditional mestizo values was developed. . . . The mestizo is a manifestation of the merger of opposite forces, a duality. Allegorically, this new hybrid is the embodiment of the east and west, the conqueror and the conquered, the Christian and the pagan, capable of creating a pathway to equality and social justice for the world.[7]

Throughout its history, Chicano art has remained Chicano-oriented and people-oriented, affirming the existence of the Chicano culture and providing purpose and identity for the Chicano artist. No matter the decade, the concept of Chicano art has been balanced between political commentary, social content, and personal expressiveness.

Murals

Ideologically linked to the broader People's Art Movement, Chicano mural art was inspired by the Mexican Mural Movement (1920–30) that followed the Mexican Revolution (1910–17), and especially by Los Tres Grandes (The Big Three Mexican modernists, José Clemente Orozco, Diego Rivera, and David Alfaro Siqueiros, all of whom executed controversial murals in the United States). Themes of the government-sponsored Mexican murals (mostly painted in a traditional fresco medium) focused on a common people's historical perspective rather than a glorified perspective of the elite and rich. Associated with the school of social realism, the Mexican murals used a visual language of symbols and images easily read by the general public. No longer exclusive or academic, Mexican art was enlivened by a special accent of *mexicanidad*, celebrating the Mexican-ness of the people. These early Mexican muralists stimulated the creation of the Public Works of Art Project (Franklin D. Roosevelt's New Deal program initiated in 1933), which provided work for countless unemployed American artists while recording the idealism of the New Deal era on the walls of public buildings. Prior to this, mural art in the United States primarily had been controlled by private interests. The People's Art Movement of the 1960s revived America's interest in public art, but now it was more accessible and demystified a people's expression.

The creation of Chicano murals in the 1960s involved the active and eager participation of neighborhood artists and residents. They took political and social issues to the streets by painting their history and culture on public walls, thus reclaiming their immediate environment. Many of the earliest murals were produced on a shoestring budget independent of governmental funds, underscoring their revolutionary intent. Painted mostly in urban centers, such as Chicago, Denver, Detroit, El Paso, Los Angeles, San Antonio, San Diego, San Francisco, and Santa Fe, Chicano murals were invigorated by the civil rights, student, and women's rights movements; Chicano labor and politics; and the counterculture. Creativity became a metaphor for the freedom of personal and group expression guaranteed to all Americans, but often denied to women and people of color.

Early Chicano murals communicated contemporary themes of race, class, and ethnicity[8] that spoke specifically to the diverse Chicano experience, while addressing issues relevant to poor and working-class Americans of all colors. Depending heavily on figurative and representational painting styles easily read by the masses, Chicano muralists often combined visual elements found in early Mesoamerican history (to underscore indigenousness) with images of controversial figures from popular culture to represent current issues. In one of the earliest documented Chicano murals, Antonio Bernal's 1968 *Untitled* mural (located on the front of Teatro Campesino's office in Del Rey, California) adopted the recognizable narrative style of Mayan art (directly borrowing from the Mayan Bonampak mural cycle [c. 800 A.D.]) to portray a victory procession of symbolic Mexican revolutionary figures (La Adelita, Francisco Villa, and Emiliano Zapata) alongside American and Chicano civil rights leaders (Martin Luther King, Jr., and César Chávez). In 1975, José Gamaliel González led youth of Westtown, Chicago, in painting *Raza de Oro* (Race of Gold), which also utilized the form of a Mayan relief lintel (725 A.D.) from Yaxchilón to create a vision of the plumed serpent, symbolizing the common struggle of Chicanos as an emerging golden race, a new "people of the sun."

Like the early Mexican muralists, early Chicano artists symbolically repossessed the original home of the Mexico/Nahua Indians, Aztlán (the birthplace of the Aztecs, "People of the Sun"). The Indian became the symbol of the oppressed and of social consciousness, drawing diverse elements in the community to a common cause or shared American heritage. By painting their people's symbolic exodus, they hoped to reclaim a place of honor in the American landscape on behalf of dispossessed Mexicans and Chicanos, who at one time dominated much of the Mexican territory now known as the U.S. Southwest. In 1978, Martín Moreno's *Vibrations of a New Awakening* (Adrian, Michigan) combined Michigan state history with Aztec mythology to depict agricultural and industrial workers crucified and stripped of individual identity to the point of becoming androids. Upon "awakening," some workers escape exploitation and climb onto the back of the feathered serpent Quetzalcoatl, symbolizing a rebirth of consciousness for Indian and Chicano mestizo alike and a return to a common origin or land base.

Some Chicano artists (many from the working class) assumed the role of cultural worker, devoting their art to the Movimiento and the enlightenment and education of Chicano workers in recognition of their contributions to the economic development of American enterprise and industry. Chicano civil rights leaders and labor groups invited artists to support the Chicano revolution by creating a people's art that was reflective of *chicanismo* cultural values and the principles of self-identification and self-determination. Chicano murals and posters became the popular vehicles of mass communication that appealed to a ready-made audience created by the revolution. Muralists such as Moreno (who now lives in Phoenix, Arizona, where he creates murals, sculpture, and paintings) stressed the organic creative process rather than the end product,

inviting the community to participate with neighborhood artists: "The creation of murals has become a national artistic phenomenon. Thus . . . the creation of the mural is not a simple matter of applying paint to a dreary wall. But it is instead a process by which a muralist and the community are guided into communication with each other by the experience of working together. By leaving reflections of the community, [artists] are leaving a small part of themselves."[9]

As Chicano muralists began to study more varied forms of expression in world art, such as Renaissance and Byzantine mural art, more sophisticated and contemporary styles began to appear, such as classical representation, photo realism, expressionism, and abstraction. They also began to discover more permanent paint materials and advanced design and technologies.

Art Groups

Soon, Chicano art became a cause unto itself, an art *movimiento* calling for cultural equality for Chicano artists and urging mainstream artists to create works that were reflective of nonwestern styles using Mexican and Chicano sources.[10] Fortunately, the early history of Chicano art was being documented by emerging scholars of the time, such as Jacinto Quirarte and Raymond Barrio.[11]

Chicano murals appeared in urban centers throughout the United States during the late sixties and well into the seventies. In the early days, many artists were consumed with the immediate message in mural art and were not worried about receiving public funding or specialized art training. As time went by, artists began consolidating their efforts by organizing into mural groups that could provide training for aspiring young artists as well as seek local and federal funding for more ambitious projects. Additionally, some artists introduced the portable mural (moveable panels innovated by the Mexican muralists) to carry the visual message into otherwise-restricted or new spaces.

In the 1970s Chicano art groups arose throughout the nation to formalize various art theories and to concentrate their creative activities by working in mural groups or collectives such as Artes Guadalupanos de Aztlán in New Mexico; Mujeres Muralistas in San Francisco (one of the earliest Chicana mural groups); ASCO and Los Four (Charles Almaraz, Robert de la Rocha, Gilbert Luján, and Frank Romero) in California; Con Safo in San Antonio, Texas; Raza Art/Media Collective in Ann Arbor, Michigan; and the Association of Hispanic Arts in New York City. In addition, the Royal Chicano Air Force in Sacramento, Galería de la Raza in San Francisco, La Raza Graphic Center in San Antonio, and Self Help Graphics in Los Angeles promoted poster art/printmaking and its production. In the late 1970s, a network of these individual art groups came together in a national coalition of Hispanic organizations to encourage funding of minority arts by federal and state governments.

One of the most significant of the Chicano alternative art groups was ASCO (Spanish for "nausea" or "disgust"). Founded in 1972 in Los Angeles by Willie Herrón, Harry Gamboa, Jr., Gronk (born Gluglio Gronk Nicandro), and Patssi Valdez, the vanguard group experimented with numerous radical styles and new media, including visually striking social-commentary murals executed in abstract and expressionistic styles; alternative murals; street theater; film and video; and multimedia conceptual, performance, and installation art. Their murals extracted unlikely popular cultural elements from an urban environment to create new images and forms, ranging from the 1972 *Walking Mural* (a performance/alternative mural worn in public by ASCO members, see figure 1) to the 1979 *Black and White Mural* (which incorporated graffiti painted into the design by neighborhood youth). Despite harsh criticism, ASCO's daring brand of art was a sharp knife that cut boldly to create new Chicano urban expressions to delight new tastes in neosurrealism and vanguard art. According to Gronk, "That urban sensibility gave a hard core to our work. We did our work despite what some people said, 'It's [the] worst thing being done,' or '[T]hat's ugly!' But we continued our work. That was gumption. . . . We were not passive."[12]

Chicano artists in Chicago eventually aligned with non-Chicano artists, forming mural collectives or syndicates to expedite the support and production of murals through citywide mural projects. Murals most often were produced by multicultural community-oriented arts organizations, such as the Public Arts Workshop directed by Mark Rogovin and the Chicago Mural Group founded by Bill Walker (an African American artist who painted the earliest community murals in Chicago) and John Weber. Movimiento Artístico Chicano, a group of Chicano muralists, graphic artists, filmmakers, educators, and photographers, joined citywide efforts to celebrate art, not only in the Chicano community but throughout the city as well.

Posters and Prints as Graphic Art

The satirical newspaper illustrations of José Guadalupe Posada and Manuel Manilla, popular turn-of-the-century Mexican printmakers, inspired a longstanding tradition in Mexican graphic art and later Chicano graphic art. In 1937 the Taller de Gráfica Popular was formed by Leopoldo Méndez, Luis Arenal, and Pablo O'Higgins, a graphic arts collective whose purpose was to produce art devoted to social realism and to teach graphic techniques, both traditional and new. (Some members also were in the Mexican Mural Movement.) Borrowing directly from Posada, Diego Rivera, and Mexican photographer Agustín Casasola, Chicano artists reproduced Mexican revolutionary figures to serve as heroes of the Chicano movement as well. For instance, Casasola's famous photograph

Figure 1. ASCO members with *The Walking Mural.* From left: Patssi Valdez, Gronk, and Willie Herrón. Los Angeles, California, December 24, 1972. (Photograph by Harry Gamboa, Jr.)

of Zapata was copied by the United Farm workers (UFW) Graphic Center in a 1970 poster, with the declaration, "Viva la Revolución."

Early Chicano posters also were influenced by the bold, bright, and "flat" design characteristics of Cuban posters of the 1960s. In 1964, the Cuban postrevolutionary government began employing its artists to create posters of Castro and Ché Guevara as a form of popular propaganda. Later, when the government-owned film industry employed them to make movie posters, the artists began to experiment with psychedelic colors and designs found in the hippie movement, creating some of their most interesting work. America's walls and kiosks were thickly layered with Cuban-influenced posters containing images of heroes of the New Left counterculture such as Ché, Bob Dylan, Malcolm X, and Zapata.[13]

Printmaking is still a powerful medium because good-quality multiple copies can be produced at a reasonable cost, making it possible to get a visually striking message across to masses of people. Posters, usually linoleum-cut or wood-cut, silk-screen, or lithographic prints, allowed Chicano artists of the sixties and seventies to mass-produce affordable, portable art for an eager Chicano audience. Chicano posters and flyers announced important exhibitions, mural unveilngs, and rallies, and were distributed free or at a nominal charge.

Graffiti Art

Sharing the stage of public expression with murals and graphic arts, graffiti utilize a special sign language that resembles mysterious cult symbols or ancient petroglyphs. Historically, Chicano graffiti are linked to the *pachucos* (the Mexican American "zoot-suiters" of the 1930s and 1940s). Their *placa* (a distinctive calligraphic writing style), unusual tattoos, hand signs, and fashions reflected an alternative lifestyle of intense Mexican ethnic pride, whose influence still can be seen in contemporary gang graffiti. As part of the signage found in the urban landscape, graffiti act as pictographs, unique pictures representing a word, an idea, or a record in hieroglyphic symbols. Modernists such as Pablo Picasso and Jean Dubuffet were inspired by graffiti, as are Chicano artists such as Charles "Chaz" Bojórquez, John Valadez, José Gálvez, Antonio Pérez, and members of ASCO.

To those outside Chicano street culture, graffiti may appear as indecipherable scribbling at best, vandalism at worst. To insiders, graffiti are seen as individual acts of pride or protest, gang declarations of territory or challenge, and weapons in a class war. Regardless of the issue of "Is it art?" graffiti are a cheap medium that provide instant public communication for those in society who perceive themselves as powerless. For many rebellious elements in Chicano culture, graffiti are the only accessible medium to communicate with in the urban forum.

In the 1960s Chicano graffiti artists joined other youths in a visual assault against authority figures and slumlords. "Taggers" scrawled their spray-painted nicknames or "tags" on buildings, police cars, and subways as a demonstration of their bravado and anger. In the 1970s taggers began combining felt-tip markers with their spray-paint techniques, treating a bold new calligraphy affected by *cholo* (new Chicano street culture), hip-hop, and rap cultures. Latino culture crossed over into the black American experience, producing cultural hybrids in music, film, and public art and inspiring new voices in both cultures.

The Emergence of Chicana Art

With Chicano art heavily male-dominated, the emergence of a women's or Chicana art was nothing short of a miracle. Chicanas defined positive cultural identities that embraced the traditional elements in the Chicano community while asserting their womanhood with figures denoting empowerment, independence, and unity.

Early women artists who broke into a previously exclusive Chicano mural scene include Judith Baca, who organized the monumental historical project *The Great Wall of Los Angeles* (1976–84), and Yolanda M. López, who guided high-school girls in painting one of the first murals created by women at Chicano Park in San Diego, a "people's park" that was heavily decorated with mural art throughout the 1970s.

Chicanas used graphic art to focus on feminist concerns, perhaps because they could easily access printmaking to speak their minds with more artistic freedom than they could in the more male-dominated public mural arena. Chicanas produced challenging, exciting images of women that could be easily packaged and distributed to an emerging women's market and to other interested consumers. In 1979 Isabel Castro (Santa Monica, California) made a series of color photocopies entitled "Women Under Fire," which places a young Latina in the cross-hairs of a rifle's telescope to symbolize those Mexicanas/Chicanas who were involuntarily sterilized while undergoing childbirth at a Los Angeles hospital.

Many Chicanas, including Amalia Mesa-Bains (known for her altars), Carmen Lomas Garza (painter/printmaker), and Yreina Cervántez (muralist/painter), explored heroines such as the Virgen de Guadalupe, La Malinche (Hernán Cortés's Mexican Indian mistress and translator), and Frida Kahlo and used their images to illustrate a feminist perspective in Chicano history and contemporary culture. Artists Patssi Valdez (ASCO) and Kathy Vargas (Con Safo) experimented with multimedia installation, performance art, photo-collage, and other approaches to create new images of women in traditional and innovative spaces.

Individual Chicanas, struggling to gain greater exposure in a male-controlled art world, formed their own groups to produce art and promote feminist causes. Following the lead of Mujeres Muralistas in San Francisco, Las Mujeres Muralistas del Valle was organized in Fresno in the mid-1970s to paint community murals using a women's perspective. In 1977, Chicanas founded Mujeres Artísticas del Suroeste in Austin to represent Chicanas and Latinas from Austin, San Antonio, Laredo, and other cities in central and south Texas.

1980s: Expansion into the Contemporary Art Movement

By the 1980s, the features of Chicano art changed with the emerging "new" Chicanos, who were no longer largely poor or working class, but middle class, educated, economically mobile, and recognized consumers. Chicano artists expanded into new territories, investigating other artistic theories and media and organizing groups to address issues affecting the United States and Mexico as well as Latin American and Third/Fourth World countries. Chicano art in its new and often avant-garde forms was labeled "Nueva Onda" (New Wave art) and included conceptual and performance art, mixed-media sculpture and assemblage, video and filmmaking (rapidly becoming a popular medium of mass communication), and anti-art, to name a few of the more contemporary expressions. Houston photographer Guillermo Pulido documented his ritualized initiation into Incan Indian culture in an installation work. Gloria Maya (Oakland, California) ritualized her family's Christmas dinner in an assemblage of sculptures consisting of turkey bones, which acknowledge life by accepting death. Meanwhile, Chicana video/filmmakers Sylvia Morales, Lourdes Portillo, and Susan Racho were breaking into that male-dominated medium.

Artists continued using mural art as a popular medium of communication to the community and the larger society to promote Chicano culture, to correct cultural ignorance about Chicanos, and simply to beautify neighborhoods. For some artists the struggle to make murals turned into a struggle against institutional censorship. In the case of Los Angeles artist Barbara Carrasco, her *L.A. History—A Mexican Perspective* (a portable 16-by-80-foot mural that features the face of the artist, her braids interwoven with historical scenes and images of women and people of color, see figure 2) was censored by officials of the 1984 Summer Olympics in Los Angeles. They had charged that scenes depicting the internment of Japanese Americans during World War II and a mass lynching of Chinese workers in the late 1800s would insult Asian visitors. Even though Carrasco received letters from Asian Americans supporting her interpretation of their history, the officials would not budge, insisting that she whitewash the "offensive" areas of the work. Rather than compromise her mural, Carrasco found an alternative site to display her work.[14] She compared her mural controversy with that experienced by David Alfaro Siqueiros when he painted his fresco mural *Tropical America* (1932) in Los Angeles's Sonora Town (so-called because of its large Mexican population). It was whitewashed by city fathers, who were upset by an image of a crucified Mexican Indian/peón.[15]

At this time, Chicano art recognized (and sometimes rejected) the canons of postmodernism and yet supported the radical aspect of the vanguard, not refuting history, but (re)discovering it by inventing and constructing new art for a new society. While maintaining self-discovery and community contact with Chicano culture, Chicano artists tore down the stereotypical images of Chicano separatist rhetoric of the Movimiento in order to create space for new cultural images of Chicanos as Americans alive with new attitudes about themselves and their struggles. With the bonfire of protest from the sixties and seventies still smoldering, Chicano artists in the 1980s celebrated contemporary life (despite the setbacks suffered by women and people of color, the poor, and the middle-class during the years of the Reagan administration), proudly affirming their Mexican roots while embracing their new American identity.

Chicano artists started crossing over into new commercial art markets. Ester Hernández had her popular 1982 "Sun Mad Raisins" silk-screen (an image of a skeleton "Sun Maid" wearing a sun bonnet and holding a basket of grapes) printed on postcards and T-shirts in an effort to educate a larger audience (especially targeting children and women) about the inherent dangers of chemical insecticides to both farmworkers and consumers. In 1986, painter Nora Mendoza (born in Texas, currently living in

Michigan) was commissioned by César Chávez to produce a series of colorful greeting cards honoring migrant workers and their families that later were exhibited at the George Mcaney Labor Center in Silver Springs, Maryland.

After the heyday of Chicano politics in the sixties and seventies, Chicano graphic artists were implementing new visions without compromising the ongoing Chicano struggle. In 1988–89, the Wight Gallery at UCLA, along with Self Help Graphics of Los Angeles, organized the National Chicano Screenprint Taller (funded by the Metropolitan Life Foundation). The collection of silk-screen prints displays unexpected humor, along with typical commentary. The common thread of the complex Chicano experience can easily be discovered in this collection of contemporary works. Larry Yáñez's "Cocina Jaiteca" indulges the false pride of many Latina housewives: a "high-tech" *cocina* (kitchen) with an old-fashioned refrigerator, stove, etc. Ester Hernández underscores feminist pride in "La Ofrenda," which pictures a tattoo of the Virgen de Guadalupe on the bare back of a confident young Chicana with a radical short hairstyle. Carlotta Espinoza demonstrates against institutionalized racism and oppression in "Broken Treaties," symbolized by a nude Chicana who is trapped in a web made of barbed wire and her own hair. She holds a dove in her hand (like a Greek kore statue), while behind her, the colors of the U.S. flag run and fade away.

Chicano art also became connected with a healthy trend toward pluralism/multiculturalism in American art. Chicano artists began a dialogue with other American artists of color and immigrants from Latin America and Asia, many of whom were in exile from tyranny in their native lands.[16] Chicano artists increasingly related to the experience of Latin American artists, who were also searching for a new identity and a renewed sense of historical presence in their American environment. In 1981 the Museum of Modern Art at the Institute of Fine Arts in Mexico City published a special issue of *Artes Visuales* that reported an update of Chicano visual arts as represented by artists who were "exploring new possibilities, trying to escape imposed clichés . . . to produce art at the margin of what is officially acceptable."[17] The Mexican publication also stressed the continuation of a dialogue between Chicano artists and those from Latin America to better conceptualize "the role of art in politics, and politics in art."[18]

Individual Chicano artists who exemplified the spirit of a new wave or neo-Chicano art included performance/installation artist and photographer Jerry Dreva (Los Angeles), who organized a series of performance events (including tattooing his body) to celebrate the two-hundredth anniversary of the founding of Los Angeles; performance/body artist Sylvia Salazar Simpson (born in Santa Fe), who wore a headdress of living green plants and flowers populated by earthworms in her piece entitled "Antes/Before"; computer/video artist René Yáñez (San Francisco), who

Figure 2. Barbara Carrasco, *L.A. History—A Mexican Perspective* (1981–83). Mural located in Los Angeles, California. (Photograph by Barbara Carrasco.)

explored three-dimensional animation in hologram art in "Pachuco," about a young girl flirting with a *pachuco*; multimedia artist Jack Vargas (born in Santa Paula, California), who, in *Breakfast with Evaristo Altamirano*, projects video images alongside text, inventing new "Chicano-speak" words such as "Jiffy Beanzales" and "Mexi-Queen."

Although many new artists appeared on the scene, some drifted away and others matured, moving into new avenues. The founding members of ASCO, for example, headed down different artistic paths. By 1987, they no longer worked together as a group, leaving a prominent gap in Chicano art. Looking historically at the face of Chicano art, ASCO was the "jawline, because we could take the punches!"[19] Gronk explains. With ASCO now dismantled, according to Gamboa, "[t]here was no oasis in the urban desert."[20]

1990s: The Era of New Chicano Art

That Chicano art has survived into the 1990s should not be a surprise, given the increase in the Chicano population and its marked socioeconomic impact on the United States. As America rediscovers itself, it also discovers new Chicano art, despite its limited inclusion in museums. In the 1960s Chicano art primarily was aimed at Chicanos and other oppressed people, but in the 1990s its appeal extended to the broader American audience. Chicano artists who once condemned or boycotted the consumption of grapes, lettuce, and wine have crossed over into the mainstream graphic arts/advertising industry. Carmen Lomas Garza's popular illustrations of Chicano family life now appear in full-page magazine advertisements sponsored by Anheuser-Busch and Budweiser beer distributors. A photographic image by Gronk has been reproduced in an advertisement for the California State Lottery. The crossover of some Chicano artists into the corporate business world is significant, underscoring the acceptance of Chicanos in mainstream society.

New Chicano art signifies a new reality for Chicanos. Performance artist Rubén Guevara represents the new Chicano orientation of reality:

> I am born of magic, fire, water, earth, wind, bullets, blood, and betrayal: Grandson of Hernán Cortés and Malintzin, La Malinche un hijo de la chingada a child of Conquest. . . . My name is Xicanoatl. . . . I am a post-quincentennial cultural anti-hero—a Chicano Xicano concept: An intergalactic, interdimensional, intercultural, interdisciplinary, performance Mestizo. A powerful blend Arabian-Spain, with the mystery of Africa and Asia, fused with the mysticism of Native America. Indigenous mysticism merging with modern technology, creating a new man, a new woman, a new reality.[21]

Contemporary Chicano art mirrors the new Chicano psychology. Yes, racism and prejudice still exist, yet Chicanos themselves must invent a new paradigm of empowerment to liberate both themselves and the oppressor. As facilitators and mediators, Chicano artists today offer a new mirror of creative transformation to replace the old mirror of oppression. Without a doubt, Chicano art is still grounded in the traditions of social commentary, thriving in Chicano urban centers as an art of conscience and activism; but now when Americans see contemporary Chicano art, they appreciate it as a new American expression without disputing the quality,[22] intent, or market value of the work. More fluid, organic, multifaceted, and multicultural, Chicano art today describes a fresh worldview of unlimited possibilities and is less strictly nationalistic.

Still defined by a history and an urban iconography that are distinctly Chicano in spirit and content, Chicano art also represents American popular art. It is infused with a strong sense of pluralism, speaking to a broader cross-section of American culture as Chicanos themselves discover the shared American dream and legacy. Increasingly, Chicano art also is becoming an important part of multicultural education as more Chicano teachers and students expect to see a reflection of their presence in U.S. society. Artists/teachers such as Diana Alva (mixed-media artist from Detroit, Michigan) depend on art to educate, enlighten, and empower Chicano children. Alva asserts, "When a child learns that he or she can transform a piece of paper into something beautiful, or mold a mound of clay into an object of his/her choice, then that child can learn to have control over even bigger things, such as one's life."[23] Currently, this new model in Chicano art is open and ready for a new definition, role, and purpose to be applied by individual artists and their communities. However, this open model is inevitably tied to the Chicano's dual cultural identity as it cultivates a universal sensibility or cosmic view. In the words of painter/ceramist Gloria Osuna Pérez (El Paso), "The reality of Mexican and Chicano communities, wherever they may be, is the theme for my work. I show people and their lives, emphasizing the positive, seeking the external reality, enlarging the reality into a universal scale that invites a participation with the details. From a particular individual I fictionalize an abstract image that reaches into the heart of the viewer. My supra portraits attempt to transcend the impersonal anonymity of humanity, to invite the outsider to come and partake of our humanity."[24]

Chicano artists in the vanguard continually innovate ways to communicate with their old and new audiences. Ingenious video artists such as Gamboa and Juan Garza are inventing new visual texts to interpret the new Chicano reality by experimenting with film, video, and computer technologies for mass communication.

Today's Chicano graphic art is more sophisticated and is being produced by both established and emerging artists. Posters include familiar subjects, new images of the contemporary Chicano lifestyle, and crossovers of pop cultural influences such as graffiti art and street culture. A spectrum of technologies is used, from the traditional to more recent innovations such as photo silk-screen, photocopy, and computer graphics. Despite technological advancements that encourage individual expression, collectives or workshops are still in popular demand, perpetuating the communal spirit of the Mexican graphic art tradition. As in the past, Chicano posters and prints are affordable for individuals, private collectors, and museums alike, and can be easily stored and exhibited.

Certainly, printmaking in the 1990s prospers under mature artists such as Rupert García, Luis Jiménez, Carmen Lomas Garza, Martín Moreno, José Narezo, and Patssi Valdez. The 1995 touring exhibition "Chicano Connection" presented a group vision of diverse and unfolding identities in the Chicano community and the world.[25] The collection of silk-screen prints addresses varied artistic interests and themes. Pat Gómez's "War Stories" places a family narrative in a thematic setting, beautifully framing it with roses and sacred hearts. Mario Calvano's "Portrait with Text" presents a human figure with indirect references to Columbus and the conquest, forcing the viewer to read between the lines regarding personal and political realities.

According to purists, graffiti art in the 1990s is distinguished by the exclusive use of cans of spray paint, although some graffiti artists also explore the use of spray guns and air compressors. Graffiti artists (many of whom are former taggers) have attempted to elevate graffiti, also known as aerosol art or "spray-fiti," to a popular and valid creative expression by channeling antisocial behavior into positive architectural decoration and community comment. New graffiti artists utilize fast-drying, longer-lasting paint and brighter colors to create vivid images protesting street gangs and other social ills, paying tribute to murdered or lost youth or just inventing tags for fun. Disavowing "studio graffiti" and destructive tagging, new graffiti artists organize competitions to encourage the "good stuff"—a controlled, tight, and original script that identifies the artist's character, community, and even region. Today, some graffiti artists enter public mural competitions.

With Chicanos slowly entering into mainstream art, the overall acceptance of Chicano art in the 1990s has only slightly improved. Currently, only a handful of galleries, collectors, historians, and museums accept it as a vital part of contemporary expression. Nonetheless, the success of the touring "Chicano Art: Resistance and Affirmation" (CARA) exhibition indicates the American public's growing interest in Chicano art. New attendance records were set during the 1990–93 tour at the sponsoring museums in Albuquerque, Denver, El Paso, Fresno, Los Angeles, New York City, San Antonio, and Tucson. Excited crowds viewed a kaleidoscopic survey of Chicano art from 1965–85, displayed within a historical framework.[26] The vol-

ume and diversity of the collection were awesome, with works including paintings, graphic prints, photographs, sculptures, installations, *altarcitos* (altar installations), graffiti-inspired art, and hologram art by a multitude of artists from all walks of life. According to Gaspar Enríquez (El Paso artist included in the exhibit who was instrumental in bringing it to El Paso), CARA's success was based on the fact that such a display of Chicano art and history never had been assembled before and that community involvement was emphasized at all exhibition sites.

In El Paso, CARA was introduced to new audiences (many of whom lived in the city but had never set foot in the El Paso Art Museum) by a parade (that included mariachi bands, low-riders, high-school bands, Chicano labor groups, and Mexican immigration support organizations) and by a series of community events (lectures, films, and museum tours, for example) on Chicano art. For some viewers, the art depicted the familiar, for others, the unfamiliar and fantastic, but it was all reflective of the Chicano experience and was stimulating for all viewers, regardless of their artistic or cultural orientation.

Speaking for a major ethnic group that has been marginalized in society and ignored in cultural institutions, CARA's high impact across the country was twofold: CARA validated Chicano history and culture for many Chicanos, confirming a sense of group identity while inspiring youth to rediscover their roots; and it enlightened other Americans about Chicanos through a sampling of their art, unveiling a rich, diverse, and often spontaneous American expression.

The popularity of CARA with the U.S. museum establishment demonstrated this group's interest in Chicano art as well. The community's intense involvement in CARA underscored the emerging role of museums in educational outreach to a community that increasingly wants to see exhibits that reflect its racial/ethnic makeup. For some museum staffs, CARA proved to be both a rich learning process and a challenging professional experience, from mounting the show to organizing the numerous tours and educational programs. Additionally, placing Chicano art within a museum environment made it more palatable for some critics to digest and made it easier to dismiss the intense messages of social protest as outdated issues. If the huge success rates at sponsoring museums are indicators of CARA's social acceptance, Chicano art has indeed "arrived."

Although Chicano art means street culture or community expression for many artists, for others it stands for vanguard thought and form, confronting old ideas with a cutting-edge visual art. Brief biographies on seven such cutting-edge artists who have experienced and participated in the Chicano art movement from different vantage points follows. These selected artists often use interdisciplinary, multicultural approaches that cross over into indigenous and world cultures, expanding the definition of "community." The mixing of ethnic groups and crossover influences often results in never-before-seen forms and symbols that defy conventional description. These artists are part of the vanguard in Chicano and American art, representing the hybridization of new Chicano ideas and forms and their commitment to the continued development of a people's art.

Gaspar Enríquez

A Bowie High School art teacher, Gaspar Enríquez has dedicated his life to the El Paso community, where he was born in 1942. With a degree in arts education and a master's degree in metalwork, he has exhibited throughout the United States. Enríquez promotes Latino culture through his public art projects and community involvement. For more than twenty years he has provided young artists with scholarships and dozens of mural projects throughout the city. Drawing identity and artistic inspiration for his murals from the best elements of his bicultural background, Enríquez declares, "I am an American with a Mexican (Chicano) culture. . . . The form of my creations and their execution integrate both cultures. I do not abandon either culture completely: I just reorder and use them in new ways, and sometimes I transform them."[27] He believes that the unique experience of life on the border gives border artists a singular artistic perspective, but finds it hard to define, "I live with it every day, and take it for granted, using these special images in my art."

His murals and metalwork are sophisticated and technically complex, with an emphasis on permanence and excellence in public art. Enríquez feels that new technologies have not been fully explored by Chicano artists, including himself, especially computer technology, which is rapidly becoming a more accessible and desirable medium or tool. He credits Luis Jiménez for bringing Chicano art into the arena of more "permanent statements" with his fiber-glass sculptural creations. He also admires Jiménez's professional integrity and vision, which have endured despite continuous criticism surrounding his public works. (In June of 1995 the city of El Paso finally dedicated a fiber-glass sculpture-fountain, *Plaza de los Lagartos*, by Luis Jiménez after years of bureaucratic shuffling and community controversy.)

In his mural *History of the Mission Valley* (1994) Enríquez focused on the Salt War of 1877,[28] one of the darkest chapters in Texas history, offering a (re)interpretation of the bloody rebellion in El Paso, which is usually blamed on Mexicans. Painted with the help of five University of Texas, El Paso, students[29] on an old silo (32 feet in circumference by 47 feet high) near a Big-8 Supermarket (the sponsor), the mural was executed in sign painter's paint, using both paintbrush and spray gun (figure 3). The pre-Columbian history of the area is introduced with stenciled images of ancient petroglyphs (a thunderbird and a feathered serpent) and painted images of corn. The Spanish discovery is represented by conquistadors' hel-

Figure 3. Gaspar Enríquez, *History of the Mission Valley* (1994). Mural painted on a silo near a Big-8 Supermarket in El Paso, Texas. (Photograph by George Vargas.)

mets. El Paso's three missions (Ysleta, Socorro, and San Elizario) wrap around the upper portion of the silo. American settlers in wagons are pictured above bales of cotton. The flags of Mexico, the United States, and Texas signify the complex, and often violent, political history of El Paso.

In his recent mixed-media installation *La Rosa Dolorosa* (1995, his first mixed-media installation), Enríquez presents a realistic portrait of a young Chicana Madonna holding a single rose and radiating love and compassion to a dying Chicano youth and his girlfriend below. Sharing the title with a poem by Chicano poet Juan Contreras, written expressly for this sculpture, Enríquez stirs our human emotions and spiritual or inner self. We see the Madonna offering solace to the "Bronzed Barrio

Warrior fallen by a drive-by"[30] who grasps a rose in his right hand, while his girlfriend cradles his upper body in a scene resembling Michelangelo's *Pieta*. The two human figures are two-dimensional, or flat, black-and-white cut-outs mounted on foam board, whereas the young Mother Goddess is brilliantly painted and illuminated to create a three-dimensionality that is further enhanced by the Mexican baroque-like altar and columns. In this bittersweet vignette, the artist instructs and enlightens Chicanos and others about our common culture and destiny without preaching to us.

> *Now, let us see,*
> *un nuevo amanecer/a new awakening,*
> *envision a tomorrow*
> *minus life's tragedies*
> *and afflictions, minus years of tears,*
> *minus the rain of pain,*
> *where we can love one another . . .*[31]

Harry Gamboa, Jr.

Balancing on the razor's edge of Chicano avant-garde, Harry Gamboa, Jr., observes the tragic side of humanity and satirizes its predicaments and pratfalls. Born in 1951 in Los Angeles, the self-taught artist calls himself an "intermedia artist," whose body of work includes essays, poems, film/video, photography, performance/installation art, conceptual art, and anti-art. He revels in the ridiculous, absurd, and dark side of Chicano urban life, and mocks our contemporary cultural icons. "I like those who ridicule reality, or make reality ridiculous," he states simply.

Obsessed with the invisible "fallen angels" of Los Angeles, Gamboa dissects the stark contradictions of America's so-called city of the future—diverse and cosmopolitan, yet possessing the largest Chicano barrio in the United States. He points to social issues affecting Mexicans/Chicanos who, despite their great historical presence in California, are generally perceived as the "phantom culture,"[32] according to Gamboa. He served as both ideologue and documenter for ASCO, whose members collectively attempted to relate to the violence and tragedy in Los Angeles by creating new art that broke away from the paralyzing stereotypes of Chicanos and other Americans. The group also satirized American pop culture and "safe" or "no-risk" artists, receiving harsh criticism but eventually universal praise for their neodadaist/neosurrealist works.

During the last two decades, Gamboa has practiced his pure art, gaining critical attention in the form of major grants, fellowships, and commissions for his individual films/videos and literary works/plays. As a videographer, Gamboa has created new video texts for the 1990s, such as his *Vis-a-Vid* (1991–92) series, which won the "Premio Mesquite for Best Experimental Work" at the San Anto-

nio Cinefestival in 1992. The series also was shown as an example of a "video mural" at the first Contemporary Latino Mural Conference at the University of Texas at El Paso. It reveals the changing nature of Chicanos and their relationships with humanity. Shown in both the United States and Mexico, Gamboa's work involves the latest video techniques and Day-Glo colors to paint intriguing vignettes of Chicanos as real people living in a contemporary world. *Cold Java* depicts an angst-ridden Latino man who, while staring into a cup of coffee, realizes that his life, like his coffee, has grown cold. "Something is wrong with the coffee. . . . I can't drink. I can't think," he complains. *Disconnected* features Barbara Carrasco, who is being chased by a real or imagined stalker (or an angry lover?) in an eerie Los Angeles cityscape that resembles the lonely emptiness of Godard's *Alphaville*. Produced by Dr. Eloy Rodríguez (Biological Sciences at Cornell University), Gamboa's next episode, *Fire Medicine*, presents a humorous and scientific view of the Mexican/Chicano culture's fascination with chile peppers. Using relatives, friends (such as Los Angeles artist John Valadez), and the "man on the street," Gamboa gives Chicanos a chance to laugh at themselves (a man tells us about a chile pepper seed stuck in his eye), while teaching others about the strange culinary delights of the Chicano culture. In the episode *El Mundo L.A.*, actor Humberto Sandoval's character rants and raves the psychobabble of one suffering from "burnout." Yet like truths blurted out by drunks and madmen, the musings by Everyman/Sandoval about Los Angeles and the Chicano movement sound almost reasonable. Like a Chicano Travis Bickle (from the movie *Taxi Driver*), who loathes the filth and disintegration of Chicano culture, he blames the disorientation of Chicanos on L.A.'s lack of Mexican pyramids and accuses blacks of not "sharing the pie," thus denying him the "good life." The viewer prays that Everyman's fate is not ours and that he is a liar, but we fear otherwise.

Although ASCO no longer exists, the spirit of bold experimentation and intense social protest survives in the Chicano neodadaist Gamboa, whose works prophesied the present decade of social alienation, violent upheaval, and cataclysmic change that confronts humanity's future.

Margarita "Mago" Gándara

A highly trained artist (she studied under Urbici Soler, Spanish master sculptor and friend of Picasso) and teacher (with a master's degree in bicultural arts education), Margarita "Mago" Gándara was born of Spanish/Mexican parents in El Paso, Texas, in 1929. Resembling a Mexicanized Georgia O'Keeffe, she currently resides and works on both sides of the El Paso/Juárez border. Since 1973, she has been producing monumental mosaic murals for a bicultural, international community.[33]

As a young artist, wife, and mother in California, Mago lived a "hidden life," raising five children, all the while making art without the approval of her husband. Newly divorced, in 1973 she returned to El Paso to complete her degree and create murals, paintings, and sculptures. She also designed and built her adobe studio in Mexico. Calling herself an art warrior, Mago (appropriately nicknamed the "Magician") especially speaks to people who feel dispossessed of homeland and heritage. The powerful beings in her murals (always executed with the help of young apprentices whom she pays) are benevolent guardians (Mexican mythical figures and traditional icons) that protect people who are overwhelmed with survival on the physical plane and that remind them of their spiritual life.

In 1992, a blend of fate and coincidence brought Mago to her most ambitious, and best-received, mosaic mural commission, *La Niña Cósmica/ The Cosmic Child* (figure 4), which is mounted above the entrance to the student cafeteria at Frederick Douglass Elementary School in El Paso (on a wall measuring 12 feet in height by 72 feet in length). A modest materials budget allowed Mago to use store-bought pieces of colored tile, stained glass, and mirror instead of her usual recycled materials, giving her the pleasure of a full range of color and texture.

She wanted the semiabstract mural to be about the Great Mother, manifest as Coatlicue, a mythical figure present throughout Aztec history who symbolizes life, death, and regeneration. The mural scene depicts a brown-skinned goddess dancing through cosmic space, her mantle of stars and serpents billowing around her. She lovingly holds her own creations, the sun (Huitzilopochtli) and moon (Coyolxuahqui), in her outspread hands. As the mural progressed, Mago frequently told stories of Coatlicue to the children and their parents, school officials, teachers, and staff. All became part of Mago's world as she labored day after day, at first spreading out the giant mural on the floor inside the cafeteria, and later working outside on scaffolding above its entrance.

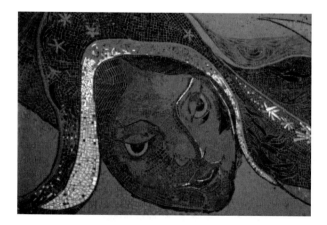

Figure 4. Mago Gandara, *La Niña Cósmica/The Cosmic Child* (1992–93). Mosaic located at Frederick Douglass Elementary School, El Paso, Texas. (Photograph by George Vargas.)

To organize this masterfully executed mosaic, Mago utilized the sensuous "**S**-curve," a technique used to organize ancient Teotihuacán architecture and murals and found in the works of Praxiteles and Diego Rivera, who called it the "wave."[34] The curving motion of *La Niña's* undulating mantle and her graceful limbs bring an organizing rhythm to the vast space. These flowing, serpentine lines hold the artist's dazzling palette of colored glass and tile. The occasional use of bits of mirror in *La Niña's* halo and mantle of stars bring glittering movement to the mural's surface, as each piece independently reflects the trees blowing in the wind or the movement of passersby. Mago found herself wanting others to participate in the creative process, incorporating ideas from her assistants, visiting friends, Girl Scouts who came to help, and mothers and teachers passing through the school. "Mosaic mural [art] is exciting to me because it is cooperative in nature. It is not just a great 'I AM' . . . everyone has a chance to express [themselves] within the structure of the original design—not hodgepodge, not paint thrown on a wall. . . . We need to involve the public, always [remembering that] the artist is the prime soul of the design."[35]

On November 24, 1993, Mago finally celebrated *La Niña Cósmica's* completion with a community festival. More than 1,000 people packed the cafeteria to inaugurate or baptize the mural. Mago appeared in a long black dress decorated with colorful ribbons, a purple scarf artfully wrapped around her flowing long hair. When the festivities were over, Mago was filled with a sense of serenity and peace because her project had clearly brought spiritual unity and joy to the neighborhood for which it was created.

Overcoming the inevitable obstacles that materialize while making giant public works, Mago persisted in her vision, demonstrating to observers that anyone (especially the "hidden individual") can be a warrior or hero/heroine. Art, she believes, is central to the process of cultivating a unified border community, with a shared culture and common values, utilizing ideas that are universal. "We look down on a new order like astronauts. We are greeting spiritual liberation in quantum leaps." On a feminist level, Mago's murals act as implicit metaphors to illustrate her own journey: a woman's unique life experience at the border, "having to be brave, bold, and courageous in a society that does not necessarily nurture women."[36]

Nora Mendoza

Currently living in Michigan, Nora Mendoza was born in Westlaco, Texas, in 1932. She matured as an artist in Michigan after moving to Detroit in 1953 with her husband, who was completing his medical internship. While raising two children and serving in the role of doctor's wife, Mendoza still made time to study art. In the early 1970s she trained individually under respected Michigan abstract artists Richard Koslow and Ljubo Biro. When she divorced in 1975, determined to succeed as both a single mother and a working artist, she began selling her paintings in local malls, eventually gaining attention in galleries.

When necessary, Mendoza labels herself an abstract impressionist. Infused with rich color and hidden images, her paintings are now sold in galleries throughout the nation and abroad, and they decorate both private homes (such as Aretha Franklin's) and corporate offices (Ford, Rockefeller). She has been commissioned by various Chicano groups and individuals, including former UFW leader César Chávez, University of Minnesota Chicano historian Dennis Nodin Valdés, and Michigan State University linguist and Latin American historian Lucia Fox Lockert.

A Chicana feminist, Mendoza helped found early key Latino arts organizations such as Nuestras Artes de Michigan (an umbrella arts organization) and its offshoot, the Michigan Hispanic Cultural/Art Association (MHCAA). She also has served as consultant and advisor for New Detroit, Inc., and the Michigan Council for the Arts, helping to initiate vital support for minority artists and community organizations.

Having spent time in Nicaragua, Hawaii, and most recently Germany, Mendoza finds it exciting to cross over into other cultures in exhibiting her paintings and community murals. Following the 1992–95 touring exhibition "Crossing Bridges," which was organized by the MHCAA and featured seventeen Latino artists, Mendoza visited most of the nine German cities that the exhibit traveled to.[37] She was asked to return to Herrlingen, Germany, to produce an acrylic-on-wood portable mural with the help of local youth. As a certified elder member of Kanto de la Tierra/Medicine Eagles Gathering (a nonprofit intertribal council that brings people from many Indian Nations together to pray for the Earth's healing), she taught the German students about America's indigenous family, including Chicanos.

Her most recent work, *Spirits of the Fourth World* (figure 5), combines Chicano images and symbols with those of indigenous people. In this way Mendoza celebrates her own Indian heritage as a Chicana. This series proudly speaks of Indian culture, protests the ongoing political trials and tribulations of Indians around the Fourth World, and captures the struggles of and changes made by Mexicans and Chicanos. Her new works serve to heal her wounds of depression and pain while acknowledging the guilt and pain experienced by other Chicanos. She believes that many youths hurt themselves and others because, "[If] you've been lied to for so many years, there's a lot of hurt, pain, and anger."[38] She believes that art can heal the pain, empowering us to improve our own lives and to help others.

From the beginning of her career as a Chicana artist to the present, Mendoza has always aimed to be true to her artistic and feminist identity. To better involve the

Figure 5. Nora Mendoza, from the *Spirits of the Fourth World* series (1992). Acrylic and mixed-media painting, 20 inches by 24 inches. (Photograph by Nora Mendoza.)

viewer and call attention to social issues, she explains, "I have tried to express my deepest inner feelings and my own reality, which include the issues and struggles of our people, particularly women."[39]

Martín Moreno

Adept at both sculpture and mural painting (over his career he has directed more than eighty public art projects), Phoenix artist/art teacher Martín Moreno devotes much of his time to public service through community arts. Born in Adrian, Michigan (a predominantly Latino-populated farming and manufacturing community), in 1951, he was raised in Sunnyside, a Mexican/Chicano barrio, attended local schools and colleges, and worked in the fields and factories. His working-class background provides him with special memories and inspiration that are still visible in his work today. "My earliest memories are [those] of the fields—sitting in the back of a pickup truck with my family watching row upon row of corn and tomatoes form a visual pattern of rhythm," Moreno recalls. "Realities of superstition told by the elders, stories of La Llorona, the Earth, my glorious past—all the images come to life in stone, paint, and canvas, and walls."[40]

Moreno (whose works were included in the CARA exhibition) organizes public art projects in Phoenix, Tucson, and other cities in Arizona, specializing in working with youth. The CBS television network commissioned Moreno to paint a mural titled *In the Killing Fields of America* as a companion piece to a 1994 documentary of the same name, about the plague of violence that is destroying our youth and neighborhoods. Moreno led a dozen Phoenix-area children, who painted simple portraits of ten Americans who have died in "inner-city wars," including a two-year-old girl from Phoenix, above the U.S. stars and stripes on the wall of a local YMCA. Moreno insisted that all participants read short biographies of the people they were portraying. "We were all brought to tears,"[41] admits Moreno with sadness. A mural, according to Moreno, must be designed and executed with the community, because the finished product will become public property and part of that community's environment. The art form must reflect the character of the community and, through architectonics, complement the cultural and architectural environment.

Moreno most recently has received a major commission in Phoenix to sculpt a memorial monument to César Chávez (to date untitled). Two other professionals will also be working on the project, which is currently in the planning stage.[42] Mexican architect Dalinda Jimenez will design the landscape and a structure that will contain a larger-than-life-size romanticized portrait of the UFW leader by Chicano artist Zarco Guerrero (mask-maker, sculptor, and muralist living in Mesa, Arizona). Moreno will decorate the wall enclosure with relief work. The $100,000 public artwork (to be dedicated in April to coincide with Chávez's birthday) will further demonstrate the proficiency and inventiveness of Chicano artists who increasingly work in permanent public art. According to Moreno, this new opportunity represents a great honor to participate in the movement to immortalize Chávez and his accomplishments and a "chance to articulate my artistic perspective in permanent monumental sculpture."

Moreno continues to cross boundaries into new fields and to experiment with new media. For example, he has produced a series of "borderland" prints that were exchanged with Mexican artists in an effort to promote goodwill between the United States and Mexico and to explore the influence of borderland culture on both Chicano and Mexican artists. He recognizes and nurtures the ability of Chicano art to heal and inspire Chicanos and other Americans, offering optimism to both participants in his projects and to the viewers who "activate" his art by seeing a true reflection of themselves in his murals and sculpture.

Gluglio Gronk Nicandro

Born Gluglio Gronk Nicandro in 1954 in Los Angeles, Gronk is an internationally recognized Chicano artist who, without formal training, excels in easel painting, performance art, and installation art.[43] He initially gained notoriety through his work with ASCO. Often satirical, his present work reflects his long-time fascination with mass media, the results of juxtaposing images of high culture with low culture, and the constant shift of linear time from present to past. Gronk's installations are destroyed after their completion to demystify the art object by stressing the impermanence of the physical material. He welcomes visitors at his work site to participate in the creative process while he constructs his installation, encouraging personal interaction to humanize the artist and enhance a feeling of community involvement.

Above all, Gronk treasures the process of making art for and with the community, wherever that community may be. His 1992 piece, *Fascinating Slippers No. 3* (an installation that was painted at the University of Texas at El Paso over a five-day period, see figure 6), was important to the artist for two reasons: It drew countless university students and community members who engaged with the artist in the creative process, thus stimulating interesting artistic and personal dialogue, and it evolved into other pieces for the artist.

> This was the first time that I had done a landscape painting. I did a landscape that wrapped around the walls like the mountains that wrap around El Paso. I also painted in lungs in the middle, because you have ASARCO [a local smelting industry] spewing all those gases into the air. The lungs unify the painting with all the land. After all, what are wars fought about? Usually land. What do people return to? Land. You have all these issues about land. What is Chiapas [the agrarian rebellion in Mexico] all about? The row of K-Mart plastic buckets [in front of the main painted wall] symbolizes the borderland and the Rio Grande, and the water inside them speak[s] to the universal issue of water. All those kind[s] of ideas of connection come from this piece in El Paso, some of this has gone out to other pieces that I've worked on.[44]

Gronk contends that the artist needs to invent and reinvent him/herself over and over again to avoid mediocrity and stagnation. Change is necessary in the creation of new art.

> My work has changed and transformed. I talk with other artists, and I think that there's a younger generation of artists who don't have to repeat things from the past. Looking at Diego Rivera many say, "Oh, look at what he did, he brought the Indians to the attention of the people!" I think that if he were alive today, he would be doing CD-ROM or videos. He wouldn't necessarily be doing murals. You utilize what is around, and you try different possibilities of communication.[45]

Figure 6. Gronk's site-specific installation *Fascinating Slippers No. 3* (1992). Painted at the University of Texas at El Paso. This photograph was taken during an early stage of the artwork's creation. (Photograph by George Vargas.)

Consequently, Gronk represents the cutting edge of contemporary expression, never looking back but constructing ambitious installations, prints, and paintings, all seemingly taking different routes to reach new ways to define Chicano art. This diverse range in expression characterizes Gronk's work, which is all interrelated. Gronk elaborated on his new mixed-media projects in an interview with this author.

> For myself, I do a diversity of projects, experimenting with painting and other media, perhaps such as music. In the piece done with Kronos String Quartet ["Tormenta Cantata," performed at UCLA, May 14, 1995, and dedicated to Gronk's dark-haired heroine who appears in some of his major work] . . . you have a string quartet trained in classical music, a soprano, and an artist with a paintbrush amplified for sound . . . and you create a visual element to a musical entity. This is opening up new possibilities for me as an artist. I learn from collaboration with different artists, different groups. I've been doing a lot of music projects. An opera [*Journey to Córdova,* performed at Dorothy Chandler Pavilion, Los Angeles, 1995], this string quartet piece, and the Disney movie. I'm working on *Fantasia,* part two, on Beethoven's Fifth using computer animation. Very advanced stuff in the state-of-the-art. I take from that experience and incorporate it into my own work. I don't have a set of ideas [or know] where it's leading to. I research and include all that is in my journey, in my exploration.[46]

Pointing to the limited success of Chicano art in mainstream art, he appreciates that academics have documented its progress but notes that the majority of galleries and museums do not exhibit minority artists and do not have minorities employed as staff.[47] In defining where Chicano artists are now, Gronk downplays his own notable success in the mainstream because he is more concerned with the art-making process over the end product. He feels that he will be fully accepted when Chicano artists as a group are accepted and recognized within mainstream art. Commenting on Chicano art's role as avant-garde or vanguard expression:

> I consider myself more a part of the vanguard. I can't give myself that label "avant-garde." But I do think that if you're doing art on the cutting edge that doesn't quite fit, that challenges notions as to what is or should be, to me that's avant-garde. *Avant* means "front" in French. For every front, there must also be a rear! . . . The rear is the conservatism in the arts today. I feel that avant-garde means an artist who has stayed to work in the community, to make a real change in the community where he's producing art. To me that's avant, not necessarily what you read in books, not what you see in a museum or gallery.[48]

José "Match" Fernández

Attempting to correct society's misconception about graffiti, El Paso artist José "Match" Fernández uses graffiti as a vehicle of social commentary infused with fresh street culture and comic-book imagery. Born in 1955 in Ciudad Juárez, Mexico, Match moved to El Paso, where he attended Bowie High School and was instructed in art by Gaspar Enríquez.[49] He remembers being influenced by Grateful Dead posters when he moved to California and later by El Paso's *placa,* though he never was a tagger himself. A former sign painter who considers himself a street artist and border artist, Match treasures the process or public "show" of making a graffiti mural, which temporarily beautifies the environment, but eventually is painted over. Faithfully every Christmas, Match and other graffiti artists collaborate to create a special holiday mural for the El Paso community.

Since 1989, Match, Frank Molina, and others have created a graffiti mural that changes every month on the wall of El Paso's old Pershing Theater. With the permission of the building's owner, they invite emerging young graffiti artists to move away from gang vandalism and drug abuse by exploring alternative mural art with them. In 1992, the Pershing mural (at the time called *Stop the Killing*) received support from Los Murales (a Junior League-sponsored project dedicated to the proliferation and preservation of El Paso's murals), marking their first contribution to graffiti art.

However, Match's proudest community achievement was his participation in the *Gene K. Wilson Memorial Mural* project in 1994. Using only black and white spray paint, he painted a huge permanent portrait of Wilson, a popular local artist/activist, on the wall of the Goeting Clinic/Planned Parenthood Center. Because the realistic painting faithfully captures the spirit of Wilson, many viewers are amazed that the portrait was done solely with spray cans.

Match predicts that computer/digital technology and graphics software will become a greater presence in graffiti art. Computer-generated designs and lettering are emerging influences among the youth, who, for example, now use "slice and shift" digitized lettering instead of the once-popular balloon letters or the "wild style." Finally, he believes that the future of Chicano art will be discovered in the street, where youth and other members of the Chicano community congregate and celebrate their uniqueness.

Conclusion: The Future

Challenging in theme and content, with styles uniquely Chicano and yet often urbane, international, even chic, Chicano art still is intertwined with the Chicano experience of U.S. society within the context of American history. It inevitably changes as American society changes, while maintaining a link to its Mexican roots. No matter its intent, the very nature of Chicano art is cultivated from a historical continuity of diverse artistic traditions and cultural rituals that flow from a deep communal well of creativity.

Many of the artists from the early Chicano Movimiento now are established artists, art teachers, and community leaders. They have moved from making immediate neighborhood art, often with recycled and impermanent materials, to making permanent monumental public art and exploring new media such as computer technologies. Whereas the artists of the 1960s looked toward Mexico for inspiration, today's young Chicano artists have role models living and working right in their own neighborhoods. Many of these young artists are producing murals, still the most accessible vehicle of visual communication, while others explore new avenues of expression. Additionally, as the women's liberation movement left its imprint on American society, the number of Chicanas entering the art scene has increased, bringing provocative feminine visions into the limelight.

Chicano art, for better or worse, is synonymous with social movement and artistic change. Chicano artists still encounter resistance to their ideas because they are the messengers of progressive change, a message often met with resistance, as it apparently is human nature to fear that which we do not understand. Nonetheless, Chicanos represent the inevitable movement of people of color into the U.S. mainstream, much like outsiders and immigrants of previous times, and reflect the ethnic diversity that binds all Americans together. The formal influences to be discovered in Chicano art are derived from North American, Latin American, and European art movements, testifying to the migration of a people that continues between Mexico and the United States and creating local neighborhoods in a global community. Chicano artists and Latin American artists increasingly are drawn to each other's art in their shared Latin(o) American search for a new identity in the American landscape. Chicano art and Latin American art serve as reference points on a cultural bridge that spans the new world and the old one.

Today, political commentary still is quite popular in Chicano art, sometimes overshadowing the newer, more personal, expressions simply because many still expect Chicano art to be polemic, maybe even confrontational, by nature. Growing numbers of scholars and laypersons have documented, interpreted, and repeatedly interconnected Chicano art at multiple levels to broader art and political movements. Chicano art historians such as Amalia Mesa-Bains, Chon Noriega, Víctor Sorell, and Tomás Ybarra-Frausto join other scholars in deciphering the language of Chicano art to help us better understand its unfolding nature.

In earlier times there were few publications on Chicano artists and their artworks, and even fewer art historians in the field to document, research, and analyze the role and meaning of Chicano art. Many early Chicano historians met the same resistance that confronted the artists. Even today, they continue to receive criticism for their academic studies. The general public has expressed a greater interest in Chicano culture than before, including a growing number of Chicanos who want to see their history and culture on display. Adopting a no-risk attitude, most museums and galleries give Chicano art little or no attention. Denied traditional spaces, Chicano artists often turn to alternative spaces such as community centers and churches to exhibit their work. Specialized museums such as the Mexican Art Museum in San Francisco and the Mexican Art Center in Chicago have been created, directed, and staffed by professionals who generally are knowledgeable in both the Western aesthetic and the Latino aesthetic.

The future of Chicano art will continue to relate to the historical condition of the Chicano people as an emerging ethnic population inside an American sociopolitical system. Like jazz and abstract expressionism, Chicano art increasingly will be accepted as an American cultural product, as more Chicano artists cross over into mainstream society. Chicano art also will become recognized internationally as Chicanos themselves traverse international borders. Because of the increasing importance of the trade between Mexico and the United States, cities located on or near the U.S.Mexico border, such as El Paso, Phoenix, San Diego, and Tucson, are becoming more important, as are the expressions of contemporary Mexican/Chicano culture that characterize most border towns. Ironically, once ignored by the business sector, Chicano art now is gradually being displayed alongside cowboy art and Indian art throughout the Southwest in an attempt to commercialize the unique cultures of North America's last frontier.

Just like any other transformative art, Chicano art can help unify us. How we read the messages will be increasingly interrelated to the destiny of Chicano Americans in the information age, and to their interrelationship with other Americans and the rest of the world. To better understand the state of Chicano art is to better comprehend the changes in the Chicano mind as it searches for a new identity and renewed family and societal associations. Like visionaries, Chicano artists at the cutting edge connect with the present by recalling the past while peering into the future. Chicano art in this sense is a consciousness-raising expression that has the power to enlighten, liberate, and heal while advancing the precious American ideal of individual freedom and creative liberty. Chicano art provides a practical framework of cultural reality for a people's America of the future. As such, the new open model of Chicano art increasingly will serve as a visual mirror of change and popular culture in a new American frontier.

Notes

1. Ursula R. Murray, ed., *Latino Artists: Michigan. U.S.A., Crossing Bridges* (Detroit: Michigan Hispanic Cultural/Art Association, 1991).

2. Murray, *Latino Artists*.

3. The racial/ethnic trunk of the Americas also is distinctly *mestizo*, constituting the majority of the American population. Edmund Stephen Urbanski, *Hispanic America and Its Civilizations* (Norman, Okla.: University of Oklahoma Press, 1978), 84–85.

4. Armando Durón et al., "Ester Hernández," in *Encuentro: Invasion of the Americas and the Making of the Mestizo* (Venice, Calif.: Social and Public Art Resource Center, 1991), 19.

5. Murray, *Latino Artists*.

6. The immediate cultural reality for artists in the United States, especially in the borderlands, is truly mestizo, not exclusively Mexican or Chicano. "*Mestizaje,* not *Chicanismo,* is the reality of our lives," declares feminist writer Gloria Anzaldúa. "We bleed in mestizaje, we eat, sweat, and cry in mestizaje." Gloria Anzaldúa, "Chicana Artists," *NACLA Report on the Americas* 27, no. 1 (1993): 40.

7. Durón, et al., *Encuentro,* 14.

8. Shifra M. Goldman, "The Iconography of Chicano Self-Determination: Race, Ethnicity, and Class," in *Dimensions of the Americas: Art and Social Change in the Americas* (Chicago: University of Chicago Press, 1994), 398–408. For a summary on early Chicano murals, see also Goldman, "Resistance and Identity: Street Murals of Aztlán," in *Dimensions of the Americas,* 118–22; and Eva Cockcroft and John Weber, *Toward a People's Art: The Contemporary Mural Movement* (New York: E.P. Dutton & Company, 1977). Also, for an update on California mural art and Chicanos, see Eva Sperling Cockcroft and Holly Barnet-Sánchez. eds., *Signs from the Heart: California Chicano Murals* (Venice, Calif.: Social and Public Art Resource Center, 1990; also published by University of New Mexico Press, 1993 and 1996).

9. *National Council of La Raza/NCLR Exhibition* (Detroit: National Council of La Raza, 1993).

10. One of the first reports on Chicano art as an art movement was Manuel J. Martínez's "The Art of the Chicano Movement and the Movement of Chicano Art" (1972) reprinted in *Speaking for Ourselves: American Ethnic Writing,* ed. Lillian Faderman (Glenview, Ill.: Scott, Foresman and Company, 1975), 314–16. Mildred Monteverde was one of the first historians to contextualize Chicano art within a Chicano aesthetic and an historical chronology. See Mildred Monteverde, "Contemporary Chicano Art" (1972), reprinted in *Chicano Art History: A Book of Selected Readings,* ed. Jacinto Quirarte (San Antonio: Research Center for the Arts and Humanities, University of Texas at San Antonio, 1984), 80–83.

11. The first books on Chicano art history were authored by Jacinto Quirarte, *Mexican American Artists* (Austin: University of Texas Press, 1973); and Raymond Barrio, *Mexico's Art and Chicano Art* (Sunnyvale, Calif.: Ventura Press, 1975). Additionally, Quirarte documented the beginnings of Chicano art, including writings by artists, activists, and scholars on Chicano identity, Chicano manifestos, and the roles of Chicano art in *Chicano Art History: A Book of Selected Writings* (San Antonio: University of Texas, San Antonio, 1984).

12. Gronk, tape-recorded interview by George Vargas, El Paso, Texas, June 11, 1995.

13. For a review of posters as revolutionary art and its relationship to the New Left, read Eva Cockcroft's chapter on "The United States and Socially Concerned Latin American Art 1920–1970," in *The Latin American: Art and Artists in the United States,* eds. Luis Cancel, Jacinto Quirarte, et al. (New York: Harry N. Abrams, Inc., 1988), 184–221.

14. Víctor Valle, "Chicano Art: An Emerging Generation," in *Southern California's Latino Community,* eds. George Ramos et al. (Los Angeles: *Los Angeles Times,* 1983), 94–97. Also, note the reproduction of Carrasco's mural that includes a portrait of David Alfaro Siqueiros's painting *Tropical America,* in Shifra M. Goldman's article, "How, Why, Where, and When It All Happened: Chicano Murals of California," in *Signs from the Heart,* 32.

15. Mario Micheli, *Siqueiros* (Milan, Italy: Secretaría de Educación Pública, 1968), 5–51. Also see Shifra M. Goldman, "Siqueiros and

Three Early Murals in Los Angeles," (1974), reprinted in Quirarte, *Chicano Art History,* 56–63.

16. Installation/performance/earthbody artist Ana Mendieta, who was separated from her parents during Castro's revolution and sent to the United States, identified with Chicanos and other Latinos searching for their roots. (She returned to Cuba in 1980 to reclaim her roots through new works, but she tragically died in 1985.) "The condition of all Latin American artists that live in the United States is similar, although this condition is not one of my preoccupations, I recognize that, through it, a kind of search—a collision—of our roots is imposed [on] us, a search that is not necessarily the same for each one nor requires the same channels." Carla Stellweg et al., eds., *Artes Visuales* (Mexico City, Mexico: Museum of Modern Art, 1981), 69.

17. Roberto Gil de Montes, "Presentation," in *Artes Visuales, 9.*

18. Gil de Montes, "Presentation." For more information on multiculturalism and the conduits existing between Chicano and Latin American artists, see Lucy R. Lippard, *Mixed Blessings: New Art in a Multicultural America* (New York: Pantheon Books, 1990).

19. Gronk interview (1995).

20. Harry Gamboa, Jr., "In the City of Angels, Chameleons, and Phantoms: ASCO, A Case of Chicano Art in Urban Tones (or ASCO was a Four-Member Word)," in *Chicano Art: Resistance and Affirmation/CARA,* eds. Richard Griswold del Castillo et al. (Los Angeles: Wight Art Gallery, UCLA, 1991), 129. Also see S. Zaneta Kosiba-Vargas, "Harry Gamboa and ASCO: The Emergence and Development of a Chicano Art Group, 1971–1987" (Ph.D. dissertation, University of Michigan, 1988).

21. Durón et al., eds., *Encuentro,* 18.

22. Lippard argues that, unfortunately, the element of quality in art "is identifiable only by those in power . . . [caretakers] overwhelmingly white, middle-class, and-in the upper echelons—usually male." According to this "lofty view, racism has nothing to do with it. . . . Quality will transcend boundaries and prevail; so-called minorities just haven't got it yet." Artists of color and women dedicated to revising the notion of quality have been turned away at the gates of mainstream art "by this garlic-and-cross strategy." Lippard, *Mixed Blessings,* 7.

23. Murray, *Latino Artists*.

24. Gloria Osuna Pérez, *Rethinking La Malinche* (Austin, Tex.: Mixec-Arte Museum, 1995).

25. "Chicano Connection" is a touring collection of prints by Self Help Graphics (a collective/gallery in East Los Angeles) curated by the Salt River Artistic Movement (alternative art space in Phoenix) and funded by the Arizona Commission on the Arts.

26. For more detailed information on the artists, their works, and the history of Chicano art, see Griswold del Castillo et al., *Chicano Art.*

27. Griswold del Castillo et al., *Chicano Art,* 348.

28. For a complete account of the Salt War, see C. L. Sonnichsen, *The El Paso Salt War of 1877* (El Paso: Texas Western Press, 1961). See also Arnoldo de León, *They Called Them Greasers* (Austin: University of Texas Press, 1983), 99–101.

29. University of Texas, El Paso, students who worked on the silo mural include Diana Capital, Donna Haynes, Mauricio Olague, Steve Salazar, and Alfonso Valenzuela.

30. Juan Contreras, "La Rosa Dolorosa," reproduced in "La Rosa Dolorosa Exhibition" gallery sheet, El Paso Museum of Art, 1995.

31. Contreras, "La Rosa Dolorosa."

32. See Max Benavídez, "A Battle of Wills" *Los Angeles Times,* 9 June 1991. Also see his article "Latino Dada: Savage Satire from Harry Gamboa, Jr.," *L.A. Weekly,* 16–22 May 1986.

33. Summarized from an article by George Vargas, "Mago Gándara: A Woman Artist at the Border" (El Paso: Center for Inter-American and Border Studies, 1995).

34. Diego Rivera, "Dynamic Detroit—An Interpretation," *Creative Artist,* April 1933, 289.

35. Mago Gándara, videotaped interviews by George Vargas, El Paso, Texas, 1993.

36. Gándara interview (1993).

37. "Crossing Bridges" successfully toured Germany (part of which at that time was still under Communism), extending its initial schedule because of its popularity with large European audiences. Latino artists from Michigan were offered low fares by the German airline, Lufthansa, to encourage them to attend the exhibition's numerous

receptions in order to provide informal talks to curious yet sincere audiences.

38. Linda Ann Chomin, "Her Canvases Exude Her Indian Heritage," *The Observer* (Livonia, Michigan), 6 September 1995.

39. Nora Mendoza, letter to George Vargas, 16 September 1995.

40. *National Council of La Raza/NCLR Exhibition* (Detroit: National Council of La Raza, 1993).

41. Alita Corcos, "Portraits of the City," *Phoenix Magazine*, August 1995, 102.

42. Martín Moreno, telephone interview by George Vargas, El Paso, Texas, 17 September 1995.

43. For more background information on Gronk and ASCO, see Lippard, *Mixed Blessings*, 29, 227–29.

44. Gronk interview (1995).

45. Ibid.

46. Ibid.

47. Ibid. Regarding the noticeable lack of minority artists and staff in major museums, see David Ross et al., *Race, Ethnicity and Culture in the Visual Arts* (New York: American Council for the Arts, 1992).

48. Gronk interview (1995).

49. José "Match" Fernández, taped interview by George Vargas, El Paso, Texas, 23 August 1995.

El Mundo Femenino: Chicana Artists of the Movement—A Commentary on Development and Production

Amalia Mesa-Bains

Cultural transformation requires an expansion of an aesthetic language. Consequently, in the search for new concepts to describe America's broadening cultural diversity, we critics, scholars, and historians must begin to address those groups whose artistic production challenges old labels and limits. In particular we must try to understand the conditions and concerns that shape the work of Chicana artists, as well as the means by which these issues constitute a specificity of gender expressiveness.

Heritage, origin, family values, and cultural practices reside deep within the world view of Chicanas. Chicanas have renegotiated the domestic and community roles they fulfill as they migrate, become educated, and interact with their culture and the larger society. Their social roles are often in conflict, and this collision has recast the borders and boundaries of geography and identity. To begin to describe the cultural production and aesthetic language of Chicana artists, we must be willing to view their visual voice as a multiple text composed of shifting layers of meaning. This multiple text asserts a relationship between form and content. The work of these artists during the Movement was the result of the historical moment in which they found themselves; as such, it reflects an intention born of the social, cultural, and sexual realities of their lives.

To understand the aesthetic production of Chicanas, we must place their cultural development in its historical framework. The twenty-five years following the mid-1960s were an era in which all Chicanos sought to define themselves and to understand the sources of their identity. The sense of alienation and struggle that marked the discrimination experienced by Chicanos also fueled the resistance so characteristic of Chicano and Chicana art.

The Chicana Focus on Cultural Identity

During the Chicano Movement, the resistance of Chicanas to the cultural oppression of the majority was matched by their resistance to the intracultural roles through which males dominated many aspects of family life and the arts community. Chicana artists focused on their cultural identity using the female lenses of narrative, domestic space, social critique, and ceremony, which filtered these nutrient experiences, contradictory roles, and community structures.

Narrative

Broad categories of cultural content provide a context for examining the work of specific Chicana artists. Narration is particularly significant in the artistic effort of Chicanas to restate family histories. The feminist critic Griselda Pollock asserts that through language women are continually produced as elements in the social and economic structure of patriarchy.[1] Consequently, the narrative in Chicana art alters the relationship of women to domination by affirming positive histories so often denied in the larger society and by relocating women in a central, emancipated position.

The telling of family tales and the recording of daily events through recuerdos, diaries, letters, and home altars call upon women to remember the details of a personal and familial reality. Since their roles center on relationships, women are entrusted with teaching values through the oral traditions of storytelling, sayings, songs, and family histories. These are the sources of the cultural narration found in the work of many Chicana artists.

Within an emancipated dialogue, Chicanas positioned women as figures of power and control, while maintaining some of the familial and regional elements that affirmed the culture of the larger Chicano community. Rural and urban settings produced widely varying narratives that were often linked only by the role of women.

Chicano Art: Resistance and Affirmation, 1965-1985, edited by Griswold del Castillo, McKenna and Yarbo-Bejarano. Reprinted by permission of Wight Art Gallery-University of California.

Domestic Space

In addition to the narrative intention, the need to circumscribe space in the community is a driving force in the work of women artists, who have, for example, used neighborhood walls for their murals. Another kind of re-appropriation of territory is found in works that spring from a domestic space. The day-to-day experience of working-class Chicanas circumscribes space within the domestic sphere through home embellishments, home altars, healing traditions, and personal feminine poses or styles. The phenomenon of the home altar is perhaps the most prevalent.

Established through pre-Hispanic continuities of spiritual belief, the family altar functions for women as a counterpoint to male-dominated rituals within Catholicism. Often located in bedrooms, the home altar presents family history and cultural belief systems. Women arrange bric-a-brac, memorabilia, devotional icons, and decorative elements, and in doing so exercise a familial aesthetic. Constant formal elements include images of saints, flowers (plastic, dried, natural, and synthetic), family photographs, mementos, historic objects (military medals and flags), candles, and offerings. Characterized by accumulation, display, and abundance, altars allow history, faith, and personal objects to commingle. Formal structures and techniques include nichos (niches), retablos (boxlike containers highlighting special icons), innovative uses of Christmas lights and reflective material, and miniaturization.

Like the family life of women, the box form occupies space. If so-called feminine space seeks to gather, encircle, bind, link, and therefore circumscribe site, location, and activity, then box art and installation work break feminine space and refashion domestic enclosures.

Chicana rasquache, which I call domesticana, is like its male counterpart, the product of resistance to the majority culture and affirmation of other cultural values.[2] It also grows out of women's restrictions within the culture. Female rasquachismo defies the cultural identity imposed by Anglo Americans and defies the restrictive gender identity imposed by the Chicano culture. In the work of Chicana artists, techniques of subversion play with traditional imagery and cultural material, and together they characterize domesticana.

Social Critique

The social defiance that characterizes Chicano art in general finds a unique gender expression among Chicanas. Through the use of inversion, satire, reversals, and juxtapositions, Chicanas express a kind of resistant feminine commentary. These devices of subversion take benign symbols of North American culture and present them as signs of exploitation. The resulting social indictment is driven by women's political consciousness, desire for social change, and maternal sense of responsibility for the generations to come.

In an intracultural critique, artists take shared female images of everyday family life and manipulate them to question the limits of the feminine. In this sense, the work of many Chicanas does not simply reflect ideology, it constructs ideology. Their social critique provokes the viewer to see the benign and often domesticated versions of the feminine in new ways.

The Ceremonial

Spirituality, religiosity, spectacle, and pageantry are a prevailing aesthetic dimension of the work of many Chicana artists, who use, in particular, the shrine, ofrenda, altar, retablo, and nicho box forms. This ceremonial aspect highlights belief, healing, and celebration as elements in the ongoing lexicon of women's work. Maintaining the traditional place of women in spiritual practices, artists use ceremonial forms to expand their painting and mixed-media work. For example, the need to mediate death and transform the spiritual in celebrating El Día de los Muertos (the Day of the Dead) inspires a new body of work reflecting ritual and pageantry. The sources and sensibilities of folk practices, curanderismo, and the Catholic Baroque are fragments of the ceremonial intention expressed by Chicana artists.

Chicana Artists

The elements of the narrative, the circumscription of domestic space, the social critique, and the ceremonial are never discrete and monodimensional influences. They are, instead, memories and experiences, layered and scattered in a multiple text within each work. Overlapping and polysemous references permeate the work of Chicana artists.

Signifiers of their era, the following artists represent different outlooks and generations within the Chicano Movement. Despite their differences they are artistic pioneers of their epoch and, as such, cross boundaries. Their production lends insight into the major themes, aesthetic vocabulary, and multiple realities that characterize the larger Chicano identity and struggle for rights. Their personal development is complex and must be viewed within a historical framework. Their world view, cultural practices, social context, and early artistic influences thus determine and reflect their particular aesthetic. The nutrient experiences and sensibilities that express their intention as artists must be located in the historical moment of their group. The following women are but a few of the Chicanas whose presence as leaders, activists, and artists has been critical to achieving large-scale social change.

Judith Baca

Judith Baca's work, primarily the production of murals, is part of a large-scale, publicly engaged process that employs both narration and social critique. Baca's methods of solving problems and involving the community in her work arise from her early collective struggles in the family and neighborhood. Raised in a strong female household, Baca uses her family of women as a model for structures of feminist empowerment. The family model also inspires her to involve youth gangs in her work as a public muralist. Her conceptualization and production of murals involve historians, cultural informants, storytellers, neighborhood residents, young artists, and others in a collaborative venture to identify issues, images, and narratives.

The Great Wall of Los Angeles, located in the Tujunga Wash Drainage Canal in the San Fernando Valley, California, began in 1967 as the project of an artists' collective and became over many years the longest mural in the world (over half a mile long). In its portrayal of the history of Los Angeles the mural presents a panorama of the social struggle and disenfranchisement of diverse racial and ethnic groups. Each year youths of all races, under Baca's direction, learned about events such as the Japanese American Internment, the Freedom Bus Rides, and the Dust Bowl Journey as they worked on the mural.

Baca is committed to engaging gang youth in work that helps them define themselves and their culture because she was challenged as a youth growing up in Chicano barrios in the Pacoima area to define her self. Her installation piece *Las Tres Marías* (1976; cat. no. 33) plays on the multiple roles that the pachuca of the 1940s (proper left panel) and the chola or ruca of the 1970s (proper right panel) have assumed over time. This piece, whose title recalls the Three Marys of the crucifixion, sets up a good woman/bad woman satire by positioning a mirror so that it captures the viewer in the center of these extremes. Baca, seen dressed in a pachuca costume in the proper left panel, used this work as a performance piece in 1976.

Through her work, Baca focuses primarily on redefining social history and repositioning women in roles of power. She founded the Social and Public Art Resource Center in 1976, a center organized and run by women to document and preserve mural images, in part as a response to the male exclusivity of much of the mural movement. Baca's artistic association with Suzanne Lacy and Judy Chicago was at that time one of the few instances in which Chicana artists were in direct contact with the White feminist art movement. In general, Chicana artists were located within the broader cultural reclamation movement of the Chicano community while espousing a critical discourse related to women's issues. As artists deeply imbedded in their own communities, women disagreed with their male counterparts within the greater cultural dialogue. *Uprising of the Mujeres,* (1979; cat. no. 106), a sketch for a larger mural project, reflects the concerns of Chicanas in an emblematic construction of images of women.

In the largest perspective, Baca's contribution has been to develop structures and ideology using the mural. The *Great Wall* project is a multiracial, not just a Chicano,

chronicle of history. Strong social critique. investigative indictment, and a cine-documentary perspective characterize her work. Baca applies her style of mural painting to socially charged theories, but her murals are only one product of her art; the process of empowering Chicanos and reclaiming neighborhood space is equally important.

Santa Barraza

Santa Barraza was raised in Kingsville, Texas, which is located on the vast King Ranch of southern Texas. Her ancestors have lived in this region for generations, an area known for its historic oppression of Mexican and Chicano communities. Her personal experience of continuity and history placed Barraza in the pivotal role of cultural chronicler. Her early photorealist work, which forms an archive of cultural narrative, provides Chicanos with strong visual support affirming their own reality in the face of a hostile Anglo culture. In depicting the characters and events of her region in painstaking detail, Barraza traces the events and memories of her own life and family: first holy communions, healing ceremonies, and familiar figures, landscapes, and neighborhoods. Barraza's *Renacimiento* is a classic Chicano work that blends myth, spirituality, and family sustenance in a symbolically coded layering.

Her pastel on paper, *El Descanso Final o la Entrada* (1980 - 84; cat. no. 81), narrates her grandmother's death by overlapping the memories of generations and fusing the icon of Zapata with the Chicano soldier boys and the image of la Abuelita. Barraza's grandmother, an emancipated figure, was the first person to drive a Model-T on the ranch. Her family relationships formed the basis of her healing world view.

> My father's sister, a curandera, would go to Mexico the first Tuesday of each month to see her master. She would train, and it was an all day thing. I would go with her to keep her company. This master curandera was about four feet tall and very heavy, with real short, black hair. There was an energy about her. She had this separate mud house, and she was always sitting on her bed. In the main house lived her daughters and husband, but she lived in this little hut. There was one bed right in the center of the room and then her altar. They would talk for hours, and I could see all this incense going out through the doors, burning up. Then once they invited me in. Though I never understood why, they performed a ritual on me. I think it was like going into womanhood because I was at that age. They dug a hole in the center, of the room. She summoned one of the little boys to go out to the field and get some plants to burn. She put some coal in the pit and had the smoke going, and I had to stand over it and open my legs. I would rotate around it, and she would perform the chants. I didn't understand what was going on, but when they finished, they took the ashes and buried them so I knew it was a very important ritual.[3]

Barraza internalizes this world view within the context of a folk belief that joins the mind, body, and soul and does not distinguish clearly between the natural and the supernatural. Objects of power, herbs, and talismans are the common currency of such healing. The blending of this often secret curing with the maintenance of home altars stands as a powerful parallel to the allegory of the mass and the ritual of Catholicism.

These themes remained part of Barraza's work even as she shifted from photorealism to expressionism. Like many Chicanas, she moved away from collective and historical imagery and toward a personal visual representation as an organic part of her own development. In the 1980s she began to work in mixed media and printmaking, using an intimate and highly charged feminine imagery. Dreams, healing gestures, death, and sexuality permeate her later work. The mixed-media folding book *Una Vida,* for example, presents and preserves the deep continuity of the generations of women of her family: the spirituality that links cultural practices, religiosity, and curanderismo and that centers her world view as an artist.

Carmen Lomas Garza

The distinctive monitos paintings of Carmen Lomas Garza depict stylized figures in a South Texas community. These cultural narratives present her childhood in a Kingsville, Texas, barrio. As in Barraza's work, the historical element is felt intimately and personally in Lomas Garza's paintings. Her visual storytelling offers varied groupings of characters engaged in the everyday events and festivities, of their community. Images of the cakewalk, la cena, and el curanderismo form the memories of a generation of rural Chicanos. The details of Lomas Garza's narratives signify the collective memories that make up an important regional Chicano experience. Along with Barraza, Lomas Garza has brought to a wider audience her remembrances of a rural Texas landscape of community pastimes like the cumpleaños party, the loteria games, and the healing traditions of important figures such as Don Pedrito Jaramillo, a curandero known for his legendary cures.

In her paintings she also recreates the folk-ethos of everyday life. She incorporates popular art forms, such as papel picado, in her paintings and reclaims her regional history by affirming the artistic legacy of artesanías. The multiple voices of her experience help us to understand the universe of her paintings and to renew our own memories.

In the sociopolitical sense, Lomas Garza's use of memory stands against the historical erasure of Chicano culture. Within the greater society, her cultural narrative recreates the lived reality of a community. She remembers what we can never forget and thereby subverts the dominance of Anglo society. As critic Víctor Zamudio-Taylor reminds us, the alternative chronicle only has power in the

anecdote, or chisme. Walter Benjamin refers to the power of the anecdote when he writes:

> Anecdote brings them closer to us in space, allows them to enter our lives. Anecdote represents the extreme opposite of History . . . the true method of making things present is to image them in our own space.[4]

As an alternative chronicler, Lomas Garza offers a history that is an antidote to the institutional Texas histories. She creates in her paintings the sense of another time and uses this device to jar our memory and declare her resistance. Hers is not the history of the Alamo or Sam Houston; hers is the community record of the American G.I. Forum, the miraculous apparitions of the Virgen de Guadalupe, and the healing cures of Don Pedrito Jaramillo. Throughout this litany of recuerdos, Lomas mother, and curandera attest to Garza's grandmother, mother, and curandera attest to the powerful attributes of women. In many respects, the sequence of Lomas Garza's paintings resembles the pages of a family album or a young woman's diary.[5] They are the events that marked her. Hers is an alternative chronicle where culture and gender interpenetrate. Lomas Garza's device of flattening the figures is often perceived to be part of an unconscious, naive folk style. It is, instead, a deliberate technique that reduces the external, formal elements that might distract from the storytelling itself.

Both Ybarra-Frausto and Zamudio-Taylor note that the setting of Lomas Garza's paintings is often tinged with the sinister and the disquieting, with details such as knives and traces of blood. Most prevalent is what Zamudio-Taylor refers to as the "uncanny": the presence of a temporal reality magnified through minute details.[6]

Her gouache painting *Camas para Sueños* (1985: cat. no. 123) uses a somber palette to depict a remembered vignette of Carmen and her sister Margie lying on the roof under the moon while their mother prepares their bed in the house below. The painting commemorates the dreams and aspirations in which their mother encouraged them to indulge while she provided protection and sustenance. In this sense her narratives tell of both a sociocultural and internal psychology of gender identity.

Throughout Lomas Garza's chronicle we glimpse the artist as a young girl struggling against a world filled with discrimination and hostility. She has recalled:

> They would make snide remarks about your dresses and your being dirty. "Look at you, your dress is torn and hand-me-down. Why don't you ever set your hair? Don't you ever carry a purse?"[7]

Reconciling the past history and the anticipated future is the great task of each individual seeking to create an inner identity. Lomas Garza, like others of her generation, has had to mediate vastly disparate worlds. Beyond that she has had to locate her potential as a woman and as an artist within the cultural roles assigned to females. *Camas para Sueños* shows how that reconciliation was made possible within the family context.

Ester Hernández

Ester Hernández is of both Yaqui and Mexican descent. The influences of her parents, and particularly her grandmother, infuse her work with an ongoing set of images. Although imbued with the familial, her works provoke and defy the viewer. From her earliest association with the Mujeres Muralistas in the 1970s through her portraits in serigraphy and oil pastels, Hernández has consistently indicted society through her powerful and memorable images. Her classic print, *Sun Mad,* (1982; cat. no. 115). which transforms the smiling Sun Maid of the commercial raisin box into a skeleton, is a stinging and disturbing icon of death. *Sun Mad* not only recalls the satirical tradition of Mexican artists, such as the nineteenth-century printmaker Guadalupe Posada, but also conveys her own rage at having been unknowingly contaminated by poisonous pesticides used in the fields where she worked.

The serigraph *Tejido de los Desaparecidos* (1984; cat. no. 121) potently blends an innocent pattern of folkloric weaving with the subtle but alarming images of calaveras, helicopters, and blood. Hernández has mastered the disquieting technique of juxtaposing the seemingly benign domestic symbol with horrifyingly unexpected elements.

Equally important is how she reworks the female image. Marked by the early family models of mother and grandmother as well as the festivities of the local Guadalupana society, she has articulated the gender issue in a series of portraits, such as those of Lydia Mendoza and Frida Kahlo as calaveras. Her Guadalupe karate fighter in the print *La Virgen de Guadalupe Defendiendo los Derechos de los Xicanos (*1975; cat. no. 100), in particular, breaks the traditional role of the Virgen de Guadalupe as icon and repositions her as a feminist assertion. Her Guadalupe karate fighter and *La Llorona* are two of the signature pieces of her generation.

Crucial to her visual commitment to the issues of empowerment is her lived commitment to social service among the elderly, the disabled, and the farmworkers within the cultural institutions of her community. Like most of her Chicana peers, she produces works of art and is of service within the community. Hernández, along with Yolanda López, restructures the feminine through social critique. She subverts, recontextualizes, and thus transforms culturally traditional images into a series of feminist icons.

Yolanda López

The potential of feminine images to emancipate women is best realized in the landmark Guadalupe series by Yolanda López (1978; cat. nos. 103, 104, 105). López restates the Virgin of Guadalupe by removing the traditional figure from the halo of rays and replacing it with powerful images of family and self. The traditional icon is customarily portrayed as a passive and submissive figure. López's Guadalupes are mobile, hardworking, assertive, working-class images of the abuela as a strong, solid nurturer, mother as a family-supporting seamstress, and daughter as a contemporary artist and powerful runner. This repositioning becomes both satire and provocation, while retaining the transfigurative liberation of the icon. By breaking the bonds of Guadalupe and setting her free, López attests to the internal familiarity of the image and the powerful influence of her own family members. The art in this series does not simply reflect an existing ideology; it actively constructs a new one. It attests to the critique of traditional Mexican women's roles and religious oppression in a self-fashioning of new identities.

López works with a variety of forms, including prints, posters, drawings, videos, and installations Throughout this range of forms, her intent is to indict, analyze, and critique. From her earliest commitment to the farmworkers' struggle, to the cause of Los Siete—the seven political activists from San Francisco's Mission District who were charged with and later aquitted of killing a policeman in 1969—to examining conditions existing along the border, López melds her personal and political activism in the aesthetic of her community.

Her early experience with cultural conflict, Anglo discrimination, and even adolescent conflict itself sets the stage for her efforts to redefine the feminine in a feminist context. López has stated:

> The ideal was white, and I was not. I didn't understand it in those terms as such, but I knew very well that I didn't look like that. So I never considered myself pretty or anything like that. Like all thirteen and fourteen-year-olds, I worked very hard at grooming myself.[8]

López's close relationship with her grandmother connected her with a cultural memory unavailable through her young working mother. The family tales of migration and change were gifts of history from her abuela and later served as text for her installation work. Becoming a mother herself also heightened and expanded her concern with and focus on,the family and the future. López uses cultural memory to connect the generations of her family, and this adds a new dimension to socially charged work. Currently, she has moved into both community and domestic discourse on object and image, politics and power in her analysis of Mexican kitsch and her video work on Mexicana stereotypes.

Patricia Rodríguez

Early in the Chicano Movement, Rodríguez, like others, was mentored by artists such as Esteban Villa and José Montoya. Nevertheless, Rodríguez, like many other Chicanas, recognized an element of male exclusivity that required women to form their own collectives. The impulse to make a collective commitment was great in the early period of the Movement. Rodríguez recalled:

> You understood what discrimination was about . . . . I felt that I had a responsibility. I had a duty as part of this younger generation with this kind of consciousness to try and correct some of those things. It was like enlisting in the army. If I had to have art become part of that duty for X amount of time, then it would, because it was simply something that I would have felt terrible if I had not done.[9]

For Rodríguez, as for many other artists, el Movimiento offered hope for a generation raised within discrimination and conflict. It created new models and a new sense of their potential as artists. The Movement focused on collective, publicly accessible, and socially committed work, and Las Mujeres Muralistas was driven by these values. The traditional male model of the individual artist was too limiting, and Rodríguez turned to women's traditions for a model that could strengthen her life as an artist and cultural worker. Las Mujeres Muralistas was formed to give working artists a support structure and only included women. Together, Irene Pérez, Graciela Carrillo, Consuelo Méndez, and Rodríguez worked as a team on the arduous and sometimes hazardous task of painting murals in public spaces. Circumscribing public space was rarely associated with the work of women, and Las Mujeres Muralistas was a revolutionary effort. Their structure resembled that of other organizations in the Movement whose work was publicly accessible, antielitist, and collective in nature. Their formula was feminist, however, and therefore unique. Although short-lived as a collective force, Las Mujeres Muralistas exerted a considerable impact on Chicano and Chicana art and artists.

In the years after Las Mujeres Muralistas, Rodríguez turned to a more private and intimate form of art, yet one deeply marked by the ceremonial and enduring memories of her rural childhood: her retablo box pieces. In these boxes, Rodríguez represents private space within public discourse. She elaborates and retells stories of childhood festivities, rural celebrations, and patterns of kinship and community in satirical stagings within the small box tableau. She persistently uses memory as device of emancipation.

Rodríguez's *Sewing Box* includes the predictable elements of feminine portraiture, such as threads, bits of fabric, milagros, and toy doll limbs. Compartmentalized in distinct enclosures with drawers partially opened, small plastic soldiers, representing the dominant patriarchy, are offered in juxtaposition to the feminine materials. She reminds us of the segregated roles of girl and boy and of nurturing and aggression through these phenomena of discarded experience. Tokens of love and narratives of domesticity and ruin are presented as a secret exposed to us, but from which we are ultimately excluded.

Retablo, or box art, has a strong tradition among both Chicano and Chicana artists, due in part to the persistence of the venerated pre-Hispanic and Catholic reliquaries. As Tomás Ybarra-Frausto writes:

> These sacred objects were venerated religious items such as a supposed thorn from the crown of the crucifixion, a piece of the true cross or vials of blood or mummified anatomical parts of a holy personage displayed behind glass in elaborate containers. As worshipers touched or venerated them, their aura or power was transferred to the supplicant.[10]

The creative reconstruction of these reliquaries through domesticana retrieves memory and captures in permanent imagery the ephemeral and temporal remembrances of things past. In assemblage, bricolage, miniaturization, and small sculpture, Rodríguez creates a mimetic worldview that retells her feminine past from a new position. The rasquache attitude of making the most from the least in dazzling displays of popular decorative art marks much of Rodríguez's work, including the box portrait *José Montoya,* (1973; cat. no. 60). Similar to the function of home altars, Rodríguez's ceremonial works document, accrue, and detail events of family relations through arrangements often characterized by a subtle sense of the seductive, the veiled, and the contained. Like small stage sets they present themes of passion, death, healing, ancestry, and the everyday, and serve as narrative junctures for broader cultural themes.

Patssi Valdez

The early work of Patssi Valdez was integrally tied to the urban conceptual group Asco. Raised in Los Angeles, Valdez faced many of the problems common to urban life: poverty, violence, alienation, and family fragmentation. Detached from traditional rural experiences, Valdez and the other members of Asco sought the meaning of the Chicano experience in their own inner-city environment.

Along with Gronk, Harry Gamboa, Jr., and Willie Herrón, Valdez articulated a visual and conceptual language of her own urbanism. Like a tierra incognita, the Los Angeles context inspired works such as *The Instant Mural* (1974), *The Walking Mural* (1972), the No Movies, and other satirical, iconoclastic gestures of impermanence. Valdez, the only woman participating in Asco's aesthetic of alienation, developed a feminine iconography out of her own need to create instant glamour in an impoverished world. Using herself as an object of art, she collaborated on producing a series of images of her own persona through the media of pageantry, urban spectacle, and photomontage. Like other artists who shared her Los Angeles experience, she used fragments of television, film, fashion, and theater to produce satirical statements on America's throw-away society.

Asco produced a counterpoint to the traditional regional cultural politics of the Chicano Movement. Their alienated urban focus often clashed with the more idealized family and community narratives of the Southwest. Valdez began to construct her own ephemeral installations composed of urban discards, party materials, and her own photographic studies. Through her installations Valdez contributed to an urban feminine rasquache that could only be created from the remnants of a metropolis. Her reference points were the glamorous industries of cinema, television, and fashion and their spontaneous obsolescence. In the company of the other members of Asco, who were much like a family, Valdez formed part of a larger social indictment of the violent, disturbing conditions facing Chicanos: la Migra, police harassment, homelessness, and psychological isolation.

In her installation work Valdez reminds us of the sincere and innocent longing for an inaccessible world of beauty and festivity that contrasts with the lived reality of ruination, destruction, and loss. In site-specific homages to the Black Virgin, she uses the discards of pop culture, the remnants of party materials, and the hyperfeminine gestures of the glamorous to represent the polarities of purity and debasement. She combines and recombines jewelry, kitchenware, toiletries, saints, holy cards, and milagros to create the spectacle of the modern metropolis. She juxtaposes the patriarchal polarities of the good woman and the bad woman and thus transgresses the controlling masculine gaze. This transgression brings redemption and enunciates the language of domesticana as both the product and the pose of rasquachismo.

In her later development, Patssi Valdez turned to a more intimate and private domain. Images of her domestic world include introspective and provocative self-portraits. Her details of private landscapes present a kind of feminine diary and replace the instant glamour of her earlier works. She now presents a more permanent perspective of the enduring objects of her everyday world.

Summary

These artists continuously negotiate the narrative in their work, an effort that binds their strikingly diverse work. The diversity of region and generation, which directly affects their choice of themes, materials, and forms, brings richness to their output. In the 1960s and 1970s, working within the demands of the larger Chicano Movement to produce socially charged work, many of these artists also redefined their own roles within Mexican/Chicano culture. They reorchestrated, for example, the positive strengths of mother and grandmother to emancipate the roles of women. The idiom of feminist Chicanas inhibited the traditional roles and images, a change that called for negotiation within the cultural group. This reorchestration was problematic. The balancing of enduring, sustaining aspects of cherished cultural roles and practices, and the strengthening of emancipatory devices is never accomplished easily. Tradition and innovation are intertwined and reflected in the degree to which Chicanas drew images, themes, and content from the apparently constricting and contradictory roles. Armed with a contemporary understanding of the struggles facing them, these artists used ancestry, ceremony, mass media, social subversion, and critique to fashion an aesthetic and reconstruct ideologically a new language of liberation for themselves. Perhaps the greatest hallmark is that disparate views of a single cultural phenomenon, such as Yolanda López's representation of the Virgen de Guadalupe and the traditional Virgen image, have been able to coexist in Chicana art.

Exploring a new aesthetic vocabulary is the first step in establishing a context for Chicana artists, although that vocabulary is neither fixed nor singular. Narration, the circumscription of domestic space and spirit, indictment, and ceremony are often fissured in a constantly shifting language. These artists move freely within broad sensibilities and intentions, breaking the preexisting categories and enlarging the vocabulary of the feminine. Reclaiming our past and marking our experiences through our culture and lives have been the real contributions of Chicana artists. Their work continually recasts an open identity where tradition and innovation must live together.

Notes

1. See Griselda Pollock, *Vision and Difference—Femininity, Feminism and the Histories of Art* (London and New York: Routledge Press, 1988).
2. For an introduction to the concept of rasquache from the larger cultural perspective, see essay by Tomás Ybarra-Frausto, "Rasquachismo: A Chicano Sensibility."
3. Santa Barraza, interview with the author, 1982.
4. Walter Benjamin, *Illuminations* (New York: Harcourt, Brace & World, 1968).
5. Lomas Garza has in fact recently published a selection of her paintings as a children's book with short bilingual narratives, *Family Pictures* (San Francisco: Children's Book Press, 1990).
6. Víctor Zamudio-Taylor, "Allegory, Memory & History," lecture presented at the Museum of Hispanic Art, New York, 1990.
7. Carmen Lomas Garza, interview with the author, 1982.
8. Yolanda López, interview with the author, 1982.
9. Patricia Rodríguez, interview with the author, 1982.
10. Tomás Ybarra-Frausto, "Cultural Context," in *Ceremony of Memory* (Santa Fe, New Mexico: Center for Contemporary Arts of Santa Fe, 1988), 11.

Chicano Literary Folklore

María Herrera-Sobek

U p to the present the formulation of an exact definition for the term "folklore" has been a difficult and elusive goal. The *Standard Dictionary of Folklore, Mythology and Legend* incorporates no less than twenty-one separate definitions submitted by experts in the field. A cursory examination of these definitions, however, does show a certain consistency in the general framework of their constructs. We note, for example, that certain key words are repeatedly utilized in the descriptions of this cultural phenomenon. Scholars generally agree that folklore encompasses the *oral traditions* (as opposed to the written traditions) of a people that have been handed down from generation to generation. Traditions considered under the field of folkloristics include:

1. prose narratives (myths, folktales, legends, memorates, *casos,* jests);
2. folksongs (ballads, *canciones, décimas, coplas);*
3. folk speech;
4. proverbs and proverbial expressions;
5. folk drama;
6. children's songs and games;
7. riddles;
8. beliefs and folk medicine;
9. folk festivals;
10. folk arts and crafts;
11. folk dance; and
12. folk gestures. In this study we focus on the first eight genres subsumed under the category of literary folklore.

We define Chicano folklore as that folklore belonging to the group of people of Mexican-American descent residing in the United States; the majority living mainly in the American Southwest: Texas, California, Arizona, New Mexico, and Colorado. Interest in Chicano folklore scholarship began early in the twentieth century with the efforts of Aurelio M. Espinosa (from New Mexico) who collected, analyzed, and published articles and books related to Hispanic folklore. Espinosa contributed serious articles and books on New Mexican-Spanish romances, folktales, children's songs and games, and other related areas. Generally regarded as an "Españolista," Espinosa was principally concerned with demonstrating that the folklore evidenced in New Mexico was a direct descendant of the folklore the original Spanish settlers introduced in the area and that it had not been "contaminated" by Mexican influences. This thesis was of course debunked by later scholars, but his collections and studies nevertheless first pointed out the richness of oral traditions extant in the Southwest. Espinosa is particularly remembered for his studies on the New Mexican romance. In his collections are included such famous romances as "La aparición," "Gerineldo," "Estaba señor don Gato," "El piojo y la liendre," and others. The following is a short version of "La esposa infiel":

Andándome yo paseando
por las orillas del mar
me encontré una chaparrita
y me puse a platicar
"¡Mi marido, mi marido!
¡Válgame Dios! ¿Qué haré yo?"
 "Siéntese aquí en ese catre.
Déjeme ir a conversar yo?"
"¿De quién es ese caballo
que en mi corral relinchó?"
"Ese es de un hermano tuyo
que tu padre te lo mandó
pa que vayas al casorio
de un hermano que se casó."
"Ya me puedes ir diciendo
que caballos tengo yo."
 La mujer murió a la una
y el hombre murió a las dos.[1]

While I was traveling
along the seashore
I met a petite woman
and we started to talk
"My husband, my husband!"
O my God! What shall I do?"
"Sit down on this cot.
I will talk to him."
"Whose horse it that
Which hee-hawed in my corral?"
"It belongs to your brother.
Your father sent it to you,
so you could attend the wedding
of one of your brothers."
"You can tell me now
which horses belong to me."
The wife died at one o'clock,
the man died at two.

Other scholars from New Mexico, such as Arthur León Campa and Aurora Lucero-White Lea, continued to collect and analyze the folklore of New Mexico in the decades that followed. Succeeding authors, however, began to acknowledge the great influence Mexican folklore has had on Chicano folklore. Research activity also flourished in Texas with such publications as J. Dobie's *Puro Mexicano* and Mody C. Boatright's *Mexican Border Ballads and Other Lore* in the 1930s and 1940s.

The foremost Chicano folklore scholar, however, is no doubt Américo Paredes from Texas, who has been at the forefront of folklore scholarship in general and Mexican-American folklore research in particular since the publication in 1958 of his book *With His Pistol in His Hand: A Border Ballad and Its Hero.* In the three decades since then, Paredes has published close to one hundred articles and books dealing specifically with Mexican-America folklore. His expertise and intimate knowledge of the Chicano experience led him to examine such wide ranging topics as the *corrido,* the *décima,* folk speech, folk medicine, the jest, the proverb, as well as other Chicano-related issues. His clarity of thought, perceptiveness, and incisive logic provided him with the proper tools to make serious, original contributions to the field in general and to Chicano studies in particular.

In recent years the turbulent 1960s and 1970s initiated a new awareness of the Chicano experience. The social upheavals and confrontations of this era were no doubt directly responsible for stimulating research related to and dealing with Mexican-American issues. Chicano folklore benefited directly from this upsurge in interest; the numerous books and articles published in the 1960s in various genres of folklore attest to this fact. In an issue of *Aztlán* dedicated to Mexican-American folklore and art, Américo Paredes elaborates in no uncertain terms that:

folklore is of particular importance to minority groups such as the Mexican Americans because their basic sense of identity is expressed in a language with an "unofficial" status, different from the one used by the official culture. We can say, then, that while in Mexico the Mexican may well seek lo mexicano in art, literature, philosophy, or history—as well as in folklore—the Mexican American would do well to seek his identity in his folklore.[2]

No doubt Chicano folkloristics will continue to prosper in the future and will prove profitable in the understanding and elucidation of the Chicano character and experience.

Prose Narrative

The categories subsumed under the broad umbrella of "prose narratives" include myths, folktales, legends, *casos,* memorates, and jests. There are no "true" Chicano myth narratives as such; myths evidenced in Chicano literature derived mainly from Aztec and Mayan sources. These myths proved vitally important in the Chicano's quest for self-definition and identity in the past twenty years. It should not be surprising that Aztec myths found fertile ground in the creative thought processes of Chicanos, who, having been denied their Indian heritage in previous decades, suddenly felt a renovated affiliation with that heritage. Thus, a new political meaning was grafted into the old myth of Aztlán, the land of the Chicanos' mythic Aztec ancestors who dwelled in the American Southwest before migrating south, to Tenochtitlán (Mexico City). Early Chicano political activists and creative writers renovated these Aztec myths in their groping for a reaffirmation of their centuries-old roots in America, sense of identity which they perceived to be not wholly Mexican, not wholly American, but Chicano. *Lo indio, lo azteca, lo maya* was no longer a source of embarrassment or something to be ashamed of, but a source of pride. Through the breathtakingly beautiful myths of the Ancients, one could perceive that brown was indeed beautiful. Alurista, one of the most prominent poets of the Chicano literary renaissance, liberally sprinkles his verses with the themes of Quetzalcóatl, priest-god of the Toltecs; Kukulcán, Mayan god; Coatlicue, an Aztec mother goddess; and many other Aztec and Mayan deities to effectively convey this new-found pride.

The folktale, on the other hand, bears the stamp of both an Indian and Spanish heritage and is a rich source of Chicano folklore. The European-Spanish heritage surfaces in the fairytale or märchentype of narratives. *María Cenicienta, Caperucita Roja, Blancanieves, The Little Horse of Seven Colors, Juan y las habichuelas,* and others of this type are obviously of European origin having migrated with the Spaniards to the New World. It was inevitable, however, that contact with a large Indian population would eventually produce a syncretism of European tales with Native American ones. In addition, a significant number of Meso-American Indian tales integrated themselves into the general Mexican and Mexican-American folktale repertoire. Thus an important number of animal tales such as those pertaining to the coyote cycle originate from Native American stock.

A similar statement can be formulated for the legends. Although many came from Europe, particularly the religious legends, a good number derive from Meso-American Indian lore. Others demonstrate a decided syncretism in the type of motifs found in the structural framework. A good example of this process is evident in the *La Llorona* legend. Two strands exist and intermingle in this legend: one Mexican and one Aztec. According to the former version, *Llorona* was originally a beautiful young mestizo woman madly in love with a wealthy Spanish caballero. The fruit of this love resulted in various children (one to nine, the number varies) out of wedlock; the Spaniard having promised to eventually marry her. It came to pass that one night the young mestizo's mother was informed of her caballero's impending wedding. On the night of her lover's wedding, after peeking through the window of her lover's house witnessing the wedding scene, she returns to her own home intensely distraught. There, in a fit of rage and/or insanity, she kills all her children. Having realized her deed, she madly rushes out of her house screaming "¡Ayyyyy, mis hijos!" As punishment for this barbaric deed, she roams the waterways, any dark street or road screeching, "¡Ayyyyy, mis hijos!" forever in search of her lost children. According to the Aztec version, on the other hand, *La Lórona* was a woman who, before the conquest, predicted the fall of the Aztec empire and was seen in the streets of the Aztec capital in a white dress, long hair in disarray and screaming in anguish, "¡Ayyyy, mis hijos!" in anticipated pain of the loss to come.

Some excellent work has been done on the Mexican/Chicano legend and folktale. Juan Rael published a large collection of tales from Colorado. Stanley L. Robe from UCLA has done extensive research on tales and legends from various parts of Mexico and the Southwest. Elaine Miller published a collection of folktales from the Los Angeles area called *Mexican Folk Narrative from the Los Angeles Area* (1973). Her collection includes religious narrative such as La Virgen de Talpa and El Santo Niño de Atocha, devil narratives, the return of the dead-that is, legends depicting the apparition of dead persons, another very popular type being the dead person that returns to pay a *manda* (promise) to some saint—buried treasure, *duendes,* as well as traditional tales (animal tales, tales of magic, stupid ogre tales, and others).

Américo Paredes amply explains the usefulness of legends in exploring the character of Mexicans and Mexican Americans. In an incisive article entitled "Mexican Legendry and the Rise of the Mestizo" published in 1971,[3] Paredes proposes that the "rise of the mestizo as representative of the Mexican nationality may be illuminated by the study of Mexican legendry" (p. 98). According to the author, before the "rise of the mestizo" (prenineteenth-century Mexico), legends dealt generally with supernatural, miraculous events such as the apparition of saints. As the mestizo seized power, legend content leaned toward the recounting of the deeds of flesh and blood heroes such as Heraclio Bernal, Gregorio Cortez and later, during the Mexican Revolution of 1910, the deeds and actions of the revolutionary heroes such as Pancho Villa, Emiliano Zapata, Francisco I. Madero, and others.

Recently, scholars are grappling with the new concepts of caso and memorate. These new terms are designed to meet the ever-increasing problem of defining in more precise terms the large corpus of prose narrative present in all cultures. More and more scholars are realizing that the old terminology (folktale, legend, märchen) is inadequate and too broadly based to meet the needs of rigorous scientific analysis. The terms caso, memorate, and personal experience narrative are currently used to classify a large body of narratives extant in the Mexican/Chicano folklore. The above terms generally encompass narratives that happened to the informant or to someone the informant knows. Joe Graham provides the following definition:

> a relatively brief prose narrative, focusing upon a single event, supernatural or natural, in which the protagonist or observer is the narrator or someone the narrator knows and vouches for, and which is normally used as evidence or as an example to illustrate that "this kind of thing happens."[4]

Graham offers fourteen types of casos discernible by their theme and structure in Chicano folklore. The following is an example:

Caso Type I

A Mexican American becomes ill and is taken to a doctor, who either treats him, with no visible results, or says that the person is not ill. The person is taken to a *curandero* or folk practitioner, who provides the proper remedy, and the patient gets well. (p. 31)

These new areas of endeavor in folklore, such as the caso, memorate, and personal experience narrative, illustrate the richness and complexity of Mexican/ Chicano culture.

An equally significant area of folklore is the *chiste* or jest. Again, Américo Paredes undertook seminal research in this genre and provided a theoretical construct for understanding the underlying basis of much of Chicano folklore in general, and Chicano jokes in particular. Paredes' basic thesis underscores the element of cultural conflict as the principal moving force generating Chicano folklore.

Much of Chicano humor derives from the confrontation of two cultures: one Mexican, Catholic, Spanish-speaking; the other Anglo, Protestant, English-speaking. A large corpus of jokes, for example, relies on Mexican-Anglo conflicts using the linguistic differences between the two cultures as points of departure. Notice the following:

A gringo was traveling on a rural Mexican road in his Cadillac when suddenly a man and his burro block his path. The gringo gets down from his car, takes off his glove, and slaps the Mexican in the face with the glove yelling, "Son-of-a-bitch!" Whereupon' the Mexican takes off his huarache, slaps the gringo in the face and yells, "B.F. Goodrich!"[5]

Here, although the Mexican does not understand the insult, he manages to outsmart the Anglo by striking the hardest blow. It is typical of Chicano humor in general that the Mexican/Chicano protagonist comes out the best in the exchange.

There is a cycle of jokes, however, where the protagonist (a Mexican immigrant) is the butt of the joke. This cycle of jokes portrays the difficulties recently arrived Mexicans have due to the differences in language. A good example of this type of joke follows:

A recently arrived Mexican immigrant who cannot read English wants to buy a coke. He sees a coke machine and takes the smallest coin he has which is a dime and inserts it in the slot. A red light flashes out reading *DIME*. The man reads it in Spanish with its equivalent meaning of "Tell me!" So the fellow looks around and whispers: "¡Dame una coca!" ("Give me a coke!")[6]

These jokes told by immigrants themselves to other immigrants serve cathartic function of relieving the stress and anxiety concomitant with moving to a foreign country.

A second basic factor that characterizes many Chicano jokes is the bilingualism expressed within the jokes as evidenced in the two examples given above. Many Chicano jokes require an understanding of both Spanish and English due to the fact that the structure of the jokes utilizes the misunderstanding of one or both languages to deliver its intended humor and punch line.

Folksongs

Two of the most researched genres of Chicano folksongs are corrido and the décima. Both Arthur L. Campa and Américo Paredes have contributed substantial scholarly articles and collections of these two types of folklore.

The corrido or ballad has been and continues to be an important means of self-expression for the Chicano community. In fact, the corrido, according to Américo Paredes' theory on the renaissance of this genre, experiences its rebirth as a result of the bloody conflict between Mexicans and Anglos in the Mexican-American War of 1848. A conquered people, having been denied access to the printing press of the dominant culture, seized the corrido as a valid form of self-expression, historical documentation, and information dissemination.[7]

Most scholars agree that the corrido originally derived from the Spanish romances. Imported to America during the fifteenth and sixteenth centuries, it languished in the area until the nineteenth century; at this point in time historical events propelled it to the center stage where it became the literary instrument of protest and revolt par excellence. Paredes posits that it was the clash of cultures in the Lower Rio Grande Valley where men of Mexican descent were forced "defender su derecho con su pistola en la mano" (to defend their right with a pistol in their hand). The heroic deeds and actions of these valiant, fearless men were duly recorded in the oral history and expressive folklore of the people. Corridos were lustily and proudly sung from ranch to ranch and pueblo to pueblo, the lyrics of these depicting the exploits of Chicanos who resisted the encroachment and heavy hand of the Anglo settlers.

Paredes incisively analyzes one of these corridos in his seminal book *With His Pistol in His Hand: A Border Ballad and Its Hero*. The corrido examined in this work depicts the legend of Gregorio Cortez who, having been unjustly accused of killing a Texas sheriff, was hunted down through the state of Texas until he voluntarily surrendered to the Texas Rangers (after realizing his family had been imprisoned).

Another example of the Chicano/Anglo conflict-type corridos that vividly portrays this state of affairs is the "Corrido de Joaquín Murieta."

Yo no soy americano
pero comprendo el inglés.
Yo lo aprendí con mi hermano
al derecho y al revés.
A cualquier americano
lo hago temblar a mis pies.

Cuando apenas era un niño
huérfano a mí me dejaron.
Nadie me hizo ni un cariño,
a mi hermano lo mataron.
Y a mi esposa Carmelita,
cobardes la asesinaron.

Yo me vine de Hermosillo
en busca de oro y riqueza.
Al indio pobre y sencillo
lo defendí con fiereza.
Y a buen precio los sherifes
pagaban por me cabeza.

A los ricos avarientos,
yo les quité su dinero.
Con los humildes y pobres
yo me quité mi sombrero.
Ay, que leyes tan injustas
fue llamarme bandolero.

A Murieta no le gusta
lo que hace no es desmentir.
Vengo a vengar a mi esposa,
y lo vuelvo a repetir,
Carmelita tan hermosa,
como la hicieron sufrir.

Por cantinas me metí,
castigando americanos.
"Tú serás el capitán
que mataste a mi hermano.
Lo agarraste indefenso,
orgulloso americano."

Mi carrera comenzó
por una escena terrible.
Cuando llegué a setecientos
ya mi nombre era temible.
Cuando llegué a mil doscientos
ya mi nombre era terrible.

Yo soy aquel que domina
hasta leones africanos.
Por eso salgo al camino
a matar americanos.
Ya no es otro mi destino
¡pongan cuidado, parroquianos!

Las pistolas y las dagas
son juguetes para mí.

I am not an American
but I understand English.
I learned it with my brother
forwards and backwards.
And any American
I make tremble at my feet.

When I was barely a child
I was left an orphan.
No one gave any love,
they killed my brother,
And my wife Carmelita,
the cowards assassinated her.

I came from Hermosillo
in search of gold and riches.
The Indian poor and simple
I defended with fierceness
And a good price the sheriffs
would pay for my head.

From the greedy rich,
I took away their money.
With the humble and poor
I took off my hat.
Oh, what laws so unjust
to call me a highwayman.

Murieta does not like
to be falsely accused.
I come to avenge my wife,
and again I repeat it,
Carmelita so lovely
how they made her suffer.

Through bars I went
punishing Americans.
"You must be the captain
who killed my brother.
You grabbed him defenseless
you stuck-up American."

My career began
because of a terrible scene.
When I got to seven hundred
[killed]
then my name was dreaded.
When I got to twelve hundred
Then my name was terrible.

I am the one who dominates
even African lions.
That's why I go out on the road
to kill Americans.
Now my destiny is no other,
watch out, you people!

Pistols and daggers
are playthings for me.

Balazos y puñaladas,
carcajadas para mí.
Ahora con medios cortados
ya se asustan por aquí.

No soy chileno ni extraño
en este suelo que piso.
De México es California,
porque Dios así lo quiso.
Y en mi sarape cosida
traigo mi fe de bautismo.

Que bonito es California
con sus calles alineadas,
donde paseaba Murieta
con su tropa bien formada,
con su pistola repleta,
y su montura plateada.

Me he paseado en California
por el año del cincuenta.
Con mi montura plateada,
y mi pistola repleta.
Y soy ese mexicano
de nombre Joaquín Murieta.

Bullets and stabbings
big laughs for me.
With their means cut off
they're afraid around here.

I'm neither a Chilean nor a
stranger
on this soil which I tread.
California is Mexico's
because God wanted it that way,
And in my stitched serape,
I carry my baptismal certificate.

How pretty is California
with her well-laid-out streets
where Murieta passed by
with his troops,
with his loaded pistol,
and his silver-plated saddle.

I've had a good time in California
through the year of '50 [1850].
With my silver-plated saddle
and my pistol loaded
I am that Mexican
by the name of Joaquín Murieta.[8]

Early corridos from the Lower Rio Grande Valley in Texas served as paradigms for the *guerrillero,* rebel corridos that surfaced in Mexico during Porfirio Díaz's repressive regime, one of the most famous of these corridos being "El corrido de Heraclio Bernal." The events of the Mexican Revolution of 1910 provided further material for corrido productions. The heroes of the revolution were immortalized in the lyrics of the corrido: Pancho Villa, Emiliano Zapata, Benjamín Argumedo, Francisco I. Madero, Venustiano Carranza, La Adelita, and many others.

The ever-present stream of Mexican immigrants to the United States in search of work continually replenishes the general repertoire of Chicano folk songs with Mexican corridos. Thus, literally thousands of corridos exist in the southwestern part of the United States with as varied themes as Mexican immigrant corridos ("El deportado," "Corrido de Pennsylvania," "Corrido de Texas"), corridos whose main subject is horses ("El potro lobo gatiado"), those depicting the exploits of drug and tequila smugglers ("El tequilero"), love-tragedy corridos ("Rosita Alvírez," "La 'Güera' Chavela," "Rafaelita"), those extolling the life and death of political figures such as the Kennedy corridos, and those dealing with protest. During César Chávez's farmworkers' union movement of the 1960s and 1970s, numerous songs appeared depicting the hardships and aspirations of the farmworkers. These are frequently sung at protest rallies and serve as an effective means of uniting the people in a common cause. At

present the corrido is very much a vital force in ethnic identification and in expressing through its lyrics the continuing struggle for achieving social justice in America.

La décima, on the other hand, experienced its apogee in the eighteenth and nineteenth century in both Mexico and the Southwest. Américo Paredes has several articles on the décima in Texas and Arthur L. Campa has a significant collection of décimas from New Mexico. Its rigid form, however (in contrast to the flexible form of the corrido), doomed it to be discarded in favor of the more flexible corrido.

Folk Speech

Chicano Spanish has recently been the focus of intense study, particularly by linguists and those interested in bilingual education. The realization by American schools and by linguists that the Spanish spoken in the Southwest differed markedly from that spoken in Spain, Mexico, and other Latin-American countries, led to a flurry of research. The most comprehensive bibliography on Chicano speech is Richard V. Teschner, Garland D. Bills, and Jerry R. Craddock's *Spanish and English of United States Hispanos: A Critical, Annotated, Linguistic Bibliography* (1975), which cites 675 items. The most fruitful work undertaken is on the aspect of code-switching (switching in the middle of a phrase, sentence, or paragraph from English to Spanish or vice versa), but the most outstanding area of research from a folklorist's point of view has been neglected. Thus, little in-depth research is available on *caló* (the jargon of the underworld or the pachuco) or other areas of folk speech. A seminal work by George C. Baker "Pachuco: An American-Spanish Argot and Its Social Function in Tucson, Arizona" (1975) [9] is still one of the best works in the field. Baker studied the speech of *pachucos* from Tucson and related this speech to the social function it played within the in-group and the out-group. Some of these words include: *carnal* (brother), *jaina* (girlfriend), *chante* (house), *ruca* (girl), *birrea* (beer), *cantón* (house), *chale* (no), *lisa* (shirt), *simón* (yes) and *refinar* (to eat). The lack of studies in this genre is indeed deplorable. José Limón, a scholar on folklore, has amply demonstrated the importance of this area in his article "The Folk Performance of 'Chicano' and the Cultural Limits of Political Ideology." Limón analyzes the failure of the folk term *Chicano* to gain widespread acceptance in the community and posits the thesis that *"in part* this failure may be attributed to the unintentional violation of the community's rules about the socially appropriate use of the term—rules keyed on the community's definition of the performance of the term as belonging to the folklore genres of nicknaming and ethnic slurs."[10] It is fairly easy to deduce from this study that if political movements are to succeed, the leaders of these movements must have an intimate and working knowledge of the people they propose to represent. One way to accomplish this is through an in-depth understanding of the cultural vectors (such as folklore) operative in the community.

Proverbs and Proverbial Expressions

Proverbs and proverbial expressions, entities intimately related to folk speech, form an integral part of Chicano folklore. Although used most frequently by the older generation, a recent study undertaken by Shirley Arora[11] demonstrates that the younger generations of Chicanos are indeed aware of proverbs, having been raised by a mother, father, or other family member who interspersed their speech with these colorful expressions.

A proverb may be defined as a short, succinct expression that encompasses within its words a philosophical wisdom. Examples include:

1. Más vale pájaro en mano que ver un ciento volar. (Better a bird in hand than two in the bush.)
2. Dime con quién andas y te diré quién eres. (Tell me who your friends are and I'll tell you who you are.)
3. De tal palo tal astilla. (A chip off the old block.)
4. El que con lobos anda a aullar se enseña. (He who runs around with wolves will learn how to howl.)
5. En boca cerrada no entran moscas. (In a closed mouth no flies can enter.)

6. Todo cabe en un jarrito sabiéndolo acomodar. (All can be filled in a mug if you know how to place things right.)
7. Al que madruga Dios lo ayuda. (He who rises early God helps.)
8. Dios dice: "Ayúdate que yo te ayudaré." (God helps those who help themselves.)
9. El que con niños se acuesta mojado se levanta. (He who sleeps with children wakes up wet.)[12]

The proverb, as other folklore genres prove to be, is yet another important area in which the philosophy or worldview of a people can be profitably explored. Américo Paredes, however, advised extreme caution when attempting to analyze the character of a people and warns against literal interpretation of proverbs and/or deducing Mexican/Chicano traits when taken out of context. Analysis of proverbs must be undertaken in the context in which these expressions are uttered. Otherwise, the social scientist or folklorist may be, albeit unwittingly, misled to make totally false and harmful generalizations about the character of a people. Valuable information regarding the Chicano experience can be gleaned from careful research of these entities and their use in Chicano households as demonstrated by Shirley Arora's article "Proverbs in Mexican American Tradition." Her study provides key insights into status and usage of proverbs by Chicanos in Los Angeles. For example, Arora found that frequent use of proverbs is most noticeable in the area of child-rearing, "from the inculcation of table manner—El que come y canta loco se levanta, la mano larga nunca alcanza—to the regulation of social relationships and dating behavior" (p. 59). Arora also indicates that proverbs have a potential and may indeed be already employed for purposes of ethnic identification and group solidarity. Needless to say, more in-depth studies on proverb usage need to be undertaken to better comprehend this particular aspect of Chicano folklore.

Shirley Arora has also undertaken extensive research on proverbial comparisons in the Los Angeles area in her work *Proverbial Comparisons and Related Expressions in Spanish.* The comparison may be defined as a phrase in which the following formulaic structures appear:

está como . . .
tan . . . como
tan . . . que

The exaggeration likewise employs the formulaic structures of:

más . . . que

Arora interviewed 517 informants and collected thousands of entries. Some examples follow.

1. Más aburrido que un abogado (more boring than a lawyer) (p. 37).
2. Tan flaca que si se traga una aceituna parece que está preñada (so skinny that if she swallows an olive she looks pregnant) (p. 38).
3. Más alegre que un día de pago (as happy as payday) (p. 172).
4. Es tan avaro que no da ni los buenos días (he's so stingy that he doesn't even give a good morning) (p. 172).
5. Se repite como disco rayado (he repeats himself like a scratched record) (p. 179).

The humorous nature and originality of many of these proverbial expressions, together with the large number collected within a relatively small geographic area (greater Los Angeles), indicate the amazing creativity present in the speech of the Chicano community. It is evident in the large number of entries of both proverbs and proverbial expressions collected by Arora that a great premium is placed on language skills and language dexterity by Chicanos. Arora found in her study that more often than not people with a large repertoire of proverbial expressions elicited admiration and respect from the community.

Proverbs and proverbial expressions provide a strong affectivity factor toward the Spanish language and are no doubt one important reason for the high premium placed on preserving the Spanish language. The wealth of Spanish proverbs and the witticism inherent in proverbial expressions contribute to the widespread folk belief that Spanish is one of the most delightful languages in the world. This folk belief in turn brings us to closer understanding of why a conquered people, after one hundred years of political and cultural domination, tenaciously clings to one of their cultural manifestations-the Spanish language.

Folk Theatre

The folk theatre of the Chicano, like Mexican- and Latin-American theatre, traces its roots to the Spanish *conquistadores* and their religious plays. The early missionaries, interested in converting the Indians of the New World, discovered that, due to the differences in language representations of biblical and religious stories, drama provided an effective means of indoctrinating them into the Catholic faith. Thus, early theatrical works in the western hemisphere were religious plays in which the Indians themselves played major roles and which were extremely popular with the faithful. These plays generally took place in the church atrium and were presented to the populace on specific holy days such as Christmas or Easter Sunday. When New Mexico was settled in the seventeenth century, works that had been successful in Mexico migrated with the Spanish and Mexican settlers into what is now the American Southwest. Arthur Campa and Aurora Lucero-White Lea have both collected folk plays from this region. Among those collected is *Coloquio de los Pastores*, which, according to Lea, "represents that older type of traditional Nativity play which was presented in the village church on Christmas Eve in lieu of Midnight Mass when that village had no resident priest."[14]

Other popular plays collected include: *La aurora del nuevo día, Adán y Eva, Los tres reyes, El niño perdido, Las cuatro apariciones de Nuestra Señora de Guadalupe, and Los moros y cristianos*. One should also mention the pastorelas or shepherd's plays performed during the Christmas season and which are still being enacted today. Folk theatre influenced to some extent present-day Chicano theatre, particularly that of Luis Valdez. Like the corrido, present-day Chicano theatre is being effectively used as a vehicle to convey and express the injustices perpetuated on the Mexican/Chicano by Anglo society.

Children's Songs and Games

As is true of most of the other genres of folklore, children's songs and games from the Chicano Southwest evidence basically the same categories and specimens as those from Spain. A rather flexible division of songs and games played or sung by or for children is attempted in the following major categories:

1. *canciones de cuna* (lullabyes) "Duérmete mi niño";
2. *canciones de manos y dedos* "Tortillitas" (hand and finger games);
3. *rondas* "Naranja dulce";
4. *retahilas* "El castillo de Chuchurumbel";
5. *canciones* "La muñeca";
6. *conjuros* "Sana, sana colita de rana"; and
7. miscellaneous "escondidas," "matatena," "los encantados," "rayuela."

Those of us who grew up in a Spanish-speaking environment can nostalgically remember songs and games of yore such as:

Duérmete mi niño
que tengo que hacer
lavar los pañales
ponerme a coser.

Tortillitas de manteca
pa mamá que está contenta.
Tortillitas de cebado
pa papá que está enojado.

Naranja dulce
limón partido
dame un abrazo
que yo te pido.

Doña Blanca está encerrada
en pilares de oro y plata
romperemos un pilar
para que salga Doña Blanca.

Go to sleep my child
I have work to do
wash the diapers
and some sewing too.

Little tortillas made of lard
for mommy, for happy is she.
Little tortillas made of barley
for daddy, for angry is he.

Sweet orange
lemon is cut
Give me a hug
I ask of you.

Doña Blanca is imprisoned
within pillars of gold and silver
let us break one of these pillars
so Doña Blanca can be free.[15]

Paredes made a revealing observation with regard to children's songs, and games and cultural conflict—the basic thread that runs throughout Chicano folklore. As innocuous and free from anxiety and conflict as children's games may appear, the opposite state of affairs is discovered upon close analysis. Experts agree that children oftentimes express their fears and anxieties through play. Paredes pointed this out in a game played by Chicano children that exemplifies the point. The game is "la roña" also known as "la mancha" (tag). In this game children flee from the one that has "la roña" and the latter in turn tries to "touch" or "tag" the others. In Texas the game is known as "la correa," a name given to immigration officers. Thus, by implication, the Texas children enact the real-life situation of Immigration and Naturalization Services officers trying to capture undocumented workers.[16]

Riddles

Riddles comprise another area of Chicano folklore. Archer Taylor, a folklorist from Berkeley, provides us with the classic definition of a "true riddle:" "questions that suggest an object foreign to the answer and confound the hearer by giving a solution that is obviously correct and entirely unexpected."[17]

More recently, Elli Kongas-Maranda has suggested that "the riddle is a structural unit, which necessarily consists of two parts: the riddle image and the riddle answer. In a riddling situation, these two parts are 'recited' by two different parties."[18] *La adivinanza,* as it is called in Spanish, is an integral part of the expressive culture of the Chicano. However, few studies have been undertaken on Chicano riddling habits. An exception is John M. McDowell's *Children's Riddling* (1979). McDowell's in-depth study offers extremely relevant conclusions as to the function of riddles in children's ludic activities. For McDowell,

> Riddles in the modern, industrial society serve as models of synthetic and analytic thinking. They encourage children to discover the archetypical set of commonalities binding diverse experimental realms into a single, coherent world view; and at the same time, they require children to confront the tentative status of conceptual systems, thereby fostering a flexibility of cognition evidently of some utility in a great many cultural settings.[19]

The following are some popular examples of riddles common throughout Mexico, Latin America, and the Southwest:[20]

Agua pasa por mi casa
cate de mi corazón.
Si no me adivinas ésta
eres puro burro cabezón.
        (aguacate)

Adivíname esta adivinanza
que se pela por la panza.
        (la naranja)

Una vieja larga y seca
que le escurre la manteca.
        (la vela)

Tito, Tito capotito
sube al cielo
y tira un grito.
        (el cohete)

Water passes through my house
my beloved.
If you do not answer this one
you are a thick-headed donkey.
        (avocado)

Answer this riddle for me:
You peel it from the tummy.
        ([navel] oranges)

A tall, skinny old lady
that drips lard.
        (the candle)

Tito, Tito, little cape
fly up in the sky
and give out a scream.
        (the firecracker)

As is apparent, the adivinanza challenges the intellect and the reasoning processes by offering descriptions that are close enough to resemble the objects yet so hidden between the texture (metaphors, similes) of the words as to yield them difficult to answer. The riddle, a thoroughly social act in itself in that at least two people are required for it to function, provides the players with an excellent instrument to play with language. Different opportunities are offered: rhyming schemes (nos. 1-5); disconnecting and connecting various morphemes (nos. 1 and 5); deceiving metaphorical images (nos. 2 and 3) and alliterative, onomatopoetic sounds (no. 4).

McDowell perceived two different sets of riddles in the repertoire of the children interviewed (Chicano children from a barrio in Austin, Texas in 1972).

1. a collection of riddles learned at school, from Anglo children, from the media (television, radio) and
2. a set of more traditional ones learned at home from parents, relatives, and/or peers.

One significant function deduced in this Texas study is the proposition that riddles serve enculturation purposes, (enculturation being defined as "the process of induction, wherein the individual acquires competency in his own culture, or the kinds of knowledge requisite to fulfillment of recognized social roles."[21]) In the acquisition of the riddling/habits of the dominant society one is also being acculturated into this dominant culture. The riddle, then, aside from serving the pleasure function manifest in all ludic play, equally serves other cognitive endeavors.

Folk Belief and Folk Medicine

The folk-belief system of the Chicano community, particularly as it deals with folk medicine and curanderismo, is one of the most controversial areas of scholarship in Chicano folklore. In a revealing article by

Beatrice A. Roeder, "Health Care Beliefs and Practices Among Mexican Americans: A Review of the Literature,"[22] the author identified four stages in the trajectory of folk, belief scholarship vis-à-vis Mexican Americans. These stages include:

1. works dealing with the sources and historical development of Mexican folk medicine,
2. pioneer works of documentation—that is, collections done between 1894-1954,
3. the 1950-1960s—Lyle Saunders and his follower's era (who seek to understand Mexican American health practices by placing them in their cultural context), and
4. the 1970s—includes revisionist Chicano scholars who vigorously challenge previous research findings and take a socioeconomic approach to understanding Mexican medical practices as opposed to a "cultural context" approach.

The basic controversy between the last two major groups centers upon the question of whether the Mexican-American folk belief system is largely responsible for the Chicano's "inability" or reluctance to utilize and take advantage of modern "scientific" medical services. In other words, this perspective posits that it is the Chicanos' own cultural restraints that hamper them in obtaining adequate medical services. Chicano revisionists such as Nick C. Vaca, Miguel Montiel, and Armando Morales argue on the other hand that the culture-as-culprit thesis, or "cultural determinism" as they label it, is a "myth" propagated by and used as a rationalization tool by the Anglo-dominant society, which, through institutionalized racism (such as segregated schools, lack of bilingual personnel), prevents Chicanos from attaining proper medical care. A glaring example is found in Joe S. Graham's article "The Role of the *Curandero* in the Mexican American Folk Medicine System in West Texas." In his introductory remarks he states:

> In West Texas the term "scientific medicine" became almost synonymous with "Anglo medicine"—and still is. To my knowledge, there is not one licensed Mexican American doctor practicing in the whole rural region between Del Rio and El Paso, separated by over four hundred miles—this in spite of the fact that over half of the population is Mexican American.[23]

What Graham failed to do in this otherwise sensitive article was to point out

1. that Texas has had a de facto segregated system (Chicano schools are generally much inferior to all white schools),
2. that medical schools in the United States previous to the 1970s had racial quotas and it was next to impossible for a black, Mexican American, or a woman to be admitted, and
3. that border-area residents in Texas did heavily utilize Spanish-speaking Mexican doctors from Mexico (who in addition tend to be less expensive than their American counterparts).

The above issues were totally neglected in the article, which instead zeroed in on the culture-as-culprit theory.

As can be deduced from the expressed concerns of the above investigators, folk medicine has been largely studied from a social scientist's perspective and is very much the concern of the anthropologist and sociologist.

The inclusion of belief and folk medicine in this study, however, is due to their close proximity to the legend, the caso, the memorate, and personal-experience narrative. Folk beliefs cover a wide range of cosmological and human experiences and are perceived by some scholars as man's attempt at "scientific" explanation for an otherwise incomprehensible event. Beliefs are interconnected with prose narratives in the sense that for any, given belief there may be a "story" explaining this belief. In addition to a narrative explicating the belief, additional narratives corroborating the truthfulness or efficacy of this belief may be present. These narratives may surface in

1. the form of a personal experience,
2. an experience that happened to a close relative or acquaintance, or
3. an experience that happened to some unknown person.

For example, numerous folk beliefs are associated with the Catholic religion.

A common belief is the following:

> *A manda* (promise) to a saint is sacred. One must always keep these promises or suffer the consequences.

Generally, when the above belief is stated, a narrative or series of narratives will illustrate this specific point. The casos described earlier are frequently corroborating stories of a belief. There are literally thousands of beliefs. The following are but a few examples:

1. belief in the existence of witches *(brujas)*
2. belief in *curanderas (os)* or folk healers
3. belief in the devil
4. belief in la Llorona
5. belief in ghosts, evil spirits, *duendes,* werewolves, vampires, headless riders, *espantos* (supernatural beings both good and bad), poltergeists, kobolds, bewitched areas or places *(lugares encantados)*
6. belief in buried treasures
7. belief in objects to put hexes or prevent bewitchment
8. belief in folk medicine and folk ailments such as *susto* (shock*), empacho, aire (*air*), caída de la mollera* (fallen fontenelle), *mal puesto* (bewitched)

For each of the above entities there are thousands of narratives in existence detailing how in fact such an event was witnessed by someone or how it actually happened to a specific individual. All of these narratives, of course, are jewels in the rough that when discovered by a literary genius can transform them into, veritable gems. For example, the Colombian novelist Gabriel García Márquez utilized hundreds of folk beliefs in the process of constructing the magical-fantastic universe of his masterpiece *One Hundred Years of Solitude (1967).* One needs to mention only three well-known Chicano works—" *. . . y no se lo tragó la tierra"* by Tomás Rivera; *Bless Me, Ultima* by Rudolfo Anaya; and *El diablo en Texas* by Aristeo Brito—to realize the impact of folk beliefs on Chicano literature. Folk beliefs, then, are an integral and significant element in Chicano folklore (and of course in the folklore of all cultures) and certainly merit continued investigation.

This necessarily short introduction to Chicano folklore provides the reader with a greater appreciation of the cultural phenomenon called folklore and with a better understanding of the richness of Chicano culture.

Notes

1. Aurelio M. Espinosa, *Romancero de Nuevo México* (Madrid: Consejo Superior de Investigaciones Científicas, 1953), P. 66.
2. Américo Paredes, "Folklore, Lo Mexicano and Proverbs," *Aztlàn*, vol. 13, nos. 1 and 2 (Spring and Fall 1982), p. 1.
3. Américo Paredes, "Mexican Legendry and the Rise of the Mestizo," in Wayland D. Hand, ed., *American Folk Legend: A Symposium* (Los Angeles: University of California Press, 1971), pp. 97–107.
4. Joe Graham, "The Caso: An Emic Genre of Folk Narrative," in Richard Bauman and Roger D. Abrahams, eds., *"And Other Neighborly Names" Social Process and Cultural Image in Texas Folklore* (Austin: University of Texas Press, 1981), p. 19.
5. Collected from the personal repertoire of a student in my folklore class at the University of California at Irvine in 1980.
6. María Herrera-Sobek, "Verbal Play and Mexican Immigrant Jokes," *Southwest Folklore*, vol. 4 (Winter 1980), p. 16. See also María Herrera-Sobek, *The Bracero Experience: Elitelore Versus Folklore* (Los Angeles: UCLA Latin American Center Publications, 1979).
7. For further discussion on the topic, see Américo Paredes, "The Mexican Corrido, Its Rise and Fall," in Mody C. Boatright, Wilson M. Hudson, and Allen Maxwell, eds., *Folk Travelers* (Austin: Texas Folklore Society Publications, 1957), pp. 91–105.
8. "Corrido de Joaquín Murieta," collected by Philip Sonnichsen and printed in "Texas-Mexican Border Music," vols. 2 and 3, corridos 1 and 2, Arhollie Records, 1975.
9. This particular study appears in Eduardo Hernández-Chávez, A. D. Cohen, and A.F. Beltrano, eds. *El lenguaje de los chicanos* (Arlington: Center for Applied Linguistics, 1975).
10. José Limón, "The Folk Performance of 'Chicano' and the Cultural Limits of Political Ideology," in Bauman and Abrahams, eds., *"And Other Neighborly Names,"* p. 197.
11. Shirley Arora, "Proverbs in Mexican American Tradition," *Aztlán*, vol. 13, nos. 1 and 2 (Spring and Fall 1982), pp. 43-69.
12. Collected from my grandmother Susana Escamilla de Tarango.
13. Shirley Arora, *Proverbial Comparisons and Related Expressions in Spanish* (Berkeley: University of California Press, 1977).
14. See Aurora Lucero-White Lea, *Literary Folklore of the Hispanic Southwest* (San Antonio: Naylor Company, 1953), p. 5.
15. Collected from my grandmother Susana Escamilla de Tarango.
16. Américo Paredes, "El folklore de los grupos de origen mexicano," *Folklore Americano*, no. 14, año 16 (1966), p. 158.
17. As quoted in John Holmes McDowell, *Children's Riddling* (Bloomington: Indiana University Press, 1979), p. 18.
18. Elli Kongas-Maranda is quoted in McDowell, *Children's Riddling*, p. 20.
19. McDowell, *Children's Riddling*, p. 20.
20. Collected from my grandmother Susana Escamilla de Tarango.
21. McDowell, *Children's Riddling*, p. 222.
22. This article appears in *Aztlán*, vol. 13, nos. 1 and 2 (Spring and Fall 1982), pp. 223–56.
23. Joe S. Graham, "The Role of the *Curandero* in the Mexican American Folk Medicine System in West Texas," in Wayland D. Hand, ed., *American Folk Medicine* (Berkeley: University of California Press, 1976), p. 176.

On Chicano Music in the U.S.

Carlos F. Ortega

This essay explores the notion of Chicano music. It is a term long in use and is applied to music and artists with a connection to the Chicano community. Growing up in Los Angeles, my experience is involved with Chicano music: As a musician, a teacher in Chicano Studies, developing musical projects on radio, and writing on the subject of music. Over the years I have also had questions regarding what we mean by 'Chicano music.' There has always been as sense of ambiguity regarding the term. Is there an exact definition or is it a working concept? Are there reference points? Does it refer to an era? Is it a sound? These questions led to the development of this essay in order to answer or attempt to answer these questions and perhaps leave a clear sense of what Chicano music can mean.

The most obvious of my concerns is the manner by which the term Chicano music is used. Some authors use the term in a broad context and without clear definitions or clear parameters, which locates the term within its historical and political context, making it confusing. José Angel Gutiérrez, for example, writing on the roots of Chicano music paints a broad canvass of what appears to be every musical influence from the indigenous, to European, and African experience in Mexico and the Southwest United States as a source of Chicano music.[1]

He starts with indigenous music, beginning with the Olmecs who lived in the present day Mexican states of Veracruz and Tabasco almost 1,200 years ago. The conch or *caracol*, made from a seashell was used primarily for signaling others and not music per se. Later the Olmecs did develop a drum and over time it became an integral part of Mesoamerican religious functions.

From this vantage point, Gutiérrez moves linearly as he discusses African and Spanish influences (drumming and guitar/song styles respectively). With Gutiérrez we move into the present era. Key artists are discussed who presumably help to develop Chicano music. I say presumably, because he never really says who or when this occurred. He refers to the great Tejana singer, Lydia Mendoza, for example, as a "Chicana recording star." I wonder if Mrs. Mendoza saw herself this way in the decades of the 1930s, 40s, 50s, or even 60s.

While we can identify these influences, in contemporary music, indigenous roots (in terms of instrumentation) are not clearly evident in Chicano music—played traditionally or with new arrangements. Perhaps the closest we come is with Los Lobos, whose recording of 'La Bamba,' as close to the Ritchie Valens version as one can find, segues into *son jarocho* as the rock version fades out. Or listen to 'Be Still,' which uses the *huapango* style effectively.[2] Yet, even these renditions reflect the fusion of European instruments and African rhythms by indigenous peoples and not the pre-Columbian rhythms played by groups such as the Olmecs.

In reading his essay I searched for a location where one could say, "This is where Chicano music begins," but this was never really made clear.

Another essay, which moves with broad strokes, is one by Robert Rivera-Ojeda. He writes: "The history of música Chicana dates back to the mid 1800s; prior to and after the Mexican American War. In reality, it dates back to the landing of Cortez at Veracruz in 1519."[3] He cites Américo Paredes as his source and I went back to check what Paredes said. In fact, Paredes was speaking of Mexico as a "cultural entity" that began with the arrival of Cortez, though not necessarily in the context of music.[4] The rest of Ojeda's essay addresses the emergence of Tejano music and for the most part he covers this history quite well, but like Gutiérrez, Rivera-Ojeda subtly gives this entire history the moniker of Chicano music. The problem I feel is his use of the term Chicano music within the historical context of Tejano conjunto music. His perspective defines Chicano music as early as the 1920s.[5] While the need to categorize social phenomena is a feature of academic writing, I cannot help but wonder how Narciso Martínez, Bruno Villareal and Santiago Jiménez, Sr. identified themselves. And while there was a stage in Tejano music referred to as *La Onda Chicana*, it did not emerge until the late 1960s. Now some Tejanos might agree (with his assessment) that

Chicano music is a Texas creation, but Chicanos in California would say otherwise.

In addition to using Chicano music in a broad context, the term can also be contradictory and ambiguous, depending on whom you talk to. Chicano music is viewed as a dynamic fusion of musical influences, or an attempt to reclaim the past, especially in musical genres. Chicano music is also tied to the use of language within its lyrics. That is, the use of English, Spanish and Spanglish within the context of a song. I will explore these possibilities further on in the essay. Reyes and Waldman, for example, add to this concern when they write:

> While not all these musicians and bands—and their audiences—called or call themselves 'Chicanos,' they come from Mexican American backgrounds or offer a blend of American and Latino sound that we call Chicano rock 'n' roll.[6]

Another insight comes from Rafael Pérez-Torres who writes that according to some critics: "Cultural Mestizaje at times has been viewed as a type of assimilation." He cites Manuel Peña's notion of how Tejano music "oscillates" between 'authenticity' and 'assimilation.'[7] In Peña's 1985 book, *The Texas-Mexican Conjunto*, he depicts the conjunto style as a resilient cultural product of the working class and orquesta music as an "example of assimilationist desires" sought by the middle class. In other words, Peña believes conjunto music (made up of the accordion, bajo sexto, upright bass or tololoche, and drums) is more 'organic' and rooted in the lives of the working class and the upscale orquesta (consisting of a fifteen to twenty piece orquestra, without accordion and bajo sexto, and rooted in the styles of American swing bands), which represents a form of cultural disloyalty. Pérez-Torres writes: "This disloyalty stems from the contradictory position of an emergent Chicano middle class that does not identify with the working class but that, in turn, is not accepted by a xenophobic American society."[8]

Instead of cultural disloyalty let's consider other possibilities. Is it possible to conceive that musical forms are ascribed ideological positions as Peña asserts? Or is it also possible to conceive that cultural influences shape the ideological contours of a musician's choice to play certain types of music?[9] The notion of cultural change is the subject of tremendous literature, which is too extensive to address here but one can assume is a common reality. The question is whether that change is the result of conquest, accident or choice. To say disloyalty is to draw a picture of something planned, an attempt to abandon an aspect of culture, which is considered more authentic. For some time now, anthropologists and sociologists have worked with the concept of 'transculturation' as a means of understanding what or why change occurs. Ethnomusicologist Margaret Kartomi has defined 'transculturation' as a "process of cultural transformation marked by the influx of new cultural elements and the loss or alteration of existing ones."[10] For many, the "alterations" are real. They can be felt from generation to generation. Yet, depending on the individual it is possible to situate oneself between those changes in order to create a bicultural experience.

Let us also define our terms. Gutiérrez places music within its cultural context. He writes: "Each succeeding generation and civilization builds upon that of the previous one in such areas as musical form, rhythm, instrumentation, composition, arrangement, and utility."[11] There is no disloyalty here, just a process that is felt in all cultures. Another term that needs to be clarified is: 'Chicano.' It is a concept, an expression of a people's history. In Mexico, the word was used to refer to the poor and/or uneducated. But 'Chicano,' according to musician Rubén Guevara, became a "statement of pride and defiance by student activists in the sixties."[12]

We'll come back to this notion momentarily, but for now let us assume that if Guevara is right, and I believe he is, then this definition (of Chicano) must be understood in order to clearly visualize the concept of Chicano music. While one can say Chicano music is "anything that has to do with Mexicans" or based on 'lo mexicano,' or is an 'East L.A. thing,' we still need a better sense of the term.

The Dimensions of Chicano Music

Determining what constitutes Chicano music requires a sound concept enabling the student or researcher to zero in on the parameters of the subject of study. Pérez-Torres has come as close as anyone I know at achieving this level of exactness. He uses the term Chicano music:

> . . . to indicate music that thematically—in terms of both lyrics and music—situates itself within a context of Chicano cultural production. The music forms a kind of hybrid creation, one that acknowledges both African American and Latino art forms and that evokes a cultural as well as at times, historical and political connection to Chicano and Latino social communities.[13]

From this vantage point we can begin to narrow down our search for meaning in Chicano music. Pérez-Torres uses the word, hybridity, a tendency to absorb musical influences while at the same time expressing a unique Chicano sound and connection to Chicano identity and place. He points to Los Lobos in their 1978 debut album *Just Another Band from East L.A.* or Kid Frost in his 1992 album *East Side Story*. In each case the artists utilize influences as diverse as Tejano, rock, and the blues, as did Los Lobos, or hip hop and rap, as did Kid Frost. In the latter, language use by Kid Frost demonstrates a concern with "the naming and placing of self through linguistic mixture." As such Chicano artists have used English, Spanish, Caló, and street slang in order to accomplish this connection.

Chicano music then is characterized by the fusion of music to create a synthesis and can also be reflected in how language is used; straight ahead English, Spanish, slang, or Caló. There is also language mixing within a song, a process referred to as code-switching, the practice of using two languages simultaneously. Thematically, Chicano music contains social and/or political lyrics that speak to concerns affecting the Chicano community. Pérez-Torres analyzes the work of numerous groups, such as Rage Against the Machine and determines that within the context of their lyrics, musical influences and political positions, they constitute Chicano music.

Add to this the idea of the word Chicano referring to a statement of pride and defiance, then we have, a situation where musical artists strive to create a sound reflecting their community and the use of language that leads to a cultural connection. No one else may get it, but within the community, the music speaks loud and clear. However, whereas Pérez-Torres speaks to contemporary musical developments and examples like Los Lobos and Kid Frost in determining what he means by Chicano music, it is just as important to turn back the pages and search those locations directing us to the creation of Chicano music.

Corridos and Songs

According to Luis Leal, Professor of Chicano Studies at the University of California, Santa Barbara and the late Américo Paredes, Professor of English and Folklore, University of Texas, Austin, the corrido has a long and diverse history in the American Southwest. Early Spanish explorations saw the creation of settlements providing a cultural base for individuals to create different forms of cultural expression. In his study of the corrido, Leal makes mention of the 'corrido in Aztlán,' no doubt reflecting his understanding of the concept within the literature of the Chicano movement.[14] Aztlán meant more than just the legendary homeland of the Aztecs; in the Chicano Movement, Aztlán came to mean the Southwest. That is, he distinguishes between the Mexican corrido and the Chicano corrido.

The Chicano corrido has all the characteristics of the Mexican corrido but, now and then, slight changes emerge reflecting the experiences of Chicanos and Anglos, which help lay the foundation for the use of hybridity that Pérez-Torres writes about. One corrido, 'La Guerra Mundial' ('The World War') from the early twentieth century shows the effects of this encounter:

Cantando desde el 'number one'
Cantando hasta el 'number two'
No era el 'Spanish influenza'
Era el 'American flu.'

Paredes wrote numerous studies regarding the border corrido. One example concerned the "corrido of intercul-

tural conflict," a corrido that focused on the Mexican experience with Anglo Americans in Texas. This particular corrido took on many themes and whether the individual Mexican was guilty or not, within the text of these corridos became a hero. Paredes writes:

Not all border men who shot it out with the law were completely blameless individuals defending their rights. But so keen was the Mexican sense of injustice against Anglo domination, so vivid the pattern of intercultural in the corrido, that sometimes an outlaw with no conscience of social or political justice was elevated into a hero of border conflict.[15]

This style of corrido becomes the hallmark for capturing the Chicano experience of the twentieth century.

Another type of corrido that Paredes collected was one that addressed the issue of assimilation. These songs were usually humorous but also reflected the experience of culture change. The use of the word *pocho*, especially in the 1950s, reflected a particular disdain for U.S.-born Mexican Americans. In 'Los Mexicanos que Hablan Inglés,' however, the composer captures the experiences of Mexican immigrants who attempt to use English:

Y jau-dididu mai fran
En ayl si yu tumora
Para decir 'diez reales'
Dicen dola yene cuora.

And 'how-dee-do, my friend,
And I'll see you tomorrow.'
When they want to say 'diez reales,'
They say 'dollar and a quarter.'[16]

Corridos were at their greatest peak in the late nineteenth century and early twentieth century. Thematically, corridos of intercultural conflict reflected a sense of resistance and a stand against the perceived or real injustice that existed at the time.

Songs of the Chicano Experience

The late Guillermo Hernández, professor of English at the University of California, Los Angeles, collected songs for a study that illuminated the diversity of the Chicano experience. Urbanization, effects of culture change through language, cultural transitions from oral traditions to written composition, effects of war, pachucos, and the war hero were some of the themes one might hear in the first half of the twentieth century. He writes:

The effects of culture change can be clearly observed in the linguistic varieties employed in the two dialogues that form part of this collection ('Street Dialogue' and the 'Pachuco and the Tarzan'). In both of these, standard Spanish speech alternates with regionalisms, archaisms, slang, and Anglicisms; in their bilingual humor they convey interesting examples of attitudes towards languages and cultures in contact.[17]

Do the songs illustrated by Hernández constitute Chicano music? I am not sure. However, these themes are important for they capture events that impacted on the community—all driven by politics, economics, and culture. Here again is a clear attempt to capture the conditions faced by Chicanos as seen through culture change and intercultural conflict. Some of these issues would again emerge during the Chicano movement. Perhaps such themes then set the stage for what was to come during the decades of the sixties and seventies. It does make sense since during the period under review, Chicanos were essentially excluded from the larger U.S. society.

Musical Fusion

During the 1940s, music had a tremendous impact on Latino communities but also on the larger musical community. From the standpoint of commercial radio and recordings, music was as popular and diverse as one could imagine. In different ways, the Chicano community would be affected by these musical trends, and a close look at these developments highlights the strengthening of the musical foundations that created Chicano music two decades later.

From the east coast came the emerging orchestra of Machito and His Afro-Cubans. From the start of the decade, Machito and his musical director Mario Bauza developed a unique orchestra sound that pushed the mambo onto dance floors around the country. Rooted in a West African Congolese cult, Machito developed a powerful rhythm section that was Afro Cuban at heart, added strong brass arrangements that can still be heard in salsa music today, and perfected the *son montuno*, an improvisational section that came to influence jazz musicians of the day. The popularity of the mambo was evident throughout the decade and in the fifties was still going strong thanks to the efforts of Tito Puente and Pérez Prado.[18]

U.S. musicians were also riding high on the popularity of swing music and a piano style that made its way from New Orleans, called boogie woogie. Both of these developments were to capture dancing audiences throughout the country, although for a time, the boogie was more rooted to the Black musical experience. The swing bands of Benny Goodman and others hit stages in Los Angeles. Their recordings were available. Even segregated Los Angeles, however, could not keep this music away from young Mexican Americans and Afro Americans. They went deep into this music as a form of cultural expression. On the boogie side of things, a brilliant saxophonist named Louis Jordan landed in Los Angeles after playing some years with the Count Basie Orquestra in Kansas City. He was looking for a sound that was not as big as that of an orchestra, but effective enough to cause the audience to jump and dance. Because he was long connected to the blues, Jordan began to experiment with his new five piece band and ended up creating what is known as 'jump blues,' a style that many now believe was the forerunner to rock 'n' roll in the 1950s.[19]

Another popular form emerging from the east coast was a street style known as doo-wop. Grounded in harmony and acapella singing, this sound remained popular throughout the early sixties. What some writers characterize as a Black sound, it should be noted that many east coast groups were racially mixed, Blacks, Latinos and Whites. They were not bothered by the segregationist attitudes of the day and joined together to form very hip music for young people.

All these ingredients need to be mentioned because they formed the base of sounds young Mexican Americans would begin to fuse and synthesize during the late 1940s. As music progressed into the 1950s, the next generation of Mexican Americans would continue the mix, and rock music, which was now popular, would become part of the fusion.

Thus, when Pérez-Torres speaks of hybridity, musically or linguistically, we can see it is a process that has been at work through much of the twentieth century, and it is with this knowledge that we can now move into the early stages of what became known as Chicano music.

The Foundations of Chicano Music

During the 1940s, Los Angeles was awash in bitter racial battles with young Mexican Americans who called themselves Pachucos. Strident in their cultural space they did not fit into the world of their parents. They had seen too much of 'the other side'—the world of popular music, dance, and film. They were part of a world where English seemed to be everywhere; if not at home then at school, magazines, radio and the movie house. This is not to say they did not speak Spanish because the great majority did. They were bilingual and now bicultural. The problem was they were not accepted by the larger society. They were segregated in school, from popular dance halls, from restaurants in Hollywood. So they created their own form of expression, manifested through the zoot suit, linguistically through the use of Caló—which has unfortunately been characterized as criminal speech. Then, there was the music. While Pachucos could sit with anyone and sing rancheras or corridos, they began to express their musicality through their tastes in swing music, the mambo and, as Pachucos shared more of their experiences with young Afro Americans (who also knew something about being segregated), they learned the blues and boogie woogie.

Soon musicians like Lalo Guerrero and Don Tosti began organizing bands in order to compose, record and perform music that would speak to the Mexican-origin community in Los Angeles.[20] This would eventually find expression in different parts of the Southwest. Lalo Guerrero, for example, had been in Los Angeles for over a decade and during this time sang with Mexican trios, usually in restaurants or at cultural activities. He found it confining to be a musician relegated to the same style, the same venues. He wanted to explore other avenues of style and interest, in spite of segregation and racial attitudes. In the early forties, Don Tosti was fortunate to have been asked to join Jack Teagarden's jazz band and, because of his skill with the upright bass, toured for almost eight years and was also heard on hundreds of recordings. He also played with the orchestras of Charlie Barnett, Les Brown and Jimmy Dorsey. But he returned to Los Angeles tired of the road and looking for other possibilities. The L.A. club scene provided an avenue for jazz expressions. Both of these men knew of the Sleepy Lagoon Murder Case, which in 1942 had caused great fear in the community due to the scandalous trial that ensued. They also understood the fallout that existed in the city following the Zoot Suit Riots in 1943. To be Pachuco was not viewed in a positive light. The city even went so far as to ban the wearing of the Zoot Suit in order to keep things calm!

Yet both of these men formed bands that in the late 1940s went into studios to record songs that would put a unique slant on the social realities of Los Angeles. Both artists borrowed from the popularity of the mambo, swing, boogie, and jump blues. Lyrically, both utilized Pachuco Caló and also lyrics that were considered risqué by the morally upstanding community of the day. Guerrero y Sus Cinco Lobos released 'Chicas Patas Boogie,' which was later heard in Luis Valdez's play and film, *Zoot Suit*. 'Muy Sabroso Blues,' and 'Mambito' all demonstrate Guerrero's ability to fuse various styles of music and arranged each in such a way so as to speak to young and old. Don Tosti and his Pachuco Boogie Boys recorded 'Pachuco Boogie' (1948).[21] 'Pachuco Boogie' eventually sold two million copies, unique for a record that upheld the Pachuco experience five years after the Zoot Suit riots and six years after the Sleepy Lagoon Murder Case. Besides the use of Caló, Don Tosti used scat-singing and blues harmonies. While some Spanish-language radio stations refused to play the song, Anglo DJs who programmed black R & B aimed at White teenagers, put the song on their play lists.[22]

By the mid-fifties, the development of Chicano rock was about to begin. Since the previous decade, Afro Americans and Mexican Americans had worked together in bands, had been influenced by their own music, so the fusion continued at a very natural gait. Chicanos listened to doo-wop performers like Johnny Ace and the Drifters. Groups forming in Los Angeles in the 1950s fused doo-wop, R & B, and rock. This should be no surprise. The level of segregation created an environment where blacks and Chicanos attended similar dance halls and continued to borrow musically from each other. Songs like 'Hey Señorita' by the Penguins and 'Pachuko Hop' by Chuck Higgins made reference to Chicano culture and language.[23]

Both Guerrero and Don Tosti were still working in Los Angeles; the mambo was stronger than ever in California and the Southwest thanks to the touring of Pérez Prado. The next foundational stage in Chicano music was about to take place.

In 1956, Johnny Otis discovered Lil' Julian Herrera and they began to work together. Otis had moved to Los Angeles from Oakland, California in 1943, where he worked with African American bands playing the music he so dearly loved. His association with boogie and blues has lasted fifty years. He has been a band leader, composer, DJ, author and mentor. Herrera grew up in East Los Angeles. Together they composed 'Lonely Lonely Nights.' It was a local hit. Guevara writes: "It's an elegant doo-wop ballad, very much in the black style, but something about it—the accent, the voice, the 'attitude'—made it different. It was Chicano rock."[24] I'm not sure if doo-wop can be linked to rock because of the style's musical roots, but be that as it may, Guevara was pointing to a beginning that was to have a key impact on musicians on the east side of Los Angeles.

If Lil' Julian Herrera was about attitude, then Ritchie Valens was about fusion at its best. Much has been written about his life and work so I will summarize key points regarding his influence on Chicano music. In his short life Valens had learned from numerous styles: traditional Mexican, country, black R & B, and rock. These influences were partly shaped by the musical environment that was post-war Los Angeles.[25] Many of my teaching colleagues have always mentioned, when the subject comes up, at how impressed they are at Ritchie's composition of 'La Bamba.' And I'm always amused when they go into shock upon learning that Valens did not write the song but in fact recorded a treasured piece of Mexican folklore. John Storm Roberts found that 'La Bamba' was performed as early as 1755 in Mexico City by a *jarocho* group from the Mexican state of Veracruz.[26] What's more, it is in the state of Veracruz that African rhythms are nurtured by the Mexican community, thanks to the musical influence of African slaves, as well as early Afro Cuban rhythms from the Caribbean. Indigenous groups and mestizo musicians borrowed from European-stringed instruments by developing the harp, a four-stringed, guitar-shaped instrument called the *requinto* as well as a rhythm instrument called the *jarana*. Valens took the lyrics of the song, arranged a brilliant rock rhythm and lead-solo part to create the first Chicano rock song: 'La Bamba.' And if one listens carefully, they will hear the Cuban 2-3 reverse clave rhythm.[27]

Finally, in Texas, Tejano groups were themselves going through musical changes that would eventually tie into Chicano music. Stylistically, the traditional conjunto was characterized by the group's instruments: the accordion, the bajo sexto, the upright bass or tololoche, and the drums. But as early as the late 1940s, musicians began to form orquestas that began to perform the popular swing music of the time. Peña has discussed this development as reflecting the assimilation and upwardly mobile status of Tejanos during the war years. This process led audiences to demand a newer music, something that left conjunto in the past. Eventually orquestas began to include Tejano music but without the traditional instruments. The music of Beto Villa and Isidro López provided the key development of the Orquesta mosaic at the time. Essentially, one could attend a dance and hear Tejano music in a very different light. By the late fifties, younger musicians, better trained musically, began to merge into the Orquesta tradition but they brought different influences to the table: they were influenced by rock. Little Joe Hernández and Sunny Ozuna are the prime movers of this tradition. And Little Joe in particular is going to be most affected by developments taking shape in the late sixties and early seventies.[28]

It is the developments, already influenced by the hybridity of musical growth beginning in the 1940s, that will bring Chicano music into its own.

Chicano Music Hits Its Stride

The Chicano Movement emerged in the mid 1960s when César Chávez began the grape boycott in California. The action of Chávez, Dolores Huerta and others galvanized the community against the tactics of grape growers, but also set off political activity in urban areas as well. The work of Reies López Tijerina and his struggles to reclaim land grants lost in the nineteenth century, the Crusade for Justice in Denver, Colorado, and La Raza Unida in Crystal City, Texas, were the key areas of work throughout the Southwest. It is a misconception, however, to leave the impression these were the only areas of work. The energy of the movement affected all areas of the Southwest. Slates of political, social and cultural issues were addressed. Armando Navarro writes:

> The Chicano Movement was a heterogeneous political reform movement comprised of 'multiple' leaders, organizations, competing ideologies, and protest mobilization strategies and tactics. While some organizations within its ranks perceived themselves as revolutionary, ultimately its modus operandi proved to be essentially reformist in orientation.[29]

When Guevara wrote that Chicano was a term reflecting pride and defiance, he expressed the influence of nationalism within the Chicano Movement. In recent years writers have criticized the movement's failure to be more revolutionary because of its reformist tendencies and clinging nature to nationalism. Manuel Peña has said the *movimiento* was driven by romantic nationalism, with a developed political and cultural agenda, with a focus on creating a separatist community, centered and shaped by a cultural renaissance found in literary, musical, theatrical, and filmic expressions. Peña refers to the Chicano agenda as 'ethnocentrist,' which connects to the notion of romantic nationalism.[30] But opposed to what?

The impression Peña and other critics leave is of a movement entirely naïve and entirely lacking in political maturity. From this vantage point the only nationalism one can embrace is romantic. On the other hand, Anthony D. Smith writes:

> Romance, mystery, drama—this is the stuff of any nationalist salvation—drama. It is important because it helps to teach us 'who we are,' to impart the sense of being, a link in a chain which stretches back over the generations to bind us to our ancestors and our descendents.

Add to this the historical context: As Rodolfo Acuña has expressed, it was okay to be anything but Mexican.[31] What the Chicano Movement illustrated was the importance of first accepting oneself. This stage was a necessity; call it romantic or naïve. Moreover, nationalism was a vehicle, a strategy and, in some degree, essential. Remember, Chicanos were responding to pressures to assimilate to social injustice, exclusion and outright disdain. The pressure to eliminate one's culture had been felt in the schools, among academics and other spokespersons who felt Mexicans were in the way. The Chicano Movement and its nationalism was a reaction to this experience. Nationalism was able to direct Chicanos towards the question of identity and self-determination. Thus, a strategy to redefine who we are as a people was created.

It is this perspective that leads to the Chicano Renaissance in literature, art, film, and music. For musicians, their choice of style would be dictated by influence and preferences, but always a connection to the community. While the movement may have been reformist, naïve, and lacking in political maturity, in many cases there was a strong leadership, commitment to the Chicano community, and a desire to see change occur.

Thus when Los Lobos played a show and focused on traditional Mexican music, it became a wake-up call to young people: this is what we come from. Folkloric or commercial, people made the connection. Or take the experience of Danny Valdez: Though never achieving the commercial success of other groups, Valdez stuck to his guns by composing and playing music rooted in the corrido and ranchera tradition. His lyrics though spoke to the contemporary issues of the day and related clearly to farm workers. But when he composed 'Primavera' and went on tour, his band delivered an Afro Cuban set of rhythms along with the more traditional Mexican ones. Clearly, while delivering a political message, the music reflected multiple influences that had been present in the Chicano community for some time.

As Estevan César Azcona writes:

> It was the activist nature of movimiento music—and the groups linked to it—that ultimately defined it from its brethren in the commercial realm. This was not

music for the market or for its critics but rather music for and from an emerging 'Chicano public sphere.'[32]

The insight from Azcona is made stronger when placed in its historical context: Music, according to Dorothea E. Hast, James R. Cowdery, and Stan Scott, has provided vehicles for presenting political messages. From the Psalms of David, the epics of Homer, from the Yugoslavian nationalist whose songs capture the glory of past heroes against ethnic groups who were viewed as enemies, to a Chicano activist whose songs speak to social injustice. Music also serves to critique government: The songs of Robin Hood, to outlaw ballads celebrating Pretty Boy Floyd and Jesse James, to the punk anthems by the Clash, all speak to injustice and oppression at the hands of social institutions. Songs of protest and resistance, topical songs, which thematically have covered subjects such as anti-rent wars in the nineteenth century, the abolition of slavery, the labor movement, the civil rights movement, and the anti-war movement, serve to illustrate the power of music to inspire and encourage people to take a stand.[33]

I discuss the Chicano Movement because its energy was great and musicians were clearly affected by this. But then they also expressed this influence in different ways. Azcona makes clear that Chicano Music is given birth to by the Chicano Movement. Viewed in this way, we can eliminate some of the confusion with what we call Chicano music: Besides hybridity, it must be acknowledged that the Chicano Movement lends inspiration to the influences that shape the perspectives of Chicano musicians on the more commercial side of industry. The rest of this section will be devoted to examining how the Chicano Movement influenced music in the late 1960s and early 1970s, specifically, I will examine music of the Chicano Movement, rock music in the late 60s and 70s, and *La Onda Chicana* from Texas. Building on what happened in the decades of the forties and fifties; we can then determine how Chicano music emerged as a genre all of its own; with different forms of instrumentation, style, and lyrical content.

Música del Movimiento

The Chicano Movement was more than a mass political struggle. Within the mass movements, there was also a need for cultural expression, which found its home in different realms. Literature, art (particularly, the mural movement), theatre, film and music, all provided a way for Chicanos to express the realities, cultural and political, encountered within the movement. Three different styles of Movement music were prominent: Huelga songs addressing the experience of farm workers in California and Texas; Corridos, the narrative ballads that stylistically centered on heroes of the movement and experiences of intercultural conflict; and Movimiento music, which were protest songs written by Chicanos participating in the movement but also influenced by larger struggles such as those of Viet Nam and Mexico.[34]

Daniel Valdés, as a member of El Teatro Campesino, the United Farmer Worker Theatre, began adding musical themes that related to the struggle in the fields. By using the corrido and the ranchera rhythms, he was able to utilize lyrics that spoke to the striking members of the union. 'Huelga en General,' 'El Picket Sign,' 'El Corrido de Dolores Huerta,' and 'El Corrido de César Chávez' were sung at rallies, marches, and protests that were not even tied to the farm workers struggle.

In the urban areas like Los Angeles, 'Yo Soy Chicano' became an important anthem for organizing youth and to spear energy at marches. 'Yo Soy Chicano' was musically borrowed from 'La Rielera,' one of the more famous corridos of the Mexican Revolution. Ramón "Chunky" Sánchez wrote some memorable pieces like 'Trilingual Corrido,' 'Chorizo Sandwich' and 'Chicano Park Samba.'[35]

Movimiento music reflects the numerous struggles that took place in the Southwest by Chicanos in the mid 1960s to 1980. Each piece collects an event, an individual or issue where Chicanos took to heart. Like the hymns, which energized the African American Civil Rights struggle, such as 'We Shall Overcome,' Chicanos used music to propel the nature of their struggle. In fact, on the 1977 recording of the album, 'Sí Se Puede,' a key song is 'No Nos Moverán,' 'We Shall Overcome' Chicano style.[36]

The lyric found in a Movement song is a clear cry, a reaching out to the community: A call to organize and confront the institutions responsible for our oppression! Political lyrics over the centuries have had the same goal: inform and get people involved. From this perspective songs of the Chicano Movement can be classified as Chicano music. And it is the energy of the music and the *movimiento* in general that inspires commercial musicians to borrow ideology, image, language and sensibility, then fuse it with their own form of musical expression.

Rockin' from the Eastside

Chicano artists between the 1950s and 1968—with the probable exception of Ritchie Valens—did not draw attention to their ethnicity, or so say Reyes and Waldman. Perhaps there was pressure to adapt to industry desires, such as when Ritchie Valens is told by his manager that his proper name, Ricardo Valenzuela, will not do. Hence, his stage name 'Ritchie Valens.' But Lipsitz sees clearly that these groups also came to taste the vicious nature of discrimination and segregation. During the 1960s, Black and Anglo artists composed and recorded numerous songs with a clear political content; nothing of the sort existed within the Chicano community. Guevara tells us that this changed or began to change when a local group, the VIP's changed their name to El Chicano.[37] After 1968, there was a deliberate change. Bands now chose Spanish names (for their bands), used Mexican dress, or sang songs about conditions in the barrio, police brutality, the INS, or the Viet Nam War. The source of this change was the emphasis on ethnic nationalism, which was in opposition to assimilation. Also, the criticism of the Mexican American generation placed the Chicano Movement within the context of the generational revolt evident in the 1960s.[38]

While Chicano rock was developing in the East side, developments were also shaping music in Texas. But while these groups did not build on the imagery or political themes often used by Chicano groups in the East side, they too fused with different musical styles. Specifically, they borrowed from the Tejano conjunto sound. While they did not use the accordion, the Vox farfisa organ carried the same melodic movement and the bass lines played on the farfisa reflected the bass lines played on the bajo sexto. The important groups in this regard were the Sir Douglas Quintet (She's About a Mover), led by Doug Sham; ? and the Mysterians, young musicians whose parents worked the migrant trails, actually recorded their hit song '96 Tears' in Michigan; and Sam the Sham and the Pharaohs 'Wooly Bully.' The intro to that song has Sam (Samudio) saying, "one, two, one, two, tres, cuatro . . ."[39] Artists such as the late Freddy Fender, recorded country-inspired songs that became popular: 'Wasted Days and Wasted Nights' and 'Before the Next Teardrop Falls' were regularly heard on radio and the latter tune was aided in its popularity because it was sung bilingually.

La Onda Chicana

As previously mentioned, the orquesta tradition in Texas emerged as a response to the process of assimilation. The early stage was an attempt to mimic the music of swing bands popular in the 1940s. In the 1950s, orquestas led by Isidro López provided a spin on the original orquestas by developing a new Tejano sound that came to define the nature of Tejano music. By the late fifties, the third generation of *orquesta* leaders began to emerge. Little Joe and Sunny Ozuna took the helm of their respective groups and by the mid 1960s each brought his own form of expressing the *orquesta* sound. Little Joe and the Latinaires utilized R & B, while Sunny focused his act on English-language covers and originals; all within the *orquesta* sound.

By the early sixties it appeared as if Sunny and the Sunglows would be the top *orquesta* group. His rendition of 'Talk to Me,' originally recorded by Little Willie John, shot into the top 10, garnered him incredible exposure and a spot on the American Bandstand lineup. His success further drove home the point that Tejano would not be part of his musical career. But by the late sixties, Sunny was doing Tejano songs, especially in the local performances and Little Joe and the Latinaires were touring California. For Little Joe, the political activity and mobilization within the Chicano Movement had an affect on him. Little by little, he began to reflect on the issues being addressed and in 1968 the climate was intense. By the time he re-

turned to Texas he was already planning to reinvent himself.

As early as 1967, Johnny González of Zarape Records used the label, *La Onda Chicana*, as a way of "linking the new style of Little Joe and the Latinaires to the ethnocentered consciousness emerging among Mexican Americans."[40] The connection to *La Onda Chicana* is what Manuel Peña refers to as 'compound bimusicality,' a process "interacting with politico-ideological activity." This is seen in Little Joe with an aesthetic transformation beginning with a Chicano look, a new name (La Familia), a counterculture lifestyle and a shift toward the ideology of Chicanismo. This led to a unique display of music by Little Joe which has yet to be equaled. Peña writes:

> Para la Gente (1970) was the first LP by any Texas group to exploit what I earlier called a 'compound' form of bimusicality—where styles identifiable as Mexican ranchero and those identifiable as sophisticated American swing-jazz were yoked together within the same musical piece to create, in effect, a hybrid or synthetic music in a relation homologous to compound bilingualism. Several of the tunes prominently displayed 'intrasentential code-switching' between ranchero and sophisticated.

This bimusicality, alternating ranchero with American 'jaiton' styles within the same musical piece—is at the center of hybridity and synthesis. It was also heard on 'Las Nubes,' which led off Little Joe's *Para la Gente* album.[41]

Much of the success of *La Onda Chicana* was helped by the exposure gained through the Johnny Canales Show. Popular in the southwest, Mexico and parts of the U.S., Canales brought exposure to Tejano music by presenting new and established artists such as Al Hurricane from New Mexico and Selena from South Texas. He promoted *La Onda Chicana* and the use of code-switching.

Chicano Cultural Production

In the end, what we call Chicano music can be understood as a musical style with roots in the intercultural conflicts and experiences between Mexicans and Anglos. A review of what Leal calls Chicano corridos and other song forms provide insight with respect to what was on the minds of composers. Whether social in content or linguistically mixed, this was the first stage of development.

By the middle of the twentieth century, we see Mexican Americans borrowing for diverse styles such as the mambo, jazz, swing, the blues, boogie-woogie, doo-wop and rock. Forms such as Pachuco Boogie, R & B stylings and rock interpretations by Ritchie Valens signal the development of musical fusion or bimusicality and linguistic playfulness. But it is still not Chicano music.

It is not until the rise of the Chicano Movement and concurrently, the renaissance in literature, the arts, music and film, that we begin to see the influence of a Chicano perspective in these fields. With music one is affected by the lyrics as well as the use of traditional musical forms like the corrido and ranchera. These elements influence Little Joe, El Chicano, Thee Midnighters and others to adopt a Chicano image in music.

According to George Lipsitz:

> (Chicanos) were neither assimilationist nor separatist, they drew on 'families of resemblance'—similarities to the experiences and cultures of other groups—to fashion a 'unity of disunity.' In that way, they sought to make alliances with other groups by cultivating the ways in which their particular experiences spoke with special authority about the ideas and alienations felt by others.[42]

Moreover, the emphasis of popular music "supports the contention of ethnic studies scholars who see cultural production not only as an integral part of oppositional politics, but as an 'important register' of social and political change."[43] The socio-historical relationships between Blacks and Chicanos in Los Angeles are joined by political, economic and culture change. When we listen to Los Lobos, Rage Against the Machine and Ozomatli, we become the beneficiaries of this relationship. For Beverly Johnson, it represents the development of multiethnic identities, gender, and geographic space that leads to the development of cross border music.[44]

The role of Chicano cultural production is a vast array of genres, attitudes, experiences and solidarity with the community. The individual expressions by artists reflect their understanding and depth of connection to Chicano music. I have tried to show that understanding Chicano music, as a concept requires the student and listener to grasp characteristics of fusion, tradition, lyrical expression, whether political or cultural, sound, and attitude. It is tied to political movements such as the Chicano Movement; it is tied to generational expression whether in rock, punk or hip-hop. Cajun musician Jo-El Sonnier, who I remember well during his stint in Los Angeles once, commented to a journalist:

> I've sold myself as French, as R & B, as country, and as rock. But I want to do it all if I can; I think we could open doors for this music. Look at what Los Lobos has done for ethnic music, and they got signed without really changing. It can't just be that all people want is Madonna and punk music! All I've ever wanted to do is bring my music and my culture to the people. I have a message about the preservation of it. I feel like if I let my culture die, I die with it.[45]

Conclusion

Bonnie Wade writes: "Worldwide integration through technology and market exchange is the hallmark of globalization, and we are beginning to understand that many, if not most, music has emerged from processes of hybridization or fusion."[46] She is of course addressing the idea of transnationalization. It is a process that is taking us to other places or bringing other places to us and the more we open up to influences from the outside, we will see changes culturally and in our forms of cultural expression.

But this is not new; it is only more evident, more powerful and more encompassing. Guevara writes:

> There are now many sounds, many subcultures, from hip-hop to traditional Mexican, from sixties soul traditionalists in the car clubs to punk bands that helped to start the whole L.A. punk scene. From Spanish to English and all shades in between.[47]

In the end, what makes Chicano music a unique set of sounds, genres, linguistic mixing, political thought and poetry, historical insight, and cultural capital, is the fact that it moves people—to sing and dance, to higher levels of analysis, to emotional power. The quality of Chicano music is that it reigns in the collective identity of Chicanos, as diverse as that may be. "Memories tell us who we are, and music is one of the most powerful tools for evoking memory. Music helps us to recall ideas and events, and serves to make particular occasions memorable."[48] Thus researchers who study the issue of immigration can find a wealth of musical material that clearly details the experience of crossing borders. This type of data connects us to experiences that to date continue to educate. Memory shapes identity within groups, within nations, around ethnic and cultural communities that live within and across political borders. At the personal level, friends and family members help us to understand our past express memory.

So Chicano music then draws from the past. It is our foundation. It is expressed through political lyrics and content with respect to the Chicano experience. And for those not always engaged at the political level, Chicano music is expressed in its ideological symbolism, as with *La Onda Chicana* or East L.A. rock bands. There is the experience of Mark Guerrero, son of Lalo Guerrero, who majored in Chicano Studies at California State University, Los Angeles, who continues to perform and has written songs like, 'Pre-Columbian Dreams.' Tierra, a band that utilizes, jazz, Mexican melodies and R & B, becomes a staple at political events in East L.A. As we continue to move into the twenty-first century, Chicano music will continue to evolve. The historical styles will always be there. The oldies and *La Onda Chicana* will continue to be emotional connections, the political verve will inspire as long as the community is affected by social injustice.

As styles make their impact, Chicano music will continue to hybridize and synthesize new sounds for new generations.

"Go on; tírame una rola."

Notes

1. José Angel Gutiérrez, "Chicano Music: Evolution and Politics to 1950," *The Roots of Texas Music,* eds. Laurence Clayton and Joe W. Specht (College Station: Texas A & M Press, 2003) 146–174.
2. Los Lobos, "La Bamba," *La Bamba Soundtrack,* LP, Slash Records, 1987 and, Los Lobos, "Be Still," *The Neighborhood,* CD, Slash Records, 1990.
3. Robert Rivera-Ojeda, "Chicano Music: A Perspective," *Mexican and Chicano Music,* ed. José "Pepe" Villarino, 2nd ed. (New York: Primus Custom Publishing, 1999) 93.
4. Américo Paredes, *A Texas-Mexican Cancionero* (Austin: University of Texas Press, 1976) 3.
5. Ojeda 94.
6. David Reyes and Tom Waldman, *Land of a Thousand Dances: Chicano Rock 'n' Roll from Southern California* (Albuquerque: University of New Mexico Press, 1998) viii.
7. Rafael Pérez-Torres, *Mestizaje* (Minneapolis: University of Minnesota Press, 2006) 93.
8. In fact, Peña does mention that upwardly mobile Mexican Americans never quite broke away from their conjunto roots. See Manuel Peña, *A Texas-Mexican Conjunto* (Austin: University of Texas Press, 1996) 10–14.
9. Pérez-Torres 94.
10. As quoted in Bonnie C. Wade, *Thinking Musically: Experiencing Music, Expressing Culture* (New York: Oxford University Press, 2004) 146.
11. Gutiérrez 146.
12. Rubén Guevara, "The View from the Sixth Street Bridge: the History of Chicano Rock," *The Real World of Rock and Roll* ed. Dave Marsh (New York: Pantheon, 1984) 113.
13. Pérez-Torres 87–88.
14. Luis Leal, "El Corrido" *Xalman* (1980): 24.
15. Paredes 30.
16. Paredes 163–64.
17. Guillermo Hernández, *Canciones de la Raza: Songs of the Chicano Experience* (Berkeley: El Fuego de Aztlán, 1978) 2.
18. John Storm Roberts, *The Latin Tinge* 2nd. ed. (New York: Oxford University Press, 1998) 101.
19. On boogie woogie piano styles, see Marshall Stearns, *The Story of Jazz* (New York: The New American Library, 1958) 122–23. On jump blues, see Steve Loza, *Barrio Rhythm: Mexican Music in Los Angeles* (Urbana: University of Illinois Press, 1993) 80–81.
20. Ed Morales, *The Latin Beat* (New York: De Capo Press, 2003) 283.
21. *Pachuco Boogie,* CD, Arhoolie Records, 2002.
22. George Lipsitz, "Chicano Rock: Crusing Around the Historical Bloc," *Rockin the Boat: Mass Music and Mass Movements* ed. Reebee Garofolo (Boston: South End Press, 1992) 271.
23. Morales 284.
24. Guevara 118.
25. Lipsitz 273. Also see, Beverly Mandheim, *Ritchie Valens: the First Chicano Rocker* (Tempe: Bilingual Review Press, 1987).
26. Roberts 20.
27. Morales 284.
28. See chapters 3 and 4 in Manuel Peña, *The Mexican American Orquesta* (Austin: University of Texas Press, 1999).
29. Armando Navarro, *Mexicano Political Experience in Occupied Aztlán: Struggle and Change* (Walnut Creek: Altamira Press, 2005) 303–04.
30. Manuel Peña, *Música Tejana* (College Station: Texas A & M Press, 1999) 160.
31. Anthony D. Smith, *The Ethnic Origins of Nations* (New York: Blackwell Publishers, Inc. 1988) 180, and Rodolfo F. Acuña, *Anything But Mexican: Chicanos in Contemporary Los Angeles* (New York: Verso Press, 1996).
32. Esteban César Azcona, liner notes, *Rolas de Aztlán,* CD, Smithsonian Folkways Recordings, 2005, 3.
33. Dorothea E. Hast, James R. Cowdery, and Stan Scott, *Exploring the World of Music* (Dubuque: Kendall/Hunt Publishers, 1999) 38.
34. Azcona 4–6.
35. José "Pepe" Villarino, "The Blending of Two Cultures Through Music," *Mexican and Chicano Music* ed. José "Pepe" Villarino 2nd ed. (New York: Primus Custom Publishing, 1999) 105.
36. *Si Se Puede,* LP, Brown Bag Records, 1977.
37. Guevara 122.
38. Reyes and Waldman 112 and Lipsitz 275.
39. Morales 290–91.
40. Peña, *Música* 162.
41. Peña, *Música* 168.
42. Lipsitz 270.
43. Gaye T.M. Johnson, "A Sifting of Centuries: Afro-Chicano Interaction and Popular Musical Culture in California, 1960–2000," *Decolonial Voices: Chicana and Chicano Cultural Studies in the 21st Century* (Bloomington: Indiana University Press, 2002) 317.
44. Johnson 327.
45. Judy Raphael, "Ragin Cajun: Jo-El Sonnier's Last Stand," *LA Weekly* 8 (15) (1985): 57 as quoted by Lipsitz 278.
46. Wade 148.
47. Guevara 125.
48. Hast, Cowdery, Scott 52.

Imagined Borders: Locating Chicano Cinema in America/América

Chon A. Noriega

In this essay, I will examine the articulation and development of a "Chicano cinema" as an expression of the Chicano civil rights movement. To some extent, this is a history that has been told a number of times already, first by the filmmakers themselves, and later by programmers and scholars.[1] And it is a history that has been told within a metanarrative of cultural resistance that defines *lo chicano* according to its oppositional "experience," "expression," and "identity." Nonetheless, in these accounts, my own included, Chicano cinema inevitably occupies an ambiguous location within the national culture, caught between the conflicting egalitarian and communitarian goals of both its practitioners and its academic critics.[2] This conflict marks the underlying conditions for the production of both Chicano films and the critical discourse on them (in short, race relations), while the metanarrative of cultural resistance requires that, as a practical matter, such social contradictions be addressed at the allegorical level. Although an institutional critique of either Chicano cinema or Chicano studies is beyond the scope of this essay, I do want to raise the ambiguous location of Chicano cinema to the level of historiographic operation. One can find a precursor in Coco Fusco's writings on Black and Latino media in the late 1980s.[3] Working not as an academic but as a media professional actively involved in the object of her study—curator, writer, and program officer—Fusco voiced pragmatic concerns as she sought to define a historical moment of "minority" intellectual or cultural production. If more academic accounts necessarily diverted these concerns to an allegorical level, Fusco bristled against her location as the representative for the underrepresented, as the insider for the outsiders, and, consequently, as the outsider who was inside. This ambiguous or dual location, then, became the very methodology by which she read against the grain of oppositional thinking and of "minority" texts. In a similar fashion, I want to raise several ques-

tions about the function of "Chicano cinema" within various discourses—nationalist, postnationalist and American, pan-American—in order to make a distinction between the idea of "Chicano cinema" (as category) and its practice. In some respects, the category preceded the practice insofar as it created the possibilities for special admissions, trainee programs, public affairs series, production grants, distribution agencies, exhibition slots, and so on. From this discursive origin, "Chicano cinema" constructed itself in opposition to Hollywood and in alliance with New Latin American Cinema.[4] Although framed as a matter of either/or choice, this strategy actually provided new terms within which access could be negotiated. As a final matter, I want to suggest that "Chicano cinema" developed not just vis-à-vis Hollywood and New Latin American Cinema (as well as cinema and television), but through the disavowal of an avant-garde tradition within Chicano cultural production. The focus of this essay will be on the period of the Chicano civil rights movement (1965–75), during which the first generation of Chicano filmmakers went from student activists to film and television professionals. I will pay special attention to Jesús Salvador Treviño and his pivotal role as filmmaker, organizer, advocate, and polemicist.

The Chicano Civil Rights Movement

As the story is told, the first generation of Chicano filmmakers emerged out of the context of the farmworkers' struggle and the student movement. In the first years of the Chicano movement, the farmworkers' struggle would in some sense define its political, class, and rhetorical orientations, providing the basis for a categorical shift away from the perceived middle-class, accommodationist, and integrationist strategies of the Mexican American Generation.[5] Under the leadership of César Chávez, the United Farm Workers (UFW), founded in 1962, gained national attention when it joined the grape strike in Delano, California, on September 16, 1965, the anniversary of Mexican independence from Spain in 1810. Both

Mexican-based historical references and cultural production played a pivotal role in these social protests (and their political resonance), incorporating more subtle allusions to American political history. Luis Valdez, writer and director of *Zoot Suit* (1981) and *La Bamba* (1987), was especially important in developing this bicultural political rhetoric in the mid-1960s. In 1965, he founded El Teatro Campesino in order to rally striking farmworkers, developing collaborative agitprop *actos* (skits) that were performed on the flatbeds of trucks. Then, in March 1966, he wrote the influential "Plan of Delano," a manifesto that announced the grape strike as the start of a "social movement"—done in the rhetorical style of the U.S. Declaration of Independence and Black gospel à la Martin Luther King Jr.—which it then rooted in the Virgin of Guadalupe, Benito Juárez, and the Mexican Revolution of 1910.[6] In this manner, Valdez created a unique expression that coupled together seemingly opposed egalitarian and communitarian goals, so that the call for equal justice within the United States justified an affirmation of a Mexican past and culture that then made such equality its inevitable outcome. As a Chicano rhetorical strategy, Valdez's "Plan of Delano" would have a direct impact on other plans ("El Plan Espiritual de Aztlán" and "El Plan de Santa Barbara"), epic poems ("I Am Joaquín"), films (in particular, Valdez's *I Am Joaquín* [1969] and *Los Vendidos: The Sellouts* [1972]), and—in a more indirect fashion—film manifestos.[7]

By the late 1960s, the emphasis of the Chicano movement shifted from rural to urban issues, and from farmworkers to students, and Los Angeles became a major focal point. In East Los Angeles, some ten thousand high school students undertook a series of "Blow Outs" (or walkouts) in March 1968 to protest institutional racism and poor education. The Blow Outs were initiated by high school teacher Sal Castro, who joined the students, and were coordinated by members of United Mexican American Students (UMAS), including UCLA students and future filmmakers Moctesuma Esparza and Francisco Martínez. In June, Castro and Esparza were among the "L.A. Thirteen" indicted on conspiracy charges for their organizational role in the Blow Outs, an act that resulted in increased Chicano student activism and radicalism within the next year.[8] In March and April 1969, student conferences in Denver and Santa Barbara consolidated the student movement, uniting the four major Mexican American student groups under one banner: M.E.Ch.A., or El Movimiento Estudiantil Chicano de Aztlán (The Chicano Student Movement of Aztlán). The rejection of the self-designation "Mexican American" in favor of "Chicano," and the fact that *mecha* is vernacular Spanish for "match," underscored the student movement's militant nationalism.

The first Chicano film, *I Am Joaquín* (1969), embodies these transitions in the Chicano movement and represents the culmination of an intertextual dialogue between the movement's rural and urban visionaries: Luis Valdez

and Rodolfo "Corky" Gonzales. Like Valdez, Gonzales had been actively involved in the Democratic Party, but became disenchanted in the early 1960s. In 1965, Gonzales resigned from the party and founded the Crusade for Justice, a civil rights organization located in Denver. The film is Valdez's adaptation of Gonzales's epic poem of the same title, written in 1967, and widely distributed through chapbooks and mimeograph copies.[9] The poem itself, however, draws upon the rhetorical style of Valdez's "Plan of Delano," ending with the first person singular expression of phrases that punctuate the earlier manifesto: "I SHALL ENDURE. I WILL ENDURE."[10] The major shift between plan and poem occurs in terms of the subject of their "poetic consciousness."[11] The "Plan of Delano," although grounded in key figures and moments from Mexican history, addressed a multiethnic membership (mostly Mexican and Filipino), then focused on one class-based social movement rooted in the farmworkers' struggle, but ultimately aimed at uniting "all of the races that comprise the oppressed minorities in the United States," including "poor whites." Furthermore, in defining the role of theater and other cultural expressions within that movement, Valdez himself made a clear-cut distinction between its symbolic politics (both theater and demonstrations) and "actual hardass, door to door, worker to worker organizing."[12] If community had to be imagined for a national audience, local politics required an interpersonal expression and organization of that community. In contrast to the "Plan of Delano," Gonzales's "I Am Joaquín" envisioned a mestizo historical genealogy for the broad-based Chicano movement, articulating a series of bipolar parameters for Chicano identity—of race, religion, class, and, more insidiously, gender—that could be subordinated to nationalism. For Gonzales—as echoed in the words of "El Plan Espiritual de Aztlán"—"nationalism as the key to organization transcends all religious, political, class, and economic factions" within the Chicano community.[13] Nationalism, then, gave a singular political meaning to *mestizaje*. Whereas Valdez used nationalist icons in order to argue for historical justification as well as internal unity within a working-class struggle, Gonzales turned nationalism itself into the "key" for uniting an admittedly heterogeneous group of Mexican descent.

By the time "I Am Joaquín" was written, Valdez had realized the need to develop the aesthetic and political dimensions of El Teatro Campesino beyond direct involvement with the United Farm Workers. At stake for Valdez was a question of professionalism and the potential for a national audience for an artistic practice that had begun as a component within grassroots politics. Valdez's film adaptation exemplifies his own artistic shift from community-based organizing to addressing a mass audience for which community must be imagined. Before the adaptation, El Teatro Campesino had developed a slide show that combined the photographs of George Ballis, who worked with the United Farm Workers, with a dramatic reading of the poem. Shortly thereafter, Ballis's photographs were shot and edited together into a film, with Luis Valdez's narration and Daniel Valdez's improvised music recorded in a sound studio in Los Angeles.[14] The film was shown at both farmworkers' rallies and within the urban barrio (as with earlier dramatic readings of the poem and the slide show), but it also reached classrooms, festivals, and a national television audience. Thus, the film—like the poem—brought together the diverse aspects of the Chicano movement, while it also expanded the domain for Chicano expressions into the mass media of film and television.[15] In this manner, the film adaptation of "I Am Joaquín" signaled both the professional reorientation of El Teatro Campesino (and Chicano arts in general), Luis Valdez's own shift from rural/local/grassroots to mass media forms, and "a new era in Chicano self-determination in film and television."[16]

From Protests to Trainee Programs, 1967–69

Although *I Am Joaquín* is symptomatic of the struggle for Chicano self-representation within film and television—both as an organizing tool and as a means of representing the Chicano movement to a national audience—more structural changes would come about as a result of the combined efforts of social protests, federal regulation, and foundation initiatives. From these efforts emerged a number of industry trainee programs and film school admissions policies that brought in the first generation of would-be Chicano filmmakers. In the summer of 1968, for example, the U.S. Office of Economic Opportunity funded a program called New Communicators that was designed to train minorities for employment in the film industry. With a board of directors comprised of various progressives within Hollywood, the program "recruited about twenty students, largely Blacks and Chicanos, with a few Indians and one or two token hippie-type white guys."[17] Through intensive hands-on training with film graduates from the University of Southern California, the students were to advance from Super-8 to 16mm over the course of one year. Although the program fell apart within eight months because of internal conflicts, it nonetheless provided several Chicanos with their first exposure to the film industry: Jesús Treviño, Esperanza Vásquez, Francisco Martínez, and Martín Quiroz. Treviño, who by this time had become involved in the Educational Issues Coordinating Committee (EICC) formed within the Chicano community after the Blow Outs of March 1968, used a Super-8 (and later a 16mm) camera from the New Communicators to document subsequent Blow Outs as well as EICC activities. In particular, he documented the Sal Castro hearings before the board of education, and the EICC sit-in and arrests after the board refused the appeal to reinstate Castro.[18] In addition to the ten to twelve hours of unedited footage collected, Treviño edited together several films in early 1969 as part of his training at New Communicators. These include *La Raza Nueva* (The new people), on Super-8 with sound and narration on a separate tape cassette, and *¡Ya Basta!* (Enough already!), on 16mm. *La Raza Nueva* documents the March 1968 Blow Outs, the conspiracy trial of the "L.A. Thirteen," and the Castro hearings and sit-in. In *¡Ya Basta!*, Treviño experiments with jump cuts, dramatic recreations, and multiple story lines, which reemerge in Treviño's later television documentaries such as *Yo Soy Chicano* (1972). The "free-form" docudrama intercuts blown-up footage from *La Raza Nueva* with a dramatic sequence about a teenage boy with troubles at home and school. By the end of the film the boy's death is coded as a direct outcome of the board of education's refusal to reinstate Castro. Although these films appear "primitive" and incoherent according to mass-media conventions, their effective use within the EICC and the Chicano community at the time suggests another way of understanding early artistic expressions within the movement. As Treviño himself argues, the "free-form" style of *¡Ya Basta!* relied upon the fact that "so much of this was self-evident to the audience."[19] Thus, the film served the needs of an audience whose main concern was the organization of a "community" and not the craft of an autonomous, objective, or artistic statement. To that extent, watching a "Chicano" film about an event experienced firsthand by many of the audience members played a role in community building, becoming more important than the actual form and content of the film, and more important than its ability to function within the mass media.

Chicano Public Affairs Series, 1970–74

The limited or distorted media coverage of social protests and community concerns motivated a number of student activists to become filmmakers able to work within the mass media itself. Meanwhile, Chicano media advocates and activist groups, including Carissma and Justicia, aggressively pushed for Chicano-produced local television shows in the Los Angeles area.[20] Overall, these local television shows or specials provided initial, albeit contested, outlets for Chicano-produced film related to the issues, protests, and goals of the Chicano movement. But as producers attempted to address these issues within the television industry, they confronted both economic and ideological constraints. In fact, program budgets did not provide for more than a "talking heads" format, while station managers suppressed their efforts to use television for social critique. An examination of two series produced by Treviño reveals the extent to which Chicano filmmakers were able to subvert these constraints.

The *¡Ahora!* series—funded by the Ford Foundation as part of an initiative at PBS affiliate KCET in Los Angeles—was perhaps the first television show to document and discuss current issues within the Chicano community. Given the prior absence of local media coverage on Chicanos, members of the community were hostile to the series, then in development, even though politically active Chicanos were in the role of producers. Various community meetings were held, and at one such meeting some two hundred people voted on whether or not to support the program. Treviño attempted to intervene: "I gave this impassioned plea, like, at least give us a chance, don't you trust me, et cetera. And the vote . . . there were four people who voted for me: my wife, two friends and myself! [Laughing] It was really tense in those days."[21] In the first week, the program featured "every single major [Chicano] group," and by the end of the year, "whenever we would have a major news event happening, the local news stations would come to our studio, because we would have the people there. We would get them before anyone else."[22] Because of the close relationships Treviño established within the community, *¡Ahora!* could also provide immediate coverage for planned protests and other events. Treviño quickly became the associate producer, writer, and on-air host for the show, which aired live weeknights at 7:00 p.m. for 175 episodes. In addition to the political issues dealt with in talk-show format or documented through live remotes, *¡Ahora!* scheduled regular episodes on cultural and historical dimensions of the Chicano experience. These included a three-part series on Mexican Americans in Hollywood.[23] Treviño also hired Luis Torres, a high school senior (later a producer for the National Latino Communications Center), to research and write a weekly episode on "la raza history." On Fridays, the show usually aired live performances of Latino music and drama. In this manner, in its weekly programming, *¡Ahora!* wove together current events, history, culture, and entertainment, providing an integrated vision of the Chicano community and its political struggle.

Taken as a whole, Treviño's programming on *¡Ahora!* can be seen as congruent with "El Plan Espiritual de Aztlán" and its demand for cultural expressions that would "strengthen our identity and the moral backbone of the movement." The Plan made explicit the movement's assumption about the role of cultural production within political struggle, and, more generally, the way in which cultural nationalism mediated between the Chicano family and dominant society: "our culture unites and educates the family of La Raza towards liberation with one heart and one mind." The Plan then articulated seven "organizational goals" for the movement, calling upon "writers, poets, musicians, and artists" to assist this process by defining the "cultural values" of the family and home as a "powerful weapon" against the "gringo dollar value system." But while the role of cultural expression was central to the organization of the movement, it was also the only

"organizational goal" that was absent from the "action" or public sphere portion of the Plan. To some extent, this can be explained by the way in which the Plan equated cultural expression with the private domain of the family and home. Thus, although the Chicano family served as a model for political organization and "nation" building, its patriarchal and hierarchical structure served to keep the issues associated with family *entre familia* (literally, "between family members," or not for public discussion). These issues were, namely, those of gender, generation, and sexuality. Within the terms of the Plan, cultural production was expected to maintain this status quo—to reaffirm the traditional family—as a central element within an oppositional Chicano politics.

Despite its location within mass media, *¡Ahora!* worked within the terms of the Plan, since the public affairs series used broadcast television to reach the homes of Chicano families just after dinner, informing that audience about political events, but also cultivating cultural and historical awareness that was, in the words of the Plan, both "appealing" and "revolutionary." As an example of prime-time access programming, *¡Ahora!* was situated between the six o'clock news and prime-time entertainment, drawing upon both forms of television discourse, but serving a specific segment of the station's market. Thus, although ratings were generally above average for its time slot, the viewership was constituted along the lines of local and ethnic needs (what would now be called narrowcasting). As such, this type of show was at odds with commercial television, which sold advertising time based on reaching a percentage of a broadcast audience. This narrowcasting strategy would typify minority public affairs series throughout the 1970s until deregulation brought an end to prime-time access, shifting the few remaining shows to Sunday mornings.

When Ford Foundation support ended in 1970, Trevino had to apply activist strategies within the station in order to secure another show that addressed the concerns of the Chicano community. He organized the fifteen to twenty "Spanish surnamed" employees of the station—janitors, secretaries, and various technicians—"to sign a petition that said, unless the Chicano community had a weekly television show, we were all going to resign en masse. . . . and that was the birth of *Acción Chicano* [sic]."[24] By the time *Acción Chicano* first aired in 1972, Treviño had decided that "the problem with our programming was that it kept being ghettoized and relegated to the corner." His response was to reproduce the "high production values" of the station's other shows, even though this meant that he had to stick to a talk-show or performance format given the limited budgets (about fifteen hundred dollars per week/episode). Even with these limitations, however, Treviño and other Chicano filmmakers could draw upon various strategies in order to introduce political commentary, and to find alternative ways to "run the whole spectrum of programming."[25]

One effective strategy used by Treviño and others was to speak from behind the mask of a "folk" ethnicity, in particular through *teatro* performances that included variations on the folk music of the Mexican Revolution. In this manner, the "folkloric" appearances satisfied station managers who might otherwise have been concerned about the unsubtitled Spanish. In one episode of *Acción Chicano*, Treviño featured a performance by Los Mascarones (The Masquers), a Mexican *teatro* group similar in style and politics to El Teatro Campesino. The episode was sent to PBS for national release, and, "they thought this was a nice folkloric kind of stuff . . . and went along with it." It was during the national airing that PBS discovered the content of the Spanish-language episode (with no subtitles), since numerous Cuban exiles in Miami called in to protest. The Los Mascarones performance ends with the theme song of the Cuban Revolution, with added lines that place the civil rights struggles of Chicanos, Puerto Ricans, and Blacks within its radical framework.[26] In the 1970s, many of the Chicano and Latino television series and specials would use Spanish as a way to communicate ideas and information that might have been censored in English.[27] Other examples of *teatro*-based programs that relied on Spanish-language dialogue and code switching, included *Los Vendidos: The Sellouts* (1972), *Guadalupe* (1976), and *El Corrido* (1976).

Using *Acción Chicano* as a base from which to pool resources and expand his audience, Treviño was also able to produce some of the first film documentaries. "I would tape two or three shows and make them all talk shows so that I could take that budget and invest it in film stock." These films included *La Raza Unida* (1972), *Yo Soy Chicano* (1972), *Carnalitos* (1973), and *Somos Uno* (1973). Treviño also used these films as a way to train other Chicano filmmakers, such as Bobby Páramo, who coproduced *Carnalitos*.[28] Finally, in a move that would have national repercussions, in 1972 *Acción Chicano* pooled resources with a new Puerto Rican series in New York City, *Realidades*, wherein the two shows traded five episodes each for local rebroadcast. This became a first step in the development of pan-Latino advocacy and organization at the national level.

"Our Own Institutions"

In 1975, *Realidades* became the first national Latino television series, and subsequently commissioned numerous Chicano films, including Severo Pérez's *Cristal* (1975), Susan Racho's *Garment Workers* (1975), José Luis Ruiz's *Guadalupe* (1976), Bobby Páramo's *Salud and the Latino* (1976), Ricardo Soto's *Cosecha* (1976), *Migra* (1976), and *Al Otro Paso* (1976), and Adolfo Vargas's *Una Nación Bilingüe* (1977). The program stood in contrast to the earlier occasional national feeds of local material, and provided a pan-Latino forum for Chicano and Puerto Rican films. Several works dealt with national Latino issues, with

footage shot on both coasts and in the Midwest: *Garment Workers,* Jay Ojeda's *De Colores* (1975), *Salud and the Latino*. *Realidades* was created in 1972, when members of the Puerto Rican Education and Action Media Council took over the studio of PBS affiliate WNET-TV (New York) during the station's pledge drive. In its first two years, the series was similar to the concurrent *Acción Chicano* (also created through protest), with which it exchanged programs.[29] In 1974, the Corporation for Public Broadcasting (CPB) awarded *Realidades* sixty thousand dollars to produce a one-hour pilot for national broadcast. In its two years as a national series, *Realidades* received $553,687 from the CPB, and produced twenty-three half-hour programs. The monies from CPB represented less than 3 percent of the CPB total production budget; after the series ended, that level dropped to 1 percent for Latino projects.[30]

Despite its short-lived success, *Realidades* revealed the need for a national pan-Latino organization in order to secure greater continuity of reforms, while it also provided a national network of producers associated with the series. With the waning of public protests in the early 1970s, Chicano/Latino filmmakers began to develop national institutions within the industry. These included the Latino Consortium (since 1974; now, National Latino Communications Center), which syndicates Latino-themed and -produced works on public television; the Chicano Film Festival in San Antonio, Texas (since 1975; now, CineFestival), which provides a national forum for public exhibition, as both a community-based event and a professional one; and the National Latino Media Coalition (1975–80), formed by Humberto Cintrón, executive producer of *Realidades*, which lobbied for federal funding. Echoing "El Plan Espiritual de Aztlán," Treviño identified these various efforts as an attempt to create "our own institutions."[31] These were, however, institutions that attempted to speak on behalf of both the community and media professionals from within the mass media, rather than institutions whose domain was that of the community itself. In contrast to *¡Ahora!* and other eclectic format series whose primary audience was the Chicano community, these "institutions" worked at the crossroads of a Chicano/Latino audience and a national one, primarily within the domain of educational programming rather than that of entertainment. Overall these efforts represented a significant shift from social protest strategies to professional advocacy within the industry and the independent sector. But, as Trevino and other filmmakers have noted, Hollywood studios and television networks remained intransigent in the face of these internal pressures.[32]

Locating Chicano Cinema

The move to professionalism, however, did not occur in a political vacuum; rather, despite limited success with studios and networks, it represented a significant maneuver within a larger strategy to locate Chicano culture.

Throughout the 1960s and 1970s, contacts with Latin America via postrevolutionary Cuba provided an essential framework for the development of the movement's radical politics as well as its reformist achievements. Even before the Chicano movement, in 1964, Luis Valdez traveled to Cuba as a member of a Progressive Labor Party delegation. Valdez, like many Chicano student activists, had been involved in reformist efforts directed at the Democratic Party, such as the Mexican American Political Association (MAPA), and had been active in the "Viva Kennedy!" clubs. Upon his return from Cuba, however, Valdez coauthored one of the first radical student manifestos, "Venceremos! Mexican American Statement on Travel to Cuba," which anchored its rejection of reformist politics in a pan-American solidarity.[33] Chicano political discourse continued to look to Mexico, Cuba, and, more generally, the "Bronze Continent" as the necessary backdrop of its efforts to imagine an ethnic community within the political, socioeconomic, and legal structures of the United States. This "imagined" location in the Americas became the context for local political action as well as professional reform within the U.S. film and television industries.

Perhaps the most lasting impact has been the result of Treviño's involvement with New Latin American Cinema. In 1974, Treviño was recruited into the Cuban-sponsored Comité de Cineastas de América Latina (Latin American Filmmakers Committee), an international committee of a dozen filmmakers committed to the advancement of New Latin American Cinema. The committee met six mimes between 1974 and 1978, and worked toward the organization of the Annual Festival of New Latin American Cinema, which premiered in December 1979 in Havana, Cuba. At its sixth meeting (in Havana, July 12–17, 1978), the committee issued a declaration about the festival, and, in the second paragraph, spelled out the relationship of the Chicano filmmakers to New Latin American Cinema:

> We also declare our solidarity with the struggle of Chicano cinema, the cultural manifestation of a community that combats the oppression and discrimination within the United States in order to affirm its Latin American roots. This reality remains almost or entirely unknown by most of our people, or reaches them through the distortions of the imperialist news media. Yet today the Chicano community has its own filmmakers and films, and demands of us the commitment to strengthen the cultural-historical ties that join us together, by contributing to the dissemination of their films, their experiences, and their struggles.[34]

Treviño and the Chicano Cinema Coalition led a delegation of Chicano filmmakers and media advocates to the first festival. As he explains, "It was a real eye-opener experience for a lot of Chicanos that went, because for the first time they were seeing a lot of Latin American, not just Cuban, cinema."[35] Although the experience seemed to confirm the predictions of the earlier film manifestos, the social context for racial and radical politics in the United States had changed quite a bit since the heyday of the Chicano movement and New Latin American Cinema. Nonetheless, the contacts with Cuba and Latin America did foster an increased international political perspective in the 1980s, although it is difficult to separate this from the filmmakers' increased awareness of and attention to the international film market and festival circuit.[36] In this respect, the festival served an important symbolic role in doubling the "location" of Chicano cinema, making it into a movement that was at once reformist and revolutionary. But rather than constitute a contradiction, this dual location provided Chicano filmmakers with an effective political strategy within the United States. Clearly, many of the early successful reforms came about as a result of shifting the center leftward during public protests and press statements, providing filmmakers with a vantage point from which to negotiate.

By the late 1970s, this strategy rang hollow after national and international "movement" politics came to a violent end. Chicano filmmakers would, for the most part, shift to a politics of "professionalism" within the industry and the independent sector. Still, "Chicano cinema" persists as a quasi-national category within international film festivals in Latin America and Europe, and is generally tied to a "minority" cultural politics.[37] Since the late 1970s, Chicano filmmakers have continued to articulate and develop connections to New Latin American Cinema as well as Spanish-language cinema in general. These filmmakers also initiated various efforts to integrate both Hollywood and the independent sector in order to produce and distribute Chicano-themed feature films and documentaries. Thus, if Treviño and others located "Chicano cinema" within both New Latin American Cinema and Hollywood, it was as the functional synthesis of ostensible contradictions, one that allowed the practice to follow upon the idea and the possibilities it created.

What stands outside these efforts to walk the line between reform and revolution—the bipolar terms of the Chicano movement—was the simultaneous emergence of a Chicano avant-garde in the mid-1960s and early 1970s, one split between the modernist aesthetics of a personal, visionary cinema and the postmodern parody of an alienated television generation.[38] Taking this work into account challenges the prevailing history of Chicano cinema with its equivalence between body, politics, and aesthetics as well as its ambivalence about institutional location. Indeed, *I Am Joaquín* is not the "first" Chicano film in the strict sense of the word, since there are at least two earlier avant-garde films: Ernie Palomino's *My Trip in a '52 Ford* (1966), also a film poem, but one that follows in the tradition of Beat counterculture rather than the neo-indigenist *floricanto* (Chicano poetry); and Severo Pérez's *Mozo: An Introduction into the Duality of Orbital Indecision* (1968), a pot-induced send-up of the trance film that circulated as part of the Texas Underground National Tour. Most filmmakers and critics, however, continue to identify *I Am Joaquín* as the "first" Chicano film, in the same manner that poets and literature scholars identify Gonzales's "I Am Joaquín" as the "first" Chicano poem: both are seen as the first articulations of a political, historical, and poetic consciousness about the "Chicano experience." Unlike the experimental films with their interracial, cross-cultural, and transcendental concerns, *I Am Joaquín* contributed to the idea of a "Chicano cinema" that operated within clearly marked borders (for community, for identity) that were defined by the exigencies of the Chicano civil rights movement. Like Gonzales's poem, which recontained its ambivalence within stable bipolar terms, Chicano cinema both juxtaposed and straddled two locations: America and América. Again, this was not so much a matter of an either/or choice (even though it was presented as such), but rather an attempt to define tightly coupled oppositional terms—nationalism and assimilation; revolution and reform—so that the one would inevitably produce the other. Without a doubt, such a strategy put Chicano cinema on the map in both a literal and a figurative sense, constructing an alternative to Hollywood. But it was an alternative in both senses of the word, something different from Hollywood, yet something that also aspired to take its place.

Notes

1. Of the filmmakers, Jesús Salvador Treviño has been the most prolific and influential, publishing in Europe and the Americas, and in some ways setting the terms for subsequent scholarship. See, for example, Treviño's articles "Cinéma Chicano aux Etats-Unis," in *Les Cinémas de l'Amérique Latine*, ed. Guy Hennebelle and Alfonso Gumucio-Dagron (Paris: Nouvelles Editions Pierre Lherminier, 1981), 493–99; "Chicano Cinema," *New Scholar* 8 (1982): 167–80; and "El desarrollo del cine chicano," in *Hojas de cine: testimonios y documentos del nuevo cine latinoamericano* (México: Fundación del nuevo cine latinoamericano, 1986), n.p. Books on Chicano cinema include Gary D. Keller, ed., *Chicano Cinema: Research, Reviews, and Resources* (Binghamton, N.Y.: Bilingual Review/Press, 1985); Chon A. Noriega, ed., *Chicanos and Film: Representation and Resistance* (Minneapolis: University of Minnesota Press, 1992); Rosa Linda Fregoso, *The Bronze Screen: Chicana and Chicano Film Culture* (Minneapolis: University of Minnesota Press, 1993); and Gary D. Keller, *Hispanics and United States Film: An Overview and Handbook* (Tempe, Ariz.: Bilingual Press, 1994).
2. I draw upon Mario Barrera's insightful analysis of the historical role of egalitarian (integrationist) and communitarian (cultural nationalist) goals in the Mexican-origin community. See Mario Barrera, *Beyond Aztlán: Ethnic Autonomy in Comparative Perspective* (Notre Dame, Ind.: University of Notre Dame press, 1988), chapters 1–6.
3. Coco Fusco, "Fantasies of Oppositionality: Reflections on Recent Conferences in Boston and New York," *Screen* 29 (autumn 1988): 80–93; and "Ethnicity, Politics and Poetics: Latinos and Media Art," in *Illuminating Video: An Essential Guide to Video Art*, ed. Doug Hall and Sally Jo Fifer (New York: Aperture/BAVC, 1990), 304–16.
4. Chon A. Noriega, "Between a Weapon and a Formula: Chicano Cinema and Its Contexts," in Noriega, ed., *Chicanos and Film*, 141–67.
5. See Carlos Muñoz Jr., *Youth, Identity, Power: The Chicano Movement* (New York: Verso, 1989).
6. The "Plan of Delano" is reprinted in Armando B. Rendón, *Chicano Manifesto* (New York: Macmillan, 1971), 327–30. Rendón reprints the "Plan of Delano" with three other manifestos under the appendix title "Four Declarations of Independence."

7. As I discuss later, this can be seen in the use of specific phrases as well as rhetorical strategies. The "Plan Espiritual de Aztlán" is reprinted in Rudolfo A. Anaya and Francisco Lomelí, eds., *Aztlán: Essays on the Chicano Homeland* (Albuquerque, N.M.: Academia/El Norte Publications, 1989), 1–6. The "Plan de Santa Barbara" is reprinted in Muñoz, *Youth, Identity, Power*, 191–202. Three film manifestos from the 1970s are reprinted in Noriega, ed., *Chicanos and Film*, 275–307.
8. The charges against the "L.A. Thirteen" were dismissed as unconstitutional after two years of appeals (Rodolfo Acuña, *Occupied America: A History of Chicanos*, 3d ed. [New York: HarperCollins, 1988], 388).
9. *I Am Joaquín* was later annotated and reissued by Bantam Books in 1972. Film and poem appear in Spanish and English versions.
10. "I/WE SHALL ENDURE" appears in capital letters in both texts.
11. See Tomás Ybarra-Frausto, "The Chicano Movement and the Emergence of a Chicano Poetic Consciousness," *New Scholar* 6 (1977): 81–109.
12. Luis Valdez, "Notes on Chicano Theater" (1970), in *Luis Valdez—Early Works* (Houston: Arte Público Press, 1990), 8.
13. "El Plan Espiritual de Aztlán," in Anaya and Lomelí, eds., *Aztlán*, 2. See also Gonzales, "Chicano Nationalism: The Key to Unity for la Raza," *Militant*, March 30, 1970.
14. The production dates cited for the film range from 1967 to 1970. In his article "Cinéma Chicano aux Etats-Unis," Treviño—based on interviews with the Valdez brothers—states that the film was shot and recorded "[o]n a hot summer evening in 1967," the same year the poem was written. The film itself has a 1969 copyright, which may indicate that the film was shown before it was copyrighted, or that it took over a year to edit the film.
15. See Rolando Hinojosa's comments on the changes made in the film in order to make it more commercial (Hinojosa, "*I Am Joaquín*: Relationships between the Text and the Film," in Keller, ed., *Chicano Cinema*, 142–45). The United Farm Workers Service Center continued to document events on film, and produced at least two Spanish-language documentaries for internal use: *Nosotros Venceremos* (1971; *We Will Overcome*), which uses photographic stills to relate UFW struggles and goals; and *Sí, se puede* (1973; *Yes, We Can*), on César Chávez's hunger strike in Arizona.
16. Jesús Salvador Treviño, "Chicano Cinema Overview," *Areíto* 37 (1984): 40.
17. Personal interview with Treviño, May 28, 1991.
18. Ibid.
19. Ibid.
20. Treviño, "Chicano Cinema": 170–71; and Harry Gamboa Jr., "Silver Screening the Barrio," *Equal Opportunity Forum* 6.1 (November 1978): 6–7.
21. Personal interview with Treviño, May 28, 1991.
22. Ibid.
23. An unauthorized reprint appears in Cine-Aztlán, "The Treviño/Ahora Survey: A Historical Profile of the Chicano and Latino in Hollywood Film Productions," in *La Raza Film Bibliography* (Santa Barbara, Calif.: Cine-Aztlán, 1974), 9–16.
24. Personal interview with Treviño, May 28, 1991. In Spanish, adjectives usually conform to the gender of the noun. Thus, the correct title would be *Acción Chicana*. Treviño, however, "purposely changed it to *Chicano*," since "I basically, at that time, thought that *Chicana* would read that it was a show only for women, and I wanted to make it clear that this was for the whole community." That there would have been such confusion owes more to the decreased Spanish-language maintenance within the Chicano generation than to sexism. In fact, Treviño himself was not fluent in Spanish at the time.
25. Ibid.
26. Ibid.
27. In Lubbock, Texas, for example, the Spanish-language series *Aztlán* (1976–79), produced by Héctor Galán, "got away with murder, because the station didn't understand" (statement by Héctor Galán during the roundtable "In the Public Eye: A Dialogue on Chicano Media Arts," Dialogues in Movement: A Chicano Media Arts Retrospective, San Antonio, Texas, July 13, 1991).
28. Bobby Páramo, "*Cerco Blanco, The Balloon Man*, and *Fighting City Hall*: On Being a Chicano Filmmaker," *Metamorfosis* 3.2 (1980–81): 77–82.

29. José García Torres, "José García Torres & *Realidades*," interview by Aurora Flores and Lillian Jiménez, *Centro Bulletin* 2.8 (spring 1990): 30–43.

30. "Pensamientos: Latinos and CPB," *Chicano Cinema Newsletter* 1.6 (August 1979): 2–3, 2.

31. Quoted in Antonio José Guernica, "Chicano Production Companies: Projecting Reality, Opening the Doors," *Agenda: A Journal of Hispanic Issues* 8.1 (January-February 1978): 12–15, 13.

32. Jesús Salvador Treviño, "Lights, Camera, Action," *Hispanic* (August 1992): 76.

33. Luis Valdez and Roberto Rubalcava, reprinted in Luis Valdez and Stan Steiner, eds., *Aztlán: An Anthology of Mexican American Literature* (New York: Alfred A. Knopf, 1972): 215–16.

34. "Declaración del Comité de Cineastas de América Latina," *Cine Cubano* 8.3 (1977–78): 45–46; translation mine. The declaration was translated by Ralph Cook and reprinted in *Cineaste* 9.1 (fall 1978): 54. In Cook's version, he inserts references to the Chicano movement. The original text, however, refers to the Chicano "community," and not the "movement," whose militant phase had already come to an end.

35. Personal interview with Treviño, May 28, 1991.

36. See, for example, David Rosen's chapter on *The Ballad of Gregorio Cortez* in *Off-Hollywood: The Making and Marketing of Independent Films* (New York: Grove Weidenfeld, 1990), 1–22.

37. See my forthcoming article, "On Curating," *Wide Angle* 17.1–4.

38. These two tendencies are exemplified by the work of Willie Varela and Harry Gamboa Jr., respectively. See Chon A. Noriega, "Willie Varela," *New American Film and Video Series* 72, program note (New York: Whitney Museum of American Art, 1994); and the section on Gamboa in my article "Talking Heads, Body Politic: The Plural Self of Chicano Video," in *Resolutions: Contemporary Video Practices,* ed. Michael Renov and Erika Suderburg (Minneapolis: University of Minnesota Press, in press.). For the filmmakers' own accounts, see Gamboa, "Past Imperfecto," *Jump Cut* 39 (June 1994): 93–95, and Varela, "Chicano Personal Cinema," *Jump Cut* 39 (June 1994): 96–99.

Section 5: Literature, Art, Folklore, Music, and Cinema
Assessment and Application

1. Identify and describe each of Ortego's historical developmental stages of Chicano literature and provide examples of each period.

2. Name the four principal reasons why literary production was limited during the pre-Chicano period.

3. How is Chicano literature different from Mexican, Latin-American or Euro-American literature?

4. Discuss the importance of gender and sexuality in Chicano feminist literature according to Yarbro-Bejarano.

5. Identify the major differences between literature, oral history or tradition, and folklore.

6. Provide various examples of Chicano folklore that would be useful to providers of social services, educators, or business persons in your community.

7. Contrast and compare the images, cultural icons, norms, values, and beliefs manifested by a Chicana and a Chicano author.

8. After reading Vargas' essay, identify some salient murals in your community.

9. Take photographs of selected murals in your community and produce a 20-minute socio-ethnographic presentation illustrating each mural, its painter, and the themes addressed by each mural. Preface your presentation with a socio-economic and historical overview of the areas where these murals are found. What cultural messages do you find? How is ethnic identity depicted by the murals?

10. How does Amalia Mesa-Bains define the political and feminist work of Chicana artists?

11. How does Chicana art differ from Chicano art?

12. Select two Chicano and two Chicana artists from your community and organize a panel presentation in which they can discuss their artistic contributions and relevant gender issues.

13. According to Ortega, what are some of the key conceptual features of Chicano Music?

14. Why is the Chicano Movement a catalyst for Chicano music, especially with the use of lyrics?

15. Describe how Noriega links the expression of Chicano cinema with the Chicano Movement.

Section 5: Suggested Readings

Abarca, Meredith E. (2006). *Voices in the Kitchen: Views of Food and the World from Working-Class Mexican and Mexican American Women.* College Station, TX: Texas A&M University Press.

Anzaldúa, Gloria. (1998). Chicana Artists: Exploring Nepantla, el Lugar de la Frontera. In Antonia Darder & Rodolfo Torres, (Eds.). *The Latino Studies Reader: Culture, Economy and Society.* Malden, MA: Blackwell Publishers.

Arrizón, Alicia. (1999). *Latina Performance: Traversing the Stage.* Bloomington, IN: Indiana University Press.

Broyles-González, Yolanda. (1994). *El Teatro Campesino: Theater in the Chicano Movement.* Austin, TX: University of Texas Press.

Byrd, Bobby and Mississippi Byrd, Susannah. (Eds.). (1996). *The Late Great Mexican Border: Reports from a Disappearing Line.* El Paso, TX: Cinco Puntos Press.

Cantú, Norma E. and Nájera-Ramírez, Olga. (2002). *Chicana Traditions: Continuity and Change.* Champaign, IL: University of Illinois Press.

Castro, Rafaela G. (2001). *Chicano Folklore: A Guide to the Folktales, Traditions, Rituals and Religious Practices of Mexican Americans.* New York, NY: Oxford University Press.

Chew Sánchez, Martha I. (2006). *Corridos in Migrant Memory.* Albuquerque, NM: University of New Mexico Press.

Clayton, Lawrence and Specht, Joe W. (2003). *The Roots of Texas Music.* College Station, TX: Texas A&M University Press.

Cull, Nicholas J. and Carrasco, David. (2004). *Alambrista and the U.S.-Mexico Border: Film, Music, and Stories of Undocumented Immigrants.* Albuquerque, NM: University of New Mexico Press.

Edberg, Mark Cameron. (2004). *El Narcotraficante: Narcocorridos & the Construction of a Cultural Persona on the U.S.–Mexico Border.* Austin, TX: University of Texas Press.

Gaspar de Alba, Alicia. (1998). *Chicano Art Inside/Outside the Master's House.* Austin, TX: University of Texas Press.

Gaspar de Alba, Alicia. (2003). *Velvet Barrios: Popular Culture & Chicana/o Sexualities.* New York, NY: Palgrave Macmillan.

Griswold del Castillo, Richard; McKenna, Teresa, and Bejarano, Yvonne. (1991). *Chicano Art: Resistance and Affirmation, 1965–1985.* Los Angeles, CA: Wight Gallery, University of California, Los Angeles.

Guerrero, Lalo and Mente, Sherilyn Meece. (2002). *Lalo: My Life and Music.* Tucson, AZ: University of Arizona Press.

Gutiérrez-Jones, Carl. (2004). *Rebellious Reading: The Dynamics of Chicana/o Cultural Literacy.* Santa Barbara, CA: Center for Chicano Studies, University of California, Santa Barbara.

Hernández, Guillermo. (1978). *Canciones de la Raza: Songs of the Chicano Experience.* Berkeley, CA: El Fuego de Aztlán.

Hernández-Gutiérrez, Manuel de Jesús and Foster, David William. (Eds.). (1997). *Literatura Chicana, 1965–1995: An Anthology in Spanish, English, and Caló.* New York, NY: Garland Publishing.

Herrera-Sobek, María. (1996). *Chicana Creativism and Criticism: New Frontiers in American Literature.* Albuquerque, NM: University of New Mexico Press.

Herrera-Sobek, María. (1993). *Northward Bound: The Mexican Experience in Ballad and Song.* Bloomington, IN: Indiana University Press.

Huerta, Jorge A. (1982). *Chicano Theater: Themes and Forms.* Tempe, AZ: Bilingual Review Press.

Joysmith, Claire. (Ed.). (1995). *Las Formas de Nuestras Voces: Chicana and Mexicana Writers in México.* México, D.F.: Centro de Investigaciones sobre América del Norte, Universidad Autónoma de México.

Kanellos, Nicolás, et al. (2002). *En Otra Voz: Antología de la Literatura Hispana de los Estados Unidos.* Houston, TX: Arte Público Press.

Keller, Gary D. (1997). *A Biographical Handbook of United States Film.* Tempe, AZ: Bilingual Review Press.

Keller, Gary D. et al. (2002). *Contemporary Chicana and Chicano Art, Vol. I: Artists, Works, Culture and Education.* Tempe, AZ: Bilingual Review Press.

Keller, Gary D. et al. (2002). *Contemporary Chicana and Chicano Art, Vol. II: Artists, Works, Culture and Education.* Tempe, AZ: Bilingual Review Press.

Keller, Gary D. (2005). *Triumph of Our Communities: Four Decades of Mexican American Art.* Tempe, AZ: Bilingual Review Press.

López, Miguel R. (2001). *Chicano Timespace: The Poetry and Politics of Ricardo Sánchez.* College Station, TX: Texas A&M University Press.

Loza, Steven. (1993). *Barrio Rhythm: Mexican American Music in Los Angeles.* Urbana, IL: University of Illinois Press.

Loza, Steven. (1993). *Mexican American Music in Los Angeles.* Urbana, IL: University of Illinois Press.

Maciel, David R.; Ortiz, Isidro D., and Herrera-Sobek, María. (2000). *Chicano Renaissance: Contemporary Cultural Trends*. Tucson, AZ: University of Arizona Press.

Mendoza, Louis Gerard. (2001). *Historia: The Literary Making of Chicana & Chicano History*. College Station, TX: Texas A&M University Press.

Morton, Carlos. (1994). *The Many Deaths of Danny Rosales and Other Plays*. Houston, TX: Arte Público Press.

Noriega, Chon A. and López, Ana M. (1996). *The Ethnic Eye: Latino Media Arts*. Minneapolis, MN: University of Minnesota Press.

Peña, Manuel. (1999). *Música Tejana: The Cultural Economy of Artistic Transformation*. College Station, TX: Texas A&M University Press.

Peña, Manuel. (1985). *The Texas-Mexican Conjunto: History of a Working-Class Music*. Austin, TX: University of Texas Press.

Pérez-Torres, Rafael. (2006). *Mestizaje: Critical Uses of Race in Chicano Culture*. Minneapolis, MN: University of Minnesota Press.

Pérez-Torres, Rafael. (1995). *Movements in Chicano Poetry: Against Myths, Against Margins*. New York, NY: Cambridge University Press.

Portales, Marco. (2000). *Crowding Out Latinos: Mexican Americans in the Public Consciousness*. Philadelphia, PA: Temple University Press.

Quirarte, Jacinto. (Ed.). (1984). *Chicano Art History: A Book of Selected Readings*. San Antonio, TX: Research Center for the Arts and Humanities.

Rebolledo, Diana Tey. (2005). *The Chronicles of Panchita Villa and Other Guerrilleras: Essays on Chicana/Latina Literature and Criticism*. Austin, TX: University of Texas Press.

Rebolledo, Diana Tey and Rivero, Eliana S. (1993). *Infinite Divisions: An Anthology of Chicana Literature*. Tucson, AZ: University of Arizona Press.

Reyes, David and Waldman, Tom. (1998). *Land of a Thousand Dances: Chicano Rock 'n' Roll from Southern California*. Albuquerque, NM: University of New Mexico Press.

Richmond Ellis, Robert. (1997). *The Hispanic Homograph: Gay Self-Representation in Contemporary Spanish Autobiography*. Urbana, IL: University of Illinois Press.

Sheey, Daniel. (2006). *Mariachi Music in America: Experiencing Music, Expressing Culture*. New York, NY: Oxford University Press.

Shirley, Carl R. and Shirley, Paula W. (1988). *Understanding Chicano Literature*. Columbia, SC: University of South Carolina Press.

Storm Roberts, John. (1979). *The Latin Tinge: The Impact of Latin American Music on the United States*. New York, NY: Oxford University Press.

Tejeda, Juan and Valdez, Avelardo. (2001). *Puro Conjunto: An Album in Words & Pictures*. Austin, TX: University of Texas Press.

Vázquez, Francisco H. and Torres, Rodolfo D. (2003). *Latino/a Thought: Culture, Politics and Society*. New York, NY: Rowman & Littlefield Publishers.

Vila, Pablo. (1996). Catholicism and Identity on the U.S.-Mexico Border. *Occasional Papers in Chicano Studies*. (8). El Paso, TX: Chicano Studies, University of Texas at El Paso.

Section 5: Suggested Films and Videos

Al Otro Lado/To the Other Side, 2006
Natalia Almada/Altamura Films
50 South 4th St., Suite 402, Brooklyn, NY 11211

The Bronze Screen: 100 Years of the Latino Image
    in Hollywood, 2002
Insight Media
2162 Broadway, New York, NY 10024-0621

Border Brujo/The Shaman, 1990
Cine West
Coronado, CA
New York, NY

Chicano Park, 1989
Cinema Guild
130 Madison Ave., 2nd Floor, New York, NY 10016

Chulas Fronteras, 1976
Rower Films
El Cerrito, CA

El Contrato/The Contract, 2003
Films for the Humanities and Sciences
P.O. Box 2053, Princeton, NJ 08543-2053

Corridos!: Tales of Passion and Revolution, 1987
KQED, Inc./El Teatro Campesino
San Juan Bautista, CA

Countdown: Reflections of a Life Dance, 2005
American Public Television
55 Summer Street, Boston, MA 02110

Crossing Arizona, 2006
The Cinema Guild
130 Madison Ave., 2nd Floor, New York, NY 10016

El Día de Los Muertos/Day of the Dead, 1991
Institute of Texan Cultures
San Antonio, TX

Exploring Borderlands, 2003
Insight Media
2162 Broadway, New York, NY 10024-0621

Fandango, 2006
Los Centzoles Mexican Arts Center
13108 San Pablo Ave., San Pablo, CA 94805

Hispanic Art & Culture
An instructional unit that includes a video, a book, 14 slides
    and a bilingual guide.
Produced by the Smithsonian National Museum of Art.
Social Studies School Service
10200 Jefferson Blvd., Room 1611
P.O. Box 802, Culver City, CA 90232-0802

Hispanic Excellence: Arts and Entertainment, 1993
Conrad & Associates Inc./Tuoka Productions, Inc.

Hispanics in the Media
Films for the Humanities and Sciences
P.O. Box 2053, Princeton, NJ 08543-2053

La Ofrenda: The Days of the Dead, 1989
Direct Cinema, LTD

La Pastorela: The Sheperd's Tale, 1991
El Teatro Campesino
San Juan Bautista, CA

Limón: A Life Beyond Words, 2005
Dance Conduit
35 5th Street, Frenchtown, New Jersey 00825

Madres Unidas: Parents Researching for Change, 2003
Berkeley Media LLC
2600 Tenth St., Suite 626, Berkeley, CA 94710

Mujeres, 1989
Women Make Movies
New York, NY

Paño Arte: *Images From Inside* and the Bilingual
    Documentary
About Time Productions.

Quinceañera: Princess for a Day, 1993
Mexicana Imágenes de México
México, D.F.
Rancho California (Por Favor), 2003
Berkeley Media LLC
2600 Tenth St., Suite 626, Berkeley, CA 94710

Real Women Have Curves, 2002
HBO Independent Productions

Recuerdos de Flores Muertas, 1982
Willie Varela
7541 Medano, El Paso, TX 79912

Rolas de Aztlán, 2005
Smithsonian Folkways Recordings
750 9th St. NW, Suite 4100, Washington D.C. 20560-0953

Salt of the Earth, 1953
Independent Productions and the
International Union of Mine, Mill & Workers
Oak Forest, IL

Songs of the Homeland: History of Tejano Music
Films for the Humanities and Sciences
P.O. Box 2053, Princeton, NJ 08543-2053

The Piñata Makers, 1988
Barr Films
Irwindale, CA

Tapestry II, 1996
Martin Recording
El Paso, TX

Two Documentaries on Key Moments and Figures in
    Chicano Art: 1) Los Four, 2) Murals of Aztlán: The Street
    Painters of East Los Angeles.
Chicano Cinema and Media Art Series (UCLA)
193 Haines Hall, Los Angeles, CA 90095-1544

Los Vendidos, 1972
El Teatro Campesino
San Juan Bautista, CA

Visiones, Latino Art & Culture, 2004
Galán, Inc.
5524 Bee Caves Rd. Suite B-5, Austin, TX 78746

Walls that Speak: A Video about El Paso's Murals, (1994)
The Junior League of El Paso
The El Paso Hispanic Chamber
El Paso, TX

Zoot Suit, 1981
Universal Pictures

Appendix A
Organizations and Entities Concerned with the Mexican Origin Population

The ASPIRA Association
www.aspira.org

Center for Hispanic Entrepreneurship
organizations.utep.edu/cfhe

Las Comadres Para Las Américas
www.lascomadres.org

The Congressional Hispanic Caucus Institute (CHCI)
www.chci.org

The Environmental Defense Fund (EDF)
www.environmentaldefense.org

Hispanic Business Magazine
www.hispanicbusiness.com

Hispanic Engineer National Achievement Awards Corporation (HENAAC)
www.henaac.org

The Hispanic Association of Colleges and Universities (HACU)
www.hacu.net

Inter-University Program for Latino Research (IUPLR)
www.nd.edu/~iuplr/

Labor Council for Latin American Advancement
www.lclaa.org

League of United Latin American Citizens (LULAC)
www.lulac.org

The Mexican American Legal Defense and Educational Fund (MALDEF)
www.maldef.org

Mexican American National Association: A National Latina Organization: (MANA)
www.hermana.org

Mexican Fine Arts Center Museum
www.mfacmchicago.org

Mexico-North Research Network, Inc.
www.mexnor.org

Mujeres Activas en Letras y Cambio Social (MALCS)
Women Active in Letters and Social Change
www.malcs.net/

National Association for Bilingual Education (NABE)
www.nabe.org

National Association for Chicana and Chicano Studies (NACCS)
www.naccs.org

The National Association of Hispanic Journalists (NAHJ)
www.nahj.org

National Association of Latino Arts and Culture (NALAC)
www.nalac.org

National Association of Latino Elected and Appointed Officials (NALEO)
www.naleo.org

National Association for Multicultural Education (NAME)
www.nameorg.org

National Compadres Network
www.nationalcompadresnetwork.com

National Council of La Raza (NCLR)
www.nclr.org

National Hispanic Cultural Center (NHCC)
www.nhccnm.org

National Hispanic Medical Association
www.nhmamd.org

National Latino Education Network
nlen.csusb.edu

National Network for Immigrant and Refugee Rights (NNIRR)
www.nnirr.org

The Pan American Health Organization (PAHO)
www.paho.org

The PEW Hispanic Center
pewhispanic.org

REFORMA: The Association to Promote Library and Information Services to Latinos and the Spanish Speaking
www.reforma.org

Smithsonian Center for Latino Initiatives
www.latino.si.edu

Society for Advancement of Chicanos and Native Americans in Science (SACNAS)
www.sacnas.org

Southwest Voter Registration Project (SVREP)
www.svrep.org

The Texas Association of Chicanos in Higher Education (TACHE)
www.tache.org

The Tomás Rivera Policy Institute (TRPI)
www.trpi.org

United States Hispanic Chamber of Commerce Foundation (USHCC)
www.ushccfoundation.org

United States-México Border Health Commission
www.borderhealth.org

The University of California Institute for Mexico and the United States (UC MEXUS)
www.ucmexus.ucr.edu